Financial Instruments – IFRS 9 and related Standards

iGAAP 2016

Financial Instruments – IFRS 9 and related Standards

VOLUME B

Deloitte.

Wolters Kluwer

As used in this book, Deloitte refers to one or more of Deloitte Touche Tohmatsu Limited ("DTTL"), a UK private company limited by guarantee, and its network of member firms, each of which is a legally separate and independent entity. Please see **www.deloitte.co.uk/about** for a detailed description of the legal structure of DTTL and its member firms.

Deloitte LLP is the United Kingdom member firm of DTTL.

Published by Wolters Kluwer (UK) Ltd
145 London Road
Kingston upon Thames KT2 6SR
United Kingdom
Telephone +44 (0)844 561 8166
Facsimile +44 (0)208 247 2638
Email: cch@wolterskluwer.co.uk
Website: www.cch.co.uk

ISBN 978-1-78540-232-6

British Library Cataloguing-in-Publication Data

A catalogue record for this book is available from the British Library

Typeset by Innodata Inc., India.

Printed and bound by CPI Group (UK) Ltd, Croydon, CR0 4YY

Foreword

It is a pleasure once again to introduce *iGAAP*, Deloitte's guide to International Financial Reporting Standards. A significant enhancement in the content this year is the introduction of Volume D, an online volume containing disclosure examples drawn from a wide sample of IFRS reporters globally.

Although no major IFRSs have been issued since the release of our last edition, the past year has seen significant activity in many areas of financial reporting. In particular, many companies have started to prepare for the transition to two recently-completed Standards, IFRS 9 *Financial Instruments* and IFRS 15 *Revenue from Contracts with Customers*. Following an amendment to IFRS 15, both Standards are now effective from 1 January 2018 – which sounds a long way off but will be upon us before we know it. Both Standards are important and both will present significant implementation challenges.

Revenue is one of the most significant measures used by investors and the implementation of IFRS 15 will be a major exercise for many. IFRS 15 should result in a consistent measure of revenue irrespective of industry or jurisdiction. It provides more guidance than previous Standards and requires an appropriate use of professional judgement. A joint IASB/FASB Transition Resource Group (TRG), bringing together preparers, auditors, standard-setters and others, has been working to identify, evaluate and resolve implementation issues so as to ease transition and ensure consistent application.

Financial services entities are keenly focused on the implementation of IFRS 9, but this Standard should not be overlooked by others. The rules on impairment apply to all financial assets, including trade accounts and investments. IFRS 9 allows for the consideration of a broader range of information in determining credit loss estimates, and requires recognition of lifetime expected credit losses for those loans that have experienced a significant increase in credit risk. Here, too, the IASB has established the Impairment Transition Resource Group (ITG), whose remit is similar to the TRG established for IFRS 15.

Both IFRS 9 and IFRS 15 will require management and audit committees to consider the transition to the new Standards holistically, because both will require changes to information systems, business processes, compensation and other contractual arrangements. IFRS 15 provides for either a fully retrospective or a modified retrospective transition, and that choice will require careful evaluation. The transition to IFRS 9 will also need careful planning, particularly in deciding whether to continue to apply IAS 39 to hedging relationships. Presentation and disclosure in the financial statements will also be critical for both IFRSs.

Looking forward, two significant projects are nearing completion: *Leases* and *Insurance Contracts*. For the leases Standard, much hinges on the definition of a lease, which is still being refined as we go to press. All leases, as defined and subject to the short-term lease exception, will be on-balance sheet, with the accounting being similar to IAS 17's finance lease requirements. Lessor accounting will not change significantly from that in IAS 17.

Having made significant progress, the IASB expects to issue the insurance Standard late in 2016. The interaction between this IFRS and IFRS 9, in particular how to manage the gap between the effective dates of the two Standards, is a current concern. The IASB has recently issued proposals to mitigate this issue (including a possible deferral of the effective date of IFRS 9 for particular entities), with any amendment to IFRS 9 expected in mid-2016.

In financial reporting more generally, the IASB's Disclosure Initiative continues to bear fruit, with a draft Practice Statement on Materiality released in October 2015 and a major discussion paper on the Principles of Disclosure expected in early 2016.

Our aim in writing iGAAP is to provide you with a clear, practical guide to applying IFRSs, helping you get to grips with the issues and complexities that arise. The interpretative guidance provided draws on the wealth of experience of IFRS specialists and clients from around the globe. Our thanks to them for their generous and valuable input.

Veronica Poole

Global IFRS Leader
Deloitte

Principal authors

Veronica Poole

Veronica is a Senior Accounting Technical Partner at Deloitte. She is the UK National Head of Accounting and Corporate Reporting and the firm's Global IFRS Leader. Veronica is a member of the UK Accounting Council, the Financial Reporting Advisory Board to HM Treasury, CBI Companies Committee and the Hundred Group Financial Reporting Committee. She also chairs the Financial Reporting Faculty Advisory Board at the ICAEW.

Andrew Spooner

Andrew is the lead partner on IFRS financial instruments globally across Deloitte. He is a partner of the UK firm advising UK and multinational clients, with particular focus on financial services. Andrew is also a member of the European Securities and Markets Authority's Consultative Working Group for the Corporate Reporting Standing Committee, the Technical Expert Group of the European Financial Reporting Advisory Group and the Financial Reporting Faculty Board of the ICAEW.

Phil Barden

Phil is a partner in Deloitte's UK IFRS Centre of Excellence, assisting UK and multinational clients on a wide range of financial reporting issues. He is a member of the IASB/FASB Joint Transition Resource Group for Revenue Recognition and leads Deloitte's global Expert Advisory Panel on revenue recognition. Phil chairs the Financial Reporting Editorial Board of the ICAEW, and is a member of the Institute's Financial Reporting Committee.

Kush Patel

Kush is a partner in Deloitte's UK IFRS Centre of Excellence and specialises in the accounting for financial instruments. He advises financial and non-financial corporates on complex transactions and emerging accounting issues. He is a member of the ICAEW Financial Instruments Working Group and Deloitte's global Expert Advisory Panel on financial instruments.

Ken Rigelsford

Ken is the Director responsible for UK statutory reporting in Deloitte's UK technical department. He has been closely involved in the development of the new UK GAAP and is a member of the FRC's UK GAAP Technical Advisory Group. Ken is a member of the Financial Reporting, Business Law and Company Law Committees of the ICAEW. He chairs the Distributable Profits Working Party (a joint working party of the ICAEW and the ICAS) and is regarded as one of the leading experts in this field.

Norma Hall

Norma Hall is the team leader of the author team. She is a Director in Deloitte's IFRS Global Office and Editor of the firm's International Accounting Manual. She was formerly a partner in Deloitte's Hong Kong office, with extensive experience of the application of IFRSs to commercial transactions.

Amy Haworth

Amy Haworth is the team leader for UK GAAP volumes. She is a member of the UK IFRS Centre of Excellence and of Deloitte's global Expert Advisory Panel on revenue recognition.

Contributors

The authors would like to express their thanks to Deloitte's Global IFRS Leadership Team and the members of the UK technical department, with particular appreciation to the following for their contributions.

Kristin Bauer (USA)
Hanna Ben Fekih (France)
Jens Berger (Germany)
Mark Bolton (USA)
Robert Carroll (UK)
Evangelina Chatzitsakou (UK)
Chris Chiriatti (USA)
Elizabeth Chrispin (UK)
Brandon Coleman (USA)
Svetlana Cox (UK)
Anna Crawford (Australia)
Mark Crowley (USA)
Chris Cryderman (USA)
Kerry Danyluk (Canada)
Eric Dard (France)
Trevor Derwin (South Africa)
Shivanthi Edwards (USA)
Trevor Farber (USA)
Colin Fleming (UK)
Candy Fong (China)
Adrian Geisel (Germany)
Claudio Giaimo (Argentina)
Richard Gillin (UK)
Tracey Gordon (UK)
Clair Grindley (Canada)
Markus Hahn (UK)
Karen Higgins (Canada)
Tom Hopkins (UK)
Shinya Iwasaki (Japan)
Ryszarda Kingston (UK)
Tim Kolber (USA)
Frank Kroesch (USA)
Nadine Kusche (UK)
Christine Lallouette (France)
An Lam (Canada)
Elise Lambert (USA)
Sarah McWhirter (UK)
Miguel Millan (Mexico)
Jane Miller (Chile)
Jo Mithen (UK)
Robert Morris (USA)
Anthony Mosco (USA)
Rogerio Mota (Brazil)
Shan Nemeth (USA)
Magnus Orrell (USA)
Martine Pelletier (France)
Disna Perera (UK)
Sean Prince (USA)
Linda Riedel (UK)
Laurence Rivat (France)
Estela Rodenstein (UK)
James Rogers (UK)
Helen Shaw (UK)
Melissa Sim (Australia)
Amanda Swaffield (UK)
Nura Taef (Canada)
Stephen Taylor (China)
Alan Texeira (UK)
Jeffrey Thomas (USA)
Vicki Tibbitts (UK)
Robert Uhl (USA)
Maryse Vendette (Canada)
Henri Venter (Australia)
Debra Wan (Australia)
Peter Westaway (UK)
Kenichi Yoshimura (Japan)

Standards covered

This book covers the following Standards that are effective for reporting periods beginning on or after 1 January 2015:

- International Accounting Standard 32 – *Financial Instruments: Presentation* (IAS 32)
- International Financial Reporting Standard 1 – *First-time Adoption of International Financial Reporting Standards* (IFRS 1)
- International Financial Reporting Standard 7 – *Financial Instruments: Disclosures* (IFRS 7)
- International Financial Reporting Standard 9 – *Financial Instruments* (IFRS 9)
- International Financial Reporting Standard 13 – *Fair Value Measurement* (IFRS 13)

This book incorporates relevant discussions from meetings of the International Accounting Standards Board and IFRS Interpretations Committee that took place up to 1 September 2015.

Table of Contents

B1 Scope

Contents

1 Introduction

In IFRS accounting literature, three Standards deal with the accounting for financial instruments.

- IAS 32 *Financial Instruments: Presentation* deals with the presentation and classification of financial instruments as financial liabilities or equity, and sets out the requirements regarding the offset of financial assets and financial liabilities in the statement of financial position.
- IFRS 7 *Financial Instruments: Disclosures* sets out the disclosures required in respect of financial instruments.
- IFRS 9 *Financial Instruments* contains the guidance on the recognition, derecognition, classification and measurement of financial instruments, including impairment and hedge accounting.

IFRS 9 *Financial Instruments* was published as a completed Standard in July 2014. Prior to that IFRS 9 was issued in stages in November 2009 and subsequently amended in October 2010 and November 2013. The Standard supersedes IAS 39 *Financial Instruments: Recognition and Measurement*. IFRS 9 is effective for annual periods beginning on or after 1 January 2018, with earlier application permitted.

The version of IFRS 9 issued in July 2014 superseded the earlier versions of IFRS 9 issued in 2009, 2010 and 2013. Yet, if the entity's date of initial application is before 1 February 2015 an entity may choose to apply those earlier versions of IFRS 9 instead of the finalised and completed version issued in July 2014. [IFRS 9(2014):7.3.2] For the purpose of this publication it is assumed the entity is applying IFRS 9(2014) in full including all aspects of hedge accounting.

iGAAP 2016 Financial Instruments: IAS 39 and related Standards – Volume C, Deloitte's companion volume for this manual, provides guidance for entities that have not yet adopted any of the requirements of IFRS 9.

Chapter B13 provides guidance for entities that already apply IFRSs but that are adopting the requirements of IFRS 9 for the first time.

The definition of a financial instrument is broad; a financial instrument is defined as any contract that gives rise to a financial asset of one entity and a financial liability or equity instrument of another entity. Trade receivables and payables, bank loans and overdrafts, issued debt, ordinary and preference shares, investments in securities (e.g. shares and bonds), and various derivatives are just some examples of financial instruments. In addition, some contracts to buy and sell non-financial items that would not meet the definition of financial instruments are specifically brought within the scope of the financial instruments Standards on the basis that they behave and are used in a similar way to financial instruments (see **section 2.5**).

This chapter explains which items that meet the definition of a financial instrument are scoped out of IAS 32, IFRS 7 and IFRS 9. The detailed scope exclusions of IFRS 7 are discussed in more detail in **section 2** of **chapter B11**.

All three Standards have detailed scoping paragraphs that exclude from their scope certain financial instruments. The scoping paragraphs of the three Standards (IAS 32, IFRS 7 and IFRS 9) differ slightly so that:

- all financial instruments that are scoped out of IAS 32 are also scoped out of IFRS 9;
- financial instruments that an entity issues with a discretionary participation feature are accounted for under IFRS 4 *Insurance Contracts* and are scoped out of IFRS 9. Such instruments are within the scope of IFRS 7 and IAS 32 except that, for such contracts, the requirements of IAS 32 regarding the distinction between financial liabilities and equity instruments are not applicable;
- IFRS 9 have some additional scope exclusions that go beyond the scope exclusions in IAS 32 (see **section 3**);
- Although the scope of IFRS 9 excludes some loan commitments, the impairment and derecognition requirements of IFRS 9 apply to loan commitments not otherwise within scope of that standard; and
- IFRS 9 exclude all instruments classified as equity from their scope, whereas IFRS 7 appears to exclude only those derivatives over own equity, puttable instruments and instruments that impose on the entity an obligation to deliver a pro rata share of the net assets upon liquidation that are classified as equity, making no reference to other non-derivative instruments such as ordinary shares. It appears that this difference does not have any practical effect (see **3.1**).

2 Financial instruments scoped out of IAS 32, IFRS 7 and IFRS 9

The following table summarises the scope of IAS 32, IFRS 7 and IFRS 9 with respect to financial instruments only.

Financial instrument	**Within scope of IAS 32?**	**Within scope of IFRS 7?**	**Within scope of IFRS 9?**
Interests in subsidiaries, associates and joint ventures accounted for in accordance with IAS 27, IAS 28,or IFRS 10	No	No	No
Interests in subsidiaries, associates and joint ventures accounted for in accordance with IFRS 9 as permitted by IAS 27:10(b), IAS 28:44 or IFRS 10:31	Yes	Yes	Yes
Investments in equity securities	Yes	Yes	Yes
Investments in debt securities	Yes	Yes	Yes
Trade receivables and payables	Yes	Yes	Yes
Finance lease receivables of a lessor	Yes	Yes	No (1)
Construction contract receivables that do not qualify as financial instruments and are accounted for under IFRS 15 *Revenue from Contracts with Customers* (see **2.7**)	No	No	No
Cash and cash equivalents	Yes	Yes	Yes
Borrowings and other financial liabilities (e.g. preference shares classified as financial liabilities)	Yes	Yes	Yes
Derivatives (and non-closely related embedded derivatives)	Yes	Yes	Yes
Derivatives over interests in subsidiaries, associates and joint ventures in individual financial statements	Yes	Yes	Yes
Derivatives over interests in associates and joint ventures in consolidated financial statements	Yes	Yes	Yes
Contracts over non-financial items that do not meet the purchase, sale or usage exemption in IFRS 9:2.4	Yes	Yes	Yes

Financial instrument	Within scope of IAS 32?	Within scope of IFRS 7?	Within scope of IFRS 9?
Contingent consideration in a business combination (acquirer or vendor) (2)	Yes	Yes	Yes
Deferred consideration in a business combination (acquirer or vendor)	Yes	Yes	Yes
Financial guarantee contracts for the writer that are not accounted for as insurance contracts	Yes	Yes	Yes
Finance lease obligations of a lessee	Yes	Yes	No(3)
Own equity shares	Yes	No(4)	No
Derivatives over own equity shares that are classified as equity (including derivatives over shares in non-controlling interest in the consolidated financial statements)	Yes	No	No
Forward contracts between an acquirer and a vendor in a business combination to buy or sell an acquiree at a future date	Yes	Yes	No
Loan commitments that cannot be settled net in cash or another financial instrument, are not designated as financial liabilities at fair value through profit or loss, or are not a loan commitment at a below market rate of interest	Yes	Yes	No(5)
Employer's rights and obligations under employee benefit plans covered by IAS 19	No	No	No
Share-based payment arrangements covered by IFRS 2	No	No	No
Insurance contracts for the writer or holder of insurance (settled in cash or other financial assets)	No	No	No

(1) Except for the requirements on derecognition, impairment and embedded derivatives.

(2) Assumes that IFRS 3 *Business Combinations* (as revised in 2008) is being applied. Contingent consideration in a business combination is not in the scope of any of the three Standards for the acquirer if it arose in a business combination accounted for under the previous version of IFRS 3. Contingent consideration is always in the scope of all three Standards for the vendor.

(3) Except for the requirements on derecognition and embedded derivatives.

(4) Scope exclusion refers only to derivatives over own equity, certain puttable instruments and instruments that impose on the entity an obligation to deliver a pro rata share of the net assets upon liquidation but can be applied broadly to all equity instruments of the issuer – see **3.1**.

(5) The derecognition and impairment requirements of IFRS 9 apply to loan commitments that are otherwise outside the scope of those standards

IAS 32 applies to all financial instruments except for the following:

- interests in subsidiaries, associates and joint ventures (see **section 2.1**);
- employers' rights and obligations under employee benefit plans (see **2.2**);
- rights and obligations arising under insurance contracts as well as financial instruments that are within the scope of IFRS 4 because they contain a discretionary participation feature (see **2.3**); and
- financial instruments, contracts and obligations under share-based payment arrangements (see **2.6** for further guidance and exceptions).

IFRS 9 also scope out these instruments, but have some additional scope exemptions (see **section 3**).

In addition, all three standards include within their scopes some contracts to buy or sell non-financial assets (see **section 2.5**) even though they do not meet the definition of a financial instrument.

Each of the above is considered in turn.

2.1 Interests in subsidiaries, associates and joint ventures

Interests in subsidiaries, associates and joint ventures that are accounted for under IAS 27 *Separate Financial Statements*, IAS 28 *Investments in Associates and Joint Ventures or* IFRS 10 *Consolidated Financial Statements* are not within the scope of IAS 32. However when, in the circumstances specified by those standards an entity accounts for its interests in subsidiaries, associates and/or joint ventures in accordance with IFRS 9, then those interests in subsidiaries, associates and/or joint ventures are also brought within the scope of IAS 32 and IFRS 7 (see **2.1.1**). In such circumstances, the relevant disclosure requirements of IAS 27 and IFRS 12 *Disclosure of Interests in Other Entities* apply in addition to those of IFRS 7. For example, in the parent's separate financial statements, if the parent chooses to recognise its investment in its subsidiary in accordance with IFRS 9 as at fair value through profit or loss or designated as at fair value through other comprehensive income, then that investment, having been clearly scoped into IFRS 9, also falls into the scope of IFRS 7.

Derivatives that are linked to interests in subsidiaries, associates and joint ventures are always within the scope of IAS 32. If a derivative on an interest in a subsidiary meets the definition of equity in the consolidated financial statements in accordance with IAS 32 (see **chapter B3**) that derivative is scoped out of IFRS 7 and IFRS 9 and is accounted for as equity under IAS 32. This treatment applies for a derivative over shares in a subsidiary when the derivative will be settled by delivery of a fixed amount of shares for a fixed amount of cash or other financial asset. The derivative meets the definition of equity in the consolidated financial statements because shares in a subsidiary in the consolidated financial statements are presented as non-controlling interests which are part of consolidated equity. In contrast, shares in an associate or joint venture are never considered part of equity in the consolidated financial statements and, therefore, in consolidated financial statements a derivative over an interest in an associate or joint venture will never meet the definition of equity and, consequently, will always be within the scope of IFRS 7 and IFRS 9.

When derivatives over interests in subsidiaries, associates and joint ventures are within the scope of IFRS 9 they are covered by the normal measurement requirements for derivatives as detailed in **chapter B4**.

Example 2.1A

Written call over equity of subsidiary (1)

Parent X and Subsidiary Y are part of Group Z.

Subsidiary Y writes a call option to an entity outside the group over a fixed number of its own equity shares that is exclusively physically settled in all cases and the strike price of the option is a fixed amount of cash. For Subsidiary Y, the written call option meets the definition of equity in accordance with IAS 32 and, therefore, in the financial statements of Subsidiary Y it is treated as an equity item.

In the consolidated financial statements of Group Z, the instrument is within the scope of IAS 32 because it is a derivative over an interest in a subsidiary. It is outside the scope of IFRS 7 and IFRS 9 because the instrument meets the definition of equity in the financial statements of Subsidiary Y in accordance with IAS 32 and, therefore, it is presented within non-controlling interests in the consolidated financial statements of Group Z.

Example 2.1B

Written call over equity of subsidiary (2)

The facts are as in **example 2.1A** except that Parent X writes the call option over a fixed number of shares in Subsidiary Y for a fixed amount of cash.

In the separate financial statements of Parent X, the written call option is a derivative that is in the scope of IFRS 7 and IFRS 9 because it does not meet the definition of equity in Parent X's financial statements (because the derivative does not relate to Parent X's equity).

In the consolidated financial statements of Group Z, the written call option is within the scope of IAS 32 because it is a derivative over an interest in a subsidiary which is presented within non-controlling interests. The instrument is outside the scope of IFRS 7 and IFRS 9 because the instrument meets the definition of equity.

In October 2012 the IASB issued *Investment Entities – Amendments to IFRS 10, IFRS 12 and IAS 27*. The amendments require that Investment Entities shall not consolidate entities that they control subject to meeting specified criteria. Instead, Investment Entities shall measure those entities, along with their interests in associates and joint ventures, at fair value through profit or loss in accordance with IFRS 9.

2.1.1 Investments in subsidiaries, associates and joint ventures in separate financial statements

When an entity prepares separate financial statements (as defined in IAS 27), an investment in a subsidiary, associate or joint venture should be accounted for either:

[IAS 27:10]

(a) at cost;

(b) in accordance with IFRS 9; or

(c) using the equity method as described in IAS 28.

In August 2014, the IASB amended IAS 27 to allow an entity preparing separate financial statements to account for investments in subsidiaries, joint ventures and associates using the equity method as described in IAS 28. Prior to this an entity could only account for these investments at cost or in accordance with IFRS 9. The amendments apply retrospectively for annual periods beginning on or after 1 January 2016. Earlier application is permitted in which case disclosure that the entity has applied the requirements for an earlier period is required.

The entity is required to apply the same accounting for each category of investments.

If the investment is accounted for in accordance with IFRS 9, then it will either be classified as at fair value through profit or loss or designated as at fair value through other comprehensive income (see **5.3** of **chapter B2**).

Investments that cease to be subsidiaries, but that do not become associates or joint ventures, are accounted for in accordance with IFRS 9 from the date they cease to be subsidiaries.

Similarly, investments that cease to be associates, but that do not become subsidiaries or joint ventures, are accounted for in accordance with IFRS 9 from the date the entity ceases to have significant influence. Investments that cease to be joint ventures, but that do not become subsidiaries or associates, are accounted for in accordance with IFRS 9 from the date the entity ceases to have joint control.

Venture capital organisations, mutual funds, unit trusts, investment-linked insurance funds and similar entities may, upon initial recognition, choose to measure their interests in associates and joint ventures as at fair value through profit or loss in accordance with IFRS 9, in the entity's individual or consolidated financial statements. [IAS 28:18] A venture capital organisation or similar entity is not permitted to apply IFRS 9 to its investments in subsidiaries in the consolidated financial statements.

2.1.2 *Investments in subsidiaries, associates and joint ventures partially held by a venture capital organisation or similar entity*

A group may consist of a venture capital entity (or similar) and other operations. This is common in large financial institutions when the organisation consists of a venture capital business as well as other banking operations, such as retail and investment banking.

IAS 28:19 states when an entity has an investment in an associate, a portion of which is held indirectly through a venture capital organisation, or a mutual fund, unit trust and similar entities including investment-linked insurance funds, the entity may elect to measure that portion of the investment in the associate at fair value through profit or loss in accordance with IFRS 9 regardless of whether the venture capital organisation, or the mutual fund, unit trust and similar entities including investment-linked insurance funds, has significant influence over that portion of the investment. If the entity makes that election, the entity shall apply the equity method to any remaining portion of its investment in an associate that is not held through a venture capital organisation, or a mutual fund, unit trust and similar entities including investment-linked insurance funds.

In October 2012 the IASB issued *Investment Entities – Amendments to IFRS 10, IFRS 12 and IAS 27*. The amendments require that Investment Entities shall not consolidate entities that they control subject to meeting specified criteria. Instead, Investment Entities shall measure those entities, along with their interests in associates and joint ventures, at fair value through profit or loss in accordance with IFRS 9. The amendments do not permit a parent to not consolidate an entity it controls if the parent is not itself an investment entity. Therefore a parent that is not an investment entity, but has investment entities in its group, must consolidate all entities it controls and cannot apply the investment entity exemption.

2.2 Employers' rights and obligations under employee benefit plans

Employers' rights and obligations under employee benefit plans are outside the scope of IAS 32, IFRS 7 and IFRS 9. They are within the scope of IAS 19 *Employee Benefits*. IAS 19:153(a) specifically notes that 'other long-term employee benefits' include long-service benefits. Consequently, these liabilities should follow the accounting and disclosure requirements set out in IAS 19, and not IAS 32.

2.3 Rights and obligations arising under insurance contracts

Contracts that meet the definition of an insurance contract in IFRS 4 *Insurance Contracts* are outside the scope of IAS 32, IFRS 7and IFRS 9 (see **2.3.1**).

In addition, financial instruments that are within the scope of IFRS 4 because they contain a discretionary participation feature are outside the scope of IAS 32 and IFRS 9. A discretionary participation feature is the right to receive, in addition to guaranteed benefits, significant further benefits that are at the discretion of the issuer and are based on the performance of a specified pool of contracts, investment returns or profit or loss of a company, fund or other entity that issues the contract. [IFRS 4:2 & Appendix A] The issuer of such instruments is exempt from applying the paragraphs in IAS 32 with respect to the distinction between financial liabilities and equity instruments. However, these instruments are subject to all of the other requirements of IAS 32. Furthermore, IAS 32 applies to derivatives embedded in these instruments that are required to be separately accounted for in accordance with IFRS 9 (see **2.3.2**).

2.3.1 Definition of an insurance contract

An insurance contract is defined in IFRS 4 as a contract under which one party (the insurer) accepts significant insurance risk from another party (the policyholder) by agreeing to compensate the policyholder if a specified uncertain future event (the insured event) adversely affects the policyholder. [IFRS 4:Appendix A] An insurance risk is a pre-existing risk that the policyholder transfers to the insurer and is a risk other than financial risk, i.e. other than a risk of a possible future change in either a financial variable (e.g. interest rate, commodity price, credit rating) or a non-financial variable that is not specific to a party to the contract. The insurance risk has to be significant; it has to have a discernible effect on the economics of the transaction, i.e. significant additional benefits including claims handling and assessment costs could become payable. An adverse effect on a policyholder as a result of an insured event is a precondition for payment; however, the payment itself does not have to be limited to the financial loss suffered by the policyholder.

IFRS 4 contains numerous examples of insurance contracts, and also examples of contracts that do not meet the definition of an insurance contract and may fall within the scope of IAS 32, IFRS 7 and IFRS 9.

Example 2.3.1

Insurance risk

A life insurance contract in which the insurer bears no significant mortality risk and that creates financial assets or financial liabilities will be in the scope of IFRS 9. [IFRS 4:B19]

2.3.2 Derivatives embedded in insurance contracts

Derivatives embedded within insurance contracts are within the scope of IAS 32, IFRS 7 and IFRS 9 if they are required to be separated in accordance with IFRS 9. The only exception is if a derivative embedded in an insurance contract is itself an insurance contract. [IFRS 4:7]

Example 2.3.2

Embedded derivatives in insurance contracts

[IFRS 4:IG4, Example 2.16]

A contractual feature within an insurance contract provides a return that is contractually linked (with no discretion) to the return on specified assets. The embedded derivative is not an insurance contract and is not closely related to the contract (IFRS 9:B4.3.8(h)). Fair value measurement is required [*i.e. the embedded derivative will be separated from the insurance contract and fair valued*].

2.3.3 Financial guarantee contracts (issuer accounting)

If an entity has issued a financial guarantee to a third party, the entity will need to consider whether that instrument meets the definition of a financial guarantee contract as set out in Appendix A of IFRS 9. The Standard defines such contracts as those that require the issuer to make specified payments to reimburse the holder for a loss it incurs because a specified debtor fails to make payment when due in accordance with the original or modified terms of a debt instrument. The issuer of such a contract should, in accordance with the requirements of IFRS 9, initially recognise the financial guarantee contract at fair value and subsequently measure it at the higher of:

[IFRS 9:4.2.1(c)]

- the amount of the loss allowance determined in accordance with section 5.5 of IFRS 9; and
- the amount initially recognised less, when appropriate, the cumulative amount of income recognised in accordance with the principles of IFRS 15 *Revenue from Contracts with Customers*.

This treatment in respect of initial recognition and subsequent measurement applies with the following three exceptions:

- if the financial guarantee contract was entered into or retained on a transfer of a financial asset and prevented derecognition of the financial asset or resulted in continuing involvement (see **3.3** and **3.4** in **chapter B8** for further details); [IFRS 9:4.2.1(b)]
- if the financial guarantee contract was designated as at fair value through profit or loss at inception (see **7.1.2** in **chapter B3** for further details); [IFRS 9:4.2.1(a)] and
- if the issuer has previously asserted explicitly that it regards such contracts as insurance contracts and has used accounting applicable to insurance contracts; in such circumstances, the issuer may elect to apply either IFRS 9 or IFRS 4 *Insurance Contracts*. This election may be made on a contract-by-contract basis, but once made it is irrevocable. [IFRS 9:2.1(e)]

An entity may have written financial guarantee contracts but not as a core business activity. It may have historically considered these contracts as insurance and asserted that they were insurance contracts or, alternatively, it may have made such an assertion at the time of transition to IFRSs.

The following decision tree summarises the treatment of issued financial guarantees.

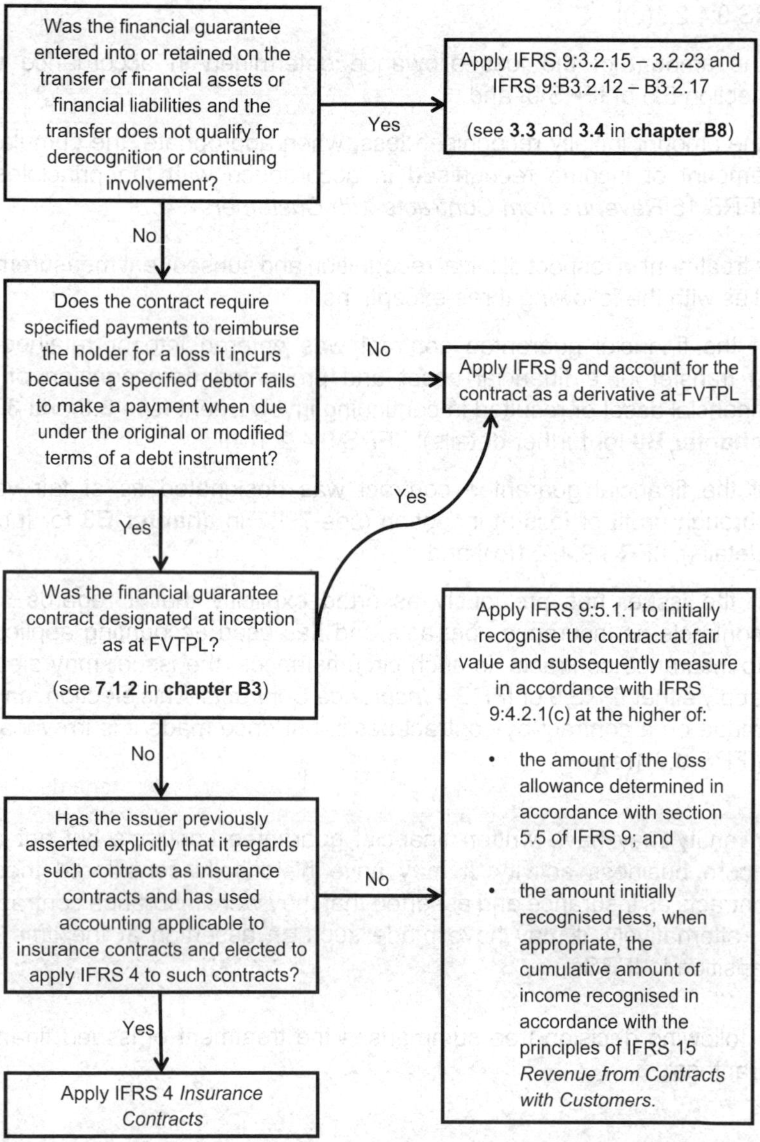

Example 2.3.3A

Financial guarantee contracts (1)

Entity A owns CU100 million of Entity X bonds that mature in 20 years. Entity X is rated BBB by the rating agencies. Entity A is concerned that Entity X may be downgraded, resulting a decline in value for the bonds. To protect against such a decline, Entity A enters into a contract with Entity B that will pay Entity A for any decline in the fair value of the Entity X bonds related to a credit downgrade to BB or below. The contract is for a five-year period, and Entity A pays CU2 million to enter into the contract. Because the contract pays Entity A in the event of a downgrade, and not in the event of a failure by Entity X to meet its payment obligations under the issued bonds, it is a derivative instrument within the scope of IFRS 9 for Entity A and Entity B.

Example 2.3.3B

Financial guarantee contracts (2)

Entity X owns CU100 million of single family residential mortgage loans. Entity X is concerned that defaults may increase as a result of a recession and, consequently, purchases a guarantee contract from Entity B, a mortgage insurance entity. The contract requires Entity B to pay Entity X for losses suffered as a result of mortgage defaults when Entity X forecloses on the mortgage. The contract has a CU5 million cap. Entity X pays Entity B a CU2 million fee for the contract. Because the contract provides for specified payments to be made to reimburse Entity X for a loss it incurs in the event of a failure of a specified debtor to pay when due, the contract meets the definition of a financial guarantee contract.

For the writer of the financial guarantee contract (Entity B), the instrument is within the scope of IFRS 9. Unless the contract is designated as at fair value through profit or loss at inception, the contract will be recognised initially at fair value and then measured at the higher of the loss allowance determined in accordance with section 5.5 of IFRS 9 and the amount initially recognised less, when appropriate, the cumulative amount of income recognised in accordance with the principles of IFRS 15 *Revenue from Contracts with Customers*. However, if Entity B has previously asserted explicitly that it regards such contracts as insurance contracts and used accounting applicable to insurance contracts, it could elect to apply either IFRS 9 or IFRS 4 to the specific contract. If such an election is made, it is irrevocable in respect of the contract with Entity X but it does not affect Entity B's options for the treatment of other similar contracts.

Example 2.3.3C

Financial guarantee contracts (3)

Entity A has a wholly-owned subsidiary, Entity B. Entity B enters into a third-party bank loan. Entity A writes a financial guarantee contract to the bank over the loan. In the separate financial statements of Entity A, the financial guarantee contract is accounted for as set out in **example 2.3.3B**. In the consolidated financial statements of Group A, the financial guarantee contract is not separately recognised because the group as a single entity has simply borrowed money from a third party.

If Entity A instead provides a guarantee directly to Entity B in respect of its bank loan, in the separate financial statements of Entity A the guarantee is not recognised separately. The arrangement is such that Entity A has agreed to contribute more money to its subsidiary which will generally be accounted for as a capital contribution as and when it is contributed. The promise by the parent to inject money at a future date is not recognised up-front.

2.3.4 Financial guarantee contracts (holder accounting)

IFRS 9 does not specifically address the accounting by a holder of a financial guarantee contract (such as Entity X in **example 2.3.3B**). However, prior to the consequential amendments to IAS 39 made when IFRS 9 was revised in October 2010, IAS 39:IN6 was explicit that financial guarantee contracts held, as opposed to those issued, were outside the scope of IAS 39. The consequential amendments resulted in the deletion of IAS 39:IN6, along with all the introductory paragraphs in IAS 39. IAS 39:IN6 was not carried over into the introductory paragraphs of IFRS 9. However, given that IAS 39 and IFRS 9 scope out 'rights' under a financial instrument that meets the definition of an insurance contract in IFRS 4, it is reasonable to conclude that purchased financial guarantee contracts are outside the scope of IFRS 9.

The scope exclusion does not state which Standard should be applied for purchased financial guarantee contracts. Given that financial guarantee contracts held are not in the scope of IFRS 9, they are generally recognised as an asset equal to the premium paid and the asset is amortised to profit or loss over the period in which the benefit of the guarantee is obtained. Only if the entity considers it virtually certain that its claim under the financial guarantee contract will be successful will the asset be remeasured upwards to reflect the claim in accordance with IAS 37. The contract is not accounted for in accordance with IFRS 4 because that Standard only applies to the accounting by the issuer of insurance contracts, not the holder.

2.3.5 General guarantees of subsidiary obligations

In some jurisdictions, regulatory or statutory requirements state that an ultimate parent company or subsidiary (the guarantor) must, or can elect to, make representations that it will make payments to unspecified parties outside the group if a subsidiary (the obligor) fails to make payments under its obligations to those parties. The guarantor agrees to make a payment to the creditor equal to the amount that the obligor has failed to pay. The representation is open-ended (i.e. it relates to all currently recognised obligations as well as to all obligations that the subsidiary may enter into in the future) and does not have a specified counterparty. Care needs to be taken in determining whether such representations by the guarantor are financial guarantee contracts in the guarantor's financial statements.

Before considering whether the representation meets the definition of a financial guarantee contract in accordance with Appendix A of IFRS 9, the entity must consider whether the instrument meets the definition of a financial instrument. If it does not, the instrument is not within the scope of IFRS 9 and cannot be a financial guarantee contract.

Representations to unspecified parties do not meet the definition of a financial instrument because they are not a contractual arrangement between the guarantor and a specified third party or parties. IAS 32:13 states that a contract is "an agreement between two or more parties that has clear economic consequences that the parties have little, if any, discretion to avoid, usually because the agreement is enforceable by law". A representation to meet the subsidiary's obligations if the subsidiary fails to do so is a representation of unspecified amounts held by unspecified parties. As such, the representation is not a contractual arrangement and is outside the scope of IAS 32 and IFRS 9. In addition, IAS 32:AG12 clarifies that "liabilities or assets that are not contractual (such as income taxes that are created as a result of statutory requirements imposed by governments) are not financial liabilities or financial assets". Therefore, the guarantor would apply IAS 37 and recognise a provision in accordance with the requirements of that Standard if the criteria in IAS 37:14 are met.

If the representation is a contractual arrangement between the guarantor and a specified third party over a specified amount and, therefore, it does meet the definition of a financial instrument and is within the scope of IFRS 9, the entity must consider whether the instrument meets the definition of a financial guarantee contract in Appendix A of IFRS 9. A financial guarantee contract only exists when the guarantor agrees to make specified payments to reimburse the holder for a loss it incurs because a specified debtor fails to make payment when due in accordance with the original or modified terms of a debt instrument. If the guarantor has not explicitly stated that it regards financial guarantee contracts as insurance contracts under IFRS 4, it must measure the contract as described earlier in this section.

A contractual arrangement that does meet the definition of a financial instrument but does not meet the definition of a financial guarantee contract is measured at fair value through profit or loss because the contractual arrangement meets the definition of a derivative in Appendix A of IFRS 9. Such a contractual arrangement meets the definition of a derivative because: (1) the initial investment received by the guarantor is small compared with the amount that could be required to be paid if a claim is made under the contractual arrangement, (2) the fair value of the arrangement is driven by the credit risk of the obligor, and (3) the arrangement will be settled either at a future date (if the holder make a claim against the guarantor) or at its maturity (because expiration at maturity is a form of settlement). [IFRS 9:Guidance on Implementation B.7]

2.3.6 *Parent committed to future contributions to subsidiary (separate financial statements)*

An arrangement whereby a parent agrees to make future contributions or to lend to a subsidiary is not a financial guarantee contract for the parent in its separate financial statements because the parent is not agreeing to make payments in the event that the subsidiary suffers loss on a specified debt instrument. Even if the subsidiary only makes a claim from the parent when it is in financial difficulty, the exercise of the claim is more in the nature of a claim under a loan commitment (and written and purchased loan commitments are outside the scope IFRS 9 – see **section 3.5**) or a commitment for a capital contribution which by analogy to loan commitment accounting would also be considered outside the scope of IFRS 9.

2.3.7 *Obligation to make payments when the counterparty to a derivative contract fails to make payment*

A contract that requires an entity to make payments when the counterparty to a derivative contract (e.g. a foreign currency forward contract or an interest rate swap) fails to make payment is not a financial guarantee contract. A financial guarantee contract is a contract "that requires the issuer to make specified payments to reimburse the holder for a loss it incurs because a specified debtor fails to make payment when due in accordance with the original or modified terms of a debt instrument". [IFRS 9: Appendix A] Because a derivative is not a debt instrument, the contract does not meet the definition of a financial guarantee contract.

2.3.8 *Weather derivatives*

Contracts requiring payments based on climatic, geological or other physical variables are inside the scope of IFRS 4 if they meet the definition of an insurance contract. Those based on climatic variables are sometimes referred to as 'weather derivatives'. Examples of climatic, geological and other physical variables include:

- the number of inches of rainfall or snow in a particular area;
- temperature in a particular area or for a specified period of time; and
- the severity of earthquakes.

If these contracts are not within the scope of IFRS 4, and they meet the definition of a derivative in **chapter B4**, they are within the scope of IAS 32, IFRS 7 and IFRS 9.

2.3.9 Instruments issued by Real Estate Investment Trusts (REITs)

In January 2010, the IFRIC (now the IFRS Interpretations Committee) issued an agenda decision on IFRS 4 and IAS 32, *Scope Issue for Investments in REITs*. In some jurisdictions, a Real Estate Investment Trust (REIT) is a tax or regulatory designation used for an entity investing in real estate that meets certain criteria, for example to attain preferential income tax status. The contractual terms of the ownership units of some such REITs require them to distribute 90% of their total distributable income; distribution of the remaining 10% of distributable income is at the discretion of management. The IFRIC received a request to provide guidance on whether the discretion to distribute the remaining 10 per cent of total distributable income met the definition of a discretionary participation feature as defined in IFRS 4. If the discretionary participation feature definition is met, IFRS 4 permits the ownership units to be classified as liabilities, rather than assessing the instrument for financial liability and equity components in accordance with IAS 32.

The IFRIC noted that the objective of IFRS 4 is to specify the financial reporting for insurance contracts and that the definition of discretionary participation feature in Appendix A of IFRS 4 requires, among other things, that the instrument provides the holder with guaranteed benefits and that the discretionary participation feature benefits are additional to those guaranteed benefits. Further, the IFRIC noted that there must be guaranteed benefits to the holder for the definition to be met and that such guaranteed benefits are typically those present in insurance activities. The IFRIC noted that providing guidance on this issue would be in the nature of application guidance, rather than interpretative guidance. Consequently, the IFRIC decided not to add the issue to its agenda.

2.4 Contracts for contingent consideration in a business combination

Under IFRS 3(2008), contracts for contingent consideration which meet the definition of a financial instrument are within the scope of IAS 32, IFRS 7 and IFRS 9 for both the acquirer and the seller. Paragraph BC349 in the Basis for Conclusions accompanying IFRS 3(2008) states that "the boards noted that most contingent consideration obligations are financial instruments, and many are derivative instruments".

Contracts for contingent consideration in a business combination that relate to business combinations accounted for in accordance with IFRS 3(2004) are excluded from IAS 32, IFRS 7 and IFRS 9. They are subject to the requirements of IFRS 3(2004). This exemption applies only to the acquirer, not to the seller.

Improvements to IFRSs, issued by the IASB in May 2010, amended IFRS 3(2008) to make clear that contingent consideration balances arising from business combinations for which the acquisition date preceded the adoption of IFRS 3(2008) remain subject to the requirements of IFRS 3(2004) and, therefore, are not within the scope of IAS 32, IFRS 7 or IFRS 9.

Irrespective of whether IFRS 3(2008) has been adopted, a seller's contract for contingent consideration is within the scope of IAS 32, IFRS 7 and IFRS 9. The seller will recognise a financial asset arising from the contract for contingent consideration. The measurement of this financial asset will depend on the facts and circumstances of the contractual arrangement. Because the cash flows under the contract for contingent consideration are often derived from an underlying such as the future performance of the entity that has been sold, the asset will often meet the definition of a derivative in its entirety (see **chapter B4**) and will therefore be measured at fair value through profit or loss. Alternatively, the contingent consideration asset may be a non-derivative financial asset that fails the amortised cost and fair value through other comprehensive income criteria as the cash flows are not solely payments of principal and interest on the principal outstanding (see **chapter B2**) and therefore will be measured at fair value through profit or loss.

2.5 Contracts to buy or sell non-financial items

IAS 32, IFRS 7 and IFRS 9 deal primarily with contracts that are financial items; however, they also capture some contracts to buy or sell non-financial items. Contracts to buy or sell non-financial items that can be settled net (either in cash or by exchanging financial instruments) are within the scope of IAS 32, IFRS 7 and IFRS 9 unless they were entered into, and continue to be held, for the purpose of the receipt of the non-financial item in accordance with the entity's expected purchase, sale or usage requirements. [IFRS 9:2.4]

IFRS 9 permits a contract to buy or sell a non-financial item that can be settled net in cash or another financial instrument, or by exchanging financial instruments, as if the contract was a financial instrument, to be irrevocably designated as measured at fair value through profit or loss (FVTPL) even if it was entered into for the purpose of the receipt or delivery of a non-financial item in accordance with the entity's expected purchase, sale or usage requirements. This designation is available only at inception of the contract and only if it eliminates or significantly reduces a recognition inconsistency (sometimes referred to as an 'accounting mismatch') that would otherwise arise from not recognising that contract because it is excluded from the scope of IFRS 9. [IFRS 9:2.5]

2.5.1 Net settlement

Net settlement can be in cash, another financial instrument, or by exchanging financial instruments. It can be achieved in many ways:

[IFRS 9:2.6]

(a) the contractual terms may permit either party to settle net in cash or by exchanging financial instruments;

(b) settlement may not be explicit under the terms of the contract, but the entity may have a past practice of net settling similar contracts (see **2.5.3**);

(c) for similar contracts, the entity may have a past practice of taking delivery of the underlying and selling it within a short period after delivery for the purpose of generating a profit from short-term price fluctuations or from dealer's margin; or

(d) the non-financial item that is the subject of the contract may be readily convertible to cash.

2.5.2 Non-performance penalties

The terms of a contract need to be evaluated in detail because net settlement provisions may be implicit rather than explicit.

A non-performance penalty in a purchase order, when the amount of the penalty is calculated by reference to changes in the price of the item that is the subject of the contract, is an example of an implicit net settlement provision.

Example 2.5.2A

Non-performance penalty equivalent to net settlement

Entity A enters into a forward purchase agreement with Entity B to buy 100 units of a commodity at CU1.00 per unit. Entity A defaults on the forward contract when the prevailing market price of the commodity is CU0.75 per unit. Under the terms of the contract, Entity A is required to pay Entity B a non-performance penalty of CU25, i.e. 100 x (CU1.00 - CU0.75). The non-performance penalty represents an implicit net settlement provision.

Conversely, fixed penalties or normal handling fees do not amount to net settlement.

Example 2.5.2B

Non-performance penalty not equivalent to net settlement

Entity A enters into a contract to purchase wheat which will be used in its manufacturing operations. The delivery contract requires a non-performance penalty of CU1 million if Entity A fails to take delivery of the wheat. This is a fixed penalty and does not provide for net settlement because the amount of CU1 million is not based on changes in the price of wheat (the reference asset).

2.5.3 Past practice

Contracts where there is a past practice of either net settling or purchasing and selling the underlying within a short period after delivery with a view to making a short-term profit (i.e. (b) or (c) in the list in **2.5.1**) are always within the scope of the financial instruments Standards. It cannot be argued that such contracts have been entered into and continue to be held for the purpose of the receipt or delivery of the non-financial item in accordance with the entity's expected purchase, sale or usage requirements, because the entity's activities clearly indicate that this is not the case.

Example 2.5.3A

Rolling contracts until physical delivery

Entity C is in the business of milling maize and using it in its production process. Entity C's procurement strategy for maize includes purchasing futures on a futures exchange. Due to the significant quantity of maize needed, Entity C enters into forward purchases of maize to secure the level required for the running of its business. The intention at the outset is to take physical delivery of the maize under these contracts.

In January 20X6, Entity C secures maize for its 20X6 requirements. The longest available maturity of maize futures contracts is to July 20X6. Entity C's purchasing policy requires it to secure maize at least for 9 months, i.e. as far out as September 20X6. Accordingly, Entity C enters into a larger number of July 20X6 contracts with a view to rolling some of them to September 20X6.

In April 20X6, Entity C will close out some of its July 20X6 futures at market value at the time, and take out September 20X6 futures. As a result, Entity C will take physical delivery of the maize under the September contracts only.

Entity C's practice of net settling some of its July futures contracts (i.e. its practice of net settling similar contracts) prevents it from arguing that it enters into futures contracts for the receipt of maize in accordance with its expected purchase, sale or usage requirements. Accordingly, both the July and September contracts are within the scope of IFRS 9.

Example 2.5.3B

Choice of cash or physical settlement (1)

[Extract from IFRS 9:Guidance on Implementation A.1]

Entity XYZ enters into a fixed price forward contract to purchase one million kilograms of copper in accordance with its expected usage requirements.

The contract permits XYZ to take physical delivery of the copper at the end of twelve months or to pay or receive a net settlement in cash, based on the change in fair value of copper.

If XYZ intends to settle the contract by taking delivery and has no history for similar contracts of settling net in cash or of taking delivery of the copper and selling it within a short period after delivery for the purpose of generating a profit from short-term fluctuations in price or dealer's margin, the contract is not accounted for as a derivative under IFRS 9. Instead, it is accounted for as an executory contract [*i.e. outside the scope of IFRS 9*] (unless the entity irrevocably designates it as measured at fair value through profit or loss in accordance with paragraph 2.5 of IFRS 9).

Example 2.5.3C

Choice of cash or physical settlement (2)

Entity A is a copper manufacturer. Entity A enters into forward contracts to sell its copper cathode to its customers. The forward contracts are homogenous and permit Entity A to either:

- provide physical delivery of copper at the end of the contract; or
- pay or receive a net settlement in cash based on the change in fair value of copper.

Based on its inventory levels and its production capacity, Entity A is able to meet the obligation to deliver copper if it decides to provide physical delivery of copper for all of its outstanding forward sales contracts.

The stated intention in entering into the forward sales contracts is for the purpose of delivery of copper in accordance with its sales requirements. Historically, Entity A has a practice of net settling a portion of similar forward contracts, provided that the contracts are in the money. For contracts that are out of the money, historically Entity A has opted for physical delivery.

These contracts are all homogenous and the fact that Entity A has a past practice of net settling a portion of similar forward contracts means that it cannot assert that the contracts are held for the purpose of the delivery of copper in accordance with its expected sale requirements. Accordingly, the forward contracts are in the scope of IFRS 9 and will be accounted for as derivatives at FVTPL.

In some circumstances, an entity will net settle as part of its normal operating cycle, as opposed to net settling in order to generate profits from short-term movements in prices. This is particularly common for utility entities that need to balance the demand from their customers with their supply contracts. For example, a retail gas supplier purchases gas under long-term take-or-pay contracts where if it does not take physical delivery of gas it has to pay a fixed monetary amount per unit. The buyer's intent is to use the contracted volumes it takes delivery of to serve its customers. However, the demand in certain periods (usually in the summer months) may fall below the minimum required contractual take. In this case, the buyer is forced to settle net, i.e. pay amounts without receiving gas, because the relative scarcity of natural gas storage capacity makes it difficult to store it for later use (storage of electricity is effectively impossible, so a similar situation is likely under a power contract). This 'balancing' activity is common for gas and power entities serving retail customers because customer demand forecasts cannot be precise. The practice of net settling similar contracts needs to be considered in determining whether the long-term contracts meet the definition of own-use requirements contracts for the purpose of applying the IFRS 9 scope exemption.

It is a matter of judgement what is past practice of net settlement. An entity will need to consider its historical behaviour, reasons for past net settlement, and relative frequency. In some cases, it may be argued that an occurrence of a net settlement in the past was the result of an isolated non-recurring event that could not have been reasonably anticipated.

2.5.4 Written options

In addition to the restriction on contracts when there is a past practice of settling net or a practice of taking delivery of the underlying and selling it within a short period after delivery, a written option to buy or sell a non-financial item that can be settled net contractually or when the non-financial item is readily convertible to cash is always within the scope of IFRS 9.

Example 2.5.4A

Written call option with no net settlement

Entity XYZ owns an office building. It writes Entity ABC an option, allowing Entity ABC to purchase the office building for a fixed price on a future date. The terms of the contract do not allow for it to be net settled, and the office building is not readily convertible to cash. Therefore, although Entity XYZ has written an option, the option does not fall within the scope of IFRS 9.

Example 2.5.4B

Written put with possible net settlement

[Extract from IFRS 9:Guidance on Implementation A.2]

Entity XYZ owns an office building. Entity XYZ enters into a put option with an investor that permits XYZ to put the building to the investor for CU150 million. The current value of the building is CU175 million. The option expires in five years. The option, if exercised, may be settled through physical delivery or net cash, at XYZ's option.

XYZ's accounting depends on XYZ's intention and past practice for settlement. Although the contract meets the definition of a derivative, XYZ does not account for it as a derivative [*i.e. the contract would not be in the scope IFRS 9*] if XYZ intends to settle the contract by delivering the building if Entity XYZ exercises its option and there is no past practice of settling net (IFRS 9:2.4; but also IFRS 9:2.5).

The investor, however, cannot conclude that the option was entered into to meet the investor's expected purchase, sale or usage requirements because the investor does not have the ability to require delivery (IFRS 9:2.7). In addition, the option may be settled net in cash. Therefore, the investor has to account for the contract as a derivative [*i.e. within the scope of IFRS 9*]. Regardless of past practices, the investor's intention does not affect whether settlement is by delivery or in cash. The investor has written an option, and a written option in which the holder has a choice of physical settlement or net cash settlement can never satisfy the normal delivery requirement for the exemption from IFRS 9 because the option writer does not have the ability to require delivery.

IFRS 9 does not define a written option, with only limited discussion of written options provided in the context of hedge accounting.

There are different schools of thought as to what is considered to be a written option in the context of contracts over non-financial items. Some focus on the existence of a premium received. This treatment is analogous to the approach described in the hedge accounting guidance, under which the receipt of a premium (whether up-front or over the life of the option) indicates that the party to the option is taking on a greater risk of loss and, therefore, is being compensated by a premium. However, in the context of contracts over a non-financial item, this approach has its difficulties, largely because it can be extremely difficult to ascertain whether a premium is received over the life when this 'premium' may be included in the pricing of the non-financial item that will be delivered under the contract.

An alternative approach is to consider whether the holder of the option has the ability to exercise the option in order to make a profit. This approach assesses the pay-off characteristics of the contract. In circumstances where the behaviour of the holder in exercising the option is independent of price (i.e. the holder exercises the option for reasons other than the value of the underlying being greater than the strike price under the option), it could be argued that the holder exercises the option not in order to profit, but to take delivery of the non-financial item so as to meet the expected purchase, sale or usage requirements. Examples of this are electricity supply contracts to retail customers because generally electricity is considered to be readily convertible to cash in the hands of the writer of the option. As the holder of the option, the retail customer has no ability to take delivery of the electricity, store it, and sell the electricity on at a profit (i.e. the holder is unable to realise a profit from the contract). The holder's behaviour is driven simply by the need for electricity to meet its usage requirements. From the perspective of the writer of the option (i.e. the electricity seller), it can then be argued that it has not written an option.

In March 2007, the IFRIC (now the IFRS Interpretations Committee) issued an agenda decision on IAS 39, *Written Options in Retail Energy Contracts*. The IFRIC discussed what is meant by a 'written option' within the context of IAS 39:7 (now IFRS 9:2.7). The discussion was primarily concerned with the accounting for energy supply contracts to retail customers. The agenda decision states that, following an analysis of such contracts, the IFRIC believes that in many situations these contracts do not meet the net settlement criteria laid out in IAS 39:5 & 6 (now IFRS 9:2.4 & 2.6) and, if this is the case, such contracts would not be considered to be within the scope of IAS 39 (now IFRS 9). It is not entirely clear from the IFRIC's agenda decision whether they considered these contracts as written options over an underlying that is not readily convertible into cash (and, therefore, not net settled per IAS 39:6(d) (now IFRS 9:2.6(d)), or whether they did not consider them written options at all (and, therefore, viewed an analysis of ready convertibility of the underlying into cash as irrelevant).

In March 2010, the IFRIC (now the IFRS Interpretations Committee) issued an agenda decision on IAS 39, *Unit of Account for Forward Contracts with Volumetric Optionality*. The IFRIC had received a request to provide guidance on whether a contract that:

(a) obliges an entity to deliver (sell) at a fixed price a fixed number of units of a non-financial item that is readily convertible to cash and

(b) provides the counterparty with the option to purchase, also at a fixed price, a fixed number of additional units of the same item

can be assessed as two separate contracts for the purpose of applying IAS 39:5 - 7 (now IFRS 9:2.4 - 7).

For example, an entity enters into an agreement to buy 100 units of a non-financial item that is readily convertible into cash, which includes a right to purchase a further 15 units at the same contracted price. These contracts are often referred to as having 'volumetric flexibility'.

The IFRIC recognised that diversity exists in practice and noted that the Board has accelerated its project to develop a replacement for IAS 39. At the time of its decision the IFRIC expected the IASB to issue a comprehensive replacement Standard by the end of 2010. The agenda decision stated the Board will consider the scope of IAS 39, including the guidance about contracts to buy or sell non-financial items in IAS 39:5 - 7, as part of the replacement Standard. Consequently, the IFRIC decided not to add this issue to its agenda.

Since IFRIC's discussion IFRS 9 has been completed and this particular issue was not deliberated as part of the finalisation of the new standard and consequently no further guidance has been provided in this area. Given IFRS 9 assesses financial instruments on a contract-by-contract basis, when assessing whether the terms of the arrangement meet the own use and net settlement requirements in IFRS 9:4 - 7, it is appropriate to view the unit of account as the whole contract. Using the example described above, if the seller concludes that the option on the 15 units is a written option, then the whole contract for 115 units is a written option. The contract is a single contract over 115 units and, therefore, it is not appropriate to split it into: (1) a forward over 100 units classified as a normal usage requirements contract outside the scope IFRS 9; and (2) a written option over 15 units within the scope of IFRS 9.

2.5.5 Expected purchase, sale and usage requirements

Non-optional contracts or purchased options over non-financial items where either the terms of the contract permit net settlement, or where the non-financial item that is subject to the contract is readily convertible to cash (e.g. many commodity contracts) must be assessed to see if they were entered into for the receipt or purchase of the item in accordance with the entity's expected purchase, sale or usage requirements.

Example 2.5.5

Purchase contract with possible net settlement

Entity X enters into a fixed price forward contract to purchase one million tonnes of copper. Copper is traded on the London Metals Exchange and is readily convertible to cash. The contract permits Entity X to take physical delivery of the copper at the end of 12 months or to pay or receive a net settlement in cash, based on the change in fair value of copper. Entity X does not have a practice of settling similar contracts net or taking physical delivery of copper and selling it within a short period after delivery for the purposes of generating a profit from short-term fluctuations in price.

In order for the contract to be scoped out of IFRS 9, Entity X needs to demonstrate that the contract was entered into and continues to be held for the purpose of the receipt of copper in accordance with its expected purchase or usage requirements. In addition to past practice, factors like the quantities involved, quality and grades of the commodity, and delivery locations would need to be considered.

If the reporting entity, rather than the counterparty, has the choice of net cash settlement, the reporting entity may be able to demonstrate that it does not intend to exercise its right to net cash settlement and, therefore, the existence of the net cash settlement feature does not result in the arrangement being scoped into IFRS 9. If the choice of net cash settlement is with the counterparty, it will generally not be possible for the reporting entity to demonstrate that the non-financial item will be delivered under the contract because the reporting entity does not control the cash settlement decision. If the reporting entity cannot insist that the counterparty delivers the non-financial item, the reporting entity cannot demonstrate that it intends to receive the non-financial item in accordance with its expected purchase, sale or usage requirements.

Each contract must be evaluated in its entirety. For example, an entity may have a contract for 100 units, but its expected usage requirement is only 80 units. The entity intends to net settle the part of the contract it does not need in its normal course of business. Such partial net settlement can be achieved in different ways (e.g. by entering into an offsetting contract for 20 units, or by taking delivery of all 100 units and selling 20 immediately). The entire contract falls within the scope of FRS 9 because the entire contract cannot be argued to be in accordance with the entity's expected usage requirements.

The following decision tree illustrates how to evaluate whether contracts to buy or sell non-financial items are within the scope of IAS 32, IFRS 7 and IFRS 9.

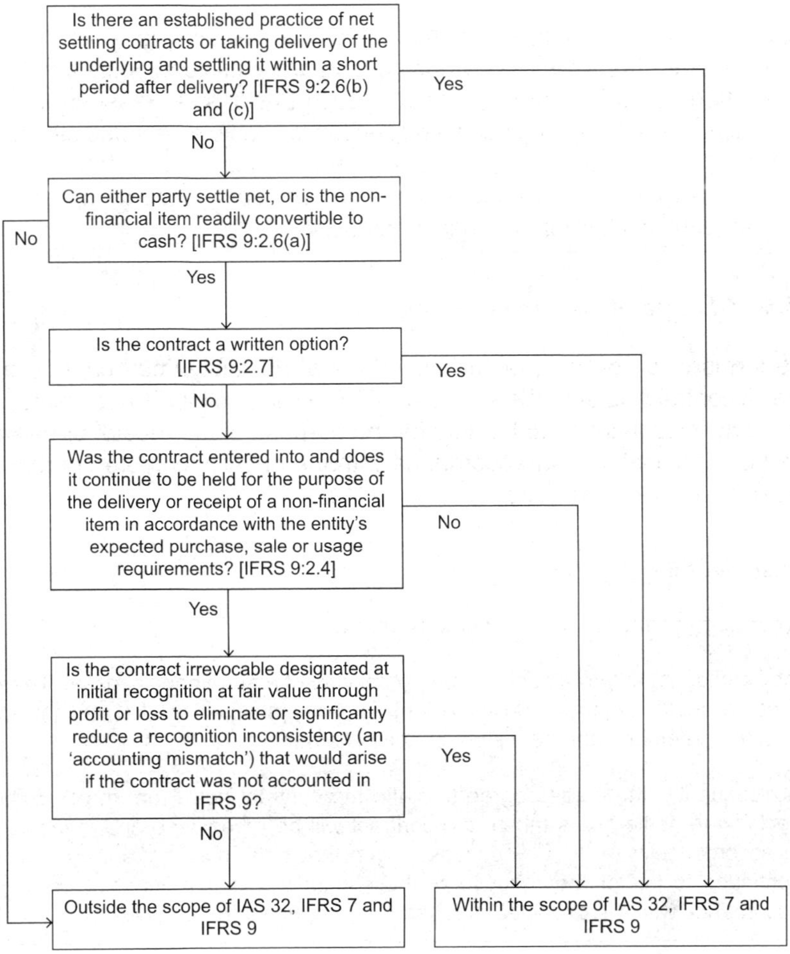

Entities may enter into multiple contracts with the same contractual terms for different reasons. Care needs to be taken in determining whether the contracts themselves should have the same accounting treatment or not. One subsidiary in a group may enter into contracts to buy non-financial items that are used in the group's production processes for the provision of finished goods and that are always physically delivered. A separate part of the group may enter into contractual arrangements with the same contractual terms but that are not always physically delivered (e.g. this separate business may cash settle the contracts or enter into offsetting contracts as part of a trading strategy). From a group perspective, it may be possible to differentiate the two portfolios of contracts in the two separate businesses and, therefore, account for them differently; such differentiation will only be appropriate if: (1) the contracts are entered into separately and not in contemplation of each other; (2) there are no transfers between the businesses within the group; (3) the businesses are managed independently of each other; and (4) the strategies of the businesses are sufficiently different that the different settlement behaviour of each business is reasonable. In practice, it is unlikely that such a distinction is possible because different parts of a group often choose to transact with each other rather than entering separately into offsetting transactions outside the group, which would result in additional transaction costs.

2.5.6 Change of settlement terms

The terms of a contract, or the intentions of an entity, may change over time. A contract outside the scope of IFRS 9 will continue to be treated as such only if it continues to be held for the purpose of the receipt or delivery of a non-financial item in accordance with the entity's expected purchase, sale or usage requirements.

Example 2.5.6

Change of terms to include net settlement

Two parties enter into a contract for the delivery of a non-financial asset. There is no net settlement provision in the contract, no established market mechanism or side agreement, and no history of net settlement.

Subsequently, the parties agree to settle the contract net. From the time the decision to settle net is taken, the contract will be recognised and measured in accordance with IFRS 9 because, from that time, the contract no longer continues to be for the purpose of the receipt of the non-financial asset in accordance with the expected purchase, sale or usage requirements.

2.6 Share-based payments

IAS 32, IFRS 7 and IFRS 9 exclude from their scope financial instruments, contracts and obligations under share-based payment arrangements to which IFRS 2 *Share-based Payment* applies, except for contracts over non-financial items that are within the scope of IFRS 9 (see **section 2.5**). However, the scope of IAS 32 makes it clear that treasury shares that are purchased, sold, issued or cancelled in connection with employee share option plans, employee share purchase plans, and all other share-based payment arrangements are in the scope of IAS 32 (see **section 5** of **chapter B3**).

2.7 Construction contract receivables

Construction contract receivables are measured and presented in accordance with IFRS 15 *Revenue from Contracts with Customers*. The financial instruments Standards do not specifically scope out these contracts and, therefore, consideration must be given as to whether such receivables are financial instruments. A right to cash or another financial asset is a critical component of the definition of a financial asset. In construction contract arrangements, the amount of work carried out by the contractor may be in excess of the amount that is billed. Where only the passage of time is required before consideration is due, IFRS 15:108 requires that a receivable is recognised in the statement of financial position. Where there is a further conditional requirement before payment is due, for example certification of work done, IFRS 15:107 requires that a contract asset is recognised in the statement of financial position. In either case the amount recognised is subject to the impairment requirements of IFRS 9. An entity must consider whether the amount recognised in accordance with IFRS 15 can be contractually billed or recovered.

Example 2.7

Gross amount due from customer for contract work

Entity A has entered into a contract with Entity B for the construction of a building. The contract is within the scope of IFRS 15, and is specifically not within the scope of IFRIC 12 *Service Concession Arrangements*. Entity A has assessed that the revenue from the contract will be recognised over time in accordance with IFRS 15. At the end of the reporting period, costs incurred plus recognised profits (less recognised losses) exceed progress billings and Entity A presents a contract asset in its statement of financial position.

Under the terms of the contract, Entity A is only able to invoice Entity B when specific work performed by Entity A has been certified as completed. These invoiced amounts are recognised in the statement of financial position as a separate financial asset because they represent a contractual right to receive cash and, therefore, meet the definition of a financial asset in IAS 32:11. Until that point the contract asset is not a financial asset because it is not "a contractual right... to receive cash or another financial asset from another entity". [IAS 32:11]

IFRS 9 and IFRS 7 do not apply to an asset that is not a financial instrument as defined in IAS 32.

3 Additional scope exclusions of IFRS 9

In addition to the scope exclusions discussed above, IFRS 9 set out a number of further exemptions as follows:

- financial instruments issued by the entity that meet the definition of equity instruments in accordance with IAS 32 (see **3.1**);
- forward contracts to buy or sell an acquiree in a business combination (see **3.2**);
- certain reimbursement rights (see **3.3**);

- rights and obligations under leases, although in certain circumstances the derecognition, impairment and embedded derivative requirements of IFRS 9 apply (see **3.4**); and
- certain loan commitments other than the impairment and derecognition requirements of IFRS 9 (see **section 3.5**).

Each of these items is considered in turn in the following sections.

3.1 Equity instruments of the entity

Financial instruments issued by an entity that meet the definition of equity instruments in IAS 32 (see **section 2** of **chapter B3**) are outside the scope of IFRS 9. This exemption includes stand-alone equity instruments (e.g. ordinary shares), as well as derivatives over own equity that exchange a fixed amount of cash or other financial asset for a fixed number of equity instruments. The exemption applies only to the issuer of the equity instrument. The holder of the instrument should apply the recognition and measurement criteria of IFRS 9.

Example 3.1

Classification of equity instruments held as an economic hedge

Entity F is a large financial institution whose shares are included in the FTSE 100 index. Entity F issues a bond whose principal amount varies with the movement in the FTSE 100 share index (an 'index tracker bond'). In order to hedge economically the equity derivative that is embedded in the bond, Entity F purchases a portfolio of the shares contained in the FTSE 100 index and wishes to classify them as held for trading. However, because IFRS 9:2.1(d) excludes instruments that meet the definition of equity in IAS 32 from the scope of the Standard, Entity F cannot recognise its own purchased shares as financial assets. IAS 32 requires that treasury shares be presented in the statement of financial position as a deduction from equity and not as financial assets, and that no gain or loss should be recognised in profit or loss on such equity instruments.

Following the amendment to IAS 32 *Puttable Financial Instruments and Obligations Arising on Liquidation*, issued in February 2008, some instruments previously classified as financial liabilities are classified as equity (see **2.1.2.1** and **2.1.3** in **chapter B3**). The IAS 32 amendment also amended IFRS 7 to exclude these instruments classified as equity from the scope of IFRS 7. [IFRS 7:3(f)]

IFRS 7 scopes out derivatives over own equity that meet the definition of equity. IFRS 7 does not appear to have a scope exception for non-derivative instruments classified as equity, such as ordinary shares. This appears to be an oversight in the drafting of the Standard because IFRS 7:BC8 states that the scope of IFRS 7 is intended to be the same as IAS 32 (which included disclosure requirements for financial instruments prior to IFRS 7 being issued) with one exception, namely "derivatives based on interests in subsidiaries, associates or joint ventures if the derivatives meet the definition of an equity instrument in IAS 32". The Basis for Conclusions justifies the exclusion of such derivatives by stating that these instruments are not remeasured and hence "do not expose the issuer to balance sheet and income statement risk" and that the disclosures about the significance of financial instruments for financial position and performance are not relevant to equity instruments. In addition, IFRS 7:BC8 states that these instruments are excluded from the scope of IFRS 7, but they are within the scope of IAS 32 for the purpose of determining whether they meet the definition of equity instruments. It appears reasonable to conclude that the scope exclusions for derivatives over own equity that meet the definition of equity also applies to non-derivatives that meet the definition of equity because the justification in the Basis for Conclusions of IFRS 7 would be equally relevant.

3.2 Forward contracts to buy or sell an acquiree in a business combination

Forward contracts between an acquirer and a selling shareholder in a business combination to buy or sell an acquiree that will result in a business combination within the scope of IFRS 3 *Business Combinations* are outside the scope of IFRS 9. The term of the forward contract should not exceed a reasonable period normally necessary to obtain any required approvals and to complete the transaction. The application of IFRS 9:2.1(f) is assessed at the time the holder enters into the derivative contract. If the contract is a forward contract, whether partly prepaid or not, which will lead to a certain business combination, the exemption applies and the forward contract is outside the scope of IFRS 9. Contracts that have settlement alternatives that may not result in all cases in the delivery of shares to the acquirer will be within the scope of IFRS 9 because the exemption within IFRS 9:2.1(f) will not apply.

The above scenarios should be distinguished from contracts between an acquirer and vendor that are options to buy or sell a business in the future. IFRS 10 requires an assessment of whether substantive potential voting rights alone, or in combination with other rights, can give an investor the current ability to direct the relevant activities of the entity and potentially control the entity. For IFRS 10, if control does exist, the parent's proportion of the acquiree in the consolidated financial statements is determined taking into account the present ownership interests which do not reflect the possible exercise or conversion of potential voting rights. In such circumstances, the ownership interest that excludes the exercise of the currently exercisable option is a subsidiary because there is control and, therefore, it will be necessary to consider whether the currently exercisable option (to acquire a non-controlling interest) meets the definition of equity in the consolidated financial statements (see **section 6** in **chapter B3**). If the option meets the definition of equity, it is outside the scope of IFRS 9. Otherwise, it will be within the scope of IFRS 9 and the exemption in IFRS 9:2.1(f) does not apply.

If the option is currently exercisable and it gives the holder the ability to control the target entity, and it is an in-substance present ownership interest, then in accordance with IFRS 10:B90 control exists and the parent's proportion of the acquiree in the consolidated financial statements is determined reflecting the in substance present ownership interest. The option is not subject to the requirements of IFRS 9 in such circumstances because it is treated as a present ownership interest rather than being a derivative to acquire such an interest in the future.

If the option is not currently exercisable and would give the holder the ability to control the target entity only when it becomes exercisable, the scope exemption within IFRS 9:2(f) also does not apply. The option will not always result in a business combination to buy or sell an acquiree at a future date and therefore is in the scope of IFRS 9.

The IFRS 9:2.1(f) exemption applies equally to the acquirer and the vendor. Therefore, if the acquirer applies the exemption on the basis that the contract will result in a future business combination, the vendor equally applies the exemption and scopes out its contract to sell its subsidiary to the acquirer in its consolidated financial statements. Irrespective of IFRS 9:2.1(f), the contract may be outside the scope of IFRS 9 for the vendor because the contract may meet the definition of equity when the contract is a forward sale of shares in a subsidiary for a fixed amount of functional currency.

In 2007, the IFRIC (now the IFRS Interpretations Committee) was asked to interpret whether the IAS 39:2(g) (now IFRS 9:2.1(f)) scope exemption applies only to binding contracts to acquire shares that constitute a controlling interest in another entity within the period necessary to complete a business combination, or if it applies more widely, and also whether it applies to similar transactions, such as those to acquire an interest in an associate. In January 2008, the IFRIC acknowledged that the wording in IAS 39:2(g) (now IFRS 9:2.1(f)) was ambiguous and could lead to diversity in practice. For this reason, the IFRIC referred the issue to the IASB. In April 2009, the IASB issued *Improvements to IFRSs*, which amended IAS 39:2(g) (now IFRS 9:2.1(f)). As amended, IAS 39:2(g) (now IFRS 9:2.1(f)) states that the scope exception applies only to forward contracts between an acquirer and a selling shareholder to buy or sell an acquiree that will result in a business combination at a future acquisition date. The term of the forward contract should not exceed a reasonable period normally necessary to obtain any required approvals and to complete the transaction.

Following the amendment made by *Improvements to IFRSs*, IAS 39:BC24D makes clear that the exception in IAS 39:2(g) (now IFRS 9:2.1(f)) should not be applied by analogy to investments in associates and similar transactions because an investment in an associate does not represent an acquisition of the constituent assets of the investee. The purpose of IAS 39:2(g) (now IFRS 9:2.1(f)) is to exempt from the provisions of IAS 39 and IFRS 9 contracts for business combinations that are firmly committed to be completed. Once the business combination is consummated, the entity follows the requirements of IFRS 3. IAS 39:2(g) (now IFRS 9:2.1(f)) applies only when completion of the business combination is not dependent on further actions of either party (and only the passage of a normal period of time is required). This contrasts with option contracts, which allow one party to control the occurrence or non-occurrence of future events depending on whether the option is exercised.

3.3 Certain reimbursement rights

Rights to payments to reimburse the entity for expenditure it is required to make to settle a liability that it recognises as a provision in accordance with IAS 37 *Provisions, Contingent Liabilities and Contingent Assets*, or for which, in an earlier period, it recognised a provision in accordance with IAS 37, are outside the scope of IFRS 9. [IFRS 9:2.1(i)] Such rights are within the scope of IAS 37 and are recognised as a separate asset when, and only when, it is virtually certain that the reimbursement will be received if and when the entity settles the liability. [IAS 37:53]

3.4 Rights and obligations under lease contracts

Rights and obligations under lease contracts may meet the definition of a financial instrument. In a finance lease, a lease receivable recognised by the lessor represents the lessor's right to receive a stream of cash flows. This receivable is substantially the same as blended payments of principal and interest under a loan agreement. Accordingly, a finance lease is a contract that gives rise to a financial asset from the lessor's perspective and also gives rise to a financial liability from the lessee's perspective. Operating leases, on the other hand, are generally regarded as uncompleted contracts whereby lessors provide the use of assets in exchange for a fee for their service. Accordingly, an operating lease is not regarded as a financial instrument (except as regards individual payments currently due and payable). This continues to be the case even if the operating lease is regarded as an onerous contract and a provision has been recognised in accordance with IAS 37. IAS 17 *Leases* sets out the accounting framework for leases and, consequently, leases are, for the most part, outside of the scope of all three financial instruments Standards. However:

- lease receivables recognised by a lessor are subject to the derecognition requirements and impairment requirements of IFRS 9 (see **section 3** of **chapter B8** and **chapter B6** respectively);
- finance lease payables recognised by a lessee are subject to the derecognition requirements of IFRS 9 (see **section 3** of **chapter B8**);
- derivatives embedded in lease contracts are subject to the embedded derivative requirements of IFRS 9 (see **section 9** of **chapter B5**); and
- finance leases are subject to the disclosure and presentation requirements of IFRS 7 and IAS 32.

3.5 Loan commitments

Loan commitments are potentially in the scope of IFRS 9. In some cases all of the Standard applies, for example, when the loan commitment is measured at fair value through profit or loss, and in other cases only part of the Standard applies, such as the impairment and derecognition requirements only. For all loan commitments, the derecognition and impairment requirements contained in IFRS 9 apply. [IFRS 9:2.1(g)]

Loan commitments that cannot be settled net in cash or another financial instrument are outside the scope of IFRS 9, unless the entity designates them as financial liabilities at fair value through profit or loss. If an entity has a past practice of selling the asset resulting from a loan commitment shortly after its origination, it should apply IFRS 9 to all loan commitments in the same class. [IFRS 9:2.3(a)]

Loan commitments that can be settled net in cash or another financial instrument are derivatives that are classified as at fair value through profit or loss within the scope of IFRS 9. Instalment payments do not constitute net settlement. Thus, for example, a mortgage construction loan that is paid out in instalments in line with the progress of the construction is not within the scope of IFRS 9. [IFRS 9:2(b)]

A financial institution may write a loan commitment to a large corporate borrower as a lead lender with the expressed intention of selling part of the loan to other financial institutions immediately when lent. The intention to sell part of the loan is part of the financial institution's predetermined credit risk management. At the inception of the loan commitment, the financial institution cannot assert that it does not have a past practice of selling the asset resulting from a loan commitment shortly after its origination and, therefore, it cannot consider the loan commitment wholly outside the scope of IFRS 9. The financial institution may be able to demonstrate that, consistent with its predetermined credit risk management, only part of the loan that may be originated from the loan commitment is intended to be sold and, if so, that only that proportion of the loan commitment is in the scope of IFRS 9 and is measured at fair value through profit or loss. If the loan is originated, the part of the loan commitment that is measured at fair value through profit or loss will be derecognised and will be incorporated into the initial carrying amount of the resulting loan.

If an entity commits to providing a loan at a below-market interest rate, it should initially recognise the written commitment at fair value. Subsequently, the commitment is measured at the higher of:

[IFRS 9:4.2.1(d)]

(i) the amount of the loss allowance determined under section 5.5 of IFRS 9; and

(ii) the amount initially recognised less, when appropriate, the amount initially recognised less, when appropriate, the cumulative amount of income recognised in accordance with the principles of IFRS 15 *Revenue from Contracts with Customers*.

Below is a summary of the accounting for loan commitments:

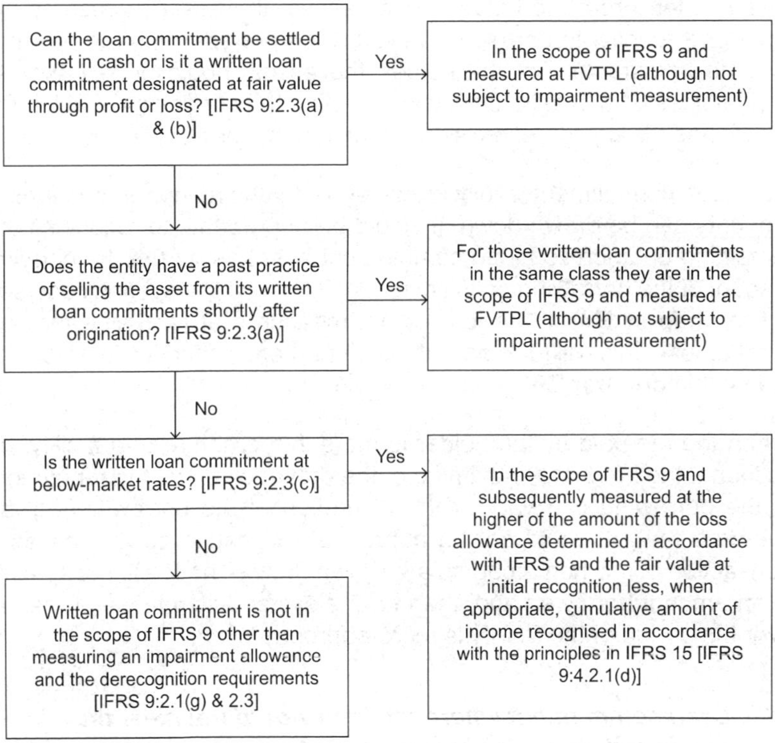

Loan commitments can either be optional (i.e. provide a borrower with the right to borrow in the future from a specified lender) or non-optional (i.e. the borrower must borrow from the specified lender). In all cases, the lender will lend funds to the borrower either when the borrower exercises its right to borrow or, in the case of non-optional loan commitments, in accordance with the specified conditions in the contract. If a contract requires or gives an option for an entity to *acquire* a debt instrument, as opposed to lending funds to the borrower under the commitment, this arrangement is not a loan commitment because a lending will not take place. The arrangement is a derivative financial instrument which will be measured at fair value through profit or loss except if it meets the regular way exemption as described in **2.2** in **chapter B8**.

If a loan commitment is not within the scope of IFRS 9, the writer of the loan commitments accounts for it in accordance with IFRS 15.

3.5.1 Measurement of loan commitment outside the scope of IFRS 9 (holder)

IFRSs do not provide specific guidance on the measurement of a loan commitment that is outside the scope of IFRS 9 from the perspective of the holder. When the holder of the loan commitment pays the writer of the loan commitment compensation for entering into the loan commitment, the fair value of the compensation should be recognised as an asset. From the holder's perspective, the asset represents the right for the entity to borrow in the future on pre-specified terms which may be favourable. For the holder, the asset should be released to profit or loss on a systematic basis reflecting the periods over which the holder has the right to exercise the loan commitment.

If the loan commitment is fully drawn down by the holder and no further amounts can be drawn down, it would be appropriate to recognise the remaining unamortised loan commitment asset as part of the carrying amount of the borrowing on initial recognition as a transaction cost (see **2.1** in **chapter B6**). If the loan is not measured at fair value through profit or loss, this will form part of the instrument's effective interest rate (see **4.1** in **chapter B6**).

When the fee paid by the holder is more in the nature of a facility fee such that the amounts and timing of the draw-down and the repayment of the borrowing can vary at the discretion of the borrower (e.g. an overdraft fee), it would not be appropriate to capitalise the fee as a transaction cost when amounts are drawn down. The fee is not specific to an amount borrowed and, therefore, a systematic release of the fee over the period of the facility is more appropriate.

3.5.2 Loan commitment where the loan would not meet the amortised cost or FVTOCI criteria for the lender or would include a non-closely related embedded derivative for the borrower

When the loan to be originated under a loan commitment will be in the scope of IFRS 9 but for the lender, the contractual terms of the loan will not give rise solely to payments of principal and interest on the principal amount outstanding, or for the borrower, IFRS 9 would require separation of a non-closely related embedded derivative, the question arises as to whether it is still permissible for the loan commitment to be scoped out of IFRS 9 for the writer and holder of the loan commitment.

Once the loan is originated, the loan will be measured in its entirety at fair value through profit or loss for the lender or wholly or partly (in the case of separated embedded derivatives) measured at fair value for the borrower. It could be argued that applying the scope exemption in such circumstances creates a measurement inconsistency between the measurement of the loan commitment (outside the scope of IFRS 9 and not measured at fair value) and the subsequent measurement of the loan (within the scope of IFRS 9 and either wholly at fair value through profit or loss if so designated or in part measured at fair value in the case of a separately recognised embedded derivative for the borrower, or wholly measured at fair value through profit or loss within the scope of IFRS 9 for the lender). However, it should be noted that IFRS 9 already allows such a measurement inconsistency when a loan commitment that will result in a borrowing not containing any embedded derivatives is outside the scope of IFRS 9 (and not measured at fair value) and the borrowing arising from under the commitment is designated at fair value through profit or loss if the qualifying conditions are met. Similarly, for the lender, if a loan's contractual terms give rise solely to payments of principal and interest on the principal amount outstanding, it may be measured at amortised cost or fair value through other comprehensive income (FVTOCI), or an entity may choose to designate the loan on origination at fair value through profit or loss rather than measure it at amortised cost or FVTOCI if measurement at amortised cost or FVTOCI would result in an accounting mismatch. It seems, therefore, appropriate that the scope exemption for loan commitments that will result in borrowings with separately accounted embedded derivatives or lending with contractual terms that do not give rise solely to payments of principal and interest on the principal amount outstanding should still apply if the relevant conditions are met (i.e. the loan commitment cannot be settled net in cash, the entity has not designated it as at fair value through profit or loss, and the entity does not have a past practice of selling the assets resulting from loan commitments shortly after origination).

To illustrate, Entity X may enter into a firm commitment to lend to Entity Y. The loan to be originated under the commitment will be a loan that the lender can convert into a fixed number of equity shares of the borrower. Once originated, the lender will be required to measure the entire instrument at fair value through profit or loss and the analysis in the paragraph above would apply. For Entity X the loan commitment would be outside the scope of IFRS 9.

From Entity Y's perspective, the loan commitment is a right jointly to borrow cash and issue a derivative over its own equity. The loan commitment is partly a derivative over debt and partly a derivative over a derivative over own equity. The definition of a financial liability (see **section 2** in **chapter B3**) makes it clear that a derivative over a derivative over own equity would itself not meet the definition of equity and, therefore, it could be argued that the loan commitment can be considered to be within the scope of IFRS 9. However, economically speaking all loan commitments are derivatives yet many are specifically excluded from the scope of IFRS 9. Consequently, it is reasonable to consider such a loan commitment for Entity Y as also being outside the scope of IFRS 9.

B2 Financial assets

Contents

1 Introduction

IFRS 9 *Financial Instruments* was published as a completed Standard in July 2014. Prior to that IFRS 9 was issued in stages, firstly in November 2009 and subsequently amended in October 2010 and November 2013.

IFRS 9(2009) introduced new requirements for the classification and measurement of financial assets which were different to those in IAS 39 *Financial Instruments: Recognition and Measurement*. These new classification and measurement requirements for financial assets were subsequently amended in the final version of IFRS 9 issued in July 2014.

The version of IFRS 9 issued in July 2014 superseded the earlier versions of IFRS 9 issued in 2009, 2010 and 2013. However, if the entity's date of initial application is before 1 February 2015 an entity may choose to apply those earlier versions of IFRS 9 instead of the finalised and completed version issued in July 2014. For the purpose of this guide it is assumed the entity is applying IFRS 9(2014) in full.

One of the objectives of IFRS 9 is to establish principles for financial reporting of financial assets that will present relevant and useful information to users of financial statements for their assessment of the amounts, timing and uncertainty of the entity's future cash flows.

Under IFRS 9, financial assets are classified as being subsequently measured at either amortised cost or fair value. Gains and losses on assets measured at fair value are recognised either in profit or loss ('fair value through profit or loss') or in other comprehensive income ('fair value through other comprehensive income'). The classification of financial assets is based on the business model within which they are held and their contractual cash flow characteristics.

2 Interaction with IAS 32, IFRS 7 and IFRS 13

IAS 32 *Financial Instruments: Presentation* also applies to entities that apply IFRS 9. Specifically, the IAS 32 definition of a financial asset (see **section 3**) and the IAS 32 requirements regarding the offset of financial assets and financial liabilities (see **section 6** in **chapter B11**) are applicable. IAS 32 also applies to determine whether a derivative over own equity is an equity instrument or an asset or liability in the scope of IFRS 9 (e.g. a purchased or written call option over own shares, see **section 6** in **chapter B3**).

IFRS 9 addresses the recognition and derecognition of financial instruments, their classification and measurement, including impairment, as well as hedge accounting. In addition, the disclosure requirements of IFRS 7 *Financial Instruments: Disclosures*, after consequential amendments arising from IFRS 9, are applicable (see **chapter B11**). Further, IFRS 13 *Fair Value Measurement* defines fair value, provides guidance on fair value measurement and requires fair value disclosures (see **chapters B7** and **B11**).

3 Definition of a financial asset

A financial asset is "any asset that is:

[IAS 32:11]

(a) cash;

(b) an equity instrument of another entity;

(c) a contractual right:

  (i) to receive cash or another financial asset from another entity; or

  (ii) to exchange financial assets or financial liabilities with another entity under conditions that are potentially favourable to the entity; or

(d) a contract that will or may be settled in the entity's own equity instruments and is:

  (i) a non-derivative for which the entity is or may be obliged to receive a variable number of the entity's own equity instruments; or

  (ii) a derivative that will or may be settled other than by the exchange of a fixed amount of cash or another financial asset for a fixed number of the entity's own equity instruments. For this purpose the entity's own equity instruments do not include puttable financial instruments classified as equity instruments in accordance with IAS 32:16A and 16B, instruments that impose on the entity an obligation to deliver to another party a pro rata share of the net assets of the entity only on liquidation and are classified as equity instruments in accordance with IAS 32:16C and 16D, or instruments that are contracts for the future receipt or delivery of the entity's own equity instruments".

A deposit of cash with a bank or similar institution is a financial asset because it represents the contractual right of the depositor to obtain cash from the institution or to draw a cheque or similar instrument against the balance in favour of a creditor in payment of a financial liability.

Common examples of financial assets that represent a contractual right to receive cash in the future are trade accounts receivable, notes and loans receivable, and investments in debt securities. An example of a financial asset that represents a contractual right to receive a financial asset other than cash is a note payable in treasury bonds which gives the holder the contractual right to receive treasury bonds.

Gold bullion is not a financial instrument, it is a commodity. Although bullion is highly liquid, there is no contractual right to receive cash or another financial asset inherent in the bullion. [IFRS 9:IG.B.1] When the anticipated future economic benefit is the receipt of goods or services (e.g. in the case of prepaid expenses), the asset is not a financial asset. Also, assets that represent rights to receive cash that are not contractual (e.g. tax receivables) are not financial assets because they arise from statutory requirements. [IAS 32:AG12]

The definition of a financial asset as set out above (in combination with the scope requirements of IFRS 9 detailed in **chapter B1**) results in the following contractual arrangements being financial assets within the scope of IFRS 9:

- investments in equity instruments;
- investments in debt instruments;
- trade receivables;
- cash and cash equivalents;
- derivative financial assets;
- interests in subsidiaries, associates and joint ventures accounted for in accordance with IFRS 9; and
- deferred or contingent consideration receivable in a business combination (seller).

The definition of a financial asset also includes some derivative and non-derivative contracts indexed to, or settled in, an issuer's equity instruments, as illustrated in **example 3**.

Example 3

Derivative financial asset

On 1 February 20X0, Entity E enters into a contract with Entity F under which Entity E will receive the fair value of 1,000 of its own ordinary shares in exchange for a payment of CU104,000 in cash (i.e. CU104 per share) on 31 January 20X1. Under the terms of the contract, settlement will be net in cash. The market price per share of Entity E's ordinary shares on 1 February 20X0 is CU100.

The fair value at initial recognition of the forward contract on 1 February 20X0 is zero. On 31 December 20X0, Entity E's share price has increased and, as a result, the fair value of the forward contract has increased to CU6,300. Entity E revalues the derivative asset to CU6,300 at 31 December 20X0.

For further detail on the classification of contracts indexed to or settled in an entity's own equity instruments as derivative assets or liabilities, gross liabilities or equity, by the issuer, see **section 6** in **chapter B3**.

4 Initial recognition and initial measurement of financial assets

4.1 Initial recognition

An entity should only recognise a financial asset in its statement of financial position when it becomes party to the contractual provisions of the instrument. [IFRS 9:3.1.1] For a more detailed discussion of IFRS 9's requirements regarding the initial recognition of financial assets, see **section 2** of **chapter B8**.

Under IFRS 9:3.1.2, a 'regular way' purchase or sale of financial assets can be recognised (and derecognised) using either trade date or settlement date accounting (see **2.2** of **chapter B8**).

4.2 Initial measurement

IFRS 9 requires that a financial asset (except for certain trade receivables) should be measured at initial recognition at its fair value plus, for financial assets not subsequently measured 'at fair value through profit or loss' (see **section 5.5**), transaction costs that are directly attributable to the acquisition of the financial asset (see **section 2** of **chapter B6**). Trade receivables that do not have a significant financing component (determined in accordance with IFRS 15 *Revenue from Contracts with Customers*) are not initially measured at fair value, rather they are initially measured at their transaction price. [IFRS 9:5.1.1 & 5.1.3]

Example 4.2

Transaction costs

[IFRS 9:B5.2.2]

An entity acquires an asset for CU100 plus a purchase commission of CU2 that is measured at fair value through other comprehensive income (see **section 5.3**). Initially, the entity recognises the asset at CU102. The reporting period ends one day later, when the quoted market price of the asset is CU100. If the asset were sold, a commission of CU3 would be paid. On that date, the entity measures the asset at CU100 (without regard to the possible commission on sale) and recognises a loss of CU2 in other comprehensive income. If the financial asset is a debt instrument measured at fair value through other comprehensive income the transaction costs are amortised to profit or loss using the effective interest method.

IFRS 9's requirements regarding initial measurement are described in more detail in **chapters B6** and **B7**; the discussion includes the definition of fair value (see **section 3** of **chapter B7**), the appropriate accounting for transaction costs on initial recognition (see **2.1** of **chapter B6**) and guidance regarding the recognition of 'day 1 P&L' (see **7.1** of **chapter B7**).

5 Classification and measurement of financial assets

Subsequent to initial recognition, IFRS 9 requires all assets within its scope to be measured at:

[IFRS 9:5.2.1]

- amortised cost (see **section 5.2**);
- fair value through other comprehensive income (FVTOCI) (see **section 5.3**); or
- fair value through profit or loss (FVTPL) (see **section 5.5**).

Except for financial assets that are designated at initial recognition as at FVTPL, a financial asset is classified on the basis of both:

[IFRS 9:4.1.2 and 4.1.2A]

- the entity's business model for managing the financial assets (see **5.1**); and
- the contractual cash flow characteristics of the financial asset (see **section 5.4**).

In addition, the impairment requirements (see **chapter B6**) apply to financial assets measured at amortised cost and those financial instruments that are debt instruments measured at FVTOCI. Further, the hedge accounting requirements also apply to a financial asset that is designated as a hedged item or hedging instrument (see **chapter B9**).

IFRS 9 precludes the separation of any embedded derivatives from a hybrid contract when the host contract is a financial asset within its scope (see **section 2** of **chapter B5**). Instead, the entire hybrid financial asset is classified into one of the three categories listed above.

The flow chart below summarises the classification model at initial recognition only.

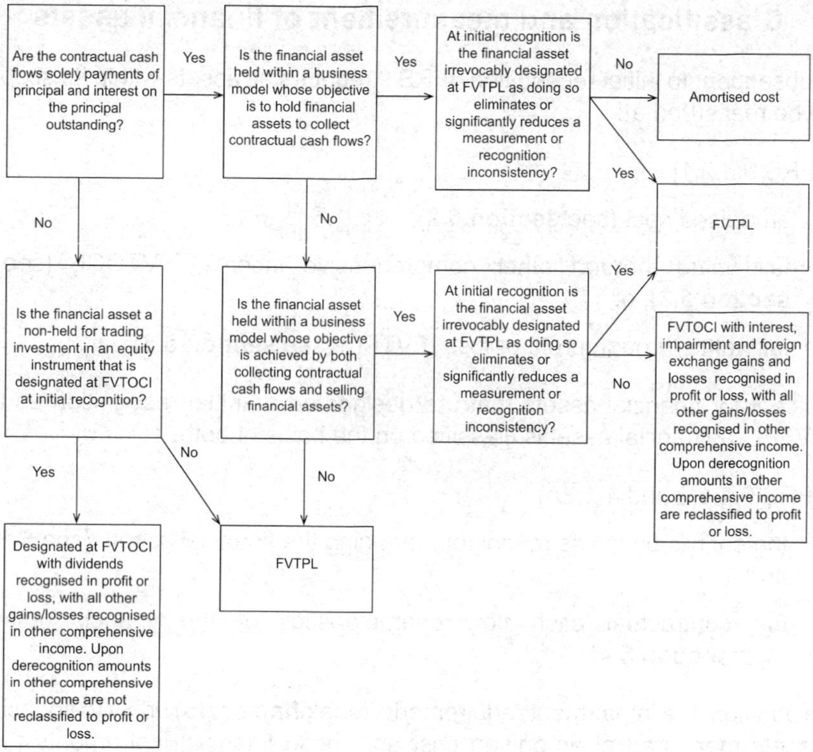

Subject to meeting certain criteria after initial recognition, IFRS 9 requires reclassification between FVTPL, FVTOCI and amortised cost, and vice versa (see **section 7**). Reclassifications are expected to be very infrequent.

The classification categories that are possible for different financial assets are summarised below:

	Type of financial asset		
Measurement category	Derivative instrument*	Investment in an equity instrument **	Investment in a debt instrument ***
Amortised cost			■
FVTOCI			
– classified			■
– elected at initial recognition		■	
FVTPL			
– classified	■	■	■
– elected at initial recognition			■

* a derivative instrument is an asset that meets the definition of a derivative in Appendix A of IFRS 9 (see **section 2** in **chapter B4**).

** an investment in an equity instrument is a non-derivative financial asset that meets the definition of equity in IAS 32 from the perspective of the issuer. This does not include puttable instruments that contain a financial obligation but that are presented as equity by the issuer (see **5.3.2**).

*** other financial assets in the scope of IFRS 9 are investments in debt instruments (e.g. loans, receivables, debt securities).

5.1 Business model assessment

An assessment of business models for managing financial assets is fundamental to the classification of financial assets.

For a financial asset to be measured at amortised cost it must be held within a business model whose objective is to hold financial assets in order to collect contractual cash flows (see **5.2.1**). [IFRS 9:4.1.2(a)]

For a financial asset that is a debt instrument to be measured at FVTOCI it must be held within a business model whose objective is achieved by both collecting contractual cash flows and selling financial assets (see **5.3.1**). [IFRS 9:4.1.2A(a)]

Financial assets held in a business model that do not meet one of the two criteria described above are required to be measured at FVTPL, unless the instrument is an investment in an equity instrument that meets the criteria for designating at FVTOCI, see **5.3.2**.

An entity's business model is determined at a level that reflects how groups of financial assets are managed together to achieve a particular business objective. The entity's business model does not depend on management's intentions for an individual instrument. Accordingly, this condition is not an instrument-by-instrument approach to classification and should be determined at a higher level of aggregation. However, a single entity may have more than one business model for managing its financial instruments. Therefore, classification need not be determined at the reporting entity level. For example, an entity may hold a portfolio of investments that it manages in order to collect contractual cash flows and another portfolio of investments that it manages in order to sell to realise fair value changes. Similarly, in some circumstances, it may be appropriate to separate a portfolio of financial assets into subportfolios in order to reflect the level at which an entity manages those financial assets. For example, that may be the case if an entity originates or purchases a portfolio of mortgage loans and manages some of the loans with an objective of collecting contractual cash flows and manages the other loans with an objective of selling them. [IFRS 9:B4.1.2]

Example 5.1A

More than one business model

Entity A has a retail banking business whose objective is to collect the contractual cash flows of its loan assets. Entity A also has an investment banking business whose objective is to realise fair value changes through the sale of loan assets before their maturity.

Entity A's financial instruments held in the retail banking business qualify for amortised cost measurement even if similar financial instruments in the investment banking business do not.

An entity's business model refers to how an entity manages its financial assets in order to generate cash flows. That is, the entity's business model determines whether cash flows will result from collecting contractual cash flows, selling financial assets or both. Consequently, this assessment is not performed on the basis of scenarios that the entity does not reasonably expect to occur, such as so-called 'worst case' or 'stress case' scenarios. For example, if an entity expects that it will sell a particular portfolio of financial assets only in a stress case scenario, that scenario would not affect the entity's assessment of the business model for those assets if the entity reasonably expects that such a scenario will not occur. If cash flows are realised in a way that is different from the entity's expectations at the date that the entity assessed the business model (e.g. if the entity sells more or fewer financial assets than it expected when it classified the assets), that does not give rise to a prior period error in the entity's financial statements (see IAS 8) nor does it change the classification of the remaining financial assets held in that business model (i.e. those assets that the entity recognised in prior periods and still holds) as long as the entity considered all relevant information that was available at the time that it made the business model assessment. However, when an entity assesses the business model for newly originated or newly purchased financial assets, it must consider information about how cash flows were realised in the past, along with all other relevant information. [IFRS 9:B4.1.2A]

Example 5.1B

Assessment of business model at initial recognition

Entity B has a portfolio of loans that are held within a business whose objective is to hold to collect contractual cash flows. Entity B has disposed of some of its loans over the period but continues to regard the business that holds the remaining loans as having an objective to hold to collect contractual cash flows.

Entity B purchases a new portfolio of loans. Entity B must consider the objective of the business that acquired the loans and in doing so it considers whether the disposals of previously held loans in the period indicate a different business objective for holding financial assets.

An entity's business model for managing financial assets is a matter of fact and not merely an assertion. It is typically observable through the activities that the entity undertakes to achieve the objective of the business model. An entity will need to use judgement when it assesses its business model for managing financial assets and that assessment is not determined by a single factor or activity. Instead, the entity must consider all relevant evidence that is available at the date of the assessment. Such relevant evidence includes, but is not limited to:

[IFRS 9:B4.1.2B]

(a) how the performance of the business model and the financial assets held within that business model are evaluated and reported to the entity's key management personnel;

(b) the risks that affect the performance of the business model (and the financial assets held within that business model) and, in particular, the way in which those risks are managed; and

(c) how managers of the business are compensated (e.g. whether the compensation is based on the fair value of the assets managed or on the contractual cash flows collected).

An entity will need to reassess its business model each reporting period to determine whether the business model has changed since the preceding period. Increasing levels of sales of financial assets held within a business that previously met the amortised cost or FVTOCI criteria may be evidence that the business model has changed and, therefore, warrant reclassification of financial assets (see **section 7**).

When sales of financial assets measured at amortised cost become more frequent, but the business model is itself unchanged, the remaining assets in the business will continue to be measured at amortised cost. However, this would not be the case if the business model assessment underlying the amortised cost classification in the previous financial statements was incorrect based on the information available as of the date of the original assessment as this would be an error; in such circumstances, IAS 8 *Accounting Policies, Changes in Accounting Estimates and Errors* would require the financial assets to be restated to be as at FVTPL or FVTOCI.

As described above, an entity may have multiple business models. At initial recognition, care should be taken in determining whether newly recognised financial assets are part of an existing business model or whether they reflect the commencement of a new business model; if they are considered to reflect the commencement of a new business model, they will be assessed separately for the purpose of the amortised cost criteria.

There may be a difference between the entity's management of the assets within a business unit versus the strategic decisions management make in respect of the business unit itself. An example would be the decision to divest a complete business unit that includes financial assets along with other recognised and unrecognised assets and liabilities. The business model assessment may be to hold financial assets in order to collect contractual cash flows even though management's intent is to dispose of the business unit.

Example 5.1C

Intended disposal of a business unit

Bank A is a diversified global financial group offering multiple services (e.g. investment banking, retail banking, private equity investments, insurance). Within its retail banking service, Bank A operates a business unit that provides loans for cars. The objective of the car loan business unit, as determined by Bank A's key management personnel, is to hold the loans in order to collect the contractual cash flows. Consequently, the 'business model test' under IFRS 9:4.1.2(a) is met. Assume also that the 'contractual cash flows characteristics' condition in IFRS 9:4.1.2(b) is satisfied in respect of the terms of the car loans (see **section 5.4**). Accordingly, the car loans are measured at amortised cost.

Following a significant market event, the Board of Directors of Bank A announces its intention to divest certain of its business units to reduce its exposures to certain businesses. This will involve multiple business units being sold off over a number of years. One of the business units to be disposed of is the car loan business unit.

In the period prior to its disposal, the car loan business unit continues to operate as before and it continues to originate new business (i.e. to make new car loans). It is intended that the business unit will be sold in its entirety as a going concern (i.e. including financial assets as well as intangible assets and infrastructure).

The intention and/or decision to sell a business unit does not in itself represent a change in business model. In the circumstances under consideration, the activities of the business unit following the decision to sell are exactly the same as previously. In the period prior to its disposal, the business unit continues to originate new car loans and to service the loans with the aim of collecting the cash flows from the loans (as opposed to realising a profit through selling or trading the financial assets). IFRS 9 refers to "managing the financial assets" and it is at the business unit level that the assets continue to be managed to collect the contractual cash flows. When it is eventually sold, the car loan business will be sold as an operating business unit rather than as a portfolio of financial assets.

This can be contrasted to the example in IFRS 9:B4.4.1(b) in which a financial services firm decides to shut down its mortgage business, as a result of which it will no longer accept new business and is actively marketing the mortgage loan portfolio for sale. In that case, the business unit ceases operating and the financial assets in the business are intended to be sold and not held to collect contractual cash flows. IFRS 9 states that this is an example of circumstances in which the assets no longer meet the amortised cost criteria and therefore should be reclassified to FVTPL.

This conclusion is not affected by whether the business unit meets the definition of a disposal group held for sale under IFRS 5 *Non-current Assets Held for Sale and Discontinued Operations*.

Business models are likely to remain unchanged for prolonged periods. When an entity's business model does change, IFRS 9 requires financial assets to be reclassified (see **section 7**) and also requires extensive disclosures (see **4.1.4** in **chapter B11**).

5.2 Amortised cost

Except for financial assets that are designated at initial recognition as at FVTPL (see **5.5.3**) a financial asset is measured at amortised cost only if both of the following conditions are met:

[IFRS 9:4.1.2]

(a) the financial asset is held within a business model whose objective is to hold financial assets in order to collect contractual cash flows (the *business model test*, see **5.1**) and

(b) the contractual terms of the financial asset give rise on specified dates to cash flows that are solely payments of principal and interest on the principal amount outstanding (the *contractual cash flows characteristics test*, see **section 5.4**).

If a financial asset satisfies both of these conditions, it is required to be measured at amortised cost unless it is designated as at FVTPL on initial recognition (see **5.5.3**).

Financial assets that do not meet the condition in IFRS 9:4.1.2(b) are required to be subsequently measured at FVTPL except for investments in equity instruments not held for trading that are elected at initial recognition to be measured at FVTOCI (see **5.3.2**). A financial asset that does meet the condition in IFRS 9:4.1.2(b) but does not meet the condition in in IFRS 9:4.1.2(a) may meet the criteria to be measured at FVTOCI (see **5.3.1**).

Because both conditions (the business model test and the contractual cash flows characteristics test) must be met for amortised cost measurement, the order in which the tests are performed is irrelevant. However, in practice it is likely that the business model test will be considered first because it is performed at a higher level of aggregation and not for each financial asset individually.

5.2.1 Business model assessment for amortised cost measurement

For amortised cost measurement financial assets must be held within a business model whose objective is to hold financial assets in order to collect the contractual cash flows. [IFRS 9:4.1.2(a)]

Financial assets that are held within a business model whose objective is to hold assets in order to collect contractual cash flows are managed to realise cash flows by collecting contractual payments over the life of the instrument. That is, the entity manages the assets held within the portfolio to collect those particular contractual cash flows (instead of managing the overall return on the portfolio by both holding and selling assets). [IFRS 9:B4.1.2C]

Example 5.2.1A

Trade receivables

Entity B sells goods to customers on credit. Entity B typically offers customers up to 60 days following the delivery of goods to make payment in full. Entity B collects the cash in accordance with the contractual cash flows of the trade receivables and has no intention to dispose of the receivables.

Entity B's objective is to collect the contractual cash flows from the trade receivables and, therefore, the trade receivables meet the business model test for the purpose of classifying the financial assets at amortised cost.

In determining whether cash flows are going to be realised by collecting the financial assets' contractual cash flows, it is necessary to consider the frequency, value and timing of sales in prior periods, the reasons for those sales and expectations about future sales activity. However sales in themselves do not determine the business model and therefore cannot be considered in isolation. Instead, information about past sales and expectations about future sales provide evidence related to how the entity's stated objective for managing the financial assets is achieved and, specifically, how cash flows are realised. An entity must consider information about past sales within the context of the reasons for those sales and the conditions that existed at that time as compared to current conditions. [IFRS 9:B4.1.2C]

Although the objective of an entity's business model may be to hold financial assets in order to collect contractual cash flows, the entity need not hold all of those instruments until maturity. Thus an entity's business model can be to hold financial assets to collect contractual cash flows even when sales of financial assets occur or are expected to occur in the future. [IFRS 9:B4.1.3]

IFRS 9's business model test is not equivalent to IAS 39's criteria for qualification as held-to-maturity investments; that is to say, eligibility for amortised cost measurement under IFRS 9 is not dependent on the entity holding the assets until their maturity. However, the objective of the entity's business model must be to collect the contractual cash flows, rather than to realise the value of the financial assets through sale.

IFRS 9 does not specifically define what is meant by the expression "to hold assets in order to collect contractual cash flows", although it does provide application guidance on how this condition should be applied. The business model test in IFRS 9 is not the inverse of the held for trading definition in IFRS 9:Appendix A. However, if financial assets meet IFRS 9's definition for 'held for trading' (see **5.5.2**) they will not pass the business model test for amortised cost or FVTOCI because the objectives for holding held for trading assets are inherently inconsistent with the concept of holding the financial assets to collect the contractual cash flows, or holding financial assets to collect the contractual cash flows and to sell them.

The business model may be to hold assets to collect contractual cash flows even if the entity sells financial assets when there is an increase in the assets' credit risk. To determine whether there has been an increase in the assets' credit risk, the entity considers reasonable and supportable information, including forward looking information. Irrespective of their frequency and value, sales due to an increase in the assets' credit risk are not inconsistent with a business model whose objective is to hold financial assets to collect contractual cash flows because the credit quality of financial assets is relevant to the entity's ability to collect contractual cash flows. Credit risk management activities that are aimed at minimising potential credit losses due to credit deterioration are integral to such a business model. Selling a financial asset because it no longer meets the credit criteria specified in the entity's documented investment policy is an example of a sale that has occurred due to an increase in credit risk. However, in the absence of such a policy, the entity may demonstrate in other ways that the sale occurred due to an increase in credit risk. [IFRS 9:B4.1.3A]

Example 5.2.1B

Managing credit risk of financial assets

[IFRS 9:B4.1.4, Example 1]

An entity holds investments to collect their contractual cash flows. The funding needs of the entity are predictable and the maturity of its financial assets is matched to the entity's estimated funding needs.

The entity performs credit risk management activities with the objective of minimising credit losses. In the past, sales have typically occurred when the financial assets' credit risk has increased such that the assets no longer meet the credit criteria specified in the entity's documented investment policy. In addition, infrequent sales have occurred as a result of unanticipated funding needs.

Reports to key management personnel focus on the credit quality of the financial assets and the contractual return. The entity also monitors fair values of the financial assets, among other information.

Although the entity considers, among other information, the financial assets' fair values from a liquidity perspective (i.e. the cash amount that would be realised if the entity needs to sell assets), the entity's objective is to hold the financial assets and collect the contractual cash flows.

Sales would not contradict that objective if they were in response to an increase in the assets' credit risk, for example if the assets no longer meet the credit criteria specified in the entity's documented investment policy. Infrequent sales resulting from unanticipated funding needs (e.g. in a stress case scenario) also would not contradict that objective, even if such sales are significant in value.

Example 5.2.1C

Sales of assets to minimise credit losses

Entity Q is a financial institution that holds for the long term a portfolio of debt investments with a high credit quality. Entity Q expects to collect the contractual cash flows on the instruments. However, Entity Q's internal guidelines require that if a debt instrument's credit rating falls below a specified level, and its fair value falls below 60 per cent of its par value, Entity Q is required to sell the asset (a 'stop loss feature').

Even though Entity Q's business model requires the debt instruments to be sold when specified trigger events occur, it may still be appropriate for Entity Q to regard its business as holding the assets to collect the contractual cash flows. Sales of assets are not expected to be frequent and they are only carried out in order to limit losses in circumstances when there is significant deterioration in the credit quality of a particular instrument.

Sales that occur for other reasons, such as sales made to manage credit concentration risk (without an increase in the assets' credit risk), may also be consistent with a business model whose objective is to hold financial assets in order to collect contractual cash flows. In particular, such sales may be consistent with a business model whose objective is to hold financial assets in order to collect contractual cash flows if those sales are infrequent (even if significant in value) or insignificant in value both individually and in aggregate (even if frequent). [IFRS 9:B4.1.3B]

IFRS 9 distinguishes between selling financial assets in response to an increase in the asset's credit risk and selling in response to credit concentration risk. The IASB noted that the notion of credit concentration risk is applied fairly broadly in practice and may include changes in the entity's investment policy or strategy that are not related to credit deterioration. The IASB noted that frequent sales that are significant in value and labelled as 'due to credit concentration risk' (but that are not related to an increase in the assets' credit risk) are likely to be inconsistent with the objective of collecting contractual cash flows. [IFRS 9:BC4.147]

Example 5.2.1D

Unexpected sales and impact on business model assessment

Entity F holds a portfolio of debt instruments with the objective of collecting the contractual cash flows from those instruments. Entity F measures the debt instruments at amortised cost.

Entity F sells some of the debt instruments prior to their maturity to fund the settlement of a legal claim which was not previously expected to be settled.

Notwithstanding the unforeseen sale of the debt instruments, Entity F can continue to assert that its business model is to collect the contractual cash flows on its debt instruments because the sales were unexpected and are not customary. This business model assessment is applicable to debt instruments that continue to be recognised in the business as well as new debt instruments recognised by the business.

If more than an infrequent number of such sales are made out of a portfolio and those sales are more than insignificant in value (either individually or in aggregate), the entity needs to assess whether and how such sales are consistent with an objective of collecting contractual cash flows. Whether a third party imposes the requirement to sell the financial assets, or that activity is at the entity's discretion, is not relevant to this assessment. An increase in the frequency or value of sales in a particular period is not necessarily inconsistent with an objective to hold financial assets in order to collect contractual cash flows, if an entity can explain the reasons for those sales and demonstrate why those sales do not reflect a change in the entity's business model. In addition, sales may be consistent with the objective of holding financial assets in order to collect contractual cash flows if the sales are made close to the maturity of the financial assets and the proceeds from the sales approximate the collection of the remaining contractual cash flows. [IFRS 9:B4.1.3B]

Example 5.2.1E

Financial assets held for liquidity purposes

[IFRS 9:B4.1.4, Example 4]

A financial institution holds financial assets to meet liquidity needs in a 'stress case' scenario (e.g. a run on the bank's deposits). The entity does not anticipate selling these assets except in such scenarios.

> The entity monitors the credit quality of the financial assets and its objective in managing the financial assets is to collect the contractual cash flows. The entity evaluates the performance of the assets on the basis of interest revenue earned and credit losses realised.
>
> However, the entity also monitors the fair value of the financial assets from a liquidity perspective to ensure that the cash amount that would be realised if the entity needed to sell the assets in a stress case scenario would be sufficient to meet the entity's liquidity needs. Periodically, the entity makes sales that are insignificant in value to demonstrate liquidity.
>
> The objective of the entity's business model is to hold the financial assets to collect contractual cash flows.
>
> The analysis would not change even if during a previous stress case scenario the entity had sales that were significant in value in order to meet its liquidity needs. Similarly, recurring sales activity that is insignificant in value is not inconsistent with holding financial assets to collect contractual cash flows.
>
> In contrast, if an entity holds financial assets to meet its everyday liquidity needs and meeting that objective involves frequent sales that are significant in value, the objective of the entity's business model is not to hold the financial assets to collect contractual cash flows.
>
> Similarly, if the entity is required by its regulator to routinely sell financial assets to demonstrate that the assets are liquid, and the value of the assets sold is significant, the entity's business model is not to hold financial assets to collect contractual cash flows. Whether a third party imposes the requirement to sell the financial assets, or that activity is at the entity's discretion, is not relevant to the analysis.

An entity may determine that financial assets are held for the purpose of collecting contractual cash flows even if those cash flows are hedged (whether merely economically hedged or in a hedge accounting relationship). When debt instruments are held with a view to collecting the contractual cash flows, but the business also makes use of derivatives to manage risk (e.g. interest rate or foreign currency swaps), this does not necessarily alter the assessment regarding whether the debt instruments meet the business model test for the purpose of measurement at amortised cost. This is the case even if the cash inflows from the debt instruments (e.g. interest) are received under the contractual terms of the debt instrument and are concurrently paid out gross (or net of receipts under the derivative) to the counterparty of the derivative. Because the assets are held by the business with a view to receiving the contractual cash flows, the business model test for the purpose of classifying the financial assets at amortised cost may still be met.

Example 5.2.1F

Financial assets with incurred credit losses that are hedged

[IFRS 9:B4.1.4, Example 2]

An entity's business model is to purchase portfolios of financial assets, such as loans. Those portfolios may or may not include financial assets that are credit-impaired.

If payment on the loans is not made on a timely basis, the entity attempts to realise the contractual cash flows through various means - for example, by contacting the debtor by mail, telephone or other methods. The entity's objective is to collect the contractual cash flows and the entity does not manage any of the loans in this portfolio with an objective of realising cash flows by selling them.

In some cases, the entity enters into interest rate swaps to change the interest rate on particular financial assets in a portfolio from a floating interest rate to a fixed interest rate.

The objective of the entity's business model is to hold the financial assets and collect the contractual cash flows.

The same analysis would apply even if the entity does not expect to receive all of the contractual cash flows (e.g. some of the financial assets are credit-impaired at initial recognition).

Moreover, the fact that the entity enters into derivatives to modify the cash flows of the portfolio does not in itself change the entity's business model.

5.3 Fair value through other comprehensive income

Except for financial assets that are designated at initial recognition as at FVTPL (see **5.5.3**) a financial asset is measured at FVTOCI if both of the following conditions are met:

[IFRS 9:4.1.2A]

(a) the financial asset is held within a business model whose objective is achieved by both collecting contractual cash flows and selling financial assets (the *business model test*, see **5.3.1**); and

(b) the contractual terms of the financial asset give rise on specified dates to cash flows that are solely payments of principal and interest on the principal amount outstanding (the *contractual cash flows characteristics test*, see **section 5.4**).

Financial assets that do not meet the condition in IFRS 9:4.1.2A(b) are required to be subsequently measured at FVTPL or in the case of certain investments in equity instruments may be elected at initial recognition to be measured at FVTOCI (see **5.3.2**). A financial asset that does meet the condition in IFRS 9:4.1.2A(b) but does not meet the condition in IFRS 9:4.1.2A(a) may meet the criteria to be measured at amortised cost (see **5.2.1**).

The FVTOCI category consists of two subsets of financial assets. The first includes those financial assets that are debt instruments that meet the criteria in IFRS 9:4.1.2A. The second subset includes financial assets that do not meet the criteria in IFRS 9:4.1.2A or the amortised cost criteria in IFRS 9:4.1.2 and are designated at initial recognition at FVTOCI. This option to designate a financial asset at FVTOCI is restricted to investments in equity instruments that are neither held for trading nor contingent consideration recognised by an acquirer in a business combination to which IFRS 3 *Business Combinations* applies (see **5.3.2**).

As the FVTOCI category includes both debt instruments that are required to be measured at FVTOCI (absent electing them to be classified as at FVTPL at initial recognition) and those investments in equity instruments that are designated as at FVTOCI at initial recognition, the use of term *FVTOCI* can be confusing. The key distinction is whether the instrument is *required* to be measured at FVTOCI because it is a debt instrument that meets the contractual cash flows characteristics test, or is a holding of an equity instrument that is *designated* at FVTOCI. The distinction is important because debt instruments measured at FVTOCI, have interest recognised in profit or loss using the effective interest rate, are measured for impairment, have foreign currency gains or losses recognised in profit or loss, and result in reclassification of gains and losses from other comprehensive income to profit or loss on derecognition. This compares with investments in equity instruments designated at FVTOCI for which only dividend income is recognised in profit or loss but all other gains and losses are recognised in other comprehensive income without reclassification on derecognition.

Because both conditions (the business model test and the contractual cash flows characteristics test) must be met for FVTOCI measurement for financial assets that are debt instruments, the order in which the tests are performed is irrelevant. However, in practice it is likely that the business model test will be considered first because it is performed at a higher level of aggregation and not for each financial asset individually.

5.3.1 Business model assessment for FVTOCI measurement

For a financial asset that is a debt instrument to be measured at FVTOCI it must be held within a business model whose objective is achieved by both collecting contractual cash flows and selling financial assets. [IFRS 9:4.1.2A(a)]

An entity may hold financial assets in a business model whose objective is achieved by both collecting contractual cash flows and selling financial assets. In this type of business model, the entity's key management personnel have made a decision that both collecting contractual cash flows and selling financial assets are integral to achieving the objective of the business model. There are various objectives that may be consistent with this type of business model. For example, the objective of the business model may be to manage everyday liquidity needs, to maintain a particular interest yield profile or to match the duration of the financial assets to the duration of the liabilities that those assets are funding. To achieve such an objective, the entity will both collect contractual cash flows and sell financial assets. [IFRS 9:B4.1.4A]

Compared to a business model whose objective is to hold financial assets to collect contractual cash flows, this business model will typically involve greater frequency and value of sales. This is because selling financial assets is integral to achieving the business model's objective instead of being only incidental to it. However, there is no threshold for the frequency or value of sales that must occur in this business model because both collecting contractual cash flows and selling financial assets are integral to achieving its objective. [IFRS 9:B4.1.4B]

Example 5.3.1A

Financial assets held to fund capital expenditure with sales to achieve a higher return

[IFRS 9:B4.1.4C, Example 5]

An entity anticipates capital expenditure in a few years. The entity invests its excess cash in short and long-term financial assets so that it can fund the expenditure when the need arises. Many of the financial assets have contractual lives that exceed the entity's anticipated investment period. The entity will hold financial assets to collect the contractual cash flows and, when an opportunity arises, it will sell financial assets to re-invest the cash in financial assets with a higher return.

The managers responsible for the portfolio are remunerated based on the overall return generated by the portfolio.

The objective of the business model is achieved by both collecting contractual cash flows and selling financial assets. The entity will make decisions on an ongoing basis about whether collecting contractual cash flows or selling financial assets will maximise the return on the portfolio until the need arises for the invested cash.

In contrast, consider an entity that anticipates a cash outflow in five years to fund capital expenditure and invests excess cash in short-term financial assets. When the investments mature, the entity reinvests the cash in new short-term financial assets. The entity maintains this strategy until the funds are needed, at which time the entity uses the proceeds from the maturing financial assets to fund the capital expenditure. Only sales that are insignificant in value occur before maturity (unless there is an increase in credit risk). The objective of this contrasting business model is to hold financial assets to collect contractual cash flows (see **5.2.1**).

Example 5.3.1B

Financial assets held for liquidity purposes with active management of the portfolio

[IFRS 9:B4.1.4C, Example 6]

A financial institution holds financial assets to meet its everyday liquidity needs. The entity seeks to minimise the costs of managing those liquidity needs and therefore actively manages the return on the portfolio. That return consists of collecting contractual coupon payments as well as gains and losses from the sale of financial assets.

As a result, the entity holds financial assets to collect contractual cash flows and sells financial assets to reinvest in higher yielding financial assets or to better match the duration of its liabilities. In the past, this strategy has resulted in frequent sales activity and such sales have been significant in value. This activity is expected to continue in the future.

The objective of the business model is to maximise the return on the portfolio to meet everyday liquidity needs and the entity achieves that objective by both collecting contractual cash flows and selling financial assets. In other words, both collecting contractual cash flows and selling financial assets are integral to achieving the business model's objective.

Example 5.3.1C

Financial assets held by an issuer to fund insurance liabilities with regular buying and selling

[IFRS 9:B4.1.4C, Example 7]

An insurer holds financial assets in order to fund insurance contract liabilities. The insurer uses the proceeds from the contractual cash flows on the financial assets to settle insurance contract liabilities as they come due. To ensure that the contractual cash flows from the financial assets are sufficient to settle those liabilities, the insurer undertakes significant buying and selling activity on a regular basis to rebalance its portfolio of assets and to meet cash flow needs as they arise.

The objective of the business model is to fund the insurance contract liabilities. To achieve this objective, the entity collects contractual cash flows as they come due and sells financial assets to maintain the desired profile of the asset portfolio. Thus both collecting contractual cash flows and selling financial assets are integral to achieving the business model's objective.

5.3.2 Designation of equity instruments as at FVTOCI

At initial recognition, an entity may make an irrevocable election to present in other comprehensive income subsequent changes in the fair value of an investment in an equity instrument that is not held for trading nor contingent consideration recognised by an acquirer in a business combination to which IFRS 3 *Business Combinations* applies. [IFRS 9:5.7.5] A financial asset is held for trading if:

[IFRS 9: Appendix A]

(a) it is acquired principally for the purpose of selling it in the near term;

(b) on initial recognition it is part of a portfolio of identified financial instruments that are managed together and for which there is evidence of a recent actual pattern of short term profit-taking; or

(c) it is a derivative (except for a derivative that is a financial guarantee contract or a designated and effective hedging instrument).

The definition of a derivative is included in **section 2** in **chapter B4**.

An investment in an equity instrument can be interpreted to be broadly consistent with the definition of equity contained in IAS 32:11 (see **section 2** in **chapter B3**); however, there are two notable differences.

- IAS 32 requires that certain derivatives that result in the delivery of equity instruments are classified as equity in the issuer's financial statements. An example is an option that upon exercise by the holder of the option requires the issuer to deliver to the holder a fixed number of the issuer's own non-derivative equity instruments in return for the holder paying the issuer a fixed amount of cash or another financial asset (denominated in the issuer's functional currency). The holder of the option cannot designate the financial asset as at FVTOCI, even though from the issuer's perspective it is classified as an equity instrument, because from the investor's perspective it meets the definition of a derivative and, therefore, also meets the definition of held for trading.
- Also, certain issued puttable instruments meeting specified strict criteria are presented as equity of the issuer even though they convey a financial obligation to deliver cash or another financial asset; such instruments are not eligible for designation as at FVTOCI from the perspective of the holder. IFRS 9:BC5.21 states that puttable instruments presented as equity in IAS 32 do not meet the definition of an equity instrument for the purposes of classification in IFRS 9.

The election to designate an investment in an equity instrument at FVTOCI is made on an instrument-by-instrument basis. If the election is made, only dividend income that does not clearly represent a recovery of part of the cost of the investment is recognised in profit or loss, with all other gains and losses (including those relating to foreign exchange) recognised in other comprehensive income. These gains and losses remain permanently in equity and are not subsequently reclassified to profit or loss, even on derecognition. However, the entity may transfer the cumulative gain or loss within equity as a reserve movement. [IFRS 9:B5.7.1]

The IASB noted that reclassification of gains and losses to profit or loss would create a similar treatment to that applied to the available-for-sale category in IAS 39 and would necessitate the requirement to assess the equity instrument for impairment, which had previously led to application problems. As such, it would not significantly improve or reduce the complexity of the financial reporting for financial assets. Accordingly, the IASB decided to prohibit reclassification of gains and losses from equity to profit or loss when an equity instrument is derecognised. [IFRS 9:BC5.25(b)]

Dividends are recognised in profit or loss only when:

[IFRS 9:5.7.1A]

(a) the entity's right to receive payment of the dividend is established;

(b) it is probable that the economic benefits associated with the dividend will flow to the entity; and

(c) the amount of the dividend can be measured reliably.

However, if the dividend income clearly represents a recovery of part of the cost of investment, the dividend is not recognised in profit or loss. [IFRS 9:B5.7.1]

Dividends are defined in IFRS 9:Appendix A as '[d]istributions of profits to holders of equity instruments in proportion to their holdings of a particular class of capital."

IFRS 9:B5.7.1 is unambiguous that if dividend income clearly represents a recovery of part of the cost of investment in an equity instrument designated as at FVTOCI, the dividend is not recognised in profit or loss. However, the Standard does not elaborate on when a dividend is considered to clearly represent a recovery of part of the cost of the investment.

As part of the Basis for Conclusions on dividends arising from assets designated as at FVTOCI, IFRS 9:BC5.25(a) makes reference to dividends that are a 'return of investment' as opposed to those that are a 'return on investment'. Although these terms are not used in the main body of the Standard, it appears the Board's intention was to distinguish between dividends that clearly represent a return of investment (and, therefore, are akin to a partial liquidation of the holder's initial investment in the equity instrument) and other dividends.

Most dividends are a return on investment rather than a return of investment and, consequently, they will be recognised in profit or loss. However, a thorough understanding of the facts and circumstances surrounding the payment of the dividend is required in order to make this assessment. Judgement will be required when assessing whether a dividend is a 'return of' rather than a 'return on' investment and, consequently, whether recognition of the dividend in profit or loss is prohibited.

Example 5.3.2

Return of investment versus a recovery of cost

Entity A invested in an equity security for CU100 many years ago; the investment was designated as at FVTOCI when the entity first applied IFRS 9. At the current reporting date, the fair value of the equity instrument is CU300. A cumulative gain of CU200 has been recognised in other comprehensive income.

The issuer of the equity security distributes a dividend worth CU150 and, concurrently, the fair value of the equity instrument declines by CU150. There is no evidence that the dividend represents a partial liquidation or return of capital of Entity A's initial investment.

In accordance with IFRS 9:B5.7.1, the dividend is recognised in profit or loss because the dividend is not clearly a recovery of part of the cost of its investment. The fact that the dividend is relatively large in comparison to Entity A's initial cost of the investment and Entity A's post-acquisition cumulative gain is not of itself evidence that part of the cost of the investment is clearly being recovered.

The following journal entries are recorded.

		CU	CU
Dr	Cash	150	
Cr	Profit or loss		150

To recognise the dividend in profit or loss

Dr	Other comprehensive income	150	
Cr	Financial asset		150

To recognise the decrease in fair value in other comprehensive income

5.4 Contractual cash flows characteristics test

For a financial asset that is a debt instrument to be measured at amortised cost or fair value through comprehensive income, its contractual terms must give rise on specified dates to cash flows that are solely payments of principal and interest on the principal amount outstanding. [IFRS 9:4.1.2(b)

& 4.1.2A(b)] For the purpose of applying this requirement, principal is the fair value of the financial asset at initial recognition, however that principal amount may change over the life of the financial asset (e.g. if there are repayments of principal). [IFRS 9:4.1.3(b) & B4.1.7B] Interest consists of consideration for the time value of money, for the credit risk associated with the principal amount outstanding during a particular period of time and for other basic lending risks and costs, as well as a profit margin. [IFRS 9:4.1.3]

The assessment of whether contractual cash flows are solely payments of principal and interest is made in the currency in which the financial asset is denominated. [IFRS 9:B4.1.8] See **5.4.10** for the classification of dual-currency bonds.

In practice only financial assets that are debt instruments are capable of meeting the contractual cash flows characteristics test in IFRS 9:4.1.2(b) & 4.1.2A(b). Derivative assets and investments in equity instruments will not meet the criteria.

Contractual cash flows that are solely payments of principal and interest on the principal amount outstanding are consistent with a basic lending arrangement. In a basic lending arrangement, consideration for the time value of money and credit risk are typically the most significant elements of interest. However, in such an arrangement, interest can also include consideration for other basic lending risks (e.g. liquidity risk) and costs (e.g. administrative costs) associated with holding the financial asset for a particular period of time. In addition, interest can include a profit margin that is consistent with a basic lending arrangement. In extreme economic circumstances, interest can be negative if, for example, the holder of a financial asset either explicitly or implicitly pays for the deposit of its money for a particular period of time (and that fee exceeds the consideration that the holder receives for the time value of money, credit risk and other basic lending risks and costs). However, contractual terms that introduce exposure to risks or volatility in the contractual cash flows that is unrelated to a basic lending arrangement, such as exposure to changes in equity prices or commodity prices, do not give rise to contractual cash flows that are solely payments of principal and interest on the principal amount outstanding. An originated or an acquired financial asset can be a basic lending arrangement irrespective of whether it is a loan in its legal form. [IFRS 9:B4.1.7A]

5.4.1 Consideration for the time value of money

Time value of money is the element of interest that provides consideration for only the passage of time. That is, the time value of money element does not provide consideration for other risks or costs associated with holding the financial asset. In order to assess whether the element provides consideration for only the passage of time, an entity applies judgement and considers relevant factors such as the currency in which the financial asset is denominated and the period for which the interest rate is set. [IFRS 9:B4.1.9A]

5.4.2 Fixed cash flows

A non-prepayable fixed rate instrument that has a fixed return provides the holder with consideration for the time value of money.

A fixed return may consist solely of the contractual coupon in the case when a debt instrument is initially recognised at an amount equal to the par amount due at redemption, or include an implicit fixed return when the financial asset is initially recognised at a discount or premium to the par amount due at redemption, or both an implicit fixed return arising from a discount or premium and a fixed contractual coupon. As the principal amount is defined as the fair value of the financial asset at initial recognition, and all financial assets (except certain trade receivables) are initially recognised at fair value, the discount or premium to par at initial recognition forms part of the return on the financial asset.

Example 5.4.2A

Fixed rate loan

Entity Q lends CU10 million to Entity P. The terms of the loan require repayment of CU10 million by Entity P in three years and is not prepayable. The interest rate on the loan is 7% on CU10 million payable in arrears at the anniversary date of the lending. There are no other features in the contractual terms that result in any variability in the contractual cash flows.

For Entity Q, the loan gives rise on specified dates to cash flows that are solely payments of principal and interest on the principal amount outstanding. Consequently, the contractual cash flows characteristics test is met.

Example 5.4.2B

Zero coupon bond

Entity W acquires a zero coupon bond that was originally issued by Entity X. The terms of the bond require repayment of CU10 million by Entity X in three years and is not prepayable. The terms of the bond do not include a contractual interest rate.

Whether Entity W acquired the zero coupon bond at the date it was originally issued by Entity X or at a later date does not affect the assessment as to whether the asset can be classified at amortised cost or FVTOCI by Entity W. At the date of acquisition, Entity W has a financial asset that provides a fixed return of interest and repayment of principal. The fixed return is the difference between the amount paid to acquire the bond and the amount due from Entity X at redemption.

A loan that consists entirely of fixed cash flows (being fixed interest and principal), whether initially recognised at its par amount, or a discount or premium to its par amount, does not automatically pass the contractual cash flows characteristics test. If the fixed rate loan is prepayable or extendable, consideration will need to be given as to whether these prepayment and extension features meet the contractual cash flows characteristics test (see **5.4.4** and **5.4.5**).

5.4.3 Variability in timing and amount of cash flows

Financial assets may have contractual cash flows that vary in amount and/or timing. The contractual cash flow characteristics test requires an analysis of the contractual cash flows that could arise both before, and after, the change in contractual cash flows, to determine whether the contractual cash flows that could arise over the life of the instrument are solely payments of principal and interest on the principal outstanding. [IFRS 9:B4.1.10]

When the amount and/or timing of contractual cash flows are contingent on a future event consideration must be given to the nature of the event. While the nature of the contingent event in itself is not a determinative factor in assessing whether the contractual cash flows are solely payments of principal and interest, it may be an indicator. IFRS 9:B4.1.10 makes a comparison between an instrument with an interest rate that is reset to a higher rate if the debtor misses a particular number of payments to a financial instrument with an interest rate that is reset to a higher rate if a specified equity index reaches a particular level. The Standard notes that it is more likely in the former case that the contractual cash flows over the life of the instrument are solely payments of principal and interest on the principal amount outstanding because of the relationship between missed payments and an increase in credit risk.

Judgement is needed in assessing whether a payment (or non-payment) of a contractual cash flow that only arises as a result of the occurrence or non-occurrence of a contingent event leads to the instrument failing the contractual cash flow characteristics test. An entity should consider what is the risk that leads to the contingent event happening and whether that risk is consistent with risks associated with a basic lending arrangement. The risk cited in IFRS 9:B4.1.10 is equity price risk which is not a risk consistent with basic lending arrangements.

A financial asset that has a variable rate of interest that consists of consideration for the time value of money, the credit risk associated with the principal amount outstanding during a particular period of time (the consideration for credit risk may be determined at initial recognition only, and so may be fixed) and other basic lending risks and costs, as well as a profit margin, will meet the contractual cash flow characteristics test. [IFRS 9:B4.1.11(a)]

Example 5.4.3A

Floating rate loan

Entity S lends €10 million to Entity T. The terms of the loan require Entity T to repay €10 million in three years and the loan is not prepayable. The interest rate on the loan is based on EURIBOR plus 2% on €10 million payable in arrears at the anniversary date of the lending. The rate of EURIBOR is determined in advance at the start of each annual period. There are no other features in the contractual terms that result in any variability in the contractual cash flows.

Even though the interest on the loan is partly fixed and partly variable, the variable element is determined by reference to a market interest rate and therefore, for Entity S, the loan gives rise on specified dates to cash flows that are solely payments of principal and interest on the principal amount outstanding. Consequently, the contractual cash flows characteristics test is met.

The contractual floating rate on a loan is not required to be based on an observable market index (e.g. LIBOR) for it to be regarded as compensation for the time value of money and credit risk of the borrower. It is common for financial institutions to price their lending based off an internal interest rate index (e.g. the lender's 'standard variable rate'). The lender may add a further fixed premium to the internal interest rate index depending on the relative credit risk of the borrower. When the contractual interest rate on a loan is linked to a lender's internal interest rate index, the loan may still be regarded as having cash flows that are solely payments of principal and interest on the principal amount outstanding if the interest is consideration for the time value of money and for the credit risk of the borrower, and the contractual terms of the loan do not include variability due to risks that are inconsistent with a basic lending arrangement.

Consistent with the view that a contractual return on a debt instrument can be fixed or floating, or a combination thereof and pass the contractual cash flow characteristics test, a floating contractual return, subject to a cap or floor, can also pass the test.

Example 5.4.3B

Capped variable rate instrument with a stated maturity date

[IFRS 9:B4.1.13 Instrument C]

Instrument C is a bond with a stated maturity date and pays a variable market interest rate. That variable interest rate is capped.

The contractual cash flows of both:

(a) an instrument that has a fixed interest rate and

(b) an instrument that has a variable interest rate

are payments of principal and interest on the principal amount outstanding as long as the interest reflects consideration for the time value of money, for the credit risk associated with the instrument during the term of the instrument and for other basic lending risks and costs, as well as a profit margin (See IFRS 9:B4.1.7A).

Therefore, an instrument that is a combination of (a) and (b) (e.g. a bond with an interest rate cap) can have cash flows that are solely payments of principal and interest on the principal amount outstanding. Such a contractual term may reduce cash flow variability by setting a limit on a variable interest rate (e.g. an interest rate cap or floor) or increase the cash flow variability because a fixed rate becomes variable.

A floating contractual interest rate would not be regarded as consideration for the time value of money and for the credit risk of the borrower if the changes in the contractual floating interest rate do not move in the same direction as the interest rate index (i.e. when the interest rate index increases the contractual floating interest rate decreases, and vice versa).

Example 5.4.3C

Loan with inverse floating interest rate

[IFRS 9:B4.1.14 Instrument G]

Instrument G is a loan that pays an inverse floating interest rate (i.e. the interest rate has an inverse relationship to market interest rates).

The contractual cash flows are not solely payments of principal and interest on the principal amount outstanding.

The interest amounts are not consideration for the time value of money on the principal amount outstanding.

Loan arrangements may have a coupon that changes in response to the borrower's credit quality. Such contractual terms may meet the contractual cash flows characteristics test if they compensate the lender for the credit risk associated with the principal amount outstanding during a particular period of time.

Example 5.4.3D

Adjustments to the coupon for changes in credit risk of the issuer

Entity Q lends CU10 million to Entity P. The terms of the loan require repayment of CU10 million by Entity P in five years.

The interest rate is payable yearly in arrears and is calculated as follows:

- fixed rate of 6 per cent (considered to be compensation for the time value of money per IFRS 9:4.1.3); plus
- a credit margin that initially reflects the credit risk of the borrower at the date the loan is originated and is automatically adjusted on an annual basis during the loan term to reflect changes in the borrower's credit risk.

Assuming that all contractual terms other than automatically adjusting the credit margin represent solely payments of principal and interest the inclusion of credit risk adjusted margin would result in the instrument passing the contractual cash flow characteristics test.

IFRS 9:B4.1.11(a) notes that a floating interest rate containing a credit margin that may be fixed at the date of lending may meet the contractual cash flow characteristics test. In practice, the credit margin is generally fixed at the date of lending and is not subsequently adjusted. However, in the circumstances described, the contractual interest rate consists of a fixed element reflecting the time value of money, plus a variable element reflecting the credit risk. A floating interest rate containing a variable credit margin will meet the contractual cash flow characteristics test as long as the total contractual interest payments do not include variability due to risks that are inconsistent with a basic lending arrangement.

The contractual cash flows characteristics assessment should consider all the contractual terms of the instrument, not just those contractual cash flows that are most likely to be due. When an asset may be prepaid, the contractual cash flow characteristics assessment must assess the contractual cash flows both before and after the timing of the prepayment option irrespective of the probability that the instrument may be repaid prior to maturity.

Example 5.4.3E

Increased interest rate if issuer redemption option not exercised

Entity B invests in a debt security that bears a floating interest rate (e.g. interest rate index plus 2 per cent) for the first three years. At the end of Year 3, the issuer has the option to redeem the note at principal plus unpaid contractual interest. If the issuer does not redeem, the interest rate margin on the floating interest rate increases by a fixed amount (i.e. the same interest rate index plus increased margin) until maturity at the end of Year 5.

The financial asset contains no other terms that would fail the contractual cash flow characteristics test in IFRS 9:4.1.2(b) & 4.1.2A(b).

Although there is optionality regarding the life of the instrument, with a linked change in interest rate, under either option the cash flows of the instrument represent principal and interest on the principal amount outstanding. A similar instrument (i.e. with the margin over the floating rate index stepping up after a point in time) which did not include an issuer redemption option would meet the condition in IFRS 9:4.1.2(b) & 4.1.2A(b). The addition of the issuer redemption option does not alter this conclusion. For further guidance on prepayment options see **5.4.4**.

In some cases, the time value of money element may be modified (i.e. imperfect). That would be the case, for example, if a financial asset's interest rate is periodically reset but the frequency of that reset does not match the tenor of the interest rate (e.g. the interest rate resets every month to a one-year rate) or if a financial asset's interest rate is periodically reset to an average of particular short-term and long-term interest rates. In such cases, an entity must assess the modification to determine whether the contractual cash flows represent solely payments of principal and interest on the principal amount outstanding. In some circumstances, the entity may be able to make that determination by performing a qualitative assessment of the time value of money element whereas, in other circumstances, it may be necessary to perform a quantitative assessment. [IFRS 9:B4.1.9B]

When assessing a modified time value of money element, the objective is to determine how different the contractual (undiscounted) cash flows could be from the (undiscounted) cash flows that would arise if the time value of money element was not modified (the benchmark cash flows). For example, if the financial asset under assessment contains a variable interest rate that is reset every month to a one-year interest rate, the entity would compare that financial asset to a financial instrument with identical contractual terms and the identical credit quality except the variable interest rate is reset monthly to a one-month interest rate. If the modified time value of money element could result in contractual (undiscounted) cash flows that are significantly different from the (undiscounted) benchmark cash flows, the financial asset does not meet the contractual cash flow characteristics test. To make this determination, the entity must consider the effect of the modified time value of money element in each reporting period and cumulatively over the life of the financial instrument. The reason for the interest rate being set in this way is not relevant to the analysis. If it is clear, with little or no analysis, whether the contractual (undiscounted) cash flows on the financial asset under the assessment could (or could not) be significantly different from the (undiscounted) benchmark cash flows, an entity need not perform a detailed assessment. [IFRS 9:B4.1.9C]

When assessing a modified time value of money element, an entity must consider factors that could affect future contractual cash flows. In doing this, an entity must consider only reasonably possible scenarios instead of every possible scenario. For example, if an entity is assessing a bond with a five-year term and the variable interest rate is reset every six months to a five-year rate, the entity cannot conclude that the contractual cash flows are solely payments of principal and interest on the principal amount outstanding simply because the interest rate curve at the time of the assessment is such that the difference between a five-year interest rate and a six-month interest rate is not significant. Instead, the entity must also consider whether the relationship between the five-year interest rate and the six-month interest rate could change over the life of the instrument such that the contractual (undiscounted) cash flows over the life of the instrument could be significantly different from the (undiscounted) benchmark cash flows. If an entity concludes that the contractual (undiscounted) cash flows could be significantly different from the (undiscounted) benchmark cash flows, the financial asset does not meet the condition in IFRS 9:4.1.2(b) and 4.1.2A(b) and therefore cannot be measured at amortised cost or FVTOCI. [IFRS 9:B4.1.9D]

Example 5.4.3F

Modified interest rate where the borrower chooses the reset period

[IFRS 9:B4.1.13 Instrument B]

Instrument B is a variable interest rate instrument with a stated maturity date that permits the borrower to choose the market interest rate on an ongoing basis. For example, at each interest rate reset date, the borrower can choose to pay three-month LIBOR for a three-month term or one-month LIBOR for a one-month term.

The contractual cash flows are solely payments of principal and interest on the principal amount outstanding as long as the interest paid over the life of the instrument reflects consideration for the time value of money, for the credit risk associated with the instrument and for other basic lending risks and costs, as well as a profit margin (see IFRS 9:B4.1.7A). The fact that the LIBOR interest rate is reset during the life of the instrument does not in itself disqualify the instrument.

However, if the borrower is able to choose to pay a one-month interest rate that is reset every three months, the interest rate is reset with a frequency that does not match the tenor of the interest rate. Consequently, the time value of money element is modified. Similarly, if an instrument has a contractual interest rate that is based on a term that can exceed the instrument's remaining life (e.g. if an instrument with a five-year maturity pays a variable rate that is reset periodically but always reflects a five-year maturity), the time value of money element is modified. That is because the interest payable in each period is disconnected from the interest period.

In such cases, the entity must qualitatively or quantitatively assess the contractual cash flows against those on an instrument that is identical in all respects except the tenor of the interest rate matches the interest period to determine if the cash flows are solely payments of principal and interest on the principal amount outstanding. (But see IFRS 9:B4.1.9E for guidance on regulated interest rates).

For example, in assessing a bond with a five-year term that pays a variable rate that is reset every six months but always reflects a five-year maturity, an entity considers the contractual cash flows on an instrument that resets every six months to a six-month interest rate but is otherwise identical.

The same analysis would apply if the borrower is able to choose between the lender's various published interest rates (e.g. the borrower can choose between the lender's published one-month variable interest rate and the lender's published three-month variable interest rate).

In some jurisdictions, the government or a regulatory authority sets interest rates. For example, such government regulation of interest rates may be part of a broad macroeconomic policy or it may be introduced to encourage entities to invest in a particular sector of the economy. In some of these cases, the objective of the time value of money element is not to provide consideration for only the passage of time. However, despite IFRS 9:B4.1.9A - B4.1.9D, a regulated interest rate shall be used as a proxy for the time value of money element for the purpose of applying the condition in IFRS 9:4.1.2(b) & 4.1.2A(b) if that regulated interest rate provides consideration that is broadly consistent with the passage of time and does not provide exposure to risks or volatility in the contractual cash flows that are inconsistent with a basic lending arrangement. [IFRS 9:B4.1.9E]

The IASB noted that in some jurisdictions the government or regulatory authority establishes interest rates and, in some cases, the objective of the time value of money element may not be to provide consideration for only the passage of time. However, the IASB decided that such a regulated interest rate is a *proxy* for the time value of money element if that interest rate provides consideration that is broadly consistent with the passage of time and does not provide exposure to risks or volatility in the contractual cash flows that are inconsistent with a basic lending arrangement. [IFRS 9:BC4.179]

The IASB acknowledged that this approach for regulated interest rates is broader than the approach for interest rates that are established freely by market participants. However, the IASB noted that these regulated rates are set for public policy reasons and thus are not subject to structuring to achieve a particular accounting result. For example, the IASB noted that French retail banks collect deposits on special 'Livret A' savings accounts. The interest rate is determined by the central bank and the government according to a formula that reflects protection against inflation and an adequate remuneration that incentivises entities to use these particular savings accounts. This is because legislation requires a particular portion of the amounts collected by the retail banks to be lent to a governmental agency that uses the proceeds for social programmes. The IASB noted that the time value element of interest on these accounts may not provide consideration for only the passage of time; however the IASB believes that amortised cost would provide relevant and useful information as long as the contractual cash flows do not introduce risks or volatility that are inconsistent with a basic lending arrangement. [IFRS 9:BC4.180]

When the contractual return on a debt instrument is not derived from an interest rate index, care is required in assessing whether the contractual return is consideration for the time value of money and the credit risk of the borrower. IFRS 9 provides examples of the application of the contractual cash flows characteristics test when the return is based on a non-interest rate index.

Example 5.4.3G

Bonds with a stated maturity date

[IFRS 9:B4.1.13 Instrument A]

Instrument A is a bond with a stated maturity date. Payments of principal and interest on the principal amount outstanding are linked to an inflation index of the currency in which the instrument is issued. The inflation link is not leveraged and the principal is protected.

The contractual cash flows are solely payments of principal and interest on the principal amount outstanding. Linking payments of principal and interest on the principal amount outstanding to an unleveraged inflation index resets the time value of money to a current level. In other words, the interest rate on the instrument reflects 'real' interest. Thus, the interest amounts are consideration for the time value of money on the principal amount outstanding.

However, if the interest payments were indexed to another variable such as the debtor's performance (e.g. the debtor's net income) or an equity index, the contractual cash flows are not payments of principal and interest on the principal amount outstanding (unless the indexing to the debtor's performance results in an adjustment that only compensates the holder for changes in the credit quality of the instrument, such that contractual cash flows are solely payments of principal and interest). That is because the contractual cash flows reflect a return that is inconsistent with a basic lending arrangement (see IFRS 9:B4.1.7A).

Example 5.4.3H

Euro-inflation linked bonds

Within the Eurozone, governments issue inflation-linked bonds with one of the following characteristics:

- the inflation index is tied to the specific issuing country and the bond is denominated in Euros (e.g. a bond issued by the French government denominated in Euros where the interest is determined as fixed interest multiplied by the official French inflation index); or
- the inflation index is based on the Eurozone inflation rate and the bond is denominated in Euros (e.g. a bond issued by the French government denominated in Euros where the interest is determined as fixed interest multiplied by the official Eurozone inflation index).

Assuming that all other contractual terms represent solely payments of principal and interest on the principal outstanding, the linking to inflation in the instruments described above meet the contractual cash flows characteristics test.

Irrespective of whether the inflation referenced in the bond is the domestic inflation of a particular issuing country within the Eurozone, or the Eurozone inflation itself, the interest amounts can be considered to compensate the holder for the time value of money because the interest rate on the instrument reflects a 'real' interest rate for that economic environment.

IFRS 9 does not specifically address whether an inflation-linked bond must be principal protected (i.e. in the case of cumulative deflation over the life of the instrument, the principal must be paid back in full) in order to qualify for amortised cost measurement. The example included in IFRS 9 refers to the principal on the inflation-linked bond being protected but does not refer to the protection of the principal as being relevant in the accounting analysis.

It is reasonable to conclude that as long as the contractual interest on the inflation-linked bond reflects the possibility of a reduced principal due to the risk of cumulative deflation over the instrument's life, the instrument's contractual terms are regarded as having cash flows that are solely payments of principal and interest on the principal outstanding. Generally, the possibility of cumulative deflation (and, therefore, the risk of a reduction in the principal) will result in a higher contractual interest return when compared to an inflation-linked bond with principal protection. As long as the overall return on both instruments provides the holder with interest that is regarded as consideration for the time value of money and the credit risk of the borrower, both types of inflation-linked bonds would meet the contractual cash flows characteristics test.

5.4.4 Prepayment options

A contract may permit the issuer to prepay, or the holder to put back, a debt instrument before maturity. Whether a prepayment option passes the contractual cash flows characteristics test will depend on what events are needed to occur that then permit the issuer to prepay or the holder to put back, and the prepayment amount. Generally, both factors are important in determining whether the financial asset gives rise only to contractual cash flows that are a return of principal and interest on the principal outstanding.

As noted in **5.4.3** when the amount and/or timing of contractual cash flows are contingent on a future event consideration must be given to the nature of the event. While the nature of the contingent event in itself is not a determinative factor in assessing whether the contractual cash flows are solely payments of principal and interest, it may be an indicator. [IFRS 9:B4.1.10]

Therefore, a prepayment option that is exercisable only when an event happens that is unrelated to the risks associated with a basic lending arrangement, for example, a return not based on the time value of money, credit risk of the borrower and liquidity risk of the instrument, may not pass the contractual cash flows characteristics test. The inclusion of risks unrelated to a basic lending arrangement may not provide a return of principal and interest on the principal outstanding.

Example 5.4.4A

Prepayment option linked to credit quality of the borrower

Entity F borrows CU10m from a bank. The borrowing agreement permits the bank to demand early repayment if Entity F's credit rating slips three notches relative to the rating when the loan was made.

The contingent feature within the early repayment term is consistent with a return of principal and interest on the principal outstanding as the contingent event is directly linked to the credit risk of the borrower. The credit risk of the borrower is a risk that is reflected in a basic lending arrangement.

Example 5.4.4B

Lender's option to demand early repayment contingent on covenant breach

Entity E lends CU10 million to Entity F at a fixed interest rate; the loan is repayable in three years. Entity E has the right to demand early repayment at par plus accrued interest if Entity F's interest cover ratio (ratio of profit before interest cost to interest cost) falls below a specified level.

Even though the prepayment option is contingent on a future event (i.e. the future interest cover ratio), the prepayment option does not breach the contractual cash flows characteristics test because the feature protects the lender from the risk of non-payment by the borrower in circumstances when the borrower is subject to low profitability.

Where the issuer's right to prepay, or holder's right to demand repayment, is exercisable without being subject to a contingent event, other than the passage of time, then the analysis is simpler. Consideration only needs to be given to whether the prepayable amount is solely a return of principal and interest on the principal outstanding.

IFRS 9:B4.1.11 provides an example of when a prepayment option is considered a contractual cash flow that is solely payments of principal and interest on the principal outstanding. The example given is where the issuer is permitted to prepay, or the holder is permitted to require the issuer to prepay, when the prepayment amount substantially represents an unpaid amount of principal and interest on the principal amount outstanding, which may include reasonable additional compensation for the early termination of the contract.

The example included in IFRS 9:B4.1.11 illustrates the principle that the prepayment term should merely accelerate the timing of the principal that is due at maturity. Additional compensation above the principal amount often represents compensation for interest rate risk.

In the case of floating rate debt instruments the issuer and borrower are indifferent to changes in interest rates in terms of when to exercise the prepayment option as the debt instrument is continuously being reset to a market interest rate. Therefore, it is unlikely that compensation will be included for changes in interest rates other than the compensation for any contractual coupon that has accrued but not been settled.

Compensation for early termination of the contact will be common when the debt instrument has a fixed rate and market interest rates have fallen since the debt was issued. If the issuer prepays the debt early the holder will often be compensated for the interest rate risk benefit it previously had in holding debt with an interest rate higher than the interest rate that would be achieved if investing in debt at the prepayment date. The compensation may be calculated by comparing the remaining contractual coupons with the return that would be achieved by the holder investing in a debt instrument with a comparable credit rating with the same time to maturity. The interest rate differential is compared and the difference is present valued. Compensation in cases like this is often referred to as a 'make-whole' provision.

Example 5.4.4C

Borrower's option to prepay at par

Entity A lends CU10 million to Entity B at a fixed interest rate; the loan is repayable in three years. Entity B has the right to prepay the loan after the first anniversary of the loan at CU10 million plus any accrued interest.

The prepayment option written by Entity A as part of the loan to Entity B does not breach the contractual cash flows characteristics test because the right to prepay merely results in the acceleration of the payment of principal outstanding plus accrued interest since the last interest payment date.

Example 5.4.4D

Borrower's option to prepay at a premium

Entity B lends CU10 million to Entity C at a fixed interest rate; the loan is repayable in three years. Entity C has the right to prepay the loan after the first anniversary of the loan at CU10 million plus any accrued interest plus a prepayment penalty.

The prepayment option written by Entity B as part of the loan to Entity C does not breach the contractual cash flows characteristics test because the right to prepay merely results in the acceleration of the payment of principal outstanding. Compensation for accrued interest and a reasonable penalty which aims to compensate Entity B for reinvestment risk (because Entity C is more likely to prepay the loan when interest rates have fallen) would not breach the contractual cash flows characteristics test.

Example 5.4.4E

Borrower's option to prepay at a variable premium

Entity C lends CU10 million to Entity D at a fixed interest rate; the loan is repayable in three years. Entity D has the right to prepay the loan at an amount equal to the present value of the remaining contractual interest and principal payments (i.e. payments due up to including the end of Year 3) discounted by the original effective interest rate adjusted for changes in interest rates since origination if the risk-free market interest rate is lower than the equivalent risk-free market interest rate at origination. The prepayment penalty (otherwise known as a 'make-whole' provision) aims to compensate the lender for decreases in market interest rates since the loan was originated.

Because the exercise of the prepayment feature provides the lender with compensation for unpaid amounts of principal and interest on the principal amount outstanding, the prepayment feature does not breach the contractual cash flows characteristics test.

Example 5.4.4F

Lender's option to demand early repayment contingent on change in tax law

Entity F lends CU10 million to Entity G at a fixed interest rate; the loan is repayable in three years. Entity F has the right to demand early repayment at par plus unpaid accrued interest from Entity G if there is a change in tax law that has a negative impact on Entity F's post-tax internal rate of return on its lending.

Similarly, Entity G may have the right to repay the loan if a change in tax law adversely affects the post-tax cost of its borrowing from Entity F.

In either case, because the prepayment option is contingent on a change in relevant taxation that is designed to protect the borrower or lender from adverse effects of changes in taxation, and in doing so, protect the post-tax interest return on the principal amount outstanding, the prepayment feature does not breach the contractual cash flows characteristics test.

Example 5.4.4G

Lender's option to demand early repayment contingent on a change of control

Entity G lends CU100 million to Entity H at a fixed interest rate; the loan is repayable in five years. Entity G has the right to demand early repayment at par plus unpaid accrued interest from Entity H if there is a change in control of Entity H. The change of control provision provides protection to Entity G should Entity H be acquired by a group with a worse credit quality.

Because the prepayment option is contingent on a change in control that provides the lender with protection from adverse changes in credit quality of the borrower, the prepayment feature does not breach the contractual cash flows characteristics test.

Example 5.4.4H

Lender's option to demand early repayment contingent on change in credit rating

Entity X lends CU10 million to Entity Y at a fixed interest rate; the loan is perpetual. Entity X has the right to demand early repayment at par plus unpaid accrued interest from Entity Y if Entity Y's credit rating falls by more than three notches compared with the rating at origination.

Because the prepayment option is contingent on a change in credit rating of the borrower that is designed to provide the lender with protection from adverse changes in credit quality of the borrower, the prepayment feature does not breach the contractual cash flows characteristics test.

Example 5.4.4I

Mortgage loan with put option linked to the loan-to-value ratio

Entity Q lends CU10 million to Entity P. The terms of the loan require repayment of CU10 million plus interest by Entity P in five years.

The loan is secured on real estate. When the loan is originated, the principal borrowed represents 50 per cent of the appraised value of the real estate (i.e. the loan-to-value ratio is 50 per cent). Entity Q has the right to demand early repayment of the loan at par plus accrued interest if the loan-to-value ratio exceeds 70 per cent during the five-year term (i.e. Entity Q has a contingent prepayment option).

For lenders, a lower loan-to-value ratio means lower credit risk. An increase in the loan-to-value ratio since the date of lending may be evidence of higher credit risk. Therefore, in the circumstances described, it might be argued that the prepayment option triggered by a deterioration in the loan-to-value ratio is designed to protect Entity Q against the credit deterioration of Entity P. However, whether this is the case is a matter requiring careful judgement based on the specific facts and circumstances. If the loan-to-value ratio that forms part of the terms of the contractual arrangement is a reasonable measure to protect the lender against the credit deterioration of the borrower (e.g. defaults, credit downgrades or loan covenant violations) then it passes the contractual cash flow characteristics test.

Circumstances in which the loan-to-value ratio might be considered a reasonable measure to protect the lender against the credit deterioration of the borrower include (but are not limited to):

- the change in the loan-to-value ratio which triggers repayment indicates a credit deterioration of the borrower (e.g. in circumstances when the assets available to creditors at liquidation of the borrower consist primarily of the collateral, i.e. the real estate); and
- if the loan is a non-recourse instrument such that the lender's claim is limited to the real estate financed, additional consideration should be given to the guidance in IFRS 9:B4.1.16-17 in determining whether the instrument gives rise to contractual cash flows that are solely payments of principal and interest.

IFRS 9:B4.1.11(a) & (b) include examples where the contractual provisions permit the issuer (i.e. the debtor) to prepay a debt instrument or permit the holder (i.e. the creditor) to put a debt instrument back to the issuer before maturity. Other than in the specific exemption in IFRS 9:B4.1.12 the Standard does not specifically refer to contractual terms that *require* the instrument to be repaid prior to maturity, i.e. early repayment is not optional.

Where the provision for early repayment is automatic, and not an option, the provision should be assessed against the criteria in IFRS 9:B4.1.10 - 12 as if it was an option. For example, if an automatic prepayment provision protects the holder against the credit deterioration of the issuer then this provision would pass the contractual cash flow characteristics test.

Example 5.4.4J

Loan with an automatic provision to prepay

Entity R lends CU10 million to Entity S. The terms of the loan require repayment of CU10 million plus interest by Entity S in five years.

If Entity S breaches any term of the loan agreement, the principal outstanding and any accrued interest become immediately repayable. When a breach occurs, no action by Entity R is required; the acceleration of the repayment date is automatic.

It is established that the acceleration of the repayment date represents a protection for Entity R against the credit deterioration of Entity S.

Economically speaking, the triggering of an automatic acceleration of the repayment date that protects the lender from credit risk of the borrower is similar to a prepayment option where the lender has an option to require the borrower to repay the loan prior to maturity in the case of an increase in the credit risk of the borrower. Provided that the link to the contingent event that accelerates the repayment date is to protect the lender (Entity R) against the credit deterioration of the borrower (Entity S), an 'automatic' acceleration should be treated in the same way as an acceleration instigated by the holder.

Therefore, assuming that all contractual terms other than the automatic prepayment provision represent solely payments of principal and interest on the principal outstanding, the inclusion of the automatic prepayment provision does not breach the contractual cash flow characteristics test.

IFRS 9 includes a specific criterion for certain prepayable loans which are acquired or originated at a premium or discount to the contractual par amount. IFRS 9:B4.1.12 states that if all other contractual cash flows of the financial asset pass the contractual cash flow characteristics test other than the prepayment feature, and despite the requirements in IFRS 9:B4.1.10 that require an assessment of the contingent event in the case where the prepayment option is subject to a contingent event, the instrument will pass the contractual cash flow characteristics test if:

[IFRS 9:B4.1.12]

(a) The entity acquires or originates the financial asset at a premium or discount to the contractual par amount;

(b) The prepayment amount substantially represents the contractual par amount and accrued (and unpaid) contractual interest, which may include reasonable additional compensation for the early termination of the contract; and

(c) When the entity initially recognises the financial asset, the fair value of the prepayment feature is insignificant.

The specific criteria included in IFRS 9:B4.1.12 were originally designed to permit certain acquired prepayable distressed debt to pass the contractual cash flow characteristics test. In developing IFRS 9 the IASB considered that if distressed debt was acquired at a discount to the contractual par amount because of credit deterioration since the debt was originally issued, and that the issuer had the right to prepay the debt (or holder right to demand the issuer prepay), that the prepayment option should not result in the contractual cash flow characteristics test being breached. The logic being that the right of the issuer to prepay, or right of the holder to demand repayment is of little consequence given that at initial recognition the borrower has limited ability to repay the debt given its deterioration in credit standing since the debt was originally issued. On further deliberation the IASB concluded that the argument in favour of passing the contractual cash flow characteristics test for certain prepayable distressed debt equally applied to non-distressed debt that was purchased (or originated) at a premium to the contractual par amount.

IFRS 9:B4.1.12(a) & (b) refer to the 'contractual par amount'. This is the par amount (or principal amount) as stated in the contract. This is not to be confused with the 'principal amount' used throughout IFRS 9 which as noted in IFRS 9:4.1.3 is the fair value of the financial asset at initial recognition.

Example 5.4.4K

Prepayable debt security purchased at an amount above the contractual par amount

Entity A purchases a debt security in the secondary market that is repayable at par on maturity and that pays interest at a fixed rate throughout its life. The issuer may prepay the debt security at par plus unpaid interest at any time during the life of the security plus additional compensation in the form of a 'make-whole' provision when market interest rates are lower at the prepayment date than when the debt was originally issued. The prepayment feature had an insignificant fair value when Entity A acquired the debt security.

Interest rates had fallen since the debt was issued and the issuer's credit quality had remained stable and therefore Entity A purchased the debt security at a premium above the contractual par amount when the fair value of the prepayment was insignificant.

For Entity A the debt security passes the contractual cash flow characteristics test even though the debt was acquired at a premium above the contractual par amount, because the prepayment amount substantially represents the contractual par amount, plus accrued interest, with compensation for lower interest rates and the fair value of the prepayment feature was insignificant when Entity A initially recognised it.

5.4.5 Extension options

A contract may permit the issuer to extend the term of the borrowing, or permit the holder to extend the term of its lending. Whether an extension option passes the contractual cash flows characteristics test will be influenced by what events are needed to occur that then permits the issuer or holder to extend the term of the instrument, and what are the terms of the instrument following extension and for the remaining life. Both factors are important in determining whether the financial asset gives rise only to contractual cash flows that are a return of principal and interest on the principal outstanding.

As noted in **5.4.3** when the amount and/or timing of contractual cash flows are contingent on a future event, consideration must be given to the nature of the event. While the nature of the contingent event in itself is not a determinative factor in assessing whether the contractual cash flows are solely payments of principal and interest, it may be an indicator. [IFRS 9:B4.1.10]

Therefore, an extension option that is exercisable only when an event happens that is unrelated to the risks associated with a basic lending arrangement, for example, a return not based on the time value of money, credit risk of the borrower or liquidity risk of the instrument, may not pass the contractual cash flows characteristics test. The inclusion of risks unrelated to a basic lending arrangement may not provide a return of principal and interest on the principal outstanding.

Example 5.4.5A

Term extension option with a borrower's right to choose the basis of interest

Entity T lends CU10 million to Entity U at a fixed interest rate; the loan is repayable in three years. Entity U has the right to extend the term of the borrowing by an additional two years. If Entity U wishes to exercise its right to extend its borrowing, it must make the election in the final year prior to maturity.

The interest on the loan after extension for Years 4 and 5 is either a fixed market rate of interest determined at the start of Year 4 or 3-month LIBOR plus a 100 basis points reset every three months. Entity U must decide the basis of interest on the day it exercises the option to extend the maturity of its borrowing.

The extension option inherent in the loan does not breach the contractual cash flows characteristics test because after the term has been extended it will result in a debt instrument that provides solely for payments of principal and interest on the principal amount outstanding. The fact that Entity U can choose the basis of interest prior to the loan being extended is not a violation of the contractual cash flows characteristics test because the interest on the loan is solely compensation to the lender for the time value of money and the credit risk of the borrower. Entity U is effectively the holder of a loan commitment to draw down a loan in the future at a pre-specified interest rate.

Example 5.4.5B

Term extension option where extended loan is not derived from an interest rate index

Entity U lends CU10 million to Entity V at a fixed interest rate; the loan is repayable in three years. Entity V has the right to extend the term of the borrowing by a further two years. If Entity V wishes to exercise its right to extend its borrowing, it must make the election in the final year prior to maturity.

The principal of the loan payable in Year 5 (i.e. after extension) will be based on the movements in the FTSE-100 equity price index from the start of Year 4.

The extension option inherent in the loan breaches the contractual cash flows characteristics test because, although the option is not contingent on future events, the extended loan would not provide Entity U with payments of only principal and interest on the principal amount outstanding because the principal return is derived from an equity price index. In effect, Entity U has written an option inherent in the original loan for Entity V to issue an equity linked note at a specified date in the future, consideration for which is non-payment of the principal at the end of Year 3.

5.4.6 Perpetual debt instruments

The fact that an instrument is perpetual (i.e. it has no stated maturity date) does not in itself mean that the contractual cash flows are not payments of principal and interest on the principal amount outstanding. Consideration will need to be given to the contractual interest rate, which will include whether it provides for consideration for the time value of money, credit risk of the borrower, liquidity risk, and a profit margin for the lender. Variability in the contractual cash flows due to factors other than this will generally result in the instrument failing the contractual cash flows characteristics test.

IFRS 9:B4.1.14 Instrument H describes a perpetual instrument and notes that a perpetual instrument is like a stream of continuous (multiple) extension options (see **5.4.5** for extension options). Such options will result in contractual cash flows that are payments of principal and interest on the principal amount outstanding if the contractual cash flows following each interest payment (i.e. each extension option) are themselves considered solely payments of principal and interest on the principal amount outstanding.

A perpetual interest may also be prepayable by the issuer, or the holder may demand early repayment. The prepayment feature shall be considered in the same way as a prepayment feature on debt with a maturity date, i.e. one that is not perpetual and has a specified term (see **5.4.4** for prepayment options).

Example 5.4.6

Callable perpetual fixed rate debt security

Entity A issues floating rate debt for €100m that has a coupon equal to EURIBOR plus 200 basis points on contractual par amount of €100m. Entity A may repay the debt at its contractual par amount on the anniversary of the issue date.

Entity B acquires the debt in the secondary market at €95m, at a discount to the contractual par amount, following a deterioration in the credit quality of Entity A since the security was issued, when the fair value of the prepayment option is insignificant.

The financial asset passes the contractual cash flows characteristics test as the prepayment amount is equal to the contractual par amount and the prepayment option at initial recognition is considered as having an insignificant fair value. The contractual cash flows, representing the floating rate coupon compensate the holder for the time value of money.

5.4.7 Contractual return not based on an interest rate index

Instruments that provide the holder with an economic interest or participation in a risk that is not consistent with a basic lending arrangement will generally not pass the contractual cash flows characteristics test. Examples include equity price risk and commodity price risk.

Example 5.4.7

Convertible bond

[IFRS 9:B4.1.14 Instrument F]

Instrument F is a bond that is convertible into a fixed number of equity instruments of the issuer.

The holder would analyse the convertible bond in its entirety.

The contractual cash flows are not payments of principal and interest on the principal amount outstanding because they reflect a return that is inconsistent with a basic lending arrangement (see IFRS 9:B4.1.7A); i.e. the return is linked to the value of the equity of the issuer.

5.4.8 Collateral or security

The right of the lender to access collateral or security of the borrower in the case of non-payment under the contractual terms of the loan does not in itself prevent the loan from meeting the contractual cash flows characteristics test. A loan may be unsecured, fully secured (i.e. the security value is equal to or in excess of the amount due from the borrower), or partly secured (i.e. the security is less than the amount due from the borrower). Under- or over-collateralisation does not mean that a loan cannot meet the contractual cash flows characteristics test if the contractual interest rate charged reflects the credit risk associated with the borrower.

When assessing the impact of collateral or security on financial asset classification, consideration should be given to the non-recourse provisions in IFRS 9 described in **5.4.13**.

Example 5.4.8A

Full recourse loan secured by collateral

[IFRS 9:B4.1.13 Instrument D]

Instrument D is a full recourse loan and is secured by collateral.

The fact that a full recourse loan is collateralised does not in itself affect the analysis of whether the contractual cash flows are solely payments of principal and interest on the principal amount outstanding.

When the terms of a loan are such that the interest or principal is not contractually required to be paid due to reasons other than the borrower's ability to meet the contractual obligations (i.e. the borrower's credit risk) and there is no concurrent adjustment for further compensation for deferred payment of interest or principal, such terms will generally not be regarded as giving rise to cash flows that are solely payments of principal and interest on the principal amount outstanding as the lender does not receive compensation for the time value of money and credit risk of the borrower when the payments are deferred. This is illustrated in **example 5.4.8B**.

Example 5.4.8B

Perpetual instrument with issuer call option

[IFRS 9:B4.1.14 Instrument H]

Instrument H is a perpetual instrument but the issuer may call the instrument at any point and pay the holder the par amount plus accrued interest due.

Instrument H pays a market interest rate but payment of interest cannot be made unless the issuer is able to remain solvent immediately afterwards.

Deferred interest does not accrue additional interest.

The contractual cash flows are not payments of principal and interest on the principal amount outstanding. That is because the issuer may be required to defer interest payments and additional interest does not accrue on those deferred interest amounts. As a result, interest amounts are not consideration for the time value of money on the principal amount outstanding.

If interest accrued on the deferred amounts, the contractual cash flows could be payments of principal and interest on the principal amount outstanding.

[...]

Also, the fact that Instrument H is callable does not mean that the contractual cash flows are not payments of principal and interest on the principal amount outstanding unless it is callable at an amount that does not substantially reflect payment of outstanding principal and interest on that principal amount outstanding. Even if the callable amount includes an amount that reasonably compensates the holder for the early termination of the instrument, the contractual cash flows could be payments of principal and interest on the principal amount outstanding (see **5.4.4**).

5.4.9 Leverage

Leverage is a contractual cash flow characteristic of some financial assets. Leverage increases the variability of the contractual cash flows with the result that they do not have the economic characteristics of interest. Stand-alone option, forward and swap contracts are examples of financial assets that include such leverage. Thus, such contracts do not meet the contractual cash flow characteristics test and cannot be subsequently measured at amortised cost or FVTOCI. [IFRS 9:B4.1.9] Such instruments will be classified as at FVTPL (unless designated in certain hedge relationships, see **chapter B9**).

Leverage is regarded as a multiple greater than one. Therefore, a contractual cash flow that is linked to, say, LIBOR multiplied by 1.1 would be regarded as leveraged.

Example 5.4.9

Contractual leveraged return

Entity L invests in a debt instrument that has an interest rate linked to LIBOR. The contractual return is LIBOR plus 100 basis points except when LIBOR is greater than 6%. For the period when LIBOR is greater than 6%, the contractual interest return changes to LIBOR multiplied by 1.5 (i.e. if LIBOR was 7%, the contractual interest return would increase to 10.5%). The debt instrument is not regarded as having contractual terms that give rise on specified dates to cash flows that are solely payments of principal and interest on the principal outstanding and, therefore, must be measured subsequent to initial recognition at FVTPL.

5.4.10 Foreign currency

If the denomination of the interest and principal paid on an asset are different from the functional currency of the investor, this would not prevent the asset from passing the contractual cash flow characteristics test. However, if the currency denominations of the interest and the principal differ such that the currency in which the interest is denominated does not match the currency in which the principal is denominated (i.e. dual currency bonds), the disconnect would give rise to cash flows that are not solely payments of principal and interest and, consequently, prevent the financial asset from being measured at amortised cost.

Example 5.4.10

Dual currency bond

Entity D invests in a dual currency bond. The bond's principal is to be repaid in a fixed amount of Euros and periodic floating interest payments are denominated in and paid in US Dollars. Because the interest in US Dollars is derived from a US Dollar principal, but the principal due under the bond is denominated in Euros, the instrument is not regarded as having contractual terms that give rise on specified dates to cash flows that are solely payments of principal and interest on the principal outstanding and, therefore, must be measured subsequent to initial recognition at FVTPL.

5.4.11 Non-genuine and de minimis contractual terms

A contractual cash flow characteristic does not affect the classification of the financial asset if it could have only a de minimis effect on the contractual cash flows of the financial asset. To make this determination, an entity must consider the possible effect of the contractual cash flow characteristic in each reporting period and cumulatively over the life of the financial instrument. In addition, if a contractual cash flow characteristic could have an effect on the contractual cash flows that is more than de minimis (either in a single reporting period or cumulatively) but that cash flow characteristic is not genuine, it does not affect the classification of a financial asset. A cash flow characteristic is not genuine if it affects the instrument's contractual cash flows only on the occurrence of an event that is extremely rare, highly abnormal and very unlikely to occur. [IFRS 9:B4.1.18]

The use of the term 'genuine' in IFRS 9 is similar to the use of the term non-genuine in IAS 32:25 when considering the classification of financial instruments with contingent settlement provisions (see **2.1.7** in **chapter B3**).

5.4.12 Non-contractual terms

The contractual cash flows characteristics test should consider only those provisions that form part of the contractual arrangement. In some cases, the return to the holder receives may depend on a non-contractual term, for example, a statutory right which impacts the amount of contractual cash flows that the holder receives. IFRS 9 includes an example of such a feature where a national resolving authority has the right to enforce non-payment by the issuer and in doing so forces losses onto the holder. If this feature is as a result of a statutory provision enforced by a government, or similar body, then the feature is not considered in assessing the contractual cash flows for the purposes of classification of the financial asset by the holder.

Example 5.4.12

Non-contractual terms enforced by national resolving authority

[IFRS 9:B4.1.13 Instrument E]

Instrument E is issued by a regulated bank and has a stated maturity date. The instrument pays a fixed interest rate and all contractual cash flows are non-discretionary.

However, the issuer is subject to legislation that permits or requires a national resolving authority's power to impose losses on the holders of particular instruments, including Instrument E, in particular circumstances. For example, the national resolving authority has the power to write down the par amount of Instrument E or to convert it into a fixed number of the issuer's ordinary shares if the national resolving authority determines that the issuer is having severe financial difficulties, needs additional regulatory capital or is 'failing'.

The holder would analyse the contractual terms of the financial instrument to determine whether they give rise to cash flows that are solely payments of principal and interest on the principal amount outstanding and thus are consistent with a basic lending arrangement.

That analysis would not consider the payments that arise only as a result of the national resolving authority's power to impose losses on the holders of Instrument E. That is because that power, and the resulting payments are not contractual terms of the financial instrument.

In contrast, the contractual cash flows would not be solely payments of principal and interest on the principal amount outstanding if the contractual terms of the financial instrument permit or require the issuer or another entity to impose losses on the holder (e.g. by writing down the par amount or by converting the instrument into a fixed number of the issuer's ordinary shares) as long as that contractual term is genuine, even if the probability is remote that such a loss will be imposed.

5.4.13 Non-recourse debt instruments

In some circumstances, a financial asset may have contractual cash flows that are described as principal and interest but those cash flows do not represent the payment of principal and interest on the principal amount outstanding as described in IFRS 9:4.1.2(b), 4.1.2A(b) & 4.1.3. [IFRS 9:B4.1.15]

This may be the case if the financial asset represents an investment in particular assets or cash flows and hence the contractual cash flows are not solely payments of principal and interest on the principal amount outstanding. For example, if the contractual terms stipulate that the financial asset's cash flows increase as more automobiles use a particular toll road, those contractual cash flows are inconsistent with a basic lending arrangement. As a result, the instrument would not satisfy the contractual cash flows characteristics test. This could be the case when a creditor's claim is limited to specified assets of the debtor or the cash flows from specified assets (e.g. some 'non-recourse' financial assets). [IFRS 9:B4.1.16]

However, the fact that a financial asset is non-recourse does not in itself necessarily preclude the financial asset from meeting the contractual cash flows characteristics test. In such situations, the creditor is required to assess ('look through to') the particular underlying assets or cash flows to determine whether the contractual cash flows of the financial asset being classified are payments of principal and interest on the principal amount outstanding. If the terms of the financial asset give rise to any other cash flows or limit the cash flows in a manner inconsistent with payments representing principal and interest, the financial asset does not meet the contractual cash flows characteristics test. Whether the underlying assets are financial assets or non-financial assets does not in itself affect this assessment. [IFRS 9:B4.1.17]

When a debt instrument's contractual cash flows are specifically derived from specified assets of the borrower, care needs to be exercised in assessing whether the cash flows arising from the debt instrument represent solely a return of principal and interest on the principal outstanding. For example, if the contractual return on a loan is dependent on the performance of a property, such that the 'principal' repayment is linked to the proceeds realised on disposal of that property, the compensation is other than for the time value of money and credit risk of the borrower because the loan represents a synthetic interest in a property.

In circumstances where cash flows are repayable by the borrower only when received on certain non-derivative assets (e.g. finance lease receivables), the 'interest' may be regarded as compensation for the time value of money and the credit risk of the borrower if the underlying assets, to which the lender has recourse, exhibit characteristics equivalent only to compensation for the time value of money and the credit risk of the borrower (in this example, the lease receivables). If the cash flows on a debt instrument were dependent on a portfolio of assets that did not represent principal and interest on the principal outstanding (e.g. a portfolio of equity investments only), the debt instrument could not qualify for amortised cost measurement.

5.4.14 Subordinated instruments

An instrument that is subordinated to other instruments may meet the contractual cash flows characteristics test if the debtor's non-payment is a breach of contract and the holder has a contractual right to unpaid amounts of principal and interest on the principal amount outstanding even in the event of the debtor's bankruptcy. [IFRS 9:B4.1.19]

For example, a trade receivable where the creditor is ranked as a general creditor would meet the test. This is the case even if the debtor issued loans that are collateralised which, in the event of bankruptcy, would give the loan holders priority over the claims of the general creditor in respect of the collateral, but do not affect the contractual right of the general creditor to unpaid principal and other amounts due. [IFRS 9:B4.1.19]

5.4.15 Contractually linked subordinated instruments

In some types of transactions, an issuer may prioritise payments to the holders of financial assets using multiple contractually linked instruments that create concentrations of credit risk (tranches). Each tranche has a subordination ranking that specifies the order in which any cash flows generated by the issuer are allocated to the tranche. In such situations, the holders of a tranche have the right to payments of principal and interest only if the issuer generates sufficient cash flows to satisfy higher-ranking tranches. [IFRS 9:B4.1.20]

An example of a contractually linked subordinated instrument is a tranche issued by a structured investment vehicle in a 'waterfall' structure that prioritises the payments by the issuer to the holders of the different tranches. Such structures specify the order in which any losses that the issuer incurs are allocated to the tranches. [IFRS 9:BC4.26]

In developing IFRS 9 the IASB proposed alternative approaches in the accounting for contractually linked instruments. As part of those deliberations, as evidenced in the Basis for Conclusions to IFRS 9, the IASB made clear that subordination in itself should not preclude passing the contractual cash flow characteristics test. IFRS 9:BC4.28 states that the ranking of an entity's instruments is a common form of subordination that affects almost all lending transactions. Commercial law (including bankruptcy law) typically sets out a basic ranking for creditors. This is required because not all creditors' claims are contractual (e.g. claims regarding damages for unlawful behaviour and for tax liabilities or social insurance contributions). Although it is often difficult to determine exactly the degree of leverage resulting from this subordination, the Board believed that it is reasonable to assume that commercial law does not intend to create leveraged credit exposure for general creditors such as trade creditors. Thus, the Board believed that the credit risk associated with general creditors does not preclude the contractual cash flows representing the payments of principal and interest on the principal amount outstanding. Consequently, the credit risk associated with any secured or senior liabilities ranking above general creditors should also not preclude the contractual cash flows from representing payments of principal and interest on the principal amount outstanding.

Although the IASB made changes to the criteria for determining the contractual cash flow characteristics test for contractually linked instruments compared with the exposure draft, the concept that subordination of itself does not preclude passing the contractual cash flow characteristics test still stands in IFRS 9.

IFRS 9 states that an investment in a tranche of contractually linked instruments meets the contractual cash flows characteristics test only if all of the following three criteria are met:

(i) the tranche must only have contractual cash flow characteristics that are solely payments of principal and interest without looking through to the underlying pool of instruments (e.g. the interest rate is not linked to, say, a commodity index); [IFRS 9:B4.1.21(a)]

In many instances, tranches, such as investments in collateralised debt obligations (CDOs), have a fixed and/or floating contractual interest return and, therefore, may meet this condition. In cases where the tranche has contractual cash flows linked to risks or indices that are not based on interest rates (e.g. equity price risks or commodity price risks), the investor's tranche will not pass the contractual cash flow characteristics test.

(ii) the underlying pool of instruments held by the entity issuing the tranche must contain one or more financial assets whose contractual cash flows are only payments of principal and interest. [IFRS 9:B4.1.23] The underlying pool of instruments can contain other instruments (e.g. derivatives), but these must only reduce the cash flow variability of the pool of instruments held whose contractual cash flows are solely payments of principal and interest or align the fixed or floating nature of the interest rate, foreign currency risk, or timing difference of the cash flows of the tranches and the cash flows of the underlying pool of financial instruments. [IFRS 9:B4.1.24(a) & (b)] When derivatives are used to reduce the cash flow variability of instruments in the pool, the combined cash flows must give rise to payments of principal and interest for this condition to be satisfied;

If an issuer of a tranche invests exclusively in derivative financial instruments, the investor's tranche would not meet the contractual cash flows characteristics test because the pool of financial instruments held by the issuer does not contain financial assets whose contractual cash flows are only payments of principal and interest on the principal outstanding.

In most instances, the issuer (a structured entity) will invest in a pool of instruments that includes at least one financial asset that would meet the contractual cash flows characteristics test. Examples include cash, receivables and debt securities such as government bonds or corporate bonds.

It is common for a structured entity that issues tranches to enter into derivative financial instruments in order to align the contractual cash flows of its pool of financial assets (e.g. loans, credit card receivables, corporate bonds) with the contractual cash flows of the tranches it issues. Derivatives that merely align the cash flows of the pool of assets with the tranches (e.g. interest rate and currency swaps) do not generally cause a tranche to fail the contractual cash flow characteristics test. When derivatives result in leverage in the structure (e.g. the notional of the interest rate swaps or currency swaps is larger than the aggregate notional of the pool of financial assets), the tranches are exposed to cash flows from derivatives which do not merely align the cash flows on the pool of assets with the tranches. The derivatives in this case do not reduce cash flow variability and, therefore, would prevent the investor's interest in the tranche passing the contractual cash flow characteristics test. The investor's interest in the tranche would therefore be required to be measured subsequent to initial recognition at FVTPL.

When the issuer of the tranche enters into multiple derivative instruments to reduce cash flow variability of the pool of assets or to align the cash flows on the pool of financial assets with the contractual cash flows of the tranche (e.g. when the issuer enters into a combination of interest rate swaps and foreign currency swaps), it is the combination of both types of derivatives that is considered in determining whether the derivatives align the cash flows of the assets with those of the tranches and thereby reduce cash flow variability.

As part of its strategy to reduce cash flow variability of the pool of assets or to align the cash flows of the pool of assets with the cash flows of the tranches, the issuer may purchase options rather than entering into solely non-optional derivative instruments. The issuer may enter into options to hedge the prepayment risk that arises when some or all of the pool of assets held by the issuer prepays. Also, interest rate or currency swaps may contain 'knock-out' features so that, if the pool of assets prepays, the swaps are extinguished in order to avoid a scenario where the issuer is 'over-hedged' (i.e. the issuer is exposed to derivatives that do not align the cash flows on the assets with those of the tranches).

An issuer may invest in assets that have a shorter term than the issued tranches. When assets have a shorter life than the tranches used to fund the assets, it is expected that the issuer will have a predetermined reinvestment strategy so that the tranche holders know in advance the assets in which the issuer will reinvest when the shorter term assets mature. This will be the case in many asset backed securitisations when the issuer invests in a programme of short-term receivables (e.g. credit card receivables or short-term unsecured loans), where the issuer has an agreement with an originator of the loans to buy more loans from the originator. It is necessary to have an understanding of the replacement assets that the issuer may purchase in order to ensure that the issuer always has at least some financial assets whose contractual cash flows are only payments of principal and interest. Additionally, the issuer may enter into derivative instruments (e.g. interest rate swaps), to hedge the forecasted cash flows on short-term recognised assets and on assets in which it intends to reinvest. For example, an issuer may issue long-term fixed rate tranches while the underlying pool of financial instruments held by the issuer consists of short-term floating rate assets and a long-term interest rate swap. The fact that the interest rate swap has a longer term than the recognised assets in the underlying pool held by the issuer does not in itself fail the contractual cash flow characteristics test for the holder of the tranches as long as the combination of the interest rate swap, the recognised assets and the forecast reinvestment in assets aligns with the cash flows due on the tranches.

In synthetic CDO structures, the structured entity typically invests in highly rated non-derivative financial assets (such as government bonds) as well as writing credit default swaps over the credit quality of referenced corporate bonds. The investor in the tranche has a synthetic interest in the performance of the corporate bonds in which the structured entity has referenced its credit default swaps. In this case, the credit default swaps neither reduce the cash flow variability of the pool of assets nor do they align the cash flows between the pool of financial assets and the tranches. Instead, they result in the structured entity failing to pay the principal on the tranche due to losses arising on the credit default swaps because the referenced corporate bonds default. The investor's interest in the tranche in the synthetic CDO, therefore, does not pass the contractual cash flow characteristics test and must be measured subsequent to initial recognition at FVTPL.

It is a requirement for the investor in the tranche to understand the operations of the structured entity, and to be able to 'look through' the structured entity in order to pass the contractual cash flow characteristics test. The investor must be able to assert that the conditions in IFRS 9:B4.1.21 & B4.1.23 – B4.1.24 will be met throughout the life of the tranche. Failure to meet any criterion will result in the tranche being measured subsequent to initial recognition at FVTPL.

(iii) the exposure to credit risk in the underlying pool of financial instruments inherent in the tranche is equal to or lower than the exposure to credit risk of the underlying pool of financial instruments (e.g. the credit rating of the tranche being assessed for classification is equal to or higher than the credit rating that would apply to a single tranche that funded the underlying pool of financial instruments). [IFRS 9:B4.1.21(c)]

The credit risk assessment in IFRS 9:B4.1.21(c) is an attempt to differentiate between tranches that have average, or less than the average, exposure to credit losses of the pool of financial instruments held by the issuer and those that have more than the average exposure to credit losses. Those that have an exposure equal to the average credit losses, or less, may pass the contractual cash flow characteristics test while those tranches that have more than the average are required to be measured subsequent to initial recognition at FVTPL.

If an investor holds the most senior, and therefore the most secure, tranche issued by the issuing entity it would typically meet the condition in IFRS 9:B4.1.21(c) for that tranche and, therefore, potentially pass the contractual cash flow characteristics test. Conversely, if the investor holds the most junior, and therefore the least secure, tranche (often referred to as an 'equity tranche') it would typically not meet the condition in IFRS 9:B4.1.21(c) for that tranche. Investments in tranches that rank between the most senior and the most junior in the issuer's credit waterfall will require a thorough analysis to assess whether the credit risk inherent in the tranche is equal to the average, or less than the average credit risk of the pool of financial instruments held by the issuer. An investor in such a tranche would be expected to perform a sophisticated analysis of various probability weighted credit events on the portfolio of financial instruments held by the issuer in order to determine which tranche bears those credit losses. Only then can the investor assert that the tranche held has an exposure to the average or less than the average credit risk of the pool of financial instruments held by the issuer and thereby potentially pass the contractual cash flow characteristics test.

If any of the three conditions described above is not met, the contractually linked subordinated instrument will not meet the contractual cash flows characteristics test and, therefore, the investor will be required to measure the instrument subsequent to initial recognition at FVTPL.

To perform this assessment, a detailed instrument-by-instrument analysis of the pool may not be necessary. However, an entity must use judgement and perform sufficient analysis to determine whether the instruments in the pool meet the conditions in IFRS 9:B4.1.23 & B4.1.24 (see **5.4.11** for guidance on contractual cash flow characteristics that have only a de minimis effect). [IFRS 9:B4.1.25]

Example 5.4.15A

Contractually linked subordinated instruments (1)

Entity D issues contractually linked subordinated instruments (tranches) to various investors. The different tranches contain a different contractual priority to receive cash flows from Entity D. Entity D invests in a portfolio of equity securities. Entity D is obligated to pay amounts to the various tranches in order of priority when dividends are received on the underlying equity securities or when equity securities are sold and the proceeds are not invested in new equity securities. The tranches do not have a specified fixed or floating contractual return because the coupon on the tranches is dependent on the amount and timing of dividends on the equity securities.

From the perspective of the investors, none of the tranches is eligible for amortised cost or FVTOCI measurement because (i) investments in equity securities are not financial assets whose contractual cash flows are only payments of principal and interest on the principal outstanding and (ii) the contractual terms of the tranches do not give rise to cash flows that are solely payments of principal and interest on the principal outstanding because the coupon is not compensation for only the time value of money and the credit risk of the borrower.

An entity must look through until it can identify the underlying pool of instruments that are creating, rather than passing through, the cash flows. This is the underlying pool of financial instruments. [IFRS 9:B4.1.22] If it is impracticable to assess the underlying pool of instruments, the tranche must be classified at initial recognition as at FVTPL.

Example 5.4.15B

Contractually linked subordinated instruments (2)

Entity A invests in tranches issued by Entity X. Entity A 'looks through' into Entity X to discover that Entity X invests in tranches issued by Entity Y. If Entity A is unable to look through into Entity Y to determine whether the tranches issued by Entity Y to Entity X would meet the contractual cash flows characteristics test for the holder of those tranches, Entity A cannot assert that its tranches pass the contractual cash flows characteristics test.

When the underlying pool of instruments can change, all possible instruments must be considered as part of the assessment. If the underlying pool of instruments can change after initial recognition so that the pool may not meet the conditions outlined above, the tranche must be measured subsequent to initial recognition at FVTPL. However, if the underlying pool includes instruments that are collateralised by assets that do not meet the conditions in IFRS 9:B4.1.23 & 24, the ability to take possession of such assets shall be disregarded for the purposes of applying this paragraph unless the entity acquired the tranche with the intention of controlling the collateral. [IFRS 9:B4.1.26]

For example, if the underlying pool, at initial recognition of the tranche, does not include written credit derivatives, but the underlying pool could include these instruments in the future, then the tranche will not pass the contractual cash flow characteristics test. Alternatively, if the underlying pool includes, or could include in the future, financial assets that are secured on property which is only available to the holder in the case of foreclosure of the financial asset as a result of default of the borrower, and default is not probable at the date the financial asset is acquired, then the inclusion of such financial assets in the pool will not fail the contractual cash flow characteristics test.

5.5 Fair value through profit or loss

Any financial asset that does not qualify for amortised cost measurement (see **section 5.2**) or measurement at FVTOCI (see **section 5.3**) must be measured subsequent to initial recognition at FVTPL (except if it is an investment in an equity instrument designated at FVTOCI, see **5.3.2**).

5.5.1 Financial assets that fail the contractual cash flows characteristics test

The following are some examples of the types of instruments that will be required to be measured subsequent to initial recognition at FVTPL as they fail the contractual cash flows characteristics test in IFRS 9:4.1.2(b) and 4.1.2A(b) (the list is not exhaustive):

- investments in equity instruments (unless irrevocably designated as at FVTOCI – see **5.3.2**);
- derivative financial assets (including embedded derivative assets required to be separated in accordance with IFRS 9 – see **chapters B4** & **B5**);
- an investment in a convertible bond or loan note;
- a purchased option to buy a financial asset;
- a foreign currency forward contract to buy one currency and sell a different currency at a specific time and amount in the future that, at the period end, has a positive fair value (i.e. is a financial asset), and is not designated as an effective cash flow hedge or hedge of a net investment in a foreign operation;
- an investment in a dual currency bond or loan note;
- an investment in an equity-linked note where, at redemption, the principal repaid to the holder is derived from movements in a specified equity price index;
- an investment in a property loan where the amount repayable at redemption is derived from the proceeds realised on the disposal of the property by the issuer;
- an investment in the most junior tranche issued by a structured entity in an asset-backed securitisation; and
- an investment in a debt security where the contractual return in certain circumstances is a multiple of LIBOR (greater than 1.0).

5.5.2 Business models that result in measurement at FVTPL

Financial assets that do not meet the business model assessment for holding to collect the contractual cash flows in IFRS 9:4.1.2(a) or holding to collect contractual cash flows and selling financial assets in IFRS 9:4.1.2A(a) are required to be subsequently measured at FVTPL. Examples include:

[IFRS 9:B4.1.5 & B4.1.6]

- When an entity manages the performance of a portfolio of financial assets with the objective of realising cash flows through the sale of the assets. The entity makes decisions based on the assets' fair values and manages the assets to realise those fair values. In this case, the entity's objective will typically result in active buying and selling. Even if the entity will collect contractual cash flows while it holds the financial assets, the objective of such a business model is not achieved by collecting contractual cash flows and selling financial assets. This is because the collection of contractual cash flows is not integral to achieving the business model's objective; instead, it is incidental to it.
- A portfolio of financial assets that is managed and whose performance is evaluated on a fair value basis. The primary focus is fair value information and that information is used to assess the assets' performance and to make decisions
- A portfolio of financial assets that meets the definition of held for trading (see immediately below). The collection of contractual cash flows is only incidental to achieving the business model's objective.

IFRS 9:Appendix A defines held for trading as a financial asset or financial liability that:

(a) is acquired or incurred principally for the purpose of selling or repurchasing it in the near term;

(b) on initial recognition is part of a portfolio of identified financial instruments that are managed together and for which there is evidence of a recent actual pattern of short-term profit-taking; or

(c) is a derivative (except for a derivative that is a financial guarantee contract or a designated and effective hedging instrument).

Example 5.5.2A

Sale of assets to maximise yield

Entity P invests in a portfolio of debt instruments with varying maturities. Entity P's objective is to maximise the yield on its debt instruments by buying and selling bonds issued by entities in certain industry sectors. Entity P's investment mandate within each of the industry sectors is broad and, therefore, Entity P will take opportunities to maximise its yield by buying and selling bonds within an industry sector.

Entity P's business is not to hold financial assets to collect contractual cash flows nor hold to collect contractual cash flows and to sell financial asset because its time horizon for holding financial assets is unknown and is dependent on movements in market prices. Entity P's investments in debt instruments cannot qualify for amortised cost or FVTOCI measurement and therefore must be measured subsequent to initial recognition at FVTPL.

Example 5.5.2B

Sale of loans to securitisation vehicle

[IFRS 9:B4.1.4, Example 3]

An entity has a business model with the objective of originating loans to customers and subsequently selling those loans to a securitisation vehicle. The securitisation vehicle issues instruments to investors.

The originating entity controls the securitisation vehicle and thus consolidates it.

The securitisation vehicle collects the contractual cash flows from the loans and passes them on to its investors.

It is assumed for the purposes of this example that the loans continue to be recognised in the consolidated statement of financial position because they are not derecognised by the securitisation vehicle.

The consolidated group originated the loans with the objective of holding them to collect the contractual cash flows.

However, the originating entity has an objective of realising cash flows on the loan portfolio by selling the loans to the securitisation vehicle, so for the purposes of its separate financial statements it would not be considered to be managing this portfolio in order to collect the contractual cash flows.

IFRS 9 does not specifically address whether an entity can claim that its business is to collect the contractual cash flows of its financial assets when the business expects to 'transfer' the assets (in accordance with IFRS 9:3.2.4, see **3.1.4** in **chapter B8**) but, following the transfer, the financial assets will continue to be recognised in the transferor's statement of financial position.

Example 5.5.2C

Sale of instruments that continue to be recognised

Entity C holds investments in debt instruments that it intends to 'repo' (i.e. to sell the assets and concurrently enter into an obligation to repurchase the assets at a specified time and specified price). The repurchase arrangements require the transferee to pay all the cash flows it receives on the transferred assets to Entity C in return for receiving a predetermined fixed amount of cash. At the maturity of the repo Entity C intends to hold the asset to collect the contractual cash flows.

Entity C does not derecognise the assets at the date of transfer because it has retained substantially all the risks and rewards of ownership via the repo. Entity C recognises a collateralised borrowing for the proceeds received upon entering into the repo (see **chapter B8**).

In this fact pattern it is reasonable for Entity C to claim that its business is to collect the contractual cash flows on its assets subject to repo because, even though the assets are intended to be temporarily legally transferred to the transferee, Entity C continues to recognise the assets and continues to receive cash flows from the transferee equivalent to the cash flows it would have received had it not transferred the assets and following maturity of the repo Entity C intends to collect the contractual cash flows from the assets.

When an entity expects, as part of its business model, to transfer the contractual rights to cash flows on its financial assets, but to retain substantially all the risks and rewards of ownership of those financial assets (e.g. by writing a guarantee over their performance or through buying from the transferee a subordinated interest in them), it is less clear whether the entity can claim that its business is to collect the contractual cash flows on its assets. In such circumstances, the entity will not necessarily continue to receive the same cash flows that it would have received if the assets had not been transferred because some or all of those cash flows may be retained by the transferee. IFRS 9 does not address whether continued recognition of the asset is sufficient in itself for an entity to claim that the assets are held to collect the contractual cash flows, or whether a transferor that continues to recognise transferred assets also needs to argue that the expectation is to collect substantially the same cash flows under the assets as would have been received had it not transferred the assets. It will be necessary to exercise judgement in determining whether the entity's business is the collection of the contractual cash flows.

5.5.3 Designation as at FVTPL

An entity may irrevocably elect on initial recognition to designate a financial asset that meets the conditions for amortised cost measurement in accordance IFRS 9:4.1.2 (see **section 5.2**) or FVTOCI measurement in accordance with IFRS 9:4.1.2A (see **section 5.3**) as at FVTPL if that designation eliminates or significantly reduces an accounting mismatch that would have occurred if the financial asset had been measured at amortised cost or fair through other comprehensive income respectively. [IFRS 9:4.1.5]

The following are examples of the application of the fair value option.

- An entity has liabilities under insurance contracts whose measurement incorporates current information (as permitted by paragraph 24 of IFRS 4 *Insurance Contracts*), and related financial assets that would otherwise be measured either at amortised cost or FVTOCI. Designating the assets as at FVTPL means that changes in the fair value of the financial assets are recognised in profit or loss in the same period as related changes in the value of the liabilities. [IFRS 9:B4.1.30(a)]

- An entity has financial assets, financial liabilities, or both, that share a risk (e.g. interest rate risk) that gives rise to opposite changes in the fair value of those assets and liabilities that tend to offset each other. Only some of the instruments (e.g. derivatives, or assets held for trading) are measured at FVTPL. Also, the requirements for hedge accounting may not be met (e.g. because the requirements for hedge effectiveness are not met). Designating the assets and liabilities as at FVTPL will achieve an accounting offset that reflects the existing natural economic offset. [IFRS 9:B4.1.30(b)]
- An entity has financial assets, financial liabilities, or both, that share a risk (e.g. interest rate risk) that gives rise to opposite changes in the fair value of those assets and liabilities that tend to offset each other. The assets and liabilities may be measured on a different basis and hedge accounting cannot be applied because none of the instruments are measured at FVTPL. Designating the assets and liabilities as at FVTPL will achieve an accounting offset that reflects the existing natural economic offset. For example, the entity has financed a specified group of loans by issuing traded bonds whose changes in fair value tend to offset each other. If, in addition, the entity regularly buys and sells the bonds but rarely, if ever, buys and sells the loans, reporting both the loans and the bonds at FVTPL eliminates the inconsistency in the timing of recognition of gains and losses that would otherwise result from measuring them both at amortised cost and recognising a gain or loss each time a bond is repurchased. [IFRS 9:B4.1.30(c)]

Example 5.5.3A

Fair value option: fixed rate loan

Entity A originates a fixed rate loan and, at origination, it economically hedges that loan with an interest rate swap with matching terms, which swaps the fixed interest rate to a floating rate. Assuming the conditions for amortised cost or FVTOCI measurement are met, measuring the loan asset at amortised cost or FVTOCI would create an accounting mismatch with the interest rate swap measured at FVTPL. In this case, the loan could be designated at initial recognition as at FVTPL to reduce the measurement mismatch that arises from measuring the loan at amortised cost or FVTOCI and, consequently, provide more relevant information.

Example 5.5.3B

Fair value option: intragroup derivative

A subsidiary acquires a 5-year fixed rate bond which at initial recognition meets the criteria for amortised cost or FVTOCI measurement. To hedge against the interest rate risk, it enters into a pay fixed receive variable interest rate swap with its parent. In the subsidiary's financial statements, the bond is designated as at FVTPL using the fair value option. The designation cannot be applied in the consolidated financial statements because the interest rate swap is eliminated on consolidation. If the parent or another group entity had entered into an interest rate swap with a third party, a different designation could be made for the bond in the consolidated financial statements provided that the designation is made upon initial recognition.

In the examples above, for practical purposes, the entity need not have entered into all of the assets and liabilities giving rise to the measurement or recognition inconsistency at exactly the same time. The fair value option is available provided that each transaction is designated as at FVTPL at its initial recognition and, at that time, any remaining transactions are expected to occur. [IFRS 9:B4.1.31]

It would not be acceptable to designate only some of the financial assets and financial liabilities giving rise to the inconsistency as at FVTPL if to do so would not eliminate or significantly reduce the inconsistency and would therefore not result in more relevant information. However, it would be acceptable to designate only some of a number of similar financial assets or financial liabilities as at FVTPL if to do so would achieve a significant reduction (and possibly a greater reduction than other allowable designations) in the inconsistency. [IFRS 9:B4.1.32]

Example 5.5.3C

Fair value option: lack of accounting mismatch

Entity A borrows (through a single instrument) CU1,000,000 from a third-party bank and, at the same time, uses some of the loan to acquire 10 similar financial assets each of a value of CU50,000 which are all measured subsequent to initial recognition at FVTPL. Entity A wishes to reduce the measurement inconsistency by designating the bank loan as at FVTPL. IFRS 9 does not permit part, only all, of a financial instrument to be designated at FVTPL. However, if all of the loan were designated at FVTPL, Entity A would create an accounting mismatch in profit or loss related to the portion of the bank loan (CU500,000) not matched by the financial assets measured at FVTPL. This accounting mismatch is comparable to the mismatch that would have arisen if the fair value option were not applied in the first place. Therefore, Entity A cannot apply the fair value option to the loan because it would not significantly reduce the accounting mismatch between the financial assets and the financial liability.

An entity is not permitted to designate a financial asset as at FVTPL after initial recognition. The guidance appears less clear as to whether an entity is required to de-designate out of FVTPL, if previously designated as at FVTPL at initial recognition, when there is a change in the business model that would result in the instrument no longer meeting the business model qualification criteria. IFRS 9:4.4.1 requires reclassification in the case of a change in business model (see **section 7**) and does not specifically distinguish between assets that are *classified by default* at FVTPL and those that met at initial recognition the amortised cost criteria in IFRS 9:4.1.2 or FVTOCI criteria in IFRS 9:4.1.2A but were instead *designated* as at FVTPL. Because IFRS 9:BC5.25(d) refers to the option to designate a financial asset at fair value as irrevocable, it is appropriate to conclude that the requirements to reassess classification due to changes in business model for assets described in IFRS 9:4.4.1 do not apply for assets designated as at FVTPL. Consequently, if the financial asset was designated as at FVTPL at initial recognition, an entity is not permitted to reclassify out of FVTPL to amortised cost or FVTOCI should the business model change and thereby require other non-designated at FVTPL assets included in the same business to be reclassified from FVTPL to amortised cost or FVTOCI.

6 Measurement of unquoted equity investments

IFRS 9 requires all investments in equity investments to be measured at fair value. However, the Standard also recognises that, in some limited circumstances, cost may be an appropriate estimate of fair value for an unquoted equity investment. This may be the case if insufficient more recent information is available to measure fair value, or if there is a wide range of possible fair value measurements and cost represents the best estimate of fair value within that range. [IFRS 9:B5.2.3] Cost is never the best estimate of fair value for investments in quoted equity instruments (or contracts on quoted equity instruments). [IFRS 9:B5.2.6]

Indicators that cost might not be representative of fair value include:

[IFRS 9:B5.4.15]

- a significant change in the performance of the investee compared with budgets, plans or milestones;
- changes in expectation that the investee's technical product milestones will be achieved;
- a significant change in the market for the investee's equity or its products or potential products;
- a significant change in the global economy or the economic environment in which the investee operates;
- a significant change in the performance of comparable entities, or in the valuations implied by the overall market;
- internal matters of the investee such as fraud, commercial disputes, litigation, changes in management or strategy; or
- evidence from external transactions in the investee's equity, either by the investee (such as a fresh issue of equity), or by transfers of equity instruments between third parties.

This list is not exhaustive. An entity is required to use all information about the performance and operations of the investee that becomes available after the date of initial recognition. To the extent that any relevant factors indicate that cost may not be representative of fair value, the entity is required to measure fair value. [IFRS 9:B5.4.16] Further, the IASB noted that for particular entities such as financial institutions and investment funds the cost of equity investments cannot be considered representative of fair value. [IFRS 9:BC5.18]

7 Reclassification

An entity is required to reclassify financial assets when it changes its business model for managing financial assets. [IFRS 9:4.4.1]

Investments in equity instruments that are designated as at FVTOCI at initial recognition cannot be reclassified because IFRS 9:5.7.5 and BC5.25(d) are clear that the election to designate as at FVTOCI is irrevocable.

As previously described in **5.5.3**, it is not appropriate for financial assets that are *designated* as at FVTPL to be reclassified after initial recognition.

Reclassifications are expected to be very infrequent. Such changes must be determined by the entity's senior management as a result of external or internal changes and must be significant to the entity's operations and demonstrable to external parties. Accordingly, a change in an entity's business model will occur only when an entity either begins or ceases to perform an activity that is significant to its operations; for example, when the entity has acquired, disposed of or terminated a business line. [IFRS 9:B4.4.1]

Example 7A

Portfolio of commercial loans resulting in a change in business model

[IFRS 9:B4.4.1(a)]

An entity has a portfolio of commercial loans that it holds to sell in the short term. The entity acquires a company that manages commercial loans and has a business model that holds the loans in order to collect the contractual cash flows. The portfolio of commercial loans is no longer for sale, and the portfolio is now managed together with the acquired commercial loans and all are held to collect the contractual cash flows.

Example 7B

Closure of retail mortgage business resulting in a change in business model

[IFRS 9:B4.4.1(b)]

A financial services firm decides to shut down its retail mortgage business. The retail mortgage business no longer accepts new business and the financial services firm is actively marketing its mortgage loan portfolio for sale.

The following are not considered to be changes in business model:

[IFRS 9:B4.4.3]

- a change in intention related to particular financial assets (even in circumstances of significant changes in market conditions);
- a temporary disappearance of a particular market for financial assets; or
- a transfer of financial assets between parts of the entity with different business models.

If there has been no change in the business model for managing financial assets, if the terms of a financial asset remain unchanged, or the terms of a financial asset change but the asset is not derecognised, reclassification is not permitted. If the terms of an instrument change sufficiently to warrant derecognition, this would not be a reclassification; instead, the old asset is derecognised and a new one is recognised. In cases where terms inherent in the instrument expire or take effect during the instrument's life, and the asset continues to be recognised, the changing terms would not change the classification assessment made at initial recognition.

Example 7C

Terms of instrument unchanged

Entity D lends CU10 million to Entity E; the loan is repayable in five years. The contractual return on the loan for the first three years is derived from movements in a specified equity price index. In Years 4 and 5, the contractual return is 5% of par.

At initial recognition, Entity D classifies the loan as a financial asset measured as at FVTPL because the loan does not pass the contractual cash flows characteristics test (see **5.4**). The contractual return is linked to equity prices and, therefore, is not consistent with a basic lending arrangement.

Entity D is not permitted to reclassify the financial asset after Year 3, the point at which the contractual linkage to equity prices ceases, because the terms of the instrument have not changed since initial recognition and the original asset continues to be recognised.

When an asset converts into a different asset during the instrument's life, the entity must consider whether the original asset should continue to be recognised or whether, on conversion, the old instrument is derecognised and a new one is recognised.

Example 7D

Reclassification versus recognition and derecognition

Entity X invests in a convertible bond issued by Entity Y. Upon conversion, Entity X will receive a predetermined number of Entity Y's non-derivative equity instruments in exchange for giving up its right to receive the principal on the bond. On conversion, the convertible bond is derecognised and ceases to be measured at FVTPL. The equity instruments recognised may be classified as at FVTPL or designated as at FVTOCI at their initial recognition. The conversion does not give rise to a reclassification because the original instrument is derecognised.

If an entity reclassifies financial assets, it is required to apply the reclassification prospectively from the reclassification date, defined as the first day of the first reporting period following the change in business model that results in the entity reclassifying financial assets. [IFRS 9:Appendix A] The reclassification applies prospectively from the reclassification date and therefore previously recognised gains, losses (including impairment gains or losses) or interest are not restated. [IFRS 9:5.6.1]

A change in the objective of the entity's business model must be effected before the reclassification date. [IFRS 9:B4.4.2]

Example 7E

Date of reclassification

[IFRS 9:B4.4.2]

A financial services firm decides on 15 February to shut down its retail mortgage business and thus must reclassify all affected financial assets on 1 April (i.e. the first day of the entity's next reporting period). The entity must not accept new retail mortgage business or otherwise engage in activities consistent with its former business model after 15 February.

IFRS 9 is not explicit as to how to interpret the 'first day of the first reporting period following the change in business model' in the context of interim financial statements. Specifically, it is not clear whether the 'first reporting period following the change in business model' is the next interim financial reporting period or the next annual financial reporting period.

On balance, it is appropriate to regard an interim reporting period as a "reporting period" for this purpose. Therefore, when the next financial reporting period is an interim financial period, the start of that period will be the reclassification date. This is supported by Improvements to IFRSs issued in May 2010, which amends IAS 34 *Interim Financial Reporting* to clarify that disclosure is required in interim reports of "changes in the classification of financial assets as a result of a change in the purpose or use of those assets".

Example 7F

Date of reclassification for interim financial statements

Entity A changes its business model on 15 February 20X0 and, as a result, must reclassify all affected financial assets at the reclassification date (being the first day of the entity's next reporting period) from amortised cost to FVTPL.

Entity A has the following period-ends:

- half-year interim period end: 31 March 20X0;
- third-quarter interim period end: 30 June 20X0; and
- annual period end: 30 September 20X0.

The reclassification date should be 1 April 20X0, being the first day of the entity's next reporting period following the change in business model. Therefore, the third-quarter interim financial statements will reflect the effect of the reclassification of financial assets at 1 April 20X0. Further, it would not be appropriate to have multiple reclassification dates for a change in one business model. Therefore, the reclassification date of 1 April 20X0 also applies in the annual financial statements ending 30 September 20X0.

Financial statements	**Measurement basis of financial assets subject to reclassification**
Half-year interim financial statements ending 31 March 20X0	Amortised cost
Third-quarter interim financial statements ending 30 June 20X0	FVTPL
Annual financial statements ending 30 September 20X0	Six months at amortised cost and six months at FVTPL

IFRS 7 requires extensive disclosures if financial assets are reclassified (see **4.1.4** in **chapter B11**).

7.1 Measurement at the date of reclassification

IFRS 9:5.6.2 to 5.6.7 contains detailed requirements as to how to measure a financial asset when it reclassified from one classification category to another. Below is a summary of the measurement requirements that apply at the reclassification date.

		Reclassified to		
		Amortised cost	FVTOCI	FVTPL
Reclassified from	Amortised cost		Recognise at fair value with the difference between fair value and closing amortised cost recognised in other comprehensive income. The effective interest rate and the measurement of expected credit losses are not adjusted. [IFRS 9:5.6.4 & B5.6.1]	Recognise at fair value with the difference between fair value and closing amortised cost recognised in profit or loss. [IFRS 9:5.6.2] An effective interest rate or impairment gains or losses are not required to be separately recognised following reclassification. [IFRS 9:B5.6.2]
	FVTOCI	Closing fair value plus/less the cumulative amount in other comprehensive income at the reclassification date becomes the new amortised cost gross opening carrying amount. The effective interest rate and the measurement of expected credit losses are not adjusted. This adjustment affects other comprehensive income but does not affect profit or loss and therefore is not an IAS 1 reclassification adjustment. [IFRS 9:5.6.5]		Continue to measure at fair value with the cumulative amount in other comprehensive income reclassified immediately to profit or loss as an IAS 1 reclassification adjustment. [IFRS 9:5.6.7] An effective interest rate and impairment gains or losses are not required to be separately recognised following reclassification. [IFRS 9:B5.6.2]

	Reclassified to			
	FVTPL	Closing fair value becomes the new amortised cost opening gross carrying amount. At the reclassification date a new effective interest rate and measurement of expected credit losses will be determined. [IFRS 9:5.6.3]	Continue to measure at fair value with a new effective interest rate and measure a loss allowance for expected credit losses determined at the reclassification date. [IFRS 9:5.6.6]	

Example 7.1A

Measurement at date of reclassification (1)

At initial recognition, Entity H classifies a portfolio of loans at amortised cost. At initial recognition, the amortised cost is equal to fair value, CU10 million. The effective interest rate on the loans is 10%.

After initial recognition, the portfolio of loans is reclassified to FVTPL. At the date of reclassification, being the start of the reporting period immediately following the period when there was the change in the objective of the business model, the amortised cost was CU10 million. The fair value at that date was CU11 million.

At the date of reclassification, Entity H recognises a gain of CU1 million, and discloses this as a separate line item in its statement of comprehensive income.

Example 7.1B

Measurement at date of reclassification (2)

At initial recognition, Entity M classifies a portfolio of loans as at FVTPL; the loans do not qualify for amortised cost measurement because they fail the business model test. The beginning of Entity M's reporting period is 1 January 20X1. Subsequent to initial recognition, in November 20X1, the business model changes and the loans are required to be reclassified to amortised cost.

At 1 January 20X2, Entity M reclassifies the loans that were previously classified as at FVTPL to amortised cost. The fair value at 1 January 20X2 becomes the new opening gross carrying amount at amortised cost and, therefore, no gain or loss is recognised at that date. Entity M estimates the remaining contractual cash flows of the reclassified loans and determines the effective interest rate which will be applied in measuring the assets at amortised cost in future period(s).

When a financial asset is reclassified from amortised cost to FVTOCI (or vice versa) the measurement of expected credit losses will not change as both classification categories apply the same impairment approach. However, the presentation and disclosure of the impairment allowance will differ. If a financial asset is reclassified out of FVTOCI to amortised cost measurement, for presentation purposes, a loss allowance would be recognised as an adjustment to the gross carrying amount of the financial asset from the reclassification date. If a financial asset is reclassified out of amortised cost to FVTOCI measurement, for presentation purposes, a loss allowance would be derecognised (and thus would no longer be recognised as an adjustment to the gross carrying amount) but instead would be recognised as an accumulated impairment amount (of an equal amount) in other comprehensive income and would be disclosed from the reclassification date. [IFRS 9:B5.6.1(b)]

If an entity reclassifies a financial asset from amortised cost to FVTPL, it must disclose as a separate line item in its statement of comprehensive income any gain or loss arising from a difference between the previous carrying amount and its fair value on reclassification in accordance with IAS 1:82(ca). Similarly, if an entity reclassifies a financial asset from FVTOCI to FVTPL, it must disclose as a separate line in its statement of comprehensive income any gain or loss arising from reclassifying the previously recognised amount in other comprehensive income to profit or loss in accordance with IAS 1:82(cb).

Example 7.1C

Reclassification of financial assets

[IFRS 9:IE104 - 114]

An entity purchases a portfolio of bonds for its fair value (gross carrying amount) of CU500,000.

The entity changes the business model for managing the bonds in accordance with IFRS 9:4.4.1. The fair value of the portfolio of bonds at the reclassification date is CU490,000.

If the portfolio was measured at amortised cost or at fair value through other comprehensive income immediately prior to reclassification, the loss allowance recognised at the date of reclassification would be CU6,000 (reflecting a significant increase in credit risk since initial recognition and thus the measurement of lifetime expected credit losses).

The 12-month expected credit losses at the reclassification date are CU4,000.

For simplicity, journal entries for the recognition of interest revenue are not provided.

Scenario 1: Reclassification out of the amortised cost measurement category and into the fair value through profit or loss measurement category

Bank A reclassifies the portfolio of bonds out of the amortised cost measurement category and into the fair value through profit or loss measurement category. At the reclassification date, the portfolio of bonds is measured at fair value. Any gain or loss arising from a difference between the previous amortised cost amount of the portfolio of bonds and the fair value of the portfolio of bonds is recognised in profit or loss on reclassification.

	Debit	Credit
Bonds (FVTPL assets)	CU490,000	
Bonds (gross carrying amount of the amortised cost assets)		CU500,000
Loss allowance	CU6,000	
Reclassification loss(profit or loss)	CU4,000	

(To recognise the reclassification of bonds from amortised cost to fair value through profit or loss and to derecognise the loss allowance.)

Scenario 2: Reclassification out of the fair value through profit or loss measurement category and into the amortised cost measurement category

Bank A reclassifies the portfolio of bonds out of the fair value through profit or loss measurement category and into the amortised cost measurement category. At the reclassification date, the fair value of the portfolio of bonds becomes the new gross carrying amount and the effective interest rate is determined based on that gross carrying amount. The impairment requirements apply to the bond from the reclassification date. For the purposes of recognising expected credit losses, the credit risk of the portfolio of bonds at the reclassification date becomes the credit risk against which future changes in credit risk shall be compared.

	Debit	Credit
Bonds (gross carrying amount of the amortised cost assets)	CU490,000	
Bonds (FVTPL assets)		CU490,000
Impairment loss (profit or loss)	CU4,000	
Loss allowance		CU4,000

(To recognise reclassification of bonds from fair value through profit or loss to amortised cost including commencing accounting for impairment.)

Scenario 3: Reclassification out of the amortised cost measurement category and into the fair value through other comprehensive income measurement category

Bank A reclassifies the portfolio of bonds out of the amortised cost measurement category and into the fair value through other comprehensive income measurement category. At the reclassification date, the portfolio of bonds is measured at fair value. Any gain or loss arising from a difference between the previous amortised cost amount of the portfolio of bonds and the fair value of the portfolio of bonds is recognised in other comprehensive income. The effective interest rate and the measurement of expected credit losses are not adjusted as a result of the reclassification. The credit risk at initial recognition continues to be used to assess changes in credit risk. From the reclassification date the loss allowance ceases to be recognised as an adjustment to the gross carrying amount of the bond and is recognised as an accumulated impairment amount, which would be disclosed.

	Debit	**Credit**
Bonds (FVTOCI)	CU490,000	
Bonds (gross carrying amount of amortised cost assets)		CU500,000
Loss allowance	CU6,000	
Other comprehensive income *	CU4,000	

(To recognise the reclassification from amortised cost to fair value through other comprehensive income. The measurement of expected credit losses is however unchanged.)

* For simplicity, the amount related to impairment is not shown separately. If it had been, this journal entry (i.e. DR CU4,000) would be split into the following two entries: DR Other comprehensive income CU10,000 (fair value changes) and CR other comprehensive income CU6,000 (accumulated impairment amount).

Scenario 4: Reclassification out of the fair value through other comprehensive income measurement category and into the amortised cost measurement category

Bank A reclassifies the portfolio of bonds out of the fair value through other comprehensive income measurement category and into the amortised cost measurement category. The portfolio of bonds is reclassified at fair value. However, at the reclassification date, the cumulative gain or loss previously recognised in other comprehensive income is removed from equity and adjusted against the fair value of the portfolio of bonds. As a result, the portfolio of bonds is measured at the reclassification date as if it had always been measured at amortised cost. The effective interest rate and the measurement of expected credit losses are not adjusted as a result of the reclassification. The credit risk at initial recognition continues to be used to assess changes in the credit risk on the bonds. The loss allowance is recognised as an adjustment to the gross carrying amount of the bond (to reflect the amortised cost amount) from the reclassification date.

	Debit	Credit
Bonds (gross carrying value of the amortised cost assets)	CU490,000	
Bonds (FVTOCI assets)		CU490,000
Bonds (gross carrying value of the amortised cost assets)	CU10,000	
Loss allowance		CU6,000
Other comprehensive income *		CU4,000

(To recognise the reclassification from fair value through other comprehensive income to amortised cost including the recognition of the loss allowance deducted to determine the amortised cost amount. The measurement of expected credit losses is however unchanged.)

* The cumulative loss in other comprehensive income at the reclassifi cation date was CU4,000. That amount consists of the total fair value change of CU10,000 (i.e. CU500,000 – 490,000) offset by the accumulated impairment amount recognised (CU6,000) while the assets were measured at fair value through other comprehensive income.

Scenario 5: Reclassification out of the fair value through profit or loss measurement category and into the fair value through other comprehensive income measurement category

Bank A reclassifies the portfolio of bonds out of the fair value through profit or loss measurement category and into the fair value through other comprehensive measurement category. The portfolio of bonds continues to be measured at fair value. However, for the purposes of applying the effective interest method, the fair value of the portfolio of bonds at the reclassification date becomes the new gross carrying amount and the effective interest rate is determined based on that new gross carrying amount. The impairment requirements apply from the reclassification date. For the purposes of recognising expected credit losses, the credit risk of the portfolio of bonds at the reclassification date becomes the credit risk against which future changes in credit risk shall be compared.

	Debit	Credit
Bonds (FVTOCI)	CU490,000	
Bonds (FVTPL assets)		CU490,000
Impairment loss (profit or loss)	CU4,000	
Other comprehensive income		CU4,000

(To recognise the reclassification of bonds from fair value through other comprehensive income including commencing accounting for impairment. The other comprehensive income amount reflects the loss allowance at the date of reclassification (an accumulated impairment amount relevant for disclosure purposes) of CU4,000.)

Scenario 6: Reclassification out of the fair value through other comprehensive income measurement category and into the fair value through profit or loss measurement category

Bank A reclassifies the portfolio of bonds out of the fair value through other comprehensive income measurement category and into the fair value through profit or loss measurement category. The portfolio of bonds continues to be measured at fair value. However, the cumulative gain or loss previously recognised in other comprehensive income is reclassified from equity to profit or loss as a reclassification adjustment (see IAS 1 *Presentation of Financial Statements*).

	Debit	**Credit**
Bonds (FVTPL)	CU490,000	
Bonds (FVTOCI assets)		CU490,000
Reclassification loss (profit or loss)	CU4,000	
Other comprehensive income*		CU4,000

(To recognise the reclassification of bonds from fair value through other comprehensive income to fair value through profit or loss.)

* The cumulative loss in other comprehensive income at the reclassification date was CU4,000. That amount consists of the total fair value change of CU10,000 (i.e. CU500,000 – 490,000) offset by the loss allowance that was recognised (CU6,000) while the assets were measured at fair value through other comprehensive income.

B3 Financial liabilities and equity

Contents

1 Introduction

IAS 32 *Financial Instruments: Presentation* requires an issuer of a financial instrument to classify the financial instrument, or its component parts, as a financial liability or as equity in accordance with the substance of the contractual arrangement and the definitions of a financial liability and an equity instrument. The overriding principles are that when the issuer does not have an unconditional right to avoid the obligation to deliver cash or another financial asset, and when the contract does not, in substance, evidence a residual interest in the net assets of the issuer after deducting all of its liabilities, the instrument is not an equity instrument (see **section 2**).

A more complex area, in respect of which the Standard provides additional guidance, is the treatment of derivative and non-derivative contracts indexed to, or settled in, an entity's own equity instruments. The definitions of a financial asset and a financial liability also include certain contracts on own equity and are applied to evaluate whether such contracts are, in substance, equity, financial liabilities or derivatives (derivatives can be either financial assets or financial liabilities). For example, a written put option on own shares that will be settled, if the option is exercised by the holder, by delivering cash in exchange for the entity's own shares, is a financial liability because the entity will have an obligation to deliver cash (see **section 6**).

IAS 39 *Financial Instruments: Recognition & Measurement* is superseded by IFRS 9 *Financial Instruments* which is effective for annual reporting periods beginning on or after 1 January 2018. The characteristics of financial liabilities and equity as detailed in IAS 32 are unchanged following the introduction of IFRS 9. The IASB has included financial instruments with characteristics of equity as part of its research agenda (see **section 9**).

This chapter addresses the application of the financial liability and equity definitions to various types of financial instruments issued in practice and contracts indexed to and settled in an entity's own equity. It also indicates the implications of classification as either debt, equity or a derivative for the measurement of that contract or its component parts.

2 Principles of liability/equity classification

A financial instrument or its component parts should be classified upon initial recognition as a financial liability or an equity instrument according to the substance of the contractual arrangement, rather than its legal form, and the definitions of a financial liability and an equity instrument. [IAS 32:15 & 18] For some financial instruments, although their legal form may be equity, the substance of the arrangements is that they are liabilities. A preference share, for example, may display either equity or liability characteristics depending on the substance of the rights attaching to it.

The appropriate classification as a financial liability, equity or a combination of both, is determined by the entity when the financial instrument is initially recognised and that classification is not generally changed subsequently unless the terms of the instrument change. As exceptions to this general principle, **section 8** discusses a number of circumstances in which reclassification may be appropriate even though the terms of the instrument have not changed. In addition, when the specific requirements for puttable instruments and instruments that contain an obligation to deliver a pro rata share of net assets at liquidation described in **2.1.2.1** and **2.1.3** respectively no longer apply or start to apply, reclassification may be appropriate.

When classifying a financial instrument in consolidated financial statements, an entity should consider all of the terms and conditions agreed upon between members of the group and the holders of the instrument. For example, a financial instrument issued by a subsidiary could be classified as equity in the subsidiary's individual financial statements and as a liability in the consolidated financial statements if another group entity has provided a guarantee to make payments to the holder of the instrument.

IAS 32 defines a financial liability as any liability that is:

[IAS 32:11]

(a) a contractual obligation:
  - (i) to deliver cash or another financial asset to another entity (e.g. a payable); or
  - (ii) to exchange financial assets or financial liabilities with another entity under conditions that are potentially unfavourable to the entity (e.g. a financial option written by the entity); or

(b) a contract that will or may be settled in the entity's own equity instruments and is:
  - (i) a non-derivative contract for which the entity is or may be obliged to deliver a variable number of its own equity instruments (e.g. an instrument that is redeemable in own shares to the value of the carrying amount of the instrument); or
  - (ii) a derivative contract over own equity that will or may be settled other than by the exchange of a fixed amount of cash (or another financial asset) for a fixed number of the entity's own equity instruments (e.g. a net-share settled written call over own shares). For this purpose, rights, options or warrants to acquire a fixed number of the entity's own equity instruments for a fixed amount of any currency are equity instruments if the entity offers the rights, options or warrants pro rata to all of its existing owners of the same class of its own non-derivative equity instruments. Also for these purposes, the entity's own equity instruments do not include puttable financial instruments that are classified as equity instruments in accordance with IAS 32:16A and 16B, instruments that impose on the entity an obligation to deliver to another party a

pro rata share of the net assets of the entity only on liquidation and are classified as equity instruments in accordance with IAS 32:16C and 16D, or instruments that are contracts for the future receipt or delivery of the entity's own equity instruments.

As an exception, an instrument that meets the definition of a financial liability is classified as an equity instrument if it has all the features and meets the conditions in IAS 32:16A and 16B or IAS 32:16C and 16D.

The Standard defines an equity instrument as any contract that represents a residual interest in the assets of an entity after deducting all of its liabilities.

In May 2008, the IFRIC (now the IFRS Interpretations Committee) issued an agenda decision on IAS 32, *Deposits on Returnable Containers*. The IFRIC was asked to provide guidance on the accounting for the obligation to refund deposits on returnable containers. In some industries, entities that distribute their products in returnable containers collect a deposit for each container delivered and have an obligation to refund this deposit when containers are returned by the customer. The issue is whether the obligation should be accounted for in accordance with IAS 39 (now IFRS 9).

The IFRIC noted that IAS 32:11 defines a financial instrument as "any contract that gives rise to a financial asset of one entity and a financial liability or equity instrument of another entity". Following delivery of the containers to its customers, the seller has an obligation only to refund the deposit for any returned containers. In circumstances in which the containers are derecognised as part of the sale transaction, the obligation is an exchange of cash (the deposit) for the containers (non-financial assets). Whether that exchange transaction occurs is at the option of the customer. Because the transaction involves the exchange of a non-financial item, it does not meet the definition of a financial instrument in accordance with IAS 32. In contrast, when the containers are not derecognised as part of the sale transaction, the customer's only asset is its right to the refund. In such circumstances, the obligation meets the definition of a financial instrument in accordance with IAS 32 and is therefore within the scope of IAS 39 (now IFRS 9). In particular, IFRS 13:47 states that "the fair value of a financial liability with a demand feature (e.g. a demand deposit) is not less than the amount payable on demand, discounted from the first date that the amount could be required to be paid."

2.1 Contractual obligation to deliver cash or another financial asset

The key feature in determining whether a financial instrument is a liability is the existence of a contractual obligation of one party (the issuer) to deliver cash or another financial asset to another party (the holder), or to exchange financial assets or liabilities under conditions that are potentially unfavourable. In contrast, in the case of an equity instrument (e.g. ordinary shares) the right to receive cash in the form of dividends or other distributions is at the issuer's discretion and, therefore, there is no obligation to deliver cash or another financial asset to the holder of the instrument. There is an exception to this rule for certain puttable instruments and instruments with an obligation to deliver a pro rata share of net assets only at liquidation (see **2.1.2.1** and **2.1.3**).

Items such as deferred revenue and warranty obligations require delivery of goods or services rather than an obligation to deliver cash or another financial asset and, therefore, are not financial liabilities. [IAS 32:AG11] Obligations to pay tax, company registration fees and other similar charges are obligations to pay cash. However, these are statutory rather than contractual requirements and, therefore, they are not financial liabilities. Similarly, constructive obligations (as defined in IAS 37 *Provisions, Contingent Liabilities and Contingent Assets*) do not arise from contracts and are not financial liabilities. [IAS 32:AG12]

Liability characteristics are established in practice in a number of ways, as discussed in the following sections.

In November 2012 the IFRS Interpretations Committee received a request to clarify the classification of the liability for prepaid cards issued by a bank in the bank's financial statements and accounting for the unspent balance of the prepaid cards with the following contractual features:

(a) no expiry date;

(b) cannot be refunded, redeemed or exchanged for cash;

(c) redeemable for goods or services only;

(d) redeemable only at selected merchants, which, depending upon the card programme, range from a single merchant to all merchants that accept a specific card network; and

(e) no back-end fees, which means that the balance on the prepaid card does not reduce unless spent by the holder.

The Interpretations Committee was asked to consider whether the liability for those prepaid cards is a non-financial liability because the issuing bank does not have an obligation to deliver cash to the cardholder.

At its November 2014 meeting, the Interpretations Committee discussed the submission and observed that the liability for prepaid cards with features as explained above would meet the definition of a financial liability, because the issuing bank has a contractual obligation to deliver cash to the merchant that is conditional upon the cardholder using the prepaid card to purchase goods or services. In such a circumstance, an issuing bank would apply the guidance in IFRS 9 to determine when to derecognise the liability for prepaid cards. However, the Interpretations Committee was concerned about other similar arrangements, such as customer loyalty programmes or prepaid cards issued by a non-banking entity that can be redeemed for goods or services of the issuing entity or of other entities, and requested the staff to analyse those other similar arrangements.

In January 2015, the Interpretations Committee discussed the staff's analysis and requested further analysis on more complex arrangements which, at the time of writing, had yet to be presented to the Interpretations Committee.

2.1.1 *Mandatory redemption and/or mandatory interest payments*

When an instrument requires mandatory redemption by the issuer for a fixed or determinable amount, a contractual obligation to deliver cash at redemption exists and, therefore, the instrument includes, and is presented as, a liability. An exception to this principle applies for certain puttable instruments and certain instruments that contain an obligation to deliver a pro rata share of net assets at liquidation as described in **2.1.2.1** and **2.1.3**.

Example 2.1.1A

Mandatorily redeemable preference shares

Entity A issues preference shares that are mandatorily redeemable at par in ten years. A contractual obligation to deliver cash exists for the repayment of principal – the issuer cannot avoid the outflow of cash in Year 10. Therefore, the preference shares should be classified as a financial liability.

Perpetual instruments provide the holder with no right to require redemption. However, the terms of such instruments often require the issuer to make coupon payments into perpetuity. A perpetual instrument with a mandatory coupon is a liability in its entirety because the whole of its value is derived from the stream of future coupon payments.

Example 2.1.1B

Perpetual coupon-bearing preference shares

A perpetual instrument is issued at a par amount of CU100 million requiring coupon payments of 6 per cent to be made annually. Provided that 6 per cent is the market rate of interest for this type of instrument when issued, the issuer has assumed a contractual obligation to make a future stream of 6 per cent interest payments. The net present value of the interest payments is CU100 million and represents the fair value of the instrument. The preference shares should be classified as a financial liability.

Many traditional debt instruments such as bonds and bank loans involve both mandatory redemption and mandatory interest payments.

Other instruments may require a mandatory distribution of a percentage of the profits of an entity (to the extent that such profits are generated) rather than of a traditional interest payment. Such an instrument meets the definition of a liability because it is a contractual obligation of the issuer to deliver cash or another financial asset to the holder. The issuer has no discretion over paying out a percentage of its profits.

A distinction must be drawn between those circumstances in which the issuer genuinely contractually has no discretion over payment of interest (or dividends) and those in which payment may be avoided but this decision will have consequences (even if significant). For example, an entity may issue instruments under which it contractually retains the discretion regarding the distribution of a percentage of profits but, if the distribution is not paid, the entity ceases to benefit from a favourable tax treatment. Such arrangements are common for Real Estate Investment Trusts (REITs) in some jurisdictions. In such circumstances, although the entity may intend to pay dividends in order to retain the significant tax benefits, it has no contractual obligation to deliver cash (or another financial asset) to the holder of the instrument and, therefore, the instrument is not a financial liability.

The terms of shares issued by REITs may differ and each situation should be assessed on its own merits. The scope of REITs from the perspective of the issuer is also discussed in **2.3.9** in **chapter B1**.

2.1.2 Puttable instruments

A puttable instrument is defined as a financial instrument that gives the holder the right to put the instrument back to the issuer for cash or another financial asset or that is automatically put back to the issuer on the occurrence of an uncertain future event or the death or retirement of the instrument holder. [IAS 32:11]

2.1.2.1 Puttable instruments presented as equity

Because puttable instruments contain a contractual obligation for the issuer to deliver cash or another financial asset to the holder, such instruments are generally classified as financial liabilities. However, certain puttable instruments that meet specified criteria must be presented as equity. The criteria for equity classification are extensive and restrictive.

The requirements regarding equity classification for some puttable instruments originated from an amendment to IAS 32 issued in February 2008, *Puttable Financial Instruments and Obligations Arising on Liquidation*. The purpose of the amendment was to provide a limited scope exception to the definition of a financial liability that would apply to certain financial instruments that contain obligations but that, in the IASB's view, also represent a residual interest in the net assets of the issuing entity. The exception applies to puttable instruments (described in this section) as well as to instruments containing an obligation to deliver a pro rata share of the net assets of the entity only on liquidation (see **2.1.3**). Because the requirements of the amendment are designed as an exception, they should be applied narrowly and should not be used by analogy (IAS 32:96B). Failure to meet one of the requirements results in failure to qualify for the exception, in which case the instrument will not meet the criteria for classification as equity.

A puttable instrument is classified as equity if it meets all of the following criteria:

[IAS 32:16A]

(a) the holder is entitled to a pro rata share of the entity's net assets in the event of the entity's liquidation;

The entity's net assets are those assets that remain after deducting all other claims on its assets. A pro rata share is determined by: (i) dividing the entity's net assets on liquidation into units of equal amount; and (ii) multiplying that amount by the number of the units held by the financial instrument holder. The IASB decided that the instrument must entitle the holder to a pro rata share of the net assets on liquidation because the net assets on liquidation represent the ultimate residual interest in the entity. [IAS 32:BC57]

An instrument that has a preferential right on liquidation of the entity is not an instrument with an entitlement to a pro rata share of the net assets of the entity. An instrument has a preferential right on liquidation, for example, if it entitles the holder to a fixed dividend on liquidation, in addition to a share of the entity's net assets, when other instruments in the subordinate class with a right to a pro rata share of the net assets of the entity do not have the same right on liquidation. [IAS 32:AG14C]

(b) the instrument is in the class of instruments that is subordinate to all other classes of instruments;

For an instrument to be in the most subordinate class, the financial instrument must have no priority over other claims to the assets of the entity on liquidation and must not need to be converted into another instrument before it is in the class of instruments that is subordinate to all other classes of instruments. [IAS 32:BC58] The instrument must be in the class of instruments that is subordinate to all other classes of instruments on liquidation in order to represent the residual interest in the entity.

When determining whether an instrument is in the subordinate class, an entity evaluates the instrument's claims on liquidation as if liquidation were to occur on the date when the instrument is classified. The initial classification should be reassessed if there is a change in relevant circumstances. For example, if the entity issues or redeems another financial instrument, this may affect whether the instrument under consideration is in the class of instruments that is subordinate to all other classes. [IAS 32:AG14B]

If an entity has only one class of financial instruments, that class is treated as if it were subordinate to all other classes. [IAS 32:AG14D]

In some circumstances, the most subordinate class of instruments is immaterial compared to the overall capital structure of the entity. This is particularly so when the most subordinate instruments are 'founder shares' (i.e. shares issued when the entity was formed) but the entity is capitalised by other issued instruments (e.g. puttable instruments issued after the founder shares were issued). The founder shares in this case, although immaterial, cannot be ignored in determining whether the puttable instruments should be classified as equity. Because the puttable instruments are not the most subordinate instruments issued by the entity, they are not classified as equity.

Example 2.1.2.1A

Immaterial founder shares

Entity A is capitalised principally by issue of puttable instruments whose contractual terms meet the requirements of IAS 32:16A for classification as equity except for the criterion of IAS 32:16A(b) that such an instrument be subordinate to all other classes of instruments. This is due to the existence of 'founder shares' (i.e. shares issued when Entity A was formed), the value of which is immaterial compared to the puttable instruments and the overall capital structure of the entity. The puttable instruments rank ahead of the ordinary shares on liquidation of Entity A.

Entity A should classify the puttable instruments as liabilities. IAS 32:16A(b) requires that, for a puttable instrument to be classified as equity, it must be in the class of instruments that is subordinate to all other classes of instruments.

In the circumstances described, although immaterial, the founder shares cannot be ignored in determining whether the puttable instruments should be classified as equity. Because the puttable instruments are not the most subordinate instruments issued by Entity A, they should not be classified as equity.

(c) all financial instruments in the class of instruments that is subordinate to all other classes of instruments have identical features. For example, they must all be puttable, and the formula or other method used to calculate the repurchase or redemption price is the same for all instruments in that class;

In January 2009, the IFRIC (now the IFRS Interpretations Committee) issued an agenda decision on IAS 32, *Classification of Puttable and Perpetual Instruments*. The IFRIC considered whether a puttable instrument is subordinate to all other classes of instruments when an entity also has perpetual instruments that meet the definition of equity instruments.

The IFRIC noted that a financial instrument is first classified as a liability or equity instrument in accordance with the general requirements of IAS 32. That classification is not affected by the existence of puttable instruments. As a second step, if a financial instrument would meet the general definition of a liability because it is puttable to the issuer, the entity considers the conditions in IAS 32:16A & 16B to determine whether it should be classified as equity. Consequently, the IFRIC noted that IAS 32 does not preclude the existence of several classes of equity.

The IFRIC also noted that IAS 32:16A(c) applies only to "instruments in the class of instruments that is subordinate to all other classes of instruments". IAS 32:16A(b) specifies that the level of an instrument's subordination is determined by its priority in liquidation. Accordingly, the existence of the put option does not of itself imply that the puttable instruments are less subordinate than the perpetual instruments.

(d) apart from the contractual obligation for the issuer to repurchase or redeem the instrument for cash or another financial asset, the instrument does not include any contractual obligation to deliver cash or another financial asset to another entity, or to exchange financial assets or financial liabilities with another entity under conditions that are potentially unfavourable to the entity, and it is not a contract that will or may be settled in the entity's own equity instruments as set out in subparagraph (b) of the definition of a financial liability; and

Limiting equity classification to instruments where the only obligation in the instrument is the put right held by the holder ensures that the limited scope exception does not apply to instruments with other obligations. To include puttable instruments with obligations other than the put right within the limited scope exception would include instruments that may not represent a residual interest of the entity because the holder may have a claim to some of the net assets in preference to other instrument holders. [IAS 32:BC60]

(e) the total expected cash flows attributable to the instrument over the life of the instrument are based substantially on the profit or loss, the change in the recognised net assets or the change in the fair value of the recognised and unrecognised net assets of the entity over the life of the instrument (excluding any effects of the instrument).

Profit or loss and the change in the recognised net assets should be measured in accordance with relevant IFRSs. [IAS 32:AG14E]

For a puttable instrument to be classified as equity, in addition to meeting the above criteria in IAS 32:16A, the issuer must have no other financial instrument or contract that has:

[IAS 32:16B]

(a) total cash flows based substantially on the profit or loss, the change in the recognised net assets or the change in the fair value of the recognised and unrecognised net assets of the entity (excluding any effects of such instrument or contract); and

(b) the effect of substantially restricting or fixing the residual return to the puttable instrument holders.

When applying IAS 32:16B(a) and (b), the issuer is not required to consider non-financial contracts with a holder of an instrument described in IAS 32:16A that have contractual terms and conditions that are similar to the contractual terms and conditions of an equivalent contract that might occur between a non-instrument holder and the issuing entity.

The application guidance issued with IAS 32 (which is an integral part of the Standard) provides guidance on how to determine whether transactions and arrangements were entered into by the instrument holder other than as an owner of the entity. The general principle is that a transaction or arrangement between the instrument holder and the issuing entity will only be considered to have been entered into by the instrument holder in a capacity other than as an owner if the cash flows and contractual terms and conditions of the transaction or arrangement are similar to an equivalent transaction that might occur between a non-instrument holder and the issuing entity; in other words, the arrangement must be similar to an arrangement that could have been entered into with a non-owner.

If an instrument holder is also an employee of the issuing entity, the cash flows payable to the instrument holder in his or her capacity as an employee are ignored because those cash flows do not arise in their capacity as an owner. Similarly, a profit- or loss-sharing arrangement that allocates profit or loss to the instrument holders on the basis of services rendered or business generated during the current or prior years are arrangements with instrument holders in a non-owner role and should not be considered when assessing the features listed in IAS 32:16A. However, if the profit- or loss-sharing arrangement allocates profit or loss based on the nominal amount of the instrument holder's interest relative to others in the class, this would represent an arrangement with the holders in their capacity as owners and should be considered when applying IAS 32:16A. [IAS 32:AG14H]

IAS 32:AG14G provides a further example of a partnership structure where some partners provide a guarantee to the entity and are remunerated for that guarantee. In determining whether the partners' interests in the partnership are identical, the guarantee is ignored because the guarantee is not provided by the partners in their capacity as owners.

IAS 32:AG14J provides examples of some instruments and arrangements that, when entered into on normal commercial terms with unrelated parties, are unlikely to prevent instruments that otherwise meet the criteria in IAS 32:16A from being classified as equity:

(a) instruments with total cash flows substantially based on specific assets of the entity;

(b) instruments with total cash flows based on a percentage of revenue;

(c) contracts designed to reward individual employees for services rendered to the entity; and

(d) contracts requiring the payment of an insignificant percentage of profit for services rendered or goods provided.

In May 2010, the IFRS Interpretations Committee considered a request for clarification of guidance relating to the classification of puttable financial instruments that include contractual obligations to provide pro rata distributions. The request proposed an amendment to the guidance in IAS 32 as part of *Improvements to IFRSs* to clarify that a puttable instrument can be classified as equity if it has a contractual obligation to deliver cash, or another financial asset, to all existing holders of the instrument on a pro rata basis.

The Interpretations Committee decided not to propose an amendment to IAS 32 because they considered that the identified unique circumstances that justified amending IAS 32, titled *Classification of Rights Issues* (see **6.1.1**), did not apply in this case. Further, an amendment to IAS 32 in this regard would introduce an additional exception to the general definition of a financial liability, which would be beyond the scope of the annual improvements process. At the date the decision was made, the Committee considered that an amendment would only be effective for annual periods beginning on or after 1 January 2012 and this was expected to be after the IASB had issued a final *Financial Instruments with Characteristics of Equity* (FICE) Standard.

Since the IFRIC reached the agenda decision the FICE project has been deferred and has been included in the IASB's research programme. See future developments in **section 9**.

If a puttable instrument is presented as equity, IAS 1 *Presentation of Financial Statements* requires the following disclosures:

[IAS 1:136A]

- summary quantitative data about the amount classified as equity;
- the entity's objectives, policies and processes for managing its obligation to repurchase or redeem the instruments when required to do so by the instrument holders, including any changes from the previous period;
- the expected cash outflow on redemption or repurchase of that class of financial instruments; and
- information about how the expected cash outflow on redemption or repurchase was determined.

When a puttable instrument is presented as equity, but subsequently fails to meet any of the criteria detailed in IAS 32:16A & 16B, the entity should reclassify it from the date when the instrument ceases to have all of the features or meet all of the conditions set out in those paragraphs. The financial liability should be measured at the instrument's fair value at the date of reclassification with any difference between the carrying amount of the equity instrument and the fair value of the financial liability at the date of reclassification recognised in equity. Similarly, if an entity redeems all of its issued non-puttable instruments and any puttable instruments that remain outstanding have all of the features and meet all of the conditions in IAS 32:16A & 16B, the entity should reclassify the puttable instruments as equity instruments from the date when it redeems the non-puttable instruments. The reclassification to equity should be at the carrying amount of the financial liability at the date of reclassification. [IAS 32:16E & 16F]

IAS 1 requires that when an entity reclassifies a puttable financial instrument between financial liabilities and equity, it should disclose the amount reclassified into and out of each category, and the timing and reason for that reclassification. [IAS 1:80A(a)]

Because the presentation of some puttable instruments as equity, rather than as financial liabilities, is an exception to the principles in IAS 32, the Standard does not permit the extension of this amendment to the classification of non-controlling interests in the consolidated financial statements. Therefore, puttable instruments presented as equity in the separate or individual financial statements that represent non-controlling interests in the consolidated financial statements are classified as financial liabilities in the consolidated financial statements.

Example 2.1.2.1B

Puttable instruments held by non-controlling interests

Entity P controls Entity Q, which therefore is included in Entity P's consolidated financial statements. Entity Q's capital structure consists of puttable instruments (partly held by Entity P and partly by other external investors) which meet the requirements for equity classification in its individual financial statements. Entity P's interest in the puttable instruments is eliminated on consolidation. Even though the puttable instruments held by the non-controlling interests meet the definition of equity in Entity Q's individual financial statements, they are presented as a financial liability in the consolidated financial statements of Entity P.

The prohibition on equity classification in the consolidated financial statements for certain puttable instruments presented as equity in the subsidiary financial statements appears at odds with the general principles in IFRS 10 *Consolidated Financial Statements* under which equity instruments issued by subsidiaries not held by the parent are presented as non-controlling interests. This is further evidence that the requirement to present certain puttable instruments as equity is a limited scope exception that not only overrides the general definition of a financial liability, but also overrides other principles within IFRSs.

2.1.2.2 Puttable instruments presented as financial liabilities

A puttable instrument that does not meet the definition of equity as described in **2.1.2.1** will be classified either wholly as a financial liability, or partly as a financial liability in the case of an instrument that is a compound instrument (i.e. the instrument consists partly of a financial liability and partly an equity component). In considering whether an instrument is a financial liability or equity, an entity must first apply the criteria in **2.1.2.1** to determine whether the instrument is equity. If it is not, this section is relevant.

The fact that the contractual put right in a puttable instrument is conditional upon the holder exercising its right to require redemption does not negate the existence of a financial liability, because the issuer does not have the unconditional right to avoid delivering cash or another financial asset. [IAS 32:19(b)] An obligation is not negated if the instrument gives the holder the right to a residual interest in the assets of the issuer as is the case, for example, for a unit in a mutual fund. [IAS 32:18(b)]

Example 2.1.2.2A

Preference shares puttable at par

An entity issues preference shares that are puttable at par for cash at the option of the holder at a particular date.

The preference shares contain a financial liability element which should be measured at the present value of the obligation to redeem the preference shares for par in cash.

The fact that the contractual put right in a puttable instrument is conditional upon the holder exercising its right to require redemption does not negate the existence of a financial liability element, because the issuer does not have the unconditional right to avoid delivering cash or another financial asset. Further, the instrument does not meet the exception to the definition of a financial liability in IAS 32:16A & 16B to be presented as equity.

Example 2.1.2.2B

Instrument puttable at net asset value

Entity A issues Class B shares which allow the holder to put the shares back to Entity A at any time at a price equal to the holder's proportional share of the net assets of Entity A. This price is calculated as the number of Class B shares owned, divided by the total number of Class B shares outstanding, multiplied by the net assets of Entity A (excluding the Class B shares from the net asset calculation).

The Class B shares do not entitle the holder to a pro rata share of Entity A's net assets in the event of liquidation and are not the most subordinate class of shares. As such, the criteria of IAS 32:16A are not met.

Although Class B shareholders might receive returns that would typically be associated with equity holders in that they participate in the performance of the net assets of Entity A, the fact that Entity A has a contractual obligation to pay the holder of the Class B shares cash if the holder chooses to put the instrument back to Entity A, and the fact that the terms of the Class B shares do not meet the criteria to be classified as equity in IAS 32:16A, mean that Entity A should classify the Class B shares as financial liabilities.

Example 2.1.2.2C

Discretion to refuse redemption

Entity A has instruments in issue that allow the holders to request redemption of their instrument at specified dates and amounts. Entity A's governing charter states that the entity has a choice whether or not to accept the holder's request. There are no other conditions on the level of redemptions or any limitations on the entity's discretion to redeem or make payments to holders. In its history, Entity A has never refused to redeem the instruments when requested to do so by a holder. All other characteristics of the instrument are equity.

Because Entity A has no obligation to transfer cash or another financial asset, the instrument should be classified as equity. A history of, or intention to make, discretionary payments does not trigger liability classification. [IAS 32:AG26]

Under IAS 32, interests in many open-ended mutual funds, unit trusts, partnerships and some co-operative entities, which embody the right of the holder to require the issuer to redeem the interests for a cash amount equivalent to their share of net assets, but which do not meet the narrow criteria for equity classification described in **2.1.2.1**, should be classified as financial liabilities. This may lead to a situation where some entities have no equity capital in their financial statements. IAS 32 permits the use of an appropriate description of the line item relating to puttable instruments and provides an illustrative example of such presentation, which is reproduced below.

Example 2.1.2.2D

Presentation of an entity without equity

[Extracts from IAS 32 Illustrative Examples: Example 7]

Statement of financial position as at 31 December 20X1

		20X1		20X0
	CU	CU	CU	CU
ASSETS				
Non-current assets (classified in accordance with IAS 1)	91,374		78,484	
Total non-current assets		91,374		78,484
Current assets (classified in accordance with IAS 1)	1,422		1,769	
Total current assets		1,422		1,769
Total assets		92,796		80,253
LIABILITIES				
Current liabilities (classified in accordance with IAS 1)	647		66	
Total current liabilities		(647)		(66)
Non-current liabilities excluding net assets attributable to unitholders (classified in accordance with IAS 1)	280		136	
		(280)		(136)
Net assets attributable to unitholders		91,869		80,051
Statement of comprehensive income for the year ended 31 December 20X1				
Revenue		2,956		1,718
Expenses (classified by nature or function)		(644)		(614)
Profit from operating activities		2,312		1,104
Finance costs:				
– other finance costs		(47)		(47)
– distributions to unitholders		(50)		(50)
Change in net assets attributable to unitholders		2,215		1,007

When an entity has no instruments classified as equity, the usual requirements for presenting specified gains and losses in other comprehensive income continue to apply. For example, the effective portion of hedging gains and losses on cash flow hedges and net investment hedges (see **chapter B9**), and gains and losses on financial assets measured as at fair value through other comprehensive income (see **chapter B2**) are recognised in other comprehensive income following the general recognition and measurement rules.

IFRIC Interpretation 2 *Members' Shares in Co-operative Entities and Similar Instruments* provides guidance on the application of IAS 32's principles to the classification of members' shares in a co-operative entity as liabilities. The Interpretation clarifies the following.

- The contractual right of a member to request redemption of contracts identified as members' shares does not, in itself, give rise to a liability. Rather, the entity must consider all of the terms of the contract in determining classification as a liability or equity (including relevant local laws, regulations and the entity's governing charter in effect at the date of the classification). However, expected future amendments to those laws, regulations or the entity's charter should not be considered. [IFRIC 2:5]
- Members' shares that give the member a right to request redemption are equity of the entity if the entity has an unconditional right to refuse redemption. [IFRIC 2:7]
- Local laws, regulations or the entity's governing charter can impose prohibitions on the redemption of members' shares that are unconditional or dependent on certain conditions being met (or not met) (e.g. prohibitions based on liquidity criteria). If redemption is unconditionally prohibited, members' shares are equity. However, provisions in local laws, regulations or the entity's governing charter that prohibit redemption only if conditions (e.g. liquidity constraints) are met (or not met) do not result in members' shares being equity. [IFRIC 2:8]
- An unconditional prohibition may be absolute (i.e. all redemptions are prohibited) or partial (i.e. redemption of members' shares prohibited if redemption would cause the number of shares or paid-in capital from members' shares to fall below a specified level). In the case of a partial prohibition, members' shares in excess of the prohibition against redemption are liabilities, unless the entity has an unconditional right to refuse redemption, or the members' shares meet the criteria allowing certain puttable instruments (see **2.1.2.1**) and obligations arising on liquidation (see **2.1.3**) to be classified as equity. [IFRIC 2:9]

Example 2.1.2.2E

Limited discretion to refuse redemption

Local laws governing the operation of co-operatives prohibit co-operative entities from redeeming members' shares if, by such redemption, an entity would reduce paid-in capital from members' shares below 90 per cent of the highest amount of paid-in capital from members' shares. The highest amount for a particular co-operative is CU1,000,000. With the exception of the 90 per cent restriction, the paid-in capital for this co-operative is redeemable at the option of the member.

At 31 December 20X0 the balance of paid-in capital represented by the issued shares is CU900,000; at 31 December 20X1, the balance has increased to CU950,000.

At 31 December 20X0, the entire balance of CU900,000 is classified as equity.

At 31 December 20X1, CU900,000 is classified as equity and CU50,000 as a financial liability.

In some cases, the number of shares or the amount of paid-in capital subject to a redemption prohibition may change over time. If this is the case, such a change may lead to a transfer between financial liabilities and equity. [IFRIC 2:9]

Example 2.1.2.2F

Reclassification due to change in local law

Continuing with the **example 2.1.2.2E**, at 31 December 20X2, the local laws governing the operation of co-operatives are amended so that redemption of members' shares is permitted up to 20 per cent of the highest amount of members' shares, rather than 10 per cent. If, at that date, the entire balance of paid-in capital remained unchanged from 31 December 20X1 at CU950,000, the entity would reclassify an additional CU100,000 from equity to financial liabilities so that CU800,000 is classified as equity and CU150,000 is classified as a financial liability, with no gain or loss resulting at the date the transfer is made. The entity should disclose separately the amount, timing and reason for the transfer.

Consistent with the requirements of IFRS 9, demand deposits, including current accounts, deposit accounts and similar contracts that arise when members act as customers, are financial liabilities of the entity. [IFRIC 2:6]

2.1.3 Instruments containing an obligation to deliver a pro rata share of the net assets of the entity only on liquidation

When liquidation of an entity is certain to occur and is outside the control of the entity (e.g. an entity with a limited life) or is not certain to occur but is at the option of the holder of an instrument issued by the entity (e.g. in some partnership interests), the entity has a contractual obligation to pay cash or another financial asset that the entity cannot avoid. Therefore, such entities will generally recognise a financial liability with respect to the amounts payable by the entity on liquidation. However, IAS 32 has an exception for certain instruments, or components of instruments, when the issuer has an obligation to deliver to another party a pro rata share of the net assets of the entity only on liquidation. This limited scope exception was introduced at the same time as the equivalent limited scope exception for puttable instruments described in **2.1.2.1**.

The criteria for equity classification are similar to, but not the same as, the criteria described in IAS 32:16A & 16B for puttable instruments. The instrument must meet all of the following criteria to be presented as equity:

[IAS 32:16C]

(a) it entitles the holder to a pro rata share of the entity's net assets in the event of the entity's liquidation;

(b) it is in the class of instruments that is subordinate to all other classes of instruments; and

(c) all financial instruments in the class of instruments that is subordinate to all other classes of instruments must have an identical contractual obligation for the issuing entity to deliver a pro rata share of its net assets on liquidation.

The three criteria above are equivalent to the criteria in IAS 32:16A(a) - (c) for puttable instruments. The shaded boxes that accompany the criteria described in **2.1.2.1** apply equally to the criteria in IAS 32:16C reproduced immediately above.

For an instrument, or component of a financial instrument, containing an obligation to deliver a pro rata share of the net assets of the entity only on liquidation, to be classified as equity, in addition to meeting the above criteria in IAS 32:16C, the issuer must have no other financial instrument or contract that has:

[IAS 32:16D]

(a) total cash flows based substantially on the profit or loss, the change in the recognised net assets or the change in the fair value of the recognised and unrecognised net assets of the entity (excluding any effects of such instrument or contract); and

(b) the effect of substantially restricting or fixing the residual return to the instrument holders.

When applying (a) and (b) above, the issuer should not consider non-financial contracts with a holder of an instrument described in IAS 32:16C that have contractual terms and conditions that are similar to the contractual terms and conditions of an equivalent contract that might occur between a non-instrument holder and the issuing entity. If the entity cannot determine that this condition is met, it should not classify the instrument as an equity instrument.

IAS 32:16D reproduced immediately above is equivalent to IAS 32:16B for puttable instruments. The guidance and shaded boxes that accompany IAS 32:16B for puttable instruments, and the inability to classify puttable instruments held by non-controlling interests as equity in the consolidated financial statements (as described in **2.1.2.1**), apply equally to instruments containing an obligation to deliver a pro rata share of the net assets of the entity only on liquidation.

The Board acknowledged in its Basis for Conclusions that many of those requirements, and the reasons for them, are similar for puttable financial instruments and instruments that contain an obligation to deliver a pro rata share of the net assets only at liquidation. As highlighted in IAS 32:BC67, the criteria for the latter instruments differ from the former because:

(a) there is no requirement that there be no other contractual obligations;

(b) there is no requirement to consider the expected total cash flows throughout the life of the instrument; and

(c) the only feature that must be identical among the instruments in the class is the obligation for the issuing entity to deliver to the holder a pro rata share of its net assets on liquidation.

The Standard explains that the reason for the differences is the timing of settlement of the obligation. In the case of obligations settled only on liquidation, the life of the financial instrument is the same as the life of the issuing entity because the extinguishment of the obligation can occur only on liquidation. Therefore, the IASB concluded that it was appropriate to focus only on the obligations that are triggered on liquidation. The instrument must be subordinate to all other classes of instruments and represent the residual interests only at that point in time. However, if the instrument contains other contractual obligations, those obligations may need to be accounted for separately in accordance with the requirements of IAS 32 (i.e. the instrument may be a compound instrument containing a financial liability and equity component).

IAS 1 requires that when an entity reclassifies between financial liabilities and equity an instrument that imposes on the entity an obligation to deliver to another party a pro rata share of the net assets of the entity only on liquidation, it should disclose the amount reclassified into and out of each category (financial liabilities or equity), and the timing and reason for that reclassification. [IAS 1:80A(b)]

In the case of a limited life entity, disclosure is required of information regarding the length of the entity's life. [IAS 1:138(d)]

2.1.4 Restrictions on ability to satisfy contractual obligation

A restriction on the contractual obligation of the entity to deliver cash or another financial instrument, such as the need to obtain regulatory approval for payment, does not in itself negate that obligation. In such cases, the entity does not have an unconditional right to avoid delivering cash or another financial asset. [IAS 32:19(a)]

Example 2.1.4

Inability to satisfy put feature

Entity A issued preference shares that are puttable for CU1 million by the holders to Entity A at any time after a specified date. Under the terms of the shares, Entity A is required to satisfy its obligation under the put option from its distributable reserves.

The preference shares include a liability that reflects the put option feature that creates an obligation for Entity A. The possibility that Entity A might not be in a position to satisfy the obligation under the put option if it were to find that it has insufficient distributable reserves does not negate the obligation (however likely this is to occur).

2.1.5 Contractual obligation that is not explicit

An obligation may be established indirectly through the instrument's terms and conditions. IAS 32 gives two examples of how such an obligation could be created.

- A financial instrument may contain a non-financial obligation that must be settled if, and only if, the entity fails to make distributions or to redeem the instrument. If the entity can avoid a transfer of cash or another financial asset only by settling the non-financial obligation, the financial instrument is a financial liability. [IAS 32:20(a)]
- A financial instrument is a financial liability if it provides that, on settlement, the entity will deliver either cash or another financial asset, or its own shares whose value is determined to exceed substantially the value of the cash or other financial asset. Although the entity does not have an explicit obligation to deliver cash or another financial asset, the holder of the asset has in substance been guaranteed a minimum amount equal to at least the cash/other financial asset settlement option amount. [IAS 32:20(b)]

In March 2006, the IFRIC (now the IFRS Interpretations Committee) discussed the role of contractual and economic obligations in the classification of two different financial instruments under IAS 32. The first instrument was an irredeemable, callable financial instrument with dividends payable only if dividends are paid on the ordinary shares of the issuer which included a 'step-up' dividend clause that would increase the dividend at a pre-determined date in the future unless the instrument had previously been called by the issuer. The second instrument was an irredeemable, callable financial instrument with dividends that must be paid if interest is paid on another, linked, instrument.

The IFRIC agreed that IAS 32 is clear that a contractual financial obligation was necessary in order that a financial instrument be classified as a liability (ignoring the classification of financial instruments that may or will be settled in the issuer's own equity instruments). Such a contractual obligation could be established explicitly or indirectly. However, the obligation must be established through the *terms and conditions* of the financial instrument. IFRIC also noted that IAS 32 is clear that an economic obligation (commonly known as *economic compulsion*), by itself, would not result in a financial instrument being classified as a liability. The IFRIC also discussed the role of 'substance' in the classification of financial instruments. It noted that IAS 32 restricted the role of 'substance' to consideration of the contractual terms of an instrument, and that anything outside the contractual terms was not considered for the purpose of assessing whether an instrument should be classified as a liability under IAS 32. These points were subsequently confirmed by the IASB through their discussions in June 2006.

In September 2013 the IFRS Interpretations Committee dealt with a request to clarify how an issuer would classify three financial instruments in accordance with IAS 32. None of the financial instruments had a maturity date but each gave the holder the contractual right to redeem at any time. The holder's redemption right was described differently for each of the three financial instruments; however in each case the issuer had the contractual right to choose to settle the instrument in cash or a fixed number of its own equity instruments if the holder exercised its redemption right. The issuer was not required to pay dividends on the three instruments but could choose to do so at its discretion.

The Interpretations Committee noted that IAS 32:15 requires the issuer of a financial instrument to classify the instrument in accordance with the substance of the contractual arrangement. Consequently, the issuer cannot achieve different classification results for financial instruments with the same contractual substance simply by describing the contractual arrangements differently.

IAS 32:11 sets out the definitions of both a financial liability and an equity instrument. IAS 32:16 describes in more detail the circumstances in which a financial instrument meets the definition of an equity instrument.

The Interpretations Committee noted that a non-derivative financial instrument that gives the issuer the contractual right to choose to settle in cash or a fixed number of its own equity instruments meets the definition of an equity instrument in IAS 32 as long as the instrument does not establish an obligation to deliver cash (or another financial asset) indirectly through its terms and conditions. IAS 32:20(b) provides the example that an indirect contractual obligation would be established if a financial instrument provides that on settlement the entity will deliver either cash or its own equity instruments whose value is determined to exceed substantially the value of the cash.

The Interpretations Committee also acknowledged that financial instruments, in particular those that are more structured or complex, require careful analysis to determine whether they contain equity and non-equity components that must be accounted for separately in accordance with IAS 32.

The Interpretations Committee noted that if the issuer has a contractual obligation to deliver cash, that obligation meets the definition of a financial liability.

The Interpretations Committee considered that in the light of its analysis of the existing IFRS requirements, an interpretation was not necessary and consequently decided not to add the issue to its agenda.

In January 2014 the IFRS Interpretations Committee dealt with a request to clarify how an issuer would classify in accordance with IAS 32 a financial instrument that is mandatorily convertible into a variable number of shares (subject to a cap and a floor) but gives the issuer the option to settle by delivering the maximum (fixed) number of shares

The Interpretations Committee discussed how an issuer would assess the substance of a particular early settlement option included in a financial instrument in accordance with IAS 32. The instrument has a stated maturity date and at maturity the issuer must deliver a variable number of its own equity instruments to equal a fixed cash amount, subject to a cap and a floor. The cap and the floor limit and guarantee, respectively, the number of equity instruments to be delivered. The issuer is required to pay interest at a fixed rate. The issuer has the contractual right to settle the instrument at any time before maturity. If the issuer chooses to exercise that early settlement option, it must:

(i) deliver the maximum number of equity instruments specified in the contract; and

(ii) pay in cash all of the interest that would have been payable if the instrument had remained outstanding until its maturity date.

The Interpretations Committee noted that the definitions of financial asset, financial liability and equity instrument in IAS 32 are based on the financial instrument's contractual rights and contractual obligations. However, IAS 32:15 requires the issuer of a financial instrument to classify the instrument in accordance with the substance of the contractual arrangement. Consequently, the Interpretations Committee noted that if a contractual term of a financial instrument lacks substance, that contractual term would be excluded from the classification assessment of the instrument.

The Interpretations Committee noted that the issuer cannot assume that a financial instrument (or its components) meets the definition of an equity instrument simply because the issuer has the contractual right to settle the financial instrument by delivering a fixed number of its own equity instruments. The Interpretations Committee noted that judgement will be required to determine whether the issuer's early settlement option is substantive and thus should be considered in determining how to classify the instrument. If the early settlement option is not substantive, that term would not be considered in determining the classification of the financial instrument.

The Interpretations Committee noted that the guidance in IAS 32:20(b) is relevant because it provides an example of a situation in which one of an instrument's settlement alternatives is excluded from the classification assessment. Specifically, the example in that paragraph describes an instrument that the issuer will settle by delivering either cash or its own shares and states that one of the settlement alternatives should be excluded from the classification assessment in some circumstances.

The Interpretations Committee noted that to determine whether the early settlement option is substantive, the issuer will need to understand whether there are actual economic or other business reasons that the issuer would exercise the option. In making that assessment, the issuer could consider, along with other factors, whether the instrument would have been priced differently if the issuer's early settlement option had not been included in the contractual terms. The Interpretations Committee also noted that factors such as the term of the instrument, the width of the range between the cap and the floor, the issuer's share price and the volatility of the share price could be relevant to the assessment of whether the issuer's early settlement option is substantive. For example, the early settlement option may be less likely to have substance– especially if the instrument is short-lived–if the range between the cap and the floor is wide and the current share price would equate to the delivery of a number of shares that is close to the floor (i.e. the minimum). That is because the issuer may have to deliver significantly more shares to settle early than it may otherwise be obliged to deliver at maturity.

The Interpretations Committee considered that in the light of its analysis of the existing IFRS requirements, neither an interpretation nor an amendment to a Standard was necessary and consequently decided not to add the issue to its agenda.

Example 2.1.5

Perpetual instrument with coupon step-up and dividend pusher

Bank A issues a perpetual instrument with the following terms.

- €100 million notional with annual 8 per cent interest payments for 8 years. Bank A has a call option embedded in the instrument that allows the instruments to be repurchased at the end of Year 8, and each year thereafter, for €100 million.
- If the instrument is not called by Bank A at the end of Year 8, the interest on the instrument increases to 14 per cent per annum (commonly referred to as a 'step-up' feature).
- The interest payments (both before and after the call date) are only payable if Bank A pays a dividend on its ordinary shares (commonly referred to as a 'dividend pusher'); the ordinary shares are classified wholly as equity.

Bank A has consistently chosen to pay dividends on its ordinary shares. When the perpetual instrument is issued, Bank A's cost of borrowing for a similar debt instrument is approximately 8 per cent.

Bank A does not have an indirect or a direct obligation to deliver cash or another financial asset in respect of the perpetual instrument. The instrument is therefore classified wholly as equity.

Bank A has no obligation to pay interest because it can always avoid paying interest by exercising its discretion and not paying dividends on its ordinary shares. Bank A has no obligation to exercise its right to call the instrument at the end of Year 8 because the call right is an option and Bank A can always choose not to exercise that right. Because the instrument is perpetual, there is no redemption date and, therefore, the instrument does not contain any contractual obligation to deliver cash or another financial asset.

In determining the substance of the contractual arrangement, an entity must assess whether the terms of the instrument provide the issuer with discretion as to whether to deliver cash or another financial asset. In the circumstances described, Bank A has discretion as to whether or not it wishes to pay an ordinary dividend. Even though it may be highly likely that Bank A will choose to pay ordinary dividends and, as a result, will be required to pay interest under the perpetual instrument, the high likelihood is of itself not sufficient for the instrument to be classified as a financial liability. Similarly, although it may be very likely that Bank A will pay interest on the perpetual instrument and will exercise its call option at the end of Year 8 (thus making the instrument economically equivalent to an 8-year loan), this likelihood of itself is not sufficient for the instrument to be classified as a financial liability.

2.1.6 Shares to the value of, or issuer settlement option

Some instruments may contain an obligation for the issuer to deliver a variable number of its own equity instruments such that the fair value of the entity's own equity delivered under the arrangement equals the amount of the contractual obligation. The amount of the contractual obligation may be fixed or may fluctuate in part or in full in response to a variable other than the market price of the issuer's own equity.

Such instruments do not meet the definition of equity because the issuer is merely using its own shares as currency to extinguish its obligation. The contract therefore does not evidence a residual interest in the entity's assets after deducting all of its liabilities. [IAS 32:21]

Example 2.1.6A

Variable number of shares to the value of a fixed obligation

Entity A issues CU0.01 nominal preference shares that will pay out CU1 over three years. Entity A will pay the CU1 in its own ordinary shares so that the number of shares issued will vary to equate to CU1 in value.

The instrument is a financial liability because Entity A issues shares such that the fair value of the shares delivered is always equal to the amount of the contractual obligation (i.e. a variable number of shares).

Example 2.1.6B

Variable number of shares to the value of a variable obligation

Entity B issues an instrument for CU100 that pays no interest before maturity. At maturity, Entity B is required to deliver as many of its own equity instruments as are equivalent in value to the original issue price of CU100 plus a supplemental redemption amount depending on whether a designated share price index has increased between issuance of the instrument and the maturity date. The supplemental amount is determined as a multiple of the percentage increase in the share price index from the date of issue of the instrument to maturity and the original issue price. If the share price index has fallen over the life of the instrument, equity instruments equivalent in value to CU100 are delivered.

The instrument is a financial liability in accordance with IAS 32:11 because the instrument will be settled by delivery of a variable number of Entity B's equity instruments.

As stated in IFRS 9:B4.3.5(c) equity-indexed payments are not closely related to a debt instrument in which they are embedded. Accordingly, this feature needs to be separated out from the host contract and accounted for separately in accordance with IFRS 9:4.3.

2.1.7 Contingent settlement provisions

Financial instruments may be structured such that the obligation to deliver cash or another financial instrument arises only on the occurrence or non-occurrence of uncertain future events (or on the outcome of uncertain circumstances) that are beyond the control of both the issuer and the holder of the instrument. The issuer does not have an unconditional right to avoid the obligation to deliver cash or another financial instrument and, therefore, such instruments are financial liabilities of the issuer unless:

[IAS 32:25]

- the contingent settlement provision that could require payment in cash or another financial asset is not genuine; or
- settlement in cash or another financial asset can only be required in the event of liquidation of the issuer; or
- the instrument meets the specified criteria for a puttable instrument or an obligation arising on liquidation to be classified as equity (see **2.1.2.1** and **2.1.3** respectively).

'Genuine' is generally understood to be not spurious or counterfeit, i.e. a genuine provision is one that is authentic and has commercial substance. A provision that is extremely rare, highly abnormal and very unlikely to occur is not considered genuine. [IAS 32:AG28]

Future events that are beyond the control of both the issuer and the holder of the instrument include:

(a) a change in macroeconomic, industry and other indices such as a stock market index, consumer price index, growth in Gross Domestic Product or total sector production;

(b) changes in law, government regulations, and other regulatory requirements (such as changes in taxation, pricing controls or accounting requirements); and

(c) changes in the key performance indicators of the issuer that are beyond the control of both the issuer and the holder such as revenues, net income or debt to equity ratio.

Example 2.1.7A

Contingent settlement provisions: change in accounting or tax law

Entity A issues preference shares bearing 5 per cent non-cumulative dividends payable at the discretion of the issuer. The shares will be redeemed if the applicable taxation or accounting requirements were to change.

The contingent event of a change in taxation or accounting requirements is deemed to be genuine.

The requirement for redemption on change of taxation or accounting requirements represents a contingent settlement provision (i.e. it is an uncertain future event beyond the control of both the issuer and the holder of the instrument).

Because the contingent event is genuine and can result in the issuer having to deliver cash or another financial asset at a time other than Entity A's liquidation, the instrument is classified as a financial liability. [IAS 32:25].

However, the 5 per cent dividend is payable at the discretion of Entity A and, consequently, is equity of Entity A. Therefore, the preference share contains both debt and equity features, i.e. it is a compound instrument (see **section 3**).

Example 2.1.7B

Contingent settlement provisions: shares redeemable on initial public offering

Entity B issues shares for CU1 million. Dividends are discretionary. Entity B is obligated to redeem the shares for par in the event of a flotation/initial public offering (IPO) of the entity. Entity B cannot guarantee a successful flotation/IPO, but it does have discretion as to whether to instigate proceedings to float or to seek an IPO. Given that Entity B can avoid redeeming the shares by avoiding a flotation/IPO, the instrument is classified as equity.

Example 2.1.7C

Contingent settlement provisions: shares redeemable in the absence of an initial public offering

Entity C issues shares for CU1 million. Entity C is obligated to redeem the shares at par in the event that Entity C is not subject to a successful flotation/ Initial Public Offering (IPO) within five years from the date of issue of the shares. Entity C cannot guarantee a successful flotation/IPO, but it does have discretion as to whether to instigate proceedings to float or to seek an IPO.

Given that the contingent event (a successful flotation/IPO) is not in the control of Entity C, it is a contingent settlement provision. The contingent settlement provision is considered genuine, it is potentially payable other than at liquidation, and the shares do not meet the puttable exception in IAS 32 and therefore IAS 32:25 applies. Because Entity C cannot avoid redeeming the shares for cash, the instrument contains an obligation to pay cash that creates a financial liability.

Example 2.1.7D

Contingent settlement provisions: change of control

Entity D issues preference shares for CU1 million. Entity D is obligated to redeem the preference shares at par in the event that control of Entity D changes. A change in control is defined in the terms of the preference shares as a change in ownership of at least 51 per cent of the ordinary shares of Entity D.

Given that the contingent event (the sale of ordinary shares in Entity D by one set of shareholders to another) is not in the control of the Entity D, it is a contingent settlement provision. Because Entity D cannot avoid redeeming the preference shares for cash, the instrument contains an obligation to pay cash that creates a financial liability.

2.2 Equity instruments

In classifying a financial instrument as a liability or equity, equity classification is appropriate only if the instrument fails the definition of a financial liability as detailed in **section 2**.

The key requirement in determining whether an instrument is equity is the issuer's unconditional ability to avoid delivery of cash or another financial asset. That ability is not affected by:

- the history of making distributions;
- an intention to make distributions in the future;
- a possible negative impact on the price of ordinary shares of the issuer if the distributions are not made on the instrument concerned;
- the amount of the issuer's reserves;
- an issuer's expectations of a profit or loss for the period; or
- an ability or inability of the issuer to influence the amount of its profit or loss for the period.

Provided that dividends are at the discretion of the issuer, it is irrelevant whether dividends are cumulative or non-cumulative. [IAS 32:AG26]

Once a dividend is properly declared and the issuer is legally required to pay it, a contractual obligation to deliver cash comes into existence and a financial liability for the amount of the declared dividend should be recognised. Similarly, a liability arises upon liquidation to distribute to the shareholders the residual assets in the issuer, i.e. any remaining assets after satisfying all of its liabilities.

The existence of an option whereby the issuer can redeem equity shares for cash does not trigger liability classification because the issuer retains an unconditional right to avoid delivering cash or another financial asset. A contractual obligation would only arise at the point when the issuer exercised its right to redeem. This principle applies to all instruments that are not derivatives over own equity.

Specific rules apply to derivatives over own equity. For example, a purchased call option over a fixed number of shares will allow the issuer to buy back shares at a fixed price in the future. The issuer always has a choice as to whether it wishes to pay cash, because it always has a choice as to whether it wishes to exercise its option. However, this instrument is only treated as equity if it is gross physically settled in all cases when the issuer chooses to exercise, i.e. the option can never be net settled.

Instruments are frequently issued with a link to dividend payments on other types of instruments, most commonly ordinary shares. A 'dividend stopper' is a contractual term that requires no dividend to be paid on the ordinary shares if the payment is not made on another specified instrument. A 'dividend pusher' is a term that requires a dividend to be paid on a specified instrument if a dividend payment is made on ordinary shares.

Provided that the link is to the dividends on an instrument like an ordinary share where the issuer has discretion as to whether or not to pay a dividend, neither a 'dividend pusher' nor a 'dividend stopper' of itself result in the instrument concerned being classified as a liability. This is because the issuer retains discretion as to whether or not to pay on the instrument, albeit that the decision will need to be made in conjunction with the decision on whether to pay dividends on ordinary shares. The issuer continues to have an unconditional right to avoid the outflow of cash (or other financial assets).

Example 2.2A

Dividend stopper

Entity Y issues 6 per cent cumulative, non-redeemable preference shares with discretionary dividends that are subject to the availability of distributable reserves. The directors of Entity Y decide at each period end whether and the extent to which a dividend will be paid on the preference shares. The terms of the instrument include a dividend stopper, i.e. if no dividend is paid on the preference shares, then no dividend is paid on Entity Y's ordinary shares.

The payment of dividends on the preference shares is entirely at Entity Y's discretion (albeit the decision will need to be made in conjunction with the decision regarding whether to pay dividends on ordinary shares). For this reason, Entity Y continues to have an unconditional right to avoid an outflow of cash (or another financial asset) and, therefore, the preference shares should be classified as equity.

Example 2.2B

Dividend pusher

Entity M issues non-redeemable preference shares bearing 6 per cent discretionary non-cumulative dividends that are subject to the availability of distributable reserves. The directors of Entity M decide at each period end whether and the extent to which a dividend will be paid on the preference shares. The payment of dividends on Entity M's ordinary shares is also discretionary. However, the terms of the instrument include a dividend pusher, i.e. if a dividend is paid on Entity M's ordinary shares, then a dividend must be paid on the preference shares.

Because the payment of dividends on its ordinary shares is discretionary, Entity M continues to have an unconditional right to avoid an outflow of cash (or another financial asset) and, therefore, the preference shares should be classified as equity.

In March 2010, the IFRIC (now the IFRS Interpretations Committee) issued an agenda decision *IAS 32 Financial Instruments: Presentation – Shareholder Discretion*, in response to a request for guidance on whether a financial instrument in the form of a preference share that includes a contractual obligation to deliver cash is a financial liability or equity, if the payment is at the ultimate discretion of the issuer's shareholders.

The IFRIC noted that:

- IAS 32:AG26 identifies that when distributions to holders of preference shares are at the discretion of the issuer, the shares are equity instruments;
- diversity may exist in practice in assessing whether an entity has an unconditional right to avoid delivering cash if the contractual obligation is at the ultimate discretion of the issuer's shareholders and, consequently, whether a financial instrument should be classified as a financial liability or equity; and
- the IASB is currently undertaking a project to improve and simplify the financial reporting requirements for financial instruments with characteristics of equity. The main objectives of this project are to develop a better distinction between equity and non-equity instruments and converge IFRSs and US GAAP.

Consequently, the IFRIC recommended that the IASB address this issue as part of the current project on *Financial Instruments with Characteristics of Equity* (FICE). At that time, the IASB's project was expected to address the distinction between equity and non-equity instruments in a shorter period than the IFRIC would require to complete its due process. The IFRIC therefore decided not to add this issue to its agenda.

Since the IFRIC reached the agenda decision the FICE project has been deferred and has been included in the IASB's research programme. See future developments in **section 9**.

3 Compound instruments

The terms of a financial instrument may be structured such that it contains both equity and liability components (i.e. the instrument is neither entirely a liability nor entirely an equity instrument). Such instruments are defined in IAS 32 as compound instruments. An example of a compound instrument is a bond that is convertible, either mandatorily or at the option of the holder, into a fixed number of equity shares of the issuer. Compound instruments come in many forms and are not restricted solely to convertible instruments.

The liability and equity components of a compound instrument are required to be accounted for separately. [IAS 32:28]

The requirement to separate out the equity and financial liability components of a compound instrument is consistent with the principle that a financial instrument must be classified in accordance with its substance, rather than its legal form. A compound instrument takes the legal form of a single instrument, while the substance is that both a liability and an equity instrument exist.

For example, a convertible bond that pays fixed coupons and is convertible by the holder into a fixed number of ordinary shares of the issuer has the legal form of a debt contract; however, its substance is that of two instruments:

- a financial liability to deliver cash (by making scheduled payments of coupon and principal) which exists as long as the bond is not converted; and
- a written call option granting the holder the right to convert the bond into a fixed number of ordinary shares of the entity.

The economic effect of the instrument is substantially the same as issuing simultaneously (i) a debt instrument with an early settlement provision and (ii) warrants to issue ordinary shares.

Example 3

Instrument exchangeable into equity of a subsidiary

Entity P issues to independent investors, zero coupon guaranteed exchangeable bonds for cash of CU2 billion. The bonds are exchangeable into the existing ordinary shares of a subsidiary of Entity P, Entity S, at a fixed conversion price of CU25 per share (80 million shares). The functional currency of both Entity P and Entity S is Currency Units (CU).

At maturity, the bondholders will choose to either (1) redeem the bonds in cash at 109.10 per cent of their issued amount, or (2) convert the bonds into equity shares of Entity S at the fixed exercise price. If the bond holders choose to convert the bonds into equity, Entity P will deliver existing ordinary shares of Entity S, reducing Entity P's interest in Entity S from 100 per cent to a minimum of 90 per cent.

The conversion option is classified as equity in Entity P's consolidated financial statements because it provides for the exchange of a fixed amount of cash for a fixed number of Entity S's shares. IAS 32:22 states that "a contract that will be settled by the entity (receiving or) delivering a fixed number of its own equity instruments in exchange for a fixed amount of cash or another financial asset is an equity instrument." In consolidated financial statements, this applies to equity instruments of a subsidiary as well as of the parent entity.

Assuming that Entity P does not lose control of Entity S, any transfer of Entity S's shares on conversion of bonds will be accounted for as an equity transaction in accordance with IFRS 10:23.

The treatment of a convertible bond denominated in a currency that is not the functional currency of the entity that issued the instrument and/or the entity whose shares will be delivered on conversion is discussed in **3.8.1**.

3.1 Separating the liability and equity components

Separation of the instrument into its liability and equity components is made upon initial recognition of the instrument and is not subsequently revised. The method used is as follows:

- firstly, the fair value of the liability component is calculated, and this fair value establishes the initial carrying amount of the liability component; and
- secondly, the fair value of the liability component is deducted from the fair value of the instrument as a whole, with the resulting residual amount being recognised as the equity component.

This method of allocating the liability and equity components is consistent with the definition of equity as a residual interest in the assets of an entity after deducting all of its liabilities. It ensures that no gain or loss arises on the initial recognition of the two components.

The fair value of the liability component on initial recognition is the present value of the contractual stream of future cash flows (including both coupon payments and redemption amount) discounted at the market rate of interest that would have been applied to an instrument of comparable credit quality with substantially the same cash flows, on the same terms, but without the conversion option.

Example 3.1A

Convertible debt

Entity A issues 2,000 convertible bonds on 1 January 20X5. The bonds have a 3-year term, and are issued at par with a face value of CU1,000 per bond, resulting in total proceeds of CU2 million. Interest is payable annually in arrears at an annual interest rate of 6 per cent. Each bond is convertible, at the holder's discretion, at any time up to maturity into 250 ordinary shares. When the bonds are issued, the market interest rate for similar debt without the conversion option is 9 per cent.

On initial recognition, the contractual cash flows of the liability component are valued first, and the difference between the proceeds of the bond issue (being the fair value of the instrument in its entirety) and the fair value of the liability is assigned to the equity component. The present value (i.e. fair value) of the liability component is calculated using a discount rate of 9 per cent (i.e. the market interest rate for similar bonds with the same credit standing having no conversion rights). The calculation, which excludes the income tax entries, is illustrated below.

	CU
Present value of principal at the end of 3 years*	1,544,367
Present value of interest (CU120,000 payable annually in arrears for 3 years**)	303,755
Total liability component (B)	1,848,122
Residual equity component (A-B)	151,878
Proceeds of bond issue (A)	2,000,000

* present value of principal amount at 9%:

2,000,000/(1.09)^3 =	1,544,367

** present value of interest (CU120,000) payable at the end of each of 3 years:

interest at end of year 1: 120,000/1.09 =	110,092
interest at end of year 2: $120{,}000/(1.09)^2$ =	101,002
interest at end of year 3: $120{,}000/(1.09)^3$ =	92,661
Total net present value of interest payments	**303,755**

Upon initial recognition of the convertible instrument in the financial statements of the issuer, the following entries are recorded.

		CU	CU
Dr	Cash	2,000,000	
Cr	Financial liability		1,848,122
Cr	Equity		151,878

To recognise the recognition of convertible instrument.

Any transaction costs are allocated between the debt component and the equity component using their relative fair values.

The financial liability component will be subsequently measured in accordance with the measurement requirements in IFRS 9 depending on its classification (either as a financial liability at FVTPL, or as an 'other' liability, measured at amortised cost using the effective interest method).

The equity component will not be remeasured.

Example 3.1B

Perpetual interest-bearing preference shares

Entity A, a CU functional currency entity, issues non-redeemable preference shares. The preference shares have a cumulative, mandatory dividend fixed at CU424 per share per year. If earnings are not sufficient to cover the dividend in any given year, such dividends will be paid in future years. Additional dividends may be declared but only if dividends of the same amount are declared on the other classes of shares.

The preference share is a compound financial instrument that contains both liability and equity components. The liability is the contractual obligation by the issuer to deliver cash (CU424 per year), while the equity component is represented by the holder's right to receive an equity return in the form of additional dividends, if declared.

The fair value of the liability will be calculated as the present value of the mandatory dividend of CU424 per share per year in perpetuity discounted at the market interest rate for a similar instrument that does not entitle the holder to additional discretionary dividends. The equity component is calculated as the residual amount after deducting from the fair value of the instrument as a whole the amount separately determined for the liability component.

3.2 Separating the liability and equity components when the instrument has embedded derivatives

In addition to the financial liability and equity components, a compound instrument may also have embedded derivatives (see **chapter B5**). For example, the instrument may contain a call option exercisable by the issuer. The value of any such embedded derivative features must be allocated to the liability component. [IAS 32:31] Thus, the carrying amount of the liability component is established by measuring the fair value of a similar liability (with similar terms, credit status and embedded non-equity derivative features) but without an associated equity component. The carrying amount of the equity component is then determined by deducting the fair value of the liability component from the fair value of the compound instrument as a whole.

A further assessment is required to establish whether the embedded derivative is closely related to the liability component (see **chapter B5**). This assessment is made before separating the equity component. No gain or loss arises from initially recognising the components of the instrument separately.

Example 3.2A

Convertible debt with issuer call

A CU functional currency entity issues a bond with a principal amount of CU60 million carrying a coupon of 5 per cent payable annually in arrears. The instrument is issued for proceeds of CU60 million. The instrument is convertible into a fixed number of equity shares of the issuer after a specified date. The instrument has no fixed maturity. However, it contains an issuer call option that allows the issuer to redeem the bond at par at any point in time.

It is established that the value of a similar bond (of similar credit status with similar features except that it does not contain a call or equity conversion option) at current market rates would be CU57 million. Based on an option pricing model, it is further determined that the value of the issuer purchased call option on a similar bond without a conversion option is an asset of CU2 million.

The value allocated to the liability and equity components should be as follows.

Liability component: CU55 million (CU57 million less CU2 million)

This reflects the inclusion of the value of the additional embedded derivative feature (asset) in the liability component.

Equity component: CU5 million (CU60 million – CU55 million)

This represents the equity residual arrived at by subtracting from the fair value of the whole instrument the fair value of the liability component (which includes the value of the embedded derivative feature in the form of the purchased call feature).

The guidance in IFRS 9:B4.3.1 - B4.3.8 will need to be considered in assessing whether the embedded derivative is closely related to the host contract or whether, subsequent to issuance of the bond, it will be accounted for separately at fair value through profit or loss.

In **example 3.2A**, the initial amortised cost of the financial liability is established as the fair value of issued callable debt. Assuming the call feature over the debt instrument is not separated, the effective interest rate applied at inception and throughout the life of the instrument is the same rate of interest that would apply to plain callable debt. To the extent that interest rates change subsequent to issue, this will impact the likelihood that the callable debt will be called by the issuer and, therefore, the carrying amount will be updated (see **4.1** in **chapter B6**).

Example 3.2B

Convertible debt with issuer call and holder put

Entity X issued a convertible debt instrument in May 20X1 with a contractual maturity of 8 years. One bond allows the holder to obtain, at any time, one share

> of the issuer (the conversion option). The coupon is 2 per cent payable annually. The issue price is 100 per cent and the redemption price is 140 per cent.
>
> The instrument is puttable by the holders on three different dates during the life of the instrument (May 20X3, May 20X5 and May 20X7).
>
> The instrument is also callable by the issuer, starting 20X3, if the price of the issuer's shares increases beyond 125 per cent of the redemption price.
>
> In the case of exercise of the put/call option, the redemption price is equivalent to the amortised cost of the issued instrument (prior to the equity conversion option being separated). The embedded call/put options, therefore, are closely related to the instrument and are not accounted for as derivatives with changes in fair value recognised in profit or loss. On initial recognition, Entity X considers that there is a very high probability that the instrument will be redeemed by the holders on the first exercise date of the put (i.e. 20X3), given the low price of its shares.
>
> Entity X will account for the issued bond as a compound instrument. On initial recognition, Entity X needs to consider the contractual cash flows in order to measure the value of the debt component of the compound instrument.
>
> The fair value of the plain debt instrument without a call/put or equity conversion option is equivalent to the present value of the contractually determined stream of future cash flows until maturity (in this case 20X9) discounted at the rate of interest that applies to instruments of comparable credit quality and providing substantially the same cash flows on the same terms but without the call, put or conversion option (i.e. debt instruments with a 20X9 maturity date).
>
> Entity X then determines the value of the call and put options embedded in the debt instrument using an option pricing model. The call and put options are valued as if they were a call and a put embedded in a debt instrument that did not have any equity conversion feature. Both the purchased call and the written put are deducted and added to the debt in order to obtain the fair value of the total liability component.
>
> Finally, Entity X determines the value of the embedded conversion option (equity component) by subtracting the total liability component from the total net proceeds received on issuance.

If the financial liability is not designated as at FVTPL, the effective interest rate must be applied in determining amortised cost. If an entity designates financial instruments as at FVTPL, it should have a policy as to whether it recognises the effective interest rate in profit or loss separately for such items (see **4.3.1** in **chapter B11**). An issuer must apply the effective interest rate to the financial liability ignoring the likelihood that the financial liability may be forgiven if the equity conversion is exercised. This treatment is consistent with the principle that the likelihood of conversion is reflected in the value of the conversion option and is recognised as a separate financial instrument in equity.

3.3 Conversion of a compound instrument

Upon conversion of a compound instrument, equity is issued and the liability component is derecognised. The original equity component recognised at inception remains in equity (although it may be reclassified from one line item of equity to another). No gain or loss is recognised on conversion. [IAS 32:AG32]

Example 3.3A

Convertible debt: issue of new shares

Assume the facts are as in **example 3.1A**, but the date now is 31 December 20X6 (i.e. the end of Year 2 of the instrument's life). Assume that, due to a rapid rise of Entity A's share price, all holders of the bonds exercise their right to convert their holdings into a fixed number of equity instruments of Entity A at 31 December 20X6.

The liability has been accounted for at amortised cost using the effective interest method (see **4.1** in **chapter B6**).

At 31 December 20X6, the following applies:

- the amortised cost carrying amount of the liability (determined using the effective interest method) immediately prior to conversion is CU1,944,954;
- the original equity component immediately prior to conversion still stands at the original CU151,878; and
- upon conversion, 500,000 equity shares will be issued (250 equity shares per bond x 2,000 bonds issued) with each equity share having a nominal value of CU1.

The accounting entries on conversion are as follows.

		CU	CU
Dr	Bond liability	1,944,954	
Cr	Equity		1,944,954

To remove the liability from the statement of financial position and recognise the issue of shares as a result of conversion.

The original component of equity, CU151,878, may be reclassified to another line item within equity.

Example 3.3B

Convertible debt: issue of treasury shares

Assume the facts are as in **example 3.1A** except that, instead of issuing new shares upon conversion, Entity A satisfies the requirement for equity shares to be delivered to the bondholders through the use of treasury shares. Rather than issuing 500,000 new equity shares, Entity A delivers to the bondholders upon conversion 500,000 of its own shares that it had previously repurchased and held as treasury shares.

The accounting entries in these circumstances would be as follows.

		CU	CU
Dr	Bond	1,944,954	
Cr	Equity		1,944,954

To remove the liability from the statement of financial position as a result of conversion and remove the treasury shares from equity.

The original component of equity (CU151,878) and the amount deducted from equity (as required by IAS 32:33) on acquisition of the treasury shares may be reclassified to another line item within equity upon conversion.

3.4 Early redemption of a compound instrument

When an entity redeems or repurchases a convertible instrument before its maturity through a tender offer (without altering the conversion feature) through a tender offer, the consideration paid (including any transaction costs) is allocated to the liability and equity components at the date of the early redemption/early repurchase. The method used to make this allocation is the same as that used to make the original allocation of the proceeds of the issue of the instrument between the liability and equity components upon initial recognition. [IAS 32:AG33]

To the extent that the amount of the consideration allocated to the liability component exceeds the carrying amount of the liability component at that time, a loss is recognised in profit or loss. Conversely, to the extent that the consideration allocated to the liability component is smaller than its carrying amount, a gain is recognised in profit or loss.

The amount of consideration allocated to equity is recognised in equity with no gain or loss being recognised (the equity component that is not eliminated may be reclassified to another line item within equity).

Example 3.4

Convertible debt: repurchase

Assume the facts are as in **example 3.1A** and that one year has elapsed since the convertible bonds were issued and it is now 31 December 20X5.

In respect of the first year (year ended 31 December 20X5), the following accounting entries will have been recorded.

		CU	CU
Dr	Interest expense	166,331	
Cr	Bond liability		166,331

To recognise the interest expense and amortised cost of the bond using an effective interest rate of 9 per cent.

		CU	CU
Dr	Bond liability	120,000	
Cr	Cash		120,000

To recognise the payment of interest in cash.

This gives a carrying amount for the liability at the end of the first year of CU1,894,453.

	CU
Initial carrying amount at inception	1,848,122
Accretion in Year 1 using the effective interest method	166,331
Cash coupon payment at end of Year 1	(120,000)
Carrying amount at end of Year 1	1,894,453

At the end of the first year, Entity A repurchases the convertible bonds for a cash amount of CU2,100,000. It is established that, at the date of repurchase, Entity A could have issued a non-convertible instrument with a term of 2 years bearing a coupon rate of 7 per cent.

The consideration paid is allocated to the liability and equity components using the same method as was used on initial recognition of the convertible bonds; the fair value of consideration paid is first allocated to the liability component with the residual being assigned to the repurchase of the equity component:

	Fair value of repurchase consideration	**Carrying amount prior to repurchase**	**Difference**
	CU	**CU**	**CU**
Liability component:			
Present value of two remaining interest payments of CU120,000 discounted at 7 per cent and 9 per cent respectively	216,963	211,093	
Present value of principal amount due in two years' time of CU2 million discounted at 7 per cent and 9 per cent respectively	1,746,877	1,683,360	
	1,963,840	1,894,453	69,387
Equity component	136,160*	151,878	(15,718)
Total	2,100,000	2,046,331	53,669

* The amount of CU136,160 represents the difference between the repurchase price of CU2,100,000 and the amount of the consideration paid allocated to the liability component.

Having completed the allocation of the repurchase price, the following entries are recorded by Entity A in respect of the repurchase of the bonds.

		CU	CU
Dr	Bond liability	1,894,453	
Dr	Debt extinguishment loss (profit or loss)	69,387	
Cr	Cash		1,963,840

To recognise the repurchase of the bond liability and the resulting loss.

		CU	CU
Dr	Equity	136,160	
Cr	Cash		136,160

To recognise the portion of the cash paid in respect of the repurchase of the equity component.

The remaining balance of CU15,718 for the equity component may be reclassified to another line item within equity upon redemption.

3.4.1 Early redemption of convertible bond by the issuer exercising an embedded call option

Repurchase of convertible debt through a tender offer is explicitly addressed in the application guidance to IAS 32 as described above, but early redemption via the issuer exercising an embedded call option is not. This is considered in the following example.

Example 3.4.1

Early redemption of convertible bond by the issuer exercising an embedded call option

Entity B (whose functional currency is CU) issues a convertible bond for CU10 million on 1 January 20X0. The bond is redeemable at the par amount of CU10 million at 31 December 20X9. The bond pays interest of 4 per cent on the par amount on 31 December throughout its life. The holder can convert the bond into a fixed number of equity shares at any point from 1 January 20X5 to 31 December 20X9. In addition, under the terms of the call option embedded in the convertible bond, Entity B may redeem the instrument early by paying the par amount of CU10 million at any point between 1 January 20X5 and 31 December 20X9. Once notice is given that the call option is to be exercised the call option is settled immediately thereafter.

The convertible bond is classified as a compound instrument with a financial liability and equity components. The call option is deemed to be closely related to the debt instrument (see **7.1** in **chapter B5**) and is therefore not separately accounted for on the basis of a comparison of the exercise price of the option (amount repayable if called) to the amortised cost of the instrument before separating the equity component under IAS 32.

Entity B exercises its call option on 1 January 20X5 and redeems the instrument under the terms of the option at this date.

One way of accounting for the exercise of the call option would be to account for it as part of the debt instrument to which it is closely related. This would necessitate remeasuring the amortised cost of the financial liability component of the convertible debt under IFRS 9:B5.4.6. This would involve discounting the revised estimate of cash flows payable under the instrument (to include the CU10 million that will be payable immediately under the terms of the option) at the original effective interest rate established at initial recognition of the financial liability component of the convertible debt. The difference between the previous amortised cost carrying amount and the newly remeasured amount would be recognised in profit or loss. This would have the effect of recognising a loss equal to par less the carrying amount from the prior reporting period.

Alternatively, it may be argued that the guidance under IAS 32:AG33 should be applied because this refers to redemption. Under this approach, the consideration paid to redeem the convertible debt would be allocated to the financial liability and equity components upon early redemption using the same method as that used to make the allocation between the financial liability and equity component on initial recognition of the compound instrument. However, because the fair value of the financial liability component once the option has been exercised is likely to be equal to the redemption price, this method would allocate all of the consideration (i.e. the redemption price) to the financial liability component. Therefore, the effect would be likely to be substantially the same as the remeasurement under IFRS 9:B5.4.6 as discussed in the previous paragraph.

3.5 Amendment of the terms of a compound instrument to induce early conversion

An entity may amend the terms of a convertible instrument during its life so as to make conversion more attractive through either offering a more favourable conversion ratio, paying additional consideration in the event of conversion before a specified date, or a combination of both. In such circumstances, the difference between the fair value of the consideration that the holder receives upon conversion under the revised terms and the fair value of the consideration that the holder would have received upon conversion under the original terms, measured at the date when the terms are amended, should be recognised in profit or loss as a loss. [IAS 32:AG35]

Example 3.5

Convertible debt: inducement to convert

Assume the facts are as in **example 3.1A**, but at 31 December 20X5 (i.e. the end of Year 1 of the instrument's life), to induce holders to convert promptly,

Entity A amends the terms in one of two ways in respect of conversions that take place prior to 1 March 20X6.

Scenario 1: Entity A alters the terms such that each of the 2,000 bonds converts into 300 equity shares of Entity A, instead of 250 equity shares as under the original conversion terms (assume the market value of the equity shares at the date of the amendment is CU5).

Scenario 2: Entity A states that it will pay an additional CU1 in cash in relation to each share converted.

The liability and equity components have the following carrying amounts in the statement of financial position at 31 December 20X5:

	CU
Liability component:	
– present value of two remaining interest payments of CU120,000 discounted at 9 per cent	211,093
– present value of principal amount of CU2 million due in two years' time discounted at 9 per cent	1,683,360
	1,894,453
Equity component	151,878*
Total	**2,046,331**

* The equity component remains unchanged since the allocation on initial recognition.

The following entries will be needed to recognise the amendment of the terms of the convertible bonds.

Scenario 1

Number of equity shares to be issued to bondholders under the *amended* conversion terms:	
– number of bonds issued	2,000
– number of shares to be issued per bond on conversion	300
Total number of equity shares to be issued on conversion	600,000
Number of equity shares to be issued to bondholders under *original* conversion terms:	
– number of bonds issued	2,000
– number of shares to be issued per bond on conversion	250
Total number of equity shares to be issued on conversion	500,000

Number of incremental equity shares to be issued to bondholders upon conversion: 100,000

Value of incremental equity shares to be issued to bondholders upon conversion:

100,000 x CU5 = CU500,000

Therefore, the entry needed to record the amendment of the terms is as follows.

		CU	CU
Dr	Expense on amendment of terms of convertible bonds (profit or loss)	500,000	
Cr	Equity		500,000

To recognise the amendment of the terms of the convertible bonds.

Upon conversion, the accounting would follow the approach laid out in **example 3.3A**. If the instrument were not converted, no further gain or loss would be recognised.

Scenario 2

The additional consideration to be paid in the event of conversion would amount to: 500,000 × CU1 = CU500,000

This would be recognised through the following entry upon amendment of the terms of the convertible bonds.

		CU	CU
Dr	Expense on amendment of terms of convertible bonds (profit or loss)	500,000	
Cr	Financial liability		500,000

To recognise the amendment of the terms of the convertible bonds.

On conversion, the accounting would follow the approach laid out in **example 3.3A** except that an additional entry would be required to recognise the payment of the additional cash inducement as follows.

		CU	CU
Dr	Financial liability	500,000	
Cr	Cash		500,000

To record the payment of the additional cash inducement.

If the instrument were not converted, an entry would be required to derecognise the inducement that the holder has not exercised.

		CU	CU
Dr	Financial liability	500,000	
Cr	Gain upon non-exercise of inducement (profit or loss)		500,000

To derecognise the liability for the inducement that has not been exercised.

As described in **3.3**, upon conversion of a compound instrument, equity is issued and the liability component is derecognised. The original equity component recognised at inception remains in equity (although it may be reclassified from one line item of equity to another) and no gain or loss is recognised on conversion. This treatment equally applies for conversion of a compound instrument where previously there was an inducement and an expense in profit or loss and increase in equity was recognised. Upon conversion of the compound instrument, the financial liability is derecognised and reclassified to equity. Equity will therefore consist of the original equity component recognised on issue of the compound instrument, the amount recognised in equity as a result of the inducement, plus the reclassification of the liability upon conversion. Amounts may be transferred within equity from one line item to another upon conversion of the compound instrument.

3.6 Treatment of mandatorily convertible instruments

An entity may issue an instrument that at the end of its life is mandatorily convertible into a fixed number of its equity shares (rather than conversion being at the option of the holder). This instrument is, in substance, a prepaid forward purchase of the entity's equity shares. Because the instrument carries an obligation for the issuer to make fixed interest payments during the life of the mandatorily convertible instrument, the instrument includes a financial liability component. The following example illustrates the entries for a mandatorily convertible debt instrument.

Example 3.6

Mandatorily convertible instrument

A CU functional currency entity issues a mandatorily convertible instrument for CU100,000 on 1 January 20X5. The instrument obliges the entity to make cash coupon payments of CU5,000 on both 31 December 20X5 and 31 December 20X6. On 31 December 20X6, the instrument will mandatorily convert into 5,000 ordinary shares of the entity.

At the inception of the instrument, the following two elements will be separated.

- A liability component arising from the coupon payments of CU5,000 to be made on both 31 December 20X5 and 31 December 20X6. This will be determined as the present value of the payments discounted at the rate that would have been applicable if the entity had issued a debt instrument with similar features and of similar credit standing, but without the mandatory conversion feature.
- An equity component representing the delivery of equity in the future. This amount will be determined as the residual amount after the liability component is deducted from the fair value of the whole compound instrument at inception (CU100,000).

If, using this methodology, it is determined that the liability component at inception is, for example, CU9,000 (based on a discount rate of 7.32 per cent), the following entries will be required on initial recognition of the instrument.

		CU	CU
Dr	Cash	100,000	
Cr	Financial liability		9,000
Cr	Equity		91,000

To recognise the mandatorily convertible instrument.

Over the life of the instrument, the following entries will be made with respect to the liability so that, by the end of the instrument's life, the liability component will have been extinguished.

Year end 31 December 20X5

		CU	CU
Dr	Interest expense	659	
Cr	Financial liability		659

To recognise the interest expense to account for the liability at amortised cost using the effective interest rate of 7.32 per cent.

		CU	CU
Dr	Financial liability	5,000	
Cr	Cash		5,000

To record the cash coupon payment of CU5,000.

Year end 31 December 20X6

		CU	CU
Dr	Interest expense	341	
Cr	Financial liability		341

To recognise the interest expense to account for the liability at amortised cost using the effective interest rate of 7.32 per cent.

		CU	CU
Dr	Financial liability	5,000	
Cr	Cash		5,000

To reflect the cash coupon payment of CU5,000.

Upon mandatory conversion of the instrument into 5,000 ordinary shares of the entity via the issue of new shares, local company law may require some reclassification of the balance within equity. However, no gain or loss is recognised on conversion in accordance with IAS 32:AG32.

In May 2014, the IFRS Interpretations Committee issued a final agenda decision on IAS 32, *Classification of a financial instrument that is mandatorily convertible into a variable number of shares upon a contingent 'non-viability' event.*

The Interpretations Committee discussed how an issuer would classify a particular mandatorily convertible financial instrument in accordance with IAS 32. The financial instrument did not have a stated maturity date but was mandatorily convertible into a variable number of the issuer's own equity instruments if the issuer breached the Tier 1 Capital ratio (i.e. described as a 'contingent non-viability event'). The financial instrument is issued at par and the value of the equity instruments that will be delivered at conversion is equal to that fixed par amount. Interest payments on the instrument are payable at the discretion of the issuer.

Specifically the Interpretations Committee discussed the following issues:

(i) whether the financial instrument meets the definition of a financial liability in its entirety or must be classified as a compound instrument comprised of a liability component and an equity component (and, in the latter case, what those components reflect); and

(ii) how the financial liability (or liability component) identified above in bullet (i) would be measured.

The Interpretations Committee decided not to add this issue to its agenda. The Interpretations Committee noted that the scope of the issues raised in the submission is too broad for it to address in an efficient manner.

3.7 Convertible debt with multiple settlement options

Throughout **section 3** so far, it has been assumed that the equity conversion option can only be gross physically settled, i.e. a fixed number of shares is delivered on conversion of the bond. However, this may not always be the case. As explained in **section 6**, if the settlement of the call option can be achieved in ways other than by delivery of a fixed number of shares for a fixed amount of cash, the call option is treated as a derivative and is carried at fair value with gains and losses recognised in profit or loss.

Some convertible debt instruments include cash settlement options. The contractual terms of such an instruments allow that if the holder of the instrument invokes the conversion option, the issuer has a choice over the manner in which the call option is settled: the issuer may deliver either a fixed number of shares to the holder, or an amount of cash equal to the market value of the fixed number of shares on the date of conversion or an average price in a period before conversion. Because the issuer will not always deliver a fixed amount of equity for receipt of a fixed amount of cash upon conversion, the conversion feature does not meet the definition of equity. The written call option is accounted for as a derivative liability.

The convertible debt is a hybrid instrument containing a host debt contract and an embedded derivative liability (written call option over own shares). The embedded derivative is measured at fair value with changes in fair value recognised in profit or loss. The treatment of hybrid instruments is explained in **chapter B5**.

Example 3.7

Convertible debt: cash settlement choice at conversion

On 1 January 20X1, Entity X issues a convertible bond with a face value of CU10 million at par. The instrument has a maturity of 10 years and pays an annual coupon of 5 per cent on 31 December. The bond is convertible at maturity at the discretion of the holder. However, if the holder exercises the right to convert, Entity X can either:

- deliver a fixed number of Entity X's ordinary shares; or
- pay an amount of cash equal to the fixed number of shares under the conversion option multiplied by the average share price of Entity X's ordinary shares in the 10 days immediately preceding maturity.

IAS 32:26 states that when a derivative financial instrument gives one party a choice regarding how it is settled, it is a financial asset or a financial liability unless all of the settlement alternatives would result in it being an equity instrument.

In the circumstances described, Entity X has an obligation to pay cash for interest payments and to redeem the instrument at maturity and, because the written call option within the convertible instrument may be settled in cash rather than through the delivery of a fixed number of shares, the equity conversion feature does not meet the definition of equity. The convertible debt is therefore a financial liability in its entirety.

Entity X does not designate the instrument at initial recognition as at fair value through profit or loss, therefore the hybrid instrument must be separated between a debt host contract measured at amortised cost and the equity conversion feature measured at fair value through profit or loss.

The difference between the fair value of the total hybrid instrument and the fair value of the embedded derivative is assigned to the host contract, with the host accounted for at amortised cost.

Assuming that the fair value of the written call option is CU1.5 million at 1 January 20X1, the entries on that date would be as follows.

		CU	CU
Dr	Cash	10,000,000	
Cr	Financial liability (host contract)		8,500,000
Cr	Derivative financial liability		1,500,000

To recognise the convertible debt and written call option.

Entity X will account for the host contract at amortised cost by applying the effective interest rate of 7.15 per cent, and the derivative will be remeasured to its fair value. On 31 December 20X1, the amortised cost of the host debt contract is CU9,107,750 and the fair value of the embedded derivative is CU2,450,000. Therefore, the entries required are as follows.

		CU	CU
Dr	Interest expense	607,750	
Cr	Financial liability (host contract)		607,750
Dr	Financial liability (host contract)	500,000	
Cr	Cash		500,000

To recognise the interest expense on the host debt contract measured at amortised cost using the effective interest rate of 7.15 per cent and payment of contractual coupon.

		CU	CU
Dr	Derivative loss	950,000	
Cr	Derivative financial liability		950,000

To recognise the fair value movement on the embedded derivative in profit or loss.

3.8 Foreign currency denominated convertible debt

An entity may issue an instrument denominated in a foreign currency (a currency other than the functional currency of the entity) that is convertible into a fixed number of ordinary shares of the entity. Such an instrument contains a written option to exchange a fixed number of equity instruments for a fixed amount of cash that is denominated in a foreign currency.

As explained in **section 6**, a derivative contract over an entity's own equity is accounted for as equity only when it will be settled exclusively by the entity delivering (or receiving) a fixed number of its own equity instruments in exchange for a fixed amount of cash or another financial asset.

For foreign currency denominated convertible debt, the question arises as to whether the equity conversion option meets the definition of equity when the consideration the issuer receives for issuing a fixed number of shares is forgiveness of a debt instrument that is variable in functional currency terms. The same question also applies to freestanding instruments (e.g. a stand-alone physically settled written call over own shares that will be settled at exercise through an exchange of a fixed number of own shares for a fixed amount of foreign currency cash).

A gross physically settled derivative over a fixed number of own equity shares meets the definition of equity only if the amount of cash or financial assets paid or received is fixed in the *functional currency* of the issuer (the one exception relates to certain rights issues as described in **6.1.1**). The following guidance is relevant.

- A derivative over a fixed number of equity shares that is exchanged for a variable amount of cash is a derivative, and not equity. For example, an instrument that requires an exchange of a fixed number of equity shares for a variable amount of cash calculated to equal the value of 100 ounces of gold is a derivative because the fair value of the derivative is driven from movements in the gold price as well as the equity price. [IAS 32:24]
- IFRS 9 considers that, although foreign denominated monetary items and foreign currency forecast transactions are fixed in foreign currency terms, they are variable in functional currency terms and, therefore, they are eligible to be designated in a cash flow hedge. [IFRS 9:IG.E.3.3 & E.3.4]

Applying this guidance to foreign currency denominated convertible debt, it is clear that (1) the foreign currency convertible, while fixed in foreign currency terms, is variable in functional currency terms and, therefore, a fixed number of shares will be delivered in exchange for a variable amount of cash; and (2) conversion will occur based on the interaction of not only the equity price, but also the foreign currency value of the bond that is forgiven.

The IFRIC (now the IFRS Interpretations Committee) referred the classification of foreign currency denominated convertible debt to the IASB and, in September 2005, the Board explored whether to amend IAS 32 to permit contracts to be classified as equity if they are to be settled by an entity delivering a fixed number of its own equity instruments for a fixed amount of cash or another financial asset denominated in a foreign currency. The Board noted that the amendment would result in equity and foreign exchange features whose values are interdependent being recognised in equity, and that excluding from equity the value attributable to the foreign exchange features would require arbitrary rules. The Board also noted that allowing dual indexed contracts (to share price and foreign exchange rates) to be classified as equity would require additional and detailed guidance to avoid structuring opportunities aimed at obtaining a desired accounting result. The Board therefore decided not to proceed with an amendment to IAS 32.

Example 3.8

Foreign currency denominated convertible debt

Entity A has a functional currency of Sterling. Entity A issues a convertible bond denominated in US dollars that, if converted, will result in the gross physical delivery of a fixed number of Entity A's shares.

The convertible bond will be classified in its entirety as a financial liability because, upon conversion, a fixed amount of shares will be delivered in exchange for a variable amount of functional currency cash, being the forgiveness of the bond obligation.

3.8.1 Different entities in a group issue convertible debt and the shares delivered on conversion when debt is in a foreign currency

A convertible debt instrument might be issued under which the shares to be delivered on conversion will not be those of the legal entity that issued the instrument, but those of another entity in the same group (e.g. the parent or subsidiary of the issuer). Further, the debt may be denominated in a currency that is different from the functional currency of either the entity that issued the instrument, the entity whose shares will be delivered on conversion, or both.

If a parent and subsidiary have the same functional currency and either the parent issues a foreign currency denominated convertible bond that is convertible into a fixed number of the subsidiary's shares, or the subsidiary issues a foreign currency convertible bond that is convertible into a fixed number of the parent's shares, the instrument in both cases would be classified wholly as a liability in the consolidated financial statements because a fixed number of shares is exchanged for a variable amount of functional currency cash.

The accounting for convertible debt issued by an entity in the group that is convertible into a fixed number of equity instruments of another entity in the group is more complex when the two entities have different functional currencies and the bond is denominated in one of those currencies. The IFRIC (now the IFRS Interpretations Committee) discussed this scenario but did not take the issue onto its agenda because the issue was considered to be too narrow. In the absence of specific guidance, it is not clear whether a group should look to the functional currency of the issuer of the fixed number of shares or the functional currency of the issuer of the convertible bond. For the purpose of assessing such convertible instruments, a group should establish a policy as to how it determines what is a fixed amount of functional currency cash when different entities in the group issue the convertible instrument and the shares. This policy should be applied consistently to all similar instruments.

3.8.2 Functional currency of the issuer 'pegged' to the currency of the debt

When the functional currency of the issuer is 'pegged' to the currency in which the convertible debt instrument is denominated, the currency in which the convertible debt is denominated is not regarded as a 'foreign' currency.

Example 3.8.2

Functional currency of the issuer 'pegged' to the currency of the debt

A Hong Kong dollar functional entity issues a convertible debt instrument denominated in US dollars. At the date of issue, the Hong Kong dollar and US dollar are subject to a fixed peg (i.e. the exchange rate between the US dollar and the Hong Kong dollar is fixed).

Because there is no variability in the carrying amount of the US dollar financial liability in the functional currency of the issuer, the US dollar is not regarded as a foreign currency. Accordingly, the convertible debt is treated as a compound instrument containing a financial liability and an equity component.

As discussed in **section 8**, there is no clear guidance on when it is appropriate to reconsider the liability/equity classification in circumstances when there has been no change in the terms of the instrument. Thus, if following the issue of the convertible debt, the Hong Kong dollar and the US dollar cease to be subject to a fixed peg, resulting in the US dollar being regarded as a foreign currency, the issuer should determine an appropriate accounting policy and apply it consistently.

3.9 Anti-dilutive provisions in convertible debt

Convertible bonds will often include anti-dilutive provisions within the contractual terms of the instrument to ensure that the bondholder's potential interest in the equity of the issuer is not diluted in specified circumstances. If these provisions are triggered, the number of shares that would be delivered to the bondholder is adjusted.

For an equity conversion feature to be considered equity, it must result in the exchange of a fixed amount of cash or other financial asset for a fixed number of equity instruments (the 'fixed-for-fixed criterion').

IAS 32 does not provide any guidance on which types of anti-dilutive provision in convertible debt result in the equity conversion feature failing equity treatment.

Many anti-dilutive provisions are structured so as to 'make-whole' the holder of the convertible bond if specified events occur such that the holder of the convertible debt instrument remains in the same position relative to existing ordinary shareholders before and after the event. If this is the case, such provisions are not deemed to breach the fixed-for-fixed criterion. A different conclusion would be reached if the adjustment to the conversion ratio benefited the convertible bondholder at the expense of the existing ordinary shareholders.

To the extent that shares are issued at a discount or repurchased at a premium (i.e. the shares are not issued or repurchased at their fair value), the convertible bondholders that are potential shareholders of the entity will be disadvantaged relative to the existing shareholders. An anti-dilutive provision that makes-whole for the discount on issue or premium on repurchase will not breach the fixed-for-fixed criterion. Consider the following examples:

Conversion option adjusted for bonus issue of shares to existing ordinary shareholders

If the issuer decides to issue additional ordinary shares to existing ordinary shareholders while the convertible debt is outstanding (e.g. through a bonus issue for nil consideration), the conversion feature will be adjusted to reflect the increased number of shares in issue. This adjustment attempts to put the convertible debt holder in the same economic position relative to existing ordinary shareholders as was the case immediately prior to the issue of the new shares and, as such, does not breach the fixed-for-fixed criterion.

Conversion option adjusted for share buyback

The same principle can be applied when the number of shares under the conversion option is reduced due to the issuer entering into a buyback of its own shares at a premium to their market price when the convertible debt is outstanding. If the adjustment to the conversion ratio only reflects the degree to which the shares are purchased a premium to their market price and so the convertible bondholder does not gain any advantage, the existence of the anti-dilution feature would not breach the fixed-for-fixed criterion.

Conversion option is adjusted for special dividends

Anti-dilutive provisions linked to dividend payments are also common. If the issuer pays dividends on its existing ordinary shares, there may be an adjustment to the conversion ratio which attempts to compensate the holder of the convertible debt when dividends paid are in excess of a specified level. Such provisions attempt to compensate the holder of the convertible bond when a 'special dividend' is paid which is in the nature of a return of capital to the existing ordinary shareholders. In such circumstances, the conversion ratio that was determined when the convertible bond was issued assumes a certain level of dividend payments between the date when the instrument was issued and the date when conversion can occur. The adjustment to the conversion feature makes whole the difference between the amount of the special dividend and the amount of the dividends expected to be paid.

Alternatively, the number of shares under the conversion feature may be adjusted for the actual dividend paid in a period while the convertible bond is outstanding. In this instance, the conversion ratio that was determined when the convertible bond was issued assumed no dividend payments between the date when the instrument was issued and the date when conversion can occur. The number of shares to be delivered under the conversion feature is adjusted so that the conversion price is equal to that which would have been determined had the issuer known at inception exactly what dividends would be paid in the future. Neither of these anti-dilutive provisions is considered to breach the fixed-for-fixed criterion because they both exist to retain parity between the existing ordinary shareholders (who have received dividends) and holders of the convertible debt (who have not).

Down-round protection

An example of a provision that would breach the fixed-for-fixed criterion is 'down-round protection'. Under these arrangements, the number of shares receivable under the conversion option increases if the strike price of the conversion option is adjusted downwards or if shares are subsequently issued at a lower price. Such arrangements are designed to protect the holders of convertible debt from adverse movements in share price at the expense of the existing ordinary shareholders and, as such, result in a transfer of value (in relative terms) from the existing ordinary shareholders to convertible debt holders. For this reason, they are not purely 'anti-dilutive' in nature and result in the equity conversion feature not meeting the definition of equity.

3.10 Other variations in convertible debt

It is not practicable to provide an exhaustive list of different variations in conversion features in convertible debt. However, some further examples and discussion of the accounting analysis are set out below.

3.10.1 Discounted convertible debt

Convertible debt may be issued such that the investor receives some of the interest on the instrument in the form of fixed cash coupons and some in the form of accretion up to the par amount. The accretion up to the par amount is not regarded as variable, i.e. not fixed, consideration and therefore will not breach the 'fixed-for-fixed' criterion. This is because, firstly, the par amount remains constant and, therefore, the nominal value of the bond remains unchanged (as referred to in IAS 32.22, the bond has a 'fixed stated principal amount'). Secondly, the unwinding of the discount to par is part of the interest on the bond component. When compared to conventional fixed rate convertible debt issued at par (i.e. without a discount), the conversion option always results in the holder giving up a variable amount of future interest receipts. As the instrument's life shortens, the amount of interest forgiven by the holder reduces. Such variability in the amount forgiven by the holder is not considered variability in cash in determining whether the conversion option meets the definition of equity.

Example 3.10.1

Discounted convertible debt

Entity A issues convertible debt for CU90 that is convertible into a fixed number of equity shares at any time and pays an annual cash coupon of 1 per cent based on the par amount of CU100. If the holder does not choose to convert the instrument into the fixed number of equity shares, the bond will be redeemed at maturity for the par amount of CU100. Consequently, the holder of the instrument receives some of the interest on the instrument in the form of fixed cash coupons and some in the form of the additional CU10 received following accretion up to the par amount.

The conversion option meets the fixed-for-fixed criterion and should be classified as equity because the nominal amount of the bond given up on conversion is fixed.

3.10.2 Convertible debt: interest linked to benchmark interest rate

Convertible debt usually carries a fixed rate of interest or, as described above, it may be partly issued at a discount and, therefore, economically pays a fixed amount of interest at maturity. If the interest on convertible debt is linked to a benchmark interest rate (e.g. LIBOR) and the instrument is not issued at a discount, then all interest flows are variable. It could be argued that the conversion feature breaches the 'fixed cash' criterion because the interest forgiveness is always changing. Similar to the analysis above for a discounted convertible bond, it would be inappropriate to consider variable interest as a breach of the 'fixed cash' criterion. Firstly, the par amount remains constant (as referred to in IAS 32.22, the bond has a 'fixed stated principal amount'). Secondly, IAS 32:22 specifically states that "changes in the fair value of a contract arising from variations in market interest rates that do not affect the amount of cash or other financial assets to be paid or received … on settlement of the contract" do not preclude equity classification. If the fixed cash is considered the par amount and the variable interest is considered to be merely servicing, the 'fixed cash' criterion is not breached. Such an instrument would therefore be treated as a compound instrument that contains a financial liability and an equity component.

If the interest payments were driven not by a benchmark interest rate but, instead, by another variable that was not a market rate of interest (e.g. changes in the profitability of the entity), the same conclusion would not be appropriate and, therefore, the instrument would be treated as a financial liability in its entirety. The issuer would need to consider whether the variable basis of interest payments was a closely related embedded derivative if the instrument was not classified as at FVTPL. Guidance on embedded derivatives is set out in **chapter B5**.

3.10.3 Convertible debt: conversion to a variable number of shares dependent on the share price at the date of conversion

Convertible debt that permits the holder to convert the instrument into a variable number of shares dependent on the share price at the date of conversion is not a compound instrument. For example, the conversion feature may be forgiveness of a fixed amount of functional currency debt (i.e. principal and any future interest) for a fixed number of shares (say 10.0 shares if the share price is above CU100 but below CU110, but 9.5 shares if the share price is above CU110 but below CU120, and 9.0 shares if the share price is above CU120). The number of shares to be delivered is based on a sliding scale that reduces as the share price increases. In such circumstances, the conversion feature does not meet the definition of equity because the conversion does not result in the delivery of a fixed number of shares.

In the example set out in the previous paragraph, it is not appropriate to consider the conversion feature as three separate conversion features that each have a right to convert the same fixed amount of cash (being principal and interest) for a fixed amount of shares because the conversion features are mutually exclusive. Only one conversion feature can ever be exercised (equally, there can only ever be one fixed amount of cash that is forgiven as consideration for the issue of shares) because, once conversion has occurred, the instrument is extinguished.

3.10.4 Convertible debt: conversion to a fixed number of shares or variable number of shares to the value of the debt component

Consider an example where convertible debt permits the holder to convert into a fixed number of shares before the debt's contractual maturity date when the share price is above a specified level, but also allows the holder to forgive the debt component (being principal and interest) by electing for a variable number of shares equal to the par value of the debt component when the share price is below that specified level. On the face of it, and consistent with the example described in **3.10.3**, because the instrument does not always result in the delivery of a fixed number of shares, it could be argued that the instrument does not have any equity element (i.e. the entire instrument is a financial liability).

However, the right for the holder to require repayment of debt in a variable number of shares equal in value to the debt component is not itself a conversion feature; rather, it is a settlement alternative inherent in the debt component. The payment of interest and principal, regardless of whether it is settled in cash or in shares of an equal value, is a financial liability. The inclusion of a feature that permits the holder to early redeem the instrument by requiring the issuer to deliver a variable number of shares equal in value to the par amount of the debt when the share price is below a specified level is merely an early redemption option. Put another way, when the share price is below a specified level, the holder can require the convertible debt to be early redeemed and the issuer is required to use its own shares as currency for this early redemption.

The right to convert into a fixed number of shares when the share price is above the specified level is an equity instrument because it permits the holder to require the issuer to deliver a fixed amount of shares in exchange for a fixed amount of cash (being the principal and interest, and the 'shares to the value of' settlement alternative on that principal and interest).

3.10.5 Convertible debt: convertible only on the occurrence of a contingent event

The issuer of convertible debt that is convertible only upon the occurrence of a contingent event that is outside the control of the holder and the issuer must first determine whether, if the event occurs, the conversion would result in the delivery of a fixed number of equity instruments for a fixed amount of functional currency cash. Put another way, ignoring the contingent element, would the instrument be a compound instrument with an equity and a debt component? If the answer to this question is yes, then the fact that the holder can only convert if a contingent event occurs does not prevent the conversion feature being presented as equity.

The inclusion of the contingency merely reduces the likelihood of the conversion occurring and, therefore, for a stated amount of proceeds would result in the residual amount of net proceeds allocated to the equity component being lower when compared to an equity component of convertible debt without the contingency. This is because the fair value of the debt component would be higher due to a corresponding higher contractual interest rate on the debt component when the conversion option is contingent compared to when it is not.

3.10.6 Convertible debt: conversion into a variable number of shares but subject to a specified minimum and/or maximum number of equity shares

In May 2014, the IFRS Interpretations Committee issued a final agenda decision on IAS 32, *Accounting for a financial instrument that is mandatorily convertible into a variable number of shares subject to a cap and a floor*.

The Interpretations Committee discussed how an issuer would account for a particular mandatorily convertible financial instrument in accordance with IAS 32 or IFRS 9. The financial instrument has a stated maturity date and, at maturity, the issuer must deliver a variable number of its own equity instruments to equal a fixed cash amount – subject to a cap and a floor, which limit and guarantee, respectively, the number of equity instruments to be delivered.

The Interpretations Committee noted that the issuer's obligation to deliver a variable number of the entity's own equity instruments is a non-derivative that meets the definition of a financial liability in IAS 32:11(b)(i) in its entirety. IAS 32:11(b)(i) of the definition of a liability does not have any limits or thresholds regarding the degree of variability that is required. Therefore, the contractual substance of the instrument is a single obligation to deliver a variable number of equity instruments at maturity, with the variation based on the value of those equity instruments. Such a single obligation to deliver a variable number of own equity instruments cannot be subdivided into components for the purposes of evaluating whether the instrument contains a component that meets the definition of equity. Even though the number of equity instruments to be delivered is limited and guaranteed by the cap and the floor, the overall number of equity instruments that the issuer is obliged to deliver is not fixed and therefore the entire obligation meets the definition of a financial liability.

Furthermore, the Interpretations Committee noted that the cap and the floor are embedded derivative features whose values change in response to the price of the issuer's equity share. Therefore, assuming that the issuer has not elected to designate the entire instrument under the fair value option, the issuer must separate those features and account for the embedded derivative features separately from the host liability contract at fair value through profit or loss in accordance with IFRS 9. The Interpretations Committee considered that in the light of its analysis of the existing IFRS requirements, an Interpretation was not necessary and consequently decided not to add the issue to its agenda.

Example 3.10.6

Convertible bond convertible into a variable number of shares but subject to a specified minimum and/or maximum number of equity shares

Entity A (CU functional currency) issues a convertible debt instrument with a maturity of five years that pays interest at 5 per cent on a nominal value of CU10,000. At the option of the holder, the instrument may be converted at maturity into ordinary shares of Entity A as follows:

- if the ordinary share price is under CU100 at the convertible instrument's maturity date, into 100 ordinary shares; or
- if the ordinary share price is above CU150 at the convertible instrument's maturity date, into 67 ordinary shares; or
- if the ordinary share price is between CU100 and CU150 at the convertible instrument's maturity date, into the number of ordinary shares that are equivalent in value to CU10,000.

The ordinary shares meet the definition of equity instruments in IAS 32.

The convertible debt instrument is entirely a financial liability as the number of equity instruments to be delivered on conversion is not fixed. The variability in the number of shares to be issued is limited; Entity A may actually deliver a fixed number of shares such as a minimum (floor) or maximum (cap) number of shares depending on its future ordinary share price. However, the conversion feature of the instrument still fails the definition of equity because the number of shares to be delivered on conversion varies.

It is not appropriate to consider the instrument as containing three separate conversion features, two of which convert into a fixed number of shares (being the cap and the floor), because the conversion features are mutually exclusive. Only one of the three possible conversion features can ever arise on exercise because, following conversion, the debt instrument (including the other two conversion features) is extinguished.

Consequently, the convertible instrument is a hybrid financial liability in its entirety consisting of two separate obligations: (1) an obligation to pay interest at 5 per cent on a principal of CU10,000 throughout the life of the instrument and to repay the principal of CU10,000 at maturity and (2) a derivative conversion option that fails the definition of equity because the issuer is obliged to deliver a variable number of equity instruments if the holder exercises the conversion option.

If the instrument is not measured at fair value through profit or loss in its entirety, the appropriate accounting for Entity A in accordance with IFRS 9 is as follows:

- the derivative conversion feature should be separated out as a non-closely related embedded derivative and measured at fair value through profit or loss; and
- the debt host contract (i.e. the obligation to pay interest and principal) should be measured at amortised cost.

3.10.7 Convertible debt: change of control clauses

Many convertible debt instruments contain change of control protection clauses. One common example of a protection clause attempts to provide the convertible bondholder with an enhanced conversion ratio following a change of control of the issuer in order to compensate the convertible bondholder for the loss of time value in the option in the event that the bondholder chooses to exercise the conversion option early. Such instruments will often grant to the issuer a right to redeem the convertible bond early, at par, for a period immediately following a change of control. It is this issuer call option that may incentivise the convertible bondholder to convert early and, in doing so, receive an additional number of shares to reflect the fact that, absent conversion, the issuer will buy back the convertible bond at par and the convertible bondholder will lose the remaining value of the conversion option.

The terms and conditions of the instrument will generally either stipulate a predetermined adjusted conversion ratio which varies depending on when the change of control occurs during the life of the instrument (with the adjustment to the conversion ratio being reduced the closer the date of the change of control is to the maturity date of the instrument) or include a formula which attempts to determine the value of the remaining time value in the conversion option at the date of change of control and adjusts the conversion ratio to reflect this value.

Change of control clauses vary considerably and it is not possible to generalise as to their effect on the classification of convertible debt. The terms and objective of the clause must be carefully considered to determine whether the objective of the change in the conversion ratio is to preserve the rights and value of the bondholders following a change of control by providing additional shares on conversion equal to the remaining time value of the conversion option on the date of change of control. If this is the case, this feature would not breach the fixed-for-fixed criterion.

3.11 Reverse convertible instruments

A conventional convertible bond entitles the holder to convert the bond into shares of the issuer. If the conversion option meets the definition of equity, the conversion option is recognised in equity and the bond component is recognised as a financial liability. The accounting treatment for this is clear in IAS 32 and reflects the fact that, until conversion, the issuer always has an obligation to pay the bond component, which will either be settled by paying cash or another financial asset or be forgiven by the holder if the holder choose to exercise its conversion option.

The accounting treatment under IAS 32 is less clear for 'reverse' convertible instruments where the issuer (rather than the holder) has the choice as to whether to settle a bond with cash or another financial asset or to deliver a fixed number of shares. In this case, the holder does not have a choice as to whether to convert. This raises the question as to whether the issuer ever has an obligation to pay cash because the issuer can always choose to deliver shares.

Example 3.11

Reverse convertible bond

Entity X is a CU functional currency entity and issues a reverse convertible instrument for CU100 million. The instrument has a maturity of five years. The instrument has non-discretionary annual interest payments over its life of CU10 million. At maturity, the issuer has a choice of either:

(i) paying cash equal to the principal amount (CU100 million); or

(ii) issuing a fixed number of 15 of its own equity shares. The value of 15 shares at issue of the instrument does not substantially exceed the value of the cash settlement alternative under (i).

Given the lack of clear guidance in IAS 32, two approaches are considered to be acceptable. Whichever approach is adopted, Entity X should apply it consistently as an accounting policy choice.

Approach 1

From Entity X's perspective, the instrument is a compound instrument analysed as (a) an obligation to pay cash as interest during the life and principal at maturity, which is a financial liability, and (b) a purchased put option over its own shares (i.e. an option to exchange the obligation to pay CU100 million for a fixed number of shares), which is equity. Economically, the high interest payments represent the interest rate on a plain vanilla bond (without the conversion feature) plus the option premium in respect of the purchased put spread over the life. This approach is consistent with the approach taken for conventional convertible debt where the holder has the choice of conversion. The equity component of the reverse convertible bond will be determined as the difference between the fair value of the instrument as a whole and the fair value of the financial liability (comprising the obligation to pay cash in relation to interest and principal).

Approach 2

From Entity X's perspective, the instrument is a compound instrument analysed as (a) an obligation to pay cash in respect of interest over the life and (b) an option to either pay CU100 million or issue 15 shares at maturity in settlement of the principal. Because Entity X can avoid paying cash in relation to the principal amount through delivery of a fixed number of own equity shares, this feature does not give rise to a financial liability.

This approach views the reverse convertible bond as different from a conventional convertible bond under which the holder has the choice regarding conversion and the issuer always has an obligation to pay the principal in cash because it cannot control whether the conversion option is exercised. In the case of the reverse convertible bond, the issuer can avoid the outflow of cash by exercising its right to convert and delivering the fixed number of equity shares.

Supporters of this approach view it as being consistent with IAS 32:20(b), which states that an entity has a financial liability if the terms of the instrument provide that, on settlement, the entity will deliver either:

(i) cash or another financial asset; or
(ii) its own shares whose value is determined to exceed substantially the value of the cash or other financial asset.

Because IAS 32:20(b) only requires financial liability treatment if the value of the shares is determined to exceed substantially the value of the cash alternative, the settlement choice at maturity for this reverse convertible bond is not a financial liability.

The equity component of the reverse convertible bond will be determined as the difference between the fair value of the instrument as a whole and the fair value of the financial liability (comprising only the obligation to pay cash in relation to interest).

In some cases, careful judgement is needed in order to determine whether a contractual arrangement is a derivative over own equity, and therefore is equity if it meets the 'fixed-for-fixed' requirements (see **section 6**) or whether it is a non-derivative, and therefore is equity if it is contains no obligation to pay cash or another financial asset.

Consider the following example. Entity A enters into an arrangement with an investor whereby it receives CU100 on Day 1. Under the terms of the arrangement, Entity A has a choice of either delivering a fixed number of equity shares of Entity A to the potential investor or returning the CU100 to the investor.

This arrangement is most akin to a reverse convertible bond and, as such, two different approaches are considered to be acceptable.

The first approach is to view the arrangement as an instrument that will be settled by Entity A either delivering cash or issuing a fixed number of own shares and not to apply the rules regarding derivatives over own equity. Viewed in this way, the arrangement should, on initial receipt of CU100, be accounted for as equity because Entity A has the unconditional right to avoid delivering cash by choosing to deliver own shares. This is the case only if the value of the alternative to deliver shares instead of cash is not determined to exceed substantially the value of the cash alternative. [IAS 32:21] A financial liability would only be recognised at the point when Entity A has chosen not to deliver own shares and has therefore incurred an obligation to deliver cash. If the value of the share settlement was determined to exceed substantially the value of the cash, the instrument would be considered a financial liability because, in substance, the holder has been guaranteed receipt of an amount that is at least equal to the cash alternative.

The second approach is to view the instrument as a debt host contract (being the obligation to deliver CU100) and an embedded purchased put option which permits the issuer to deliver its own equity shares as extinguishment for the debt host contract. Because the number of shares delivered by the issuer and the debt host contract forgiven is fixed, the purchased put option would meet the definition of equity.

4 Treatment of interest, dividends, gains and losses and other items

The classification of a financial instrument or a component of a financial instrument as either a financial liability or an equity instrument determines the treatment of interest, dividends, and other gains and losses relating to that instrument or component of that instrument. Interest, dividends, losses and gains relating to a financial liability, or to a component of a compound instrument that is a financial liability, are recognised as income or expense in profit or loss. Distributions to holders of equity instruments shall be recognised by the entity directly in equity. Similarly, transaction costs of an equity transaction are accounted for as a deduction from equity. [IAS 32:35] Income tax relating to distributions to holders of an equity instrument and to transaction costs of an equity transaction shall be accounted for in accordance with IAS 12 *Income Taxes*. [IAS 32:35A]

The following items are treated as income or expense in profit or loss:

[IAS 32:35 - 37]

- interest payments on a bond issued by an entity;
- dividend payments on preference shares that are classified as financial liabilities;
- gains and losses associated with redemption or refinancing an instrument classified as a financial liability (notwithstanding the fact that the instrument may take the legal form of a share);
- gains and losses related to the carrying amount of an instrument that is a financial liability notwithstanding the fact that the instrument gives the holder a right to participate in the residual interest of an entity (e.g. certain puttable instruments such as units in a mutual fund that fail equity classification); and
- costs of an equity transaction that is abandoned.

Dividends classified as an expense in profit or loss may be presented either with interest on other liabilities or as a separate item.

Dividends that are non-discretionary represent a financial liability (or, depending on the other terms of the shares, a component of a larger financial liability) to provide cash (or another financial asset) to shareholders. In accordance with IAS 32:35, such dividends are recognised as income or expense in profit or loss.

The obligation to pay non-discretionary dividends will be measured either at amortised cost (using the effective interest method) or at fair value depending on the classification of the financial liability to which the dividends relate. Unlike discretionary distributions to holders of equity instruments, recognition does not depend on declaration of the dividend.

The following items are accounted for within equity:

[IAS 32:35 & 37]

- dividend payments on shares classified wholly as equity; and
- incremental directly attributable costs incurred in successfully issuing or acquiring an entity's own equity instruments (including transaction costs, regulatory fees, amounts paid to regulatory, legal, accounting and other professional advisers, printing costs, stamp duties).

The amount of transaction costs accounted for as a deduction from equity in the period is disclosed in line with the requirements of IAS 1 *Presentation of Financial Statements*. [IAS 32:39] IAS 32 does not specify where in equity the transaction costs should be recognised and this may depend on local legal requirements.

In May 2012, the IASB issued *Annual Improvements to IFRSs 2010-2012 Cycle* which clarified the intention of IAS 32 was to follow the requirements in IAS 12 for accounting for income tax relating to distributions to holders of an equity instrument and to transaction costs of an equity transaction. Paragraph 35A was added and paragraph 39 amended in order to do this.

Example 4A

Effective interest rate and dividends for a compound instrument

Entity A issues a non-cumulative preference share that is mandatorily redeemable for cash of CU10 million in 10 years' time. During the life of the instrument, dividends are payable at the discretion of Entity A. The non-cumulative preference share is issued for CU8 million.

The non-cumulative redeemable preference share is a compound instrument. The liability component is determined as the present value of the eventual redemption amount of CU10 million discounted at the rate at which the entity could issue a similar instrument with a similar credit standing but without the feature of discretionary dividends during its life.

Assuming the liability component is equal to CU7.8 million, the residual amount of CU0.2 million will be treated as the equity component. The unwinding of the discount (between the redemption of CU10 million and its present value of CU7.8 million) on the liability component is accounted for using the effective interest method as an interest expense and reported in profit or loss. Any discretionary dividends declared and paid are treated as relating to the equity component and, therefore, are classified as an equity distribution.

Transaction costs that are incremental and directly attributable to the issue of a compound financial instrument (i.e. they would have been avoided if the compound instrument had not been issued) are allocated to the liability and equity components in proportion to the allocation of the proceeds (see **3.1**). Costs that relate jointly to more than one transaction (for instance a joint and concurrent offering of some equity instruments and an issue of instruments classified as liabilities) are allocated using a basis that is rational and consistent with similar transactions. [IAS 32:38]

Example 4B

Transaction costs: placing and new issue of shares

Entity B places its privately held ordinary shares that are classified as equity with a stock exchange and simultaneously raises new capital by issuing new ordinary shares on the stock exchange. Transaction costs are incurred in respect of both transactions. Because the issue of new shares is the issue of an equity instrument, but the placing of the existing equity instruments with the exchange is not, the transaction costs will need to be allocated between the two transactions. Transaction costs in respect of the new shares issued will be recognised in equity whereas the transaction costs incurred in placing the existing shares with the stock exchange will be recognised in profit or loss.

In July 2008, the IFRIC (now the IFRS Interpretations Committee) issued an agenda decision on IAS 32, *Transaction Costs to be Deducted from Equity*. The IFRIC received a request for guidance on the extent of transaction costs to be accounted for as a deduction from equity in accordance with IAS 32:37 and on how the requirements of IAS 32:38 to allocate transaction costs that relate jointly to more than one transaction should be applied. The issue related specifically to the meaning of the terms 'incremental' and 'directly attributable'.

The IFRIC noted that only incremental costs directly attributable to issuing new equity instruments or acquiring previously outstanding equity instruments are considered to be related to an equity transaction under IAS 32. The IFRIC also noted that judgement will be required to determine which costs are related solely to other activities undertaken at the same time as issuing equity, such as becoming a public company or acquiring an exchange listing, and which costs are related jointly to both activities and, therefore, are required to be allocated in accordance with IAS 32:38. In view of the existing guidance, the IFRIC decided not to add this issue to its agenda.

5 Treasury shares

When an entity reacquires its own shares, those shares (known as treasury shares) are deducted from equity. No gain or loss is recognised in profit or loss on the purchase, sale, issue or cancellation of an entity's own equity instruments. The acquisition and subsequent resale by an entity of its own equity instruments represents a transfer between owners (specifically between those who have given up their equity interest and those who continue to hold an equity instrument) rather than a gain or loss to the entity. Accordingly, any consideration paid or received is recognised in equity. [IAS 32:33]

Example 5A

Acquisition of equity

Entity A buys back 100,000 of its own equity shares in the market for CU5 a share. The shares will be held as treasury shares to enable Entity A to satisfy its obligations under its employee share option scheme. The following entry will be made to recognise the purchase of the treasury shares as a deduction from equity.

		CU	CU
Dr	Equity	500,000	
Cr	Cash		500,000

To recognise treasury shares as a deduction from equity.

Example 5B

Treasury shares held as an economic hedge

Entity F is a large financial institution whose shares are included in the FTSE 100 index. Entity F issues a bond whose principal amount varies with the movement in the FTSE 100 share index (an 'index tracker bond'). In order to hedge economically the equity derivative that is embedded in the bond, Entity F purchases a portfolio of the shares contained in the FTSE 100 index and wishes to classify them as held for trading. Within that portfolio are a number of Entity F's own shares.

Entity F cannot classify its own purchased shares as held for trading in order to hedge economically the index tracker bond. IFRS 9 excludes from its scope instruments issued by an entity that meet the definition of equity in IAS 32.

Furthermore, IAS 32 requires that treasury shares be presented in the statement of financial position as a deduction from equity and not as assets, and that no gain or loss should be recognised in profit or loss on such shares.

The amount of treasury shares held is disclosed separately either in the statement of financial position or in the notes in accordance with IAS 1. An entity provides disclosure in accordance with the requirements of IAS 24 *Related Party Disclosures* when an entity reacquires its own equity instruments from related parties. [IAS 32:34]

When an entity holds its own shares on behalf of others (as is the case when a financial institution holds its own shares on behalf of a client as a custodian), this represents an agency relationship and, consequently, the shares are not included in the statement of financial position of the entity. [IAS 32:AG36]

6 Derivatives over own equity

A derivative contract over an entity's own equity is accounted for as equity *only* when it will be settled by the entity delivering (or receiving) a fixed number of its own equity instruments and receiving (or delivering) a fixed amount of cash or another financial asset. Any consideration received (such as the premium received in relation to written options over own shares or warrants on the entity's own shares that satisfy the above condition) is added directly to equity. Similarly, any consideration paid for such an instrument (such as premium paid for a purchased option that satisfies the above condition) is deducted from equity. Changes in fair value of the equity instrument are not recognised in the financial statements. [IAS 32:22] At a group level, derivatives over own equity include derivatives over shares of subsidiaries.

In January 2010, the IFRIC (now the IFRS Interpretations Committee) issued an agenda decision titled *IAS 32 Financial Instruments: Presentation – Application of the 'Fixed-for-Fixed' Condition*. The IFRIC received requests for guidance on the application of IAS 32:22 which states that "except as stated in paragraph 22A, a contract that will be settled by the entity (receiving or) delivering a fixed number of its own equity instruments in exchange for a fixed amount of cash or another financial asset is an equity instrument" (often referred to as the 'fixed-for-fixed' condition).

As part of the IFRIC's discussions grouped the questions on the fixed-for-fixed condition into two broad groups: those related to the denomination of the fixed amount of cash being in a foreign currency and those where the fixed amount of cash or shares is not fixed, but predetermined. The IFRIC identified that diversity may exist in practice in the application of the fixed-for-fixed condition to these situations and also other situations. However, the IFRIC decided not to add this item to its agenda in anticipation of finalisation of the Board's *Financial Instruments with Characteristics of Equity* (FICE) project. Since the IFRIC reached the agenda decision the FICE project has been deferred and has been included in the IASB's research programme. See future development in **section 9**.

Example 6A

Purchased call option

On 1 February 20X5, Entity A, a CU functional currency entity, purchases for CU5,000 a call option over 1,000 of its own ordinary shares. The option is exercisable at a strike price of CU102 per share only on 31 January 20X6 (i.e. it is a 'European type' option).

The option is gross physically settled, i.e. Entity A takes delivery of 1,000 of its own shares in exchange for an amount of cash paid to the counterparty equal to the option exercise price of CU102,000 (CU102 per share × 1,000 shares).

1 February 20X5

On inception of the contract, the following entry will be recorded in order to recognise the cash paid in exchange for the right to receive a fixed number of own shares in exchange for a fixed amount of cash.

		CU	CU
Dr	Equity	5,000	
Cr	Cash		5,000

To recognise the call option.

The premium is recognised in equity because the call option gives a right to receive a fixed number of the entity's own shares in exchange for a fixed amount of cash and, therefore, meets the definition of an equity instrument.

31 December 20X5

No entry is recorded on 31 December 20X5 because no cash is paid or received. The fair value of the option is irrelevant because the equity instrument is not remeasured.

31 January 20X6

The entity exercises the call option and the contract is gross physically settled through the entity taking delivery of 1,000 of its own shares in exchange for a payment of CU102,000 to the counterparty. This is recognised with the following entry.

		CU	CU
Dr	Equity	102,000	
Cr	Cash		102,000

To record the exercise of the call option.

With the exception of instruments that meet the exception from financial liability presentation in IAS 32:16A & 16B, or IAS 32:16C & 16D, a contract that contains an obligation for an entity to purchase its own equity instruments for cash or another financial asset gives rise to a financial liability for the present value of the redemption amount (for example, for the present value of the forward repurchase price, option exercise price or other redemption amount). This is the case even if the contract itself is an equity instrument. [IAS 32:23] This is commonly referred to as 'gross obligation accounting'.

Examples of instruments that give rise to a liability include forward contracts to buy own equity and written put options that allow the holder to put the shares back to the entity at a fixed or variable amount (e.g. a fixed amount plus inflation). At inception, such contracts are recognised at an amount equal to the present value of the obligation inherent in the contract. This treatment is required notwithstanding the fact that the contract itself may be an equity instrument (as it can be settled only through the entity delivering a fixed amount of cash in exchange for a fixed number of its own shares). [IAS 32:23] This is similar to taking delivery of own shares today but with an obligation to still pay the cash under the share buy-back to the counterparty.

IAS 32:23 requires the financial liability arising from the obligation to buy back own equity to be measured at the *present value* of the redemption amount but does not specify the discount rate that should be used in deriving the present value. In the absence of specific guidance a reasonable approach would be to reflect in the discount rate:

- interest rate risk – being the benchmark interest rate for the term to the earliest redemption date for the relevant currency of the obligation; and
- the credit risk associated with the issuer because the issuer is the obligor under the arrangement.

The discount rate should not reflect:

- the risk associated with potential changes in cash flows, to the extent that this risk is already taken into consideration in developing the cash flows used to establish the redemption price and by adjusting the liability each period for the change in variability of cash flows; or
- the likelihood that the option will be exercised, because the basis for the measurement of liability assumes the amount is payable.

The financial liability is subsequently remeasured through profit or loss (i.e. interest is accrued in accordance with the effective interest method up to the share redemption amount). In the case of a gross liability based on a variable amount of cash, the remeasurement of the amount of the eventual liability (e.g. for changes in inflation) would also be recognised through profit or loss.

If the contract expires without delivery, the carrying amount of the financial liability is reclassified to equity; amounts recognised in profit or loss up to the date of extinguishment are not reversed in profit or loss.

Recognition of a gross obligation for the present value of the redemption amount is required where the contract is exclusively gross physically settled by the entity delivering cash or another financial asset in exchange for the entity's equity instruments or if the counterparty to the arrangement has the right to require the entity to pay the counterparty cash or another financial asset in exchange for the entity's equity instruments.

Where the entity has a choice how the contract is settled and one of the settlement choices is for the entity (not the holder) to choose gross physical settlement, IAS 32 is less clear how the contract should be presented. There are two acceptable approaches and an entity should choose an approach as an accounting policy applied consistently to all similar transactions.

Presentation as a derivative at FVTPL

This presentation may be applied on the basis that:

- the entity can choose not to gross settle and therefore is not obligated to settle the contract by delivering cash or another financial instrument in acquiring its own equity instruments; and
- the settlement alternatives other than gross physical settlement will not result in the exchange of a fixed number of equity instruments for a fixed amount of cash or another financial asset and therefore meet the definition of a financial asset and financial liability in IAS 32:11.

Presentation as a gross obligation

Presentation as a gross obligation equal to the present value of the amount potentially payable under the contract may be applied on the basis that:

- if the contract may be gross settled, irrespective of which party may choose that settlement choice, the entity has a potential obligation to pay cash or another financial asset in acquiring its equity instruments; and
- the illustrative examples in the implementation guidance of IAS 32, specifically IAS 32:IE6 and IAS 32:IE31, include a forward purchase

and written put over equity instruments with settlement alternatives where one of the settlement choices is gross settlement. Both examples state: "[i]f one of the settlement alternatives is to exchange cash for shares, Entity A recognises a liability for the obligation to deliver cash. Otherwise, Entity A accounts for the forward contract as a derivative." The examples do not distinguish between gross settlement at the choice of the entity or choice of the holder.

Example 6B

Forward purchase contract

Assume the facts are as in **example 6A** except that, instead of purchasing a call option over own shares that will be gross physically settled, on 1 February 20X5 Entity A enters into a forward contract to buy 1,000 of its own ordinary shares on 31 January 20X6 for CU104 per share.

This contract will be gross physically settled, i.e. Entity A will take delivery of 1,000 of its own shares in exchange for paying to the counterparty a share redemption amount of CU104,000 (CU104 per share × 1,000 shares).

1 February 20X5

The entity has an unconditional obligation to deliver CU104,000 in cash in one year's time to the counterparty in exchange for a fixed number of its own equity shares. The following entry is made to recognise this obligation to deliver CU104,000 in one year at its present value of CU100,000 discounted using an appropriate interest rate which is determined to be 4 per cent.

		CU	CU
Dr	Equity	100,000	
Cr	Liability		100,000

To recognise the forward contract.

31 December 20X5

The following journal entry is made to accrue interest in accordance with the effective interest method.

		CU	CU
Dr	Interest expense	3,660	
Cr	Liability		3,660

To accrue interest at the effective interest rate of 4 per cent.

31 January 20X6

The following journal entry is made to accrue interest for the month of January 20X6 in accordance with the effective interest method.

		CU	CU
Dr	Interest expense	340	
Cr	Liability		340

To accrue interest at the effective interest rate of 4 per cent.

On the same date, the following entry is made to recognise the settlement of the liability for the share redemption amount.

		CU	CU
Dr	Liability	104,000	
Cr	Cash		104,000

To recognise payment of the share redemption amount.

Local company law may also require some reclassification of the balance within equity on receipt by Entity A of its own shares.

Example 6C

Written put option

On 1 February 20X5, Entity A writes a put option over 1,000 of its own ordinary shares and receives in exchange a premium of CU5,000. The option is exercisable at a strike price of CU98 per share only on 31 January 20X6 (i.e. it is a European type option). The option will be gross physically settled, i.e. if the option is exercised, the entity will receive 1,000 of its own shares in exchange for paying to the counterparty an amount equal to the option exercise price of CU98,000 (CU98 per share × 1,000 shares).

1 February 20X5

At the inception of the contract, the following entry is recorded to recognise the cash received in exchange for writing the put option and the present value of the CU98,000 obligation to be settled on 31 January 20X6 (discounted using an appropriate interest rate determined to be 3.2 per cent) giving the counterparty the right to receive a fixed amount of cash in exchange for a fixed number of Entity A's shares.

		CU	CU
Dr	Cash	5,000	
Dr	Equity	90,000	
Cr	Liability		95,000

To recognise the premium received and the present value of the liability under the put option.

31 December 20X5

The following entry is recorded to accrue interest on the liability in accordance with the effective interest method.

		CU	CU
Dr	Interest expense	2,745	
Cr	Liability		2,745

To accrue interest at the effective interest rate of 3.2 per cent.

31 January 20X6

The following journal entry is recorded to accrue interest on the liability for the remaining month of January 20X6 in accordance with the effective interest method.

		CU	CU
Dr	Interest expense	255	
Cr	Liability		255

To accrue interest at the effective interest rate of 3.2 per cent.

On the same date, if the written put option is exercised by the counterparty, the following entry is recorded to recognise the settlement of the liability for the strike price of the written put option.

		CU	CU
Dr	Liability	98,000	
Cr	Cash		98,000

To recognise payment of the strike price.

If the written put option is not exercised by the counterparty, the following entry is recorded instead.

		CU	CU
Dr	Liability	98,000	
Cr	Equity		98,000

To record the expiry of the put option.

When an acquirer acquires less than 100 per cent of the shares of a subsidiary in a business combination, it is common also to enter into a written put option with the seller that permits the seller to put its remaining interest in the subsidiary to the acquirer at a specified price. These put options are written by the acquirer to allow the seller an exit mechanism for the remaining shares. The acquisition of shares that results in the interest being recognised as a subsidiary will be accounted for in accordance with IFRS 3 *Business Combinations*. If the written put option can be physically settled (i.e. the subsidiary's shares are physically delivered and paid for by cash or other financial asset), irrespective of whether the strike price of the put option is a fixed or variable price, a gross obligation must be recognised at an amount equal to the present value of the amount that could be required to be paid to the counterparty in accordance with IAS 32. Changes in the measurement of the gross obligation due to the unwinding of the discount or changes in the amount that the acquirer could be required to pay are always recognised in profit or loss. It is not acceptable to adjust these gains or losses against the goodwill that arose on the acquisition because changes in the value of the gross obligation relate to the potential *future* purchase of the remaining shares in the subsidiary.

In November 2006, the IFRIC (now the IFRS Interpretations Committee) considered the classification and presentation of written put options and forward purchase arrangements entered into by a parent over shares of a subsidiary, otherwise known as puts and forwards over non-controlling interests (previously known as 'minority interests'). The IFRIC confirmed that in the consolidated financial statements, a financial liability must be recognised in accordance with IAS 32:23 for the obligation to pay cash in the future to purchase the shares held by non-controlling interests (NCI), even if the payment of that cash is conditional on the option being exercised by the holder. After initial recognition, any liability to which IFRS 3 is not being applied will be accounted for in accordance with IAS 39 (now IFRS 9). The parent will reclassify the liability to equity if the put option expires unexercised.

The IFRIC recognised that there is likely to be divergence in practice in how the related debit to equity is presented. However, the IFRIC did not believe that it could reach a consensus on this matter on a timely basis and, therefore, it decided not to add this item to its agenda.

The debit recognised in equity on initial recognition of the written put or forward purchase over an NCI may be presented as either a deduction from NCI or from other reserves alongside NCI. The subsequent attribution of profit or loss and other comprehensive income between the equity of the ultimate parent and NCI may be affected by this decision.

In May 2010, the IFRS Interpretations Committee started to discuss how an entity should account for changes in the carrying amount of a financial liability for a put option written over NCI. The request to the Interpretations Committee focused on the accounting for an NCI put option after the amendments to IFRS 3 *Business Combinations* and IAS 27 *Consolidated and Separate Financial Statements* in 2008 and IAS 39 (now IFRS 9). The request considered whether there was a potential conflict between these amendments and the financial instruments guidance.

In September 2010, the IFRS Interpretations Committee issued a tentative decision not to take the issue on to its agenda. That tentative decision stated that the Committee observed that IAS 32:23 requires the financial liability recognised for an NCI put option to be subsequently measured in accordance with IAS 39 (now IFRS 9). The Committee observed that IAS 39:55 & 56 (equivalent to IFRS 9:5.7.1 & 5.7.2) require changes in the carrying amount of financial liabilities to be recognised in profit or loss. However, the Committee noted that additional accounting concerns exist relating to the accounting for NCI put options and that these would be best addressed as part of the IASB's *Financial Instruments with Characteristics of Equity* (FICE) project.

Many respondents to the tentative agenda decision did not agree with the Interpretations Committee's approach. Further, as the Board did not have the capacity to devote time necessary to deliberate issues relating to the FICE project the Committee decided to add the issue to its agenda with the objective of addressing on a timely basis the current significant diversity that exists in practice.

In January and March 2011 the Interpretations Committee discussed possible ways to resolve the issue through a potential scope exception from IAS 32 for written put options over NCI. The scope exclusion would change the measurement basis of NCI puts to that used for other derivative contracts, i.e. FVTPL, thereby not recognising a financial liability at the present value of the option exercise price as currently required by IAS 32:23. The scope exclusion would apply only to the consolidated financial statements of the controlling shareholder. In addition, the scope exclusion would apply only to NCI puts with the following features:

- the NCI put is not embedded in another contract, and
- the NCI put contains an obligation for an entity in the consolidated group to settle the contract by delivering cash or another financial asset in exchange for the interest in the subsidiary.

The Interpretations Committee recommended that the Board should consider making an amendment to the scope of IAS 32. The proposal was rejected by the IASB. The Board noted that, ideally, the accounting for derivatives written on an entity's own equity instruments should be addressed comprehensively within the context of its project on *Financial Instruments with Characteristics of Equity*. Although the Board decided not to amend IAS 32 to change the accounting for NCI puts at this time, it asked the Interpretations Committee to address the issue that was submitted by clarifying the existing accounting requirements for the subsequent measurement of the financial liability that is recognised for an NCI put.

The Interpretations Committee responded to the Board's request by issuing Draft IFRIC Interpretation DI/2012/2 *Put Options Written on*

Non-controlling Interests in May 2012. The draft IFRIC Interpretation states for written puts on NCI a financial liability is initially measured at the present value of the redemption amount in the parent's consolidated financial statements. Subsequently, the financial liability is measured in accordance with IFRS 9. IFRS 9:5.7.1 & 5.7.2 require that changes in the measurement of that financial liability are recognised in profit or loss. The changes in the measurement of that financial liability do not change the relative interests in the subsidiary that are held by the parent and the non-controlling-interest shareholder and therefore are not equity transactions (i.e. they are not transactions with owners in their capacity as owners) as described in IFRS 10:23.

Feedback received on the Draft IFRIC was reported by the Interpretations Committee to the IASB, which in June 2014 decided that this project should be incorporated into the broader project looking at the distinction between liabilities and equity (see **section 9**).

Example 6D

Written put option over equity of subsidiary

On 1 January 20X8, Entity Q, the ultimate parent of Group Q, acquires a 60 per cent interest in Entity P from Entity O. As part of the acquisition agreement, Entity Q also writes a put option over the remaining 40 per cent of shares in Entity P to Entity O. Entity Q pays CU1,000 million under the purchase agreement. The written put option allows Entity O to put the 40 per cent interest in Entity P to Entity Q at CU275 million plus 20 per cent of Entity P's post-acquisition cumulative profits. The put option can be exercised by Entity O at 1 July 20Y0 and at every anniversary thereafter until 1 July 20Y2. Cumulative profits are determined based on audited financial statements of Entity P up to the year ended immediately prior to exercise of the put option. Group Q's reporting period end is 31 December.

At 1 January 20X8, the fair value of 60 per cent of the shares in Entity P is CU1,100 million and the fair value of the written put option is CU100 million. At that date, Group Q measures non-controlling interests at CU200 million, which is their proportionate share of the acquiree's identifiable net assets. Entity Q's estimation of profits of Entity P for the two-year period ending 31 December 20X9 is CU50 million. Entity Q determines that an appropriate discount rate for use in measuring the financial liability relating to the put option is 10 per cent.

At 31 December 20X8, the fair value of the written put option is CU90 million. Entity Q revises its estimate of Entity P's profits for the two-year period ending 31 December 20X9 to CU80 million.

Entity Q separate financial statements

The written put option is over a third party's equity and, therefore, it does not meet the definition of equity for Entity Q. The put option will therefore be classified as at fair value through profit or loss (FVTPL).

1 January 20X8

		CU million	CU million
Dr	Cost of investment	1,100	
Cr	Cash		1,000
Cr	Written put option – FVTPL		100

To recognise the cost of investment in the subsidiary and the written put option at fair value at initial recognition.

31 December 20X8

		CU million	CU million
Dr	Written put option – FVTPL	10	
Cr	Gain (profit or loss)		10

To recognise the remeasurement of the put option.

Group Q consolidated financial statements

The written put option permits a third party, Entity O, to put up to 40 per cent of the shares in a subsidiary of Group Q to Group Q. Because Group Q could be required to pay cash or other financial assets as settlement for the acquisition of shares in a subsidiary (in this case, non-controlling interests in the group), Group Q is required to recognise a gross obligation for the potential future acquisition of these equity shares.

1 January 20X8

At the date of acquisition, Group Q consolidates Entity P and recognises a 40 per cent non-controlling interest (NCI). The fair value of consideration used to acquire 60 per cent of the shares in Entity P for the purposes of determining any goodwill arising on acquisition is CU1,100 million. The difference between this amount and the total consideration paid to Entity O is the premium that Entity Q received for writing the put option.

The estimated present value of the amount Group Q could be required to pay Entity O should Entity O exercise its put option on 1 July 20Y0 is CU225 million. This is determined as follows: [CU275 million + (CU50 million x 20 per cent)] x $1/(1.1^{2.5})$.

		CU million	CU million
Dr	Net assets acquired and goodwill	1,300	
Cr	NCI		200
Dr	Equity	125	
Cr	Cash		1,000
Cr	Gross obligation under put option		225

To recognise the acquisition of the subsidiary and the recognition of the present value of the gross obligation under the written put option over the non-controlling interest.

The debit recognised in equity on initial recognition of the written put option over Entity P's shares may be presented as either a deduction from NCI or from other reserves (within Entity Q's equity) alongside NCI. The subsequent attribution of profit or loss and other comprehensive income between the equity of Entity Q and NCI may be affected by this decision.

31 December 20X8

The estimated present value of the amount Group Q could be required to pay Entity O, should Entity O exercise its put option at the earliest opportunity, being 1 July 20Y0, is CU252 million. This is determined as follows: [CU275 million + (CU80 million x 20 per cent)] x $1/(1.1^{1.5})$.

		CU million	**CU million**
Dr	Profit or loss	27	
Cr	Gross obligation under put option		27

To recognise the remeasurement of the present value of the gross obligation under the written put option over the non-controlling interest.

All derivatives over own equity (other than forward purchases and written puts) where settlement is not exclusively by the exchange of a fixed number of equity shares for a fixed amount of cash (or another financial asset) are treated as derivatives (derivative financial assets or liabilities) and are accounted for in accordance with the requirements of IFRS 9; the fair value of the instrument is recognised in the statement of financial position with changes in fair value recognised in profit or loss unless it is designated as an effective hedging instrument in a cash flow hedge or a hedge of a net investment in a foreign operation. A forward purchase or a written put option that may result in the entity receiving its own equity shares and being obligated to deliver cash (or another financial asset) is recognised as a financial liability that represents the entity's gross obligation to deliver cash or another financial asset to the counterparty. All other forward purchase and written put option contracts over own shares are measured at fair value through profit or loss.

Therefore, the following derivatives over own equity are accounted as derivatives that are fair valued through profit or loss:

- those that are exclusively net settled in cash (or other financial assets);
- those that are exclusively net settled in own equity shares; and
- any derivative over own equity which gives either party a choice over how it is settled unless all the settlement alternatives result in the exchange of a fixed number of own shares for a fixed amount of cash or another financial asset (or in the case of a forward purchase or written put over own shares where one of the settlement alternatives can require the issuer to gross physically settle).

Example 6E

Forward sale contract: net share settlement

On 1 February 20X5, Entity A, a CU functional currency entity, enters into a forward sale contract over 1,000 of its own ordinary (equity) shares on 31 January 20X6 at a fixed price of CU18 per share. The terms of the contract are that it will be net settled in shares, i.e. on 31 January 20X6. Entity A will receive (if the share price is below CU18) or deliver (if the share price is above CU18) shares with an aggregate market value equal to 1,000 times the difference between the market price per share at that date and the fixed price in the contract of CU18.

1 February 20X5

The price per share when the contract is entered into on 1 February 20X5 is CU18. The initial fair value of the forward contract on 1 February 20X5 is zero. Therefore, no entry is recorded because the fair value of the derivative is zero and no cash is paid or received.

31 December 20X5

On 31 December 20X5, the market price per share has increased to CU24 and, as a result, the fair value of the forward contract has decreased to a liability of CU6,000 [(CU24-CU18) x 1,000)].

The following entry is recorded to recognise the decrease in the fair value of the forward contract.

		CU	CU
Dr	Loss (profit or loss)	6,000	
Cr	Forward liability		6,000

To recognise the decrease in the fair value of the forward contract.

31 January 20X6

On 31 January 20X6, the market price per share has decreased to CU20. The fair value of the forward contract is a liability of CU2,000 ([(CU20 – CU18) x 1,000]. Therefore, the following entry is recorded to recognise the decrease in the fair value of the forward liability.

		CU	CU
Dr	Forward liability	4,000	
Cr	Gain (profit or loss)		4,000

To recognise the decrease in the fair value of the forward liability.

On the same day, the contract is settled net in shares (with Entity A delivering 100 of its own shares to the counterparty to settle its obligation to deliver shares with an aggregate value of CU2,000). The following entry is therefore recorded to recognise the settlement of the contract net in own equity shares.

		CU	CU
Dr	Forward liability (100 shares x CU20)	2,000	
Cr	Equity		2,000

To recognise the settlement of the contract net in own equity shares.

For illustrative purposes only, the effect of time value is excluded from the calculation of the fair value of the forward contract.

Example 6F

Total return swap

An entity enters into a total return swap ('TRS') over 1,000 of its own equity shares on 1 February 20X5. The contract matures on 31 January 20X6. Due to the nature of the total return swap (whose fair value is driven by changes in the entity's share price), gross settlement is not possible and it will be settled net (either in cash or in a variable number of shares). Therefore, the instrument does not qualify as an equity instrument and it will be accounted for as a derivative.

1 February 20X5

The initial fair value of the swap on 1 February 20X5 is zero. No entry is recorded because the fair value of the derivative is zero and no cash is paid or received.

31 December 20X5

The fair value of the swap at 31 December 20X5 is CU4,500; therefore, the following entry is required to record the increase in fair value.

		CU	CU
Dr	Swap asset	4,500	
Cr	Profit or loss		4,500

To recognise the increase in fair value of the swap asset.

31 January 20X6

The fair value of the swap at 31 January 20X6 is CU3,750; therefore, the following entry is recorded to recognise the decrease in fair value.

		CU	CU
Dr	Profit or loss	750	
Cr	Swap asset		750

To recognise the decrease in fair value of the swap asset.

The entries to be recorded upon settlement will depend on which of the two methods of net settlement is chosen. If net share settlement is chosen, the following entry will be made.

		CU	CU
Dr	Equity	3,750	
Cr	Swap asset		3,750

To recognise the net share settlement.

In this scenario, settlement will take place through the entity taking receipt of 150 of its own shares (CU3,750/CU25) (the market value of the entity's share on this date is CU25).

If net cash settlement is chosen, the following entry will be made at settlement of the contract.

		CU	CU
Dr	Cash	3,750	
Cr	Swap asset		3,750

To recognise the net cash settlement.

The following decision tree summarises the classification of derivatives over own equity instruments. In making this determination, it should also be noted that:

- in consolidated financial statements, derivatives over the equity of subsidiaries are treated in the same way as derivatives over the equity of the parent entity;
- recognition of a financial liability for an obligation to purchase own equity for cash (or another financial asset) is required even if the obligation is conditional on the holder exercising its right to sell the shares to the entity and notwithstanding the fact that the contract itself may be an equity instrument (because it can be settled only through the entity delivering a fixed amount of cash in exchange for a fixed number of its own shares); [IAS 32:23] and
- a derivative over own equity when the underlying equity instrument meets the requirements for equity classification in accordance with either IAS 32:16A & 16B (puttable instruments) or IAS 32:16C & 16D (instruments that impose on the entity an obligation to deliver to another party a pro rata share of the net assets of the entity only on liquidation) of IAS 32 cannot be classified as equity. [IAS 32:22A]

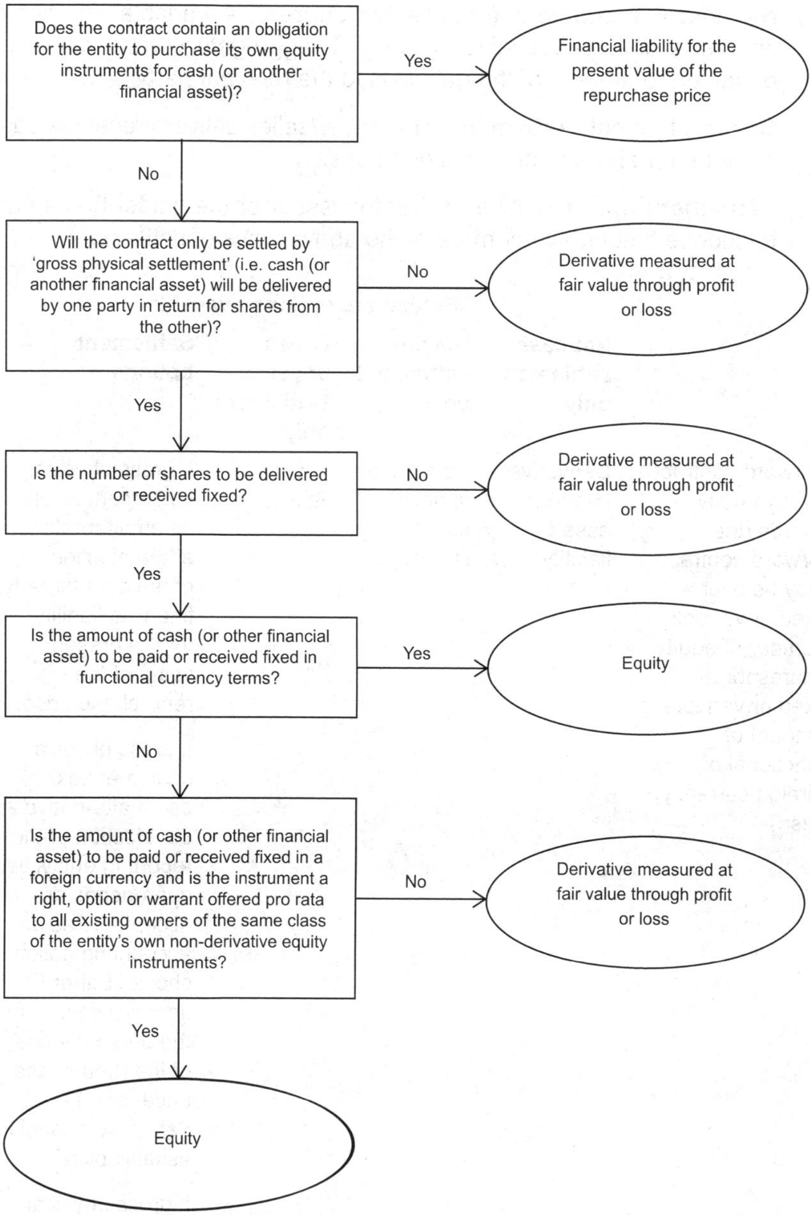

The following table illustrates the application of IAS 32 to different derivatives over own equity, with different settlement mechanisms. The settlement mechanisms are described as follows.

(1) **Net cash settlement.** When one party's net gain/loss is settled in cash and no shares are exchanged.

(2) **Net share settlement (shares for shares).** A variable number of shares is delivered/received having an aggregate current fair value equal to the amount of the gain/loss to the relevant party.

(3) **Gross physical settlement.** The buyer/seller delivers/receives cash in return for shares from the seller/buyer.

(4) **Settlement options.** When either the issuer or the holder has a right to choose among two or more of the above ways of settlement.

	Settlement options available			
	Net cash settlement only	**Net share settlement only**	**Gross physical settlement only**	**Settlement options**
Forward contract to buy equity shares (the forward contract may be over a fixed or variable number of equity shares for a fixed or variable amount of functional or foreign currency cash)	Derivative financial asset/ liability	Derivative financial asset/ liability	Gross liability	If gross physical settlement exists as an alternative at the election of the counterparty, financial liability for the present value of the repurchase price. If gross physical settlement exists as an alternative at the election of the reporting entity, two approaches are acceptable as an accounting policy choice. Either (i) financial liability for the present value of the repurchase price, or (ii) derivative financial asset/liability. If gross physical settlement does not exist as an alternative for either party, treat as a derivative financial asset/ liability.

	Settlement options available			
	Net cash settlement only	**Net share settlement only**	**Gross physical settlement only**	**Settlement options**
Forward contract to sell a fixed number of equity shares for a fixed amount of functional currency cash	Derivative financial asset/ liability	Derivative financial asset/ liability	Equity	Derivative financial asset/liability
Forward contract to sell a fixed number of equity shares for a fixed or variable amount of foreign currency cash or a variable amount of functional currency cash	Derivative financial asset/ liability	Derivative financial asset/ liability	Derivative financial asset/ liability	Derivative financial asset/liability
Forward contract to sell a variable number of equity shares for a fixed or variable amount of functional or foreign currency cash	Derivative financial asset/ liability	Derivative financial asset/ liability	Derivative financial asset/ liability	Derivative financial asset/liability
Purchased call option on a fixed number of equity shares for a fixed amount of functional currency cash	Derivative financial asset	Derivative financial asset	Equity	Derivative financial asset
Purchased call option on a fixed number of equity shares for a fixed or variable amount of foreign currency cash or variable amount of functional currency cash	Derivative financial asset	Derivative financial asset	Derivative financial asset	Derivative financial asset

	Settlement options available			
	Net cash settlement only	**Net share settlement only**	**Gross physical settlement only**	**Settlement options**
Purchased call option on a variable number of equity shares for a fixed or variable amount of functional or foreign currency cash	Derivative financial asset	Derivative financial asset	Derivative financial asset	Derivative financial asset
Written call option on a fixed number of equity shares for a fixed amount of functional currency cash	Derivative financial liability	Derivative financial liability	Equity	Derivative financial liability
Written call option on a fixed number of equity shares for a fixed or variable amount of foreign currency cash or a variable amount of functional currency cash	Derivative financial liability	Derivative financial liability	Derivative financial liability	Derivative financial liability
Written call option on a fixed number of equity shares for a fixed amount of foreign currency cash that is offered pro rata to all of the issuer's existing owners of the same class of its own non-derivative equity instruments. See **6.1.1**.	Derivative financial liability	Derivative financial liability	Equity	Derivative financial liability

	Settlement options available			
	Net cash settlement only	**Net share settlement only**	**Gross physical settlement only**	**Settlement options**
Written call option on a fixed number of equity shares for a fixed amount of foreign currency cash that is *not* offered pro rata to all of the issuer's existing owners of the same class of its own non-derivative equity instruments. See **6.1.1**.	Derivative financial liability	Derivative financial liability	Derivative financial liability	Derivative financial liability
Written call option on a variable number of equity shares for a fixed or variable amount of functional or foreign currency cash	Derivative financial liability	Derivative financial liability	Derivative financial liability	Derivative financial liability
Purchased put option on a fixed number of equity shares for a fixed amount of functional currency cash	Derivative financial asset	Derivative financial asset	Equity	Derivative financial asset
Purchased put option on a fixed number of equity shares for a fixed or variable amount of foreign currency cash or variable amount of functional currency cash	Derivative financial asset	Derivative financial asset	Derivative financial asset	Derivative financial asset

	Settlement options available			
	Net cash settlement only	**Net share settlement only**	**Gross physical settlement only**	**Settlement options**
Purchased put option on a variable number of equity shares for a fixed or variable amount of functional or foreign currency cash	Derivative financial asset	Derivative financial asset	Derivative financial asset	Derivative financial asset
Written put option on equity shares (the option may be over a fixed or variable number of equity shares for a fixed or variable amount of functional or foreign currency cash)	Derivative financial liability	Derivative financial liability	Gross liability	If gross physical settlement exists as an alternative at the election of the counterparty, financial liability for the present value of the repurchase price. If gross physical settlement exists as an alternative at the election of the reporting entity (issuer), two approaches are acceptable as an accounting policy choice. Either (i) financial liability for the present value of the repurchase price, or (ii) derivative financial liability. If gross physical settlement does not exist as an alternative for either party, treat as a derivative financial liability.

6.1 Other variations of terms of derivatives over own equity

As described immediately above, the guidance on multiple settlement alternatives for stand-alone derivatives over own equity is consistent with the multiple settlement alternatives guidance for convertible debt described in **3.7**. The guidance is consistent because, in order to determine whether an equity conversion option in convertible debt is considered to be equity for the issuer, the guidance regarding derivatives over own equity is applied. As a result, the guidance on foreign currency convertible debt described in **section 3.8** equally applies to stand-alone derivatives over own equity, i.e. for a derivative over own equity to meet the definition of equity it must be an exchange of a fixed number of shares for a fixed amount of functional currency cash. The one exception to this is the accounting for certain rights denominated in a foreign currency (see **6.1.1**). The guidance on anti-dilutive provisions in **3.9** also applies to stand-alone derivatives over own equity.

It is not possible to provide an exhaustive list of different variations in the terms of derivatives over own equity. However, some examples and the accounting analysis are included below.

6.1.1 Foreign currency denominated rights issues

In October 2009, the IASB issued an amendment to IAS 32 titled *Classification of Rights Issues*. The amendment changes the presentation for certain rights issues denominated in a foreign currency that prior to the amendment would have failed the definition of equity and would have been presented as a financial liability. Following the amendment, rights, options and warrants that will be settled only by the issue of a fixed number of shares for a fixed amount of cash or other financial asset *in any currency* are presented in equity if the entity offers the rights, options or warrants pro rata to all of its existing owners of the same class of its own non-derivative equity instruments. [IAS 32:11(b)(ii)] Prior to the amendment, rights, options and warrants that result in the receipt of currency other than the functional currency of the issuing entity would not meet the definition of equity and would therefore be presented as a derivative financial liability as at FVTPL.

It is common for rights issues to have an exercise price in a currency other than the functional currency of the issuer if the issuer is listed in more than one jurisdiction or might be required to do so by law or regulation. As part of its deliberations, the IASB agreed that a contract with an exercise price denominated in a foreign currency would not result in the entity receiving a fixed amount of cash and, therefore, would fail the definition of equity. However, the IASB considered that with respect to foreign currency denominated rights issues the accounting treatment was inconsistent with the substance of the transaction because the Board considered such transactions to partially resemble dividends paid in shares as the rights issue is offered only to existing shareholders on the basis of the number of shares they already own. In addition, the Board considered that such arrangements are a transaction with an entity's owners in their capacity as owners and, therefore, the transaction should be recognised in equity with no impact in comprehensive income. It is for these reasons that the IASB decided to make an 'extremely narrow amendment' (IAS 32:BC4J) by amending the definition of a financial liability to exclude such arrangements.

Example 6.1.1

Foreign currency denominated rights issue

Entity D's ordinary shares are listed on multiple stock exchanges. Entity D offers all its existing shareholders the right to buy one ordinary share in Entity D for every two shares held (a '1 for 2' rights issue). The price payable to Entity D for the issue of ordinary shares under the rights issue (the strike price) is at a 30% discount to the share price at the rights offer date (a fixed price in the currency of the strike price). Because Entity D's ordinary shares are listed on multiple stock exchanges, Entity D structures the rights issue so that the strike price for the rights in a particular jurisdiction matches the currency of that jurisdiction.

The rights issue should be classified as equity because the discounted shares are offered pro rata to all ordinary shareholders and therefore the condition in IAS 32:11(b)(ii) is met.

The limited amendment to IAS 32 only relates to 'rights, options and warrants'. [IAS 32:11(b)(ii)] Therefore, contractual arrangements that are non-optional (e.g. forward contracts or other arrangements where the counterparty is not given the choice as to whether to acquire equity instruments of the issuer) are not subject to the exemption included in the amendment. Because the amendment to IAS 32 only applies to certain rights issues that meet the specific criteria for equity classification, it is not possible to analogise to other arrangements that do not meet these criteria and classify those arrangements as equity.

6.1.2 Contracts under which the number of own equity shares or amount of cash is predetermined but still subject to variability

Derivatives over own equity may be structured so that they can be exercised at various points in time and the number of shares or the amount of cash is predetermined up-front but varies with time. One must consider whether such derivatives involve an exchange of a fixed amount of cash or other financial asset for a fixed amount of equity. The following example illustrates this point.

Entity A, which has a currency unit (CU) functional currency, enters into two stand-alone contracts to deliver its own equity to a third party.

- Contract 1 is a written call option that gives the counterparty the right to buy equity of Entity A for CU100 on any of three fixed dates over a 3-year period. The number of shares that will be delivered to the counterparty on exercise will depend on when the counterparty exercises the option. If the counterparty exercises the option one year after issuance, 10 shares will be delivered; if two years after issuance, 11 shares; and, if three years after issuance, 12 shares. If the option is not exercised on any of these dates, the call option will expire and there is no further right to buy shares under the arrangement.

- Contract 2 is also a written call option that gives the counterparty the right to buy equity of Entity A for CU100 on any of three fixed dates over a 3-year period. The number of shares that will be delivered to the counterparty on exercise will depend on when the counterparty exercises the option and the rate of LIBOR on that date. If the counterparty exercises the option one year after issuance, the number of shares delivered is 10 × (1 + LIBOR); if two years after issuance, 10 × $(1 + LIBOR)^2$ and, if three years after issuance, 10 × $(1 + LIBOR)^3$. If the option is not exercised on any of these dates, the call option will expire and there is no further right to buy shares under the arrangement.

Contract 1 meets the definition of an equity instrument because, if exercised, the issuer will receive a fixed amount of cash for delivering a fixed amount of its own equity. Even though the number of shares that the instrument may be converted into varies, it only varies with the passage of time and not with other variables (i.e. the number of shares is fixed at inception of the contract). The arrangement is considered to be an exchange of a fixed number of shares for a fixed amount of cash. Therefore, the premium received for writing the call option is credited to equity and subsequent changes in the fair value of the instrument are not recognised in the financial statements.

Contract 2, on the other hand, does not meet the definition of equity because, if exercised, the issuer will deliver a variable number of shares for a fixed amount of cash. Even though the number of shares is determinable (i.e. it is determined by a specified index, in this case LIBOR), the number of shares is not fixed in advance and varies due to factors other than the passage of time (in this case, interest rates). The contract is not, therefore, an exchange of a fixed number of shares for a fixed amount of cash. The written option meets the definition of a derivative in IFRS 9:Appendix A and should be measured at fair value through profit or loss.

6.1.3 Contract to exchange a fixed number of shares of a parent for a fixed number of shares in a subsidiary

In the consolidated financial statements, a contract to exchange a fixed number of shares of a parent for a fixed number of shares in a subsidiary is an exchange of a fixed number of shares of the issuer (the parent), which are equity instruments, for a fixed number of shares of a subsidiary (held by a non-controlling interest), which are also equity of the group. IAS 32 does not address this fact pattern because the Standard assumes that, for a derivative over equity, to be classified as equity the exchange will always involve receipt or delivery of a fixed amount of cash (or other financial asset) for a fixed amount of equity. Because the arrangement is an exchange of a fixed number of two equity instruments, at the consolidated level it is reasonable that the instrument be presented as equity because the holder is exchanging one fixed amount of residual interest in one group entity for another.

6.2 Share buy-back arrangements

An entity may enter into arrangements with a third party, usually with a financial institution, for that third party to buy back the entity's equity shares in the market for delivery to the entity. It is important to determine for such arrangements whether the third party is acting as principal or as an agent for the entity. If the third party is acting as agent, then the contractual arrangement between the entity and the third party is not a financial instrument. In such cases, only when shares are acquired by the third party will the entity recognise a financial liability to pay the third party and a debit in equity for the shares to be delivered; and when the shares are delivered to the entity will the entity settle the financial liability with cash or other financial asset and re-present within equity that treasury shares have been acquired or shares cancelled.

Example 6.2

Share buyback arrangement

Entity A enters into an arrangement immediately prior to its period end which allows a financial institution to acquire equity shares in Entity A in the market and then deliver these shares to Entity A at the price the financial institution paid subject to a fee.

The financial institution must acquire a number of shares between a minimum (the 'floor') and maximum (the 'cap') amount, and there is a maximum number of shares which may be acquired in a trading day. Within these boundaries, the financial institution has full discretion to buy shares and Entity A cannot refuse to purchase those shares once they are acquired by the financial institution.

Entity A enters into this arrangement to ensure that its share buyback programme continues during the 'quiet period', (the period, also referred to as a 'close period' between the entity's period end and the release of its financial results) without breaching regulatory rules.

At the period end, Entity A will need to recognise a financial liability for the obligation to acquire its own equity (i.e. a 'gross obligation'). This financial liability will be initially recognised at the present value of the maximum amount that Entity A could be required to pay to the financial institution, with a corresponding debit in equity.

Changes in the present value of this liability (e.g. due to the unwinding of any discount applied or to changes in the market price of the Entity A's shares), will be recognised in profit or loss.

> If the arrangement limits the maximum amount the entity can pay to the financial institution, the financial liability will be initially measured at the present value of this amount. In this case, Entity A may not have variability in the amount it will pay due to changes in its share price because Entity A could always be required to pay the maximum amount to the financial institution.
>
> When the financial institution buys the shares in the market and delivers them to Entity A, and Entity A settles the obligation with cash or another financial asset, Entity A will derecognise the part of the financial liability equal to the amount that has been paid.
>
> If, at the end of the buyback period, the financial institution has not acquired the maximum amount of shares or utilised the maximum amount that Entity A can spend on buying back shares, the financial liability remaining at that point should be reversed with a corresponding credit in equity to show that it has been extinguished.

7 Classification of financial liabilities

All financial liabilities are required to be classified and subsequently measured at amortised cost using the effective interest rate method (see **section 4** of **chapter B6**), except for:

[IFRS 9:4.2.1]

- financial liabilities at fair value through profit or loss (FVTPL) (see **section 7.1**);
- financial liabilities that arise when a transfer of a financial asset does not qualify for derecognition or when the continuing involvement approach applies (see **7.2** and **3.4** of **chapter B8**);
- financial guarantee contracts not designated as at FVTPL that are not accounted for under IFRS 4 *Insurance Contracts* (see **2.3.3** of **chapter B1**); and
- commitments to provide a loan at a below-market interest rate (see **3.5** of **chapter B1**).

Financial liabilities that are designated as hedged items are subject to the hedge accounting requirements (see **chapter B9**).

7.1 Financial liabilities at FVTPL

This category of financial liabilities can further be divided into the following two sub-categories:

- financial liabilities classified as held for trading; and
- financial liabilities designated by the entity as at FVTPL.

7.1.1 Financial liabilities classified as held for trading

A financial liability is held for trading if it falls into one of the following categories:

[IFRS 9: Appendix A]

- financial liabilities incurred principally for the purpose of repurchasing them in the near term;
- financial liabilities that on initial recognition form part of a portfolio of identified financial instruments that are managed together and for which there is evidence of a recent actual pattern of short-term profit-taking; and
- derivative liabilities, unless the derivative is a financial guarantee contract or it forms part of a designated and effective hedging relationship (see **chapter B9**).

The fact that a liability is used to provide funding for trading activities does not of itself mean that liability is to be classified as held for trading. [IFRS 9:BA.8] Thus, a borrowing that a bank uses to fund its trading portfolio of debt and equity securities is not automatically classified as held for trading.

The following are examples of liabilities that would be classified as held for trading and thus included in the FVTPL category:

- an interest rate swap that has negative fair value and is not accounted for as a hedging instrument;
- a derivative liability incurred upon writing a foreign exchange option that is not accounted for as a hedging instrument;
- an obligation to deliver financial assets borrowed by a short seller (i.e. an entity that sells financial assets it has borrowed and does not yet own); and
- a quoted debt instrument that the issuer plans to buy back in the near term depending on movements in the debt instrument's fair value, i.e. a financial liability that is incurred with an intention to repurchase it in the near term.

7.1.2 Financial liabilities designated as at FVTPL

The option to designate a financial liability as at FVTPL is available in limited circumstances notwithstanding the fact that, in the absence of such a choice, the liability would have been classified and measured other than at FVTPL. A financial liability can only be designated as at FVTPL when it meets one of three specified criteria (see below). The designation is irrevocable so that, once it has been made, the liability cannot subsequently be reclassified into another category during its life.

There are many reasons why an entity might wish to designate a financial liability as at FVTPL, for example if:

- it eliminates or significantly reduces an accounting mismatch;
- it allows an entity to avoid the burden of hedge accounting requirements such as the requirements to designate, assess and measure effectiveness (see **chapter B9**), because classification of both the hedging instrument and the hedged item as at FVTPL achieves a similar result as if fair value hedge accounting had been applied;
- it de-emphasises interpretative issues regarding when an item is appropriately considered to be 'held for trading'; or
- when applied to hybrid instruments (see **chapter B5**), it eliminates the burden of separating embedded derivatives that are not considered to be closely related to the host contract because the fair value of the whole contractual arrangement is then recognised in profit or loss.

The term 'designated as at fair value through profit or loss' has been carried forward from IAS 39 to IFRS 9. However, the term is slightly misleading in an IFRS 9 context because, unlike IAS 39, not all fair value gains or losses are recognised in profit or loss. IFRS 9 requires that changes in the fair value of a non-derivative financial liability designated at FVTPL that are attributable to changes in the credit risk of that liability should be recognised in other comprehensive income, not profit or loss, except in limited circumstances when all fair value gains or losses are recognised in profit or loss. This treatment is discussed in detail in **7.1.2.5**.

A financial liability may upon initial recognition be designated as at FVTPL only in one of the following circumstances:

[IFRS 9:4.2.2]

- it eliminates or significantly reduces a measurement or recognition inconsistency that would otherwise arise from measuring assets or liabilities or recognising the gains and losses on them on different bases (commonly referred to as an 'accounting mismatch') (see **7.1.2.1**);
- a group of financial assets, financial liabilities or both is managed and its performance is evaluated on a fair value basis, in accordance with a documented risk management or investment strategy, and information about the group is provided internally on that basis to the entity's key management personnel (as defined in IAS 24 *Related Party Disclosures*) (see **7.1.2.2**); or

[IFRS 9:4.3.5]

- in the case of a hybrid financial liability containing one or more embedded derivatives, an entity may designate the entire hybrid (combined) contract as a financial liability as at FVTPL unless:
  - (a) the embedded derivative does not significantly modify the cash flows that otherwise would be required by the contract; or
  - (b) it is clear with little or no analysis when a similar hybrid instrument is first considered that separation of the embedded derivative is prohibited (e.g. a prepayment option embedded in a loan that permits the holder to prepay the loan for approximately its amortised cost) (see **7.1** in **chapter B5**). This requirement is discussed in more detail in **7.1.2.3**.

Note that the criteria for designating financial liabilities as at FVTPL differ from the fair value option criteria for financial assets as detailed in **5.5.3** in **chapter B2**.

The election to designate a financial liability as at FVTPL has to be made at initial recognition of the financial instrument and cannot subsequently be revoked. This is the case even if the instrument giving rise to an accounting mismatch is derecognised.

The decision by an entity to designate a financial liability as at FVTPL is similar to an accounting policy choice in that the result of applying the fair value option should provide reliable and more relevant information about the effects of transactions, other events and conditions on the entity's financial position, financial performance or cash flows. [IFRS 9:B4.1.28] However, an important difference between an accounting policy choice and the fair value option is that the latter is applied on an instrument-by-instrument basis. The fair value option must be applied to a financial liability in its entirety – it cannot be applied to only part of a financial liability.

The fair value option can only be applied to financial liabilities within the scope of IFRS 9 and, therefore, it is not available for financial liabilities that are not in the scope of IFRS 9 (e.g. finance lease obligations).

7.1.2.1 Eliminates or significantly reduces an accounting mismatch

The following are examples of the application of the fair value option so as to significantly reduce a measurement or recognition inconsistency.

- An entity may have financial assets, financial liabilities, or both, that share a risk (e.g. interest rate risk) that gives rise to opposite changes in fair value that tend to offset each other. Yet, often only some of the instruments (e.g. derivatives) are measured at FVTPL. The requirements for hedge accounting may not be met (e.g. because the requirements for effectiveness are not met). Designating the assets and liabilities as at FVTPL will achieve an accounting offset that reflects the existing natural economic offset. [IFRS 9:B4.1.30(b)]

- An entity may have financial assets, financial liabilities, or both, that share a risk (e.g. interest rate risk) that gives rise to opposite changes in fair value for those assets and liabilities that tend to offset each other. The assets and liabilities may be measured on a different basis and hedge accounting cannot be applied because none of the instruments is a derivative. Designating the assets and liabilities as at FVTPL will achieve an accounting offset that reflects the existing natural economic offset. For example, the entity has financed a specified group of loans by issuing traded bonds whose changes in fair value tend to offset each other. If, in addition, the entity regularly buys and sells the bonds but rarely, if ever, buys and sells the loans, reporting both the loans and the bonds at FVTPL eliminates the inconsistency in the timing of recognition of gains and losses that would otherwise result from measuring them both at amortised cost and recognising a gain or loss each time a bond is repurchased. [IFRS 9:B4.1.30(c)]

Example 7.1.2.1A

Fair value option: issued fixed rate debt

Entity A issues fixed rate debt. In order to economically hedge the fair value risk associated with interest payments on the fixed rate debt, Entity A concurrently enters into an interest rate swap with a bank (receive fixed, pay floating), which has the same terms and payment dates as the debt. The interest rate swap is a derivative that must be measured at FVTPL. Entity A does not wish to apply fair value hedge accounting because it does not wish to prepare any hedge documentation and it does not have the processes in place to monitor hedge effectiveness. By designating the fixed rate debt as at FVTPL on initial recognition, the entity will achieve a substantial offset in profit or loss against the fair value movements on the held for trading derivative. Because the instruments share a common risk (interest rate risk), Entity A will seek to demonstrate that applying the fair value option results in more relevant information because it significantly reduces a measurement inconsistency that would otherwise arise from measuring the derivative at FVTPL and measuring the debt at amortised cost.

Example 7.1.2.1B

Fair value option: intragroup derivative

A subsidiary issues a five-year fixed rate bond. To hedge against the interest rate risk, it enters into a pay variable receive fixed interest rate swap with its parent. In the subsidiary's financial statements, the bond is designated as at FVTPL. The designation cannot be applied in the consolidated financial statements because the interest rate swap is eliminated on consolidation. If the parent or another group entity had a derivative instrument with a third party that shares a common risk with the bond, a different designation could be made for the bond in the consolidated financial statements provided that the designation is made upon initial recognition.

In the examples above, the entity need not have entered into all of the assets and liabilities giving rise to the measurement or recognition inconsistency at exactly the same time. The fair value option is available provided that (1) each instrument is designated as at FVTPL at its initial recognition, (2) the delay between entering into the separate transactions is reasonably short, and (3) when each instrument is initially recognised, any remaining transactions are expected to occur. [IFRS 9:B4.1.31]

It would not be acceptable to designate only some of the financial assets and financial liabilities giving rise to the inconsistency as at FVTPL if to do so would not eliminate or significantly reduce the inconsistency and would therefore not result in more relevant information. However, it would be acceptable to designate only some of a number of similar financial assets or financial liabilities if to do so would achieve a significant reduction (and possibly a greater reduction than other allowable designations) in the inconsistency. [IFRS 9:B4.1.32]

Example 7.1.2.1C

Fair value option: lack of accounting mismatch

Entity A borrows (through a single instrument) €1,000,000 from a third-party bank and, at the same time, uses some of the borrowing to acquire 10 similar financial assets each of a value of €50,000 which are all classified as at FVTPL. Entity A wants to reduce the measurement inconsistency by designating the liability as at FVTPL. However, if all of the borrowing were accounted for at FVTPL, Entity A would create an accounting mismatch in profit or loss related to the portion of the borrowing (€500,000) not matched by the financial assets measured at FVTPL. This accounting mismatch is comparable to the mismatch that would arise by not applying the fair value option in the first place. Therefore, Entity A cannot apply the fair value option to its financial liabilities because it would not significantly reduce the accounting mismatch between the assets and the liability.

7.1.2.2 Managed and performance evaluated on a fair value basis

An entity may manage and evaluate the performance of a group of financial liabilities or financial assets and financial liabilities in such a way that measuring that group at FVTPL results in more relevant information. The focus in this instance is on the way the entity manages and evaluates performance, rather than on the nature of its financial instruments. [IFRS 9:B4.1.33]

Applying the fair value option to financial liabilities at their initial recognition would be appropriate when financial assets and financial liabilities share one or more risks and those risks are managed and evaluated on a fair value basis in accordance with a documented policy of asset and liability management. For example, an entity could have issued 'structured products' containing multiple embedded derivatives and could be managing the resulting risks on a fair value basis using a mix of derivative and non-derivative financial instruments. Because the designation is based on managing and evaluating a group of financial instruments, all of the eligible financial liabilities that are managed and evaluated together must be designated. [IFRS 9:B4.1.34 & 35]

The entity's strategy for managing the group of financial instruments must be documented, although documentation need not be extensive. For example, if the performance management system as approved by the entity's key management personnel clearly demonstrates that the performance is evaluated on a total return basis, no additional documentation is required. The documentation does not need to be on an item-by-item basis (it may be on a portfolio basis), or at the level of detail required for hedge accounting. [IFRS 9:B4.1.36]

7.1.2.3 Contracts containing one or more embedded derivative

As detailed in **7.1.2** above, IFRS 9:4.3.5 permits a financial liability in the scope of IFRS 9 that is a hybrid contract containing one or more embedded derivatives to be designated in its entirety as at FVTPL. Designation is permitted unless the embedded derivative does not significantly modify the cash flows that otherwise would be required by the contract; or it is clear with little or no analysis when a similar hybrid instrument is first considered that separation of the embedded derivative is prohibited.

Example 7.1.2.3

Fair value option: commodity-linked debt

Entity Q issues a debt instrument that has interest payments linked to a basket of commodity prices. The linking to commodity prices is considered to be a non-closely related embedded derivative that would require separation and measurement at FVTPL. Entity Q may choose at initial recognition to designate the whole debt instrument as at FVTPL to avoid separating out the embedded derivative.

IFRS 9 generally only applies to financial instruments within its scope. However, certain of its requirements (such as those in respect of embedded derivatives) apply to a wider range of contracts. For example, an operating lease that is not a financial instrument may have an embedded derivative that is separately recognised in the statement of financial position. The question arises as to whether the fair value option provisions can be extended to hybrid contracts when the host contract is a non-financial item or a financial item outside the scope of IFRS 9. In March 2007, the IFRIC (now the IFRS Interpretations Committee) was asked to consider this question with respect to IAS 39. In November 2007, the IFRIC recommended that the IASB should clarify IAS 39:11A (equivalent to IFRS 9:4.3.5) by specifying whether it applies only to contracts with embedded derivatives that have financial hosts, or whether the fair value option can be applied to all contracts with embedded derivatives. In August 2008, the IASB issued an exposure draft, *Improvements to IFRSs*, which proposed amending IAS 39 to clarify that the fair value option could only apply to financial instruments within the scope of IAS 39. In the Basis for Conclusions to the exposure draft, the Board acknowledged that the wording in IAS 39:11A was not clear. The Board noted that prior to June 2005 IAS 39 had an unrestricted fair value option which could only be applied to financial instruments within the scope of IAS 39. The objective of the fair value option that was introduced in June 2005 (and subsequently included in IFRS 9 in October 2010), was to restrict, not broaden, an entity's ability to designate financial instruments as at FVTPL. At its January 2009 meeting, the IASB decided to defer its redeliberations on the fair value option for a future period.

At its January 2010 meeting, the IFRIC decided to remove the item, without finalisation, from the Annual Improvements project. The IFRIC believed that the issue would be incorporated as part of the Board's broader decisions on replacing IAS 39 and, therefore, should not be considered on a piecemeal basis. Since that decision, IFRS 9 has been finalised with respect to classification and measurement of financial liabilities. The wording included in IAS 39, that some regarded as ambiguous, was simply transferred to IFRS 9 unchanged in October 2010 because the Board agreed to only make limited amendments to the text previously included in IAS 39 regarding financial liability classification and measurement. It could therefore be argued that the ambiguity that existed in IAS 39 remains in IFRS 9.

However, it would be surprising to reach a conclusion that financial liabilities outside the scope of IFRS 9 could be eligible to be designated as at FVTPL based on criteria in IFRS 9. If this designation were permitted, it would mean that any host contract that is outside the scope of IFRS 9 (and that, in many cases, has been specifically excluded from IFRS 9), could be measured at FVTPL; this would override the recognition and measurement guidance included in more specific Standards, such as IAS 17 *Leases*, IFRS 4 *Insurance Contracts* and IAS 11 *Construction Contracts*. It would also mean that executory host contracts (e.g. sale and purchase contracts) would be 'grossed up' in the statement of financial position. It is of note that the fair value option with respect to financial liabilities in IFRS 9 only relates to those contractual arrangements that are wholly within the scope of that Standard.

Further, the rules on embedded derivatives contained in non-financial host contracts were introduced as an anti-abuse measure to stop entities from stapling financial instruments on to non-financial contracts. Once the embedded derivative is separated, that part of the hybrid instrument is in the scope of IFRS 9 but the host contract always remains outside the scope of IFRS 9. The fair value option provisions are contained in IFRS 9, the Standard that deals with financial instruments and contracts that behave like financial instruments is IFRS 9, and, therefore, it seems logical that the fair value option is restricted only to contracts that are in the scope of IFRS 9.

IFRS 9:B4.3.11 (which incorporates the text formally included in IFRIC 9 *Reassessment of Embedded Derivatives*) requires an entity to reconsider whether an embedded derivative is closely related only if there is a change in the terms of the contract that significantly modifies the cash flows that otherwise would be required under the contract. Because the fair value option can only be applied at initial recognition, only if the cash flows are modified sufficiently for the original instrument to be derecognised would an entity be able to designate the modified instrument as at FVTPL (see **section 3** in **chapter B5**).

IFRS 3 *Business Combinations* states that if a contractual arrangement is acquired as part of a business combination, the acquirer must determine what is the classification of the contractual arrangement at the date of acquisition because this is the date of initial recognition in the group financial statements. At the date of acquisition, the acquirer will need to consider whether the contractual arrangement has any embedded derivatives that require separation. The acquirer is not *reassessing* an embedded derivative at this point because the acquirer is recognising the contractual arrangement for the first time and will be able to apply the fair value option election as appropriate.

7.1.2.4 Fair valuing through alternative designations

In some cases, an entity could achieve fair value accounting through profit or loss by using alternative designation strategies. The choice of that designation strategy must be made when the instruments concerned are first recognised.

Example 7.1.2.4

Fair value option: alternative designations

Bank A issues structured notes that contain non-closely related embedded derivatives linked to specific securities. Bank A manages the risk of these embedded derivatives by immediately investing in the underlying securities (which do not meet the definition of held for trading). Bank A also manages the performance of the portfolio of underlying securities and issued structured notes on a fair value basis.

Bank A has a number of choices. It can:

(a) designate the portfolio of financial assets (underlying securities) and financial liabilities (structured notes) as at FVTPL because it is managed on a fair value basis; or

(b) designate the hybrid financial liabilities (structured notes) as at FVTPL because they contain non-closely related embedded derivatives; or

> (c) designate the financial assets (underlying securities) as at FVTPL because there is an accounting mismatch with the embedded derivative that is separately accounted for at FVTPL; or
>
> (d) designate the financial assets (underlying securities) as at FVTPL because there is an accounting mismatch with the financial liabilities if they are designated as at FVTPL under (b) above.

In some scenarios, a particular choice of designation will produce more meaningful information about the effects of transactions, other events and conditions on the entity's financial position, financial performance or cash flows. Because the decision to designate an instrument is similar to an accounting policy choice, the entity should choose the designation strategy that results in reliable and the *most* relevant information.

If an entity has designated a financial liability as at FVTPL, it is required to disclose separately the amount of the change in its fair value that is due to credit risk which can be determined as the amount of change that is not attributable to changes in market conditions that give rise to market risk (i.e. benchmark interest rate). [IFRS 7:10] (See **4.1.3** in **chapter B11**.)

7.1.2.5 Fair value movements due to changes in credit risk

Gains or losses on a financial liability (other than a loan commitment or a financial guarantee contract) designated as at FVTPL are required to be presented as follows:

[IFRS 9:5.7.7 & 8]

(a) the amount of the change in the fair value of the financial liability that is attributable to changes in the credit risk of that liability should be presented in other comprehensive income; and

(b) the remainder of the change in the fair value of the liability should be presented in profit or loss unless the treatment of the effects of changes in the liability's credit risk described in (a) would create or enlarge an accounting mismatch in profit or loss (in which case all gains or losses are recognised in profit or loss).

All gains and losses on loan commitments and financial guarantee contracts that are designated as at FVTPL are recognised in profit or loss. [IFRS 9:5.7.9]

In making the determination of whether recognising changes in the liability's credit risk in other comprehensive income will create or enlarge an accounting mismatch in profit or loss an entity must assess whether it expects that the effects of changes in the liability's credit risk will be offset in profit or loss by a change in the fair value of another financial instrument measured at fair value through profit or loss. Such an expectation must be based on an economic relationship between the characteristics of the liability and the characteristics of the other financial instrument. [IFRS 9:B5.7.6] That determination is made at initial recognition and is not reassessed.

For practical purposes the entity need not enter into all of the assets and liabilities giving rise to an accounting mismatch at exactly the same time. A reasonable delay is permitted provided that any remaining transactions are expected to occur. An entity must consistently apply its methodology for determining whether presenting in other comprehensive income the effects of changes in the liability's credit risk would create or enlarge an accounting mismatch in profit or loss. However, an entity may use different methodologies when there are different economic relationships between the characteristics of the liabilities designated as at fair value through profit or loss and the characteristics of the other financial instruments. [IFRS 9:B5.7.7]

As part of the IASB's deliberation in developing the requirements for changes in own credit risk of financial liabilities designated at FVTPL they undertook research to see what examples in practice might meet the requirement to recognise all fair value gains and losses in profit or loss. The IASB found one example related to mortgage funding where an accounting mismatch may arise. In that example, Danish mortgage banks lend to customers and fund each individual loan by selling a bond with identical terms (i.e. outstanding balance, term, currency, and repayment terms) to that of the mortgage loan. The mortgage loan term permits borrowers to prepay their loan by retiring their specific outstanding bond at fair value. There is a contractual linkage between the effects of changes in credit risk of the bond and fair value changes in the mortgage loan. As a result of using the fair value option, if the mortgage bank recognises changes in the fair value due to changes in credit risk of the bond through other comprehensive income while recognising the full change in fair value of the loan through profit and loss, this would create an accounting mismatch.

IFRS 7 defines credit risk as "the risk that one party to a financial instrument will cause a financial loss for the other party by failing to discharge an obligation". This relates to the risk that the issuer will fail to perform on a particular liability and it does not necessarily relate to the creditworthiness of the issuer. For example, if an entity issues a collateralised liability and a non-collateralised liability that are otherwise identical, the credit risk of those two liabilities will be different, even though they are issued by the same entity. The credit risk on the collateralised liability will be less than the credit risk of the non-collateralised liability. The credit risk for a collateralised liability may be close to zero. [IFRS 9:B5.7.13]

In cases where amounts payable under an obligation are only paid when amounts are due on specified assets (e.g. with some asset-backed securities), care is required in differentiating between credit risk and asset-specific performance risk. IFRS 9:B5.7.14 is clear that asset-specific performance risk is not related to the risk that an entity will fail to discharge a particular obligation but rather it is related to the risk that a single asset or a group of assets will perform poorly (or not at all). The differentiation between credit risk and asset-specific performance risk is important because, in some circumstances, a financial liability may have little or no credit risk, and substantially all the changes in the fair value of the liability may be attributable to asset-specific performance risk (and, therefore, those changes should be recognised in profit or loss, not other comprehensive income).

IFRS 9 provides two examples of instruments with asset-specific performance risk.

[IFRS 9:B5.7.15]

- A liability with a unit-linking feature whereby the amount due to investors is contractually determined on the basis of the performance of specified assets. The effect of that unit-linking feature on the fair value of the liability is asset-specific performance risk, not credit risk.
- A liability issued by a structured entity with the following characteristics. The entity is legally isolated so that the assets in the entity are ring-fenced solely for the benefit of its investors, even in the event of bankruptcy. The entity enters into no other transactions and the assets in the entity cannot be hypothecated. Amounts are due to the entity's investors only if the ring-fenced assets generate cash flows. Thus, changes in the fair value of the liability primarily reflect changes in the fair value of the assets. The effect of the performance of the assets on the fair value of the liability is asset-specific performance risk, not credit risk.

What is evident from the above examples of asset-specific performance risk is that the entity does not have any obligation to make payments if the assets to which the obligation is contractually linked fail to perform. For example, an entity may issue a note that is contractually linked to specified financial assets (e.g. corporate bonds) which themselves have credit risk (i.e. that the issuer of the corporate bonds fails to perform under its obligation). However, the entity's issued note may have little or no credit risk if the entity has no obligation to make payments unless amounts are received on the corporate bonds.

Depending on how the obligation of the entity, and the entity itself, is structured there may still be some credit risk in circumstances where there is also asset-performance risk. In cases where amounts received on the assets are not immediately payable to the counterparty of the obligation, the entity will owe amounts to the counterparty even when the asset has performed. Depending on whether the entity is able to utilise the cash received on the assets for purposes other than to pay its obligations under the financial liability, there may be some residual credit risk. In some cases this may be minimal.

Asset-specific performance risk is relevant when amounts payable on the financial liability are only due if amounts are received on the specified assets. For many collateralised financial liabilities (i.e. non-recourse arrangements) this will not be the case. Amounts due under a borrowing that is secured, say, on a property or on financial assets may be payable irrespective of the performance of the security. The security (collateral) reduces the credit risk associated with the obligation relative to an uncollateralised financial liability, but it does not equate to asset-specific performance risk because, irrespective of the performance of the security, the entity will still owe amounts under the obligation. The security merely permits the counterparty to the obligation to secure that asset if the entity fails to otherwise meet its obligation.

IFRS 9 describes in some detail how the change in the fair value of a financial liability that is attributable to changes in the credit risk of that liability should be calculated. This amount may be determined:

[IFRS 9:B5.7.16 & 17]

(a) as the amount of change in the fair value of the liability that is not attributable to changes in market conditions that give rise to market risk. This includes changes in a benchmark interest rate, the price of another entity's financial instrument, a commodity price, a foreign exchange rate or an index of prices or rates; or

(b) using an alternative method the entity believes more faithfully represents the amount of the change in the liability's fair value that is attributable to changes in its credit risk.

When the only significant relevant changes in market conditions for a liability are changes in an observed (benchmark) interest rate, which could be the case for a fixed rate borrowing with standard terms and conditions, the changes in fair value attributable to credit risk can be estimated as follows.

[IFRS 9:B5.7.18]

(a) First, the entity computes the liability's internal rate of return at the start of the period using the fair value of the liability and the liability's contractual cash flows at the start of the period. It deducts from this rate of return the observed (benchmark) interest rate at the start of the period, to arrive at an instrument-specific component of the internal rate of return.

(b) Next, the entity calculates the present value of the cash flows associated with the liability using the liability's contractual cash flows at the end of the period and a discount rate equal to the sum of (i) the observed (benchmark) interest rate at the end of the period and (ii) the instrument-specific component of the internal rate of return as determined in (a).

(c) The difference between the fair value of the liability at the end of the period and the amount determined in (b) is the change in fair value that is not attributable to changes in the observed (benchmark) interest rate. This is the amount to be presented in other comprehensive income in accordance with IFRS 9:5.7.7(a).

The method described immediately above assumes that changes in fair value arising from factors other than changes in the instrument's credit risk or changes in observed (benchmark) interest rates are not significant. This method would not be appropriate if changes in fair value arising from other factors are significant. In those cases, an entity is required to use an alternative method that more faithfully measures the effects of changes in the liability's credit risk. For example, if the instrument in the example contains an embedded derivative, the change in fair value of the embedded derivative is excluded in determining the amount to be presented in other comprehensive income in accordance with IFRS 9:5.7.7(a). [IFRS 9:B5.7.20]

As with all estimates of fair value, an entity's measurement method for determining the portion of the change in the liability's fair value that is attributable to changes in its credit risk must make maximum use of market inputs. [IRS 9:B5.7.20]

The own credit requirements in IFRS 9 are available for early application in isolation, i.e. without also early applying the other requirements in IFRS 9 (see **section 3** in **chapter B13**).

7.2 Financial liabilities arising from continuing involvement accounting and failed derecognition

When an entity transfers an asset but neither retains nor transfers substantially all of the risks and rewards of ownership of a financial asset, and retains control of that asset, the entity continues to recognise the asset to the extent of its continuing involvement (see **3.4** in **chapter B8**). A corresponding liability is also recognised in accordance with IFRS 9:3.2.17 and measured so that the net carrying amount of the asset and the liability is:

- the amortised cost of the rights and obligations retained, if the asset is measured at amortised cost; or
- the fair value of the rights and obligations retained (if the asset is measured at fair value).

The specific measurement guidance as described above means that a continuing involvement liability cannot be classified as at FVTPL. This is reinforced in IFRS 9:3.2.21 which states that, if the transferred asset is measured at amortised cost, an entity is prohibited from designating the associated financial liability as at FVTPL.

When an entity transfers an asset but retains substantially all the risks and rewards of ownership of the asset, a financial liability is recognised equal to the consideration received. IFRS 9 is not clear whether this 'failed sale' financial liability can be designated as at FVTPL. The recognition of such financial liabilities is common in the case of repurchase obligations ('repos') or in structured transactions when an asset is legally transferred but the risks and rewards related to the transferred asset are passed back to the transferor via guarantees and/or derivatives. IFRS 9:4.2.1 requires all financial liabilities to be measured at amortised cost with some exceptions that include liabilities measured at fair value through profit or loss (whether held for trading or designated as at FVTPL) and financial liabilities that arise when a transfer of a financial asset does not qualify for derecognition. In the case of a financial liability initially recognised at the fair value of the consideration received on a failed derecognition transaction, the terms of the liability are imputed from the transfer arrangement and the liability is regarded as an in-substance collateralised borrowing. IFRS 9:3.2.15 states that the transferor should recognise any income on the transferred asset that continues to be recognised in the transferor's statement of financial position "and any expense incurred on the financial liability". Because the Standard is not clear whether 'expense' is limited to interest expense only on the deemed collateralised borrowing or whether it could include fair value gains/losses, it is reasonable that an entity can designate the financial liability as at FVTPL if all the criteria for designation are met.

7.3 Reclassification

Reclassifications of financial liabilities in and out of the FVTPL category are prohibited. The following changes in circumstances are not reclassifications:

[IFRS 9:4.4.3]

- a derivative that was previously a designated and effective hedging instrument in a cash flow hedge or net investment hedge no longer qualifies as such; and
- a derivative becomes a designated and effective hedging instrument in a cash flow hedge or net investment hedge.

7.4 Classification of financial liabilities acquired in a business combination

When financial liabilities are assumed in a business combination, those liabilities must be classified in the consolidated financial statements of the acquirer into one of the permitted categories described in **section 7** above. It is entirely possible that the classification of a financial liability for these purposes may differ from its classification in the financial statements of the acquiree. For example, the acquirer in its consolidated financial statements may choose to designate a financial liability as at FVTPL at initial recognition even though the acquiree may have classified it otherwise when it first recognised the liability. These differences can arise because 'initial recognition' from the acquirer's perspective is the date of acquisition of the subsidiary and its classification decisions are made at that date.

IFRS 3 *Business Combinations* provides clear guidance stating that, at the acquisition date, the acquirer should make any classifications, designations concerning financial assets acquired or financial liabilities assumed in a business combination in accordance with pertinent conditions (e.g. contractual terms, economic conditions, acquirer's operating or accounting policies) at that date.

8 Reassessing classification

The liability-equity classification made at initial recognition is reconsidered if there are changes to the contractual terms of the instrument. In November 2006, the IFRIC (now the IFRS Interpretations Committee) issued an agenda decision that included a reassessment of liability-equity classification in the case of a change in terms of the instrument that resulted in a financial liability being reclassified to equity. IFRIC 2:5 also states that in determining liability-equity classification, the entity should consider all terms and conditions at the date of classification "but not expected future amendments to those laws, regulations or charter". The IFRIC noted that Example 3 in IFRIC 2 provides an example of reclassification from equity to financial liability following a change in the entity's governing charter.

IAS 32 is less clear in what circumstances it is appropriate to reconsider the liability-equity classification in circumstances where the terms of the instrument do not change. Generally, an entity would not reconsider the classification of the arrangement. However, there are instances where it is acceptable to reconsider classification, and other cases where it is required.

Reconsideration as an accounting policy choice

Where there is a change in the functional currency of the issuer of convertible debt following the initial recognition of the instrument by the issuer IAS 32 is not clear whether the financial liability and equity classification should be reconsidered. This could be the case where the fixed amount of cash nominally received under the conversion option in the convertible debt is in the functional currency of the issuer when the instrument is issued, but following initial recognition the cash is deemed to be in a foreign currency because the functional currency of the issuer changes. Another example is where the fixed amount of cash nominally received under the conversion option in the convertible debt is in a foreign currency when the instrument is issued, but following initial recognition is in the functional currency of the issuer because the functional currency of the issuer changes.

We consider there are two acceptable approaches in these circumstances and an entity should determine an appropriate accounting policy and apply it consistently in accordance with IAS 8 *Accounting Polices, Changes in Accounting Estimates and Errors*.

One approach is that the classification of the convertible debt should not be reconsidered after initial recognition if the terms of the instrument do not change. This view is supported by the fact that IAS 32 only prescribes that an entity should classify the instrument, or its component parts, on initial recognition, and that the Standard is silent regarding any requirement to re-assess the original classification after initial recognition when there is no change in the contractual terms of the instrument.

The second approach is that the classification of the convertible debt should be reconsidered after initial recognition if the terms of the instrument do not change. This view focuses on the requirement under IFRS 9:3.3.1 that an entity should derecognise a financial liability (or part of a financial liability) when, and only when, it is extinguished (i.e. when the obligation specified in the contract is discharged or cancelled or expires). When a change in functional currency above occurs and, as a consequence, the conversion feature no longer meets the definition of financial liability, reclassification is considered to be appropriate because the obligation has been discharged or cancelled. Further, if the equity component recognised at initial recognition no longer meets the definition of equity following the change in functional currency this supports the view that it should be reclassified as a financial liability.

The accounting policy would equally apply in the case of a standalone derivative over equity shares (rather than a conversion feature within a debt instrument as described above).

Examples of the application of the two approaches are included in **example 8A**.

Example 8A

Convertible debt with change in functional currency

Entity B, a US dollar functional currency entity, issues a Euro denominated convertible bond that is convertible at the holder's choice into a fixed number of equity shares of Entity B. Because the conversion feature is not in the functional currency of Entity B, it will not be settled by the exchange of a fixed amount of functional currency cash for a fixed number of shares and the conversion feature is classified as a derivative financial liability in accordance with IAS 32:11.

One year after the date of issue, Entity B's functional currency changes to the Euro. The terms of the convertible bond do not change. Following the change in functional currency, the conversion feature will be settled by the exchange of a fixed amount of functional currency cash (Euros) for a fixed number of shares.

If Entity B's functional currency had been the Euro at the date of issue of the bond, the instrument would have been classified as a compound instrument under IAS 32:28 because the conversion feature would have met the definition of equity.

Entity B needs to determine an accounting policy in accordance with IAS 8 whether to reclassify its financial liability and equity classification in response to a change in functional currency and apply it consistently.

- Policy one would not reclassify the convertible bond after initial recognition.
- Policy two would be to require reclassification of the convertible bond after initial recognition.

If the fact pattern is reversed so that Entity B's functional currency at the date of issue of the bond is the Euro, the convertible bond is classified as a compound instrument at the date of issue. If Entity B's functional currency subsequently changes to US dollar, the same accounting policy choice is available.

Where the number of equity instruments to be delivered under a standalone derivative (or a derivative embedded in another instrument) is variable for a specified period, but with certainty will be fixed in a following period and that period runs until the end of the instrument's life, IAS 32 is not clear whether the entity is permitted, or is required, to reassess the financial liability and equity classification in the second period when the number of equity shares is known to be fixed. Similar to the change of functional currency described above there is no change in terms of the contract and consequently we consider it is acceptable to determine a consistently applied accounting policy in accordance with IAS 8 as to whether the financial liability and equity classification should be reassessed after initial recognition of the instrument.

Example 8B

Convertible debt with conversion price becoming fixed with passage of time

On 1 January 20X1, Entity Y, a CU functional currency entity, issued CU denominated convertible bonds with a par value of CU30 million. The convertible bonds will mature on the third anniversary of the date of issue at par unless they are converted into ordinary shares prior to maturity. The conversion price is the lower of CU4 and 133 per cent of the issue price of ordinary shares issued for less than CU3 by Entity Y between 1 January 20X1 and 1 January 20X3. In effect, therefore, the conversion price is subject to variability until 1 January 20X3 and becomes fixed from that date onwards.

On initial recognition of the instrument on 1 January 20X1, the equity conversion option will not result in the delivery of a fixed amount of cash for a fixed number of equity shares and, therefore, does not meet the definition of equity. Because the number of shares that may be delivered under the instrument is variable, the instrument is not a compound instrument; it is a hybrid financial instrument wholly in the scope of IFRS 9. The equity conversion option is an embedded derivative that is not closely related to the debt host contract. Accordingly, unless the convertible bond is designated as at FVTPL, it will be recognised separately from the debt host contract and measured at FVTPL with the debt host contract measured at amortised cost.

On 1 January 20X3 the number of shares that will be delivered under the conversion option ceases to be variable. Therefore, there is a question as to whether at this point in time Entity Y should reconsider its liability-equity classification of the conversion option. In the absence of specific guidance in IAS 32 and IFRS 9 two approaches are considered acceptable. Whichever approach is selected by Entity Y, it should be applied consistently as an accounting policy choice.

Approach 1 – no reconsideration of classification

Entity Y could choose a policy of not reconsidering the classification when the contractual terms of the instrument do not change and there has been no change in the circumstances of the entity. If this accounting policy is adopted, Entity Y should continue to account for the equity conversion option as a non-closely related embedded derivative measured at FVTPL.

Approach 2 – reconsideration of classification

Entity Y could choose a policy of reconsidering the classification when the contractual terms of the instrument do not change and there has been no change in the circumstances of the entity. This approach would be justified on the basis that the liability classification of the conversion option at initial recognition was based on the presence of the contractual feature that gave rise to variability in the number of shares. Because this feature expires at 1 January 20X3 purely with the passage of time, although there has been no change to the contractual terms of the instrument, the contractual terms that are effective for the remainder of the life of the conversion option have changed. Under this approach the change in the effective terms makes it appropriate to reconsider the classification. At 1 January 20X3 the conversion option meets the definition of equity because it will always result, if converted, in the exchange of a fixed number of shares for a fixed amount of functional currency cash. If this accounting policy is adopted, Entity Y will reclassify the embedded derivative financial liability (representing the conversion option) to equity at its fair value with no gain or loss in profit or loss at the date of reclassification.

Reconsideration required

An alternative fact pattern that we consider would require reconsideration of the financial liability and equity classification where the terms have not changed is where the underlying shares to be delivered under a derivative (or derivative embedded in another instrument) cease, or start, to be a non-controlling interest in the consolidated financial statements after the instrument is initially issued. An example would be a convertible bond where the shares to be delivered upon conversion are a fixed number of shares of a subsidiary. In the consolidated financial statements the conversion feature meets the definition of equity, however, if after initial classification of the convertible debt the consolidated entity disposes of its subsidiary, the shares to be delivered under the convertible debt no longer meet the definition of equity as they are no longer shares of a non-controlling interest. It would not be appropriate to regard the conversion feature as meeting the definition of equity when the shares to be delivered under the conversion feature are no longer an equity instrument.

Example 8C

Derivative over interest in a subsidiary with subsequent disposal of the subsidiary

Entity C is a CU functional currency entity. It has a 60 per cent owned subsidiary, Entity D, that currently has 1 million equity shares in issue. Entity C acquires a call option enabling it to purchase a further 100,000 equity shares of Entity D; the option is not exercisable until the end of Year 2. The option can only be exercised through gross physical settlement (i.e. through receipt of a fixed number of shares for a fixed amount of CU cash).

Upon entering into the call option, Entity C determines that the call option meets the definition of equity in the consolidated financial statements because it will be settled exclusively through the exchange of a fixed amount of functional currency cash for a fixed number of equity shares.

Subsequent to entering into the call option but before the option is exercisable at the end of Year 2, Entity C disposes of half of its 60 per cent interest in Entity D such that, following the disposal it has a 30 per cent shareholding and the pre-existing purchased call option over 100,000 shares (equivalent to an additional 10 per cent). Control is lost at the date of disposal, but Entity C retains significant influence over Entity D.

Following the disposal, the purchased call option is no longer considered to be an option over the group's own equity instruments because Entity D is no longer a member of Entity C's group (its status has changed from a subsidiary to an associate). Consequently, the purchased call option no longer meets the definition of equity in Entity C's consolidated financial statements.

At the date of disposal, the purchased call option must be reclassified from equity to a derivative measured at fair value through profit or loss. Any difference between the fair value at the date of reclassification and the original amount recognised in equity is retained in equity because it is analogous to a cancellation of the equity instrument.

Although, in the circumstances described, there has been no change in the terms of the purchased call option, this fact cannot be used as a basis for not reclassifying the option (unlike in circumstances such as those discussed in **example 8A** (change of functional currency) and **example 8B** (conversion price becoming fixed with the passage of time) when the transaction/event only affects whether the 'fixed for fixed' criterion is met). This is because the disposal has affected the 'nature' of the option such that it is no longer an option over the entity's own shares.

If Entity C's interest in Entity D were originally an investment in an associate, the purchased call option would have not met the definition of equity at initial recognition and would have been measured at fair value through profit or loss.

If Entity C subsequently acquired a further 30 per cent interest in Entity D (independent of the call option), and thus acquired control of Entity D, the purchased call option would at that point meet the definition of equity and would be reclassified to equity at its fair value at the date of acquisition.

9 Future developments

In response to the views received on the 2011 Agenda Consultation the IASB agreed in May 2012 to initiate a research programme that would include financial instruments with the characteristics of equity. At the date of writing the research project was in the development stage which means the IASB has completed its assessment work, has begun its discussions, and the next step is likely to be the issuance of a discussion paper.

B4 Derivatives

Contents

1 Introduction

The classification and measurement requirements for financial assets and financial liabilities in IFRS 9 *Financial Instruments*, described in **chapters B2** and **B3** respectively, require that all derivatives are accounted for in the statement of financial position at fair value, irrespective of whether they are used as part of a hedging relationship. Changes in fair value are recognised in profit or loss unless the contract is designated in an effective hedging relationship under which some or all of the derivative gains and losses are required to be presented in other comprehensive income (e.g. in a cash flow hedge or a hedge of a net investment in a foreign operation, see **chapter B9** on hedge accounting).

Because the definition of a derivative is so broad (see **section 2**), many contracts are likely to be caught and, therefore, will have to be accounted for at fair value. For example, certain contracts to buy or sell non-financial items fall within the scope of IFRS 9 and meet the definition of a derivative (see **2.5** in **chapter B1**).

A fixed price commitment to buy or sell a financial instrument at a future date meets the definition of a derivative financial instrument. However, as a practical expedient, these are not accounted for as derivatives as at FVTPL if the commitment has a short duration accepted by market convention. Such commitments are referred to as 'regular way' purchases or sales. Regular way contracts are subject to special accounting rules dealt which are discussed in **2.2** in **chapter B8**.

2 Definition of a derivative

IFRS 9 defines a derivative as a financial instrument or other contract within the scope of the Standard with all three of the following characteristics:

[IFRS 9: Appendix A]

- its value changes in response to the change in a specified interest rate, financial instrument price, commodity price, foreign exchange rate, index of prices or rates, credit rating or credit index, or other variable, provided in the case of a non-financial variable that the variable is not specific to a party to the contract (sometimes called the 'underlying');
- it requires no initial net investment or an initial net investment that is smaller than would be required for other types of contracts that would be expected to have a similar response to changes in market factors; and
- it is settled at a future date.

The definition of a derivative is important for a number of reasons. Firstly, IFRS 9:4.2.1 requires that a financial liability must be classified as at FVTPL if it is a *derivative*. Secondly, IFRS 9 requires in some cases the separation of embedded derivatives from contracts that are themselves non-derivatives subject to meeting specified criteria (see **chapter B5**). Thirdly, the hedge accounting requirements permit certain *derivatives* to be designated as hedging instruments.

Although IFRS 9 is not explicit that a financial asset that meets the definition of a derivative must be measured at FVTPL, the classification guidance requirements for financial assets contained in IFRS 9 would lead to that conclusion. A derivative asset would by default be classified as at FVTPL, unless designated as an effective hedging instrument, because derivatives do not contain cash flows that are solely payments of principal and interest and, therefore, (1) they are not eligible for amortised cost measurement (IFRS 9:4.1.2(b)), and (2) they are not equity instruments and, therefore, they are not eligible for designation as at fair value through comprehensive income (IFRS 9:5.7.5).

2.1 Underlying

An underlying is a variable that, along with either a notional amount or a payment provision, determines the settlement amount of a derivative.

Examples of underlyings include:

- a security price or security price index;
- a commodity price or commodity price index;
- an interest rate or interest rate index;
- a credit rating or credit index;
- a foreign exchange rate or foreign exchange rate index;
- an insurance index or catastrophe loss index;
- a climatic or geological condition (e.g. temperature, earthquake severity or rainfall), another physical variable, or a related index; or
- another variable (e.g. volume of sales).

The value or cash flows of all assets, liabilities, and purchase and sale commitments change in response to changes in the market factors in which they are founded. There is nothing unique in this regard about derivatives, except that the market factor is referred to as an index, a variable or an underlying and, in many instances, the referenced underlying is not delivered at settlement but is used as a basis for computing a settlement amount, usually in cash.

Prior to the issue of IFRS 4 *Insurance Contracts*, IAS 39 (the financial instruments standard that predated IFRS 9) scoped out derivatives when the variable is based on climatic, geological and other physical variables.

However, when IFRS 4 was issued, IAS 39 was amended so that these contracts were within its scope unless they meet the definition of an insurance contract (see **2.3** in **chapter B1**). When IFRS 9 was issued, the scope paragraphs previously included in IAS 39 with respect to these contractual arrangements were unchanged. If an insurance contract contains an embedded derivative that needs to be separately accounted for, then it is only the embedded derivative part of the insurance contract that will be accounted for as a derivative in accordance with IFRS 9. Embedded derivatives are considered in **chapter B5**.

Additionally, a derivative where the underlying is a specific commodity (e.g. oil) may be scoped out of IFRS 9 if the contract is considered a normal purchase, sale or usage requirement contract (see **2.5** in **chapter B1**). Whether the instrument is scoped in or out of IFRS 9 is dependent on the entity's normal business requirements as well as the settlement terms of the instrument, the entity's past practice, and whether the instrument is a written option and the underlying is readily convertible to cash.

The definition of a derivative was amended by the IASB when it issued IFRS 4 *Insurance Contracts* to scope out contracts over non-financial variables that are specific to a party to the contract. This amendment was required to ensure that insurance risk was scoped out of IAS 39 (now IFRS 9) and instead accounted for in accordance with IFRS 4.

Yet since then there have been differing views as to whether the term 'non-financial variable specific to a party to the contract' is limited to scoping just insurance contracts or is broader than that.

In October 2007, the IASB issued an exposure draft, *Improvements to International Financial Reporting Standards*, which proposed to amend IAS 39's definition of a derivative by deleting the term 'non-financial variable specific to a party to the contract', so that contracts linked to non-financial variables specific to a party to a contract would be within the scope of the definition. In its Basis for Conclusions on those proposed amendments, the IASB observed that the phrase highlighted above was introduced when IFRS 4 Insurance Contracts was issued "to exclude from the scope of IAS 39 contracts within the scope of IFRS 4".

Following feedback on the exposure draft, in October 2008, the IASB tentatively decided not to proceed with the amendment, noting that the Board will consider the issue in a future project. Yet, in issuing IFRS 9 in 2009 and 2010, the IASB did not specifically consider the issue and carried forward the existing definition in IAS 39.

In September 2012, the IFRS Interpretations Committee considered various accounting questions in respect of the restructuring of Greek Government Bonds. As part of the restructuring the holders of these bonds received a security issued by the Hellenic Republic for which the return was indexed to the country's GDP. The Committee noted that the fact pattern submitted was based on the assumption that indexation to the issuer's GDP is a non-financial variable specific to a party to the contract. IFRIC Update September 2012 states:

> "The Interpretations Committee noted that the question of what constitutes an underlying that is a non-financial variable specific to a party to the contract had been considered on several previous occasions by itself and by the IASB. Consequently, the Interpretations Committee was concerned that it would not be able to resolve the issue efficiently within the confines of existing IFRSs and the Conceptual Framework and the demands of the Interpretation process and that it was not likely that it would be able to reach a consensus on the issue on a timely basis. The Interpretations Committee therefore considered that the question of whether the assumption in the submission is appropriate would remain open."

IFRS 9 nor any other IFRS provides a clear answer as to whether the term 'non-financial variable specific to a party to the contract' in the definition of a derivative is limited to the scoping out of insurance contracts or is broader. Both the IASB and the IFRS Interpretations Committee have considered this question in the past, but to date no clarifying guidance has been issued.

Given the lack of specific guidance on this topic and the IFRS Interpretations Committee's decision to leave open the assumption made in the submission received on Greek Government Bonds, it is acceptable to adopt either of the approaches set out below as an accounting policy choice. In developing the accounting policy, entities may need to take into consideration specific requirements by local regulators, if any.

Accounting policy one

The inclusion of the term 'non-financial variable specific to a party to the contract' is limited to excluding insurance contracts from the definition of a derivative. Therefore, unless a contract meets the definition of an insurance contract in IFRS 4, the contract is not scoped out of the definition of a derivative if the contract is either fully (or partly, in the case of an embedded derivative) in the scope of IFRS 9.

This approach is consistent with the IASB's tentative view included in the 2007 exposure draft (see above). It is also supported by:

- IFRS 9 Guidance on Implementation A.2 *Option to put a non-financial asset where an option to put an office building* that can be either physically settled or net cash settled is a derivative,
- IFRS 9 Guidance on Implementation B.8 *Definition of a derivative: foreign currency contract based on sales volume* where a contract based on foreign currency and sales volume is a derivative.

Accounting policy two

The inclusion of the term 'non-financial variable specific to a party to the contract' is broader than simply excluding insurance contracts from the definition of a derivative. Therefore, a contract (other than an insurance contract) that is either fully or partly in the scope of IFRS 9 may have a non-financial variable that is specific to a party to the contract and, consequently, it may be excluded from the definition of a derivative.

This approach, in line with the agenda decision noted in the September 2012 IFRIC Update, recognises that because the IASB has not fully resolved this question different views could validly be held.

If such an approach is applied, it is then necessary to assess what is 'specific to a party' and which variables are considered 'non-financial' (as these terms are not defined by IFRSs).

For an underlying to be specific to a party to the contract the underlying must be unique to the party. For example, an entity's real estate is a non-financial that is specific to the party to the contract. However, commodities may not be specific to the party when they are readily tradable and are homogenous. An entity's inventory of gold may not be specific to the party to the contract as it is not distinguishable from a different party holding the same commodity.

For some variables the determination of non-financial may be relatively straightforward when the variable has no financial element to it (for example, the tonnage of ore extracted from a mine or the number of units sold by a motor vehicle manufacturer). It is less straightforward whether a variable based on an amount derived from the financial statements of a party to the contract (for example, revenue, EBITDA or net assets) is 'non-financial'. Again, the views of local regulators may need to be considered in developing a policy.

2.2 Notional amounts and payment provisions

While neither a notional amount nor a payment provision is an essential characteristic of a derivative instrument , derivative instruments usually contain a notional amount or a payment provision each of which may interact with the underlying to determine the settlement amount of the derivative instrument. A notional is often an amount of currency, a number of shares, a number of units of weight or volume or other units specified in the contract. A payment provision is a provision which requires a fixed payment or payment of an amount that can change (but not proportionally to a change in the underlying) as a result of some future event that is unrelated to a notional amount.

Example 2.2A

Payment provision based on interest rates

Entity ABC receives CU200 to enter into a contract that requires it to pay CU500 if 6-month LIBOR increases by 75 basis points over the next six months. Even though this contract does not have a notional amount, it contains a payment provision that does not move proportionally with the underlying.

Example 2.2B

Payment provision based on share price

Entity XYZ enters into a contract that requires it to pay CU10 million if Entity ABC's share price increases by CU5 per share during a 6-month period; conversely Entity XYZ will receive CU10 million if Entity ABC's share price decreases by CU5 per share during the same six-month period.

In this example, the underlying is the price of Entity ABC's shares. There is no notional amount to determine the settlement amount. Instead, there is a payment provision that does not move proportionally with the underlying. The absence of a notional amount does not preclude the instrument from meeting the definition of a derivative because there is a payment provision.

It is sometimes the case that a contract has neither a notional amount nor a fixed payment provision. In addition, a contract may have multiple underlyings.

Example 2.2C

Foreign currency forward contract linked to sales

Entity X, a Euro functional currency entity, sells products in Switzerland. The sales are denominated in Swiss francs. Entity X enters into a contract with an investment bank to convert Swiss francs to Euros at a fixed exchange rate. The contract requires Entity X to remit Swiss francs based on its sales volume in Switzerland in exchange for Euros at a fixed exchange rate of 1.60.

The contract with the bank has two underlyings (sales volume and the Euro/Swiss franc exchange rate). The contract does not have a specified notional amount or a fixed payment provision, but still meets the definition of a derivative.

2.3 Interaction of notional amounts with the underlying

The settlement amount of a derivative instrument with a notional amount is determined by the interaction of that notional amount with the underlying. The interaction may be simple multiplication, or it may involve a formula with leverage factors or other constants.

Example 2.3

Interest rate swap

XYZ enters into an interest rate swap that requires XYZ to pay a fixed rate of interest and receive a variable rate of interest. The fixed interest rate amount is 7.5 per cent, while the variable interest rate amount is 3-month LIBOR, reset on a quarterly basis. The notional amount of the swap is CU100 million.

The underlying is an interest rate index, 3-month LIBOR. Net regular settlements are calculated by applying the difference between 7.5 per cent and 3-month LIBOR to the notional amount of CU100 million.

2.4 Initial net investment

The second part of the definition of a derivative is that there is either no initial net investment, or that any initial investment is smaller than would be required for other contracts that are expected to have a similar response to changes in market factors. This is a comparative measure, and excludes any margin accounts (which are instead treated as collateral). Various examples are set out in the following sections.

2.4.1 Interest rate swaps

Example 2.4.1

Interest rate swap

Entity B enters into a contract with a counterparty that requires it to pay a LIBOR-based variable rate of interest, and receive a fixed rate of 8 per cent. The contract is an interest rate swap with a notional amount of ¥10 billion. Entity B did not pay or receive cash at inception (i.e. the contract is at market at inception) and, therefore, does not require an initial net investment by either party.

In some instances, the terms of the interest rate swap may be favourable or unfavourable and may require one of the parties to make an up-front initial investment in the contract. If the initial investment represents a premium or discount for market conditions, the initial net investment would normally still be smaller than the notional amount on the debt instrument from which the interest rate cash flows are derived, and so would satisfy the initial net investment criterion of a derivative.

2.4.1.1 Interest rate swap with fixed leg prepaid

Example 2.4.1.1

Prepaid fixed leg

Entity X enters into an 8-year pay fixed at 7 per cent, receive LIBOR interest rate swap on CU100 million. It prepays the fixed leg at inception. The amount it pays is calculated as CU7 million (CU100 million x 7 per cent) for eight years, discounted at market rates.

This initial payment is significantly less than the amount Entity X would have to pay to acquire an instrument that would have a similar response to changes in market factors. Entity X would need to acquire CU100 million debt with a LIBOR return in order to replicate the return on the floating rate leg of the swap. Therefore, the swap with a prepaid fixed leg will still meet the definition of a derivative.

If the fixed rate payment obligation on the interest rate swap is prepaid after initial recognition, the payment would be considered termination of the old swap and an origination of a new instrument that would need to be classified for the first time. [IFRS 9 Guidance on Implementation B.4]

2.4.1.2 Interest rate swap with floating leg prepaid

Example 2.4.1.2

Prepaid floating leg

Entity A enters into a 6-year pay LIBOR, receive fixed 5 per cent interest rate swap on CU100 million. It prepays the variable leg at inception. The cash inflows that the entity continues to receive are akin to those of a financial instrument with a fixed annuity of 5 per cent per year for the next six years.

Because the amount prepaid will be about the same as what would have been paid to purchase a fixed annuity instrument paying 5 per cent over the next six years, the initial net investment test is failed. The contract will not be accounted for as a derivative, but instead as a loan made by Entity A. [IFRS 9 Guidance on Implementation B.5]

2.4.2 Options

For an option, the premium paid could be significant. However, it is likely to be smaller than the amount that would be required to buy an instrument with a similar response to changes in market factors, i.e. the underlying instrument to which the option relates.

Example 2.4.2A

Deep in the money option (1)

Entity A purchases, for CU1.1 million, an option to buy 80,000 shares in Entity B at CU75 per share in three months' time. When Entity A purchases the option, Entity B's shares are trading at CU70 per share. The cost of the option, CU1. 1 million, is less than what it would cost to buy 80,000 shares in Entity B, so it meets this part of the definition. This will even be the case for many deep in the money options, as demonstrated below.

Example 2.4.2B

Deep in the money option (2)

Entity XYZ purchases a deep in the money call option on Entity ABC shares. Entity ABC's share price is €100 per share. The option is an American option with a 180-day maturity. The option has a strike price of €10 per share and Entity XYZ pays a premium of €91. The initial investment in the option of €91 is less than the notional amount applied to the underlying, i.e. €100 (the notional amount is one share and the underlying is €100 per share).

Although the option has a significant initial net investment, it is smaller than the investment that would be required for other types of contracts that would be expected to have a similar response to changes in market factors. The invested amount of €91 does not approximate the notional amount applied to the underlying (€100) and, therefore, the option meets the initial net investment criterion for a derivative instrument.

2.4.3 Currency swap

Currency swaps typically require an initial exchange of currencies. These swaps will still satisfy the initial net investment criterion because the exchange is of amounts with an equal fair value, so that on a net basis the fair value at inception is zero.

Example 2.4.3

Currency swap

Entity X enters into a 3-year currency swap with Bank Z. At inception, when the Sterling/Euro exchange rate is 1.5, the swap results in Entity X paying Bank Z £100 million and Bank Z paying Entity X €150 million. Although there has been an exchange of cash, the amounts exchanged are of equal fair value.

2.4.4 Prepaid forward contract

Example 2.4.4

Prepaid forward contract

Entity X enters into a forward contract to purchase one million ordinary shares in Entity T in one year. The current market price of Entity T's shares is €50 per share, and the 1-year forward price is €55 per share. Entity X prepays the forward contract at inception with a €50 million payment.

The initial net investment approximates the investment that would be required for other types of contracts that would be expected to have a similar response to changes in market factors because one million of Entity T's shares could be purchased at inception for the same price of €50 million. Accordingly, the prepaid forward contract does not meet the initial net investment criterion for a derivative instrument. [IFRS 9 Guidance on Implementation B.9]

2.4.5 Offsetting loans

Two or more non-derivative contracts should be considered together when the substance of the aggregate position is that of a derivative. [IFRS 9 Guidance on Implementation B.6] states that indicators of such a situation are when the contracts are:

- entered into at the same time and in contemplation of each other;
- have the same counterparty;
- relate to the same risk; and
- there is no apparent economic need or substantive business purpose for structuring the transactions separately that could not also have been accomplished in a single transaction.

Example 2.4.5

Offsetting loans

Entity A makes a 5-year fixed rate loan to Entity B on market terms. Simultaneously, Entity B makes a 5-year variable rate loan to Entity A on market terms over the same notional amount. The combination of these two loans is similar in effect to an interest rate swap. Even if amounts are exchanged at inception of the two loans, the net fair value of the amounts exchanged is zero. Therefore, the loans should be considered together, and the entire arrangement accounted for as a derivative.

2.5 Future settlement

The third part of the definition of a derivative is that it is settled at a future date. Settlement can occur in different ways, either gross or net [IFRS 9 Guidance on Implementation B.3], and does not just mean exchange of cash. For example, it may be expected that an out of the money option will not be exercised. However, expiry of the contract is a form of settlement, even if at maturity of the instrument no cash or underlying changes hands. [IFRS 9 Guidance on Implementation B.7]

3 Scoped-in contracts

Certain contracts to buy or sell non-financial items are within the scope of IFRS 9 (see **2.5** in **chapter B1**). If a contract to buy or sell a non-financial item is within the scope of IFRS 9 and meets the definition of a derivative, it will be recognised at fair value.

Example 3

Contract over a non-financial item

Entity A enters into a futures contract to purchase 1,000 bushels of corn for CU1 per bushel in three months. No cash is paid at inception. Assuming the contract is within the scope of IFRS 9 (i.e. because it is not entered into for the purpose of the receipt of the corn bushels or it is entered into for the purpose of the receipt of the corn bushels but Entity A elects at initial recognition to designate the contract at fair value through profit or loss), the contract meets the definition of a derivative.

It has an underlying (the price of corn bushels), there is no initial investment, and the contract will be settled in the future. The contract must be recognised in Entity A's statement of financial position at fair value, with changes in fair value recognised in profit or loss unless the contract qualifies as a hedging instrument in an effective hedge relationship.

4 Examples of contracts that meet the definition of a derivative

Some common examples of derivatives are set out in the following table.

Contract	Notional amount/ payment provision	Underlying	Initial investment	Future settlement
A futures contract to buy 1,000 barrels of crude oil at $60 a barrel in one month and the contract is not entered into for the physical delivery of oil for the entity's normal business usage requirements	1,000 barrels of crude oil	Price of oil barrels	$0	Yes – one month
A forward to buy $500 for £300 in one year	$500 (or £300)	£/$ exchange rate	£0	Yes – one year
An option to buy 80,000 shares in Entity B at CU75 per share in one month. The option costs CU1.1m	80,000 shares	Entity B's share price	CU1.1m	Yes – one month
A pay LIBOR + 25 basis points, receive fixed 5% interest rate swap over CU100m, settled quarterly	CU100m	LIBOR	CU0	Yes – quarterly
A pay floating £ on £100m, receive floating US$ on $170m currency swap, settled annually	£100m or $170m	£/$ exchange rate	£0	Yes – annually
A contract to receive CU10m if Entity A's share price increases by CU5 per share at the end of six-months. The initial investment is CU1.0m	Payment provision	Entity A's share price	CU1.0m	Yes – six months
A pay variable Euro amount based on the entity's sales, receive £ at a fixed exchange rate of €1.5:£1 based on the entity's sales, settled monthly	Variable notional	€/£ exchange rate and sales volume	£0	Yes – monthly

Contract	Notional amount/ payment provision	Underlying	Initial investment	Future settlement
A 5-year interest rate cap over CU100m. The cap will pay if LIBOR increases beyond 8%. The premium paid to enter into the cap is CU1.0m.	CU100m	LIBOR	CU1.0m	Yes – if, during the 5-year period, LIBOR exceeds 8%.

The definition of a derivative is very broad and, therefore, can capture many contractual arrangements that traditionally would not be considered derivatives. One example is bets in the gaming industry. A bookmaker will take a bet from a customer on the outcome of a specified event (e.g. a horse race, general election or football match) in cash for stated or variable odds. When the event occurs, depending on the outcome, the bookmaker will pay any winnings to the customer. The contract for the bet is no different from a derivative contract without a notional amount and with a payment provision. The bookmaker has written an option to the customer, where the bookmaker will receive an up-front premium in return for bearing potential downside risk should the uncertain event occur.

When the customer does not 'fix' the odds (i.e. has variable odds), the derivative will be far less sensitive to changes in the probability of the uncertain event occurring and, therefore, the derivative will be far less sensitive to changes in market prices. However, when the holder of the bet 'fixes' the odds, the fair value of the bet will change with changes in the probability of the uncertain event occurring.

The bookmaker will take bets on many different outcomes for one event and expects to make a profit irrespective of that event's outcome. If a bookmaker has taken too many bets from customers on one outcome, it may 'lay off' bets with another bookmaker (i.e. it enters into an offsetting bet to lay off the risk). This is a form of economic hedging. The bookmaker cannot apply hedge accounting because a derivative is not a qualifying hedged item (see **chapter B9**). As such, in accordance with IFRS 9, bookmakers should recognise all bets, whether written or purchased, as derivative assets and liabilities measured at fair value through profit or loss.

In May 2007, the IFRIC (now the IFRS Interpretations Committee) issued a rejection notice on gaming transactions stating that an unsettled wager is likely to meet the definition of a derivative and will therefore be accounted for under IAS 39 (now IFRS 9). The IFRIC recognised that, in other situations, a gaming institution does not take a position against a customer but instead provides services to manage the organisation of games between two or more gaming parties. In these circumstances, the gaming institution earns a commission regardless of the outcome of the wager and, therefore, it is likely that the commission would meet the definition of revenue and would be recognised when the conditions in IAS 18 *Revenue* (now IFRS 15 *Revenue from Contracts with Customers*) were met.

5 Presentation of derivatives

5.1 Current versus non-current

Where assets and liabilities are not presented in the statement of financial position in order of liquidity, derivatives will need to be presented as current and non-current assets, and current and non-current liabilities in accordance with IAS 1 *Presentation of Financial Statements*.

A derivative that has a maturity of less than 12 months from the end of the reporting period or has a maturity greater than 12 months but is expected to be settled 12 twelve months should be presented as a current asset or liability in the statement of financial position. A derivative that has a maturity of more than 12 months from the end of the reporting period and is not intended to be settled within 12 months will be presented as a non-current asset or liability.

Prior to the issue of *Improvements to IFRSs* in May 2008, there was ambiguity as to whether derivatives with a maturity greater than twelve months that are not intended to be settled within twelve months and were not part of a designated and effective hedge accounting relationship could be presented as non-current because these instruments also met the definition of held for trading in IFRS 9:AppendixA. An amendment to IAS 1 included as part of *Improvements to IFRSs* clarified that, in such instances, the derivatives should be presented as non-current because the derivative is not held primarily for trading purposes.

For guidance on the presentation of embedded derivatives see **section 13** of **chapter B5**.

5.2 Presentation in profit or loss

5.2.1 Fair value gains and losses on derivatives in hedge accounting relationships

IAS 39 and IFRS 9 provide limited guidance on the appropriate presentation in profit or loss of gains and losses on derivatives in highly effective hedge accounting relationships. However, an analogy can be drawn with the principle in IFRS 9 Guidance on Implementation G.2 that describes how cash flows arising from hedging instruments should be classified in statements of cash flows. The implementation guidance states that cash flows arising from hedging instruments are classified as operating, investing or financing activities on the basis of the classification of the cash flows arising from the hedged item. Therefore, it appears appropriate that gains and losses in highly effective hedge accounting relationships are presented in the same line in the statement of comprehensive income as the hedged item affects profit or loss. If gains and losses are material, separate presentation of those gains and losses in profit or loss would be required. An item that is not sufficiently material to warrant separate presentation on the face of the statement of comprehensive income may nevertheless be sufficiently material for it to be presented separately in the notes. [IAS 1:30]

5.2.2 Fair value gains and losses on derivatives that are economic hedges

IFRS 9 requires gains and losses on derivatives to be reported in profit or loss when hedge accounting is not applied. However, the Standard does not specify where such gains and losses would be presented within profit or loss.

Example 5.2.2

Presentation of non-hedge accounting derivative

Entity A enters into a derivative contract (forward contract) to hedge a foreign currency cash flow under a highly probable forecast revenue stream. The entity does not apply hedge accounting.

Presentation of the gains and losses on the derivative within revenue or elsewhere in operating profit is not precluded, provided that the chosen presentation is applied consistently from period to period to all similar items and follows the nature of the transaction to which it is linked. The policy adopted should be disclosed in the financial statements.

B5 Embedded derivatives

Contents

1 Introduction

The definition of an embedded derivative and the principle of separation of embedded derivatives are relatively simple, but the application is complicated because most of the guidance in IFRS 9 is provided by means of examples. Furthermore, the scope is wide because an entity will need to consider whether embedded derivatives may reside in contracts other than financial instruments. Embedded derivatives can be found in any contract other than a financial asset within the scope of IFRS 9, such as a lease, an insurance contract, or a sale or a purchase contract.

The challenge extends beyond searching for all embedded derivatives. Once an embedded derivative has been found, it must then be determined whether the embedded derivative needs to be separately accounted for under IFRS 9. Not all embedded derivatives are required to be separated out from the host contract in which they reside.

Embedded derivatives that are required to be separated are accounted for in the same way as stand-alone derivatives, i.e. at fair value with gains and losses recognised in profit or loss at each measurement date, unless the embedded derivative qualifies as an effective hedging instrument in a cash flow or a net investment hedge of a foreign operation.

Embedded derivative may potentially require separation in any contractual arrangement, except when the host contract is a financial asset in the scope of IFRS 9. For financial assets in the scope of IFRS 9, an entity is not required to assess embedded derivatives because the classification model in IFRS 9 requires the entire instrument to either be measured at amortised cost or fair value. IFRS 9 does not permit an embedded derivative to be separated and recognised separately from the financial asset. This chapter is therefore relevant in the accounting for contractual arrangements where the host contract is outside the scope of IFRS 9, or within the scope of IFRS 9 but is a financial liability.

2 Definitions

IFRS 9 states that an embedded derivative is a component of a hybrid (combined) instrument that also includes a non-derivative host contract that is not an asset within the scope of IFRS 9 – with the effect that some of the cash flows of the combined instrument vary in a way similar to a stand-alone derivative. An embedded derivative causes some or all of the cash flows that otherwise would be required by the contract to be modified according to a specified interest rate, financial instrument price, commodity price, foreign exchange rate, index of prices or rates or other variable (provided in the case of a non-financial variable that the variable is not specific to a party to the contract, see **2.1** in **chapter B4**). [IFRS 9:4.3.1]

The hybrid contract is the entire contract, within which is an embedded derivative. The host contract is the main body of the contract, excluding the embedded derivative. The diagram and examples below illustrate the application of these terms.

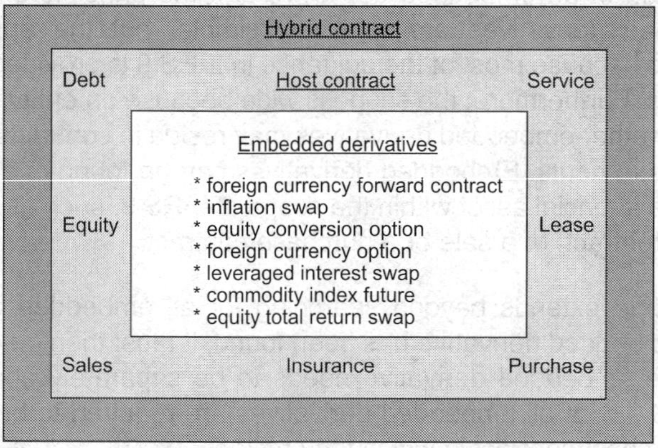

Example 2A

Debt host contract

Entity X issues a bond that is convertible into ordinary shares of Entity Y. The hybrid contract is the convertible bond; the host contract is the bond liability, and the embedded derivative is the conversion option.

Example 2B

Lease host contract

Entity A enters into a lease with an inflation factor, such that each year rentals are adjusted for changes in a retail price index. The hybrid contract is the entire lease; the host is the lease contract, and the embedded derivative is the adjustment to the retail price index.

Example 2C

Executory host contract

Entity T, a UK entity whose functional currency is Sterling, enters into a contract to sell a non-financial item in US dollars. The hybrid contract is the entire sale contract which will be settled in US dollars; the host contract is the Sterling sale contract; the embedded derivative is the foreign exchange Sterling/US dollar forward contract.

A derivative that is attached to a financial instrument but is contractually transferable independently of that instrument, or has a different counterparty from that instrument, is not an embedded derivative but a separate financial instrument. [IFRS 9:4.3.1]

Example 2D

Contractually separate derivative

Entity A issues floating rate debt. To protect itself against rising interest rates, it purchases an interest rate cap, capping interest payable at 8 per cent. The cap is contractually separate from the debt, so that it is not an embedded derivative but a free-standing derivative.

Entity A could have instead issued floating rate debt, where the debt instrument itself is capped such that, once interest rates rise above 8 per cent, interest payable is restricted to 8 per cent until rates fall below that level. In this case, there is an embedded derivative within the debt (i.e. the interest rate cap), and this cap would need to be assessed to see if it should be separately accounted for.

3 Separation conditions

Not all embedded derivatives should be separated from their host contracts. An embedded derivative is separated from its host contract and accounted for separately as a stand-alone derivative if the host contract is not an asset in the scope of IFRS 9 and all of the following criteria are met:

[IFRS 9:4.3.3]

(a) the economic characteristics and risks of the embedded derivative are not closely related to the economic risks and characteristics of the host contract;

(b) a separate instrument with the same terms as the embedded derivative would meet the definition of a derivative; and

(c) the hybrid instrument is not measured at fair value with changes in fair value recognised in profit or loss (i.e. a derivative that is embedded in a financial liability at fair value through profit or loss is not separated).

Condition (b) above means that an embedded feature should only be separated from its host contract if it meets the definition of a derivative, i.e.:

- it has an underlying;
- it involves no initial net investment (or an initial net investment that is smaller than would be required for other types of contracts that would be expected to have a similar response to changes in market factors); and
- it is settled at a future date.

See **section 2** of **chapter B4** for a detailed discussion on the definition of a derivative.

Example 3A

No underlying

A lease contract contains a provision that rentals increase by CU100 each year. The price adjustment feature does not meet the definition of a derivative on a stand-alone basis because its value does not change in response to changes of some 'underlying'; there is no underlying.

The condition in IFRS 9:4.3.3(c) (see above) means that any financial liability that is held at fair value with changes in fair value recognised through profit or loss should not be assessed to see if it contains any embedded derivatives. Any embedded derivative that is not closely related to its host and meets the definition of a derivative will be accounted for as if it were a stand-alone derivative – i.e. measured at fair value, with changes in fair value recognised in profit or loss. If the entire contract is currently accounted for at fair value, the embedded derivative is automatically accounted for at fair value and, therefore, it is not required to be separated.

An entity can elect to designate a financial liability in the scope of IFRS 9 as at FVTPL at initial recognition even though the instrument would not meet the definition of held for trading (see **7.1.2** in **chapter B3**). This option is available when the financial liability is a hybrid contract containing one or more embedded derivatives, unless:

[IFRS 9:4.3.5]

(a) the embedded derivative does not significantly modify the cash flows that otherwise would be required by the contract; or

(b) it is clear with little or no analysis when a similar hybrid instrument is first considered that separation of the embedded derivative is prohibited, as in the case of a prepayment option embedded in a loan that permits the holder to prepay the loan for approximately its amortised cost (see **7.1**).

Designating a hybrid financial liability as at FVTPL may provide benefit to entities with more complex instruments where the search for and analysis of embedded derivatives significantly increases the cost of compliance with IFRS 9. This approach will also benefit entities that issue structured products (e.g. equity-linked notes or callable range-accrual notes) which may contain more than one embedded derivative that is not closely related to the host liability contract. For issuers of these instruments who normally invest in derivatives as an economic hedge of the issued notes, measuring the hybrid instrument at fair value reduces the accounting mismatch that would have resulted had the host contract been measured at amortised cost. Furthermore, for these more complex instruments, the fair value of the combined contract may be significantly easier to measure and, therefore, provide more reliable information than the fair value of only those embedded derivatives that are required to be separated. [IFRS 9:BCZ4.69]

Example 3B

FVTPL measurement of a contract over a non-financial item

An entity enters into a forward contract to purchase wheat. The contract meets the definition of a derivative, but does not meet the 'expected purchase, sale or usage requirements' scope exemption because the entity has a history of net cash settling similar contracts (see **2.5** in **chapter B1**). Embedded in the forward contract is a price adjustment feature that if the retail price index increases by 3 per cent during the term of the contract, the contracted price will be doubled.

Because the contract is within the scope of IFRS 9 and meets the definition of a derivative, it will be accounted for at FVTPL. The embedded derivative will automatically be accounted for at FVTPL and, therefore, no further consideration of embedded derivatives is necessary.

The condition in IFRS 9:4.3.3(a) (see above) is the most difficult of the three bifurcation criteria to assess because there is no definition of 'closely related'. Rather than define 'closely related', Appendix B to IFRS 9 provides two illustrative lists: one of examples of embedded derivatives that are closely related to their hosts and the other of examples of embedded derivatives that are not closely related to their hosts.

When an embedded derivative is not included in one of these two lists, a significant degree of judgement will be required and conclusions may need to be drawn by analogy to the specific examples given. Ultimately, the conclusion reached should be consistent with the underlying principle that an embedded derivative should be separated from its host contract when its economic characteristics and risks differ from those of the host contract.

In summary, the following decision tree can be used to determine whether an embedded derivative needs to be separated from its host contract.

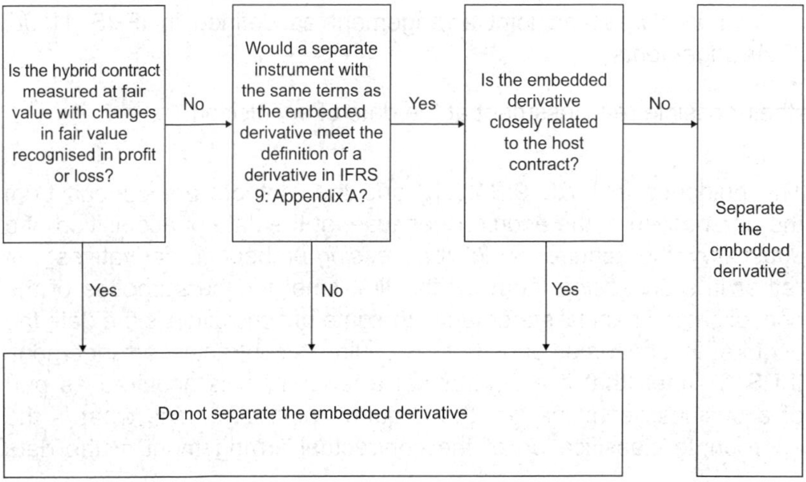

If it is determined that an embedded derivative is closely related to the host contract, it should not be separated from the host contract because the entire hybrid contract is accounted for in accordance with the relevant Standard that deals with the host contract. For example, if an embedded derivative in a lease contract is deemed to be closely related to the lease host, then the entire contract is accounted for in accordance with IAS 17 *Leases*.

If an identified embedded derivative is not closely related to the host contract, then it must be separately accounted for as if it were a free-standing derivative. This is considered further in **section 12**.

IFRS 9:B4.3.11 provides guidance on whether an entity should assess whether embedded derivatives are closely related at the time the entity first becomes a party to the contract or on an ongoing basis. IFRS 9 prohibits reassessment of whether an embedded derivative is closely related unless there is a change in the terms of the contract that significantly modifies the cash flows that would otherwise be required under the (original) contract. The significance of the change in cash flows is evaluated by considering the extent of the change in the cash flows of the embedded derivative, the host contract or both, and whether these changes are significant relative to the previously expected cash flows of the contract.

The guidance in IFRS 9:B4.3.11 described immediately above does not apply to embedded derivatives acquired in:

[IFRS 9:B4.3.12]

(a) a business combination (as defined in IFRS 3 *Business Combinations*);

(b) a combination of entities or businesses under common control as described in IFRS 3; or

(c) the formation of a joint venture as defined in IAS 31 *Interests in Joint Ventures* and joint arrangement as defined in IFRS 11 *Joint Arrangements*

or their possible reassessment at the date of acquisition.*

The guidance in IFRS 9:B4.3.12 and the footnote are curious from the perspective of the acquirer because, at the date of acquisition of a subsidiary, the acquirer is not *reassessing* embedded derivatives, but rather it is *assessing* them for the first time; for the purposes of the consolidated financial statements, the date of acquisition is the date the acquirer first becomes party to the acquiree's contractual arrangement. IFRS 3 states that if a contractual arrangement is acquired as part of a business combination, the acquirer must determine what is the appropriate classification of the contractual arrangement at the date

* IFRS 3 addresses the acquisition of contracts with embedded derivatives in a business combination.

of acquisition because this is the date of initial recognition. At the date of acquisition, for contracts that are not measured at fair value through profit or loss, the acquirer will need to consider whether the contractual arrangement includes any embedded derivatives that require separation.

For the acquiree, the accounting for a hybrid contract is not affected by the acquisition as in the acquired entity the contractual arrangements in the acquiree continue to be recognised, i.e. the acquisition date is not the initial recognition date for the acquiree. Unless the terms of the hybrid contract are changed as a result of the acquisition, with the effect that the cash flows are significantly modified, any embedded derivative will not be reassessed.

The acquirer's determination as to whether or not an embedded derivative is closely related to a host contract at the date of acquisition may differ to the determination arrived at by the acquiree when it first recognised the same contract. Differences are not uncommon because the determinations are based on the economic conditions and particular circumstances at different dates.

A first-time adopter of IFRSs is required to make its assessment on the basis of conditions existing at the later of the date it first became a party to the contract and the date a reassessment is required. In all cases, IFRS 9:B4.3.11 should be applied retrospectively.

Example 3C

Reassessment of embedded derivatives: common currency

Entity G operates in Country Y and had entered into long-dated supply contracts denominated in US dollars. When Entity G entered into the contracts, an assessment was made as to whether the US dollar was considered to be a 'common currency' per IFRS 9:B4.3.8(d)(iii) with a view to establishing whether an embedded derivative would need to be separated out. At the time Entity G entered into the contracts, the US dollar was considered a common currency for Country Y. The functional currency of Entity G and the counterparty to the contracts is not US dollars.

At the end of the current reporting period, the US dollar is no longer considered a common currency in Country Y. Entities within that country now use the domestic currency instead because the domestic currency is now traded cross-border and is considered a 'hard' currency by other countries.

Entity G should not revisit the embedded derivative assessment it made when it originally entered into the contracts because the terms of the arrangement have not changed. The accounting treatment is unchanged even though, if Entity G entered into the same contract at the end of the current reporting period, the US dollar would not be considered a common currency and an embedded derivative would need to be recognised.

It should be noted that, as part of the IASB's annual improvements project, the Board proposed amending the requirements of IFRS 9:B4.3.8(d)(iii). However, after issuing the exposure draft of annual improvements, the IFRIC (now the IFRS Interpretations Committee) agreed to remove the issue from its agenda (see **10.5**).

Example 3D

Reassessment of embedded derivatives: change in correlation of energy prices

Entity T, a coal-fired power station, entered into contracts to supply electricity prior to the deregulation of the energy market. The price paid for the supply of electricity was partly linked to the gas price. Entity T always intended to physically deliver electricity to the counterparty and, therefore the supply contract was always considered to be an executory contract that was outside the scope of IFRS 9. At the date the contract was entered into, the prices for gas and electricity were highly correlated and, therefore, Entity T considered the linkage to gas prices was a closely related embedded derivative.

Following deregulation of the market, the two prices are no longer highly correlated and, if Entity T entered into the contract today, it would conclude that the linkage to gas prices is an embedded derivative that is not closely related to the electricity supply contract. Entity T does not revisit its assessment regarded embedded derivatives made when it entered into the electricity supply contract because the terms of the arrangement are unchanged. This is the case even though, if Entity T entered into the same contract today, it would conclude that the embedded derivative should be separated.

Example 3E

Reassessment of embedded derivatives: novation within group

Group A has a US dollar functional currency subsidiary, Subsidiary B, which enters into contracts to sell non-financial items at a fixed future date with a Euro functional third-party counterparty, outside of Group A, called Entity D. The contract is denominated in US dollars.

The foreign currency embedded derivative is not separately recognised because Subsidiary B has a US dollar functional currency and is a substantial party to the contract. In Group A's consolidated financial statements, the same treatment is applied.

Sometime later, Subsidiary B novates the contract to a fellow subsidiary, Subsidiary C, which has a Sterling functional currency. At the date of novation, there are no changes to the terms of the contract other than that Subsidiary C has stepped into Subsidiary B's place as the seller. Subsidiary C is a principal to the transaction following the novation.

In the individual financial statements of Subsidiary C, at the novation date it becomes a party to the contract for the first time and, therefore, must consider whether the contract has any embedded derivatives. The contract is not denominated in either Subsidiary C's or Entity D's functional currency and, therefore, a non-closely related embedded derivative must be recognised by Subsidiary C, being a currency forward contract between Sterling and US dollar.

In Group A's consolidated financial statements, because the group is presented as a single economic entity, there has been no change in the contractual terms of the contract and, therefore, the group would not reassess the embedded derivative assessment it made when Subsidiary B entered into the arrangement.

IFRS 9 does not address remeasurement issues arising from a reassessment of embedded derivatives. This will require careful consideration depending on particular facts and circumstances.

Example 3F

Reassessment of embedded derivatives: modification to terms

Entity B, a Euro functional currency entity is party to a contract to purchase a fixed quantity of electricity at a future date for £10 million (€12 million at the spot rate at inception of the contract of €1.2:£1). The electricity will always be physically delivered under the contract and will be used for Entity B's production processes. The contract is a hybrid contractual arrangement containing a host contract that is an executory contract to purchase electricity in Euros and a non-closely related embedded foreign currency derivative based on the guidance in **10.5**. The two elements are:

(i) non-closely related embedded €/£ forward with an initial fair value of zero to buy €12 million, sell £10 million; and

(ii) host purchase contract to buy a set quantity of electricity with a purchase price of €12 million (that matches the Euro leg of the foreign currency forward in (i) above).

Upon entering into the contract, Entity B separates out the non-closely related foreign currency embedded derivative and measures it at FVTPL.

At a later date, there is a contractual modification to the terms such that the currency in which the contract is denominated changes to the functional currency of Entity B, i.e. Euro. The embedded derivative had a negative fair value at the date of modification of €1 million. Due to the redenomination of the currency of the contract, Entity B pays the counterparty €1 million which is equal to the value of the change in contractual terms of the arrangement. Entity B derecognises the embedded derivative.

The change in denomination of the contract in this case is a significant modification of the contract's cash flows that triggers reassessment under IFRS 9. Because the denomination of the contract after modification is in the functional currency of Entity B, the contract no longer has a non-closely related embedded derivative and the entire arrangement will be accounted for prospectively as an executory contract outside the scope of IFRS 39.

Care is needed in determining how the carrying amount of an embedded derivative is treated when the embedded derivative is no longer closely related. This is particularly relevant when the modification occurs without cash consideration or when the cash consideration differs from the value of the embedded derivative derecognised. The carrying amount of the embedded derivative, being its fair value, at the date of modification of the contract, will be recognised in profit or loss, remain in the statement of financial position or be recognised in other comprehensive income in the period or future periods depending on the substance of the modified terms of the contract. Consideration will need to be given as to whether the pricing of the remaining contract is modified to reflect the value of the change in terms of the arrangement; whether any other goods or services are provided or received as part of the modification; or an equity transaction occurs between the entity and the counterparty.

Consideration will also need to be given to the substance of the modification when a non-closely related embedded derivative is recognised for the first time following the modification of a contract where previously the embedded derivative was closely related. The substance of the arrangement will determine whether, having recognised the derivative at fair value, the counter-entry affects profit or loss, the statement of financial position or other comprehensive income.

4 Terms of the embedded derivative and the debt host contract

The term 'debt host contract' that is applied below refers to debt instruments that are issued by an entity (and that, therefore, are financial liabilities).

The terms of the host contract must reflect the stated or implied terms of the hybrid contract (i.e. the embedded feature must be clearly present in the hybrid contract). In the absence of implied or stated terms a judgement may have to be made, but an entity cannot create cash flows that do not contractually exist.

Example 4A

Fixed versus floating debt host contract (1)

Entity A issues floating rate debt. The contract cannot be seen as fixed rate debt with an embedded interest rate swap that swaps fixed rate cash flows into floating rate cash flows. The terms of the contract do not contain any fixed cash flows, so there can be no embedded feature with fixed rate cash flows.

Example 4B

Fixed versus floating debt host contract (2)

A 5-year debt instrument has fixed annual payments, and a principal repayment at the end of the contract which is conditional on changes in the FTSE 100 index. This instrument must be treated as a host fixed rate debt contract with an embedded equity feature. It cannot be classified as floating rate debt with an embedded equity swap that has an offsetting floating rate leg. The host is a fixed rate contract because there are no variable interest rate payments in it.

Embedded non-optional derivatives must be determined so that they have a fair value of zero at inception of the contract. If this was not stipulated, it would be possible to split one instrument into an infinite number and variety of hosts with embedded derivatives. This could be done by separating embedded derivatives with terms that create leverage, asymmetry or another risk exposure that does not exist in the hybrid contract. [IFRS 9:B4.3.3 & IFRS 9 Guidance on Implementation C.1]

Embedded optional derivatives will not necessarily have a fair value (or intrinsic value) of zero at inception. The fair value of such an embedded derivative will depend on its strike price or rate. Therefore, the separation of an option from a hybrid contract should be based on the stated terms of the option feature. [IFRS 9:B4.3.3 & IFRS 9 Guidance on Implementation C.2)]

5 Determination of host contract: debt vs. equity

If a hybrid contract has both debt and equity features, a determination must be made as to whether the host contract is debt or equity. Often, this will be a relatively straightforward task because the 'majority' of the contract will behave either more like debt or more like equity.

If the host contract has no stated or predetermined maturity and represents a residual interest in the net assets of the issuer, then its economic characteristics and risks are those of an equity instrument. Any embedded derivative would need to possess equity characteristics related to the same entity to be regarded as closely related. If the host contract is not an equity instrument and meets the definition of a financial instrument, then its economic characteristics and risks are those of a debt instrument. [IFRS 9:B4.3.2]

More commonly, the host contract will not represent a residual interest in an entity and, thus, the economic characteristics and risks of a financial host contract will be considered that of a debt instrument. For example, even though an overall hybrid instrument may provide for repayment of the principal linked to the market price of the issuer's ordinary shares, the host contract may not involve any existing or potential residual rights in the net assets of the issuer (i.e. rights of ownership) so would not be an equity instrument. The host contract is a debt instrument, and the embedded derivative, the indexation to the market price of the issuer, is not closely related to the host contract.

Example 5A

Debt host contract (1)

Entity A issues a five-year 'debt' instrument purchased by Entity B with a principal amount of CU1 million that is indexed to the share price of Entity C. At maturity, Entity B will receive from Entity A the principal amount plus or minus the change in the fair value of 10,000 shares of Entity C. No separate interest payments are made by Entity A. Entity A does not classify the debt instrument as at FVTPL. Entity A concludes that the instrument is a hybrid instrument with an embedded derivative because of the equity-indexed principal.

The host contract is a debt instrument because the hybrid instrument has a stated maturity, i.e. it does not meet the definition of an equity instrument (IAS 32:11 and IAS 32:16). The embedded non-optional derivative is separated so as to have an initial fair value of zero (See IFRS 9 Guidance on Implementation C.1). Because the embedded derivative has a fair value of zero, an amount equal to the issue proceeds, being the fair value of the entire instrument at initial recognition, is recognised as a debt instrument. The debt instrument is accounted for as a zero coupon debt instrument. Thus, in accounting for the host instrument, Entity A imputes interest over five years being the difference between the amount allocated to the debt instrument at initial recognition and the redemption amount of the debt host contract.

Example 5B

Debt host contract (2)

Entity A issues an instrument to Entity B that has the legal form of shares, and embedded within the shares is a put option allowing Entity B to put the 'shares' back to Entity A for the higher of:

(i) the fair market value of the shares; and

(ii) an amount based on the initial investment with compounded interest based on LIBOR.

The option is exercisable five years after the initial investment is made.

While the instruments have the legal form of shares, they do not evidence a residual interest in Entity A. Entity B will receive a rate of return that is at least equal to the return on a debt instrument. Entity A should account for the instruments as a debt host contract with an embedded derivative not closely related to the host contract.

6 Multiple embedded derivatives

It is possible for a contract to contain more than one embedded derivative. In such circumstances, each embedded derivative should to be individually assessed to see if it is closely related to the host contract.

Example 6A

Conversion feature and put option

Entity A issues convertible bonds under which the conversion feature may result in Entity A issuing its equity shares to the holder of the bonds. The conversion feature fails the definition of equity in IAS 32 and, therefore, it is not a compound instrument; rather it is a financial liability in its entirety. In addition to the conversion feature, the holder of the bonds can choose to put the bonds back to Entity A. When Entity A assesses for embedded derivatives, it will be necessary to consider both the conversion option and the put option.

When contracts contain multiple embedded derivatives, they are generally treated as a single compound embedded derivative. Only if the embedded derivatives relate to different risk exposures and are readily separable and independent of each other are they accounted for separately from each other. [IFRS 9:B4.3.4]

IFRS 9:B4.3.4 clearly states that the embedded derivatives should only be accounted for separately from each other when (1) they relate to different risk exposures and (2) they are readily separable and independent of each other. However, it is not clear whether the requirement to treat multiple embedded derivatives as a single compound derivative applies both to the assessment of whether the embedded derivatives are closely related to the host contract and the accounting for bifurcated derivatives, or whether it applies solely to the accounting for bifurcated derivatives. Accordingly, two accounting treatments are acceptable.

The first approach is to regard IFRS 9:B4.3.4 as applying to the assessment of the embedded derivatives and the accounting for bifurcated derivatives. The second approach is to regard IFRS 9:B4.3.4 as applying only in accounting for bifurcated derivatives. Because both approaches can be supported under IFRSs, an entity should determine as an accounting policy choice whether multiple embedded derivatives should be assessed as a single compound instrument or assessed individually. The accounting policy selected should be applied consistently to all hybrid instruments.

Example 6B

Multiple embedded derivative with the same risk

Entity Y issues debt for CU100 with a par value of CU100 and a maturity of 10 years. Key terms of the debt instrument are as follows.

- Interest rate – the interest rate is a floating rate of 3-month LIBOR plus a fixed margin.
- Interest rate floor (embedded derivative 1) - the interest rate will not be lower than X per cent for any period. The rate is set such that the interest rate floor is in the money at issuance of the debt (i.e. the floor is above the market rate of 3-month LIBOR plus the fixed margin at issuance of the contract).
- Prepayment options (embedded derivative 2) – Entity Y may at any time, voluntarily prepay the principal and related accrued interest outstanding in whole or in part plus a penalty amount of 1 per cent of the amount prepaid.

The entire instrument is not accounted for at fair value through profit or loss (FVTPL) because it is neither held for trading nor designated as at FVTPL. Other than the two embedded derivatives described, there are no other embedded derivatives and no transaction costs associated with the instrument.

A question arises whether both embedded derivatives should be assessed as a single compound instrument in determining if they are closely related to the host contract, or should they be assessed individually?

Approach 1 – IFRS 9:B4.3.4 applies to the assessment of the embedded derivatives and the accounting for bifurcated derivatives.

If this approach is applied in the circumstances described, the two embedded derivatives should be assessed as a single compound embedded derivative because they both relate to the same risk (interest rate risk), and they are not independent of each other because the likelihood of the prepayment option being exercised depends on whether the interest rate floor is in the money. Because a component of the compound embedded derivative (the interest rate floor) is not closely related (based on the floor being in the money at inception and the guidance in IFRS 9:B4.3.8(b) (see **7.7.3**), the compound embedded derivative as a whole is assessed as not closely related and bifurcated from the host contract (assuming the other criteria in IFRS 9:4.3.3 are met). Applying this approach, the prepayment option is not individually assessed to determine if it is closely related.

Approach two – IFRS 9:B4.3.4 applies only in accounting for bifurcated derivatives.

Under this approach, only embedded derivatives that individually meet all of the criteria for separation under IFRS 9:4.3.3 should be treated as embedded derivatives subject to separation. IFRS 9:B4.3.4 only applies to the resulting embedded derivatives that meet all of the IFRS 9:4.3.3 criteria for separation (i.e. it applies after assessment of what needs to be separated and not before).

When assessed individually, the interest floor is determined not to be closely related (based on the floor being in the money at inception and the guidance in IFRS 9:B4.3.8(b). Therefore, assuming that the other IFRS 9:4.3.3 criteria are met, the interest rate floor should be accounted for separately from the host debt contract. The prepayment option also needs to be assessed individually to determine if it is closely related on the basis of the guidance in IFRS 9:B4.3.5(e)(i) (see **7.1**). Only if that individual assessment results in the prepayment option being considered not closely related will the floor and the prepayment option be viewed as a compound embedded derivative.

Assuming Entity Y chooses as its accounting policy to assess the two embedded derivatives individually (i.e. approach two above) the interest rate floor that has been identified as a non-closely related embedded derivative will be separated. However, when assessing whether the prepayment option is individually closely related, IFRS 9:B4.3.5(e)(i) requires a comparison of the exercise price of the option to the "amortised cost of the host debt instrument". For the purpose of this assessment, should the host debt contract include the non-closely related interest rate floor?

IFRS 9:B4.3.5(e) states that the assessment of whether a call or put option is closely related to the host contract is made before separating the equity element of a convertible debt instrument in accordance with IAS 32 *Financial Instruments: Presentation*. However, it is not clear whether this paragraph establishes a specific exception that applies only in the case of an issuer of a compound instrument when an equity element is separated or whether this paragraph can be applied by analogy to other situations. Accordingly, two accounting treatments are acceptable.

Approach (a) – IFRS 9:B4.3.5(e) applies only in the case of an issuer of a compound instrument when an equity element is separated. Under this approach, the exception in IFRS 9:B4.3.5(e) is not relevant in this scenario and the prepayment option is assessed against the host contract excluding the interest rate floor. This is consistent with the general principle that the interest rate floor will be accounted for separately and therefore should not form part of the assessment of the remaining terms (i.e. the debt host including the prepayment option but without the floor).

The effect of excluding the floor from the host debt contract is that the amortised cost of the host instrument for the purpose of applying IFRS 9:B4.3.5(e)(i) would be determined as the difference between the fair value of the entire hybrid contract and the fair value of the embedded interest rate floor (liability) written by Entity Y. In the circumstances described, this results in an increased risk of the prepayment option being assessed as not closely related because the amortised cost of the host contract (excluding the floor) will be smaller.

Approach (b) – IFRS 9:B4.3.5(e) can be applied by analogy to other circumstances. Under this approach, the amortised cost of the instrument should include the interest rate floor. In the circumstances described, this would mean the amortised cost of the host contract for the purposes of the assessment under IFRS 9:B4.3.5(e) would start at the amortised cost of the entire hybrid contract (CU100) even though the interest rate floor will be recognised separately on the statement of financial position at initial recognition.

Because both approaches can be supported under IFRSs, an entity should determine an accounting policy choice to be applied consistently to all hybrid instruments.

If an embedded derivative must be separated from its host contract, but it cannot be valued, the entity must first determine both the fair value of the whole contract and the fair value of the host contract. The difference represents the fair value of the derivative instrument to be separated. [IFRS 9:B4.3.7] If an entity is unable to compute the fair value of the derivative on this basis, the entity must designate the entire instrument as at FVTPL. [IFRS 9:4.3.6]

7 Embedded derivatives in debt host contracts

Entities are required to assess for embedded derivatives in financial liabilities. Financial liabilities are discussed at some length in **chapter B3**. These include traditional debt contracts like bonds and bank borrowings, and also certain other securities that are in substance liabilities (e.g. mandatorily redeemable preference shares).

7.1 Put, call and prepayment options

Contractual terms that allow either party to terminate the contract early and accelerate the repayment of the outstanding principal, either in whole or in part, are often embedded derivatives. Examples of such terms include call options of the issuer, put options of the holder, and prepayment features.

These embedded derivatives are not closely related to the host debt contract unless the exercise price is approximately equal to the debt host contract's amortised cost on each exercise date. [IFRS 9:B4.3.5(e)(i)]

From the perspective of the issuer of a convertible debt instrument with an embedded call or put option feature, the assessment of whether the call or put option is closely related to the host debt contract is made before separating the equity element under IAS 32 as discussed in **section 3** of **chapter B3**. [IFRS 9:B4.3.5(e)]

Example 7.1A

Issuer call option

Entity A issues a five-year zero-coupon bond for CU75 million, with a face value of CU100 million. Embedded in the debt is a call option allowing Entity A to repay the debt after three years for CU90 million, when its amortised cost will be CU89 million. Because the repayment amount is approximately equal to its amortised cost on that date, the call option is closely related to the host contract and so is not separated from it.

If the terms were instead such that Entity A could call the debt at any time, but would have to redeem it at a fixed amount (e.g. at par of CU100 million), the call option would not be closely related because the repayment amount would not approximately equal the amortised cost on each date that the call can be exercised. For example, the week after issuing the bond (when the bond's amortised cost is approximately CU75 million), Entity A could call it back but would have to pay CU100 million to do so. This situation arises because the bond was issued at a substantial discount and, therefore, its amortised cost will not approximate to its par value except in the years close to its maturity.

Example 7.1B

Investor put option

Entity X issues 10-year bonds with a par value of CU1 million for proceeds of CU1 million. The bonds have a coupon of 10 per cent. Embedded in the bonds is a clause that allows the investors to put the bonds back to Entity X for CU1 million in the event the FTSE declines by 5 per cent. It is reasonably possible that the FTSE will decline by 5 per cent in the near future. The issue costs are insignificant.

The embedded put option would not be accounted for separately, even though the put option is contingent on an event that is not related to the host instrument (i.e. a trigger other than interest rates or credit). The tests in IFRS 9 relate to the exercise price (settlement amount), not the trigger. The likelihood of the put option being exercised is also irrelevant in determining whether the embedded derivative is closely related, although this will affect valuation. In this case, the bonds will be put back at an amount that approximates amortised cost. It is not relevant that the put option only becomes exercisable if an equity index performs in a particular manner.

Example 7.1C

Investor contingent put option

Entity A issues CU100 million 7 per cent cumulative preference shares. Dividends are payable quarterly subject to the availability of distributable profits. Issue costs are insignificant. The preference shares are puttable at par to Entity A for cash if interest rates move by 150 basis points. Any dividend that remains accumulated and not paid becomes payable when the shares are put to Entity A.

The embedded put option would not be separated from the host contract under the embedded derivative requirements. The preference shares are classified as a liability under IAS 32 (see **chapter B3**). The put feature is an option that is considered to be closely related to the host because the exercise price of the put option is the amortised cost of the preference shares.

Sometimes derivatives may be 'embedded' subsequent to the issuance of the instrument.

Example 7.1D

Remarketable put bonds

Entity X issues 10-year bonds with a 6 per cent coupon to a bank and receives proceeds of €103 million. The debt is puttable by the holder at the end of three years. The 3-year debt rate for vanilla debt instruments (i.e. those without put or call features) is 6 per cent. The bank staples a call option and sells the two instruments to an investor. This call option enables the bank to reacquire the bonds in the event that it wishes to exercise its put option inherent in the bond issued by Entity X.

A party other than the issuer (i.e. the bank) has stapled the call option into the debt instrument. Therefore, Entity X does not have to consider the accounting for the call option because Entity X is not a party to the call option.

A debt instrument that may be called by the issuer or put or prepaid by the holder must be assessed in order to determine whether these features are considered to be closely related. The outcome of this assessment is dependent on comparing the strike price under the option (i.e. the amount the issuer would pay the holder on exercise of the option) with the amortised cost of the debt host contract instrument. What is less clear is whether call, put and prepayment options that are likely to be exercised should be taken into account in determining amortised cost.

Consider the following example. A fixed rate debt instrument is issued at par with a 10-year term. The debt can be put by the holder any time after Year 5 for an amount equal to 110 per cent of par. If the issuer at initial recognition considers it likely that the holder will put at Year 5, the host contract could be considered a 10-year host redeeming at 100 per cent or a 5-year host that early redeems at 110 per cent. If the former approach is taken, the put option is not closely related because 110 per cent is not approximately equal to 100 per cent whereas, if the latter approach is taken, the put option would be closely related because 110 per cent would be equal to 110 per cent.

The above example illustrates that when a significant penalty is payable on early redemption, the accounting can differ depending on which approach is taken. Ironically, if an entity did take into account a put option that is likely to be exercised in determining the host contract it would result in that put option not being recognised. If the put option were less likely to be exercised, it would result in the put option being recognised.

Extending the example above, assume the holder can put at any time in the 10 years for an amount equal to 110 per cent of par. The issuer still believes it is most likely the holder will put at Year 5. If the issuer were to consider the 5-year put option as part of the amortised cost of the host contract, and thereby not recognise an embedded derivative for that put option, it would still need to consider whether the put options from Years 2 to 4 are closely related. If the host contract is considered a discounted instrument, issued for 100 per cent and redeemable at 110 per cent at Year 5, then some of the put options between Years 2 to 4 would be non-closely related embedded derivatives because their exercise price of 110 per cent would not be approximately equal to amortised cost.

If an early redemption in a debt instrument is reflected in the host contract's amortised cost when determining whether that features is closely related, it is not clear how an entity should account for the instrument if there is a subsequent change in the likelihood that the early redemption feature will be exercised. Applying the example above, if the issuer subsequently estimated the put option was now likely to be exercised after Year 5, two views exist. The first view is that the change in timing of cash flows is simply a remeasurement of estimated cash flows and the revised changes in cash flows should be discounted by the original effective interest rate in accordance with IFRS 9:B5.4.6. An alternative view is that the host contract is deemed a five year instrument; therefore, the right for the holder to put the instrument after Year 5 is equivalent to a term extension option which, if the extension is not at market interest rates, would be considered a non-closely related embedded derivative.

Certain prepayment options embedded in a debt host contract that are designed to ensure the lender is compensated for loss of interest when the borrower prepays are closely related to the debt host contract. Such prepayment options are not equal to the amortised cost of the debt host contract because the amount prepaid will include an adjustment to reflect the then market interest rate. IFRS 9:B4.3.5(e)(ii) states that a prepayment option is closely related to the host debt contract if the exercise price of the prepayment option reimburses the lender for an amount up to the approximate present value of lost interest for the remaining term of the host contract. Lost interest is the product of the principal amount prepaid multiplied by the interest rate differential. The interest rate differential is the excess of the effective interest rate of the host contract over the effective interest rate the entity would receive at the prepayment date if it reinvested the principal amount prepaid in a similar contract for the remaining term of the host contract.

A further consideration is whether the option is a prepayment option over an interest-only or a principal-only strip. The embedded derivative will be closely related provided that the host contract:

[IFRS 9:B4.3.8(e)]

(i) initially resulted from separating the right to receive contractual cash flows of a financial instrument that itself did not contain an embedded derivative; and

(ii) does not contain any terms not present in the original host debt.

IAS 39:AG33(e) was carried over unchanged from IAS 39 to IFRS 9, as IFRS 9:B4.3.8(e), when the embedded derivative guidance in IAS 39 was included in IFRS 9 in October 2010. This guidance was relevant when a prepayable loan was split into a principal and an interest only strip after origination and the holder applied IAS 39 in classifying and measurement the principal and/or interest only strip at initial recognition. However, this paragraph does not appear to be relevant for an entity applying IFRS 9 because the splitting of a loan into a principal and an interest only strip arises after origination of the lending and, therefore, would only be applicable to a holder of the principal and interest only strips. Because financial assets within the scope of IFRS 9 (such as loans, principal and interest only strips held) are not assessed for embedded derivatives, this paragraph does not appear to be relevant. Further, the borrower would owe the same amounts under its obligation after the loan has been split by a holder as it did prior to the split; consequently, its obligation would appear to be unchanged and, therefore, also would not be reassessed for embedded derivatives.

7.2 Term-extending features

When the term of the debt is extendable, and there is no concurrent adjustment to the approximate current market rate of interest at the time of the extension, the embedded term-extension option is not closely related to the host debt contract. To be closely related, the reset to market rates must result in a reset of both current interest rates and current credit spread for the issuer.

If an entity issues a debt instrument and the holder of that debt instrument writes a call option on the debt instrument to a third party, the issuer regards the call option as extending the term to maturity of the debt instrument provided that the issuer can be required to participate in or facilitate the remarketing of the debt instrument as a result of the call option being exercised. [IFRS 9:B4.3.5(b)]

Example 7.2A

Term-extension feature (1)

Entity X issues CU10 million fixed rate debt with an 8 per cent coupon and maturity of five years. At the end of five years, Entity X has an option to extend the term for an additional three years. If extended, the coupon will remain at 8 per cent. If the option is exercised, it will significantly extend the term of the debt and the coupon will not reset to current market rates. Therefore, this term-extending option is an embedded derivative that is not closely related to the host contract.

Example 7.2B

Term-extension feature (2)

Entity X issues debt of CU10 million with an 8 per cent coupon and a maturity of five years. If LIBOR increases by 200 basis points within any one year, the maturity of the bonds will be extended for another three years at the same 8 per cent coupon rate. The embedded derivative would be accounted for separately from the host contract because the coupon following extension does not reset to the current market rate.

The likelihood of LIBOR increasing by 200 basis points in a year is not a consideration when determining whether the embedded derivative is closely related. It will, however, affect the valuation of the embedded derivative. If the possibility of LIBOR increasing by 200 basis points is considered low, the value of the embedded derivative will be relatively small.

5-year fixed rate debt with an option to extend for three years (as described in **example 7.2A**) is economically no different from 8-year fixed rate debt that is puttable at the end of five years. However, the criteria for determining whether there is an embedded derivative in these instruments are different. As IFRS 9 has specific guidance on the accounting for prepayment options and term extension options, and that guidance differs, two instruments that are economically the same may be treated differently. An entity cannot separate a prepayment option if the debt is prepayable at its amortised cost, but would be required to separate out a term-extending option if that option did not result in the interest being reset to market rates.

An alternative accounting treatment for term-extension options is to treat them as loan commitments that may be outside the scope of IFRS 9. A term-extension option is a right to extend existing financing for a new period and therefore it can be argued is akin to a commitment to lend. Although a loan commitment meets the definition of a derivative, if it were to also meet the definition of a loan commitment and be outside the scope of IFRS 9 as described in IFRS 9:2.3 then it would not be subject to the embedded derivative requirements in IFRS 9 as an embedded derivative only requires separation if it is a derivative in the scope of IFRS 9. Such an approach would result in not applying the guidance on term-extension options as described above and detailed in IFRS 9:B4.3.5(b).

If an entity elects to apply the loan commitment exemption to term-extending features, this election should be a consistently applied accounting policy to all similar term-extending features that in the absence of applying that policy would be subject to IFRS 9:B4.3.5.(b).

7.3 Indexed interest and principal payments

When interest or principal payments in a debt contract are indexed to changes in a specified security price, commodity price, foreign exchange rate, or index of prices or rates, the host debt contract contains an embedded derivative.

Such an embedded derivative will not be closely related to the host debt contract if the amounts of interest or principal are indexed to the price of a commodity or to the change in value of an equity instrument. [IFRS 9:B4.3.5(b) & (c)]

Example 7.3A

Commodity price adjustment

Entity X issues 10-year notes with no stated coupon. Embedded in the notes is a clause that adjusts the interest paid by reference to changes in the price of corn.

The embedded derivative would be accounted for separately because the adjustment to interest payments based on changes in corn prices is not closely related to the host debt instrument.

Example 7.3B

Equity price adjustment

Entity X issues 10-year notes to a bank. The terms of the notes require interest paid to be adjusted based on changes in the share price of Entity Y.

The embedded derivative will be separated because the interest payments are indexed to changes in the share price of Entity Y and, therefore, the adjustment is not closely related to the host debt instrument.

Generally, an embedded derivative that adjusts interest and/or principal amounts paid on the debt contract will not be closely related to the host debt when the underlying that drives the value of the derivative is different from the economic factors that drive the value of the host debt contract. The guidance would equally apply to indexation to a basket of commodities or share indices like the FTSE 100.

Example 7.3C

Equity index adjustment

A bank issues 10-year notes with a coupon of 5 per cent to an entity. At maturity, the entity receives cash equal to the higher of the initial proceeds and an amount based on the Standard and Poor's 500 (S&P 500).

The embedded cash-settled S&P 500 call option is an embedded derivative that is not closely related to the host debt contract.

Even if the interest or principal payments are determined by changes in underlyings that are typically associated with debt (e.g. interest rates, inflation or creditworthiness of the issuer), there may still be an embedded derivative that is not closely related to the host debt contract (e.g. when interest or principal repayments are determined based on leveraged, complex or formulaic features).

With respect to interest rate and interest rate index features these features must be such that *either* the holder would not recover substantially all of its recognised investment *or* the issuer would pay more than twice the market rate of the host contract at inception (of issuing the instrument) *and* could result in a rate of return that is at least twice what the market return would be for a similar host contract (sometimes referred to as the 'double-double test'). [IFRS 9:B4.3.8(a)] The embedded derivative assessment is applied to the issuer of the debt instrument even though the assessment considers what is the return or loss to the investor.

Example 7.3D

Recovery of recognised investment (1)

Entity X issues CU10 million in debt with an 8 per cent coupon. However, if LIBOR increases by 500 basis points within any one year, the bonds mature and the holder receives CU8 million in total.

An embedded derivative exists and should be separately accounted for because there is a payment provision that may cause the holder not to recover substantially all of its recognised investment if LIBOR increases by 500 basis points.

In **example 7.3D**, the likelihood of LIBOR increasing by 500 basis points is not relevant when making this determination. The test in IFRS 9 is based around the possibility of the holder not recovering its recognised investment or obtaining double its initial rate of return. Even if it is unlikely that LIBOR will increase by 500 basis points, the contingent embedded derivative must be separated from the host contract. However, if the probability of this event occurring is low then the fair value of the embedded derivative at inception will be relatively small compared to the fair value of the host contract.

The condition that the holder will not recover substantially all of its recognised investment is only met if the holder can be forced to accept a settlement amount that is substantially below its recognised investment. If the terms of the contract permit, but do not require, the holder to settle the instrument in such a manner, then the feature is closely related to the host contract.

The 'double-double test' is performed at the date that the hybrid instrument is initially recognised. The first step is to determine whether there is a possible future interest rate scenario, no matter how remote, in which the embedded derivative would at least double the investor's initial return on the host contract. In making this assessment, it is important to differentiate the return on the host contract from the return on the hybrid contract. The host contract has terms identical to the hybrid contract being tested, except that it does not contain the embedded derivative. IFRS 9:B4.3.8(a) describes this step as requiring that the embedded derivative could at least double the holder's initial rate of return on the host contract. An embedded derivative that does not breach this threshold would be considered closely related to its host. If the embedded derivative does breach the threshold, a second step must be performed to determine whether it is closely related to the host contract. The second step is to review each interest rate scenario identified in the first step for which the investor's initial rate of return on the host contract would be doubled, and determine whether, for any of the scenarios, the embedded derivative would at the same time result in a rate of return that is at least twice what otherwise would be the then-current market return for a contract that has the same terms as the host contract and that involves a debtor with a credit quality similar to the issuer's credit quality at inception. If the embedded derivative does not breach the threshold, it would be considered closely related to its host contract. If the threshold is breached in any one of the scenarios then the embedded derivative would be considered not closely related to the host contract and it must be separated.

A vanilla variable rate debt instrument does not contain an embedded derivative even though the investor could pay a rate more than twice the rate at inception. A rate that is always equal to the current market rate is not an embedded derivative.

Example 7.3E

Double-double interest rate test (1)

On 1 January 20X1, an entity issues a bond where interest payments are linked to LIBOR. The bond also incorporates an interest rate cap whereby if LIBOR equals or exceeds 8 per cent at any interest rate reset date, the investor will receive a return of 10 per cent. On the date the entity issues the bond, it also could issue at par a variable rate bond not containing a cap that pays LIBOR minus 1 per cent. At 1 January 20X1, LIBOR is 5 per cent. The bond cannot be contractually settled such that the investor would not recover substantially all of its initial recorded investment in the bond.

To perform the first test in paragraph IFRS 9:B4.3.8(a), the issuer must determine whether there is any interest rate scenario, no matter how remote, under which the embedded derivative (the cap) would at least double the investor's initial rate of return on the host contract. This analysis is summarised in the following table.

A Interest rate change	B Return reflecting the effect of the cap	C Initial rate of return on the host (LIBOR - 1%)	D Initial rate of return on the host doubled	Is the first test met, i.e. is B > D?
0 – 7.99%	0 – 7.99%	4%	8%	No
8% and up	10%	4%	8%	Yes

Because the first test is met, the issuer must perform the second test described in paragraph IFRS 9:B4.3.8(a) to determine whether the embedded cap is closely related to its bond host. For this test, the issuer must determine, for each interest rate scenario identified above for which the investor's initial rate of return on the host contract would be doubled, whether the embedded cap would simultaneously result in a rate of return that is at least twice what otherwise would be the then-current market return for a contract that has the same terms as the host contract (i.e. has the same credit quality as the issuer at inception). The analysis for this test can be summarised as follows.

A Interest rate scenario identified in the first test above for which the cap would at least double the investor's initial rate of return on the host contract	B Return reflecting the effect of the cap under the interest rate scenario in A	C Current market rate of return for the host contract under the interest rate scenario in A (LIBOR - 1%)	Is the second test met (i.e. is B at least twice C for any scenario)?
8% and up	10%	7%	No

Because the first test in IFRS 9:B4.3.8(a) is met, but the second test is not, the embedded cap is considered closely related to the bond host.

Example 7.3F

Double-double interest rate test (2)

Entity B issues a 30-year variable rate debt to Entity A. The debt is indexed to the 3-month LIBOR rate plus 4 per cent. As of the date of issuance, the 3-month LIBOR rate was 2 per cent. The debt's terms also specify that if the 3-month LIBOR rate increases to 5 per cent, the debt issuer is required to pay 23 per cent for the remaining term of the bonds. The bond cannot be contractually settled such that the investor would not recover substantially all of its initial recorded investment in the bond.

If Entity B were to issue 30-year variable rate debt without any embedded derivatives (i.e. the interest rate reset feature), it would pay a coupon of 3-month LIBOR plus 6 per cent. Consequently, the initial rate of return on the host contract is 8 per cent (3-month LIBOR of 2 per cent plus 6 per cent). It is necessary to determine whether the embedded derivative could at least double the investor's initial rate of return on the host contract, which was 8 per cent at the date of issuance, in any of the possible interest rate environments. Therefore, when 3-month LIBOR increases to 5 per cent, the 23 per cent interest rate feature more than doubles the initial rate of return of 8 per cent on the host contract.

It is then necessary to perform an analysis to determine whether the embedded derivative results in a rate of return that is at least twice what otherwise would be the then-current market rate of return for a host contract when 3-month LIBOR is at 5 per cent. When 3-month LIBOR increases to 5 per cent, the rate of return on the host contract would be 11 per cent (3-month LIBOR of 5 per cent plus 6 per cent) for a bond of similar credit quality that does not contain any embedded derivatives. Therefore, when 3-month LIBOR increases to 5 per cent, the 23 per cent interest rate feature is more than twice the then-current market rate of return of the host contract of 11 per cent (3-month LIBOR of 5 per cent plus 6 per cent.)

Entity B would be required to treat the feature as a non-closely related embedded derivative.

Example 7.3G

Double-double interest rate test (3)

Entity A issues CU10 million debt with a coupon of 8 per cent and a term of 10 years. Entity A's market rate for 10-year debt is 8.25 per cent. Embedded in the debt is an interest rate adjustment that resets the interest rate to 16.40 per cent if 3-month LIBOR increases to 7 per cent or greater during the first three years of the debt.

The adjustment feature is an embedded derivative, but it would not be accounted for separately. The derivative could not cause the rate of return on the host contract to double.

Example 7.3H

Recovery of recognised investment (2)

Entity X issues CU10 million in debt with a coupon of 8.25 per cent and a term of 10 years. Entity X's market rate for 10-year debt is 8 per cent. Embedded in the debt is a clause stating that, if interest rates increase beyond a specified level, the holder of the debt must give the issuer an additional CU1 million in borrowings maturing in 10 years on which the holder will receive no interest.

The adjustment feature is a written option issued by the holder. The issuer pays for this option through a higher interest cost when compared to debt without the option. The embedded derivative would not be accounted for separately by the issuer because the holder will recover all of its recognised investment, being CU10 million advanced at inception and CU1 million if it is advanced at a later date. In all cases, the investor will recover all its recognised investment. There is no circumstance that can result in the issuer paying a rate that is more than double the market rate of the host contract at inception.

Note the 'recognised investment' is based on the amount advanced by the holder. The likelihood of the option being exercised and the present value of the loan are not considered when determining whether the holder will recover its recognised investment.

7.4 Inflation features

IFRS 9 does not specifically address whether an inflation feature within a debt contract that is in the scope of IFRS 9 is closely related to the host contract. When an embedded derivative is not specifically addressed by the Standard, significant judgement will need to be used. In these situations, drawing analogies to specific examples given will often prove helpful.

IFRS 9 does address inflation features within lease contracts. Finance lease contracts are similar to debt contracts and, therefore, the guidance below is based on the examples given for contracts with lease hosts.

Example 7.4

Inflation-linked bond

Entity X issues an inflation-linked bond. The bond pays a coupon of 4 per cent annually, with a repayment of principal on maturity of the bond. The principal payment is indexed to the domestic retail price index but cannot decrease below par.

Because the bond is denominated in the local currency, the indexation of the principal payment to domestic inflation rates is closely related to the host contract.

An inflation feature in a host debt contract in the scope of IFRS 9 is closely related to the host provided that the inflation index is not leveraged, cannot cause the investor not to recover substantially all of its initial investment, and is the inflation rate of the economic environment for the currency in which the debt is denominated.

Inflation features that are leveraged will not be closely related to a host debt contract. This is discussed further in the context of a lease host contract in **9.1**.

7.5 Credit derivatives and liquidity features

IFRS 9 does not explicitly address adjustments to the terms of a debt instrument in the scope of IFRS 9 as a result of issuer default, changes in the issuer's credit rating or creditworthiness. It does, however, provide guidance on embedded credit derivatives that relate to other reference entities. Further, certain credit sensitive contracts embedded in other instruments may meet the definition of a financial guarantee contract (see **2.3.3** in **chapter B1**).

7.5.1 Adjustment for issuer's credit risk

IFRS 9 does not provide specific guidance when the cash flows on debt instruments in the scope of IFRS 9 are adjusted for changes in the issuer's creditworthiness.

It is reasonable to conclude that credit features that relate to the credit quality of the issuer (e.g. the issuer's credit rating, default or ratios indicative of its credit status) should be viewed as closely related to the host debt contract if the credit feature is not leveraged and is designed to reflect the approximate credit risk borne by the lender. In economic terms, such features directly affect the value of the host debt contract.

Example 7.5.1A

Interest adjustment: debt covenants

Entity X issues bonds with a BBB rating. The terms of the bond are such that if Entity X violates a specified debt-to-equity ratio covenant, or Entity X's credit rating is downgraded, the interest rate will reset to the then-current market rate for Entity X.

The interest rate reset is considered to be closely related to the host contract because it relates to default in a credit risk-related covenant and Entity X's own credit rating and, therefore, the embedded derivative would not be accounted for separately.

Example 7.5.1B

Interest adjustment: credit risk and share price

Entity Y issues bonds with a BBB rating. The terms of the bond are such that if both of the following conditions are met, the coupon on the bond will be reduced by 50 basis points:

(a) the rating of the bonds by a specific rating agency is upgraded to at least BBB+; and

(b) the average share price of the ordinary shares of Entity Y exceeds a specified level over a specified 20-day period.

Because the adjustment to the interest payments only occurs if both conditions are met, it is appropriate to consider the provision as a single embedded derivative in line with IFRS 9:B4.3.4 as discussed in **section 6**, rather than two embedded derivatives. Although one of the underlyings of the derivative is related to credit quality of the issuer (i.e. Entity Y's credit rating) and the other underlying relates to Entity Y's equity price, the whole derivative would be considered not to be closely related to the host debt contract. This is because one of the underlyings (i.e. equity price) is considered not to be closely related to the economic characteristics and risks of debt (see **7.3**).

By contrast, if the feature operated such that there were two independent adjustments to the interest paid on the bond (of 25 basis points each), one of which is triggered by changes to Entity Y's credit rating and the other by movements in Entity Y's equity price, it would be appropriate to treat the two features as separate embedded derivatives. The credit-rating triggered feature would be closely related but the equity-triggered feature would not be closely related to the debt host contract and, as a consequence, would be accounted for separately at FVTPL.

7.5.2 Adjustment for liquidity of issuer's debt

IFRS 9 does not provide specific guidance when the cash flows of a debt instrument in the scope of IFRS 9 are adjusted for changes in the relative liquidity of that debt instrument. Provided that the adjustments are not leveraged, the adjustment is likely to be closely related to the debt host contract because the liquidity of the instrument is inherent in the debt host contract.

Example 7.5.2

Interest adjustment: liquidity

Entity X issues a debt instrument that is repayable at par at maturity that pays a fixed rate of interest. On issue of the debt, the instrument is not listed. The debt instrument contains a contractual provision specifying that if the debt instrument ever becomes listed the rate of interest payable on the instrument will decrease by 0.5 per cent. The interest rate will be reset to its initial level in the event that the debt instrument is subsequently delisted.

The listing of the debt instrument is likely to increase the liquidity of the debt instrument. The lower liquidity of an unlisted instrument is a cost borne by the holders because it limits their ability to sell their holding of the debt instrument when the borrower's ability to meet its obligations as they fall due is in question. The listing of the debt instrument is likely to improve its liquidity and to provide the holders with an exit mechanism before maturity. The holder's willingness to accept a reduction in the interest rate in exchange for increased liquidity would be considered closely related to the host debt contract.

7.5.3 Adjustment for third party credit

IFRS 9 views a credit derivative that transfers credit risk of a particular reference asset (which the entity, the 'beneficiary', may not own) to another party (the 'guarantor') as not closely related to the host debt contract when the host is in the scope of IFRS 9. [IFRS 9:B4.3.5(f)]

Example 7.5.3A

Credit-linked note

Entity X issues credit-linked bonds. The bonds are linked to the performance of a portfolio of third-party corporate bonds held by a third-party bank. The bonds pay a rate of interest in excess of Entity X's normal cost of funds because, in the event that one of the referenced corporate bonds defaults, Entity X will pay a reduced principal to the holders.

The embedded credit-related provision would be accounted for separately because the credit of a third party entity is not considered to be closely related to the debt host contract issued by Entity X.

Example 7.5.3B

Cash versus synthetic credit default obligations

Collateralised debt obligation (CDO) special purpose entities (SPEs) are set up to issue notes to investors which pay based on the performance of specified named corporate debt. The interest and principal on the assets is used to service and repay the CDO liability. If there is default under the named corporate debt, then the investors of the CDO notes will suffer loss. The losses are shared by investors in a pre-agreed manner, often with the most junior notes suffering most of the expected loss.

There are two types of structures:

- the assets in the SPE are actual corporate debt (e.g. GM & Ford corporate bonds), referred to as 'cash CDOs' because the SPE has to own the actual cash instruments; or
- the assets in the SPE are derivatives over the corporate debt (e.g. credit default swaps (CDS) over GM & Ford), referred to as 'synthetic CDOs' because the SPE will or may hold synthetic instruments rather than holding cash instruments.

A CDO is illustrated below.

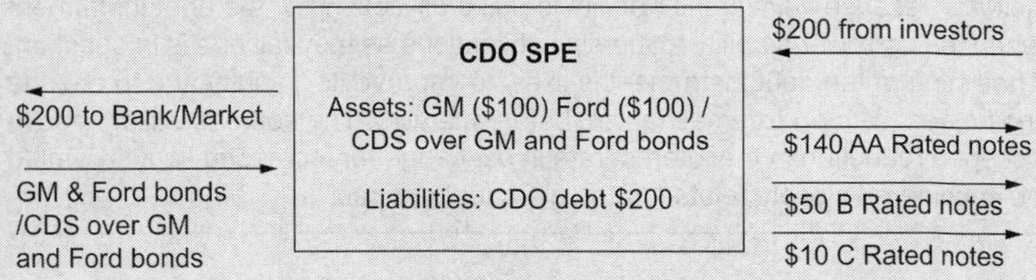

Whether the CDO structure is cash or synthetic will affect the accounting for the notes.

Cash CDO

If an issued CDO liability is not measured at FVTPL, the SPE will need to assess whether the CDO liability has embedded credit derivatives that require separation. Because the entity must own the underlying cash instruments, the issued CDO liability does not have a credit derivative that requires separation. The beneficiary (the SPE) is transferring the credit risk of its referenced assets to a guarantor (the investor in the CDO notes).

Synthetic CDO

Because the SPE is required to pay returns on the CDO liability that is linked to the performance of corporate bonds, but without actually needing to own these cash instruments (e.g. it can purchase credit derivatives over the reference corporate bonds), the notes issued by the SPE have credit embedded derivatives that require separation. The beneficiary (the SPE) is transferring the credit risk of referenced assets to a guarantor (the investor of the CDO notes) but does not own the underlying referenced assets.

7.6 Foreign currency features

Debt contracts in the scope of IFRS 9 may require the issuer to make payments of interest or principal in a foreign currency. An example of such a contract is a dual currency bond where the principal is paid in a foreign currency but interest is paid in the entity's functional currency. The foreign currency feature in a dual currency bond is an embedded derivative (foreign currency swap or foreign currency forward) but it is not separated from the host debt instrument because foreign currency gains and losses on a dual currency bond are already recognised in profit or loss following the requirements of IAS 21 *The Effects of Changes in Foreign Exchange Rates*.

Certain currency features may need to be separated. A debt contract may, for example, include a provision that would allow the holder to choose to receive interest payments in an alternative currency. This provision is a foreign currency option, written by the issuer.

Foreign currency option features are generally viewed by IFRS 9 as taking on an additional foreign currency risk that is not normally present in transactions and will not be fully reflected by the requirements of IAS 21. Such an option in a debt host contract is not closely related and needs to be accounted for separately.

7.7 Caps, floors and collars on interest rates

Floating rate debt contracts often include features that 'cap', 'floor' or 'collar' the amount of interest payable on the debt.

7.7.1 Definitions

A 'cap' is an option contract that puts an upper limit on a floating interest rate. The purchaser of the cap is paid the difference between the current floating interest rate and the strike rate of the cap whenever the current floating rate exceeds the strike rate.

Example 7.7.1

Interest rate cap

Entity A purchases an interest rate cap, paying a premium of CU1 million. The cap has a notional amount of CU100 million and a strike rate of 6 per cent. Currently, LIBOR is 4.5 per cent.

The cap will pay Entity A the difference between LIBOR and 6 per cent whenever LIBOR exceeds 6 per cent. Thus, if LIBOR moves to 6.5 per cent, the cap will pay Entity A CU500,000, i.e. 0.5 per cent (the difference between LIBOR and 6 per cent) applied to the notional amount of the cap (CU100 million).

A 'floor' is an option contract that puts a lower limit on a floating interest rate. The writer of the floor will pay the difference between the current floating interest rate and the strike rate of the floor whenever the current floating rate drops below the strike rate. A floor is effectively the opposite of a cap. The writer of a floor will receive a premium which compensates it for the risk it has taken on (i.e. the risk that rates drop below a certain level).

Entities often want to protect themselves against rises in interest rates, so they purchase caps. However, these can be expensive. To reduce or limit the cost, entities will often simultaneously write a floor. Thus, they have achieved an interest rate collar. A 'collar' is an instrument that combines a cap and a floor. The holder of an interest rate collar will be exposed to interest rate movements only within a specified range. It protects the holder against a significant rise in interest rates, but limits the benefits of a drop in interest rates.

7.7.2 'In the money' and 'out of the money' caps, floors and collars

A cap is 'in the money' if its strike rate is lower than the market rate of interest. It is 'out of the money' if its strike rate is higher than the market rate of interest. If a cap has a strike rate of 6 per cent, it will be in the money whenever interest rates are above 6 per cent and out of the money whenever interest rates are below 6 per cent.

A floor is in the money if its strike rate is higher than the market rate of interest. It is out of the money if its strike rate is lower than the market rate of interest. If a floor has a strike rate of 4 per cent, it will be in the money whenever interest rates are below 4 per cent and out of the money whenever interest rates are above 4 per cent.

A collar has two strike prices, the upper and lower limits. A collar is out of the money if interest rates are between these two strike rates; it is in the money otherwise.

7.7.3 Embedded caps, floors and collars

An embedded cap or floor on the interest rate of a debt instrument, where the cap or floor is not leveraged, is closely related to the host debt contract provided that the cap is at or above the market interest rate and the floor is at or below the market interest rate when the instrument is issued. The assessment as to whether an embedded cap or floor is closely related to a host debt contract is made at issuance and is not subsequently revised. [IFRS 9:B4.3.8(b)]

Example 7.7.3

Embedded interest rate cap

Entity X issues CU100 million debt with a 5-year maturity. The interest is payable at LIBOR plus a credit spread of 150 basis points. LIBOR at issuance is 4.5 per cent and, therefore, the rate at inception of the debt is 6 per cent. There is a provision in the debt contract that if LIBOR were to rise, the rate payable on the debt would not rise above 7 per cent.

The cap is an embedded derivative that is closely related to the host debt contract because, at the time of the issuance of the debt, the cap is out of the money.

While the Standard does not specifically address a collar embedded in a debt contract, a simple analogy to caps and floors can be made. If a debt contract has an embedded collar which caps interest rates at 7 per cent and has a floor of 4 per cent, the collar will be closely related to the host debt contract provided that both the cap and the floor are out of the money when the debt is issued and the collar is not leveraged.

7.8 Conversion and equity features

A conversion feature that allows the holder of the debt contract to convert the outstanding amount into equity of the issuer is an embedded derivative that is not closely related to the host debt contract for the issuer if the conversion feature fails the definition of equity. Assessing whether the conversion feature meets the definition of equity is complex and is addressed in **chapter B3**.

Example 7.8

Equity conversion feature

Entity X issues debt that is convertible into a fixed number of its ordinary shares in five years. The conversion feature represents an embedded written call option on the shares of Entity X, settled in a fixed number of shares.

For Entity X, because the conversion feature meets the definition of equity, the convertible debt is a compound instrument that should be split into its liability and equity components. Entity X will not account for the written call option as an embedded derivative because the option is an equity instrument of Entity X (see **chapter B3**).

Another form of equity embedded derivative is an 'equity kicker'. These are debt instruments which provide for the lender to receive shares of the borrower for nothing, or a very low amount, if the borrower lists its shares on a stock exchange. The debt remains outstanding following the delivery of the shares. Typically, the lender is a venture capitalist. Similar to convertible debt, debt with an equity kicker carries a coupon that is lower than the rate on a comparable debt without the equity kicker.

The equity kicker meets the definition of a derivative because its value will change in response to changes in the borrower's share price, it has little initial net investment, and it is settled at a future date. This is true even though the right to receive the shares is contingent on an unrelated event. [IFRS 9 Guidance on Implementation C.4]

For the issuer, if the equity kicker fails the definition of equity, it will be recognised as an embedded derivative that is not closely related to the host debt contract and therefore will require separation at FVTPL.

7.9 Non-cash settlement of interest or principal

Debt contracts that allow for the payment of interest or principal in non-cash consideration may contain embedded derivatives that are not closely related to the host debt contract. In some cases the embedded derivative feature may be outside the scope of IFRS 9 because it results in the delivery of a non-financial item in accordance with the entity's purchase, sale or usage requirements (see **2.5** in **chapter B1**).

Example 7.9

Non-cash settlement of interest

Entity A lends Entity B, a newspaper publisher, CU10 million for 10 years. Each year instead of paying interest, Entity B agrees to give Entity A a predetermined amount of free advertising space in a newspaper. For Entity B, selling newspaper advertising space falls within its normal sale requirements and, therefore, that part of the contractual arrangement is outside the scope of IFRS 9. The debt instrument, excluding the fair value of the free advertising space, is in the scope of IFRS 9 and will be measured at fair value at initial recognition. The fair value of the debt instrument will be less than the proceeds borrowed reflecting the fair value of the non-cash consideration included in the loan agreement.

If the sale of advertising space did not meet the normal purchase, sale or usage requirements exemption for Entity B (e.g. because Entity B was not a newspaper publisher), then that feature would be in the scope of IFRS 9. The delivery of non-cash consideration embedded in the loan meets the definition of a derivative because it has an underlying (the price of the advertising space), no initial net investment, and it will be settled at future dates. The economic characteristics and risks of the embedded derivative and debt are not closely related and, therefore, the non-cash consideration feature would be separated and measured at FVTPL.

7.10 Unit linking features embedded in host debt instrument

A unit-linking feature embedded in a host debt instrument in the scope of IFRS 9 is closely related to the host debt instrument if the unit-denominated payments are measured at current unit values that reflect the fair values of the assets of the fund. A unit-linking feature is a contractual term that requires payments denominated in a unit of an internal or external investment fund. [IFRS 9:B4.3.8(g)]

IFRS 4:IG Example 2: 2.15 provides the example of a policyholder option to surrender a contract for account value equal to the fair value of a pool of equity investments, possibly after deducting a surrender charge. The example makes reference to IFRS 9:B4.3.8(g) and states that if such a feature is embedded in a host investment contract then, if the insurer regards the account value as the amortised cost or the fair value of that portion of its obligation, no further adjustment is needed for the option (unless the surrender value differs significantly from the account value). Otherwise the embedded derivative feature would be required to be classified separately as at FVTPL. A host investment contract is described in IFRS 4:IG4 as a financial instrument that does not meet the definition of an insurance contract.

The above guidance suggests that unit-linking features would only be considered closely related where the unit denominated payments are measured in such a way that they reflect the fair value of the assets of the fund to which they are linked. In any case, even if the unit-linking feature is determined to be closely related to a debt host contract IFRS 9:B5.4.6 would be applicable for subsequent measurement of the hybrid instrument if it was measured at amortised cost (see **4.1.2** in **chapter B6**). Applying IFRS 9:B5.4.6 would result in the carrying amount of the hybrid instrument reflecting the amount expected to be paid or received which would incorporate the unit linking feature.

7.11 Further examples of embedded derivatives in issued host debt contracts

The table below provides further examples of derivative instruments embedded in issued debt host contracts.

Type of instrument	Economic characteristics	Embedded derivative	Closely related?
Inverse floater	Bond accrues interest at 5.25 per cent for three months to July 20X4; thereafter, at 10.75 per cent less 6-month LIBOR to January 20X5.	Forward starting fixed-to-floating rate interest rate swap	No. Para B4.3.8(a)
Leveraged inverse floater	Bond accrues interest at 6 per cent to June 20X5; thereafter, at 14.55 per cent - (2.5 × 3-month LIBOR).	Forward starting leveraged interest rate swap	No. Para B4.3.8(a)
Ratchet floater	Bond accrues interest at 3-month LIBOR + 50 basis points. In addition to having a lifetime cap of 7.25 per cent, the coupon will be collared each period between the previous coupon and the previous coupon plus 25 basis points. 3-month LIBOR at inception is 4 per cent.	Combinations of purchased and written options that create changing caps and floors	Yes. Para B4.3.8(b)
Fixed-to-floating note	A bond that pays a varying coupon (first-year coupon is fixed; second- and third-year coupons are based on LIBOR).	Forward-starting interest-rate swap	Yes. Para B4.3.8(a)
Equity-indexed note	A bond for which the return of interest, principal, or both is tied to a specified equity security or index (e.g. the Standard and Poor's 500 (S&P 500) index). This instrument may contain a fixed or varying coupon rate and may place all, or a portion, of principal at risk.	Forward exchange contracts or option contracts	Yes. Para B4.3.5(d)

Type of instrument	Economic characteristics	Embedded derivative	Closely related?
Variable principal redemption bond	A supplemental principal payment will be paid to the investor, at maturity, if the final S&P 500 closing value (determined at a specified date) is less than its initial value at date of issuance and the 10-year constant maturity treasuries (CMT) is greater than 2 per cent as of a specified date. In all cases, the minimum principal redemption will be 100 per cent of face amount.	Option contract	No. Para B4.3.5(d)
Crude-oil knock-in note	A bond that has a 1 per cent coupon and guarantees repayment of principal with upside potential based on the strength of the oil market.	Option contract	No. Para B4.3.5(e)
Gold-linked bull note	A bond that has a fixed 3 per cent coupon and guarantees repayment of principal with upside potential if the price of gold increases.	Option contract	No. Para B4.3.5(e)
Step-up bond	A bond that provides an introductory above-market yield that is less than twice the market rate at inception and steps up to a new coupon, which will be below then-current market rates or, alternatively, the bond may be called, at an amount that approximates the amortised cost of the debt instrument, in lieu of the step-up in the coupon rate.	Interest rate swap and call option	Yes. B4.3.5(g) and B4.3.8(a)
Credit-sensitive bond	A bond that has a coupon rate of interest that resets based on changes in the issuer's credit rating.	Conditional exchange contract or option	Yes. Para B4.3.8(a)

Type of instrument	Economic characteristics	Embedded derivative	Closely related?
Inflation bond	A bond with a contractual principal amount that is indexed to the non-leveraged inflation rate of the economic environment of the issuer, but cannot decrease below par; the coupon rate is below that of traditional bonds of a similar maturity.	Inflation-linked swap with embedded floor	Yes. Para B4.3.8(a) & (f)(i)
Specific equity-linked bond	A bond that pays a coupon slightly below that of traditional bonds of similar maturity; however, the principal amount is linked to the stock market performance of an equity investee of the issuer.	Series of forward contracts or option contracts	No. Para B4.3.5(d)
Dual currency bond	A bond providing for repayment of principal in one currency (e.g. Euro) and periodic interest payments denominated in a different currency (e.g. Yen).	Foreign currency forward	Yes. Para B4.3.8(c)
Short-term loan with foreign currency option	A US lender issues a loan at an above-market interest rate. The loan is made in US dollars, the borrower's functional currency, and the borrower has the option to repay the loan in US dollars or in a fixed amount of a specified foreign currency.	Foreign currency option	No. Para B4.3.5(g)

8 Embedded derivatives in equity host contracts

Embedded derivatives are not limited to debt hosts; they can also be embedded in equity host contracts. **chapter B3** provides guidance on identifying the host contract as either debt or equity because sometimes it may be difficult to determine whether the host contract is debt or equity.

From the perspective of an issuer, it is very uncommon to issue a host contract that meets the definition of equity and contains an embedded derivative that needs to be separated out as a financial asset or liability as at fair value through profit or loss (see **example 8**). In some cases both the embedded derivative and the host contract meet the definition of equity as neither conveys any obligation to pay cash or other financial assets.

Example 8

Contingent cash payment based on interest rates

Entity A issues US$100 million of perpetual, irredeemable preference shares that pay a discretionary, fixed dividend rate of 8 per cent. Because the entity has true discretion as to whether or not, and the extent to which, dividends are paid, that part of the shares meets the definition of equity in IAS 32. Embedded in the shares is a provision that states if LIBOR increases to 12 per cent or more, the holders will become entitled to receive a one-off payment of cash calculated by a predetermined formula.

The issuer cannot avoid an outflow of cash in respect of the amount prescribed by the formula if LIBOR reaches 12 per cent, i.e. the embedded feature is an embedded derivative liability. Entity A will account for this derivative separately from the host instrument at FVTPL.

9 Embedded derivatives in lease contracts

Embedded derivatives can exist in lease contracts, whether an entity is acting as a lessee or a lessor in either a finance or an operating lease.

9.1 Inflation factors

An embedded derivative in a host lease contract is closely related to the host contract if the embedded derivative is an inflation-related index (e.g. if lease payments are indexed to a retail price index), provided that the index is not leveraged, and the index relates to inflation in the entity's own economic environment. [IFRS 9:B4.3.8(f)(i)]

9.1.1 Entity's economic environment

IFRS 9 does not give any guidance as to what constitutes 'the entity's own economic environment'. It is reasonable to assume that when an entity operates in a certain country and enters into a lease agreement on, say, a property located in that country, the inflation of the country concerned will be the relevant inflation index because that index is related to the value of the lease and is present in the environment in which the entity operates.

Example 9.1.1

Inflation-adjusting lease payments

Entity X, a UK entity, has extensive operations in Europe and the US. Entity Y, Entity X's subsidiary, leases property in Paris with a lease term of 10 years. The functional currency of Entity Y is the Euro. Lease payments are to be made in Euros. Embedded in the lease is a provision that requires the lease payments to be adjusted every two years for the change in the UK consumer price index, which is not the index of the economic environment of Entity Y.

The embedded inflation indexed payment would be accounted for separately because, although the rate of inflation is not leveraged, the inflation index is in a different economic environment from the entity entering into the lease.

9.1.2 Leverage factors

The second consideration when assessing whether an inflation adjustment in a lease contract is an embedded derivative that should be separately accounted for is leverage. IFRS 9 does not define leverage in the context of inflation. However, the concept of leverage is used in the assessment of the features present in debt contracts. For debt contracts, a leverage feature that can double the holder's initial rate of return and could result in a rate of return that is at least twice what the market return would be for a contract with the same terms as the host contract is not closely related to the host debt contract.

By analogy, it can be argued that an inflation adjustment for two times or more of the inflation index will be seen as leveraged. Careful consideration of the terms of the lease is required for a decision on whether any inflation adjustment included in it is indeed leveraged.

Example 9.1.2

Leveraged inflation-adjusting lease payments

Entity X, a UK entity, leases property in London with a lease term of 10 years. Lease payments are to be made in Sterling. Embedded in the lease is a provision that requires the lease payment to be adjusted annually for three times the changes in UK's retail price index.

The embedded inflation adjustment is not closely related to the host contract and will be accounted for separately because it is leveraged.

In **example 9.1.2**, it is quite clear that there is a leveraged inflation feature that needs to be separated. However, what is less clear is whether the derivative that needs separation is the total inflation adjustment (i.e. three times the retail price index) or just the leveraged portion (i.e. two times the retail price index).

The argument for the latter is that adjustment by the retail price index is seen as closely related. However, there are two counter-arguments to that: firstly, separation of only a portion of the embedded derivative amounts to splitting the derivative into two parts which is not generally permitted under IFRS 9; secondly, separation could be argued to create cash flows that are not evident in the contract, which also is not the general practice under IFRS 9. Accordingly, the total inflation adjustment (i.e. three times the retail price index) should be split out.

9.2 Foreign currency features

There are no specific rules addressing currency features in lease contracts. There are two pieces of guidance included in IFRS 9 which analyse foreign currency features embedded in contracts: foreign currency derivatives embedded in host debt instruments; and foreign currency derivatives embedded in a host contract that is not a financial instrument.

For the former, the foreign currency feature is not separately accounted for because the instrument is a monetary item and, under IAS 21, foreign currency gains and losses are already recognised in profit or loss. For the latter, the assessment is more complicated. A foreign currency derivative embedded in a host contract that is not a financial instrument is closely related to the host provided it is not leveraged, does not contain an option, and requires payments denominated in:

- the functional currency of any substantial party to the contract;
- the currency in which the price of the related good or service that is acquired or delivered is routinely denominated in commercial transactions around the world; or
- a currency that is commonly used in contracts to purchase or sell non-financial items in the economic environment in which the transaction takes place.

It can be argued that trade receivables and payables recognised under finance leases are in the nature of a debt host and, therefore, are covered by the same requirements in IAS 21 to recognise foreign currency gains and losses in profit or loss on monetary items. Therefore, it would be reasonable to analogise from the foreign currency guidance on debt contracts when considering foreign currency features in finance lease payables and receivables.

Operating leases are non-financial instruments. Therefore, the considerations that apply to non-financial items detailed in **10.5** will equally apply to operating leases. These considerations include foreign currency options, leverage factors, the functional currency of substantial parties to the contract, and the currency that is commonly used in contracts in the economic environment in which the transaction takes place.

9.2.1 Examples of embedded foreign currency features

The following examples apply the analysis in **9.2**.

Example 9.2.1A

Operating lease denominated in functional currency of a party

Entity X, a Dutch entity, leases property from Entity Y, a UK entity, under an operating lease. The lease payments are denominated in Sterling. The functional currency of Entity X is the Euro and the functional currency of Entity Y is Sterling.

The denomination of the lease payments in Sterling would not require separate accounting because Sterling is the functional currency of a substantial party to the contract, Entity Y.

Example 9.2.1B

Operating lease not denominated in functional currency of a party

Entity X, a New Zealand entity, leases property under an operating lease from Entity Y, an Australian entity. The lease payments are denominated in US dollars. The functional currency of Entity X is the New Zealand dollar and the functional currency of Entity Y is the Australian dollar.

The denomination of the lease payments in US dollars would require separate accounting because it is not the currency of the primary economic environment of either counterparty to the contract, and the price of this asset is not denominated routinely in that currency in international commerce.

If the property were leased under a finance lease (which is a financial instrument), the lease payments would represent monetary items and, therefore, be within the scope of IAS 21. The embedded derivative would not be separated.

Example 9.2.1C

Choice of settlement in foreign currencies

A lease contract between Entity A (Sterling functional currency) and Entity B (US dollar functional currency) whereby the lessee can choose to make payments in either Sterling or US dollars, contains an embedded option that is not closely related to the host lease contract. This is true even though both of the settlement currencies are functional currencies of one of the counterparties to the lease. This answer would apply regardless of whether the lease was an operating or finance lease.

9.2.2 Substantial party

A 'substantial party' to the contract in the examples above is a party acting as a principal under the contract. The criterion for a 'substantial party' would not be satisfied if the party is an agent that is being engaged by one of the transacting entities solely to comply with the requirement that payments be denominated in the functional currency of any substantial party to the contract.

Example 9.2.2

Substantial party

Entity X would like to lease property from Entity Y under an operating lease and have the payments denominated in US dollars. The functional currency of both entities is Sterling. To accomplish a US dollar-denominated lease, Entity Y leases the property to an investment bank whose functional currency is US dollars. The investment bank then subleases the property to Entity X. The sublease agreement requires Entity X to pay US dollars. The investment bank is indemnified by Entity for any losses incurred due to a default by Entity X. The investment bank is acting solely as an agent for Entity X and, accordingly, is not at risk. The bank cannot be viewed as a substantial party to the lease. Therefore, the embedded foreign currency derivative requires separate accounting.

9.3 Referenced underlyings

A lease with contingent rentals that are based on related sales or on variable interest rates contain an embedded derivative (linkage to sale or interest) which is deemed to be closely related to the host lease contract. [IFRS 9:B4.3.8(f)(i) & (ii)]

9.3.1 Contingent rentals based on variable interest rates

Example 9.3.1

Lease linked to interest rates

Entity A, a UK entity, enters into a lease under which the payments are indexed to 6-month LIBOR. The embedded derivative does not need to be separated because the indexation is to interest rates inherent in Entity A's local economy.

IFRS 9 does not provide guidance on what constitutes a variable interest rate. It is reasonable to assume that when an entity operates in a particular jurisdiction and enters into a lease agreement in that jurisdiction, a variable interest rate would be similar to the benchmark interest rate that would be payable on a debt instrument where the proceeds received from the debt instrument are invested in the leased asset and the debt is secured on the leased asset.

9.3.2 Contingent rentals based on related sales

Example 9.3.2A

Lease linked to sales

Entity X leases a property, which it uses as a retail outlet, selling custom-made umbrellas. Embedded in the lease is a clause requiring lease payments to increase for each additional 1,000 umbrellas sales after the first 100,000.

Contingent rentals based on related sales are considered to be closely related to the host lease contract; accordingly, so the sales-related derivative should not be separated from the lease.

Example 9.3.2B

Lease linked to throughput

Entity Y leases shop premises in an airport terminal on an operating lease. The lease payments are contingent on the number of passengers who pass through the terminal.

While the contingent rentals are not based directly on related sales, it is clear that sales are directly affected by the number of passengers passing through the terminal. Therefore, the embedded derivative is closely related to the host lease contract and separate accounting is not required.

9.3.3 Contingent rentals based on other measures

IFRS 9 states that contingent rentals based on related sales are closely related to the host lease contract. However, no guidance is given on contingent rentals based on other measures, such as profit or net assets or based on ratios. Entities will need to consider their accounting policy with respect to the definition of derivative, see **2.1** in **chapter B4**, in determining whether contingent rentals linked to such measures are a "non-financial variable that is specific to a party to the contract". The application of the accounting policy may in some cases lead to a conclusion that the contingent feature does not meet the definition of a derivative and therefore cannot be considered an embedded derivative.

Example 9.3.3

Lease linked to profits

Entity Z, a UK entity, leases a retail unit in a large shopping mall located in the UK. Under the lease, lease payments will increase for each £1,000 profit after tax made over £1,000,000.

Under Entity Z's accounting policy it does not regard its own profits as a 'non-financial variable specific to a party to the contract' and therefore a separate contract with contingent payments linked to profits would meet the definition of a derivative (see **2.1** in **chapter B4**).

While contingent rentals based on related sales are closely related to a host lease contract, the same is not true of contingent rentals based on profit after tax. Several of the balances that are added together to reach profit after tax (such as cost of sales and tax) do not have economic characteristics and risks similar to those of the lease contract. Therefore, the embedded derivative is not closely related to the host lease contract and separate accounting is required.

9.3.4 Other referenced underlyings

A lease contract under which payments are determined by changes in a referenced underlying that is not generally connected with the normal pricing of a traditional lease contains an embedded derivative that is required to be separated. Examples of referenced underlyings include security prices, commodity prices, an unrelated index of prices or rates, credit ratings or a credit index.

Example 9.3.4

Lease linked to share price index

Entity A has several investments in FTSE 100 shares. It enters into a lease contract and negotiates a clause whereby lease payments are indexed to changes in the FTSE 100.

Contingent rentals based on changes in FTSE 100 are not closely related to the host lease contract; consequently, the embedded derivative would need to be separated from the host lease.

10 Embedded derivatives in purchase, sale and service contracts

There is very little guidance on assessing embedded derivatives in executory contracts that either are not net settleable or meet the own use scope exception, particularly service contracts. The appropriate accounting will need to be determined by analogising from the guidance and principles applicable to other host contracts.

10.1 Adjustments for ingredients

Pricing of sales, purchase and service contracts is often structured so as to pass on to customers the cost of an ingredient used in the production or delivery of an asset or service.

There is no guidance from which to draw an analogy. Hence, the assessment of a particular contract should be based on an analysis of the economic characteristics and risks of that contract. This should include a combination of qualitative and quantitative factors.

For example, a physically delivered contract to purchase electricity is assessed and found to be a purchase, sale and usage requirement contract that is outside the scope of IFRS 9. However, there is a pricing adjustment with respect to a different commodity, gas. Gas is used as an ingredient in the production of the electricity that will be physically delivered. The pricing adjustment is achieved through a formula that incorporates many other pricing inputs and variables. The prices of gas and electricity in this case are not highly correlated.

Commodity-based contracts that are entered into and continue to meet the entity's expected purchase, sale, or usage requirements are outside the scope of IFRS 9 and are therefore not financial instruments. (This is discussed further in **2.5** of **chapter B1**.) However, even if a contract is not a financial instrument in its entirety, it may include an embedded derivative that is potentially required to be accounted for separately.

The guidance in IFRS 9 focuses on economic characteristics and risks in determining whether the embedded derivative is closely related. The guidance does not specifically refer to a purely quantitative assessment, nor does it refer to a purely qualitative assessment of the relationship. Therefore an entity would need to determine whether both quantitative and qualitative factors are relevant in determining whether the pricing adjustment is closely related to the host contract or not.

In the circumstances described a quantitative assessment would establish that the economic characteristics are different, due to a lack of correlation between the pricing adjustment and the price of the commodity that is delivered under the contract. However, this quantitative assessment is not necessarily the only factor in the determination as to whether the embedded derivative is closely related, because qualitative factors may also be relevant to the decision. If the supplier of the electricity (who is the counterparty to the arrangement) is a gas-powered power station, then this qualitative characteristic is relevant in determining whether the pricing adjustment should be separately accounted for. Because the pricing adjustment is specifically relevant to the production of the commodity to be delivered under the contract, then the pricing adjustment is considered to be closely related to the host contract. However, if it cannot be demonstrated that the pricing adjustment is directly relevant to the counterparty, (e.g. the counterparty is an electricity exchange/broker and did not use the indexed commodity (gas) in the production of the commodity (electricity) that was to be physically delivered, or the counterparty is a nuclear-powered electricity supplier and does not use gas in the production of the electricity), then this pricing adjustment does not have qualitative merit and, therefore, a quantitative assessment should take precedence.

10.2 Inflation factors

There is no specific guidance on inflation factors within purchase, sale or service contracts, but an analogy can be established with lease contracts. An embedded inflation-related index in a host lease contract is closely related to the host contract provided that the index is not leveraged and the index relates to inflation in the entity's own economic environment.

Example 10.2

Executory contract linked to inflation

Entity A, a UK entity, enters into a long-term service contract under which it agrees to clean and maintain specified buildings owned by Entity B for the next 10 years. All the buildings are located within the UK. Entity A receives a fixed annual fee. Embedded in the contract is a clause providing for a one-off adjustment half-way through the contract such that the fee receivable is adjusted for changes in the UK's retail price index from the beginning of the contract. Thereafter, the fee remains fixed at the new amount.

The embedded-inflation indexed payment is closely related to the host service contract because the rate of inflation is not leveraged, and the inflation index is that of the local economic environment.

In determining whether the inflation feature within a sale, purchase or service contract is leveraged or is that of the entity's local environment, similar considerations to those used when assessing host lease contracts should be applied (see **9.1**).

10.3 Adjustments for unrelated factors

Purchase and sales contracts in which payments are determined by changes in a referenced underlying that is not generally connected with the normal pricing of such a contract contain embedded derivatives that need to be separated. Examples of pricing adjustments of this type include adjustments by reference to interest rates, security prices, unrelated commodity prices, and various indices of prices or rates.

Example 10.3

Executory contract linked to share price index

Entity A contracts to buy goods from Entity B for a fixed amount plus or minus an indexation feature linked to movements in the FTSE 250. The embedded derivative based on the FTSE 250 is not closely related to the host contract and would need to be separated from the host purchase contract.

10.4 Caps, floors and collars

In some purchase, sales and service contracts, the price is set as a market price at the time of the payment, but is 'capped', 'floored', or 'collared' within a range. The concepts of caps, floors and collars are explained in the context of interest rates in **7.7**.

Similar consideration can be applied here, i.e. terms included in a contract to purchase or sell an asset that establish a cap and a floor on the price to be paid or received for the asset are closely related to the host contract if both the cap and the floor are out of the money at inception and are not leveraged. [IFRS 9:B4.3.8(b)] This can be extended to collars included in purchase and sales contracts, i.e. collars are closely related to the host contract if they are out of the money at inception.

The assessment is made at inception of the contract, and is not subsequently revised.

Whilst IFRS 9 does not specifically mention caps, floors and collars embedded in service contracts, it is reasonable to analogise to the guidance given on purchase and sales contracts.

Example 10.4

Executory contract with embedded cap

Entity A enters into a contract to purchase tin in 12 months at the market price of tin at the date of purchase. Embedded in the contract is a cap that puts an upper limit on the price Entity A will be required to pay. The cap is out of the money at inception of the contract (i.e. the cap is set above the current price for tin).

The cap is closely related to the host purchase contract and, accordingly it will not be separated. The cap is closely related to the host contract for the life of the contract, irrespective of whether tin prices rise so that the cap becomes in the money.

10.5 Foreign currency features

An embedded foreign currency derivative in a host contract that is not a financial instrument is closely related to the host contract provided that it is not leveraged, does not contain an option feature and requires payments denominated in one of the following currencies:

[IFRS 9:B4.3.8(d)]

(i) the functional currency of any substantial party to the contract;

(ii) the currency in which the price of the related good or service that is acquired or delivered is routinely denominated in commercial transactions around the world (such as the US dollar for crude oil transactions); or

(iii) a currency that is commonly used in contracts to purchase or sell non-financial items in the economic environment in which the transaction takes place (e.g. a relatively stable and liquid currency that is commonly used in local business transactions or external trade).

The three criteria in IFRS 9:B4.3.8(d) are not mutually exclusive. For example, an entity in Country Y may export oil in US dollars. One, two or all three of the following may apply: the exporting entity may have the US dollar as its functional currency; oil is considered a non-financial item that is routinely denominated in US dollars throughout the world; and the US dollar may be a common currency for either internal or external transactions for Country Y.

The term 'substantial party' is discussed further in **9.2.2**.

The assessment of the functional currency of a substantial party to the contract in (i) above requires careful consideration. For example, a substantial party to a contract may be a subsidiary of a larger group. The presentation currency of the group (see IAS 21 *The Effects of Changes in Foreign Exchange Rates*) is not relevant to this assessment, because it is the functional currency of the subsidiary that is relevant. In many cases, judgement will be required when the subsidiary is in a jurisdiction that does not produce individual entity financial statements under IFRSs or an equivalent GAAP and, therefore, its functional currency is not evident. Too much reliance should not be placed on the country of incorporation or geographical location of a substantial party to the contract because the evaluation of the functional currency in IAS 21 includes many other factors.

A currency in which the price of the related goods or services is routinely denominated in commercial transactions around the world can only be a currency that is used for similar transactions all around the world, not just in one local area. For example, if cross-border transactions in natural gas in North America are routinely denominated in US dollars and such transactions are routinely denominated in Euros in Europe, neither the US dollar nor the Euro is the currency in which the goods or services are routinely denominated in commercial transactions around the world. [IFRS 9 Guidance on Implementation C.9]

By definition, a currency in which the price of goods or services is routinely denominated around the world has to be one currency. However, the existence of a relatively small proportion of transactions in one or two markets, or in a particular jurisdiction, that are denominated in a local currency does not preclude a non-financial item from being considered to be routinely denominated in a particular currency in commercial transactions around the world.

The number of non-financial items that would qualify under IFRS 9:B4.3.8(d)(ii) is likely to be limited. In practice, such items will primarily be commodities that are traded in US dollars in commercial transactions throughout the world.

For certain types of commodity transactions, contracts may be based on a dominant currency (such as the US dollar) but may be denominated in local currencies in certain markets for regulatory or other reasons, i.e. the price is translated at the spot rate into local currencies (a 'convenience translation' mechanism). For example, although the dominant currency for crude oil transactions as noted in IFRS 9:B4.3.8(d)(ii) is the US dollar, some contracts for crude oil may be denominated in Canadian dollars in Canada, when the Canadian dollar price is a convenience translation of the US dollar crude oil price. A simple convenience translation into a local currency of the price of a commodity that is routinely denominated in a dominant currency would not negate the view that the commodity is routinely denominated in a single currency in commercial transactions around the world. On the other hand, if a commodity transaction is regularly denominated in various currencies in commercial transactions around the world where such foreign currency prices are not convenience translations of a dominant currency price, that price of that commodity would not be considered to be routinely denominated in a particular currency.

The existence of an organised commodity exchange where a commodity is traded in a single currency provides a useful starting point in determining the dominant currency in which transactions in that commodity are denominated and, accordingly, whether the price of the commodity can be considered to be 'routinely denominated' in that particular currency. The organised commodity exchanges may establish liquid markets for commodities quoted in a particular currency, and transactions between counterparties that are not conducted through the exchange are also denominated in that particular currency, because to do otherwise would present arbitrage opportunities. For example, copper and gold are traded in US dollars on organised commodity exchanges and transactions between various counterparties that are not conducted through the exchange are also denominated in US dollars given the liquid markets established by the exchanges.

Certain commodities are not traded on organised exchanges, but global pricing forums exist that publish 'spot' prices denominated in a dominant currency for that particular commodity. Transactions between market participants are based on those published spot prices. For example, certain organisations independently may monitor market activities and publish US dollar prices that have become generally accepted as spot prices for the given commodity. Contracts between market participants are denominated in US dollars based on these published spot prices. In Japan and Europe, transactions may be conducted in Japanese Yen or Euros, respectively, but such Yen and Euro price equivalents are convenience translations of the US dollar spot price. Accordingly, in such circumstances, the price of the given commodity would be considered to be routinely denominated in US dollars in commercial transactions around the world.

The concept of a currency that is commonly used in contracts to purchase or sell non-financial items in the economic environment in which the transaction takes place' as described in IFRS 9:B4.3.8(d)(iii) was introduced to address situations where entities operate in economies in which it is common for business contracts to be denominated in a foreign currency. [IFRS 9:BCZ4.95]

'Economic environment' should be considered for the country concerned as a whole. It may be the case that more than one currency is commonly used. The Standard provides an example of a common currency as a "relatively stable and liquid currency that is commonly used in local business transactions *or* external trade" (emphasis added). Therefore, a currency that is common for *either* external or internal transactions will be considered common for that country.

Looking at external trade, it may be possible that a country has multiple currencies that are commonly used to purchase or sell non-financial items. For instance, import and export transactions in and out of a small country (with counterparties in other small countries) may be commonly denominated in a range of internationally liquid, stable currencies (such as the Euro and the US dollar) rather than just one internationally liquid, stable currency. In such circumstances, if there is a significant level of transactions in each of the currencies, it may be possible that more than one currency is commonly used in the economic environment of external trade for that country.

Similarly, it may be possible that in certain hyperinflationary economies more than one foreign currency is used in local business transactions (because large sections of the general population view amounts in terms of one foreign currency and significant other sections of the population view amounts in another foreign currency). Also, this may be the case where a particular industry dominates the economy and commonly uses a foreign currency in local business transactions while the entirety of the remaining part of the economy uses the local currency. The judgement as to whether there is more than one common currency will depend on how significant the use of a particular currency is with respect to the local or external trade transactions of the country as a whole.

In determining whether a currency is common in a particular jurisdiction, the analysis should focus on *all* transactions in that jurisdiction. For example, in determining whether external trade is commonly denominated in Euros, transactions with the Euro zone should not be excluded from the analysis. Equally, if an entity is determining whether a country with large oil exports is considered to have US dollars as a common currency, the analysis of that country should not exclude exports of oil which would be expected to be denominated in US dollars because oil is routinely denominated in US dollars throughout the world.

In May 2007, the IFRIC (now the IFRS Interpretations Committee) published a tentative rejection notice in response to a submission on the application of IAS 39:AG33(d)(iii) (now IFRS 9:B4.3.8(d)(iii)) regarding, in particular, what is the economic environment when determining whether a currency is commonly used in contracts to buy or sell non-financial items. In the draft rejection notice, the IFRIC noted that the paragraph requires an entity to identify where the transaction takes place and to identify currencies that are commonly used in the economic environment in which the transaction takes place. The IFRIC was proposing not to take the issue on to its agenda because any guidance developed would be more in the nature of application guidance than an interpretation.

Following responses by constituents and further debate at IFRIC, the IFRIC agreed to refer the matter to the Board for amendment to clarify the Standard and eliminate any diversity in practice. At its December 2007 meeting, the IASB noted that IFRS 9:B4.3.8(d)(iii) is intended to prohibit the separation of embedded foreign currency derivatives if the embedded derivatives are integral to the contractual arrangement. The IASB noted that embedded foreign currency derivatives are likely to be integral to the contractual arrangement if the foreign currency has one or more of the characteristics of a functional currency as set out in IAS 21:9. Accordingly, the Board decided to amend IFRS 9:B4.3.8(d)(iii) to refer to a currency that has one or more of the characteristics of a functional currency as set out in IAS 21:9.

At its January 2009 meeting, the Board decided to defer its redeliberations of the proposal relating to the bifurcation of an embedded foreign currency derivative to a future period.

At its January 2010 meeting, the IFRIC decided to remove the item, without finalisation, from the Annual Improvements project. The IFRIC believe that the issue will be incorporated as part of the Board's broader decisions on replacing IAS 39 and, therefore, should not be considered on a piecemeal basis. However, this issue was not brought back to the Board's attention as part of its deliberations in replacing IAS 39. The IASB transferred all the guidance on embedded derivatives from IAS 39 to IFRS 9 in October 2010 as part of its project to replace IAS 39 but this guidance was left unchanged.

The following examples demonstrate the application of the guidance in IFRS 9:B4.3.8(d).

Example 10.5A

Routinely denominated currency (1)

Two entities, both of whose functional currency is the Japanese Yen, enter into a 3-year supply contract. If payments were either denominated in or linked to the US dollar, and the US dollar is not the currency in which the service is routinely denominated in commercial transactions around the world, the embedded foreign currency forward would need to be separated from the host supply contract.

When a transaction is denominated in a currency that is a common currency in the economic environment of one or both of the substantial parties to the contract, it is reasonable to consider the currency denomination of the contract is closely related for both parties.

Contracts where a party has the option over which currency the contract may be settled in contain foreign currency features that are not closely related to the host purchase or sale contract.

Example 10.5B

Choice of settlement in foreign currencies

Entity A, a car dealership, contracts to purchase cars from Entity B, a car manufacturer. The functional currencies of Entities A and B are Sterling and Euro respectively. The purchase agreement allows Entity A to choose whether to settle the contract in a fixed amount of either Sterling or Euros.

The embedded foreign currency option must be separated from the host purchase contract. This treatment applies even though both settlement currencies are functional currencies of counterparties to the sales agreement.

Example 10.5C

Leveraged foreign currency adjustment

Entity X, a UK entity, enters into a sales contract with Entity Z, a US entity. Payments are in US dollars, but embedded in the contract is a clause such that payments are adjusted for twice the change in the US dollar exchange rate for the period that the payment is outstanding.

The sales contract contains an embedded derivative that is not closely related to the host sales contract because leveraged foreign currency features are not closely related to host sales contracts.

Example 10.5D

Routinely denominated currency (2)

Entity A, a UK entity, contracts to buy oil from Entity B, also a UK entity. The functional currency of both entities is Sterling; however, the contract is to be settled in a fixed number of US dollars.

The embedded foreign currency feature is closely related to the host purchase contract, even though it is not in the functional currency of either counterparty to the contract. This is because the price of oil is routinely denominated in US dollars in commercial transactions around the world. Therefore, two Sterling functional currency entities can transact in oil in US dollars and the foreign currency embedded derivative is deemed to be closely related to the host purchase or sale contract.

Example 10.5E

Common currency in local economic environment

Entity A operates in a South American country that is assessed as having a high inflation economy. Like all other local businesses, it chooses to conduct its business in US dollars, a relatively stable currency. Thus, all purchase and sales contracts are denominated in US dollars.

The embedded foreign currency derivative does not need to be separated from the host purchase or sales contract because these contracts are denominated in a currency that is commonly used in the local economic environment.

If Entity A chose to use the Euro when all other local businesses used the US dollar, this exemption would not be available. To avoid separation of the embedded derivative, Entity A would have to demonstrate that it met one of the other exemptions noted above.

Example 10.5F

Common currency: sales contract indexed to a foreign currency

Two entities based in Country A both have a functional currency of US Dollars. The entities enter into a construction contract whose price is fixed at the inception in Euros. Progress billings under the contract will be invoiced and paid in US Dollars. The amount of US Dollars payable/receivable will vary and be equal to the fixed Euro amounts converted to US Dollars based on the Euro/US Dollar exchange rate at each payment date. The Euro is the currency commonly used in contracts in the economic environment in which the transaction takes place.

As the amount of US Dollars varies to equal the fixed amount of Euros at the payment date, the contract is considered a Euro denominated contract.

The contract contains an embedded derivative because the payment terms are equivalent to entering into the contract in US Dollars and then entering into a Euro/US Dollars foreign currency derivative. However, the embedded derivative is considered to be closely related and, therefore, does not need to be accounted for separately as a derivative in accordance with IFRS 9:B4.3.8(d)(iii) because the Euro is a currency that is commonly used in the economic environment in which the transaction takes place.

Determination of contractual terms of the separated embedded derivative should be done by reference to the contractual terms of the non-financial host contract. For example, if a foreign currency derivative that is required to be separated is embedded in a purchase contract of a non-financial item which specifies delivery in two months' time, the maturity of the foreign currency derivative is two months.

The purchase contract stops being an executory (non-financial) contract once the delivery of the non-financial item takes place and a financial instrument (a foreign currency payable) comes into existence. The foreign currency translation of the payable is recognised in profit or loss in accordance with IAS 21 because it is a foreign currency denominated monetary item. When the non-financial item is recognised, the embedded derivative is derecognised and its carrying amount is included in the cost of the non-financial item (see **section 12**).

11 Embedded derivatives in insurance contracts

As discussed at **2.3** in **chapter B1**, derivatives embedded in insurance contracts are within the scope of IFRS 9 if they require separation in accordance with IFRS 9, except if a derivative embedded in an insurance contract is itself an insurance contract. [IFRS 4:7] An insurance contract is a contract under which one party (the policyholder) accepts significant insurance risk from another party by agreeing to compensate the policyholder if a specified uncertain future event adversely affects the policyholder.

As an exception to IFRS 9, an insurer is not required to separate and measure at fair value a policyholder's option to surrender an insurance contract for a fixed amount (or for an amount based on a fixed amount and an interest rate), even if the exercise price differs from the carrying amount of the host insurance liability. However, the requirement in IFRS 9 does apply to a put option or cash surrender option embedded in an insurance contract if the surrender value varies in response to the change in a financial variable (such as an equity or commodity price or index), or a non-financial variable that is not specific to a party to the contract. Furthermore, this requirement also applies if the holder's ability to exercise a put option or cash surrender option is triggered by a change in such a variable (e.g. a put option that can be exercised if a stock market index reaches a specified level). This applies equally to options to surrender a financial instrument containing a discretionary participation feature. [IFRS 4:8 & 9]

IFRS 4:IG Example 2: 2.15 provides the example of a policyholder option to surrender a contract for account value equal to the fair value of a pool of equity investments, possibly after deducting a surrender charge. The example makes reference to IFRS 9:B4.3.8(g) and states that if such a feature is embedded in a host insurance contract and if the insurer measures that portion of its obligation at account value, no further adjustment is needed for the option (unless the surrender value differs significantly from account value). Otherwise the embedded derivative is to be measured separately as at FVTPL.

A unit-linking feature embedded in a host insurance contract is closely related to the host contract if the unit-denominated payments are measured at current unit values that reflect the fair values of the assets of the fund. A unit-linking feature is a contractual term that requires payments denominated in a units of an internal or external investment fund. [IFRS 9:B4.3.8(g)] For equivalent guidance on debt host contracts, see **7.10**.

This is a complex area, and must be considered in conjunction with IFRS 4 *Insurance Contracts*. The following examples are applications of embedded derivative features in insurance contracts.

Example 11A

Surrender value indexed to share price index

A policyholder has an option to surrender an insurance contract for a surrender value based on the FTSE 100. The option is not closely related to the host contract (unless the option is life-contingent to a significant extent) and should be separated from the host contract and accounted for as a derivative.

Example 11B

Death benefit linked to share price index

A host insurance contract contains a death benefit linked to equity prices or equity index, payable only on death or annuitisation and not on surrender or maturity. The equity-index feature is an insurance contract (unless the life-contingent payments are insignificant), because the policyholder benefits from it only when the insured event occurs. Thus, the contract is outside the scope of IFRS 9.

Example 11C

Surrender value linked to interest rates

A host insurance contract contains an embedded guarantee of minimum interest rates to be used in determining its surrender or maturity values.

If the guarantee is in the money on issue, or is leveraged, then the embedded guarantee is not an insurance contract (unless the embedded guarantee is life-contingent to a significant extent) and should be separated from the host contract.

Example 11D

Dual-indexed payout feature

Entity A purchases an insurance contract that contains a dual trigger such that payment is contingent on a breakdown in power supply that adversely affects the holder (first trigger) and a specified level of electricity prices (second trigger). The contingent payment is made only if both triggering events occur.

The embedded derivative is an insurance contract (unless the first trigger lacks commercial substance). A contract that qualifies as an insurance contract, whether at inception or later, remains an insurance contract until all rights and obligations are extinguished or expire. Therefore, although the remaining exposure is similar to a financial derivative after the insured event has occurred, the embedded derivative is still an insurance contract.

A derivative embedded in an insurance contract is closely related to the host insurance contract if the embedded derivative and host insurance contract are so interdependent that an entity cannot measure the embedded derivative separately (i.e. without considering the host contract). [IFRS 9:B4.3.8(h)]

12 Measurement of embedded derivatives at initial recognition

If an embedded derivative is separated from its host contract (because it is not closely related to the host), then it must be accounted for as if it were a free-standing derivative. The embedded derivative should be recognised in the statement of financial position at fair value, with changes in fair value recognised in profit or loss as they arise, unless it is designated as an effective hedging instrument in a cash flow or a net investment hedge (see **chapter B9**).

The host contract is accounted for under IFRS 9 if it is a financial instrument within the scope of those Standard; otherwise it is accounted for under the appropriate Standard (e.g. under IAS 17 if it is a lease contract).

Example 12

Accounting for foreign currency derivative embedded in executory contract

Entity A, a UK-based entity with Sterling as its functional currency, enters into a contract to purchase cocoa from a local supplier, Entity B, in six months for a fixed amount of US dollars. The US dollar is not the functional currency of either party to the transaction. The cocoa will be delivered and used over a reasonable period in the normal course of business.

Because the cocoa will be physically delivered and is for use in the normal course of business, the contract qualifies for the purchase requirements scope exception and therefore is not wholly in the scope of IFRS 9. This means that the entire contract is not a derivative recognised in the statement of financial position at fair value with changes in fair value recognised in profit or loss.

The contract still needs to be assessed for embedded derivatives. The contract contains an embedded foreign currency forward that is not closely related because the contract will be settled in US dollars and US dollars is neither the functional currency of either counterparty to the contract nor the currency in which the price of cocoa is routinely denominated in commercial transactions throughout the world. It is also not the currency commonly used in contracts to purchase or sell non-financial items in the UK. This embedded derivative must be separated from the host purchase contract and accounted for in the statement of financial position at fair value. Changes in fair value (arising from changes in the Sterling/US dollar exchange rate) will be recognised in profit or loss.

Assume the contract is entered into on 1 January 20X5. The contract is over a specified amount of cocoa for US$150,000. The 6-month forward exchange rate is US$1.5:£1. The 3-month forward exchange rate on 31 March 20X5 (Entity A's year end) is US$1.2:£1, and the spot exchange rate on 30 June 20X5 (when the cocoa is delivered) is US$1.25:£1. From the point of view of Entity A, the contract will be accounted for as a foreign currency forward contract to sell US dollars and buy Sterling, and an unrecognised executory contract to sell Sterling and buy inventories.

There are no entries on 1 January because the embedded derivative is a non-optional derivative with a fair value of zero at inception. At 31 March, the forward exchange rate has moved and so Entity A now expects US$150,000 to be equivalent to £125,000, rather than £100,000. There is a fair value loss on the forward contract, so the entry is as follows.

		£	£
Dr	Profit or loss	25,000	
Cr	Forward liability		25,000

To record the remeasurement of the forward liability.

On 30 June, the forward liability has decreased in value, because US$150,000 will cost £120,000. The entry is as follows.

		£	£
Dr	Forward liability	5,000	
Cr	Profit or loss		5,000

The record the remeasurement of the forward liability.

Entity A now pays US$150,000 to buy the cocoa under the purchase contract.

		£	£
Dr	Inventories	120,000	
Cr	Cash		120,000

To record the purchase of cocoa.

Entity A must also remove the embedded derivative from its statement of financial position.

		£	£
Dr	Forward liability	20,000	
Cr	Inventories		20,000

To eliminate the embedded derivative.

The inventories are recognised in the statement of financial position at £100,000. This is US$150,000 translated at the forward rate contracted on 1 January. When the inventories are sold, the cost of sales will be £20,000 lower than expected (based on cash paid on 30 June). This is because a £20,000 loss has already been recognised in profit or loss as a result of fair valuing the embedded derivative.

Note: for illustrative purposes only, this example ignores the time value of money for the purpose of valuing the forward contract.

12.1 Allocating proceeds to the embedded derivative at inception

At inception, an entity must determine the fair value of the embedded derivative first. The difference between the consideration paid or received to acquire the entire contract and the fair value of the embedded derivative is assigned to the host contract.

Example 12.1

Allocating the proceeds to the embedded derivative

Entity A issues for CU1 million an exchangeable bond. The holder of the exchangeable bond has the right to exchange the bond for shares of an entity that is not the issuer of the bond, Entity B. The bond has a coupon of 6 per cent, a maturity of five years, and is exchangeable into a fixed number of shares of Entity B at maturity of the bond. Using a Black-Scholes model, it is determined that the fair value of the option to exchange is CU100,000. For Entity A, assuming that the entire bond is not carried at FVTPL, separation of the embedded derivative is necessary. The amount assigned to the bond is determined by subtracting the fair value of the option from the consideration received from the issuance of the bond. Entity A would record the following entry upon issuance.

		CU	CU
Dr	Cash	1,000,000	
Cr	Option to exchange		100,000
Cr	Bond		900,000

To record the issue of the exchangeable bond.

It will not always be easy to establish the fair value of embedded derivatives, but there is little room for manoeuvre. If an embedded derivative needs to be separately accounted for, but the entity is unable to determine reliably the fair value of the embedded derivative on the basis of its terms and conditions (e.g. because the embedded derivative results in the delivery of an unquoted equity investment), the entity must determine the fair value of the whole contract and the fair value of the host contract, and the balance represents the derivative instrument. [IFRS 9:4.3.7] If an entity is unable to do this, the entity must designate the whole contract as at FVTPL. [IFRS 9:4.3.6]

13 Presentation of embedded derivatives

IFRSs do not provide specific guidance on the presentation of embedded derivatives in the statement of financial position or in profit or loss. IFRS 9:4.3.4 has an explicit statement articulating that IFRS 9 does not address whether an embedded derivative should be presented separately in the statement of financial position.

It seems appropriate for an entity to choose as an accounting policy whether it presents a hybrid contract in its statement of financial position as a single contractual arrangement or non-closely related embedded derivatives as separate financial assets or liabilities. The policy should be applied consistently to all hybrid contracts.

If an entity chooses to present the embedded derivative(s) and the host contract as a single contractual arrangement, it must still comply with IFRS 7:8 and 20(a), which require an analysis of the carrying amounts of financial instruments, and of gains or losses in the period, by IFRS 9 classification category. Irrespective of the policy adopted for presentation (as discussed in the previous paragraph), the embedded derivative component will always be classified as at FVTPL for measurement purposes (except if it is designated in a qualifying and effective hedge relationship); the host contract, if it is a financial liability in the scope of IFRS 9, will be measured at amortised cost using the effective interest method.

In addition, an entity must determine if the embedded derivative is current or non-current under IAS 1 *Presentation of Financial Statements* when an entity does not present assets and liabilities in order of liquidity. Two accounting policies are considered acceptable, as set out below.

Policy 1

Separate presentation of the host and the embedded derivative, but assessment regarding classification as current or non-current based on the cash flows of the whole hybrid arrangement because embedded derivatives cannot be settled separately from the host contract.

Policy 2

No separate presentation of the host and the embedded derivative, and assessment regarding classification as current or non-current based on the cash flows of the whole hybrid arrangement because embedded derivatives cannot be settled separately from the host contract.

Example 13

Presentation of embedded derivative in the statement of financial position

Consider the application of the two policies described immediately above in the following five examples in which the embedded derivative would be separately accounted for under IFRS 9:

Scenario 1

Issued debt with maturity in five years with a separated embedded put option that allows the holder to put the debt instrument back to the issuer every six months' time at an amount not approximately equal to the debt host contract's amortised cost.

Scenario 2

Same as Scenario 1 except that the issuer has a call option (rather than the holder having a put option). The issuer does not expect the call to be exercised in the next 12 months.

Scenario 3

Issued debt with maturity in five years with no put or call options but principal payment depends on the performance of a specified equity index.

Scenario 4

An executory contract to buy a non-financial item in five years when the price paid is based on a non-closely related foreign currency. The non-financial host contract is treated as an executory contract outside the scope of IFRS 9. The embedded non-closely related foreign currency derivative is separately recognised at fair value through profit or loss.

Scenario 5

An operating lease with five years to maturity with a non-closely related embedded inflation derivative (e.g. the lease rentals are linked to leveraged inflation).

Depending on the entity's accounting policy, the presentation options are as follows.

	Policy 1	**Policy 2**
Scenario	Separate presentation of host contract and derivative, but assessment of current/non-current based on the whole hybrid arrangement because the embedded cannot be settled separately from the host contract.	No separate presentation of host contract and embedded, and assessment of current/non-current based on the whole hybrid arrangement because the embedded cannot be settled separately from the host contract.
1 Debt with written put	Derivative (D): current liability; Host (H): current liability	Whole instrument: current liability
2 Debt with purchased call	D: non-current asset*; H: non-current liability	Whole instrument: non-current liability*

	Policy 1	Policy 2
3 Debt linked to equity index	D: non-current asset/ liability; H: non-current liability	Whole instrument: non-current liability
4 Executory contract with foreign currency derivative	D: non-current asset/liability; H: not recognised	D: non-current asset/liability; H: not recognised
5 Operating lease with inflation derivative	D: non-current asset/liability; H: not recognised	D: non-current asset/liability; H: not recognised

* Because the issuer does not expect to call the debt in the 12 months after the reporting date, the derivative and host contract are both non-current. If the issuer expected to call the debt in the 12 months following the reporting date the derivative and host contract would be both presented as current in the statement of financial position.

The list of scenarios above is not intended to be exhaustive.

B6 Measurement

Contents

1 Introduction

IFRS 9 has a different measurement approach at initial recognition and for subsequent measurement for certain financial instruments. The Standard requires all financial instruments to be measured at initial recognition at fair value (except for certain trade receivables), but for subsequent measurement it requires a mixed measurement model with some assets and liabilities measured at fair value and others at amortised cost. This model is based on the classification of financial assets and liabilities as discussed in **chapters B2** and **B3**.

The requirements on fair value measurement at initial recognition and for financial instruments subsequently measured at fair value are contained in **chapter B7**. That chapter covers the requirements of IFRS 13 *Fair Value Measurement*.

This chapter focuses on the measurement of financial instruments measured at amortised cost, fair value through other comprehensive income (FVTOCI) and fair value through profit or loss (FVTPL), including the detailed impairment requirements.

This chapter begins with the guidance on how to account for transaction costs at initial recognition before moving onto the subsequent measurement requirements.

2 Initial recognition

2.1 Transaction costs

IFRS 9:5.1.1 to 5.1.3 require that, except for trade receivables that do not have a significant financing component (determined in accordance with IFRS 15 *Revenue from Contracts with Customers*), all financial instruments are initially recognised at fair value (see **section 3** in **chapter B7**) plus or minus, in the case of a financial asset or liability that is not classified as at FVTPL, transaction costs that are directly attributable to the acquisition or issue of the asset or liability. Trade receivables that do not have a significant financing component are initially recognised at their transaction price.

The consequences of this requirement are summarised below:

(a) For debt instruments that are measured subsequent to initial recognition at amortised cost or FVTOCI, transaction costs are included in the calculation of the effective interest rate – in effect, they are amortised through profit or loss over the term of the instrument.

(b) For investments in equity instruments designated as at FVTOCI (see **5.3.2** in **chapter B2**), the transaction costs remain in equity and are not subsequently reclassified to profit or loss. An entity may choose to reclassify within equity the cumulative gain or loss (which includes transaction costs), for example when the investment in equity instruments is derecognised. [IFRS 9:B5.7.1]

(c) For financial instruments classified as at FVTPL, transaction costs are recognised in profit or loss immediately on initial recognition.

If the fair value of a financial instrument at initial recognition differs from the transaction price, an entity should apply IFRS 9:B5.1.2A (see **7.3** of **chapter B7** for more guidance).

Transaction costs are defined as incremental costs that are directly attributable to the acquisition, issue or disposal of a financial asset or a financial liability. An incremental cost is one that would not have been incurred if the entity had not acquired, issued or disposed of the financial instrument. [IFRS 9:Appendix A]

Transaction costs include fees and commissions paid to agents (including employees acting as selling agents), advisers, brokers and dealers, levies by regulatory agencies and security exchanges, and transfer taxes and duties. However, debt premiums or discounts, financing costs, internal administrative costs and holding costs are not transaction costs. [IFRS 9:B5.4.8] In practice, the interpretation of this definition may require significant judgement.

2.2 Settlement date accounting

The accounting for regular way trades is considered at **2.2** in **chapter B8**. When an entity uses settlement date accounting for an asset that is subsequently measured at amortised cost, movements in fair value between trade and settlement date are not recognised and no accounting entries are required during that time except for impairment losses, see **5.1.1**. The effective interest rate is applied from the settlement date.

For assets measured subsequent to initial recognition at fair value, the change in fair value between trade and settlement date is recognised in profit or loss if the asset is measured at FVTPL and in other comprehensive income if the asset is measured at FVTOCI. [IFRS 9:5.7.4]

3 Subsequent measurement

3.1 Financial assets

The classification of financial instruments determines how they are subsequently measured. As discussed in **section 5** of **chapter B2**, IFRS 9 requires financial assets to be classified into one of three categories: FVTPL (**3.1.1**), amortised cost (**3.1.2**) and FVTOCI (**3.1.3**).

3.1.1 Financial assets at fair value through profit or loss (FVTPL)

Assets classified as at FVTPL are measured at fair value. All gains and losses that arise as a result of changes in fair value are recognised in profit or loss, except for hedging instruments that are designated in certain hedge relationships (e.g. cash flow hedges or hedges of a net investment in a foreign operation). **chapter B7** contains guidance on the appropriate determination of fair value.

Gains and losses that arise between the end of the last reporting period and the date an instrument is derecognised do not constitute a separate 'profit/loss on disposal'. Such gains and losses will have arisen prior to disposal, while the item is still being measured at FVTPL, and should be recognised in profit or loss when they occur.

3.1.2 Amortised cost

The amortised cost classification category only applies to debt instrument financial assets that meet the specified criteria in IFRS 9:4.1.2 (described in more detail in **5.1** in **chapter B2**). Amortised cost measurement requires the application of the effective interest method, as discussed in **section 4**.

Amortised cost of a financial instrument is defined as the amount at which the financial asset or financial liability is measured at initial recognition minus the principal repayments, plus or minus the cumulative amortisation using the effective interest method of any difference between that initial amount and the maturity amount and, for financial assets, adjusted for any loss allowance. [IFRS 9:Appendix A] Loss allowances for expected credit losses are discussed further in **section 5**.

Gains or losses resulting from fluctuations in fair value are not recognised for financial assets classified in the amortised cost category.

3.1.3 Fair value through other comprehensive income (FVTOCI)

Two types of financial assets are measured at FVTOCI. The first type is non-held for trading investments in equity instruments that are designated at initial recognition as measured at FVTOCI. The second type, similar to the amortised cost classification, only applies to debt instrument financial assets that meet the specific criteria in IFRS 9:4.1.2A (see **5.2** in **chapter B2**).

3.1.3.1 Exception to presenting changes in fair value in profit or loss for certain equity instruments

IFRS 9 permits an entity to make an irrevocable election at initial recognition for investments in equity instruments that do not meet the definition of held for trading, which would otherwise be measured at FVTPL, to present changes in fair value in other comprehensive income. [IFRS 9:4.1.4]

Reclassification of amounts recognised in other comprehensive income and accumulated in equity to profit or loss is not permitted for equity investments designated at FVTOCI. This applies throughout the life of the instrument and also at derecognition. Furthermore, such investments will not be subject to the impairment requirements.

Dividends on investments in equity instruments with gains and losses irrevocably presented in other comprehensive income are recognised in profit or loss if the dividend is not a return on investment when:

[IFRS 9:5.7.1A]

(a) the entity's right to receive payment of the dividend is established;

(b) it is probable that the economic benefits associated with the dividend will flow to the entity; and

(c) the amount of the dividend can be measured reliably.

Instead of being paid in cash, a dividend may be structured so that it is payable in shares of the issuer. This is often termed a 'stock dividend', a 'share dividend' or a 'scrip dividend'. When the dividend is payable on a pro-rata basis exclusively in shares of the issuer (i.e. there is no cash or other settlement alternative), the investor does not regard the dividend as revenue in profit or loss. Rather, the pro-rata receipt of additional shares in the issuer, from the investor's perspective, is in the nature of a bonus issue of shares whereby the investor's economic interest remains unchanged. The number of shares held by the investor increases, but the value of its total interest is unchanged because its economic interest is distributed over a greater number of shares (i.e. the increase in the number of shares results in a concurrent reduction in the value of each share).

When the investor is given a choice of settlement between shares of the issuer or cash (or another settlement alternative that is not shares of the issuer) then the investor treats the dividend as revenue in profit or loss when the dividend becomes unconditional from the perspective of the issuer. Between the dates the revenue is recognised and the date the holder makes its election of receiving further shares or cash (or another settlement alternative), this is likely to meet the definition of a derivative that will be required to be measured at FVTPL.

When the dividend is structured so that it is certain that all shareholders will decide to take the shares rather than cash (i.e. the cash alternative does not have substance), the dividend is in effect a pure stock dividend and should be accounted for accordingly. When the market value of the share alternative is above the cash alternative, the dividend is often referred to as an 'enhanced stock dividend'. Careful judgement will be necessary, based on the specific facts and circumstances, to determine whether a dividend involving an enhanced stock dividend is in substance a distribution to owners recognised in profit or loss or a pure stock dividend.

3.1.3.2 Debt instrument measured at FVTOCI

For debt instruments measured at FVTOCI, changes in fair value should be recognised in other comprehensive income, except for:

[IFRS 9:5.7.10]

- interest calculated using the effective interest rate method (see **section 4.1**);
- foreign exchange gains or losses (see **section 3.3**); and
- impairment gains or losses (see **section 5**),

until the financial asset is derecognised or reclassified.

When the financial asset is derecognised, the cumulative gain or loss previously recognised in other comprehensive income is reclassified from equity to profit or loss as a reclassification adjustment (see IAS 1 *Presentation of Financial Statements*). [IFRS 9:5.7.10] See **7.1** of **chapter B2** for the accounting of gains or losses when an item is reclassified out of the FVTOCI measurement category.

If a debt instrument asset is measured at FVTOCI, the amounts that are recognised in profit or loss are the same as the amounts that would have been recognised in profit or loss if the financial asset had been measured at amortised cost. [IFRS 9:5.7.11]

3.1.4 Hedged items

IFRS 9 includes specific requirements to be applied when accounting for a financial asset that is a hedged item. These requirements are discussed in detail in **chapter B9**.

3.1.5 Instruments whose fair value is 'unreliable'

If IFRS 9 requires a financial instrument to be measured at fair value, there is no exception from measurement on that basis. In all cases fair value is deemed to be reliable. See **chapter B7** for more guidance on fair value measurement.

3.1.6 Reclassifications

The measurement consequences of reclassifying financial assets at the date of reclassification are discussed in detail in **7.1** of **chapter B2**. The measurement guidance after the date of reclassification is generally consistent with the measurement guidance that would have applied had the financial asset been initially measured in accordance with the classification category to which it has been reclassified. However as an exception for reclassifications out of FVTPL the effective interest rate is determined at the date of reclassification rather than at initial recognition.

3.1.7 *Negative fair value*

If the fair value of a financial instrument accounted for at FVTPL previously recognised as a financial asset falls below zero, it becomes a financial liability and is measured as discussed in **section 3.2**.

3.2 Financial liabilities

Financial liabilities are measured at amortised cost using the effective interest method (see **section 4.1**), with the following exceptions:

[IFRS 9:4.2.1]

(a) financial liabilities at FVTPL (see **3.2.1**);

(b) financial liabilities that arise when a transfer of a financial asset does not qualify for derecognition or when the continuing involvement approach applies (see **3.2.2**);

(c) written financial guarantee contracts not designated as at FVTPL that are not accounted for under IFRS 4 *Insurance Contracts* (see **2.3.3** of **chapter B1**);

(d) commitments to provide a loan at a below-market interest rate (see **3.5** of **chapter B1**);

(e) hedged items (see **3.2.3**); and

(f) contingent consideration recognised by an acquirer in a business combination to which IFRS 3 applies. Such contingent consideration shall subsequently be measured at fair value with changes recognised in profit or loss.

3.2.1 *Financial liabilities at fair value through profit or loss*

Financial liabilities that are measured at FVTPL include those classified as held for trading and derivative liabilities that are not designated as effective hedging instruments, contingent consideration recognised by an acquirer in a business combination to which IFRS 3 *Business Combinations* applies, *and* those financial liabilities that are designated as at FVTPL. [IFRS 9:4.2.1(a) & (e)] Fair value gains and losses are recognised in profit or loss except in the case of certain financial liabilities that are designated as at FVTPL where changes in the liability's credit risk are included in other comprehensive income with all other gains and losses recognised in profit or loss (see **7.1.2.5** in **chapter B3**).

A consequence of financial liabilities being in this category is that the effect of changes in an entity's own credit risk will be reflected in the entity's performance (i.e. profit or loss, or other comprehensive income). For example, if an entity that has elected to measure its issued debt at fair value experiences financial difficulties, it is likely to recognise a gain in other comprehensive income or, in some specified, exceptional cases, in profit or loss, reflecting the instrument's worsening creditworthiness. Whereas for a derivative liability, all gains and losses, including those attributable to credit risk, are reflected in profit or loss unless it is designated in a certain type of hedge relationship (e.g. a cash flow hedge or hedge of a net investment in a foreign operation).

3.2.2 Financial liabilities arising on the transfer of a financial asset

A liability may arise when a transfer of a financial asset does not qualify for derecognition or is accounted for using the 'continuing involvement' approach. The approach required for measuring such liabilities is discussed in **chapter B8**.

3.2.3 Hedged items

IFRS 9 includes specific requirements to be applied when accounting for a financial liability that is a hedged item. These requirements are discussed in detail in **chapter B9**.

3.3 Foreign currency

When a financial asset or financial liability is a monetary item, foreign exchange gains and losses should be recognised in profit or loss in accordance with IAS 21 *The Effects of Changes in Foreign Exchange Rates*. Monetary items are defined as units of currency held and assets and liabilities to be received or paid in a fixed or determinable number of units of currency. [IAS 21:8]

For the purpose of recognising foreign exchange gains or losses under IAS 21, a financial asset measured at FVTOCI under IFRS 9:4.1.2A is treated as a monetary item. Accordingly, such a financial asset is treated as an asset measured at amortised cost in the foreign currency. Exchange differences on the amortised cost are recognised in profit or loss. [IFRS 9:B5.7.2A] Consequently, the impact in profit or loss in respect of foreign currency translation is the same whether a debt instrument is measured at amortised cost or measured at FVTOCI.

A non-held for trading investment in an equity instrument that is designated as at FVTOCI fails the definition of a monetary item and therefore is non-monetary. Fair value is determined first in the foreign currency in which the item is denominated and then the foreign currency amount is translated into the functional currency using the closing rate. Changes in foreign currency exchange rates are included in the financial asset's fair value that is recognised in other comprehensive income. The foreign currency element will never affect profit or loss because no fair value amounts accumulated in equity related to equity instruments designated as at FVTOCI are permitted to be subsequently reclassified to profit or loss.

3.3.1 Financial assets and liabilities measured at FVTPL

For financial assets and liabilities that are measured as at FVTPL, the requirement to recognise foreign currency gains or losses is straightforward because all gains and losses are recognised in profit or loss as part of the fair value gain or loss. The fair value is determined firstly in the foreign currency in which the item is denominated and that foreign currency amount is subsequently translated into the entity's functional currency using the closing rate. The accounting treatment is the same irrespective of whether the item is monetary or non-monetary.

3.3.2 Amortised cost and debt instruments measured at FVTOCI

For financial assets and financial liabilities measured at amortised cost as well as debt instruments measured at FVTOCI (which for the purposes of calculating foreign currency translation in profit or loss are treated as if they were amortised cost) are monetary items and so foreign currency gains or loss are calculated by determining the amortised cost in the foreign currency in which the item is denominated and the foreign currency amount is subsequently translated into the entity's functional currency using the closing rate. Such foreign currency gains and losses are recognised in profit or loss.

As the foreign currency element recognised in profit or loss for a debt instrument measured at FVTOCI is the same as if it was measured at amortised cost, the residual foreign currency element based on the translation of the carrying value (at fair value) is recognised in other comprehensive income.

3.3.3 Hedged items and hedging instruments

IAS 21 specifically excludes from its scope the measurement of foreign currency items that are subject to hedge accounting because IFRS 9 is more specific on how to recognise gains or losses when hedge accounting is applied. If a financial asset or financial liability is designated as a hedged item in a fair value hedge of the exposure to changes in foreign currency rates under IFRS 9 the hedged item is remeasured for changes in foreign currency rates even if it would otherwise have been recognised using a historical rate under IAS 21. [IFRS 9:6.5.8] This exception applies to non-monetary items that are carried in terms of historical cost in the foreign currency and are hedged against exposure to foreign currency rates. [IAS 21:23(b)] For example, an investment in a subsidiary that is measured at cost is fair value hedged for foreign currency risk.

Foreign currency gains or losses on monetary items are recognised in profit or loss except if the monetary item is designated as a hedging instrument in either a cash flow hedge or a hedge of a net investment in a foreign operation (see **chapter B9**). [IFRS 9:B5.7.2] If there is a hedging relationship between a non-derivative monetary asset and a non-derivative monetary liability, changes in the foreign currency component of those financial instruments are presented in profit or loss. [IFRS 9:B5.7.4]

3.3.4 Summary of foreign currency accounting

A summary of how foreign currency is treated for the various financial asset classifications is set out in the following table.

Classification	**Monetary or non-monetary item**	**Foreign currency gains and losses from remeasurement (prior to its disposal)***
Amortised cost (whether a financial asset or financial liability)	Monetary item, calculated on the instrument's amortised cost.	Profit or loss
Debt instruments held that are fair valued through other comprehensive income	Monetary item, calculated on the instrument's amortised cost.	Profit or loss (with the foreign currency element that is not based on amortised cost, being the translation on the difference between the fair value and the amortised cost is recognised in other comprehensive income along with the other fair value gains or losses)
Equity instruments held that are fair valued through other comprehensive income	Non-monetary item	Other comprehensive income
Fair value through profit or loss (whether a financial asset or financial liability)	Monetary or non-monetary	Profit or loss as part of the fair value gains and losses on the entire instrument

* Assumes that the item is not being hedged for foreign currency risk, or is not a hedging instrument in a foreign currency hedge.

3.3.5 Dual currency bonds issued

IFRS 9:B4.3.8(c) states that a foreign currency derivative that provides a stream of principal or interest payments denominated in a foreign currency and that is embedded in a host debt instrument (e.g. a dual currency bond) is closely related to the host debt instrument. Such a derivative is not separated from the host instrument because IAS 21 requires foreign currency gains and losses on monetary items to be recognised in profit or loss. This is relevant for all dual currency bonds issued that are not measured as at FVTPL.

Neither IFRS 9 nor IAS 21 provides specific guidance regarding how to measure dual currency bonds that are financial liabilities. Because IFRS 9 states that the foreign currency gains and losses are accounted for under IAS 21, it is reasonable to assume that the accounting treatment is equivalent to isolating the foreign currency cash flows and measuring them as if they were a separate instrument. For example, if interest is denominated in a foreign currency, but the principal is not, an entity could measure the interest flows as if it was a foreign currency denominated interest rate strip and apply the effective interest rate method and treat the principal cash flow as a functional currency denominated zero coupon bond. Conversely, if the principal is denominated in a foreign currency, but the interest is not, an entity could measure the principal as if it was a foreign currency denominated zero coupon bond and apply the effective interest rate method and treat the interest flows as a functional currency denominated interest rate strip (see **example 3.3.5**).

Example 3.3.5

Accounting for a dual currency bond

Entity A, a Sterling functional currency entity, issues a dual currency bond on 1 January 20X4 under which the interest is denominated in Sterling but the principal is denominated in US dollars. The bond has a notional amount of US$200m, has a maturity of three years and is issued at par.

Entity A determines the carrying amount of a US$-denominated 3-year zero coupon bond at inception by discounting US$200m by the 3-year US$ zero coupon rate reflecting Entity A's credit quality which is 10% (US$200m / 1.1^3 = US$150.26m). Entity A then converts this amount into its functional currency at the US$:£ spot rate at inception (US$150.26m / US$2:£1 = £75.13m). The difference between this amount and the functional currency equivalent net proceeds received from issuing the dual currency bond is allocated to the functional currency interest only strip [(US$200m / US$2:£1) – £75.13m = £24.87m]. Each period, the US$ effective interest rate of 10% is applied to the US$-denominated zero coupon bond in US$ and this US$ carrying amount is converted into Sterling in accordance with IAS 21.

Entity A determines the Sterling effective interest rate for the interest only strip which is the 3-year interest rate for an equivalent 3-year amortising loan. For illustration purposes, this interest rate is also assumed to be 10% (although, in practice, the interest rates for the respective currencies will differ).

The foreign exchange rates for the three periods are as set out below.

	Period end rate (US$:£)	Average rate (US$:£)
20X3	2.00	–
20X4	1.80	1.90
20X5	2.10	1.95
20X6	1.90	2.00

The carrying amount of the foreign currency zero coupon bond in US$ is determined by applying the US$ effective interest rate in US$.

	20X4	20X5	20X6
Opening carrying amount (US$)	150.26	165.29	181.82
Interest at 10% (US$)	15.03	16.53	18.18
Closing carrying amount (US$)	165.29	181.82	200.00

The carrying amount of the foreign currency zero coupon bond in Sterling is determined by converting the opening carrying amount in US$ at the opening rate, adding interest at the average rate, adding/subtracting foreign exchange gains or losses so that the closing value in Sterling is equal to the US$ closing value at the period end rate.

	20X4	20X5	20X6
Opening carrying amount (£)	75.13	91.83	86.58
Interest at average rates (£)	7.91	8.48	9.09
Foreign currency (gains) losses (£)	8.79	(13.72)	9.59
Closing carrying amount (£)	91.83	86.59	105.26

The carrying amount of the interest only strip in Sterling is determined by adding the effective interest rate and deducting the cash payments for each period.

	20X4	20X5	20X6
Opening carrying amount (£)	24.87	17.36	9.10
Interest at 10% (£)	2.49	1.74	0.90
Less cash paid (£)	(10.00)	(10.00)	(10.00)
Closing carrying amount (£)	17.36	9.10	–

The entries are summarised below.

	Description	Cash	Debt	Interest expense	Foreign currency gain/(loss)
		£	£	£	£
1/1/X4	Issue debt	100.00	(100.00)		
20X4	Interest on US$ zero coupon bond		(7.91)	7.91	
	Foreign currency movement		(8.79)		(8.79)
	Interest on interest only strip	(10.00)	7.51	2.49	

	Description	Cash	Debt	Interest expense	Foreign currency gain/(loss)
		£	£	£	£
20X5	Interest on US$ zero coupon bond		(8.48)	8.48	
	Foreign currency movement		13.72		13.72
	Interest on interest only strip	(10.00)	8.26	1.74	
20X6	Interest on US$ zero coupon bond		(9.09)	9.09	
	Foreign currency movement		(9.59)		(9.59)
	Interest on interest only strip	(10.00)	9.10	0.90	
31/12/X6	Repayment of dual currency bond	(105.26)	105.26		

3.3.6 Dual currency bonds held

Dual currency bonds held as financial assets are regarded as failing the amortised cost and FVTOCI criteria because IFRS 9:B4.1.8 requires that an entity assesses whether contractual cash flows are solely payments of principal and interest on the principal amount outstanding in the currency in which the financial asset is denominated. In the case of a dual currency bond, the interest receipts are based on a principal that is not the contractual principal of the instrument and, therefore, the contractual cash flows of the assets are not "solely payments of principal and interest on the principal amount outstanding" [IFRS 9:4.1.2 to 4.1.3]. Therefore, dual currency bonds held are always classified as at FVTPL and any foreign currency component is included in the fair value movement recognised in profit or loss.

4 Amortised cost

On acquisition or at issue, the carrying amount of a financial instrument, being its fair value (except for trade receivables that do not have a significant financing component determined in accordance with IFRS 15 *Revenue from Contracts with Customers* which are initially measured at the transaction price), represents the discounted amount of the expected future cash flows that will arise under that instrument. For financial assets and liabilities measured at amortised cost and debt instrument assets measured at FVTOCI, the unwinding of that discount is included in profit or loss as interest income or interest expense. See **chapter B7** for a full discussion on fair value measurement at initial recognition.

For this section 'amortised cost' measurement is not only relevant for financial assets and financial liabilities measured at amortised cost.

IFRS 9 requires debt instruments measured at FVTOCI to impact profit or loss in the same way as if they were measured at amortised cost. Therefore it is necessary to determine the amortised cost measurement of assets at FVTOCI in order to determine the appropriate amounts to recognise in profit or loss with the difference between the amortised cost and fair value of the asset recognised in other comprehensive income.

Amortised cost is defined as the amount at which the financial asset or financial liability is measured at initial recognition minus principal repayments, plus or minus the cumulative amortisation using the effective interest method of any difference between that initial amount and for financial assets, adjusted for any loss allowance. [IFRS 9: Appendix A]

The effective interest method is discussed in **section 4.1**.

For financial assets or financial liabilities at FVTPL, interest is effectively wrapped up in the fair value adjustment that is included in profit or loss in each accounting period and is not required to be separately disclosed, although an entity may choose to do so as an accounting policy choice.

4.1 The effective interest method

IFRS 9 requires that the amortised cost of a financial asset or liability is calculated using the 'effective interest method'. This method allocates interest income/expense over the relevant period by applying the 'effective interest rate' to the carrying amount of the asset or liability. This applies for financial assets and financial liabilities measured at amortised cost as well as for determining interest revenue for debt instrument assets measured at FVTOCI.

The effective interest rate is applied to the gross carrying amount of a financial asset (the carrying amount of a financial asset, before adjusting for any loss allowance) except for:

[IFRS 9:5.4.1]

- purchased or originated credit-impaired financial assets (i.e. purchased or originated financial assets that are credit-impaired on initial recognition). For those financial assets, the entity should apply the credit-adjusted effective interest rate to the amortised cost of the financial asset (i.e. to the amount net of any loss allowance) from initial recognition; and
- financial assets that are not purchased or originated credit-impaired financial assets but subsequently have become credit-impaired financial assets. For those financial assets, the entity should apply the effective interest rate to the amortised cost of the financial asset in subsequent reporting periods (i.e. to the amount net of any loss allowance).

IFRS 9 defines the effective interest rate as the rate that exactly discounts estimated future cash payments or receipts through the expected life of the financial asset or financial liability to the gross carrying amount of a financial asset or to the amortised cost of a financial liability. When calculating the effective interest rate, an entity should estimate the expected cash flows by considering all the contractual terms of the financial instrument (for example, prepayment, extension, call and similar options) but should not consider the expected credit losses. The calculation includes all fees and points paid or received between parties to the contract that are an integral part of the effective interest rate, transaction costs, and all other premiums or discounts. There is a presumption that the cash flows and the expected life of a group of similar financial instruments can be estimated reliably. However, in those rare cases when it is not possible to reliably estimate the cash flows or the expected life of a financial instrument (or group of financial instruments), the entity should use the contractual cash flows over the full contractual term of the financial instrument (or group of financial instruments). [IFRS 9:Appendix A]

Because transaction costs are taken into account when determining the initial carrying amount, their recognition in profit or loss is effectively spread over the life of the instrument. Transaction costs include fees and commission paid to agents (including employees acting as selling agents), advisers, brokers and dealers, levies by regulatory agencies and security exchanges, and transfer taxes and duties. Transaction costs do not include debt premiums or discounts, financing costs or internal administrative or holding costs. [IFRS 9:B5.4.8]

Example 4.1

Effective interest rate

On 1 January 20X0, an entity acquires a bond for CU90, incurring additional transaction costs of CU5. Interest of CU4 is receivable annually over the following five years (31 December 20X0 to 31 December 20X4). The bond has a G20X4. The bond is measured at amortised cost.

Year	Gross carrying amount at the start of the period	Interest income at 6.96%	Cash flow	Gross carrying amount at the end of the period
	CU	CU	CU	CU
20X0	95.00	6.61	(4.00)	97.61
20X1	97.61	6.79	(4.00)	100.40
20X2	100.40	6.99	(4.00)	103.39
20X3	103.39	7.19	(4.00)	106.58
20X4	106.58	7.42	(114.00)	0.00

The effective interest rate of 6.96 per cent is the rate that discounts the expected cash flows on the bond to the initial gross carrying amount, i.e.:

$4/1.0696 + 4/1.0696^2 + 4/1.0696^3 + 4/1.0696^4 + 114/1.0696^5 = 95$

The above calculations are based on the gross carrying amount of the asset. To derive the amortised cost of the asset, the loss allowance for expected credit losses (calculated separately, see **section 5**) is deducted from the gross carrying amount.

The effective interest rate is determined based on the initial carrying amount of the financial asset or liability. Therefore, the effective interest rate applied to any financial instrument is not recalculated to reflect fair value changes in the carrying amount of the asset or liability.

As noted in IFRS 9:5.4.1 the effective interest rate does not apply to purchased or originated credit-impaired financial assets. Instead a different effective interest rate, the *credit-adjusted effective interest rate* is applied which is defined as the same as the effective interest rate except that it *includes,* rather than excludes, expected credit losses. In other words, the initial expected credit losses are included in the estimated cash flows when calculating the credit-adjusted effective interest rate. A financial asset may be considered credit-impaired at initial recognition because the credit risk is very high, and in the case of a purchase it is acquired at a deep discount. However, this does not mean that a credit-adjusted effective interest rate should be applied solely because the financial asset has high credit risk at initial recognition. [IFRS 9:B5.4.7]

When financial assets that are not purchased or originated credit-impaired financial assets subsequently become credit-impaired financial assets, the effective interest rate in subsequent reporting periods is applied to the net carrying amount after deduction of the loss allowance (i.e. the amortised cost). If in the future the situation reverses, so that it ceases to be credit-impaired and the improvement can be related objectively to an event occurring after it became credit-impaired (such as an improvement in the borrower's credit rating) the interest revenue is determined using the effective interest rate applied to the gross carrying amount in subsequent reporting periods (i.e. an amount not adjusted for a loss allowance). [IFRS 9:5.4.2] **Section 5** discusses the requirements for impairment in more detail.

Under some economic conditions, the overall effective interest rate on some financial assets may be negative. For example, during an economic downturn, strong demand for 'safe harbour' assets can increase their prices sufficiently to result in negative yields. Another example of this phenomenon arises in jurisdictions where, as a matter of monetary policy, negative central bank interest rates are set, resulting in the origination of financial assets with negative interest rates.

In January 2015, the Interpretations Committee issued a final agenda decision on IAS 39 and IAS 1 *Presentation of Financial Statements*, regarding the presentation, in the statement of comprehensive income, of income and expenses arising on financial instruments with a negative yield. The agenda decision equally applies to IFRS 9.

The Interpretations Committee noted that interest resulting from a negative effective interest rate on a financial asset does not meet the definition of interest revenue in IAS 18 *Revenue*, because it reflects a gross outflow, instead of a gross inflow, of economic benefits (the same conclusion would apply under IFRS 15 *Revenue from Contracts with Customers*). Consequently, the expense arising on a financial asset because of a negative effective interest rate should not be presented as interest revenue, but in an appropriate expense classification. The Interpretations Committee noted that in accordance with IAS 1:85 and 112(c), the entity is required to present additional information about such an amount if that is relevant to an understanding of the entity's financial performance or to an understanding of this item.

The Interpretations Committee considered that in the light of the existing IFRS requirements an interpretation was not necessary and consequently decided not to add the issue to its agenda.

4.1.1 Cash flows

When calculating the effective interest rate, the *estimated* cash flows arising from the asset or liability (or, where relevant, the group of assets or liabilities) should be used. IFRS 9 explicitly states that all contractual terms of the instrument (e.g. prepayment, call and similar options) should be considered, but that expected credit losses should not be taken into account. This is because the gross carrying amount is adjusted for a loss allowance for expected credit losses which is not part of the effective interest rate calculation. The gross carrying amount less the allowance for credit losses equals the amortised cost.

In contrast, credit losses that have already been incurred on an instrument by the time it is acquired by the reporting entity should be taken into account when calculating the credit-adjusted effective interest rate. This might be the case when a financial asset is acquired at a deep discount because credit losses that have occurred are reflected in the transaction price.

If a debt instrument liability has a prepayment, put, or call feature embedded in the terms of the instrument, the entity must firstly determine whether that feature is an embedded derivative that needs to be separately accounted for. See **7.1** in **chapter B5** for further guidance on embedded derivatives. Briefly, such embedded derivatives will be separately accounted for unless the option's exercise price is approximately equal to the instrument's amortised cost on each exercise date, or the exercise price of the prepayment option reimburses the lender for an amount up to the approximate present value of lost interest for the remaining term of the host contract. [IFRS 9:B4.3.5(e)]

If the embedded derivative is accounted for separately, the impact on the timing and amount of the cash flows of this feature must not be used in determining the estimated cash flows of the debt host contract when determining the effective interest rate. If the timing and amount of the cash flows associated with the prepayment feature was taken into account in determining the timing and amount of the cash flows of the host contract, it would result in double counting of the prepayment feature in profit or loss because it would be included in the effective interest rate on the debt host contract as well as in the fair value movements of the embedded derivative.

4.1.2 Changes in cash flows

For floating rate instruments, when cash flows are re-estimated to reflect movements in market rates of interest, the effective interest rate is updated. If the instrument is initially recognised at an amount equal to the amount receivable or payable on maturity, re-estimating future cash flows for this reason will not normally have a significant effect on the carrying amount of the instrument. [IFRS 9:B5.4.5]

The re-estimation of future cash flows for any other reason, including a renegotiation or modification that does not result in the derecognition of that financial asset, or in the case of an instrument that is not a floating rate instrument will normally result in a change in carrying amount because the revised estimated cash flows are discounted at the instrument's original effective interest rate, the credit-adjusted effective interest for purchased or originated credit-impaired financial assets or the revised effective interest rate in the case where the item is fair value hedged. The required adjustment is recognised in profit or loss. [IFRS 9:5.4.3 and B5.4.6]

The difference in approach in IFRS 9:B5.4.5 and B5.4.6 reflects the fact that varying interest receipts/payments are a contractual term of a floating rate instrument. In this situation, it would be inappropriate to determine at inception a single rate to discount estimated future cash flows. Instead, the Standard requires an entity to reflect changes in the interest rate in profit or loss as such changes occur.

4.1.2.1 Changes in cash flows linked to changes in an inflation index

In 2008, the IFRIC (now the IFRS Interpretations Committee) received a request for guidance on the application of the effective interest method to a financial instrument with future cash flows linked to changes in an inflation index. The IFRIC did not add the issue to its agenda but recommended that the Board should consider clarifying or expanding the relevant guidance in IAS 39. As part of its annual improvements project, in October 2008 the IASB decided tentatively that under IAS 39 a floating rate financial instrument is an instrument with contractual variable cash flows arising from changes in market variables. The Board decided not to define the term market variable. When IFRS 9 was published as finalised it largely copied the guidance on the effective interest rate from IAS 39 to IFRS 9. Under IAS 39, given the lack of guidance, entities determined an accounting policy as to whether inflation-linked debt is treated as a floating rate debt (with guidance applied that is equivalent to IFRS 9:B5.4.5) or whether it is not a floating rate debt (with guidance applied that is equivalent to IFRS 9:B5.4.6). Given the same lack of specific guidance in IFRS 9 an accounting policy choice should be applied consistently to similar instruments.

Consider an example of a Sterling functional currency entity that has issued a Sterling denominated bond where principal and interest payments are indexed to unleveraged UK inflation. The inflation-linking feature is considered a closely related embedded derivative (see **7.4** in **chapter B5**). If the entity chooses to apply IFRS 9:B5.4.6, the effective interest rate will be calculated at initial recognition of the bond as the rate that exactly discounts the expectations of inflation at initial recognition to the initial carrying amount (being fair value less transaction costs). This effective interest rate is never updated. At the end of each subsequent reporting period, the cash flows are re-estimated, reflecting the then current expectations of future inflation, and are discounted using the original effective interest rate. Any difference between the carrying amount of the instrument before and after such re-estimation is recognised in profit or loss.

If the entity chooses to apply IFRS 9:B5.4.5, it may follow one of two possible approaches. One approach is to update the expected cash flows at each period end in line with changes in expectations of inflation in the same way as applying IFRS 9:B5.4.6 but, unlike under IFRS 9:B5.4.6, the changes in expectations do not result in an immediate gain/loss in profit or loss. Instead, the effective interest rate is revised each period (i.e. the gain/loss is spread forward). At initial recognition, the effective interest rate is calculated at a rate that discounts the estimated cash flows of principal and interest (which include the estimation of future inflation) to the initial carrying amount. That initial effective interest rate is used to account for the instrument at amortised cost until the end of the next reporting period. The carrying amount at the end of the first reporting period will be equal to the initial carrying amount, plus the effective interest on the carrying amount, less any cash payments/receipts in the period. The entity then determines a new effective interest rate as the rate that discounts the new estimated cash flows of the instrument (taking into account the revised estimation of future inflation) back to the period end carrying amount. This new effective interest rate is applied for the new reporting period. This approach is repeated at each subsequent reporting period until the instrument is derecognised.

An alternative approach in applying IFRS 9:B5.4.5 is for profit or loss to reflect only the accrued inflation for the period up to the reporting date (i.e. the effective interest rate is not determined by looking forward to expectations of future inflation). This approach is consistent with the tentative conclusion of the IASB at its Board meeting in October 2008 where the Board tentatively agreed that expectations (and changes in expectations) of future cash flows are not considered when calculating the effective interest rate for floating rate instruments under IAS 39.

Applying one of the IFRS 9:B5.4.5 approaches described above will result in a less volatile profit or loss when compared to applying IFRS 9:B5.4.6. The application of the latter approach results in changes in expectations of future inflation impacting profit or loss immediately at each re-estimation date.

4.1.2.2 'Interest' determined as a proportion of the profits of the issuer

In May 2009, the IFRIC (now the IFRS Interpretations Committee) issued an agenda decision on IAS 39, *Participation Rights and Calculation of the Effective Interest Rate*. The IFRIC was asked for guidance regarding how an issuer should account for a financial liability that contains participation rights under which the instrument holder's return is determined as a proportion of the results of the issuer. In the specific circumstances considered (1) the holder received a percentage of the issuer's net income and was allocated a proportionate share of the issuer's losses, (2) losses were applied to the nominal value of the instrument to be repaid on maturity, and (3) losses allocated to the holder in one period could be offset by profits in subsequent periods.

The IFRIC considered the issue without reconsidering the assumptions described in the request, namely that the financial liability:

- does not contain any embedded derivatives;
- is measured at amortised cost using the effective interest method; and
- does not meet the definition of a floating rate instrument.

The IFRIC noted that IAS 39:AG6 & AG8 (now IFRS 9:B5.4.4 and B5.4.6) provide the relevant application guidance for measuring financial liabilities at amortised cost using the effective interest method. The IFRIC also noted that it is inappropriate to analogise to the derecognition guidance in IAS 39 (now in IFRS 9) because the liability has not been extinguished. Because specific application guidance already exists, the IFRIC decided not to add this issue to its agenda.

Guidance on the accounting treatment of financial instruments where interest is determined as a proportion of profit of the issuer is referred to at **2.1** in **chapter B4** with respect to the definition of a derivative. This guidance is relevant for financial liabilities. Financial assets within the scope of IFRS 9 that contractually receive a proportion of the issuer's profits will not meet the criteria for amortised cost or FVTOCI classification because the linkage to profits is not regarded as risks associated with a basic lending arrangement. Such assets will be classified as at FVTPL and, therefore, the holder is not required to calculate an effective interest rate.

4.1.2.3 Changes in expected cash flows due to embedded prepayment, put or call options

Changes in any expected cash flows that relate to an embedded prepayment, put or call option may not have an effect on the carrying amount for a hybrid financial liability because one of the following two circumstances may apply.

(i) The embedded derivative is separately accounted for. As discussed in **4.1.1**, this means that the derivative is ignored when determining the effective interest rate of the host contract.

(ii) The embedded derivative is not separately accounted for because the option's exercise price is approximately equal to the instrument's amortised cost on each exercise date. In this situation, because prepayment/put/call can only occur at an amount (approximately) equal to amortised cost, the discounted amount of future cash flows will be (approximately) unaffected by any change in expectations with respect to the exercise of said options.

This statement is not applicable for embedded prepayment, put or call options embedded in compound instruments with a separated equity component because of the unique way in which the embedded prepayment, put or call options are assessed as being closely related and the way the liability component is separated from the instrument as a whole (see **3.2** in **chapter B3**).

For financial assets, if the embedded prepayment, put or call option is regarded as contractual cash flows that are solely payments of principal and interest on the principal outstanding, the financial asset may be measured at amortised cost or FVTOCI if the other amortised cost or FVTOCI criteria are met. If the debt instrument asset is measured at amortised cost or FVTOCI, the holder of the instrument will apply the effective interest method in determining amortised cost and, in doing so, estimate the future contractual cash flows that will include the terms of the prepayment, put or call feature. The probability that the prepayment, put or call feature will be exercised will form part of the holder's assessment of the estimated contractual cash flows. IFRS 9 does not permit separate accounting for the prepayment, put or call option in the case of the holder of the instrument.

When a prepayment, put or call option is embedded in an issued compound instrument, the assessment of whether the prepayment, put or call option is considered closely related to the debt host contract is made *prior* to the instrument being split into liability and equity components (see **3.2** in **chapter B3**). If the exercise price of the prepayment, put or call option is approximately equal to the amortised cost (prior to splitting the instrument into its liability and equity parts), or the exercise price of the prepayment option reimburses the lender for an amount up to the approximate present value of lost interest for the remaining term of the host contract, it is closely related and, therefore, it is not separately recognised. If the embedded derivative is not separately recognised, the embedded prepayment, put or call option is taken into account in determining the timing and amount of the expected cash flows for the liability component when determining its amortised cost in future periods. Because the liability is initially recognised at a discount to the proceeds of the instrument as a whole, yet in most cases it can be early redeemed at an amount equal to the proceeds of the instrument as a whole, changes in the likelihood that the prepayment, put or call option will be exercised will affect the liability's carrying amount.

Example 4.1.2.3A

Issuer call option and holder put option in convertible debt

Entity X issued a convertible debt instrument in May 20X2 with a contractual maturity of 16 years. Each bond allows the holder to convert, at any time, into one share of Entity X. The issue price is 100 per cent and redemption price at maturity is 140 per cent.

The instrument is puttable by the holders on three different dates during the life of the instrument (May 20X6, May 20Y0 and May 20Y4) at the amortised cost of the instrument prior to the equity conversion option being separated plus a penalty of 3 per cent of the redemption amount. At initial recognition, Entity X considers that there is a very high probability that the instrument will be redeemed by the holders at the first put date (i.e. May 20X6) given the low price of its shares. The instrument is also callable by Entity X, starting May 20X6, if the price of the issuer's shares increases beyond 125 per cent of the redemption price. Entity X does not expect to call the instrument.

All the embedded call and put options over the instrument (excluding the conversion option that is treated as equity) are considered closely related to the debt component because the exercise prices are approximately equal to the amortised cost of the instrument prior to the equity conversion option being separated. The embedded call and put options are therefore not separated and form part of the debt component recognised as a financial liability. The financial liability is not designated as at FVTPL; rather, it is subsequently measured at amortised cost.

The fair value of the debt component at initial recognition is the contractual cash flows of the instrument (i.e. interest and principal at maturity) discounted by the entity's normal borrowing rate for a term of 16 years, plus the fair value of the written put option less the fair value of the purchased call option. The effective interest rate is the rate that exactly discounts this carrying amount with the estimated early redemption payment, in this case at May 20X6. This is the instrument's *original* effective interest rate. The difference between the total liability that includes the written put option and the purchased call option and the net proceeds at issue is assigned to the equity component.

Assuming that the expectation of repayment in May 20X6 does not change, the carrying amount of the debt component will change only for the application of the effective interest rate, i.e. it will increase by the difference between the effective interest rate and interest paid in the period. At May 20X6, the carrying amount of the liability will therefore equal the redemption amount. If the put option is exercised as expected, the early redemption will result in nil gain or loss.

If, however, expectations of repayment were to change (e.g. a change in market conditions were to cause the issuer to consider that the bond will be put back to the issuer on May 20Y0 instead of May 20X6), a recalculation of the carrying amount of the liability component would be required. The new carrying amount of the liability would be the re-estimated cash flows, being interest up to, and principal payable in, May 20Y0, discounted by the *original* effective interest rate. Any difference between the new carrying amount and the old carrying amount will be recognised in profit or loss.

Example 4.1.2.3B

Example of calculating amortised cost: prepayable debt instrument asset

[IFRS 9:Guidance on Implementation.B.26]

Entity A purchases a debt instrument with five years remaining to maturity for its fair value of CU1,000 (including transaction costs). The instrument has a contractual par amount of CU1,250 and carries fixed interest of 4.7 per cent that is paid annually (CU1,250 × 4.7% = CU59 per year). The contract also specifies that the borrower has an option to prepay the instrument at par and that no penalty will be charged for prepayment. At inception, the entity expects the borrower not to prepay (and, therefore, the entity determines that the fair value of the prepayment feature is insignificant when the financial asset is initially recognised).

It can be shown that in order to allocate interest receipts and the initial discount over the term of the debt instrument at a constant rate on the carrying amount, they must be accrued at the rate of 10 per cent annually. The table below provides information about the gross carrying amount, interest revenue and cash flows of the debt instrument in each reporting period.

Year	(a) Gross carrying amount at the beginning of the year	(b = a x 10%) Interest income	(c) Cash flows	(d = a + b – c) Gross carrying amount at the end of the year
20X0	1,000	100	59	1,041
20X1	1,041	104	59	1,086
20X2	1,086	109	59	1,136
20X3	1,136	113	59	1,190
20X4	1,190	119	1,250 + 59	–

On the first day of 20X2 the entity revises its estimate of cash flows. It now expects that 50 per cent of the contractual par amount will be prepaid at the end of 20X2 and the remaining 50 per cent at the end of 20X4. In accordance with IFRS 9:B5.4.6, the gross carrying amount of the debt instrument in 20X2 is adjusted. The gross carrying amount is recalculated by discounting the amount the entity expects to receive in 20X2 and subsequent years using the original effective interest rate (10 per cent). This results in the new gross carrying amount in 20X2 of CU1,138. The adjustment of CU52 (CU1,138 – CU1,086) is recorded in profit or loss in 20X2. The table below provides information about the gross carrying amount, interest revenue and cash flows as they would be adjusted taking into account the change in estimate.

Year	(a) Gross carrying amount at the beginning of the year	(b = a x 10%) Interest income	(c) Cash flows	(d = a + b – c) Gross carrying amount at the end of the year
20X0	1,000	100	59	1,041
20X1	1,041	104	59	1,086
20X2	1,086 + 52	114	625 + 59	568
20X3	568	57	30	595
20X4	595	60	625 + 30	–

4.1.3 Fees

The definition of the effective interest rate states that "[t]he calculation includes all fees and points paid or received between parties to the contract that are an integral part of the effective interest rate". [IFRS 9:Appendix A]

IFRS 9:B5.4.1 includes a note of caution that the description of fees for financial services may not be indicative of the nature and substance of the services provided. Fees that are an integral part of the effective interest rate of a financial instrument include:

[IFRS 9:B5.4.2]

Origination fees arise on the creation or acquisition of a financial asset or are received on issuing financial liabilities measured at amortised cost. For assets this may include compensation for activities such as evaluating the borrower's financial condition, evaluating and recording guarantees, collateral and other security arrangements, negotiating the terms of the instrument, preparing and processing documents and closing the transaction. These fees are an integral part of generating an involvement with the resulting financial instrument. Origination fees received on issuing financial liabilities measured at amortised cost are included in the effective interest rate if they are an integral part of generating an involvement with a financial liability. Fees and costs should be distinguished between those that are an integral part of the effective interest rate for the financial liability from origination fees and transaction costs relating to the right to provide services, such as investment management services.

Commitment fees are received on origination of a loan when the loan commitment is not measured at FVTPL (see **3.5** in **chapter B1**) and it is probable that the entity will enter into a specific lending arrangement. These fees are regarded as compensation for an ongoing involvement with the acquisition of a financial instrument. If the commitment expires without the entity making the loan, the fee is recognised as revenue on expiry.

Fees that are not an integral part of the effective interest rate of a financial instrument and are accounted for in accordance with IFRS 15 *Revenue from Contracts with Customers* include:

[IFRS 9:B5.4.3]

(a) fees charged for servicing a loan;

(b) commitment fees to originate a loan when the loan commitment is measured at FVTPL and it is unlikely that a specific lending arrangement will be entered into; and

(c) loan syndication fees received by an entity that arranges a loan and retains no part of the loan package for itself (or retains a part at the same effective interest rate for comparable risk as other participants).

4.1.4 Amortisation period

The definition of the effective interest rate (see **4.1**) requires the amortisation of premiums/discounts, fees, points paid or received and transaction costs (those that are taken into account in calculating the effective rate) over "the expected life of the financial instrument or, when appropriate, a shorter period". A shorter period will be appropriate if it is the period to which the relevant premiums/discounts, fees, points paid or received or transaction costs relate. [IFRS 9:B5.4.4] For example, if a fee is received as compensation for a discounted interest rate over an initial period (which ends with a repricing to market interest rates), then that fee should be amortised over that initial period rather than the expected life of the instrument. In general, when the variable to which the fee, transaction costs, discount or premium relates is repriced to market rates before the expected maturity of the instrument, a shorter period will be used. If, however, the premium or discount results from a change in the credit spread over the floating rate specified in the financial instrument, or other variable that are not reset to the market rates, it is amortised over the expected life of the financial instrument.

4.1.5 Measurement

There is a presumption that it will be possible to estimate reliably the cash flows and expected life of an instrument or group of similar instruments, such that the effective interest rate can be determined. However, in those rare cases when this is not possible, the rate should be calculated based on the contractual cash flows over the full contractual term of the instrument. [IFRS 9:Appendix A]

The application of the effective interest method is illustrated in the examples below.

Example 4.1.5A

Example of calculating amortised cost: debt instruments with stepped interest payments

[IFRS 9:Guidance on Implementation B.27]

On 1 January 20X0, Entity A issues a debt instrument for a price of CU1,250. The principal amount is CU1,250 and the debt instrument is repayable on 31 December 20X4. The rate of interest is specified in the debt agreement as a percentage of the principal amount as follows: 6.0 per cent in 20X0 (CU75), 8.0 per cent in 20X1 (CU100), 10.0 per cent in 20X2 (CU125), 12.0 per cent in 20X3 (CU150), and 16.4 per cent in 20X4 (CU205). In this case, the interest rate that exactly discounts the stream of future cash payments through maturity is 10 per cent. Therefore, cash interest payments are reallocated over the term of the debt instrument for the purposes of determining amortised cost in each period. In each period, the amortised cost at the beginning of the period is multiplied by the effective interest rate of 10 per cent and added to the amortised cost. Any cash payments in the period are deducted from the resulting number. Accordingly, the amortised cost in each period is as follows:

Year	(a) Gross carrying amount at the beginning of the year	(b = a x 10%) Interest income	(c) Cash flows	(d = a + b – c) Gross carrying amount at the end of the year
20X0	1,250	125	75	1,300
20X1	1,300	130	100	1,330
20X2	1,330	133	125	1,338
20X3	1,338	134	150	1,322
20X4	1,322	133	1,250 + 205	–

An illustration of changes in the estimate of future cash flows for a prepayable asset is included in **example 4.1.2.3B**.

Example 4.1.5B

Accounting for a loan with a separated embedded derivative

On 1 January 20X0, Entity B borrows CU100. Interest of CU4 is payable annually over the next five years (on 31 December 20X0 to 31 December 20X4). The loan is repayable at an amount of CU110 on 31 December 20X4. However, Entity B can prepay the borrowing at CU111 plus accrued interest for the year at any time. Because the prepayment option will result in the borrowing potentially being prepaid by Entity B at an amount that is not approximately equal to the amortised cost and the exercise price could compensate the lender for more than the approximate present value of lost interest for the remaining term of the host contract, the prepayment option is separately accounted for as an embedded derivative. The prepayment option is effectively an option written by the lender allowing Entity B to repay the borrowing at any time. Economically, Entity B can be expected to prepay the liability if the fair value of the instrument rises above CU111 (plus accrued interest).

On 1 January 20X0, the fair value of the prepayment option for Entity B is a CU3 asset. Therefore, the remaining balance of CU103 is the host contract liability.

(1) Initial recognition at 1 January 20X0

		CU	CU
Dr	Prepayment option	3.00	
Dr	Cash	100.00	
Cr	Liability		103.00

To recognise the borrowing.

The effective interest rate on the host contract is 5.11 per cent (calculated as the rate that exactly discounts interest of CU4 and principal of CU110 to the carrying amount of CU103).

At the end of 20X0, interest rates have fallen slightly, and the fair value of the option has risen from CU3 to CU5. The following entries are recorded in 20X0.

(2) Interest expense

		CU	CU
Dr	Interest expense	5.26	
Cr	Liability		5.26

To recognise interest expense.

Interest expense is determined at the effective interest rate of 5.11 per cent (5.11% x CU103.00).

(3) Interest payment

		CU	CU
Dr	Liability	4.00	
Cr	Cash		4.00

To record payment of interest.

The carrying amount of the loan as at 31 December 20X0 is therefore CU104.26.

(4) Embedded derivative

		CU	CU
Dr	Embedded derivative asset	2.00	
Cr	Profit or loss		2.00

To record the remeasurement of the embedded derivative.

By the end of 20X1, interest rates have fallen further, so on 31 December 20X1 Entity B repays the borrowing early. At the year end, the fair value of the prepayment option is CU6.

(5) Interest expense

		CU	CU
Dr	Interest expense	5.33	
Cr	Liability		5.33

To recognise interest expense.

Interest expense is determined at the effective interest rate of 5.11 per cent (5.11% x CU104.26).

(6) Interest payment

		CU	CU
Dr	Liability	4.00	
Cr	Cash		4.00

To record payment of interest.

The carrying amount of the loan prior to early repayment is therefore CU105.59.

(7) Embedded derivative

		CU	CU
Dr	Embedded derivative asset	1.00	
Cr	Profit or loss		1.00

To record the remeasurement of the embedded derivative.

(8) Early repayment of loan

		CU	CU
Dr	Liability	105.59	
Dr	Profit or loss	11.41	
Cr	Cash		111.00
Cr	Embedded derivative asset		6.00

To record the repayment of the borrowing.

The debit in profit or loss on early repayment of the loan represents the cumulative catch-up of the fair value of the host contract. Because the host contract is not measured at fair value during its life, this results in a loss in profit or loss when the instrument is terminated, due to the impact of movements in interest rates that have not previously been recognised in the financial statements. Because interest rates have fallen considerably, the fair value of the host contract has risen.

Example 4.1.5B assumes that, at inception, the borrower considers that the put option is not likely to be exercised. If the put option was considered likely to be exercised, there is an argument that the likely exercise of the put option would form part of the instrument's amortised cost and, therefore, it would result in the terms of the host contract being identified differently (see **7.1** in **chapter B5**).

Example 4.1.5C

Effective interest rate for fixed rate perpetual debt

An entity issues a perpetual debt instrument for consideration of CU100. Interest of CU6 is payable annually in perpetuity. The instrument is not redeemable. The effective rate (i.e. the rate that discounts CU6 annually in perpetuity to CU100) is 6 per cent. Interest of CU6 is recognised in profit or loss and there is no amortisation of the principal amount. This would also be the case for a floating rate instrument because, as discussed in **section 4.1.2**, the effective rate is adjusted for changes in market rates for floating rate instruments.

Example 4.1.5D

Effective interest rate for stepped fixed rate perpetual debt

An entity issues a perpetual debt instrument; the interest rate is fixed at 10% for the first 10 years and 8% for each year thereafter.

The 10% interest payments in the first ten years represent a part payment of principal. Consequently, when these payments are made, the difference between 10% and 8% is treated as a reduction in the carrying amount of the liability. In the period from Year 10, the effective interest will be recognised at 8% because all payments relate to interest and not repayment of principal.

An alternative way of considering the higher payments in the first 10 years is the sum of the differential between the 10% and 8% represents repayments on an amortising loan. The value of the amortising loan at inception less the proceeds from the instrument as a whole represents the carrying amount of the perpetual debt instrument.

IFRS 9:IG.B.25 has a similar fact pattern as **example 4.1.5D** except that after Year 10 the interest rate reduces to zero. The implementation guidance states that the amortised cost is zero after Year 10 because the present value of the stream of future cash payments in subsequent periods is zero.

An alternative argument to that used in the implementation guidance is that, after the final payment is made at Year 10, the financial liability is derecognised because the entity has fully discharged any obligation to pay cash or other financial asset.

4.1.6 Interaction of effective interest rate and fair value hedge accounting

When an entity applies fair value hedge accounting to a hedge of a debt instrument, the carrying amount of the debt is adjusted for movements in the hedged risk. Fair value hedge accounting is explained in detail at **chapter B9**. IFRS 9:6.5.10 requires the fair value adjustment to be amortised to profit or loss beginning at the earliest when the adjustment is made and no later than when the hedged item ceases to be fair value adjusted. This amortisation is included as part of the revised effective interest rate.

If an entity chooses to amortise the fair value adjustment as soon as the adjustment is made, then assuming the fair value adjustment changes for each subsequent reporting period because there is a change in the fair value of the hedged risk and the hedge continues to meet the hedge effectiveness requirements, a revised effective interest rate will need to be determined at the start of each reporting period.

If an entity chooses to start to amortise the adjustment when hedge accounting ceases, the entity will only need to recalculate the effective interest rate at that point. Failing to begin amortisation of the hedge adjustment prior to maturity would give rise to a gain or loss at maturity in the case where a fair value hedge begins after the hedged item is initially recognised. This is because the cumulative adjustment does not include changes in fair value for the initial unhedged period, resulting in the debt instrument's carrying value not equalling its settlement amount at maturity.

5 Impairment

If all financial instruments were measured at FVTPL there would be no need for any impairment requirements as any exposure to credit risk would be reflected in the instrument's fair value and recognised immediately in profit or loss. However, under IFRS 9 a number of financial instruments that expose an entity to credit risk are not measured at FVTPL and for these instruments an impairment model is necessary to appropriately recognise credit losses on a timely basis. As noted in **5.1**, the IFRS 9 impairment model is also applied to some assets not otherwise in scope of IFRS 9 for recognition and measurement.

Under IFRS 9, an 'expected loss' impairment model applies which requires a loss allowance to be recognised based on expected credit losses. With the exception of purchased or originated credit-impaired financial assets, a loss allowance is recognised on initial recognition of a financial asset in scope of the impairment requirements.

The guidance in this section considers the:

- scope of the impairment requirements, see **section 5.1**;
- recognition requirements for expected credit losses, see **section 5.2**; and
- measurement requirements for expected credit losses, see **section 5.3**.

5.1 Scope of the impairment requirements

The following instruments are in scope of the impairment requirements under which a loss allowance for expected credit losses must be recognised:

[IFRS 9:5.5.1]

- financial assets that are measured at amortised cost or debt instruments assets measured at FVTOCI (see **section 5** in **chapter B2**);
- lease receivables under IAS 17 *Leases*;
- contract assets recognised under IFRS 15 *Revenue from Contracts with Customers;*

- written loan commitments that are not measured at FVTPL (see **3.5** in **chapter B1**); and
- written financial guarantee contracts that are not measured at FVTPL that are in the scope of IFRS 9 (see **2.3.3** in **chapter B1**).

Investments in equity instruments

The impairment requirements do not apply to equity investments designated at FVTOCI because fair value gains and losses, except dividend income, are permanently recognised in other comprehensive income without reclassification to profit or loss, see **5.3.2** in **chapter B2**. Equity instruments at FVTPL, like all financial instruments at FVTPL, are not in scope of the impairment requirements.

Loan commitments

Written loan commitments not at FVTPL are in scope of the impairment requirements because the issuer is committed to providing credit and there is a risk from the commitment date that any advance may not be repaid by the borrower. The credit risk to the issuer of the loan commitment is similar to that of an entity that has already lent money and therefore it is logical that the same impairment model applies from the commitment date.

For written loan commitments to provide a loan at a below-market interest rate, not measured at FVTPL, the impairment requirements form part of a 'higher of' test with regard to the measurement of the instrument, i.e. the loan commitment is measured subsequent to initial recognition at the higher of:

[IFRS 9:4.2.1(d)]

(i) the amount of the loss allowance determined in accordance with IFRS 9; and

(ii) the amount initially recognised less, when appropriate, the cumulative amount of income recognised in accordance with the principles of IFRS 15 *Revenue from Contracts with Customers*.

It is noteworthy that the impairment requirements extend beyond measurement of loss allowances for loan commitments at below-market interest rates as all other loan commitments that are outside the scope of IFRS 9 will have a loss allowance for expected credit losses.

The term 'loan commitment' is not defined in IFRS 9 or any other Standard; however, IFRS 9:BCZ2.2 describes loan commitments as "firm commitments to provide credit under pre-specified terms and conditions".

Firm commitments to provide credit can take a number of forms. For example, the following two commitments include the provision of credit:

- a commitment by a lessor to commence a finance lease at a date in the future (i.e. a commitment to transfer the right to use an asset at the lease commencement date in return for a payment or series of payments in the future); and
- a commitment by a retailer through the issue of a store account to provide a customer with credit when the customer buys goods or services from the retailer in the future.

However, IFRS 9's impairment requirements do not apply to all agreements that include a firm commitment to provide credit, instead, they apply to an agreement that includes a commitment to provide credit if all of the following apply:

- the agreement meets the description of a loan commitment in IFRS 9:BCZ2.2 (i.e. a firm commitment to provide credit under pre-specified terms and conditions);
- the agreement that contains the commitment meets the definition of a financial instrument as set out in IAS 32 *Financial Instruments: Presentation*; and
- there is not a specific scope exemption that results in the commitment being outside the scope of IFRS 9's impairment requirements.

In the case of a commitment by a lessor to commence a finance lease at a date in the future, the lease agreement contains a loan commitment because the lessor gives a firm commitment to provide credit under pre-specified terms and conditions. However, the finance lease commitment does not meet the definition of a financial instrument in IAS 32:11. Before commencement of the lease, the agreement represents an executory contract over a non-financial item that cannot be net settled or by exchanging financial instruments and consequently it does not represent a financial instrument (see **section 2.5** in **chapter B1**). Upon commencement of the lease, the lease receivable will represent a financial asset and come within the scope of IFRS 9's impairment requirements.

Likewise, in the case of a retailer's commitment to provide credit through the issuance of a store account, the retailer's commitment to selling goods or services on credit represents an executory contract over a non-financial item that cannot be net settled or by exchanging financial instruments and consequently it does not represent a financial instrument. For that reason it would not be within the scope of IFRS 9's impairment requirements. If the retailer is not committed to selling goods or services to the customer, the agreement would also fail the second condition above; it would not represent a loan commitment because the retailer can choose not to sell the goods or services and therefore avoid providing credit.

This issue of identifying loan commitments in scope of the IFRS 9 impairment requirements was one of the issues discussed by the IFRS Transition Resource Group for Impairment of Financial Instruments (established by the IASB to discuss transition issues surrounding the IFRS 9 impairment model) at its meeting in April 2015.

Financial guarantee contracts issued

Issued financial guarantee contracts not measured at FVTPL are in scope of the impairment requirements because the risks they expose the issuer to are similar to the non-payment risks that a lender is exposed to. In effect it is the lender's exposure to default on a financial asset which is transferred to the guarantor.

Similar to loan commitments, the impairment requirements apply to the subsequent measurement of financial guarantee contracts which are measured at the higher of:

[IFRS 9:4.2.1(c)]

(i) the amount of the loss allowance determined in accordance with IFRS 9; and

(ii) the amount initially recognised less, when appropriate, cumulative amount of income recognised in accordance with the principles of IFRS 15 *Revenue from Contracts with Customers*.

The table below summarises the requirements to recognise a loss allowance for expected credit losses under IFRS 9.

Financial assets	**Loss allowance required?**
Investment in debt instruments	
Fair value through profit or loss	No
Amortised cost financial assets	Yes
Fair value through other comprehensive income	Yes
Investment in equity instruments	
Fair value through profit or loss	No
Fair value through other comprehensive income	No

Financial assets	**Loss allowance required?**
Derivative instruments (including embedded derivatives separated out as required by IFRS 9)	
Fair value through profit or loss	No
Contract assets under IFRS 15	Yes
Lease receivables under IAS 17	Yes

Financial liabilities	**Loss allowance required?**
Written loan commitment measured at fair value through profit or loss	No
Written loan commitment not measured at fair value through profit or loss	Yes (for loan commitments below market rates the impairment allowance forms part of the 'higher of' test in IFRS 9:4.2.1(d)) (see **3.5** in **chapter B1**)
Written financial guarantee contracts measured at fair value through profit or loss	No
Written financial guarantee contracts not measured at fair value through profit or loss	Subject to higher of test (see **2.3.3** in **chapter B1**) with potential recognition of a loss allowance

5.1.1 Trade date vs settlement date accounting

A regular way purchase or sale of a financial asset is recognised using either trade date accounting or settlement date accounting (see **2.2** in **chapter B8**). When trade date accounting is used, the financial asset is recognised at the trade date. Consequently, for debt instrument assets measured at amortised cost or FVTOCI, if there is a reporting date between the trade date and the settlement date, a loss allowance would be recognised in the statement of financial position at the reporting date because the asset is clearly in scope of the IFRS 9 impairment requirements. If, on the other hand, settlement date accounting is used, the financial asset would not be recognised in the statement of financial position at the same reporting date. This raises the question of whether a loss allowance should be recognised at the reporting date. Given that the entity is exposed to the same credit risk regardless of whether it applies trade date accounting or settlement date accounting and the

IFRS 9 impairment requirements apply to loan commitments which can be seen as similar to the commitment to buy a loan asset, a loss allowance should be recognised.

5.2 Recognition of expected credit losses

The impairment approach in IFRS 9 is based on expected credit losses. Therefore, it is not necessary for a loss event to have occurred before credit losses are recognised. Instead, a loss allowance is always recognised for expected credit losses and is remeasured at each reporting date for changes in those expected credit losses. The only exception is for purchased or originated credit-impaired financial assets where a different impairment approach applies (see **5.2.5.3**).

IFRS 9 has a general approach for impairment which distinguishes between 12-month expected credit losses and lifetime expected credit losses (see **5.2.1**). Determining whether a loss allowance should be based on 12-month expected credit losses or lifetime expected credit losses depends on whether there has been a *significant increase in credit risk* of the financial instrument since initial recognition (or the commitment date).

Given the difference between 12-month and lifetime expected credit losses, the concept of a *significant increase in credit risk* is fundamental to the application of the general approach. Consequently, there is a significant amount of guidance included in the Standard to help determine whether there has been a significant increase in credit risk since the initial recognition of a financial asset (see **5.2.2**).

In addition, IFRS 9 includes guidance on how to apply the general approach to specific situations such as:

- how to apply the general model to financial assets that have been modified (see **section 5.2.3**); and
- how to apply the general approach to financial assets measured at FVTOCI (see **5.2.4**).

To ensure that the general approach can be applied practically, IFRS 9 includes some exceptions and simplifications to the general approach. These include:

- a simplification from the general approach for financial instruments that have low credit risk at the reporting date (see **5.2.5.1**);
- a simplification from the general approach for trade receivables, contract assets and lease receivables (see **5.2.5.2**); and
- an exception to the general approach for purchased or originated credit-impaired financial assets (see **5.2.5.3**).

The implementation guidance in IFRS 9 provides a decision tree which summarises the discussions in **section 5.2** which is reproduced below:

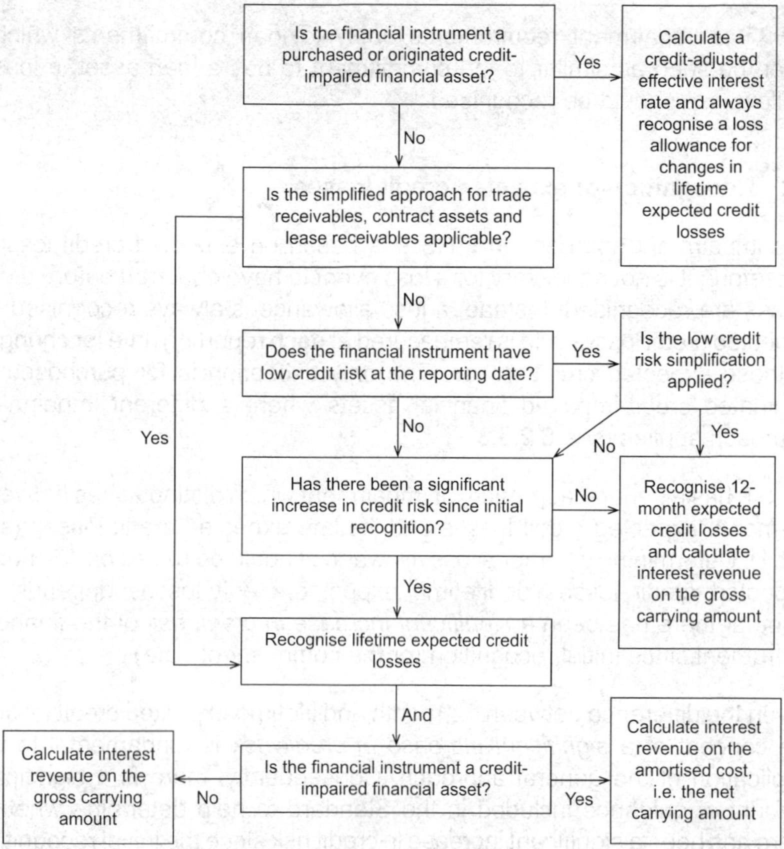

5.2.1 General approach

Under the general approach, a loss allowance for lifetime expected credit losses is recognised for a financial instrument if there has been a significant increase in credit risk since initial recognition (see **5.2.2**). This assessment must consider all reasonable and supportable historic and forward-looking information. [IFRS 9:5.5.4]

If, at the reporting date, the credit risk on a financial instrument has not increased significantly since initial recognition, a loss allowance for 12-month expected credit losses is recognised. [IFRS 9:5.5.5]

For a business combination involving the acquisition of financial assets, accounted for under IFRS 3 *Business Combinations*, the question arises as to whether the loss allowance should be recognised as part of the initial carrying amount of the asset. IFRS 3:B41 is clear that an acquirer should not recognise a loss allowance as of the acquisition date for a financial asset acquired in a business combination that is measured at its acquisition date fair value because the effects of uncertainty about future cash flows are included in the fair value measure. Consequently, the financial asset's fair value is used in the goodwill calculation (rather than its amortised cost on initial recognition) and the impairment loss arising from recognising the loss allowance is recognised in the first reporting period following the business combination.

Therefore, the general approach has two bases on which to measure *expected credit losses*:

[IFRS 9:Appendix A]

- *lifetime expected credit losses* are the expected credit losses that result from all possible default events over the expected life of a financial instrument; and
- *12-month expected credit losses* are the portion of the lifetime expected credit losses that represent the expected credit losses that result from default events on a financial instrument that are possible within the 12 months after the reporting date.

Expected credit losses are defined in Appendix A of IFRS 9 as the weighted average of credit losses with the respective risks of default occurring as the weights.

The term 12-month expected losses might intuitively sound like a provision for the cash shortfalls that an entity expects in the next 12 months. This is not the case. IFRS 9:B5.5.43 states that the 12-month expected credit losses are a portion of the lifetime expected credit losses and represent the lifetime cash shortfalls that will result if a default occurs in the 12 months after the reporting date (or a shorter period if the expected life of a financial instrument is less than 12 months), weighted by the probability of that default occurring. Therefore, 12-month expected credit losses are neither the lifetime expected credit losses that an entity will incur on financial instruments that it predicts will default in the next 12 months nor the cash shortfalls that are predicted over the next 12 months.

Example 5.2.1

12-month expected credit losses

Entity D has determined the following probabilities with respect to its loan asset:

(i) The probability of the loan being in default over the life of the loan is 3 per cent and the present value of the contractual cash flow over the life of the loan that will not be recovered given the default is CU100.

(ii) The probability of the loan being in default over the next 12 months is 1 per cent and the present value of the contractual cash flows due in the next 12 months that will not be recovered given the default is CU5.

(iii) The probability of the loan being in default over the next 12 months is 1 per cent and the present value of the contractual cash flows over the life of the loan that will not be recovered given the default is CU30.

Entity D will use (i) when calculating lifetime expected credit losses and will use (iii) when calculating 12-month expected credit losses.

The probability described in (ii) is not appropriate as it only reflects the cash shortfalls in the next 12-months, not the cash shortfalls over the life of the loan arising from a default in the next 12 months.

Because the trigger for recognising lifetime expected credit losses is a *significant increase in credit risk*, the assessment of credit risk is a *relative* assessment rather than an absolute assessment. In other words, lifetime expected credit losses is not recognised simply because the credit risk of an instrument is high; it is only recognised if the credit risk at the reporting date has increased significantly *relative* to the credit risk at initial recognition. As a result, the credit risk at initial recognition is an essential measure in applying the impairment requirements. For written loan commitments and financial guarantee contracts, the date that the entity becomes a party to the irrevocable commitment should be considered to be the date of initial recognition for the purposes of applying the impairment requirements. [IFRS 9:5.5.6]

The loss allowance may be measured at an amount equal to lifetime expected credit losses in one period and in the following period be based on 12-month expected credit losses, or vice versa. The change in basis for measuring the loan allowance is a function of whether the criteria for lifetime expected credit losses is met at the reporting date.

An impairment loss (gain) is recognised in profit or loss for the amount of expected credit losses (or reversal) needed to adjust the loss allowance at the reporting date to the required amount. [IFRS 9:5.5.8]

5.2.2 Significant increase in credit risk

Whether the loss allowance is based on 12-month expected credit losses or lifetime expected credit losses will depend on whether, at the reporting date, there has been a significant increase in credit risk since initial recognition.

A significant increase in credit risk is not a defined term and it will require significant judgment to apply this term in practice. To aid comparability and give transparency on an entity's approach, IFRS 7 requires disclosures about how an entity has determined whether the credit risk of a financial instrument has increased significantly since initial recognition (see **5.2.1** in **chapter B11**).

Because the assessment of significant increase in credit risk is performed *at* the reporting date it is important that entities make use of information that is available without undue cost and effort up to the reporting date. It is equally important that events and new information after the reporting date are dealt with appropriately with due consideration of IAS 10 *Events After the Reporting Period* which distinguishes between adjusting and non-adjusting events. This is discussed further in **5.3.5** in the context of both the assessment of significant increase in credit risk and measurement of expected losses.

Under the IFRS 9 model it is important to note that a change in credit risk is a measure of the change in the risk of a default occurring over the expected life of the financial instrument and not a measure of the change in the amount of expected credit losses. [IFRS 9:5.5.9] For example, it is possible for the expected credit losses on a collateralised loan asset to fall because of an increase in the value of the collateral at the same time as the credit risk of the instrument goes up because the borrower has become unemployed leading to an increased risk of default.

The term 'default' is not defined in IFRS 9 and an entity will have to establish its own policy for what it considers a default, and apply a definition consistent with that used for internal credit risk management purposes for the relevant financial instrument. This should consider qualitative indicators (e.g. financial covenants) when appropriate. The Standard includes a rebuttable presumption that a default does not occur later than when a financial asset is 90 days past due unless an entity has reasonable and supportable information to demonstrate that a more lagging default criterion is more appropriate. The definition of default used for these purposes should be applied consistently to all financial instruments unless information becomes available that demonstrates that another default definition is more appropriate for a particular financial instrument. [IFRS 9:B5.5.37]

To assess the credit risk, an entity should compare the risk of a default occurring on the financial instrument as at the reporting date with the risk of a default occurring on the financial instrument as at the date of initial recognition. Applying this to loan commitments, an entity considers changes in the risk of a default occurring on the loan to which a loan commitment relates and for financial guarantee contracts, an entity considers the changes in the risk that the specified debtor will default on the contract. [IFRS 9:B5.5.8]

Given that a significant increase in credit risk since initial recognition is a relative measure, a given change, in absolute terms, in the risk of a default occurring will be more significant for a financial instrument with a lower initial risk of a default occurring compared to a financial instrument with a higher initial risk of a default occurring. [IFRS 9:B5.5.9]

Example 5.2.2A

Absolute credit risk versus relative change in credit risk

At the reporting date Entity A has two financial assets that both have a probability of default of 7 per cent. At initial recognition financial instrument X had a probability of default of 6 per cent whereas financial instrument Y had a probability of default of 2 per cent. Even though both financial assets have the same absolute probability of default at the reporting date, Entity A considers that for financial instrument Y the credit risk has increased significantly since initial recognition whereas for financial instrument X it has not.

If a financial instrument was repriced to reflect a significant increase in credit risk, it could be argued that such a financial instrument should continue to have a loss allowance measured at an amount equal to the 12-month expected credit loss. As explained in IFRS 9:BC5.152 -153, this is because the contractual interest rate has been repriced to reflect the entity's expectations about credit losses and is similar to the economic position on initial recognition of a similar financial instrument with a similar credit risk at origination. However, under IFRS 9 the assessment of whether lifetime expected credit losses should be recognised should be based solely on the increase in the risk of a default occurring since initial recognition. Consequently, an entity should recognise a loss allowance measured at an amount equal to lifetime expected credit losses when there is a significant increase in credit risk, irrespective of whether the instrument's terms are repriced to reflect a significant increase in credit risk.

There are a variety of approaches that could be used to assess whether the credit risk on a financial instrument has increased significantly since initial recognition. In some cases (e.g. for some financial institutions), detailed quantitative information about the probability of default of a financial instrument (see **5.2.2.3** & **5.2.2.4**) or formal credit rating will be available which could be used to compare changes in credit risk. However, probability of default measures and credit ratings are not the only basis on which a significant change in credit risk can be identified. In some cases, qualitative and non-statistical quantitative information may be sufficient to identify a significant increase in credit risk (see **5.2.2.5**). [IFRS 9:B5.5.18] These can include methods that make use of internal risk ratings (see **5.2.2.6**) and assessments of counterparty credit risk (see **5.2.2.7**).

Approaches not directly based on the probability of default (e.g. a credit loss rate approach), can be consistent with the requirements in IFRS 9, provided changes in the risk of a default occurring are considered separately from changes in other drivers of expected credit losses, such as collateral, and the following is also considered when making the assessment:

[IFRS 9:B5.5.12]

(a) the change in the risk of a default occurring since initial recognition;

(b) the expected life of the financial instrument; and

(c) reasonable and supportable information that is available without undue cost or effort and that may affect credit risk.

The guidance in IFRS 9:B5.5.12 (and IFRS 9:B5.5.22, see **5.2.5.1**) explains that collateral is not taken into account when *assessing* credit risk. Instead recoveries from collateral are taken into account when *measuring* expected credit losses (see **5.3**). In addition, Example 3 from the illustrative examples accompanying IFRS 9 (see **example 5.3**), which deals with a highly collateralised financial asset, states that the ability to reduce cash shortfalls through the enforcement of collateral does not reduce the risk of default occurring on the financial instrument.

This same guidance equally applies to other credit enhancements such as financial guarantees integral to a financial asset. The recoveries from such guarantees are taken into account in the *measurement* of expected credit losses.

It should be noted, however, that *changes* in the value of collateral and the quality of financial guarantees (and other credit enhancements) can affect the risk of default which is discussed further in **5.2.2.5**.

This issue was one of the issues discussed by the IFRS Transition Resource Group for Impairment of Financial Instruments (established by the IASB to discuss transition issues surrounding the IFRS 9 impairment model) at its meeting in April 2015.

Example 5.2.2B

Assessing whether there has been a significant increase in credit risk on a guaranteed loan

Bank H has a loan receivable from Entity J. The loan agreement includes a financial guarantee from Guarantor K that is integral to the contractual terms of the loan. If Entity J fails to pay, Bank H can seek recovery from Guarantor K under the terms of the loan.

In accordance with IFRS 9:5.5.9, at each reporting date Bank H is required to assess whether the credit risk on its loan to Entity J has increased significantly since initial recognition. In making this assessment, Bank H is required to consider the change since initial recognition in the risk of a default occurring on the loan.

In making its assessment under IFRS 9:5.5.9, Bank H should not take into account its ability to seek recovery from Guarantor K in the event of a default.

Consistent with the treatment of collateral, recoveries from integral financial guarantee contracts are not considered when assessing whether there has been a significant increase in credit risk.

Whichever method of assessing significant increase in credit risk is used, an entity considers reasonable and supportable information that is available without undue cost or effort (see **5.2.2.1**) and considers the characteristics of the financial instrument (or group of financial instruments) and the default patterns in the past for comparable financial instruments. [IFRS 9:5.5.9 & B5.5.13]

IFRS 9 includes a rebuttable presumption that the credit risk on a financial asset has increased significantly since initial recognition when contractual payments are more than 30 days past due (see **5.2.2.8**). However, lifetime expected credit losses are generally expected to be recognised before a financial instrument becomes past due. This is because credit risk typically increases significantly before a financial instrument becomes past due. Therefore when reasonable and supportable information that is more forward-looking than past due information is available without undue cost or effort, it must be used to assess changes in credit risk. [IFRS 9:B5.5.2]

When forward-looking information is not available for an individual instrument, an entity is required to consider whether forward-looking information is available at a higher aggregated level (i.e. for a group or sub-group of instruments, see **5.2.2.2**).

5.2.2.1 Undue cost or effort and forward looking information

Past due information is generally a lagging indicator of a significant increase in credit risk as it is likely that a significant increase in credit risk has arisen before an asset becomes past due. Consequently, if reasonable and supportable forward-looking information is available without undue cost or effort, an entity cannot rely solely on past due information when determining whether credit risk has increased significantly since initial recognition. However, when such information is not available without undue cost or effort (either on an individual or a collective basis), an entity may use past due information to determine whether there has been significant increases in credit risk since initial recognition. [IFRS 9:5.5.11]

In practice there will be many different sources of credit information about financial instruments in scope of the IFRS 9 impairment model. However, an entity is not expected to undertake an exhaustive search for information when determining whether credit risk has increased significantly since initial recognition. [IFRS 9:B5.5.15]

IFRS 9 describes credit risk analysis as a multifactor and holistic analysis. Assessing whether a specific factor is relevant, and assessing what weight to give it compared to other factors, will depend on, amongst other factors, the:

- type of product,
- characteristics of the financial instruments and the borrower; and
- geographical region.

Reasonable and supportable information that is available without undue cost or effort and that is relevant for the particular financial instrument being assessed must be considered.

Because "undue cost" and "undue effort" are very subjective terms, entities may have to exercise significant judgment in determining what reasonable and supportable forward looking information is available without undue cost or effort. The outcome of applying this requirement can give rise to different results for different entities. For example, due to its risk management processes and regulatory requirements, a large international financial institution is likely to have more access to relevant credit information without undue cost or effort than a small private entity.

When factors or indicators are not identifiable on an individual financial instrument basis, collective assessments should be used to determine whether lifetime expected credit losses need to be recognised for a group or sub-group of items (see **5.2.2.2**). [IFRS 9:B5.5.16]

5.2.2.2 Applying the general approach on a collective or individual assessment basis

As noted in **section 5.3**, the *measurement* of expected credit losses is based on the *weighted average* credit loss. As a result, the *measurement* of the loss allowance should be the same regardless of whether it is measured on an individual basis or a collective basis (although measurement on a collective basis may be more practical for large portfolios of items).

When it comes to the *assessment* of whether there has been a significant increase in credit risk it may be *necessary* to perform the assessment of significant increases in credit risk on a collective basis. [IFRS 9:B5.5.1] This is because an entity may not be able to identify significant changes in credit risk for individual financial instruments before the financial instrument becomes past due (e.g. there may be little or no information for an individual retail loan until a customer fails to pay). If changes in the credit risk for individual financial instruments are not captured before they become past due, a loss allowance based only on credit information at an individual financial instrument level would not faithfully represent the changes in credit risk since initial recognition. [IFRS 9:B5.5.3]

When assessing for significant increases in credit risk and recognising a loss allowance on a collective basis, financial instruments can be grouped on the basis of shared credit risk characteristics to enable significant increases in credit risk to be identified on a timely basis (information should not be obscured by grouping financial instruments with different risk characteristics). Examples of shared credit risk characteristics may include, but are not limited to, the:

[IFRS 9:B5.5.5]

- instrument type;
- credit risk ratings;

- collateral type;
- date of initial recognition;
- remaining term to maturity;
- industry;
- geographical location of the borrower; and
- the value of collateral relative to the financial asset if it has an impact on the probability of a default occurring (for example, non-recourse loans in some jurisdictions or loan-to-value ratios).

The grouping of financial instruments could mean that the credit risk for the whole group is considered to have increased significantly since initial recognition. However, if this is not the case, lifetime expected credit losses should be recognised on a portion (e.g. 20 per cent) of the financial instruments for which credit risk is deemed to have increased significantly. Furthermore, the grouping of financial instruments to assess credit risk on a collective basis may change over time as new information becomes available on groups of, or individual, financial instruments. [IFRS 9:B5.5.6] For example, a sub-group of financial instruments may be identified due to an event that affects only the sub-group of borrowers such that the entire sub-group has exhibited a significant increase in credit risk and should be considered separately because of its shared risk characteristics. These different considerations are illustrated in **example 5.2.2.2**.

Example 5.2.2.2

Responsiveness to changes in credit risk

[IFRS 9: IE29 - IE39 – Example 5]

Bank ABC provides mortgages to finance residential real estate in three different regions. The mortgage loans are originated across a wide range of loan-to-value 'LTV' criteria and a wide range of income groups. As part of the mortgage application process, customers are required to provide information such as the industry within which the customer is employed and the post code of the property that serves as collateral on the mortgage.

Bank ABC sets its acceptance criteria based on credit scores. Loans with a credit score above the 'acceptance level' are approved because these borrowers are considered to be able to meet contractual payment obligations. When new mortgage loans are originated, Bank ABC uses the credit score to determine the risk of a default occurring as at initial recognition.

At the reporting date Bank ABC determines that economic conditions are expected to deteriorate significantly in all regions. Unemployment levels are expected to increase while the value of residential property is expected to decrease, causing the LTV ratios to increase. As a result of the expected deterioration in economic conditions, Bank ABC expects default rates on the mortgage portfolio to increase.

Individual assessment

In Region One, Bank ABC assesses each of its mortgage loans on a monthly basis by means of an automated behavioural scoring process. Its scoring models are based on current and historical past-due statuses, levels of customer indebtedness, LTV measures, customer behaviour on other financial instruments with Bank ABC, the loan size and the time since the origination of the loan. Bank ABC updates the LTV measures on a regular basis through an automated process that re-estimates property values using recent sales in each post code area and reasonable and supportable forward-looking information that is available without undue cost or effort.

Bank ABC has historical data that indicates a strong correlation between the value of residential property and the default rates for mortgages. That is, when the value of residential property declines, a customer has less economic incentive to make scheduled mortgage repayments and less incentive to make the repayments, increasing the risk of a default occurring.

Through the impact of the LTV measure in the behavioural scoring model, an increased risk of a default occurring due to an expected decline in residential property value adjusts the behavioural scores. The behavioural score can be adjusted as a result of expected declines in property value even when the mortgage loan is a bullet loan with the most significant payment obligations at maturity (and beyond the next 12 months). Mortgages with a high LTV ratio are more sensitive to changes in the value of the residential property and Bank ABC is able to identify significant increases in credit risk since initial recognition on individual customers before a mortgage becomes past due if there has been a deterioration in the behavioural score.

When the increase in credit risk has been significant, a loss allowance at an amount equal to lifetime expected credit losses is recognised. Bank ABC measures the loss allowance by using the LTV measures to estimate the severity of the loss, ie the loss given default (LGD). The higher the LTV measure, the higher the expected credit losses all else being equal.

If Bank ABC was unable to update behavioural scores to reflect the expected declines in property prices, it would use reasonable and supportable information that is available without undue cost or effort to undertake a collective assessment to determine the loans on which there has been a significant increase in credit risk since initial recognition and recognise lifetime expected credit losses for those loans.

Collective assessment

In Regions Two and Three, Bank ABC does not have an automated scoring capability. Instead, for credit risk management purposes, Bank ABC tracks the risk of a default occurring by means of past-due statuses. It recognises a loss allowance at an amount equal to lifetime expected credit losses for all loans that have a past due status of more than 30 days past due. Although Bank ABC uses past due status information as the only borrower-specific information, it also considers other reasonable and supportable forward-looking information that is available without undue cost or effort to assess whether lifetime expected credit losses should be recognised on loans that are not more than 30 days past due.

This is necessary in order to meet the objective in IFRS 9:5.5.4 of recognising lifetime expected credit losses for all significant increases in credit risk.

Region Two

Region Two includes a mining community that is largely dependent on the export of coal and related products. Bank ABC becomes aware of a significant decline in coal exports and anticipates the closure of several coal mines. Because of the expected increase in the unemployment rate, the risk of a default occurring on mortgage loans to borrowers in these areas who are employed by the coal mines is determined to have increased significantly, even if those customers are not past due at the reporting date. Bank ABC therefore segments its mortgage portfolio by the industry within which customers are employed (using the information recorded as part of the mortgage application process) to identify customers that rely on coal mining as the dominant source of employment (i.e. a 'bottom up' approach in which loans are identified based on a common risk characteristic). For those mortgages, Bank ABC recognises a loss allowance at an amount equal to lifetime expected credit losses while it continues to recognise a loss allowance at an amount equal to 12-month expected credit losses for all other mortgages in Region Two (except for those mortgages that are determined to have significantly increased in credit risk based on an individual assessment, such as those that are more than 30 days past due – lifetime expected credit losses would also be recognised on those mortgages). Newly originated mortgages to borrowers who rely on the coal mines for employment in this community would, however, have a loss allowance at an amount equal to 12-month expected credit losses because they would not have experienced significant increases in credit risk since initial recognition. However, some of these mortgages may experience significant increases in credit risk soon after initial recognition because of the expected closure of the coal mines.

Region Three

In Region Three, Bank ABC anticipates the risk of a default occurring and thus an increase in credit risk, as a result of an expected increase in interest rates during the expected life of the mortgages. Historically, an increase in interest rates has been a lead indicator of future defaults on mortgages in Region Three – especially when customers do not have a fixed interest rate mortgage. Bank ABC determines that the variable interest-rate portfolio of mortgages in Region Three is homogenous and that unlike for Region Two, it is not possible to identify particular sub portfolios on the basis of shared risk characteristics that represent customers that are expected to have increased significantly in credit risk. However, as a result of the homogenous nature of the mortgages in Region Three, Bank ABC determines that an assessment can be made of a proportion of the overall portfolio that has significantly increased in credit risk since initial recognition (i.e. a 'top down' approach can be used). Based on historical information, Bank ABC estimates that an increase in interest rates of 200 basis points will cause a significant increase in credit risk on 20 per cent of the variable interest-rate portfolio. Therefore, as a result of the anticipated increase in interest rates, Bank ABC determines that the credit risk on 20 per cent of mortgages in Region Three has increased significantly since initial recognition. Accordingly Bank ABC recognises lifetime expected credit losses on 20 per cent of the variable rate mortgage portfolio and a loss allowance at an amount equal to 12-month expected credit losses for the remainder of the portfolio (except for those mortgages that are determined to have significantly increased in credit risk based on an individual assessment, such as those that are more than 30 days past due – lifetime expected credit losses would also be recognised on those mortgages).

5.2.2.3 Changes in risk of default as time to maturity reduces

The general approach to impairment hinges on appropriately identifying when a significant increase in credit risk has occurred as this determines when an entity recognises a loss allowance based on lifetime expected credit losses instead of 12-month expected credit losses.

One approach for identifying when there has been a significant increase in credit risk is to analyse the probability of default of the financial instrument. Other approaches may use external credit ratings or internal risk ratings. Whichever method is used to measure credit risk, it is important to make sure that credit risk at the reporting date is compared to the credit risk at initial recognition for the instrument with the same time to maturity as that at the reporting date.

The relevance of this is highlighted by the fact that the risk of a default occurring on an AAA-rated bond with an expected life of 10 years is higher than that on an AAA-rated bond with an expected life of five years. [IFRS 9:B5.5.10]

Therefore, the change in credit risk cannot be assessed simply by comparing the change in the absolute risk of a default occurring over time. For example, if the risk of a default occurring for a financial instrument with an expected life of 10 years at initial recognition is identical to the risk of a default occurring on that financial instrument when its expected life in a subsequent period is only five years, that may indicate an increase in credit risk. This is because the risk of a default occurring over the expected life usually decreases as time passes if the credit risk is unchanged and the financial instrument is closer to maturity. However, for financial instruments that only have significant payment obligations close to the maturity of the financial instrument (e.g. a zero-coupon bond) the risk of a default occurring may not necessarily decrease as time passes. [IFRS 9:B5.5.11]

Example 5.2.2.3

Lifetime expected credit losses recognised for a written financial guarantee contract despite the absolute credit risk remaining the same

Entity K writes a financial guarantee contract over a long-dated bond issued by Entity P.

When the financial guarantee contract is issued by Entity K the probability of default on the bond issued by Entity P is 5 per cent. At each reporting date Entity K reassesses the probability of default of Entity P's bond.

At a subsequent reporting date when the bond is due to mature in one year's time, Entity K, estimates that the probability of default is 5 per cent. Despite the probability of default, in absolute terms, being the same as at inception of the guarantee, Entity K considers the credit risk of the bond to have increased significantly since inception. This is because Entity K determines the credit risk at the reporting date with one year to maturity of the bond is significantly higher than the credit risk of the bond at inception of the guarantee for the same bond with one year to maturity. This is illustrated in the diagram below (note that the probability of default (PD) for other exposures may develop differently over time):

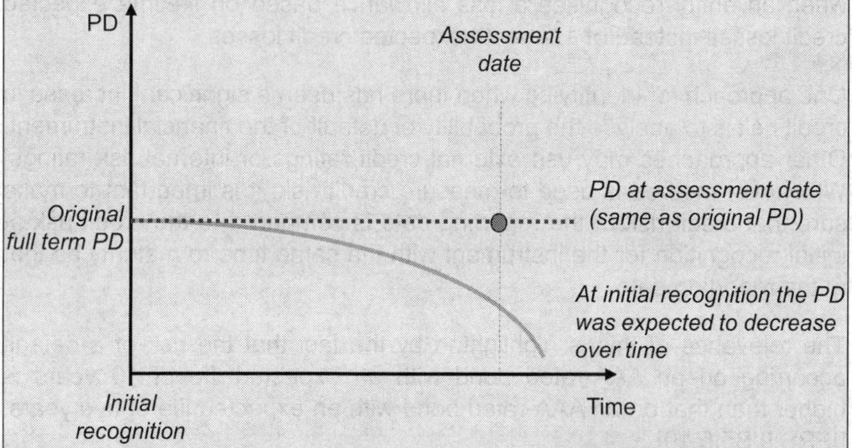

5.2.2.4 Using a 12-month probability of default as a proxy for lifetime probability of default

For financial instruments for which default patterns are not concentrated at a specific point during the expected life of the financial instrument, changes in the risk of a default occurring over the next 12 months may be a reasonable approximation of the changes in the lifetime risk of a default occurring and could be used to determine whether credit risk has increased significantly since initial recognition. [IFRS 9:B5.5.13]

The appropriateness of using changes in the risk of a default occurring over the next 12 months to determine whether lifetime expected credit losses should be recognised will depend on the specific facts and circumstances. For example, it may not be a suitable basis for determining whether credit risk has increased on a financial instrument with a maturity of more than 12 months when:

[IFRS 9:B5.5.14]

- the financial instruments only have significant payment obligations beyond the next 12 months;
- changes in relevant macroeconomic or other credit-related factors occur that are not adequately reflected in the risk of a default occurring in the next 12 months; or

- changes in credit-related factors only have an impact on the credit risk of the financial instrument (or have a more pronounced effect) beyond 12 months.

5.2.2.5 Other indicators of changes in credit risk

In practice there are many indicators, both quantitative and qualitative, to consider when assessing whether there has been a significant increase in credit risk. The following are various indicators (from IFRS 9:B5.5.17) that could be relevant in assessing whether there has been a significant increase in credit risk since initial recognition:

- **Significant changes in the terms of the same instrument** if it were issued at the reporting date that indicate a change in credit risk since initial recognition, e.g.:
  - increase in credit spread;
  - more stringent covenants;
  - increased amounts of collateral or guarantees; or
  - higher income coverage.

Any assessment of the changes in terms that would arise if the same instrument were issued at the reporting date will need to carefully consider the underlying reasons for those changes in terms because, in practice, there could be many reasons for the instrument to have different terms which do not relate to changes in the risk of default of the borrower. For example, a lender may change the terms of the loans it offers in response to changes in general underwriting practices or because it wants to increase or decrease its market presence in a particular market segment.

- **Significant changes in external market indicators of credit risk** for the same financial instrument (or similar instrument of the borrower), e.g.:
  - credit spread;
  - credit default swap prices;
  - length of time or the extent to which the fair value of a financial asset has been less than its amortised cost;
  - other market information related to the borrower, such as changes in the price of a borrower's debt and equity instruments; or
  - external credit rating (actual or expected).

Any market information used to judge a significant increase in credit risk will have to be considered carefully because a change in market indicators of credit risk will often also be influenced by other factors not specifically related to the risk of default. For example, credit spreads and credit default prices may change due to changes in market liquidity, or market repricing of credit risk, or due to expected recoveries from collateral or guarantees (which form part of measurement of expected losses rather than assessment of credit risk, see **5.3**).

When external credit ratings are used, the timing of when the rating was issued should be considered because such ratings are typically lagging indicators of credit risk and will not necessarily capture all forward looking information that is available without undue cost or effort at the reporting date.

- **Internal credit rating downgrade for the borrower or decrease in behavioural scoring** used to assess credit risk internally. Internal credit ratings and internal behavioural scoring are more reliable when they are mapped to external ratings or supported by default studies.
- **Changes in the entity's credit management approach** in relation to the financial instrument (e.g. based on emerging indicators of changes in the credit risk of the financial instrument, the entity's credit risk management practice is expected to become more active or focused on managing the instrument, including the instrument becoming more closely monitored or controlled, or the entity specifically intervening with the borrower).
- Actual or expected adverse changes in:
  - **business, financial or economic conditions** significantly affecting borrower's ability to meet its debt obligations (e.g. increase in interest rates or unemployment rates).
  - **operating results of the borrower** (e.g. declining revenues or margins, increasing operating risks, working capital deficiencies, decreasing asset quality, increased balance sheet leverage, liquidity, management problems or changes in the scope of business or organisational structure (such as the discontinuance of a segment of the business) that results in a significant change in the borrower's ability to meet its debt obligations.
  - **regulatory, economic, or technological environment** of the borrower that results in a significant change in the borrower's ability to meet its debt obligations (e.g. a decline in the demand for the borrower's sales product because of a shift in technology).
- significant changes in the:
  - **value of collateral or in the quality of third-party guarantees or credit enhancements**, which are expected to reduce the borrower's economic incentive to pay or otherwise effect the probability of default (e.g. if the value of collateral declines because house prices decline, borrowers in some jurisdictions have a greater incentive to default on their mortgages).

- **quality of a guarantee provided by a shareholder (or an individual's parents)** if the shareholder (or parents) have an incentive and financial ability to prevent default by capital or cash infusion.

IFRS 9:B5.5.17(j) refers to information regarding "increased amounts of collateral or guarantees" and "significant changes in the value of collateral supporting the obligation or in the quality of third-party guarantees or credit enhancements" as information that may be relevant in assessing changes in credit risk. However, these factors are only relevant to an assessment of credit risk to the extent that they affect the risk of the borrower defaulting. For example, a borrower under a mortgage loan may have an increased incentive to default if the value of the mortgage property has fallen significantly below the value of the loan. Another example is an individual borrower whose loan is guaranteed by a family member, when the family member may have an incentive and the financial ability to prevent default by providing the borrower with cash rather than allowing default and paying under the guarantee. The likelihood of the guarantor funding the debtor directly versus paying the lender for a claim under the guarantee does affect the probability of default and, consequently, the assessment of credit risk.

This issue was one of the issues discussed by the IFRS Transition Resource Group for Impairment of Financial Instruments (established by the IASB to discuss transition issues surrounding the IFRS 9 impairment model) at its meeting in April 2015.

- expected **changes in the loan documentation** (e.g. breach of contract leading to covenant waivers or amendments, interest payment holidays, interest rate step-ups, requiring additional collateral or guarantees).
- significant **changes in the expected performance and behaviour of the borrower**, including changes in the payment status of borrowers in the group (e.g. increase in delayed contractual payments or number of credit card borrowers expected to approach or exceed their credit limit or who are expected to be paying the minimum monthly amount).
- **past due information**, including the rebuttable presumption that the credit risk on a financial asset has increased significantly since initial recognition when contractual payments are more than 30 days past due (see **5.2.2.8**).

Example 5.2.2.5A

Significant increase in credit risk

[IFRS 9:IE7 - IE11 – Example 1]

Company Y has a funding structure that includes a senior secured loan facility with different tranches. (The security on the loan affects the loss that would be realised if a default occurs, but does not affect the risk of a default occurring, so it is not considered when determining whether there has been a significant increase in credit risk since initial recognition as required by IFRS 9:5.5.3). Bank X provides a tranche of that loan facility to Company Y. At the time of origination of the loan by Bank X, although Company Y's leverage was relatively high compared with other issuers with similar credit risk, it was expected that Company Y would be able to meet the covenants for the life of the instrument. In addition, the generation of revenue and cash flow was expected to be stable in Company Y's industry over the term of the senior facility. However, there was some business risk related to the ability to grow gross margins within its existing businesses.

At initial recognition, because of the considerations outlined above, Bank X considers that despite the level of credit risk at initial recognition, the loan is not an originated credit-impaired loan because it does not meet the definition of a credit-impaired financial asset in Appendix A of IFRS 9.

Subsequent to initial recognition, macroeconomic changes have had a negative effect on total sales volume and Company Y has underperformed on its business plan for revenue generation and net cash flow generation. Although spending on inventory has increased, anticipated sales have not materialised. To increase liquidity, Company Y has drawn down more on a separate revolving credit facility, thereby increasing its leverage ratio. Consequently, Company Y is now close to breaching its covenants on the senior secured loan facility with Bank X.

Bank X makes an overall assessment of the credit risk on the loan to Company Y at the reporting date by taking into consideration all reasonable and supportable information that is available without undue cost or effort and that is relevant for assessing the extent of the increase in credit risk since initial recognition. This may include factors such as:

- Bank X's expectation that the deterioration in the macroeconomic environment may continue in the near future, which is expected to have a further negative impact on Company Y's ability to generate cash flows and to deleverage.
- Company Y is closer to breaching its covenants, which may result in a need to restructure the loan or reset the covenants.
- Bank X's assessment that the trading prices for Company Y's bonds have decreased and that the credit margin on newly originated loans have increased reflecting the increase in credit risk, and that these changes are not explained by changes in the market environment (for example, benchmark interest rates have remained unchanged). A further comparison with the pricing of Company Y's peers shows that reductions in the price of Company Y's bonds and increases in credit margin on its loans have probably been caused by company-specific factors.
- Bank X has reassessed its internal risk grading of the loan on the basis of the information that it has available to reflect the increase in credit risk.

Bank X determines that there has been a significant increase in credit risk since initial recognition of the loan in accordance with IFRS 9:5.5.3 (see **5.2.1**). Consequently, Bank X recognises lifetime expected credit losses on its senior secured loan to Company Y. Even if Bank X has not yet changed the internal risk grading of the loan it could still reach this conclusion; the absence or presence of a change in risk grading in itself is not determinative of whether credit risk has increased significantly since initial recognition.

Example 5.2.2.5B

No significant increase in credit risk

[IFRS 9:IE12 - IE17 – Example 2]

Company C, is the holding company of a group that operates in a cyclical production industry. Bank B provided a loan to Company C. At that time, the prospects for the industry were positive, because of expectations of further increases in global demand. However, input prices were volatile and given the point in the cycle, a potential decrease in sales was anticipated.

In addition, in the past Company C has been focused on external growth, acquiring majority stakes in companies in related sectors. As a result, the group structure is complex and has been subject to change, making it difficult for investors to analyse the expected performance of the group and to forecast the cash that will be available at the holding company level. Even though leverage is at a level that is considered acceptable by Company C's creditors at the time that Bank B originates the loan, its creditors are concerned about Company C's ability to refinance its debt because of the short remaining life until the maturity of the current financing. There is also concern about Company C's ability to continue to service interest using the dividends it receives from its operating subsidiaries.

At the time of the origination of the loan by Bank B, Company C's leverage was in line with that of other customers with similar credit risk and based on projections over the expected life of the loan, the available capacity (i.e. headroom) on its coverage ratios before triggering a default event, was high. Bank B applies its own internal rating methods to determine credit risk and allocates a specific internal rating score to its loans. Bank B's internal rating categories are based on historical, current and forward-looking information and reflect the credit risk for the tenor of the loans. On initial recognition, Bank B determines that the loan is subject to considerable credit risk, has speculative elements and that the uncertainties affecting Company C, including the group's uncertain prospects for cash generation, could lead to default. However, Bank B does not consider the loan to be originated credit-impaired because it does not meet the definition of a purchased or originated credit-impaired financial asset in IFRS 9:Appendix A.

Subsequent to initial recognition, Company C has announced that three of its five key subsidiaries had a significant reduction in sales volume because of deteriorated market conditions but sales volumes are expected to improve in line with the anticipated cycle for the industry in the following months. The sales of the other two subsidiaries were stable. Company C has also announced a corporate restructure to streamline its operating subsidiaries. This restructuring will increase the flexibility to refinance existing debt and the ability of the operating subsidiaries to pay dividends to Company C.

Despite the expected continuing deterioration in market conditions, Bank B determines, in accordance with IFRS 9:5.5.3 (see **5.2.1**), that there has not been a significant increase in the credit risk on the loan to Company C since initial recognition. This is demonstrated by factors that include:

- Although current sale volumes have fallen, this was as anticipated by Bank B at initial recognition. Furthermore, sales volumes are expected to improve, in the following months.
- Given the increased flexibility to refinance the existing debt at the operating subsidiary level and the increased availability of dividends to Company C, Bank B views the corporate restructure as being credit enhancing. This is despite some continued concern about the ability to refinance the existing debt at the holding company level.
- Bank B's credit risk department, which monitors Company C, has determined that the latest developments are not significant enough to justify a change in its internal credit risk rating.

As a consequence, Bank B does not recognise a loss allowance at an amount equal to lifetime expected credit losses on the loan. However, it updates its measurement of the 12-month expected credit losses for the increased risk of a default occurring in the next 12 months and for current expectations of the credit losses that would arise if a default were to occur.

5.2.2.6 Comparing credit risk at the reporting date to the maximum initial credit risk

The impairment model requires a comparison of the risk of default at the reporting date with the risk of default at initial recognition. In some cases a practical way to readily identify a significant increase in credit risk may be to compare the credit risk at the reporting date to the maximum initial credit risk of a financial instrument. Using this approach an entity may determine that any financial instrument with a risk of default at the reporting date above a set absolute measure has exhibited a significant increase in credit risk since initial recognition. This is illustrated in the following example.

Example 5.2.2.6

Comparison to maximum initial credit risk

[IFRS 9:IE40 - IE42 – Example 6]

Bank A has two portfolios of automobile loans with similar terms and conditions in Region W. Bank A's policy on financing decisions for each loan is based on an internal credit rating system that considers a customer's credit history, payment behaviour on other products with Bank A and other factors, and assigns an internal credit risk rating from 1 (lowest credit risk) to 10 (highest credit risk) to each loan on origination. The risk of a default occurring increases exponentially as the credit risk rating deteriorates so, for example, the difference between credit risk rating grades 1 and 2 is smaller than the difference between credit risk rating grades 2 and 3. Loans in Portfolio 1 were only offered to existing customers with a similar internal credit risk rating and at initial recognition all loans were rated 3 or 4 on the internal rating scale. Bank A determines that the maximum initial credit risk rating at initial recognition it would accept for Portfolio 1 is an internal rating of 4. Loans in Portfolio 2 were offered to customers that responded to an advertisement for automobile loans and the internal credit risk ratings of these customers range between 4 and 7 on the internal rating scale. Bank A never originates an automobile loan with an internal credit risk rating worse than 7 (i.e. with an internal rating of 8-10).

For the purposes of assessing whether there have been significant increases in credit risk, Bank A determines that all loans in Portfolio 1 had a similar initial credit risk. It determines that given the risk of default reflected in its internal risk rating grades, a change in internal rating from 3 to 4 would not represent a significant increase in credit risk but that there has been a significant increase in credit risk on any loan in this portfolio that has an internal rating worse than 5. This means that Bank A does not have to know the initial credit rating of each loan in the portfolio to assess the change in credit risk since initial recognition. It only has to determine whether the credit risk is worse than 5 at the reporting date to determine whether lifetime expected credit losses should be recognised in accordance with IFRS 9:5.5.3.

However, determining the maximum initial credit risk accepted at initial recognition for Portfolio 2 at an internal credit risk rating of 7, would not meet the objective of the requirements as stated in IFRS 9:5.5.4 (see **5.2.1**). This is because Bank A determines that significant increases in credit risk arise not only when credit risk increases above the level at which an entity would originate new financial assets (i.e. when the internal rating is worse than 7). Although Bank A never originates an automobile loan with an internal credit rating worse than 7, the initial credit risk on loans in Portfolio 2 is not of sufficiently similar credit risk at initial recognition to apply the approach used for Portfolio 1. This means that Bank A cannot simply compare the credit risk at the reporting date with the lowest credit quality at initial recognition (for example, by comparing the internal credit risk rating of loans in Portfolio 2 with an internal credit risk rating of 7) to determine whether credit risk has increased significantly because the initial credit quality of loans in the portfolio is too diverse. For example, if a loan initially had a credit risk rating of 4 the credit risk on the loan may have increased significantly if its internal credit risk rating changes to 6.

5.2.2.7 Using an assessment of counterparty credit risk

The impairment model requires an entity to consider the credit risk of the specific financial instrument for which the loss allowance is determined. Therefore, it will not be appropriate to only consider changes in the assessment of counterparty credit risk without relating this back to the specific financial instrument being assessed. An illustration of how counterparty credit risk could be used appropriately is provided in the following two examples.

Example 5.2.2.7A

Counterparty assessment of credit risk

[IFRS 9:IE43 & IE 44 – Example 7]

Scenario 1

In 20X0 Bank A granted a loan of CU10,000 with a contractual term of 15 years to Company Q when the company had an internal credit risk rating of 4 on a scale of 1 (lowest credit risk) to 10 (highest credit risk). The risk of a default occurring increases exponentially as the credit risk rating deteriorates so, for example, the difference between credit risk rating grades 1 and 2 is smaller than the difference between credit risk rating grades 2 and 3. In 20X5, when Company Q had an internal credit risk rating of 6, Bank A issued another loan to Company Q for CU5,000 with a contractual term of 10 years. In 20X7 Company Q fails to retain its contract with a major customer and correspondingly experiences a large decline in its revenue. Bank A considers that as a result of losing the contract, Company Q will have a significantly reduced ability to meet its loan obligations and changes its internal credit risk rating to 8.

Bank A assesses credit risk on a counterparty level for credit risk management purposes and determines that the increase in Company Q's credit risk is significant. Although Bank A did not perform an individual assessment of changes in the credit risk on each loan since its initial recognition, assessing the credit risk on a counterparty level and recognising lifetime expected credit losses on all loans granted to Company Q, meets the objective of the impairment requirements as stated in IFRS 9:5.5.4. This is because, even since the most recent loan was originated (in 20X7) when Company Q had the highest credit risk at loan origination, its credit risk has increased significantly. The counterparty assessment would therefore achieve the same result as assessing the change in credit risk for each loan individually.

Scenario 1 in **example 5.2.2.7A** illustrates that it is not possible to assess whether there has been a significant increase in credit risk solely by considering counterparty credit risk in absolute terms. Such an approach has the potential to ignore the degree to which credit risk has increased since initial recognition of the loan. In the scenario described, for both loans there has been a significant increase in credit risk for Bank A as the increase in credit risk, as noted in the change in credit ratings, is significant for the loan that had the highest credit risk at origination.

Example 5.2.2.7B

Counterparty assessment of credit risk

[IFRS 9:IE45 - 47 – Example 7]

Scenario 2

Bank A granted a loan of CU150,000 with a contractual term of 20 years to Company X in 20X0 when the company had an internal credit risk rating of 4. During 20X5 economic conditions deteriorate and demand for Company X's products has declined significantly. As a result of the reduced cash flows from lower sales, Company X could not make full payment of its loan instalment to Bank A. Bank A re-assesses Company X's internal credit risk rating and determines it to be 7 at the reporting date. Bank A considered the change in credit risk on the loan, including considering the change in the internal credit risk rating and determines that there has been a significant increase in credit risk and recognises lifetime expected credit losses on the loan of CU150,000.

Despite the recent downgrade of the internal credit risk rating, Bank A grants another loan of CU50,000 to Company X in 20X6 with a contractual term of 5 years, taking into consideration the higher credit risk at that date.

The fact that Company X's credit risk (assessed on a counterparty basis) has previously been assessed to have increased significantly, does not result in lifetime expected credit losses being recognised on the new loan. This is because the credit risk on the new loan has not increased significantly since the loan was initially recognised. If Bank A only assessed credit risk on a counterparty level, without considering whether the conclusion about changes in credit risk applies to all individual financial instruments provided to the same customer, the objective in IFRS 9:5.5.4 would not be met.

As illustrated in scenario two of **example 5.2.2.7B**, determining whether there has been a significant increase in credit risk on a financial asset is based on the credit risk of the loan at initial recognition. Whether existing loans have experienced significant increases in credit risk does not impact the assessment for new loans. Equally, a decision to extend another loan, while there has been a significant increase in credit risk on existing loans does not change the fact that there has been a significant increase in credit risk on existing loans.

5.2.2.8 Rebuttable presumption if more than 30 days past due

Regardless of the way in which an entity assesses significant increases in credit risk, there is a rebuttable presumption that the credit risk on a financial asset has increased significantly since initial recognition when contractual payments are more than 30 days past due. The rebuttable presumption is not an absolute indictor that lifetime expected credit losses should be recognised, but is presumed to be the latest point at which lifetime expected credit losses should be recognised even when using forward-looking information (including macroeconomic factors on a portfolio level). Consequently, when an entity determines that there have been significant increases in credit risk before contractual payments are more than 30 days past due, the rebuttable presumption does not apply. [IFRS 9:5.5.11 & B5.5.19]

An entity can rebut this presumption if the entity has reasonable and supportable information that is available without undue cost or effort, that demonstrates that the credit risk has not increased significantly since initial recognition even though the contractual payments are more than 30 days past due. [IFRS 9:5.5.11] For example when:

[IFRS 9:B5.5.20]

- non-payment was an administrative oversight instead of resulting from financial difficulty of the borrower; or
- an entity has access to historical evidence that demonstrates that there is no correlation between significant increases in the risk of a default occurring and financial assets on which payments are more than 30 days past due, but that evidence does identify such a correlation when payments are more than (for example) 60 days past due.

An entity is not required to rebut the presumption on an instrument-by-instrument basis but can rebut it if the entity has information that indicates that, for a particular product, region or customer type, more than 30 days past due is not representative of the point at which credit risk increases significantly. [IFRS 9:BC5.194]

Given the objective of assessing whether there is a significant increase in credit risk, an entity cannot align the timing of significant increases in credit risk and the recognition of lifetime expected credit losses to when a financial asset is regarded as credit-impaired (see **5.2.5.3**) or an entity's internal definition of default (see **5.2.2**). [IFRS 9:B5.5.21]

5.2.3 Applying the general approach to modified financial instruments

Borrowers can seek to renegotiate debt instruments for a variety of reasons. Sometimes, the borrower seeks more favourable terms from the lender. Sometimes, the borrower might be in financial difficulty and needs to alter the terms of the instrument such as the maturity or coupon payments. The lender would need to consider whether the modification results in the derecognition of the existing instrument and the recognition of a new instrument. Derecognition for financial assets is detailed in **chapter B8**. IFRS 9 provides guidance on how to apply the impairment requirements to scenarios when a modification leads to derecognition and to scenarios when modification does not lead to derecognition.

5.2.3.1 Modifications that lead to derecognition

Where the renegotiation or modification of the contractual cash flows of a financial asset lead to the derecognition of the existing financial asset in accordance with IFRS 9 the modified asset is considered a 'new' financial asset for the purposes of IFRS 9. [IFRS 9:B5.5.25] Accordingly, the date of the modification should be treated as the date of initial recognition of that financial asset when applying the impairment requirements to the modified financial asset. This typically means measuring the loss allowance at an amount equal to 12-month expected credit losses until the criteria for the recognition of lifetime expected credit losses is met (see general approach in **5.2.1**). [IFRS 9:B5.5.26]

However, in some unusual circumstances following a modification that results in derecognition of the original financial asset, there may be evidence that the modified financial asset is credit-impaired at initial recognition, and thus, the financial asset should be recognised as an originated credit-impaired financial asset. This might occur, for example, in a situation in which there was a substantial modification of a distressed asset that resulted in the derecognition of the original financial asset. In such a case, it may be possible for the modification to result in a new financial asset which is credit-impaired at initial recognition (see **5.2.5.3**). [IFRS 9:B5.5.26]

Example 5.2.3.1

Debt modification leading to derecognition

Bank B originates a loan to Entity C. For Bank B the loan is not credit-impaired at origination.

In subsequent reporting periods Bank B renegotiates the loan with Entity C because of severe financial difficulties of the borrower. At the date of renegotiation Bank B has recognised a loss allowance equal to lifetime expected credit losses.

Bank B assesses the extent to which the modified loan has changed and determines that the modification leads to derecognition of the original loan. A gain or loss is recognised on derecognition of the original loan as the difference between the fair value of the new loan initially recognised and the carrying value of the original loan derecognised (which includes the cumulative loss allowance).

At initial recognition of the new loan Bank B determines whether the new loan is originated credit-impaired or not. If the new loan is not originated credit-impaired Bank B recognises a loss allowance equal to 12-month expected credit losses under the general approach. If the new loan is considered originated credit-impaired then Bank B does not recognise a loss allowance at initial recognition of the new loan, rather Bank B determines a credit-adjusted effective interest rate that will apply subsequent to initial recognition that reflects incurred credit losses that relate to the modified contractual cash flows on the new loan.

5.2.3.2 Modifications that do not lead to derecognition

If the contractual cash flows on a financial asset have been renegotiated or modified and the financial asset is not derecognised, an entity should assess whether there has been a significant increase in the credit risk of the financial instrument by comparing:

[IFRS 9:5.5.12]

(a) the risk of a default occurring at the reporting date (based on the modified contractual terms); and

(b) the risk of a default occurring at initial recognition (based on the original, unmodified contractual terms).

When assessing whether there has been significant increases in credit risk since initial recognition an entity should use all reasonable and supportable information that is available without undue cost or effort. This includes historical and forward-looking information and an assessment of the credit risk over the expected life of the financial asset, which includes information about the circumstances that led to the modification. [IFRS 9:B5.5.27]

If the contractual cash flows on a financial asset have been renegotiated or otherwise modified, but the financial asset is not derecognised, that financial asset is not automatically considered to have lower credit risk. Evidence that the criteria for the recognition of lifetime expected credit losses are no longer met may include a history of up to date and timely payment performance against the modified contractual terms. Typically a customer would need to demonstrate consistently good payment behaviour over a period of time before the credit risk is considered to have decreased. For example, a history of missed or incomplete payments would not typically be erased by simply making one payment on time following a modification of the contractual terms. [IFRS 9:B5.5.27]

Example 5.2.3.2

Modification of contractual cash flows

[IFRS 9:IE66 - IE73 – Example 11]

Bank A originates a five-year loan that requires the repayment of the outstanding contractual amount in full at maturity. Its principal amount is CU1,000 with an interest rate of 5 per cent payable annually. The effective interest rate is 5 per cent. The loan is not a purchased or originated credit-impaired financial asset as defined in Appendix A of IFRS 9. At the end of the first reporting period (Period 1), Bank A recognises a loss allowance at an amount equal to 12-month expected credit losses because there has not been a significant increase in credit risk since initial recognition. A loss allowance balance of CU20 is recognised.

In the subsequent reporting period (Period 2), Bank A determines that the credit risk on the loan has increased significantly since initial recognition. As a result of this increase, Bank A recognises lifetime expected credit losses on the loan. The loss allowance balance is CU30.

At the end of the third reporting period (Period 3), following significant financial difficulty of the borrower, Bank A modifies the contractual cash flows on the loan. It extends the contractual term of the loan by one year so that the remaining term at the date of the modification is three years. The modification does not result in the derecognition of the loan by Bank A.

As a result of that modification, Bank A recalculates the gross carrying amount of the financial asset as the present value of the modified contractual cash flows discounted at the loan's original effective interest rate of 5 per cent. In accordance with IFRS 9:5.4.3, the difference between this recalculated gross carrying amount and the gross carrying amount before the modification is recognised as a modification gain or loss. Bank A recognises the modification loss (calculated as CU300) against the gross carrying amount of the loan, reducing it to CU700, and a modification loss of CU300 in profit or loss.

Bank A also remeasures the loss allowance, taking into account the modified contractual cash flows and evaluates whether the loss allowance for the loan should continue to be measured at an amount equal to lifetime expected credit losses. Bank A compares the current credit risk (taking into consideration the modified cash flows) to the credit risk (on the original unmodified cash flows) at initial recognition. Bank A determines that the loan is not credit-impaired at the reporting date but that credit risk has still significantly increased compared to the credit risk at initial recognition and continues to measure the loss allowance at an amount equal to lifetime expected credit losses. The loss allowance balance for lifetime expected credit losses is CU100 at the reporting date.

Period	**Beginning gross carrying amount**	**Impairment (loss)/gain**	**Modification (loss)/ gain**	**Interest revenue**	**Cash flows**	**Ending gross carrying amount**	**Loss allowance**	**Ending amortised cost amount**
	A	B	C	D Gross: A × 5%	E	F = A + C + D − E	G	H = F − G
1	CU1,000	(CU20)		CU50	CU50	CU1,000	CU20	CU980
2	CU1,000	(CU10)		CU50	CU50	CU1,000	CU30	CU970
3	CU1,000	(CU70)	(CU300)	CU50	CU50	CU700	CU100	CU600

At each subsequent reporting date, Bank A evaluates whether there is a significant increase in credit risk by comparing the loan's credit risk at initial recognition (based on the original, unmodified cash flows) with the credit risk at the reporting date (based on the modified cash flows), in accordance with IFRS 9:5.5.12.

Two reporting periods after the loan modification (Period 5), the borrower has outperformed its business plan significantly compared to the expectations at the modification date. In addition, the outlook for the business is more positive than previously envisaged. An assessment of all reasonable and supportable information that is available without undue cost or effort indicates that the overall credit risk on the loan has decreased and that the risk of a default occurring over the expected life of the loan has decreased, so Bank A adjusts the borrower's internal credit rating at the end of the reporting period. Given the positive overall development, Bank A re-assesses the situation and concludes that the credit risk of the loan has decreased and there is no longer a significant increase in credit risk since initial recognition. As a result, Bank A once again measures the loss allowance at an amount equal to 12-month expected credit losses.

5.2.4 Applying the general approach to financial assets measured at FVTOCI

The general approach for recognising and measuring a loss allowance is the same for financial instruments measured at amortised cost and those debt instruments that are measured at FVTOCI. However, unlike amortised cost, the loss allowance should be recognised in other comprehensive income and should not reduce the carrying amount of the financial asset in the statement of financial position. [IFRS 9:5.5.2] This ensures that the carrying value of the asset is always measured at fair value in the statement of financial position, irrespective of the size of the loss allowance, and that the amount recognised in profit or loss is the same as if the financial asset was measured at amortised cost.

Example 5.2.4

Debt instrument measured at fair value through other comprehensive income

[IFRS 9:IE78 - IE81 – Example 13]

An entity purchases a debt instrument with a fair value of CU1,000 on 15 December 20X0 and measures the debt instrument at fair value through other comprehensive income. The instrument has an interest rate of 5 per cent over the contractual term of 10 years, and has a 5 per cent effective interest rate. At initial recognition the entity determines that the asset is not purchased or originated credit-impaired.

		CU	CU
Dr	Financial asset at fair value through other comprehensive income	1,000	
Cr	Cash		1,000

To recognise the debt instrument measured at its fair value.

On 31 December 20X0 (the reporting date), the fair value of the debt instrument has decreased to CU950 as a result of changes in market interest rates. The entity determines that there has not been a significant increase in credit risk since initial recognition and that expected credit losses should be measured at an amount equal to 12-month expected credit losses, which amounts to CU30. For simplicity, journal entries for the receipt of interest revenue are not provided.

		CU	CU
Dr	Impairment loss (profit or loss)	30	
Dr	Other comprehensive income	20	
Cr	Financial asset at fair value through other comprehensive income		50

To recognise the expected losses and other fair value changes on the debt instrument.

Disclosure would be provided about the accumulated impairment amount of CU30.

On 1 January 20X1, the entity decides to sell the debt instrument for CU950, which is its fair value at that date.

		CU	CU
Dr	Cash	950	
Cr	Financial asset at fair value through other comprehensive income		950
Dr	Loss (profit or loss)	20	
Cr	Other comprehensive income		20

To derecognise the fair value through other comprehensive income asset and recycle amounts accumulated in other comprehensive income to profit or loss.

5.2.5 *Simplifications and an exception to the general approach*

To ensure the general approach to impairment in IFRS 9 can be applied practically, IFRS 9 introduces a number of simplifications and an exception to the general approach discussed in **5.2.1**.

5.2.5.1 *Simplified approach for financial instruments that have low credit risk at the reporting date*

An entity may assume that the credit risk on a financial instrument has not increased significantly since initial recognition, and therefore the loss allowance is measured at an amount equal to 12-month expected credit losses, if the financial instrument is determined to have low credit risk at the reporting date. [IFRS 9:5.5.10]

This operational simplification was introduced by the IASB because they observed that for financial instruments with low credit risk, the effect of this simplification on the timing of recognition and the amount of expected credit losses should be minimal. [IFRS 9:BC5.180]

However, it was noted that for some entities assessing whether a lifetime loss allowance is required based on both a relative measure per the general approach and an absolute measure for those financial instruments with low credit risk could introduce operational complexities. As a result, the low credit risk simplification is a choice that can be applied on an instrument by instrument basis. [IFRS 9:BC5.184]

The credit risk on a financial instrument is considered low if:

[IFRS 9:B5.5.22]

- the financial instrument has a low risk of default;
- the borrower has a strong capacity to meet its contractual cash flow obligations in the near term; and
- adverse changes in economic and business conditions in the longer term may, but will not necessarily, reduce the ability of the borrower to fulfil its contractual cash flow obligations.

To determine whether a financial instrument has low credit risk, an entity may use its internal credit risk ratings or other methodologies that are consistent with a globally understood definition of low credit risk and that consider the risks and the type of financial instruments that are being assessed. An external rating of 'investment grade' is an example of a financial instrument that may be considered as having low credit risk. However, financial instruments are not required to be externally rated to be considered to have low credit risk. They should, however, be considered to have low credit risk from a market participant perspective taking into account all of the terms and conditions of the financial instrument. [IFRS 9:B5.5.23]

When using a credit rating to identify whether a financial instrument is low credit risk an entity should ensure the credit rating used is reflective of the conditions at the reporting date. For example, an entity should not simply assume that the credit rating issued before or after the reporting date is reflective of the credit risk *at* the reporting date since there may be important developments in credit risk that have not been included in ratings issued before the reporting date or have been included in ratings issued after the reporting date. The timing of the credit rating being issued and other available information will be relevant in this assessment.

Furthermore, lifetime expected credit losses are not recognised on a financial instrument simply because it was considered to have low credit risk in the previous reporting period and is not considered to have low credit risk at the reporting date. In such a case, an entity should determine whether there have been significant increases in credit risk since initial recognition and thus whether lifetime expected credit losses are required to be recognised in accordance with the general approach (see **5.2.1**). [IFRS 9:B5.5.24]

For example, a financial instrument might go from being marginally below the low credit risk threshold to marginally above the low credit risk threshold and this may not represent a significant increase in credit risk.

The Standard makes clear that the credit risk on a financial instrument is not considered low simply because:

[IFRS 9:B5.5.22]

- the value of collateral and the financial instrument without that collateral would not be considered low credit risk; or
- the financial asset has a lower risk of default than the entity's other financial instruments or relative to the credit risk of the jurisdiction within which an entity operates.

Example 5.2.5.1

Public investment-grade bond

[IFRS 9: IE24 - IE28 – Example 4]

Company A is a large listed national logistics company. The only debt in the capital structure is a five-year public bond with a restriction on further borrowing as the only bond covenant. Company A reports quarterly to its shareholders. Entity B is one of many investors in the bond. Entity B considers the bond to have low credit risk at initial recognition in accordance with IFRS 9:5.5.10. This is because the bond has a low risk of default and Company A is considered to have a strong capacity to meet its obligations in the near term. Entity B's expectations for the longer term are that adverse changes in economic and business conditions may, but will not necessarily, reduce Company A's ability to fulfil its obligations on the bond. In addition, at initial recognition the bond had an internal credit rating that is correlated to a global external credit rating of investment grade.

At the reporting date, Entity B's main credit risk concern is the continuing pressure on the total volume of sales that has caused Company A's operating cash flows to decrease.

Because Entity B relies only on quarterly public information and does not have access to private credit risk information (because it is a bond investor), its assessment of changes in credit risk is tied to public announcements and information, including updates on credit perspectives in press releases from rating agencies.

Entity B applies the low credit risk simplification in IFRS 9:5.5.10. Accordingly, at the reporting date, Entity B evaluates whether the bond is considered to have low credit risk using all reasonable and supportable information that is available without undue cost or effort. In making that evaluation, Entity B reassesses the internal credit rating of the bond and concludes that the bond is no longer equivalent to an investment grade rating because:

(a) The latest quarterly report of Company A revealed a quarter-on-quarter decline in revenues of 20 per cent and in operating profit by 12 per cent.

(b) Rating agencies have reacted negatively to a profit warning by Company A and put the credit rating under review for possible downgrade from investment grade to non-investment grade. However, at the reporting date the external credit risk rating was unchanged.

(c) The bond price has also declined significantly, which has resulted in a higher yield to maturity. Entity B assesses that the bond prices have been declining as a result of increases in Company A's credit risk. This is because the market environment has not changed (for example, benchmark interest rates, liquidity etc are unchanged) and comparison with the bond prices of peers shows that the reductions are probably company specific (instead of being, for example, changes in benchmark interest rates that are not indicative of company-specific credit risk).

While Company A currently has the capacity to meet its commitments, the large uncertainties arising from its exposure to adverse business and economic conditions have increased the risk of a default occurring on the bond. As a result of the factors described above, Entity B determines that the bond does not have low credit risk at the reporting date. As a result, Entity B needs to determine whether the increase in credit risk since initial recognition has been significant. On the basis of its assessment, Company B determines that the credit risk has increased significantly since initial recognition and that a loss allowance at an amount equal to lifetime expected credit losses should be recognised in accordance with IFRS 9:5.5.3 (see **5.2.1**).

5.2.5.2 Simplified approach for trade receivables, contract assets and lease receivables

The impairment model does not require the general approach (under which changes in credit risk since initial recognition must be monitored, see **5.2.1**) to be applied for all trade receivables, contract assets (in scope of IFRS 15 *Revenue from Contracts with Customers*) and lease receivables (resulting from transactions that are within the scope of IAS 17 *Leases*).

Instead a simplified approach can apply for these assets under which a lifetime expected loss allowance is *always* recognised (i.e. a loss allowance for 12-month expected losses is not initially or subsequently recognised). As a result there is no need to identify significant increases (or decreases) in credit risk for the purpose of measuring the impairment allowance in the statement of financial position as required under the general approach. This can make the application of the impairment model more operational. However, a consequence of always recognising a loss allowance for lifetime expected losses for assets with a term longer than 12 months is that it can give rise to a larger loss allowance and larger impairment loss on initial recognition (because lifetime expected losses for an asset with a term longer than 12 months is expected to be greater than 12-month expected losses).

In some cases the simplified approach is required and in other cases it is an accounting policy choice. For trade receivables and contract assets that do not contain a financing component (see below), it is a requirement to recognise a lifetime expected loss allowance. For other trade receivables, other contract assets, operating lease receivables and finance lease receivables it is an accounting policy choice that can be separately applied for each type of asset (but applies to all of that type of asset), as summarised below. [IFRS 9:5.5.15 & 16]

	Lifetime expected loss allowance *always* recognised
Trade receivables and contract assets that *do not contain a significant financing component*	Requirement
Trade receivables that contain a significant financing component	Accounting policy choice (for *all* such trade receivables)
Contract assets that contain a significant financing component	Accounting policy choice (for *all* such contract assets)
Operating lease receivables	Accounting policy choice (for *all* operating lease receivables)
Finance lease receivables	Accounting policy choice (for *all* finance lease receivables)

A significant financing component exists if the timing of payments agreed to by the parties to the contract (either explicitly or implicitly) provides the customer or the entity with a significant benefit of financing the transfer of goods or services to the customer. [IFRS 15:60] A contract with a customer would not have a significant financing component if any of the following factors exist:
[IFRS 15:62]

(a) the customer paid for the goods or services in advance and the timing of the transfer of those goods or services is at the discretion of the customer.

(b) a substantial amount of the consideration promised by the customer is variable and the amount or timing of that consideration varies on the basis of the occurrence or non-occurrence of a future event that is not substantially within the control of the customer or the entity (for example, if the consideration is a sales-based royalty).

(c) the difference between the promised consideration and the cash selling price of the good or service arises for reasons other than the provision of finance to either the customer or the entity, and the

> difference between those amounts is proportional to the reason for the difference. For example, the payment terms might provide the entity or the customer with protection from the other party failing to adequately complete some or all of its obligations under the contract.
>
> Further, IFRS 15:63 has a practical expedient whereby an entity need not adjust the promised amount of consideration for the effects of a significant financing component if the entity expects, at contract inception, that the period between when the entity transfers a promised good or service to a customer and when the customer pays for that good or service will be one year or less.

IFRS 9 includes an example illustrating how a provision matrix approach could be used to practically measure expected credit losses on trade receivables (see **example 5.3.5.5**).

5.2.5.3 Exception to the general approach for purchased or originated credit-impaired financial assets

Purchased or originated credit-impaired financial assets are those that at the date of initial recognition are credit-impaired. A financial asset is credit-impaired when one or more events that have a detrimental impact on the expected future cash flows of that financial asset have occurred. Evidence of credit-impairment includes observable data about the following events:

[IFRS 9:Appendix A]

- significant financial difficulty of the issuer or the borrower;
- a breach of contract, such as a default or past due event;
- the lender(s) of the borrower, for economic or contractual reasons relating to the borrower's financial difficulty, having granted to the borrower a concession(s) that the lender(s) would not otherwise consider;
- it becoming probable that the borrower will enter bankruptcy or other financial reorganisation;
- the disappearance of an active market for that financial asset because of financial difficulties; or
- the purchase or origination of a financial asset at a deep discount that reflects the incurred credit losses.

It may not be possible to identify a single discrete event – instead the combined effect of several events may have caused financial assets to become credit-impaired.

If a financial asset is purchased or originated credit-impaired then at the reporting date only the cumulative changes in lifetime expected credit losses since initial recognition are recognised as a loss allowance. [IFRS 9:5.5.13]

The amount of the change in lifetime expected credit losses should be recognised as an impairment gain or loss in profit or loss. An entity should recognise favourable changes in lifetime expected credit losses as an impairment gain, even if the lifetime expected credit losses are less than the amount of expected credit losses that were included in the estimated cash flows on initial recognition. [IFRS 9:5.5.14]

Impairment gains recognised in profit or loss arise from two sources.

Firstly, for all financial instruments that are in the scope of the impairment requirements an impairment gain arises when there is a reduction in the loss allowance leading to gain in profit or loss, i.e. a reversal of previously recognised impairment losses.

Secondly, for purchased or originated credit-impaired financial assets only, impairment gains can arise which are not reversals of previously recognised impairment losses. For these financial assets credit losses are built into the expected cash flows that determine the credit-adjusted effective interest rate when the asset is initially recognised. Consequently when there is an improvement in credit quality beyond the level that was estimated when the asset was initially recognised this will lead to impairment gains and a loss allowance that is negative (i.e. it increases the carrying amount of the asset). This approach does not apply to written financial guarantee contracts, written loan commitments and financial assets that are not purchased or originated credit-impaired because for these instruments the loan allowance must always be at least equal to 12-month expected credit losses and the loss allowance cannot be negative.

Example 5.2.5.3

Purchased credit-impaired financial asset

On 1 January 20X1, Entity A purchases, for CU6m, a fixed rate bond with four years to maturity, a contractual coupon of 10 per cent and a par amount of CU10m. The bond had originally been issued for its par amount. The deep discount to the par amount is because the issuer of the bond is in significant financial difficulty and consequently, Entity A determines the bond to be purchased credit-impaired.

On initial recognition Entity A recognises the asset at fair value less transaction costs (assumed to be nil for illustrative purposes) in accordance with IFRS 9:5.1.1. Entity A holds the asset within a business model with an objective to collect the contractual cash flows and therefore it subsequently measures the asset at amortised cost. Because the asset is purchased credit-impaired, in accordance with IFRS 9:5.5.13, Entity A does not recognise a loss allowance for lifetime expected credit losses, and instead recognises the cumulative change in lifetime credit losses since initial recognition as a loss allowance.

Because the loss allowance is nil on initial recognition of a purchased credit-impaired financial asset, the initial fair value, less transaction costs represents the amortised cost on initial recognition.

In accordance with IFRS 9:5.4.1, Entity A calculates the credit-adjusted effective interest rate (EIR), which it will use subsequently to calculate interest revenue by applying that rate to the amortised cost from initial recognition.

The credit-adjusted EIR is the rate that exactly discounts the estimated future cash receipts, to the asset's amortised cost. The expected future cash receipts are estimated considering all contractual cash flows and expected credit losses. [IFRS 9:Appendix A]

Entity A calculates the credit-adjusted EIR to be 7.46 per cent based on its estimate that it expects to receive a single cash flow of CU8m on maturity of the bond (i.e. it does not expect to receive any interest payments during the remaining term of the bond and does not expect payment of the full par amount).

The following is a description of the amounts recognised in profit or loss and the statement of financial position for each reporting period. It can be seen from this that the impairment gain or loss in any period is equivalent to the present value of the undiscounted change in the lifetime expected losses since the last reporting period end. This is because any change in the loss allowance due to the unwinding of discount is included as part of interest income, rather than impairment gain/loss because the amortised cost on which interest income is calculated includes the loss allowance.

31 December 20X1

At the end of the first reporting period following acquisition of the bond, Entity A continues to expect to receive CU8m at maturity of the bond. It therefore recognises interest income of CU447k in the period (7.46% × CU6m) resulting in an amortised cost of CU6,447k at the reporting date. Since there has been no change in the undiscounted lifetime expected credit losses, the loss allowance is nil at the reporting date.

31 December 20X2

At the end of the second reporting period following acquisition of the bond, Entity A now expects to receive CU9m at maturity of the bond. This results in a favourable change in lifetime expected credit losses. Entity A recognises interest income of CU481k in the period (7.46% × CU6,447k) and an impairment gain of CU866k. CU866k represents the cumulative change in undiscounted lifetime expected losses of CU1m, discounted by 7.46 per cent for two years. This results in a *negative* loss allowance of CU866k and an amortised cost of CU7,794k. This equates to CU8m less a *negative* loss allowance of CU1m (i.e. summing to CU9m), discounted by 7.46 per cent for two years.

31 December 20X3

At the end of the third reporting period following acquisition of the bond, Entity A now expects to receive CU7m at maturity of the bond. This results in an unfavourable change in lifetime expected credit losses giving rise to a revised (now positive) loss allowance of CU931k. CU931k represents the cumulative change in lifetime expected losses of CU1m, discounted by 7.46 per cent for one year. The unfavourable change in lifetime expected losses of CU1,861k (CU931k - (CU866k*(1+0.074))) is recognised in profit or loss. CU1,861k represents the difference between the revised loss allowance and the previous loss allowance after the unwinding of discount. The unwinding of discount is recognised as part of interest income. Entity A also recognises interest income of CU581k in the period (7.46% × CU7,794k). The result of recognising the impairment loss and interest income is that the amortised cost at the reporting date is CU6,514k (CU8m less CU1m discounted by 7.46 per cent for one year).

31 December 20X4

At the end of the fourth reporting period following acquisition of the bond, the bond matures and Entity A receives CU7m as it had expected at the last reporting date. In the period there is no change in lifetime expected credit losses except for the unwinding of discount from CU931k to CU1m recognised as part of interest income in the period of CU486k (7.46% × CU6,514k). This results in an amortised cost of CU7m immediately before settlement (the original carrying value of CU8m less the cumulative change in the loss allowance of CU1m).

Summary

CU ('000)	31 Dec 20X1	31 Dec 20X2	31 Dec 20X3	31 Dec 20X4
Opening amortised cost	6,000	6,447	7,794	6,514
Accrued interest on amortised cost at 7.46%	447	481	581	486
Impairment gain or (loss)	Nil[1]	866[2]	(1,861)[3]	Nil[4]
Closing amortised cost	6,447	7,794	6,514	7,000[5]
Loan loss allowance reconciliation:				
Opening loss allowance	Nil	Nil	866	(931)
Unwind of interest on opening balance (recognised as part of accrued interest)	Nil	Nil	64	(69)
Impairment gain or (loss)	Nil	866	(1,861)	Nil
Closing loss allowance	Nil	866	(931)	(1,000)[6]

1 This amount is nil because there was no change in the undiscounted lifetime loss allowance from initial recognition (i.e. the present value of the undiscounted change in the lifetime expected losses is nil).

2 This amount is calculated as the present value of the undiscounted change in the lifetime expected losses, i.e. undiscounted lifetime expected losses changed by CU1m, which when discounted by two years at 7.46% equates to CU866k.

3 This amount is calculated as the present value of the undiscounted change in the lifetime expected losses, i.e. undiscounted lifetime expected losses changed by CU2m, which when discounted by one year at 7.46% equates to CU1,861k.

4 This amount is nil because there was no change in the undiscounted lifetime loss allowance from the prior year (i.e. the present value of the undiscounted change in the lifetime expected losses is nil).

5 & 6 Balances shown immediately before settlement.

5.3 Measurement of expected credit losses

Expected credit losses are a probability-weighted estimate of credit losses (i.e. the present value of all cash shortfalls) over the expected life of the financial instrument. A cash shortfall is the difference between the cash flows that are due to an entity in accordance with the contract and the cash flows that the entity expects to receive. Because expected credit losses consider the amount and timing of payments, a credit loss arises even if the entity expects to be paid in full but later than when contractually due. [IFRS 9:B5.5.28]

For the purposes of measuring expected credit losses, the estimate of expected cash shortfalls reflects the cash flows expected from collateral and other credit enhancements that are part of the contractual terms and are not recognised separately by the entity. The estimate of expected cash shortfalls on a collateralised financial instrument reflects the amount and timing of cash flows that are expected from foreclosure on the collateral less the discounted costs of obtaining and selling the collateral, irrespective of whether foreclosure is probable (i.e. the estimate of expected cash flows considers the probability of a foreclosure and the cash flows that would result from it). Consequently, any cash flows that are expected from the realisation of the collateral beyond the contractual maturity of the contract are included in this analysis. Any collateral obtained as a result of foreclosure is not recognised as an asset that is separate from the collateralised financial instrument unless it meets the relevant recognition criteria for an asset in IFRS 9 or other IFRSs. [IFRS 9:B5.5.55]

Example 5.3

Highly collateralised financial asset

[IFRS 9:IE18 - IE23 – Example 3]

Company H owns real estate assets which are financed by a five-year loan from Bank Z with a loan-to-value (LTV) ratio of 50 per cent. The loan is secured by a first-ranking security over the real estate assets. At initial recognition of the loan, Bank Z does not consider the loan to be originated credit-impaired as defined in IFRS 9:Appendix A.

Subsequent to initial recognition, the revenues and operating profits of Company H have decreased because of an economic recession. Furthermore, expected increases in regulations have the potential to further negatively affect revenue and operating profit. These negative effects on Company H's operations could be significant and ongoing.

As a result of these recent events and expected adverse economic conditions, Company H's free cash flow is expected to be reduced to the point that the coverage of scheduled loan payments could become tight. Bank Z estimates that a further deterioration in cash flows may result in Company H missing a contractual payment on the loan and becoming past due.

Recent third party appraisals have indicated a decrease in the value of the real estate properties, resulting in a current LTV ratio of 70 per cent.

At the reporting date, the loan to Company H is not considered to have low credit risk in accordance with IFRS 9:5.5.10 (see **5.2.5.1**). Bank Z therefore needs to assess whether there has been a significant increase in credit risk since initial recognition in accordance with IFRS 9:5.5.3, irrespective of the value of the collateral it holds. It notes that the loan is subject to considerable credit risk at the reporting date because even a slight deterioration in cash flows could result in Company H missing a contractual payment on the loan. As a result, Bank Z determines that the credit risk (i.e. the risk of a default occurring) has increased significantly since initial recognition. Consequently, Bank Z recognises lifetime expected credit losses on the loan to Company H.

Although lifetime expected credit losses should be recognised, the measurement of the expected credit losses will reflect the recovery expected from the collateral (adjusting for the costs of obtaining and selling the collateral) on the property as required by IFRS 9:B5.5.55 and may result in the expected credit losses on the loan being very small.

5.3.1 Measurement of expected credit losses for financial assets

For financial assets, a credit loss is the present value of the difference between:

[IFRS 9:B5.5.29]

(a) the contractual cash flows that are due to an entity under the contract; and

(b) the cash flows that the entity expects to receive.

For a financial asset that is credit-impaired at the reporting date, but that is not a purchased or originated credit-impaired financial asset, the expected credit losses are measured as the difference between the asset's gross carrying amount and the present value of estimated future cash flows discounted at the financial asset's original effective interest rate. Any adjustment is recognised in profit or loss as an impairment gain or loss. [IFRS 9:B5.5.33]

IFRS 9:B5.5.33 excludes purchased or originated credit-impaired financial assets as for these assets the general approach to impairment is not applied (see **5.2.5.3**). For purchased or originated credit-impaired financial assets impairment measurement is always based on lifetime expected losses and the estimate of lifetime expected losses at initial recognition is reflected in a credit-adjusted effective interest rate. As the estimate of cash flows that forms the effective interest rate at initial recognition includes lifetime expected credit losses then impairment gains or impairment losses only arise when there are changes in the estimate of expected credit losses different to that estimated when the asset was initially recognised.

5.3.2 Measurement of expected credit losses for loan commitments

For written undrawn loan commitments, a credit loss is the present value of the difference between:

[IFRS 9:B5.5.30]

(a) the contractual cash flows that are due to the entity if the holder of the loan commitment draws down the loan; and

(b) the cash flows that the entity expects to receive if the loan is drawn down.

An entity's estimate of expected credit losses on loan commitments should be consistent with its expectations of drawdowns on that loan commitment, i.e. it should consider the expected portion of the loan commitment that will be drawn down within 12 months of the reporting date when estimating 12-month expected credit losses, and the expected portion of the loan commitment that will be drawn down over the expected life of the loan commitment when estimating lifetime expected credit losses. [IFRS 9:B5.5.31]

For loan commitments, the period over which expected credit losses should be measured is discussed in **5.3.5** and the discount rate used to present value the expected credit losses is discussed in **5.3.5.2**.

5.3.3 Measurement of expected credit losses for financial guarantee contracts

For written financial guarantee contracts payments only arise in the event of a default by the debtor in accordance with the terms of the debt instrument that is guaranteed. Accordingly, cash shortfalls are the expected payments to reimburse the holder of the debt instrument for a credit loss that it incurs less any amounts that the entity expects to receive from the holder, the debtor or any other party. If the asset is fully guaranteed, the estimation of cash shortfalls for a financial guarantee contract would be consistent with the estimations of cash shortfalls for the asset subject to the guarantee. [IFRS 9:B5.5.32]

5.3.4 Lease receivables

When measuring a loss allowance for a lease receivable, the cash flows used for determining the expected credit losses should be consistent with the cash flows used in measuring the lease receivable in accordance with IAS 17 *Leases*. [IFRS 9:B5.5.34]

5.3.5 The principles for measuring expected credit losses

An entity should measure expected credit losses of a financial instrument in a way that reflects: [IFRS 9:5.5.17]

(a) an unbiased and probability-weighted amount that is determined by evaluating a range of possible outcomes (see **5.3.5.1**);

(b) the time value of money (see **5.3.5.2**); and

(c) reasonable and supportable information that is available without undue cost or effort at the reporting date about past events, current conditions and forecasts of future economic conditions (see **5.3.5.3**).

When measuring expected credit losses, an entity need not necessarily identify every possible scenario. However, it should consider the risk or probability that a credit loss occurs by reflecting the possibility that a credit loss occurs and the possibility that no credit loss occurs, even if the possibility of a credit loss occurring is very low. [IFRS 9:5.5.18]

IFRS 9:5.5.18 makes clear that an entity cannot simply assume that the most likely outcome is payment of the contract in full and therefore expected credit losses are nil. Such an approach does not include within the probability assessment the possibility that a credit loss could occur. The aim of a probability weighted approach in IFRS 9 is to ensure that credit losses, regardless of how likely, form part of the measurement of the loss allowance.

IFRS 9:5.5.17(c) requires that the measurement of expected credit losses should reflect reasonable and supportable information available without undue cost or effort *at the reporting date* about past events, current conditions and forecasts of future economic conditions.

Therefore, reasonable and supportable information of events and current conditions and forecasts of future economic conditions that become available *before* the end of the reporting period are required to be reflected in the assessment of significant increases in credit risk and the measurement of expected credit losses at the reporting date.

In certain cases an entity may measure loan losses in advance of its reporting date. In such cases the information it uses prior to the reporting date should be updated to reflect conditions at the reporting date.

Entities will also have to carefully consider information that becomes available *after* the reporting date. Events and new information after the reporting period end should be assessed under IAS 10 *Events After the Reporting Period*, which distinguishes between:

- adjusting events – being those that provide evidence of conditions that existed at the end of the reporting period; and
- non-adjusting events – being those that are indicative of conditions that arose after the reporting period.

Determining expected credit losses at the reporting period end is inherently dependent upon reasonable and supportable estimates and forecasts at the reporting date. Forward looking effects will be determined at the reporting date through assumptions based upon expert judgement and models that will produce estimates.

Furthermore, paragraph 32 of IAS 8 *Accounting Policies, Changes in Accounting Estimates and Errors* acknowledges that, as a result of uncertainties inherent in business activities, many items in financial statements cannot be measured with precision but can only be estimated. Loan loss allowances in respect of financial instruments represent one of these items. The nature of estimates is such that actual outcomes are often different. It is therefore crucial that the estimates at the reporting date are based on reasonable and supportable forward looking information available at the reporting date determined through a robust and well-governed process. IAS 8:34 confirms that revisions of estimates due to changes in circumstances or as a result of new information do not relate to prior periods.

The timing of forecasts of future economic conditions and whether information that becomes available after the reporting date is an adjusting event was one of the issues discussed by the IFRS Transition Resource Group for Impairment of Financial Instruments (established by the IASB to discuss transition issues surrounding the IFRS 9 impairment model) at its meeting in April 2015.

Example 5.3.5A

Forecasts of future economic conditions – new information *before* the reporting date

Bank A has a 31 December year end and takes into account forward looking forecasts of future economic conditions when determining significant increases in credit risk and when measuring expected credit losses. This process uses inputs and assumptions that are developed in November each year in order to meet its financial reporting deadlines.

Bank A has a US dollar loan receivable from Entity B. Entity B's local currency is pegged to the US Dollar. Entity B's revenue is predominantly earned in its local currency.

The central bank in Entity B's jurisdiction has consistently issued policy statements that it will continue to support the US Dollar peg, and it confirms this policy publicly in November 20X0. In December 20X0, despite its November confirmation to the contrary, the central bank in Entity B's jurisdiction ceases to support the currency peg and the value of the currency immediately falls relative to the US Dollar.

In its assessment of significant increase in credit risk and the measurement of expected credit losses at 31 December 20X0 Bank A should incorporate the actions of the central bank in December 20X0.

This is because:

- IFRS 9:5.5.9 requires that the assessment as to whether there has been a significant increase in credit risk to be performed at each reporting date and consider reasonable and supportable information that is available without undue cost or effort; and
- IFRS 9:5.5.17(c) requires that the measurement of expected credit losses to reflect reasonable and supportable information available without undue cost or effort *at the reporting date* about past events, current conditions and forecasts of future economic conditions.

The maximum period to consider when measuring expected credit losses is the maximum contractual period (including extension options) over which the entity is exposed to credit risk and not a longer period, even if that longer period is consistent with business practice. [IFRS 9:5.5.19] For loan commitments and financial guarantee contracts, this is the maximum contractual period over which an entity has a present contractual obligation to extend credit. [IFRS 9:B5.5.38]

Where an extension option is in the control of the borrower the lender must reflect the credit risk potentially arising on the contractual cash flows if the loan would be extended, even if the probability of the loan being extended is low. If the lender has the ability to decline the borrower's right to extend then the lender is not exposed to credit risk for the extended period of the loan and so the maximum contractual period which the lender is exposed to is the period up to the date that borrower can elect to extend.

However, there is an exception for financial instruments that include both a loan and an undrawn commitment component and the entity's contractual ability to demand repayment and cancel the undrawn commitment does not limit the entity's exposure to credit losses to the contractual notice period. For such financial instruments only, the expected credit losses are measured over the period that the entity is exposed to credit risk and expected credit losses would not be mitigated by credit risk management actions, even if that period extends beyond the maximum contractual period. [IFRS 9:5.5.20]

The exception was included in the Standard as an acknowledgement that whilst it is contractually possible that a lender could demand immediate repayment and cancel the loan commitment and therefore limit its exposure to credit losses, practically, in cases of credit deterioration of the borrower which the lender may be unaware of, it is more likely the borrower will choose to draw down their undrawn commitment and in doing so expose the lender to greater credit risk. In cases as described in IFRS 9:5.5.20 the lender will need to estimate the usage behaviour of the borrower in drawing down the commitment in assessing the exposure to credit risk. This is discussed in greater detail in **5.3.5.4**.

Example 5.3.5B

Maximum period to consider when measuring credit losses

A lender has a portfolio of mortgage loans under which a fixed amount is advanced at the inception of each loan. Each loan has a stated maturity of six months but, immediately before maturity, each loan is automatically extended for a further six months subject to the lender not objecting to the extension. Individual credit reviews are not conducted at the time of such extensions and the lender would only object if it was aware of information about an adverse credit event in respect of the specific borrower.

Because the borrower under the mortgage loan does not have the unilateral right to extend the term of the loan and the lender has the contractual right to object to the extension the maximum period to which the lender is contractually exposed to credit risk is six months and this is the maximum period that should be considered when measuring expected credit losses. If, however, the borrower held an extension option that could force the lender to continue extending credit, this would have the effect of lengthening the maximum contractual period of credit exposure.

Although IFRS 9:5.5.20 provides an exception to IFRS 9:5.5.19 when a financial instrument includes both a loan and an undrawn commitment component, this exception does not apply to the mortgage loans under consideration because there is not the potential for both a loan and an undrawn commitment component.

Furthermore, IFRS 9:BC5.254 to BC5.261 summarise the IASB's deliberations leading to the requirement in IFRS 9:5.5.20 and clarify that the exception is designed for revolving credit facilities such as credit cards and overdraft facilities (i.e. where the borrower has flexibility in how frequently they make drawdowns on the facility and consequently it is possible that the facility could be fully drawn down or fully undrawn at the reporting date). The example above is not a revolving credit facility.

Notwithstanding the above conclusions, consistent with the general application of IFRSs (as discussed in paragraph BC3.26 in the Conceptual Framework for Financial Reporting), only substantive contractual terms of the loan are considered when determining the maximum contractual period over which the entity is exposed to credit risk. For example, a situation in which a lender is legally prevented from exercising a contractual right may result in that contractual right not being substantive.

This issue was one of the issues discussed by the IFRS Transition Resource Group for Impairment of Financial Instruments (established by the IASB to discuss transition issues surrounding the IFRS 9 impairment model) at its meeting in April 2015.

5.3.5.1 Probability-weighted outcome

The purpose of estimating expected credit losses is neither to estimate a worst-case scenario nor to estimate the best-case scenario. Instead, an estimate of expected credit losses always reflects the possibility that a credit loss occurs and the possibility that no credit loss occurs even if the most likely outcome is no credit loss. [IFRS 9:B5.5.41]

As described in **5.3.5** IFRS 9 requires the estimate of expected credit losses to reflect an unbiased and probability-weighted amount that is determined by evaluating a range of possible outcomes. In practice, this may not need to be a complex analysis. In some cases, relatively simple modelling may be sufficient, without the need for a large number of detailed simulations of scenarios. For example, the average credit losses of a large group of financial instruments with shared risk characteristics may be a reasonable estimate of the probability-weighted amount. In other situations, the identification of scenarios that specify the amount and timing of the cash flows for particular outcomes and the estimated probability of those outcomes will probably be needed. In those situations, the expected credit losses should reflect at least two outcomes, being the probability that a credit loss occurs and that it does not occur. [IFRS 9:B5.5.42]

Example 5.3.5.1

12-month expected credit loss measurement using an explicit 'probability of default' approach

[IFRS 9:IE49 - IE52 – Example 8]

Scenario 1

Entity A originates a single 10 year amortising loan for CU1 million. Taking into consideration the expectations for instruments with similar credit risk (using reasonable and supportable information that is available without undue cost or effort), the credit risk of the borrower, and the economic outlook for the next 12 months, Entity A estimates that the loan at initial recognition has a probability of default (PD) of 0.5 per cent over the next 12 months. Entity A also determines that changes in the 12-month PD are a reasonable approximation of the changes in the lifetime PD for determining whether there has been a significant increase in credit risk since initial recognition.

At the reporting date (which is before payment on the loan is due – for simplicity it is assumed that there is no amortisation of the loan), there has been no change in the 12-month PD and Entity A determines that there was no significant increase in credit risk since initial recognition. Entity A determines that 25 per cent of the gross carrying amount will be lost if the loan defaults (i.e. the LGD is 25 per cent). This example does not illustrate the time value of money as the LGD represents a percentage of the present value of the gross carrying amount. Entity A measures the loss allowance at an amount equal to 12-month expected credit losses using the 12-month PD of 0.5 per cent. Implicit in that calculation is the 99.5 per cent probability that there is no default. At the reporting date the loss allowance for the 12-month expected credit losses is CU1,250 (0.5% × 25% × CU1,000,000).

Scenario 2

Entity B acquires a portfolio of 1,000 five year bullet loans for CU1,000 each (i.e. CU1million in total) with an average 12-month PD of 0.5 per cent for the portfolio. Entity B determines that because the loans only have significant payment obligations beyond the next 12 months, it would not be appropriate to consider changes in the 12-month PD when determining whether there have been significant increases in credit risk since initial recognition. At the reporting date Entity B therefore uses changes in the lifetime PD to determine whether the credit risk of the portfolio has increase significantly since initial recognition.

Entity B determines that there has not been a significant increase in credit risk since initial recognition and estimates that the portfolio has an average LGD of 25 per cent. Entity B determines that it is appropriate to measure the loss allowance on a collective basis in accordance with IFRS 9. The 12-month PD remains at 0.5 per cent at the reporting date. Entity B therefore measures the loss allowance on a collective basis at an amount equal to 12-month expected credit losses based on the average 0.5 per cent 12-month PD. Implicit in the calculation is the 99.5 per cent probability that there is no default. At the reporting date the loss allowance for the 12-month expected credit losses is CU1,250 (0.5% × 25% × CU1,000,000).

5.3.5.2 Time value of money

Expected credit losses are discounted to the reporting date (not to the expected default or some other date) using the effective interest rate determined at initial recognition or an approximation thereof. If a financial instrument has a variable interest rate, expected credit losses are discounted using the current effective interest rate determined in accordance with IFRS 9:B5.4.5 (see **section 4.1**). [IFRS 9:B5.5.44]

For purchased or originated credit-impaired financial assets, expected credit losses are discounted using the credit-adjusted effective interest rate determined at initial recognition (see **section 4.1**). [IFRS 9:B5.5.45]

Expected credit losses on lease receivables are discounted using the same discount rate used in the measurement of the lease receivable in accordance with IAS 17 *Leases*. [IFRS 9:B5.5.46]

The expected credit losses on a loan commitment are discounted using the effective interest rate, or an approximation thereof, that will be applied when recognising the financial asset resulting from the loan commitment. This is because for the purpose of applying the impairment requirements, a financial asset that is recognised following a draw down on a loan commitment should be treated as a continuation of that commitment rather than as a new financial instrument. The expected credit losses on the financial asset are therefore measured considering the initial credit risk of the loan commitment from the date that the entity became a party to the irrevocable commitment. [IFRS 9:B5.5.47]

There is no requirement to disclose the effective interest rate in profit or loss for debt instruments that are measured at FVTPL, e.g. loan commitments that will lead to origination of debt instruments that will be measured at FVTPL. However, if the loan commitment is in the scope of the impairment requirements, because it is not measured at FVTPL, the effective interest rate for the loan that may be drawn down under the loan commitment will still need to be determined for the purposes of measuring the impairment allowance on the loan commitment even though when the loan is drawn down an effective interest rate is not required to be disclosed. The effective interest rate on the future draw down is needed to discount the expected credit losses on the loan commitment.

When a lender has a past practice of selling the assets resulting from its loan commitment shortly after origination, determining the effective interest rate on the future draw down is not necessary as the loan commitment will be outside the scope of the impairment requirements as IFRS 9:2.3(a) will require the loan commitment to be measured at FVTPL (see **3.5** in **chapter B1**)

Expected credit losses on financial guarantee contracts or on loan commitments for which the effective interest rate cannot be determined should be discounted by applying a discount rate that reflects the current market assessment of the time value of money and the risks that are specific to the cash flows but only if, and to the extent that, the risks are taken into account by adjusting the discount rate instead of adjusting the cash shortfalls being discounted. [IFRS 9:B5.5.48]

5.3.5.3 Reasonable and supportable information

When measuring expected credit losses an entity must use reasonable and supportable information that is available without undue cost or effort at the reporting date about past events, current conditions and forecasts of future economic conditions. [IFRS 9:5.5.17(c)] Although expected credit losses reflect an entity's own expectations of credit losses, they should also consider observable market information about the credit risk of the particular financial instrument or similar financial instruments. [IFRS 9:B5.5.54] Information that is available for financial reporting purposes is considered to be available without undue cost or effort. [IFRS 9:B5.5.49]

It is not a requirement to incorporate forecasts of future conditions over the entire expected life of a financial instrument. The degree of judgement that is required to estimate expected credit losses depends on the availability of detailed information. As the forecast horizon increases, the availability of detailed information decreases and the degree of judgement required to estimate expected credit losses increases. The estimate of expected credit losses does not require a detailed estimate for periods that are far in the future – for such periods, an entity may extrapolate projections from available, detailed information. [IFRS 9:B5.5.50]

An exhaustive search for information need not be undertaken, however, it should consider all reasonable and supportable information that is available without undue cost or effort and that is relevant to the estimate of expected credit losses, including the effect of expected prepayments. The information should include factors that are specific to the borrower, general economic conditions and an assessment of both the current as well as the forecast direction of conditions at the reporting date. Both internal (entity-specific) and external data sources may be used. Possible data sources include internal historical credit loss experience, internal ratings, credit loss experience of other entities and external ratings, reports and statistics. Entities that have no, or insufficient, sources of entity-specific data may use peer group experience for the comparable financial instrument (or groups of financial instruments). [IFRS 9:B5.5.51]

Historical information is an important anchor or base from which to measure expected credit losses. However, it should be adjusted to reflect the effects of the current conditions and forecasts of future conditions that did not affect the period on which the historical data is based, and to remove the effects of the conditions in the historical period that are not relevant to the future contractual cash flows. In some cases, the best reasonable and supportable information could be the unadjusted historical information, depending on the nature of the historical information and when it was calculated, compared to circumstances at the reporting date and the characteristics of the financial instrument being considered. Estimates of changes in expected credit losses should reflect, and be directionally consistent with, changes in related observable data from period to period (such as changes in unemployment rates, property prices, commodity prices, payment status or other factors that are indicative of credit losses on the financial instrument or in the group of financial instruments and in the magnitude of those changes). The methodology and assumptions used for estimating expected credit losses should be regularly reviewed to reduce any differences between estimates and actual credit loss experience. [IFRS 9:B5.5.52]

When using historical credit loss experience in estimating expected credit losses, it is important that information about historical credit loss rates is applied to groups that are defined in a manner that is consistent with the groups for which the historical credit loss rates were observed. Consequently, the method used should enable each group of financial assets to be associated with information about past credit loss experience in groups of financial assets with similar risk characteristics and with relevant observable data that reflects current conditions. [IFRS 9:B5.5.53]

Example 5.3.5.3

12-month expected credit loss measurement based on loss rate approach

[IFRS 9:IE53 - IE57 – Example 9]

Bank A originates 2,000 bullet loans with a total gross carrying amount of CU500,000. Bank A segments its portfolio into borrower groups (Groups X and Y) on the basis of shared credit risk characteristics at initial recognition. Group X comprises 1,000 loans with a gross carrying amount per client of CU200, for a total gross carrying amount of CU200,000. Group Y comprises 1,000 loans with a gross carrying amount per client of CU300, for a total gross carrying amount of CU300,000. There are no transaction costs and the loan contracts include no options (for example, prepayment or call options), premiums or discounts, points paid, or other fees.

Bank A measures expected credit losses on the basis of a loss rate approach for Groups X and Y. In order to develop its loss rates, Bank A considers samples of its own historical default and loss experience for those types of loans. In addition, Bank A considers forward-looking information, and updates its historical information for current economic conditions as well as reasonable and supportable forecasts of future economic conditions. Historically, for a population of 1,000 loans in each group, Group X's loss rates are 0.3 per cent, based on four defaults, and historical loss rates for Group Y are 0.15 per cent, based on two defaults.

	Number of clients in sample	**Estimated per client gross carrying amount at default**	**Total estimated gross carrying amount at default**	**Historic per annum average defaults**	**Estimated total gross carrying amount at default**	**Present value of observed loss**	**Loss rate**
Group	A	B	C = A × B	D	E = B × D	F	G = F ÷ C
X	1,000	CU200	CU200,000	4	CU800	CU600	0.3%
Y	1,000	CU300	CU300,000	2	CU600	CU450	0.15%

In accordance with IFRS 9:5.5.17(b), expected credit losses should be discounted using the effective interest rate. However, for the purposes of this example, the present value of the observed loss is assumed.

At the reporting date, Bank A expects an increase in defaults over the next 12 months compared to the historical rate. As a result, Bank A estimates five defaults in the next 12 months for loans in Group X and three for loans in Group Y. It estimates that the present value of the observed credit loss per client will remain consistent with the historical loss per client.

On the basis of the expected life of the loans, Bank A determines that the expected increase in defaults does not represent a significant increase in credit risk since initial recognition for the portfolios. On the basis of its forecasts, Bank A measures the loss allowance at an amount equal to 12-month expected credit losses on the 1,000 loans in each group amounting to CU750 and CU675 respectively. This equates to a loss rate in the first year of 0.375 per cent for Group X and 0.225 per cent for Group Y.

	Number of clients in sample	**Estimated per client gross carrying amount at default**	**Total estimated gross carrying amount at default**	**Expected defaults**	**Estimated total gross carrying amount at default**	**Present value of observed loss**	**Loss rate**
Group	A	B	C = A × B	D	E = B × D	F	G = F ÷ C
X	1,000	CU200	CU200,000	5	CU1,000	CU750	0.375%
Y	1,000	CU300	CU300,000	3	CU900	CU675	0.225%

In accordance with IFRS 9:5.5.17(b), expected credit losses should be discounted using the effective interest rate. However, for the purposes of this example, the present value of the observed loss is assumed.

Bank A uses the loss rates of 0.375 per cent and 0.225 per cent respectively to estimate 12-month expected credit losses on new loans in Group X and Group Y originated during the year and for which credit risk has not increased significantly since initial recognition.

5.3.5.4 Exception from using the contractual period to estimate expected credit losses

The maximum period over which expected credit losses should be measured is the maximum contractual period over which the entity is exposed to credit risk. However, some financial instruments include both a loan and an undrawn commitment component and the entity's contractual ability to demand repayment and cancel the undrawn commitment does not limit the entity's exposure to credit losses to the contractual notice period. [IFRS 9:B5.5.39] For those financial instruments only, expected credit losses are measured over the period that the entity is exposed to credit risk and expected credit losses would not be mitigated by credit risk management actions, even if that period extends beyond the maximum contractual period. [IFRS 9:5.5.20]

For example, revolving credit facilities, such as credit cards and overdraft facilities, can be contractually withdrawn by the lender with as little as one day's notice. However, in practice lenders continue to extend credit for a longer period and may only withdraw the facility after the credit risk of the borrower increases, which could be too late to prevent some or all of the expected credit losses. These financial instruments generally have the following characteristics as a result of the nature of the financial instrument, the way in which the financial instruments are managed, and the nature of the available information about significant increases in credit risk:

[IFRS 9:B5.5.39]

- the financial instruments do not have a fixed term or repayment structure and usually have a short contractual cancellation period (for example, one day);
- the contractual ability to cancel the contract is not enforced in the normal day-to-day management of the financial instrument and the contract may only be cancelled when the entity becomes aware of an increase in credit risk at the facility level; and
- the financial instruments are managed on a collective basis.

IFRS 9 is clear that a financial instrument must include both a loan and an undrawn commitment component to be able to use a period different to the contractual period for the purposes of measuring expected credit losses. Examples of such instruments would be revolving credit facilities such as credit cards and overdraft facilities. This should not be confused with situations where an entity has past practice (but not a contractual obligation) to extend credit after the contractual term has ended. The practice of extending credit beyond the contractual terms is not the same as instruments that contractually include both loan and undrawn commitment components. For example, when a loan commitment expires at a specific date and an entity decides to renew or extend its commitment to extend credit, it will be a new instrument for the purposes of applying the impairment guidance (see IFRS 9:BC5.260).

When determining the period over which the entity is expected to be exposed to credit risk, but for which expected credit losses would not be mitigated by the entity's normal credit risk management actions, an entity should consider factors such as historical information and experience about:

[IFRS 9:B5.5.40]

- the period over which the entity was exposed to credit risk on similar financial instruments;
- the length of time for related defaults to occur on similar financial instruments following a significant increase in credit risk; and
- the credit risk management actions that an entity expects to take once the credit risk on the financial instrument has increased, such as the reduction or removal of undrawn limits.

Example 5.3.5.4

Revolving credit facilities

[IFRS 9:IE58 - IE65 – Example 10]

Bank A provides co-branded credit cards to customers in conjunction with a local department store. The credit cards have a one-day notice period after which Bank A has the contractual right to cancel the credit card (both the drawn and undrawn components). However, Bank A does not enforce its contractual right to cancel the credit cards in the normal day-to-day management of the instruments and only cancels facilities when it becomes aware of an increase in credit risk and starts to monitor customers on an individual basis. Bank A therefore does not consider the contractual right to cancel the credit cards to limit its exposure to credit losses to the contractual notice period.

For credit risk management purposes Bank A considers that there is only one set of contractual cash flows from customers to assess and does not distinguish between the drawn and undrawn balances at the reporting date. The portfolio is therefore managed and expected credit losses are measured on a facility level.

At the reporting date the outstanding balance on the credit card portfolio is CU60,000 and the available undrawn facility is CU40,000. Bank A determines the expected life of the portfolio by estimating the period over which it expects to be exposed to credit risk on the facilities at the reporting date, taking into account:

- the period over which it was exposed to credit risk on a similar portfolio of credit cards;
- the length of time for related defaults to occur on similar financial instruments; and
- past events that led to credit risk management actions because of an increase in credit risk on similar financial instruments, such as the reduction or removal of undrawn credit limits.

On the basis of the information listed in IFRS 9:IE60 Bank A determines that the expected life of the credit card portfolio is 30 months.

At the reporting date Bank A assesses the change in the credit risk on the portfolio since initial recognition and determines in accordance with IFRS 9:5.5.3 (see **5.2.2**) that the credit risk on a portion of the credit card facilities representing 25 per cent of the portfolio, has increased significantly since initial recognition. The outstanding balance on these credit facilities for which lifetime expected credit losses should be recognised is CU20,000 and the available undrawn facility is CU10,000.

When measuring the expected credit losses in accordance with IFRS 9:5.5.20, Bank A considers its expectations about future draw-downs over the expected life of the portfolio (i.e. 30 months) in accordance with IFRS 9:B5.5.31 and estimates what it expects the outstanding balance (i.e. exposure at default) on the portfolio would be if customers were to default. By using its credit risk models Bank A determines that the exposure at default on the credit card facilities for which lifetime expected credit losses should be recognised, is CU25,000 (i.e.

the drawn balance of CU20,000 plus further drawdowns of CU5,000 from the available undrawn commitment). The exposure at default of the credit card facilities for which 12-month expected credit losses are recognised, is CU45,000 (i.e. the outstanding balance of CU40,000 and an additional draw down of CU5,000 from the undrawn commitment over the next 12 months).

The exposure at default and expected life determined by Bank A are used to measure the lifetime expected credit losses and 12-month expected credit losses on its credit card portfolio.

Bank A measures expected credit losses on a facility level and therefore cannot separately identify the expected credit losses on the undrawn commitment component from those on the loan component. It recognises expected credit losses for the undrawn commitment together with the loss allowance for the loan component in the statement of financial position. To the extent that the combined expected credit losses exceed the gross carrying amount of the financial asset, the expected credit losses should be presented as a provision (in accordance with IFRS 7 *Financial Instruments: Disclosure*).

Entities typically enter into agreements that allow a borrower to draw down funds from a facility as needed. In other words, there are two components to such a financial instrument; there is a loan (i.e. the amount once drawn down) and the loan commitment (the undrawn amount). Because the period over which an entity should measure the expected credit losses is the period over which the entity has a present contractual obligation to extend credit, the assessment of whether there has been a significant increase in credit risk also applies over the same period. For example, if a borrower has not drawn down any funds from a facility but an entity determines that there has been a significant increase in credit risk from the date that the entity became a party to the irrevocable commitment, it should measure the loss allowance based on lifetime expected credit losses. If the borrower subsequently draws down funds from the facility, this loan is not considered a 'new' instrument for the purposes of applying the impairment guidance in IFRS 9 (i.e. it is not measured at 12-month expected credit losses). That is because IFRS 9:B5.5.47 specifies that for the purposes of applying the impairments requirements, a financial asset that is recognised following draw down on a loan commitment shall be treated as a continuation of that commitment instead of as a new financial instrument. Consequently, when the new loan is drawn down and recognised, it will still form part of the same loss allowance measurement at lifetime expected credit losses that was applicable to the undrawn loan commitment that preceded it. As stated in IFRS 9:BC5.259 the expected credit losses on the loan amount are not estimated separately from the loan commitment, they are estimated on a facility level.

5.3.5.5 *Practical expedients*

Practical expedients may be used when measuring expected credit losses if they are consistent with the principles of measuring expected credit losses in IFRS 9:5.5.17 (see **section 5.3.5**). For example, calculating expected credit losses on trade receivables using a provision matrix. Such a matrix might be supported by historical credit loss experience of trade receivables, adjusted as appropriate to reflect current conditions and estimates of future economic conditions), for example, fixed provision rates depending on the number of days that a trade receivable is past due (say 1 per cent if not past due, 2 per cent if less than 30 days past due, 3 per cent if more than 30 days but less than 90 days past due, 20 per cent if 90–180 days past due etc). Depending on the diversity of its customer base, the entity would use appropriate groupings if its historical credit loss experience shows significantly different loss patterns for different customer segments. Examples of criteria that might be used to group assets include geographical region, product type, customer rating, collateral or trade credit insurance and type of customer (such as wholesale or retail). [IFRS 9:B5.5.35]

Example 5.3.5.5

Provision Matrix

[IFRS 9:IE74 - IE77 – Example 12]

Company M, a manufacturer, has a portfolio of trade receivables of CU30 million in 20X1 and operates only in one geographical region. The customer base consists of a large number of small clients and the trade receivables are categorised by common risk characteristics that are representative of the customers' abilities to pay all amounts due in accordance with the contractual terms. The trade receivables do not have a significant financing component in accordance with IFRS 15 Revenue from Contracts with Customers. In accordance with IFRS 9:5.5.15 (see **5.2.5.2**) the loss allowance for such trade receivables is always measured at an amount equal to lifetime expected credit losses.

To determine the expected credit losses for the portfolio, Company M uses a provision matrix. The provision matrix is based on its historical observed default rates over the expected life of the trade receivables and is adjusted for forward-looking estimates. At every reporting date the historical observed default rates are updated and changes in the forward-looking estimates are analysed. In this case it is forecast that economic conditions will deteriorate over the next year.

On that basis, Company M estimates the following provision matrix:

	Current	1–30 days past due	31–60 days past due	61–90 days past due	More than 90 days past due
Default rate	0.3%	1.6%	3.6%	6.6%	10.6%

The trade receivables from the large number of small customers amount to CU30 million and are measured using the provision matrix.

	Gross carrying amount	Lifetime expected credit loss allowance (Gross carrying amount x lifetime expected credit loss rate)
Current	CU15,000,000	CU45,000
1-30 days past due	CU7,500,000	CU120,000
31-60 days past due	CU4,000,000	CU144,000
61-90 days past due	CU2,500,000	CU165,000
More than 90 days past due	CU1,000,000	CU106,000
	CU30,000,000	**CU580,000**

5.3.6 *Interaction of impairment with FVTOCI measurement, foreign currency translation and fair value hedge accounting*

The measurement of impairment losses is the same whether the financial asset is measured at amortised cost or is a debt instrument measured at FVTOCI. However, when an asset is measured at amortised cost in the statement of financial position the loss allowance shall reduce the gross carrying value to make the amortised cost carrying value; when a debt instrument is measured at FVTOCI the loss allowance is not deducted from the carrying value of the asset in the statement of financial position as the asset must be recognised at fair value – consequently, the other side of the entry recognised in profit or loss is to other comprehensive income.

The retranslation of monetary items from a foreign currency to the functional currency, such as debt instruments held, whether measured at amortised cost or FVTOCI, is based on a carrying value that assumes it is measured at amortised cost. For financial assets measured at amortised cost this is intuitive. However, for debt instruments measured at FVTOCI the amortised cost amount is calculated which is then translated from the foreign currency to the functional currency of the entity in order to determine the foreign currency gain or loss to recognise in profit or loss. Foreign currency gains or losses on debt instruments measured at FVTOCI other than the amount recognised in profit or loss are recognised in other comprehensive income along with other fair value gains and losses.

IFRS 9 includes an example that illustrates the interaction of the impairment requirements for a foreign currency denominated debt instrument that is measured at FVTOCI and is also subject to a fair value hedge of interest rate risk. This is reproduced below. In the example, because the financial asset is measured at fair value there are no fair value adjustments to the hedged item as a result of applying fair value hedge accounting, instead the fair value gains or losses associated with changes in interest rates that are hedged are recognised in profit or loss rather than other comprehensive income.

Example 5.3.6

[IFRS 9:IE82 - IE102 – Example 14]

This example illustrates the accounting relating to a debt instrument denominated in a foreign currency, measured at fair value through other comprehensive income and designated in a fair value hedge accounting relationship. The example illustrates the interaction with accounting for impairment.

An entity purchases a debt instrument (a bond) denominated in a foreign currency (FC) for its fair value of FC100,000 on 1 January 20X0 and classifies the bond as measured at fair value through other comprehensive income. The bond has five years remaining to maturity and a fixed coupon of 5 per cent over its contractual life on the principal amount of FC100,000. On initial recognition the bond has a 5 per cent effective interest rate. The entity's functional currency is its local currency (LC). The exchange rate is FC1 to LC1 on 1 January 20X0. At initial recognition the entity determines that the bond is not purchased or originated credit-impaired. In addition, as at 1 January 20X0 the 12-month expected credit losses are determined to be FC1,200. Its amortised cost in FC as at 1 January 20X0 is equal to its gross carrying amount of FC100,000 less the 12-month expected credit losses (FC100,000 – FC1,200).

The entity has the following risk exposures:

- fair value interest rate risk in FC: the exposure that arises as a result of purchasing a fixed interest rate instrument; and
- foreign exchange risk: the exposure to changes in foreign exchange rates measured in LC.

The entity hedges its risk exposures using the following risk management strategy:

- for fixed interest rate risk (in FC) the entity decides to link its interest receipts in FC to current variable interest rates in FC. Consequently, the entity uses interest rate swaps denominated in FC under which it pays fixed interest and receives variable interest in FC; and
- for foreign exchange risk the entity decides not to hedge against any variability in LC arising from changes in foreign exchange rates.

The entity designates the following hedge relationship: a fair value hedge of the bond in FC as the hedged item with changes in benchmark interest rate risk in FC as the hedged risk. The entity enters into an on-market swap that pays fixed and receives variable interest on the same day and designates the swap as the hedging instrument. The tenor of the swap matches that of the hedged item (i.e. five years).

For simplicity, in this example it is assumed that no hedge ineffectiveness arises in the hedge accounting relationship. This is because of the assumptions made in order to better focus on illustrating the accounting mechanics in a situation that entails measurement at fair value through other comprehensive income of a foreign currency financial instrument that is designated in a fair value hedge relationship, and also to focus on the recognition of impairment gains or losses on such an instrument.

The entity makes the following journal entries to recognise the bond and the swap on 1 January 20X0:

	Debit LC	**Credit LC**
Financial asset - FVTOCI	100,000	
Cash		100,000
(To recognise the bond at its fair value)		
Impairment loss (profit or loss)	1,200	
Other comprehensive income		1,200
(To recognise the 12-month expected credit losses)*		
Swap	Nil	
Cash		Nil
(To recognise the swap at its fair value)		

* In case of items measured in the functional currency of an entity, the journal entry recognising expected credit losses will usually be made at the reporting date.

As of 31 December 20X0 (the reporting date), the fair value of the bond decreased from FC100,000 to FC96,370 because of an increase in market interest rates. The fair value of the swap increased to FC1,837. In addition, as at 31 December 20X0 the entity determines that there has been no change to the credit risk on the bond since initial recognition and continues to carry a loss allowance for 12-month expected credit losses at FC1,200 (for the purposes of simplicity, the example ignores the impact of discounting when computing expected credit losses). As at 31 December 20X0, the exchange rate is FC1 to LC1.4. This is reflected in the following table:

	1 January 20X0	**31 December 20X0**
Bond		
Fair value (FC)	100,000	96,370
Fair value (LC)	100,000	134,918
Amortised cost (FC)	98,800	98,800
Amortised cost (LC)	98,800	138,320
Interest rate swap		
Interest rate swap (FC)	–	1,837
Interest rate swap (LC)	–	2,572

	1 January 20X0	31 December 20X0
Impairment – loss allowance		
Loss allowance (FC)	1,200	1,200
Loss allowance (LC)	1,200	1,680
FX rate (FC:LC)	1:1	1:1.4

The bond is a monetary asset. Consequently, the entity recognises the changes arising from movements in foreign exchange rates in profit or loss in accordance with IAS 21:23(a) and IAS 28:28 and recognises other changes in accordance with IFRS 9. For the purposes of applying IAS 21:28 the asset is treated as an asset measured at amortised cost in the foreign currency.

As shown in the table, on 31 December 20X0 the fair value of the bond is LC134,918 (FC96,370 × 1.4) and its amortised cost is LC138,320 (FC(100,000 – 1,200) × 1.4).

The gain recognised in profit or loss that is due to the changes in foreign exchange rates is LC39,520 (LC138,320 – LC98,800), i.e. the change in the amortised cost of the bond during 20X0 in LC. The change in the fair value of the bond in LC, which amounts to LC34,918, is recognised as an adjustment to the carrying amount. The difference between the fair value of the bond and its amortised cost in LC is LC3,402 (LC134,918 – LC138,320). However, the change in the cumulative gain or loss recognised in other comprehensive income during 20X0 as a reduction is LC4,602 (LC 3,402 + LC 1,200).

A gain of LC2,572 (FC1,837 × 1.4) on the swap is recognised in profit or loss and, because it is assumed that there is no hedge ineffectiveness, an equivalent amount is recycled from other comprehensive income in the same period. For simplicity, journal entries for the recognition of interest revenue are not provided. It is assumed that interest accrued is received in the period.

The entity makes the following journal entries on 31 December 20X0:

	Debit LC	Credit LC
Financial asset—FVTOCI	34,918	
Other comprehensive income	4,602	
Profit or loss		39,520
(To recognise the foreign exchange gain on the bond, the adjustment to its carrying amount measured at fair value in LC and the movement in the accumulated impairment amount due to changes in foreign exchange rates)		
Swap	2,572	
Profit or loss		2,572
(To remeasure the swap at fair value)		

	Debit LC	Credit LC
Profit or loss	2,572	
Other comprehensive income		2,572
(To recognise in profit or loss the change in the fair value of the bond due to change in the hedged risk)		

In accordance with IFRS 7:16A, the loss allowance for financial assets measured at fair value through other comprehensive income is not presented separately as a reduction of the carrying amount of the financial asset. However, disclosure would be provided about the accumulated impairment amount recognised in other comprehensive income.

As at 31 December 20X1 (the reporting date), the fair value of the bond decreased to FC87,114 because of an increase in market interest rates and an increase in the credit risk of the bond. The fair value of the swap increased by FC255 to FC2,092. In addition, as at 31 December 20X1 the entity determines that there has been a significant increase in credit risk on the bond since initial recognition, so a loss allowance at an amount equal to lifetime expected credit losses is recognised (for simplicity, this example assumes that credit risk does not dominate the fair value hedge relationship). The estimate of lifetime credit losses as at 31 December 20X1 is FC9,700. As at 31 December 20X1, the exchange rate is FC1 to LC1.25. This is reflected in the following table:

	31 December 20X0	31 December 20X1
Bond		
Fair value (FC)	96,370	87,114
Fair value (LC)	134,918	108,893
Amortised cost (FC)	98,800	90,300
Amortised cost (LC)	138,320	112,875
Interest rate swap		
Interest rate swap (FC)	1,837	2,092
Interest rate swap (LC)	2,572	2,615
Impairment – loss allowance		
Loss allowance (FC)	1,200	9,700
Loss allowance (LC)	1,680	12,125
FX rate (FC:LC)	1:1.4	1:1.25

As shown in the table, as at 31 December 20X1 the fair value of the bond is LC108,893 (FC87,114 × 1.25) and its amortised cost is LC112,875 (FC(100,000 − 9,700) × 1.25).

The lifetime expected credit losses on the bond are measured as FC9,700 as of 31 December 20X1. Thus the impairment loss recognised in profit or loss in LC is LC10,625 (FC(9,700 – 1,200) x 1.25).

The loss recognised in profit or loss because of the changes in foreign exchange rates is LC14,820 (LC112,875 – LC138,320 + LC10,625), which is the change in the gross carrying amount of the bond on the basis of amortised cost during 20X1 in LC, adjusted for the impairment loss. The difference between the fair value of the bond and its amortised cost in the functional currency of the entity on 31 December 20X1 is LC3,982 (LC108,893 – LC112,875). However, the change in the cumulative gain or loss recognised in other comprehensive income during 20X1 as a reduction in other comprehensive income is LC11,205 (LC3,982 – LC3,402 + LC 10,625).

A gain of LC43 (LC2,615 – LC2,572) on the swap is recognised in profit or loss and, because it is assumed that there is no hedge ineffectiveness, an equivalent amount is recycled from other comprehensive income in the same period.

The entity makes the following journal entries on 31 December 20X1:

	Debit LC	Credit LC
Financial asset—FVTOCI		26,025
Other comprehensive income	11,205	
Profit or loss	14,820	
(To recognise the foreign exchange gain on the bond, the adjustment to its carrying amount measured at fair value in LC and the movement in the accumulated impairment amount due to changes in foreign exchange rates)		
Swap	43	
Profit or loss		43
(To remeasure the swap at fair value)		
Profit or loss	43	
Other comprehensive income		43
(To recognise in profit or loss the change in the fair value of the bond due to change in the hedged risk)		
Profit or loss (impairment loss)	10,625	
Other comprehensive income (accumulated impairment amount)		10,625
(To recognise lifetime expected credit losses)		

On 1 January 20X2, the entity decides to sell the bond for FC 87,114, which is its fair value at that date and also closes out the swap at fair value. The foreign exchange rate is the same as at 31 December 20X1. The journal entries to derecognise the bond and reclassify the gains and losses that have accumulated in other comprehensive income would be as follows:

	Debit LC	Credit LC
Cash	108,893	
Financial asset—FVTOCI		108,893
Loss on sale (profit or loss)	1,367	
Other comprehensive income		1,367
(To derecognise the bond)		
Swap		2,615
Cash	2,615	
(To close out the swap)		

The CU1,367 loss on sale consists of the changes in fair value of the swap, the accumulated impairment amount and the changes in foreign exchange rates recognised in other comprehensive income (LC2,572 + LC1,200 + LC43 + LC10,625 – LC4,602 – LC11,205 = -LC1,367, which is recycled as a loss in profit or loss).

5.3.7 Measurement of the loss allowance on derecognition of an asset at amortised cost of FVTOCI

Measurement of expected credit losses at the date of derecognition of an asset at amortised cost is necessary because:

- IFRS 9:3.2.12 requires the difference between the 'carrying amount' measured at the date of derecognition and the consideration received to be recognised in profit or loss; and
- paragraphs 82(aa) and 82(ba) of IAS 1 *Presentation of Financial Statements* require that separate line items be presented for gains and losses arising from derecognition and impairment losses and reversals.

For the purposes of IFRS 9:3.2.12, the 'carrying amount' refers to amortised cost, which should be adjusted for any loan loss allowance. Therefore, it is necessary to re-measure the loan loss allowance for an amortised cost asset at the date of derecognition to ensure that the gain or loss on derecognition is appropriately measured. IFRS 9 does not define 'carrying amount', but does define the gross carrying amount as "[t]he amortised cost of a financial asset, before adjusting for any loss allowance". [IFRS 9: Appendix A] Amortised cost is further defined as "[t]he amount at which the financial asset or financial liability is measured at initial recognition minus the principal repayments, plus or minus the cumulative amortisation using the effective interest method of any difference between that initial amount and the maturity amount and, for financial assets, adjusted for any loss allowance" (emphasis added). [IFRS 9: Appendix A]

Consequently, the 'carrying amount' referred to in IFRS 9:3.2.12 in respect of a financial asset measured at amortised cost will be the amortised cost of that financial asset measured at the date of derecognition. Because the definition of amortised cost includes an adjustment for any loss allowance, an entity would be required to re-measure the loss allowance at that date.

This would apply to both financial assets measured at amortised cost in accordance with IFRS 9:4.1.2 and also financial assets measured at FVTOCI under IFRS 9:4.1.2A. This is because, as noted by IFRS 9:5.7.11 and B5.7.1A, the FVTOCI measurement category recognises information in profit or loss as if the financial asset were measured at amortised cost.

This issue was one of the issues discussed by the IFRS Transition Resource Group for Impairment of Financial Instruments (established by the IASB to discuss transition issues surrounding the IFRS 9 impairment model) at its meeting in April 2015.

5.4 Disclosure

IFRS 7 *Financial Instruments: Disclosure* requires extensive disclosure of financial instruments subject to the impairment requirements. These are discussed in detail in **chapter B11**.

B7 Fair value measurement of financial instruments

Contents

1 Introduction

IAS 32, IFRS 7 and IFRS 9 all permit or require the use of fair value measurement for initial recognition, subsequent measurement or disclosure of financial instruments. Fair values are central to the measurement of financial instruments because IFRS 9 requires that all financial assets and financial liabilities are measured initially on the basis of 'fair value'. Fair value is also stipulated as the on-going measurement basis for all instruments that are held for trading, for derivatives and investments in equity investments, and for many debt instruments held as financial assets.

Detailed information about *when* a fair value measurement is required for financial instruments can be found in **chapters B2** and **B3**. This chapter primarily addresses *how* fair value is measured. This is relevant for fair value measurements of financial instruments recognised in the statement of financial position as well as fair value measurements for disclosure purposes. Guidance on fair value measurement of non-financial items is included in **chapter A6** of **Volume A** of this manual.

Prior to the issue of IFRS 13 *Fair Value Measurement* in May 2011, guidance on how to measure fair value for financial instruments was primarily included in the application guidance of IFRS 9 (previously in IAS 39); guidance on the measurement of fair value for non-financial items was available in a number of other IFRSs. Most guidance on fair value measurement has been replaced by the requirements of IFRS 13, which is a comprehensive Standard applicable to the measurement of fair value for assets, liabilities and an entity's own equity instruments except as noted in IFRS 13:6 (see **section 2**). IFRS 13 also includes disclosure requirements applicable to all assets and liabilities measured at fair value after initial recognition except those listed in IFRS 13:7 (see **section 2**). These disclosure requirements replace many of the fair value measurement disclosures previously required under IFRS 7 as well as introducing additional disclosures. The disclosure requirements for financial instruments are discussed in **chapter B11**.

IFRS 13 incorporates into IFRSs, for the first time, authoritative guidance and requirements regarding fair value measurement "when the volume or level of activity for an asset or a liability has significantly decreased" [IFRS 13:B37] Previously similar guidance was set out in the October 2008 report by the IASB's Expert Advisory Panel titled *Measuring and Disclosing the Fair Value of Financial Instruments in Markets that are no Longer Active*, which had only educational status.

1.1 Summary of IFRS 13 framework

The table and flow chart below set out a step-by-step approach to applying the basic measurement principles of IFRS 13 to financial instruments. The table also provides a high level summary of some of the key concepts underlying IFRS 13 and illustrates the framework for measuring fair value. The summary does not address all of the requirements of the Standard – users should refer to the more detailed discussions later in this chapter and to the text of the Standard for a fuller understanding.

Note that Steps 2 to 4 do not necessarily occur in the order set out in the table and flow chart (i.e. they are inter-related).

#	Step	Explanation
1.	Identify the 'asset' or 'liability' being measured (i.e. the unit of account) (see **section 3.2**)	IFRS 13 notes that the asset or liability measured at fair value may be (1) a stand-alone financial asset or liability, (2) a group of financial assets or a group of financial liabilities, or (3) a group of assets and liabilities. The level at which fair value is measured will depend on the 'unit of account' specified in other IFRSs (typically, the level at which the asset or liability is aggregated or disaggregated for recognition or disclosure purposes). Under IFRS 9, the unit of account is generally an individual financial instrument.
2a.	For financial assets and financial liabilities with offsetting market risks or counterparty credit risk, evaluate the criteria for the fair value exception and establish a policy (see **section 6**)	IFRS 13 permits an exception to the general fair value measurement requirements for financial assets and financial liabilities if an entity: • manages the group of assets and liabilities on the basis of its net exposure to market risks or counterparty credit risk; provides information on that basis to key management personnel; and • measures those assets and liabilities at fair value in the statement of financial position. In summary, the exception permits an entity to measure the fair value of the group of assets and liabilities (i.e. the portfolio) rather than the individual assets and liabilities within the portfolio. Details of the exception, including the detailed criteria for qualification, are set out in IFRS 13:48 - 56

#	Step	Explanation
		The application of this exception is an accounting policy choice in accordance with IAS 8 *Accounting Policies, Changes in Accounting Estimates and Errors* and must be applied consistently from period to period for a particular portfolio. This exception does not change the *unit of account* (which continues to be the individual instrument determined under IFRS 9), but changes the *unit of measurement* from the individual financial instrument to the group (portfolio) of financial instruments.
2b.	For financial liabilities and an entity's own equity instruments, assume the financial liabilities or equity instruments are transferred to market participants at the measurement date (see **section 5**)	IFRS 13 requires that the fair value of a financial liability or an entity's own equity instrument be based on an assumed transfer to a market participant even if the entity does not intend to transfer the liability or equity instrument to a third party or it is unable to do so. Under this assumption, the fair value of a financial liability should be measured on the basis that the liability would remain outstanding and the transferee would be required to fulfil the obligation; it should not be assumed that the financial liability would be settled or otherwise extinguished. Similarly, the fair value of an entity's own equity instrument should be measured on the basis that the equity instrument would remain outstanding and the transferee would take on the rights and responsibilities associated with the instrument; it should not be assumed that the instrument would be cancelled or otherwise extinguished. In addition, the measurement of financial liabilities and own equity instruments depends on whether identical liabilities or equity instruments are held by other parties as assets.

#	Step	Explanation
		However, an entity must measure the liability or equity instrument from the perspective of a market participant that holds the identical item as an asset if (a) a quoted price for an identical or similar instrument is not available and (b) the identical item is, in fact, held by another party (or by other parties) as an asset.
3.	Identify the market in which to price the financial asset or financial liability – i.e. either (1) the principal market or (2) if no principal market exists, the most advantageous market (see **section 3.3**)	The principal market is "[t]he market with the greatest volume and level of activity for the asset or liability". The most advantageous market is "[t]he market that maximises the amount that would be received to sell the asset or minimises the amount that would be paid to transfer the liability…". If there is a principal market for the financial asset or financial liability, the fair value measurement should reflect the price in that market, even if the price in a different market is potentially more advantageous at the measurement date. In the absence of evidence to the contrary, the market in which an entity would normally enter into a transaction to sell the asset or to transfer the liability is presumed to be the principal (or most advantageous) market. Therefore, an entity is permitted to use the price in the market in which it normally enters into transactions unless there is evidence that the principal (or most advantageous) market and that market are not the same. A market cannot be identified as the principal (or most advantageous) market unless the entity has access to that market at the measurement date.
4.	Develop assumptions that market participants in the principal (or most advantageous) market would use when pricing the financial asset or financial liability (see **section 3.3**)	'Market participants' are buyers and sellers in the principal (or most advantageous) market for the asset or liability that are (1) independent of each other, (2) knowledgeable, (3) able to enter into a transaction for the asset or liability, and (4) willing to enter into such a transaction.

#	Step	Explanation
		An entity need not identify specific market participants, but should identify characteristics that distinguish market participants generally.
5.	Estimate fair value using appropriate valuation techniques and related inputs (see **sections 8** & **9** below)	When the price for a financial asset or a financial liability cannot be observed directly, it must be estimated using a valuation technique. Entities should use valuation techniques that are appropriate in the circumstances and for which sufficient data are available to measure fair value, maximising the use of relevant observable inputs and minimising the use of unobservable inputs. Highest priority should be given to unadjusted quoted prices in active markets for identical assets or liabilities. IFRS 13 refers to three widely used valuation techniques: • the market approach (see IFRS 13:B5-B7); • the cost approach (see IFRS 13: B8-B9); and • the income approach (see IFRS 13:B10-B30). Any valuation technique used to measure fair value should be consistent with one or more of these approaches. IFRS 13 does not set out a hierarchy of valuation techniques because particular valuation techniques may be more appropriate in some circumstances than in others. The two most common valuation techniques used for financial instruments are the market approach and the income approach. The use of multiple valuation techniques may be appropriate in certain circumstances. In those cases, the results should be evaluated considering the reasonableness of the range of values indicated by those results. A fair value measurement is the point within that range that is most representative of the fair value in the circumstances.

#	Step	Explanation
		Once a valuation technique has been selected, it should be applied consistently. A change in a valuation technique or its application (e.g. a change in its weighting when multiple valuation techniques are used or a change in an adjustment applied to a valuation technique) is only appropriate if the change results in a measurement that is equally or more representative of fair value in the circumstances. An entity should evaluate the factors listed in IFRS 13:B37 (see **9.5**) to determine whether there has been a significant decrease in the volume or level of activity for the asset or liability relative to normal market activity. When such a decrease has occurred, this will affect the entity's selection of techniques and/or inputs and the weight placed on quoted prices.
6.	If the exception in Step 2a applies, allocate the fair value calculated in Step 5 (which might include several units of account) to the individual units of account that are the subject of the fair value measurement (as determined in Step 1 above) (see **section 6**)	If the fair value calculated in Step 5 is for multiple units of account, the fair value should be allocated to the individual units of account that are the subject of the fair value measurement on a reasonable and consistent basis.
7.	Classify the fair value measurement within the fair value hierarchy (see **section 10**) and prepare the disclosures required by IFRS 13 (see **chapter B11**)	IFRS 13 establishes a fair value hierarchy that categorises into three levels the inputs to valuation techniques used to measure fair value (see IFRS 13:72 - 90 for details). When several inputs are used to measure the fair value of an asset or a liability, those inputs may be categorised within different levels of the fair value hierarchy (e.g. the valuation may be based on some Level 2 and some Level 3 inputs). In such circumstances, the categorisation of the fair value measurement in its entirety is based on the lowest level input that is significant to the entire measurement.

#	Step	Explanation
		IFRS 13 sets out disclosure requirements in respect of fair value measurements. The disclosures vary depending on whether the assets or liabilities are measured at fair value on a recurring or non-recurring basis.

Fair value measurement framework

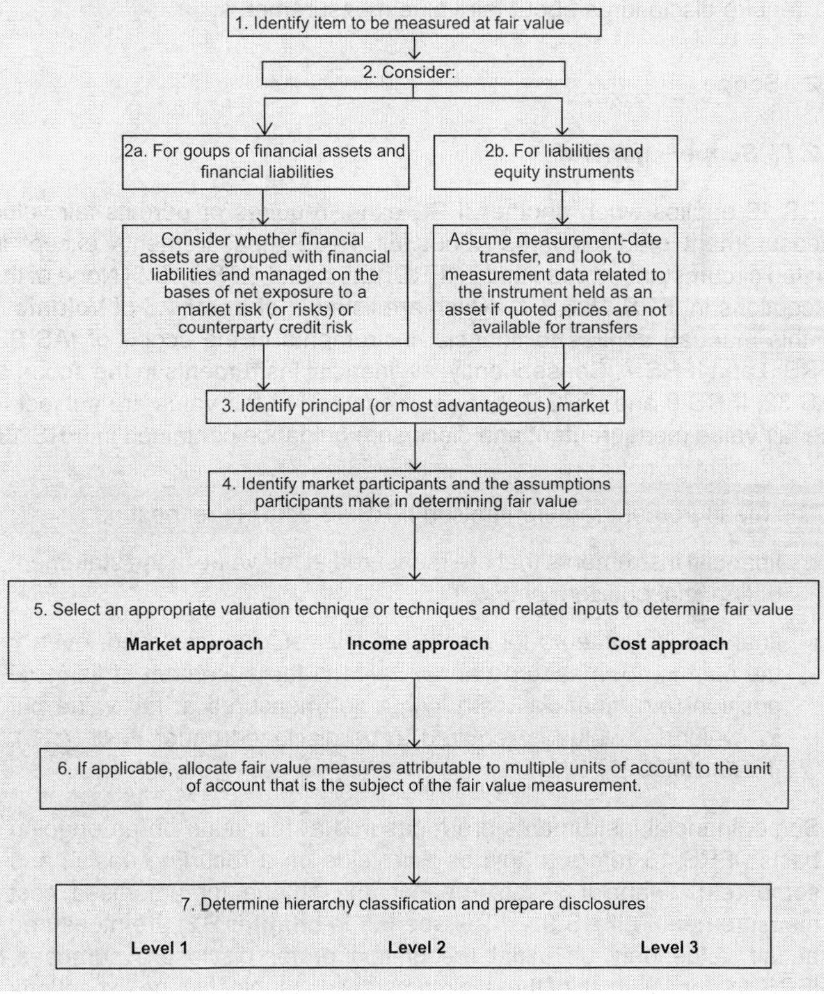

2 Objective and scope

2.1 Objective

The objective of IFRS 13 is to:

[IFRS 13:1]

- define fair value;
- set out in a single IFRS a framework for measuring fair value; and
- require disclosures about fair value measurements.

2.2 Scope

2.2.1 Scope – general

IFRS 13 applies when another IFRS either requires or permits fair value measurement or disclosures about fair value measurements except in limited circumstances specified in IFRS 13:6 and 7. [IFRS 13:5] None of the exceptions in IFRS 13:6 & 7 (which are listed in **chapter A6** of **Volume A** of this manual) applies to financial instruments in the scope of IAS 32, IFRS 9 and IFRS 7. Consequently, all financial instruments in the scope of IAS 32, IFRS 9 and IFRS 7 that are measured at fair value are subject to the fair value measurement and disclosure guidance contained in IFRS 13.

The measurement requirements in IFRS 13 apply in respect of:

- financial instruments that are measured at fair value in the statement of financial position; and
- financial instruments for which the fair value is disclosed, even if the item is not measured at fair value in the statement of financial position (e.g. financial instruments not measured at fair value but for which fair value is required to be disclosed under IFRS 7:25). [IFRS 13:BC25]

Some financial instruments are measured at fair value on an ongoing basis (IFRS 13 refers to this as 'fair value on a recurring basis') and some (e.g. financial assets meeting the criteria for amortised cost measurement in IFRS 9:4.1.2 – see **5.1** in **chapter B2**) are measured at fair value only on initial recognition or for disclosure purposes. IFRS 13 applies in all of these circumstances (subject to the exceptions in IFRS 13:6 & 7).

2.2.2 Application of IFRS 13 to receivables and payables measured at initial recognition using present value techniques

All recognised financial instruments that are within the scope of IFRS 9, excluding certain trade receivables, are required to be measured at fair value on initial recognition. This requirement applies irrespective of how the instrument is subsequently measured. The exception is for trade receivables that do not have a significant financing component (determined in accordance with IFRS 15 *Revenue from Contracts with Customers*) that are not initially measured at fair value, rather they are initially measured at their transaction price. In the case where receivables and payables are initially measured at fair value but subsequently measured at amortised cost, because fair value generally cannot be observed directly, present value techniques are used to estimate fair value at initial recognition. Accordingly, IFRS 13 (including the guidance in IFRS 13:B12-B30 regarding the use of present value techniques to measure fair value) applies to such initial measurements.

Note, however, that IFRS 13's disclosure requirements do not apply to fair value measurements at initial recognition (see IFRS 13:91 & BC184).

2.2.3 Application of IFRS 13 to financial assets measured at amortised cost that are determined to be impaired

When a financial asset is determined to be impaired, expected credit losses are measured using an unbiased and probability-weighted amount that is determined by evaluating a range of possible outcomes, reflecting the time value of money and based on reasonable and supportable information (see IFRS 9:5.5.17).

When the financial asset is measured at amortised cost in the statement of financial position IFRS 13 does not apply when an impaired financial asset is measured using this approach. The recognition of an impairment loss using the approach described results in the financial asset being remeasured at the present value of expected future cash flows discounted at the original effective interest rate (or an approximation thereof). This amount may not be equivalent to fair value because a fair value measurement would incorporate a current market discount rate. Accordingly, the measurement and disclosure requirements of IFRS 13 do not generally apply to an impaired financial asset measured at amortised cost.

However, IFRS 7:25 requires an entity to disclose the fair value of each class of financial assets and financial liabilities. Consequently, the fair value of financial assets measured at amortised cost is required to be disclosed. The amount disclosed should be measured in accordance with IFRS 13 and the disclosures required under IFRS 13:97 should be provided.

2.2.4 Application of IFRS 13 to a hedged item in a fair value hedge

Hedged items in a fair value hedge are not measured at fair value in the statement of financial position. The hedged item may be accounted for under an IFRS that specifies a measurement basis other than fair value (e.g. a debt instrument measured at amortised cost under IFRS 9). In such circumstances, under the fair value hedge accounting rules, the underlying carrying amount of the hedged item is adjusted for relevant changes in the fair value of the hedged risk. The hedged risk could be (i) changes in the fair value of the hedged item (see **example 2.2.4A**) or (ii) changes in a portion of the fair value of the hedged item specific to a hedged risk (see **example 2.2.4B**). In both cases, the fair value hedge adjustment applied to the hedged item results in a 'hybrid' carrying amount for the hedged item.

In such circumstances, the fair value measurement principles in IFRS 13 should be used in determining the amount of the fair value hedge adjustment (i.e. the amount of the relevant changes in the fair value of the hedged risk).

When the relevant IFRS requires disclosure of the fair value of a hedged item that is not measured at fair value in its entirety in the statement of financial position:

- the measurement requirements of IFRS 13 apply to the amount disclosed as fair value; and
- the disclosure requirements of IFRS 13:97 apply.

Example 2.2.4A

Application of IFRS 13 to a hedged item in a fair value hedge (1)

On 1 January 20X1, Company A (which is not a broker-dealer) measures oil inventories of 100,000 barrels under IAS 2 *Inventories* at its cost of US$60 per barrel (US$6 million). The spot price for oil is US$65 per barrel. At that date, Company A enters into and designates oil futures contracts to sell 100,000 barrels of oil at US$65 per barrel as a fair value hedge of its oil inventories. The fair value of the oil futures contracts on 1 January 20X1 is zero. The oil futures contracts are measured at fair value at subsequent reporting dates in accordance with IFRS 9.

At 31 December 20X1, the spot price for oil is US$63 per barrel. Assume, for simplicity, that Company A did not purchase or sell any oil in the period. The IAS 2 measurement of the oil inventories is unchanged, because the current spot price of US$63 per barrel is higher than the carrying amount of $60 per barrel (i.e. cost). However, as a result of the fall in the spot price from US$65 to US$63 per barrel, the fair value of the oil futures contract on 31 December 20X1 is an asset of US$200,000. For illustrative purposes, assuming Company A has a perfectly effective fair value hedge, the carrying amount of the inventories is therefore adjusted by US$200,000, resulting in an adjusted carrying amount of US$5.8 million (i.e. US$6 million less the fair value hedge adjustment of US$200,000).

This adjusted carrying amount of US$5.8 million is not the fair value of the inventories, and IAS 2 does not require that the fair value of the inventories be disclosed. Consequently, neither the measurement nor the disclosure requirements of IFRS 13 apply in respect of the inventories.

However, the fair value measurement principles in IFRS 13 should be used in determining the amount of the fair value hedge adjustment because the fair value hedge adjustment represents an adjustment for fair value movements in the hedged risk. In addition, both the measurement and the disclosure requirements of IFRS 13 apply in respect of the oil futures contracts because they are derivatives measured at fair value.

Example 2.2.4B

Application of IFRS 13 to a hedged item in a fair value hedge (2)

Entity Z issues fixed-rate debt at 6 per cent, which includes a credit spread of 100 basis points (i.e. the rate comprises a LIBOR rate of 5 per cent and a credit spread of 1 per cent). To hedge its exposure to interest rate movements, Entity Z enters into a receive-fixed rate at 5 per cent, pay-floating rate at LIBOR swap. The LIBOR portion of the 6 per cent fixed-rate debt is designated as the hedged item. At subsequent reporting dates, the interest rate swap is remeasured to fair value in accordance with IFRS 9, with the fair value movement recognised in profit or loss. The carrying amount of the debt is adjusted for changes in the fair value of the debt arising from changes in the benchmark interest rate, LIBOR.

This adjusted carrying amount is not the fair value of the debt. Consequently, the measurement requirements of IFRS 13 do not apply to that carrying amount. However, the fair value measurement principles in IFRS 13 should be used in determining the amount of the fair value hedge adjustment because the fair value hedge adjustment represents an adjustment for fair value movements in the hedged risk.

Because the entity is required to disclose the fair value of the debt under IFRS 7:

- the measurement requirements of IFRS 13 apply to the amount disclosed as fair value; and
- the disclosure requirements of IFRS 13:97 also apply.

Both the measurement and the disclosure requirements of IFRS 13 apply in respect of the interest rate swap because it is a derivative measured at fair value.

2.2.5 Application of the disclosure requirements of IFRS 13 to assets and liabilities measured at fair value and included within a disposal group classified as held for sale

Under IFRS 5 *Non-current Assets Held for Sale and Discontinued Operations*, assets and liabilities that are excluded from the scope of the measurement requirements of that Standard may nevertheless be included within a disposal group classified as held for sale and the disposal group as a whole is subject to the measurement requirements and the classification and presentation requirements of IFRS 5 (see **section 2** of **chapter A20** of **Volume A** of this manual).

Items included within a disposal group that are not subject to the measurement requirements of IFRS 5 are measured in accordance with applicable IFRSs; some items (e.g. financial instruments) may be measured at fair value. If assets and liabilities that are measured at fair value on a recurring or non-recurring basis are part of a disposal group classified as held for sale, the question arises as to whether the disclosure requirements of IFRS 13 apply to those assets and liabilities.

The extent to which the disclosure requirements of other IFRSs apply to assets or liabilities included within disposal groups classified as held for sale is addressed in IFRS 5:5B which states that "[d]isclosures in other IFRSs do not apply to [non-current assets held for sale] (or disposal groups) unless those IFRSs require . . . disclosures about measurement of assets and liabilities within a disposal group that are not within the scope of the measurement requirement of IFRS 5".

For assets and liabilities excluded from the scope of the measurement requirement of IFRS 5 that are included within a disposal group classified as held for sale and that are measured at fair value, the effect of IFRS 5:5B is that the disclosure requirements of IFRS 13 apply *to the extent that those disclosure requirements relate to measurement*.

Given that IFRS 13 as a whole is concerned with the measurement of fair value, and with disclosures regarding the measurement of fair value, all of the disclosure requirements of IFRS 13 relate to 'measurement' and, consequently, should be applied.

When determining the classes of assets and liabilities as required by IFRS 13:94 (see **section 3** in **chapter B11**), and preparing the fair value measurement disclosures, an entity should distinguish assets and liabilities that are part of a disposal group classified as held for sale from its other assets and liabilities. The classes determined in accordance with IFRS 13:94 should be consistent with the major classes of assets and liabilities disclosed separately in accordance with IFRS 5:38 (see **7.3.1** in **chapter A20** of **Volume A** of this manual).

3 Definition of fair value

3.1 Definition of fair value – general

Fair value is defined as "[t]he price that would be received to sell an asset or paid to transfer a liability in an orderly transaction between market participants at the measurement date". [IFRS 13:Appendix A]

This basis for measuring fair value is commonly referred to as an *exit price* approach because it reflects the price at which a market participant that holds the asset or owes the liability could *exit* that asset or liability by selling the asset or transferring the liability to a third party.

Note that the definition assumes a hypothetical and orderly exchange transaction (i.e. it is not an actual sale or a forced transaction or distress sale). [IFRS 13:BC30]

Fair value as defined above is a market-based measurement (not an entity-specific value). [IFRS 13:2] It is therefore measured using the assumptions that market participants would use when pricing the asset or liability, including assumptions about risk. Consequently, an entity's intention to hold an asset or to settle or otherwise fulfil a liability is not relevant when measuring fair value. [IFRS 13:3]

IFRS 13's definition clarifies that fair value should reflect current market conditions (which reflect the current expectations of market participants about future market conditions, rather than those of the reporting entity). [IFRS 13:BC31]

The extent to which market information is available can vary between different types of assets and liabilities. For some assets and liabilities, observable market transactions or market information may be available. For other assets and liabilities, observable market transactions and market information may not be available. However, the objective under IFRS 13 in both circumstances is the same – to estimate the price at which an orderly transaction to sell the asset or to transfer the liability would take place between market participants at the measurement date under current market conditions. [IFRS 13:2] When a price for an identical asset or liability is not observable, an entity measures fair value using another valuation technique that maximises the use of relevant observable inputs and minimises the use of unobservable inputs. [IFRS 13:3]

A fair value measurement requires an entity to determine all of the following:

[IFRS 13:B2]

- the particular asset or liability that is the subject of the measurement (consistently with its unit of account);

- the principal (or most advantageous) market for the asset or liability; and
- the valuation technique(s) appropriate for the measurement, considering the availability of data with which inputs that represent the assumptions market participants would use when pricing the asset or liability and the level of the fair value hierarchy within which the inputs are categorised.

Key elements of the definition of fair value are discussed in the following sections, namely:

- the asset or liability that is being measured (see **section 3.2**);
- the market in which the transaction is assumed to occur (see **section 3.3**);
- the market participants that are assumed to enter into the transaction (see **section 3.4**); and
- the 'price' at which the transaction is assumed to occur (see **section 3.5**).

3.2 Identifying the asset or liability

3.2.1 Determining the appropriate unit of account

The asset or liability being measured at fair value may be (1) a stand-alone asset or liability (e.g. a financial instrument), (2) a group of assets or a group of liabilities, or (3) a group of assets and liabilities. The level at which fair value is measured will depend on the 'unit of account' (typically, the level at which the asset or liability is aggregated or disaggregated for recognition or disclosure purposes). [IFRS 13:13 and Appendix A]

The unit of account is determined in accordance with the IFRS that requires or permits the fair value measurement, except as provided in IFRS 13. [IFRS 13:14] For financial instruments, the unit of account is determined in accordance with IAS 32, IFRS 9 or IFRS 7.

IFRS 13 does not generally prescribe the unit of account. The IASB concluded that IFRS 13 should describe *how* to measure fair value, not *what* is being measured at fair value. Other IFRSs specify whether a fair value measurement considers an individual asset or liability or a group of assets or liabilities (i.e. the unit of account). For example, under IFRS 9 the unit of account is generally an individual financial instrument. [IFRS 13:BC47]

As IFRS 9 requires that assets and liabilities be recognised and measured in accordance with their contractual terms the unit of account guidance in IFRS 9 is therefore based on a stand-alone asset or liability rather than based on a group of assets and/or liabilities. Therefore, in applying IFRS 13 to financial instruments fair value is generally determined on a stand-alone basis. However, as described in **section 6**, IFRS 13 permits financial instruments that are managed together and that have offsetting risks to be valued based on the group of financial instruments rather than the fair value of individual financial instruments.

In September 2014, the IASB issued Exposure Draft ED/2014/4 *Measuring Quoted Investments in Subsidiaries, Joint Ventures and Associates at Fair Value*. The ED considers the unit of account for the purposes of measuring the fair value of investments in subsidiaries, joint ventures and associates when the investment is quoted in an active market. This issue is relevant in the following circumstances:

- an entity chooses to measure such investments at fair value in accordance IFRS 9 in its separate financial statements;
- an acquirer acquires the controlling interest in an investee where the previously-held interest is required to be measured at fair value;
- an investment entity parent measures its investments in subsidiaries (other than subsidiaries that provide investment-related services or activities) at fair value in accordance with IFRS 10; and
- an entity is required to measure the fair value of its investment in a subsidiary, joint venture or associate as part of an impairment assessment in accordance with IAS 36.

In the ED, the IASB proposes that the unit of account for investments in subsidiaries, joint ventures and associates is the investment as a whole, and that the fair value measurement of an investment composed of financial instruments quoted in an active market should be the product of the quoted price of the financial instrument (P) multiplied by the quantity (Q) of instruments held (i.e. P × Q) without adjustments. This is on the basis that the quoted prices in an active market provide the most reliable evidence of fair value. The comment period for the ED ended in January 2015 and at the time of writing the IASB was in the redeliberation phase of the project.

Given the ongoing debate there are two acceptable approaches to fair valuing interests in subsidiaries, joint ventures and associates when the individual investment is quoted in an active market. The unit of account can be considered the individual investment and therefore the interest is fair valued as the quantity multiplied by the price of an individual instrument (i.e. P x Q), or alternatively the unit of account can be considered as a whole and thus potentially the P x Q valuation can be adjusted to reflect the premium that would be paid for control, joint control or significant influence over an investee. It should be noted that any such adjustment would be unobservable (i.e., a 'Level 3' input). If significant, this would result in the entire fair value measurement being categorised as 'Level 3' and, therefore, additional disclosures stipulated by IFRS 13 with regard to Level 3 fair value measurement (for example, a description of the valuation process and inputs used and of sensitivity to changes in the unobservable input used) would be required. An entity should select its approach as an accounting policy and apply it consistently in fair valuing interests in subsidiaries, joint ventures and associates where the individual investment is quoted in an active market.

The following examples set out considerations for determining the appropriate unit of account for equity interests held by an entity in various scenarios and how the fair value of those interests should be measured.

Scenario	Unit of account prescribed in the applicable IFRS
Scenario 1 Entity A owns a 16 per cent equity interest in Entity B (160 million ordinary shares). Entity B's ordinary shares are traded in an active market. The share price of each ordinary share at the measurement date is CU0.5. Entity A accounts for the 16 per cent equity interest at fair value at initial recognition and at the end of each reporting period in accordance with IFRS 9.	 IFRS 9 is the applicable Standard that requires the fair value measurement. IFRS 13:80 specifically discusses a scenario where an entity holds a position in a single asset or liability (including a position comprising a large number of identical assets or liabilities) and the asset or liability is traded in an active market; in such circumstances, the unit of account is the individual financial instrument (see **section 10.3**). The fair value of such a holding of financial instruments is required to be measured within Level 1 as the product of the quoted price (P) for the individual financial instrument and the quantity (Q) held by the entity (i.e. P x Q). Therefore, in this scenario, the fair value of the 16 per cent equity interest in Entity B is measured as 160 million x CU0.5 = CU80 million.

Scenario	Unit of account prescribed in the applicable IFRS
Scenario 2	
Entity C owns a 54 per cent equity interest in Entity D (300 million ordinary shares). Entity D is a subsidiary of Entity C. Entity D's ordinary shares are traded in an active market. The share price of each ordinary share at the measurement date is CU0.5. In its separate financial statements, Entity C has chosen to account for its investments in subsidiaries in accordance with IFRS 9 at fair value at initial recognition and at the end of each reporting period.	Based on Entity C's accounting policy, IFRS 9 is the applicable Standard that requires the fair value measurement in Entity C's separate financial statements. Entity's C's accounting policy for fair valuing interests in subsidiaries, joint ventures and associates is to consider the unit of account as the individual investment. Therefore, the unit of account for Entity C's investment in Entity D is the individual share in Entity D, and the fair value of the 54 per cent equity interest in Entity D is determined as the product of the quoted price (P) for the individual shares and the quantity (Q) held by Entity C (i.e. P x Q = 300 million x CU0.5 = CU150 million). Note that this question concerns measurement in the separate financial statements of Entity C only. The accounting in the consolidated financial statements is specified in IFRS 10 *Consolidated Financial Statements*.

3.2.2 Determining the characteristics of an asset or a liability to be taken into account

3.2.2.1 Characteristics of an asset or a liability to be taken into account – general

When measuring fair value, the characteristics of an asset or a liability that should be taken into account are those that market participants would consider when pricing that asset or liability at the measurement date. Such characteristics could include, for example:

[IFRS 13:11]

- the condition and location of an asset; and
- restrictions, if any, on the sale or use of an asset.

The effect on the measurement arising from a particular characteristic will differ depending on how that characteristic would be taken into account by market participants. [IFRS 13:12]

3.2.2.2 Restrictions on the sale or use of an asset

Following the principle set out in IFRS 13:11 (see **3.2.2.1**), a legal or contractual restriction on the sale or use of an asset should be incorporated in the asset's fair value measurement if (1) the restriction is a characteristic of the asset, and (2) market participants would take the effect of the restriction into account when pricing the asset.

Example 8 accompanying IFRS 13, reproduced as **example 3.2.2.2**, illustrates the effect of restrictions on the fair value measurement of an asset. Example 8 considers a restriction that is a characteristic of the asset being measured and that would transfer to market participants with the asset; such restrictions should be taken into account when measuring the fair value of the asset. In contrast, a restriction that is specific to the entity holding the asset and that would not transfer to market participants should not be taken into account when measuring the fair value of the asset.

Example 3.2.2.2

Restriction on the sale of an equity instrument

[IFRS 13:IE28 – Example 8]

An entity holds an equity instrument (a financial asset) for which sale is legally or contractually restricted for a specified period. (For example, such a restriction could limit sale to qualifying investors.) The restriction is a characteristic of the instrument and, therefore, would be transferred to market participants. In that case, the fair value of the instrument would be measured on the basis of the quoted price for an otherwise identical unrestricted equity instrument of the same issuer that trades in a public market, adjusted to reflect the effect of the restriction. The adjustment would reflect the amount market participants would demand because of the risk relating to the inability to access a public market for the instrument for the specified period. The adjustment will vary depending on all the following:

(a) the nature and duration of the restriction;

(b) the extent to which buyers are limited by the restriction (e.g. there might be a large number of qualifying investors); and

(c) qualitative and quantitative factors specific to both the instrument and the issuer.

Sometimes it is immediately clear whether a restriction is a characteristic of an asset and would transfer to market participants. In other circumstances, significant judgement may be required to make the assessment and it may be necessary to obtain expert advice.

Consistent with **example 3.2.2.2**, when a restriction needs to be taken into account when measuring the fair value of the asset, this is achieved by adjusting the fair value of an identical unrestricted asset to reflect the 'compensation' that a market participant would require because of the restriction. The adjustment will vary depending on (1) the nature and duration of the restriction, (2) the extent to which buyers are limited by the restriction, and (3) qualitative and quantitative factors specific to the asset (including factors specific to the issuer of the asset, as appropriate).

When categorising the fair value measurement for the purposes of the fair value hierarchy under IFRS 13:72, an entity will need to evaluate the significance of any adjustment made to reflect a restriction on the sale or use of the asset (see **10.3.3.2** for additional guidance regarding such evaluations).

The following are additional common examples of restrictions on the sale of assets.

Restriction on the sale of securities specified in contractual terms When a restriction on the sale of securities (e.g. prohibiting sale of the securities to specified groups of investors or only permitting the securities to be sold to specified groups of investors) is embedded in the contractual terms of the securities, the restriction is a characteristic of the securities and would transfer to market participants. Consequently, the fair value measurement of the securities should reflect the asset-specific restriction.

Founders' shares Founder shareholders may be contractually prevented from selling their shares immediately following an initial public offering (IPO). Such a restriction may be outlined in the IPO prospectus. Assuming that the restriction is not embedded in the contractual terms of the shares (and, accordingly, would not transfer to a market participant in a hypothetical sale of the shares), the restriction is specific to the founder shareholders and is not a characteristic of the shares. In such circumstances, the restriction on the sale of the shares would not be taken into account when measuring the fair value of the shares.

Directors' shareholdings Assume that Company A owns ordinary shares issued by Company B and Company A is entitled to appoint a member of its management team to Company B's board of directors. Because Company A appoints a director of Company B, Company A is restricted from selling any of its shares in Company B during the period surrounding Company B's periodic release of earnings. Other market participants that are not directors of Company B or that do not have a right to appoint directors of Company B would not be subject to this restriction. Because the restriction is entity-specific (i.e. it is not a characteristic of the shares) and would not transfer with the shares, Company A should not reflect the effect of the restriction in the fair value measurement of its investment in Company B.

Assets pledged as collateral An entity may enter into a borrowing arrangement that requires assets to be pledged as collateral. The borrowing arrangement may restrict the entity from selling or transferring the assets during the term of the arrangement. Other market participants, however, would not be subject to this restriction. Because the restriction is entity-specific (i.e. it is not a characteristic of the assets) and would not transfer with the assets, it should not be reflected in the fair value measurement of the pledged assets.

3.3 Identifying the market in which to price the asset or liability

3.3.1 Principal market versus most advantageous market

IFRS 13 requires an entity to consider the market in which the sale of an asset or the transfer of a liability will take place. The Standard introduces the concepts of a 'principal market' and a 'most advantageous' market. Both terms are important in establishing the market in which the particular asset will be sold or the liability transferred and, consequently, in determining what price will be achieved if the sale or transfer occurs in that market at the measurement date.

A fair value measurement assumes that the transaction to sell the asset or transfer the liability takes place either:

[IFRS 13:16]

- in the principal market for the asset or liability; or
- in the absence of a principal market, in the most advantageous market for the asset or liability.

The *principal market* is the market with the greatest volume and level of activity for the asset or liability. The *most advantageous market* is the market that maximises the amount that would be received to sell the asset or minimises the amount that would be paid to transfer the liability, after taking into account transaction and transport costs. [IFRS 13:Appendix A].

Note that, although transaction costs are not deducted (for an asset) or added (for a liability) when measuring fair value, they are considered when identifying the most advantageous market for an asset or a liability (see **3.5.3**).

The principal market should be identified on the basis of the volume or level of activity for the asset or liability rather than the volume or level of activity of the reporting entity's transactions in a particular market. [IFRS 13:BC52] Therefore, the assessment as to which of two or more accessible markets is the principal market is made from the perspective of market participants rather than the entity.

Equally, in the absence of a principal market, the most advantageous market is identified using the assumptions that market participants would use.

A principal market may not exist, for example, when the volume or level of activity for the asset or liability is the same in two different markets to which the entity has access, or when there is no observable market for the asset or liability. In such circumstances, an entity needs to identify the most advantageous market or develop assumptions from the perspective of a market participant in a hypothetical most advantageous market.

IFRS 13 does not require an entity to conduct an exhaustive search of all possible markets to identify the principal market or (in the absence of a principal market, the most advantageous market) but an entity is required to take into account all information that is reasonably available. In the absence of evidence to the contrary, the market in which the entity would normally enter into a transaction to sell the asset or to transfer the liability is presumed to be the principal market (or most advantageous) market. [IFRS 13:17]

Therefore, an entity is permitted to use the price in the market in which it normally enters into transactions unless there is evidence that the principal market and that market are not the same. [IFRS 13:BC53]

If there is evidence that the market in which an entity would normally transact is not the principal (or most advantageous) market, the principal (or most advantageous) market should be identified by:

- firstly, identifying other markets to which the entity has access; and
- secondly, when relevant, assessing which of two or more accessible markets is the principal (or most advantageous) market.

If there is a principal market for the asset or liability, the fair value measurement should reflect the price in that market even if the price in a different market is potentially more advantageous at the measurement date. [IFRS 13:18]

3.3.2 Access to the market

To use the price in the principal (or most advantageous) market as the basis for measuring fair value, an entity must have access to that market at the measurement date. Because different entities (and businesses within those entities) with different activities may have access to different markets, the principal (or most advantageous) market for the same asset or liability might be different for different entities (and businesses within those entities). Therefore, the principal (or most advantageous) market should be considered from the perspective of the entity, thereby allowing for differences between and among entities with different activities. [IFRS 13:19]

Example 7 accompanying IFRS 13 (summarised at **section 7**) illustrates a scenario in which two entities measure the same instrument differently because each identifies its principal market on the basis of the market to which it has access.

Although an entity must be able to access the market, the entity does not need to be able to sell the particular asset or transfer the particular liability on the measurement date to be able to measure fair value on the basis of the price in that market. [IFRS 13:20]

For example, as discussed in **example 3.2.2.2**, an entity may be restricted from selling a particular asset at the measurement date. Nevertheless, if the entity has access to the principal market at that date, the entity could measure the asset's fair value using observed prices for sales of similar (but unrestricted) assets in that market. If the restriction is a characteristic of the asset (i.e. it would transfer with the asset in a hypothetical sale), an entity should make an adjustment to observed market prices for similar (but unrestricted) assets to reflect the restriction (see **3.2.2.2** for further discussion).

3.3.3 Measuring fair value when no apparent exit market exists

Even when there is no observable market to provide pricing information about the sale of an asset or the transfer of a liability at the measurement date, a fair value measurement should assume that a transaction takes place at that date, considered from the perspective of a market participant that holds the asset or owes the liability. That assumed transaction establishes a basis for estimating the price to sell the asset or to transfer the liability. [IFRS 13:21]

When an observable market for an asset or a liability does not exist, an entity must assume a hypothetical transaction at the measurement date. This is consistent with the fair value objective in IFRS 13 to measure fair value as "the price that would be received to sell an asset or paid to transfer a liability in an orderly transaction between market participants at the measurement date". [IFRS 13:Appendix A] See **3.4.3** for guidance on how an entity might identify market participants when no apparent exit market exists.

3.3.4 Factors indicating a change in the principal (or most advantageous) market

While it is presumed that the market in which an entity normally transacts is the principal (or most advantageous) market (see **3.3.1**), an entity should reassess the principal (or most advantageous) market for an asset or a liability at each measurement date based on reasonably available information. Factors indicating that there may have been a change in the principal (or most advantageous) market include the following (the list is not exhaustive):

- a significant change in market conditions;
- a decrease in the volume or level of activity relative to other markets;
- the development of a new market (see below);
- a change in the entity's ability to access particular markets (e.g. an entity loses access to a market or gains access to a market to which it did not previously have access); and
- when there is no principal market, a change in value such that the price for the asset or liability in a market previously considered most advantageous is no longer the most advantageous.

Events such as those listed above may indicate that there has been a change in the principal (or most advantageous) market for the asset or liability, or that circumstances have changed such that there is no longer a principal market for the asset or liability (in which case the entity should refer instead to the most advantageous market).

When a market first develops (e.g. for a new form of securities), it may operate primarily as a principal-to-principal or over-the-counter market. However, the volume and level of activity in the exchange market may increase over time. As the volume and level of activity change, and the balance of market activity shifts, an entity should take this into account when reassessing the principal (or most advantageous) market for an asset or a liability.

3.4 Market participants

3.4.1 Definition of market participants

Market participants are defined as "[b]uyers and sellers in the principal (or most advantageous) market for the asset or liability that have all of the following characteristics:

(a) They are independent of each other, i.e. they are not related parties as defined in IAS 24, although the price in a related party transaction may be used as an input to a fair value measurement if the entity has evidence that the transaction was entered into at market terms.

(b) They are knowledgeable, having a reasonable understanding about the asset or liability and the transaction using all available information, including information that might be obtained through due diligence efforts that are usual and customary.

(c) They are able to enter into a transaction for the asset or liability.

(d) They are willing to enter into a transaction for the asset or liability, i.e. they are motivated but not forced or otherwise compelled to do so". [IFRS 13:Appendix A]

3.4.2 Use of assumptions that market participants would use

IFRS 13 requires an entity to use the assumptions that market participants would use when pricing the asset or liability, assuming that market participants act in their economic best interest. [IFRS 13:22]

In developing those assumptions, an entity is not expected to identify specific market participants, but is expected to identify characteristics that distinguish market participants generally, considering factors specific to:

[IFRS 13:23]

- the asset or liability;
- the principal (or most advantageous) market for the asset or liability; and
- market participants with whom the entity would enter into a transaction in that market.

Example 3.4.2A

Use of assumptions that market participants would use

Entity F uses a discounted cash flow model to measure the fair value of a financial asset. Entity F has obtained information about the assumptions that market participants would use to measure the fair value of the asset. However, Entity F believes that some of those assumptions are not appropriate.

Entity F is not permitted to rely on its own internal data rather than use the assumptions that market participants would use. A fair value measurement is a market-based measurement and not entity-specific. IFRS 13:22 requires that the fair value of an asset or a liability should be measured using the assumptions that market participants would use when pricing the asset or liability, assuming that market participants act in their economic best interest.

When using a discounted cash flow model to measure the fair value of a financial asset, Entity F should incorporate relevant observable inputs whenever available. Any unobservable inputs used in the fair value measure (e.g. estimated future cash flows or risk adjustments incorporated into the discount rate) should be based on management's estimate of assumptions that market participants would use in pricing the asset in a current transaction at the measurement date. If market data from transactions involving comparable assets indicate, for example, that a significant liquidity discount applies at the measurement date to compensate for the difficulty in selling assets under current market conditions, Entity F should incorporate that information in its cash flow model (e.g. through an adjustment to the discount rate) even if management's internal data would not result in such a liquidity adjustment.

Example 3.4.2B

Use of assumptions that market participants would use

Entity A uses a discounted cash flow model as a valuation technique to measure the fair value of its investment in the debt securities of Entity X. No quoted price for identical securities is available. Entity A's valuation technique requires assumptions about default rates as inputs. Default rate assumptions can be readily derived from current relevant observable market data: for example, actively traded credit default swaps (CDSs) on publicly traded bonds of Entity X, or asset swap spreads (the differential between the bond yield and the LIBOR curve expressed in basis points) or issuer spreads on the basis of recent notes issuances.

In applying its valuation technique to measure fair value, Entity A should maximise the use of relevant observable inputs. Therefore, it cannot rely solely on its own historical default data for issuers with a credit quality similar to that of Entity X or on its own default assumptions, even if the default assumptions are 'stressed' (e.g. by changing the inputs to other reasonably possible alternative assumptions). Instead, Entity A should use the relevant default rate assumptions that are observable in the market.

Example 3.4.2C

Fair value measurement of loans and receivables – requirement to consider the credit standing of the borrower

Entity A (a lender) has a loan receivable from Entity B (a borrower). When measuring the fair value of the loan receivable, Entity A should take into account the credit standing of Entity B.

A lender is required to take into account a borrower's credit standing when measuring the fair value of a loan receivable in accordance with IFRS 13.

IFRS 13.22 states that "[a]n entity shall measure the fair value of an asset or a liability using the assumptions that market participants would use when pricing the asset or liability, assuming that market participants act in their economic best interest".

Market participants would incorporate the effect of a borrower's credit standing into the valuation of a loan receivable because the borrower's credit standing can be indicative of the amount that will be collected on the loan. Therefore, Entity A should make appropriate adjustments to the fair value measurement of its loan and receivable to reflect Entity B's credit standing.

These requirements are relevant when Entity A measures the loan receivable at fair value on initial recognition and/or at subsequent reporting dates. They are also relevant when Entity A measures the receivable at amortised cost at subsequent reporting dates because, subject to limited exceptions, IFRS 7 requires that the fair value of financial instruments be disclosed at each reporting date. The amount disclosed should be measured in accordance with IFRS 13 and the disclosures required under IFRS 13:97 should be provided.

3.4.3 Identifying market participants when no apparent exit market exists

IFRS 13:21 requires that, even when there is no observable market to provide pricing information about the sale of an asset or the transfer of a liability at the measurement date, a fair value measurement should assume that a transaction takes place at that date, considered from the perspective of a market participant that holds the asset or owes the liability. That assumed transaction establishes a basis for estimating the price to sell the asset or to transfer the liability (see **3.3.3**).

In such circumstances, the entity is not required to identify specific market participants. Instead, the entity should consider the characteristics of potential market participants who would purchase the asset or accept a transfer of the liability being measured. In addition, the entity should identify the assumptions that such market participants would make in a transaction that maximises the amount received to sell an asset or minimises the amount paid to transfer a liability.

Potential market participants for financial instruments include counterparties to a derivative instrument, investors maximising return, investors trying to establish a strategic relationship with an investee, or a range of other participants with a specific objective.

When identifying a potential market participant, care should be taken to ensure that the unit of account from the perspective of the market participant is consistent with the unit of account of the item being measured.

When developing assumptions that market participants would use in such a hypothetical transaction, an entity may start with its own assumptions and make adjustments for factors specific to the asset or liability being measured, including (the list is not exhaustive):

- growth rates and risk adjustments to reflect market participant assumptions; and
- performance and risk indicators (e.g. delinquencies, defaults, prepayment speeds and interest rates).

Market participant assumptions that are developed when no apparent market exists may be based on unobservable inputs or adjustments. An entity needs to evaluate the significance of these inputs or adjustments when determining the appropriate level in the fair value hierarchy within which the measurement should be categorised (see **10.3.3.2** for additional guidance regarding such evaluations).

3.5 The price at which a transaction is assumed to occur

3.5.1 Characteristics of the price at which a transaction is assumed to occur

The price at which a transaction is assumed to occur in the principal or most advantageous market is the price:

[IFRS 13:24]

- in an 'orderly' transaction (see **3.5.2**); and
- under current market conditions at the measurement date.

The price may be directly observable or estimated using another valuation technique (see **section 8**). [IFRS 13:24]

The price should not be adjusted for 'transaction costs', but it should be adjusted for 'transport costs' in specified circumstances (see **3.5.3**). [IFRS 13:25 & 26]

3.5.2 An 'orderly' transaction

A fair value measurement assumes that the asset or liability is exchanged in an 'orderly' transaction in the principal (or most advantageous) market. An orderly transaction is defined as "[a] transaction that assumes exposure to the market for a period before the measurement date to allow for marketing activities that are usual and customary for transactions involving such assets or liabilities; it is not a forced transaction (e.g. a forced liquidation or distress sale)". [IFRS 13:Appendix A]

Appendix B to the Standard provides additional guidance regarding the identification of orderly transactions (see **9.6**).

3.5.3 Transaction costs and transport costs

Transaction costs are defined as "[t]he costs to sell an asset or transfer a liability in the principal (or most advantageous) market for the asset or liability that are directly attributable to the disposal of the asset or the transfer of the liability and that meet both of the following criteria:

- They result directly from and are essential to that transaction.
- They would not have been incurred by the entity had the decision to sell the asset or transfer the liability not been made (similar to costs to sell, as defined in IFRS 5)". [IFRS 13:Appendix A]

Transaction costs do not include transport costs. [IFRS 13:26] Transport costs are defined as "[t]he costs that would be incurred to transport an asset from its current location to its principal (or most advantageous) market". [IFRS 13:Appendix A]

IFRS 13 specifies that, when measuring fair value, the relevant market price should *not* be adjusted for transaction costs. Because such costs are specific to a transaction and will differ depending on how an entity enters into a transaction for an asset or a liability, they are not considered to be a characteristic of the asset or liability. [IFRS 13:25]

Note, however, that transaction costs are considered when identifying the most advantageous market for an asset or a liability (see **3.3.1** and **example 3.5.3**).

The appropriate treatment for transaction costs should be determined in accordance with other relevant IFRSs. [IFRS 13:25] For financial instruments, transaction costs are accounted for in accordance with the requirements in IAS 32 and IFRS 9 (see **2.1** in **chapter B6**). [IFRS 13:24 & 25]

In contrast, the price in the principal (or most advantageous) market used to measure the fair value of the asset or liability *is* adjusted for costs that would be incurred to transport the asset from its current location to that market *if* location is a characteristic of the asset. [IFRS 13:26]

Transport costs are relevant in determining the fair value of non-financial items. Because certain contracts that include the delivery or receipt of non-financial items are scoped into IAS 32, IFRS 9 and IFRS 7 (see **2.5** in **chapter B1**), transport costs may be relevant in determining the fair value of a contract that is in the scope of the financial instruments Standards. This may be the case in determining the fair value of a commodity for delivery to a particular location where location is an attribute of the contract.

The appropriate treatments for transaction and transport costs are illustrated in the following example.

Example 3.5.3

Level 1 principal (or most advantageous) market

[IFRS 13:IE19-IE22, Example 6]

An asset is sold in two different active markets at different prices. An entity enters into transactions in both markets and can access the price in those markets for the asset at the measurement date. In Market A, the price that would be received is CU26, transaction costs in that market are CU3 and the costs to transport the asset to that market are CU2 (i.e. the net amount that would be received is CU21). In Market B, the price that would be received is CU25, transaction costs in that market are CU1 and the costs to transport the asset to that market are CU2 (i.e. the net amount that would be received in Market B is CU22).

If Market A is the principal market for the asset (i.e. the market with the greatest volume and level of activity for the asset), the fair value of the asset would be measured using the price that would be received in that market, after taking into account transport costs (CU24).

If neither market is the principal market for the asset, the fair value of the asset would be measured using the price in the most advantageous market. The most advantageous market is the market that maximises the amount that would be received to sell the asset, after taking into account transaction costs and transport costs (i.e. the net amount that would be received in the respective markets).

Because the entity would maximise the net amount that would be received for the asset in Market B (CU22), the fair value of the asset would be measured using the price in that market (CU25), less transport costs (CU2), resulting in a fair value measurement of CU23. Although transaction costs are taken into account when determining which market is the most advantageous market, the price used to measure the fair value of the asset is not adjusted for those costs (although it is adjusted for transport costs).

IFRS 13 requires entities to ensure fair value measurements reflect characteristics specific to the asset or liability. Consequently, *if* location is a characteristic of an asset, an entity should consider transport costs when measuring the fair value of the asset.

4 Measuring the fair value of non-financial assets – highest and best use

The application of IFRS 13's requirements under this heading is limited to non-financial assets. This concept is not relevant for financial assets, liabilities or an entity's own equity instruments because those items do not have alternative uses as contemplated in IFRS 13. [IFRS 13:BC63] Consequently, this topic is not dealt with in this chapter but is discussed in **section 4** of **chapter A6** of **Volume A** of this manual.

5 Measuring the fair value of financial liabilities and an entity's own equity instruments

5.1 Measuring the fair value of liabilities and an entity's own equity instruments – general

5.1.1 General principles

The fair value of a financial liability or an entity's own equity instruments (e.g. an equity share issued as part of the consideration in a business combination) is measured based on the assumption that the liability or equity instrument is transferred to a market participant at the measurement date. [IFRS 13:34]

For a financial liability, it is assumed that the liability would remain outstanding and the market participant transferee would be required to fulfil the obligation. It would not be settled with the counterparty or otherwise extinguished on the measurement date. [IFRS 13:34(a)]

IFRS 13 is clear that the fair value of a liability is based on a transfer amount, i.e. the amount the reporting entity would need to pay a third party to take on the obligation, and that obligation remains outstanding and contractually unaltered before and after transfer. Fair value is therefore *not* based on the premise of settling the liability with the counterparty at the measurement date.

For an entity's own equity instrument, it is assumed that the equity instrument would remain outstanding and the market participant transferee would take on the rights and responsibilities associated with the instrument. The instrument would not be cancelled or otherwise extinguished on the measurement date. [IFRS 13:34(b)]

IFRS 13 requires that the fair value measurement be based on an assumed transfer to a market participant even if an entity does not intend to transfer its liability or own equity instrument to a third party (e.g. because the entity has advantages relative to the market that make it more beneficial for the entity to fulfil the liability using its own internal resources) or it is unable to do so (e.g. because the counterparty would not permit the liability to be transferred to another party). [IFRS 13:BC81 & 82]

Even when there is no observable market to provide pricing information about the transfer of a liability or an entity's own equity instruments (e.g. because contractual or other legal restrictions prevent the transfer of such items), there might be an observable market for such items if they are held by other parties as assets (see **5.1.2**). [IFRS 13:35]

Consistent with the objective of fair value measurement and the prioritisation in the fair value hierarchy (see **section 10**), when measuring the fair value of a liability or an entity's own equity instrument at fair value, the entity should maximise the use of relevant observable inputs and minimise the use of unobservable inputs.[IFRS 13:36]

5.1.2 Liabilities and equity instruments held by other parties as assets

When a quoted price for the transfer of an identical or a similar financial liability or an entity's own equity instruments is not available, and the identical item is held by another party as an asset, an entity is required to measure the fair value of the financial liability or equity instrument from the perspective of a market participant that holds the identical item as an asset at the measurement date. [IFRS 13:37] This requirement could be relevant, for example, when measuring the fair value of corporate bonds or a call option on an entity's shares. [IFRS 13:35]

Determining the fair value of a financial liability or an entity's own equity instrument from the perspective of the counterparty holding the same instrument as an asset reinforces the notion that the fair value ascribed to the contract is the same irrespective of whether the entity is the issuer or the holder. This is based on the theory that fair value is based on a transaction in which the contract is transferred, as opposed, to being settled or extinguished with the holder. In all cases the fair value is based on the premise that the instrument remains outstanding and therefore is a theoretical transfer value.

In the circumstances described above, the appropriate bases for measuring the fair value of the liability or the entity's own equity instrument are listed below, in descending order of preference:

[IFRS 13:38]

(a) using the quoted price in an active market (see below) for the identical item held by another party as an asset, if that price is available;

(b) if that price is not available, using other observable inputs, such as the quoted price in a market that is not active for the identical item held by another party as an asset; and

(c) if the observable prices in (a) and (b) above are not available, using another valuation technique, such as:

   (i) an income approach (e.g. a present value technique that takes into account the future cash flows that a market participant would expect to receive from holding the liability or equity instrument as an asset; see **section 8.6**); or

   (ii) a market approach (e.g. using quoted prices for similar liabilities or equity instruments held as assets; see **8.4**).

An active market is defined as "[a] market in which transactions for the asset or liability take place with sufficient frequency and volume to provide pricing information on an ongoing basis". [IFRS 13:Appendix A]

A quoted price of a liability or an entity's equity instrument held by another party as an asset should be adjusted only if there are factors specific to the asset that are not applicable to the fair value measurement of the liability or equity instrument. An entity should ensure that the price of the asset does not reflect the effect of a restriction preventing the sale of an asset. [IFRS 13:39]

The Standard provides the following examples of factors that might indicate that the quoted price of the asset should be adjusted.

[IFRS 13:39]

- The quoted price for the asset relates to a similar (but not identical) liability or equity instrument held by another party as an asset. For example, the liability or equity instrument may have a particular characteristic (e.g. the credit quality of the issuer) that is different from that reflected in the fair value of the similar liability or equity instrument held as an asset.

- The unit of account for the asset is not the same as for the liability or equity instrument. For example, for liabilities, in some cases the price for an asset reflects a combined price for a package comprising both the amounts due from the issuer and a third-party credit enhancement. If the unit of account for the liability is not for the combined package, the objective is to measure the fair value of the issuer's liability, not the fair value of the combined package. In such circumstances, the entity would adjust the observed price for the asset to exclude the effect of the third-party credit enhancement.

5.1.3 Liabilities and equity instruments not held by other parties as assets

5.1.3.1 Liabilities and equity instruments not held by other parties as assets – general

When a quoted price for the transfer of an identical or a similar liability or entity's own equity instrument is not available, and the identical item is not held by another party as an asset, the fair value of the liability or equity instrument is required to be measured using a valuation technique from the perspective of a market participant that owes the liability or has issued the claim on equity. [IFRS 13:40]

For example, when applying a present value technique, an entity might take into account either of the following:

[IFRS 13:41]

- the future cash outflows that a market participant would expect to incur in fulfilling the obligation, including the compensation that a market participant would require for taking on the obligation; or
- the amount that a market participant would receive to enter into or issue an identical liability or equity instrument, using the assumptions that market participants would use when pricing the identical item (e.g. having the same credit characteristics) in the principal (or most advantageous) market for issuing a liability or an equity instrument with the same contractual terms.

5.1.3.2 Estimating future cash outflows

IFRS 13's general guidance regarding the use of present value techniques is discussed in detail in **8.6.1** to **8.6.3**. This section covers the Standard's specific guidance for applying present value techniques to liabilities and an entity's own equity instruments not held by other parties as assets.

When using a present value technique to measure the fair value of a liability that is not held by another party as an asset, an entity should, among other things, estimate the future cash outflows that market participants would expect to incur in fulfilling the obligation. [IFRS 13:B31]

Those future cash outflows should include:

[IFRS 13:B31]

- market participants' expectations about the costs of fulfilling the obligation; and
- the compensation that a market participant would require for taking on the obligation.

The compensation that a market participant would require for taking on the obligation should include the return that a market participant would require for the following:

[IFRS 13:B31]

- undertaking the activity (i.e. the value of fulfilling the obligation – for example by using resources that could be used for other activities); and
- assuming the risk associated with the obligation (i.e. a risk premium that reflects the risk that the actual cash outflows might differ from the expected cash outflows).

IFRS 13 defines a risk premium (also referred to as a 'risk adjustment') as "[c]ompensation sought by risk-averse market participants for bearing the uncertainty inherent in the cash flows of an asset or a liability". [IFRS 13:Appendix A] A risk premium can be included in the fair value measurement of a liability or an entity's own equity instrument that is not held by another party as an asset in one of the following ways:

[IFRS 13:B33]

- by adjusting the cash flows (i.e. as an increase in the amount of cash outflows); or
- by adjusting the rate used to discount the future cash flows to their present values (i.e. as a reduction in the discount rate).

An entity should ensure that it does not double-count or omit adjustments for risk. For example, if the estimated cash flows are increased to take into account the compensation for assuming the risk associated with the obligation, the discount rate should not be adjusted to reflect that risk. [IFRS 13:B33]

5.2 Non-performance risk

5.2.1 Requirement to reflect the effect of non-performance risk

The fair value of a liability reflects the effect of non-performance risk. [IFRS 13:42]

Non-performance risk is defined as "[t]he risk that an entity will not fulfil its obligation. Non-performance risk includes, but may not be limited to, the entity's own credit risk". [IFRS 13:Appendix A] IFRS 7:Appendix A defines credit risk as "[t]he risk that one party to a financial instrument will cause a financial loss for the other party by failing to discharge an obligation".

Non-performance risk is assumed to be the same before and after the transfer of the liability. [IFRS 13:42]

The IASB acknowledges in the Basis for Conclusions of IFRS 13 that it is unlikely that non-performance risk is the same before and after the transfer of the financial liability. However, the IASB concluded that such an assumption was necessary when measuring the fair value of a financial liability in order for the transfer concept to apply. If the transferee, acting as a market participant, had a different credit standing to the transferor it would not take on the obligation of the transferor because either (1) in the case of the transferee's credit standing being worse than the transferor's, the counterparty to the obligation would not permit the transfer to take place, or (2) in the case of the transferee's credit standing being better than the transferor's, the transferee would not choose to take on the obligation without renegotiating the terms to reflect the difference in credit standing.

Furthermore, if it is assumed that market participants have different credit standings, this would result in fundamentally different valuations depending on the identity of the transferee. It was also noted that those that hold the entity's obligations as assets do consider the effect of an entity's credit risk and other risk factors when pricing those assets and, therefore, this effect should be equally reflected in the fair value of the entity's obligations to those holders of assets. [IFRS 13:BC94]

When evaluating the non-performance risk (including credit risk) of a financial liability for the purpose of measuring its fair value, it is useful to refer to the October 2008 report issued by the IASB's Expert Advisory Panel titled *Measuring and Disclosing the Fair Value of Financial Instruments in Markets That Are No Longer Active*. The report describes practices entities use when measuring financial instruments at fair value. In paragraph 35 of the report, the Panel noted that "[u] nderstanding the credit risk of a debt instrument involves evaluating the credit quality and financial strength of both the issuer and the credit support providers".

Paragraph 35 of the report also lists the following as some of the more common factors that an entity should consider.

"(a) **Collateral asset quality**: the assets to which the holder of an instrument has recourse in the event of non-payment or default could be either all of the assets of the issuing entity or specified assets that are legally separated from the issuer (ring-fenced). The greater the value and quality of the assets to which an entity has recourse in the event of default, the lower the credit risk of the instrument. Measuring the fair value of a debt instrument therefore involves assessing the quality of the assets that support the instrument (the collateral) and the level of the collateralisation, and evaluating the likelihood that the assigned collateral will generate adequate cash flows to make the contractual payments on the instrument.

(b) **Subordination**: the level of subordination of an instrument is critical to assessing the risk of non-payment of an instrument. If other more senior instruments have higher claims over the cash flows and assets that support the instrument, this increases the risk of the instrument. The lower the claim on the cash flows and assets, the more risky an instrument is and the higher the return the market will demand on the instrument.

(c) **Non-payment protection**: many instruments contain some form of protection to reduce the risk of non-payment to the holder. In measuring fair value, both the issuer and the holder of the instrument consider the effect of the protection on the fair value of the instrument, unless the entity accounts for the protection as a separate instrument. Protection might take the form of a guarantee or a similar undertaking (e.g. when a parent guarantees the debt of a subsidiary), an insurance contract, a credit default swap or simply the fact that more assets support the instrument than are needed to make the payments (this is commonly referred to as over-collateralisation). The risk of non-payment is also reduced by the existence of more subordinated tranches of instruments that take the first losses on the underlying assets and therefore reduce the risk of more senior tranches absorbing losses. When protection is in the form of a guarantee, an insurance contract or a credit default swap, it is necessary to identify the party providing the protection and assess that party's creditworthiness (to the extent that the protection is not accounted for separately). The protection will be more valuable if the credit risk of the protection provider is low. This analysis involves considering not only the current position of the protection provider but also the effect of other guarantees or insurance contracts that it might have written. For example, if the provider has guaranteed many correlated debt securities, the risk of its non-performance might increase significantly with increases in defaults on those securities. In addition, the credit risk of some protection providers moves as market conditions change. Thus, an entity evaluates the credit risk of each protection provider at each measurement date."

Although paragraph 35 of the Expert Advisory Panel report refers to the valuation of a 'debt instrument', the factors listed above would also be relevant in determining the non-performance risk for a derivative.

Example 5.2.1A

Impact of a guarantee by an acquirer on the fair value of an acquiree's loan

Entity A acquires 100 per cent of Entity B from Entity C in a business combination. One of the identifiable liabilities of Entity B is a loan owed to a third party. The loan was originally guaranteed by Entity C as part of the loan terms. However, as a result of the business combination, the terms of the loan are revised so that Entity A becomes the guarantor of the loan (i.e. the guarantee by Entity A becomes part of the revised loan terms).

IFRS 3 *Business Combinations* requires that the third party loan is measured at fair value at the date of acquisition. The measurement requirements of IFRS 13 apply.

There are no quoted prices available for the transfer of an identical or a similar liability.

When measuring the fair value of the loan at the date of acquisition for the purpose of preparing consolidated financial statements, Entity A should take into account the effect of its own guarantee of the loan because the guarantee is part of the loan terms.

As discussed in **5.1.1**, IFRS 13:37 requires that when a quoted price for the transfer of an identical or a similar liability is not available, and the identical item is held by another party as an asset, an entity should measure the fair value of the liability from the perspective of a market participant that holds the identical item as an asset at the measurement date.

In the circumstances described, the loan is guaranteed by Entity A from the date of acquisition. From the perspective of a market participant holding the loan as an asset, the fact that the loan is guaranteed by Entity A would be taken into account when measuring the fair value of the loan receivable because the market participant would expect to recover the loan from Entity A if Entity B defaulted on the loan. Consequently, when measuring the fair value of the loan, a market participant would take into account (1) the credit standing of Entity B, and (2) the guarantee provided by Entity A.

This is also consistent with the requirement in IFRS 13:43 (see below) that an entity should take into account the effect of its own credit risk (credit standing) and any other factors that might influence the likelihood that the obligation will or will not be fulfilled.

The effect of an entity's credit standing and any other factors that might influence the likelihood that the obligation will or will not be fulfilled may differ depending on the nature of the liability (e.g. whether it is a financial or a non-financial liability, or whether any credit enhancements are attached). [IFRS 13:43]

To understand non-performance risk, consideration has to be given to the specific terms of the instrument rather than simply looking at the overall credit rating or quality of the entity in its entirety. Looking at the latter will generally obscure the particular credit characteristics of the instrument itself, like credit enhancements, or fail to reflect the relative seniority or subordination of the liability relative to the liabilities of the entity.

Example 5.2.1B

Fair value of a financial liability – impact of credit rating

[IFRS 13:IE32]

Entity X and Entity Y each enter into a contractual obligation to pay cash (CU500) to Entity Z in five years. Entity X has a AA credit rating and can borrow at 6 per cent, and Entity Y has a BBB credit rating and can borrow at 12 per cent. Entity X will receive about CU374 in exchange for its promise (the present value of CU500 in five years at 6 per cent). Entity Y will receive about CU284 in exchange for its promise (the present value of CU500 in five years at 12 per cent). The fair value of the liability to each entity (i.e. the proceeds) incorporates that entity's credit standing.

Example 5.2.1C

Fair value of a financial liability – structured note

[IFRS 13:IE34 – Example 10]

On 1 January 20X7 Entity A, an investment bank with a AA credit rating, issues a five-year fixed rate note to Entity B. The contractual principal amount to be paid by Entity A at maturity is linked to an equity index. No credit enhancements are issued in conjunction with or otherwise related to the contract (i.e. no collateral is posted and there is no third-party guarantee). Entity A has designated this note as at fair value through profit or loss. The fair value of the note (i.e. the obligation of Entity A) during 20X7 is measured using an expected present value technique. Changes in fair value are as follows:

(a) Fair value at 1 January 20X7. The expected cash flows used in the expected present value technique are discounted at the risk-free rate using the government bond curve at 1 January 20X7, plus the current market observable AA corporate bond spread to government bonds, if non-performance risk is not already reflected in the cash flows, adjusted (either up or down) for Entity A's specific credit risk (i.e. resulting in a credit-adjusted risk-free rate). Therefore, the fair value of Entity A's obligation at initial recognition takes into account non-performance risk, including that entity's credit risk, which presumably is reflected in the proceeds (and is the same as the transaction price).

(b) Fair value at 31 March 20X7. During March 20X7 the credit spread for AA corporate bonds widens, with no changes to the specific credit risk of Entity A. The expected cash flows used in the expected present value technique are discounted at the risk-free rate using the government bond curve at 31 March 20X7, plus the current market observable AA corporate bond spread to government bonds, if non-performance risk is not already reflected in the cash flows, adjusted for Entity A's specific credit risk (i.e. resulting in a credit-adjusted risk-free rate). Entity A's specific credit risk is unchanged from initial recognition. Therefore, the fair value of Entity A's obligation changes as a result of changes in credit spreads generally.

Changes in credit spreads reflect current market participant assumptions about changes in non-performance risk generally, changes in liquidity risk, and the compensation required for assuming those risks.

(c) Fair value at 30 June 20X7. As of 30 June 20X7 there have been no changes to the AA corporate bond spreads. However, on the basis of structured note issues corroborated with other qualitative information, Entity A determines that its own specific creditworthiness has strengthened within the AA credit spread. The expected cash flows used in the expected present value technique are discounted at the risk-free rate using the government bond yield curve at 30 June 20X7, plus the current market observable AA corporate bond spread to government bonds (unchanged from 31 March 20X7), if non-performance risk is not already reflected in the cash flows, adjusted for Entity A's specific credit risk (i.e. resulting in a credit-adjusted risk-free rate). Therefore, the fair value of the obligation of Entity A changes as a result of the change in its own specific credit risk within the AA corporate bond spread.

Example 5.2.1D

Fair value of a financial liability – debt obligation: quoted price

[IFRS 13:IE40-42 – Example 12]

On 1 January 20X1 Entity B issues at par a CU2 million BBB-rated exchange-traded five-year fixed rate debt instrument with an annual 10 per cent coupon. Entity B designated this financial liability as at fair value through profit or loss.

On 31 December 20X1 the instrument is trading as an asset in an active market at CU929 per CU1,000 of par value after payment of accrued interest. Entity B uses the quoted price of the asset in an active market as its initial input into the fair value measurement of its liability (CU929 [CU2 million CU1,000] = CU1,858,000).

In determining whether the quoted price of the asset in an active market represents the fair value of the liability, Entity B evaluates whether the quoted price of the asset includes the effect of factors not applicable to the fair value measurement of a liability, for example, whether the quoted price of the asset includes the effect of a third-party credit enhancement if that credit enhancement would be separately accounted for from the perspective of the issuer. Entity B determines that no adjustments are required to the quoted price of the asset. Accordingly, Entity B concludes that the fair value of its debt instrument at 31 December 20X1 is CU1,858,000. Entity B categorises and discloses the fair value measurement of its debt instrument within Level 1 of the fair value hierarchy.

Example 5.2.1E

Fair value of a financial liability – debt obligation: present value technique

[IFRS 13:IE43-47 – Example 13]

On 1 January 20X1 Entity C issues at par in a private placement a CU2 million BBB-rated five-year fixed-rate debt instrument with an annual 10 per cent coupon. Entity C designated this financial liability as at fair value through profit or loss.

At 31 December 20X1 Entity C still carries a BBB credit rating. Market conditions, including available interest rates, credit spreads for a BBB-quality credit rating and liquidity, remain unchanged from the date the debt instrument was issued. However, Entity C's credit spread has deteriorated by 50 basis points because of a change in its risk of non-performance. After taking into account all market conditions, Entity C concludes that if it was to issue the instrument at the measurement date, the instrument would bear a rate of interest of 10.5 per cent or Entity C would receive less than par in proceeds from the issue of the instrument.

For the purpose of this example, the fair value of Entity C's liability is calculated using a present value technique. Entity C concludes that a market participant would use all of the following inputs (consistently with paragraphs B12–B30 of the IFRS) when estimating the price the market participant would expect to receive to assume Entity C's obligation:

(a) the terms of the debt instrument, including all of the following:
   (i) coupon of 10 per cent;
   (ii) principal amount of CU2 million; and
   (iii) term of four years.
(b) the market rate of interest of 10.5 per cent (which includes a change of 50 basis points in the risk of non-performance from the date of issue).

On the basis of its present value technique, Entity C concludes that the fair value of its liability at 31 December 20X1 is CU1,968,641.

Entity C does not include any additional input into its present value technique for risk or profit that a market participant might require for compensation for assuming the liability. Entity C's obligation is a financial liability, hence, Entity C concludes that the interest rate already captures the risk or profit that a market participant would require as compensation for assuming the liability. Furthermore, Entity C does not adjust its present value technique for the existence of a restriction preventing it from transferring the liability.

The fair value measurement for a liability should reflect the effect of non-performance risk based on the unit of account for financial reporting purposes specified in relevant IFRSs (see also **3.1**). The issuer of a liability issued with an inseparable third-party credit enhancement (e.g. a third-party guarantee of debt) that is accounted for separately from the liability should not include the effect of the credit enhancement in the fair value measurement of the liability; in such circumstances, the fair value measurement should reflect the credit standing of the issuer and not that of the third-party guarantor. [IFRS 13:44]

As required under IFRS 13:44, when an entity has a liability with a third-party guarantee, and the liability and the guarantee are accounted for separately under relevant IFRSs, the fair value of the liability should not reflect the effect of the guarantee. In such circumstances, the fair value of the liability from the issuer's perspective will not equal its fair value as a guaranteed liability held by another party as an asset. [IFRS 13:BC98]

5.2.2 Effect of collateral on fair value measurement of liabilities

When an entity has provided collateral in respect of a liability, this will affect the fair value measurement of the liability under IFRS 13. As discussed at **5.2**, IFRS 13:42 requires that the fair value of a liability should reflect the effect of non-performance risk, and that non-performance risk is assumed to be the same before and after the transfer of the liability. The definition of non-performance risk in IFRS 13:Appendix A (see **section 5.2**) clarifies that it encompasses an entity's own credit risk (credit standing) and any other factors that might influence the likelihood that the obligation will be fulfilled. One factor specifically mentioned in IFRS 13:43(b) is "the terms of credit enhancements related to the liability, if any".

Collateral is a form of credit enhancement that is contractually linked to a liability (i.e. the terms of the obligation require a lien on the collateral until settlement of the obligation). The fact that an entity has provided collateral typically means that the stated terms of the liability (e.g. the interest rate charged) differ from the terms of an identical liability that is not supported by collateral. The collateral is a characteristic of the liability and, consequently, it should be reflected in the fair value measurement of the collateralised liability.

Example 5.2.2 illustrates how collateral might affect the fair value of a liability on initial recognition.

Example 5.2.2

Effect of collateral on fair value measurement of liabilities

On 1 January 20X1, Company A borrows CU10 million repayable in five years. The fixed interest rate is one-year LIBOR plus 125 basis points. Company A is required to pledge specified property interests as collateral. Management estimates that Company A could have arranged a similar loan with no collateral at a 200 basis point spread to LIBOR. On 1 January 20X1, the one-year LIBOR rate is 1.5 percent. For simplicity, transaction costs are ignored.

At 1 January 20X1, the fair value of the loan (including any impact from the collateral) is CU10 million. The present value of the loan's contractual cash flows, discounted at Company A's unsecured borrowing rate of 3.5 percent (i.e. 1.5 percent LIBOR plus 200 basis points), is CU9.7 million.

This example illustrates that the effect of an issuer's credit standing as well as the effect of credit enhancements should be taken into account in measuring the fair value of the liability. If Company A ignored the reduction in the interest rate attributable to the collateral, it would mistakenly conclude that the fair value of its debt was CU9.7 million rather than CU10 million.

5.2.3 Effect of changes in non-performance risk

Changes in the fair value of collateral or an entity's credit standing should be taken into account in measuring the fair value of a liability on an ongoing basis. This is to ensure that the fair value measurement reflects market participant assumptions at the measurement date.

Examples 5.2.3A and **5.2.3B** illustrate the effect of some of these factors on the fair value of collateralised obligations.

Example 5.2.3A

Effect of a decline in the fair value of collateral

On 1 January 20X1, Company B issues CU100 million of bonds collateralised by a portion of its aircraft fleet. On 30 September 20X3, there has been a substantial decline in the fair value of the aircraft that serve as collateral for the bonds. Assume that Company B's credit standing remains unchanged and all other stated terms of the bonds represent current market conditions for the remaining term of the obligation.

When measuring the fair value of the bonds at 30 September 20X3, Company B must do so from the perspective of a market participant that holds the bonds as an asset (i.e. a bondholder) – see **5.1.1**. [IFRS 13:37] A market participant would reflect the reduced level of collateral in the price at which a transfer of the bond would take place.

Company B determines that the hypothetical market participant would be willing to transfer the liability for only CU80 million. In other words, the fair value of the bonds has decreased by CU20 million due to the decline in value of the collateral even though Company B's credit standing remains unchanged.

Example 5.2.3B

Effect of a decline in the borrower's credit standing

Assume the same facts as in **example 5.2.3A** except that, at 30 September 20X3, the fair value of the aircraft pledged as collateral remains unchanged. Instead, the credit standing of Company B has declined from AAA to AA-.

When measuring the fair value of the bonds at 30 September 20X3, Company B is required to consider the effect of the decline in its credit standing but also the fact that the fair value of the collateral has not changed.

Company B observes that the wider credit spread for uncollateralised AA- corporate bonds suggests that the fair value of the bonds has declined by 10 per cent (i.e. to CU90 million). However, because the fair value of the collateral has not changed, the note remains well collateralised. Consequently, the fair value of the note may not have declined by as much as 10 per cent. Company B determines that the increase in non-performance risk arising from the decline in its own credit standing is partially offset by the collateral. Based on credit spreads observed for similar, collateralised bonds, Company B concludes that the fair value of the notes has decreased by CU7 million to CU93 million.

5.3 Restriction preventing the transfer of a liability or an entity's own equity instrument

When measuring the fair value of a liability or an entity's own equity instrument, no separate input or adjustment to other inputs should be included to reflect the existence of a restriction that prevents the transfer of the item. The effect of a restriction that prevents the transfer of a liability is either implicitly or explicitly included in the other inputs to the fair value measurement. [IFRS 13:45]

For example, at the transaction date for a liability, both the creditor and the obligor accepted the transaction price for the liability with full knowledge that the obligation includes a restriction that prevents its transfer. As a result of the restriction being included in the transaction price, a separate input or an adjustment to an existing input is not required at the transaction date to reflect the effect of the restriction on transfer. Similarly, a separate input or an adjustment to an existing input is not required at subsequent measurement dates to reflect the effect of the restriction on transfer. [IFRS 13:46]

5.4 Financial liability with a demand feature

The fair value of a financial liability with a demand feature (e.g. a demand deposit) is not less than the amount payable on demand, discounted from the first date that the amount could be required to be paid. [IFRS 13:47]

6 Measuring the fair value of financial assets and financial liabilities with offsetting positions in market risks or counterparty credit risk

An entity that holds a group of financial assets and financial liabilities is exposed to market risks (as defined in IFRS 7) and to the credit risk (as defined in IFRS 7) of each of the counterparties. If the entity manages that group of financial assets and financial liabilities on the basis of its net exposure to either market risks or credit risk, the entity is permitted to apply an exception to the general requirements of IFRS 13 for measuring fair value.

The exception permits an entity to measure the fair value of a group of financial assets and financial liabilities on the basis of the price that would be received to sell a net long position (i.e. an asset) for a particular risk exposure or to transfer a net short position (i.e. a liability) for a particular risk exposure in an orderly transaction between market participants at the measurement date under current market conditions. This fair value measure for the group of financial assets and financial liabilities should be consistent with how market participants would price the net risk exposure at the measurement date. [IFRS 13:48] This exception only applies to financial assets, financial liabilities and other contracts within the scope of IFRS 9. [IFRS 13:52]

In December 2013 the IASB issued *Annual Improvements to IFRSs 2011–2013* Cycle that amended IFRS 13:52 to clarify that the portfolio exception applies to all contracts within the scope of IFRS 9 regardless of whether they meet the definitions of financial assets or financial liabilities as defined in IAS 32. The clarification was in response to questions raised about whether the scope included contracts that are accounted for as if they were financial instruments, but that do not meet the definitions of financial assets or financial liabilities in IAS 32, such as contracts to buy or sell a non-financial item that can be settled net in cash or another financial instrument, or by exchanging financial instruments, as if the contracts were financial instruments.

An entity shall apply that amendment for annual periods beginning on or after 1 July 2014. An entity shall apply that amendment prospectively from the beginning of the annual period in which IFRS 13 was initially applied. Earlier application is permitted. If an entity applies that amendment for an earlier period it shall disclose that fact. [IFRS 13:C4]

An entity is permitted to apply the measurement exception in IFRS 13:48 to a portfolio that contains ***only*** financial assets (as opposed to a group of financial assets and financial liabilities) provided that the financial instruments have offsetting positions in market risks or counterparty credit risk and that the detailed conditions in IFRS 13:49 (see below) are met.

An example of a portfolio containing only financial assets is a portfolio of bonds measured at fair value and purchased credit default swaps also measured at fair value. The credit default swaps may provide an offset to the credit risk associated with the specific bonds.

An entity is permitted to use this exception only if the entity does all of the following:

[IFRS 13:49]

- it manages the group of financial assets and financial liabilities on the basis of the entity's net exposure to a particular market risk (or risks) or to the credit risk of a particular counterparty in accordance with the entity's documented risk management or investment strategy;
- it provides information on that basis about the group of financial assets and financial liabilities to the entity's key management personnel, as defined in IAS 24 *Related Party Disclosures*; and
- it is required or has elected to measure those financial assets and financial liabilities at fair value in the statement of financial position at the end of each reporting period.

This exception does not apply for financial statement presentation. When the basis for the presentation of financial instruments in the statement of financial position differs from the group basis for the measurement of financial instruments (e.g. if IAS 32 does not require the group of financial instruments to be presented on a net basis) an entity may need to allocate the portfolio-level adjustments to the individual instruments that make up the group. That allocation should be performed on a reasonable and consistent basis using a methodology appropriate in the circumstances. [IFRS 13:50]

A common example of an adjustment made at the portfolio level as contemplated in IFRS 13:48 is a credit valuation adjustment (CVA). An entity might incorporate the effect of exposure to a particular counterparty's credit risk by netting its derivative asset and liability contracts with a given counterparty in accordance with a master netting arrangement and then calculate a CVA on the basis of the net position with the counterparty.

Another example of a portfolio-level adjustment is a 'mid-to-bid' or 'mid-to-ask' adjustment. A derivatives dealer might initially compute the value of a portfolio of both its long (buy) and short (sell) derivative positions with the same underlying risk using the mid-point in the bid-ask spread. The derivatives dealer would then make a 'mid-to-bid' or 'mid-to-ask' adjustment at the portfolio level effectively to move the net open position of the portfolio to the bid or ask price depending on whether the portfolio is net long or net short by period.

The question arises as to how should an entity allocate a portfolio-level adjustment to the individual financial assets and financial liabilities in the portfolio.

IFRS 13:50 requires that an entity should allocate a portfolio-level adjustment to the individual financial assets and financial liabilities in the portfolio on a reasonable and consistent basis using a methodology appropriate in the circumstances.

The following table illustrates one approach to allocating a CVA to a group of derivative contracts under a master netting arrangement with a single counterparty.

	Asset/(Liability) in CU	**Hierarchy level (prior to allocation of CVA)**
Contract A	100	2
Contract B	200	3
Contract C	(175)	3
Net position before CVA	125	Not applicable
Credit valuation adjustment	(10)	See discussion below
Fair value of portfolio	115	Not applicable

The unit of account, in this example, is each individual derivative contract in its entirety. Accordingly, the CU10 CVA must be allocated to the units of account within the portfolio. For example, the entity might allocate the CU10 CVA on the basis of the relative fair value of the asset positions (Contracts A and B in the example above). The resulting fair value of Contract A would be CU97 (i.e. CU100 less 100/300 x CU10). The resulting fair value of Contract B would be CU193 (i.e. CU200 less 200/300 x CU10). Other approaches may also be appropriate depending on the circumstances.

When a portfolio-level adjustment is allocated to individual assets and/or liabilities in the circumstances described, this will affect the classification of the assets and/or liabilities within IFRS 13's fair value hierarchy (see **section 10**). An allocated portfolio adjustment is an input to the measurement of the fair value of the asset or liability. If such an input is not based on observable data and has a significant effect on the measurement of the fair value of an individual asset or liability, the fair value measurement is categorised in Level 3 of the fair value hierarchy.

Assume in the example above that, before the allocation of the CVA, the inputs used in determining the fair value of Contract A were based on observable market data. However, if the effect of the counterparty's credit risk is not considered observable market data, the allocated amount of CVA is a Level 3 input. In determining the classification of Contract A within the hierarchy, the entity must determine whether the amount of CVA allocated to Contract A is significant to the measurement of Contract A in its entirety (see **10.3.3.1** for discussion). Because the CVA is unobservable, if the allocated portion of the CVA for Contract A is considered significant, then Contract A would be classified in Level 3 in its entirety.

During the IASB and FASB's deliberations it was noted that some respondents requested additional guidance for allocating the bid-ask and credit adjustments to the individual assets and liabilities that make up the group of financial assets and financial liabilities. The Boards noted that although any allocation method is inherently subjective, it was concluded that a quantitative allocation would be appropriate if it was reasonable and consistently applied. Therefore, the Boards decided not to require a particular method of allocation. [IFRS 13:BC131]

The application of this exception is an accounting policy choice in accordance with IAS 8 and, when selected, should be applied consistently from period to period (including the entity's policy for allocating any portfolio adjustments). [IFRS 13:51]

In May 2013 the Interpretations Committee received a request to clarify the interaction between the use of Level 1 inputs and the portfolio exception set out in IFRS 13. The portfolio exception in IFRS 13 permits an entity to measure its net exposure to either market risks or credit risk arising from a group of financial assets and financial liabilities in specified circumstances. The portfolio exception was intended to align the valuation of financial instruments for financial reporting with an entity's internal risk management practices. In particular, the issue that was discussed by the Interpretations Committee was whether an entity is:

(a) permitted to apply the portfolio exception in IFRS 13 to measure the resulting net risk exposure of a portfolio made up solely with identical Level 1 instruments; or

(b) required to measure the financial assets and the financial liabilities of such a portfolio on an individual basis, using the corresponding Level 1 prices for each financial instrument.

In its discussions, the Interpretations Committee observed that, in relation to (a) above, the main question that needs to be addressed is whether an entity:

(a) would be required to measure such a net risk exposure on the basis of the Level 1 prices for the individual instruments that comprise that net risk exposure; or

(b) would be allowed to consider the net risk exposure as a whole and, consequently, consider adjusting it with any appropriate premiums or discounts.

The Interpretations Committee noted that there was insufficient guidance in the Standard for it to be able to answer this question and so it decided that this issue needs to be considered by the IASB. Accordingly it asked the staff to present the Interpretations Committee's concerns to the IASB.

The IASB also noted that this issue has similarities with the issue of the interaction between the use of Level 1 inputs and the unit of account that arises when measuring the fair value of investments in subsidiaries, joint ventures and associates (discussed above). Consequently, the IASB included this issue in Exposure Draft ED/2014/4 *Measuring Quoted Investments in Subsidiaries, Joint Ventures and Associates at Fair Value* issued in September 2014. In the ED the IASB included an illustrative example to illustrate the application of IFRS 13:48 to a group of financial assets and financial liabilities whose market risks are substantially the same and whose fair value measurement is categorised within Level 1 of the fair value hierarchy.

As part of the IASB's redeliberations following the publication of the ED, the illustrative example was discussed by the IASB in April 2015 when it decided that the example appropriately illustrates the application of IFRS 13:48. That is, if an entity elects to use the exception in IFRS 13:48, the appropriate fair value measurement of the net risk exposure arising from a group of financial assets and financial liabilities whose market risks are substantially the same, and whose fair value measurement is categorised within Level 1 of the fair value hierarchy, would be determined by multiplying the financial instruments included in the resulting net position by the corresponding unadjusted Level 1 price.

The IASB noted that the proposed illustrative example to IFRS 13 is non-authoritative, and the comments received did not reveal significant diversity in practice. Accordingly, the IASB concluded that it was unnecessary to publish the proposed illustrative example in IFRS 13 as a separate document. Therefore the illustrative example is not due to be published by the IASB.

The example below is taken from the IASB staff paper that was discussed by the IASB in April 2015 (agenda reference 6). It is based on the illustrative example from the ED but also includes changes proposed by the IASB staff following feedback received on the ED.

Example 6

Measuring the fair value of a portfolio of Level 1 financial assets and financial liabilities with offsetting risk positions

Entity A holds a group of financial assets and financial liabilities consisting of a long position of 10,000 financial assets and a short position of 9,500 financial liabilities whose market risks are substantially the same. Entity A manages that group of financial assets and financial liabilities on the basis of its net exposure to market risks. The fair value measurement of all financial instruments in the group is categorised within Level 1 of the fair value hierarchy.

The bid-ask spread is CU98-CU102, with the mid-price being CU100. The most representative bid price is CU99 and the most representative ask price is CU101.

Entity A applies the exception in IFRS 13:48 that permits Entity A to measure the fair value of the group of financial assets and financial liabilities on the basis of the price that would be received to sell, in this particular case, a net long position (i.e. an asset) for the exposure to market risks in an orderly transaction between market participants at the measurement date under current market conditions.

Since the market risks arising from the financial instruments are substantially the same, the measurement of the net exposure to market risks arising from the group of financial assets and financial liabilities coincides with the measurement of the net long position (500 financial assets). Consequently, Entity A measures the group of financial assets and financial liabilities on the basis of the price that it would receive if it would exit its outstanding net exposure to market risks as follows:

	Quantity held (Q)	Level 1 price (CU) (P)	(CU) P × Q
Net exposure to market risks, which in this case coincide with the measurement of the net long position	500	99	49,500

Entity A would also have achieved the same measurement of CU49,500 by measuring the net exposure to market risks at the mid-price (i.e. CU100 × 500 = CU50,000) adjusted by a bid-offer reserve (CU1 × 500 = CU500).

Since the basis for the presentation of the financial instruments in the statement of financial position differs from the basis for their measurement, Entity A subsequently allocates the portfolio-level adjustments (i.e. CU49,500) to the individual (10,000) financial assets and (9,500) financial liabilities. In accordance with IFRS 13:50 and 51, Entity A performs this allocation on a reasonable basis that is consistent with previous allocations of that nature using a methodology appropriate to the circumstances.

6.1 Exposure to market risks

Consistent with the normal fair value measurement requirements, when measuring the fair value of a group of assets and liabilities based on the net exposure to one or more market risks, IFRS 13 requires an entity to apply the price within the bid-ask spread that is most representative of fair value in the circumstances to the entity's net exposure to those market risks. [IFRS 13:53]

In order to measure a group of financial assets and financial liabilities on a net basis for a particular market risk, it is necessary for that market risk within that group of financial assets and financial liabilities to be substantially the same. For example, an entity would not combine the interest rate risk associated with a financial asset with the commodity price risk associated with a financial liability because doing so would not mitigate the entity's exposure to interest rate risk or commodity price risk. [IFRS 13:54]

In some cases, the market risk parameters will not be identical due to basis differences. In those cases the basis risk should be taken into account in the fair value measurement of the financial assets and financial liabilities within the group. [IFRS 13:54]

Similarly, the term of the entity's exposure to market risk arising from the financial assets and financial liabilities should be substantially the same. For example, an entity that uses a 12-month futures contract against the cash flows associated with 12 months' worth of interest rate risk exposure on a five-year financial instrument within a group made up of only those financial assets and financial liabilities measures the fair value of the exposure to 12-month interest rate risk on a net basis and the remaining interest rate risk exposure (i.e. Years 2–5) on a gross basis. [IFRS 13:55]

6.2 Exposure to the credit risk of a particular counterparty

When applying the fair value measurement exception described in **section 6** above for financial instruments with the same counterparty, the entity should include the effect of the entity's net exposure to the credit risk of that counterparty or the counterparty's net exposure to the credit risk of the entity in the fair value measurement when market participants would take into account any existing arrangements that mitigate credit risk exposure (e.g. a master netting agreement with the counterparty or an agreement that requires the exchange of collateral on the basis of each party's net exposure to the credit risk of the other party) in the event of default. The fair value measurement should reflect market participant expectations about the likelihood that such an arrangement would be legally enforceable in the event of default. [IFRS 13:56]

Reflecting in the fair value measurement of the portfolio of items the net credit risk exposure with the same counterparty is appropriate where the two parties have an agreement that requires that in the case of default the reporting entity is only required to pay or receive the net amount of the various contracts that are owed to and due from the counterparty. Applying the fair value measurement exception in this case reduces the extent of credit risk included in the measurement of the portfolio of items relative to including credit risk in the measurement of each of the individual items and summing the assets and liabilities together.

Netting the credit risk exposure with the counterparty and reflecting only the credit risk associated with the net open credit risk position is often referred to as a CVA (credit valuation adjustment, or a 'positive CVA') in the case where the reporting entity has a net credit exposure to the counterparty, i.e. where the reporting entity is net owed amounts by the counterparty; or as a DVA (debit valuation adjustment, or a 'negative CVA') in the case where the counterparty has a net credit exposure to the reporting entity, i.e. where the reporting entity owes amounts to the counterparty.

7 Fair value measurement at initial recognition

7.1 Potential for difference between the transaction price and fair value at initial recognition

IFRS 9:5.1.1 requires that all financial assets and financial liabilities, except certain trade receivables, should be recognised initially on the basis of 'fair value'. The exception applies to trade receivables that do not have a significant financing component (determined in accordance with IFRS 15 *Revenue from Contracts with Customers*) that are not initially measured at fair value, rather they are initially measured at their transaction price.

If the asset has been acquired, or the liability assumed, in a market transaction, it might be assumed that the transaction price (i.e. the price paid to acquire an asset or received to assume a liability) can be taken to be the fair value of the asset or the liability. However, the price paid to acquire an asset, or received to assume a liability, is an *entry* price and, consequently, it is not necessarily the same as the fair value of the asset or liability for IFRS 13 purposes (which is an *exit* price – see **section 3**). The Standard notes that entities do not necessarily sell assets at the prices paid to acquire them; nor do they necessarily transfer liabilities at the prices received to assume them. [IFRS 13:57]

7.2 Indicators that the transaction price differs from fair value at initial recognition

When determining whether the fair value at initial recognition equals the transaction price, an entity should take into account factors specific to the transaction and to the asset and liability. [IFRS 13:59]

In many cases the transaction price and the fair value will be equal (e.g. when the transaction date is the same as the measurement date and the asset is acquired in the market in which the asset would be sold). [IFRS 13:58] However, when the amounts are not equal, the asset or liability should be measured at fair value and the difference between the transaction price and fair value (generally referred to as a 'day 1 gain or loss', 'day 1 profit or loss' or as 'day 1 p&l') is required to be recognised as a gain or loss in profit or loss unless the relevant IFRS specifies otherwise. [IFRS 13:60] See **7.3** for the appropriate treatment of 'day 1 p&l' under IFRS 9.

IFRS 13:B4 lists a number of factors which may suggest that the transaction price is not the fair value of the asset or liability at initial recognition.

The following table repeats the factors listed in IFRS 13:B4 and provides examples for each. Note that this list of indicators is not exhaustive, and other factors may exist that should be considered in evaluating whether a transaction price represents fair value (see IFRS 13:BC133).

Factor (IFRS 13:B4)	Example
The transaction is between related parties, although the price in a related party transaction may be used as an input into a fair value measurement if the reporting entity has evidence that the transaction was entered into at market terms.	An entity purchases a portfolio of troubled loans from an unconsolidated investee. The parties meet the definition of related parties under IAS 24 *Related Party Disclosures*. The fact that the parties are related may indicate that the transaction price does not reflect fair value. However, this alone would not be determinative. Evidence that the transaction was entered into at market terms may include: • the appointment of third parties to negotiate or measure fair value; or • the terms of the transaction are consistent with available market data for similar transactions between unrelated parties; or • there is no evidence that one of the parties to the transaction is under duress (see the next factor).
The transaction takes place under duress or the seller is forced to accept the price in the transaction (e.g. if the seller is experiencing financial difficulty).	A hedge fund must sell all of its non-marketable assets in response to a spike in redemptions that may lead to a liquidity crisis. A liquidity crisis may be an indicator of financial difficulty. The factors in IFRS 13:B43 indicating that a transaction is not orderly (see **9.6**) may also indicate that the transaction price does not represent fair value.

Factor (IFRS 13:B4)	Example
The unit of account represented by the transaction price is different from the unit of account for the asset or liability measured at fair value. For example, this might be the case if the asset or liability measured at fair value is only one of the elements in the transaction (e.g. in a business combination), if the transaction includes unstated rights and privileges that are measured separately in accordance with another IFRS, or if the transaction price includes transaction costs.	IFRS 13:14 requires that the unit of account for an asset or a liability should be determined in accordance with the IFRS that requires or permits the fair value measurement, except as provided in IFRS 13 (see **3.2.1**). The following example illustrates a scenario in which the unit of account for the asset is different from the unit of account represented by the transaction price. On 30 June 20X1, Company A acquires a 3 per cent equity interest (3 million shares) in Company B from an independent third party. Quoted prices in an active market are available for Company B's shares. Company A pays CU100 million for the entire 3 per cent equity interest (the transaction price is determined based on a negotiated arm's length price for the entire 3 per cent equity interest). The quoted price for Company B's shares on 30 June 20X1 is CU36 per share. Company A needs to identify the unit of account in order to measure the fair value of the 3 per cent equity interest on initial recognition. In identifying the unit of account for fair value measurement purposes, IFRS 9 is the applicable Standard. IFRS 13:BC47 states, in part, that "[i]n IAS 39 and IFRS 9 the unit of account is generally an individual financial instrument". This guidance is also consistent with the guidance set out in IFRS 13:80 which states that "[i]f an entity holds a position in a single asset… and the asset… is traded in an active market, the fair value of the asset… shall be measured within Level 1 as the product of the quoted price for the individual asset… and the quantity held by the entity".

Factor (IFRS 13:B4)	Example
	Therefore, notwithstanding the fact that Company A paid a transaction price of CU100 million for the entire 3 million shares, the unit of account in this example is each individual share, not the entire 3 per cent equity interest acquired. Specifically, the fair value of the 3 per cent equity interest in Company B is measured as the product of the quoted price for each individual share and the quantity held ('P x Q') (i.e. CU108 million = 3 million shares x CU36 per share).
The market in which the transaction takes place is different from the principal market (or most advantageous market). For example, those markets might be different if the entity is a dealer that enters into transactions with customers in the retail market, but the principal (or most advantageous) market for the exit transaction is with other dealers in the dealer market.	*Entity A (a retail counterparty) enters into an interest rate swap in a retail market with Entity B (a dealer) for no initial consideration (i.e. the transaction price is zero). Entity A can access only the retail market. Entity B can access both the retail market (i.e. with retail counterparties) and the dealer market (i.e. with dealer counterparties). From the perspective of Entity A, the fair value at initial recognition is zero because Entity A does not have access to the dealer market. From Entity B's perspective, the transaction price of the interest rate swap (i.e. zero) does not represent fair value at initial recognition if prices observed or market participant assumptions in the dealer market (i.e. Entity B's principal market) indicate that fair value is something other than zero. Note: This final scenario is a summary of Example 7 from the illustrative examples accompanying IFRS 13 (see IFRS 13:IE24-IE26).

7.3 Day 1 profit or loss

When there is a difference between the fair value at initial recognition and the transaction price, IFRS 13:60 states that any resulting gain or loss should be recognised in profit or loss unless another IFRS specifies otherwise.

With respect to financial instruments, an entity should understand the reason for any difference between the fair value at initial recognition and the transaction price. This difference may represent consideration for goods or services between the two entities or a capital contribution or deemed distribution in circumstances when one party is acting in its capacity as an owner. Other IFRSs will determine how such amounts are accounted for.

Example 7.3A

Interest-free loan (1)

On 1 January 20X0, Parent A grants a non-callable interest-free loan of CU100 to a wholly-owned subsidiary, Subsidiary B. The loan is repayable on 31 December 20X0 and is not callable prior to that date by Parent A. The market rate of interest for a loan to the subsidiary would be 8 per cent. Consideration paid is made up as follows:

(i) CU92.59 is the fair value of the financial asset (i.e. CU100/1.08).

(ii) CU7.41 is a capital contribution. This amount represents the fair value of Parent A's providing Subsidiary B with interest-free finance. The amount should be recognised by Subsidiary B directly in equity as a capital contribution because it does not meet the definition of income under paragraph 4.25 of the *Conceptual Framework for Financial Reporting*.

Example 7.3B

Interest-free loan (2)

On 1 January 20X0, Subsidiary C grants a non-callable interest-free loan of CU100 to its parent, Parent A. The loan is repayable on 31 December 20X0 and is not callable prior to that date by Subsidiary C. The market rate of interest for a loan to Parent A would be 8 per cent. Consideration paid is made up as follows:

(i) CU92.59 is the fair value of the financial asset (i.e. CU100/1.08).

(ii) CU7.41 is in substance a distribution from Subsidiary C to Parent A. This amount represents the fair value of the Subsidiary C's providing its parent with interest-free finance. The amount should be recognised by Subsidiary C directly in equity as a deemed distribution because it does not meet the definition of an expense under paragraph 4.25 of the *Conceptual Framework for Financial Reporting*.

When the difference is not consideration for goods or services, or a capital contribution or deemed distribution, IFRS 9 sets out specific guidance as to whether that difference (often referred to as 'day 1 p&l') may be recognised in profit or loss at initial recognition.

If, in an arm's length transaction, the transaction price differs from fair value at initial recognition, the appropriate accounting for the difference depends on how fair value is determined in those circumstances. If the fair value is evidenced by a quoted price in an active market for an identical asset or liability (i.e. a Level 1 input) (see **10.2.1**) or based on a valuation technique that uses only data from observable markets, then the difference is recognised as a gain or loss on initial recognition (i.e. day 1 profit or loss). In all other cases, the fair value at initial recognition is adjusted to bring it in line with the transaction price. Consequently, the 'day 1 p&l' is deferred by including it in the initial carrying amount of the asset or liability. After initial recognition, the entity shall recognise that deferred difference as a gain or loss only to the extent that it arises from a change in a factor (including time) that market participants would take into account when pricing the asset or liability. [IFRS 9:B5.1.2A(b)]

Example 7.3C

Day 1 p&l (1)

Bank A sells a 30-year cash-settled forward-sale contract over a commodity to Entity B.

Forward prices for the specific commodity are freely quoted in the market for 10, 15, and 20 year periods. Bank A uses an extrapolation technique and its proprietary pricing system to estimate the 30-year forward rate and incorporates an additional premium on top of this internal price. Some of the premium may be received in cash at inception and some may be included in the contracted price of the forward contract.

The valuation technique uses both the available forward prices and Bank A's estimates of the commodity prices between years 20 and 30. Because some of the inputs are entity-specific and not observable, a day 1 profit cannot be recognised.

Example 7.3D

Day 1 p&l (2)

Bank X issues credit-linked notes to institutional investors.

The credit-linked notes are debt instruments with an interest rate higher than normal bonds issued by Bank X because the performance of the notes is linked to the performance of a basket of underlying corporate bonds. The terms require that if a corporate bond in the basket defaults, then the notional principal will be reset on the next payment date to reflect the outstanding value of the remaining bonds in the basket. This term is commonly referred to as 'first-to-default', because it is the first bond in the basket that defaults that results in the early repayment of the notes at an amount less than was originally invested by the holder.

Bank X does not actually hold the corporate bonds that the credit-linked notes are linked to. Instead Bank X purchases a large number of credit default options over the individual corporate bonds. These purchased options serve as an economic hedge in case any of the referenced credits default. The remaining proceeds from issuing the credit-linked notes are invested in high quality government debt.

If the credit-linked notes are not traded in an active market, then Bank X must use a valuation technique to measure the financial liability. At inception the proceeds received from the issuance of the notes are equal to their fair value.

It would not be possible to recognise an up-front profit on initial recognition of the credit-linked notes, even if the sum paid to purchase the government bonds and the credit options is less than the proceeds from the notes if:

- there are no other observable current market transactions in the same credit-linked notes with the same terms over the same portfolio of corporate credits; or
- if the valuation of the credit-linked notes includes non-observable market data, e.g. default correlation data between the different corporate credits where this data is not sourced from observable markets.

The deferred gain or loss should be released to profit or loss such that it reaches a value of zero at the time when the entire contract can be valued using active market quotes or verifiable objective market information. IAS 39:BC222(v)(ii) (which was not carried over to IFRS 9) notes that straight-line amortisation may be an appropriate method in some cases, but it will not be appropriate in others. In circumstances when the item acts in a non-linear fashion (e.g. option-based contracts), non-linear amortisation may be appropriate. An entity should determine a policy for amortisation. The following policies may be appropriate:

(i) calibrate unobservable inputs to the transaction price and recognise the deferred gain or loss as the best estimates of those unobservable inputs change based on observable information; or

(ii) release the day 1 gain or loss in a reasonable fashion based on the facts and circumstances.

Example 7.3E

Day 1 p&l (3)

Entity A writes a call option over a specified financial asset to Entity B and receives a premium from Entity B. The option can be exercised by Entity B at any time during the instrument's life. The written call option meets the definition of a derivative and is classified by Entity A as at FVTPL. Entity A uses its proprietary valuation model to fair value the written option because the instrument is not traded in an active market. The model uses observable inputs to the extent possible but also includes significant unobservable inputs. Entity A is not permitted to recognise an up-front gain or loss at initial recognition and measures the derivative at the transaction price. Per IFRS 9:B5.4.9, Entity A should recognise in profit or loss changes in the fair value of the derivative that have occurred subsequent to initial recognition.

To illustrate, Entity A received CU500 for the written call option and the entity's proprietary model valued the instrument at CU300. Entity A initially recognises a derivative liability at CU500 equivalent to the consideration received. At the next measurement date, using the same proprietary model, the fair value of the instrument has fallen by CU100 and this fair value gain is recognised in profit or loss.

Entity A must determine an accounting policy that is consistent with IFRS 9:B5.1.2A for subsequent recognition of the initial difference of CU200 (CU500 – CU300) in profit or loss. Any amounts not recognised in profit or loss before the date of exercise or maturity will be recognised in profit or loss on that date.

8 Valuation techniques

8.1 Valuation techniques required to maximise the use of observable inputs

When the price for an asset or a liability cannot be observed directly, it must be estimated using a valuation technique. When used in the context of fair value measurement, 'valuation technique' is a generic term and its application is not limited to complex fair valuation models. For example, valuing an asset or a liability using quoted prices in an active market for identical assets and liabilities is a valuation technique. In other cases, when prices cannot be observed directly and more judgement is required, it will be appropriate to use more complex valuation techniques.

An entity is required to use valuation techniques that are appropriate in the circumstances and for which sufficient data are available to measure fair value, maximising the use of relevant observable inputs and minimising the use of unobservable inputs. [IFRS 13:61]

Observable inputs are defined as "[i]nputs that are developed using market data, such as publicly available information about actual events or transactions, and that reflect the assumptions that market participants would use when pricing the asset or liability". [IFRS 13:Appendix A]

Unobservable inputs are defined as "[i]nputs for which market data are not available and that are developed using the best information available about the assumptions that market participants would use when pricing the asset or liability". [IFRS 13:Appendix A]

8.2 Widely used valuation techniques

IFRS 13 refers to three widely used valuation techniques:

[IFRS 13:62]

- the market approach (see **8.4**);
- the cost approach (sometimes referred to as 'replacement cost') (see **8.5**); and
- the income approach (see **section 8.6**)

Any valuation technique used to estimate fair value should be consistent with one or more of the above approaches. [IFRS 13:62]

The two common valuation techniques used for financial instruments are the market approach and the income approach .

8.3 Selecting an appropriate valuation technique

IFRS 13 does not set out a hierarchy of valuation techniques; this is because particular valuation techniques might be more appropriate in some circumstances than in others. [IFRS 13:BC142]

Each valuation technique has its own merits and may or may not be suitable for measuring the fair value of a specified item or items in the given circumstances. In practice, different valuation techniques can give rise to different estimates of fair value and, therefore, it is important to select the most appropriate methodology for the particular circumstances.

Choosing a valuation technique requires judgement and involves the selection of a method, formulae and assumptions. The reliability of a fair value measurement derived from a valuation technique is dependent on both the reliability of the valuation technique and the reliability of the inputs used. Consequently, when selecting a valuation technique, it will be important to consider the availability of reliable inputs for that valuation (see **section 9**). In addition to selecting a technique that maximises the use of relevant observable inputs and minimises the use of unobservable inputs, an entity must also ensure that the best possible evidence is used to support unobservable inputs.

In assessing the appropriateness of each valuation technique, an entity should also evaluate all available inputs significant to the valuation technique and compare the technique with other valuation techniques. For example, in a given situation, an entity may conclude that it is appropriate to use a market approach rather than an income approach because the market approach uses superior market information as inputs.

An entity should consider using a valuation specialist.

See **8.7** for a discussion of when it is appropriate to use multiple valuation techniques.

Example 8.3 illustrates how an entity might approach the selection of a valuation technique (or techniques) for unquoted equity securities in specified circumstances.

Example 8.3

Selecting an appropriate valuation technique or techniques for unquoted equity securities

Company A holds equity investments in the following two entities – Company B and Company C. Company A measures these investments at fair value on a recurring basis.

- Company B is a clothing retailer that operates in the niche market of the baby clothing industry. Quoted prices are not available for Company B's shares. Most of Company B's competitors are either privately held or are subsidiaries of larger publicly traded clothing retailers. Company B is similar to two other organisations, whose shares are thinly traded in an observable market.
- Company C is a retailer that operates in the competitive consumer electronics industry. Although quoted prices are not available for Company C's shares, Company C is comparable to many entities whose shares are actively traded.

Because the prices of Company B's and Company C's shares cannot be observed directly, Company A must measure the fair value of these investments using a valuation technique (or techniques).

Company A is considering a market approach, an income approach or a combination of these two approaches. The market approach and the income approach are common valuation techniques for equity investments that are not publicly traded. Under the market approach, entities use prices and other relevant information generated by market transactions involving identical or comparable securities. Under the income approach, future amounts are converted into a single present amount (e.g. discounted cash flows model). Company A is not considering the cost approach to value its equity securities because it is not considered relevant. (See **8.4-8.6** for detailed descriptions of these valuation techniques. See also **8.7** for a discussion of when it is appropriate to use multiple valuation techniques.)

Company A should select the valuation technique (or techniques) that is (are) appropriate in the circumstances and for which sufficient data are available to measure fair value, maximising the use of relevant observable inputs and minimising the use of unobservable inputs.

Investment in Company B

Using a market approach, the fair value measurement of Company A's investment in Company B would involve an analysis of market prices and other relevant information for the two similar organisations that are traded (albeit thinly) in an observable market. It is likely that the observable market data would need to be adjusted to reflect differences between Company B and the two similar organisations that are traded. For example, Company A might consider that market participants would incorporate significant entity-specific adjustments into the valuation of Company B's shares (e.g. adjustments to reflect the relative illiquidity of Company B's shares, profitability, net assets, unrecognised assets such as internally generated intangible assets, and differences in business model between Company B and the two traded organisations). These adjustments would be made using Company A's own assumptions. Consequently, in such circumstances, a market approach would rely on unobservable inputs that are significant to the fair value measurement.

Using an income approach based on discounted cash flows, the fair value measurement of Company A's investment in Company B would also be based on significant entity-specific assumptions in forecasting Company B's future cash flows. As a result, the income approach would also rely on unobservable inputs that are significant to the fair value measurement.

Based on the above information, it is likely that Company A would conclude that both the market approach and the income approach are appropriate techniques for measuring the fair value of its investment in Company B. In making its selection, Company A would consider the reliability of the evidence supporting the inputs used in each of the valuation techniques. Provided that relevant and reliable inputs are available, and there are no other factors indicating that one of the approaches is superior, it would seem appropriate to use a combination of both approaches, even if one approach is used only to corroborate the results of the other.

Investment in Company C

When selecting an appropriate approach to measure the fair value of its investment in Company C, Company A should perform an analysis similar to that outlined above.

Using a market approach, it is more likely that market participants would incorporate fewer unobservable adjustments into the valuation of Company C's shares because of the large number of comparable traded entities and the high trading volume of the shares of those comparable entities. However, Company A should consider whether to make an adjustment for illiquidity to reflect the fact that Company C's shares are unquoted whereas those of comparable entities in the same sector are listed and actively traded.

Using an income approach based on discounted cash flows, the fair value measurement of Company A's investment in Company C would be based on forecasted future cash flows. This forecast would include projections of future profitability and, therefore, would be likely to include entity-specific assumptions that are not observable.

As a result, it is likely that Company A would conclude that it is appropriate to measure the fair value of its investment in Company C using the market approach because it uses more observable inputs (i.e. in terms of the hierarchy described in **section 10**, 'Level 2' inputs vs. 'Level 3' inputs) with a significant effect.

8.4 Market approach

The 'market approach' is defined as "[a] valuation technique that uses prices and other relevant information generated by market transactions involving identical or comparable (i.e. similar) assets, liabilities or a group of assets and liabilities, such as a business". [IFRS 13:Appendix A]

A quoted price for an identical asset or liability in an active market that the entity can access at the measurement date provides the most reliable evidence of fair value. [IFRS 13:77] Quoted prices for the identical asset or liability are regarded as Level 1 inputs within the fair value hierarchy (see **10.2.1**). When a quoted price exists for an identical asset or liability, it should be used without adjustment, except in the circumstances described at **10.2.1**. [IFRS 13:77] When a quoted price for an asset or a liability exists in multiple active markets, it will be necessary to identify the market and price which represents fair value for the specific facts and circumstances.

Valuation techniques consistent with the market approach often use market multiples derived from a set of comparable assets or liabilities. A range of multiples may be derived, with a different multiple for each comparable asset or liability. The selection of the appropriate multiple within the range requires the exercise of judgement – with appropriate consideration of the qualitative and quantitative factors specific to the measurement. [IFRS 13:B6]

Valuation techniques consistent with the market approach include matrix pricing. Matrix pricing is a mathematical technique used principally to value some types of financial instruments, such as debt securities, without relying exclusively on quoted prices for the specific securities, but rather relying on the securities' relationship to other benchmark quoted securities. [IFRS 13:B7]

8.5 Cost approach

The 'cost approach' is defined as "[a] valuation technique that reflects the amount that would be required currently to replace the service capacity of an asset (often referred to as current replacement cost)". [IFRS 13:Appendix A] This method is often used to measure the fair value of tangible assets that are used in combination with other assets or with other assets and liabilities. [IFRS 13:B9]

> The cost approach is not generally used when measuring the fair value of financial instruments. The cost approach considers the cost to replace the service capacity of an asset, a concept that is not relevant in the context of financial instruments.

8.6 Income approach

8.6.1 Income approach – general

The 'income approach' is defined as "[v]aluation techniques that convert future amounts (e.g. cash flows or income and expenses) to a single current (i.e. discounted) amount. The fair value measurement is determined on the basis of the value indicated by current market expectations about those future amounts". [IFRS 13:Appendix A]

Income approaches that are used for measuring the fair value of financial instruments include, for example:

[IFRS 13:B11]

- present value techniques (see below); and
- option pricing models, such as Black-Scholes-Merton formula or a binomial model (i.e. a lattice model), that incorporate present value techniques and reflect both the time value and the intrinsic value of an option.

IFRS 13 describes two types of present value techniques:

- the discount rate adjustment technique (see **8.6.4.2**) and
- the expected cash flow (expected present value) technique (see **8.6.4.3**).

IFRS 13 does not specifically require that one of these present value techniques be used. The most appropriate present value technique for the measurement of fair value in a particular scenario will depend on the facts and circumstances specific to the asset or liability being measured (e.g. whether prices for comparable assets or liabilities can be observed in the market) and the availability of sufficient data. [IFRS 13:B12]

8.6.2 Components of a present value measurement

Present value is a tool used to link future amounts (e.g. cash flows or values) to a present amount using a discount rate. A fair value measurement of an asset or a liability using a present value technique captures all of the following elements from the perspective of market participants at the measurement date:

[IFRS 13:B13]

- an estimate of future cash flows for the asset or liability being measured;
- expectations about possible variations in the amount and timing of the cash flows representing the uncertainty inherent in the cash flows;
- the time value of money, represented by the rate on risk-free monetary assets that have maturity dates or durations that coincide with the period covered by the cash flows and pose neither uncertainty in timing nor risk of default to the holder (i.e. a risk-free interest rate);
- the price for bearing the uncertainty inherent in the cash flows (i.e. a risk premium);

- other factors that market participants would take into account in the circumstances;
- for a liability, the non-performance risk relating to that liability, including the obligor's own credit risk.

8.6.3 General principles underlying present value measurement

Present value techniques differ in how they capture the elements listed in **8.6.2**. However, all of the following general principles govern the application of any present value technique used to measure fair value.

[IFRS 13:B14]

- Cash flows and discount rates should reflect assumptions that market participants would use when pricing the asset or liability.
- Cash flows and discount rates should take into account only the factors attributable to the asset or liability being measured.
- To avoid double-counting or omitting the effects of risk factors, discount rates should reflect assumptions that are consistent with those inherent in the cash flows. For example, a discount rate that reflects the uncertainty in expectations about future defaults is appropriate if using contractual cash flows of a loan (i.e. a discount rate adjustment technique). That same rate should not be used if using expected (i.e. probability-weighted) cash flows (i.e. an expected present value technique) because the expected cash flows already reflect assumptions about the uncertainty in future defaults; instead, a discount rate that is commensurate with the risk inherent in the expected cash flows should be used.
- Assumptions about cash flows and discount rates should be internally consistent. For example, nominal cash flows, which include the effect of inflation, should be discounted at a rate that includes the effect of inflation. The nominal risk-free interest rate includes the effect of inflation. Real cash flows, which exclude the effect of inflation, should be discounted at a rate that excludes the effect of inflation. Similarly, after-tax cash flows should be discounted using an after-tax discount rate. Pre-tax cash flows should be discounted at a rate consistent with those cash flows.

Care should be taken in determining a pre-tax discount rate by adjusting a post-tax rate. Because the tax consequences of cash flows may occur in different periods, the pre-tax rate of return is not always the post-tax rate of return grossed up by the standard rate of tax. See **8.4.2** in **chapter A10** of **Volume A** of this manual for further guidance on how to adjust a post-tax discount rate to arrive at a pre-tax discount rate.

- Discount rates should be consistent with the underlying economic factors of the currency in which the cash flows are denominated.

8.6.4 Risk and uncertainty

8.6.4.1 Risk and uncertainty – general

A fair value measurement using present value techniques is made under conditions of uncertainty because the cash flows used are estimates rather than known amounts. In many cases, both the amount and timing of the cash flows are uncertain. Even contractually fixed amounts, such as the payments on a loan, are uncertain if there is risk of default. [IFRS 13:B15]

Market participants generally seek compensation (i.e. a risk premium) for bearing the uncertainty inherent in the cash flows of an asset or a liability. A fair value measurement should include a risk premium reflecting the amount that market participants would demand as compensation for the uncertainty inherent in the cash flows. Otherwise, the measurement would not faithfully represent fair value. In some cases, determining the appropriate risk premium might be difficult. However, the degree of difficulty alone is not a sufficient reason to exclude a risk premium. [IFRS 13:B16]

Present value techniques differ in how they adjust for risk and in the type of cash flows they use. For example the discount rate adjustment technique described in **8.6.4.2** uses contractual, promised or most likely cash flows and a risk-adjusted discount rate. [IFRS 13:B17(a)]

Expected present value techniques incorporate the effects of risk and uncertainty in one of two ways. The calculation either uses risk-adjusted expected cash flows and a risk-free rate to discount them or uses expected cash flows that are not risk-adjusted and a discount rate adjusted to include the risk premium that market participants require (see **8.6.4.3**). That rate is different from the rate used in the discount rate adjustment technique described in **8.6.4.2**. [IFRS 13:B17(b) & (c)]

8.6.4.2 Discount rate adjustment technique

The discount rate adjustment technique uses a single set of cash flows from the range of possible estimated amounts, whether contractual or promised (as is the case for a bond) or most likely cash flows. In all cases, those cash flows are conditional upon the occurrence of specified events (e.g. contractual or promised cash flows for a bond are conditional on the event of no default by the debtor). The discount rate used in the discount rate adjustment technique is derived from observed rates of return for comparable assets or liabilities that are traded in the market. Accordingly, the contractual, promised or most likely cash flows are discounted at an observed or estimated market rate for such conditional cash flows (i.e. a market rate of return). [IFRS 13:B18]

The discount rate adjustment technique requires an analysis of market data for comparable assets or liabilities. Comparability is established by considering the nature of the cash flows (e.g. whether the cash flows are contractual or non-contractual and are likely to respond similarly to changes in economic conditions), as well as other factors (e.g. credit standing, collateral, duration, restrictive covenants and liquidity). Alternatively, if a single comparable asset or liability does not fairly reflect the risk inherent in the cash flows of the asset or liability being measured, it may be possible to derive a discount rate using data for several comparable assets or liabilities in conjunction with the risk-free yield curve (i.e. using a 'build-up' approach). [IFRS 13:B19]

Example 8.6.4.2

Deriving a discount rate using a build up approach

[Based on IFRS 13:B20-B21]

Assume that Asset A is a contractual right to receive CU800 in one year (i.e. there is no timing uncertainty). There is an established market for comparable assets, and information about those assets, including price information, is available. Of those comparable assets:

(a) Asset B is a contractual right to receive CU1,200 in one year and has a market price of CU1,083. Thus, the implied annual rate of return (i.e. a one-year market rate of return) is 10.8 per cent [(CU1,200/CU1,083) – 1].

(b) Asset C is a contractual right to receive CU700 in two years and has a market price of CU566. Thus, the implied annual rate of return (i.e. a two-year market rate of return) is 11.2 per cent [(CU700/CU566)^0.5 – 1].

(c) All three assets are comparable with respect to risk (i.e. dispersion of possible pay-offs and credit).

On the basis of the timing of the contractual payments to be received for Asset A relative to the timing for Asset B and Asset C (i.e. one year for Asset B versus two years for Asset C), Asset B is deemed more comparable to Asset A. Using the contractual payment to be received for Asset A (CU800) and the one-year market rate derived from Asset B (10.8 per cent), the fair value of Asset A is CU722 (CU800/1.108). Alternatively, in the absence of available market information for Asset B, the one-year market rate could be derived from Asset C using the build-up approach. In that case, the two-year market rate indicated by Asset C (11.2 per cent) would be adjusted to a one-year market rate using the term structure of the risk-free yield curve. Additional information and analysis might be required to determine whether the risk premiums for one-year and two-year assets are the same. If it is determined that the risk premiums for one-year and two-year assets are not the same, the two-year market rate of return would be further adjusted for that effect.

When the discount rate adjustment technique is applied to fixed receipts or payments, the adjustment for risk inherent in the cash flows of the asset or liability being measured is included in the discount rate. In some applications of the discount rate adjustment technique to cash flows that are not fixed receipts or payments, an adjustment to the cash flows may be necessary to achieve comparability with the observed asset or liability from which the discount rate is derived. [IFRS 13:B22]

8.6.4.3 Expected present value technique

The expected present value technique uses as a starting point a set of cash flows that represents the probability-weighted average of all possible future cash flows (i.e. the expected cash flows). The resulting estimate is identical to expected value, which, in statistical terms, is the weighted average of a discrete random variable's possible values with the respective probabilities as the weights. All possible cash flows are probability-weighted, hence, the resulting expected cash flow is not conditional upon the occurrence of any specified event (unlike the cash flows used in the discount rate adjustment technique described in **8.6.4.2**). [IFRS 13:B23]

In making an investment decision, risk-averse market participants would take into account the risk that the actual cash flows may differ from the expected cash flows. Portfolio theory distinguishes between unsystematic (diversifiable) risk, which is the risk specific to a particular asset or liability, and systematic (non-diversifiable) risk, which is the common risk shared by an asset or a liability with the other items in a diversified portfolio. Portfolio theory holds that in a market in equilibrium, market participants will be compensated only for bearing the systematic risk inherent in the cash flows. In markets that are inefficient or out of equilibrium, other forms of return or compensation might be available. [IFRS 13:B24]

IFRS 13 describes two methods for applying the expected present value technique. Both methods are illustrated in **example 8.6.4.3**.

[IFRS 13:B25 & B26]

- Method 1 adjusts the expected cash flows of an asset for systematic (i.e. market) risk by subtracting a cash risk premium (i.e. risk-adjusted expected cash flows). Those risk-adjusted expected cash flows represent a certainty-equivalent cash flow, which is discounted at a risk-free interest rate. A certainty-equivalent cash flow refers to an expected cash flow (as defined), adjusted for risk so that a market participant is indifferent to trading a certain cash flow for an expected cash flow. For example, if a market participant was willing to trade an expected cash flow of CU1,200 for a certain cash flow of CU1,000, the CU1,000 is the certainty equivalent of the CU1,200 (i.e. the CU200 would represent the cash risk premium). In that case, the market participant would be indifferent as to the asset held.

- Method 2 adjusts for systematic (i.e. market) risk by adding a risk premium to the risk-free interest rate. Accordingly, the expected cash flows are discounted at a rate that corresponds to an expected rate associated with probability-weighted cash flows (i.e. an expected rate of return). Models used for pricing risky assets, such as the capital asset pricing model, can be used to estimate the expected rate of return. Because the discount rate used in the discount rate adjustment technique is a rate of return relating to conditional cash flows it is likely to be higher than the expected rate of return relating to expected or probability-weighted cash flows. [IFRS 13:B26]

Example 8.6.4.3

Present value techniques: Discounting risk adjusted expected cash flows by the risk-free rate vs. discounting unadjusted expected cash flows by a risk-adjusted discount rate

[Based on IFRS 13:B27-B30]

Assume that an asset has expected cash flows of CU780 in one year determined on the basis of the possible cash flows and probabilities shown below. The applicable risk-free interest rate for cash flows with a one-year horizon is 5 per cent, and the systematic risk premium for an asset with the same risk profile is 3 per cent.

Possible cash flows	Probability	Probability-weighted cash flows
CU500	15%	CU75
CU800	60%	CU480
CU900	25%	CU225
Expected cash flows:		CU780

In this simple illustration, the expected cash flows (CU780) represent the probability-weighted average of the three possible outcomes. In more realistic situations, there could be many possible outcomes. However, to apply the expected present value technique, it is not always necessary to take into account distributions of all possible cash flows using complex models and techniques. Rather, it might be possible to develop a limited number of discrete scenarios and probabilities that capture the array of possible cash flows. For example, an entity might use realised cash flows for some relevant past period, adjusted for changes in circumstances occurring subsequently (e.g. changes in external factors, including economic or market conditions, industry trends and competition as well as changes in internal factors affecting the entity more specifically), taking into account the assumptions of market participants.

In theory, the present value (i.e. the fair value) of the asset's cash flows is the same whether determined by discounting the risk adjusted expected cash flows by the risk-free rate (Method 1) or by discounting the unadjusted expected cash flows by the risk-adjusted discount rate (Method 2).

Using Method 1, the expected cash flows are adjusted for systematic (i.e. market) risk. In the absence of market data directly indicating the amount of the risk adjustment, such adjustment could be derived from an asset pricing model using the concept of certainty equivalents. For example, the risk adjustment (i.e. the cash risk premium of CU22) could be determined using the systematic risk premium of 3 per cent (CU780 – [CU780 (1.05/1.08)]), which results in risk-adjusted expected cash flows of CU758 (CU780 – CU22). The CU758 is the certainty equivalent of CU780 and is discounted at the risk-free interest rate (5 per cent). The present value (i.e. the fair value) of the asset is CU722 (CU758/1.05).

Using Method 2, the expected cash flows are not adjusted for systematic (i.e. market) risk. Rather, the adjustment for that risk is included in the discount rate. Thus, the expected cash flows are discounted at an expected rate of return of 8 per cent (i.e. the 5 per cent risk-free interest rate plus the 3 per cent systematic risk premium). The present value (i.e. the fair value) of the asset is CU722 (CU780/1.08).

When using an expected present value technique to measure fair value, either Method 1 or Method 2 could be used. The selection of Method 1 or Method 2 will depend on facts and circumstances specific to the asset or liability being measured, the extent to which sufficient data are available and the judgements applied.

8.7 Use of multiple valuation techniques

In some cases, it is appropriate to use a single valuation technique (e.g. when valuing an asset or a liability using quoted market prices in an active market for identical assets or liabilities). However, in other circumstances, it is appropriate to use multiple valuation techniques. [IFRS 13:63]

When multiple valuation techniques are used to measure fair value, the results (i.e. the fair value measurements) should be evaluated taking into account the reasonableness of the range of values indicated by those results. A fair value measurement is the point within that range that is most representative of the fair value in the circumstances. [IFRS 13:63]

In determining whether it is more appropriate to use a single approach or multiple approaches, an entity should consider the appropriateness (i.e. relevance and applicability) of each valuation technique and the observability of the available inputs that are significant to the valuation technique. If one valuation technique is clearly superior to the other techniques (e.g. because it uses more observable inputs), it may be appropriate to use a single valuation technique. Conversely, if no valuation technique is superior (e.g. because all techniques use unobservable inputs that are significant to the measurement), it may be appropriate to use a combination of valuation techniques provided that reliable and relevant inputs are available.

8.8 Calibration of valuation techniques

If the transaction price is fair value at initial recognition and a valuation technique that uses unobservable inputs will be used to measure fair value in subsequent periods, the valuation technique should be calibrated so that at initial recognition the result of the valuation technique equals the transaction price. Calibration ensures that the valuation technique reflects current market conditions, and it helps an entity to determine whether an adjustment to the valuation technique is necessary (e.g. there might be a characteristic of the asset or liability that is not captured by the valuation technique). After initial recognition, when measuring fair value using a valuation technique or techniques that use unobservable inputs, an entity should ensure that those valuation techniques reflect observable market data (e.g. the price for a similar asset or liability) at the measurement date. [IFRS 13:64]

Some IFRSs require or permit assets or liabilities to be recognised initially at fair value. When an asset is acquired or a liability assumed in a market transaction, it cannot be assumed that the price paid to acquire the asset or received to assume the liability (i.e. transaction or entry price) is the same as the fair value of the asset or liability in accordance with IFRS 13 (an exit price) (see **section 7** for further discussion).

IFRS 13:64, as discussed above, deals specifically with circumstances in which:

- a valuation technique that uses unobservable inputs is used to measure the fair value of an asset or a liability in subsequent periods; and
- the transaction price for the asset or liability *is* an appropriate measure of fair value at initial recognition in accordance with IFRS 13.

In such circumstances, IFRS 13:64 requires that the valuation technique should be calibrated (i.e. adjusted) so that, at initial recognition, the result of the valuation technique equals the transaction price.

If the transaction price is fair value at initial recognition, calibration of an entity's pricing model eliminates differences between the transaction price and the model's output (the 'inception difference'). IFRS 13 does not prescribe any specific method for the calibration of pricing models. Therefore, an entity should select the most appropriate method for the particular circumstances.

Factors to consider when selecting the calibration method include:

- the valuation technique used;
- the availability of information about market participant assumptions (e.g. relevant observable inputs, estimated timing of when unobservable inputs may become observable);
- the complexity involved (i.e. complexity in different calibration methods, or in the identification of the causes underlying differences between transaction price and fair value estimates based on the entity's pricing model);
- the terms of the instrument; and
- the nature of the entity's portfolio.

In outline, calibration might be approached in the following manner.

- **Step 1** – Identify the source of the inception difference.

- **Step 2** – Adjust the unobservable inputs or establish valuation adjustments such that the adjusted model result equals the transaction price at inception (i.e. the inception difference is eliminated).
- **Step 3** – Changes in fair value measured using the entity's pricing model will be recognised subsequent to initial recognition. The adjustments identified at Step 2 may be reversed or modified when (1) unobservable inputs become observable or (2) unobservable inputs or valuation adjustments are adjusted to reflect new information (e.g. through subsequent calibration of the model or model inputs to reflect new transaction data).

Step 2 may result in either direct adjustment to model inputs or an adjustment to the model's output (a valuation adjustment).

When calibration is achieved through direct adjustment to model inputs, an entity should consider the impact of such adjustments on the valuation of other instruments in its portfolio (e.g. instruments valued using the same or similar pricing inputs). The calibration may affect the valuation of other instruments because the calibrated inputs may replace or supersede the assumptions previously used for unobservable inputs.

When calibration is achieved through a valuation adjustment, the entity should review the valuation adjustment periodically to ensure that the adjustment reflects any new information and that it is consistent with the exit price notion in IFRS 13.

See **example 8.8** for an illustration of a model calibration approach that may be acceptable when the inception difference can be isolated to a particular unobservable model input.

Example 8.8

Calibration of models or model inputs

Entity X enters into an electricity forward contract to purchase 100 megawatts of electricity (daily) for a 10-year term. The electricity forward contract is within the scope of IFRS 9 and is measured at fair value.

No cash is exchanged between the parties at the inception of the forward contract. Using the guidance in IFRS 13:B4 (see **section 7**), Entity X determines that the transaction price equals the exit price (i.e. the fair value of the forward contract equals zero at inception).

Entity X develops its own valuation technique to measure the fair value of the forward contract at subsequent reporting dates. At inception, there are three years of observable forward prices available in the relevant market. Entity X's model uses estimated forward electricity prices beyond three years. At inception, and prior to calibration, the pricing model values the forward contract as an asset of CU1 million. Consequently, Entity X needs to calibrate its model so that the model result at inception equals the transaction price of zero.

In this simple scenario, Entity X might calibrate its model as follows.

- **Step 1** – Entity X establishes that the only unobservable input that significantly affects the model value is forward electricity prices. Consequently, Entity X attributes the inception difference of CU1 million (i.e. the difference between the model's result and the fair value of zero) to its estimate of unobservable forward electricity prices for Years 4 to 10 of the contract.
- **Step 2** – Entity X adjusts the unobservable forward price points at Years 4 to 10 on the forward price curve such that the model produces a fair value of zero. Because Entity X attributed the inception difference solely to the unobservable electricity prices in the relevant market, any calibration adjustment represents a calibration of these unobservable electricity prices to the most recent available information (the forward contract's transaction price). As a result, if Entity X owns a portfolio of contracts whose fair values are estimated using long-dated electricity prices in the same market, the calibration adjustment to the electricity forward prices would most likely also affect the fair value of those other long-dated contracts. Similar considerations are also relevant when a calibration results in valuation adjustments to the pricing model's output. In general, calibration adjustments provide updated information about assumptions used by market participants in assessing unobservable inputs or valuation adjustments. Therefore, calibration adjustments may have an effect beyond the recently executed transaction.
- **Step 3** – Assuming no other calibration adjustments are made and that observable forward prices remain available for the next three years, the calibration adjustments would be removed as the inputs for Years 4 to 10 become observable. (For example, at the end of Year 1 of the contract, observable forward prices would be available for Years 2 to 4, and unobservable inputs for Years 5 to 10 would be used. As a result, the calibration adjustments for Year 4 should be removed from the valuation as this input has become observable.) All calibration adjustments should be removed once all the unobservable inputs become observable (e.g. in the last 3 years of the contract). In addition, no calibration adjustments should remain in the model in a period in which settlement has occurred.

8.9 Changes in valuation techniques

Once a valuation technique has been selected, it should be applied consistently. A change in a valuation technique or its application (e.g. a change in its weighting when multiple valuation techniques are used or a change in an adjustment applied to a valuation technique) is only appropriate if the change results in a measurement that is equally or more representative of fair value in the circumstances. [IFRS 13:65]

The Standard provides the following examples of events that might appropriately lead to a change in valuation technique:

[IFRS 13:65]

- new markets develop;
- new information becomes available;
- information previously used is no longer available;
- valuation techniques improve; or
- market conditions change.

If a valuation technique does not use unadjusted quoted prices, and in a subsequent period a quoted price in an active market becomes available, the quoted price should be used because IFRS 13:77 states that "a quoted price in an active market provides the most reliable evidence of fair value and shall be used without adjustment to measure fair value whenever available", with limited exceptions.

Depending on the particular circumstances, a change from a valuation technique that uses unadjusted quoted prices to a different valuation technique (such as a discounted cash flow technique) may be appropriate when:

- quoted prices for an identical asset or liability are no longer available; or
- quoted prices are available, but the market is no longer active. Note, however, that prices from relevant observable transactions must be considered in determining fair value even if the market is not active (see **9.5**); or
- the entity no longer has access to the market in which the prices are quoted. The entity must be able to access the market in order to use a quote from that market without adjustment to reflect the lack of access, but the entity does not need to be able to sell the particular asset or transfer the particular liability on the measurement date (see **section 3.3** for further details); or
- quoted prices are no longer based on relevant observable market data and do not reflect assumptions that market participants would make in pricing the asset at the measurement date. As discussed at **9.7**, an entity cannot necessarily assume that a price provided by an external source is representative of fair value at the measurement date.

A decrease in the volume or level of activity in a market does not necessarily mean that the market is no longer active (see **10.2.1** for a discussion of active vs. inactive markets) and, consequently, that a change in the valuation technique is warranted.

In selecting another valuation technique, when appropriate, an entity should maximise the use of relevant observable inputs (e.g. quoted prices for a similar asset or liability with adjustments as appropriate) and minimise the use of unobservable inputs.

If there is a change in the valuation technique used or its application, any resulting difference should be accounted for as a change in accounting estimate in accordance with IAS 8 *Accounting Policies, Changes in Accounting Estimates and Errors*; however, the disclosures generally required under IAS 8 regarding a change in accounting estimate are not required for revisions resulting from a change in a valuation technique or its application. [IFRS 13:66]

9 Inputs to valuation techniques

9.1 Definition of inputs

Inputs are defined as "[t]he assumptions that market participants would use when pricing the asset or liability, including assumptions about risk, such as the following:

(a) the risk inherent in a particular valuation technique used to measure fair value (such as a pricing model); and

(b) the risk inherent in the inputs to the valuation technique". [IFRS 13:Appendix A]

Inputs may be observable or unobservable. [IFRS 13:Appendix A] Valuation techniques used to measure fair value are required to maximise the use of relevant observable inputs and minimise the use of unobservable inputs (see **section 8**). [IFRS 13:67]

Valuation inputs that are observable are more reliable than those that are unobservable (sometimes referred to as 'entity-specific' because these inputs are derived by an entity rather than by the 'market').

The inputs used should be consistent with the characteristics of the asset or liability that market participants would take into account in a transaction for the asset or liability (see **3.1**). [IFRS 13:69]

Various factors may influence the fair value of a financial instrument. Below is a non-exhaustive list of factors that may be relevant in valuing non-derivative and derivative financial instruments:

- time value of money (i.e. interest at the risk-free rate);
- credit risk (both counterparty credit risk for a financial asset and own credit risk for a financial liability);
- liquidity risk;

- foreign currency exchange rates;
- commodity prices;
- equity prices;
- volatility;
- prepayment or surrender risk; and
- servicing costs.

9.2 Observable inputs

Examples of markets in which inputs might be observable for some assets and liabilities include the following.

[IFRS 13:B34]

- **Exchange markets** In an exchange market, closing prices are both readily available and generally representative of fair value (e.g. the London Stock Exchange).
- **Dealer markets** In a dealer market, dealers stand ready to trade (either buy or sell for their own account), thereby providing liquidity by using their capital to hold an inventory of the items for which they make a market. Typically, bid and ask prices (representing the price at which the dealer is willing to buy and the price at which the dealer is willing to sell, respectively) are more readily available than closing prices. Over-the-counter markets (for which prices are publicly reported) are dealer markets. Dealer markets also exist for some other assets and liabilities, including some financial instruments, commodities and physical assets (e.g. used equipment).
- **Brokered markets** In a brokered market, brokers attempt to match buyers with sellers but do not stand ready to trade for their own account. Brokers do not use their own capital to hold an inventory of the items for which they make a market. The broker knows the prices bid and asked by the respective parties, but each party is typically unaware of another party's price requirements. Prices of completed transactions are sometimes available. Brokered markets include electronic communication networks, in which buy and sell orders are matched, and commercial and residential real estate markets.
- **Principal-to-principal markets** In a principal-to-principal market, transactions (both originations and re-sales) are negotiated independently with no intermediary. Little information about those transactions may be made available publicly.

9.3 Applying a premium or discount

In some cases, the characteristics of an asset or a liability that market participants would take into account in a transaction for the asset or liability result in the application of an adjustment, such as a premium or discount (e.g. a control premium or non-controlling interest discount). However, a fair value measurement should not incorporate a premium or discount that is inconsistent with the unit of account in the IFRS that requires or permits the fair value measurement (see **section 3.2**). [IFRS 13:69]

Premiums or discounts that reflect size as a characteristic of the entity's holding (specifically, a blockage factor that adjusts the quoted price of an asset or a liability because the market's normal daily trading volume is not sufficient to absorb the quantity held by the entity) are not permitted in a fair value measurement. [IFRS 13:69]

For example, an investor holding one share that is quoted in an active market may receive a different amount of consideration per share compared to an investor that sells 15 per cent of the total equity shares. The difference between the two holdings is simply the size of the investor's holding, which is typically not a characteristic of the financial asset and thus is not considered in the fair value measurement in this circumstance. For both investors, the fair value measurement of the shares is the price for disposing of a single share multiplied by the quantity held.

In contrast, when measuring the fair value of a controlling interest, it is appropriate to incorporate a control premium because IFRS 13 regards the control premium as a characteristic of the asset or liability. [IFRS 13:69]

In all cases, if there is a quoted market price in an active market for an asset or a liability, the entity should use that price without adjustment when measuring fair value, except as specified in IFRS 13:79 (see **10.2.1**). [IFRS 13:69]

9.4 Bid price versus ask price inputs

9.4.1 Bid price and ask price inputs – general

If an asset or a liability measured at fair value has a bid price and an ask price (e.g. an input from a dealer market), IFRS 13 requires the price within the bid-ask spread that is most representative of fair value in the circumstances to be used to measure fair value regardless of where the input is categorised within the fair value hierarchy (i.e. Level 1, 2 or 3; see **section 10**).

IFRS 13 permits, but does not require, that asset positions may be measured at bid prices and that liability positions may be measured at ask prices. [IFRS 13:70]

IFRS 13 allows an entity to use mid-market pricing or other pricing conventions that are used by market participants as a practical expedient for fair value measurements within a bid-ask spread. [IFRS 13:71]

An entity does not need to meet any specific qualifying criteria to use mid-market pricing or other pricing conventions as a practical expedient for measuring fair value, provided that the selected pricing convention:

- is used by market participants (e.g. an industry-accepted pricing convention); and
- is consistent with the fair value measurement objective of IFRS 13. For example, it would not be appropriate to use ask prices for recognised assets or bid prices for recognised liabilities because such a pricing approach would be inconsistent with the IFRS 13 objective that fair value is an exit price.

The decision to use a particular pricing convention is an accounting policy choice that should be consistently applied from period to period and for assets or liabilities with similar characteristics and risk. The policy should also be disclosed, if appropriate.

Example 9.4

Mid-market prices

Entity X and Entity Y hold the same debt security as an asset. Entity Y, a broker-dealer, is a market-maker in the debt security. Entity X is not. The debt security is traded in an active market by Entity Y (and other broker-dealers) using bid and ask prices.

Even though Entity X would most likely sell the debt security at or close to the bid price, Entity X may select a policy to use the mid-market price as the fair value of the debt security as a practical expedient. However, it would not be appropriate to use the ask price for the debt security because this would be inconsistent with the objective of fair value being an exit price.

Even though Entity Y may be able to exit at a price greater than the bid price, Entity Y may choose as its policy to measure the debt security by using the bid price as a practical expedient.

IFRS 13 also contains detailed guidance for circumstances when an entity may fair value a portfolio of similar items together that have offsetting market risks and in doing so use mid-market prices for the offsetting market risks (see **section 6**).

9.4.1 Changes in the use of bid, ask or mid-market pricing or other pricing conventions

When an entity has in the past complied with the requirements of IFRS 13:70 (see above) and measured fair value at the price within the bid-ask spread that is most representative of fair value in the circumstances, it is not generally appropriate for the entity to change its accounting policy to using the practical expedient of mid-market pricing or another pricing convention as permitted by IFRS 13:71.

Once a valuation technique has been selected, it should generally be applied consistently. A change in a valuation technique is only appropriate if the change results in a measurement that is equally or more representative of fair value in the circumstances. [IFRS 13:65]

Having established a policy of measuring fair value at the price within the bid-ask spread that is most representative of fair value in the circumstances, a change to using a practical expedient such as mid-market pricing or another pricing convention would generally be inappropriate because it would not typically result in a measurement that is equally or more representative of fair value.

9.5 Measuring fair value when the volume or level of activity for an asset or a liability has significantly decreased

IFRS 13 notes that the fair value of an asset or a liability might be affected when there has been a significant decrease in the volume or level of activity for that asset or liability in relation to normal market activity for the asset or liability (or similar assets or liabilities). [IFRS 13:B37]

The consequence of a significant decrease in the volume or level of activity could be that a transaction price or a quoted price for that item is not representative of fair value. However, a decrease in the volume or level of activity on its own may not indicate that a transaction price or quoted price does not represent fair value or that a transaction in that market is not orderly. [IFRS 13:B38]

The following are examples of factors that can help determine whether, on the basis of evidence available, there has been a significant decrease in the volume or level of activity for the asset or liability:

[IFRS 13:B37]

- there are few recent transactions;
- price quotations are not developed using current information;
- price quotations vary substantially either over time or among market-makers (e.g. some brokered markets);

- indices that previously were highly correlated with the fair values of the asset or liability are demonstrably uncorrelated with recent indications of fair value for that asset or liability;
- there is a significant increase in implied liquidity risk premiums, yields or performance indicators (such as delinquency rates or loss severities) for observed transactions or quoted prices when compared with the entity's estimate of expected cash flows, taking into account all available market data about credit and other non-performance risk for the asset or liability;
- there is a wide bid-ask spread or significant increase in the bid-ask spread;
- there is a significant decline in the activity of, or there is an absence of, a market for new issues (i.e. a primary market) for the asset or liability or similar assets or liabilities; and
- little information is publicly available (e.g. for transactions that take place in a principal-to-principal market).

In assessing whether there has been a significant decrease in the volume or level of activity, an entity should evaluate the significance and relevance of factors such as those listed above. [IFRS 13:B37]

Note that the presence of one or more of the factors listed in IFRS 13:B37 alone is not sufficient to conclude that a market is not 'active' see **10.2.1** for further discussion).

If it is concluded that there has been a significant decrease in the volume or level of activity for the asset or liability in relation to normal market activity for the asset or liability (or similar assets or liabilities), further analysis of the transactions or quoted prices is needed. If it is determined that a transaction or quoted price does not represent fair value (e.g. there may be transactions that are not orderly), an adjustment to the transactions or quoted prices will be necessary if those prices are to be used as a basis for measuring fair value. The adjustment can be significant to the fair value measurement in its entirety. [IFRS 13:B38]

Adjustments also may be necessary in other circumstances (e.g. when a price for a similar asset requires significant adjustment to make it comparable to the asset being measured, or when the price is 'stale'). [IFRS 13:B38]

IFRS 13 does not prescribe a methodology for making significant adjustments to transactions or quoted prices. Consistent with valuation techniques discussed in **section 8**, appropriate risk adjustments should be applied, including a risk premium reflecting the amount that market participants would demand as compensation for the uncertainty inherent in the cash flows of an asset or a liability. Otherwise, the measurement does not faithfully represent fair value. In some cases, determining the appropriate risk adjustment may be difficult. However, the degree of difficulty alone is not a sufficient basis on which to exclude a risk adjustment. The risk adjustment should be reflective of an orderly transaction between market participants at the measurement date under current market conditions. [IFRS 13:B39]

If there has been a significant decrease in the volume or level of activity for the asset or liability, a change in valuation technique or the use of multiple valuation techniques may be appropriate (e.g. the use of a market approach and an income approach – see **8.1** and **8.3** respectively). When weighting indications of fair value resulting from the use of multiple valuation techniques, an entity should consider the reasonableness of the range of fair value measurements. The objective is to determine the point within the range that is most representative of fair value under current market conditions. A wide range of fair value measurements may be an indication that further analysis is needed. [IFRS 13:B40]

Even when there has been a significant decrease in the volume or level of activity for the asset or liability, the objective of a fair value measurement remains the same. Fair value is the price that would be received to sell an asset or paid to transfer a liability in an orderly transaction (i.e. not a forced liquidation or distress sale) between market participants at the measurement date under current market conditions. [IFRS 13:B41]

Estimating the price at which market participants would be willing to enter into a transaction at the measurement date under current market conditions if there has been a significant decrease in the volume or level of activity for the asset or liability depends on the facts and circumstances at the measurement date and requires judgement. An entity's intention to hold the asset or to settle or otherwise fulfil the liability is not relevant when measuring fair value because fair value is a market-based measurement, not an entity-specific measurement. [IFRS 13:B42]

If an entity is unwilling to transact at a price from an external source (such as a quoted market price or a price provided by a broker, pricing service or potential buyer), the entity's unwillingness to transact at that price is not sufficient evidence for the entity to disregard that price in measuring fair value. If the best information available in the circumstances indicates that market participants would transact at a price from an external source, an entity is not permitted to disregard that price simply because it is not willing to transact at that price.

Examples 9.5A and **9.5B** explore this issue further.

Example 9.5A

Assumptions can be readily derived from current observable market data

Entity A is using a valuation model to measure the fair value of its investment in privately placed corporate debt securities issued by Entity X. No quoted price for identical securities is available. Entity A's valuation model uses assumptions about default rates and discount rates. Default rate assumptions can be readily derived from current observable market data for actively traded credit default swaps on publicly traded bonds of Entity X. When measuring the fair value of its investment, Entity A cannot disregard this market data even if Entity A would not be willing to transact at a price consistent with this market data.

Example 9.5B

Active markets for similar securities

Entity A holds distressed debt securities. Transactions in the securities occur infrequently and there is no active market for the securities, but there are active markets for similar securities. Entity A's own valuation model, which is based on observable Level 2 inputs current at the measurement date, indicates that market participants would be willing to buy and sell the debt for CU30 at the measurement date. Entity A has calibrated the model to the best information available at the measurement date (including transaction prices in similar securities and risk premiums).

At the measurement date, a potential buyer provides an unsolicited bid to buy the securities for CU20. When measuring the fair value of the debt securities, Entity A can neither disregard this bid price simply because it is not willing to transact at that price, nor can it assume that the bid price provides better evidence of fair value than its own model. Although the bid price is the price one potential buyer would be willing to pay for Entity A's asset, it may not necessarily be the price at which market participants (buyers and sellers) would be willing to transact on the measurement date.

Valuation techniques to measure fair value should maximise the use of relevant observable inputs (i.e. Level 1 and Level 2 inputs that do not require significant adjustment) and minimise the use of unobservable inputs (Level 3 inputs). If the bid price is classified as a Level 3 input, it may be appropriate for Entity A to place less weight on the bid price in measuring the fair value of its debt securities given that Entity A's own model is based on Level 2 inputs. However, if Entity A obtains several bid prices and the fair value indicated by the valuation model is not in the range of the bid prices obtained, Entity A may need to consider whether its model is valid and identify the reasons for the discrepancy between the model amount and the bid prices.

IFRS 13 provides an illustrative example of estimating a market rate of return when the volume or level of activity for a financial asset has significantly decreased (see **example 9.5C**).

Example 9.5C

Estimating a market rate of return when the volume or level of activity for an asset has significantly decreased

[IFRS 13:IE48-IE58 – Example 14]

This example illustrates the use of judgement when measuring the fair value of a financial asset when there has been a significant decrease in the volume or level of activity for the asset when compared with normal market activity for the asset (or similar assets).

Entity A invests in a junior AAA-rated tranche of a residential mortgage-backed security on 1 January 20X8 (the issue date of the security). The junior tranche is the third most senior of a total of seven tranches. The underlying collateral for the residential mortgage-backed security is unguaranteed non-conforming residential mortgage loans that were issued in the second half of 20X6.

At 31 March 20X9 (the measurement date) the junior tranche is now A-rated. This tranche of the residential mortgage-backed security was previously traded through a brokered market. However, trading volume in that market was infrequent, with only a few transactions taking place per month from 1 January 20X8 to 30 June 20X8 and little, if any, trading activity during the nine months before 31 March 20X9.

Entity A takes into account the factors in IFRS 13:B37 (see above) to determine whether there has been a significant decrease in the volume or level of activity for the junior tranche of the residential mortgage-backed security in which it has invested. After evaluating the significance and relevance of the factors, Entity A concludes that the volume and level of activity of the junior tranche of the residential mortgage-backed security have significantly decreased. Entity A supported its judgement primarily on the basis that there was little, if any, trading activity for an extended period before the measurement date.

Because there is little, if any, trading activity to support a valuation technique using a market approach, Entity A decides to use an income approach using the discount rate adjustment technique described in paragraphs IFRS 13:B18–B22 (see **8.3.3.1**) to measure the fair value of the residential mortgage-backed security at the measurement date. Entity A uses the contractual cash flows from the residential mortgage-backed security.

Entity A then estimates a discount rate (i.e. a market rate of return) to discount those contractual cash flows. The market rate of return is estimated using both of the following:

(a) the risk-free rate of interest.

(b) estimated adjustments for differences between the available market data and the junior tranche of the residential mortgage-backed security in which Entity A has invested. Those adjustments reflect available market data about expected non-performance and other risks (e.g. default risk, collateral value risk and liquidity risk) that market participants would take into account when pricing the asset in an orderly transaction at the measurement date under current market conditions.

Entity A took into account the following information when estimating these adjustments:

(a) the credit spread for the junior tranche of the residential mortgage-backed security at the issue date as implied by the original transaction price.

(b) the change in the credit spread implied by any observed transactions from the issue date to the measurement date for comparable residential mortgage-backed securities or on the basis of relevant indices.

(c) the characteristics of the junior tranche of the residential mortgage-backed security compared with comparable residential mortgage-backed securities or indices, including all of the following:

  (i) the quality of the underlying assets (i.e. information about the performance of the underlying mortgage loans such as delinquency and foreclosure rates, loss experience and prepayment rates)

  (ii) the seniority or subordination of the residential mortgage-backed security tranche held and

  (iii) other relevant factors.

(d) relevant reports issued by analysts and rating agencies.

(e) quoted prices from third parties such as brokers or pricing services.

Entity A estimates that one indication of the market rate of return that market participants would use when pricing the junior tranche of the residential mortgage-backed security is 12 per cent (1,200 basis points). This market rate of return was estimated as follows:

(a) Begin with 300 basis points for the relevant risk-free rate of interest at 31 March 20X9.

(b) Add 250 basis points for the credit spread over the risk-free rate when the junior tranche was issued in January 20X8.

(c) Add 700 basis points for the estimated change in the credit spread over the risk-free rate of the junior tranche between 1 January 20X8 and 31 March 20X9. This estimate was developed on the basis of the change in the most comparable index available for that time period.

(d) Subtract 50 basis points (net) to adjust for differences between the index used to estimate the change in credit spreads and the junior tranche. The reference index consists of subprime mortgage loans, whereas Entity A's residential mortgage-backed security consists of similar mortgage loans with a more favourable credit profile (making it more attractive to market participants). However, the index does not reflect an appropriate liquidity risk premium for the junior tranche under current market conditions. Thus, the 50 basis point adjustment is the net of two adjustments:

  (i) the first adjustment is a 350 basis point subtraction, which was estimated by comparing the implied yield from the most recent transactions for the residential mortgage-backed security in June 20X8 with the implied yield in the index price on those same dates. There was no information available that indicated that the relationship between Entity A's security and the index has changed.

  (ii) the second adjustment is a 300 basis point addition, which is Entity A's best estimate of the additional liquidity risk inherent in its security (a cash position) when compared with the index (a synthetic position).

> This estimate was derived after taking into account liquidity risk premiums implied in recent cash transactions for a range of similar securities.
>
> As an additional indication of the market rate of return, Entity A takes into account two recent indicative quotes (i.e. non-binding quotes) provided by reputable brokers for the junior tranche of the residential mortgage-backed security that imply yields of 15-17 per cent. Entity A is unable to evaluate the valuation techniques or inputs used to develop the quotes. However, Entity A is able to confirm that the quotes do not reflect the results of transactions.
>
> Entity A has multiple indications of the market rate of return that market participants would take into account when measuring fair value, hence, it evaluates and weights the respective indications of the rate of return, considering the reasonableness of the range indicated by the results.
>
> Entity A concludes that 13 per cent is the point within the range of indications that is most representative of fair value under current market conditions. Entity A places more weight on the 12 per cent indication (i.e. its own estimate of the market rate of return) for the following reasons:
>
> (a) Entity A concluded that its own estimate appropriately incorporated the risks (e.g. default risk, collateral value risk and liquidity risk) that market participants would use when pricing the asset in an orderly transaction under current market conditions
>
> (b) the broker quotes were non-binding and did not reflect the results of transactions, and Entity A was unable to evaluate the valuation technique(s) or inputs used to develop the quotes.

9.6 Identifying transactions that are not orderly

The determination as to whether a transaction is orderly is more difficult if there has been a significant decrease in the volume or level of activity for the asset or liability in relation to normal market activity. In such circumstances, it is not appropriate to conclude that all transactions in that market are not orderly (i.e. forced liquidations or distress sales). [IFRS 13:B43]

IFRS 13 does not require an entity to undertake exhaustive efforts to determine whether a transaction is orderly, although, the entity should not ignore information that is reasonably available. However, the Standard does establish a presumption that, when an entity is a party to a transaction, it has sufficient information to conclude whether the transaction is orderly. [IFRS 13:B44]

An entity is expected to evaluate the circumstances to determine whether, on the weight of the evidence available, the transaction is orderly. [IFRS 13:B43]

The Standard identifies the following circumstances that may indicate that a transaction is not orderly:

[IFRS 13:B43]

- there was not adequate exposure to the market for a period before the measurement date to allow for marketing activities that are usual and customary for transactions involving such assets or liabilities under current market conditions;
- there was a usual and customary marketing period, but the seller marketed the asset or liability to a single market participant;
- the seller is in or near bankruptcy or receivership (i.e. the seller is distressed);
- the seller was required to sell to meet regulatory or legal requirements (i.e. the seller was forced); or
- the transaction price is an outlier when compared with other recent transactions for the same or a similar asset or liability.

If a transaction price is determined not be orderly, little if any weight (compared to other indications of fair value) is placed on that transaction price. [IFRS 13:B44(a)]

If a transaction price is determined to be orderly, that transaction price is taken into accounting in estimating fair value. However, the amount of weight placed on that transaction price when compared with other indications of fair value will depend on facts and circumstances such as:

[IFRS 13:B44(b)]

- the volume of the transaction.
- the comparability of the transaction to the asset or liability being measured.
- the proximity of the transaction to the measurement date.

If there is not sufficient information available to conclude whether a transaction is orderly, the transaction price should be taken into account in estimating fair value. However, the transaction price may not represent fair value and, consequently, would not necessarily be the sole or primary basis for measuring fair value or estimating market risk premiums and less weight should be placed on it when compared with other transactions that are known to be orderly. [IFRS 13:B44(c)]

Example 9.6

Determining whether a transaction is orderly

Entity A is acting as an administrator on behalf of the creditors of Entity B, which is subject to bankruptcy proceedings. The administrator's role is to seek to maximise the return to Entity B's creditors. As part of Entity A's responsibilities, it auctions a portfolio of Entity B's financial assets. Entity A promotes the auction to interested parties with the expectation of receiving bids for the financial assets over a specified period.

Even though the financial assets are being sold as part of bankruptcy proceedings, the auction process may be considered to be an orderly transaction provided that all of the necessary conditions are met.

IFRS 13:Appendix A defines an orderly transaction as "[a] transaction that assumes exposure to the market for a period before the measurement date to allow for marketing activities that are usual and customary for transactions involving such assets or liabilities; it is not a forced transaction (e.g. a forced liquidation or distress sale)".

In the circumstances described, it seems possible that the auction process may be considered to be an orderly transaction because the sale is not immediate and there is sufficient (i.e. usual and customary) time to market the assets to other market participants.

If transactions in assets or liabilities occur between willing buyers and sellers in a manner that is usual and customary for transactions involving such assets or liabilities, these should be considered to be orderly transactions. Persuasive evidence is required to establish that an observable transaction is not an orderly transaction.

9.7 Quoted prices provided by third parties

IFRS 13 does not preclude the use of quoted prices provided by third parties, such as pricing services or brokers, if it is determined that the quoted prices provided by those parties are developed in accordance with IFRS 13. [IFRS 13:B45]

However, if there has been a significant decrease in the volume or level of activity for the asset or liability, an entity is required to evaluate whether the quoted prices provided by third parties are developed using current information that reflects orderly transactions or a valuation technique that reflects market participant assumptions (including assumptions about risk). In weighting a quoted price as an input to a fair value measurement, an entity should place less weight (when compared with other indications of fair value that reflect the results of transactions) on quotes that do not reflect the result of transactions. [IFRS 13:B46]

Furthermore, the nature of a quote (e.g. whether the quote is an indicative price or a binding offer) should be taken into account when weighting the available evidence, with more weight given to quotes provided by third parties that represent binding offers. [IFRS 13:B47]

Broker or pricing service quotes are not necessarily determinative of fair value if an active market (as defined in IFRS 13:Appendix A –

see **10.2.1**) does not exist for the item being measured. In assessing whether a broker or pricing service quote appropriately represents fair value, an entity needs to understand how the broker or pricing service has arrived at the quoted price, and the inputs and other information used.

Quote based on information from an active market

Consistent with IFRS 13:77 (see **10.2.1**), when a broker or pricing service quote represents the unadjusted price quoted for an identical asset, liability or equity instrument in an active market to which the entity has access at the measurement date, the entity is required to use the quoted price without adjustment when measuring fair value, subject to limited exceptions as discussed in IFRS 13:79. Such a quote represents a Level 1 input.

If any adjustment is made to the broker or pricing service quote in the circumstances specified in IFRS 13:79, or in the absence of an active market, a broker or pricing service quote does not represent a Level 1 input. However, it may nevertheless be determinative of fair value.

Quote based on valuation technique(s)

If a quote is based on a valuation technique that is used by market participants and uses market-observable or market-corroborated inputs that reflect the assumptions of market participants, it is determinative of fair value if no significant adjustment to the quote is needed. If a significant adjustment is needed, the quote is not determinative of fair value but it could represent a relevant observable input into the entity's fair value measurement.

General considerations

In assessing whether a quote is determinative of fair value, the entity should consider all relevant circumstances, including the following questions (the list is not exhaustive).

- Are there differences between the asset or liability being measured and the item for which a quote is available (e.g. differences in the terms or risk attributes)? Such differences may necessitate adjustments to the price quoted by the broker or pricing service.
- Does the quote reflect currently occurring orderly transactions for the asset or liability being measured? That is, are market participants currently transacting in the asset or liability at the price quoted by the broker or pricing service or does the quote reflect 'stale' information or transactions that are not orderly? IFRS 13.B46 (see above) provides specific guidance for circumstances in which there has been a significant decrease in the volume or level of activity for the asset or liability.

- Is the broker or pricing service using a valuation technique that complies with the fair value measurement principles in IFRS 13? For example, does the valuation technique used by the broker or pricing service (1) reflect market participant assumptions, including assumptions about risk, (2) maximise the use of relevant observable inputs, and (3) minimise the use of unobservable inputs? If the valuation technique does not reflect the assumptions market participants would use in pricing the asset or liability, the price quoted by the broker or pricing service may need adjustment or may not be relevant to the entity's fair value measurement.
- Is the quote provided by the broker or pricing service an indicative price or a binding offer? That is, does the broker or another market participant stand ready to transact at the price quoted by the broker or pricing service? As noted above, IFRS 13:B47 indicates that more weight should be given to quotes based on binding offers. Typically, a quote obtained from a broker or pricing service is an indicative price and not a binding offer (unless the broker is a market-maker).
- Does the quote come from a reputable broker or pricing service that has a substantial presence in the market and the experience and expertise to provide a representationally faithful quote for the asset or liability being measured? An entity may place more weight on a quote from a broker or pricing service that has more experience and expertise related to the asset or liability being measured.

As the number of market transactions decreases, brokers or pricing services may rely more on proprietary models based on their own assumptions to arrive at a quote. The entity should evaluate how the quote has been arrived at and whether it reflects market participant assumptions, including assumptions about risk. This information may be difficult to obtain if quotes are based on proprietary models that brokers or pricing services may not be willing to share. However, even when brokers or pricing services do not wish to share detailed information about their models, it may still be possible to obtain information about the nature of the assumptions and the inputs used in the model. If the quote does not reflect assumptions that market participants would use in pricing the asset or liability, the quote will most likely not be determinative of fair value because adjustments may be required. In such cases, the quote may be an input to the entity's fair value measurement, but other indications of fair value may be equally or more useful when estimating fair value (e.g. a valuation based on the entity's own estimates of the inputs that market participants would use in pricing the asset or liability).

Multiple quotes

An entity may need to perform additional analysis when quotes for an individual asset or liability are obtained from different brokers or pricing services. Multiple quotes within a narrow range constitute stronger evidence of fair value than multiple quotes that are widely dispersed.

IFRS 13:B40 states that a wide range of measurements may be an indication that further analysis is needed. The entity should consider the reasonableness of the range of fair value measurements, with the objective of determining the point within the range that is most representative of fair value under current market conditions.

In addition, if an entity's own estimate of fair value is outside the range of broker or pricing service quotes, the entity should understand the reason(s) for such a difference. If the range of quotes provides strong evidence of fair value, the entity may need to make adjustments to its valuation technique to reflect current market information.

10 Fair value hierarchy

10.1 Fair value hierarchy – general

To increase consistency and comparability in fair value measurements and related disclosures, IFRS 13 establishes a fair value hierarchy that categorises into three levels the inputs to valuation techniques used to measure fair value, as follows:

[IFRS 13:72]

- Level 1 inputs comprise unadjusted quoted prices in active markets for identical assets and liabilities that the entity can access at the measurement date (see **10.2.1**);
- Level 2 inputs comprise other observable inputs not included within Level 1 of the fair value hierarchy (see **10.2.2**); and
- Level 3 inputs comprise unobservable inputs (including the entity's own data, which are adjusted, if necessary, to reflect the assumptions market participants would use in the circumstances) (see **10.2.3**)

Observable inputs are defined as "[i]nputs that are developed using market data, such as publicly available information about actual events or transactions, and that reflect the assumptions that market participants would use when pricing the asset or liability". [IFRS 13:Appendix A]

Unobservable inputs are defined as "[i]nputs for which market data are not available and that are developed using the best information available about the assumptions that market participants would use when pricing the asset or liability". [IFRS 13:Appendix A]

The fair value hierarchy gives the highest priority to Level 1 inputs and the lowest priority to Level 3 inputs. [IFRS 13:72]

For example, if a fair value measurement for an asset is based on an unadjusted quoted price in an active market for an identical asset that the entity can access at the measurement date, this is categorised within 'Level 1' of the fair value hierarchy. In contrast, a valuation based on unobservable inputs would be categorised within 'Level 3'. [IFRS 13:72]

When an entity approaches the measurement of an asset, or a liability, or an entity's own equity instrument, at fair value, it looks at the available valuation techniques and at the inputs available for those techniques. When selecting the techniques and inputs to be used, the entity is required to maximise the use of observable inputs and minimise the use of unobservable inputs (see **section 8**). Once the selection has been made, each of the inputs is categorised within the fair value hierarchy outlined above; **section 10.2** summarises IFRS 13's requirements regarding the categorisation of inputs.

When an entity has determined the appropriate categorisation of the inputs into a fair value measurement, and has arrived at a measure of fair value using those inputs, it is then necessary to determine the appropriate categorisation of the fair value measurement in its entirety; this topic is discussed in **section 10.3**.

10.2 Categorisation of inputs to valuation techniques within the fair value hierarchy

10.2.1 Level 1 inputs

10.2.1.1 Level 1 inputs – general

Level 1 inputs are quoted prices (unadjusted) in active markets for identical assets or liabilities that the entity can access at the measurement date. [IFRS 13:76 & Appendix A]

A quoted price for an identical asset or liability in an active market provides the most reliable evidence of fair value and should be used without adjustment to measure fair value whenever available, except in any of the circumstances described in IFRS 13:79 (see below). [IFRS 13:77]

An active market is defined as "[a] market in which transactions for the asset or liability take place with sufficient frequency and volume to provide pricing information on an ongoing basis". [IFRS 13:Appendix A]

Determining whether a market is active focuses on the trading activity for the individual asset or liability being measured and not on the general levels of activity in the market in which the asset or liability is traded. For example, a security listed on the FTSE in London or HKEx in Hong Kong could be considered to be traded in an inactive market if the security itself is traded infrequently.

IFRS 13:B37 sets out a list of factors that may indicate that there has been a significant decrease in the volume or level of activity for an asset or a liability relative to normal market activity for that asset or liability (or similar assets or liabilities) (see **9.5**).The presence of one or more of the factors listed in IFRS 13:B37 alone is not sufficient to conclude that a market is not active. An entity should evaluate the relevance and significance of these factors to the individual asset or liability measured at fair value in order to determine whether the market for that asset or liability is inactive. A market is not deemed inactive simply because of insufficient trading volume relative to the size of an entity's position.

The characterisation of a market as 'active' or 'inactive' may change as market conditions change. However, a decline in the volume of transactions for a particular asset or liability does not automatically mean that the market has become inactive. A market would still be considered active as long as the frequency and volume of relevant transactions are sufficient to provide ongoing pricing information.

Further, quoted prices from a market affected by a decline in the volume or level of activity should not be ignored unless the price is associated with a transaction that is not orderly. It is not appropriate to conclude automatically that all transactions occurring in a market exhibiting a significant decline in volume or level of activity are not orderly. IFRS 13:B43 sets out a list of factors that may indicate that a transaction is not orderly (see **9.6**). Very little weight should be given to prices observed for a transaction that is not orderly; more weight may be given to a price observed for an orderly transaction. However, the entity should evaluate carefully whether an adjustment may be needed to that price to ensure the fair value measurement is consistent with the objectives in IFRS 13.

When a financial asset or financial liability is exchanged in multiple active markets (e.g. on different exchanges), the entity will need to consider which market is the most relevant for measuring fair value. IFRS 13 states explicitly that the emphasis within Level 1 is on determining both of the following:

[IFRS 13:78]

- the principal market for the asset or liability or, in the absence of a principal market, the most advantageous market for the asset or liability (see **section 3.3**); and
- whether the entity can enter into a transaction for the asset or liability at the price in that market at the measurement date.

When a quoted price in an active market is available, it should not be adjusted except in the circumstances listed below.

[IFRS 13:79]

- When an entity holds a large number of similar (but not identical) assets or liabilities (e.g. debt securities) that are measured at fair value and a quoted price in an active market is available but not readily accessible for each of those assets or liabilities individually (i.e. given the large number of similar assets or liabilities held by the entity, it would be difficult to obtain pricing information for each individual asset or liability at the measurement date). In such circumstances, as a practical expedient, an entity may measure fair value using an alternative pricing method that does not rely exclusively on quoted prices (e.g. matrix pricing – see **8.4**). However, the use of an alternative pricing method results in a fair value measurement categorised within a lower level of the fair value hierarchy.

- When a quoted price in an active market does not represent fair value at the measurement date. That might be the case if, for example, significant events (such as transactions in a principal-to-principal market, trades in a brokered market or announcements) take place after the close of a market but before the measurement date. An entity shall establish and consistently apply a policy for identifying those events that might affect fair value measurements. However, if the quoted price is adjusted for new information, the adjustment results in a fair value measurement categorised within a lower level of the fair value hierarchy.

- When measuring the fair value of a liability or an entity's own equity instrument using the quoted price for the identical item traded as an asset in an active market and that price needs to be adjusted for factors specific to the item or the asset (see **5.1.1**). If no adjustment to the quoted price of the asset is required, the result is a fair value measurement categorised within Level 1 of the fair value hierarchy. However, any adjustment to the quoted price of the asset results in a fair value measurement categorised within a lower level of the fair value hierarchy.

If an entity holds a position in a single asset or liability (including a position comprising a large number of identical assets or liabilities, such as a holding of financial instruments) and the asset or liability is traded in an active market, the fair value of the asset or liability should be measured within Level 1 as the product of the quoted price for the individual asset or liability and the quantity held by the entity. That is the case even if a market's normal daily trading volume is not sufficient to absorb the quantity held and placing orders to sell the position in a single transaction might affect the quoted price. [IFRS 13:80]

10.2.1.2 Published net asset values for open-ended investment funds as Level 1 inputs

Some open-ended investments funds not listed on a stock exchange may publish daily quotations of their net asset values (NAVs) at which redemptions or purchases of units occur without any adjustments to the published NAV. The redemptions and unit purchases may take place regularly at the quoted NAVs and there is no secondary market for the units because they are not transferrable (i.e. the sole transactions are issuances and redemptions of the units by the fund). These quoted NAVs may meet the definition of a Level 1 input provided that all of the elements of the definition in IFRS 13:76 (see **10.2.1.1**) are met.

Consequently, the following criteria must be satisfied:

- the price must be quoted in an active market (see **10.2.1.1**);
- the price must be unadjusted;
- the price must be for an asset or a liability that is identical to the asset or liability being measured; and
- the entity must have access to the price at the measurement date.

For the price to be classified as a Level 1 input, it is not required that there be an active market between the holders of the financial instrument and other potential holders that are not the issuer of the financial instrument; it is possible that the financial instrument does not have an active market other than between the holders of the financial instrument and the issuer of the financial instrument.

Careful analysis is required when assessing whether such prices meet the definition of a Level 1 input. In particular, the assessment should include: (1) whether quoted prices are readily and regularly available; (2) whether transactions occur regularly; and (3) whether the regularly occurring transactions take place at the quoted (unadjusted price) on an arm's length basis.

10.2.2 Level 2 inputs

Level 2 inputs are inputs other than quoted prices included within Level 1 that are observable for the asset or liability, either directly or indirectly. [IFRS 13:81 & Appendix A]

Level 2 inputs include the following:

[IFRS 13:82]

- quoted prices for similar assets or liabilities in active markets.
- quoted prices for identical or similar assets or liabilities in markets that are not active.
- inputs other than quoted prices that are observable for the asset or liability, for example:
  - interest rates and yield curves observable at commonly quoted intervals;

  - implied volatilities; and
  - credit spreads.
- inputs that are derived principally from or corroborated by observable market data by correlation or other means (market-corroborated inputs).

Under IFRS 13:82 (see above), when an entity measures the fair value of an asset or a liability and no Level 1 inputs are available, it may use quoted prices for 'similar' assets or liabilities in active markets as a Level 2 input. Equally, under IFRS 13:79(a) (see **10.2.1**), entities holding a large number of 'similar' assets or liabilities for which a quoted price is not accessible for all of the assets and liabilities being measured, may measure fair value using alternative pricing (e.g. matrix pricing) as a practical expedient.

IFRS 13 does not provide any specific guidance as to what is meant by 'similar' in this context. The identification of a similar asset or liability involves the exercise of judgement and requires both:

- an understanding of the terms and other factors that affect the fair values of the asset or liability being measured and the asset or liability for which the quoted price exists; and
- an identification and assessment of any differences in the terms and other factors that affect the fair values of these assets or liabilities.

In October 2008, the IASB's Expert Advisory Panel issued a report *Measuring and Disclosing the Fair Value of Financial Instruments in Markets That Are No Longer Active* which describes practices entities use when measuring financial instruments at fair value. Paragraph 32 of the report (quoted below) provides examples of the basic terms of a financial instrument with contractual cash flows. Entities may consider these terms, and any associated differences, when assessing whether the instrument for which a quoted price exists is 'similar' to the instrument being measured.

> "The basic terms of a financial instrument include, for example:
>
> (a) **the timing of the cash flows**: when the entity expects to realise the cash flows related to the instrument.
>
> (b) **the calculation of the cash flows**: for example, for a debt instrument the interest rate that applies (i.e. the coupon), or for a derivative instrument how the cash flows are calculated in relation to the underlying instrument or index (or indices).
>
> (c) **the timing and conditions for any options in the contract**: for example:
>
> (i) prepayment options (one or both parties can demand or make an early payment).
>
> (ii) extension options (one or both parties can extend the period of the instrument).

(iii) conversion options (one or both parties can convert the instrument into another instrument).

(iv) put or call options (one or both parties can exchange the instrument for a defined amount

(d) **protection of the rights of the parties to the instrument**: for example:

(i) terms relating to credit risk in debt instruments, such as collateral, event of default and margin call triggers.

(ii) subordination of the instrument, for example the priority of the instruments in the event of a winding up.

(iii) the legal enforceability of the cash flows."

Further, paragraph 33 of the report notes that "to measure the fair value of an instrument it is necessary to assess the return that market participants would require on the instrument to compensate for" certain risks. This principle is largely consistent with the fair value measurement principles in IFRS 13. Accordingly, any differences between the compensation that market participants would require for the risk associated with the instrument being measured and the compensation required for the instrument for which a quoted price exists should be considered in determining whether the instruments are similar and whether an adjustment to the quoted price is necessary.

If the asset or liability has a specified (contractual) term, a Level 2 input must be observable for substantially the full term of the asset or liability. [IFRS 13:82]

Example 10.2.2

Determining how an input is classified when the item being measured has a specified contractual term

Company X enters into a fixed-price six-year agreement to sell 50 megawatts (MW) of on-peak electricity for delivery at location ABC beginning on 1 January 20X1 and continuing through to 31 December 20X6. On 31 March 20X1, Company X is measuring the fair value of the fixed-price agreement. Active market quotes are available for forward contracts to sell electricity at location ABC for two years (31 March 20X1 to 31 March 20X3). Accordingly, Company X will use the two years of observable forward pricing data and develop an expectation for the remaining 3 years and nine months (i.e.1 April 20X3 to 31 December 20X6) using a model that relies on pricing data and weather patterns from the previous four years. The model also incorporates all relevant physical constraints (capacity of existing power plants and power plants expected to be completed near location ABC, projected supply and demand etc.).

In the circumstances described, the five-year and nine-month forward price curve represents a Level 3, rather than a Level 2, input.

An input for an item with a specified contractual term falls within Level 2 of the hierarchy only if it meets both of the following criteria:

- as required by IFRS 13:82 (see above), the input must be observable for substantially the full term of the asset or liability (see above); and
- the impact of the unobservable period must not be significant to the fair value of the asset or liability. The guidance set out in **10.3.3.2** should be applied when evaluating whether the effect of the unobservable period is significant.

IFRS 13:B35(b) cites as an example an interest rate swap with a term of 10 years and for which the fair value is determined using a swap rate based on a yield curve that is observable at commonly quoted intervals for 9 years. The swap rate input is a Level 2 input provided that any reasonable extrapolation of the yield curve for Year 10 would not be significant to the fair value measurement of the swap in its entirety.

In contrast, in the circumstances described, Company X can observe forward prices for only 24 months of the remaining 69-month term of the agreement (i.e. 35 per cent of the term). Because this does not represent substantially the full term, the first criterion above is not met. An analysis of the second criterion is unnecessary; the forward price curve is considered a Level 3 input. However, if the forward price curve had been observable for substantially the full term, Company X would need to consider the second criterion (i.e. whether the effect of the unobservable term is significant to the fair value of the agreement) to determine whether the forward price curve is a Level 2 or Level 3 input.

Adjustments to Level 2 inputs will vary depending on factors specific to the asset or liability. Those factors include the following:

[IFRS 13:83]

- the condition or location of the asset;
- the extent to which inputs relate to items that are comparable to the asset or liability (including those factors described in IFRS 13:39 – see **5.1.2**); and
- the volume or level of activity in the markets within which the inputs are observed.

An entity should consider whether adjustments to the quoted price for a similar asset or liability are necessary to reflect differences between the terms of the items being compared and other factors that may affect the fair values of those items. For example, the entity may need to make adjustments to reflect differences in the condition, location or risks (including non-performance risk and liquidity risk) of the items being compared.

Under IFRS 13:37, when a quoted price for the transfer of an identical or similar liability is not available and the identical item is held by another party as an asset, the fair value of the liability is measured from the perspective of a market participant that holds the identical item as an asset at the measurement date. The value should only be adjusted for factors specific to the asset that are not applicable to the fair value measurement of the liability. IFRS 13:39 provides a number of examples of such factors (see **5.1.2**).

In addition, if an entity uses a quoted price for a similar item in its valuation technique, the entity may need to make adjustments to reflect differences in risk, including liquidity differences. For example, the item being measured may be in shorter supply (relative to demand) than the similar item for which a quoted price exists. In this situation, a liquidity risk premium exists for the item being measured that should be factored into the fair value measurement as an adjustment to the quoted price of the similar item.

An adjustment to a Level 2 input that is significant to the entire measurement might result in a fair value measurement categorised within Level 3 of the fair value hierarchy, if the adjustment uses significant unobservable inputs. [IFRS 13:84]

IFRS 13 provides the following examples of Level 2 inputs for particular assets and liabilities.

[IFRS 13:B35]

- **Receive-fixed, pay-variable interest rate swap based on the London Interbank Offered Rate (LIBOR) swap rate** A Level 2 input would be the LIBOR swap rate if that rate is observable at commonly quoted intervals for substantially the full term of the swap.
- **Receive-fixed, pay-variable interest rate swap based on a yield curve denominated in a foreign currency** A Level 2 input would be the swap rate based on a yield curve denominated in a foreign currency that is observable at commonly quoted intervals for substantially the full term of the swap. That would be the case if the term of the swap is 10 years and that rate is observable at commonly quoted intervals for 9 years, provided that any reasonable extrapolation of the yield curve for Year 10 would not be significant to the fair value measurement of the swap in its entirety (but see **example 10.2.2** for circumstances when observable data is not available for substantially the full term of the agreement).
- **Receive-fixed, pay-variable interest rate swap based on a specific bank's prime rate** A Level 2 input would be the bank's prime rate derived through extrapolation if the extrapolated values are corroborated by observable market data, for example, by correlation with an interest rate that is observable over substantially the full term of the swap.

- **Three-year option on exchange-traded shares**. A Level 2 input would be the implied volatility for the shares derived through extrapolation to Year 3 if both of the following conditions exist:
  - (i) prices for one-year and two-year options on the shares are observable
  - (ii) the extrapolated implied volatility of a three-year option is corroborated by observable market data for substantially the full term of the option.

  In that case, the implied volatility could be derived by extrapolating from the implied volatility of the one-year and two-year options on the shares and corroborated by the implied volatility for three-year options on comparable entities' shares, provided that correlation with the one-year and two-year implied volatilities is established. [IFRS 13:B35]

10.2.3 Level 3 inputs

Level 3 inputs are unobservable inputs for the asset or liability. [IFRS 13:86 & Appendix A]

Unobservable inputs should be used to measure fair value to the extent that relevant observable inputs are not available (e.g. when there is little, if any, market activity for the asset or liability at the measurement date). However unobservable inputs should reflect the assumptions that market participants would use when pricing the asset or liability, so as to achieve the general fair value measurement objective (i.e. an exit price at the measurement date from the perspective of a market participant that holds the asset or owes the liability). [IFRS 13:87]

Unobservable inputs should reflect, among others, assumptions that market participants would make about risk. Assumptions about risk include the risk inherent in a particular valuation technique used to measure fair value (such as a pricing model) and the risk inherent in the inputs to the valuation technique. A measurement that does not include an adjustment for risk would not represent a fair value measurement if market participants would include one when pricing the asset or liability. For example, it might be necessary to include a risk adjustment when there is significant measurement uncertainty (e.g. when there has been a significant decrease in the volume or level of activity when compared with normal market activity for the asset or liability (or similar assets or liabilities) and the entity has determined that the transaction price or quoted price does not represent fair value – see **9.5** to **9.7**). [IFRS 13:88]

Unobservable inputs should be developed using the best information available in the circumstances, which might include an entity's own data. In developing unobservable inputs, an entity's own data, should be adjusted if reasonably available information indicates that other market participants would use different data or there is something particular to the entity that is not available to other market participants (e.g. an entity-specific synergy). IFRS 13 does not require an entity to undertake exhaustive efforts to obtain information about market participant assumptions. However, the entity is required to take into account all information about market participant assumptions that is reasonably available. Unobservable inputs developed in the manner described above are considered market participant assumptions and meet the objective of a fair value measurement. [IFRS 13:89]

IFRS 13 provides the following examples of Level 3 inputs for particular assets and liabilities.

[IFRS 13:B36]

- **Long-dated currency swap** A Level 3 input would be an interest rate in a specified currency that is not observable and cannot be corroborated by observable market data at commonly quoted intervals or otherwise for substantially the full term of the currency swap. The interest rates in a currency swap are the swap rates calculated from the respective countries' yield curves.
- **Three-year option on exchange-traded shares** A Level 3 input would be historical volatility, i.e. the volatility for the shares derived from the shares' historical prices. Historical volatility typically does not represent current market participant expectations about future volatility, even if it is the only information available to price an option.
- **Interest rate swap** A Level 3 input would be an adjustment to a mid-market consensus (non-binding) price for the swap developed using data that are not directly observable and cannot otherwise be corroborated by observable market data.

10.2.4 Determining the level within the fair value hierarchy when broker or pricing service quotes are used

IFRS 13 allows the use of quoted prices provided by brokers or pricing services if the entity has determined that the quoted prices provided by a broker or pricing service are developed in accordance with IFRS 13. See **9.7** for more detailed guidance regarding when a quoted price provided by a broker or pricing service can be considered to be determinative of fair value.

When quoted prices are provided by a broker or pricing service, and are used by an entity in measuring the fair value of an asset or a liability, the following considerations are relevant for the entity's assessment of the level within the fair value hierarchy in which the quoted prices fall.

Level 1 inputs

Level 1 inputs are unadjusted quoted prices in active markets for identical assets or liabilities. If the quote provided by a broker or pricing service is a Level 1 input, the quoted price should be used to measure the fair value of the asset or liability without adjustment, subject to limited exceptions as discussed in IFRS 13:79 (see **10.2.1.1**).

If an adjustment is necessary in accordance with IFRS 13:79, or if the quoted price originates from a market that is not active, the broker or pricing service quote does not represent a Level 1 input.

In January 2015, the Interpretations Committee received a request to clarify under what circumstances prices that are provided by third parties would qualify as Level 1 in the fair value hierarchy in accordance with IFRS 13. The submitter noted that there are divergent views on the level within the hierarchy in which fair value measurements based on prices received from third parties should be classified.

The Interpretations Committee noted that when assets or liabilities are measured on the basis of prices provided by third parties, the classification of those measurements within the fair value hierarchy will depend on the evaluation of the inputs used by the third party to derive those prices, instead of on the pricing methodology used. In other words, the fair value hierarchy prioritises the inputs to valuation techniques, not the valuation techniques used to measure fair value. In accordance with IFRS 13, only unadjusted quoted prices in active markets for identical assets or liabilities that the entity can access at the measurement date qualify as Level 1 inputs. Consequently, the Interpretations Committee noted that a fair value measurement that is based on prices provided by third parties may only be categorised within Level 1 of the fair value hierarchy if the measurement relies solely on unadjusted quoted prices in an active market for an identical instrument that the entity can access at the measurement date.

The Interpretations Committee also observed that the guidance in IFRS 13 relating to the classification of measurements within the fair value hierarchy is sufficient to draw an appropriate conclusion on the issue submitted. Consequently, the Interpretations Committee decided not to add this issue to its agenda.

Level 2 inputs

Level 2 inputs are inputs other than quoted prices included within Level 1 that are observable for the asset or liability, either directly or indirectly. Observable inputs are defined in IFRS 13:Appendix A as "[i]nputs that are developed using market data, such as publicly available information about actual events or transactions, and that reflect the assumptions that market participants would use when pricing the asset or liability [or own equity instrument]".

If a quote from a broker or pricing service meets any of the following criteria, it represents a Level 2 input.

- The entity can determine that the broker or pricing service quote itself represents a quoted price for similar assets or liabilities in active markets.
- The entity can determine that the quote is based on quoted prices for identical or similar assets or liabilities in markets that are not active, from transactions that are orderly and for which adjustments are based only on information that is (1) observable, or (2) market-corroborated, or (3) unobservable, but insignificant to the measurement.
- The entity can determine that the quote was established using a valuation technique and that the inputs the broker or pricing service used to arrive at the quoted price are observable or market-corroborated and any unobservable inputs do not have a significant effect on the measurement.
- The entity can corroborate the broker or pricing service quote or inputs using prices (1) from orderly transactions in an active market or (2) from orderly transactions in an inactive market for which any adjustment needed to ensure the price is representative of fair value is insignificant to the measurement.

In some circumstances, adjustments to the Level 2 inputs may be necessary, for example if the quoted price is based on a similar (but not identical) asset or liability. If an adjustment is required, an entity should determine whether the adjustment is significant to the entire measurement and whether it is based on unobservable inputs. If this is the case, the entire measurement will be categorised within Level 3.

Level 3 inputs

Level 3 inputs are unobservable inputs for the asset or liability. Broker or pricing service quotes meeting any of the following criteria are categorised in Level 3 of the fair value hierarchy.

- The entity can determine that the quote is based on a Level 1 or Level 2 input but an adjustment is required that is significant to the measurement and based on unobservable inputs.
- The entity can determine that the quote is based on unobservable inputs with a significant effect.

Regardless of whether the entity determines that the broker or pricing service quote is based on observable or unobservable inputs, it is not appropriate for an entity to accept, without further analysis, that the inputs used are appropriate in the circumstances. The entity must gain sufficient understanding of the inputs to be able to conclude that they reflect assumptions market participants would use, including assumptions about risks inherent in a particular valuation technique and the inputs used. Further, an entity must be able to conclude that the inputs used are based on the best information available. Adjustments should be made if reasonably available information, including the entity's own data, indicates that other market participants would use different inputs.

Other considerations

Depending on the asset or liability being measured at fair value, a quote from a broker or pricing service may be the only input, or one of many inputs, into an entity's fair value measurement of that asset or liability. All inputs must be considered before determining the level within the fair value hierarchy for measurement of the asset or liability (see **section 10.3**).

Other factors indicating that a broker or pricing service quote may be given more weight in the fair value measurement include that:

- the quote is binding on the entity making the quote; or
- the quote is available from more than one broker or pricing service.

Disclosure

IFRS 13:IE64(b) in the illustrative examples accompanying IFRS 13 suggests that, in order to comply with the disclosure requirements in IFRS 13:92(d), an entity may disclose "how third-party information such as broker quotes, pricing services, net asset values and relevant market data was taken into account when measuring fair value" as part of the entity's additional information about significant unobservable inputs. Further, IFRS 13:IE65(d) suggests that, in order to comply with the disclosure requirements in IFRS 13:93(g), an entity may disclose how the entity determined that third-party information, such as broker quotes or pricing services, used in the fair value measurement was developed in accordance with IFRS 13 as part of the entity's description of its valuation process for Level 3 fair value measurements.

10.3 Categorisation of fair value measurements within the fair value hierarchy

10.3.1 Categorisation of fair value measurements – general

The categorisation of a fair value measurement within the fair value hierarchy is a two-step process. Initially, the entity determines the appropriate categorisation of the inputs to the valuation techniques used in the fair value measurement (see **section 10.2**). Once the valuation techniques have been applied, and the fair value measured, it is then necessary to determine the appropriate categorisation of the fair value measurement in its entirety. This is required in order to arrive at the appropriate analysis of the fair value measurements for disclosure purposes (see **4.3.3.3** in **B11**).

As can be seen from the discussion in **10.3.1** to **10.3.2**, the appropriate categorisation of a fair value measurement is determined by the 'mix' of inputs used. For example, if only Level 1 inputs are used, the fair value measurement will be categorised as a Level 1 measurement (see **10.3.1**). The same principle applies if only Level 2 or only Level 3 inputs are used. Alternatively, the fair value measurement may be derived from several inputs from different categories, in which case it will be necessary to consider the significance of each of those inputs (see **10.3.2**).

10.3.2 Categorisation of measurements made using Level 1 inputs

A fair value measurement can only be categorised as a Level 1 measurement when only Level 1 inputs are used, and no adjustments are made.

In any of the circumstances described in IFRS 13:79 (see **10.2.1**), a Level 1 input cannot be used without adjustment. IFRS 13:79 outlines the appropriate adjustments for each circumstance. Note that any adjustment to a Level 1 input, regardless of its significance, means that the resulting fair value measurement cannot be categorised as a Level 1 measurement.

Based on the definition in IFRS 13:76 and Appendix 1 (see **10.2.1**), for a fair value measurement to be categorised in Level 1 of the fair value hierarchy, the following criteria must be satisfied:

- the only input used must be a price (or prices) quoted in an active market;
- the price must be unadjusted. IFRS 13:79 (see above) requires that any adjustment to a fair value measurement (regardless of its significance) that would otherwise meet the Level 1 criteria results in the fair value measurement being categorised as a lower-level measurement;
- the price must be for an asset or liability that is identical to the asset or liability being measured (see **examples 10.3.2A** to **10.3.2D**); and
- the entity must have access to the price at the measurement date. For example, an entity has access to the price if it has the ability to transact at that price in an exchange market. In addition, an entity has access to the price if there are dealers who stand ready to transact with the entity at that price. However, broker quotes by themselves are not sufficient evidence that the entity has access to the price if the brokers do not stand ready to transact at that price. Any adjustment made to a quoted price in an active market

because the entity has limited or no access to that market results in a Level 2 or a Level 3 measurement, depending on the nature of the adjustment. Further, although a quoted price in an active market may be available, such pricing may not be readily accessible for all of the assets and liabilities being measured, if an entity holds a large volume of similar (but not identical) instruments. As a result, the entity may measure fair value using alternative pricing (e.g. matrix pricing) as a practical expedient, which would result in a lower level measurement in the fair value hierarchy.

Example 10.3.2A

Application of Level 1 classification criteria – debt security

Entity P holds a debt security that is traded in a dealer market in which bid and ask prices are available. The market is an active market and it is the principal market for the security. The market is accessible by Entity P. No adjustments have been made to the quoted price.

If the quoted price used to measure the fair value of the debt security is for a debt security identical to that held by Entity P, the measurement of the debt security should be classified within Level 1 of the fair value hierarchy. The fact that a price is derived from a dealer market (rather than an 'exchange' market) does not in itself preclude classification as a Level 1 measurement because such dealer markets may be active and accessible to the entity.

Example 10.3.2B

Application of Level 1 classification criteria – issued debt security with identical instrument traded as an asset

Entity Q has issued an exchange-traded debt security. Entity Q has elected to account for this instrument using the fair value option under IFRS 9. A quoted price for the transfer of an identical or similar liability is not available; however, an identical instrument is currently trading as an asset in an active market. Entity Q uses the quoted price for the asset as its initial input for the fair value measurement of the issued debt security. Entity Q also evaluates whether the quoted price for the asset requires adjustment for factors, such as third-party credit enhancements, that would not be applicable to the issued debt security. Entity Q determines that no adjustments are required to the quoted price of the asset.

Because the quoted price used to measure the fair value of the issued debt security is for an identical debt security (e.g. the identical ISIN*) traded as an asset, and no adjustments to the quoted price of the instrument are required, the resulting measurement of the issued debt security should be classified as a Level 1 measurement in the fair value hierarchy.

* ISIN refers to the International Securities Identification Number, a 12-character alpha-numerical code that does not contain information characterising financial instruments but serves for uniform identification of a security at trading and settlement.

Example 10.3.2C

Application of Level 1 classification criteria – 'look-alike' forward contract

Entity R holds an over-the-counter (OTC) 'look-alike' forward contract (i.e. it mirrors another contract). The counterparty to this contract is contractually obligated to settle it on the basis of the quoted price for a similar futures contract traded on an active futures exchange. The forward contract meets the definition of a derivative and is therefore measured at fair value.

While the look-alike forward contract mirrors the exchange-traded futures contract, and the value of the look-alike forward contract is intended to approximate the quoted price for the exchange-traded futures contract, the forward and futures contracts are not identical. Even if the parties to the forward contract both have the highest credit quality (resulting in the same level of credit risk as the exchange-traded futures contract), the forward contract is not considered identical because (1) the counterparties are different, and (2) Entity R cannot sell the forward contract on the futures exchange (i.e. the forward contract has different levels of counterparty and liquidity risk when compared to the futures contract). While the quoted price for the futures contract may be a Level 1 input (when the market for it is active), the fair value measurement of the look-alike forward contract can only be classified as Level 2 or 3.

Example 10.3.2D

Application of Level 1 classification criteria – interest rate swap

Entity S is a party to an interest rate swap that is transacted on an over-the-counter (OTC) market. The OTC market does not quote prices for interest rate swaps. Entity S would determine the fair value of the swap by using either (1) a discounted cash flow approach based on market-based yield curves, or (2) the price at which a similar swap was exchanged on the OTC market. While similar swaps may have been exchanged on the OTC market, the similar swaps would have different counterparties and would, therefore, not be identical to the swap held by Entity S.

The price at which Entity S would be able to sell the swap would result from a negotiated transaction contemplating the credit standings of the two parties to the swap as well as the terms of the specific swap. Because the swap held by Entity S is not identical to any similar swap for which there may be transactions on the OTC market, the measurement of the swap by Entity S would be classified as a Level 2 or 3 measurement, depending on the inputs that are significant to the measurement.

10.3.3 Determining the level within the fair value hierarchy when several inputs are used

10.3.3.1 Determining the level within the fair value hierarchy – general

When several inputs are used to measure the fair value of an asset or a liability, those inputs may be categorised within different levels of the fair value hierarchy (e.g. the valuation may be based on some Level 2 and some Level 3 inputs). In such circumstances, the categorisation of the fair value measurement in its entirety is based on the lowest level input that is significant to the entire measurement. [IFRS 13:73] See **10.3.3.2** for a discussion of the meaning of the term 'significant'.

Example 10.3.3.1

Classification of fair value measurements within the fair value hierarchy

Entity I holds an investment in equity instruments that are not traded in an active market (e.g. equity instruments issued by a private entity). In accordance with IFRS 9, the investment is measured at fair value subsequent to initial recognition.

How should Entity I classify the fair value measurement of its investment within the fair value hierarchy (i.e. as Level 1, Level 2 or Level 3)?

The examples below illustrate the application of the guidance in IFRS 13 on the classification of measurements within the fair value hierarchy.

Note that, because the equity instruments are not traded in an active market, Level 1 inputs are not available.

Scenario 1 – Fair value is estimated based on recent transactions

If Entity I estimates the fair value of its investment based on recent transactions between independent third parties (e.g. quoted prices in an inactive market, privately negotiated acquisitions or disposals of the equity instruments etc.), these transaction prices would be considered Level 2 inputs if they meet the definition of fair value. This would be the case if the price represents an exit price for the equity instruments at the date of the transaction, the transaction is executed at terms that are consistent with how other market participants would transact, and the transaction is not executed under duress.

Similarly, prices based on recent transactions between Entity I and third parties may be considered Level 2 inputs if they meet the criteria above. For example, Entity I owns a 5 per cent equity investment in Entity X and measures that investment at fair value. Entity I acquires an additional 10 per cent of Entity X. If the transaction price for the additional 10 per cent meets the definition of fair value, Entity I may use that price as a basis for valuing its entire 15 per cent investment at the next reporting date.

In either case, it may be necessary to adjust the recent transaction price to measure the investment appropriately at fair value at the reporting date. For example, the recent transaction price should be adjusted for events or changes in the entity's financial position that have occurred since the date of the transaction that would affect the value of the equity investment in the entity. Unobservable adjustments to a Level 2 input that are significant to the entire measurement would change the categorisation to Level 3.

Scenario 2 – Fair value is determined based on a discounted cash flow technique

IFRS 13:B36(e) (see **10.2.3**) cites as an example of a Level 3 input "a financial forecast (e.g. of cash flows or earnings) developed using the entity's own data if there is no reasonably available information that indicates that market participants would use different assumptions". While certain information used in the model may be observable (e.g. interest rate curves), the entity's projected cash flows (which are not observable) would probably be significant to the entire fair value measurement. Therefore, the measurement of the investment would probably be classified as Level 3.

Scenario 3 – Fair value is determined based on a market-based multiple applied to a financial measure

IFRS 13:B35(h) (see **10.2.2**) cites as an example of a Level 2 input "a valuation multiple (e.g. a multiple of earnings or revenue or a similar performance measure) derived from observable market data, e.g. multiples derived from prices in observed transactions involving comparable (that is, similar) businesses, taking into account operational, market, financial, and non-financial factors". The market-derived multiple may thus be considered a Level 2 input. However, the historical financial measure (i.e. earnings or EBITDA) and any adjustments needed to reflect differences between the entity and comparable entities would probably be Level 3 inputs because they are entity-specific and are not considered market-observable data. Therefore, the measurement of the investment would probably be classified within Level 3 of the fair value hierarchy.

The availability of relevant inputs and their relative subjectivity might affect the selection of appropriate valuation techniques. However, the fair value hierarchy prioritises the inputs to valuation techniques, not the valuation techniques used to measure fair value. For example, a fair value measurement developed using a present value technique might be categorised within Level 2 or Level 3, depending on the inputs that are significant to the entire measurement and the level of the fair value hierarchy within which those inputs are categorised. [IFRS 13:74]

In other words, the categorisation of the fair value measurement in the fair value hierarchy is based on inputs, not on the valuation technique in which they are used.

If an observable input requires an adjustment using an unobservable input and that adjustment results in a significantly higher or lower fair value measurement, the resulting measurement is a Level 3 measurement. For example, if a market participant would take into account the effect of a restriction on the sale of an asset when estimating the price for the asset, an entity would adjust the quoted price to reflect the effect of that restriction. If that quoted price is a Level 2 input and the adjustment is an unobservable input that is significant to the entire measurement, the measurement would be categorised within Level 3 of the fair value hierarchy. [IFRS 13:75]

10.3.3.2 Determining the 'significance' of an input or an adjustment

The Standard does not expand on what is meant by 'significant' in the context of IFRS 13:73, other than to state that the assessment of the significance of a particular input to the entire measurement requires judgement, taking into account factors specific to the asset or liability. [IFRS 13:73]

To determine the level in which the fair value measurement should be categorised, an entity should aggregate the inputs to the measurement by level and determine the lowest level of inputs that are significant to the fair value measurement in its entirety. For example, a measurement that includes inputs with significant effect from Levels 2 and 3 would be classified in its entirety in Level 3, because Level 3 is the lowest level input with a significant effect.

Entities should establish a methodology for determining whether an input or aggregated inputs are significant to the measurement in its entirety. The methodology should be applied consistently.

In some cases, a qualitative assessment of the inputs used may be sufficient. For example, changes in discount rates generally have a significant effect on fair value measurements determined using a discounted cash flow model.

In other cases, a quantitative analysis of the inputs may be required. One quantitative approach might involve the following steps.

- **Step 1** – Select a threshold or percentage of the overall fair value measurement as a benchmark for significance.
- **Step 2** – Perform a sensitivity analysis, calculating the percentage change in the fair value measurement arising from reasonably possible changes to each input.
- **Step 3** – Compare the percentage change in the fair value measurement for each input calculated under Step 2 to the benchmark selected under Step 1. If the percentage change in the fair value measurement for a particular input exceeds the selected benchmark, that input would be considered significant. If none of the individual Level 3 inputs are considered significant, the combined effect of all the Level 3 inputs should be considered to determine whether they have a significant effect in aggregate on the fair value measurement.

When this approach is used, the benchmark should represent a percentage of the overall measurement and not a percentage of a particular component of the fair value measurement. In addition, the threshold should not represent a percentage of total assets, total liabilities, gains or losses, or other line items in the statement of financial position or the statement of comprehensive income because this would not be specific to the fair value measurement.

Example 10.3.3.2 illustrates this approach.

Example 10.3.3.2

Determining the significance of an input

Entity A holds a hybrid instrument which includes an embedded option. Entity A is measuring the instrument at fair value in its entirety. One of the inputs to its valuation model is the volatility of the embedded option for which market data are not available (i.e. it is unobservable and, consequently, a Level 3 input).

Entity A is evaluating whether the unobservable volatility input is significant to the overall fair value measurement for the hybrid instrument. In making its assessment, Entity A considers the significance of the volatility in relation to the hybrid instrument in its entirety and not solely in relation to the embedded option.

Entity A uses a quantitative methodology and selects a threshold or percentage of the overall fair value measurement of the hybrid instrument as a benchmark for significance. Entity A then performs a sensitivity analysis to determine how the volatility input affects the overall fair value of the hybrid instrument within a reasonably possible range of values for the volatility input.

If reasonable changes in the volatility input cause the percentage change in the fair value measurement of the hybrid instrument to exceed the selected threshold, Entity A would conclude that the unobservable volatility input is significant to the measurement in its entirety. In that case, the fair value measurement of the hybrid instrument would represent a Level 3 measurement within the fair value hierarchy.

10.3.4 Observable transactions in inactive markets

The level of market activity does not affect the IFRS 13 measurement objective, i.e. fair value is the price in an orderly transaction between market participants at the measurement date under current market conditions.

Observable transactions are relevant inputs to a fair value measurement when they reflect market participants' assumptions in orderly transactions and, thus, are representative of fair value. Relevant observable inputs should be given priority when measuring fair value in accordance with IFRS 13. IFRS 13:67 (see **section 9**) states that "[v]aluation techniques used to measure fair value shall maximise the use of relevant observable inputs and minimise the use of unobservable inputs". Further, IFRS 13:87 (see **10.2.3**) states, in part, that "[u]nobservable inputs [Level 3] shall be used to measure fair value to the extent that relevant observable inputs [Level 1 and 2] are not available…".

However, when the volume and level of activity in a market have significantly decreased and the market is not active, observable transactions may not be representative of fair value because of increased instances of transactions that are not orderly (e.g. forced liquidations or distress sales). Consequently, an entity should perform further analysis of the transactions or quoted prices available to determine whether they represent fair value. In some circumstances, a change in valuation technique or the use of multiple valuation techniques may be appropriate, as discussed below.

Transaction is not orderly

If the observable transactions are not orderly, IFRS 13:B44(a) states that "the entity shall place little, if any, weight (compared with other indications of fair value) on that transaction price" (see **9.6**). If an entity previously used quoted prices to measure fair value, and quoted prices from orderly transactions are no longer available, the entity may need to change its valuation technique or use multiple valuation techniques. If the entity measures fair value by using the price from a transaction that is not orderly, the price should be adjusted to reflect the assumptions that market participants would use in pricing the asset or liability in an orderly transaction. The resulting measurement would generally be classified as a Level 3 measurement.

Transactions are orderly

If the observable transactions are orderly, the entity should consider the transaction price when estimating fair value. However, the entity may also need to adjust the transaction price when measuring fair value to meet the measurement objective. IFRS 13:B44(b) states that the "amount of weight placed on that [orderly] transaction price when compared with other indications of fair value will depend on the facts and circumstances" (see **9.6**).

If an entity determines that it does not need to make any significant adjustment to the transaction price using unobservable inputs to arrive at the fair value of the asset or liability, the transaction price represents a relevant observable input and the measurement would be classified as a Level 2 measurement. However, if the entity determines that it needs to make a significant adjustment to the transaction price using unobservable inputs, the measurement would be classified as a Level 3 measurement.

Insufficient information to determine whether transactions are orderly

If an entity is unable to obtain, without undue cost and effort, sufficient information to determine whether the transaction is orderly, the entity must consider the transaction price in determining fair value; however, the transaction price may not be the 'sole or primary' basis for estimating fair value. In such circumstances, because the transaction price may not reflect the assumptions that market participants would use, a fair value measurement that has this price as its principal input would most likely represent a Level 3 measurement. As above, the use of multiple valuation techniques may be appropriate in this case.

B8 Recognition and derecognition

Contents

1 Introduction

The recognition requirements of IFRS 9 address the question of whether or not a financial instrument is included in the statement of financial position. Derecognition, not surprisingly, is the reverse of recognition and is the removal of a previously recognised financial instrument from the statement of financial position.

In summary, IFRS 9 stipulates that:

- a financial instrument (financial asset or financial liability) is recognised when, and only when, the entity becomes a party to the contractual provisions of the instrument;
- a previously recognised financial asset is derecognised when, and only when, either the contractual rights to the cash flows from that asset expire, or the entity transfers the asset such that the transfer qualifies for derecognition; and
- a financial liability is derecognised when, and only when, it is extinguished.

The criteria that are applied to transfers of financial assets are a mix of risks and rewards and control tests. IFRS 9 establishes a hierarchy of the tests and provides many examples to clarify the meaning of the concepts used and application of the tests to various transfer transactions.

Although the broad principles of derecognition may appear simple, a significant degree of judgement is required when applying these principles in practice.

2 Initial recognition

2.1 General principle

An entity should only recognise a financial asset or a financial liability in its statement of financial position when it becomes a party to the contractual provisions of the instrument. [IFRS 9:3.1.1]

Arrangements that are recognised as financial assets and liabilities are as follows.

- Unconditional receivables are recognised as an asset when the entity becomes a party to the contract and, as a consequence, has a legal right to receive cash. [IFRS 9:B3.1.2(a)]
- Issued debt is recognised as a liability when the entity that issues it becomes a party to the contractual terms of the debt and, consequently, has a legal obligation to pay cash to the debt holder.
- A derivative is recognised as an asset or a liability on the commitment date, rather than on the date on which settlement takes place. At

inception, the fair values of the right and obligation created by the derivative may be equal, in which case the fair value of the derivative will be zero. [IFRS 9:B3.1.2(c)]

Arrangements that are not recognised as financial assets and liabilities are as follows:

- Planned future transactions, no matter how likely, are not assets and liabilities because the entity has not become a party to a contract. [IFRS 9:B3.1.2(e)]
- Derivative contracts to buy or sell non-financial items that are scoped out of IFRS 9 are not recognised as financial assets and liabilities because they are executory contracts.
- Assets to be acquired and liabilities to be incurred as a result of a firm commitment are generally not recognised until at least one of the parties has performed under the agreement. [IFRS 9:B3.1.2(b)]

A firm commitment to acquire a non-financial item is not recognised until the asset is acquired if the commitment itself is deemed to be outside the scope of IFRS 9 (see **2.5** in **chapter B1**). A firm commitment to buy a financial asset, or a commitment to buy a non-financial item where the commitment is in the scope of IFRS 9, is generally recognised as a derivative on the date the commitment is entered into (see **chapter B4**) unless the 'regular way' exemption is applied (see **2.2**). If a previously unrecognised firm commitment is subject to a highly effective fair value hedge, changes in the fair value of the hedged risk of the firm commitment are recognised in the statement of financial position. This appears to run counter to the general principle of not recognising firm commitments. The argument for permitting such an approach is that all firm commitments are recognised, but generally at a historical cost of nil, and the fair value hedge requirements merely remeasure part of that commitment to fair value.

If an entity transfers or receives cash as collateral for an arrangement, careful consideration is needed to determine whether the cash should be recognised as a financial asset in the hands of the recipient. If the cash received by the recipient is not legally segregated from the recipient's other assets and the recipient has an unfettered right to use the cash, then the cash meets the definition of an asset. This is because the ultimate realisation of a financial asset is its conversion into cash and, therefore, no further transformation is required before the economic benefits of the cash transferred by the provider of the collateral are realised by the recipient. In this case, the recipient would recognise the cash as a financial asset and recognise an equivalent financial liability to return the cash to the provider of the collateral. The provider of the collateral would derecognise the cash and recognise a receivable from the collateral holder. [IFRS 9 Guidance on Implementation D.1.1]

Derivatives that prevent a transfer of financial assets from achieving derecognition are not recognised if recognising both the derivative and the asset that failed derecognition would amount to accounting for the same rights and obligations twice. [IFRS 9:B3.2.14] For example, if an entity transfers a financial asset but at the date of transfer agrees to repurchase the asset at a fixed price in the future, the forward contract to repurchase the asset is not recognised as a derivative at FVTPL as it is this repurchase arrangement that results in the entity retaining the risks and rewards of ownership and thereby continuing to recognise the transferred asset.

2.1.1 Linked transactions

IFRS 9 does not contain any general guidance regarding when two separate financial instruments entered into concurrently should be recognised as a single combined instrument. IFRS 9 does, however, provide specific implementation guidance in IFRS 9 Guidance on Implementation B.6 regarding when a loan receivable and a payable should be accounted for as a single transaction equivalent to an interest rate swap. It seems reasonable to apply the guidance in this example in IFRS 9 Guidance on Implementation B.6 to other transactions. Two financial instruments should therefore be recognised and measured as a single combined instrument if all of the following conditions are met:

- they are entered into at the same time and in contemplation of each other;
- they have the same counterparty;
- they relate to the same risk; and
- there is no economic need or substantive business purpose for structuring the transactions separately that could not also have been accomplished in a single transaction.

Transactions are commonly structured as two or more financial instruments, notwithstanding that their substance is that of a single arrangement, in order to generate specific tax benefits. It is difficult to see how it can be argued that structuring for the purposes of obtaining tax benefits is a substantive business purpose, particularly when those tax benefits derive from the accounting treatment adopted.

In March 2014, the IFRS Interpretations Committee issued a final agenda decision on IAS 39, *Accounting for a term-structured repo transaction*. The agenda decision equally applies to IFRS 9.

The Interpretations Committee received a request to clarify: (Issue 1) whether an entity (Entity A) should account for three transactions separately or aggregate and treat them as a single derivative; and (Issue 2) how to apply IAS 39:IG.B.6 (the equivalent paragraph in IFRS 9 is IFRS 9 Guidance on Implementation B.6 and is used in the remainder of this section) in addressing Issue 1. Some key features of the three transactions are as follows:

(a) Transaction 1 (bond purchase): Entity A purchases a bond (the bond) from another entity (Entity B).

(b) Transaction 2 (interest rate swap): Entity A enters into interest rate swap contract(s) with Entity B. Entity A pays a fixed rate of interest equal to the fixed coupon rate of the purchased bond in Transaction 1 and receives a variable rate of interest.

(c) Transaction 3 (repurchase agreement): Entity A enters into a repurchase agreement with Entity B, in which Entity A sells the same bond in Transaction 1 on the same day it purchases the bond and agrees to buy back the bond at the maturity date of the bond.

The Interpretations Committee noted that in order to determine whether Entity A should aggregate and account for the three transactions above as a single derivative, reference should be made to IFRS 9 Guidance on Implementation B.6 and C.6 and IAS 32:AG39.

The Interpretations Committee also discussed Issue 2, i.e., how to apply IAS 39:IG.B.6 in addressing Issue 1. The Interpretations Committee noted that application of the guidance in IFRS 9 Guidance on Implementation B requires judgement. It also noted that the indicators in IFRS 9 Guidance on Implementation B.6 may help an entity to determine the substance of the transaction, but that the presence or absence of any single specific indicator alone may not be conclusive.

The Interpretations Committee noted that providing additional guidance would result in the Interpretations Committee attempting to specify the accounting for a specific transaction, and that this would not be appropriate.

On the basis of the analysis above, the Interpretations Committee determined that, in the light of the existing IFRS requirements, neither an Interpretation nor an amendment to a Standard was necessary and consequently decided not to add this issue to its agenda.

2.1.2 Modification that leads to initial recognition of a new instrument

An entity may become a party to the contractual provisions of a financial instrument as a result of a substantial modification of the terms of an instrument that it already recognises in its statement of financial position. The entity will need to consider whether the modification results in derecognition of the existing instrument and recognition of a new instrument. Derecognition of financial assets is detailed in **section 3** and derecognition of financial liabilities is detailed in **section 4**.

Example 2.1.2

Initial recognition following modification

An entity had previously issued a perpetual instrument with an issuer option to redeem after 15 years. Under the terms of the instrument, the entity was entitled to defer interest payments indefinitely, except upon liquidation of the entity. The instrument met the definition of an equity instrument and was presented as equity at its net proceeds.

During the current reporting period, the entity and the holder of the instrument agree to modify the terms of the instrument so that, if a prescribed contingent event occurs any time after the date of modification, the entity will be required to pay all deferred interest and lose the right to defer future interest. This newly created contingent settlement provision is considered to be 'genuine' in accordance with IAS 32:25; consequently, after this modification, in accordance with IAS 32:25 the instrument is classified as a financial liability. The modification involves no compensation payment to the holders of the instrument and no change in the expected cash flows, and no fees in respect of the modification are paid.

All financial instruments are measured at fair value at initial recognition. In this example, the initial recognition date for the financial liability is the date of the modification because, at that date, the original equity instrument is derecognised and a new financial liability is recognised. Therefore, the entity must recognise the financial liability at its fair value, which will incorporate expectations of cash flows and market interest rates at the date of the modification. Any difference between the previous carrying amount recognised in equity and the fair value of the financial liability is recognised as an adjustment within equity.

If the entity does not designate the financial liability as at FVTPL, after initial recognition the liability is measured at amortised cost which will include any directly attributable transaction costs.

In November 2006, the IFRIC (now the IFRS Interpretations Committee) issued a rejection notice regarding changes in the contractual terms of an existing equity instrument that results in the instrument being reclassified as a financial liability for the issuer. Two issues were discussed:

(i) on what basis the financial liability should be measured at the date when the terms are changed; and

(ii) how any difference between the carrying amount of the previously recognised equity instrument and the amount of the financial liability recognised at the date when the terms are changed should be accounted for.

The IFRIC noted that the financial liability is initially recognised when the contractual terms are changed and that, on initial recognition, a financial liability is measured at its fair value in accordance with

IAS 39:43 (now IFRS 9:5.1.1). The IFRIC observed that Example 3 of IFRIC 2 *Members' Shares in Co-operative Entities and Similar Instruments* deals with a similar situation. In that example, at the time when the financial liabilities are recognised as a result of a change in terms, they are recognised at their fair value.

The IFRIC observed that the change in the terms of the instrument results in the derecognition of the original equity instrument. The IFRIC noted that IAS 32:33 states that no gain or loss should be recognised in profit or loss on the purchase, sale, issue or cancellation of an entity's own equity instruments. The IFRIC therefore concluded that, at the time when the terms are changed, the difference between the carrying amount of the equity instrument and the fair value of the newly recognised financial liability should be recognised in equity.

2.2 Trade date and settlement date accounting

Under IFRS 9:3.1.2, a 'regular way' (see below) purchase or sale of financial assets can be recognised (and derecognised) using either trade date or settlement date accounting. The method used is required to be applied consistently for all purchases and sales of financial assets that belong to the same category as defined by IFRS 9. For this purpose, assets that are mandatorily measured at FVTPL form a separate classification category from assets designated as at FVTPL. [IFRS 9:B3.1.3]

A 'regular way' purchase or sale is defined as a transaction whose contractual terms "require delivery of the asset within a timeframe established generally by regulation or convention in the marketplace concerned". [IFRS 9: Appendix A] A marketplace is not limited to a formal stock exchange or organised over-the-counter market. Rather, it means the environment in which the financial asset is customarily exchanged. An acceptable timeframe would be the period reasonably and customarily required for the parties to complete the transaction and prepare and execute closing documents. [IFRS 9 Guidance on Implementation B.28] The trade date is the date of the commitment to buy or sell the financial asset. The settlement date is the date of the delivery of the asset. If a transaction is considered 'regular way', a derivative is not recognised for the time period between the trade date and the settlement date.

When trade date accounting is applied, the entity recognises the financial asset to be received and the corresponding liability to pay for it at the trade date; on disposal, the financial asset is removed from the statement of financial position on the trade date. [IFRS 9:B3.1.5]

Under the settlement date accounting approach, the asset is recognised on the date on which it is received by the entity; on disposal, the asset is not derecognised until the asset is delivered to the buyer. When the purchase of an asset is accounted for using settlement date accounting, between the trade date and settlement date, although the asset itself is not yet recognised, the entity is required to account for changes in its fair value, applying the same measurement basis that will be used to account for the acquired asset once it is recognised; therefore, changes in fair value are recognised in profit or loss for assets to be classified or designated as at FVTPL, in other comprehensive income (OCI) for assets to be designated as at fair value through other comprehensive income, and not recognised for assets measured at amortised cost. [IFRS 9:B3.1.6]

Example 2.2A

Trade and settlement date accounting for a purchase of an asset

The following example illustrates the amounts to be recognised for a purchase of a financial asset.

The dates and fair values that are relevant to the example are:

- trade date: 29 December 20X1 (fair value of asset 1,000);
- period end date: 31 December 20X1 (fair value of asset 1,002); and
- settlement date: 4 January 20X2 (fair value of asset 1,003).

The contracted price of the asset is set as the trade date fair value of 1,000.

TRADE DATE ACCOUNTING

Journal entries	**Debt instrument measured at amortised cost**	**Investment in equity instruments designated as at FVTOCI**	**FVTPL**
29/12/20X1			
	Dr Asset 1,000	Dr Asset 1,000	Dr Asset 1,000
	Cr Liability 1,000	Cr Liability 1,000	Cr Liability 1,000
Description	*To recognise the asset and payable.*	*To recognise the asset and payable.*	*To recognise the asset and payable.*
31/12/20X1			
	–	Dr Asset 2	Dr Asset 2
	–	Cr OCI 2	Cr Profit or loss 2
Description		*To recognise the increase in fair value to date.*	*To recognise the increase in fair value to date.*
04/01/20X2			
	–	Dr Asset 1	Dr Asset 1
	–	Cr OCI 1	Cr Profit or loss 1
Description		*To recognise the increase in fair value to date.*	*To recognise the increase in fair value to date.*

TRADE DATE ACCOUNTING

Journal entries	**Debt instrument measured at amortised cost**	**Investment in equity instruments designated as at FVTOCI**	**FVTPL**
	Dr Liability 1,000	Dr Liability 1,000	Dr Liability 1,000
	Cr Cash 1,000	Cr Cash 1,000	Cr Cash 1,000
Description	*To record the payment for the asset at the contracted amount.*	*To record the payment for the asset at the contracted amount.*	*To record the payment for the asset at the contracted amount.*

SETTLEMENT DATE ACCOUNTING

Journal entries	**Debt instrument measured at amortised cost**	**Investment in equity instruments designated as at FVTOCI**	**FVTPL**
29/12/20X1			
	–	–	–
	–	–	–
31/12/20X1			
	–	Dr Receivable 2	Dr Receivable 2
	–	Cr OCI 2	Cr Profit or loss 2
Description		*To recognise the increase in fair value to date.*	*To recognise the increase in fair value to date.*
04/01/20X2			
	–	Dr Receivable 1	Dr Receivable 1
	–	Cr OCI 1	Cr Profit or loss 1
Description		*To recognise the increase in fair value to date.*	*To recognise the increase in fair value to date.*
	Dr Asset 1,000	Dr Asset 1,003	Dr Asset 1,003
	Cr Cash 1,000	Cr Cash 1,000	Cr Cash 1,000
	–	Cr Receivable 3	Cr Receivable 3
Description	*To recognise the asset and payment for the asset at the contracted amount.*	*To recognise the asset and payment for the asset at the contracted amount and its change in fair value since trade date.*	*To recognise the asset and payment for the asset at the contracted amount and its change in fair value since trade date.*

When the settlement provisions of a financial instrument differ between various active markets, the entity must apply the provisions that apply in the market in which the purchase or sale of the financial instrument actually takes place.

Example 2.2B

Regular way contracts: which customary settlement provisions apply?

[Extract from IFRS 9 Guidance on Implementation B.30]

Entity XYZ purchases one million shares of Entity ABC on a US stock exchange, for example, through a broker. The settlement date of the contract is six business days later. Trades for equity shares on US exchanges customarily settle in three business days. Because the trade settles in six business days, it does not meet the exemption as a regular way trade.

However, if XYZ did the same transaction on a foreign exchange that has a customary settlement period of six business days, the contract would meet the exemption for a regular way trade.

When the regulation or convention for settlement differs between a derivative over the underlying (e.g. a call option over a share) and the underlying itself (e.g. the share), the regulation or convention that is used to determine whether the financial instrument is regular way would be the regulation or convention specific to that instrument. For example, if the call option over the share is regularly settled within 14 days of exercise of the option in the option markets, but a direct acquisition of a share requires three day settlement, the entity will look to the options market in determining whether an option is regular way or not. [IFRS 9 Guidance on Implementation B.31]

Example 2.2C

Application of trade and settlement date accounting for different categories of financial asset

Entity P has an accounting policy of settlement date accounting for amortised cost assets and trade date accounting for investments in equity instruments designated as at FVTOCI. Entity P enters into a regular way transaction whereby it will sell a loan asset measured at amortised cost in exchange for an investment in equity instruments to be designated as at FVTOCI. At the date of entering into the arrangement, 30 March 20X8, both assets have the same fair value. The settlement date is 2 April 20X8. Entity P's reporting period is 31 March 20X8.

	Amortised cost	Fair value
	CU	CU
30 March 20X8		
Loan measured at amortised cost	10,000	
Investment in equity instrument designated as at FVTOCI		10,400

	Amortised cost	Fair value
	CU	CU
31 March 20X8		
Loan measured at amortised cost	10,005	
Investment in equity instrument designated as at FVTOCI		10,350
2 April 20X8		
Loan measured at amortised cost	10,015	
Investment in equity instrument designated as at FVTOCI		10,325

30 March 20X8

		CU	CU
Dr	Investment in equity instrument designated as at FVTOCI	10,400	
Cr	Financial liability		10,400

To recognise the investment in equity instrument designated as at FVTOCI at trade date.

31 March 20X8

		CU	CU
Dr	Other comprehensive income (equity)	50	
Cr	Investment in equity instrument designated as at FVTOCI		50

To recognise the change in fair value of the investment in equity instrument.

		CU	CU
Dr	Loan measured at amortised cost	5	
Cr	Interest income		5

To recognise the interest earned on an effective interest rate basis.

2 April 20x8

		CU	CU
Dr	Loan measured at amortised cost	10	
Cr	Interest income		10

To recognise the interest earned on an effective interest rate basis.

		CU	CU
Dr	Other comprehensive income (equity)	25	
Cr	Investment in equity instrument designated as at FVTOCI		25

To recognise the change in fair value of the investment in equity instrument.

		CU	CU
Dr	Financial liability	10,400	
Cr	Loan measured at amortised cost		10,015
Cr	Profit or loss		385

To recognise the gain on disposal of the loan at the date of derecognition. The gain represents the difference between the proceeds received (i.e. the fair value of the investment in equity instrument at the date the contract is entered into) and the amortised cost of the loan at the settlement date.

Trade or settlement date accounting for regular way transactions is not limited to exchanges of securities for cash because exchanges of large amounts of foreign currency are also subject to market convention. For example, an entity may agree to exchange an amount of foreign currency cash recognised in its statement of financial position for an amount of functional currency cash at a predetermined foreign currency exchange rate but with deferred delivery in, say, two days after the agreement date subject to normal market settlement convention.

If the market settlement convention is not deemed normal (i.e. this is not a regular way transaction), the entity would continue to recognise the foreign currency cash balance and recognise a foreign currency forward contract to sell foreign currency and buy functional currency in two days' time at FVTPL. At maturity of the foreign currency forward contract, the foreign currency cash and the foreign currency forward contract would both be derecognised and the functional currency recognised.

If the market settlement convention is deemed normal (i.e. the transaction is a regular way one), the accounting would depend on whether the entity's accounting policy is to apply trade or settlement date accounting.

Example 2.2D

Trade and settlement date accounting for an exchange of foreign currency cash

Entity A agrees to sell US$200 million that is recognised in its statement of financial position for £100 million with settlement two days after trade date ('t+2'). Entity A has a Sterling functional currency. t+2 is considered to be the normal market settlement convention for the size and type of asset being exchanged in the market in which the exchange takes place. Entity A concludes, therefore, that this is a regular way transaction.

The dates and currency rates that are relevant are as follows:

- trade date: 30 December 20X1; US$2:£1 spot rate;
- period end date: 31 December 20X1; and
- settlement date: 1 January 20X2.

If Entity A's policy is trade date accounting, the following entries would be recorded.

30 December 20X1

		£m	£m
Dr	Receivable - £	100*	
Cr	Cash – US$		100

To derecognise the US$ cash at the trade date and recognise a receivable for the Sterling amount to be received at 1 January 20X2.

* the balance should be discounted unless the effect is immaterial

31 December 20X1

Because the US$ asset has been derecognised, there is no foreign currency monetary item that requires translation (had the receipt been in a foreign currency, the receivable would be retranslated to Entity A's functional currency at the period end).

1 January 20X2

		£m	£m
Dr	Cash - £	100	
Cr	Receivable – £		100

To derecognise the Sterling receivable and recognise the Sterling cash at the settlement date.

If Entity A's policy is settlement date accounting the following entries would be recorded.

30 December 20X1

No entries are required because the US$ cash remains recognised until settlement date.

31 December 20X1

Because Entity A has agreed to sell the US$ at 1 January 20X1 at a fixed amount of Sterling, it does not have exposure to foreign currency risk. Entity A does not retranslate the US$ to Sterling after the trade date. This is consistent with IFRS 9 Guidance on Implementation D.2.2, which states "[a] change in the fair value of a financial asset that is sold on a regular way basis is not recorded in the financial statements between trade date and settlement date even if the entity applies settlement date accounting because the seller's right to changes in the fair value ceases on the trade date". Therefore, no entries are required.

1 January 20X2

		£m	£m
Dr	Cash - £	100	
Cr	Cash - US$		100

To derecognise the US$ cash and recognise the Sterling cash at the settlement date.

If an entity derecognises a financial asset using settlement date accounting but it receives a non-cash financial asset in exchange which, under the entity's generally policy for the category of non-cash financial asset received, will be recognised using trade date accounting, the entity must apply trade date accounting to the non-cash financial asset to be received.

Example 2.2E

Settlement date accounting: exchange of non-cash financial assets

[Extract from IFRS 9 Guidance on Implementation D.2.3]

On 29 December 20X2 (trade date) Entity A enters into a contract to sell Note Receivable A, which is carried at amortised cost, in exchange for Bond B, which will be classified as held for trading and measured at fair value. Both assets have a fair value of CU1,010 on 29 December, while the amortised cost of Note Receivable A is CU1,000. Entity A uses settlement date accounting for assets measured at amortised cost and trade date accounting for assets held for trading. On 31 December 20X2 (financial year-end), the fair value of Note Receivable A is CU1,012 and the fair value of Bond B is CU1,009. On 4 January 20X3, the fair value of Note Receivable A is CU1,013 and the fair value of Bond B is CU1,007. The following entries are made:

29 December 20X2

Dr	Bond B	CU1,010
Cr	Payable	CU1,010

31 December 20X2

Dr	Trading loss	CU1
Cr	Bond B	CU1

4 January 20X3

Dr	Payable	CU1,010
Dr	Trading loss	CU2
Cr	Note Receivable A	CU1,000
Cr	Bond B	CU2
Cr	Realisation gain	CU10

In January 2007, the IFRIC (now the IFRS Interpretations Committee) issued a rejection notice on accounting for short sales of securities when the terms of the short sales require delivery of the securities within the timeframe established generally by regulation or convention in the marketplace concerned. A fixed price commitment between trade date and settlement date of a short sale contract meets the definition of a derivative. Because IAS 39:AG55 and AG56 (now IFRS 9:B3.1.5 & B3.1.6) only permit a choice of trade or settlement date accounting for recognition and derecognition of financial assets traded under regular way purchases and regular way sales of long positions, the Standard would require a short sale to be recognised as a derivative until delivery of the security. The IFRIC acknowledged that an interpretation that is applied in practice is that entities choose trade date or settlement date accounting for short sales rather than treat a short sale as a derivative. Specifically, practice recognises the short sales as financial liabilities at fair value with changes in fair value recognised in profit or loss. Under the industry practice, the same profit or loss amount is recognised as would have been recognised if short sales of securities were accounted for as derivatives but the securities are presented differently in the statement of financial position. The IFRIC acknowledged that requiring entities to account for the short positions as derivatives may create considerable practical problems for entities' accounting systems and controls with little, if any, improvement to the quality of the financial information presented. For these reasons and because there is little diversity in practice, the IFRIC decided not to take the issue onto its agenda.

IFRS 9 does not provide guidance on whether the trade date exemption can be applied if an entity delivers a financial instrument under a regular way contract but the delivery date is delayed, and the asset is delivered outside the normal convention for that type of contract. For example, a contract has a delivery date of t+3 days, but there is a delay in delivery and the instrument is delivered at t+5. A delay should not preclude use of the regular way exemption if the delay is outside the control of the entity.

3 Derecognition of financial assets

A financial asset is derecognised (i.e. removed from the statement of financial position), when, and only when, either the contractual rights to the asset's cash flows expire, or the asset is transferred and the transfer qualifies for derecognition.

The decision as to whether a transfer qualifies for derecognition is made by applying a combination of risks and rewards and control tests. The risks and rewards tests seek to establish whether, having transferred a financial asset, the entity continues to be exposed to the risks of ownership of that asset and/or continues to enjoy the benefits that it generates. The control tests are designed with a view to understanding which entity controls the asset (i.e. which entity can direct how the benefits of that asset are realised).

This use of both types of tests is often criticised for being a mix of two accounting models that can create confusion in application. IFRS 9 addresses this criticism by providing a clear hierarchy for application of the two sets of tests: risks and rewards tests are applied first, with the control tests used only when the entity has neither transferred substantially all the risks and rewards of the asset nor retained them.

Inherent in the IFRS 9 derecognition model is the notion of 'stickiness', i.e. it is more difficult to remove an asset from an entity's statement of financial position than it is to recognise that asset in the first place. Derecognition cannot be achieved by merely transferring the legal title to a financial asset to another party. The substance of the arrangement must be assessed in order to determine whether an entity has transferred the economic exposure associated with the rights inherent in the asset (i.e. its risks and rewards) and, in some cases, control of those rights.

3.1 The IFRS 9 derecognition decision tree

IFRS 9 provides a decision tree, reproduced below, that clarifies the hierarchy of application of the derecognition tests.

[IFRS 9:B3.2.1]

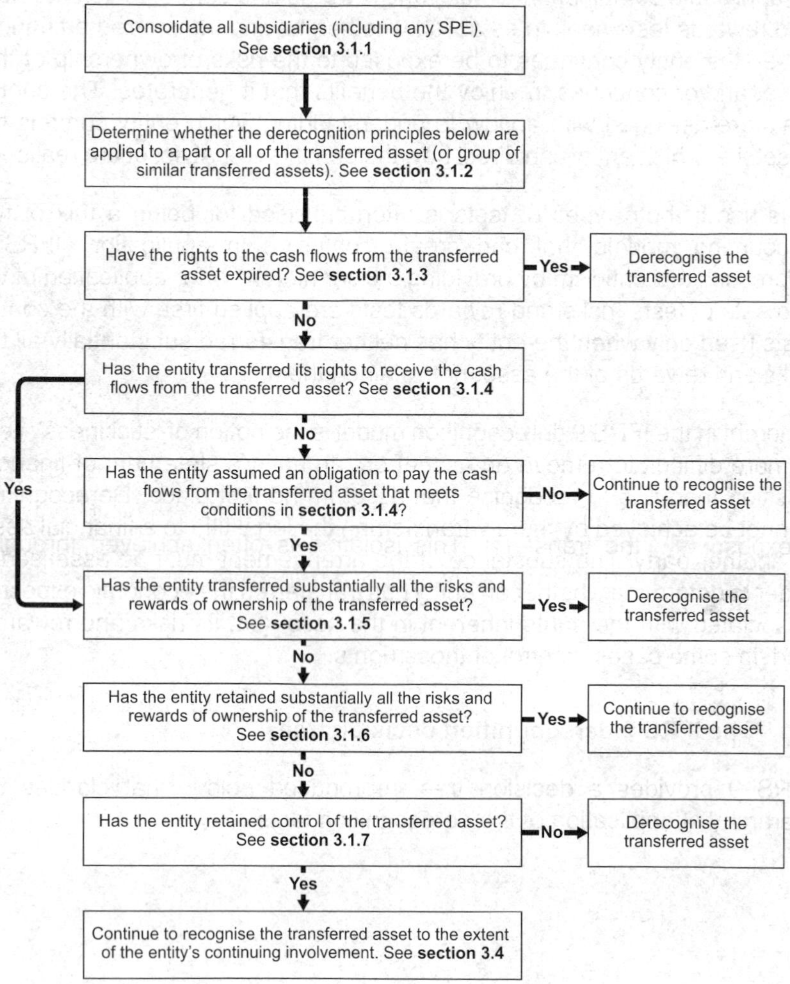

The steps of this decision tree are explained below.

3.1.1 Consolidate all subsidiaries

The first step is to define at which level the derecognition decision is to be applied – in the parent's separate financial statements or in the consolidated financial statements. When derecognition of financial assets is to be applied in the consolidated financial statements, the reporting group must first consolidate all subsidiaries in accordance with IFRS 10 *Consolidated Financial Statements*. [IFRS 9:3.2.1]

This first step ensures that the derecognition decision is consistent regardless of whether the transfer of assets is direct to investors or through a consolidated structured entity that obtains the financial assets, and, in turn, transfers those financial assets (or a portion of them) to third-party investors. [IFRS 9:BCZ3.24]

IFRS 10 requires consolidation of all entities that are controlled by the reporting entity. An investor controls an investee when it is exposed, or has rights, to variable returns from its involvement with the investee and has the ability to affect those returns through its power over the investee.

Structured entities may take the form of a corporation, trust, partnership or unincorporated entity and are often created with legal arrangements that impose strict and sometimes permanent limits on the decision-making powers of their governing board, trustees or management over the operations of the structured entity. Frequently, these provisions specify that the policy guiding the ongoing activities of the structured entity cannot be modified, other than perhaps by its creator or sponsor (i.e. they operate on so-called 'autopilot').

Structured transactions, such as securitisations and certain other asset-based financing arrangements, typically seek, as their primary economic objective, to isolate legally the assets from the party providing them (and from that party's creditors) to avoid the investor having a credit exposure to the transferor. This isolation is often achieved through a structured entity. For many sellers of financial assets, structured arrangements that isolate the assets permit access to capital markets at more favourable prices than might otherwise be available because credit agencies and investors require a lower return from structures that avoid the consequences arising from bankruptcies. This ability is particularly important for those entities whose credit ratings may reflect the adverse effects of financial, operational or environmental risks not directly attributable to the assets being transferred. However, bankruptcy isolation does not automatically lead to the conclusion that the sponsor is not required to consolidate the structured entity.

A structured entity may issue different types of beneficial interests, multiple classes of interests and classes of interests with different maturities. Several forms of structured entities are common, depending on the asset being securitised, the securities issued by the entity and the legal framework governing the entity's operations. These include grantor trusts, owner trusts, revolving trusts, master trusts, structured corporations and REMICS (Real Estate Mortgage Investment Conduits).

Typically, the structured entity is prevented from selling, assigning or pledging its direct interest in any financial asset it holds; however, the owners of the beneficial interests generally have the right to pledge or exchange their beneficial interests.

3.1.2 Determine whether the derecognition principles are applied to a part or all of an asset (or group of similar assets)

An entity needs to determine what is being evaluated for derecognition; this could be a whole financial asset, a group of financial assets, part of a financial asset, or part of a group of similar financial assets.

The derecognition principles are applied to part of a financial asset (or a group of similar financial assets) if the part comprises one of the following:

[IFRS 9:3.2.2(a)]

- specifically identified cash flows (e.g. an interest or principal strip from a debt instrument);
- a fully proportionate share of the cash flows (e.g. the rights to the cash flows on 90 per cent of all cash flows arising from a debt instrument); or
- a fully proportionate share of specifically identified cash flows (e.g. 90 per cent of the cash flows that arise on the interest strip from a debt instrument).

In all other cases, the financial asset (or the group of financial assets) is considered in its entirety. [IFRS 9:3.2.2(b)]

Example 3.1.2

Determining the part of a financial asset subject to transfer

Entity X, the transferor, transfers the right to the first CU90 of cash flows that are derived from a debt instrument; the fair value of the asset is CU100 on the date of transfer.

The transferor cannot apply the derecognition model to part of the asset because the transferor has neither transferred specifically identifiable cash flows nor a fully proportionate share of all or part of the cash flows. The transferor would apply the derecognition model to the asset in its entirety. The transferor effectively agrees to absorb the first CU10 of losses from the transferred asset.

It should be noted, however, that if the transferor had transferred a 90 per cent pro rata share of all cash flows from the asset, then the derecognition model could be applied to the part of the asset that has been transferred, i.e. 90 per cent. In that case, the transferor and the transferee would have agreed to participate in a fully proportionate share of losses.

IFRS 9 does not provide any guidance regarding what makes assets 'similar'. 'Similar' generally means that the two instruments have contractually specified cash flows that are similar in amounts and timings, and have similar risk attributes. An entity should consider the similarity of terms (e.g. prepayment features, interest rates, currency denomination). By definition, there will always be some differences between similar instruments – otherwise they would be identical. A portfolio of mortgages transferred by a bank is often deemed to contain similar financial assets. Similarly, a portfolio of corporate bonds transferred by a bank is often deemed to contain similar financial assets. However, no two portfolios are ever precisely alike. A transfer of a portfolio of mortgages would need to be assessed separately from a transfer of a portfolio of corporate bonds even if the two transfers are made at the same time. With individual equity investments, the differences are so significant that no two equity investments are ever likely to be similar – the value is affected by intangibles and other 'soft' assets (e.g. reputation) that are not recognised in the statement of financial position or measured in any consistent way, but that do affect perceptions and, therefore, market price.

In September 2006, the IASB was asked by the IFRIC (now the IFRS Interpretations Committee) for input and advice on the meaning of 'similar' for group of financial assets (in IAS 39:16, now IFRS 9:3.2.2). The Board's view (subsequently used by the IFRIC as a basis for a tentative rejection wording in November 2006) was that they believed that derivative assets (which are often transferred together with non-derivative financial assets) are not 'similar' to non-derivative financial assets. Therefore, entities should apply the derecognition tests in IAS 39 (now IFRS 9) to non-derivative financial assets (or groups of similar non-derivative financial assets) and derivative financial assets (or groups of similar derivative financial assets) separately, even if they are transferred at the same time. The Board also indicated that transferred derivatives that could be either assets or liabilities (such as interest rate swaps) would have to meet both the financial asset and the financial liability derecognition tests. This view was reaffirmed in the amendments to IAS 39, *Novation of Derivatives and Continuation of Hedge Accounting,* issued in June 2013 (which have since been incorporated into IFRS 9) where paragraph BC220B was introduced which states that "a derivative should be derecognised only when it meets both the derecognition criteria for a financial asset and the derecognition criteria for a financial liability in circumstances in which the derivative involves two-way payments between parties (i.e. the payments are or could be from and to each of the parties).

Following comments from constituents, at the IFRIC meeting in January 2007 the IFRIC decided to withdraw its tentative agenda decision and to add a project on derecognition to its agenda. However, in March 2009, the IFRIC decided to remove this topic from its agenda because the IASB accelerated its project to develop a replacement for the sections of IAS 39 on derecognition. An exposure draft was published in March 2009 with the intention of issuing a final IFRS in the second half of 2010. However, in June 2010, the IASB announced its intention to proceed with a more limited project to issue new disclosure requirements regarding derecognition. These amendments to IFRS 7, *Transfers of Financial Assets*, were issued in October 2010 (see **4.1.6** in **chapter B11**).

3.1.3 Have the rights to the cash flows from the asset expired?

An entity derecognises a financial asset when the rights to the cash flows from that financial asset expire. [IFRS 9:3.2.3]

The rights to the cash flows expire when, for example, a financial asset reaches its maturity and there are no further cash flows arising from that asset, or a purchased option reaches its maturity unexercised. An entity may have a right to receive certain or all cash flows from a financial asset over a specified period of time which may be shorter than the contractual maturity of that financial asset. In that case, the entity's right to the cash flows expires once the specified period expires.

In November 2014 the IASB's Interpretations Committee issued a final agenda decision on IAS 39 (the requirements in IAS 39 and IFRS 9 in this case are the same), titled, *Holder's Accounting for Exchange of Equity Instruments*.

The Interpretations Committee received a request about the accounting by the holder of equity instruments in the circumstance in which the issuer exchanges its original equity instruments for new equity instruments in the same entity but with different terms. Specifically, this transaction involved equity instruments issued by a central bank and the exchange of instruments was imposed on the holders as a consequence of a change in legislation.

The submitter asked whether the holders of the equity instruments should account for this exchange under IAS 39 as a derecognition of the original equity instruments and the recognition of new instruments.

The Interpretations Committee observed that: (i) because of the unique nature of the transaction, the issue is not widespread; and (ii) the submitter had not identified significant diversity in accounting for this transaction among the holders of the equity instruments in question.

For these reasons, the Interpretations Committee decided not to add this issue to its agenda.

The Interpretations Committee additionally noted requests for more guidance in IAS 39 and IFRS 9 on the derecognition of financial assets that have been modified or exchanged. The staff observed that this more general matter had been raised previously with the IASB but that it had decided not to add such a project to its agenda. The Interpretations Committee asked the staff to perform further analysis to identify whether an issue of sufficiently narrow scope could be identified to be raised with the IASB. The staff's analysis is due to be considered at a future Interpretations Committee meeting.

3.1.4 Has the entity transferred its rights to receive the cash flows from the asset?

An entity may transfer the contractual rights to the cash flows that comprise a financial asset, or it may retain the contractual rights to the cash flows but assume a contractual obligation to pass on those cash flows to one or more recipients (often referred to as a 'pass-through' arrangement).

When an entity enters into a pass-through arrangement (i.e. the entity agrees to receive cash flows and has a concurrent obligation to pay those cash flows to the eventual recipient), the entity should treat the transaction as a transfer of a financial asset if, and only if, all of the following conditions are met:

[IFRS 9:3.2.5]

- the entity has no obligation to pay amounts to the eventual recipients unless it collects equivalent amounts from the original asset (i.e. the entity does not benefit or suffer from performance or non-performance of the asset);
- the entity is prohibited by the terms of the transfer arrangement from selling or pledging the original asset other than as security to the eventual recipients for the obligation to pay them cash flows (i.e. the entity does not have control of the future economic benefits associated with the transferred asset); and
- the entity has an obligation to pass on or remit the cash flows that it has collected on behalf of the eventual recipients *without material delay*, is prohibited from reinvesting the cash flows received in the short settlement period between receiving them and remitting them to the eventual recipient in anything other than cash or cash equivalents (as defined in IAS 7 *Statement of Cash Flows*) and any interest earned on such investments must be passed on to the eventual recipients (i.e. the entity has no access to the benefits of the asset).

Transfers most commonly arise in respect of financial assets that represent a contractual right to receive cash. However, it is possible to transfer a financial asset that is a contractual right to receive a non-financial asset. For example, an entity may have a contractual right to receive oil to the value of CU100m that fails the 'own use' exemption in IFRS 9:2.4 and is accounted for under IFRS 9 as a financial asset. The transfer criteria in IFRS 9:3.2.4 state that a transfer can arise if the contractual right to receive 'cash flows' of the asset are transferred, or if the contractual right to the 'cash flows' of the financial asset are retained but a contractual obligation to pay the 'cash flows' to one or more recipients meets the pass-through conditions above. When a non-financial asset is receivable under a financial asset, that non-financial asset represents the 'cash flows' for the purpose of applying IFRS 9:3.2.4. As a result, an arrangement can fail to represent a pass-through if the obligation assumed does not require remittance of the non-financial asset. This is illustrated in the following example.

Example 3.1.4

Application of the pass-through test to an asset in the scope of IFRS 9 that is settled by the receipt of a non-financial item

Entity A has an existing offtake agreement to purchase crude oil from an oil producer, Entity B, in the future. Under this arrangement, Entity A advances to Entity B cash of CU100 million and in return Entity B is obliged to deliver to Entity A on specified dates a variable amount of oil until Entity B has delivered oil equal in value to the amount of the advance (CU100 million) plus interest accrued at a rate of 10 per cent per annum. The value of the oil is determined based on the spot price at the date of delivery.

Entity A does not intend to use the oil as part of its usage requirements; it will either sell the oil spot on receipt, or forward in the future, or retain the physical oil for speculative purposes. Consequently, the advance does not qualify for the 'own use' exemption in IFRS 9:2.4; even though it is settled with the receipt of a non-financial item, it is an asset in the scope of IFRS 9.

Entity A enters into a separate agreement with Bank C under which it 'sells' its economic interest in the asset for CU100 million. This is achieved by Entity A assuming a contractual obligation to deliver to Bank C cash equivalent to the value of oil that it receives from Entity B. Entity A retains the contractual right to receive oil. When title to oil passes from Entity B to Entity A, this immediately triggers a cash payment from Entity A to Bank C (e.g. if Entity A receives CU12 million worth of oil on a specific date, Entity A is required to pay CU12 million in cash to Bank C on the same date).

The exposure to variability in timing of delivery of oil by Entity B is passed to Bank C because Entity A's obligation to pay Bank C is not triggered until Entity A receives oil from Entity B.

The arrangement with Bank C does result in a transfer by Entity A of its asset from Entity B under the 'pass-through' requirement of IFRS 9:3.2.4(b).

Under IFRS 9:3.2.4(b), a transfer arises if an entity both retains the contractual rights to receive the cash flows of the asset and assumes a contractual obligation to pay the cash flows to one or more eventual recipients.

Because Entity A's asset due from Entity B is exclusively physically settled in oil, the 'cash flows' for the purposes of applying IFRS 9:3.2.4(b) are the contractual rights to receive oil. Therefore, in order to meet the second condition in IFRS 9:3.2.4(b), it is necessary for Entity A to assume an obligation to pay to Bank C the same 'cash flows' (i.e. an equivalent physical amount of oil). However, the arrangements are such that Entity A receives physical oil from Entity B but pays cash to Bank C. The difference in the physical nature between receiving oil and paying cash means that the criteria for 'pass-through' in IFRS 9:3.2.4(b) are not satisfied.

Entity A should instead recognise the cash proceeds from Bank C of CU100 million as a financial liability.

In September 2012 the IFRS Interpretations Committee considered the accounting treatment for various aspects of the restructuring of Greek Government Bonds (GGBs). One of the aspects the Committee received a request for guidance on was whether the restructuring of GGBs should result in derecognition of the whole asset, or only part of it, in accordance with IAS 39 (although the Interpretations Committee referred only to IAS 39 in their draft rejection notice the equivalent paragraphs in IFRS 9 apply and therefore have been included below). Specifically, the Committee was asked whether the portion of the old GGBs that are exchanged for twenty new bonds with different maturities and interest rates should be derecognised, or conversely accounted for as a modification or transfer that would not require derecognition.

The Committee noted that the request has been made within the context of a narrow fact pattern. The narrow fact pattern highlighted the diversity in views that had arisen in relation to the accounting for the portion of the old GGBs that is exchanged for twenty new bonds with different maturities and interest rates. The submitter asked the Committee to consider whether these should be derecognised, or conversely accounted for as a modification or transfer that would not require derecognition.

In addition, the Committee has been asked to consider whether IAS 8 *Accounting Policies, Changes in Accounting Estimates and Errors* would be applicable in analysing the submitted fact pattern, and whether the exchange can be considered a transfer within the scope of IFRS 9:3.2.3(b).

The Committee observed that the term 'transfer' is not defined in IFRS 9. However, the potentially relevant portion of IFRS 9:3.2.4 states that an entity transfers a financial asset if it transfers the contractual rights to receive the cash flows of the financial asset. The Committee noted that, in the fact pattern submitted, the bonds are transferred back to the issuer rather than a third party. Accordingly, the Committee believed that the transaction should be assessed against IFRS 9:3.2.3(a).

In applying IFRS 9:3.2.3(a), the Committee noted that, in order to determine whether the financial asset is extinguished, it is necessary to assess the changes made as part of the bond exchange against the notion of 'expiry' of the rights to the cash flows. The Committee also noted that, if an entity applies IAS 8 because of the absence in IFRS 9 of an explicit discussion of when a modification of a financial asset results in derecognition, applying IAS 8 requires judgement to develop and apply an accounting policy. IAS 8:11 requires that, in determining an appropriate accounting policy, consideration must first be given to the requirements in IFRSs dealing with similar and related issues. The Committee noted that, in the fact pattern submitted, that requirement would lead to the development of an analogy to the notion of a substantial change of the terms of a financial liability in IFRS 9:3.3.2.

IFRS 9:3.3.2 sets out that such a change can be effected by the exchange of debt instruments or by way of modification of the terms of an existing instrument. Hence, if this analogy to financial liabilities is applied to financial assets, a substantial change of terms (whether effected by exchange or by modification) would result in derecognition of the financial asset.

The Committee noted that if the guidance for financial liabilities is applied by analogy to assess whether the exchange of a portion of the old GGBs for twenty new bonds is a substantial change of the terms of the financial asset, the assessment needs to be made taking into consideration all of the changes made as part of the bond exchange.

In the fact pattern submitted, the relevant facts led the Committee to conclude that, in determining whether the transaction results in derecognition of the financial asset, both approaches (i.e. extinguishment under IFRS 9:3.2.3(a) or substantial change of the terms of the asset) would result in derecognition.

The Committee considered the following aspects of the fact pattern in assessing the extent of change that results from the transaction:

- A holder of a single bond has received, in exchange for one portion of the old bond, twenty bonds with different maturities and cash flow profiles as well as other instruments in accordance with the terms and conditions of the exchange transaction.
- All of the bondholders received the same restructuring deal irrespective of the terms and conditions of their individual holdings. This indicates that the individual instruments, terms and conditions were not taken into account. The different bonds (series) were not each modified in contemplation of their respective terms and conditions but instead replaced by a new uniform debt structure.
- The terms and conditions of the new bonds are substantially different from those of the old bonds; this includes many different aspects such as the change in governing law, the introduction of contractual collective action clauses and the introduction of a co-

financing agreement that affects the rights of the new bond holders, and modifications to the amount, term and coupons.

The Committee noted that the starting point that was used for its analysis was the assumption in the submission that the part of the principal amount of the old GGBs that was exchanged for new GGBs could be separately assessed for derecognition. The Committee emphasised that this assumption was more favourable for achieving partial derecognition than looking at the whole of the old bond. Hence, its conclusion that the old GGBs should be derecognised would apply even more so when taking into account that the exchange of the old GGBs, was as a matter of fact, the result of a single agreement that covered all aspects and types of consideration for surrendering the old GGBs. As a consequence, the Committee noted that partial derecognition did not apply.

Consequently, the Committee decided not to add the issue to its agenda.

3.1.4.1 Meaning of 'without material delay'

Without material delay does not mean instantaneously, nor does it imply an extended length of time. The contractual arrangement will need to be considered in full in order to make an assessment as to whether the timeframe between the collection of cash flows on the underlying assets and the point at which they are passed on to the eventual recipients is material in the context of the contractual arrangements of the transfer.

In some arrangements, the cash collected on the underlying assets occurs sporadically throughout a period of time. For example, if an entity retains the rights to the cash flows arising on a group of credit card receivables, the payments arising on those credit cards are likely to occur on any given day throughout the month. The contractual arrangement of the transfer may require that those cash flows are remitted to the eventual recipients on a weekly, monthly, quarterly or even annual basis. There is a trade-off between passing on the cash flows almost as soon as they arise and the administrative burden that goes along with passing on those cash flows. It is likely that half-yearly payments to the eventual recipients (and certainly annual payments) would be considered to be subject to a material delay because the conditions specified above fail and, therefore, derecognition would be inappropriate in these circumstances. It appears reasonable that the entity can invest the cash flows from the assets for up to three months without breaching the condition that all cash flows must be passed to the eventual recipient without material delay.

Any significant delay in passing on the cash flows of a transferred asset alters the credit risk characteristics for the eventual recipient when compared to the original transferred asset. The holder is exposed not only to the original transferred asset but to additional credit risk from the reinvestment of the cash flows from the original asset.

3.1.4.2 Pass-through arrangements structured with shares

When the contractual arrangement that passes the cash flows on the transferred asset to the eventual recipient is legally structured as a share, as opposed to a conventional obligation to a creditor, the form of the share may prevent the pass-through tests being met. For example, if a dividend under the share (i.e. the cash received under the transferred asset) is only required to be paid if there are sufficient distributable profits in the entity, then a lack of distributable profits will limit the transferor's ability to make payments to the eventual recipients without material delay. The potential for a dividend block in this case will prohibit the transferor meeting the pass-through criteria. Consideration should be given to other restrictions, either inherent in the terms of the instrument or in the articles of the entity, that would limit the entity's ability to pay amounts to the eventual recipients when due without material delay.

3.1.4.3 Consideration of the likelihood that the transferor will default

The likelihood that the transferor will default under the pass-through arrangements as a result of a default on other creditor obligations is not considered an impediment to meeting the pass-through criteria because the transferor is assumed to be a going concern. In many cases, the transferee may limit this risk by ensuring that the transferred assets reside in a bankruptcy remote structured entity so that the wider credit risk of the transferor is not borne by the transferee.

3.1.4.4 Pass-through arrangements with credit enhancement

A transferor may provide credit enhancement in a transfer arrangement so that it suffers the first loss on the asset up to a specified amount. In such circumstances, if the debtor fails to pay, the transferor absorbs the first loss fully, with the eventual recipient only suffering a loss after the first loss has been fully absorbed. A credit enhancement may be in the form of over-collateralisation or may be in the form of purchasing a subordinated interest in a consolidated structured entity (in the latter case, the entity is applying the pass-through tests at a consolidated level). Providing credit enhancement will not in itself result in failure of the pass-through tests if all cash received by the transferor on transferred assets is paid on to the eventual recipient, although the credit enhancement may result in failure of derecognition due to the transferor retaining substantially all the risks and rewards of ownership of the assets. The pass-through tests must be considered prior to considering the entity's exposure to risk and rewards.

If a greater amount of cash is realised on the assets than is needed to pay the eventual recipient (i.e. the eventual recipient's initial investment is fully paid), then the entity will retain the remainder of the cash and will not pass it on. In all cases the entity passes "any cash it collects on behalf of the eventual recipients".

Example 3.1.4.4

Pass-through arrangements with credit enhancement

Entity B enters into an arrangement with Entity C under which where Entity C pays Entity B CU0.9 million in return for receiving cash flows on CU1.0 million of assets when expected losses on the assets are 10 per cent of all cash flows (interest and principal). Entity B retains the contractual rights to receive the cash flows from the assets but assumes an obligation to pay cash flows from the asset to Entity C. The maximum cash flows that Entity C can receive under the arrangement are interest and principal on a notional of CU0.9 million. If actual credit losses are lower than expected (say, only 5 per cent), Entity B will pay Entity C interest and principal on CU0.9 million and retain interest and principal on CU0.05 million.

Entity B will apply the derecognition model to the full CU1.0 million of assets (see **3.1.2**). Entity B will pass the pass-through tests, assuming all other conditions are met, because Entity B will pass interest and principal on a notional up to CU0.9 million of the cash flows to Entity C.

However, if the form of the transaction were different, in that Entity C pays Entity B CU1.0 million for the assets and purchases a financial guarantee contract from Entity B for CU0.1 million, then the pass-through tests would not be met because Entity B will pay the eventual recipient, Entity C, even when it does not collect the equivalent amount from the original assets.

3.1.4.5 Revolving structures

In a revolving structure, cash received on the assets is reinvested in buying new receivables assets. In other words, cash 'revolves' into new assets instead of being returned immediately to the investors. Upon maturity, the reinvested assets are used to repay the beneficial interest holders. Such 'revolving' structures do not meet the pass-through tests because they involve a material delay before the original cash is passed onto the eventual recipients and the reinvestment would typically be not in cash or cash equivalents. The treatment of revolving structures described above was confirmed by the IFRIC (now the IFRS Interpretations Committee) in September 2005.

3.1.4.6 Retention of servicing rights

An entity may enter into an arrangement with a third party to transfer the contractual rights to receive the cash flows of a financial asset, but also agree to continue to act as an agent to administer collection and distribution of cash flows to the recipient (i.e. it retains servicing rights on the cash flows).

IFRS 9:3.2.4(a) focuses on whether an entity transfers the contractual rights to receive the cash flows from a financial asset. The determination as to whether the contractual rights to cash flows have been transferred is not affected by the transferor retaining the role of an agent to administer collection and distribution of cash flows. Retention of servicing rights by the entity transferring the financial asset does not, in itself, cause the transfer to fail the requirements in IFRS 9:3.2.4(a). However, careful judgement must be applied to determine whether the entity providing servicing is acting solely as an agent for the owner of the financial asset (i.e. whether it has transferred all risks and rewards).

3.1.4.7 Transfer of legal title

When the Board considered a number of derecognition issues in September 2006 at the request of the IFRIC, it discussed whether any transfer in which legal ownership of the asset is not transferred can be considered an outright transfer of contractual rights under IAS 39:18(a) (now IFRS 9:3.2.4(a)). In other words, it considered whether the pass-through test is applicable to all transfers in which legal ownership of the financial asset is not transferred. The Board indicated that a transaction in which an entity transfers *all* the contractual rights *to receive the cash flows* [emphasis added in the IASB Update] (without necessarily transferring legal ownership of the financial asset), would not be treated as a pass-through and would be considered a transfer of contractual rights under IAS 39:18(a). An example might be a situation in which an entity transfers all the legal rights to specifically identified cash flows of a financial asset (e.g. a transfer of the interest or principal of a debt instrument).Conversely, the pass-through test would be applicable to situations when the entity does not transfer all the contractual rights to cash flows of the financial asset, such as disproportionate transfers (see IAS 39:16(b), now IFRS 9:3.2.2(b)).

The Board's view in this case would mean that if an arrangement transferred all the legal rights to cash flows for a full proportionate interest in an asset (say 50 per cent of all cash flows), even though legal title of the asset was not transferred to the transferee, the transferor would apply IAS 39:18(a) (now IFRS 9:3.2.4(a)) to the transfer and, therefore, would avoid the pass-through tests in IAS 39:18(b) (now IFRS 9:3.2.4(b)).

3.1.4.8 Conditional transfers

The Board also discussed whether conditional transfers should be treated as pass-through transactions. Conditions attached to a transfer could include provisions ensuring the existence and value of transferred cash flows at the date of transfer or conditions relating to the future performance of the asset. The Board indicated that such conditions would not affect whether the entity has transferred the contractual rights to receive cash flows (under IAS 39:18(a), now IFRS 9:3.2.4(a)). However, the existence of conditions relating to the future performance of the asset might affect the conclusion related to the transfer of risks and rewards as well as the extent of any continuing involvement by the transferor in the transferred asset.

The Board's view on conditional transfers would allow the pass-through criteria to be met for a transfer of trade receivables even when there is a promise, say, to compensate the transferee should the transferor issue a credit note to the customer because the goods are returned. In this case, the transferor is obligated to pay cash to the transferee when the transferee did not collect cash from the asset.

The Board's views were included in a draft rejection notice issued by the IFRIC (now the IFRS Interpretations Committee) in November 2006. Following comments from constituents, at the IFRIC meeting in January 2007, the IFRIC decided to withdraw the rejection notice and add a project on derecognition to its agenda. However, in March 2009, the IFRIC decided to remove all of the outstanding derecognition issues from its agenda because the IASB accelerated its project to develop a replacement for the sections of IAS 39 on derecognition; the IASB published an exposure draft on this subject in March 2009 with the intention of issuing a final IFRS in the second half of 2010. However, in June 2010, the IASB announced its intention to proceed with a more limited project regarding new disclosure requirements in connection with derecognition. The resulting amendments to IFRS 7, *Transfers of Financial Assets*, were issued in October 2010 (see **4.1.6** in **chapter B11**).

3.1.5 Has the entity transferred substantially all of the risks and rewards of ownership of the asset?

Determining the extent to which the risks and rewards of the transferred asset have been transferred and retained is critical in determining the accounting outcome for a transfer. The greater the risks and rewards retained, the greater is the likelihood of continued recognition. The degree to which risks and rewards have been transferred and its effect on the accounting outcome can be illustrated as follows.

More risks and rewards transferred from transferor to transferee (↑)

Situation		Accounting treatment for transferor
Substantially all risks and rewards transferred		Derecognise transferred asset Recognise any new assets/ liabilities
Neither retained nor transferred substantially all risks and rewards of ownership	Control no longer retained by transferor – transferee can unilaterally sell the transferred asset	Derecognise transferred asset Recognise any new assets/ liabilities
	Control retained by transferor – transferee cannot unilaterally sell the transferred asset	Recognise asset and liability to the extent of continue involvement
Substantially all risks and rewards retained		Continue to recognise transferred asset Proceeds from transfer are recognised as a financial liability

When the entity transfers substantially all of the risks and rewards of ownership of the financial asset, the asset should be derecognised. The entity may have to recognise separately any rights and obligations created or retained in the transfer. [IFRS 9:3.2.6(a)]

There is no 'bright line' provided in IFRS 9 as to what is meant by a transfer of 'substantially all' of the risks and rewards of ownership, and a significant degree of judgement is required when applying the risks and rewards test.

There are other references in the Standard to various yardsticks that need to be met when applying certain paragraphs. For example, when comparing the old and new terms of a financial liability, the terms are considered to be 'substantially different' if the present value of the cash flows under the new terms is at least 10 per cent different from the discounted present value of the remaining cash flows of the original financial liability (see **4.1**).

While IFRS 9 does not apply the 90 per cent test to derecognition of financial assets, it would seem imprudent to conclude that substantially all the risks and rewards of ownership have been transferred when the computations show that the entity still retains more than 10 per cent of the exposure to the variability in present value of the expected future cash flows post transfer.

IFRS 9 provides three examples of when an entity has transferred substantially all of the risks and rewards of ownership:

[IFRS 9:B3.2.4]

- an unconditional sale of a financial asset;
- a sale of a financial asset together with an option to repurchase the financial asset at its fair value at the time of repurchase; and

- a sale of a financial asset together with a put or call option that is deeply out of the money (i.e. an option that is so far out of the money that it is highly unlikely to be in the money before expiry).

In the first example, it is clear that there has been a transfer of all the risks and rewards of ownership of the asset. In the second example, the entity has sold the asset and, although it can call the asset back, this can only be done at the fair market value of the asset at the time of re-acquisition. The entity is in the same economic position as having sold the asset outright, with the ability to go into the market to reacquire the asset (i.e. it has transferred the full price risk of the asset). In the third example, the option is highly unlikely ever to be exercised and has very little value, which is substantially the same economic position as an unconditional sale.

Pass-through arrangements that meet the criteria in **section 3.1.4** may not satisfy the test regarding the transfer of substantially all of the risks and rewards of ownership.

Example 3.1.5A

Interaction of pass-through tests and risk and reward tests

Entity A originates a portfolio of five-year interest-bearing loans of CU10,000. Entity A enters into an agreement with Entity C whereby, in exchange for a cash payment of CU9,000, Entity A agrees to pay to Entity C the first CU9,000 (plus interest) of cash collected from the loan portfolio. Entity A retains rights to the last CU1,000 (plus interest), i.e. it retains a subordinated residual interest. If Entity A collects, say, only CU8,000 of its loans of CU10,000 because some debtors default, Entity A would pass on to Entity C all of the CU8,000 collected and Entity A keeps nothing. If Entity A collects CU9,500, it passes CU9,000 to Entity C and retains CU500. Expected losses are CU500.

Even though all cash flows that derive from the portfolio of assets are passed onto Entity C up to a maximum of CU9,000, Entity A has not transferred substantially all the risks and rewards of ownership because of the subordinated retained interest. The residual interest absorbs the likely variability in net cash flows, i.e. the expected losses.

IFRS 9 acknowledges that in many cases it will be clear whether or not the entity has transferred substantially all of the risks and rewards of ownership following a transfer of an asset. When it is unclear whether or not there has been a transfer of substantially all of the risks and rewards of ownership of the financial asset, then the entity will have to evaluate its exposure before and after the transfer by comparing the variability in the amounts and timing of the net cash flows of the transferred asset. [IFRS 9:3.2.7] If the exposure to the present value of the future net cash flows from the financial asset does not change significantly as a result of the transfer, then the entity has not transferred substantially all of the risks and rewards of ownership.

The computational comparison is made using an appropriate current market interest rate as the discount rate. All reasonably possible outcomes should be considered and a greater weight given to those outcomes that are more likely to occur. This is an expected cash flow model and should include all risks inherent in the cash flows.

There is no example in IFRS 9 of the methodology to be used in performing the risks and rewards assessment. Whichever methodology is used, it should be consistently applied to all transfers that are similar in nature. It would be inappropriate to use multiple methodologies for similar transactions and to 'cherry pick' the methodology that indicated the desired degree of transfer of risks and rewards.

A common approach is to use a standard deviation statistic as the basis for determining how much variability has been transferred and retained by the transferor. To apply this approach, the transferor will need to consider various future scenarios that will impact the amount and timing of cash flows of the transferred assets and calculate the present value of these amounts both before and after the transfer. In the case of a transfer of debt instruments, scenarios will incorporate, among other factors:

- changes in the amount of cash flows due to changes in the rate of default by the borrower and recovery of any collateral in the case of default; and
- changes in the timing of when cash flows are received due to changes in prepayments rates.

The expected cash flows on the transferred assets will be allocated to the transferor and the transferee based on the rights and obligations following the transfer. For example, if the transferor guarantees part of the transferred assets or invests in a subordinated loan, a subordinated interest only strip or excess spread issued by the transferee, this will result in some of the exposure to the assets coming back to the transferor.

The transferor will need to assess the probability of the various scenarios occurring so that it can take the various present values described above and multiply them by those probabilities in order to determine probability weighted present values. These values are used for calculating the standard deviation, which can be thought of as the exposure, or volatility, that the transferor has to the transferred asset both before and after the transfer. This will form the basis for judging whether the transferor has retained or transferred substantially all the risks and rewards of ownership of the transferred assets.

The example below is aligned with the fact pattern included in the illustration in IFRS 9:B3.2.17, reproduced in **example 3.4.2**, where prepayable loans are transferred to a transferee in return for cash proceeds and an investment in a subordinated interest only strip, subordinated principal only strip, and an excess spread. The illustration in the Standard concludes that the transferor has neither retained nor transferred substantially all the risks and rewards of ownership.

Example 3.1.5B

Determining the extent of risk and reward transferred

Entity A has a portfolio of similar prepayable fixed rate loans with a remaining maturity of two years, a coupon and effective interest rate of 10%. The principal and amortised cost is CU10,000. On 1/1/X0, Entity A transfers the loans for cash consideration of CU9,115 to Entity B, an entity not consolidated in Entity A's consolidated financial statements. In order to acquire the loans, Entity B issues a senior note, linked to the performance of the transferred assets, to third parties where the holders of the notes obtain the right to CU9,000 of any collections of principal plus interest thereon at 9.5 per cent. Entity A agrees to retain rights to CU1,000 of any collections of principal plus interest thereon at 10 per cent, plus the excess spread of 0.5 per cent on the remaining CU9,000 of principal. Collections from prepayments are allocated between the transferor and the transferee proportionately in the ratio of 1:9, but any defaults are deducted from Entity A's retained interest of CU1,000 until that interest is exhausted. Entity A's retained interest is therefore subordinate to the senior notes because it suffers the loss of any defaults on the transferred assets prior to the holders of the senior notes.

Interest is due on the transferred assets annually on the anniversary of the date of transfer.

In order to determine the extent to which Entity A has retained the risks and rewards of the transferred assets, Entity A considers a number of scenarios where amounts and timings of cash flows on the transferred assets vary and assigns a probability for each scenario occurring in the future. For illustration purposes, only four scenarios are included below although, in practice, a larger number of scenarios is likely to be required. A risk-free rate of 8.5% is used to determine net present values. All amounts are denominated in CU.

Scenario		**Total**	**Senior note holders**	**Retained by Entity A**
1. All loans prepay immediately with no defaults. Probability is 20%	1/1/X0 – undiscounted	10,000	9,000	1,000
	Total net present value	*10,000*	*9,000*	*1,000*
2. All loans prepay in one year with no defaults. Probability is 30%	1/1/X0 – undiscounted	–	–	–
	1/1/X1 – undiscounted	11,000	9,855 (9.5% x 9,000) + 9,000	1,145 (0.5% x 9,000) + (10% x 1,000) + 1,000
	Total net present value	*10,138*	*9,083*	*1,055*

Scenario		Total	Senior note holders	Retained by Entity A
3. All loans run to their contractual maturity of 1/1/X2 with no defaults. Probability is 30%	1/1/X0 – undiscounted	–	–	–
	1/1/X1 – undiscounted	1,000	855 (9.5% x 9,000)	145 (0.5% x 9,000) + (10% x 1,000)
	1/1/X2 – undiscounted	11,000	9,855	1,145
	Total net present value	*10,265*	*9,159*	*1,106*
4. All loans default at 1/1/X1 and due to immediate foreclosure and sale of the collateral, a total of CU10,741 is recovered. Probability is 20%	1/1/X0 – undiscounted	–	–	–
	1/1/X1 – undiscounted	10,741	9,855	886 Proceeds from sale of collateral less amount paid to senior note holders
	Total net present value	*9,900*	*9,083*	*817*

The net present values for each scenario are multiplied by the probability of each scenario to determine a probability weighted present value. The variance before and after the transfer is determined using the profitability weighted present values as illustrated below.

Entity A's variability before the transfer

Scenario	PV of cash flows	Probability	Probability weighted PV	Variability in PV	Probability weighted variability
	a	b	c = a × b	e = a – d	f = e² × b
1	10,000	20%	2,000	(101)	2,040
2	10,138	30%	3,041	37	411
3	10,265	30%	3,080	164	8,069
4	9,900	20%	1,980	(201)	8,080
Total			10,101 [d]		18,600
Square root of f					**136**

Entity A's variability after the transfer

Scenario	PV of cash flows	Probability	Probability weighted PV	Variability in PV	Probability weighted variability
	a	b	c = a × b	e = a – d	f = e² × b
1	1,000	20%	200	(12)	29
2	1,055	30%	317	43	555
3	1,106	30%	332	94	2,651
4	817	20%	163	(195)	7,605
Total			1,012 [d]		10,840
Square root of f					**104**

Senior note holders' variability after the transfer

Scenario	PV of cash flows	Probability	Probability weighted PV	Variability in PV	Probability weighted variability
	a	b	c = a × b	e = a – d	f = e² × b
1	9,000	20%	1,800	(90)	1,620
2	9,083	30%	2,725	(7)	15
3	9,159	30%	2,748	69	1,428
4	9,083	20%	1,817	(7)	10
Total			9,090 [d]		3,073
Square root of f					**55**

Entity A determines whether substantially all of the risks and rewards of ownership of the transferred assets are retained by dividing the variability retained after the transfer by the variability of the portfolio as a whole [$^{104}/_{136}$ = 76%]. Consequently, Entity A concludes that substantially all the risks and rewards of ownership are neither transferred nor retained. Entity A would then need to address whether it has control of the transferred asset as described in detail in **3.1.7** to determine whether Entity A can derecognise the asset in full or continue to recognise its continuing involvement in the transferred assets.

It is worth noting that the sum of variability of Entity A after the transfer (CU104) plus variability of the senior note holders (CU55) is greater than the variability of the portfolio as a whole (CU136). This arises because the portfolio of loans as a whole has less risk due to the diversification of the loans within the portfolio. Some of this diversification is reversed when the portfolio is split into pieces. More complex mathematical techniques can be applied to show Entity B's variability to the loans after the transfer that includes the diversification effect that exists in the portfolio prior to the transfer. Such techniques are beyond the scope of this manual.

3.1.6 Has the entity retained substantially all of the risks and rewards of ownership of the asset?

If the entity has retained substantially all of the risks and rewards of ownership of a financial asset, the entity should continue to recognise that financial asset. [IFRS 9:3.2.6(b)]

Once again, when it is unclear whether the entity has retained substantially all of the risks and rewards of ownership of the asset, it should look at its exposure before and after the transfer by comparing the variability in the amounts and timing of the net cash flows of the transferred asset. [IFRS 9:3.2.7]

IFRS 9 provides examples of transfers where substantially all of the risks and rewards of ownership have been retained and, therefore, derecognition is not permitted:

[IFRS 9:B3.2.5]

- a sale and repurchase transaction where the repurchase price is a fixed price or the sale price plus a lender's return;
- a securities lending transaction;
- a sale of a financial asset together with a total return swap that transfers the market risk back to the entity;
- a sale of a financial asset together with a deep in-the-money written put option or purchased call option (i.e. an option that is so far in the money that it is highly unlikely to go out of the money before expiry); and
- a sale of short-term receivables in which the entity guarantees to compensate the transferee for credit losses that are likely to occur.

In a typical repurchase agreement, the entity might, for example, own government securities that it sells to a third party with an agreement to repurchase the securities at a specified price, generally within a short period of time. At inception, the lender transfers the securities to the borrower and receives cash or other consideration as collateral; if the consideration is cash, it is then invested in other assets that earn a return. At a defined date, the transferor repurchases the securities. Dollar repurchase agreements (dollar rolls) are similar transactions in which the transferor repurchases similar but not identical assets to those originally sold. Economically, the lender is motivated in these transactions by the liquidity afforded by the agreement and/or the excess returns it expects to earn on the collateral.

Repurchase agreements are commonly referred to as 'repos'. In many countries, these are actively traded on listed exchanges or in the over-the-counter market and often are used as a source of funding or yield enhancement mechanism. The terminology, however, varies from country to country and the form taken, also, can be different. In some countries, a distinction is made between a repurchase agreement where legal title passes (also known as 'sell/ buy-backs') and a 'carry' (typically, a short-term repo that is sometimes known as a classic repo) where title does not pass. Terminology also differs depending on which party is 'buying' or 'selling' the security (hence the use of terms such as 'reverse repos', 'inward carries' and 'outward carries').

In a securities lending transaction, the transferor (lender of the security) transfers a security to the transferee (borrower of the security) for a period of time. The transferee generally is required to provide collateral, which may be cash, other securities, or a standby letter of credit with a value that can be slightly higher than the value of the security borrowed (sometimes referred to as a 'haircut'). These transactions are typical when an entity needs a specific security to cover a short sale or a customer's failure to deliver securities sold. The transferor is compensated for lending the security by earning a fee or a return on the collateral invested if the collateral is cash.

A sale and repurchase transaction with a fixed price establishes a lending arrangement whereby the transferor is always going to reacquire the asset in the future. The fixed price is usually set to reflect the cost of borrowing over the period of the transaction. Because the transferor is required to reacquire the asset for a fixed price, the transferor is exposed to the market risk of the asset. The same analysis applies to a securities lending transaction. [IFRS 9:B3.2.16(a)]

A sale of a financial asset together with a total return swap that transfers the market risk back to the entity also establishes the economic equivalent of a lending arrangement. Under the terms of the total return swap, the transferor will usually pay an amount equivalent to a borrowing rate to the transferee over time and the transferee will reimburse the transferor for the performance of the asset. For example, the transferred asset may be an equity security; if the equity price goes up, the transferor receives the benefits of the rise in value of the transferred equity security from the transferee and pays an amount equivalent to a borrowing rate to the transferee; if the equity security price falls, the transferor pays an amount equivalent to a borrowing rate and, in addition, pays an amount equivalent to the fall in value of the equity security. The transferor continues to be exposed to the rise and fall in the equity security price after the transfer and hence, has retained substantially all of the risks and rewards of ownership of the asset. [IFRS 9:B3.2.16(o)]

When an entity sells an asset, but retains the right to buy the asset back at a price that is sufficiently low (option is deep in the money) that the option is highly likely to be exercised, the entity retains substantially all the risks and rewards of ownership. Similarly, when an entity sells an asset and gives the transferee the right to put the asset back at a sufficiently advantageous price (option is deep in the money) so that the option is likely to be exercised, the entity retains substantially all the risks and rewards of ownership. [IFRS 9:B3.2.16(f)]

Example 3.1.6A

Transfer of receivables with a deep in-the-money written put option (1)

Transferor X transfers receivables that are carried at amortised cost with a carrying amount of $90 and a put option which expires in 10 days to Transferee Y. Transferee Y pays $150 for the receivables, which have a fair value of $100. Under the terms of the put option, Transferee Y may put the receivables to Transferor X for $151. The possibility of the fair value of the receivables increasing to $151 in 10 days is considered remote and, therefore, exercise of the option appears virtually assured at inception.

Because, at inception, it is virtually certain that the put option will be exercised, Transferor X has retained substantially all of the risks and rewards of ownership over the receivables, and this transaction should be accounted for as a secured borrowing of $150 with the difference between the consideration received and the put strike price (i.e. $1), amortised to profit or loss using the effective interest method.

However, the same analysis is not appropriate when the option is not deep in the money and further derecognition tests should be applied.

In a sale of short-term receivables where the main risk of ownership is credit risk (i.e. the risk that the debtor will fail to pay), and the entity guarantees to compensate the transferee for credit losses that are likely to occur, the transferor has retained substantially all of the risks of ownership. [IFRS 9:B3.2.5(e)]

All the terms of a transfer need to be carefully evaluated. For example, penalty provisions attached to the agreement may affect the analysis of whether the risks and rewards have been transferred.

Example 3.1.6B

Transfer of receivables with a deep in-the-money written put option (2)

Transferor X transfers receivables with a carrying amount of $90 and a put option that expires in 10 days' time to Transferee Y. In the exchange, Transferee Y pays Transferor X $100, the fair value of the receivables. Under the terms of the put option, Transferee Y may put the receivables back to Transferor X for $101. However, if Transferee Y does not put the receivables back to Transferor X, Transferee Y must pay Transferor X an additional $50. The possibility of the fair value of the receivables increasing to $151 in 10 days is remote and, therefore, exercise of the option appears virtually assured at inception.

Because, at inception, it is virtually certain that the put option will be exercised, Transferor X has effectively retained substantially all the risks and rewards of ownership and, therefore, the transaction should be accounted for as a secured borrowing of $100 with the difference between the consideration received of $100 and the put strike price of $101 amortised to profit or loss using the effective interest method.

Typical risks included in a risk and reward analysis are interest rate risk, credit risk (i.e. risk of default) and late payment risk. In many securitisation transactions, an entity (typically a structured entity) acquires assets and issues notes that are backed by those assets. The overall securitisation has liquidity risk associated with the fact that there is a mismatch in the timing of cash inflows and outflows. It is important to recognise that liquidity risk arising in the structured entity from differences in the contractual timing of cash flows of the assets and the notes issued to acquire the assets is not part of the transferred assets. This compares to late payment risk and credit default risk which is inherent in the assets. However, if an asset pays late, the transferee may not be able to meet its obligations under the notes. This liquidity risk is not part of the transferred assets because it only arises when the assets are placed inside the securitisation structure. The liquidity risk associated with late payment risk is therefore not included in the transferor's risk and rewards assessment in determining derecognition for the transferor. However, the impact of liquidity risk will be included in determining whether an entity should consolidate that structured entity, in particular in the assessment of whether the entity is exposed, or has rights, to variable returns from its involvement with the structured entity.

Derivatives are often included in contractual arrangements that transfer financial assets and may affect the analysis of whether the risks and rewards of those assets have been transferred. Their presence and contractual terms may not be obvious and careful review of all the terms of the transfer agreement is required.

In some instances, derivatives are included in a transfer or a securitisation structure and are not explicitly defined as derivatives. For example, the terms of a securitisation may call for the allocation of all principal cash flows to outside investors, with any remainder going to the retained interest of the seller. This provision may be in the form of a call option, put option, or forward contract. Identifying the implicit derivative in this example requires a thorough understanding of the transfer structure, terms, and conditions.

Derivatives commonly found in transfers of financial assets include put options, call options, forward or repurchase contracts, forward sales contracts and swap agreements. Put options provide the transferee with the right to require the transferor to repurchase some or all of the financial assets that were sold (e.g. to repurchase delinquent receivables). Call options provide the transferor with the right to repurchase some or all of the financial assets sold to the transferee. Forward or repurchase agreements require the transferee to sell and the transferor to buy some or all of the financial assets that were sold before their scheduled maturity. Forward sales contracts require the transferor to sell and the transferee to buy additional financial assets in the future. Swap agreements effectively change one or more cash flows of the underlying transferred assets (or debt issued by a structured entity). For example, an interest rate swap may convert a variable rate asset to a fixed rate.

Derivatives can operate automatically or require exercise by one of the parties; they can be exercised freely or only after the occurrence of a future event. Such a future event may be certain of occurring (e.g. the passage of time), or may be conditional upon another event (e.g. a loan becoming delinquent). For conditional events, the certainty of occurrence varies – their occurrence may be considered to be probable, possible or remote. The exercise price of a derivative can be fixed above, below or equal to the market value of the financial assets at inception or it can be variable, equal to the market value at exercise date, or the result of a formula that is a function of market conditions or other future events. Derivatives can be combined to form different types of derivatives. Each of these factors impacts the extent to which risks and rewards have been retained by the transferor.

When a transferor transfers a fixed rate debt instrument for cash or other consideration and at the same time enters into an interest rate swap with the transferee so that the transferor receives a fixed rate and pays floating rate based on a notional equal to the par amount of the transferred debt instrument, the interest rate swap does not preclude derecognition of the debt instrument as long as payments under the swap are not conditional on payments being made on the transferred debt. [IFRS 9:B3.2.16(p)] Even though the interest rate swap results in the transferor receiving cash flows similar to the underlying cash flows it would have received under the debt instrument, this does not prevent derecognition because the transferor's exposure before and after the transfer is different. Prior to the transfer, the transferor is exposed to fixed interest only and the credit risk of the issuer of the debt instrument. After the transfer, the transferor is exposed to the net of fixed and floating interest rates and the credit risk of the transferee to the extent that the transferee owes the transferor any amounts under the interest rate swap. If the cash flows under the swap were contingent on the cash flows received under the debt instrument, then the credit risk of the interest flows under the debt instrument would be retained by the transferor and a different derecognition conclusion would be likely to result.

When a transferor transfers a prepayable fixed rate debt instrument for cash or other consideration, and at the same time enters into an amortising interest rate swap with the transferee so that the transferor receives fixed rate and pays floating rate, the transferor will have retained prepayment risk if the repayment profile on the debt instrument matches the amortising profile of the interest rate risk. In this case, the transferor will either continue to recognise fully the fixed rate debt instrument or will recognise the transferred asset to the extent of its continuing involvement. If the amortisation of the notional amount of the swap is not linked to the principal amount outstanding of the transferred asset, the swap will not result in the transferor retaining prepayment risk on the asset. [IFRS 9:B3.2.16(q)] For the same reasons as described above for non-amortising swaps, as long as the interest flows on the swap are not conditional on the cash flows under the debt instrument, and the swap does not result in the transferor retaining any other significant risks and rewards of ownership, then derecognition of the asset would be appropriate.

3.1.7 Has the entity retained control of the asset?

When an entity determines that it has neither transferred nor retained substantially all of the risks and rewards of ownership of the transferred assets, it needs to make an assessment as to whether or not it has retained control of the asset.

- If the entity has not retained control of the financial asset, the entity should derecognise the financial asset and recognise separately as assets or liabilities any rights and obligations created or retained in the transfer.
- If the entity has retained control of the financial asset, the entity should continue to recognise the financial asset to the extent of its continuing involvement in the financial asset. [IFRS 9:3.2.6(c)]

An entity controls a financial asset when it is able to sell that asset. When the transferee has the *practical ability* to sell the asset in its entirety to an *unrelated* third party and is able to exercise that ability *unilaterally* and *without* the imposition of additional *restrictions* on the transfer, the transferee controls the asset and, therefore, the transferor must have relinquished control (emphasis added). [IFRS 9:3.2.9]

When the transferred asset is traded in an active market, the transferee generally has the practical ability to sell the asset. This is because there is a ready market and the transferee can repurchase the asset if and when it is required to return the asset back to the transferor. [IFRS 9:B3.2.7]

However, the fact that the transferred asset is traded in an active market is not in itself sufficient to conclude that the transferee has the 'practical ability' to sell the asset. For example, the settlement terms of repurchase, which are driven by the market conventions, may differ significantly from the settlement terms in the transfer agreement such that the transferee will not be able to gain access to the asset quickly enough to deliver the asset to the transferor so as to comply with the contractual provisions of the transfer agreement. In this case, the transferee is forced to hold the asset in order to ensure that it can deliver the asset back to the transferor when required.

Other factors may affect the entity's practical ability to sell the asset:

- a financial asset that would satisfy the call option or forward contract may have to be purchased from a third party at a price significantly above its estimated fair value, thus indicating that the assets are not liquid;
- financial assets available to satisfy the call option or forward contract may be held by one or a small number of investors, thus indicating that the assets are not liquid; or
- the quantity of financial assets necessary to satisfy the call option or forward contract may be too large compared to that traded in the market and the terms of the transfer do not allow delivery of the assets over a period of time.

Intuitively, the wider the range of assets that may be used to satisfy the call option, the more likely it is that the entity has practical ability to sell the asset. For instance, assets identical to those originally transferred may not be readily obtainable but, if the call option permits delivery of assets that are similar to the transferred assets, they may be readily obtainable. When a call option permits settlement in cash as an alternative to delivering the financial asset, and the cash settlement alternative does not contain an economic penalty rendering it unfeasible, the transferee has the practical ability to sell the asset as cash is a readily obtainable asset.

Unilateral and unrestricted ability to sell means that there can be no 'strings' attached to the sale. If the transferee has to attach a call option over the asset when it sells it, or introduce conditions over how the asset is serviced, in order to satisfy the terms of the original transfer, then 'strings' exist and the test of 'practical ability' has failed.

The 'strings' can be created by other instruments that form a contractual part of the transfer arrangement and are sufficiently valuable to the transferee, so that if the transferee were to sell the asset it would rationally include similar features within that sale. For example, a guarantee may be included in the initial transfer and may have such potential value to the transferee that the transferee would be reluctant to sell the asset and forgo any payments that may fall due under the guarantee.

The transfer agreement may have an explicit restriction that prohibits the transferee from selling the asset. When that restriction is removed or lapses, and as a result the transferee has the practical ability to sell the asset, derecognition would be appropriate.

The fact that the transferee may or may not choose to sell the asset should not form part of the decision making process: it is the transferee's practical ability to do so that is important.

Example 3.1.7A

Transfer of readily obtainable bonds with written put option

Transferor X sells South African government bonds that are readily obtainable in the market with a carrying amount of Rand 100 to Transferee Y for Rand 103. The transfer includes an option for Transferee Y to put the assets back to Transferor X up to one year after the transfer date at Rand 103.50. Transferee Y exercises its option 30 days after the initial sale. The option had a fair value of Rand 2 at the exchange date consisting of time value of Rand 1.50 and intrinsic value of Rand 0.50.

In this example, the transferor has neither transferred nor retained substantially all the risks and rewards of ownership because the option is neither deeply in nor deeply out of the money. The transferor has not retained control because the assets are readily obtainable. This put option does not therefore preclude derecognition.

Example 3.1.7B

Transfer of mortgage loans with right to call

Transferor X transfers a portfolio of mortgage loans to a third party, Transferee Y. The transferred loans can be repurchased by Transferor X at any time prior to their maturity. The agreement contains no explicit conditions restraining Transferee Y from selling, exchanging or pledging the assets to a third party.

Transferee Y does not have the practical ability to sell the portfolio of mortgage loans because it must have access to the original mortgage loans that were transferred in the event Transferor X exercises its right under the call option and the mortgage loans cannot be readily obtained from another source.

IFRS 9 envisages circumstances when the transferee does not have the unilateral and unrestricted ability to sell the asset due to arrangements such as a call option held by the transferor. The Standard is less clear on the accounting treatment that should apply when a call option is held by a party other than the transferor. **Example 3.1.7C** illustrates this point.

Example 3.1.7C

Transfer of asset with purchased call option held by a third party

Bank A transfers loans to a non-consolidated structured entity. The funds that the structured entity used to purchase the loans were generated through a securitisation involving notes being issued by the structured entity to third parties. Bank A invests in a note that comprises an interest only strip on the transferred loans and also provides a subordinated loan to the structured entity. Bank B (an independent third party relative to Bank A) holds substantive rights to direct the relevant activities of the structured entity, has provided a larger subordinated loan and invested in the most junior notes of the structured entity. Because it has the ability to use its power to affect its returns from its involvement with the structured entity, Bank B consolidates the structured entity. Bank B has a call on the assets of the structured entity that is exercisable at a fixed price.

Because Bank A has invested in the interest only strip and provided the subordinated loan, it is considered to neither have transferred nor retained substantially all of the risks and rewards of the transferred loans. Bank A must assess whether it has retained control of the asset, i.e. whether the *transferee* has the practical ability to sell the asset in its entirety to an unrelated third party and is able to exercise that ability unilaterally and without imposition of additional restrictions.

In this example, if the structured entity is considered to be the transferee, it does not have the practical ability to sell the loans without restrictions. If it were to sell the loans, it would need to attach restrictions such that it could honour its obligations under the call option which allows Bank B to call the remaining loans. The call option written by the structured entity limits the structured entity's ability to sell the asset. However, if the transferee in this case is viewed as the consolidated group of Bank B (which, therefore, includes the structured entity) then the transferee does have the unrestricted ability to sell the assets because the call option is eliminated on consolidation. Also, it can be argued that Bank A has not retained control of the asset, given that it has no mechanism within the arrangements for buying back the loans or being forced to acquire the loans. It is appropriate, therefore, for Bank A to derecognise the loans and not to apply continuing involvement accounting (see **section 3.4**), and instead initially recognise the interest only strip and subordinated loan at fair value.

3.2 Transfers that qualify for derecognition

When an entity concludes that derecognition of a financial asset is appropriate (the rights to the cash flows from the asset expired, or the entity has transferred substantially all of its risks and rewards, or the entity no longer retains control of the asset), the asset is removed from the statement of financial position and any new financial assets obtained, financial liabilities assumed and any servicing obligation are recognised at fair value. [IFRS 9:3.2.11]

Often the transferor continues to service the transferred assets for a fee, which may take the form of part of the interest receipts on the transferred assets that an entity retains as compensation for servicing those assets.

Servicing refers to activities associated with the collection of cash flows from receivables or other financial assets after origination and the distribution of that cash to investors if the receivables are owned by other entities. Servicing may include the temporary investment and distribution to the financial asset owners of all or a portion of the cash collected. Servicing activities, also, may include monitoring delinquencies, advancing delinquent payments, restructuring receivables, and foreclosing on the collateral underlying the receivables when necessary. If the receivables are mortgage loans, servicing activities often include collecting and disbursing escrow payments for taxes and insurance. Servicing activities are inherent in all receivables; however, they do not need to be performed by the owner of the receivables. If the receivables are being serviced for another entity, the servicer generally receives a fee for performing these activities. This fee is usually a contractual amount received based on a fixed percentage of the outstanding receivables for the period. Servicers may also receive additional compensation by retaining late charges, other ancillary fees, and the float, which is the net interest earned on funds held by the servicer before disbursement. The compensation received by the servicer is referred to as the benefits of servicing.

If the benefits of servicing are not expected to cover the costs of servicing the assets, the entity should recognise a liability for the fair value of the service obligation that it has entered into as a result of the transfer. [IFRS 9:3.2.10] The servicing in this instance represents an obligation, because the servicer will either have to use its assets in the future to perform under the servicing contract or pay another entity to assume the servicing contract.

If the benefits of servicing exactly compensate the servicer for performing the servicing but provide no additional benefits, the servicer has neither an asset nor a liability and the fair value of this servicing contract is zero.

A servicing contract with a positive fair value is considered to be one that would be favourable for a substitute servicer should one be required, and includes the profit that would be demanded in the marketplace. The amount allocated to a servicing right is treated as a retained interest and the amount allocated to it is determined by allocating the carrying amount of the larger financial asset. [IFRS 9:3.2.10]

Example 3.2

Allocating consideration received between sold and retained interests

Entity A owns loans with a face amount of CU1 million that contractually yield 10 per cent interest over their life. The carrying amount of these loans after recognising impairment of CU20,000 is CU980,000. Entity A sells 90 per cent of the principal, plus the right to receive interest income of 8 per cent, without recourse to an investor for CU900,000 in cash. The part of the asset that has been transferred meets all the criteria for derecognition.

Entity A retains the right to service these loans, and the servicing contract stipulates a 1 per cent fee as compensation for performing the servicing. Entity A also retains an interest only strip for the portion of the interest coupon not sold (1 per cent). At the date of transfer, the fair value of the retained 10 per cent of the loan is CU100,000, the fair value of the servicing asset is CU15,000, and the fair value of the interest only strip is CU35,000.

The following table demonstrates the allocation of the carrying amount of the loans between the sold and retained interests assuming the entity has already determined that it has transferred substantially all the risks and rewards of ownership of the transferred assets (e.g. substantially all the credit losses and the majority of interest rate risk on the loans transferred).

Interest	Fair value	Percentage of total fair value	Allocated carrying amount[1]	Sold interests	Retained interests
	CU	%	CU	CU	CU
Loans sold	900,000	85.71	840,000	840,000	–
Loans retained	100,000	9.53	93,333		93,333
IO strip	35,000	3.33	32,667		32,667
Servicing asset	15,000	1.43	14,000		14,000
Total	1,050,000	100.00	980,000	840,000	140,000

(1) The allocated carrying amount is calculated as the percentage of total fair value multiplied by the aggregate carrying amount prior to the transfer (CU980,000).

The difference between:

- the carrying amount (measured at the date of derecognition) allocated to the part derecognised; and
- the consideration received for the part derecognised (including any new asset obtained less any new liability assumed) is recognised in profit or loss. [IFRS 9:3.2.13]

In the above example, the assets were carried at amortised cost and the amount recognised in the profit or loss is calculated as the difference between the consideration of CU900,000 and the allocated carrying amount of the derecognised asset of CU840,000.

There are likely to be instances in which allocation based on the 'relative fair value method' is difficult because it is difficult to obtain the fair value of the parts of the asset that are subject to derecognition and continued recognition. The Standard acknowledges that when an entity has a historical practice of selling parts similar to the part that is continued to be recognised, or other market transactions for such parts exist, recent prices for actual transactions would best reflect the fair value of the parts. When there are no price quotes available, the best estimate of the fair value is the difference between the fair value of the larger financial asset as a whole and the consideration received from the transferee for the part of the asset that is derecognised. [IFRS 9:3.2.14]

3.3 Transfers that do not qualify for derecognition

When a financial asset is precluded from being derecognised in its entirety (i.e. the transferor retains substantially all of the risks and rewards of ownership), the entity continues to recognise the asset in its entirety and recognises a financial liability for the consideration received. [IFRS 9:3.2.15] The asset and liability cannot be offset and, similarly, any income arising from the asset cannot be offset against any expense incurred on the liability. [IFRS 9:3.2.22] The asset's classification, measurement basis and income recognition does not change as a result of the transfer. This accounting treatment is often referred to as 'gross presentation' or 'secured borrowing' presentation.

Example 3.3

Transfer of receivables with credit guarantee

Entity X transfers short-term receivables to Entity Y and provides a credit guarantee to Entity Y over the expected losses of those receivables.

Entity X continues to recognise the receivables in its statement of financial position because it has retained substantially all the risks and rewards of ownership of the receivables. Entity X will recognise a financial liability for the proceeds received. The substance of the arrangement is that of a secured borrowing (i.e. short-term receivables provide security for the cash advanced by Entity Y).

When a derivative financial instrument forms part of the transfer arrangement and precludes the asset from being derecognised, the derivative is not accounted for separately because this would result in the rights to the cash flows being effectively counted twice. [IFRS 9:B3.2.14]

IFRS 9 does provide some guidance on the transferee's accounting in circumstances where the transferor continues to recognise the asset in its entirety. To the extent that a transfer of a financial asset does not qualify for derecognition, the transferee does not recognise the transferred asset as its asset. The transferee derecognises the cash or other consideration paid and recognises a receivable from the transferor [IFRS 9:B3.2.15]. If the transferor continues to recognise the asset and, therefore, recognises a collateralised borrowing for the consideration received, then the transferee will not recognise the asset but will instead recognise a collateralised lending to the transferor. If a derivative is entered into between the transferor and the transferee as part of the arrangement, but it is not recognised by the transferor because it is an impediment to derecognition, then similarly the derivative will not be recognised by the transferee. The terms of the collateralised lending will include the cash consideration paid at the date of transfer, the contractual cash flows of the derivative, as well as the imputed repayment of principal.

3.4 Continuing involvement in the transferred assets

When an entity neither transfers, nor retains substantially all of the risks and rewards of ownership of a financial asset, and retains control of that asset, the entity continues to recognise the asset to the extent of its continuing involvement. Continuing involvement represents the extent to which the transferor continues to be exposed to the changes in the value of the transferred asset. A corresponding liability is also recognised and measured in such a way that the *net* carrying amount of the asset and the liability is:

[IFRS 9:3.2.17]

- the amortised cost of the rights and obligations retained, if the asset is measured at amortised cost; or
- the fair value of the rights and obligations retained, if the asset is measured at fair value.

The liability that is recognised at the date of transfer will not necessarily equate to the proceeds received in transferring the asset which would ordinarily be the case if the asset continued to be fully recognised and the proceeds received were recognised as a collateralised borrowing. In some cases, the liability appears to be the 'balancing figure' that results from applying the specific guidance for continuing involvement accounting. IFRS 9 acknowledges that measuring the liability by reference to the interest in the transferred asset is not in compliance with the other measurement requirements of the Standard. [IFRS 9:3.2.17]

This requirement for consistent measurement of the asset and the associated liability means that the entity is not permitted to designate the liability as at FVTPL if the transferred asset is measured at amortised cost (see **7.2** in **chapter B3**).

The entity cannot offset the asset and the associated liability. Any subsequent changes in the fair value of the asset and the liability are measured consistently and are not offset. [IFRS 9:3.2.19] Any income on the asset to the extent of the entity's continuing involvement and any expense incurred on the associated liability are not offset. [IFRS 9:3.2.18]

When an entity transfers assets, but retains a guarantee over the transferred assets that absorb future credit losses, and that guarantee (as well as other continuing involvement) results in the transferor neither transferring nor retaining substantially all the risks and rewards of ownership, the transferor must recognise the guarantee as part of its continuing involvement. Assuming, for illustrative purposes only, that the guarantee represents the transferor's only continuing involvement in the transferred asset, then:

- the transferred asset at the date of transfer will be measured at the lower of (i) the carrying amount of the asset and (ii) the maximum amount of the consideration received in the transfer that the entity could be required to repay; and
- the associated liability is measured initially at the amount in (ii) above plus the fair value of the guarantee.

The initial fair value of the guarantee is recognised in profit or loss when (or as) the obligation is satisfied in accordance with the principles of IFRS 15 *Revenue from Contracts with Customers* and the carrying amount of the asset is reduced by any impairment losses. [IFRS 9:B3.2.13(a)]

Example 3.4A

Continuing involvement: guarantee over first default losses

Transferor X transfers an asset to Transferee Y. The carrying amount at the date of transfer is CU100, which is also the asset's fair value at that date. Transferee Y pays CU105. Transferor X provides a guarantee to Transferee Y to pay for the first default losses up to a value of CU8. The fair value of the guarantee at the date of transfer is CU5. Expected future losses on the asset are CU12. Transferor X considers that substantially all the risks and rewards of ownership have neither been transferred, nor retained. Transferee Y does not have the practical ability to sell the assets, i.e. Transferor X controls the asset.

Transferor X determines its continuing involvement as the extent to which it continues to be exposed to the changes in the value of the transferred asset, i.e. the lower of:

(i) the carrying amount of the asset (CU100); and

(ii) the maximum amount of the consideration received in the transfer that Transferor X could be required to repay ('the guarantee amount') (CU8).

Transferor X recognises its continuing involvement in the asset at CU8, and derecognises the part of the asset transferred, i.e. CU92. The associated liability is initially measured at CU13, being the guarantee amount (CU8) plus the fair value of the guarantee (CU5). Subsequently, the initial fair value of the guarantee is recognised in profit or loss on a time proportion basis.

The following entries would be recorded at the date of transfer.

		CU	CU
Dr	Cash	105	
Cr	Financial asset		92
Cr	Financial liability		13

To record the transfer of the asset and recognition of the liability associated with the guarantee.

If, at the end of the guarantee period, no amounts have been paid under the guarantee, the following entries will be recorded.

		CU	CU
Dr	Financial liability	8*	
Cr	Financial asset		8

To derecognise the continuing involvement in the asset and the liability associated with the guarantee.

* the fair value of the guarantee of CU5 will have been fully amortised by the end of the guarantee period

If, at the end of the guarantee period, the full amount of the guarantee is claimed by Transferee Y, the following entries will be recorded.

		CU	CU
Dr	Financial liability	8	
Cr	Cash		8
Dr	Profit or loss	8*	
Cr	Financial asset		8

To record the settlement of the liability associated with the guarantee and derecognition of continuing involvement in the asset.

* the fair value of the guarantee of CU5 will have been fully amortised by the end of the guarantee period

Example 3.4B

Continuing involvement: guarantee over slow payment risk

Entity A transfers short-term receivables to Bank B under a factoring arrangement. Entity A transfers the credit risk of the receivables but retains the slow payment risk up to a maximum of 120 days. If the receivable is outstanding after 120 days, the risk is absorbed by Bank B because the receivable is deemed to be in default. Entity A is charged a market interest rate of 10% for the slow payment risk on the outstanding balance for the period if it is deemed to be a slow paying receivable. At the date of transfer, receivables with a nominal value and amortised cost carrying amount of CU300 million are transferred and the fair value of the late payment guarantee is CU1 million. The total consideration received by Entity A is CU288 million.

Entity A considers that it has neither retained nor transferred substantially of all the risks and rewards of ownership and is deemed to control the receivables because Bank B does not have the practical ability to sell the transferred assets.

Entity A determines its continuing involvement as the extent to which it continues to be exposed to the late payment risk of the transferred asset, i.e. the lower of:

(i) the carrying amount of the asset (CU300 million); and

(ii) the maximum amount of the consideration received in the transfer that Entity A could be required to repay ('the guarantee amount') (CU10 million, being CU300 million x 120/360 x 10%).

Entity A recognises its continuing involvement in the asset at CU10 million, and derecognises the part of the asset transferred (i.e. CU290 million). The associated liability is initially measured at CU11 million, being the guarantee amount (CU10 million) plus the fair value of the guarantee (CU1 million). Subsequently, the initial fair value of the guarantee is recognised in profit or loss on a time proportion basis.

		CUm	CUm
Dr	Cash	288	
Dr	Continuing involvement in the transferred asset	10	
Dr	Loss on disposal (profit or loss)	13	
Cr	Receivables		300
Cr	Continuing involvement liability		11

To record the derecognition of the receivables and the recognition of the continuing involvement.

The interest in the continuing involvement asset of CU10 million less the continuing involvement liability of CU11 million is equal to the fair value of the guarantee at the date of transfer, (i.e. CU1 million).

3.4.1 Continuing involvement through options

Transfer arrangements often contain written or purchased options, or combinations thereof, so that the transferor neither retains, nor transfers substantially all the risks and rewards of ownership, and controls the transferred asset. This is the case when the option is neither deeply in, nor deeply out of the money at the date of transfer. In such transfer arrangements, with the exception of arrangements that contain a put option written by the transferor when the transferor measures the asset at fair value, the entity's continuing involvement in the asset is the amount of the transferred asset that the entity may repurchase. In the case of an arrangement containing a put option written by the transferor when the transferor measures the asset at fair value, the continuing involvement is the lower of the asset's fair value and the option exercise price. [IFRS 9:3.2.16(b)] This is because, in such a transfer arrangement, the entity has no right to increases in fair value of the transferred asset above the exercise price of the option.

The table below sets out the measurement bases for the asset and associated liability for transfers that contain written or purchased options, or combinations thereof, when the transferor continues to recognise its continuing involvement in the asset. The manner of settlement of the options, gross or net cash settled, does not affect the accounting analysis below. However, a cash settled option in of itself is less likely to restrict the transferee's practical ability to sell the transferred asset and, therefore, so may result in derecognition rather than continuing involvement accounting.

Derivative involved	Measurement basis of transferred asset prior to the transfer	Measurement basis of transferred asset after the transfer	Measurement basis of the associated financial liability
Purchased call option	Amortised cost	Amortised cost	Amortised cost: cost on initial recognition (being consideration received) is adjusted for amortisation of the difference between that cost and amortised cost of the asset on the expiration date of the option.
Written put option	Amortised cost	Amortised cost	Amortised cost: cost on initial recognition (being consideration received) is adjusted for amortisation of the difference between that cost and amortised cost of the asset on the expiration date of the option.
Purchased call option	Fair value	Fair value	When the *option is in or at the money* – the call option exercise price less the time value of the option. When the *option is out of the money* – the fair value of the transferred asset less the time value of the option. This ensures that the net carrying amount of the asset and associated liability is the fair value of the call option right.
Written put option	Fair value	Fair value (limited to the lower of the fair value of the asset and the option exercise price)	Option exercise price plus the time value of the option. This ensures that the net carrying amount of the asset and associated liability is the fair value of the put option obligation.
Collar (combination of purchased call and a written put)	Amortised cost	Amortised cost	Amortised cost: cost on initial recognition (being consideration received) is adjusted for amortisation of the difference between that cost and amortised cost of the asset on the expiration date of the options.

Derivative involved	Measurement basis of transferred asset prior to the transfer	Measurement basis of transferred asset after the transfer	Measurement basis of the associated financial liability
Collar (combination of purchased call and a written put)	Fair value	Fair value	When the *call option is in or at the money* – the sum of the call exercise price and fair value of the put option less the time value of the call option. When the *call option is out of the money* – the sum of the fair value of the asset and the fair value of the put option less the time value of the call option. This ensures that the net carrying amount of the asset and associated liability is the fair value of the options held and written.

The examples below illustrate the application of the requirements set out in the table.

Example 3.4.1

Continuing involvement: options

(a) Out-of-the money purchased call option

Entity A transfers an asset to Bank X and receives US$92. The amortised cost of the asset on the date of transfer is US$98. The amortised cost of the asset on the expiration of the option will be US$100. The fair value of the asset on the date of transfer is US$95. The exercise price of the purchased call option is US$99 (out of the money at the date of transfer) and, therefore, the premium paid to purchase the option consists entirely of the time value, being US$3, at the date of transfer.

The asset is held at amortised cost. On the date of transfer, the asset will continue to be recognised at US$98. The associated liability will be recognised at the fair value of the consideration received, US$92, with the difference between US$92 and US$100 being recognised in profit or loss using the effective interest method.

The asset is held at fair value. On the date of transfer, the asset will continue to be recognised at US$95. The associated liability will be recognised at US$92, being the fair value of the transferred asset, US$95, less the time value of the option, US$3.

(b) In- or at-the-money purchased call option

Entity A transfers an asset to Bank X and receives US$87. The amortised cost of the asset on the date of transfer is US$98. The amortised cost of the asset on the expiration of the option will be US$100. The fair value of the asset on the date of transfer is US$95. The exercise price of the purchased call option is US$90 (in the money at the date of transfer) and, therefore, the premium paid to purchase the option consists of intrinsic value, being US$5, and time value, being US$3, at the date of transfer.

The asset is held at amortised cost. On the date of transfer, the asset will continue to be recognised at US$98. The associated liability will be recognised at the fair value of the consideration received, US$87, with the difference between US$87 and US$100 being recognised in profit or loss using the effective interest method.

The asset is held at fair value. On the date of transfer the asset will continue to be recognised at US$95. The associated liability will be recognised at US$87, being the option exercise price, US$90, less the time value of the option, US$3.

(c) Written put option

Entity A transfers an asset to Bank X and receives US$95. The amortised cost of the asset on the date of transfer is US$98. The amortised cost of the asset on the expiration of the option will be US$100. The fair value of the asset on the date of transfer is US$92. The exercise price of the written put option is US$90 (out of the money at the date of transfer) and, therefore, the premium received for writing the option consists entirely of time value, being US$3.

The asset is held at amortised cost. On the date of transfer, the asset will continue to be recognised at US$98. The associated liability will be recognised at the fair value of the consideration received, US$95, with the difference between US$95 and US$100 being recognised in profit or loss using the effective interest method.

The asset is held at fair value. The asset will be recognised at the lower of its fair value and the option exercise price, i.e. at US$90. The associated liability will be recognised at US$93, being the option exercise price, US$90, plus the time value of the option, US$3.

(d) Collar

Entity A transfers an asset to Bank X and receives US$98. The amortised cost of the asset on the date of transfer is US$98. The amortised cost of the asset on the expiration of the option will be US$100. The fair value of the asset on the date of transfer is US$92. The cost of the collar at the date of transfer is zero. The exercise price of the written put is US$80 (out of the money at the date of transfer) and the exercise price of the purchased call is US$120 (out of the money at the date of transfer).

The asset is held at amortised cost. On the date of transfer, the asset will continue to be recognised at US$98. The associated liability will be recognised at the fair value of the consideration received, US$98, with the difference between US$98 and US$100 being recognised in profit or loss using the effective interest method.

The asset is held at fair value. On the date of transfer, the asset will continue to be recognised at US$92. The associated liability will be recognised at US$92, which is calculated as the sum of the fair value of the asset, US$92, and the fair value of the put option, less the time value of the call. The fair value of the put option will be equal to the time value of the call, because the put option's fair value represents only time value, and the sum of the two premiums on the options (both representing time value only) is zero.

When an option expires unexercised, the transferor derecognises financial assets that were subject to the option and also derecognises the associated liability. The transferee recognises the financial assets and eliminates the receivable due from the transferor.

3.4.2 Continuing involvement in a part of a financial asset

If an entity has a continuing involvement in only a part of a financial asset, the entity allocates the previous carrying amount of the financial asset between the part it continues to recognise under continuing involvement, and the part it no longer recognises, based on the relative fair values of those parts at the date of transfer. [IFRS 9:3.2.20]

The allocation exercise and the calculation of the gain or loss on the disposal of the part of the asset are done in the same way as is described in **3.2**. In addition to the part retained, the transferor also recognises its continuing involvement in the asset and the associated liability. IFRS 9:B3.2.17 contains a numerical illustrative example of continuing involvement in a part of an asset which is reproduced below.

Example 3.4.2

Continuing involvement: part of a financial asset

[Extract from IFRS 9:B3.2.17]

Assume an entity has a portfolio of prepayable loans whose coupon and effective interest rate is 10 per cent and whose principal amount and amortised cost is CU10,000. It enters into a transaction in which, in return for a payment of CU9,115, the transferee obtains the right to CU9,000 of any collections of principal plus interest thereon at 9.5 per cent. The entity retains rights to CU1,000 of any collections of principal plus interest thereon at 10 per cent, plus the excess spread of 0.5 per cent on the remaining CU9,000 of principal. Collections from prepayments are allocated between the entity and the transferee proportionately in the ratio of 1:9, but any defaults are deducted from the entity's interest of CU1,000 until that interest is exhausted. The fair value of the loans at the date of the transaction is CU10,100 and the estimated fair value of the excess spread of 0.5 per cent is CU40.

The entity determines that it has transferred some significant risks and rewards of ownership (for example, significant prepayment risk) but has also retained some significant risks and rewards of ownership (because of its subordinated retained interest) and has retained control. It therefore applies the continuing involvement approach.

To apply IFRS 9, the entity analyses the transaction as (a) a retention of a fully proportionate retained interest of CU1,000, plus (b) the subordination of that retained interest to provide credit enhancement to the transferee for credit losses.

The entity calculates that CU9,090 (90 per cent × CU10,100) of the consideration received of CU9,115 represents the consideration for a fully proportionate 90 per cent share. The remainder of the consideration received (CU25) represents consideration received for subordinating its retained interest to provide credit enhancement to the transferee for credit losses. In addition, the excess spread of 0.5 per cent represents consideration received for the credit enhancement. Accordingly, the total consideration received for the credit enhancement is CU65 (CU25 + CU40).

The entity calculates the gain or loss on the sale of the 90 per cent share of cash flows. Assuming that separate fair values of the 90 per cent part transferred and the 10 per cent part retained are not available at the date of the transfer, the entity allocates the carrying amount of the asset in accordance with IFRS 9:3.2.14 as follows:

	Estimated fair value	**Percentage**	**Allocated carrying amount**
Portion transferred	9,090	90%	9,000
Portion retained	1,010	10%	1,000
Total	10,100		10,000

The entity computes its gain or loss on the sale of the 90 per cent share of the cash flows by deducting the allocated carrying amount of the portion transferred from the consideration received, i.e. CU90 (CU9,090 – CU9,000). The carrying amount of the portion retained by the entity is CU1,000.

In addition, the entity recognises the continuing involvement that results from the subordination of its retained interest for credit losses. Accordingly, it recognises an asset of CU1,000 (the maximum amount of the cash flows it would not receive under the subordination), and an associated liability of CU1,065 (which is the maximum amount of the cash flows it would not receive under the subordination, i.e. CU1,000 plus the fair value of the subordination of CU65).

The entity uses all of the above information to account for the transaction as follows:

	Debit	Credit
Original asset	–	9,000
Asset recognised for subordination of the residual interest	1,000	–
Asset for the consideration received in the form of excess spread	40	–
Profit or loss (gain on transfer)	–	90
Liability	–	1,065
Cash received	9,115	–
Total	**10,155**	**10,155**

Immediately following the transaction, the carrying amount of the asset is CU2,040 comprising CU1,000, representing the allocated cost of the portion retained, and CU1,040, representing the entity's additional continuing involvement from the subordination of its retained interest for credit losses (which includes the excess spread of CU40).

In subsequent periods, the entity recognises the consideration received for the credit enhancement (CU65) on a time proportion basis, accrues interest on the recognised asset using the effective interest method and recognises any credit impairment on the recognised assets. As an example of the latter, assume that in the following year there is a credit impairment loss on the underlying loans of CU300. The entity reduces its recognised asset by CU600 (CU300 relating to its retained interest and CU300 relating to the additional continuing involvement that arises from the subordination of its retained interest for credit losses), and reduces its recognised liability by CU300. The net result is a charge to profit or loss for credit impairment of CU300.

A number of observations can be drawn from the example in IFRS 9:B3.2.17 reproduced above. A concern that is often cited is that the example advocates 'double-counting', i.e. the continuing involvement in the asset is accounted for twice. This is best illustrated using the numbers in the example above. The transferor continues to recognise a fully proportionate interest in 10% of all cash flows which equals an amortised cost of CU1,000 (being 10% x CU10,000 carrying amount) and also recognises an additional CU1,000 being the 'asset recognised for subordination or the residual interest'. This may appear odd because the interest in the assets is limited to a disproportionate interest in the transferred asset up to CU1,000. However, the reason for presenting the transferor's interest in the transferred asset 'grossed up' is to reflect that the transferor's interest in 10% of the asset is in fact subordinated (and, therefore, is not a fully proportionate interest) because any losses borne by the transferred assets continue to be borne by the transferor until their remaining interest is exhausted. In order to recognise the transferor's continuing involvement liability, the entity needs to 'gross-up' its statement of financial position by recognising a further asset.

Because the transferor's interest in the transferred asset is deemed to be a fully proportionate share of the asset (plus that interest being subordinated), the calculation of the gain/loss on partial disposal of the asset is also based on a fully proportionate basis. On the face of it, this calculation may also appear odd because the entity has not economically sold a fully proportionate share in the asset to the transferee; rather it has retained a disproportionate share of the cash flows of the asset.

The example also recognises another new asset that it refers to as the 'asset for the consideration received in the form of excess spread'. It is worth noting that the amount recognised for the excess spread is equal to the fair value of the excess spread at the date of transfer, being CU40, even though it appears the loans themselves were not originally measured at fair value (i.e. they were originally measured at amortised cost). Because the objective of accounting for continuing involvement is to ensure that the measurement of the net involvement (being the net of the continuing involvement asset and continuing involvement liability) is consistent with the measurement of the transferred assets, it is surprising that the excess spread in the example is initially recognised at fair value rather than amortised cost. It appears possible that this was an oversight when the example was developed.

3.4.3 Accounting by the transferee in the case of continuing involvement

Example 3.4.3

Accounting by the transferee in the case of continuing involvement

Bank S owns a 16 per cent equity stake in a thinly traded entity. The investment is designated as at FVTOCI by Bank S. Bank S enters into an agreement with Entity K whereby Entity K pays CU102 to Bank S in return for:

- the 16 per cent equity interest in the thinly traded entity; and
- a put option that allows Entity K to put the shares back to Bank S for a price of CU96 at a pre-specified date.

On the date of the transfer, the fair value of the shares is CU97 and the time value of the put option is CU5 (CU102 minus CU97), i.e. the option is out of the money at inception.

Transferor accounting

Bank S, the transferor, will apply continuing involvement accounting because it has neither transferred nor retained substantially all the risks and rewards of the shares and Entity K does not have the practical ability to sell the shares because it is a significant holding in an entity that is thinly-traded and, therefore, Bank S is deemed to control the shares.

Because the arrangement involves the transferor writing a put option on an asset that is measured at fair value, the extent of the continuing involvement for Bank S is limited to the lower of the fair value of the shares and the option exercise price. [IFRS 9:3.2.16(b) & B3.2.13(d)]

At the transaction date, the following entries will be recorded.

		CU	CU
Dr	Cash	102	
Cr	Investment in equity instrument designated as at FVTOCI		1
Cr	Financial liability		101

To record recognition of the liability and adjustment to the asset for continuing involvement.

This entry recognises a liability of CU101, consisting of a strike price of CU96 and time value of the put option of CU5.

The shares continue to be recognised by Bank S and measured as an investment in an equity instrument designated as at FVTOCI, although changes in their value above the strike price of CU96 are not recognised.

If the put option is exercised by Entity K because the share price is below CU96, the following entry will be recorded.

		CU	CU
Dr	Financial liability	96	
Cr	Cash		96

To record the derecognition of the liability on exercise of the put option.

The difference between the opening and the closing carrying amount of the liability of CU5 (CU101 less CU96) will be recognised in profit or loss over the life of the arrangement. Any fair value loss on the investment in the equity instrument designated as at FVTOCI below CU96 will be recognised in other comprehensive income.

If the put option is not exercised by Entity K because the share price is above CU96, the following entry will be recorded.

		CU	CU
Dr	Financial liability	96	
Cr	Investment in equity instrument designated as at FVTOCI		96

To record derecognition of the liability and the asset on expiry of the put option.

The difference between the opening and closing carrying amount of the liability of CU5 (CU101 less CU96) will be recognised in profit or loss over the life of the arrangement. Any amounts accumulated in equity as a result of movements in the fair value of the investment in the equity instrument may be reclassified within equity on derecognition.

Transferee accounting

Entity K has paid cash of CU102 in return for a right to receive cash of CU96 (through exercise of its purchased put option) and rights to all the upside on the shares above CU96 (i.e. by not exercising its put option and physically retaining the transferred shares). Entity K economically has an investment in shares with no downside risk below CU96.

However, Entity K does not have an investment in an equity instrument due to the existence of the put right and, therefore, cannot designate the asset as at FVTOCI. Further, the asset does not meet the amortised cost or FVTOCI criteria because it is not solely a receipt of principal and interest on the principal outstanding. The asset therefore must be measured at FVTPL; however, Entity K should not recognise any changes in fair value below the strike price of CU96 because Entity K has no exposure to fair value movements below this amount. This is the inverse of the accounting by the transferor, Bank S. Entity K recognises fair value changes above CU96, and Bank S recognising fair value changes below CU96.

At the date of transfer the following entry will be recorded.

		CU	CU
Dr	Asset measured at fair value through profit or loss	102	
Cr	Cash		102

To record initial recognition of the asset.

This entry will recognise the financial asset consisting of the fair value of the shares of CU97 plus the value of the purchased put option of CU5. Increases in the fair value of the asset above CU96 will be recognised in profit or loss. The asset and the purchased put will be remeasured in profit or loss. Because the purchased put option provides a 'floor' of CU96, changes in fair value of the security below this amount will not be recognised. At maturity of the option, the time value of the option will have been fully eroded resulting in the security either being put at CU96 (and, thereby, being derecognised), or continuing to be measured at fair value through profit or loss because the transferee has not exercised the put option. The put option is not separately measured because, for the transferor, it is not recognised because it is an impediment to derecognition and, for the transferee, it forms part of its involvement in the asset.

If the put option is exercised by Entity K because the share price is below CU96, the following entry will be recorded.

		CU	CU
Dr	Cash	96	
Cr	Asset measured at fair value through profit or loss		96

To record derecognition of the asset on exercise of the put option.

An amount of CU1 would have already been recognised in profit or loss when the fair value of asset had decreased to CU96. Fair value movements below CU96 are not recognised.

If the put option is not exercised by Entity K because the share price is above CU96, no further entry will be required to recognise the shares because they are already recognised in Entity K's statement of financial position. After the expiration of the option, all gains or losses on the security will be recognised in profit or loss because Entity K will be exposed to movements in the share price in both directions.

3.5 Collateral

A transfer arrangement may require a transferor to provide non-cash collateral (e.g. a debt or an equity instrument) to the transferee. The transferee's entitlement to the collateral is conditional upon the transferor's default and while the transferor continues to perform under the contract, the transferor continues to benefit from substantially all of the collateral's risks and rewards. Normal recognition and derecognition principles apply to the collateral: the transferee is not entitled to recognise the collateral until it becomes contractually entitled to it, which will not be the case until the transferor defaults under the terms of the contract; the transferor retains all of the risks and rewards of ownership of the asset pledged as collateral and, therefore, cannot derecognise it.

If the transferee has the right by contract or custom to sell or repledge the collateral, the asset that has been pledged by the transferor should be reclassified in its statement of financial position separately from its other assets and described as a loaned asset, pledged equity instrument or repurchase receivable. If the transferee uses that right and sells the collateral, it should recognise the proceeds from the sale and a liability measured at fair value for its obligation to return the collateral. [IFRS 9:3.2.23(b)]

In the event of a default by the transferor, the risks and rewards of the collateral, within the confines of the collateral agreement, are transferred to the transferee. Hence, the transferor derecognises the collateral and the transferee, who after the default becomes contractually entitled to it, recognises the collateral at its fair value, unless the transferee has already sold the collateral, in which case, it derecognises its obligation to return the collateral to the transferor.

3.6 Sale and repurchase agreements and stock lending

A sale and repurchase agreement usually takes the form of an agreement to sell a security (i.e. transfer all the rights attaching to a security) with a simultaneous agreement to repurchase it at a specified price at a fixed future date. The consideration involved is either in the form of cash or security. The repurchase price is normally structured higher than the sale price; alternatively, the two prices can be the same, but with an explicit interest rate charged instead. The transferee will require that it is assured of a lender's return on its investment and the transferor will require that the transferee earns no more than this return. In the event that the transferee is entitled to retain any coupons or dividends that are paid on the asset during the term of the repurchase agreement, the transaction price is adjusted to reflect the fact (see **3.1.6**).

The table below considers some common terms of sale and repurchase transactions and applies IFRS 9 derecognition principles to those transactions.

Features	Applying derecognition in IFRS 9
The repurchase price is an agreed price higher than the market value at the date of sale.	If the repurchase price results in a lender's return for the transferee, then the transferor has not transferred, but has retained substantially all of the risks and rewards of ownership of the asset. The lender's return earned by the transferee is consistent with the arrangement being a collateralised borrowing for the transferor, and a collateralised lending for the transferee.
The repurchase provision is an option for the transferor to repurchase the asset at a fixed price (when the call option is neither deeply in nor out of the money), and the asset is readily obtainable in the market.	The asset is derecognised because the transferor neither transferred nor retained substantially all of the risks and rewards of ownership, and has lost control over the asset since the asset is readily obtainable in the market (i.e., the transferee has the practical ability to sell the asset). The transferor will recognise a stand-alone call option in the statement of financial position at fair value with gains or losses recognised in profit or loss.

Features	Applying derecognition in IFRS 9
The repurchase provision is an option for the transferor to repurchase the asset at a fixed price (where the call option is neither deeply in nor out of the money), and the asset is *not* readily obtainable in the market.	The transferor has neither transferred nor retained substantially all of the risks and rewards of ownership but has retained control of the asset because the asset is not readily obtainable in the market (i.e. the transferee does not have the practical ability to sell the asset). Hence, the transferor continues to recognise the asset to the extent of its continuing involvement: when the asset is measured at fair value and the option is out of the money, the transferor recognises a liability for the fair value of the transferred asset less the time value of the option; when the asset is measured at fair value and the option is at or in the money, the transferor recognises a liability for the option exercise price less the time value of the option; when the asset is measured at amortised cost, the transferor recognises a liability for the consideration received and adjusts it for the amortisation between the consideration received and the amortised cost of the asset on the expiration date of the option.
The repurchase provision is a put option at a fixed price (where the put option is neither deeply in nor out of the money) and the asset is readily obtainable in the market.	The asset is derecognised because the transferor has neither retained nor transferred substantially all of the risks and rewards of ownership, and has lost control over the asset because the asset is readily obtainable in the market (i.e. the transferee has the practical ability to sell the asset). The transferor recognises a stand-alone put option in the statement of financial position at fair value with gains or losses recognised in profit or loss.
The repurchase provision is a put option at a fixed price (where the put option is neither deeply in nor out of the money) and the asset is *not* readily obtainable in the market.	The transferor has neither transferred nor retained substantially all of the risks and rewards of the asset and has retained control of the asset; hence, it continues to recognise the asset to the extent of its continuing involvement because the asset is not readily obtainable in the market (i.e. the transferee does not have the practical ability to sell the asset). When the asset is measured at fair value, the transferor recognises a liability equal to the option exercise price plus the time value of the option; when the asset is measured at amortised cost, the transferor recognises a liability for the consideration received and adjusts it for the amortisation between the consideration received and amortised cost of the asset on the expiration date of the option.

Features	Applying derecognition in IFRS 9
The asset sold is subject to the transferor receiving a deferred consideration receipt/payment based on the increases/decreases in the fair value of the asset respectively for a specified period of time.	The deferred consideration passes the changes in the fair value of the asset back to the transferor, thus the transferor has retained substantially all of the risks and rewards of ownership of the asset; hence, the transferor continues to recognise the asset and recognises a liability for the initial cash consideration received.
The asset is subject to a varying repurchase price such that original purchase price is adjusted retrospectively to pass variations in the value of the asset to the transferor.	The variation in the repurchase price so as to pass the changes in the value of the asset back to the transferor means that the transferor retains substantially all the risks and rewards of ownership; hence, the transferor continues to recognise the asset and recognises a liability for the cash consideration received.
The transferor provides a residual value guarantee to the transferee or subordinated debt to protect the transferee from falls in the value of the asset.	Provided that the asset has upside potential, the transferor has neither retained nor transferred substantially all the risks and rewards of ownership (transferred the upside, but retained the downside). The transferor continues to control the asset where the guarantee is sufficiently valuable to the transferee and limits its ability to transfer the asset and, therefore, the transferor continues to recognise the asset to the extent of its continuing involvement (i.e. at the date of the transfer the asset is measured at the lower of its carrying amount and the guarantee amount). The transferor recognises an associated liability equal to the guarantee amount plus the fair value of the guarantee. When the guarantee does not restrict the transferee's ability to sell the asset, the transferor derecognises the asset.
The repurchase price, whether put/call or forward, is the market price at the time of repurchase.	The transferor has transferred substantially all of the risks and rewards of ownership of the asset because the transferor can only repurchase it at its fair value. Hence, the asset is derecognised.

Features	Applying derecognition in IFRS 9
Asset repurchased is substantially the same as the asset that is transferred or the transferee can substitute the asset with one that is similar or is of equal fair value.	The transferor retains substantially all the risks and rewards of ownership of the asset and, therefore, derecognition is precluded.

3.7 Debt factoring

Debt factoring is used extensively as a method for obtaining one or more of the following benefits: obtaining financing, bad debt protection or sales ledger administration. A factoring transaction normally takes the form of an entity receiving cash consideration in exchange for the rights to cash collected from its receivables. In many situations, the rights to the cash flows on the receivables are subject to certain restrictions or guarantees. Sometimes the transferee may have recourse to the transferor over the performance of the receivables either up to a certain limit or to the extent to which there is a shortfall of the cash collected on the receivables. In a non-recourse transaction, there is no obligation of the transferor to make good to the transferee for any shortfall on the assets. In order to receive a market return from the receivables (the receivables are collected over time), the transferee charges interest.

The table below sets out some of the common features of debt factoring transactions and application of derecognition principles to a 'vanilla' debt factoring transaction (an entity receives cash consideration in exchange for the rights to cash collected from its receivables) with each of those features. It is assumed that the transferee cannot sell receivables (i.e. the transferor continues to control them).

Features	Applying derecognition in IFRS 9
For all receivables not recovered after a certain period (e.g. 120 days), whether due to late payment or default, the transferor provides a guarantee.	The guarantee may represent substantially all the risks of ownership of receivables (e.g. where most receivables are long term due to the credit terms offered). If so, derecognition is precluded. When the transferor has neither transferred nor retained substantially all the risks and rewards of ownership, the transferor continues to recognise receivables to the extent of its continuing involvement, i.e. to the extent that amounts may be repaid under the guarantee.

Features	Applying derecognition in IFRS 9
In the event of a receivable going bad beyond but not prior to a certain period (e.g. the period commencing after 120 days), the transferor provides credit protection on that receivable.	The credit protection may represent substantially all the risks of ownership (e.g. where credit terms are 120 days or more and thus the risk of a receivable going bad stays with the transferor). If it does, derecognition is precluded. Depending on the likelihood of default prior to 120 days and other risks transferred to the transferee, the transferor may determine that substantially all the risks and rewards of ownership are neither transferred nor retained and thus the transferor continues to recognise receivables to the extent of its continuing involvement, i.e. to the extent that amounts may be repaid under the credit protection.
The transferor receives an element of non-returnable consideration for the receivables, but either the transferor or the transferee has rights to some further sums from the other party to the transaction. This further sum depends on whether or when cash is collected from the receivables, e.g. through deferred consideration, a retrospective adjustment to the sale price or rebates of certain charges.	When the further sums from the other party are not considered to be substantially all of the risks and rewards of ownership, the transferor has neither transferred nor retained substantially all the risks and rewards of ownership and continues to recognise the receivables to the extent of its continuing involvement. The transferor derecognises receivables to the extent of the non-returnable consideration.

Features	Applying derecognition in IFRS 9
The transferor provides a warranty over the quality/condition of the receivables at the moment of transfer, e.g. at the point of delivery of the goods, the customer had not breached their credit limit.	The warranty provision may result in the transferor retaining some risks and rewards (e.g. if the transferor has to reimburse the transferee should the transferor's representations as to the quality/condition of the asset prove to be wrong). If the warranty results in the transferor neither transferring nor retaining substantially all the risks and rewards of ownership, it continues to recognise the receivables to the extent of its continuing involvement, i.e. to the extent that amounts may be repaid under the warranty. If the warranty as to quality/condition of the assets at the date of transfer results in the entity transferring substantially all the risks and rewards of ownership, then the transferor will derecognise the assets. (The IFRIC (now the IFRS Interpretations Committee) considered conditional transfers in November 2006 – see **section 3.1.4**.)
The transferor continues to service the receivables by administering the sales ledger for a fee that is based upon the total amount of receivables factored at each month end. The charge is at market price. The transferor is not subject to any recourse and the transferor has not retained any residual interest in the receivables.	A servicing arrangement at a market price with no further continuing involvement in the receivables is considered to be a transfer of substantially all of the risks and rewards of ownership of the assets, and, therefore, derecognition by the transferor is appropriate. If the charge for the servicing arrangement is not at market price such that the benefits of servicing the assets are not commensurate with the administration charges, but did not otherwise involve further transfer of exposure to risk back to the transferor, a servicing asset or servicing liability will arise and be recorded separately.
The transferor has a call option to purchase outstanding receivables from the transferee at a predetermined price when the amount of outstanding assets falls to a specified level at which the cost of servicing those assets is too high as compared to the benefits of servicing. This is sometimes known as a clean-up call.	Provided that the clean-up call results in the entity neither retaining nor transferring substantially all the risks and rewards of ownership, it precludes derecognition only to the extent of the amount of the assets subject to the call option.

3.8 Securitisations

Securitisation is a means of making use of a portfolio of assets, usually receivables held by an entity (loans, mortgages, credit cards etc.) to obtain cost effective funding. These assets are usually purchased by a transferee who then repackages the receivables as asset-backed securities and sells them on in the market to investors for cash consideration. The normal process is to repackage these securities in a vehicle specifically set up for that purpose, a structured entity (see **3.1.1**). The notes issued to the investors are secured on the underlying assets that have been transferred to the structured entity. It is usual for investors to require a form of credit enhancement which can take many forms:

- subordination: typically the transferor acquires a junior (often the most junior) note issued by the structured entity that absorbs the first losses incurred by the transferred assets;
- over-collateralisation: the face amount of the transferred assets is larger than the funding used to buy the assets;
- excess spread: after all interest has been received and paid and expenses of the structured entity settled, an amount is retained in the arrangement which will absorb first losses should they occur;
- reserve fund: similar to excess spread except a separate fund is created;
- guarantees: the structured entity may obtain guarantees either from the transferor or from third parties, for example from well rated insurance companies;
- letters of credit: the structured entity may obtain letters of credit from well rated banks where the bank will stand ready to reimburse the structured entity for losses incurred up to a specified amount; or
- cash collateral account: similar to a letter of credit except the bank lends cash upfront which is invested in highly rated short-term commercial paper. The structured entity has some credit risk on its investments but this is less than would be the case for a letter of credit where the borrower runs the risk that the lender will fail to meet its lending commitment when demanded by the borrower. Alternatively, the transferor may deposit a percentage of its proceeds from the securitisation in a cash collateral or maintenance account.

Some forms of credit enhancement, like subordination and over-collateralisation and some cash collateral accounts deposited by the transferor, transfer risks and rewards of the transferred asset back to the transferor. Others, like letters of credit and some cash collateral accounts, transfer risks and rewards to third parties. The types of risk transferred determine whether the transferor is able to achieve derecognition for the transferred assets.

As explained in **3.1.1**, it is important to determine whether or not the entity needs to consolidate the structured entity. If the structured entity is consolidated, the extent of derecognition achieved is the same irrespective of whether the transfer is direct to investors or through a consolidated structured entity that obtains the financial assets and, in turn, transfers them to third party investors.

In many securitisations, the structured entity is consolidated and the assets are not transferred to a third party (i.e. the right to receive the cash flows from the assets remains with the group). The group may assume a contractual obligation to pass on those cash flows to ultimate investors in a 'pass-through' arrangement that meets all three conditions detailed in **section 3.1.4**. Nevertheless, the group may still have retained all the risks and rewards of ownership of the assets (e.g. when credit risk is the main risk and credit enhancement provided by the group covers all expected losses) and may still need to continue to recognise the assets. The IASB recognises that many securitisations will not qualify for derecognition either because one of the three conditions in the pass-through test will not be met or because the credit enhancement required by the ultimate investors will mean that the group retains substantially all the risks and rewards of ownership of the assets. [IFRS 9:BCZ3.23] Where credit enhancement provided by the group is such that the group neither retains nor transfers all the risks and rewards of ownership, the group will continue to recognise the assets only to the extent of its continuing involvement, i.e. the credit enhancement provided.

The table below sets out some of the common features of securitisations where the structured entity that purchases the assets is *not consolidated* by the transferor and application of derecognition principles to securitisations with each of those features. It is assumed that the structured entity cannot sell receivables, i.e. the transferor continues to control them and the transferor has no exposure to the assets other than stated.

Features	**Applying derecognition in IFRS 9**
Credit enhancement is provided for the transferred receivables by an independent third party (e.g. third party credit insurance or guarantee).	The transferor has transferred the rights to receive cash flows on the assets to the structured entity and also transferred substantially all the risks and rewards of ownership of those assets; hence, full derecognition is appropriate.
As above, but the transferor acts as the servicing agent on the portfolio of the assets.	The retention of a servicing right at market price does not preclude derecognition, because substantially all of the risks and rewards of the assets have been transferred and, accordingly, derecognition is appropriate. If the charge for the servicing asset is not at market price, such that the benefits of servicing the assets are not commensurate with the administration charges but do not otherwise involve further retention of exposure to risk, a servicing asset or liability arises and is recognised separately.

Features	Applying derecognition in IFRS 9
A call option is held by the transferor that allows it to call back some of the assets from the portfolio. The transferor has the choice of which balances can be recalled but the total amount of balances that can be recalled is restricted.	Assuming the transferor is economically rational, the transferor will repurchase those assets that will yield the highest return, thereby avoiding assets that are expected to default. This interest in the assets indicates that the transferor has neither transferred nor retained substantially all the risks and rewards of ownership, and hence is required to continue to recognise the assets to the extent of its continuing involvement, i.e. the extent to which the transferred assets are subject to the call option.
The transferor has a call option enabling it to insist on the return of some specific assets from the portfolio; the amount of balances that can be recalled is restricted and the transferor cannot choose the balances to be recalled.	Assuming the call option is not deeply in or out of the money, the transferor has neither retained nor transferred all the risks and rewards of ownership and will continue to recognise the assets to the extent of its continuing involvement, i.e. the extent to which the transferred assets are subject to the call option. If the call option is deeply out of the money (e.g. the assets that can be recalled are in default), derecognition is appropriate.
The transferor services the assets and has a clean-up call to purchase outstanding receivables from the structured entity when the amount of outstanding assets falls to a specified level at which the cost of servicing those assets is too high as compared to benefits of servicing.	Provided that the clean-up call results in the transferor neither retaining nor transferring substantially all the risks and rewards of ownership, the clean-up call precludes derecognition only to the extent of the amount of the assets subject to the call option.

The table below sets out some of the common features of securitisations where the structured entity that purchases the assets is consolidated by the transferor and application of derecognition principles to securitisations with each of those features. It is assumed that the structured entity has not transferred the assets to a third party, but instead assumed a contractual obligation to pass the cash flows to external investors. Other than indicated, the pass-through tests (see **section 3.1.4**) are met and the group has not retained substantially all the risks and rewards of ownership.

Features	Applying derecognition in IFRS 9
The structured entity has provisions for a revolving investment facility (i.e. securitisation of revolving assets such as credit card receivables) in which for a given time period the structured entity reinvests cash receipts in similar assets. This is common when the receivables have a much shorter life than the securitisation programme.	The pass-through conditions are not met because the reinvestment is in assets other than cash and cash equivalents and the cash flows are not passed on without material delay. Derecognition by the group is precluded.
A rebalancing swap is taken on by the structured entity to ensure that the cash flows due on the notes are met at their predetermined payment dates as the timing of cash flows on the underlying assets is often unpredictable.	Short-term advances to the investors from the group do not violate the pass through tests as long as the investors still bear the risk of recovery of the assets. Hence, provided that the amounts paid to investors are recovered by the group if the group suffers loss on the assets and any advances are only short term, derecognition is appropriate.
The group is granted rights to cash collected from the portfolio of assets and any remaining cash after the payments due on the securities issued to the investor, e.g. deferred sale consideration, dividend payments or other fees.	This right to collect the excess cash flows is often designed to create a similar payoff profile for the group as if the group had retained a subordinated interest in a non-consolidated structured entity. The extent of subordination as compared to expected credit losses on the assets determines whether the group has retained substantially all the risks and rewards of ownership and thus continues to recognise the assets or whether the group has neither retained nor transferred substantially all of the risks and rewards of ownership and thus continues to recognise the assets only to the extent of its continuing involvement, i.e. to the extent of its subordinated interest.

3.9 Loan transfers

A loan transfer is an agreement under which payments of principal and interest collected under the original loan are passed to a transferee or transferees for an immediate cash payment. There are several ways in which a loan transfer can be enacted. The three most common ways are as follows.

(a) Novation – this is normally where the rights and obligations of the loan are cancelled or amended and renegotiated such that the identity of the lender has been changed. In this case, the borrower is released from its obligation to the transferor and instead has an obligation to the transferee.

(b) Assignment – this is a similar process to novation but the original borrower may or may not be made aware of the change in assignment depending on whether or not the assignment is statutory or equitable respectively. Any cash flows paid to the transferor are passed on to the transferee.

(c) Sub-participation – the borrower still has an obligation to the transferor but at the same time the transferor enters into a non-recourse back-to-back agreement with the transferee to pass on the cash flows collected on the original loan.

Under novation, the transferor's rights to the cash flows cease and hence the transferor has transferred the financial asset. Consideration will need to be given to whether the transferor retains some or all of the risk or rewards of ownership of the transferred asset. In an assignment or sub-participation, when the cash flows paid to the transferee reflect in full the collections from the original loan and there is no recourse to the transferor, it is likely that the pass-through tests in **section 3.1.4** are met and the transferor does not retain the risks and rewards of ownership of the assets i.e. derecognition is appropriate.

The table below sets out common features of loan sub-participations and application of derecognition principles to sub-participations with each of those features. Other than indicated, the pass-through tests are met and there is no recourse to the transferor (i.e. risks and rewards are transferred).

Features	Applying derecognition in IFRS 9
The terms of the transfer provide that additional funds that are not part of the terms of the original loan will be made available to the borrower in the event of restructuring of the debt; this facility is not provided to the transferee under the terms of the sub-participation.	In the event of restructuring, the entity will not pass all the restructured cash flows to the transferee, i.e. pass-through tests are not met and derecognition is precluded.
A proportionate share of all future cash flows on the original loan is transferred, e.g. 40 per cent.	A fully proportionate share of the cash flows from the original loan (40 per cent) constitutes part of the loan. It is assumed that the pass-through tests applied to that part of the loan are met and the transferor has transferred all the risks and rewards of ownership of that part of the loan. Hence, derecognition of the part of the loan is appropriate.

Features	Applying derecognition in IFRS 9
The transferor continues to administer the original loan for a fee.	The servicing right at market price does not preclude derecognition since substantially all of the risks and rewards of the asset have been transferred.
	If the charge for the servicing asset is not at market price such that the benefits of servicing the asset are not commensurate with the administration charges, but does not otherwise involve further transfer of exposure to risk, a servicing asset or liability arises and is recognised separately.
The assigned loan or sub-participation is floating rate, while the original loan carries a fixed rate coupon.	The pass-through tests are not met because the transferor may be required to pay amounts that are not collected on the original loan to the transferee and equally not all cash flows collected on the original loan are passed to the transferee. Hence, derecognition is precluded.
Both the original loan and the assigned loan or sub-participation are floating rate instruments but they are priced off different floating rate indices, e.g. 6 month LIBOR and 6 month EURIBOR.	The pass-through tests are not met because the transferor may be required to pay amounts that are not collected on the original loan to the transferee and equally not all cash flows collected on the original loan are passed to the transferee. Hence, derecognition is precluded.
The original loan and the assigned loan or sub-participation are in different currencies.	The pass-through tests are not met because the transferor may be required to pay amounts that are not collected on the original loan to the transferee and equally not all cash flows collected on the original loan are passed to the transferee. Hence, derecognition is precluded.

Features	Applying derecognition in IFRS 9
The sub-participation is in the same currency, but concurrently the transferor and transferee enter into a cross-currency swap over the same notional as the original loan which converts the payments made to the transferee into a different currency. If the original loan defaults the swap can be terminated at its fair value at the time; the amounts and timing of the payments on the swap are not adjusted to reflect any changes that may occur in the amounts and timing of the cash flows of the original loan.	The sub-participation qualifies for derecognition because all of the risks and rewards of ownership of the original loan are transferred to the transferee. The cross-currency swap is recognised separately as a derivative at FVTPL and may qualify for hedge accounting in the books of the transferee.

3.9.1 Loan syndication

Loan syndication is an agreement between several lenders to fund jointly a large loan. Each lender will advance a loan of a specific amount to the borrower and has the right to repayment from the borrower. Such a syndication agreement does not involve a loan transfer and should be accounted for as recognition of a financial asset by each of the lenders involved.

In some loan syndications, a lead lender may advance cash to the borrower and transfer the loan to a number of other lenders so that repayments by the borrower are made to the lead lender who then distributes the collections to the other lenders in the syndicate. Such loan syndications are just another form of a loan sub-participation and the lead lender would need to consider whether the pass-through tests are met. In other syndications, the pass-through tests are not relevant because the lead lender transfers the contractual rights to a proportion of the loan to third parties.

3.10 Transfers with total return swaps

A total return swap (TRS) is a derivative that transfers the exposure of a referenced asset between two parties. Typically, one entity would pay amounts equal to increases in the fair value of the referenced asset to the counterparty, and at the same time receive amounts equal to decreases in the fair value of the asset plus a floating rate interest return calculated on a fixed notional amount. This floating funding interest compensates the entity for the theoretical cost of borrowing cash in order to buy the referenced asset or, put another way, is equal to a cost that would have been borne by the entity if the entity had instead chosen to expose itself to the referenced asset by acquiring the referenced asset as opposed to entering into the TRS. These types of instruments are common in transfers of financial assets because they allow the transferor some or all of the participation in the underlying asset. As discussed in **3.1.6**, a transfer of an asset for cash consideration and a TRS would not result in the transferor derecognising the transferred asset as the transferor continues to be exposed to substantially all the risks and rewards of ownership as a result of the TRS. However, TRSs can be used in transfer arrangements in other ways. Below are some illustrations which explain the consideration that would need to be given in assessing whether derecognition is appropriate.

Example 3.10

Transfers of financial assets with a total return swap

(i) Transfer of a financial asset with deferred consideration and a total return swap

Transferor A transfers a debt instrument where the transfer agreement requires Transferee B to pay the transferor a fixed sum in six months' time. The transferor and the transferee also enter into a TRS whereby the transferor receives cash equal to increases in fair value of the asset from the transferee and pays cash equal to decreases in the fair value of the asset plus LIBOR plus a fixed spread every quarter based on a notional equal to the fair value of the debt instrument at the date of transfer. The transferee also pays the transferor any interest that it receives on the transferred asset.

Transferor A must first determine whether the contractual rights to cash flows have been transferred to Transferor B in accordance with IFRS 9:3.2.4(a). Because Transferee B has all rights to cash flows under the asset, the answer is yes. Transferor A must then consider whether it has transferred substantially all the risks and rewards of ownership to Transferor B. The existence of the TRS results in the transferor continuing to be exposed to the risks and rewards of ownership of the transferred asset, being both fair value risk and the interest earned. The risks and rewards are retained by the transferor and, therefore, derecognition is not appropriate even though the transferor has taken on an additional risk that it did not have prior to the transfer, being the credit risk of the transferee who has yet to pay the transferor cash consideration for the transferred asset.

Because the TRS is an impediment to derecognition, it will not be recognised by the transferor in accordance with IFRS 9:B3.2.14. Transferor A will continue to recognise the assets until maturity of the TRS. At that date, the TRS will not be an impediment to derecognition because it will have matured and, therefore, the transferor will not have retained substantially all the risks and rewards of ownership, cash consideration for the asset will be received from the transferee and a gain/loss will be recognised by the transferor on disposal.

(ii) Transfer of a financial asset with deferred delivery of the asset at maturity of a total return swap

Entity C enters into a six month TRS with Entity D over Entity C's debt instrument whereby Entity C will pay Entity D cash equal to increases in fair value of the asset and receive from Entity D cash equal to decreases in the fair value of the asset plus LIBOR plus a fixed spread every quarter based on a notional equal to the fair value of the debt instrument at the date of entering into the arrangement. Entity C will also pay Entity D any interest that it receives on the transferred asset immediately after Entity C receives the interest from the issuer of the debt instrument. If Entity C does not receive interest on the debt instrument it has no obligation to pay Entity D. Equally, Entity C does not provide Entity D with any guarantee to pay further amounts. At maturity of the TRS, Entity C will physically deliver the referenced asset to Entity D for a fixed amount of cash determined upon entering into the arrangement.

Entity C must first determine whether the contractual rights to cash flows have been transferred to Entity D in accordance with IFRS 9:3.2.4(a). Because the transferor retains all the rights to cash flows under the asset, the answer is no. Entity C must then consider whether the pass-through requirements in IFRS 9:3.2.4(b) and IFRS 9:3.2.5 are met. It is clear that *all* the contractual cash flows under the asset are not passed to Entity D because the only cash flows that are passed to Entity D are interest flows on the asset for six months. Because these interest flows are specifically identified cash flows from a financial asset, i.e. they constitute a portion of the asset, under IFRS 9:3.2.2(a)(i) and the cash flows are immediately paid by Entity C to Entity D when Entity C receives the cash, then Entity C could apply the pass-through requirements to the portion of the asset that represents the interest flows for six months only. Assuming that both the pass through and risks and rewards tests lead to the conclusion that the portion of the asset representing the interest flows for six months should be derecognised, Entity C would need to recognise a debtor from Entity D as no upfront consideration is received by Entity C. The debtor recognised would be equal to the fair value of the interest flows for the next six months and may differ in amount to the portion of the asset derecognised in the case where the asset is not measured at fair value, i.e. it is measured at amortised cost, with the difference recognised in profit or loss as a gain/loss on disposal.

The remaining portion of the financial asset is not subject to a transfer and, therefore, will continue to be recognised and measured consistently with the period prior to the transaction occurring. The TRS will be recognised at FVTPL. When the referenced asset is physically delivered to Entity D at maturity of the TRS, Entity C transfers the contractual right to cash flows under the asset and derecognises it. This scenario is illustrated below.

- Entity C's fixed rate debt instrument has an amortised cost of €100, and fair value of €110 at 1 January 20X8. The amortised cost of the remaining interest flows, being the present value discounted at the original effective interest rate, is €3, and the fair value, being the present value discounted at current market rates, is €4.
- Entity C enters into a TRS with Entity D for six months over the fixed rate debt instrument. Entity C will pay Entity D increases in fair value of the debt instrument and Entity D will pay Entity C decreases in fair value as well as a funding rate of 6-month LIBOR + 50 basis points set in advance. At the maturity of the TRS Entity C will transfer the debt instrument to Entity D for €110. LIBOR at 1 January 20X8 was 5.5%.
- At 30 June 20X8 the fair value of the debt instrument is €106.

1 January 20X8

		€	€
Dr	Receivable from Entity D	4	
Cr	Debt instrument measured at amortised cost		3
Cr	Profit or loss		1

To recognise the profit on derecognition of the portion of the debt instrument representing the 6-month interest flows that were subject to the pass-through tests.

No further entries are required at 1 January 20X8 because the contractual rights to the cash flows of the remaining portion of the asset have not been transferred and the pass-through requirements for the remaining portion of the asset do not apply.

30 June 20X8

		€	€
Dr	Total return swap asset	7	
Cr	Profit or loss		7

To recognise the TRS at FVTPL. For illustrative purposes, the fair value of the TRS is equal to the decrease in fair value of the debt instrument (€4) plus 6-month LIBOR accrued for 6 months (6% x 6/12).

		€	€
Dr	Cash	117	
Cr	Total return swap asset		7
Cr	Debt instrument		97
Cr	Receivable from Entity D		4
Cr	Profit or loss		9

To recognise the consideration received on transfer of the debt instrument with the corresponding derecognition of the TRS, the debt instrument, and the receivable that was recognised on entering into the pass-through arrangement.

The gain on disposal represents the unrealised gain on the debt instrument immediately prior to entering into the arrangement, being €10, less the gain of €1 recognised on 1 January 20X8 upon entering into the pass-through arrangement.

3.11 Write-off

Under the IFRS 9 impairment model an entity recognises a loss allowance for expected losses on debt instrument assets measured at amortised cost or fair value through other comprehensive income (see **chapter B6**). The loss allowance does not form part of the gross carrying amount of the asset but is included in the asset's amortised cost measure (i.e. the gross carrying amount of a financial asset is the amortised cost of a financial asset, before adjusting for any loss allowance, IFRS 9:Appendix A).

When an entity has no reasonable expectation of recovering the contractual cash flows on a financial asset (in its entirety or a portion of it), IFRS 9:5.4.4 requires the gross carrying amount to be reduced directly which also leads to a reduction in the required loss allowance. IFRS 9:5.4.4 further states that a write-off constitutes a derecognition event, which is reiterated in IFRS 9:B3.2.16(r) which includes write-off as an example of the application of the derecognition principles in IFRS 9.

The requirement in IFRS 9:5.4.4 was introduced into IFRS 9 as part of the 2014 amendment that introduced the expected loss impairment model into IFRS 9.

4 Derecognition of a financial liability

A financial liability is derecognised when, and only when, it is extinguished, i.e. when the obligation in the contract is *discharged*, *cancelled* or *expired*. [IFRS 9:3.3.1]

An entity discharges its obligation by paying amounts of cash, other financial assets, or by delivering other goods or services to the counterparty. An obligation may expire due to the passage of time (e.g. an unexercised written option). An obligation is cancelled when through the process of law, or via negotiation with a creditor, an entity is released from its primary obligation to pay the creditor.

Example 4A

Extinguishment of financial liabilities

Situations may arise where a liability is considered unlikely to result in an outflow of economic resources. The following examples illustrate three scenarios in which a liability might never be extinguished absent a statute of limitation in the applicable jurisdiction:

Unredeemed travellers' cheques

Entity A is in the business of issuing travellers' cheques to customers. Historical statistical analysis indicates that five per cent of travellers' cheques will never be redeemed. Travellers' cheques do not have an expiry date.

Because travellers' cheques do not have an expiry date, the entity is obliged to honour the redemption of travellers' cheques on demand. The financial liability will be measured at the amount Entity A can be required to pay on demand. This obligation may carry on indefinitely into the future unless the jurisdiction allows for legal release from that obligation when a specified period of time has passed.

Goods received but not invoiced

Entity B is a media-buying entity that purchases advertising space in newspapers, television and radio on behalf of its customers, thereby incurring a liability to pay for that advertising space. Historical analysis shows that invoices have never been received by Entity B in respect of five per cent of the advertising space purchased. The jurisdiction of Entity B contains a 'statute of limitations' under which the counterparty is no longer able legally to enforce payment if it does not claim payment from Entity B within a period of six years from the date the goods or services are provided.

Until six years have expired since the transaction, Entity B is legally obligated to pay the counterparty if a claim is made. The financial liability will be measured at the amount Entity B can be required to pay on demand. At the end of six years, Entity B should derecognise the financial liability.

Dormant bank accounts

Bank C cannot locate all its customers that deposit cash with the bank. The depositor may have moved from his or her home without notifying the bank and there have been no transactions on the account for a considerable period of time (the account is dormant). However, the depositor or their legal representatives, including the depositor's executor of the estate, have the right to claim the deposited amounts indefinitely. Historically, five per cent of dormant accounts held with the bank are never reclaimed.

In the absence of a statute of limitation in Bank C's jurisdiction, Bank C will continue to recognise the financial liability to return the cash to the depositor at the amount repayable on demand. In other jurisdictions, the law may allow the bank, or the bank may be forced, to transfer the deposit to a third party (e.g. a government body), after a specified period of time. The legal release on transfer to the government body is a legal release for the bank if the depositor has no recourse to the bank.

When an entity pays another party to assume its obligation under a contract (sometimes referred to as 'in substance defeasance'), the liability is not extinguished until a legal release from the obligation is obtained. [IFRS 9:B3.3.3]

Legal release from an obligation extinguishes the liability but if, concurrently, an entity assumes another obligation to a third party or indeed to the original creditor, the new obligation is recognised. For example, an entity may be released from its primary obligation to the creditor, but assumes a guarantee if the party assuming the primary obligation defaults, in which case it derecognises the original liability and recognises the new liability for the guarantee. [IFRS 9:B3.3.4]

When a liability is extinguished, the difference between its carrying amount and the consideration paid including any non-cash assets transferred and any new liabilities assumed is recognised in profit or loss. [IFRS 9:3.3.3] In the above example, the difference between the carrying amount of the liability and consideration paid to the creditor including the fair value of the guarantee provided to the creditor is recognised in profit or loss. When only part of a liability is extinguished (e.g. repurchased by an entity), the allocation of the previous carrying amount between the amount that continues to be recognised and the part that is derecognised is performed by reference to the relative fair values of those parts on the date of repurchase (see **3.2**).

Example 4B

Expiry of embedded written put option

Entity F issues an instrument that contains a written put option embedded in the instrument that allows the holder to redeem the instrument for par in cash three years after the instrument is issued. The instrument also contains an entitlement to a fixed coupon payable at the discretion of the entity to the extent the instrument remains outstanding. If the put option is not exercised by the holder the instrument will remain outstanding in perpetuity. The instrument contains no other financial liability component other than the written put element. In accordance with IAS 32, at initial recognition the difference between the net proceeds and the fair value of the financial liability in respect of the written put option measured at the present value of the strike price of the written put at Year 3, is recognised in equity.

If the put option is exercised by the holder at the end of Year 3, the whole instrument is extinguished and, therefore, is derecognised. Due to the unwinding of the discount on the financial liability recognised in profit or loss, the carrying amount of the financial liability will equal the exercise price of the put option and, therefore, the put option will be settled with no gain or loss.

If the put option is not exercised by the holder at the end of Year 3, the instrument remains outstanding and the written put option is extinguished because it has not been exercised by the holder and is, therefore, derecognised. The financial liability is derecognised at its closing carrying amount and reclassified to equity. In this instance, the terms of the instrument have not changed but the written put option ceases to be a financial liability and starts to be recognised as equity. No gain or loss is recognised on derecognition of the financial liability in this case because the holder has chosen not to exercise its put right to redeem the instrument but rather chose to retain the instrument and have an entitlement to a fixed coupon payable at the discretion of the issuer which is classified as equity.

4.1 Exchange or modification of a financial liability

Often entities will seek to renegotiate debt instruments for a variety of reasons. Sometimes the entity will be seeking more favourable terms from the lender. Sometimes the borrower may be in financial difficulty and need to alter the contractual terms of the liability such as the maturity of the instrument or the coupon on the instrument.

When the existing borrower and lender exchange instruments with terms that are substantially different, the exchange is accounted for as an extinguishment of the original liability and recognition of a new liability. Similarly, modification of the terms of a liability is accounted for as an extinguishment of the original liability and recognition of a new liability where the modification is substantial. [IFRS 9:3.3.2]

The terms are deemed to be substantially different if the net present value of the cash flows under the new liability, including any fees paid and received, is at least 10 per cent different from the net present value of the remaining cash flows of the existing liability, both discounted at the original effective interest rate of the original liability. Similarly, modification is deemed to be substantial if the net present value of the cash flows under the modified terms, including any fees paid or received, is at least 10 per cent different from the net present value of the remaining cash flows of the liability prior to the modification, both discounted at the original effective interest rate of the liability prior to the modification. [IFRS 9:B3.3.6]

IFRS 9:B3.3.6 is clear that *fees paid* are included as part of the cash flows of the new or modified liability when performing the 10 per cent test. However, it is not clear whether this relates only to fees paid to the lender or whether this also includes fees paid to third parties (e.g. third party legal fees). In the absence of further guidance, inclusion or exclusion of third party fees could be justified.

Excluding third-party fees from the calculation is justified based on a view that the 10 per cent test under IFRS 9:B3.3.6 is intended to compare the cash flows between the borrower and the lender before and after the modification or exchange. Some of these cash flows may be referred to as 'fees' but, in substance, they are indistinguishable from the other cash flows of the modified debt instrument. Furthermore, inclusion of directly attributable cash flows in the calculation can be justified by analogy to the definition of transaction costs to be included in the initial carrying value of a financial asset or liability which includes, according to IFRS 9:B5.4.8, fees and commissions paid to agents (including employees acting as selling agents), advisers, brokers and dealers, levies by regulatory agencies and securities exchanges, and transfer taxes and duties. Accordingly, third party fees should be considered to form part of the cash flows of the modified debt instrument.

On the other hand, fees paid to another party are distinguishable as payments for services other than lending and therefore it can be justified that such fees should not form part of the cash flows used for the purpose of the 10 per cent test.

An entity should adopt an accounting policy, to be applied consistently, to either include or exclude directly attributable fees payable to a third party other than the lender from calculation of the 10 per cent test.

When performing the 10 per cent test described above, the entity must exclude from the original effective interest rate the effects of hedge accounting (whether fair value hedging or cash flow hedging). For example, if the issuer is fair value hedge accounting the interest rate risk portion of its issued fixed rate debt, the effective interest rate on this debt will reflect current floating rates at the date of exchange. Because the terms of the original debt are fixed, not floating, the original effective interest determined at initial recognition of the debt prior to any hedge accounting, should be the rate that is used in applying the 10 per cent test.

The above treatment for fair value hedge accounting is consistent with applying the original effective interest rate at initial recognition had the issuer designated the debt as at FVTPL. Designating the debt as at FVTPL for subsequent measurement does not negate the issuer determining the original effective interest rate at the date the instrument was initially recognised for the purposes of applying the 10 per cent test.

Example 4.1A

Debt modification: change in interest and term

Entity A borrowed CU1 million on 1 January 20X0, at a fixed rate of 9 per cent per annum for 10 years. Entity A incurred issue costs of CU50,000. Interest on the loan is payable annually in arrears. The original effective interest rate (EIR) is 9.807 per cent. During 20X5, Entity A approached the lender for a modification of the terms of the debt (this modification could have been as a result of a deteriorating financial condition of the borrower or because of a fall in interest rates). The following modified terms were agreed with effect from 1 January 20X6:

- interest rate to be reduced to 7.5 per cent payable yearly in arrears; and
- the original amount, payable on maturity, to remain unchanged but the maturity of the loan to be extended by two years to 31 December 20Y1.

No fees are payable for renegotiating the finance.

	Opening	**Interest**	**Payments**	**Closing**
	CU	**CU**	**CU**	**CU**
		EIR of 9.807%	(950,000)	
31 Dec 20X0	950,000	93,166	90,000	953,166
31 Dec 20X1	953,166	93,477	90,000	956,643
31 Dec 20X2	956,643	93,818	90,000	960,461
31 Dec 20X3	960,461	94,192	90,000	964,653
31 Dec 20X4	964,653	94,604	90,000	969,257
31 Dec 20X5	969,257	95,055	90,000	**974,312**
31 Dec 20X6	974,312	95,551	90,000	979,863
31 Dec 20X7	979,863	96,095	90,000	985,958
31 Dec 20X8	985,958	96,693	90,000	992,651
31 Dec 20X9	992,651	97,349	1,090,000	0

The present value of the modified debt at the original effective interest rate is calculated as follows.

	Payments
	CU
31 Dec 20X6	75,000
31 Dec 20X7	75,000
31 Dec 20X8	75,000
31 Dec 20X9	75,000
31 Dec 20Y0	75,000
31 Dec 20Y1	1,075,000
Present value at 1 January 20X6 discounting at original EIR of 9.807%	**898,954**

The entity must determine whether the modification is considered to be an extinguishment of the original debt. [IFRS 9:3.3.2 and IFRS 9:B3.3.6] Because the difference between the amortised cost of the debt instrument at the date of modification and the present value of the new debt instrument, discounted by the original effective interest rate, is less than 10 per cent, the modification is not considered an extinguishment of the original debt. The difference (CU75,358) will be recognised in profit or loss in future periods through the revised effective interest rate.

For the avoidance of doubt, at the date of modification only, the issuer should not apply IFRS 9:B5.4.6, because this will result in an immediate gain/loss in profit or loss on modification which is contrary to the issuer not achieving derecognition. The issuer will apply IFRS 9:B5.4.6 following the date of modification if the estimates of future cash flows change. The revised cash flows must be discounted at the revised effective interest rate that was determined at the date of modification.

A modification of debt terms may include changes to any one or a combination of the following:

- stated interest rate for the remaining original life of the debt;
- maturity date or dates;
- face amount of the debt;
- accrued interest;
- recourse or non-recourse features;
- priority of the obligation;
- collateral (requirement for or changes in the type of the collateral);
- covenants and/or waivers;

- currency denomination;
- the guarantor (or elimination of the guarantor); or
- option features.

Example 4.1B

Debt modification: change in notional, interest, term

Entity P borrowed CU100 million on 1 January 20X0 at a fixed interest rate of 10 per cent per annum for 10 years. Entity P incurred no issue costs. Interest on the loan is payable annually in arrears. The original effective interest rate is 10 per cent. At the end of 20X4, Entity P is offered a number of alternatives to refinance its issued debt with effect from 1 January 20X0. The current market interest rate including a credit premium for Entity P's credit risk (which has remained unchanged) is 5 per cent for the remaining time to maturity of its existing debt, i.e. half the contractual cash flows on the original debt issued at the start of 20X0.

All proposed new borrowings are with the same counterparty and are used to buy back existing debt with the issue and buy back being in contemplation of one another. Assume for illustrative purposes only, the yield curve is flat at 1 January 20X5.

The fair value of the outstanding debt at 31 December 20X4 is determined as follows.

Period	Cash flows 10% x CU100m	Discount factor at 5%	Present value CUm
20X5	10	0.952	9.52
20X6	10	0.907	9.07
20X7	10	0.864	8.64
20X8	10	0.823	8.23
20X9	110	0.784	86.19
		Fair value	121.65

Scenario 1 – new borrowing at current market interest rate of 5% with notional amount equal to the amount needed to buy back the outstanding debt at market price

Entity P determines the present value of remaining cash flows on its existing debt at the original effective interest rate and compares this with the cash flows on the new debt also discounted at the same original effective interest rate.

The new debt has a notional amount of CU121.65 million and an interest rate of 5% and matures in 20X9.

Period	Cash flows Existing debt CUm	Cash flows New debt 5% x CU121.65m	Discount factor at 10%	Present value Existing debt CUm	Present value New debt CUm
20X5	10	6.08	0.909	9.09	5.53
20X6	10	6.08	0.826	8.26	5.03
20X7	10	6.08	0.751	7.51	4.57
20X8	10	6.08	0.683	6.83	4.15
20X9	110	127.73	0.621	68.31	79.31
				100.00	98.59

The difference between the present value of the existing and new debt discounted at the original effective interest rate is CU1.41million (1.41%). Because the difference is within the '10% test' the existing debt will not be derecognised.

Scenario 2 – same as Scenario 1 but term of new debt is extended by one year (assuming yield curve is flat)

The new debt has a notional amount of CU121.65 million and an interest rate of 5% and matures in 20Y0.

Period	Cash flows New debt 5% x CU121.65m	Discount factor at 10%	Present value New debt CUm
20X5	6.08	0.909	5.53
20X6	6.08	0.826	5.03
20X7	6.08	0.751	4.57
20X8	6.08	0.683	4.15
20X9	6.08	0.621	3.78
20Y0	127.73	0.564	72.10
			95.16

The difference between the present value of the existing and new debt discounted at the original effective interest rate is CU4.84 million (4.84%). Because the difference is within the '10% test', the existing debt will not be derecognised.

The difference in the present value calculations of the new debt in scenario 1 and new debt in scenario 2 arises because scenario 2 has an additional interest flow at current market rates and deferral of the principal by a year.

Scenario 3 – same as Scenario 2 but the yield curve is not flat in 20Y0

The yield curve remains flat until 20X9 as in scenario 2 but then falls in 20Y0 and beyond. The 6-year yield curve at 1/1/X5 (i.e. until 20Y0) is 4.85% compared to 5% in scenario 2.

Period	Cash flows New debt 4.85% x CU121.65m	Discount factor at 10%	Present value New debt CUm
20X5	5.90	0.909	5.37
20X6	5.90	0.826	4.88
20X7	5.90	0.751	4.43
20X8	5.90	0.683	4.03
20X9	5.90	0.621	3.67
20Y0	127.55	0.564	71.99
			94.37

The difference between the present value of the existing and new debt discounted at the original effective interest rate is CU5.63 million (5.63%). Because the difference is within the '10% test', the existing debt will not be derecognised.

The difference in the present value calculations of the new debt in scenario 2 and the new debt in scenario 3 has increased because, even though both scenarios 2 and 3 have the same maturity and notional amount, the effective interest rate on the new debt differs. Because the additional contractual interest flows on the new debt extending beyond the term of the existing debt are locking in a lower interest rate environment, this exaggerates the difference in present value calculations between the existing and new debt. If the term was to extend further, and/or interest rates were even lower, then the present value of the new debt may be greater than 10% of the existing debt which would result in derecognition of the existing debt and recognition of the new debt at fair value in accordance with IFRS 9:5.1.1.

It is possible in a scenario of higher interest rates that when the term of the debt is extended beyond the term of the existing date that the '10% test' is breached and derecognition of the existing debt is required.

Example 4.1C

Debt modification: change in basis of interest

Entity C issued 5 year debt at a fixed rate of interest of 7 per cent on 1/1/X3 at par for €100 million. The debt is measured at amortised cost. On 1/1/X5, the debt is exchanged with the original lender for a new debt instrument that has floating rate, LIBOR, for the remaining three year term that is set annually in advance. The current LIBOR rate is 4 per cent and the yield curve is flat for the next three years. Because interest rates have fallen from 7 per cent to 4 per cent, and credit spreads have remained unchanged, the fair value of the debt has risen above par. In order to put the current debt holders in the same economic position following the debt exchange, the issuer agrees to increase the notional amount of the new debt to €108.70 million.

Entity C applies the 10 per cent per cent test to the debt exchange. Entity C sums the cash flows on the new debt discounted by the original effective interest rate of 7 per cent:

- €4.3 million for three years (4 per cent × €108.70 million, as the LIBOR curve is flat at the date of exchange); and
- the principal of €108.70 million payable at the end of year 3.

The net present value of the new debt discounted using the original effective interest rate is €100 million.

Entity C then sums the remaining cash flows on the old debt of €7 million for three years and a principal of €100 million discounted by the original effective interest rate of 7 per cent, which is also €100 million.

The net present value of the old debt and modified debt discounted by the original effective interest rate are the same, i.e. €100 million. Entity C therefore does not derecognise the old debt.

For the remaining three years, Entity C applies a modified effective interest rate that consists of current LIBOR for the period plus the amortisation from €100 million to €108.70 million based on a constant yield. The internal rate of return for the amortisation is 2.82 per cent per year and represents the current discount to par on the modified debt. This is the same accounting as for a discounted floating rate bond. The amortisation for the remaining three years is as follows.

Period ending 31/12/X5:	2.82% × €100m	= €2.82m
Period ending 31/12/X6:	2.82% × €102.82m	= €2.90m
Period ending 31/12/X7:	2.82% × €105.72m	= €2.98m

At 31/12/X5, Entity C accrues both LIBOR for the period plus the amortisation less the LIBOR interest paid in the period. Because LIBOR is set in advance, the interest payment is €4.3 million, being 4 per cent on the modified notional of the debt of €108.70 million. The period end carrying amount is therefore €102.82 million (being €100 million + €4.3 million + €2.82 million - €4.3 million).

For illustrative purposes, the forecast LIBOR interest rate is assumed to equal to the spot LIBOR rate at the date of modification.

The period end carrying amounts for 31/12/X6 and 31/12/X7 are as follows.

	€m
1/1/X6	102.82
LIBOR	4.30
Amortisation of discount	2.90
Less cash paid	(4.30)
31/12/X6	105.72
LIBOR	4.30
Amortisation of discount	2.98
Less cash paid	(4.30)
31/12/X7	108.70

At 31/12/X7, Entity C settles the modified debt instrument for €108.70 million, being its par amount.

IFRS 9 is not clear whether an entity should forecast future floating interest rates or use the floating spot rate at the date of renegotiation when determining the amount of cash flows to include in the 10% test when either or both of the original or modified financial liability have floating interest rates. In the absence of specific guidance, it is reasonable for an entity to choose one of the two approaches as an accounting policy that should be applied consistently to all financial liability derecognition assessments.

In most instances 'substantially different' will be determined by using the 10 per cent test. However, in limited circumstances, a simple qualitative assessment will be sufficient to establish that the terms of the modified liability are substantially different from those of the original one. One example of modification where a qualitative assessment is relevant is when the denomination of the original liability is changed to a different currency such that the entity is left in a different economic position due to the new currency exposure taken on.

The guidance on renegotiations and exchanges of debt instruments in IFRSs is broadly based on the equivalent guidance in US GAAP. However, US GAAP has a greater amount of guidance in certain areas.

The following guidance included in ASC 470-50 may be relevant in applying the '10 per cent' test under IFRSs:

- the cash flows have to include all cash flows specified by the terms of the new debt instrument (plus any amounts paid by the debtor to the creditor and less any amounts received by the debtor from the creditor as part of the exchange or modification);
- if either the old or the new debt instrument or both have a variable interest rate, an entity has to use the rate effective as at the date of exchange or modification to calculate the cash flows;
- if either the old or the new debt instrument has a call or a put option then separate cash flow analyses for exercise and non-exercise has to be performed and the scenario that generates the smaller change would be used to decide whether the 10 per cent hurdle is breached;
- judgement is to be used when determining the cash flows if the instrument contains contingent payment terms or unusual interest rate terms;
- if the exchanged or modified debt instrument is exchanged or modified again within one year, the terms of the original debt should be used as starting point to perform the '10 per cent' test;

- in the case of an intermediary acting as an agent for the debtor, the assessment of the transaction should "look through" that intermediary; and
- if the intermediary is identified as acting as a principal it is treated like any other creditor.

When an investment bank is used to facilitate a debt exchange, it is important to establish all the terms of the arrangement in order to establish whether the investment bank is acting as agent or principal to the transaction. An investment bank can undertake a number of roles in debt exchanges. For example, if an entity wishes to exchange its issued debt it may request an investment bank to seek out the holders of the debt in order for those holders to be offered the new debt instrument. If the investment bank is remunerated by way of a predetermined fee for this service, it is likely the bank is acting as an agent to enable the issuer to exchange its existing debt instruments.

If the existing debt holders acquire the new debt in exchange for returning the old debt to the issuer, and the investment bank simply facilitates this exchange as an agent of the issuer, then this is considered a debt exchange between the issuer and existing debt holders and, therefore, the 10 per cent test would need to be applied by the issuer. On the other hand, if debt is transferred from one debt holder to another, the issuer's accounting is not affected as long as funds do not pass through the issuer or its agent.

In some instances, the investment bank buys the existing debt from the debt holders by using its own funds and bears market risk of the debt and, therefore, is considered principal to the original debt. If the investment bank subsequently exchanges or modifies the debt with the issuer, the investment bank is considered the original debt holder and the issuer must determine whether the debt exchange between the investment bank and the issuer breaches the 10 per cent test. The investment bank would not be acting as principal (i.e. it would be acting as an agent) if it merely places the new notes in the market and only buys the new debt that it has contractually agreed to sell to others.

If an exchange of debt instruments or modification of terms is accounted for as an extinguishment, any costs or fees incurred are recognised as part of the gain or loss on the extinguishment. When the terms of the new/modified instrument are not substantially different, then any fees or costs paid in the exchange/modification are treated as an adjustment to the carrying amount of the original liability and are amortised over the remaining life of the new/modified liability. [IFRS 9:B3.3.6]

There may be very limited circumstances when fees associated with the issue of new debt can be recognised as a reduction in the carrying amount of the new debt at its initial recognition following a substantial modification of a pre-existing debt. When the fees do not relate to the exchange or modification, but rather are an incremental cost of issuing the new debt that is payable to a party other than the lender (e.g. stamp duty or a listing fee for listing the new debt), it can be argued that these costs are a transaction cost of the new debt and, therefore, are appropriately deducted from the carrying amount of the new debt if the new debt is subsequently measured at amortised cost. Examples of this are likely to be limited as many costs incurred relate to the overall exchange or modification and, therefore, cannot be isolated and identified as being specifically related only to the issue of the new debt.

4.2 Exchange of a financial liability for equity

In November 2009, the IFRIC (now the IFRS Interpretations Committee) issued IFRIC 19 *Extinguishing Financial Liabilities with Equity Instruments*. The Interpretation addresses the accounting for entities that issue equity instruments in order to extinguish all or part of a financial liability (often referred to as 'debt for equity swaps'). Debt for equity swaps are more common when the borrower is in financial difficulty and agrees with its lender to forgive amounts due to the lender in return for the lender receiving equity in the borrower.

IFRIC 19 has a limited scope as it only deals with the accounting by the entity that issues equity instruments in order to extinguish, in full or in part, a financial liability. It does not address the accounting by the lender. In addition, the Interpretation is not to be applied in situations where:

[IFRIC 19:3]

(a) the lender is also a direct or indirect shareholder and is acting in its capacity as a direct or indirect shareholder;

(b) the lender and the entity are controlled by the same party or parties before and after the transaction and the substance of the transaction includes an equity distribution from, or contribution to, the entity; or

(c) extinguishing the financial liability by issuing equity shares is in accordance with the original terms of the financial liability.

The IFRIC concluded that the issue of equity instruments to extinguish all or part of a financial liability constitutes 'consideration paid' in accordance with IFRS 9:3.3.3. The IFRIC observed that the issue of equity instruments to extinguish financial liabilities can be seen as consisting of two transactions: (i) the issue of equity instruments for cash, and (ii) acceptance by the creditor of that amount of cash to extinguish the financial liability. In effect, whether a financial liability is exchanged for equity or equity is issued for cash and the cash is used to extinguish the financial liability, the accounting treatment should be the same.

The IFRIC also concluded that an entity should measure the equity instruments issued as extinguishment of the financial liability at their fair value on the date of extinguishment of the liability, unless that fair value is not reliably measurable. In such circumstances, the equity instruments should be measured to reflect the fair value of the liability extinguished. Therefore, it is not acceptable to simply reclassify the carrying amount of the financial liability to equity (unless the fair value of the equity instruments issued happens to equal the carrying amount of the financial liability at the date of extinguishment).

If only part of a financial liability is extinguished through the issue of equity instruments, the Interpretation states that the entity should assess whether some of the consideration paid represents a modification of the portion of the liability which remains outstanding. If it is determined that part of the consideration paid relates to a modification of the outstanding liability, the entity should apportion the consideration between the portion that has been extinguished and that which remains outstanding. Any difference between the carrying amount of the liability (or the part of the liability) extinguished and the fair value of equity instruments issued is recognised in profit or loss. When consideration is partly allocated to the portion of a liability which remains outstanding, the part allocated to this portion forms part of the assessment as to whether there has been an extinguishment or a modification of that portion of the liability. If the remaining liability has been substantially modified, the entity should account for the modification as the extinguishment of the original liability and the recognition of a new liability as required by IFRS 9:3.3.2.

Example 4.2A

Liability for equity swap (1)

Entity B issues equity instruments with a fair value of CU90 million to Lender X as extinguishment of the whole of its financial liability to Lender X.

The amortised cost carrying amount of the financial liability on the date of extinguishment is CU100 million.

The following entries would be recorded.

Dr	Financial liability	CU100m
Cr	Profit or loss	CU10m
Cr	Equity	CU90m

To record derecognition of the financial liability, recognition of the equity instruments issued at fair value at the date of issue and recognition of the difference in profit or loss.

Example 4.2B

Liability for equity swap (2)

Entity C issues equity instruments with a fair value of CU35 million to Lender Y as extinguishment of a portion of financial liability to Lender Y. The total financial liability has an amortised cost carrying amount of CU100 million. The portion extinguished has a carrying amount of CU40 million. The issue of equity instruments does not modify in any way the terms of the obligation relating to the portion of the liability which remains outstanding, whose carrying amount is CU60 million (i.e. CU100 million-CU40 million).

The following entries would be recorded.

Dr	Financial liability	CU40m
Cr	Profit or loss	CU5m
Cr	Equity	CU35m

To record derecognition of the portion of the financial liability that is extinguished, recognition of the equity instruments issued at fair value at the date of extinguishment of that portion and recognition of the difference in profit or loss. There is no modification to the remaining portion of the liability of CU60 million; therefore, this portion of the liability is not adjusted or derecognised.

Example 4.2C

Liability for equity swap (3)

Entity C issues equity instruments with a fair value of CU36 million to Lender Z as extinguishment of a portion of its financial liability to Lender Z. The total financial liability has an amortised cost carrying amount of CU100 million. The portion extinguished has a carrying amount of CU40 million. The remaining portion of the financial liability with a carrying amount of CU60 million (i.e. CU100 million - CU40 million) remains outstanding; however, Lender Z agrees to change the contractual cash flows of this portion of the liability.

Entity C determines that, of the issue of equity instruments of fair value CU36 million, CU34 million relates to the extinguishment of the portion of the liability extinguished and the remaining CU2 million is in substance a fee for the change in terms of the portion of the liability which remains outstanding. The entity assesses the new terms of the remaining financial liability, applies the 10% test, and determines that they are not substantially different from the previous terms. Therefore, the entity adjusts the effective interest rate of the portion of the liability which remains outstanding to the rate which discounts the revised future contractual cash flows to the new carrying amount of the financial liability. The fee incurred by the entity (i.e. the portion of equity instruments issued with fair value of CU2 million) adjusts the carrying amount of the liability, and is amortised over the remaining term of the modified liability in accordance with IFRS 9:B3.3.6.

The following entries would be recorded.

Dr	Financial liability	CU40m
Cr	Profit or loss	CU6m
Cr	Equity	CU34m

To record derecognition of the portion of the financial liability that is extinguished, recognition of the equity instruments issued at fair value as at the date of extinguishment and recognition of the difference in profit or loss.

Dr	Financial liability	CU2m
Cr	Equity	CU2m

To record the adjustment of the carrying amount of the remaining financial liability on modification in accordance with IFRS 9:B3.3.6, and recognition of the equity instruments issued at fair value at the date of modification. The effective interest rate of this remaining portion of the liability is recalculated to give the rate that discounts the revised future contractual cash flows to the new carrying amount of this portion of the liability.

When consideration is paid to extinguish a financial liability, and there is a concurrent modification of the remaining contractual cash flows of the financial liability, the consideration paid, in whatever form, is treated as a 'cash flow' that is attributed to the new financial liability when applying the '10% test'. For example, the consideration paid could be in the form of equity instruments issued (see **example 4.2D**). If consideration is instead *payable* in the future these amounts would be included in the 10% test as future cash flows in the relevant period and discounted using the original effective interest rate.

Example 4.2D

Liability for equity swap (4)

Entity D borrowed CU100 million, equal to its par, at an interest rate of 5% from Lender T some years ago. The borrowing matures in 20X5, in 5 years' time. The borrowing is measured at amortised cost. Entity D restructures its borrowing with Lender T by issuing equity instruments as extinguishment for part of the amount due to Lender T and modifying the contractual cash flows on the remaining amounts due.

The equity instruments issued have a fair value of CU50 million at the date of issue. The remaining contractual borrowings are modified so the par is reduced to CU38 million, the interest rate is changed to 8% and the maturity of the borrowing is extended a further year to 20X6. The fair value of the borrowing in its entirety immediately prior to the modification was CU88 million.

Entity D applies the 10% test to determine whether the modified contractual cash flows on the borrowing are substantially different from the contractual cash flows of the original financial liability.

The present value of the remaining contractual cash flows of the original financial liability discounted at the original effective interest rate (EIR) is as follows.

Period	Cash flows original debt 5% x CU100m	Discount factor at original EIR of 5%	Present value original debt CUm
20X1	5.00	0.952	4.76
20X2	5.00	0.907	4.54
20X3	5.00	0.864	4.32
20X4	5.00	0.823	4.11
20X5	105.00	0.784	82.27
			100.00

The present value of the new financial liability discounted at the original effective interest rate is as follows.

Period	Cash flows new debt 8.00% x CU38m	Discount factor at original EIR of 5%	Present value new debt CUm
20X0	50.0 (equity instruments issued)	1.000	50.0
20X1	3.04	0.952	2.90
20X2	3.04	0.907	2.76
20X3	3.04	0.864	2.63
20X4	3.04	0.823	2.50
20X5	3.04	0.784	2.38
20X6	41.04	0.746	30.64
			93.81

The difference between the present value of the original and new financial liability discounted at the original effective interest rate is CU6.19 million (CU100 million – CU93.81 million), being 6.19% of the discounted present value of the remaining cash flows of the original liability. Because the difference is within the '10% range', the modified financial liability will not be initially recognised at fair value; instead, the original financial liability will:

(i) be partly derecognised due to the issue of equity instruments; and

(ii) partly continuously recognised with a new effective interest rate used for recognising interest in future periods.

Of the total principal of CU100 million that was originally outstanding at the date of modification, CU62 million has been extinguished. In addition, all future interest payments on that proportion of principal have been extinguished.

The fair value of the proportion of the old debt that has been extinguished is CU54.56 million (CU62 million / CU100 million * CU88 million). A gain of CU7.44 million is recognised in profit or loss as the carrying amount of the old debt derecognised (CU62 million) was greater than its fair value (CU54.56 million).

The difference between the fair value of original debt extinguished (CU54.56 million) and the fair value of the total equity instruments issued (CU50 million) represents a fee for modifying the terms of the remaining financial liability which is paid via the revised interest payments and is added to the carrying amount of the liability at the date of modification.

Dr	Financial liability – derecognition of a proportion of the original liability	CU62.00m
Cr	Financial liability – fee for modification of terms of original liability	CU4.56m
Cr	Profit or loss	CU7.44m
Cr	Equity	CU50.00m

To record the derecognition of the portion of the financial liability that is extinguished, recognition of the fee for modifying the terms of the remainder of the original liability, recognition of the equity instruments issued at fair value as at the date of extinguishment and recognition of the difference in profit or loss.

The effective interest rate on the financial liability that continues to be recognised is revised to reflect the new contractual cash flows as a result of the modification. The modified effective interest rate that discounts all the remaining expected contractual cash flows to the portion of the carrying amount that continues to be recognised (being CU42.56 million at the date of modification) is 5.59%.

	Opening carrying amount	**Effective interest rate at 5.59%**	**Interest and capital paid**	**Closing carrying amount**
	CUm	**CUm**	**CUm**	**CUm**
20X1	42.56	2.38	(3.04)	41.90
20X2	41.90	2.34	(3.04)	41.20
20X3	41.20	2.30	(3.04)	40.46
20X4	40.46	2.26	(3.04)	39.68
20X5	39.68	2.22	(3.04)	38.86
20X6	38.86	2.18	(41.04)	–

If the lender is a direct or an indirect shareholder and is acting in its capacity as a direct or an indirect shareholder, or the lender and the borrower are controlled by the same party or parties before and after the transaction and the substance of the transaction includes an equity distribution from, or contribution to, the borrower, the transaction is not in the scope of IFRIC 19.

If a transaction is outside the scope of IFRIC 19 for the reasons noted above, judgement will be required in determining the appropriate accounting treatment. In such circumstances, it is possible that the fair value of consideration paid (if any) may differ significantly from the fair value of the financial liability that has been extinguished.

Provided that the effects of any significant capital contribution or bonus element are excluded from profit or loss, it will often be acceptable for the borrower to choose one of the following approaches when derecognising the liability.

- **Approach 1:** following the principles underlying IFRIC 19, the borrower may choose to recognise in profit or loss any difference between the carrying amount of the liability derecognised and its fair value at the date of derecognition (as illustrated in **examples 4.2E** and **4.2F**). In effect, this is akin to measuring the increase in equity (for shares issued, if any, as adjusted for any capital contribution or bonus element) by reference to the fair value of the financial liability that has been extinguished.
- **Approach 2:** alternatively, the borrower may choose to recognise no gain or loss on derecognition of the liability. In effect, this is akin to measuring the increase in equity (for shares issued, if any, as adjusted for any capital contribution or bonus element) by reference to the carrying amount of the financial liability that has been extinguished, rather than its fair value.

If the fair value of shares issued is significantly less than the fair value of the liability extinguished, the difference between the two should not be recognised as a gain in profit or loss, because it is instead a capital contribution from owners. Similarly, if a liability is extinguished for no consideration, the fair value of the liability extinguished should not be recognised as a gain in profit or loss, because it is instead a capital contribution from owners.

By the same logic, if the fair value of the shares issued is significantly greater than the fair value of the liability extinguished, the difference between the two should not be recognised as a loss; the difference is instead akin to a bonus issue of shares, as illustrated in **example 4.2F**, in that it represents a distribution of additional shares to a parent for no (incremental) consideration.

In some cases, the carrying amount and the fair value of the financial liability may be similar. For example, where a financial liability is repayable on demand by the lender, IFRS 9:5.4.3 indicates that its fair value is not less than the amount that is repayable on demand. In other cases, the carrying value and the fair value of the financial liability may be different, e.g. where the financial liability is not repayable on demand and the subsidiary is in financial difficulty.

Example 4.2E

Parent waives debt from subsidiary for no consideration

Scenario 1

Subsidiary T is a wholly-owned subsidiary of Parent Y. Parent Y waives a financial liability owed to it by Subsidiary T for no consideration. The carrying amount of the financial liability measured at amortised cost is £100 million. At the date of exchange the fair value of the financial liability is also £100 million.

The difference of £100 million between the fair value of the financial liability (£100 million) and the consideration paid (£nil) should not be reported in profit or loss, because it is instead a capital contribution from owners.

The following entries will be recorded by Subsidiary T.

Dr	Financial liability	£100m	
Cr	Equity		£100m

Being the derecognition of the financial liability and recognition of the capital contribution from the borrower's parent.

Scenario 2

Subsidiary T is a wholly-owned subsidiary of Parent Y. Parent Y waives a financial liability owed to it by Subsidiary T for no consideration. The carrying amount of the financial liability measured at amortised cost is £100 million. At the date of exchange the fair value of the financial liability is £90 million.

An amount should be credited to equity, to reflect the capital contribution that has been made by Parent Y. Subsidiary T should choose an appropriate accounting approach when measuring the amount to be credited to equity.

If Subsidiary T chooses to follow Approach 1, measuring the capital contribution by reference to the fair value of the financial liability that has been extinguished, the following entries will be recorded.

Dr	Financial liability	£100m	
Cr	Profit or loss (£100m – £90m)		£10m
Cr	Equity		£90m

Being the derecognition of the financial liability, recognition of the capital contribution from the borrower's parent and recognition of the difference in profit or loss.

If Subsidiary T chooses to follow Approach 2, measuring the capital contribution by reference to the carrying amount of the financial liability that has been extinguished, the following entries will be recorded.

Dr	Financial liability	£100m	
Cr	Equity		£100m

Being the derecognition of the financial liability and recognition of the capital contribution from the borrower's parent.

Example 4.2F

Liability for equity swap (5)

Scenario 1

Subsidiary T is a wholly-owned subsidiary of Parent Y. Subsidiary T issues equity instruments to its lender, Parent Y, as part of extinguishing all of its financial liability owed to Parent Y. The carrying amount of the financial liability measured at amortised cost is £100 million. At the date of exchange the fair value of the financial liability is also £100 million. The equity instruments issued to Parent Y have a fair value of £110 million.

The excess of £10 million of the consideration paid (£110 million) over the fair value and carrying amount of the financial liability (£100 million) should not be reported in profit or loss, because it is instead akin to a bonus issue to owners. Therefore, the overall amount credited to equity should be £100 million.

The following entries will be recorded by Subsidiary T.

Dr	Financial liability	£100m	
Cr	Equity (*)		£100m

Being the derecognition of the financial liability and recognition of the equity instruments issued.

(*) This can be thought of as equivalent to the issue of equity instruments at fair value (£110 million), less an element akin to a bonus issue (£10 million) being the excess of the fair value of equity instruments issued over the fair value of the consideration received (i.e. the liability derecognised).

Scenario 2

Subsidiary T is a wholly-owned subsidiary of Parent Y. Subsidiary T issues equity instruments to its lender, Parent Y, as part of extinguishing all of its financial liability owed to Parent Y. The carrying amount of the financial liability measured at amortised cost is £100 million. At the date of exchange the fair value of the financial liability is £80 million. The equity instruments issued to Parent Y have a fair value of £90 million.

An amount should be credited to equity, to reflect the equity instruments that have been issued to Parent Y (adjusted for any capital contribution or bonus element). Subsidiary T should choose an appropriate accounting approach when measuring the amount to be credited to equity.

If Subsidiary T chooses to follow Approach 1, measuring the increase in equity by reference to the fair value of the financial liability that has been extinguished, the following entries will be recorded.

Dr	Financial liability	£100m	
Cr	Profit or loss (£100m – £80m)		£20m
Cr	Equity (*)		£80m

Being the derecognition of the financial liability, recognition of the equity instruments issued to the borrower's parent and recognition of the difference in profit or loss.

(*) This can be thought of as equivalent to the issue of equity instruments at fair value (£110 million), less an element akin to a bonus issue (£10 million) being the excess of the fair value of equity instruments issued over the fair value of the consideration received (i.e. the liability derecognised).

If Subsidiary T chooses to follow Approach 2, measuring the increase in equity by reference to the carrying amount of the financial liability that has been extinguished, the following entries will be recorded.

Dr	Financial liability	£100m	
Cr	Equity		£100m

Being the derecognition of the financial liability and recognition of the equity instruments issued.

Scenario 3

Subsidiary T is a wholly-owned subsidiary of Parent Y. Subsidiary T issues equity instruments to its lender, Parent Y, as part of extinguishing all of its financial liability owed to Parent Y. The carrying amount of the financial liability measured at amortised cost is £100 million. At the date of exchange the fair value of the financial liability is £80 million. The equity instruments issued to Parent Y have a fair value of £70 million.

An amount should be credited to equity, to reflect the equity instruments that have been issued to Parent Y (adjusted for any capital contribution or bonus element). Subsidiary T should choose an appropriate accounting approach when measuring the amount to be credited to equity.

If Subsidiary T chooses to follow Approach 1, measuring the increase in equity by reference to the fair value of the financial liability that has been extinguished, the following entries will be recorded.

Dr	Financial liability	£100m	
Cr	Profit or loss (£100m – £80m)		£20m
Cr	Equity (*)		£80m

Being the derecognition of the financial liability, recognition of the equity instruments issued to the borrower's parent and recognition of the difference in profit or loss.

(*) This can be thought of as equivalent to the issue of equity instruments at fair value (£70 million), plus a capital contribution (£10 million) being the excess of the fair value of the consideration received (i.e. the liability derecognised) over the fair value of equity instruments issued.

If Subsidiary T chooses to follow Approach 2, measuring the increase in equity by reference to the carrying amount of the financial liability that has been extinguished, the following entries will be recorded.

Dr	Financial liability	£100m	
Cr	Equity		£100m

Being the derecognition of the financial liability and recognition of the equity instruments issued.

5 Future developments

In response to the global financial crisis and the recommendations made by the Financial Stability Forum, in March 2009, the IASB issued an exposure draft of proposed amendments to IAS 39 and IFRS 7, ED/2009/3 *Derecognition*. The exposure draft proposed derecognition of an asset when:

- the contractual rights to the cash flows expire;
- there is a transfer and the transferor has no continuing involvement in the asset; or
- there is a transfer and there is retention of continuing involvement, but the transferee has the practical ability to transfer the asset for its own benefit.

The exposure draft contained an 'alternative approach' proposed by a significant minority of Board members. Like the model described above, it is based on control. However, the model would require that if a transferor does not have access to *all* the cash flows the transferor recognised prior to the transfer, then the asset is derecognised and a new asset is recognised for any interest in part of the asset transferred.

After considering constituents' comments, the IASB tentatively decided in October 2009 to pursue the alternative approach described in the exposure draft. However, in June 2010, the IASB announced its intention to proceed with a more limited project to issue new disclosure requirements in connection with derecognition which were issued in October 2010 as an amendment to IFRS 7 (see **4.1.6** in **chapter B11**). These amendments are intended to improve the disclosure requirements in relation to transferred financial assets and converge with the requirements under US GAAP.

Following the finalisation of the amended derecognition disclosures the IASB and FASB have agreed not to develop an alternative derecognition model.

B9 Hedge accounting

Contents

1 Objective and scope of hedge accounting

1.1 Hedging economic exposures

Virtually all entities are exposed to risks of some kind. The nature of these risks can be diverse, ranging from business, environmental and political risk, to market, liquidity and credit risk. Often these risk exposures are retained within the business and used to generate a return for investors. On the other hand, sometimes entities choose to manage risks by using financial instruments to create an opposing exposure which, taken together with the original exposure, gives them a 'hedge' against the risk.

1.2 The need for hedge accounting

Despite the intention to reduce risk by using financial instruments for hedging purposes, when it comes to the accounting, such activities can actually create accounting volatility. This is because the underlying exposure is not necessarily recognised and measured on the same basis as the financial instrument used to hedge it. For example, a foreign currency derivative used to hedge a forecast transaction will be recognised and measured at fair value through profit or loss from inception, whereas the forecast transaction will remain unrecognised until it happens. Hence, although over the long term, the financial statements present the cumulative effect of hedging, accounting mismatches, and consequently earnings volatility can arise in the intervening reporting periods.

Hedge accounting helps to address this difference in measurement and recognition and is designed to represent in the financial statements the effect of an entity's risk management activities to manage risks that could affect profit or loss (or other comprehensive income in the case of equity investments measured at FVTOCI, see **6.4.3**). [IFRS 9:6.1.1] Through the application of hedge accounting, an entity can match, in profit or loss (or other comprehensive income), gains and losses on the financial instruments used to hedge ('hedging instruments') with losses and gains on the exposures hedged ('hedged items') to the extent the hedge is effective.

Hedge accounting does not necessarily present the full risk management picture because it only addresses situations where risks are hedged, rather than left unhedged, and is confined within the boundaries of accounting and must be consistent with established accounting principles. These principles are presented as the hedge accounting requirements and specify, amongst other things, the eligibility conditions for hedging instruments (see **section 2**) and hedged items (see **section 3**) (including groups of items, see **section 4**). Therefore, just because an entity hedges a particular risk using a financial instrument does not mean the entity will be eligible for hedge accounting. Furthermore, in those cases where gains and losses on hedging instruments and hedged items naturally offset in profit or loss hedge accounting will not be necessary.

Hedge accounting is voluntary on a hedge by hedge basis and can only be applied prospectively from the point that a hedging instrument and hedged item are formally designated in a hedging relationship and the other qualifying criteria are met, including an assessment of the expected effectiveness of the hedge (see **section 5.2**). Once a hedge is formally designated and the conditions are met, hedge accounting must be applied and is only discontinued when certain conditions are no longer met (see **section 6.3**). If for any reason a hedging relationship does not meet all of the necessary conditions, hedge accounting cannot be applied.

1.3 The mechanics of hedge accounting

The mechanics through which hedge accounting achieves offsetting of gains or losses on the hedging instrument with the hedged item varies depending on the nature of the hedge.

Generally, hedges of exposures to variability in cash flows are dealt with by deferring changes in value of the hedging instrument in other comprehensive income, with amounts later removed or reclassified and ultimately recognised in profit or loss at the same time as the hedged item. This is referred to as cash flow hedge accounting (see **section 6.5**).

Generally, hedges of existing (rather than forecast) hedged items that are hedged for changes in fair value (such as an equity investment or fixed rate loan) are matched in profit or loss with the hedging instrument by also re-measuring the hedged item through profit or loss to reflect changes in value due to the hedged risk. An exception to this is where an entity hedges an equity investment designated at FVTOCI, where the hedging instrument's gains or losses are recognised and matched in other comprehensive income. In both of these cases, this is referred to as fair value hedge accounting (see **section 6.4**).

Another type of hedge accounting is a hedge of a net investment, which applies to hedges of foreign currency risk on net investments in foreign operations and is accounted for in a similar way to cash flow hedge accounting (see **section 6.6**).

In addition to the mechanics for offsetting gains or losses, there are also specific requirements for accounting for certain costs of hedging, such as the cost or premium for purchasing an option contract (see **sections 6.8 - 6.10**).

When an entity elects to apply hedge accounting, it also brings itself into the scope of the hedge accounting disclosures in IFRS 7 (see **chapter B11**). These disclosures provide insights into the reporting entity's risk management strategies and make the effect that hedge accounting has on the financial statements more transparent.

Although the hedge accounting model in IFRS 9 allows some limited groups of hedged items to be hedge accounted, it does not include a macro hedge accounting model to cater for hedges of dynamic (open) portfolios. The IASB is undertaking a project to explore the development of a model to address the measurement inconsistencies that arise from macro hedging. Given the early stage of this project, IFRS 9 allows entities to apply the specific hedge accounting requirements in IAS 39 in respect of portfolio fair value hedging of interest rate risk (including designating as the hedged item a portion that is a currency amount and complying with the hedge effectiveness requirements of IAS 39 (see IAS 39:81A, 89A and AG114 to AG132). [IFRS 9:6.1.3] See **section 7** of **chapter C10** of *iGAAP 2016 Financial Instruments: IAS 39 and related Standards – Volume C*, Deloitte's companion volume for this manual.

In addition to this, IFRS 9 also allows those transitioning to IFRS 9 from IAS 39, as an accounting policy choice, to continue to apply the IAS 39 hedge accounting requirements, in full, in place of the requirements in Chapter 6 of IFRS 9. The rationale behind this option is to allow entities the opportunity to see the outcome of the macro hedging project before being required to adopt the new general model and hence avoid changing to the new general model and then potentially changing again to a new macro model. As such, the IASB anticipates removing this option once the macro hedging project is completed.

This chapter discusses the (general) hedge accounting model contained in Chapter 6 of IFRS 9 and follows a similar structure. **Chapter B10** includes additional detailed illustrative examples of the application of the hedge accounting requirements.

1.4 Alternative to hedge accounting

Given all of the requirements for hedge accounting and the fact that it is voluntary, some entities may choose not to apply hedge accounting and accept the accounting volatility that arises, or they may consider alternatives to hedge accounting that can achieve a similar outcome. One of these alternatives involves designating the underlying exposure at FVTPL to reduce the accounting mismatch arising from measuring financial instruments used to hedge at FVTPL.

Four specific fair value options are available when the designation eliminates or significantly reduces a recognition inconsistency that would otherwise arise (i.e. an accounting mismatch). Three of these options are only available on initial recognition and each apply separately to financial assets (see **chapter B2**), financial liabilities (see **chapter B3**) and contracts to buy or sell a non-financial item that are otherwise outside scope of IFRS 9 (see **chapter B1**).

The fourth fair value option applies to exposures hedged for credit risk, which has its own specific eligibility conditions and is more flexible in that it is available after initial recognition of the exposure and can also later be revoked (see **section 7**).

The simplicity of applying the fair value option in these cases can come at a cost. For example, with the exception of the fair value option for credit exposures, the designation must be made at inception of the contract and is irrevocable. Also, the fair value option can be less targeted than hedge accounting because the item is fair valued in its entirety rather than solely for the hedged risk as is the case with fair value hedge accounting. As a result, the fair value option can lead to more volatility in profit or loss than applying fair value hedge accounting.

2 Hedging instruments

The underlying need for hedge accounting stems from the fact that the financial instruments that are used to manage risks are not always recognised and measured on the same basis as the exposure that is hedged by them. Often, financial instruments used to hedge risks are measured at FVTPL, which can give rise to significant profit or loss volatility if the hedged item is not measured on the same basis (e.g. when the hedged item is an unrecognised future transaction or when it is recognised and measured at cost).

IFRS 9 only permits financial instruments that are within its scope to be designated as hedging instruments and allows both derivative (see **section 2.1**) and non-derivative financial instruments (see **section 2.2**) to be eligible with some specific restrictions. Generally, such instruments must be measured at FVTPL to be eligible hedging instrument with the exception of non-derivative instruments used to hedge foreign currency risk (see **2.2.1**).

For hedge accounting purposes, only contracts with parties external to the reporting entity (i.e. external to the group or individual entity being reported on) can be designated as hedging instruments. [IFRS 9:6.2.3].

2.1 Derivative hedging instruments

With the exception of some written options (see **2.1.1**), a derivative measured at FVTPL may be designated as a hedging instrument, provided in the case of an embedded derivative, it is separately accounted for as if it were a standalone derivative. [IFRS 9:6.2.1 & IFRS 9:B6.2.1]

Restricting the eligibility of hedging derivatives only to those that are measured at FVTPL prevents derivatives outside the scope of IFRS 9 from being eligible. For example, a derivative contract for the receipt or delivery of a non-financial item that meets the own use criteria (see **chapter B1**) and is not within the scope of IFRS 9 would be accounted for as an executory contract and would not be an eligible hedging instrument (but could be an eligible hedged item, see **3.3**). Furthermore, a derivative over own equity that meets the definition of equity cannot be designated as a hedging instrument because it is not a financial asset or financial liability and is not measured at FVTPL. [IFRS 9:B6.2.2].

2.1.1 Written options

IFRS 9 does not allow a written option to be designated as a hedging instrument unless it is designated as an offset to a purchased option, including one that is embedded in another financial instrument [IFRS 9:B6.2.4]. For example, a written option could be designated as a hedge of a callable liability where the issuer has the right to call the debt back early.

Example 2.1.1A

Hedging an amortised cost asset with a written call option

Entity A owns bonds issued by Entity X, an unrelated entity. It measures these bonds at amortised cost. Entity A purchased the bonds when the bond price was CU93. The bond price is currently CU96. Entity A writes a call option over the bonds allowing the purchaser of the option to acquire the bonds for CU98, and in exchange Entity A receives a premium.

Entity A may not designate the option as a hedge of its bonds in Entity X because it is a written option and is not being used to hedge a purchased option.

All hedging instruments must be assessed to consider whether they contain a written option because this may disqualify them from being designated as hedging instruments. This applies to both derivative and non-derivative hedging instruments measured at FVTPL and designated as hedging instruments.

Example 2.1.1B

Embedded written options in interest rate swaps

Entity A issues twenty-year fixed rate debt. To hedge its fair value exposure to interest rate risk, it enters into a receive fixed, pay floating interest rate swap, where all the terms of the swap match the terms of the debt. Owing to the long-term nature of the swap, the counterparty to the swap, the Bank, inserts a break clause into the swap giving the Bank the option to terminate the swap after ten years at no cost. No cash is exchanged at the start of the transaction.

Entity A has effectively written an option to the bank allowing it to terminate the swap after ten years. While no cash was exchanged up-front, Entity A will be recompensed for writing this option by receiving a favourable rate on one of the legs of the swap.

The swap cannot be designated as a hedge of the issued debt because it contains a written option. The written option cannot be split out of the swap contract (leaving a vanilla twenty year interest swap) because a derivative must be designated as a hedging instrument in its entirety (with only a limited number of specified exceptions discussed in **2.1.3** and **2.1.7**).

If the terms of the break clause resulted in termination of the swap at fair value at the time of termination, and fair value excluded any additional compensation paid/receivable to either party in excess of the interest rate swap, the swap would still contain a written option, but the value of the option would be zero. The legs of the swap would be no different from a swap without a break clause. In this case, the swap could be used as a hedging instrument.

2.1.2 Net written options

The restrictions on designating written options as hedging instruments also apply to net written options arising from a combination of a written option and a purchased option within a single contract. For example, an interest rate collar that combines a purchased option and written option would have to be assessed to determine whether it represents a net written option before designating it as a hedging instrument. [IFRS 9:6.2.6]

Similarly, two or more instruments (or proportions of them) may be jointly designated as a hedging instrument only if, in combination they are not, in effect, a net written option at the date of designation (unless designated as an offset to a purchased option). For example, the combination of a stand-alone purchased option and a stand-alone written option would have to be assessed to determine whether, in effect, it is a net written option before designating it as a hedging instrument. [IFRS 9:6.2.6]

It is clear from IFRS 9:6.2.6 that written options may be designated as hedging instruments if they are combined with purchased options (as hedging instruments) if the combination does not represent a net written option.

The assessment of whether a combination of purchased and written options is a net written option is performed at the date of designation.

IFRS 9 does not provide specific guidance on how to assess whether a combination of option contracts is a net written option. However, the IASB notes in the Basis for Conclusions on IFRS 9 that the assessment would follow established practice under IAS 39. That practice considers the following cumulative factors to ascertain that an interest rate collar or other instrument that includes a written option is not a net written option:

[IFRS 9:BC6.153]

(a) No net premium is received either at inception or over the life of the combination of options. The distinguishing feature of a written option is the receipt of a premium to compensate the writer for the risk incurred.

(b) Except for the strike prices, the critical terms and conditions of the written option component and the purchased option component are the same (including the underlying variable or variables, currency denomination and maturity date). Also, the notional amount of the written option component is not greater than the notional amount of the purchased option component.

Therefore, even when the critical terms and conditions of the written option and purchased option are largely the same, a combination of written and purchased options is deemed to be net written if:

(i) a net premium is received, either at inception or over the life of the combination of options; or

(ii) the notional on the written option exceeds that on the purchased option.

Example 2.1.2

Hedging with a collar

Entity A issues CU100 million variable rate debt. To hedge against interest rate increases, it purchases an interest rate collar at the date of issuance of the debt that hedges interest rates above 8 per cent and below 4 per cent. Current fixed interest rates for the same term as the debt are 6 per cent. The collar costs CU0.5 million as there is a greater likelihood that the purchased cap will be in the money compared to the written floor. The purchased cap at 8 per cent and written floor at 4 per cent included in the collar have the same notional of CU100 million.

Entity A may designate the collar as a cash flow hedge of the variable rate debt because there is no net premium received (there is a net premium payable of CU0.5 million) and the notional on the floor does not exceed that on the cap.

If there was a premium received on the collar, it could not have been designated as a hedging instrument. Equally, if the notional on the floor was greater than CU100 million, the collar could not have been designated as a hedging instrument.

It is not acceptable to split a single instrument that consists of a number of options (e.g. an interest rate collar) and designate just the purchased option component as a hedging instrument. IFRS 9:6.2.4 specifies that a derivative is designated as a hedging instrument in its entirety except in certain circumstances.

2.1.3 Splitting a derivative

A hedging instrument must generally be designated in its entirety, because there is usually only one fair value for a hedging instrument, and the factors contributing to that fair value are interdependent. However, IFRS 9 allows a limited number of exceptions to this rule, some of which apply solely to derivative hedging instruments as follows:

[IFRS 9:6.2.4 (a) - (b)]

(i) separating the intrinsic value and time value of an option and designating only the intrinsic element as the hedging instrument (see **section 6.8**);

(ii) separating the forward element and spot element of a forward contract and designating only the spot element as the hedging instrument (see **section 6.9**);

(iii) separating the foreign currency basis spread of a foreign currency derivative and excluding it from the designation of the hedging instrument (in the same way as excluding the forward element of a forward contract) (see **section 6.10**); and

These exceptions are permitted because the intrinsic value of an option, the spot element of a forward contract and the foreign currency basis spread of a foreign currency derivative can usually be measured separately. However, this principle of reliable separate measurement cannot be extended. Even if it can be demonstrated that a reliable measure of an element of a derivative can be determined, it cannot be excluded from the hedge designation unless it qualifies for one of the permitted exceptions.

In practice, there may be various reasons why an entity might choose to exclude one of the above components of a derivative from its designation as a hedging instrument. In many cases it will be because the excluded component represents a cost of hedging and is not regarded as an offsetting component of the hedged item. Hence excluding that component will improve hedge effectiveness. Furthermore, IFRS 9 provides for alternative accounting for the excluded component, which can avoid it being recognised in profit or loss on a fair value basis, thereby providing further incentive to exclude it from the hedge designation (see **sections 6.8 - 6.10**).

In addition to the above, an entity can choose to designate only a proportion of an entire hedging instrument, (e.g. 50 per cent of all of the cash flows of a derivative). However, a hedging instrument may not be designated for a part of its change in fair value that results from only a portion of the time period during which the hedging instrument remains outstanding (e.g. the first three years of cash flows on a derivative with a term of five years). [IFRS 9:6.2.4(c)]

In these cases, the entity could also apply one of the exceptions noted above should it wish to (e.g. designate 70% of an option and exclude the time value associated with that proportion from the designation as a hedging instrument). Designation of proportions of hedging instruments is discussed in **2.1.7**.

2.1.4 Purchased options

An entity may designate an option as a hedge of changes in the cash flows or fair value of a hedged item above or below a specified price or other variable (a one-sided risk).

The value of the option consists of its intrinsic value (as if the option was presently exercisable) and the time value of the option (reflecting its potential to be 'in the money' over time before its expiry). The time value of the option decreases to zero at an increasing rate as the option approaches expiry.

When designating an option, it is common to designate just the intrinsic value of the option as permitted by IFRS 9:6.2.4(a) and not designate the time value of the option. This approach ensures that when the option is in the money', the option is more effective at hedging the variability in cash flows of the hedged item as the fair value change associated with the time value of the option is excluded from the hedge effectiveness assessment.

The time value of the option not designated as part of the hedging relationship under IFRS 9 is considered to be a 'cost of hedging' similar to an insurance premium paid by an entity to protect it from downside risk. IFRS 9 requires specific accounting to be applied to the excluded time value component of an option involving the deferral of time value changes (to the extent they relate to the hedged item) in other comprehensive income (i.e. it is not simply recognised in profit or loss on a fair value basis). The recognition and measurement of the time value varies depending on a number of factors, including the nature of the hedged item and whether the critical terms of the option match that of the hedged item. This is discussed in more detail in **section 6.8**.

2.1.5 Forward contracts

Entities may designate forward contracts as hedging instruments in a hedge relationship. To improve hedge effectiveness, entities may separate the forward contract's forward element and spot element, with only the spot element designated as the hedging instrument. For example, an entity may wish to hedge the foreign currency risk associated with inventory of a commodity priced in a foreign currency. The inventory would give rise to spot foreign currency risk (because it is an existing item rather than a future transaction) and the risk would be more effectively hedged by the spot component of a foreign exchange contract.

When the forward element of a forward contract is excluded, there is a choice as to how it is accounted for. It may either be recognised in profit or loss on a fair value basis or it may be treated as a 'cost of hedging' in a similar way to the time value of an option. If the entity treats the excluded forward element as a 'cost of hedging', they are treated similarly to the time value of options. Under this approach, changes in value of the forward element are recognised in the other comprehensive income to the extent they relate to the hedged item. Thereafter, they impact the profit or loss differently depending on, amongst other things, the nature of the hedged item. This is discussed in more detail in **section 6.9**.

An entity may also exclude the foreign currency basis spread from the designation of a forward contract in order to improve hedge effectiveness and treat the foreign currency basis spread as a cost of hedging. This is discussed in **2.1.6**.

2.1.6 Foreign currency basis spread

A foreign currency basis spread can be described as a charge for the future exchange of one currency for another. It is inherently present, to varying degrees, in any financial instrument that exchanges one currency for another, however, it is generally more prominent in cross-currency interest rate swaps. In perfect markets, arbitrage opportunities are eliminated and a forward currency rate is a function of only the spot exchange rate plus the risk free interest rate differential between the two currencies (i.e. the forward points). However, in practice a foreign currency basis spread is included as a charge for exchanging currencies and has become more significant during times of financial crisis and more transparent pricing. The spread reflects a number of different factors, including:

- The credit, liquidity and country risks of the relevant currencies.
- The supply and demand for a particular type of cross-currency swap (e.g. the principal size, the currencies and maturities involved).
- The interaction between the spot and forward foreign exchange markets.

Example 2.1.6

Identifying a foreign currency basis spread in a cross-currency swap

Entity A has a US$ functional currency. It issues a floating rate loan with £100m principal and wishes to hedge its exposure to foreign currency risk. Entity A buys a cross-currency interest rate swap.

The terms of the swap are:

On initial exchange (based on the spot rate at inception):

Receive	US$150m
Pay	£100m
On-going settlements:	
Receive	3-month UK LIBOR + 10 basis points
Pay	3-month US LIBOR
On final exchange	
Receive	£100m
Pay	US $150m

The instrument exchanges a floating rate in one currency for a floating rate in another currency. The additional 10 basis points charged on top of the UK LIBOR rate includes the foreign currency basis spread. The actual amount of the foreign currency basis spread included within the 10 basis points can be determined by reference to quoted market data.

In using a derivative containing a foreign currency basis spread as a hedging instrument, an entity needs to assess whether the same exposure is present in the hedged item. Where the hedged item does not involve the exchange of currencies it will not contain a foreign currency basis spread, for example, if the hedged item is a foreign currency loan, it would not include a foreign currency basis spread, which would lead to some hedge ineffectiveness if the hedging instrument containing this spread is designated in its entirety. To improve hedge effectiveness an entity may exclude the foreign currency basis spread from the designation of the hedging instrument in a similar way in which the forward element of a forward may be excluded from its designation as a hedging instrument. If it is excluded, the changes in the fair value of the derivative due to foreign currency basis spread are either recognised directly in profit or loss or treated as a 'cost of hedging'. If treated as a cost of hedging, changes in the fair value of the derivative due to the foreign currency basis spread would initially be recognised in other comprehensive income (to the extent that it relates to the hedged item) and then be reclassified to profit or loss based on the nature of the hedged item (see **6.10** for further detail).

The translation of a foreign currency item to the functional currency of the reporting entity does not include an exposure to foreign currency basis spread because the translation of a foreign currency item into the reporting entity's functional currency is not a contractual exchange of currencies. Instead the foreign currency amount is simply retranslated into the functional currency of the entity using the relevant exchange rate excluding any currency basis spread. For example, a US dollar denominated loan in a Euro functional currency entity does not include an exposure to foreign currency basis spread and is translated using the US$:€ exchange rate excluding any currency basis spread. Similarly, a US dollar receive fixed, pay floating interest rate swap in a Euro functional currency entity does not include an exposure to foreign currency basis spread because there is no exchange of different currencies under the financial instrument.

2.1.7 Designation of portions and proportions of a derivative

A proportion of the entire hedging instrument may be designated as the hedging instrument in a hedge relationship. [IFRS 9:6.2.4(c)]

Example 2.1.7A

Designating part of a derivative: proportion

Entity A has a receive-variable, pay-fixed interest rate swap that it wishes to designate as hedging its issued variable rate debt. The notional on the swap is CU100 million and the notional on the debt is CU60 million. Entity A may designate CU60 million of the swap (i.e. 60 per cent) as the hedging instrument of the variable rate debt. The remaining CU40 million (i.e. 40 per cent) of the swap will be measured at FVTPL, unless it is designated as a hedging instrument in another hedge relationship.

A hedging instrument may not be designated for a part of its change in fair value resulting from only a portion of the time period that the hedging instrument is outstanding. [IFRS 9:6.2.4(c)]

Example 2.1.7B

Designating part of a derivative: portion

Entity A has a receive-variable, pay-fixed interest rate swap that it wishes to designate as hedging its issued variable rate debt. The swap has a 10-year term and the debt has a 7-year term. Entity A cannot designate seven of the ten years of the swap as the hedging instrument.

Note that designating portions of hedged items is less restrictive. For example, if the swap had a 7-year term and the debt had a 10-year term, it would be possible to hedge the debt for the first seven years of its term with the 7-year swap. This would represent a partial term hedge (see **3.11.3**).

The inability to designate part of the change in the fair value of a hedging instrument relating only to a portion of the time period that the hedging instrument remains outstanding is an extension of the rule that does not allow derivatives to be split. IFRS 9 does not permit an entity to designate part of a derivative that is not a proportion of the derivative as a whole, unless the part of the derivative excluded from the hedge relationship is the time value of an option, forward element of a forward contract or the foreign currency basis spread of a foreign currency derivative as discussed in **sections 6.8 - 6.10**. For example, an entity with a 10-year interest rate swap with monthly net settlements could not designate only the first 12 months of cash flows on the derivative as a hedging instrument and exclude the remaining 9 years of cash flows from the hedge relationship.

This should not be confused with designating all (or a proportion) of the changes in fair value of a hedging instrument for only part of its life. For example, it is possible to designate all cash flows on a 10-year interest rate swap as a hedging instrument against, say a 10-year debt instrument, even if the intention is to terminate the swap after one year.

2.1.8 Deal contingent derivatives

An entity that expects to enter into transactions whose occurrence depends on a future event sometimes enters into derivatives that mirror the possibility of non-occurrence of the future event, i.e. the derivative has a knock-out option that is exercised if the future event does not occur. These are often referred to as deal contingent derivatives. If the future event occurs the derivative remains outstanding; if the event does not occur, the derivative ceases to exist and no settlements between the parties are made. Although such instruments might be eligible hedging instruments in their own right, in practice it is unlikely that they could be designated in effective hedging relationships with the contingent hedged item as illustrated in the example below.

Example 2.1.8

Hedging with deal contingent forwards

An entity believes it will enter into a business combination at a future date where the consideration for the acquiree is specified in a foreign currency. The prospective acquirer is awaiting approval by the acquiree's current shareholders, regulatory agencies, governments, or other parties etc. The prospective acquirer chooses to hedge economically its exposure by entering into a deal contingent foreign currency forward contract, such that if the business combination does not proceed the forward is terminated with no cash settlement between the parties. The value of this derivative contract is driven not only by the foreign currency component but also by the probability of the business combination occurring.

For a forecast transaction to be eligible for hedge accounting it must be highly probable (see **3.4.1**). In this case the business combination is unlikely to be seen as being highly probable and, therefore, it would be inappropriate to designate the deal contingent forward contract as a hedge of the currency risk of the forecast business combination. The existence of a knock-out option adds strength to the argument that the business combination is not highly probable because the knock-out feature would not be needed if it was. IFRS 9 presupposes that if an entity is hedging a transaction that it claims to be highly probable it expects the transaction to occur, while here the entity is economically entering into an additional hedge: the hedge of the non-occurrence of the transaction.

The fair value of the deal contingent forward includes the probability that the business combination will not occur which, when compared to the fair value of a hypothetical derivative, a vanilla forward that assumes the transaction will occur, will be different and hence a source of hedge ineffectiveness (see **5.4.1** for guidance on hypothetical derivatives). This difference may be so significant that even if it was designated in a hedge the entity may not meet the hedge effectiveness requirements.

The ineffectiveness cannot be minimised by designating additionally the risk of non-occurrence of the transaction or excluding the knock-out feature from the deal contingent forward because:

(i) the risk of non-occurrence is considered to be a general business risk and hence is not an eligible hedged risk [IFRS 9:B6.3.1]; and

(ii) with the exceptions set out in IFRS 9:6.2.4, an entity must designate a derivative instrument in its entirety.

2.1.9 'All-in-one' hedges

A derivative instrument within the scope of IFRS 9 that will be settled by physical delivery of an underlying asset at a fixed price can be designated as the hedging instrument in a cash flow hedge of that gross settlement. Without the derivative there would be an exposure to variability in the purchase or sale price. The derivative eliminates this exposure, i.e. it acts as a hedging instrument. This hedge strategy is suitable when the underlying hedged item, when it is recognised, will not subsequently be measured at fair value through profit or loss (see **example 2.1.9A**).

The rationale for allowing hedge accounting for 'all-in-one' hedges is that an entity should not be disadvantaged by not achieving hedge accounting irrespective of whether a transaction is structured as a single instrument or as a combination of two transactions. Consider the following example.

Entity A normally sells products at variable prices. Entity A could concurrently enter into derivative transactions to fix the price of its forecast sales. Derivative instruments would be recognised at fair value with gains or losses recognised in profit or loss, unless hedge accounting is applied. Assuming the sales are highly probable and cash flow hedge accounting is applied, Entity A would recognise the gains and losses on its hedging instruments in other comprehensive income and reclassify them from equity to profit or loss when the sales occur.

Entity A now decides that it is no longer going to sell its products at variable prices and swap them back into fixed prices via derivatives, but instead is going to fix the sales price today directly with the customer. If the fixed price contract with the customer fell within the scope of IFRS 9, it would be recognised at fair value with gains and losses recognised in profit or loss. By applying an all-in-one hedge accounting strategy, Entity A can obtain the same accounting treatment (i.e. recognise gains and losses on the derivative in other comprehensive income until the sale occurs under cash flow hedging), as had been the case in the former scenario where hedge accounting was applied to the derivative and the forecast sale separately.

It is not permissible to designate in an 'all-in-one' cash flow hedge either, the acquisition of an equity investment that will be designated as at FVTOCI, or the sale of an equity investment that is already at FVTOCI. This is because IFRS 9:6.5.2(b) only permits cash flow hedging for hedged items that could impact profit or loss. An investment in an equity instrument designated as at FVTOCI will not impact profit or loss, other than for the recognition of dividends received. Equally it is not permissible to designate in an 'all-in-one' hedge the forecast acquisition of an equity investment that will be measured at FVTPL because there is no systematic basis for reclassifying amounts from equity following acquisition (see **example 2.1.9C**).

Example 2.1.9A

All-in-one hedge of a non-financial item

An entity enters into a fixed price contract to sell a commodity and that contract is accounted for as a derivative under IFRS 9. (This may be because the entity has a practice of settling similar contracts net in cash or taking delivery of the underlying and selling it within a short period after delivery for the purpose of generating a profit from short-term fluctuations in price or dealer's margin.) The entity may designate the fixed price contract as a cash flow hedge of the variability of the consideration to be received on the sale of the asset (a future transaction) even though the fixed price contract is the contract under which the asset will be sold.

Example 2.1.9B

All-in-one hedge of a debt instrument

An entity enters into a forward contract to purchase a debt instrument that will be settled by physical delivery of the debt instrument. The forward contract is a derivative in the scope of IFRS 9 because its term exceeds the regular way delivery period in the marketplace. The entity may designate the forward contract as a cash flow hedge of the variability of the consideration to be paid to acquire the debt instrument (a forecast transaction), even though the derivative is the contract under which the debt instrument will be acquired.

Example 2.1.9C

All-in-one hedge of an equity investment to be measured at FVTPL

Entity P, a US dollar functional currency entity, enters into a forward contract to buy an equity share of Entity X in six months' time at US$10 per share. The current share price of Entity X is US$10. At maturity of the forward contract, the share price is US$15 and, consequently, the forward contract has a positive fair value at maturity of US$5 per share.

Under IFRS 9, the equity share must be measured at fair value with gains and losses recognised in profit or loss unless on initial recognition the entity elects to present gains or losses in other comprehensive income.

Entity P cannot designate the forward contract as an all-in-one hedge of the future acquisition of a share in Entity X in six months' time if the shares are to be classified on initial recognition at FVTPL because there is no systematic basis in which the hedged risk affects profit or loss. To illustrate, consider the accounting entries that would result if cash flow hedging were applied:

(i) at initial recognition of the equity share, a gain of US$5 would be recognised in other comprehensive income that would require reclassification from equity to profit or loss when the hedged risk of the hedged item affects profit or loss; and

(ii) the shares would be recognised at fair value, being US$15 (Dr Shares US$15, Cr Cash US$10, Cr Derivative asset US$5).

If the share price subsequently rose or fell, and thus affected profit or loss, there would be no basis for determining how much of the gain recognised in other comprehensive income should be reclassified to profit or loss.

If the entity had expected to designate the equity instrument as at FVTOCI, the equity instrument would still not have been an eligible hedged item in an all-in-one cash flow hedge because fair value changes of the equity share would not impact profit or loss. A cash flow hedge must result in the hedged risk impacting profit or loss.

If at recognition of the equity investment an entity elects to measure it at FVTOCI, that equity investment would, subsequent to initial recognition, be an eligible hedged item in a fair value hedge in accordance with IFRS 9:6.5.3.

2.1.10 Splitting a derivative to exclude embedded financing

It is not possible to split the embedded financing from a non-optional derivative that has a fair value other than zero at the time of designation and account for it as a separate amortising loan whilst designating the zero fair value derivative as the hedging instrument.

If a non-optional derivative, such as a forward contract or swap, has a fair value other than zero at inception of the hedge, future changes in its fair value are affected by that starting value. The derivative includes an embedded financing element that contributes to its fair value movements and causes them to differ from the changes in fair value of the hedged item when the hedged item does not have an equal and opposite financing element.

IFRS 9 does not prohibit non-zero fair value non-optional derivatives being designated as hedging instruments as long as the hedge relationship meets the hedge effectiveness requirements (see IFRS 9:B6.4.15). In fact, IFRS 9:B6.5.28 allows hedging instruments to be designated part way through their lives and, therefore, it could be quite common for a derivative to have a starting value on designation other than zero.

However, the fact that a derivative is in or out of the money at inception of a hedging relationship will likely cause some hedge ineffectiveness over the term of the hedge. This is particularly the case for cash flow hedges because the 'hypothetical derivative' is deemed to be on-market at the date of designation, which for a non-optional derivative would have a fair value of zero (see **5.4.1**). This ineffectiveness arises because the embedded financing element is economically similar to a fixed rate amortising loan embedded in the derivative and this 'loan' will change in fair value as interest rates move. By the time the derivative matures, the loan will have been fully eliminated along with the derivative.

In assessing hedge effectiveness, an entity should use a method that captures the relevant characteristics of a hedging relationship including potential sources of hedge ineffectiveness. An entity would also need to consider the appropriate hedge ratio at inception of the hedge and on an on-going basis.

2.1.11 Internal derivatives

In a group that has a central treasury function, a group entity or division that wishes to enter into hedging transactions uses their central treasury function rather than using an external group counterparty. The central treasury function then aggregates all its internal positions and enters into external transactions to offset the internal ones on a net basis thereby taking advantage of any natural offsets and hedging the exposures of the group in a cost efficient way.

At a group level, if the central treasury function enters into external derivatives these can be used as hedging instruments of exposures that exist at the group level (including eligible net positions, see **section 4**).

However, in the consolidated financial statements, intragroup derivatives cannot be hedging instruments because these are not external to the reporting entity and they are eliminated on consolidation. These intragroup derivatives may be used in the entity's individual financial statements because, from the individual entity's perspective, such derivatives are with an external third party. [IFRS 9:6.2.3]

Example 2.1.11A

Hedge accounting in the group versus individual financial statements

Entity A has a 100 per cent owned subsidiary, Entity B. The group treasury policy requires that only Entity A enters into derivatives with external parties. If Entity B wishes to enter into a foreign currency forward it notifies Entity A. Entity A enters into a forward with a bank (Forward 1), and then enters into an equal and opposite forward contract with Entity B (Forward 2). Entity B is not party to any contractual arrangement with the bank.

From a consolidated perspective, only the forward contract with the bank, Forward 1, can be a designated hedging instrument. In Entity B's individual financial statements, however, Forward 2 may be designated as a hedging instrument. This would be true even if Entity A had not entered into Forward 1 with the bank.

In Entity A's individual financial statements, there will be two equal and opposite derivatives. These must be presented separately in its statement of financial position. They cannot be offset as they do not meet the offset requirements of IAS 32 (see **chapter B11**).

Entities sometimes enter into netting agreements with a bank such that derivatives held with that bank are settled on a net basis. This does not in itself preclude those instruments from being designated as hedging instruments.

Example 2.1.11B

Hedging an external gross position (1)

Entity A has several subsidiaries. Entity A acts as a central treasury function, so that if any subsidiary wants to lay off risk it must do so with Entity A. For each internal derivative, Entity A enters into an equal and opposite external contract with a bank. Thus, if it has a 3-year receive LIBOR, pay 6 per cent interest rate swap with a subsidiary, it will enter into a 3-year receive 6 per cent, pay LIBOR interest rate swap with a bank, such that all of the terms of the two contracts match. Each internal derivative is hedging a gross exposure.

The external derivatives can be designated as hedging instruments of the underlying gross exposures in the group's consolidated financial statements. This is true even if the external derivatives are settled on a net basis. Provided that the contracts are legally separate and serve a valid business purpose (such as laying off risk exposures on underlying gross positions), they qualify as hedging instruments.

Entities sometimes have external positions that offset each other. This can arise (as in the above example) because there is a policy of hedging every exposure separately (i.e. gross), or because an entity wishes to manage its external portfolio in a certain way.

Example 2.1.11C

Hedging an external gross position (2)

Continuing with **example 2.1.11B**, assume Entity A manages the portfolio of offsetting external derivatives separately from other exposures of the entity and enters into an additional, single derivative to offset the risk of the portfolio.

The individual external derivative contracts in the portfolio can still be designated as hedging instruments of the underlying gross exposures even though a single external derivative is used to offset fully the market exposure created by entering into these external contracts.

The purpose of structuring the external derivative contracts in this manner is consistent with the entity's risk management objectives and strategies. External derivative contracts that are structured separately and serve a valid business purpose qualify as hedging instruments.

2.2 Non-derivative hedging instruments

In addition to derivatives, non-derivative financial instruments can also be eligible hedging instruments. Although non-derivative financial instruments that are not measured at FVTPL can only be designated in a hedge of foreign currency risk.

2.2.1 Hedging foreign currency risk with a non-derivative

For a hedge of foreign currency risk only, the foreign currency risk component of any non-derivative financial asset or financial liability can be an eligible hedging instrument, provided that it is not an equity investment designated at FVTOCI. For hedges of foreign currency risk, the foreign currency risk component of a non-derivative hedging instrument is determined in accordance with IAS 21. [IFRS 9:6.2.2 & IFRS 9:B6.2.3]

Therefore, an entity can designate the foreign currency component of foreign currency denominated loans and deposits as hedging instruments, provided the other conditions for hedge accounting are met. A common example of a non-derivative hedging instrument is a foreign currency denominated loan liability measured at amortised cost where the foreign currency component is designated in a hedge of a net investment in a foreign operation (see **section 6.6.1**).

Example 2.2.1A

Hedging a financial asset with the foreign currency risk component of a non-derivative financial liability measured at amortised cost

Entity J, whose functional currency is Sterling, has issued US$5 million five-year fixed rate debt measured at amortised cost. It also acquired a US$5 million five-year fixed rate bond which is measured at fair value through profit or loss.

Entity J cannot designate its US dollar liability as a hedging instrument in a fair value hedge of the entire fair value exposure of its US dollar bond asset because a non-derivative not measured at fair value through profit or loss may only be used as a hedging instrument of foreign currency risk (where only the foreign currency risk component of that instrument is designated as the hedging instrument).

Entity J could consider the use of the fair value option (see **chapter B3**) at initial recognition of the liability. This designation could result in substantial offset of gains and losses in profit or loss.

If Entity J does not apply the fair value option it could designate the foreign currency component of the US$ liability as a hedge of the foreign currency component of the bond, but hedge accounting will not provide any advantage over not applying hedge accounting at all; the foreign currency gains and losses on both the monetary asset and monetary liability are already recognised in profit or loss in the period, in accordance with IAS 21 (i.e. there is already a natural offset of foreign currency risk in profit or loss).

It should be noted that if the hedged item was a foreign currency equity investment designated as at FVTOCI, the foreign exchange gains and losses on the equity investment will be included within the overall fair value changes recognised in other comprehensive income. Absent hedge accounting, the foreign exchange gains and losses from translating the monetary financial liability would be recognised in profit or loss under IAS 21. The foreign currency component of the equity investment is an eligible hedged risk in a fair value hedge as it affects other comprehensive income. If designated in a hedging relationship, the foreign exchange gains and losses from translating the monetary liability would be presented in other comprehensive income together with any hedge ineffectiveness (see **6.4.3**).

Example 2.2.1B

Hedging a firm commitment with a non-derivative

Entity X's functional currency is the Euro. It has issued a US$5 million fixed rate bond with semi-annual interest payments that matures in two years. The bond liability is measured at amortised cost. Entity X has also entered into a US$5 million fixed price sale commitment (a firm commitment) of a non-financial item that matures in two years and is not accounted for as a derivative because it meets the exemption as a contract that is entered into and continues to be held for the purpose of the delivery of a non-financial item in accordance with the entity's expected sale requirements (i.e. it meets the own use exception, see **chapter B1**).

Entity X cannot designate its US dollar liability as a hedging instrument in a fair value hedge of the entire fair value exposure of its fixed price sale commitment because a non-derivative liability, not accounted at fair value through profit or loss, can only be designated in a hedge of a foreign currency risk. Therefore, as an alternative, Entity X can designate its US dollar liability in a fair value or a cash flow hedge of the foreign currency risk of its fixed price sale commitment.

Note that Entity X cannot designate the fixed price sale commitment as the hedging instrument instead of the hedged item because it is not measured at FVTPL and is not a financial instrument in the scope of IFRS 9.

If the foreign currency component of the sale commitment was separated as an embedded derivative that was not considered to be closely related to the sale contract, the embedded derivative could be designated as a hedging instrument of the foreign currency risk of the fixed rate debt instrument. However, applying hedge accounting would not provide the entity with any presentation benefit as, in the absence of hedge accounting, both the foreign currency risk on the debt and the embedded derivative hedging instrument would be recognised in profit or loss.

2.2.2 *Hedging risks other than foreign currency risk with a non-derivative*

A non-derivative financial asset or financial liability measured at FVTPL may be designated as a hedging instrument for risks other than only foreign currency risk. To qualify, a non-derivative financial liability must have all of its change in fair value reflected in profit or loss, including the change in fair value due to changes in credit risk, hence a liability designated at FVTPL, for which changes in fair value attributable to credit risk is presented in other comprehensive income, is not an eligible hedging instrument. [IFRS 9:6.2.2]

The classification and measurement model in IFRS 9 requires FVTPL measurement for:

- non-derivative financial assets that do not qualify for amortised cost or FVTOCI measurement (see **chapter B2**);
- non-derivative financial liabilities held for trading; and
- non-derivative financial assets designated as at FVTPL
- non-derivative financial liabilities designated as at FVTPL where recognising changes in fair value due to credit risk in other comprehensive income would create or enlarge an accounting mismatch in profit or loss.

Although all of these instruments are classified as at FVTPL, not all of them would necessarily be eligible hedging instruments. Instruments designated at FVTPL under the fair value option should be assessed to ensure that the hedge designation would not contradict the original objective for invoking the fair value option (i.e. it would not recreate the accounting mismatch the fair value option was used to eliminate). For example, an instrument designated under the fair value option to reduce a measurement mismatch would not be an appropriate hedging instrument in a cash flow hedge if the other item giving rise to the original mismatch (on which the election was based) still exists, because designating it would recreate a mismatch. However, hedge accounting could be appropriate for an instrument designated at FVTPL when the item underlying the original fair value option election is subsequently sold or terminated but the instrument continues to be recognised at FVTPL (because of the irrevocability of the initial fair value election). Applying hedge accounting in these circumstances might mitigate the accounting mismatch without recreating the original one. [IFRS 9:BC6.136 - 139]

2.2.3 *Designation of portions and proportions of a non-derivative*

Consistent with the requirements for derivative hedging instruments, a proportion of an entire non-derivative hedging instrument (e.g. 50 per cent) may be designated as the hedging instrument in a hedge relationship. [IFRS 9:6.2.4(c)]

This applies to all non-derivative hedging instruments, regardless of whether the hedging instrument is a non-derivative measured at FVTPL or the foreign currency component of a non-derivative measured at amortised cost or FVTOCI.

For hedges other than hedges of foreign currency risk, when an entity designates a non-derivative financial asset or a non-derivative financial liability measured at fair value through profit or loss as a hedging instrument, it may only designate the non-derivative financial instrument in its entirety or a proportion of it. [IFRS 9:B6.2.5]

This statement could imply that for hedges of foreign currency risk, when an entity designates a non-derivative measured at FVTPL as a hedging instrument, there is additional flexibility in designating a component other than a fully proportionate amount of the instrument, for example, designating only specified cash flows. However, in light of the specific requirements in IFRS 9:6.2.4(c) it does not appear possible to designate a non-derivative hedging instrument other than either the entire instrument (or entire foreign currency component) or a proportion of the entire instrument (or proportion of the foreign currency component). Instead, this language is likely simply referring to the ability of an entity to designate only the foreign currency risk component of a non-derivative financial instrument as the hedging instrument in a hedge of foreign currency risk.

A hedging relationship may not be designated for a part of its change in fair value resulting from only a portion of the time period that the hedging instrument is outstanding. [IFRS 9:6.2.4(c)]

For example, the cash flows during the first three years of a 10-year borrowing denominated in a foreign currency cannot qualify as a hedging instrument in a cash flow hedge of the first three years of revenue in the same foreign currency. This compares with partial-term hedging where it is permitted to designate only a portion of the time period to maturity of a hedged item (see **3.11.3**).

2.3 Designating combinations of derivatives and/or non-derivatives

An entity may view in combination, and jointly designate as the hedging instrument, any combination of the following (including those circumstances in which the risk or risks arising from some hedging instruments offset those arising from others):

[IFRS 9:6.2.5]

(a) derivatives or a proportion of them; and

(b) non-derivatives or a proportion of them.

However, restrictions apply to combinations of instruments that are, in effect, a net written option (see **2.1.2**).

Common situations where two or more offsetting derivatives are designated in combination as a hedging instrument are:

- when an entity issues fixed rate debt, swaps the entirety of the debt instrument to floating, and then re-fixes some of the instrument's cash flows;
- when an entity uses a combination of long and short foreign currency forward contracts to hedge its net investments in a foreign operation (e.g. when it manages foreign currency risk on the net assets of the foreign operation where the value of those net assets changes on a frequent basis); and
- when an entity uses a combination of a basis swap and a floating to fixed interest rate swap if there is not enough liquidity directly to enter into a floating to fixed interest rate swap that has a floating leg that matches the specific risk of the hedged item.

Example 2.3A

Hedging with multiple derivatives (1)

Entity A has a forecast purchase of copper. To hedge the price risk associated with the forecast purchase, it enters into a futures contract to buy copper. However, the grade of copper in the futures contract is lower than that required by Entity A. It therefore also enters into a basis swap which swaps between the different grades of copper between the futures contracts and the forecast purchase. Subject to the other hedge accounting criteria being satisfied, Entity A may jointly designate the futures and the basis swap as hedging its forecast purchase of copper.

When a combination of derivative or non-derivative instruments is used as a hedging instrument, the hedge effectiveness of this relationship is based on the combination as a whole.

Example 2.3B

Hedging with multiple derivatives (2)

Entity X issues fixed rate 10-year debt. Entity X has a strategy of only fixing the interest rate for 12 months so when the debt is issued Entity X enters into a receive-fixed, pay-floating interest rate swap whose terms exactly match those of the debt and a 1-year receive-floating, pay-fixed interest rate swap.

Subject to the other hedge accounting criteria being satisfied, Entity X may designate both swaps as a partial term fair value hedge of interest rate risk for years 2 to 10 (even though the second swap partially offsets the effects of the first swap). Partial term hedging is discussed further in **3.11.3**.

This approach is likely to give rise to hedge ineffectiveness as the fixed rate received on the 10-year swap is unlikely to offset the fixed rate paid on the 1-year swap.

As an alternative, the entity may consider designating the first derivative in a fair value hedge for the full 10-year term and then designating the aggregated exposure consisting of the 10-year fixed rate debt and 10-year receive-fixed, pay-floating interest rate swap as the hedged item in a cash flow hedge (i.e. the 10-year debt and 10-year swap are together viewed as 10-year floating rate debt for risk management purposes). Aggregated exposures are discussed in more detail in **3.10**.

Example 2.3C

Hedging with multiple derivatives (3)

Entity C is a Euro functional currency entity. Entity C issues Mexican Peso floating rate debt. Entity C has a policy of swapping all floating rate debt into fixed and into its functional currency. Because of limited liquidity for Mexican Peso/Euro swaps, Entity C does not enter into a Receive Mexican Peso floating, Pay Euro fixed cross-currency interest rate swap. Instead, Entity C enters into a Receive Mexican Peso floating, Pay US dollar floating cross-currency swap, and a Receive US dollar floating, Pay Euro fixed cross-currency interest rate swap, and designates these two swaps in combination as a cash flow hedge of both interest rates and foreign currency of its Mexican Peso floating debt.

Example 2.3D

Hedging with derivatives and non-derivatives (1)

Entity A, a UK entity, has a US subsidiary, Entity Z. Entity A hedges its net investment in Entity Z in its consolidated financial statements using forward foreign currency contracts and loans. It manages the net asset position quarterly and, as the net asset position changes, it enters into further forward contracts to sell US$ and buy £ that cover the increased exposure (if the US$ net asset position increases), or if the exposure decreases (if the US$ net asset position falls) the entity enters into forward contracts to sell £ and buy US$. In the latter case, any sold US$ forward contracts will partially offset the purchased US$ forward contracts.

The loans and forward contracts may be viewed in combination and jointly designated as a hedge of the spot foreign currency risk of the net investment in Entity Z, even though some of the forward contract positions may offset each other.

Example 2.3E

Hedging with derivatives and non-derivatives (2)

Entity H has a 25-year fixed rate financial liability measured at amortised cost. Entity H has also invested in a 20-year bond measured at FVTPL. Entity H is unable to find suitable bonds of a longer duration to match the last 5 years of the liability's term profile. Its risk management strategy is to buy a forward starting swap that swaps fixed payments into the floating benchmark rate starting in 20 years' time. The entity may jointly designate the swap and the bond in a fair value hedge of interest rate risk of the 25-year financial liability.

Alternatively, Entity H could have elected to measure the financial liability at FVTPL to eliminate an accounting mismatch arising from the financial assets being measured at FVTPL. However, that election would have had to have been made on initial recognition of the financial liability and would have been irrevocable.

2.4 Hedging more than one risk with a single hedging instrument

A hedging instrument is often designated as hedging one risk only. However, a hedging instrument can be designated as hedging more than one risk provided that there is specific designation of the hedging instrument and the different risk positions designated as hedged items. Furthermore, the hedged items can be in different hedging relationships. [IFRS 9:B6.2.6]

If a single hedging instrument is hedging more than one risk, and each risk is being hedged using a different form of hedge accounting (e.g. one as a fair value hedge and one as a cash flow hedge), the entity will need to isolate changes in the derivative's fair value relating to each type of hedge and separate disclosures will be needed for each type of hedge in accordance with IFRS 7:24A (see **chapter B11**).

2.4.1 Hedging more than one risk in a single hedged item

A single hedged item is often subject to more than one risk and these risks can be hedged with a single instrument or multiple hedging instruments. A common example is designating a single derivative to hedge both foreign currency and interest rate risks of a single hedged item. For example, cross-currency interest rate swaps are commonly used to swap foreign currency floating rate debt into functional currency fixed rate debt, or to swap foreign currency fixed rate debt into functional currency floating rate debt.

Example 2.4.1

Hedging both interest rate and foreign currency risk

Entity A, a Sterling functional currency entity, issues floating US dollar debt. To hedge its exposure to foreign currency exchange rates and to interest rate risk,

> it enters into a cross-currency interest rate swap. The terms of the swap match those of the debt. Under the swap, Entity A receives floating US dollars and pays fixed Sterling. IFRS 9 allows the swap to be designated as a cash flow hedge of both US dollar interest rate risk and US$:£ foreign currency risk in a single hedge relationship.
>
> Similarly, Entity A could have issued fixed US dollar debt, and used a cross-currency interest rate swap to convert the position into floating Sterling debt. IFRS 9 would permit the entity to designate the swap as a fair value hedge of both the interest rate and foreign currency risk designated as a single hedge relationship. The entity incorporates two risks in a single fair value hedge and, therefore, does not need to separate notionally the derivative instrument across multiple hedge relationships.

2.4.2 Hedging more than one risk in multiple hedged items

Single or multiple hedging instruments may be designated to hedge multiple hedged items that have different hedged risks. A common example is designating a hedge of both foreign currency risk and interest rate risk where those risks reside in more than one hedged item. For example, consider an example of a Japanese Yen functional currency entity that has a 5-year floating rate US$ liability and a 10-year fixed rate £-denominated note receivable and chooses to hedge both items with a single foreign currency forward contract where it will receive US$ and pay £ in five years. Because the principal amounts of the asset and liability when converted into Japanese Yen are the same, the entity designates the dual foreign currency forward contract as hedging foreign currency risk for both items. Even though foreign currency risk is defined by reference to the entity's functional currency, and the foreign currency forward contract does not have a cash flow in the functional currency (i.e. Japanese Yen), the foreign currency forward contract may still be designated as hedging *both* foreign currencies as the exposure to both currencies has been eliminated by the forward. Put another way, if the entity entered into a receive US$ pay Japanese Yen forward, and a receive Japanese Yen pay £ forward, each forward could have been designated separately as hedging the foreign currency risk of the liability and asset respectively, and the fair value of the two Japanese Yen legs would effectively offset. In a single forward to receive US$ pay £, the receive Japanese Yen leg and the pay Japanese Yen leg do not exist but this does not create hedge ineffectiveness because the fair value of both legs offsets to zero. However, in assessing and measuring hedge effectiveness with a single forward contract, the entity will need to impute the two notional Japanese Yen legs into the hedge designation in order to determine the hedge effectiveness of the two hedges of foreign currency risk. Imputing the two notional cash flows for assessing hedge effectiveness is permitted because doing so does not create any additional cash flows, as both notional cash flows offset each other perfectly.

The example noted above is taken from the implementation guidance in IAS 39 (IAS 39:IG.F.1.13). In July 2007, the IFRIC (now the IFRS Interpretations Committee) issued a rejection notice on hedging multiple risks with a single derivative financial instrument under IAS 39. IFRIC's views on this matter under IAS 39 are equally relevant under IFRS 9. The IFRIC recognised that IAS 39's interpretative guidance does result in an entity needing to impute a notional leg as a means of splitting the fair value of the derivative into multiple components in order to assess hedge effectiveness. The IFRIC considered that this was acceptable in assessing hedge effectiveness because this conclusion did not conflict with IAS 39:IG.C.1 (equivalent to IFRS 9:IG.C.1), which prohibits an entity from recognising embedded derivatives that result in the *recognition* [emphasis added in the July 2007 *IFRIC Update*] of cash flows that do not contractually exist. The IFRIC's rejection notice highlights that, should any entity need to split notionally a derivative for assessing hedge effectiveness when that derivative is hedging multiple risks, then the process of splitting should not result in any new cash flows or any new risks arising which were not evident in the contractual terms of the derivative.

Example 2.4.2A

Hedging a net investment in a foreign operation and interest rate risk of issued debt

Parent P, a € functional currency entity, has issued a €100 million denominated fixed rate debt. Parent P consolidates Subsidiary S, a US dollar functional currency foreign operation with opening net assets of US$300 million. Parent P's objective is to hedge:

(i) the foreign currency risk of part of its foreign operation (being US$150 million of net assets); and

(ii) the fair value due to changes in interest rates on its issued debt (being interest rate risk on €100 million).

In order to minimise transaction costs, Parent P enters into a single derivative to Receive € fixed on €100 million, Pay 3m US LIBOR on US$150 million with the fair value of the cross-currency interest rate swap equal to zero at the transaction date (i.e. the derivative is on-market).

Parent P designates in the consolidated financial statements the cross-currency interest rate swap, in its entirety, as a hedge of the foreign currency risk of Subsidiary S's net assets equal to US$150 million and the fair value interest rate risk on €100 million of its €-denominated debt.

In order to measure hedge effectiveness for the net investment hedge and the fair value hedge, Parent P notionally splits the derivative into the following:

(i) Receive fixed €100m, Pay 3m-EURIBOR on €100m (notional derivative 1); and

(ii) Receive 3m-EURIBOR on €100m, Pay 3m US LIBOR on US$150m (notional derivative 2).

Parent P fair values the two notional derivatives at inception and both have a fair value of zero so the sum of the fair values equals the fair value of the actual contractual derivative. Each period, the notional derivatives are fair valued in order to measure hedge effectiveness and to ensure that the sum of these fair values equals the fair value of the actual contractual derivative entered into.

Example 2.4.2B

Hedging cash flow variability of both an asset and liability

Entity B, a Sterling functional currency entity, has issued 3m LIBOR £200 million denominated debt and has an investment in an inflation-linked bond that receives 3% + UK CPI on a notional of £200 million. The asset and liability have the same five year maturity and both are measured at amortised cost.

Entity B's objective is to hedge the cash flow variability on both its asset and its liability. In order to minimise transaction costs, the entity enters into 5-year Receive 3m-LIBOR £200 million, Pay 3% + UK CPI £200 million basis swap and designates it as a hedge of the cash flow variability of both its asset and its liability.

In order to measure hedge effectiveness, Entity B notionally splits the derivative into the following:

(i) 5-year Receive 3m LIBOR £200 million, Pay 6% £200 million (notional derivative 1); and

(ii) Receive 6% £200 million, Pay 3% + UK CPI £200 million (notional derivative 2).

Entity B fair values the two notional derivatives at inception and both have a fair value of zero so the sum of the fair values equals the fair value of the actual contractual derivative. Each period, the notional derivatives are fair valued in order to measure hedge effectiveness and to ensure that the sum of these fair values equals the fair value of the actual contractual derivative entered into.

Example 2.4.2C

Hedging cash flow variability of both a foreign currency sale and purchase

Entity C, a Euro functional currency entity, has forecast sales in US dollars and forecast purchases in Japanese Yen. Entity C enters into a series of foreign currency forward contracts under which it receives a fixed amount of Japanese Yen and pays a fixed amount of US dollars every month. The fair value of each forward contract is zero at inception as the terms are on-market at that date. Entity C's objective is to hedge the variability in functional currency cash flows of its US dollar sales and Japanese Yen purchases.

In order to measure hedge effectiveness, Entity C notionally splits the derivative into the following:

(i) receive fixed amount of Japanese Yen, pay fixed amount of Euro (notional derivative 1); and

(ii) receive fixed amount of Euro, pay a fixed amount of US dollars (notional derivative 2).

Entity C fair values the two notional derivatives at inception and both have a fair value of zero so the sum of the fair values equals the fair value of the actual contractual derivative. Each period the notional derivatives are fair valued in order to measure hedge effectiveness and to ensure that the sum of these fair values equals the fair value of the actual contractual derivative entered into.

Assuming the hedges meets the hedge effectiveness requirements, the effective gains/losses on the series of forward contracts will initially be recognised in other comprehensive income and will be recognised in profit or loss when the sales and purchases affect profit or loss. It should be noted that the timing of the impact to profit or loss of the two hedged items may differ. This is because purchases would normally result in recognition of inventory (which must be basis-adjusted when recognised, see **section 6.5.2**) and the sale of the inventory acquired in Japanese Yen could occur in a period after the sales in US dollars. The entity must allocate the fair value gains/losses accumulated in equity to the two individual hedge relationships so it can determine the appropriate amount to remove from equity to basis-adjust the acquired inventory and the amounts to be reclassified to profit or loss when the US dollar sale affects profit or loss.

Judgement is required in determining what is an appropriate split when allocating the fair value of derivatives to multiple hedged items for assessing whether the hedge effectiveness requirements are met and also for measuring hedge ineffectiveness. It would not be appropriate to create multiple notional derivatives which introduce notional legs over risks that did not exist in the contractual derivative or are not specific to the entity entering into the transaction, for example the entity's functional currency. Taking **example 2.4.2A**, the notional legs introduced are in the functional currency of the entity, the Euro, which is a reference point that is specific to the entity; the frequency of reset of EURIBOR on the notional leg is equal to the frequency of reset on the US$-LIBOR leg of the actual derivative. Taking **example 2.4.2B**, the notional legs introduced are the Sterling fixed rate for a 5-year interest rate swap priced off the Sterling 5-year LIBOR curve. In both examples, it would be unacceptable to impute notional legs which, although they could offset each other, would introduce an unrelated risk (say equity prices or an unrelated currency).

If a single hedging instrument is designated as a hedge of more than one risk, the hedge accounting criteria must be satisfied in respect of all the designated hedged risks. If the criteria are not met in respect of one of the risks being hedged, no hedge accounting treatment is allowed for the period. If one designation fails to meet the hedge effectiveness requirements or no longer exists, continuing hedge accounting would result in split accounting for the hedging instrument, treating one part as a hedge and the other as a trading instrument, which is not permitted.

3 Hedged items

IFRS 9 limits the types of exposures that are eligible for hedge accounting. As a result, not all exposures that are economically hedged for risk management purposes may be eligible hedged items for hedge accounting. Therefore, before designating an exposure as a hedged item in a hedging relationship, an entity should assess the exposure for eligibility and in some cases may need to modify how it is defined in order for it to be an eligible hedged item.

A hedged item can be a single item, a group of items (see **section 4**) or a component of a single or group of items where the item is:

[IFRS 9:6.3.1]

- a recognised asset or liability (e.g. a fixed rate loan);
- an unrecognised firm commitment (e.g. a contract to buy oil that is for 'own use');
- a forecast transaction (e.g. highly probable forecast sales in a foreign currency); or
- a net investment in a foreign operation (e.g. foreign net assets of a subsidiary consolidated into group accounts).

In all cases the hedged item must be reliably measurable and where the hedged item is a forecast transaction, that transaction must also be highly probable (see **3.4.1**). [IFRS 9:6.3.2 - 3]

The items mentioned above can be designated in their entirety (i.e. all changes in cash flows or fair value), however, in practice it is more common to hedge only components of such items (i.e. less than the entire fair value change or cash flow variability of an item). Under IFRS 9, only the following components (including combinations) are eligible hedged items:

[IFRS 9:6.3.7]

(a) only changes in the cash flows or fair value of an item attributable to a specific risk or risks (i.e. risk component), provided that, based on an assessment within the context of the particular market structure, the risk component is separately identifiable and reliably measurable (see **section 3.11**). Risk components include a designation of only changes in the cash flows or the fair value of a hedged item above or below a specified price or other variable (i.e. a one-sided risk).

(b) one or more selected contractual cash flows.

(c) components of a nominal amount, i.e. a specified part of the amount of an item (see **3.16**).

Although derivatives are usually designated as the hedging instrument (see **section 2**), under IFRS 9 a hedged item may include a derivative as part of an 'aggregated exposure'. [IFRS 9:6.3.4] The reasons why an entity may wish to designate a derivative as part of the hedged item and the necessary accounting considerations for such a hedge are covered in more detail in **3.10**.

With the exception of certain intragroup transactions that can be hedged in the consolidated financial statements (see **section 3.1**), only assets, liabilities, firm commitments or highly probable forecast transactions with a party external to the reporting entity can be designated as hedged items. It follows that hedge accounting can be applied to transactions between entities in the same group in the individual or separate financial statements of those entities. [IFRS 9:6.3.5]

3.1 Intragroup items

As a general rule only assets, liabilities, firm commitments or highly probable forecast transactions with a party external to the reporting entity can be designated as hedged items. Hence, hedge accounting is generally not permitted for intra-group transactions in the consolidated financial statements of the group because such transactions generally eliminate on consolidation. However, there are three exceptions to this general rule:

[IFRS 9:6.3.5 - 6]

- transactions between entities in the same group in the consolidated financial statements of an investment entity, as defined in IFRS 10 *Consolidated Financial Statements*, where transactions between an investment entity and its subsidiaries measured at fair value through profit or loss will not be eliminated in the consolidated financial statements.
- when the foreign currency exposure of an intragroup monetary item does not fully eliminate on consolidation under IAS 21 (see **3.1.1**).
- when the foreign currency risk of a highly probable forecast intragroup transaction will affect consolidated profit or loss (see **3.1.2**).

Within a group, an entity exposed to a hedged risk is not required to be party to the hedging instrument if hedge accounting is applied at a group level. An entity may decide not to apply hedge accounting in its individual financial statements, but hedge accounting can be applied in the consolidated financial statements that include that entity. For example, it is common in many groups that operating subsidiaries do not enter into derivative transactions; instead the corporate treasury function does so on their behalf. Unless there are internal derivative transactions between the operating subsidiary and corporate treasury, the subsidiary would not be able to apply hedge accounting in its individual financial statements because it has not entered into any hedging instruments. However, hedge accounting may be applied in the consolidated financial statements if the external hedging instrument entered into by the corporate treasury function is an effective instrument at the group level.

3.1.1 Intragroup monetary items and interest

The foreign currency risk of an intragroup monetary item (e.g. a payable/receivable between two subsidiaries) may qualify as a hedged item in the consolidated financial statements if it results in an exposure to foreign exchange rate gains or losses that are not fully eliminated on consolidation in accordance with IAS 21 *The Effects of Changes in Foreign Exchange Rates*. In accordance with IAS 21, foreign exchange rate gains and losses on intragroup monetary items are not fully eliminated on consolidation when the intragroup monetary item is transacted between two group entities that have different functional currencies. [IFRS 9:6.3.6]

Example 3.1.1

Foreign currency risk on intragroup loans

A Sterling functional currency parent entity makes a five-year US dollar denominated fixed rate interest-bearing loan to its US dollar functional currency subsidiary. The loan does not form part of the parent's investment in the US subsidiary. In the parent's separate financial statements, this loan will need to be remeasured at the end of each reporting period in accordance with IAS 21, and will give rise to an exchange gain or loss. However, there will be no corresponding foreign currency gain or loss in the subsidiary's financial statements because the loan is denominated in its functional currency.

In the consolidated financial statements, an exchange gain or loss on the intragroup balance will not be eliminated, but will be reported in profit or loss as an exchange gain or loss on a monetary item.

The parent hedges the foreign currency risk of both interest and principal by entering into a cross-currency swap with a counterparty outside of the group, under which the parent receives Sterling fixed and pays US dollar fixed on the interest payment dates of the intragroup loan with a gross exchange of US dollar for Sterling at inception and Sterling for US dollar in five years' time equivalent to the US dollar notional amount of the loan.

The loan may be designated as a hedged item in both the parent's separate financial statements and in the consolidated financial statements. In the parent's separate financial statements, the cross-currency swap is expected to meet the hedge effectiveness requirements as a cash flow hedge of the US dollar foreign currency risk arising on the interest and principal of the loan.

However, in the consolidated financial statements, the cross-currency swap will be less effective because the impact on profit or loss in the parent's separate financial statements and the consolidated financial statements differs and, therefore, the hedged risk differs. In the parent's separate financial statements, the impact on profit or loss will be the foreign currency risk associated with both interest and principal cash flows denominated in a foreign currency. In the consolidated financial statements, the hedged risk differs because part of the risk that resides in the parent's separate financial statements does not survive consolidation. The parent's interest income (measured at spot or an average rate) in the parent's separate financial statements and the subsidiary's interest expense (measured at spot or an average rate) in the subsidiary's financial statements should eliminate in the consolidated financial statements. Because the hedged risk differs, the hypothetical derivative will differ, and its fair value will differ from the actual derivative entered into by the parent (for detail on the hypothetical derivative method see **5.4.1**). The difference in the actual and hypothetical derivative will need to be determined in order to assess whether the hedge effectiveness requirements are met.

3.1.2 Foreign currency risk of a highly probable forecast intragroup transaction

The foreign currency risk of a highly probable forecast intragroup transaction may qualify as a hedged item in consolidated financial statements provided that the transaction is denominated in a currency other than the functional currency of the entity entering into that transaction and the foreign currency risk will affect consolidated profit or loss. [IFRS 9:6.3.6]

The entity can be a parent, subsidiary, associate, joint arrangement or branch. [IFRS 9:B6.3.5]

In many cases, a forecast intragroup transaction does not affect consolidated profit or loss and hence is not eligible as a hedged item. This is usually the case for royalty payments, interest payments or management charges between members of the same group, unless there is a related external transaction. By contrast, in the case of forecast sales or purchases of inventories between members of the same group when there is an onward sale of the inventories to a party external to the group, there will be an effect on consolidated profit or loss (see **example 3.1.2B**). Similarly, a forecast intragroup sale of plant and equipment from the group entity that manufactured it to a group entity that will use the plant and equipment in its operation may affect consolidated profit or loss. This could occur, for example, because the plant and equipment will be depreciated by the purchasing entity and the amount initially recognised for the plant and equipment may change if the forecast intragroup transaction is denominated in a currency other than the functional currency of the purchasing entity (see **example 3.1.2A**). [IFRS 9:B6.3.5]

If a hedge of a forecast intragroup transaction qualifies for hedge accounting, any gain or loss is recognised in, and taken out of, other comprehensive income in accordance with the cash flow hedge accounting mechanics discussed in **section 6.5**. The relevant period or periods during which the foreign currency risk of the hedged transaction affects profit or loss is when it affects consolidated profit or loss. [IFRS 9:B6.3.6]

Example 3.1.2A

Hedging foreign currency risk of intragroup transactions (1)

Entity A (a Sterling functional currency entity) is expecting, with a high degree of probability, to purchase a machine from Entity B (a Euro functional currency entity) for €10m in 1 years' time. Entity A and Entity B are part of the same group and Entity A will use the machine in its production process to make goods for external sale. The cost of the machine will be capitalised and depreciated over its useful economic life in both the individual financial statements of Entity A and the consolidated financial statements (including both Entity A and Entity B). Entity A enters into a buy Euro sell Sterling forward contract with a third party to hedge the expected foreign currency risk on the forecast purchase.

The forecast intragroup purchase will qualify as a hedged item in the consolidated financial statements in a cash flow hedge of the currency risk because:

- the purchase is highly probable;
- the purchase is denominated in a currency (Euro) other than Entity A's functional currency (Sterling); and
- the depreciation of the machine will result in the foreign currency risk of the forecast transaction affecting consolidated profit or loss. The Euro/Sterling exchange rate at the date of purchase will affect the amount initially recognised in respect of the machinery, and thus will affect the associated depreciation expense.

Example 3.1.2B

Hedging foreign currency risk of intragroup transactions (2)

In all scenarios below, the group has two subsidiaries (Entity C – Euro (€) functional currency and Entity D – US dollar (US$) functional currency).

Scenario 1

Entity C incurs external production costs in € towards goods it manufactures and sells in € to a fellow subsidiary, Entity D. This creates a foreign currency risk in Entity D to the €/US$ exchange rate with regard to its forecast purchase from Entity C (purchase of goods in €). Entity D also intends to sell the goods externally outside of the group in US$. In order to hedge the exposure associated with the forecast purchase from Entity C, Entity D enters into a forward contract with a third party (buy €/ sell US$). The group wishes to designate the forward contract as hedging the foreign currency risk of the forecast intragroup purchase by Entity D from Entity C in a cash flow hedging relationship in the consolidated financial statements.

Scenario 2

The facts are as in Scenario 1 except that the sale of goods from Entity C to Entity D is denominated in US$ and, therefore, there is foreign currency risk for Entity C on the sale of goods to Entity D. Entity C enters into a forward contract with a third party to mitigate its foreign currency risk of the forecast sale to Entity D in US$ (buy €/ sell US$). The group wishes to designate the forward contract as hedging the foreign currency risk of the forecast intragroup sale by Entity C to Entity D in a cash flow hedging relationship in the consolidated financial statements.

Scenario 3

The facts are as in Scenario 1 except that the sale of goods from Entity C to Entity D is denominated in Sterling and, therefore, there is foreign currency risk for Entity C on the sale of goods to Entity D and there is also foreign currency risk for Entity D on the purchase of goods from Entity C. Entity C enters into a buy €/ sell £ forward contract with a third party to mitigate its foreign currency risk of the forecast sale to Entity D, and Entity D enters into a buy £/sell US$ forward contract with a third party to mitigate its foreign currency risk of the forecast purchase from Entity C.

In both Scenarios 1 and 2, the internal transaction being designated is denominated in a currency other than the functional currency of the entity entering into it: in Scenario 1, the forecast intragroup purchase by Entity D (functional currency of US$) is denominated in €; in Scenario 2, the forecast intragroup sale by Entity C (functional currency of €) is denominated in US$. Also, in both cases, the onward sale of the goods by Entity D will affect consolidated profit or loss. Therefore, in both cases, the forecast intragroup transaction could be designated as the hedged item in a cash flow hedge of foreign currency risk in the consolidated financial statements, assuming all other conditions of hedge accounting are met.

In Scenario 3, in the individual financial statements of both entities, cash flow hedge accounting can be applied. With respect to the consolidated financial statements, there is the possibility of applying hedge accounting for intragroup forecast transactions for situations where one of the parties to the internal transaction passes its foreign currency risk to the other, as in Scenarios 1 and 2 above. This is the currency risk that exists and cannot be avoided because the two parties have different functional currencies. In Scenario 3, the parties to the internal transaction are taking on additional foreign currency risk and, therefore, hedge accounting cannot be applied. Furthermore, although the sum of the two derivatives result in a net buy €/ sell US$ position, these two derivatives cannot be designated in combination in the consolidated financial statements as a hedge of the external € purchases or a hedge of the external US$ sales, because Entity C does not have a US$ exposure, and Entity D does not have a € exposure.

Example 3.1.2C

Hedging foreign currency risk of intragroup transactions (3)

Entity E (Sterling functional currency entity) has a wholly-owned subsidiary, Entity F (Yen functional currency entity). Entity F generates substantial profits and regularly pays Yen dividends on its ordinary shares to Entity E. In order to hedge the Yen exposure associated with the dividend income, Entity E enters into a series of sell Yen buy Sterling forward contracts. Entity E also expects to pay dividends on its own ordinary shares (classified as equity in accordance with IAS 32 *Financial Instruments: Presentation*) using the proceeds from dividends received from its shareholding in Entity F.

The forecast intragroup transaction (the dividend income in the hands of Entity E) will not qualify as a hedged item in the consolidated financial statements of the group in a cash flow hedge of the currency risk because the foreign currency risk will not affect consolidated profit or loss. Even though Entity E may expect to make an onward declaration and payment of dividends on its own shares, IAS 32 requires that distributions to holders of an equity instrument should be recognised directly in equity and, therefore, this will not give rise to a gain or loss in consolidated profit or loss.

As an alternative, Entity E could designate the forward contracts in a net investment hedge of the net assets of Entity F in the consolidated financial statements. This alternative hedge designation reflects the fact that the dividend to be received will come from the net assets of Entity F and will be subject to foreign currency risk which is eligible for net investment hedging (see **section 6.6**).

Example 3.1.2D

Hedging foreign currency risk of intragroup transactions (4)

Entity A is a Euro functional currency entity that has a fellow subsidiary Entity B, a US dollar (US$) functional currency entity. Entity A borrows a specified amount of Euro from a party external to the group at fixed interest rates. Entity A lends the proceeds of the borrowing to Entity B on the same terms as the external borrowing. Because Entity B has borrowed in Euro at fixed rates and has a US$ functional currency, it enters into a receive Euro fixed pay US$ fixed cross-currency swap with a party external to the group to hedge the foreign currency risk of the interest and principal payments on its borrowing from Entity A.

In its separate financial statements, Entity B can designate the foreign currency risk arising from the Euro denominated interest payments and principal of its borrowing from Entity A in a hedging relationship with the hedging instrument being the external cross-currency swap.

In the consolidated financial statements, the cross-currency swap cannot be designated as a hedge of the foreign currency risk of the forecast intragroup interest payments by Entity B because the interest payments in Entity B are eliminated against the interest receipts in Entity A. Entity B's interest payments do not affect consolidated profit or loss and, therefore, cannot be designated as a hedged item in the consolidated financial statements.

The foreign currency exposure generated on the intragroup loan will not be fully eliminated on consolidation in accordance with IAS 21 because the loan is measured in Entity B in US$ but measured in Entity A in Euro. In the consolidated financial statements the swap's fair value is derived from both interest and principal payments and receipts whereas the foreign currency risk that survives consolidation is limited to Entity B's translation of the opening and closing carrying amounts of the intragroup loan.

Example 3.1.2E

Hedging foreign currency risk of highly probable forecast intragroup royalty payments

Entity A is the parent of Entity B. Entity A charges Entity B a royalty to compensate for external costs it incurs on behalf of Entity B in respect of technology, brands or other intellectual property. Entity B recovers the royalty cost through the sales price it charges externally whenever it sells the goods/services that utilise the technology, brands or other intellectual property. Entity A and Entity B have different functional currencies. Entity A's functional currency is US dollars (USD); Entity B's functional currency is Norwegian Krona (NOK). The intragroup royalty payments are denominated in Entity A's functional currency.

Scenario 1: royalty for use of manufacturing process

Entity A has incurred USD1 million in developing a manufacturing process used to make Product X. The manufacturing process is transferred to Entity B, which uses that process to manufacture Product X. Entity A charges Entity B a USD10 royalty for each unit of Product X that Entity B sells externally over a two-year period.

Entity B will sell Product X to customers outside the group at a price in NOK that is substantially in excess of the royalty cost Entity B incurs. Entity B enters into foreign currency forward contracts to hedge the foreign currency risk arising on its forecast intragroup royalty payments relating to highly probable external sales.

Scenario 2: royalty for use of an acquired brand

Entity A acquires an external brand for USD10 million. The group plans to use the newly acquired brand on new products to be sold externally. Some of the newly branded products will be sold by Entity B in NOK and Entity B will be required to pay to Entity A an intragroup royalty payment at a fixed USD amount per unit sold. The royalty payment incurred by Entity B represents no more than 20 per cent of the expected NOK external sales price.

Entity B enters into foreign currency forward contracts to hedge the foreign currency risk arising on its forecast intragroup royalty payments relating to highly probable external sales.

Scenario 3: royalty for use of patented technology

Entity A has developed a patented technology that is used by Entity B as part of its product development for products that Entity B manufactures and sells to customers outside the group in NOK. Entity B pays a USD royalty to Entity A for each unit sold externally which was set at inception of the arrangement at a fixed percentage of the then current external sales price.

Entity B enters into foreign currency forward contracts to hedge the foreign currency risk arising on its forecast intragroup royalty payments relating to its highly probable external sales.

IFRS 9:6.3.6 states that, in the consolidated financial statements, "the foreign currency risk of a highly probable forecast intragroup transaction may qualify as a hedged item in a [cash flow hedge] provided that (1) the transaction is denominated in a currency other than the functional currency of the entity entering into that transaction and (2) the foreign currency risk will affect consolidated profit or loss". Further, IFRS 9:B6.3.5 states that royalty payments, interest payments and management charges between members of the same group will not generally affect consolidated profit or loss (and, consequently, cannot qualify as a hedged item in a cash flow hedge) "unless there is a related external transaction".

In each of the scenarios described, the intragroup royalty cost is an unavoidable part of the highly probable forecasted external sale. Therefore, the foreign currency risk arising from the highly probable forecast intragroup royalty payment may qualify as a hedged item in a cash flow hedge in the consolidated financial statements because (1) the royalty is denominated in a functional currency other than Entity B's and (2) there is a related external transaction that will cause the changes in the royalty payments due to changes in exchange rates to affect consolidated profit or loss.

3.2 Unrecognised assets

Unrecognised assets (other than unrecognised firm commitments) cannot be designated as hedged items. For example, it is not possible to hedge account for an unrecognised intangible asset such as a core deposit intangible that is not recognised in the statement of financial position.

3.3 Firm commitment

A firm commitment is a binding agreement for the exchange of a specified quantity of resources at a specified price on a specified future date or dates. [IFRS 9:Appendix A]

A commitment is binding if it is enforceable either legally or otherwise. If the commitment is with a related party, consideration should be given as to whether in practice the right can be enforced. To be enforceable, the agreement should provide for remedies that are available to the parties to the contract in the event of non-performance, i.e. there is sufficient disincentive for non-performance. For example, a penalty could be specified at a fixed amount or equal to the change in market price of the item under the contract. Alternatively, the penalty may not be specifically stipulated in the agreement but may otherwise be applicable (e.g. remedies under law). When an entity that is a member of a group is preparing its individual financial statements, the entity needs to consider carefully whether transactions between group entities meet the definition of a firm commitment, because they may not be subject to remedies for non-performance either as part of the contract or under law. In many cases, particularly in the absence of non-controlling interests that may require protection from the controlling interest, an agreement between group entities would not be binding.

Example 3.3A

Hedging foreign currency risk of a firm commitment

Entity B sells machinery at fixed prices in many jurisdictions. Entity B's functional currency is Sterling. Entity B enters into an enforceable contract with Entity D, whose functional currency is the Euro, to sell machinery for delivery in six months' time at a fixed price in Euro that is determined today. In other words, Entity B has entered into a firm commitment with Entity D.

Entity B simultaneously enters into a foreign currency forward contract to hedge its future exposure to Euro arising from its firm commitment. This foreign currency forward contract can either be designated as a hedging instrument in a fair value hedge or a cash flow hedge because it is hedging the foreign currency risk of a firm commitment. [IFRS 9:6.5.4]

Example 3.3B

Fair value hedging a firm commitment

Entity E is a discount grocery chain with over 400 stores in the US, which enters into forward contracts to purchase various inventory items for its stores. On 1 June 20X0, Entity E enters into a contract to purchase 300,000 bushels of wheat from a wheat producer for a fixed price of US$1.40 per bushel on 1 August 20X0. Entity E will use the wheat in its bakery operations. Entity E intends to take physical delivery of the wheat in accordance with its expected purchase requirements. If Entity E fails to take delivery of the wheat, it would be required to pay for any decrease in the value of the wheat and legal remedies would be available to the wheat producer.

The transaction is a firm commitment because it is a binding agreement for the exchange of a specified quantity of wheat at a specified price on a specified future date. The purchase contract is not accounted for as a derivative because Entity E intends to take physical delivery of the wheat and has no past practice of settling similar contracts net. Entity E could enter into a contract to hedge the fair value exposure of the firm commitment due to the change in the price of wheat between 1 June 20X0 and 1 August 20X0 (e.g. a net cash settled forward contract to sell wheat for a fixed price on 1 August). Such a contract would qualify as a hedging instrument in a fair value hedge of a firm commitment.

3.4 Forecast transactions

A forecast transaction is an uncommitted but anticipated future transaction. [IFRS 9:Appendix A]

It is important to distinguish between forecast transactions and firm commitments because forecast transactions are always cash flow hedged, whereas firm commitments are generally fair value hedged (see **3.3**). The following table illustrates some examples of forecast transactions and also illustrates the difference between a forecast transaction and a firm commitment.

Example 3.4

Examples of forecast transactions and firm commitments

Forecast transaction	***Firm commitment***
In May 20X1 an entity forecasts the purchase of 100,000 bushels of corn to be used in its manufacturing process in October 20X1.	An entity has signed a legally binding purchase agreement to take delivery of 100,000 bushels of corn on 30 September 20X1 for US$2 per bushel.
Corporate Treasury forecasts the sale of a debt instrument measured at amortised cost at the end of the fourth quarter.	Corporate Treasury signs a legally binding agreement with a third party to sell a specific debt instrument for par on 30 December 20X1.
Corporate Treasury forecasts the purchase of a £25 million bond on 23 March 20X1 from an investment bank.	Corporate Treasury enters into a legally binding purchase agreement with a bank to take delivery of a £25 million bond for par on 23 March 20X1.

3.4.1 Highly probable

Cash flow hedge accounting can be applied to a forecast transaction only if the transaction is highly probable. [IFRS 9:6.3.3]

The term 'highly probable' is not defined in IFRS 9. The probability of occurrence must be significantly in excess of 50 per cent, but will not be as high as 100 per cent because it can never be claimed that a transaction to which an entity is not yet committed is certain to occur. Paragraph BC81 of IFRS 5 *Non-current assets Held for Sale and*

Discontinued Operations also discusses the meaning of the term 'highly probable' although in a different context. It states that for the purpose of IFRSs 'probable' is defined as "more likely than not" and that 'highly probable' is regarded as implying a significantly higher probability than 'more likely than not' and as being equivalent to the phrase "likely to occur".

The implementation guidance that predated IFRS 9 and accompanies IAS 39 provides guidance on how the term 'highly probable' should be interpreted as well as guidance on how a forecast transaction should be identified and documented (see IAS 39:IG.F.3.7, IG.F.3.10 and IG.F.3.11); this guidance can (summarised below) be considered relevant to IFRS 9.

Probability is assessed based on observable facts and the relevant circumstances. In assessing the likelihood that a transaction will occur, consideration should be given to the following:

- the frequency of similar past transactions;
- the financial and operational ability of the entity to carry out the transaction;
- substantial commitments of resources to a particular activity (e.g. a manufacturing facility that can be used in the short-run only to process a particular type of commodity);
- the extent of loss or disruption of operations that could result if the transaction does not occur;
- the likelihood that transactions with substantially different characteristics might be used to achieve the same business purpose (e.g. an entity that intends to raise cash may have several ways of doing so, ranging from a short-term bank loan to a common stock offering); and
- the entity's business plan.

In addition, both the length of time until a forecast transaction is projected to occur and the quantity of the forecast transaction should be considered in determining probability. Other factors being equal, the more distant a forecast transaction the less likely it is that the transaction would be considered highly probable and the stronger the evidence that would be needed to support an assertion that it is highly probable. For example, a forecast that a transaction will occur in five years may be less reliable than a forecast of a transaction expected to occur in one year.

Other factors being equal, the greater the physical quantity or future value of a forecast transaction, the less likely it is that the transaction would be considered highly probable and the stronger the evidence that would be required to support an assertion that it is highly probable. For example, it is easier to support forecast sales by an entity of 100,000 units in a particular month than to support forecast sales of 300,000 units in that month, when recent sales have averaged 300,000 units per month for the past three months.

To meet the 'highly probable' requirement, an entity is not required to predict and document the exact date a forecast transaction is expected to occur. However, it is required to identify and document the time period during which the forecast transaction is expected to occur within a reasonably specific and generally narrow range of time from a most probable date, as a basis for assessing hedge effectiveness.

A pattern of discovering that hedged forecast transactions are no longer expected to occur would call into question both an entity's ability to predict accurately forecast transactions and the propriety of using hedge accounting in the future for similar transactions.

A hedged forecast transaction must be identified and documented with sufficient specificity so that when the transaction occurs, it is clear whether the transaction is the designated hedged transaction. Therefore, a forecast transaction may be identified as the sale of the first 15,000 units of a specific product during a specified three-month period, but it could not be identified as the last 15,000 units of that product sold during a three-month period because the last 15,000 units cannot be identified with sufficient specificity: it could be units 20,001 to 35,000 or units 120,001 to 135,000.

For the same reason, a forecast transaction cannot be specified solely as a percentage of sales or purchases during a period.

3.5 Overall business risks

A firm commitment to acquire a business in a business combination cannot be a hedged item, except for foreign exchange risk, because the other risks being hedged cannot be specifically identified and measured. Those other risks are general business risks. [IFRS 9:B.6.3.1]

Example 3.5

Hedging foreign currency risk of a firm commitment to acquire a business

Entity D, a € functional currency entity, is the parent of Group D. Entity D enters into an agreement to acquire Entity E in two months' time for US$50 million. The consolidated financial statements of Group D will include Entity E from the date of acquisition. To hedge the US$ foreign currency risk of the purchase consideration, Entity D enters into a foreign currency forward contract to buy US$50 million and sell € at a specified foreign currency rate that matures in two months.

Because Entity D is hedging the foreign currency risk of a firm commitment, it may designate the foreign currency forward contract as a fair value hedge or as a cash flow hedge.

If Entity D designates the derivative in a fair value hedge, the gains or losses will be recognised in profit or loss, and the movements in the fair value of the firm commitment due to foreign currency risk will also be recognised in profit or loss, with the other side of the entry recognised in the statement of financial position. At acquisition, this balance will be derecognised and will adjust the amount of goodwill recognised if any.

If Entity D designates the derivative in a cash flow hedge, the gain or loss will be recognised in other comprehensive income. It will remove the gain or loss on the derivative from equity and in accordance with IFRS 9:6.5.11(d)(i) basis-adjust the goodwill that is recognised on acquisition. The amount of the basis adjustment will affect profit or loss if any resulting goodwill is impaired.

3.6 Loans measured at amortised cost

Amortised cost measurement applies to those assets and liabilities that meet the amortised cost criteria in IFRS 9 if the entity does not choose to designate the instrument as at FVTPL. Such instruments can be a hedged item in a fair value hedge or a cash flow hedge. For example, if a loan earns fixed rate interest, it could be hedged for changes in fair value due to movements in interest rates which could affect profit or loss on derecognition of the loan. Further, it is possible to hedge the cash flows that arise from its future disposal where its disposal is considered to be highly probable (i.e. a highly probable forecast sale of the fixed rate loan).

3.7 Loan assets measured at FVTOCI

Some loan assets are required to be measured at FVTOCI if they meet certain conditions under the classification and measurement requirements of IFRS 9 (see **chapter B2**), unless they are designated as at FVTPL. Although they are measured on the balance sheet at fair value, the fair value gains and losses are initially recognised in other comprehensive income and will ultimately be reclassified to profit or loss. Furthermore, any interest received on the loan asset affects profit or loss in the same way as it would for an amortised cost asset. Therefore, similar to loans at amortised cost, these assets can be a hedged item in a fair value hedge or a cash flow hedge. The key difference is that in the case of a fair value hedge, the loan asset at FVTOCI will not be adjusted as it is already carried at fair value which will include any change in fair value due to the hedged risk. Instead, the effect of applying fair value hedge accounting will be reclassifying amounts that relate to changes in the hedged risk from equity to profit or loss over the hedged period.

3.8 Investments in equity instruments

IFRS 9 requires that an investment in an equity instrument be measured at fair value. The default treatment for recognising changes in fair value is to recognise them in profit or loss (i.e. FVTPL); however, on initial recognition an entity may elect to present fair value changes in other comprehensive income (i.e. FVTOCI), with only dividend income recognised in profit or loss (see **chapter B2**).

Investments in equity instruments that are measured at FVTPL may be eligible for hedge accounting. However, because the gains and losses on the hedging instrument and the hedged item will in any case automatically be recognised in profit or loss, hedge accounting would not bring any recognition or measurement benefit.

Although the general requirement for hedge accounting to be applied is that the hedged exposure must be something that could affect profit or loss, there is an explicit exception to this rule for investments in equity instruments that are measured at FVTOCI. [IFRS 9:6.5.3] Such investments may be designated in a fair value hedge despite the fact that only dividend income is recognised in profit or loss and fair value gains or losses are presented in other comprehensive income with no subsequent reclassification. In such cases, the recognised hedge ineffectiveness is also presented in other comprehensive income (see **6.4.3**). [IFRS 9:6.5.8(b)]

3.9 Equity-method investments and investments in consolidated subsidiaries

An equity method investment cannot be a hedged item in a fair value hedge.

This is because the equity method recognises in profit or loss the investor's share of the investee's profit or loss, rather than changes in the investment's fair value.

For a similar reason, an investment in a consolidated subsidiary cannot be a hedged item in a fair value hedge. This is because consolidation recognises in profit or loss the subsidiary's profit or loss, rather than changes in the investment's fair value. [IFRS 9:B.6.3.2]

Although in the consolidated financial statements it is not possible to apply fair value hedge accounting for an equity-method investment or an investment in a consolidated subsidiary, it may be possible to apply fair value hedge accounting to such an exposure in the investor's separate financial statements if the equity method is not applied. For example, in its separate financial statements, the investor may apply fair value hedging with respect to foreign currency risk in relation to an equity investment in a foreign subsidiary denominated in a foreign currency held at cost (see **section 6.6**).

A hedge of a net investment in a foreign operation is different because it is a hedge of the foreign currency exposure, not a fair value hedge of the change in the value of the investment. [IFRS 9:B.6.3.2] Hedges of net investments in foreign operations are dealt with in **section 6.6**.

3.10 Aggregated exposures

Although derivatives are mostly designated in a hedging relationship as the hedging instrument, IFRS 9 allows an aggregated exposure, which is a combination of an exposure that could qualify as a hedged item and a derivative, to be designated as the hedged item in a hedging relationship. [IFRS 9:6.3.4]

The derivative that is included in the aggregated exposure need not be an existing derivative as aggregated exposures include forecast transactions of aggregated exposures (i.e. uncommitted but anticipated future transactions that would give rise to an exposure and a derivative) provided the aggregated exposure is highly probable and, once it has occurred and is therefore no longer forecast, is eligible as a hedged item (see **example 3.10B**). [IFRS 9:6.3.4]

Designating an aggregated exposure as the hedged item can sometimes help to better reflect the risk management objective of transacting multiple derivatives to hedge different risk exposures. For example, this can arise where:

- An exposure gives rise to more than one risk and each risk is separately hedged with different derivatives and those derivatives are transacted at different times (see **example 3.10A**).
- A forecast exposure includes a forecast derivative (see **example 3.10B**)
- An exposure is hedged by more than one derivative transacted at the same time, but each derivative is designated in a different type of hedging relationship (e.g. the first derivative is designated in a fair value hedge and the second derivative is designated in a cash flow hedge, see **example 3.10C**).
- To qualify for hedge accounting, it is necessary to notionally split a single derivative into two derivatives and designate the first component in a hedge of the exposure and the second component in a hedge of an aggregated exposure that is a combination of the first component derivative and the exposure (see **example 3.10D**).

Example 3.10A

Hedging two risks in a forecast transaction at different points in time

Entity B, with € functional currency, has a highly probable forecast purchase of 100,000 barrels of oil in 18 months' time. Because oil is priced in US$, this forecast purchase exposes Entity B to both oil price risk and foreign currency risk. Entity B's risk management strategy requires it to hedge the oil price risk on this forecast transaction 18 months before the transaction whereas the foreign currency risk must be hedged only 12 months in advance.

Entity B enters into a net settled forward contract to buy 100,000 barrels of oil at US$100 per barrel in 18 months' time and designates this in a cash flow hedge of the oil price risk in US$.

Six months later, the entity transacts a foreign currency forward contract to receive US$10 million (100,000 x $100) and pay €6 million to hedge the foreign currency risk on the combination of the forecast oil purchase and the net settled forward to buy oil (i.e. the aggregated exposure). Entity B designates the aggregated exposure in a cash flow hedge of US$/€ foreign currency risk.

Example 3.10B

Pre-hedging a forecast aggregated exposure

Entity X, with £ functional currency, is due to refinance £100 million of debt in six months' time. Instead of issuing debt in £, it plans to issue debt in US$ and concurrently swap the cash flows using a cross currency-interest rate swap (CCIRS). The swap will receive US$ cash flows that perfectly match the expected cash flows of the US$ debt and pay £ fixed rate cash flows. Both the forecast US$ debt issuance and the forecast CCIRS are highly probable. Given that both the debt and the derivative, which together make up the aggregated exposure, are forecast transactions (i.e. a forecast aggregated exposure), Entity X remains exposed to changes in UK LIBOR (i.e. as UK LIBOR changes, the fixed rate on the forecast CCIRS will change).

To hedge itself from changes in UK LIBOR, Entity X enters into a forward starting, receive UK LIBOR, pay fixed interest rate swap, with terms that closely match the forecast aggregated exposure. Entity X will close out the interest rate swap when the debt and CCIRS are issued, it will no longer be exposed to variability in UK LIBOR because the CCIRS has fixed rate £ cash flows.

Entity X designates the forecast aggregated exposure as the hedged item in a cash flow hedge of UK LIBOR interest rate risk until the issuance of the debt.

Example 3.10C

Layering a cash flow hedge on top of a fair value hedge

Entity K has a US dollar functional currency. Entity K issues fixed-rate Euro-denominated 10-year debt. It chooses to issue the debt in the Euro market because it perceives the net interest cost after hedging to be cheaper than issuing directly in the US market. At the date of issue, Entity K immediately swaps all the foreign currency cash flows on the debt into its functional currency by entering into a 10-year receive € fixed pay US dollar floating cross-currency interest rate swap (CCIRS) because it does not wish to be exposed to foreign currency risk. Because Entity K has an interest rate policy of fixing interest rates for 5 years, it also enters into a 5-year receive US dollar floating pay US dollar fixed interest rate swap to fix its interest cost for the five years after issue of the debt.

To apply hedge accounting, Entity K designates the CCIRS in a fair value hedge of both interest rate risk and foreign currency risk for the 10-year period and then designates this aggregated exposure in a cash flow hedge of interest rate risk for the first five years.

As an alternative designation, Entity K could designate the CCIRS and the interest rate swap in combination as a partial-term hedge of foreign currency risk of the debt for the first five years and a hedge of foreign currency risk and interest rate risk for the latter five years. IFRS 9 permits a combination of derivatives to be designated jointly as a hedging instrument (see **2.3**) and permits partial-term hedging (see **3.11.3**).

Example 3.10D

Splitting a derivative and designating a component as part of an aggregated exposure

Entity X issues inflation-linked debt in respect of which it pays a fixed real rate of 2 per cent plus a variable inflation rate together applied to a fixed principal amount of CU100 million. Interest is paid every six months. Entity X does not wish to be exposed to the cash flow variability of the inflation rate nor the fair value risk from the fixed real rate and enters into an inflation swap under which it receives cash flows to match the coupon on the debt and pays 6-month CU LIBOR on a fixed notional of CU100m.

Entity X notionally splits the inflation linked-swap into two component derivatives each with nil fair value.

Derivative Component 1	
Receive:	2% plus inflation
Pay:	Fixed rate of 5%
Derivative Component 2	
Receive:	Fixed rate of 5%
Pay:	CU LIBOR

Derivative Component 1 is designated in a cash flow hedge of the changes in the inflation rate. The combination of the debt and Derivative Component 1 makes the aggregated exposure that is designated in a fair value hedge for interest rate risk with Derivative Component 2.

In the examples of aggregated exposures provided above, the derivative that is part of an existing aggregated exposure is itself designated in a hedging relationship with the exposure. As a result, there are two (layers of) hedging relationships. The first (layer) is a hedging relationship of the first derivative and the exposure, and the second (layer) is a hedging relationship of the second derivative and the aggregated exposure. However, as noted in IFRS 9:BC6.167, it is not necessary for the first derivative and the exposure that make up the aggregated exposure to be designated in a hedging relationship. The IASB acknowledges that not achieving hedge accounting for the first-level relationship could make the accounting for the aggregated exposure more complicated and inferior compared to achieving hedge accounting for the first-level relationship. For example, consider the following example which is an adaptation of **example 3.10A**.

Example 3.10E

Hedging an aggregated exposure that is not in a hedging relationship

Entity B, with € functional currency, has a highly probable forecast purchase of 100,000 barrels of oil in 18 months' time. Because oil is priced in US$, this forecast purchase exposes Entity B to both oil price risk and foreign currency risk. Entity B's risk management strategy requires it to hedge the oil price risk on this forecast transaction 18 months before the transaction whereas the foreign currency risk must be hedged only 12 months in advance.

Entity B enters into a net settled forward to buy 100,000 barrels of oil at US$100 per barrel in 18 months' time but does not designate this instrument in a cash flow hedge.

Six months later, when the forward price of oil is US$90, the entity transacts a foreign currency forward contract to receive US$10 million (100,000 x US$100) and pay €6 million to hedge the foreign currency risk on the combination of the forecast oil purchase and the net settled forward to buy oil (i.e. the aggregated exposure to buy oil at US$100 per barrel). Entity B designates the aggregated exposure in a cash flow hedge of US$/€ foreign currency risk.

Because the first derivative was not designated in a cash flow hedge of the oil price risk, the derivative in the aggregated exposure affects profit or loss on a fair value basis whereas the forecast oil purchase will affect profit or loss when the goods the oil was used to produce are sold. This leads to an inferior hedge accounting result as illustrated below (the illustration ignores discounting and assumes spot and forward rates are equal).

Assume the next reporting period is six months after inception of the foreign currency hedge and the foreign currency forward contract has a fair value of €1 million due to changes in the US$/€ exchange rate since inception of the hedge. Assuming the hedge is 100 per cent effective the full €1 million is initially recognised in the cash flow hedge reserve. During the same six month period, the oil price has fallen further from US$90 to US$85 per barrel and the fair value of the oil derivative is now a liability of US$1.5 million (100,000 x (US$85 – US$100). This would imply that 15 per cent of the foreign currency risk (i.e. US$1.5 million/US$10 million) hedged by the foreign currency forward has affected profit or loss, requiring €150,000 (i.e. 15 per cent) of the €1 million recognised in the cash flow hedge reserve to be reclassified to profit or loss, leaving €850,000 in the cash flow hedge reserve.

At the next reporting period six months later and at maturity of the hedge, assume the US$/€ exchange rate remains the same and the fair value of the foreign currency forward contract remains €1 million. However, over the six months the oil price has returned to $100 per barrel and the oil derivative has nil fair value. At this point, only €850,000 remains deferred in reserves and this amount is removed from equity and recognised as a basis adjustment to the cost of oil inventory recognised from the hedged purchase. Because some of the foreign currency forward's fair value had already been recognised in profit or loss, the hedged oil purchase is not recognised at the hedged rate and the effect of hedge accounting is inferior to the effect that would have had been achieved if the first hedge with the oil derivative had been designated in a cash flow hedge. If this had been the case (and assuming the oil price hedge was 100 per cent effective) the full €1 million fair value change of the foreign currency forward would have been deferred in reserves until recognition of the oil inventory. The inventory would then have been basis adjusted by €1 million and recognised at the hedged rate.

The fact that the first-level relationship is not required to be designated in a qualifying hedging relationship means that an aggregated exposure can consist of an exposure and a derivative that is not eligible for hedge accounting in a first-level relationship. This is best illustrated with an example.

Consider an entity with £ functional currency that wishes to raise floating rate debt in US$; instead of issuing US$ directly, the entity achieves the same synthetic position by issuing floating rate £ debt and transacting a cross-currency swap that swaps the £ flows into US$ floating flows. The £ debt would not be an eligible hedged item in a hedging relationship with the cross-currency swap because the swap *creates* foreign currency exposure. Nevertheless, the entity could designate the synthetic US$ debt in a cash flow hedge of interest rate risk with a US$ interest rate swap to receive floating rates and pay fixed rates because there is no requirement for the exposure and the derivative in the aggregated exposure to be designated in a first-level hedging relationship.

When designating an aggregated exposure IFRS 9:B.6.3.4(b) imposes restrictions on the derivative that is included as part of the aggregated exposure:

- where the derivative included in the aggregated exposure is designated in a hedging relationship, the same designated amount of the derivative is included as part of the aggregated exposure (e.g., if the forward element of the first derivative is excluded from the first-level hedge relationship, then the forward element is also excluded from the aggregated exposure that is hedged as part of the second-level hedge relationship).
- where the derivative included in the aggregated exposure is not designated in a hedging relationship, the derivative included in the aggregated exposure can be the derivative in its entirety or a proportion of it (e.g,. it is not possible to exclude any other components of the

derivative such as the time value component of an option or the forward element of a forward, nor is it possible to split the derivative by risk, term or cash flows).

Given the limited restrictions on the derivative that can be included as part of the aggregated exposure, derivatives that are not eligible as hedging instruments would in many cases appear to be eligible to be included as part of an aggregated exposure. For example, a written option or net written option could be included as part of the aggregated exposure.

Assessing and measuring hedge effectiveness for an aggregated exposure is inevitably more complicated than for typical micro-hedges. To aide application, IFRS 9 provides three illustrative examples which have been reproduced with additional explanatory commentary in **section 5** of **chapter B10**. These examples, reiterate the point that when applying hedge accounting to an aggregated exposure, derivatives that are part of an aggregated exposure are recognised as separate assets or liabilities measured at fair value and 'synthetic accounting' with the derivative's fair value off balance sheet does not apply. [IFRS 9:B6.3.4(a)]

The examples considered above, as well as the examples provided in IFRS 9, only go as far as layering on one hedge relationship onto another. However, IFRS 9 does not include any explicit restriction on how many hedge relationships can be layered upon one another. For example, it could be possible to designate an aggregated exposure ('aggregated exposure two') as a hedged item with a derivative ('derivative three') where aggregated exposure two is itself a combination of a derivative ('derivative two') and an aggregated exposure ('aggregated exposure one') where aggregated exposure one is a combination of a derivative ('derivative one') and the original non-derivative exposure. Despite this possibility, in practice such hedges are expected to be rare and would need to be carefully assessed to ensure that they are consistent with the entity's risk management strategy and that the mechanics of hedge accounting are operable.

3.11 Risk components

Changes in the cash flows or fair value of an item attributable to a specific risk or risks (i.e. a risk component), can be designated as the hedged item provided that, based on an assessment within the context of the particular market structure, the risk component is separately identifiable and reliably measurable. [IFRS 9:6.3.7(a)]

The ability to designate risk components allows entities some flexibility in how the hedged risk is defined, allowing it to be defined in a way that more closely resembles the risk that is hedged from a risk management perspective. A basic example of hedging a risk component is hedging the foreign currency risk component of a highly probable forecast transaction denominated in a foreign currency and excluding from the hedge any other variability in price of that forecast transaction. More complex examples arise in practice, particularly in respect of hedging other risk components in non-financial items. Further examples are provided below.

The ability to designate risk components has important consequences when it comes to demonstrating compliance with the hedge effectiveness requirements (see **5.2**). An entity's ability to define the hedged risk in such a way that it closely matches the terms of the hedging instrument, will make it easier for the entity to demonstrate that there is an economic relationship between the hedged item and hedging instrument and identify the appropriate hedge ratio to use. Furthermore, more closely matching the designated risk component to the hedging instrument will reduce hedge ineffectiveness, and any ineffectiveness recognised will more closely align with ineffectiveness anticipated in the entity's risk management strategy. However, it is important to note that IFRS 9 does not allow an entity to simply assume that a risk component equivalent to the hedging instrument exists within the hedged item. Instead it must independently assess the hedged item to determine whether the risk component is separately identifiable and reliably measurable.

Risk components may be identified in financial or non-financial items and can be contractually specified (see **example 3.11A**) or implicit in the cash flows or fair value of an item (see **example 3.11C**). Where the risk component is contractually specified it will generally be regarded as identifiable (because it is contractually specified) and will often be reliably measurable (because its measurement will be required to establish the cash flows under the contract), however, this would not always be the case, for example where although spot prices are available for determining the contract cash flows, forward prices may not be reliably measurable.

Where a risk component is implicit in the cash flows or fair value of an item, more judgement will be required to establish whether it is separately identifiable and reliably measurable. IFRS 9 provides some guidance to assist entities in identifying what risk components qualify for designation as a hedged item, which will be particularly relevant in these cases. It notes an entity should assess such risk components within the context of the particular market structure to which the risk or risks relate and in which the hedging activity takes place. Such a determination requires an evaluation of the relevant facts and circumstances, which differ by risk and market. [IFRS 9:B6.3.9]

In circumstances when an entity hedges a physical item, (e.g. finished electrical goods) the physical components of that item, (e.g. copper components) may be a starting point used by an entity to identify risk components that could be hedged. However, the presence of a physical component in an item would not necessarily mean that such a component is eligible to be designated as a hedged item because that physical component may not be a separately identifiable and reliably measurable component of the fair value or cash flows of the item. For example, changes in the price of copper may not result in an identifiable change in the price of finished electrical goods because, given the market structure, there are many influences on the price of the finished goods and the effect of a change in the price of the copper component on the overall price is not separately identifiable and reliably measurable. That said, there will be some cases where the presence of a physical component does have an identifiable and reliably measurable impact on the price of an overall item. One such example provided in IFRS 9 is a hedge of the crude oil component of jet fuel (see **example 3.11C**). In these cases, it will be important to apply careful judgement and clearly understand the workings of the market, how prices are determined and the basis for entering into the hedge from a risk management perspective.

Risk components can be identified in a number of different ways provided the risk component is separately identifiable and reliably measurable. For example, a risk component can be identified from specific identified cash flows of an item (e.g. only hedging a risk component from the first five years of interest flows on a 10-year loan with annual interest payments). Risk components can also include only changes in the cash flows or the fair value of a hedged item:

- above or below a specified price or other variable (i.e. a one-sided risk, see **3.11.2**); and
- that are part of the term of the cash flow or fair value exposure (i.e. a partial term hedge, see **3.11.3**).

When designating a risk component as a hedged item, the hedge accounting requirements apply to that risk component in the same way as they apply to other hedged items that are not risk components. For example, the qualifying criteria, including the hedge effectiveness assessment and measurement requirements apply in the same way. [IFRS 9:B6.3.11]

Example 3.11A

Hedging contractually specified risk components

[IFRS 9:B6.3.10(a)]

Entity A has a long-term supply contract for natural gas that is priced using a contractually specified formula that references commodities and other factors (for example, gas oil, fuel oil and other components such as transport charges). Entity A hedges the gas oil component in its supply contract using a gas oil forward contract. Because the gas oil component is specified by the terms and conditions of the supply contract it is a contractually specified risk component. Hence, because of the pricing formula, Entity A concludes that the gas oil price exposure is separately identifiable. At the same time, there is a market for gas oil forward contracts. Hence, Entity A concludes that the gas oil price exposure is reliably measurable. Consequently, the gas oil price exposure in the supply contract is a risk component that is eligible for designation as a hedged item.

Example 3.11B

Hedging contractually specified and non-contractually specified risk components

[IFRS 9:B6.3.10(b)]

Entity B hedges its future coffee purchases based on its production forecast. Hedging starts up to 15 months before delivery for part of the forecast purchase volume. Entity B increases the hedged volume over time (as the delivery date approaches). Entity B uses two different types of contracts to manage its coffee price risk:

(i) exchange-traded coffee futures contracts; and

(ii) coffee supply contracts for Arabica coffee from Colombia delivered to a specific manufacturing site. These contracts price a tonne of coffee based on the exchange-traded coffee futures contract price plus a fixed price differential plus a variable logistics services charge using a pricing formula. The coffee supply contract is an executory contract in accordance with which Entity B takes actual delivery of coffee.

For deliveries that relate to the current harvest, entering into the coffee supply contracts allows Entity B to fix the price differential between the actual coffee quality purchased (Arabica coffee from Colombia) and the benchmark quality that is the underlying of the exchange-traded futures contract.

However, for deliveries that relate to the next harvest, the coffee supply contracts are not yet available, so the price differential cannot be fixed. Entity B uses exchange-traded coffee futures contracts to hedge the benchmark quality component of its coffee price risk for deliveries that relate to the current harvest as well as the next harvest.

Entity B determines that it is exposed to three different risks: coffee price risk reflecting the benchmark quality, coffee price risk reflecting the difference (spread) between the price for the benchmark quality coffee and the particular Arabica coffee from Colombia that it actually receives, and the variable logistics costs.

For deliveries related to the current harvest, after Entity B enters into a coffee supply contract, the coffee price risk reflecting the benchmark quality is a contractually specified risk component because the pricing formula includes an indexation to the exchange-traded coffee futures contract price. Entity B concludes that this risk component is separately identifiable and reliably measurable.

For deliveries related to the next harvest, Entity B has not yet entered into any coffee supply contracts (i.e. those deliveries are forecast transactions). Hence, the coffee price risk reflecting the benchmark quality is a non-contractually specified risk component. Entity B's analysis of the market structure takes into account how eventual deliveries of the particular coffee that it receives are priced. Hence, on the basis of this analysis of the market structure, Entity B concludes that the forecast transactions also involve the coffee price risk that reflects the benchmark quality as a risk component that is separately identifiable and reliably measurable even though it is not contractually specified.

Consequently, Entity B may designate hedging relationships on a risk components basis (for the coffee price risk that reflects the benchmark quality) for coffee supply contracts as well as forecast transactions.

Example 3.11C

Hedging non-contractually specified risk components in a non-financial item

[IFRS 9:B6.3.10(c)]

Entity C hedges part of its future jet fuel purchases on the basis of its consumption forecast up to 24 months before delivery and increases the volume that it hedges over time. Entity C hedges this exposure using different types of contracts depending on the time horizon of the hedge, which affects the market liquidity of the derivatives.

For the longer time horizons (12–24 months) Entity C uses crude oil contracts because only these have sufficient market liquidity. For time horizons of 6–12 months Entity C uses gas oil derivatives because they are sufficiently liquid. For time horizons up to six months Entity C uses jet fuel contracts.

Entity C's analysis of the market structure for oil and oil products and its evaluation of the relevant facts and circumstances is as follows:

(i) Entity C operates in a geographical area in which Brent is the crude oil benchmark. Crude oil is a raw material benchmark that affects the price of various refined oil products as their most basic input. Gas oil is a benchmark for refined oil products, which is used as a pricing reference for oil distillates more generally. This is also reflected in the types of derivative financial instruments for the crude oil and refined oil products markets of the environment in which Entity C operates, such as:

- the benchmark crude oil futures contract, which is for Brent crude oil;
- the benchmark gas oil futures contract, which is used as the pricing reference for distillates – for example, jet fuel spread derivatives cover the price differential between jet fuel and that benchmark gas oil; and
- the benchmark gas oil crack spread derivative (ie the derivative for the price differential between crude oil and gas oil-a refining margin), which is indexed to Brent crude oil.

(ii) The pricing of refined oil products does not depend on which particular crude oil is processed by a particular refinery because those refined oil products (such as gas oil or jet fuel) are standardised products.

Hence, Entity C concludes that the price risk of its jet fuel purchases includes a crude oil price risk component based on Brent crude oil and a gas oil price risk component, even though crude oil and gas oil are not specified in any contractual arrangement. Entity C concludes that these two risk components are separately identifiable and reliably measurable even though they are not contractually specified. Consequently, Entity C may designate hedging relationships for forecast jet fuel purchases on a risk components basis (for crude oil or gas oil). This analysis also means that if, for example, Entity C used crude oil derivatives based on West Texas Intermediate (WTI) crude oil, changes in the price differential between Brent crude oil and WTI crude oil would cause hedge ineffectiveness.

Example 3.11D

Hedging a forecast acquisition of a non-financial item: foreign currency risk

Entity D, a € functional currency entity, has a highly probable forecast transaction to purchase tyres from an external US dollar functional currency entity.

Entity D hedges the foreign currency risk that will arise from buying the tyres because the foreign currency risk between the Euro and the US dollar is separately identifiable and reliably measurable.

Example 3.11E

Hedging a forecast acquisition of a non-financial item

Entity B purchases bronze for use in the manufacture of its products. Entity B enters into a forward contract indexed to copper and wishes to designate it as a hedge of the copper component in forecasted purchases of bronze.

Entity B can designate the copper price risk component of the bronze price as the hedged item if it determines that component is a separately identifiable and reliably measurable component of bronze price risk. To determine this, Entity B would need to analyse the pricing and market structure for bronze.

Example 3.11F

Hedging a forecast acquisition of a non-financial item: basis risk

Entity E hedges the forecast purchase of cocoa using cocoa futures. The cocoa futures contracts specify cocoa of a quality grade that differs from the quality grade of the forecast purchase of cocoa. The difference in quality grades between the hedged item and the hedging instrument is referred to as basis risk. The basis risk will cause hedge ineffectiveness if the cocoa futures contract is designated as a hedge of the forecast purchase of cocoa in its entirety.

Entity E can designate a risk component of the cocoa purchase equivalent to cocoa price referenced in the futures contract if it determines that component is a separately identifiable and reliably measurable component of its forecast cocoa purchase. To determine this, Entity E would need to analyse the pricing and market structure for its forecast purchase of cocoa. Designating a risk component could result in less hedge ineffectiveness than designating the cocoa purchase in its entirety.

Example 3.11G

Hedging a forecast acquisition of a non-financial item: excluding transportation charges

Entity C acquires commodities for use in its business. It acquires the commodities at spot prices on the date it requires a commodity for use in its business. The amount it pays to the supplier for the commodity is an amount referenced to the London Metal Exchange (LME), plus a variable amount for transportation of the commodity from the supplier to the entity.

Entity C hedges the cash flow variability arising from changes in the commodity price risk using commodity derivatives. Entity C excludes transportation charges from the designated hedged risk and designates only the commodity price risk component (which is deemed to be separately identifiable and reliably measurable) in a cash flow hedge with the commodity derivative. Excluding transportation charges from the designated hedged risk improves hedge effectiveness and better reflects the risk management objective of the hedge.

Example 3.11H

Hedging a non-financial item: all risks except foreign currency

Entity O has an anticipated purchase of 1,000 barrels of oil in six months that is highly probable. The purchase price will be the market price at the date of purchase and will be priced in US dollars. Entity O's functional currency is the Australian dollar.

Entity O purchases oil futures on 500 barrels of oil to fix the price at US$60,000 for those 500 barrels. The duration (and other terms) of the forecast transaction and the futures contracts match.

The forecast purchase gives rise to two risk exposures for Entity O: oil price risk (in US dollars) and foreign currency risk (US$:AUS$).

The oil futures hedge the oil price risk only. Entity O does not hedge its exposure to the US dollar on the purchase contract.

The oil futures can be designated as a hedge of the commodity price risk of the forecast purchase of oil in US dollars, because this risk is separately identifiable and reliably measurable.

Example 3.11J

Hedging a non-contractually specified risk component in a financial item

[IFRS 9:B6.3.10(d)]

Entity D holds a fixed-rate debt instrument. This instrument is issued in an environment with a market in which a large variety of similar debt instruments are compared by their spreads to a benchmark rate (for example, LIBOR) and variable-rate instruments in that environment are typically indexed to that benchmark rate. Interest rate swaps are frequently used to manage interest rate risk on the basis of that benchmark rate, irrespective of the spread of debt instruments to that benchmark rate. The price of fixed-rate debt instruments varies directly in response to changes in the benchmark rate as they happen. Entity D concludes that the benchmark rate is a component that can be separately identified and reliably measured. Consequently, Entity D may designate hedging relationships for the fixed-rate debt instrument on a risk component basis for the benchmark interest rate risk.

Example 3.11K

Hedging interest rate risk portion (1)

Entity A wishes to issue five-year fixed rate debt. Based on market rates of interest and Entity A's credit rating, it is able to issue debt at 6.5 per cent. This comprises a five-year interest rate of 4.5 per cent, and a credit spread of 2 per cent. Entity A may designate the hedged risk as changes in the fair value of the debt associated with changes in interest rate risk only (i.e. it may exclude from the designation its own credit spread), assuming it concludes that the designated interest rate risk can be separately identified and reliably measured.

Excluding the credit spread from the designation will increase the effectiveness of the hedge relationship because the equivalent credit risk inherent in the debt is not reflected in the terms of the interest rate swap.

Example 3.11L

Hedging interest rate risk portion (2)

Entity Z has a credit rating of B. It issues fixed rate debt at 6 per cent, which includes a credit spread of 100 basis points (i.e. the rate comprises a LIBOR rate of 5 per cent and a credit spread of 1 per cent). To hedge its exposure to changes in interest rate movements, it enters into a receive-fixed, pay-floating interest rate swap.

Instead of entering into a swap where the pay leg exactly matches the equivalent of LIBOR (i.e. receive 5 per cent, pay LIBOR), Entity Z enters into a swap where the fixed leg exactly matches its debt payments. Because the receive leg is 6 per cent, the pay leg is increased correspondingly to LIBOR + 100 basis points. Because the fair value of the swap is derived from its net settlements, the receive 5 per cent, pay LIBOR swap and the receive 6 per cent, pay LIBOR + 100 basis points will have the same fair value for a given movement in interest rates. Therefore, Entity Z may still designate the LIBOR portion of its debt as the hedged item.

Example 3.11M

Ineligible portion of interest rate risk

Entity C has issued Euro denominated debt with a floating interest rate based on the European Central Bank (ECB) rate. It has also entered into a receive EURIBOR pay fixed Euro interest rate swap with a notional equal to the principal of the debt.

The receive EURIBOR pay fixed interest rate swap cannot be designated as a hedge of the portion of the ECB cash flows that is due to changes in EURIBOR. There is no EURIBOR component in the ECB variable cash flows. The interest rate risk that can be designated as the hedged risk is variability in the ECB rate.

Alternatively, Entity C could hedge the variability of the ECB floating interest rate with a EURIBOR swap; however, this is unlikely to be a perfectly effective hedging instrument even if the notional amounts of the two swaps are the same, because of the basis difference between ECB rate and EURIBOR. Changes in the cash flows of the floating interest rate on the debt will not necessarily be offset by variability in EURIBOR on the swap.

The ECB interest rate risk may be hedged for risk management purposes by continually adjusting the number of EURIBOR swaps to be equivalent to the variability in cash flows generated by variability in the ECB rate which could meet the hedge effectiveness requirements. This is a dynamic hedging strategy.

3.11.1 Hedging foreign currency risk of non-financial asset held at cost

If an entity is hedging foreign currency risk, this risk must be separately identifiable and reliably measurable. A non-financial asset that was purchased in a foreign currency cannot be hedged for foreign currency risk because foreign currency risk is not evident in that non-financial item. However, the foreign currency risk associated with a forecasted sale of that non-financial item could qualify as a hedged item.

It is important to distinguish between hedging foreign currency risk of a non-financial item and hedging foreign currency risk in relation to the forecast sale or purchase of that non-financial item.

Example 3.11.1 illustrates that it is not possible to hedge the foreign currency risk of a non-financial item because the foreign currency risk is not evident and not separately measurable. However, if an entity is purchasing or selling a non-financial item in a foreign currency, it is a fixed amount of foreign currency that will be needed to buy or will be received from selling that non-financial item, and a qualifying foreign currency exposure therefore exists.

Example 3.11.1

Hedging a non-financial item: held at cost

Entity A, a Sterling functional currency entity, acquires some plant and machinery in US$ from Entity B, an unrelated third party US dollar functional currency entity. In the financial statements of Entity A, the plant and machinery will be translated at the US$:£ exchange rate at the date of the purchase (i.e. at historical rate).

If Entity A used US dollar borrowings to finance the purchase of the plant and machinery, these US dollar borrowings cannot be used as a hedging instrument in a fair value hedge of the foreign currency risk of the plant and machinery because the hedged item does not contain any separately measurable foreign currency risk.

If Entity A was to demonstrate that the disposal of the plant and machinery will be priced in US dollars and is highly probable, then the US dollar denominated debt could be used as a hedging instrument against the forecast sale in US dollar provided that the timing of the future cash flows on the debt coincided with the timing of the future cash flow on the disposal.

3.11.2 Hedging a one-sided risk

To hedge a one-sided risk is to hedge only changes in the cash flows or fair value of a hedged item above or below a specified price or other variable. Because it is only a hedge of some of the risks of an item it is regarded as a risk component. Hedging of only one side of a risk usually arises when a risk manager wants to remain exposed to potential upside from favourable changes in a risk variable but wants protection against the potential downside. Such a hedging strategy comes at a cost, because to gain protection against only adverse changes in a risk, an entity would have to pay a premium to purchase an option, which for an out of the money option would be equivalent to the time value of the option.

The intrinsic value of a purchased option that has the same principal terms as the designated risk reflects a one-sided risk in a hedged item. For example, an entity can designate the variability of future cash flows resulting from a price increase of a forecast commodity purchase. In such a situation, the entity designates only cash flow losses that result from an increase in the price above the specified level. The hedged risk does not include the time value of a purchased option, because the time value is not a component of the forecast transaction that affects profit or loss. [IFRS 9:B6.3.12]

When measuring the hedged item using the intrinsic value of an option, IFRS 9:B6.5.5 explains that the terms of the (hypothetical) option would be derived based on an at the money or out of the money option, such that if the actual hedging instrument is in the money at the point of designation, hedge ineffectiveness will arise.

In some cases an entity may hedge two one-sided risks in the same item, such as hedging against variability in cash flows or fair value above and below two different prices. For example, an entity with a forecast purchase of oil may hedge against oil price increases above $110 per barrel and below $90 per barrel. This hedged risk would be reflected by the intrinsic value of a combination of a purchased option (to reflect the risk of price increases above $110) and a written option (to reflect the risk of price decreases below $90), often referred to as a collar (see **example 6.8.1**).

The advantage of being able to designate only a one-sided risk is that it allows an entity to exclude from the hedged item any variability that is not part of the hedge and hence allows hedge accounting to be more reflective of the risk management objective of the hedge.

3.11.3 Partial term hedging

Another type of risk component arises when instead of hedging the full term of an exposure an entity only hedges an exposure for part of the time-period that it exists. Cash flows that happen in the future can expose an entity to cash flow and/or fair value risk up until such cash flows are settled. For example, a forecast transaction to sell goods in a foreign currency in 12 months' time can give rise to cash flow variability due to changes in the foreign exchange rate for the full 12 month term until the sale takes place. Likewise a firm commitment to buy a property at a fixed price due to settle in 18 months' time can give rise to fair value risk due to changes in the property price until the contract is settled in 18 months. IFRS 9 allows an entity to designate a partial term hedge because it represents a risk component, however, as with all risk components it must be separately identifiable and reliably measurable.

There are various reasons why an entity may only hedge a part of the term of a risk exposure. For example, it may enter into a shorter dated forward contract which is more liquid and cheaper with the intention of rolling it forward into further short dated forwards until the full term of the exposure is hedged. Alternatively an entity may only want to hedge a part of the term of a risk exposure because after the initial hedged term the risk may naturally be hedged with an equal but opposite exposure.

The concept of being able to hedge on a partial term basis is driven by the relationship between spot rates and forward rates for any given yield curve. The spot rate today, and the anticipated spot rates in the future periods are used to construct the yield curve today. The yield curve is a reflection of the anticipated rates in the future based on an assessment today.

By dissecting a longer dated current yield curve into 'mini-curves', it is possible to isolate the fair value movements of a longer dated instrument due to movements in the shorter part of the yield curve.

Example 3.11.3

Partial term hedging fixed rate debt

Entity Q issues ten-year fixed rate debt. To hedge against changes in interest rates, it enters into a six-year receive-fixed pay-floating interest rate swap. Entity Q may designate the swap as hedging the fair value exposure of the interest and principal payments relating to the first six years of the yield curve.

At issuance of the bond, Entity Q can obtain the yield curve for the stated maturity of the whole instrument, in this case, a ten year yield curve.

The ten year yield curve can be dissected into mini-yield curves.

- Spot interest rate today (t_0) for interest due in a year (t_1).
- Expected spot interest rate starting in a year's time (t_1) due at the end of that year (t_2) [one-year forward rate starting in a year].
- Expected spot interest rate starting at year two (t_2) due at the end of that year (t_3) [one-year forward rate starting in year two].

If Entity Q wishes to fair value hedge for movements in the interest rate curve that matures in six years' time, it only has to consider movements in the first six years of the ten year yield curve in computing the change in the fair value of the hedged item. Because a six-year interest rate swap is priced off the six-year yield curve, in order to demonstrate hedge effectiveness, the entity discounts the hedged cash flows using the spot rates at the date hedge effectiveness is measured.

In one year's time, Entity Q will compare the change in the fair value of the derivative (with five years remaining) with the change in fair value of the hedged selected cash flows on the bond to the extent affected by changes in the spot yield curve for the next five years, and so on.

3.11.4 Financial instruments subject to prepayment

A fixed rate debt instrument that contains an embedded prepayment option may still be designated as a hedged item. However, the effect of the prepayment option should be considered when designating the hedged item and assessing whether the hedge relationship will meet the necessary hedge effectiveness requirements (see **section 5.2**).

If the entire asset or liability is designated as being hedged, the hedging instrument may have to include an equivalent option that coincides with the prepayment option in the hedged item in order for the hedge effectiveness requirements to be met. For example, for a fixed rate loan asset with a written prepayment option for the borrower to repay the loan early at par, the interest rate swap used to hedge that loan for interest rate risk may require a purchased option for the lender to terminate the swap early for nil value in order for the hedge to be effective (see **example 3.11.4C**). Inclusion of such an option in the hedging instrument ensures the fair value of the hedging instrument is sensitive to changes in the hedged interest rate risk in a similar way to the hedged item. However, hedge ineffectiveness can still arise due to factors other than interest rates influencing the decision to prepay a loan. For example, the probability a customer may repay a loan early due to a change in personal circumstances, rather than due to a change in interest rates, will not be replicated in the fair value of the interest rate swap.

Alternatively, the hedging relationship could be designated for a part of the term of the hedged item prior to the prepayment option being capable of being exercised, provided that the hedging instrument is designated for the entirety of its term. For example, if a debt instrument can be prepaid by the issuer after year five, the investor may wish to hedge the debt instrument for a period before the prepayment option can be exercised, i.e. for the first five years only.

For a hedge of a floating rate debt instrument that contains an embedded prepayment option, the hedged cash flows must be highly probable to qualify for hedge accounting.

Consequently, cash flows in the period when the prepayment option is exercisable may only qualify as highly probable if they result from a group or pool of similar assets (e.g. mortgage loans) for which prepayments can be estimated with a high degree of accuracy or if the prepayment option is significantly out of the money.

Example 3.11.4A

Hedging prepayable loans for interest rate risk (1)

Entity A purchases a perpetual debt instrument which pays a fixed rate of interest of 5 per cent on par. The issuer of the debt instrument has an option to prepay the perpetual debt at an amount that is equal to the instrument's par amount after five years. Entity A measures the instrument at amortised cost.

Entity A enters into a non-prepayable swap with Bank B to receive LIBOR and pay fixed 5 per cent for 20 years. The interest rate swap is designated as a partial term fair value hedge of the LIBOR portion of the perpetual debt instrument for 20 years. Apart from the issuer call prepayment option, all terms and conditions of the swap match those of the hedged item.

Entity A must compare the changes in fair value of the interest rate swap to the changes in the fair value of the perpetual debt instrument, where the latter includes both the change in fair value of the contractual cash flows and the change in fair value of the prepayment option. Hedge ineffectiveness will arise because the hedged item is prepayable while the hedging instrument is not. Hedge ineffectiveness could be so significant in that it could be difficult to demonstrate compliance with the hedge effectiveness requirements. If five years after the issue, the perpetual debt has not been called by the issuer, Entity A may be able to designate the interest rate swap as a partial term hedge of the LIBOR portion of the perpetual debt for the next 15 years. It is not permitted to exclude the prepayment risk from the designation of the hedging relationship because prepayment risk and interest rate risk are closely interrelated.

Example 3.11.4B

Hedging prepayable loans for interest rate risk (2)

Facts as in **example 3.11.4A**, except that Entity A enters into a swap with Bank B whereby the swap can be terminated after five years at Entity A's option. The swap will be terminated at the swap's then fair value.

Entity A must compare the changes in fair value of the interest rate swap to the changes in the fair value of the perpetual debt instrument. In both cases, the change in fair value includes both the change in fair value of the contractual cash flows as well as the change in fair value of the prepayment option which for the swap has negligible value because the swap terminates at fair value. Hedge ineffectiveness will still arise because the hedged item is prepayable at par while the hedging instrument can only be terminated at its then fair value, which will include the fair value of the expected future cash flows on the remaining 15 years of the swap. Again, hedge ineffectiveness is likely to be so significant in that it may be difficult to demonstrate compliance with the hedge effectiveness requirements.

Example 3.11.4C

Hedging prepayable loans for interest rate risk (3)

Facts as in **example 3.11.4A**, except that Entity A enters into a swap with Bank B whereby the swap can be terminated after five years at Entity A's option. The swap will be terminated at zero value.

Entity A must compare the changes in fair value of the interest rate swap to the changes in the fair value of the perpetual debt instrument due to the hedged risk. In both cases, the change in fair value includes the change in fair value of the contractual cash flows as well as the change in fair value of the prepayment option. The hedging relationship is expected to meet the hedge effectiveness requirements for the designated term because the hedging instrument and the hedged item have matching terms where the loan is prepayable at par (i.e. nil gain/loss) and the swap can be terminated for zero value (i.e. nil gain/loss).

3.11.5 Hedging the inflation component of a financial item

There is a rebuttable presumption that unless inflation risk is contractually specified, it is not separately identifiable and reliably measurable and hence cannot be designated as a risk component of a financial instrument. However, in limited cases, it is possible to identify a risk component for inflation risk that is separately identifiable and reliably measurable because of the particular circumstances of the inflation environment and the relevant debt market. [IFRS 9:B6.3.13]

Where the inflation component of a financial item is contractually specified it may be designated as a hedged item for inflation risk as long as other cash flows of the instrument are not affected by the inflation risk component. [IFRS 9:B6.3.15]. An example would be an inflation-linked bond, where the cash flows are linked to inflation such that when inflation changes, the cash flows of the bond change. Assuming that inflation is reliably measurable for the term of the hedge, the inflation component of the bond would be an eligible risk component. Hence an entity that swaps the inflation linked cash flows for fixed cash flows using an inflation swap would be able to designate the swap in a cash flow hedge of inflation risk.

Sometimes, instead of issuing inflation-linked debt, entities issue nominal rate debt and then swap the cash flows of that debt into inflation linked cash flows in order to synthetically create inflation linked debt. For example, an entity issues fixed rate debt and enters into a swap that receives fixed cash flows and pays inflation-linked cash flows. This approach is common where it is cheaper to issue synthetic inflation-linked debt rather than issue inflation linked debt directly because of supply and demand factors (i.e. overall it pays a lower interest rate under the synthetic debt compared to a direct issuance). In the absence of any hedge accounting, and assuming the debt is measured at amortised cost, profit or loss volatility arises due to the default IFRS 9 requirement for the swap to be measured at fair value through profit or loss. To avoid this volatility entities seek to apply hedge accounting between the debt and the inflation swap, on the premise that the swap is hedging a component of the nominal rate debt.

Where the nominal rate on the debt is a fixed rate, the objective of the hedge would be to hedge the fair value risk associated with the fixed inflation component of the fixed rate debt, implying that the nominal fixed rate is the sum of the real rate of interest and the inflation rate, such that when inflation rates change, the fair value of the debt will also change.

Where the nominal rate on the debt is a floating rate (e.g. LIBOR), the objective of the hedge would be to hedge the cash flow variability of the floating rate due to changes in the real rate of interest, implying that the nominal rate is the sum of a variable real rate and a variable inflation rate, where the swap fixes the real rate component of the variability (leaving debt with cash flows that change with inflation).

In both of these cases, in order to apply hedge accounting it is necessary to demonstrate that the inflation component is a separately identifiable and reliably measurable component of the relevant nominal rate, rather than inflation being simply implied in the nominal rate with the real rate component being determined as a residual component.

As noted in IFRS 9:BC6.192 - 193, the IASB initially considered prohibiting the designation of non-contractually specified inflation risk components of financial instruments as a carry-over from IAS 39, but noted an outright ban meant no room for the possibility that in some situations there might be circumstances that could support identifying an eligible risk component for inflation risk. The IASB also considered that financial markets continuously evolve and that the requirements should be capable of addressing changes in the market over time.

The IASB was nevertheless concerned that instead of being supported by the market structure and independently determined for the hedged item, inflation risk might be determined by simply projecting the terms and conditions of the inflation derivative that was actually used as the hedge onto the hedged item.

On balance, the IASB decided not to have an outright prohibition, but to avoid being misunderstood included the rebuttable presumption and guidance that in order to determine whether inflation risk is an eligible risk component, a careful analysis of the facts and circumstances is required so that the criteria for designating risk components are properly applied.

To rebut the presumption, IFRS 9 uses an example of an entity that issues debt in an environment in which inflation-linked bonds have a volume and term structure that results in a sufficiently liquid market that allows constructing a term structure of zero-coupon real interest rates. This means that for the respective currency, inflation is a relevant factor that is separately considered by the debt markets. In those circumstances the inflation risk component could be determined by discounting the cash flows of the hedged debt instrument using the term structure of zero-coupon real interest rates (i.e. in a manner similar to how a risk-free (nominal) interest rate component can be determined). [IFRS 9:B6.3.14]

Conversely, in many cases an inflation risk component is not separately identifiable and reliably measurable. For example, an entity issues only nominal interest rate debt in an environment with a market for inflation-linked bonds that is not sufficiently liquid to allow a term structure of zero-coupon real interest rates to be constructed. In this case the analysis of the market structure and of the facts and circumstances does not support the entity concluding that inflation is a relevant factor that is separately considered by the debt markets. Hence, the entity cannot overcome the rebuttable presumption that inflation risk that is not contractually specified is not separately identifiable and reliably measurable. Consequently, an inflation risk component would not be eligible for designation as the hedged item. This applies irrespective of any inflation hedging instrument that the entity has actually entered into. In particular, the entity cannot simply impute the terms and conditions of the actual inflation hedging instrument by projecting its terms and conditions onto the nominal interest rate debt. [IFRS 9:B6.3.14]

3.11.6 Hedging the credit risk component

During the development of the general hedge accounting model in IFRS 9, the IASB spent considerable time debating whether credit risk of a financial item should be an allowable risk component to designate as a hedged item in a hedge relationship (e.g. with a credit derivative such as a credit default swap).

As part of this debate, the IASB concluded that the credit risk of a financial item is not a risk component that meets the eligibility criteria for hedged items. It noted that the spread between the risk-free rate and the market interest rate incorporates credit risk, liquidity risk, funding risk and any other unidentified risk component and margin elements and, although it is possible to determine that the spread includes credit risk, the credit risk cannot be isolated in a way that would allow the change in fair value that is attributable solely to credit risk to be separately identifiable. [IFRS 9:BC6.470]

Despite reaching this conclusion as part of developing IFRS 9, it was not considered by the IASB to represent a change from IAS 39 under which a risk component of a financial item could be designated as the hedged item if it was separately identifiable and reliably measurable and hence did not give rise to any change in the specific requirements for risk component hedging. However, given the IASB's view documented in the Basis for Conclusions on IFRS 9, this effectively introduces a prohibition from designating the credit risk component of a financial item.

As an alternative to designating the credit risk component of a financial item as the hedged item, IFRS 9 contains a fair value option where the credit exposure hedged by a credit derivative may be designated as at FVTPL if specified conditions are satisfied (see **section 7**).

3.12 Foreign currency risk of a forecast foreign currency debt issuance

An entity that has a highly probable forecast debt issuance may wish to cash flow hedge the interest rates and/or the foreign currency risk associated with the issuance. Hedging the interest rate risk is permitted, however, the foreign currency risk can only be hedged if it could affect profit or loss.

IFRS 9 does not provide guidance on whether a hedge of the variability in functional currency equivalent proceeds to be received from a highly probable forecast issuance of debt (denominated in a currency other than the entity's functional currency) attributable to foreign exchange risk can qualify for hedge accounting. It would not appear to be possible to designate the variability in the functional currency equivalent cash flows of a forecast debt issuance in a foreign currency because the foreign currency risk does not affect profit or loss. Foreign currency risk only arises from the date the debt is recognised in the statement of financial position because it is translated thereafter into the entity's functional currency under IAS 21. The quantum of this foreign currency risk that will affect profit or loss following the issue of the debt bears no relation to the quantum of foreign currency risk that arises before the debt is issued.

Example 3.12

Hedging foreign currency risk of forecast foreign currency debt issuance

On 1 January, Entity C, a US dollar functional currency entity, has a highly probable forecast 10% fixed rate debt issuance of €100 million in one month's time, and wishes to hedge the variability in the US dollar equivalent proceeds that it will receive from the point in time when the hedging instrument is entered into to the point in time when the debt is issued. Entity C will enter into a foreign currency forward contract to sell €100 million and to buy an equivalent amount of US dollars, based on the forward rate for delivery when the debt is expected to be issued. At the date Entity C enters into the foreign currency forward contract, it is expected that the combination of the net cash flows from the forward contract and the Euros to be received from issuing the debt should equal US$100 million, all other things being equal.

Entity C cannot designate the changes in foreign currency risk between the date of entering into the derivative and the date the forecast debt is expected to be issued as a qualifying hedge exposure. This is because the foreign currency risk on the debt will only arise and affect profit or loss from the date it is recognised as a liability and is retranslated from Euro to Entity C's US dollar functional currency during the period it remains outstanding. The gains/losses on the forward contract prior to the debt being issued bear no relationship to the foreign currency gains/losses that will be recognised after the debt is issued. Furthermore, the functional currency amount of interest in future periods is unaffected by movements in foreign currency prior to the debt being issued, as illustrated below.

Assume the foreign currency exchange rate at 1 January is US$1:€1 and at 1 February is US$1.5:€1. Using the 1 January exchange rate, the annual interest in US dollars would be US$10 million. At the rate of exchange prevailing on 1 February, the amount of Euro proceeds necessary to raise US$100 million would be €67 million. The related annual interest, assuming constant interest rates, would be €6.7 million. However, translating € into US dollars, the annual interest is still US$10 million (because €6.7 million x 1.5 = US$10 million). As demonstrated, the annual interest expense in functional currency terms is unaffected by a change in exchange rates between the date the foreign currency forward contract is entered into and the date the debt is issued.

Once the debt is issued, it will be a recognised monetary item and will be retranslated from Euro to US dollars on an ongoing basis in accordance with IAS 21 with any resulting foreign exchange gains or losses recognised in profit or loss. Once recognised, the debt could be designated in either a cash flow or fair value hedge of foreign currency risk.

3.13 Hedging capitalised borrowing costs

Neither IFRS 9 nor IAS 23 *Borrowing Costs* provides guidance on whether an entity can cash flow or fair value hedge interest rate risk when the interest is partly or fully capitalised under IAS 23 as part of a qualifying asset. IAS 23 makes reference in its basis of conclusions to the fact that US GAAP does provide specific guidance in this area for fair value hedges. IAS 23:BC21 states that US GAAP "concludes that derivative gains and losses (arising from the effective portion of a derivative instrument that qualifies as a fair value hedge) are part of the capitalised interest cost. IAS 23 does not address such derivative gains and losses".

The capitalisation of borrowing costs in and of itself should not prohibit any entity from applying hedge accounting for interest rate risk for debt that is used to fund a qualifying asset under IAS 23. IFRS 9 requires that a hedge must result in the hedged risk affecting profit or loss (with limited exception in the case of equity investments classified as FVTOCI), which will be the case when interest on debt is capitalised because the qualifying asset will affect profit or loss either through amortisation, impairment or sale.

If an entity applies cash flow hedge accounting it is necessary to consider whether the hedged variable interest cash flows result in the recognition of a non-financial asset as contemplated in IFRS 9:6.5.11(d)(i) (see **6.5.2**). This is because IFRS 9:6.5.11(d)(i) requires that if a hedged forecast transaction subsequently results in the recognition of a non-financial asset, the amount that has been accumulated in the cash flow hedge reserve should be removed and included directly in the initial cost of the non-financial asset as a 'basis-adjustment'.

It could be argued that because the hedged interest cash flows are capitalised as part of the 'qualifying asset' (i.e. a non-financial asset) the hedged forecast interest payments result in the recognition of a non-financial asset and therefore basis-adjustment is required.

Alternatively it could be argued that IFRS 9:6.5.11(d)(i) was intended for future purchases of non-financial assets and in these circumstances the hedged item is forecast interest payments (i.e. a financial item). Therefore the hedged item is financial in nature and the fact that the interest cash flows are capitalised only changes when the hedged forecast interest cash flows affect profit or loss and does not change the financial nature of the forecast transaction. Consequently basis-adjustment under IFRS 9:6.5.11(d)(i) does not apply.

The requirements of IFRS 9 are not clear in this regard and an entity should determine as a matter of accounting policy whether the hedged variable interest cash flows required to be capitalised as borrowing costs results in the recognition of a non-financial asset as contemplated in IFRS 9:6.5.11(d)(i).

The example below sets out two scenarios where cash flow and fair value hedge accounting of interest rate risk is applied when the interest on the borrowing is capitalised under IAS 23.

Example 3.13

Hedging capitalised borrowing costs

Entity A borrows CU10 million to finance the construction of a 'qualifying asset' in accordance with IAS 23. The related borrowing costs are eligible for capitalisation.

Scenario 1: Entity A borrows at fixed rates

Entity A enters into an interest rate swap (with the same notional and term as the debt) to receive fixed pay 3m LIBOR and designates this as a hedge of the fair value exposure to changes in interest rates (say 3m LIBOR) of its debt. Entity A will capitalise under IAS 23 the synthetic floating rate borrowing costs that have been achieved as a result of entering into the effective hedge accounting relationship.

(i) Entity A will determine the effectiveness of the fair value hedge and recognise any ineffectiveness in profit or loss. If the hedge is meets the qualification requirements, the debt will be fair value adjusted for changes in interest rates with the corresponding entry in profit or loss. The fair value adjustment will be amortised to profit or loss either immediately when the adjustment is made or no later than the date the debt ceases to fair value hedge adjusted.

(ii) The synthetic floating interest rate that is achieved as a result of the hedge is capitalised. This amount will include the actual fixed rate on the debt plus the effect of swapping this fixed rate into floating rates.

Scenario 2: Entity A borrows at floating rates

Entity A enters into an interest rate swap to receive 3m LIBOR pay fixed rates (same notional and term as debt) and designates the swap as hedging the variability in its debt due to changes in 3m LIBOR. Entity A intends to cash flow hedge the variability in interest rates on its borrowings even though the interest on the borrowings is capitalised under IAS 23.

Entity A can apply cash flow hedge accounting of the interest rate risk on its variable rate borrowings but the gain/loss on the derivative that is recognised in other comprehensive income is reclassified from equity to profit or loss when the interest component of the qualifying asset affects profit or loss.

Entity A will apply the following steps in order.

(i) Capitalise the variable rate interest on the borrowing in accordance with IAS 23.

(ii) Determine the effectiveness of the cash flow hedge and recognise any ineffectiveness in profit or loss. Recognise the effective gain/loss on the derivative in other comprehensive income.

(iii) Depending on the entity's accounting policy (see the guidance immediately before this example), the amount recognised in other comprehensive income will be either: reclassified from equity to profit or loss when the hedged risk affects profit or loss; or capitalised as a basis-adjustment as part of the qualifying asset. If basis-adjustment is applied, the effect would be equivalent to the entity borrowing at fixed rates and capitalising fixed borrowing costs. If basis-adjustment is not applied, the hedged interest that is capitalised as part of the qualifying asset will affect profit or loss when the qualifying asset is amortised, impaired or is sold. Similarly, the net effect in profit or loss from this reclassification will be equivalent to the entity borrowing at fixed rates and capitalising fixed borrowing costs.

If an entity does not apply hedge accounting and, therefore, the derivatives are classified as at fair value through profit or loss, it is not appropriate for the entity to capitalise part of the derivative as part of the borrowing costs under IAS 23. All gains/losses on non-hedging derivatives must be immediately recognised in profit or loss.

3.14 Hedging own equity

Transactions in an entity's own equity cannot be designated as hedged items. An entity's own equity transactions cannot be hedged because they do not expose the entity to a risk that can affect reported profit or loss. For example, a forecast dividend payment could not be designated as a hedged item, because IAS 32 requires that distributions to owners are recognised directly in equity and, therefore, they do not affect profit or loss. However, a properly declared dividend that has not yet been paid and that is recognised as a financial liability by the payer or as a financial asset by the recipient may qualify as a hedged item for foreign currency risk if it is denominated in a foreign currency because changes in the foreign currency will affect profit or loss.

An entity may be able to designate share-based payment transactions that are exclusively cash settled in an effective hedge accounting relationship. Even though the amount of cash payable varies by reference to the entity's share price, there is a cash flow variability that will affect profit or loss.

3.15 Hedging issued convertible debt

As explained at in **chapter B3**, convertible debt that is determined to be a compound instrument is separated at issue, by the issuer, into a financial liability and an equity conversion option which is included in equity. The financial liability is recognised at the present value of the contractual interest flows and principal, discounted at an interest rate for a debt without the equity conversion option. Because the financial liability is measured as if the entity had issued a partly discounted bond, any hedge of the interest rate risk on this financial liability must also take into account this discount. In addition, because the financial liability will be extinguished when the convertible bond is converted, any hedging instrument should mirror this termination feature in order to increase hedge effectiveness.

3.16 Nominal components

Instead of designating an item in its entirety as the hedged item for a particular risk (or risks), IFRS 9 allows a proportion or layer component of an item to be designated. For example, an entity could designate a proportion of 50 per cent of the contractual cash flows of a loan, or a layer of the first FC10m of foreign currency sales in a particular month. For the same quantum of hedged item, the hedge accounting outcome can be very different depending on how the nominal component is designated. This is why IFRS 9 requires the nominal component to be designated in a way that is consistent with the risk management objective (see **example 3.16A**). [IFRS 9:B6.3.16]

A layer component may be specified from a defined, but open, population, or from a defined nominal amount. Examples include:

[IFRS 9:B6.3.18]

(a) part of a monetary transaction volume, (e.g. the next FC10 cash flows from sales denominated in a foreign currency after the first FC20 in March 201X);

(b) a part of a physical volume, (e.g. the bottom layer, measuring 5 million cubic metres, of the natural gas stored in location XYZ);

(c) a part of a physical or other transaction volume, (e.g. the first 100 barrels of the oil purchases in June 201X or the first 100 MWh of electricity sales in June 201X); or

(d) a layer from the nominal amount of the hedged item, (e.g. the last CU80 million of a CU100 million firm commitment, the bottom layer of CU20 million of a CU100 million fixed-rate bond or the top layer of CU30 million from a total amount of CU100 million of fixed-rate debt that can be prepaid at fair value (the defined nominal amount is CU100 million)).

Although the term 'nominal' is often used in practice to denote the par amount of a loan, as illustrated in the examples in IFRS 9:B6.3.18, the term is much broader.

Examples (a) - (c) above are examples of layer components from defined populations (i.e. sales in March 20X1, gas stored in location XYZ, electricity sales in June 20X1) which are regarded as open because there is no fixed defined overall volume. However, in part (d), the exposures have a defined nominal amount from which the hedged item is defined (i.e. CU100 million). When the exposure has a defined nominal amount it will be possible to designate either a proportion of the defined amount or any layer component of the defined amount except for some prepayable items discussed in **3.11.4**. However, when the exposure is from an open population, it will not be possible to designate a proportion of that exposure (e.g. 20% of foreign currency sales in April 20X5), or a layer of that exposure represented by the last volume (e.g. the last FC100 of sales in April 20X5). This is because these components of a nominal amount cannot be identified from an open population and will not be known until the population is closed (e.g. after the total sales in April 20X5 are known).

Identifying the nominal component of the hedged item will not only be important to demonstrate compliance with the hedge accounting requirements (e.g. as part of determining whether the hedged amount is highly probable or expected to occur, see **3.4.1**), but it will also have consequences on the hedge accounting mechanics. For example, for a cash flow hedge, amounts will be removed or reclassified from equity when the hedged forecast transaction occurs (see **section 6.5.2**), and for fair value hedges the fair value hedge adjustment must be recognised in profit or loss no later than when the item is derecognised. For a layer component in a fair value hedge, this requires an entity to track the nominal amount from which it is defined. For example, in IFRS 9:B6.3.18(d), the total defined nominal amount of CU100 million must be tracked in order to track the bottom layer of CU20 million or the top layer of CU30 million. [IFRS 9:B6.3.19]

Although IFRS 9 identifies components of a nominal amount as the bottom layer or top layer, these amounts are not further defined. For recognised items, a bottom layer is generally regarded as representing the last amount of the item to be derecognised. Therefore, if an entity were to hedge the top CU20 layer of a CU100 fixed rate bond, any hedge adjustment relating to that component that remains when the entity sells CU50 of bond would have to be derecognised upon sale. Whereas, if the entity had hedged the bottom layer of CU20 of that bond, the hedge adjustment would remain and continue to be accounted for as normal. For unrecognised items, such as firm commitments, an entity would have to clearly articulate which layer component is designated in the hedge. For example, if an entity hedges a layer of a firm commitment to purchase a fixed volume of a non-financial item, and part of that firm commitment is cancelled, the cancelled component would come from the top layer and hence give a different hedge accounting outcome depending on which layer was designated in the hedge.

Example 3.16A

Fair value hedging a nominal component of a non-prepayable fixed rate loan

Entity U issues CU100 million of listed non-prepayable fixed rate debt with a 10-year term. In accordance with its risk management strategy, Entity U concurrently transacts an interest rate swap with a notional amount of CU30 million under which it receives a fixed rate and pays CU LIBOR to hedge interest rate risk on CU30 million of debt. Entity U designates the swap in a 10-year fair value hedge of CU30 million of debt.

After six years, the amortised cost carrying amount of the debt is CU97 million which includes a fair value hedge adjustment of CU3 million (debit). At that time, Entity U chooses to buy back CU40 million of debt from the market for CU35 million, and meets the derecognition criteria for CU40 million nominal of its outstanding debt.

The treatment of the hedge adjustment at the time Entity U buys back CU40 million of debt depends on how the CU30 million nominal component of the debt was designated. Three different scenarios are considered below.

The different outcome in each of the different scenarios below illustrates the importance of appropriately defining the nominal component designated in the hedging relationship as the hedged item.

Scenario 1: Bottom layer of CU30 million of debt

Under this scenario, Entity U's risk management objective was to hedge the bottom layer of CU30 million of debt; consequently this nominal component of the total CU100 million of debt was designated in a hedge.

As a result, subsequent to CU40 million of debt being bought back, the fair value hedge adjustment of CU3 million continued to be recognised as part of the carrying amount of the debt which was now CU57 million. Buying back CU40 million of debt for CU35 million gave rise to a gain in profit or loss of CU5 million.

Entity U continued to hold the swap and hedge accounting continued to apply uninterrupted.

Scenario 2: Top layer of CU30 million of debt

Under this scenario, Entity U's risk management objective was to hedge the top layer of CU30 million of debt; consequently this nominal component of the total CU100 million of debt was designated in a hedge.

As a result, subsequent to CU40 million of debt being bought back, the fair value hedge adjustment of CU3 was derecognised as part of the carrying amount of the debt derecognised. The carrying amount of the remaining debt was now CU60 million. Buying back CU40 million nominal of debt with a carrying amount of CU37, for CU35 million, gave rise to a gain in profit or loss of CU2 million.

Entity U continued to hold the swap but discontinued hedge accounting because the designated hedged item no longer existed.

Scenario 3: 30 per cent proportion of CU100 million of debt

Under this scenario, Entity U's risk management objective was to hedge a 30 per cent proportion of CU100 million of debt; consequently this nominal component of the total CU100 million of debt was designated in a hedge.

As a result, subsequent to CU40 million of debt being bought back, 40 per cent of the fair value hedge adjustment of CU3 (i.e. CU1.2 million) was derecognised as part of the carrying amount of the debt derecognised. The carrying amount of the remaining debt was now CU58.2 million. Buying back CU40 million nominal of debt with a carrying amount of CU38.8 million, for CU35 million, gave rise to a gain in profit or loss of CU3.8 million.

Entity U continued to hold the swap but discontinued hedge accounting on 40 per cent of the hedge relationship because 40 per cent of the designated hedged item no longer existed. The undesignated proportion of the swap is re-designated by Entity U in a new hedging relationship of CU12 million of the debt by increasing the proportion of the debt hedged to 50 per cent (i.e. CU30/CU60) of which 30 per cent is a continuing hedge (i.e. 30 per cent of CU60 million, CU18 million) and 20 per cent is a new hedge (i.e. 20 per cent of CU60 million, CU12 million).

As noted in the examples above, designating a layer component of an existing item or contract (e.g. loan or firm commitment) can be more reflective of the risk management objective and is permitted where that component is separately identifiable and reliably measurable. IFRS 9 includes a specific example of when a layer component of an existing item or contract is not eligible and that is a layer component that includes a prepayment option if the prepayment option's fair value is affected by changes in the hedged risk, unless the designated layer includes the effect of the related prepayment option when determining the change in the fair value of the hedged item. [IFRS 9:B6.3.20]

The criteria for hedging prepayable loans in IFRS 9:B6.3.20 is designed to ensure that when determining the fair value sensitivity of the loan, the hedged risk reflects the existence of the prepayment option. Therefore, IFRS 9 does not prohibit hedge accounting of components of a nominal amount by designating the item in layers, however, the Standard requires that changes in the fair value of the prepayment option as a result of changes in the hedged risk must be included when measuring the change in fair value of the hedged item. When cash flows are subject to prepayment, those cash flows generally have interest rate sensitivity because of the existence of the right to prepay. This is the case where the amount that is prepayable is the amortised cost of the cash flows, for example, a right to repay a loan at the par amount plus accrued interest. An example where a prepayment option would not have sensitivity to changes in interest rates is where the option to prepay is at the fair value of the cash flows subject to the prepayment.

Example 3.16B

Hedging a layer of a prepayable fixed rate loan

A loan with a principal amount of CU100 and a maturity of five years that allows the debtor to repay (at par) up to CU10 at the end of each year would mean that CU40 is prepayable (at different points in time), whereas CU60 is non-prepayable and has a five-year fixed term. Because the CU60 is fixed-term debt and cannot be prepaid, its fair value does not include the effect of a prepayment option (i.e. the layer does not include the prepayment option); consequently a layer component of this amount may be designated. However, the changes in fair value related to the prepayable CU40 include a prepayment option whose fair value is affected by changes in interest rate risk. Consequently, a layer component of the CU40 would not be an eligible risk component unless the effect of the related prepayment option is included when determining changes in the fair value of the hedged item.

Example 3.16C

Distinguishing between a bottom and top layer of a prepayable loan

Entity D has a fixed rate loan receivable with a term of five years with a nominal of CU10 million. The borrower can repay a maximum of 40 per cent of the loan at the par amount plus accrued interest. Entity D does not have the right to demand early repayment from the borrower.

In determining the nominal components of the loan, the Entity D will be able to split the loan into two layers. The bottom layer can be considered a CU6 million non-prepayable fixed rate loan. Because the borrower has no right to prepay 60 per cent of the loan, that component of the nominal may be hedged for fair value changes due to changes in interest rates for the full life of the loan. The top layer can be considered a CU4 million prepayable fixed rate loan. Because the borrower has right to prepay 40 per cent of the loan, that component of the nominal may be hedged for fair value changes due to changes in interest rates but the hedged risk must include the interest rate sensitivity arising from the prepayment option. A partial prepayment of the loan by the borrower does not affect the hedge relationship for the bottom layer because it is not subject to prepayment.

If Entity D had a risk management objective of hedging the interest rate sensitivity for all the loan, then a hedging instrument that would be typical in hedging the bottom layer would be a receive fixed, pay floating, interest rate swap with a notional of CU6 million with a maturity of five years. A hedging instrument that would be typical in hedging the top layer would be a receive fixed, pay floating, interest rate swap with a notional of CU4 million with a maturity of five years that contains a knock-out option that results in the swap being early terminated for zero should the loan be prepaid.

Example 3.16D

Hedging multiple layers of a prepayable loan

Entity E has a fixed rate loan receivable with a term of six years with a nominal of CU100 million that is measured at amortised cost. The borrower can repay a maximum of 40 per cent of the loan at the par amount plus accrued interest. Entity E does not have the right to demand early repayment from the borrower.

Entity E has a risk management objective of hedging all the interest rate sensitivity of the loan on a post-prepayment basis, i.e. considering all cash flows that are not expected to be prepaid. Entity E estimates that CU10 million of the loan principal will be repaid and therefore does not economically hedge those cash flows.

Of the CU90 million of the loan not expected to be repaid early, Entity E considers there are two components of the nominal amount. Entity E determines the bottom layer ('the first layer') as all the interest and principal on a nominal of CU60 million. The next layer ('the second layer') is the interest and principal on a nominal of CU30 million, being the cash flows that are potentially subject to prepayment but which are not anticipated to be prepaid.

Entity E has a receive floating, pay fixed, six-year interest rate swap with a notional of CU90 million. It designates two-thirds of the interest rate swap, being a notional of CU60 million, as a hedge of the first layer. Entity E designates one-third of the interest rate swap, being a notional of CU30 million, together with a swaption with a notional of CU30 million (i.e. an option to enter into a swap with CU30 million notional and opposing terms to the original swap for nil consideration effectively closing out CU30 million of original swap) as a hedge of the second layer.

The first layer of the loan is adjusted for changes in the fair value attributable to changes in interest rates. The second layer of the loan is also adjusted for changes in the fair value attributable to changes in interest rates but this also includes the changes in fair value attributable to the prepayment option.

If the borrower prepays CU10 million of the loan, as Entity E expects, there will be a gain or loss on derecognition – being the difference between the amount received from the borrower and the amortised cost of the CU10 million of the loan that is prepaid. Prepayments after the first CU10 million would also result in a gain or loss on derecognition being the difference between the amount received from the borrower and the carrying amount of the portion of the second layer of the loan that is prepaid. The carrying amount of the second layer is the amortised cost amount plus or minus the unamortised cumulative fair value hedge adjustment.

IFRS 9:B6.3.19 makes clear that when fair value hedging a layer component of a nominal amount, like with **example 3.16D**, the entity must be able track the item to which the fair value hedge adjustment relates. Tracking is needed because the entity must be able to systemically release the amount of the fair value hedge adjustment to profit or loss as IFRS 9 requires that the fair value hedge adjustment must be recognised in profit or loss no later than when the item is derecognised.

3.17 Relationship between components and the total cash flows of an item

If a component of the cash flows of a financial or non-financial item is designated as the hedged item, that component must be less than or equal to the total cash flows of the entire item. However, all of the cash flows of the entire item may be designated as the hedged item and hedged for only one particular risk (e.g. only for those changes that are attributable to changes in LIBOR or a benchmark commodity price). [IFRS 9:B6.3.21]

For example, in the case of a financial liability whose effective interest rate is below LIBOR, an entity cannot designate:

[IFRS 9: B6.3.22]

(a) a component of the liability equal to interest at LIBOR (plus the principal amount in case of a fair value hedge); and

(b) a negative residual component.

However, in the case of a fixed-rate financial liability whose effective interest rate is (for example) 100 basis points below LIBOR, an entity can designate as the hedged item the change in the value of that entire liability (ie principal plus interest at LIBOR minus 100 basis points) that is attributable to changes in LIBOR. [IFRS 9:B6.3.23]

Example 3.17A

Fair value hedging sub-LIBOR fixed rate debt

Entity XYZ issues fixed rate debt at 3.75 per cent when LIBOR is 4 per cent. Entity XYZ would like to hedge its debt for interest rate risk arising from changes in the benchmark interest rate, i.e. LIBOR.

Entity XYZ *cannot* designate a LIBOR component (4 per cent) as the hedged risk as this amount is greater than the contractual cash flow on the hedged item. However, Entity XYZ can designate all of the contractual cash flows of the debt instrument as the hedged item and specify that these cash flows are hedged for changes that are attributable to LIBOR. In order for Entity XYZ to comply with the hedge effectiveness requirements, Entity XYZ will need to carefully consider the appropriate hedge ratio for the hedge relationship.

If an entity enters into a fair value hedge of a fixed rate asset or a liability after its initial recognition, IFRS 9 permits the entity to designate as the hedged item a portion of the cash flows equal to the benchmark rate (e.g. LIBOR) that is higher than the contractual fixed rate received or paid on the asset or liability, provided that the benchmark rate is less than the recalculated effective interest rate on the asset or liability calculated as if the entity had purchased or issued the instrument on the date it first designates the hedged item. [IFRS 9:B6.3.23]

Assume an entity issues a fixed rate bond at par that will redeem at par. At a later date, it enters into an interest rate swap to hedge its exposure to changes in the fair value of the liability attributable to the benchmark interest rate. If the swap has a fair value of zero at inception and interest rates have fallen since the bond was issued, the coupons on the bond will be higher than the contracted fixed receipts on the interest rate swap. Because the fixed receipts on the swap are lower than the contractual fixed rate coupons on the bond, the entity can designate as the hedged item a portion of each coupon cash flow equal to the fixed receipts of the swap. The fixed receipts of the swap and the cash flows on the designated portion of the bond will match and the hedge is likely to meet the hedge effectiveness requirements.

If interest rates have risen since the bond was issued, the coupons on the bond may be lower than the contractual fixed receipts on the interest rate swap. The entity can designate the bond as hedged for the benchmark interest rate portion of its fair value interest rate risk, provided that the benchmark rate is less than the effective interest rate of the hedged item, calculated based on the assumption that the entity had issued the bond on the date the hedge is designated. [IFRS 9:B6.3.23]

This is achieved by designating as the hedged risk both the contractual coupon payments and an amount of discount which is included in the difference between the current fair value of the bond and the amount repayable at maturity. A hedge designated in this way is likely to exhibit ineffectiveness because the fixed cash flows of the swap will have a different profile from the fixed cash flows of the hedged item; the fixed interest cash flows of the swap are composed of equal payments, while the hedged interest cash flows on the bond comprise lower contractual payments and a discount to par. The different cash flow profiles will result in different changes in fair value in response to changes in interest rates.

To minimise ineffectiveness, an entity may need to enter into a swap with a fixed leg rate equal to or lower than the contractual coupons on the bond. Such a swap does not have a zero fair value at inception because it is not entered into at market interest rates. When the upfront payment on the swap is structured to be equivalent to the discount on the bond, the swap will be more effective at hedging the bond than an on-market swap with nil fair value.

Example 3.17B

Fair value hedging fixed rate debt when interest rates have moved since issue

Entity F originated a four-year 5 per cent fixed rate loan of CU10,000 on 1 January 20X2, with a maturity date of 31 December 20X5. Of the 5 per cent coupon, 0.4 per cent represents credit spread (i.e. the market rate of interest was 4.6 per cent). Interest is receivable annually. The effective interest rate of Entity F's loan at inception is 5 per cent.

Scenario 1: Interest rates fall between 1/1/20X2 and 31/12/20X2

One year later, interest rates have fallen. At 31 December 20X2, the loan has a fair value of CU10,251. Entity F wishes to protect its loan asset against an increase in interest rates by entering into a fair value hedge of interest rate risk. The current market rate of interest is now 3.5 per cent, rather than 4.6 per cent.

Entity F enters into a receive-variable rate, pay-fixed rate of 3.5 per cent interest rate swap on 31 December 20X2 with a maturity of 31 December 20X5 to hedge its fair value interest rate exposure. The swap is on-market, i.e. it has a fair value of zero at inception.

The benchmark interest rate of 3.5 per cent is lower than the contractual cash flows of the loan and, therefore, Entity F is permitted to designate as the hedged item a portion equal to the benchmark rate (e.g. LIBOR).

Scenario 2: Interest rates increase between 1/1/20X2 and 31/12/20X2

One year later, interest rates have increased. At 31 December 20X2, the loan has a fair value of CU9,081. Entity F wishes to protect its loan asset against a further increase in interest rates by entering into a fair value hedge of the interest rate risk. The current market rate of interest is now 6 per cent, rather than 4.6 per cent.

Entity F enters into a receive-variable rate, pay-fixed rate of 6 per cent interest rate swap on 31 December 20X2 with a maturity of 31 December 20X5 to hedge its fair value interest rate exposure. The swap is on-market, i.e. it has a fair value of zero at inception.

If Entity F had originated the loan when the hedging swap was entered into, it would not have originated the loan at 5 per cent, but at 6.4 per cent, i.e. at the benchmark interest market rate plus the appropriate margin given the counterparty's credit rating, i.e. the (6 per cent + 0.4 per cent). The benchmark interest rate of 6 per cent is lower than the effective interest rate of this 'hypothetical loan' and, therefore, Entity F is permitted to designate as the hedged item a portion equal to the benchmark rate (e.g. LIBOR) that is higher than the contractual fixed rate received on the asset.

Items with contractually specified risk components and negative margins can be designated as hedged items, however, the presence of negative margins will often limit the range of variability due to embedded floors in the contract that prevent the cash flows of the contract becoming negative. Hence if such risks are hedged with derivatives that do not contain a corresponding embedded cap to limit the cash flows on the derivative, hedge ineffectiveness may arise.

Example 3.17C

Hedging a variable rate financial liability with negative margin

[IFRS 9:B6.3.24]

If a variable-rate financial liability bears interest of (for example) three-month LIBOR minus 20 basis points (with a floor at zero basis points), an entity can designate as the hedged item the change in the cash flows of that entire liability (ie three-month LIBOR minus 20 basis points – including the floor) that is attributable to changes in LIBOR. Hence, as long as the three-month LIBOR forward curve for the remaining life of that liability does not fall below 20 basis points, the hedged item has the same cash flow variability as a liability that bears interest at three-month LIBOR with a zero or positive spread. However, if the three-month LIBOR forward curve for the remaining life of that liability (or a part of it) falls below 20 basis points, the hedged item has a lower cash flow variability than a liability that bears interest at three-month LIBOR with a zero or positive spread.

Example 3.17D

Hedging a variable rate non-financial liability with negative margin

[IFRS 9:B6.3.25]

A similar example of a non-financial item is a specific type of crude oil from a particular oil field that is priced off the relevant benchmark crude oil. If an entity sells that crude oil under a contract using a contractual pricing formula that sets the price per barrel at the benchmark crude oil price minus CU10 with a floor of CU15, the entity can designate as the hedged item the entire cash flow variability under the sales contract that is attributable to the change in the benchmark crude oil price. However, the entity cannot designate a component that is equal to the full change in the benchmark crude oil price. Hence, as long as the forward price (for each delivery) does not fall below CU25, the hedged item has the same cash flow variability as a crude oil sale at the benchmark crude oil price (or with a positive spread). However, if the forward price for any delivery falls below CU25, the hedged item has a lower cash flow variability than a crude oil sale at the benchmark crude oil price (or with a positive spread).

4 Groups of hedged items

IFRS 9 permits a group of items to be designated in a hedge relationship if specified criteria are met. A group of items is eligible to be hedged as a group if the items (including a group of items that constitute a net position; see IFRS 9:B6.6.1 - B6.6.8) only if:

[IFRS 9:6.6.1]

(a) it consists of items (including components of items, see **section 3.11**) that are, individually, eligible hedged items; (see **section 3**)

(b) the items in the group are managed together on a group basis for risk management purposes; and

(c) in the case of a cash flow hedge of a group of items whose variabilities in cash flows are not expected to be approximately proportional to the overall variability in cash flows of the group so that offsetting risk positions arise:

(i) it is a hedge of foreign currency risk; and

(ii) the designation of that net position specifies the reporting period in which the forecast transactions are expected to affect profit or loss, as well as their nature and volume (see IFRS 9:B6.6.7 - B6.6.8).

The following flowchart summarises the requirements of IFRS 9:6.6.1 and clarifies when a group of hedged items is eligible to be designated in a hedge relationship:

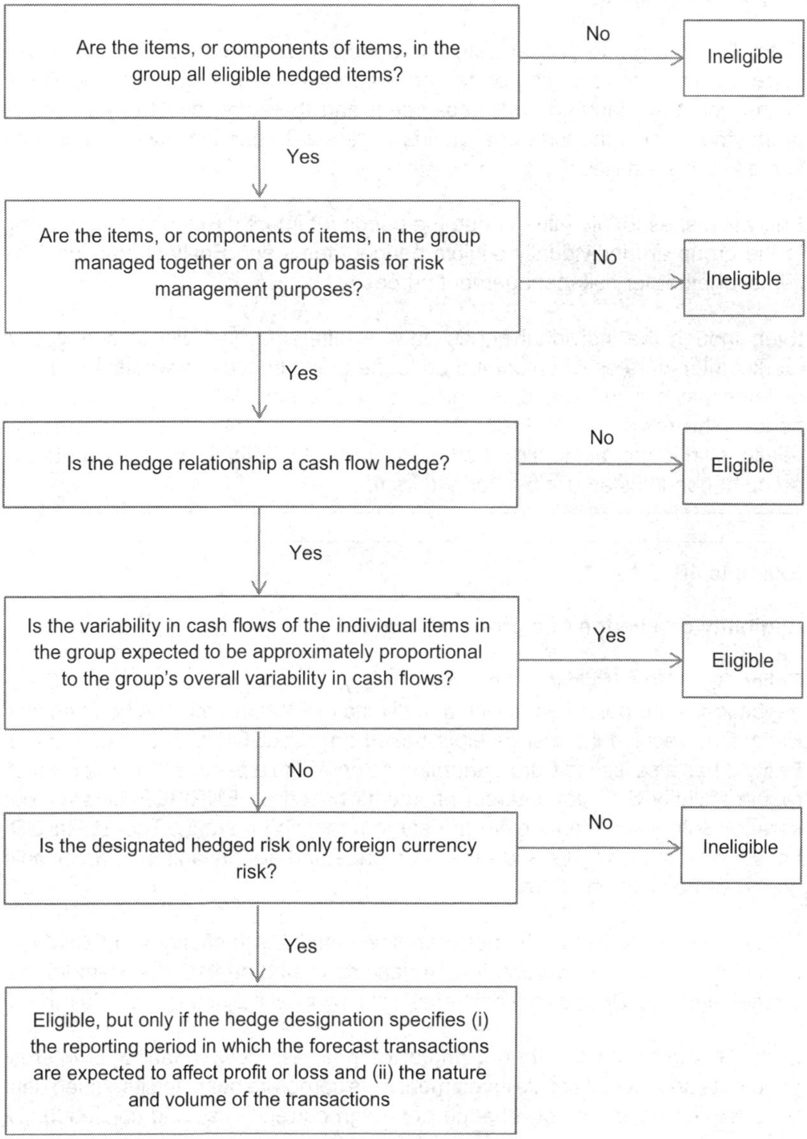

A group of items can be a group of items that form a gross position or a group of (partially) offsetting items or risks that result in a net position. However, as noted in IFRS 9:6.6.1(c) a net position is not always eligible for hedge accounting if it is a cash flow hedge as IFRS 9 restricts cash flow hedges of net positions to certain foreign currency hedges only. This restriction is not applicable for fair value hedges.

Example 4A

Eligibility of a hedge of a group of items (1)

Entity P has a group of fixed rate corporate bonds denominated in the same currency. The fixed rate corporate bonds contain different rights for the holder of the bonds to demand early repayment and therefore, due to the different prepayment risks, the individual bonds have a different sensitivity to changes in market interest rates.

Entity P wishes to fair value hedge the bonds for interest rate risk. All the items in the group are individually eligible hedged items and Entity P manages the items together for risk management purposes.

Even though the individual bonds have a different sensitivity to changes in market interest rates when compared to the group because a whole, the group of items may still be hedged as a group as the hedge relationship is a fair value hedge. The restriction in IFRS 9:6.6.1(c) does not apply because the hedge relationship is not a cash flow hedge. Accordingly, Entity P may designate the group of bonds as an eligible hedged item.

Example 4B

Eligibility of a hedge of a group of items (2)

Entity S, a Euro functional currency entity, has an investment in a Euro-denominated corporate bond with a par value of €100 million. The bond entitles Entity S to receive interest receipts based on EURIBOR plus a fixed spread. Entity S has also issued Euro-denominated debt with a par of €120 million which requires Entity S to pay interest payments based on EURIBOR plus a fixed spread. Both investments have the same remaining maturity. The EURIBOR-based interest payments and receipts reprice and are payable and receivable on the same payment dates.

Entity S wishes to hedge the net cash flow variability to changes in EURIBOR on its investment in its corporate bond and its issued debt. Entity S enters into a receive-EURIBOR, pay fixed, interest rate swap with a nominal of €20 million.

Entity S is not permitted to designate the net cash flow variability of interest payments and receipts on its investment in its corporate bond and its issued debt because the hedge is not a hedge of foreign currency risk and consequently, would breach the requirement in IFRS 9:6.6.1(c).

Entity S may instead apply an alternative designation that is eligible that is not a hedge of a group of items. Entity S could designate the interest rate swap as a hedge of the cash flow variability due to changes in EURIBOR on a sixth (€20m/€120m) of the issued debt. This designation is not a hedge of a group of items but rather a hedge of a proportion of a single item.

Where a net position is designated the entity must specify the gross items that make up the net position and designate them together as the hedged item. An entity is not permitted to merely designate an abstract net position that does not specify the items that form the group. [IFRS 9:B6.6.4]

The IASB noted that a hedge of an individual item is similar to a hedge of a group of hedged items and therefore a similar approach to hedge accounting should apply. Consequently, the IASB proposed that the eligibility criteria that apply to individual hedged items should also apply to hedges of groups of items. However, some restrictions were retained for cash flow hedges of net positions. [IFRS 9:BC6.436]

The restrictions in IFRS 9:6.6.1(c) were developed following lengthy debate by the IASB as to how to apply cash flow hedging when the items that make up the net position are expected to arise in different reporting periods. An example is a hedge of the foreign currency risk of a foreign currency denominated forecast sale and purchase. Although economically the net foreign currency risk arising from the offsetting sale and purchase is being hedged, it was noted that it was challenging how to report the amount of the sale or purchase when one arises before the other. This challenge arises for cash flow hedges as gains or losses arising from the hedging instrument are reclassified from other comprehensive income to profit and loss when the hedged item impacts profit or loss. The IASB noted that when the first forecast transaction occurs this would involve deferring in other comprehensive income the cumulative gains and losses on that forecast transaction from the time it occurred until other forecast transactions affect profit or loss in later reporting periods. When those later transactions occurred, their measurement would be adjusted for the amounts deferred in other comprehensive income on forecast transactions that had occurred earlier. [IFRS 9:BC6.444]

The IASB concluded that this would be a significant departure from the general IFRS requirements and the requirements of the hedge accounting model for hedging instruments so when the IASB produced its exposure draft that preceded the changes to IFRS 9 the IASB proposed prohibiting all cash flow hedges of net positions where the offsetting risk positions would affect profit or loss in different periods. Yet, following deliberation of the feedback on the exposure draft the IASB partially reversed its restriction for cash flow hedges of net positions of foreign currency only as they considered these hedges were most common. To reduce the risk of earnings management where an entity could use hindsight to allocate the hedging gains or losses to those items so as to achieve a particular result in profit or loss, the IASB required that the hedge designation specifies the reporting period in which the forecast transactions are expected to affect profit or loss, as well as their nature and volume. IFRS 9:BC6.455 includes an example of this where an entity would specify in the hedge documentation the nature of the forecast purchase, such as items of property, plant and equipment, including the depreciation pattern and if the nature of those items is such that the depreciation pattern could vary depending on how the entity uses those items (such as different useful lives because of being used in different production processes).

Example 4C

Cash flow hedge of a net foreign currency position when the transactions occur in the same period

Entity P has forecast sales of €10 million and a forecast purchase of property, plant and equipment (PPE) of €12 million in one year's time. Entity P has a AUS$ functional currency.

Entity P wishes to hedge the net foreign currency position of €2 million by entering into a purchase €/sell AUS$ forward contract that matures in one year.

The PPE, once recognised, will be depreciated on a straight-line basis over five years.

For illustration only, this example assumes that (1) the spot rate equals the forward rate and the currency basis spread is nil, (2) the forecast sales and (3) purchase occur in one year as expected and there is no hedge ineffectiveness.

The AUS$/€ spot rates are as follows.

At inception of the hedge	1.50
In one year's time	1.40

The following journals, in AUS$ millions, would apply:

Year 1

		AUS$m	AUS$m
Dr	Other comprehensive income	0.2	
Cr	Derivative		0.2

To recognise the change in fair value of the derivative as fully effective in hedging the net foreign currency position [(€2m @ 1.40) - (€2m@1.5) = -AUS$0.2m]

		AUS$m	AUS$m
Dr	Derivative	0.2	
Cr	Cash		0.2

To recognise the net settlement of the derivative

		AUS$m	AUS$m
Dr	Cash	14.0	
Cr	Revenue		14.0

To recognise the receipt of €10m from the sales translated at the spot rate of 1.40 AUS$/€

Dr	Other comprehensive income	1.0	
Cr	Net position hedging gain/loss*		1.0

*To reclassify the portion of the cumulative gain/loss on the hedging derivative from equity to profit or loss when the sale affects profit or loss [(€10m @1.5) – (€10m @1.4) = AUS$1.0m] and to present the effect of the net position hedging in a separate line**

		AUS$m	AUS$m
Dr	PPE	16.8	
Cr	Cash		16.8

To recognise the payment of €12m for the purchase of the PPE translated at the spot rate of 1.40 AUS$/€

		AUS$m	AUS$m
Dr	PPE	1.2	
Cr	Other comprehensive income		1.2

To remove the remaining portion of the cumulative gain/loss on the hedging derivative from other comprehensive income to include it in the initial recognition of the PPE [(€12m @1.4) – (€12m @ 1.5) = -AUS$1.2m]

Years 2 to 5

		AUS$m	AUS$m
Dr	Depreciation	3.36	
Cr	PPE		3.36

To depreciate the PPE over five years based on the initial cost of the PPE excluding the basis adjustment [(AUS$16.8m) / 5 = AUS$3.36m]

		AUS$m	AUS$m
Dr	Net position hedging gain/loss**	0.24	
Cr	PPE		0.24

To present in a separate line the effect of the net position hedging [AUS$1.2m / 5]*

Income statement (AUS$m)

	1	2	3	4	5	6	Total
Revenue	14.00						14.00
Net position hedging gain/loss	1.00	(0.24)	(0.24)	(0.24)	(0.24)	(0.24)	(0.20)
Depreciation		(3.36)	(3.36)	(3.36)	(3.36)	(3.36)	(16.80)
Profit	15.00	(3.60)	(3.60)	(3.60)	(3.60)	(3.60)	(3.00)

Statement of financial position (AUS$m)

	1	2	3	4	5	6
Cash	(3.0)	(3.0)	(3.0)	(3.0)	(3.0)	(3.0)
PPE	18.0	14.4	10.8	7.2	3.6	0

* Note that because this example is a cash flow hedge of a net position, the line items that relate to the hedged item (i.e. revenue and depreciation) remain unaffected from the application of hedge accounting because, in accordance with IFRS 9:6.6.4 (see **section 4.2**), hedging gains and losses are presented in a separate line.

Example 4D

Cash flow hedge of a net foreign currency position when the transactions occur in different periods

Entity E, a £ functional currency entity, has a foreign currency denominated purchase commitment of CAN$10 million on 31 March 20X6. It also has a foreign currency denominated sale commitment of CAN$8 million on 30 April 20X6. On 1 January 20X6, Entity E hedges the net foreign currency exposure of the group of sale and purchase commitments that constitute the net position of CAN$2 million by entering into a foreign exchange forward contract to buy CAN$2 million and sell £1.0 million; the forward contract matures on 31 March 20X6. The non-financial asset arising from the purchase is subsequently sold on 31 July 20X6.

	Spot rate	**Forward rate**	**Fair value of forward contract £**
1 January 20X6	CAN$2:£1	CAN$2:£1	
31 March 20X6	CAN$1.8:£1	CAN$1.8:£1	111,111
30 April 20X6	CAN$1.6:£1		

For illustrative purposes only, this example assumes that (1) the spot and forward rates are the same and the currency basis spread is nil, (2) there is no hedge ineffectiveness and (3) there is no discounting.

1 January 20X6

The foreign currency forward has a fair value of zero when it is entered into and therefore there are no journal entries.

31 March 20X6

		£ '000s	**£ '000s**
Dr	Asset	5,556	
Cr	Cash		5,556

To recognise the purchases of CAN$10 million at the spot rate [CAN$10m /1.8]

		£ '000s	£ '000s
Dr	Forward contract	111	
Cr	Cash flow hedge reserve		111

To recognise the change in fair value of the effective portion of the forward in the cash flow hedge reserve via other comprehensive income

		£ '000s	£ '000s
Dr	Cash flow hedge reserve	556	
Cr	Asset		556

To basis adjust the foreign currency denominated hedged purchases for the grossed up portion of the change in value of the hedging instrument relating to the hedged purchase [CAN$10m/2.0 – CAN$10m/1.8]. Following the reclassification of the hedge adjustment the Canadian Dollar purchases are recognised at £5 million, being the hedged rate. When the purchases impact the profit or loss (whether through sale or impairment) the effect of net position hedging i.e. the gain of CAN$556k must be presented in a separate line.

		£ '000s	£ '000s
Dr	Cash	111	
Cr	Forward contract		111

To recognise the cash settlement of the forward contract at maturity

30 April 20X6

		£ '000s	£ '000s
Dr	Cash	5,000	
Cr	Sales		5,000

To recognise the sales of CAN$8m at the spot rate [CAN$8m / 1.6]

		£ '000s	£ '000s
Dr	Net position hedging gain/loss*	444	
Cr	Cash flow hedge reserve		444

To reclassify a grossed up portion of the cumulative gain/loss on the hedging derivative from other comprehensive income to profit or loss [CAN$8m/2.0 – CAN$8m/1.8]. The reclassification reflects the remaining amount in the cash flow hedge reserve being a net loss on the hedge of foreign currency risk from 1 January 20X6 to 31 March 20X6 effectively representing a loss on the foreign currency denominated hedged purchase of £556k and a gain on the forward of £111k which together offsets the gain of £444k on sales over the same period.

31 July 20X6

		£ '000s	£ '000s
Dr	Cost of sales	5,556	
Cr	Net position hedging gain/loss*		556
Cr	Asset		5,000

To derecognise the asset arising from the purchase and recognise the cost of sales excluding the effect of the hedge which is presented separately.

Because the hedge was perfectly effective during the periods, the foreign currency denominated sales and purchases are both reflected in profit or loss, on a net basis, at the hedged rate.

This same group of hedged items (assuming they are firm commitments) could have been designated as a fair value hedge of a net position, where the firm commitments would have been hedge adjusted through profit or loss for changes in the hedged risk and the gain/loss on the forward would have been presented in a separate line in accordance with IFRS 9:6.6.4 (see **section 4.2**).

* Note that because this example is a cash flow hedge of a net position, the line items that relate to the hedged item (i.e. sales and cost of sales) remain unaffected from the application of hedge accounting as, in accordance with IFRS 9:6.6.4 (see **section 4.2**), hedging gains and losses are presented in a separate line.

4.1 Designation of components of nominal amounts of groups

A component of a nominal amount may be eligible as a hedged item. Further guidance is included in **3.16**. IFRS 9 also permits components of nominal amounts of groups of items to be designated in a hedge accounting relationship.

A component that is a proportion of an eligible group of items is an eligible hedged item provided that designation is consistent with the entity's risk management objective. [IFRS 9:6.6.2]

Designating a layer component of an overall group of items is more complex than hedging a fully proportionate component of a nominal amount as additional criteria need to be met. A layer component of an overall group of items (e.g. a bottom layer or a top layer) is eligible for hedge accounting only if:

[IFRS 9:6.6.3]

(a) it is separately identifiable and reliably measurable;

(b) the risk management objective is to hedge a layer component;

(c) the items in the overall group from which the layer is identified are exposed to the same hedged risk (so that the measurement of the hedged layer is not significantly affected by which particular items from the overall group form part of the hedged layer);

(d) for a hedge of existing items (e.g. an unrecognised firm commitment or a recognised asset) an entity can identify and track the overall group of items from which the hedged layer is defined (so that the entity is able to comply with the requirements for the accounting for qualifying hedging relationships); and

(e) any items in the group that contain prepayment options meet the requirements for components of a nominal amount (see IFRS 9:B6.3.20).

Example 4.1A

Hedging a fully proportionate component of a group of nominal amounts

Entity A has a portfolio of non-prepayable corporate fixed rate bonds that are denominated in the entity's functional currency. Entity A is exposed to the fair value risk of changes in market interest rates. Rather than hedge the fair value risk for all of the bonds, Entity A has a risk management strategy to hedge 30 per cent of the nominal of all corporate bonds within the portfolio, (i.e. to hedge the fair value risk associated with 30 per cent of the bonds). Rather than enter into a derivative instrument for each bond, Entity A chooses to hedge the interest risk on a portfolio basis and by doing so, matches the notional of the interest rate swap with the sum of the designated components of the nominal amounts on the bonds in the portfolio. Entity A is able to identify and track the bonds within the group because they are individually identifiable and documented.

Example 4.1B

Hedging a group of non-prepayable amortising loans

Entity B has a portfolio of non-prepayable fixed rate amortising loans issued in the same month that are denominated in the entity's functional currency. The amortisation schedule for each loan within the portfolio is the same and Entity B is able to identify the timing of the contractual cash flows of each loan. The sum of the notional amounts of all loans in the portfolio is CU1,000 million. However, Entity B has a policy of not hedging the interest rate risk on the whole portfolio; rather, its policy is to hedge a bottom layer nominal amount equivalent to 25 per cent of the total nominal amount of the group. Entity B therefore identifies the overall group of items from which it designates a bottom layer of CU250 million as the hedged item.

The IASB noted that there are additional benefits of identifying a layer component of a nominal amount of a group of items that do not apply when designating a layer component of a single hedged item. These included:

[IFRS 9:BC6.439]

(a) uncertainties such as a breach (or cancellation) of contracts, or prepayment, can be better modelled when considering a group of items;

(b) in practice, hedging layers of groups of items (e.g. a bottom layer) is a common risk management strategy; and

(c) arbitrarily identifying and designating (as hedged items) specific items from a group of items that are exposed to the same hedged risk can:

(i) give rise to arbitrary accounting results if the designated items do not behave as originally expected (while other items, sufficient to cover the hedged amount, do behave as originally expected); and

(ii) can provide opportunities for earnings management (e.g. by choosing to transfer and derecognise particular items from a group of homogeneous items when only some were specifically designated into a fair value hedge and therefore have fair value hedge adjustments attached to them).

4.2 Presentation of hedges of group of items

For a hedge of a group of items with offsetting risk positions (i.e. in a hedge of a net position) whose hedged risk affects different line items in the statement of profit or loss and other comprehensive income, any hedging gains or losses in that statement shall be presented in a separate line from those affected by the hedged items. Hence, in that statement the amount in the line item that relates to the hedged item itself (e.g. revenue or cost of sales) remains unaffected. [IFRS 9:6.6.4]

As part of the IASB's deliberations that led to the finalisation of IFRS 9 the Board concluded it was preferable to require a separate line in profit or loss or other comprehensive income for the hedging gains or losses where the hedged risk affects different line items. The alternative to a separate line item would be grossing up the hedging gains or losses and allocating them to the gross items that make up portfolio. The Board considered that such an approach would be distorting gains or losses with amounts that did not exist. [IFRS 9:BC6.458]

Examples 4C and **4D** illustrate the separate presentation of hedging gains or losses arising from hedges of net positions. As can be seen from these examples, cash flow hedging net positions of items that effect different lines in profit or loss, and in different reporting periods, requires additional tracking of hedging gains or losses in order to ensure they are separately recognised in accordance with IFRS 9:6.6.4.

For assets and liabilities that are hedged together as a group in a fair value hedge, the gain or loss in the statement of financial position on the individual assets and liabilities shall be recognised as an adjustment of the carrying amount of the respective individual items comprising the group in accordance with IFRS 9:6.5.8(b). [IFRS 9:6.6.5]

Because the treatment of gains or losses for both the hedged item and the hedging instrument in a fair value hedge is the same, the IASB did not believe any changes to the fair value hedge accounting mechanics were necessary to accommodate fair value hedges of net positions.

However, in situations in which some hedging gains or losses are considered a modification of revenue or an expense (e.g. when the net interest accrual on an interest rate swap is considered a modification of the interest revenue or expense on the hedged item), those gains or losses should be presented in a separate line when the hedged item is a net position. [IFRS 9:BC6.459]

4.3 Nil net positions

IFRS 9 has specific requirements when hedging an exposure that is a net nil position (i.e. the hedged items among themselves fully offset the risk that is managed on a group basis). In those circumstances an entity is permitted to designate that net nil position in a hedging relationship that does not include a hedging instrument, provided that:

[IFRS 9:6.6.6]

(a) the hedge is part of a rolling net risk hedging strategy, whereby the entity routinely hedges new positions of the same type as time moves on (e.g. when transactions move into the time horizon for which the entity hedges);

(b) the hedged net position changes in size over the life of the rolling net risk hedging strategy and the entity uses eligible hedging instruments to hedge the net risk (i.e. when the net position is not nil);

(c) hedge accounting is normally applied to such net positions when the net position is not nil and it is hedged with eligible hedging instruments; and

(d) not applying hedge accounting to the nil net position would give rise to inconsistent accounting outcomes, because the accounting would not recognise the offsetting risk positions that would otherwise be recognised in a hedge of a net position.

Example 4.3

Hedging a net risk exposure of nil

Entity Y economically hedges the foreign currency risk of foreign currency denominated sales and purchases. Entity Y's risk management strategy is to eliminate all foreign currency risk and it does this by hedging the net foreign currency risk exposure using foreign currency forwards. The group of foreign denominated sales and purchases are not expected to all occur in the same period. Consequently, Entity Y applies hedge accounting to the net position of sales and purchases.

Following many periods of applying hedge accounting to the net open position when the amount of foreign currency forecast sales exceeds forecast purchases, or *vice versa*, Entity Y estimates that the amount of hedged foreign currency forecast sales over the next three years will equal that of forecast purchases over the same period. Together these hedged sales and purchases represent a net nil position because Entity Y only hedges three years out.

Entity Y is permitted to apply hedge accounting to the net nil position because:

- the hedge is part of a rolling net risk hedging strategy;
- the net position changes in size over the life of the strategy;
- Entity Y normally hedges the net position when it is other than nil; and
- if Entity Y did not apply hedge accounting to the net nil position, this would have resulted in inconsistent accounting outcomes.

For example, not applying hedge accounting would result in the sales and purchases being recognised at the prevailing spot exchange rates in each year with no offsetting effect between each period which is inconsistent with the treatment applied when the net position is not nil.

The IASB considered it was justified in permitting hedge accounting for nil net positions even though there is no hedging instrument (unlike all other eligible hedge relationships) as they considered a nil net position would arise coincidentally. The IASB also noted that to prohibit hedge accounting for nil net positions could lead to distorted results for an entity that otherwise hedged (with eligible hedging instruments) and applied hedge accounting on a net basis. For example, in periods in which hedge accounting is permitted (because a net position exists and is hedged with a hedging instrument), the transactions would affect profit or loss at an overall hedged rate or price; whereas in periods in which hedge accounting would not be permitted (because the net position is nil), transactions would affect profit or loss at prevailing spot rates or prices. [IFRS 9:BC6.466]

The IASB also noted that such situations would be coincidental and hence it expected that nil net positions would be rare in practice [IFRS 9:BC6.467]

4.4 Portfolio fair value hedge of interest rate risk

Although the hedge accounting model in IFRS 9 allows some limited groups of hedged items to be hedge accounted, it does not include a model to cater for fair value hedging interest rate risk for a dynamic (open) portfolio of financial assets (e.g. a portfolio of prepayable mortgage assets) or financial liabilities. This hedging activity is often referred to as 'macro hedging'. The IASB is undertaking a project to explore the development of a model to address the measurement inconsistencies that arise from macro hedging. In the absence of an alternative model, IFRS 9 allows entities to apply the specific hedge accounting requirements in IAS 39 in respect of portfolio fair value hedging of interest rate risk (including designating as the hedged item a portion that is a currency amount and complying with the hedge effectiveness requirements of IAS 39 (see IAS 39:81A, 89A and AG114 to

AG132)). [IFRS 9:6.1.3] See **section 7** of **chapter C10** of *iGAAP 2016 Financial Instruments: IAS 39 and related Standards – Volume C*, Deloitte's companion volume for this manual.

5 Qualifying criteria for hedge accounting

In order to apply hedge accounting, the following criteria must be met from inception of the hedge and on an ongoing basis: [IFRS 9:6.4.1]

- the hedging sinstruments (see **section 2**) and eligible hedged items (see **sections 3** and **4**).
- at inception of the hedging relationship there is formal designation and documentation of the hedging relationship and the entity's risk management objective and strategy for undertaking the hedge (see **section 5.1**).
- the hedging relationship meets all of the hedge effectiveness requirements (see **section 5.2**).

Once these criteria are met, hedge accounting *must* be applied for the hedging relationship and can only be discontinued when the hedge cease to meet the qualifying criteria (see **section 6.3**).

5.1 Documenting a hedging relationship

To adopt hedge accounting for a particular hedging relationship is a choice which is available if the criteria for hedge accounting can be met and is applied prospectively once all of the requirements as satisfied. A key qualification for applying hedge accounting is that there is formal designation and documentation of the hedging relationship at inception of the hedge. This is to avoid any ambiguity as to whether hedge accounting has been adopted and reduce the risk of manipulation of the accounting results through retrospective designations. That documentation must contain each of the following components: [IFRS 9:6.4.1(b)]

- documentation of the entity's risk management strategy and objective for undertaking the hedge;
- identification of the hedging instrument;
- identification of the hedged item;
- the nature of the risk being hedged; and
- how the entity will assess whether the hedging relationship meets the hedge effectiveness requirements (including its analysis of the sources of hedge ineffectiveness and how it determines the hedge ratio) (see **section 5.2**).

Without the necessary hedge documentation, hedge accounting cannot be applied.

Example 5.1A

Designating foreign currency deposits as a hedging instrument

Bank B accepts US$-denominated deposits from its depositors; the US$ is not Bank B's functional currency. The deposits are time deposits with a short maturity which can be withdrawn by depositors at the end of their term. Based on historical experience, time deposits are withdrawn and replaced with new time deposits from different depositors or existing depositors roll over their deposits with the bank beyond the contractual maturity. Bank B asserts that the total deposit balance will not be less than US$100 million as a result of deposits being withdrawn and new deposits being made.

Bank B has an investment of US$150 million in a foreign operation that has a US$ functional currency.

Bank B cannot designate the 'first US$100 million' of foreign currency deposits as a hedging instrument in a hedge of Bank B's net investment in its foreign operation because the proposed hedging instrument is not specifically identifiable as is required by IFRS 9:6.4.1(b). The first US$100 million of foreign currency deposits is not specifically identifiable because it consists of multiple individual financial instruments that are not specified. Further, over time, the individual financial instruments change as deposits are withdrawn and new deposits are received.

An alternative hedge designation that may be permissible is when the individual deposits are specified in the hedge relationship and hedge documentation. However, because of the short-term nature of the deposits, the hedge designation would be limited to a maximum time period equal to the shortest remaining contractual term of any of the specified individual deposit, which might be one day. Consequently, Bank B would need to frequently (possibly daily) designate and document the specified individual deposits that comprise the multiple hedging instruments.

Example 5.1B

Hedge documentation for Entity XYZ

Date of designation

State the date of designation of the hedging relationship.

Risk management strategy

The risk management strategy is normally set out in a general document that is cascaded down through an entity through policies containing more specific guidelines. This may include a reference to the specific policy within an entity's policy manual. (See **5.1.1**)

Risk management objective

The risk management objective should describe how the particular hedging instrument that has been designated is used to hedge the particular exposure that has been designated as the hedged item. (See **5.1.1**)

Nature of risk hedged

Specify the risk hedged (e.g. overall fair value, commodity price risk, foreign currency (forward or spot rate), interest rate risk, specific portion (i.e. risk component) such as the benchmark interest rate.

Hedge type

State the type of the hedge, i.e. cash flow hedge, fair value hedge or net investment hedge.

Details of hedging instrument

Summarise the details of the hedging instrument. This may include the type of instrument, deal reference number, contractual parties to the agreement and key contractual terms (e.g. trade date, effective date, maturity date, notional, currency amount and timing of cash flows to be paid or received).

When only a component of an instrument is designated, identify that component. If the forward or foreign currency basis spread element of the instrument is excluded from the designation, state if the treatment in IFRS 9:6.5.15 is applied (see **sections 6.9** to **6.10**).

If necessary include attachments providing additional information for the designated hedging instrument.

Details of hedged item

Summarise the details of the hedged item including the type of item and the amount designated as the hedged item and its timing. When only a component of an item is designated identify that component.

If needed include attachments providing additional information for the designated hedged item.

Effectiveness requirements

All hedge effectiveness requirements listed below are assessed at inception of the hedging relationship, and on an ongoing basis. The ongoing assessment is performed at a minimum at each reporting date or upon a significant change in circumstances affecting the hedge effectiveness requirements, whichever comes first.

Economic Relationship

State that there is an economic relationship between the hedged item and hedging instrument. Explain why this is a case and how this will be assessed and provide a cross reference to the analysis if applicable (see **5.2.3**).

Effect of credit risk

Explain how it will be demonstrated that the effect of credit risk does not dominate the fair value changes that result from that economic relationship and provide a cross reference to the analysis if applicable (see **5.2.5**).

Hedge ratio

Explain how the hedge ratio is determined (see **5.2.6**).

Explain any update to the hedge ratio (in case of rebalancing, see **section 6.2**).

Analysis of expected sources of hedge ineffectiveness

List the expected sources of ineffectiveness (e.g. credit risk) that are expected to affect the hedging relationship during its term (see **5.2.2** and **5.2.4**).

Measurement of ineffectiveness

Explain how ineffectiveness will be measured stating the method used to measure ineffectiveness.

Hedge documentation prepared by: ________________

Hedge documentation reviewed by: ________________

5.1.1 Risk management objectives and strategies

There are no accounting rules governing an entity's risk management strategy and objective for a hedge except that, to achieve hedge accounting, an entity must have documented its strategy and objective. The hedge relationships the entity wishes to apply hedge accounting for must be consistent with these stated policies. Therefore, the policies and objectives should, as a minimum, include a list of the risks that the entity is exposed to and how the entity intends to manage those risks.

For the purposes of IFRS 9, an entity's risk management strategy is distinguished from its risk management objectives. The risk management strategy is established at the highest level at which an entity determines how it manages its risk and typically identifies the risks to which the entity is exposed and sets out how the entity responds to them. This is normally set out in a general document that is cascaded down through an entity through policies containing more specific guidelines. In contrast, the risk management objective for a hedging relationship applies at the level of a particular hedging relationship. It relates to how the particular hedging instrument that has been designated is used to hedge the particular exposure that has been designated as the hedged item. Hence, a risk management strategy can involve many different hedging relationships whose risk management objectives relate to executing that overall risk management strategy. [IFRS 9:B6.5.24]

The risk management objective is an important factor in determining whether a hedging relationship should be discontinued because a change in the risk management objective for a particular hedge (such that the original objective no longer holds) will cause a discontinuation of the hedge (see **section 6.3**). [IFRS 9:B6.5.15]

5.2 The hedge effectiveness requirements

The following three requirements together compose the hedge effectiveness requirements that must be met before hedge accounting is be applied: [IFRS 9:6.4.1(c)]

(i) there is an economic relationship between the hedged item and the hedging instrument (see **5.2.3**);

(ii) the effect of credit risk does not dominate the value changes that result from that economic relationship (see **5.2.5**); and

(iii) the hedge ratio of the hedging relationship is the same as that resulting from the quantity of the hedged item that the entity actually hedges and the quantity of the hedging instrument that the entity actually uses to hedge that quantity of hedged item. However, that designation shall not reflect an imbalance between the weightings of the hedged item and the hedging instrument that would create hedge ineffectiveness (irrespective of whether recognised or not) that could result in an accounting outcome that would be inconsistent with the purpose of hedge accounting (see **5.2.6**).

5.2.1 Frequency of hedge effectiveness assessment

An entity shall assess at inception of the hedging relationship, and on an ongoing basis, whether a hedging relationship meets the hedge effectiveness requirements. At a minimum, an entity shall perform the ongoing assessment at each reporting date or upon a significant change in circumstances affecting the hedge effectiveness requirements, whichever comes first. The assessment relates to *expectations* about hedge effectiveness and is therefore only forward-looking. [IFRS 9:B6.4.12]

IFRS 9:BC6.263 clarifies that the hedge effectiveness requirements should be met throughout the term of the hedging relationship. In some cases it may be necessary to assess hedge effectiveness more frequently than the minimum requirement. For example, for some dynamic hedges when the required hedge ratio is expected to change frequently (e.g. monthly) but the hedge is designated for a longer term (e.g. two years) and the entity only reports annually, hedge effectiveness should be assessed more frequently than the minimum requirement.

If the hedge effectiveness assessment performed at the reporting date reveals that there is no longer an economic relationship between the hedged item and hedging instrument, or the effect of credit risk dominates the value changes that result from the economic relationship, hedge accounting ceases to apply from the *beginning* of the next reporting period. This is because an entity is required to discontinue hedge accounting *prospectively* when the hedging relationship (or part of a hedging relationship) ceases to meet the qualifying criteria (after taking into account any rebalancing of the hedging relationship, if applicable). [IFRS 9:6.5.6]

Given that the hedge effectiveness assessment is only forward-looking (i.e. a prospective assessment), an entity, under IFRS 9, is not required to perform a retrospective test to assess how effective the hedge was for the reporting period. For the reporting period during which hedge accounting has been applied, hedge ineffectiveness is measured and recognised accordingly. For example, if a fair value hedge is 60 per cent effective in the reporting period (e.g. the change in value of the hedged item is CU60, whilst the change in value of the hedging instrument is CU100 in the opposite direction), hedge ineffectiveness of CU40 would automatically be recognised as a result of the applying the hedge accounting journal entries.

5.2.2 Hedge effectiveness

Hedge effectiveness is the extent to which changes in the fair value or the cash flows of the hedging instrument offset changes in the fair value or the cash flows of the hedged item. Hedge ineffectiveness is the extent to which the changes in the fair value or the cash flows of the hedging instrument are greater or less than those on the hedged item. [IFRS 9:B6.4.1]

When designating a hedging relationship and on an ongoing basis, an entity shall analyse the sources of hedge ineffectiveness that are expected to affect the hedging relationship during its term. This analysis (including any updates arising from rebalancing a hedging relationship, see **section 6.2**) is the basis for the entity's assessment of meeting the hedge effectiveness requirements. [IFRS 9:B6.4.2]

Hedge effectiveness assessment is different from hedge effectiveness measurement. An entity is required to assess prospectively whether it believes that a hedge relationship will meet the hedge effectiveness requirements. The method of assessment and analysis of the sources of hedge ineffectiveness form part of the hedge documentation that an entity needs to complete in order to qualify for hedge accounting. Determining the amount of hedge ineffectiveness involves measurement and recognition of hedge ineffectiveness in profit or loss (or OCI in the case of a fair value hedge of an equity investment designated at FVTOCI).

IFRS 9 does not provide guidance on what would constitute an appropriate analysis of the sources of hedge ineffectiveness. One approach could be to perform a qualitative analysis of the sources of hedge ineffectiveness in which an entity identifies and documents the potential different sources of hedge ineffectiveness and comments on their expected effect on the effectiveness of the hedge. This may be more appropriate when the expected hedge ineffectiveness is limited (e.g. when the critical terms of the hedged item and hedging instrument match). Another approach could be to supplement the qualitative analysis with quantitative analysis. This may be necessary when the potential hedge ineffectiveness is greater (e.g. when significant basis risk exists). Such quantitative analysis may also be used to help demonstrate an economic relationship and determine the appropriate hedge ratio. This analysis may already be performed for risk management purposes and could be used to satisfy the IFRS 9 requirements.

Since the hedge effectiveness requirements are designed to be a principles-based, forward-looking assessment, without any bright-line quantitative threshold of effectiveness, any hedge effectiveness assessment is not based on any particular level of hedge effectiveness actually achieved. However, past performance may be an indicator of the future behaviour of the hedge relationship and any unexpected hedge ineffectiveness that is experienced should be appropriately factored into any subsequent forward-looking hedge effectiveness assessment.

5.2.3 Economic relationship between the hedged item and hedging instrument

IFRS 9:6.4.1(c)(i) requires that an economic relationship exists between the hedging instrument and hedged item. This means that the hedging instrument and hedged item have values that generally move in the opposite direction because of the same hedged risk. Hence, there must be an expectation that the value of the hedging instrument and the value of the hedged item will systematically change in response to movements in either the same underlying or underlyings that are economically related in such a way that they respond in a similar way to the risk that is being hedged (e.g. Brent and WTI crude oil). [IFRS 9:B6.4.4]

If the underlyings are not the same but are economically related, there can be situations in which the values of the hedging instrument and the hedged item move in the same direction, for example, because the price differential between the two related underlyings changes while the underlyings themselves do not move significantly. That is still consistent with an economic relationship between the hedging instrument and the hedged item if the values of the hedging instrument and the hedged item are still expected to typically move in the opposite direction when the underlyings move. [IFRS 9:B6.4.5]

Although it is possible that when there is an economic relationship between the hedging instrument and hedged item the values of the hedged item, and hedging instrument could move in the same direction, this situation is likely to be very rare in practice, and when it does occur, it is likely to be in relation to relatively small changes in the overall fair value.

The assessment of whether an economic relationship exists includes an analysis of the possible behaviour of the hedging relationship during its term to ascertain whether it can be expected to meet the risk management objective. The mere existence of a statistical correlation between two variables does not, by itself, support a valid conclusion that an economic relationship exists. [IFRS 9:B6.4.6]

For example, consider an entity with € functional currency, exposed to foreign currency risk on a firm commitment to buy machinery in US$, which it hedges with a net settled derivative to buy gold. If the entity considered designating the gold derivative as a hedge of the US$ foreign currency risk, the existence of a long-term inverse statistical correlation between the price of gold and the strength of the US dollar would not be sufficient to conclude that an economic relationship exists between the hedged item and the hedging instrument. Instead it would be necessary to demonstrate that the underlyings are economically related and that the hedging instrument and the hedged item are expected to have values that generally move in the opposite direction over the term of the hedge because of changes in US$/€ exchange rate. In addition it would be necessary to analyse the sources of hedge ineffectiveness that are expected to affect the hedge during its term.

5.2.4 Sources of hedge ineffectiveness

Hedge ineffectiveness can arise from many sources. The presence of known sources of hedge ineffectiveness can impact the method used to assess hedge effectiveness (i.e. whether a qualitative or quantitative assessment is required, see **5.5.1** and **5.5.2**) and can also impact the selection of an appropriate hedge ratio to comply with the hedge effectiveness requirements (see **5.2.6**). The following sections include some of the more common sources of hedge ineffectiveness.

5.2.4.1 Basis risk

It is not always possible for an entity to find a hedging instrument with exactly the same terms as the item it wishes to hedge. Basis differences result from using a hedging instrument that is based on a specific risk that is similar, but not identical to the risk being hedged in the hedged item. For example, there may not always be an active market for the grade or location of a commodity that an entity is seeking to hedge.

For interest rate sensitive items, basis differences result from differences in interest indices (e.g. LIBOR versus US Treasury rates), in terms (e.g. three-month LIBOR versus six-month LIBOR), and in credit risk differences.

Example 5.2.4.1A

Basis risk: commodities

Entity Z has 20,000 therms of natural gas stored at its location in the United Kingdom. Entity Z ultimately intends to sell this gas to customers in continental Europe, and is concerned that prices may fall in the future. To hedge the exposure of its sales of natural gas, Entity Z sells the equivalent of 20,000 therms of natural gas under a forward contract (which Entity Z intends on net settling in cash by entering into an offsetting position in the spot market at delivery). The forward contract's price is based on delivery of natural gas at the Zeebrugge gas collection point in Belgium. Because prices in the UK (as based on the price quoted in the UK National Balancing Point, or NBP, market) and at Zeebrugge will differ as a result of regional factors (e.g. location, pipeline transmission costs, and supply and demand), basis risk will arise. The impact of this on meeting the hedge effectiveness requirements would need to be considered.

Entity Z is required to demonstrate hedge effectiveness at inception and on an ongoing basis. This could be done using the combination of a qualitative assessment supported by quantitative analysis. If such analysis does not demonstrate the existence of an economic relationship between the hedged item and hedging instrument then Entity Z cannot apply hedge accounting. If on the other hand the analysis demonstrates that an economic relationship exists, the existence of basis risk is likely to impact the necessary hedge ratio and may also result in hedge ineffectiveness.

Example 5.2.4.1B

Basis risk: interest rate resets

Entity D designates an interest rate swap as hedging a debt instrument. The interest rate swap settles every three months but is indexed to the six-month LIBOR rate and the debt settles every three months but is indexed to the three-month LIBOR rate, i.e. the three-month LIBOR index on the debt does not match the six-month LIBOR index on the swap. To the extent that the hedge effectiveness requirements are met, Entity D may designate the swap as the hedge of the interest rate risk on the debt instrument, but the different rate indexation will result in ineffectiveness that needs to be measured and recognised appropriately.

Example 5.2.4.1C

Basis risk: foreign currency risk

Entity X's functional currency is the Euro. Entity X's forecast purchase of equipment from Brazil is expected to cost R$100,000. Entity X wishes to hedge its foreign currency risk. Because the US$/ Euro currency market is more liquid than the R$/ Euro currency market, Entity X enters into a forward contract to receive US$33,300 and pay €27,000. The US$ will then be converted into Brazilian Real in the liquid spot market for payment to the supplier.

Because the bases of foreign currency for the purchase of the equipment and the foreign exchange forward contract are different (R$ vs. US$), Entity X will have to demonstrate that there is an economic relationship between the hedged item and hedging instrument at inception of the hedge and on an ongoing basis.

Given the basis difference between R$ and US$, hedge ineffectiveness will arise.

5.2.4.2 Credit risk

Credit risk is defined in Appendix A of IFRS 7 as "the risk that one party to a financial instrument will cause a financial loss for the other party by failing to discharge an obligation". Therefore, consistent with IFRS 13 *Fair Value Measurement*, credit risk reflects both the counterparty's credit risk as well as the reporting entity's own credit risk.

Credit risk will in many cases represent a source of hedge ineffectiveness.

5.2.4.3 Forecast transaction occurs earlier than expected

When the forecast transaction that an entity has designated as a hedged item in a cash flow hedge (e.g. a forecast sale of a commodity) is expected to occur in an earlier or later period than originally anticipated, the entity would need to assess whether this transaction is the same as the one that was designated as being hedged. If it is regarded as the same transaction, the change in timing of the forecast transaction does not affect the validity of the designation. Where it is regarded as the same transaction, a change in timing of the hedged transaction may affect the assessment of the effectiveness of the hedging relationship and also result in the measurement of hedge ineffectiveness.

In some cases, careful judgment will be needed to determine whether the earlier or later transaction is the same hedged transaction with different timing or whether it is a different transaction entirely.

5.2.4.4 'Late designation' of a derivative in a cash flow hedge

If a non-option derivative, such as a forward contract or swap, has a fair value other than zero at inception of the hedge, future changes in its fair value are affected by that starting value. The derivative includes an embedded financing element that contributes to its fair value movements and causes them to differ from the changes in fair value of the hedged item when the hedged item does not have a similar financing element.

IFRS 9 does not prohibit non-zero fair value derivatives being designated as hedging instruments as long as the qualifying criteria for hedge accounting are met. In practice it is quite common for a derivative to have a non-zero fair value when it is designated. Assuming hedge accounting is applied, the non-zero element of the derivative at initial designation will cause hedge ineffectiveness over the term of the hedge. This is particularly the case for cash flow hedges because the 'hypothetical derivative' used to measure hedge ineffectiveness is deemed to be on-market at the date of designation, which for a non-option derivative would equate to a fair value of zero (see **5.4.1**).

The ineffectiveness arises because the embedded financing element is economically similar to a fixed rate amortising loan embedded in the derivative and this 'loan' will change in fair value as interest rates move. By the time the derivative matures, the loan will have been fully eliminated along with the derivative.

The measurement of ineffectiveness caused by late designation in a cash flow hedge is discussed further in **5.4.3**.

5.2.5 The effect of credit risk

Because the hedge accounting model is based on a general notion of offset between gains and losses on the hedging instrument and the hedged item, hedge effectiveness is determined not only by the economic relationship between those items (i.e. the changes in their underlyings) but also by the effect of credit risk on the value of both the hedging instrument and the hedged item. [IFRS 9:B6.4.7]

The impact of credit risk on a hedge relationship is complex and needs to be considered for both the hedging instrument and the hedged item.

When a hedging instrument is a financial instrument that is designated in its entirety, it is clear that credit risk will be a valuation input that could affect its value. However, when a component of a hedging instrument is designated, credit risk may not affect the valuation of that component. For example, when the foreign currency component of a foreign bond liability measured at amortised cost is designated as a hedging instrument, the foreign currency risk component is determined in accordance with IAS 21 *The Effects of Changes in Foreign Exchange Rates* and would not be affected by changes in credit risk.

When it comes to hedged items, credit risk may not be present and consequently, would not be considered as part of the hedge effectiveness assessment. For example, when hedging a forecast sale, there is no contractual arrangement and consequently, there can be no presence of credit risk. Instead, there is the risk that the forecast transaction does not occur which could affect the assessment of whether the transaction is highly probable (see **section 3.4.1**).

However, in some other cases (e.g. in a hedge of a *financial* hedged item) credit risk may be present and consequently, must be considered. When hedging a component of such an item, credit risk is often excluded from the designation and accordingly credit risk would not typically affect the change in value of the hedged component.

Despite this, in some cases, even though credit risk is excluded from the designation of the hedged item, it may affect the valuation of the hedged risk component used in the hedge effectiveness assessment. For example, in the case of a fair value hedge of a fixed rate bond asset hedged for the benchmark interest rate component, if the asset was impaired due to a credit event, this would affect the hedged interest component despite credit risk being excluded from the hedge designation because some of the cash flows on which the interest rate risk is present are no longer expected to occur. Consequently, the effect of credit risk on the hedged item should be considered even when credit risk is excluded from the designated hedged risk.

Even if there is an economic relationship between the hedging instrument and the hedged item, the impact of credit risk could mean that the level of offset becomes erratic. This can result from a change in the credit risk of either the hedging instrument or the hedged item that is of such a magnitude that the credit risk dominates the value changes that result from the economic relationship. [IFRS 9:B6.4.7]

IFRS 9 does not provide a quantitative threshold against which the effect of credit risk can be assessed to determine whether it causes a hedge to be ineffective. Instead IFRS 9 uses a qualitative threshold whereby the effect of credit risk should not *dominate* the value changes that result from the economic relationship. [IFRS 9:6.4.1(c)(ii)] The level of magnitude that gives rise to dominance is one that would result in the loss (or gain) from credit risk *frustrating* the effect of changes in the underlyings on the value of the hedging instrument or the hedged item, even if those changes were significant. [IFRS 9:B6.4.7] The interpretation of terms such as dominate and frustrating used in the context of assessing the impact of credit risk will require the exercise of careful judgment.

An example of credit risk dominating a hedging relationship is when an entity hedges an exposure to commodity price risk using an uncollateralised derivative. If the counterparty to that derivative experiences a severe deterioration in its credit standing, the effect of the changes in the counterparty's credit standing might outweigh the effect of changes in the commodity price on the fair value of the hedging instrument, whereas changes in the value of the hedged item depend largely on the commodity price changes. [IFRS 9:B6.4.8]

If during a particular period there is little change in the underlyings, the fact that even small credit risk-related changes in the value of the hedging instrument or the hedged item might affect the value more than the underlyings does not create dominance. [IFRS 9:B6.4.7] Put another way, a high proportional impact of credit risk on the value changes on the hedged item or hedging instrument does not necessarily result in credit risk dominating the value changes from the economic relationship when the overall change in value of the hedged item or hedging instrument is relatively small.

As noted in **5.2.1**, assessing whether a hedging relationship meets the hedge effectiveness requirements is an ongoing prospective assessment performed at a minimum at the beginning of each reporting period or upon the occurrence of a significant change in the circumstances affecting the hedge effectiveness requirements, whichever comes first. If, during the term of a hedging relationship, credit risk begins to *dominate* the value changes from the economic relationship, this is likely to represent a significant change in circumstances affecting the hedge effectiveness requirements and to prompt a reassessment of the hedge effectiveness requirements. Assuming the hedge relationship has met the qualification requirements up to the point of change in circumstances, hedge accounting would be applied up to this point but be discontinued subsequently.

5.2.6 The hedge ratio

The hedge ratio is defined in Appendix A of IFRS 9 as "[t]he relationship between the quantity of the hedging instrument and the quantity of the hedged item in terms of their relative weighting". The quantity of a hedged item and hedging instrument could be measured in a variety of ways depending on their nature. For example, "£100m of principal" of a bond could be hedged by a shorter dated interest rate swap with "£105m of notional" which would give a hedge ratio of 105% or 95.2% (depending on which quantity is used as the numerator and which is used as the denominator). Another example would be "1,000 tonnes" of a commodity could be hedged by a commodity derivative referencing "950 tonnes" of the same commodity but of a different grade.

As a general principle, the hedge ratio for a hedging relationship should be the same as the hedge ratio used from a risk management perspective (i.e. the hedge ratio of the hedging relationship must be the same as that resulting from the quantity of the hedged item that the entity actually hedges and the quantity of the hedging instrument that the entity actually uses to hedge that quantity of hedged item). [IFRS 9:6.4.1(c)(iii)] In many cases the hedge ratio will be 100% because the critical terms of the hedged item will match the critical terms of the hedging instrument. However, in some cases the actual hedge ratio may not be 100%. This could be due to a variety of reasons. For example, the underlyings of the hedged item and hedging instrument may be economically related but may differ giving rise to basis risk (see **5.2.4.1**), the effect of which is accommodated by adjusting the hedge ratio.

In some circumstances, determining the 'actual' hedge ratio used for risk management purposes may be challenging and subject to judgement.

Consider a financial institution that manages interest rate risk on a net portfolio basis. When the entity transacts an interest rate swap to hedge interest rate risk, it considers the interest rate risk in the net portfolio as a whole rather than interest rate risk on a specific individual hedged item. However, given that the portfolio hedge accounting model is still under development by the IASB, designating a hedge on a gross position basis (even though actual risk management typically manages risk on a net position basis) is an eligible way to designate a hedged item. This is appropriate provided the designation reflects risk management in that it is related to the same type of risk that is being managed and the financial instruments are used for that purpose. [IFRS 9:BCE.209] Therefore an entity can apply hedge accounting at the 'micro' level using the general hedge accounting model in IFRS 9 to designate individual interest rate swaps in separate hedging relationships. In order to apply the general hedge accounting model in this way, it is necessary for the entity to identify a hedged item to designate with the transacted interest rate swap.

In the circumstances described, it is not possible to identify the hedge ratio that the financial institution 'actually uses' at the individual instrument level because the economic hedge is entered into on a portfolio basis. To comply with IFRS 9:6.4.1(c)(iii), when selecting the amount of the hedged item to designate in the hedge, the hedge ratio should not reflect an imbalance between the weightings of the hedged item and the hedging instrument that would create hedge ineffectiveness that could result in an accounting outcome that would be inconsistent with the purpose of hedge accounting.

In developing the hedge ratio requirements, the IASB considered how an entity could potentially manipulate the actual hedge ratio used for risk management purposes in order to achieve a specific accounting outcome. Consequently, the hedge ratio actually used for risk management purposes is overridden if it reflects an imbalance between the weightings of the hedged item and the hedging instrument that would create hedge ineffectiveness that could result in an accounting outcome that would be inconsistent with the purpose of hedge accounting. In such cases, an entity must adjust the hedge ratio derived from the quantities of the hedged item and the hedging instrument that the entity actually uses if such adjustment is needed to avoid an imbalance. [IFRS 9:B6.4.10]

Examples of relevant considerations in assessing whether an accounting outcome is inconsistent with the purpose of hedge accounting are:

(a) whether the intended hedge ratio is established to avoid recognising hedge ineffectiveness for cash flow hedges (i.e. purposefully under-hedging), or to achieve fair value hedge adjustments for more hedged items with the aim of increasing the use of fair value accounting, but without offsetting fair value changes of the hedging instrument; and

(b) whether there is a commercial reason for the particular weightings of the hedged item and the hedging instrument, even though that creates hedge ineffectiveness.

For example, an entity enters into and designates a quantity of the hedging instrument that is not the quantity that it determined as the best hedge of the hedged item because the standard volume of the hedging instruments does not allow it to enter into that exact quantity of hedging instrument (a 'lot size issue'). An example is an entity that hedges 100 tonnes of coffee purchases with standard coffee futures contracts that have a contract size of 37,500 lbs (pounds). The entity could only use either five or six contracts (equivalent to 85.0 and 102.1 tonnes respectively) to hedge the purchase volume of 100 tonnes. In that case, the entity designates the hedging relationship using the hedge ratio that results from the number of coffee futures contracts that it actually uses, because the hedge ineffectiveness resulting from the mismatch in the weightings of the hedged item and the hedging instrument would not result in an accounting outcome that is inconsistent with the purpose of hedge accounting. [IFRS 9:B6.4.11]

The example in IFRS 9:B6.4.11 raises the question of whether, in the case of an entity that hedges with five contracts equivalent to 85 tonnes, it could designate only 85 tonnes of coffee purchases or whether it has to designate 100 tonnes.

In developing the hedge ratio requirements, the IASB noted that the approach has the advantage of providing information about the hedge ineffectiveness in situations in which an entity uses a hedging instrument that does not provide the best fit (e.g. because of cost-efficiency considerations) and aligns hedge accounting with risk management. The IASB also noted that the hedge ratio is not a free choice for accounting purposes as it was in IAS 39 (subject to passing the 80 - 125 per cent bright line test). [IFRS 9:BC6.249]

This implies that, the entity in the circumstances described would have to designate 100 tonnes of the hedged item in the hedging relationship. However, in an alternative situation when the entity's objective is to hedge 85 tonnes of coffee purchases with five contracts equivalent to 85 tonnes and leave 15 tonnes unhedged, the hedged item would be 85 tonnes. In practice, determining whether an entity's objective is to hedge 85 tonnes and leave 15 tonnes unhedged or whether its objective is to hedge 100 tonnes with futures hedging 85 tonnes may require careful judgement.

A similar question arises when the entity transacts six contracts equivalent to 102.1 tonnes. However, in this case, the excess of

2.1 tonnes is likely to be regarded as an unavoidable consequence of hedging at least 100 tonnes and consequently, should be included in the hedge designation.

The hedge ratio is assessed at inception of a hedging relationship and on an ongoing basis. In some cases the original hedge ratio designated at inception of the hedge may no longer comply with the hedge effectiveness requirements and must be adjusted. This is referred to as rebalancing and is discussed further in **section 6.2**.

5.3 Hedging on an after-tax basis

In some cases an entity may be hedging an exposure on an after-tax basis. In these cases it would be appropriate to also base the hedge ratio on an after-tax basis because this would be consistent with the risk management objective of the hedge. For example, consider a Sterling functional currency entity with an investment in a wholly-owned Euro subsidiary. It hedges €840,000 of net assets using a forward contract which exchanges €1,200,000 for a fixed amount of Sterling. The notional on the forward contract is purposefully greater than the amount of net assets being designated to compensate for the fact that foreign currency movements on the hedged item (net assets) are not taxable whilst those on the hedging instrument are taxable at a rate of 30 per cent. Since the objective of the hedge is to offset amounts on the hedged item and hedging instrument on an after-tax basis, the same hedge ratio should be used for the purpose of hedge accounting.

5.4 Measurement of hedge ineffectiveness

When applying hedge accounting it is necessary to measure both the hedging instrument and the hedged item in order to determine the required accounting entries. If there is a difference between the value changes of the hedged item and hedging instrument, hedge ineffectiveness will arise. Hedge ineffectiveness is the extent to which the changes in the fair value or the cash flows of the hedging instrument are greater or less than those on the hedged item. [IFRS 9:B6.4.1]

Hedge ineffectiveness is measured on a present value basis and therefore the change in value of the hedged item also includes the effect of the time value of money. [IFRS 9:B6.5.4]

In some cases it will be straight forward to measure the change in value of the hedged item. For example, where an entity hedges the foreign currency spot component of a net investment in a foreign operation in a net investment hedge, the hedged item can be measured by comparing the functional currency value of the hedged amount of net assets translated at the opening and closing foreign exchange rates for the hedged period. In other cases an entity may employ the use of the hypothetical derivative method.

5.4.1 Hypothetical derivative method

The hypothetical derivative method for assessing hedge effectiveness uses a derivative with terms that match the critical terms of the hedged item to measure changes in value of the hedged item. Such a derivative could be a forward, swap, option contract or a combination of these, depending on the terms of the hedged item.

If the hedge is for a two-sided risk at the current market level, the hypothetical derivative would represent a hypothetical forward contract that is calibrated to a value of nil at the time of designation of the hedging relationship. [IFRS 9:B6.5.5]

If the hedge is for a one-sided risk, the hypothetical derivative would represent the intrinsic value of a hypothetical option that at the time of designation of the hedging relationship is at the money if the hedged price level is the current market level, or out of the money if the hedged price level is above (or, for a hedge of a long position, below) the current market level. [IFRS 9:B6.5.5]

Using a hypothetical derivative is one possible way of calculating the change in the value of the hedged item. For example, in a cash flow hedge of a forecast transaction, an entity could measure changes in value of the hedged item by present valuing the cumulative change in the hedged expected future cash flows. However, the hypothetical derivative is seen as a practical way to deriving this same value.

IFRS 9 only permits the hypothetical derivative to be used to calculate the value of the hedged item; the hypothetical derivative cannot be used to include features that only exist in the hedging instrument but not in the hedged item. An example is debt denominated in a foreign currency (irrespective of whether it is fixed-rate or variable-rate debt). When using a hypothetical derivative to calculate the change in the value of such debt or the present value of the cumulative change in its cash flows, the hypothetical derivative cannot simply impute a charge for exchanging different currencies even though actual derivatives under which different currencies are exchanged might include such a charge (e.g. cross-currency interest rate swaps; see **6.10** for the treatment of the foreign currency basis spread in such hedging instruments). [IFRS 9:B6.5.5]

In addition to using the hypothetical derivative method for measuring the hedged item and recording hedge ineffectiveness, it can also be used for the purpose of assessing whether a hedging relationship meets the hedge effectiveness requirements. [IFRS 9:B6.5.6] For example, where the critical terms of a hedging instrument and hedged item are not closely aligned and it is deemed necessary to perform a quantitative test to demonstrate that there is an economic relationship between the hedged item and hedging instrument, the valuation of the hedged item can be determined using a hypothetical derivative. Furthermore, the determination and assessment of the appropriate hedge ratio can also use the values from a hypothetical derivative to represent the hedged item.

Example 5.4.1

Identifying the hypothetical derivative

Entity P has a 4-year variable rate loan asset with a notional of €100 and a maturity of 31/12/X5. The benchmark rate on the loan (i.e. the coupon excluding credit spread) is 3-month EURIBOR. Interest is received quarterly. Entity P does not hedge its loan asset on origination, 1/01/X2.

However, at the end of 20X2, Entity P forecasts a fall in interest rates and designates a receive 5 per cent fixed, pay variable overnight indexed swap rate (OIS), interest rate swap with a notional of €100 and annual interest payments as a cash flow hedge of the interest rate risk on the loan.

Entity P formally designates the hedging relationship and meets all of the hedge accounting criteria including the hedge effectiveness requirements.

To measure the effectiveness of the hedging relationship, Entity P compares the change in fair value of the hedging receive 5 per cent fixed, pay variable OIS interest rate swap to the changes in value of the 'hypothetical derivative', i.e. the derivative with critical terms that match the hedged item which is calibrated to have nil fair value at designation. In this instance, the hypothetical derivative is a receive 5.1 per cent, pay 3-month EURIBOR interest rate swap with quarterly payment dates. The 5.1 per cent fixed rate for the remaining 3 years is the market EURIBOR swap rate.

Note that the fixed rates on the actual hedging swap and the hypothetical swap differ because they are priced off different yield curves (i.e. OIS versus EURIBOR).

5.4.2 Change in timing of forecast transaction

Hedge ineffectiveness will arise if the timing or amount of a forecast transaction changes because the cumulative change in fair value (present value) of the expected future cash flows on the hedged item from inception of the hedge will not equal the cumulative change in fair value of the hedging instrument from inception of the hedge.

Determining the degree of hedge ineffectiveness that arises from a change in the timing or amount of forecast transactions can be a complex exercise. If an entity applies the hypothetical derivative method in assessing hedge effectiveness then this method will also be reapplied when the timing or amount of the hedged item changes. For example, if the expected timing of the cash flows on the derivative hedging instrument and the hedged item aligns at inception of the hedge, and the entity uses the hypothetical derivative to measure changes in the value of the hedged item, then only to the extent that the cash flows continue to align will the hedge be fully effective (ignoring credit risk). If the timing of the forecast cash flows changes during the life of the hedge relationship then the entity will need to construct a revised hypothetical derivative that reflects the entity's revised expectations about the timing of all the forecast cash flows. Put another way, the revised hypothetical derivative is the one the entity would have determined at the inception of the hedge relationship had it been able to foresee the revised timing of the forecast cash flows. A comparison of the cumulative gain/loss on the actual hedging instrument and the revised hypothetical derivative will determine the degree of hedge effectiveness and the amount of hedge ineffectiveness to be measured under IFRS 9:6.5.11(c).

5.4.3 Gains/losses versus carrying amount

The calculation of hedge ineffectiveness is based on the relative changes in the fair value of the hedging instrument and changes in the fair value of the hedged item attributable to the hedged risk. In determining the change in fair value of the hedging instrument, an entity considers gains and losses, not the carrying amount of the hedging instrument in the statement of financial position. It is the gains/losses that are recognised in profit or loss (or other comprehensive income in the case of an equity investment designated at FVTOCI), whereas changes in the carrying amount of the hedging instrument may result from receipts or payments of cash which do not affect profit or loss (or other comprehensive income). Similarly for the hedged item, it is the impact on the hedged item attributable to the hedged risk that affects profit or loss (or other comprehensive income) that should be considered when assessing hedge effectiveness and not the carrying amount of the hedged item itself.

Example 5.4.3

Cash flow hedge ineffectiveness: off-market swaps

Entity B designates an off-market receive LIBOR, pay 7% interest rate swap in a cash flow hedge of variability on CU100m of its issued variable rate debt attributable to changes in interest rates. The interest rate swap has a notional of CU100m and matures five years after the date of designation. The interest rate swap is off-market at initial designation with a negative fair value of CU8.5m because expectations of interest rates have fallen since the swap was originally priced. The current yield curve for the remaining time to maturity is 5%.

Entity B measures hedge ineffectiveness using the hypothetical derivative method. At the date of designation it determines that a hypothetical derivative that would have a fair value of zero is the same as the actual derivative except that it would receive LIBOR, pay 5% (not receive LIBOR, pay 7%). In assessing hedge effectiveness, Entity B models the actual and hypothetical derivative under various interest rate scenarios and compares the two in reaching its conclusion that the actual derivative, even though off-market, will still meet the hedge effectiveness requirements and therefore can qualify as a hedging instrument in a qualifying hedge relationship. The 2% extra that Entity B will pay on the actual derivative compared to the hypothetical derivative (CU10m in total) will not be equal to the amount of hedge ineffectiveness that will arise in the future periods. The 2% is part of the cash flows of the actual derivative. The total amount of hedge ineffectiveness due to these cash flows over the life of the hedge will be CU1.5m (equal to the difference between the cash paid in respect of the additional 2% and the initial fair value of the derivative). However, this ineffectiveness will only be recognised in profit or loss to the extent there is an over-hedge overall. The amount of hedge ineffectiveness recognised in each period will depend on how future interest rates affect the cumulative fair value gains/losses on the actual derivative from inception of the hedge as compared to the effect they will have on the hypothetical derivative. Another way of viewing the 2% difference between the pay leg of the actual derivative and hypothetical derivative is viewing Entity B as paying loan instalments equal to 2% of the notional of the swap every period (CU2m) to the swap counterparty on an amortising loan. The cash payments on the 'loan' do not affect profit or loss, but changes in fair value of these future cash flows do.

5.5 Methods of hedge effectiveness assessment

IFRS 9 does not specify a method for assessing whether a hedging relationship meets the hedge effectiveness requirements. However, an entity shall use a method that captures the relevant characteristics of the hedging relationship including the sources of hedge ineffectiveness. Depending on those factors, the method can be a qualitative or a quantitative assessment. [IFRS 9:B6.4.13]

5.5.1 Qualitative assessment

When the critical terms (such as the nominal amount, maturity and underlying) of the hedging instrument and the hedged item match or are closely aligned, it might be possible for an entity to conclude on the basis of a qualitative assessment of those critical terms that the hedging instrument and the hedged item have values that will generally move in the opposite direction because of the same risk and hence that an economic relationship exists between the hedged item and the hedging instrument (see **5.2.3**). [IFRS 9:B6.4.14]

The fact that a derivative is in or out of the money when it is designated as a hedging instrument does not in itself mean that a qualitative assessment is inappropriate. It depends on the circumstances whether hedge ineffectiveness arising from that fact could have a magnitude that a qualitative assessment would not adequately capture. [IFRS 9:B6.4.15]

The designation of off-market non-option derivatives and the impact on hedge effectiveness is considered further in **5.2.4.4**.

5.5.2 Quantitative assessment

If the critical terms of the hedging instrument and the hedged item are not closely aligned, there is an increased level of uncertainty about the extent of offset. Consequently, the hedge effectiveness during the term of the hedging relationship is more difficult to predict. In such a situation it might only be possible for an entity to conclude on the basis of a quantitative assessment that an economic relationship exists between the hedged item and the hedging instrument. In some situations a quantitative assessment might also be needed to assess whether the hedge ratio used for designating the hedging relationship meets the hedge effectiveness requirements. An entity can use the same or different methods for those two different purposes. [IFRS 9:B6.4.16]

In some cases, determining whether a quantitative or qualitative assessment is necessary to demonstrate compliance with the hedge effectiveness requirements will require careful judgement. Because the assessment is required at inception of the hedge, before hedge accounting can commence, an entity should ensure that the selected assessment basis is adequate for demonstrating effectiveness to avoid subsequently finding the assessment was inadequate and that the requirements for hedge accounting had not been met at inception.

IFRS 9 does not provide any specific guidance regarding what types of quantitative assessments would be appropriate for demonstrating that an economic relationship exists between a hedged item and a hedging instrument. An entity's risk management is the main source of information to perform the assessment of whether a hedging relationship meets the hedge effectiveness requirements. This means that the management information (or analysis) used for decision-making purposes can be used as a basis for assessing whether a hedging relationship meets the hedge effectiveness requirements. [IFRS 9:B6.4.18] In other cases an entity would need to choose an appropriate methodology to assess whether a hedging relationship meets the hedge effectiveness requirements. Several different techniques could be used including ratio analysis and regression analysis.

Ratio analysis computes, as a percentage, the extent of the hedging instrument's effectiveness at offsetting changes in the hedged item for the designated risk over a defined period of time, i.e. the degree to which the changes in fair value of the hedging instrument and the hedged item are negatively correlated. It is relatively simple to compute and is also used to measure the level of actual offset. Assessing how changes in the hedged risk would affect the valuation of the hedged item and hedging instrument in different potential scenarios could demonstrate that there is an expectation of general offset of the changes in the values of the hedged item and hedging instrument. This could, in turn, support the existence of an economic relationship (see **5.2.3**).

Regression analysis is a statistical measurement technique for determining the validity and extent of a relationship between an independent and dependent variable. It is more complex than ratio analysis and is explained in more detail in **5.5.2.1**.

IFRS 9:B6.4.6 states that a "mere existence of a statistical correlation between two variables does not, by itself, support a valid conclusion that an economic relationship exists". This should not be read to necessarily preclude using the statistical correlation output from regression analysis to demonstrate that an economic relationship exists between a specific hedged item and specific hedging instrument for the hedged risk. Such analysis would be appropriate when the underlyings of the hedged item and hedging instrument are the same (e.g. a fixed rate bond is hedged for six month UK LIBOR risk using an interest rate swap that swaps a fixed rate for six month UK LIBOR) or similar (e.g. the underlying risk in the hedged item is one-month EURIBOR and the underlying in the hedging instrument is six-month EURIBOR) but other terms do not align (e.g. the principal and term of the hedged item are different to the principal and term of the hedging instrument). In these cases regression analysis could be used to demonstrate that the hedging instrument and hedged item have values that generally move in the opposite direction because of the same hedged risk which is the definition of an economic relationship in IFRS 9:B6.4.4 (see **5.2.3**). Such an analysis considers the expected changes in fair value of the specific hedged item and hedging instrument for the term of the hedge rather than simply the correlation between two variables.

The use of any quantitative analysis to assess hedge effectiveness would need to compare the expected change in fair value of the hedging instrument to the expected change in value of the hedged item. In some cases the hedged item could be valued directly, for example in the case of a fair value hedge of an existing item such as a bond or firm commitment. In other cases, for example where the hedged item is a forecast transaction, such valuation may not be as straightforward. The hypothetical derivative method could be used as practical expedient for measuring this expected change and also for measuring actual hedge ineffectiveness, as discussed in more detail in **5.4.1**.

IFRS 9 does not provide any specific offset threshold requirement to distinguish between a hedge where an economic relationship exists and a hedge where an economic relationship does not exist (e.g. there is no required 80 to 125 per cent threshold as there is in IAS 39). As a result an entity is not required to (but may) define a quantitative threshold. When using a specific technique of quantitative assessment an entity would need to state, at the outset, how it will evaluate whether an economic relationship exists between the hedged item and hedging instrument but is not required to define a quantified threshold of effectiveness. Since the assessment is a prospective assessment any technique used would need to consider how the hedge relationship would behave over the term of the hedge. The technique used may vary for different types of hedges.

5.5.2.1 Regression analysis

Regression analysis is a statistical measurement technique for determining the validity and extent of a relationship between an independent and dependent variable. It is more complex than ratio analysis and requires appropriate interpretation and understanding of the statistical inferences. Where regression analysis is used, the entity's documented policies for assessing effectiveness must specify how the results of the regression will be assessed.

Example 5.5.2.1

Regression analysis

Where the changes in value of a hedged item in Euros is X(t) and the change in value of the hedging instrument in Euros is Y(t), if Y is a 'good hedge' points (X, Y) should be clustered close to a straight line with a slope equal to –1 and intercept equal to the value of the hedged position, C.

$Y(t) - X(t) = C$ Or $Y = X + C$

C is the (constant) value of the hedged position.

For the purposes of illustration, assuming a constant of zero, the slope of the regression equation is equivalent to the ratio of effectiveness. A correlation coefficient, R^2, of 0.8 indicates that 80 per cent of the movement in the dependent variable is 'explained' by variation in the independent variable. As the objective of hedge effectiveness is to assess the degree of offset between two variables, a simple linear regression may be an acceptable technique to use as part of demonstrating compliance with the hedge effectiveness requirements.

The slope coefficient is the slope of the straight line of best fit of the regression. For a fully effective hedge relationship the slope coefficient will approximate to -1. A slope coefficient of -1 means that for a specified movement in the hedged item the hedging instrument will move by an equal but opposite extent. A slope coefficient of -0.85 means that for every €1 change in the hedged item it will generally result in an opposite change of €0.85 in the hedging instrument.

(a) $R^2 = 1$; slope = –1

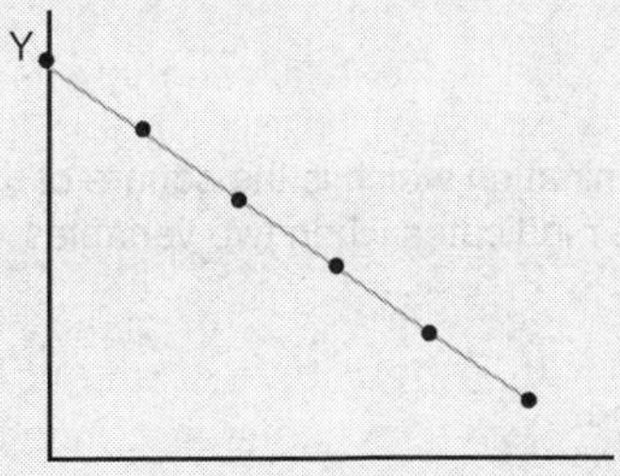

(b) $R^2 = 0$; slope = 0

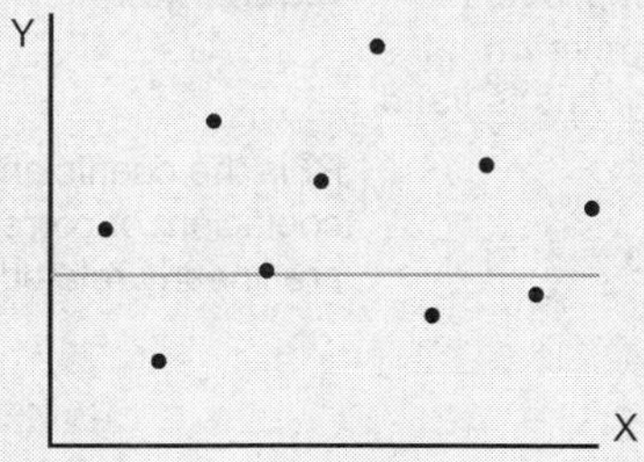

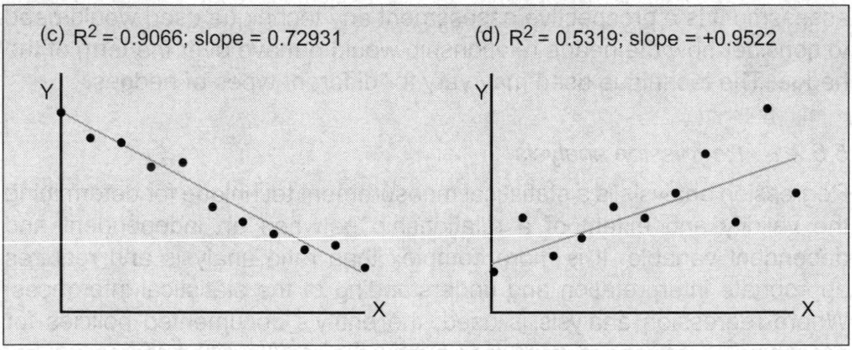

Regression analysis is best suited for measuring the strength of empirical relationships. This relationship can then be used to assess probability of offset, and establish hedge ratios. Such analysis is essential for indirect hedges, i.e. hedges with basis risk where the hedging instrument (e.g. a futures or options contract) has a different underlying to that of the hedged item or transaction (see **5.2.4.1**). A simple linear regression may establish a statistical relationship between the two variables. The most common method to determine the regression line is called the least squares method. The method finds the best-fitting equation that minimises the sum of the (squared) distances between the data points and the regression line. Where there is a valid statistical relationship, the slope of the regression line can be used to establish the hedge ratio that will maximise expected effectiveness.

The formula for a linear regression is as follows:

$y = mx + b + x1$.

where y	–	represents the dependent variable
M	–	represents the slope of the line
X	–	represents the independent variable
B	–	represents the y intercept
x1	–	represents the error term

The table below provides information on how to evaluate the validity of a linear regression.

Factors that prove a regression analysis is valid	**How to evaluate the confidence level or numerical requirement**
R^2	R^2 is the coefficient of determination which is the square of the coefficient of correlation or r. r indicates when two variables are linearly related.

Factors that prove a regression analysis is valid	How to evaluate the confidence level or numerical requirement
	The value of r can range from -1 to +1. R^2 measures the proportion of variability in y that derives from x (i.e. how much of the change of y is explained by a change in x). The higher the value the higher the indication that y is related to x. R^2 is always positive as it is a squared number and cannot exceed 1 as x cannot explain more than 100 per cent in the change of y.
m – slope factor	The slope of a line is the change in y over the change in x. An increasing or decreasing value indicates the positive or negative change in y for every change in x. For example, a slope of +1 would indicate that y is increasing at a positive rate with each change in x. In a hedging relationship, a hedge is used to achieve offsetting changes in the value of the hedged item, therefore, a regression equation for a hedging relationship should have a negative slope within the range previously specified as an entity will be long the exposure with the hedged item and short the exposure with the hedging instrument or vice versa. Additionally, 'm' represents the optimal hedge ratio for the hedge, indicating you need 'more' or 'less' of the hedging instrument to compensate for changes in the hedged item.
t – Statistic	The t statistic for the x coefficient evaluates the probability that the slope is zero. A slope of zero indicates that there is no relationship between the x and y variables. A high t statistic for the x coefficient, positive or negative, generally is a good indicator of correlation and thus a linear relationship. This statistic may be further evaluated by examining the p-value; a statistical output of the t statistic calculation. A low p-value associated with the t-statistic for the x variable, e.g. less than five per cent, indicates a low probability of the slope being zero and thus a high probability that the independent variable is useful in predicting the dependent variable.
F – Statistic	The F statistic evaluates the probability that there is no linear relationship between the x and y variables. For example, to achieve a 95 per cent confidence level, the significance of F should be less than five per cent. If the significance of F is less than five per cent then there is a less than five per cent probability that no linear relationship is present.

Users of regression must be aware of the concept of autocorrelation (i.e. serial correlation). This concept applies when the data points are correlated to each other over time, i.e. the data points are not random. One of the assumptions of a least squares regression is that the data points are uncorrelated to each other. If the data points are correlated to each other this will affect the output of the regression and will result in the R^2, m slope etc. being misstated. When data points are taken over a period of time autocorrelation can occur if the different data points are sourced from the same period. For example, if one data point is the change in fair value of a derivative from 1 June to 30 August, and the second data point is the change in fair value from 1 August to 31 October, there is autocorrelation with respect to the month of August as it overlaps in both data points. Users of regression should ensure data is taken from discrete periods to avoid the data points being correlated with each other. Statistical techniques like the Durbin-Watson test can be applied to determine whether there is autocorrelation. Other statistical techniques, like the Prais-Winsten test can be used to restate the output from the model by removing the effects of autocorrelation. As IFRS 9 provides no guidance on the use of statistical techniques, entities should use established statistical techniques that are known to provide a meaningful output that is consistent with the Standard's objective of assessing hedge effectiveness.

The data used in a regression is a series of matched-pair observations from a specified period of time. For example, an entity may wish to regress the change in fair value of an interest rate swap with the change in fair value of the interest rate portion of fixed rate debt on the first day of each month for a three year period. This will generate 36 matched-pair observations which will input into the regression model. An entity should apply a consistent number of data points as the regression is updated for each subsequent assessment.

It is common to regress observations over the same period as the length of the hedge relationship. For example, if an entity is fair value hedging 5 year fixed rate debt from the date of issue for its full term, an entity would use observations from the last 5 years to demonstrate prospectively that a 5 year receive fixed pay floating interest rate swap is expected to meet the hedge effectiveness requirements for fair value hedging the interest rate portion of the debt.

The more data points that are included in the data set will generally result in a more robust regression analysis. However, care must be taken not to include so many data points from such a long period that the data set is not representative of the expected conditions over the remaining life of the hedge relationship. It is typical to use at least 30 observations, though in theory it is possible to demonstrate compliance with the hedge effectiveness requirements with less than 30 observations when this is supported with an F-statistic and t-statistic with sufficient confidence levels if the underlying distribution can be assumed to be normal or approximately normal.

An entity will update the regression at each assessment date by adding new observations and excluding the same number of the oldest observations from the data set. This methodology ensures that the regression is consistently updated and interpreted throughout the hedge relationship.

If an entity wishes to designate a hedging relationship at initial recognition of the hedging instrument (in the case of a cash flow hedge) or at initial recognition of the hedging instrument and the hedged item (in the case of a fair value hedge) it will not necessarily have the data history for those particular instrument(s). This would be the case if the contract did not exist prior to the initial recognition date, or historical fair value data is not available for an instrument that did exist but was held by a different party. In this case the entity should consider using data from similar instruments or instead generate data points by calculating the hypothetical fair value of the instrument using historic market data assuming that instrument had existed prior to the initial recognition date.

5.5.3 Changing the method of hedge effectiveness assessment

If there are changes in circumstances that affect hedge effectiveness, an entity may have to change the method for assessing whether a hedging relationship meets the hedge effectiveness requirements in order to ensure that the relevant characteristics of the hedging relationship, including the sources of hedge ineffectiveness, are still captured. [IFRS 9:B6.4.17]

In deliberating the exposure draft *Financial Instruments: Hedge Accounting* which proposed the same prohibition on voluntary discontinuation of a hedge relationship that was finally included in IFRS 9, the IASB concluded that the proposed hedge accounting model would improve "the link between hedge accounting and risk management because the new hedge effectiveness assessment requirements would not involve a percentage band or any other bright line criterion and would result in changing the method for assessing hedge effectiveness in response to changes in circumstances as part of a *continuing hedging relationship*." [IFRS 9:BC6.316] (emphasis added)

Based on this explanation, it is reasonable to conclude that a change in circumstances that affects and prompts an entity to change its method for assessing hedge effectiveness would not cause the hedging relationship to be discontinued. The new method of assessment would apply prospectively as part of a continuing hedging relationship.

5.5.4 Documenting the method of hedge effectiveness assessment

An entity's documentation of the hedging relationship includes how it will assess the hedge effectiveness requirements, including the method or methods used. The documentation of the hedging relationship shall be updated for any changes to the methods (see **section 5.1**). [IFRS 9:B6.4.19]

6 Accounting for qualifying hedging relationships

6.1 Types of hedge relationship

Once an entity has chosen to apply hedge accounting for a particular hedging relationship and met the necessary qualification criteria it must follow the required hedge accounting "mechanics" (i.e. the journal entries) to reflect hedge accounting. The applicable hedge accounting mechanics vary depending on the specifics of the designated hedging relationship. There are a number of different factors that drive the mechanics, the main one being the type of hedging relationship.

There are three types of hedging relationships:

[IFRS 9:6.5.2 - 3]

- **fair value hedge**: a hedge of the exposure to changes in fair value of a recognised asset or liability or an unrecognised firm commitment, or a component of any such item, that is attributable to a particular risk and could affect profit or loss, unless the hedged item is an equity investment designated at FVTOCI, in which case the hedged risk must be one that could affect other comprehensive income (see **section 6.4**).
- **cash flow hedge**: a hedge of the exposure to variability in cash flows that is attributable to a particular risk associated with all, or a component of, a recognised asset or liability (such as all or some future interest payments on variable-rate debt) or a highly probable forecast transaction, and could affect profit or loss (see **section 6.5**).
- **hedge of a net investment** in a foreign operation as defined in IAS 21 (see **section 6.6**).

Since a firm commitment denominated in a foreign currency gives rise to both cash flow and fair value variability for changes in the foreign exchange rate, a hedge of the foreign currency risk of a firm commitment may be accounted for as a fair value hedge or a cash flow hedge. [IFRS 9:6.5.4]

The hedge accounting mechanics are also impacted by other features of the hedging relationship, for example:

- When hedging with option contracts where only the intrinsic value is designated, the mechanics for 'transaction related' items differ from those for 'time-period related' items (see **section 6.8**).
- When only the spot element of a forward contract is designated in a hedge, and/or the foreign currency basis spread is excluded from the designation of the hedging instrument, there is a choice over the accounting treatment for the undesignated element (see **sections 6.9** and **6.10**)

In many cases once a hedging relationship has been designated it will remain intact for the life of the hedge, however, there will be cases where circumstances change which can prompt specific accounting to be applied. For example, a hedge will be discontinued when it no longer meets all of the qualifying criteria (e.g. a hedged forecast transaction is no longer eligible for hedge accounting because it is no longer highly probable). Another example is where a hedge relationship may change due to the need to rebalance the quantities of the hedged item and hedging instrument in order to comply with the hedge ratio requirements. Since the rebalancing and discontinuation requirements are mandatory requirements that can arise in any type of hedging relationship they are considered here first before considering the specific aspects of the hedge accounting mechanics.

6.2 Rebalancing

Rebalancing of a hedging relationship is required by IFRS 9 when a hedging relationship ceases to meet the hedge effectiveness requirement relating to the hedge ratio (see **5.2.6**) but the risk management objective for that designated hedging relationship (see **5.1.1**) remains the same. In such cases an entity shall adjust the hedge ratio of the hedging relationship so that it meets the qualifying criteria again (i.e. rebalance the hedge relationship) [IFRS 9:6.5.5]

Hence, rebalancing refers to the adjustments made to the designated quantities of the hedged item or the hedging instrument of an already existing hedging relationship for the purpose of maintaining a hedge ratio that complies with the hedge effectiveness requirements. In practice, the designated quantities of a hedged item or of a hedging instrument may change for a different purpose than maintaining the hedge ratio, such as to simply hedge more or less volume of a particular exposure to comply with an entity's risk management strategy. Changes in quantities in these other such circumstances do not constitute rebalancing. [IFRS 9:B6.5.7]

If a hedging relationship is rebalanced, the adjustment to the hedge ratio can be effected by adjusting the weightings of the hedged item or hedging instrument in the following different ways: [IFRS 9:B6.5.16]

- the weighting of the hedged item can be increased by:
  - increasing the volume of the hedged item; or
  - decreasing the volume of the hedging instrument.
- the weighting of the hedging instrument can be increased by:
  - increasing the volume of the hedging instrument; or
  - decreasing the volume of the hedged item.

Changes in volume refer to the quantities that are part of the hedging relationship. Hence, decreases in volumes do not necessarily mean that the items or transactions no longer exist, or are no longer expected to occur, but that they are not part of the hedging relationship. For example, decreasing the volume of the hedging instrument can result in the entity retaining a derivative, but only part of it might remain a hedging instrument of the hedging relationship. This could occur if the rebalancing could be effected only by reducing the volume of the hedging instrument in the hedging relationship, but with the entity retaining the volume that is no longer needed. In that case, the undesignated part of the derivative would be accounted for at fair value through profit or loss (unless it was designated as a hedging instrument in a different hedging relationship). [IFRS 9:B6.5.16]

Rebalancing does not apply if the risk management objective for a hedging relationship has changed (see **5.1.1**). Instead, hedge accounting for that hedging relationship is discontinued (notwithstanding that an entity might designate a new hedging relationship that involves the hedging instrument or hedged item of the previous hedging relationship as described in IFRS 9:B6.5.28, see **section 6.3**). [IFRS 9:B6.5.15]

If the adjustment to the quantities of the hedged item or hedging instrument represents an overhaul of the existing hedging relationship, that adjustment results in the discontinuation of that hedging relationship in its entirety. An example is a hedging relationship with a hedging instrument that experiences a severe deterioration of its credit quality and hence is no longer used for risk management purposes. [IFRS 9:BC6.304] See **6.3.3** for the accounting that applies when a hedging relationship is discontinued.

Rebalancing a hedging relationship requires an entity to update its analysis of the sources of hedge ineffectiveness that are expected to affect the hedging relationship during its remaining term and update the hedge documentation accordingly. [IFRS 9:B6.5.21]

6.2.1 The aim of rebalancing

Rebalancing allows the continuation of a hedging relationship in situations in which the relationship between the hedging instrument and the hedged item changes in a way that can be compensated for by adjusting the hedge ratio. [IFRS 9:B6.5.9]

For example, an entity hedges an exposure to Foreign Currency A using a currency derivative that references Foreign Currency B and Foreign Currencies A and B are pegged (i.e. their exchange rate is maintained within a band or at an exchange rate set by a central bank or other authority). If the exchange rate between Foreign Currency A and Foreign Currency B were changed (i.e. a new band or rate was set), rebalancing the hedging relationship to reflect the new exchange rate would ensure that the hedging relationship would continue to meet the hedge effectiveness requirement for the hedge ratio in the new circumstances. In contrast, if there was a default on the currency derivative, changing the hedge ratio could not ensure that the hedging relationship would continue to meet that hedge effectiveness requirement. Hence, rebalancing does not facilitate the continuation of a hedging relationship in situations in which the relationship between the hedging instrument and the hedged item changes in a way that cannot be compensated for by adjusting the hedge ratio. [IFRS 9:B6.5.10]

Not every change in the extent of offset between the changes in the fair value of the hedging instrument and the hedged item's fair value or cash flows constitutes a change in the relationship between the hedging instrument and the hedged item. An entity analyses the sources of hedge ineffectiveness that it expected to affect the hedging relationship during its term and evaluates whether changes in the extent of offset are: [IFRS 9:B6.5.11]

(a) fluctuations around the hedge ratio, which remains valid (i.e. continues to appropriately reflect the relationship between the hedging instrument and the hedged item); or

(b) an indication that the hedge ratio no longer appropriately reflects the relationship between the hedging instrument and the hedged item.

An entity performs this evaluation against the hedge effectiveness requirement for the hedge ratio (see **5.2.6**), i.e. to ensure that the hedging relationship does not reflect an imbalance between the weightings of the hedged item and the hedging instrument that would create hedge ineffectiveness (irrespective of whether recognised or not) that could result in an accounting outcome that would be inconsistent with the purpose of hedge accounting. Hence, this evaluation requires judgement. [IFRS 9:B6.5.11]

6.2.2 Causes of rebalancing

Fluctuation around a constant hedge ratio (and hence the related hedge ineffectiveness) cannot be reduced by adjusting the hedge ratio in response to each particular outcome. Hence, in such circumstances, the change in the extent of offset is a matter of measuring and recognising hedge ineffectiveness but does not require rebalancing. [IFRS 9:B6.5.12]

Conversely, if changes in the extent of offset indicate that the fluctuation is around a hedge ratio that is different from the hedge ratio that is currently used for that hedging relationship, or that there is a trend leading away from that hedge ratio, hedge ineffectiveness can be reduced by adjusting the hedge ratio, whereas retaining the hedge ratio would increasingly produce hedge ineffectiveness. [IFRS 9:B6.5.13]

Typically, rebalancing should reflect adjustments in the quantities of the hedging instrument and the hedged item that an entity actually uses because this is generally what governs the hedge ratio required as part of the qualification criteria in IFRS 9:6.4.1(c)(iii) (see **5.2.6**). This will involve an entity monitoring its hedging relationships to identify any changes in hedge ratio arising from its risk management activities.

However, the hedge ratio will not always follow that ratio used for risk management purposes. An entity must adjust the hedge ratio that results from the quantities of the hedged item or the hedging instrument that it actually uses if: [IFRS 9:B6.5.14]

- the hedge ratio that results from changes to the quantities of the hedging instrument or the hedged item that the entity actually uses would reflect an imbalance that would create hedge ineffectiveness that could result in an accounting outcome that would be inconsistent with the purpose of hedge accounting; or
- an entity would retain quantities of the hedging instrument and the hedged item that it actually uses, resulting in a hedge ratio that, in new circumstances, would reflect an imbalance that would create hedge ineffectiveness that could result in an accounting outcome that would be inconsistent with the purpose of hedge accounting (i.e. an entity must not create an imbalance by omitting to adjust the hedge ratio).

This requirement means that in some cases rebalancing of a designated hedging relationship will be *required* despite there being no change in actual quantities of the hedging instrument or hedged item used from a risk management perspective. Conversely, in other cases, rebalancing will not be permitted because the quantities of the hedged item or hedging instrument have been adjusted to change the hedge ratio in a way that creates an inappropriate imbalance. Furthermore, there could be circumstances when there has been a change to the hedge ratio from a risk management perspective but rebalancing is required to a hedge ratio that differs from that arising from the actual quantities of hedged item and hedging instrument used because the actual hedge ratio creates an inappropriate imbalance.

An example of when this situation could arise is if an entity increases the quantity of the hedged item designated in an existing cash flow hedging relationship in order to purposefully under-hedge the exposure to reduce the amount of hedge ineffectiveness recognised (because hedge ineffectiveness from under-hedging would not impact profit or loss due to the lower of test (see **6.5.1**)). In such circumstances, IFRS 9 would require the designated hedge ratio to be different from the actual hedge ratio, to avoid an inappropriate imbalance. A similar conclusion would have been reached at the inception of the hedge if designating a hedge ratio on the basis of the quantities of the hedging instrument and hedged item actually used would create an inappropriate imbalance in the hedging relationship.

Clearly, one way of avoiding divergence between the actual hedge ratio and the ratio that should be designated is to refrain from manipulating the actual hedge ratio to derive an inappropriate accounting outcome.

However, it is also possible that such a divergence could arise after the initial designation as a result of the entity's inaction. For example, consider an entity that is exposed to foreign currency X (CX), which is pegged to foreign currency Y (CY). The exchange rate between currency X and currency Y is maintained within a range of 1.9:1 to 2.1:1 (shown as CX:CY). The entity uses a forward contract over currency Y to hedge its foreign currency exposure to CX100. Based on the managed exchange rate, the entity enters into a forward contract exchanging CY50 (CX100 divided by the average exchange rate of 2.0:1) for a fixed amount of functional currency.

During the term of the hedge, the managed exchange rate band is formally changed to 2.1:1 to 2.3:1. Accordingly, if the entity were to hedge the same exposure with a new forward contract it would transact a forward exchanging CY45 (CX100 divided by the average exchange rate of 2.2:1) for a fixed amount of functional currency. If the entity transacted a forward over CY50 in these new circumstances this would represent an imbalance and under IFRS 9:6.4.1(c) the entity would only be permitted to designate CY45 of the forward in the hedging relationship. However, given its existing circumstances, due to the cost of closing out CY5 of the existing forward, the entity chooses to retain the existing forward contract to exchange CY50 for a fixed amount of functional currency.

In these circumstances, IFRS 9:B6.5.14(b) would *require* the entity to rebalance the hedge accounting relationship when it is next assessed against the hedge effectiveness requirements. A hedge relationship is assessed against the hedge effectiveness requirements at a minimum at each reporting date or upon a significant change in circumstances affecting the hedge effectiveness requirements, see **5.2.1**). In the circumstances described, a change in the managed exchange rate band would represent a significant change in circumstances and hence prompt a hedge effectiveness assessment. At that time the hedging relationship would be rebalanced to include only CY45 of the forward contract (despite it retaining all CY50 of the forward for valid commercial reasons) because its risk management objective has not changed, and this is the quantity of hedging instrument it would transact in *new circumstances*.

This type of scenario could arise in circumstances where an entity hedges an exposure to one underlying using a hedging instrument linked to another related underlying (i.e. proxy hedging).

6.2.3 Impact of rebalancing on the accounting treatment

Rebalancing is accounted for as a continuation of the hedging relationship that remains in place and de-designation of any amount of hedged item or hedging instrument that is no longer part of the hedging relationship. On rebalancing, the hedge ineffectiveness of the hedging relationship is determined and recognised immediately before adjusting the hedging relationship for the new hedge ratio which would apply prospectively. [IFRS 9:B6.5.8]

The impact of rebalancing on the accounting of the hedge will depend on how the rebalancing is done. The impact of the four different possibilities for adjusting the hedge ratio are as follows.

6.2.4 *Adjusting the hedge ratio by increasing the volume of the hedged item*

Adjusting the hedge ratio by increasing the volume of the hedged item does not affect the measurement of the hedging instrument and the previously designated volume of the hedged item. However, from the date of rebalancing, the changes in the value of the hedged item also include the change in the value of the additional volume of the hedged item. These changes are measured starting from, and by reference to, the date of rebalancing instead of the date on which the hedging relationship was designated.

For example, if an entity originally hedged a volume of 100 tonnes of a commodity at a forward price of CU80 (the forward price at inception of the hedging relationship) and added a volume of 10 tonnes on rebalancing when the forward price was CU90, the hedged item after rebalancing would comprise two layers: 100 tonnes hedged at CU80 and 10 tonnes hedged at CU90. [IFRS 9:B6.5.17]

6.2.5 *Adjusting the hedge ratio by decreasing the volume of the hedging instrument*

Adjusting the hedge ratio by decreasing the volume of the hedging instrument does not affect the measurement of the hedged item and the volume of the previously designated hedging instrument that continues to be designated. However, from the date of rebalancing, the volume by which the hedging instrument was decreased is no longer part of the hedging relationship.

For example, if an entity originally hedged the price risk of a commodity using a derivative volume of 100 tonnes as the hedging instrument and reduces that volume by 10 tonnes on rebalancing, a nominal amount of 90 tonnes of the hedging instrument volume would remain. The 10 tonnes of derivative volume that is no longer part of the hedging relationship would be accounted for at FVTPL unless it is closed out or designated in a cash flow hedge. [IFRS 9:B6.5.18]

6.2.6 *Adjusting the hedge ratio by increasing the volume of the hedging instrument*

Adjusting the hedge ratio by increasing the volume of the hedging instrument does not affect the measurement of the hedged item and the previously designated volume of hedging instrument. However, from the date of rebalancing, the changes in the fair value of the hedging instrument also include the changes in the value of the additional volume of the hedging instrument. The changes are measured starting from, and by reference to, the date of rebalancing instead of the date on which the hedging relationship was designated.

For example, if an entity originally hedged the price risk of a commodity using a derivative volume of 100 tonnes as the hedging instrument and added a volume of 10 tonnes on rebalancing, the hedging instrument after rebalancing would comprise a total derivative volume of 110 tonnes. The change in the fair value of the hedging instrument is the total change in the fair value of the derivatives that make up the total volume of 110 tonnes. These derivatives would have different critical terms, such as their forward rates, because they were entered into at different points in time. [IFRS 9:B6.5.19]

6.2.7 Adjusting the hedge ratio by decreasing the volume of the hedged item

Adjusting the hedge ratio by decreasing the volume of the hedged item does not affect the measurement of the hedging instrument and the previously designated amount of the hedged item that continues to be designated. However, from the date of rebalancing, the volume by which the hedged item was decreased is no longer part of the hedging relationship.

For example, if an entity originally hedged a volume of 100 tonnes of a commodity at a forward price of CU80 and reduces that volume by 10 tonnes on rebalancing, the hedged item after rebalancing would be 90 tonnes hedged at CU80. The 10 tonnes of the hedged item that are no longer part of the hedging relationship would be accounted for in accordance with the requirements for the discontinuation of hedge accounting. [IFRS 9:B6.5.20]

6.3 Discontinuation of a hedging relationship

An entity is not permitted to voluntarily de-designate, and hence discontinue, a hedging relationship that continues to meet the risk management objective of the hedge (see **5.1.1**) and the qualifying criteria for hedge accounting (after any rebalancing). [IFRS 9:B6.5.23] However, if the risk management objective of the hedge or the qualifying criteria for hedge accounting cease to be met (after any rebalancing), the hedging relationship must be discontinued.

Discontinuing hedge accounting may apply to a hedging relationship in its entirety or may only apply to part of it. [IFRS 9:6.5.6] Where it only applies to a part of it, the remainder of the hedging relationship continues as normal. Discontinuation of a hedging relationship applies prospectively from when the qualifying criteria and/or the risk management objective of the hedge are no longer met. [IFRS 9:B6.5.22]

In accordance with IFRS 9:B6.5.20 (see **6.2.7**) and IFRS 9:B6.5.27(b) (see **6.3.1.3**), a reduction in the volume of hedged item designated in a hedging relationship due to rebalancing or a reduction in volume of a hedged forecast transaction designated in a hedging relationship due to some of the volume no longer being highly probable would not result in discontinuation of hedging the relationship in respect of the volume of hedged item that continues to be designated in the hedge.

6.3.1 Reasons for part or full discontinuation of a hedging relationship

In practice there may be various reasons why a hedge relationship requires part or full discontinuation. Below are some examples.

6.3.1.1 Hedging instrument expires, is sold, terminated or exercised

If the hedging instrument expires, is sold, terminated or exercised then the hedging relationship (or a part of a hedging relationship) ceases to meet the qualifying criteria (after taking into account any rebalancing of the hedging relationship, if applicable) and the hedging relationship is discontinued. For this purpose, the replacement or rollover of a hedging instrument into another hedging instrument is not an expiration or termination if such a replacement or rollover is part of, and consistent with, the entity's documented risk management objective. [IFRS 9:6.5.6] However, subject to meeting certain criteria, an exception is included in IFRS 9 for instances where a hedging instrument is novated.

6.3.1.2 Novation of the hedging instrument

A novation of a hedging instrument is not considered an expiration or termination of the hedging instrument if: [IFRS 9:6.5.6]

(a) as a consequence of laws or regulations or the introduction of laws or regulations, the parties to the hedging instrument agree that one or more clearing counterparties replace their original counterparty to become the new counterparty to each of the parties. For this purpose, a clearing counterparty is a central counterparty (sometimes called a 'clearing organisation' or 'clearing agency') or an entity or entities, for example, a clearing member of a clearing organisation or a client of a clearing member of a clearing organisation, that are acting as a counterparty in order to effect clearing by a central counterparty. However, when the parties to the hedging instrument replace their original counterparties with different counterparties the requirement in this subparagraph is met only if each of those parties effect clearing with the same central counterparty.

(b) other changes, if any, to the hedging instrument are limited to those that are necessary to effect such a replacement of the counterparty. Such changes are limited to those that are consistent with the terms that would be expected if the hedging instrument were originally cleared with the clearing counterparty. These changes include changes in the collateral requirements, rights to offset receivables and payables balances, and charges levied.

When deliberating its Exposure Draft, the IASB received an urgent request to clarify whether an entity is required to discontinue hedge accounting for hedging relationships in which a derivative has been designated as a hedging instrument when that derivative is novated to a central counterparty (CCP) due to the introduction of a new law or regulation. [IFRS 9:BC6.332] The IASB concluded that under IFRS 9 the novation of a derivative to a CCP would be accounted for as the derecognition of the original derivative and the recognition of the (new) novated derivative [IFRS 9:BC6.336]

Taking into account the conclusion of the assessment on the derecognition requirements, the IASB considered the guidance it had proposed (prior to the finalisation of the Standard) on the discontinuation of hedge accounting, which would require an entity to discontinue hedge accounting prospectively if the hedging instrument expires or is sold, terminated or exercised. [IFRS 9:BC6.337] The IASB noted that this outcome could result in more hedge ineffectiveness, particularly for cash flow hedges, compared to a continuing hedging relationship. This is because the derivative that would be newly designated as the hedging instrument would be on terms that would be different from a new derivative, i.e. it was unlikely to be 'at-market' (e.g. a non-option derivative such as a swap or forward might have a significant fair value) at the time of the novation. [IFRS 9:BC6.338]

The IASB believed that in this specific situation, accounting for the hedging relationship that existed before the novation as a continuing hedging relationship would provide more useful information to users of financial statements. [IFRS 9:BC6.339] As a consequence, it revised its proposed requirements for discontinuation of hedge accounting under IFRS 9 to provide relief from discontinuing hedge accounting in the particular circumstances described in IFRS 9:6.5.6.

As part of the IASB's deliberations it considered whether voluntary novation to a CCP should result in discontinuation of the hedging relationship. The IASB concluded that the novation does not have to be required by laws or regulations, however, for hedge accounting to continue, voluntary novation to a CCP should be associated with laws or regulations that are relevant to central clearing of derivatives and that the mere possibility of laws or regulations being introduced was not a sufficient basis for the continuation of hedge accounting. [IFRS 9:BC6.347]

The IASB acknowledged that permitting relief only where novation is directly to a CCP was too narrow. Consequently, the Board accepted that the relief would also be available if novation is undertaken with the objective of effecting clearing with a CCP. An example where this may apply is where the novation is to a clearing member in order to transact with a CCP (i.e. indirect clearing). The Board also observed that an intragroup novation also can occur in order to access a CCP;

for example, if only particular group entities can transact directly with a CCP. [IFRS 9:BC6.348 - 9]

The IASB notes in IFRS 9:BC6.352 that if an entity had previously discontinued hedge accounting, as a result of a novation, that (pre-novation) hedge accounting relationship could not be reinstated because doing so would be inconsistent with the requirements for hedge accounting (i.e. hedge accounting cannot be applied retrospectively).

6.3.1.3 Forecast transaction no longer highly probable

A hedging relationship may need to be discontinued because the hedged item is no longer eligible for hedge accounting. For example, a highly probable forecast transaction that was designated in a hedge may become only probable hence hedge accounting must be discontinued for the entire hedging relationship. In contrast, if an entity has designated a volume of forecast transactions and only *some* of the volume is no longer highly probable, hedge accounting is discontinued only for the volume that is no longer highly probable. The remaining volume continues in a hedging relationship. However, if an entity has a history of designating hedges of highly probable forecast transactions to later find that they are no longer expected to occur, the entity's ability to predict the likelihood of such forecast transactions is called into question. This affects the assessment of whether similar forecast transactions are highly probable and hence whether they are eligible for hedge accounting. [IFRS 9:B6.5.27(b)]

6.3.1.4 Hedge effectiveness requirements no longer met

When the hedge effectiveness requirements (see **section 5.2**) are no longer met, and cannot be addressed through rebalancing the hedge (see **section 6.2**), the hedge relationship is discontinued. For example, when there is no longer an economic relationship between the hedged item and the hedging instrument or the effect of credit risk starts to dominate the value changes that result from that economic relationship. [IFRS 9:B6.5.26(c)]

6.3.1.5 Rebalancing of the hedging relationship

In some cases it may be necessary to rebalance a hedging relationship in order to comply with the hedge ratio requirements (see **5.2.6**). In such cases discontinuation may apply to only part of the hedging relationship. For example, the hedge ratio might be adjusted in such a way that some of the volume of the hedged item is no longer part of a hedging relationship, hence hedge accounting is discontinued only for the volume of the hedged item that is no longer part of the hedging relationship. [IFRS 9:B6.5.27(a)]

6.3.1.6 Risk management objective of the hedge no longer applies

A hedging relationship is also discontinued if the risk management *objective* for the hedging relationship no longer applies.

As part of deliberating the impact of prohibiting voluntary discontinuation prior to the finalisation of the Standard, the IASB considered different scenarios when entities felt it beneficial to be able to voluntarily discontinue hedge accounting.

One such scenario was when a financial institution hedges on a portfolio basis but de-designates and re-designates micro hedges to emulate the effect of portfolio hedge accounting. Those portfolios were subject to constant changes and entities removed the hedge designation with the aim of adjusting the hedging relationship for new hedged items and/or hedging instruments.

Another scenario was when an entity entered into a cash flow hedge for forecast sales in a foreign currency and the risk management strategy aimed to protect the cash flows until settlement of the invoice. However, hedge accounting was only applied until the time when the sales invoice was recognised on-balance sheet, after which the entity obtained natural offset in profit or loss because of the translation of the hedged item in accordance with IAS 21 and the accounting for the hedging instrument at fair value through profit or loss.

As part of deliberating these two scenarios, the IASB noted that if the hedging relationship no longer reflected the risk management *objective* for that particular hedging relationship, discontinuation of hedge accounting was not a choice but was *required* because the qualifying criteria would no longer be met. [IFRS 9:BC6.319]

This conclusion is based on the fact that the qualifying criteria for hedge accounting require that for each hedging relationship an entity is required to formally document, at inception of the hedge, its risk management *objective* and strategy for undertaking the hedge (see **5.1.1**). It follows that if the risk management objective for that particular hedging relationship is no longer valid (e.g. because the entity has a different risk management objective for that particular hedge or because the documented risk management objective is no longer consistent with the entity's risk management strategy) the qualifying criteria for hedge accounting are no longer met.

As a consequence of the above, the IASB included specific examples in IFRS 9 to illustrate scenarios when a hedging relationship no longer reflects the risk management objective for the hedge (see **examples 6.3.1.6A** to **C**) and hedge accounting is required to be discontinued. The IASB also provided further guidance distinguishing between risk management *strategy* and risk management *objective*.

The risk management strategy is established at the highest level at which an entity determines how it manages its risk. Risk management strategies typically identify the risks to which the entity is exposed and set out how the entity responds to them. A risk management strategy is typically in place for a longer period and may include some flexibility to react to changes in circumstances that occur while that strategy is in place (e.g. different interest rate or commodity price levels that result in a different extent of hedging). This is normally set out in a general document that is cascaded down through an entity through policies containing more specific guidelines. In contrast, the risk management objective for a hedging relationship applies at the level of a particular hedging relationship. It relates to how the particular hedging instrument that has been designated is used to hedge the particular exposure that has been designated as the hedged item. Hence, a risk management strategy can involve many different hedging relationships whose risk management objectives relate to executing that overall risk management strategy. [IFRS 9:B6.5.24]

Example 6.3.1.6A

Hedging of interest rate risk where the risk management objective subsequently changes

[IFRS 9:B6.5.24(a)]

An entity has a strategy of managing its interest rate exposure on debt funding that sets ranges for the overall entity for the mix between variable-rate and fixed-rate funding. The strategy is to maintain between 20 per cent and 40 per cent of the debt at fixed-rates.

The entity decides from time to time how to execute this strategy (i.e. where it positions itself within the 20 per cent to 40 per cent range for fixed-rate interest exposure) depending on the level of interest rates. If interest rates are low the entity fixes the interest for more debt than when interest rates are high.

The entity's debt is CU100 of variable-rate debt of which CU30 is swapped into a fixed-rate exposure. The entity takes advantage of low interest rates to issue an additional CU50 of debt to finance a major investment, which the entity does by issuing a fixed-rate bond. In the light of the low interest rates, the entity decides to set its fixed interest-rate exposure to 40 per cent of the total debt by reducing by CU20 the extent to which it previously hedged its variable-rate exposure, resulting in CU60 of fixed-rate exposure.

In this situation the risk management strategy itself remains unchanged. However, in contrast the entity's execution of that strategy has changed and this means that, for CU20 of variable-rate exposure that was previously hedged, the risk management objective has changed (i.e. at the hedging relationship level).

Consequently, in this situation hedge accounting must be discontinued for CU20 of the previously hedged variable-rate exposure. This could involve reducing the swap position by a CU20 nominal amount but, depending on the circumstances, an entity might retain that swap volume and, for example, use it for hedging a different exposure or it might become part of a trading book.

Conversely, if an entity instead swapped a part of its new fixed-rate debt into a variable-rate exposure, hedge accounting would have to be continued for its previously hedged variable-rate exposure.

Example 6.3.1.6B

Micro hedges of open portfolios of debt instruments where subsequently the risk management objective ceases to apply

[IFRS 9:B6.5.24(b)]

Some exposures result from positions that frequently change, for example, the interest rate risk of an open portfolio of debt instruments. The addition of new debt instruments and the derecognition of debt instruments continuously change that exposure (ie it is different from simply running off a position that matures). This is a dynamic process in which both the exposure and the hedging instruments used to manage it do not remain the same for long.

Consequently, an entity with such an exposure frequently adjusts the hedging instruments used to manage the interest rate risk as the exposure changes. For example, debt instruments with 24 months' remaining maturity are designated as the hedged item for interest rate risk for 24 months. The same procedure is applied to other time buckets or maturity periods. After a short period of time, the entity discontinues all, some or a part of the previously designated hedging relationships for maturity periods and designates new hedging relationships for maturity periods on the basis of their size and the hedging instruments that exist at that time.

The discontinuation of hedge accounting in this situation reflects that those hedging relationships are established in such a way that the entity looks at a new hedging instrument and a new hedged item instead of the hedging instrument and the hedged item that were designated previously. The risk management strategy remains the same, but there is no risk management objective that continues for those previously designated hedging relationships, which as such no longer exist. In such a situation, the discontinuation of hedge accounting applies to the extent to which the risk management objective has changed. This depends on the situation of an entity and could, for example, affect all or only some hedging relationships of a maturity period, or only part of a hedging relationship.

Example 6.3.1.6C

Hedging foreign currency risk of forecast sales where the risk management objective no longer applies once the receivable is recognised

[IFRS 9:B6.5.24(c)]

An entity has a risk management strategy whereby it manages the foreign currency risk of forecast sales and the resulting receivables. Within that strategy the entity manages the foreign currency risk as a particular hedging relationship only up to the point of the recognition of the receivable. Thereafter, the entity no longer manages the foreign currency risk on the basis of that particular hedging relationship. Instead, it manages together the foreign currency risk from receivables, payables and derivatives (that do not relate to forecast transactions that are still pending) denominated in the same foreign currency. For accounting purposes, this works as a 'natural' hedge because the gains and losses from the foreign currency risk on all of those items are immediately recognised in profit or loss.

Consequently, for accounting purposes, if the hedging relationship is designated for the period up to the payment date, it must be discontinued when the receivable is recognised, because the risk management objective of the original hedging relationship no longer applies. The foreign currency risk is now managed within the same strategy but on a different basis. Conversely, if an entity had a different risk management objective and managed the foreign currency risk as one continuous hedging relationship specifically for that forecast sales amount and the resulting receivable until the settlement date, hedge accounting would continue until that date.

From the above examples it can be seen that, although *voluntary* discontinuation of hedge accounting is not permitted, if the risk management objective for the particular designated hedging relationship ceases to apply then hedge accounting must be discontinued. Given that there are no accounting requirements governing how an entity executes its risk management strategy, there is some flexibility around what an entity's risk management objective for a particular hedging relationship might be. This flexibility would allow an entity to specify at the outset when during the term of the designated hedging relationship the designated risk management objective will no longer apply (as per **example 6.3.1.6B** and **example 6.3.1.6C**), causing the hedge to be discontinued from that point. In other cases, the risk management objective for a particular hedge may no longer apply due to specific risk management activities in which case the hedge is discontinued from that point (as per **example 6.3.1.6A**).

As a result, in practice discontinuation of a hedging relationship is likely only to be prohibited in circumstances when the reason for discontinuation does not relate to risk management but is, say, for accounting purposes only. For example, an entity that wishes to de-designate a cash flow hedge simply to recognise subsequent gains and losses on the hedging derivative in profit or loss would not be permitted to discontinue hedge accounting if the risk management objective of the hedging relationship remains the same and the other requirements for hedge accounting continue to be met.

6.3.2 Re-designating a hedged item or hedging instrument

An entity can designate a new hedging relationship that involves the hedging instrument or hedged item of a previous hedging relationship for which hedge accounting was (in part or in its entirety) discontinued. This does not constitute a continuation of a hedging relationship but is a restart. For example: [IFRS 9:B6.5.28]

- a hedging instrument experiences such a severe credit deterioration that the entity replaces it with a new hedging instrument. This means that the original hedging relationship failed to achieve the risk management objective and is hence discontinued in its entirety. The new hedging instrument is designated as the hedge of the same exposure that was hedged previously and forms a new hedging relationship. Hence, the changes in the fair value or the cash flows of the hedged item are measured starting from, and by reference to, the date of designation of the new hedging relationship instead of the date on which the original hedging relationship was designated.
- a hedging relationship is discontinued before the end of its term. The hedging instrument in that hedging relationship can be designated as the hedging instrument in another hedging relationship (e.g. when adjusting the hedge ratio on rebalancing by increasing the volume of the hedging instrument or when designating a whole new hedging relationship).

6.3.3 Discontinuation accounting

When a hedging relationship is discontinued, various accounting requirements will apply depending on the type of hedging relationship, the hedging instrument designated, and the nature of the hedged item. The following hedge discontinuations scenarios are discussed further below.

- a cash flow hedge (see **6.5.3**)
- a fair value hedge (see **6.4.4**)
- a hedge of a transaction related hedged item with the designation of the intrinsic value of an option (see **6.8.1**)
- a hedge of a time-period related hedged item with the designation of the intrinsic value of an option (see **6.8.2**)
- a hedge with the designation of the spot element of a forward contract designated as the hedging instrument (see **6.9.1** and **6.9.2**)
- a hedging relationship where the foreign currency basis spread is excluded from the designation of a financial instrument (see **6.10**).

6.4 Fair value hedge

A fair value hedge is a hedge of the exposure to changes in fair value of a recognised asset or liability or an unrecognised firm commitment, or a component of any such item, that is attributable to a particular risk and could affect profit or loss, unless the hedged item is an equity investment designated at FVTOCI, in which case the hedged risk must be one that could affect other comprehensive income.

Fair value exposures arise from existing assets and liabilities, including firm commitments. For example, fixed rate financial assets and liabilities have a fair value exposure to changes in market rates of interest and changes in credit quality. Non-financial assets have a fair value exposure to changes in their market price (e.g. a commodity price). Some assets and liabilities have fair value exposures arising from more than one type of risk (e.g. interest rate, credit, foreign currency risk).

The following assets and liabilities are commonly fair value hedged:

- fixed rate liabilities such as loans;
- fixed rate assets such as investments in bonds;
- investments in equity securities designated at FVTOCI; and
- firm commitments to buy or sell non-financial items at a fixed price.

Examples of fair value hedges include:

- a hedge of exposure to changes in the fair value of fixed rate debt as a result of changes in market interest rates (such a hedge could be entered into either by the issuer or by the holder);
- a hedge of the foreign currency risk of an unrecognised contractual commitment (a firm commitment) by an airline to purchase an aircraft for a fixed amount of a foreign currency at a future date; and
- a hedge of the change in fuel price relating to an unrecognised contractual commitment by an electricity utility to purchase fuel at a fixed price at a specified date, with payment in its functional currency.

A fair value hedge that meets all of the hedge accounting criteria is accounted for as follows: [IFRS 9:6.5.8]

(a) the gain or loss on the hedging instrument is recognised in profit or loss except when the hedging instrument hedges an equity instrument designated at FVTOCI in which case it is recognised in OCI.

(b) the carrying amount of a recognised hedged item not already measured at fair value is adjusted for the gain or loss due to changes in the hedged risk with a corresponding entry in profit or loss. For debt instruments measured at FVTOCI, the carrying amount is not adjusted (as it is already at fair value) but the hedging gain or loss is recognised in profit or loss instead of OCI. When the hedged item is an equity instrument designated at FVTOCI the hedging gain or loss remains in OCI (to match the hedging instrument). Finally, when the hedged item is an unrecognised firm commitment (or a component thereof), the cumulative change in the fair value of the hedged item subsequent to its designation is recognised as an asset or a liability with a corresponding gain or loss recognised in profit or loss.

A detailed illustration of the mechanics of a fair value hedge of interest rate risk of fixed rate debt is included in **section 2.1** of **chapter B10**.

6.4.1 Fair value hedging firm commitments

When a hedged item in a fair value hedge is a firm commitment (or a component thereof) to acquire an asset or assume a liability, the initial carrying amount of the resulting asset or the liability is adjusted to include the cumulative change in the fair value of the hedged item that was recognised in the statement of financial position. [IFRS 9:6.5.9]

6.4.2 Fair value hedging debt instruments for which the effective interest rate is applied

When the hedged item in a fair value hedge is measured at amortised cost, any hedge adjustment to its carrying amount is amortised to profit or loss. Amortisation may begin as soon as an adjustment exists but must commence no later than when the hedged item ceases to be adjusted for hedging gains and losses (i.e. when hedge accounting no longer applies to the hedged item). The amortisation is based on a recalculated effective interest rate at the date that amortisation begins. [IFRS 9:6.5.10]

Similarly, for debt instruments measured at FVTOCI, the cumulative hedging gain or loss already recognised in profit or loss through application of fair value hedge accounting, can begin to be amortised to profit or loss through a revised effective interest rate as soon as the cumulative hedging gain or loss exists and must commence no later than when the hedging gains and losses cease to be recognised in profit or loss. [IFRS 9:6.5.10]

If amortisation begins as soon as a fair value adjustment exists, the adjustment to the carrying amount affects the effective interest rate calculation for the hedged item. In practice, to ease the administrative burden of amortising the adjustment while the hedged item continues to be fair value hedged with hedging gains and losses recognised in profit or loss, it may be easier to defer amortising the adjustment until the hedged item ceases to be fair value hedged. This is particularly true when the life of the hedge is the same as that of the hedged item. For example, if a fixed rate loan is issued at par and redeems at par, its fair value will move away from par over its life in response to changes in interest rates but it will be pulled back to par on maturity. Therefore, any hedging gains and losses will be reversed by the end of the hedge and will not require amortisation.

6.4.3 Fair value hedging equity investments designated as at FVTOCI

When certain conditions are met an entity may elect to present changes in fair value of an equity investment permanently in other comprehensive income (see **chapter B2**). Despite the fair value changes of such investments being permanently presented in other comprehensive income (with the exception of dividend income recognised in profit or loss), IFRS 9:6.5.3 permits an equity investment at FVTOCI to be an eligible hedged item in a fair value hedge. A consequence of applying fair value hedge accounting to such an investment is that any hedge ineffectiveness arising from hedge is also recorded permanently in other comprehensive income.

Example 6.4.3

Fair value hedge of an equity investment designated at FVTOCI with hedge ineffectiveness

Entity A holds 10,000 shares in Entity B which it has classified as at FVTOCI. Subsequent to the acquisition of the shares, Entity A enters into a total return swap to hedge the fair value risk of the shares for the next three years. At the time of entering into the hedge, the shares had a quoted price of CU8 per share. Under the terms of the swap, Entity A is required to pay the counterparty to the total return swap at maturity any increases in the value of the shares above CU8, with Entity A receiving from the counterparty at maturity any decreases in the share price below CU8. Entity A also receives CU400 each year on the funding leg of the total return swap. No dividends are received on the shares over the period.

Entity A designates the total return swap as a fair value hedge of the spot price of the 10,000 shares held. The hedge was designated on 1/1/X8 and hedge effectiveness is measured at the end of the annual reporting period on 31/12/X8 and the end of each annual reporting period thereafter.

End of the first reporting period

Between 1/1/X8 and 31/12/X8, the fair value of an individual share rose to CU12, giving rise to a cumulative gain on the investment of CU40,000 (CU12 – CU8 × 10,000). This gain was recognised in other comprehensive income.

The fair value of the total return swap at the end of the period, immediately before receipt of the funding charge, is a negative fair value of CU39,100 – resulting in a fair value loss on the total return swap of CU39,100 (the difference between an opening fair value of CU0 and a closing negative fair value of CU39,100).

The fair value change of the derivative is not equivalent to the fair value change of the shares in the period because of the funding charge and the fact that the derivative is a liability at the period end and there has been an increase Entity A's credit risk. In accordance with IFRS 9:6.5.8(a), all of the fair value change in the total return swap is recognised in other comprehensive income. Consequently, hedge ineffectiveness of CU900 (credit) is recognised in other comprehensive income.

End of the second reporting period

During the next reporting period ending 31/12/X9, the fair value of an individual share fell to CU7, giving rise to a cumulative loss on the investment of CU10,000 (CU8 – CU7 × 10,000). The loss of CU50,000 in the period (the difference between the opening price for the period of CU12 and the closing price for the period of CU7 multiplied by 10,000 shares) was recognised in other comprehensive income.

The fair value of the total return swap at the end of the period, immediately before the receipt of the funding charge, was a positive fair value of CU10,600 – resulting in a fair value gain on the total return swap of CU50,100 (the difference between an opening negative fair value of CU39,100 and a closing positive fair value of CU10,600; plus receipt of the CU400 funding charge from the prior year).

The fair value change of the derivative is not equivalent to the fair value change of the shares in the period because of the funding charge and the fact that the derivative has changed from being a liability to being an asset and there is an improvement in the credit risk of the counterparty to the total return swap. In accordance with IFRS 9:6.5.8(a), all of the fair value change in the total return swap is recognised in other comprehensive income.

Consequently, hedge ineffectiveness of CU100 (credit) is recognised in other comprehensive income.

End of the third reporting period and the term of the hedge

During the next reporting period ending 31/12/Y0, the fair value of an individual share fell to CU6, giving rise to a cumulative loss on the investment of CU20,000 (CU8 – CU6 x 10,000). The loss of CU10,000 in the period (the difference between the opening price for the period of CU7 and the closing price for the period of CU6 multiplied by 10,000 shares) was recognised in other comprehensive income.

The fair value of the total return swap at the end of the period, immediately prior to settlement at maturity, was a positive fair value of CU20,400 – resulting in a fair value gain on the total return swap of CU10,200 in the period (the difference between an opening positive fair value of CU10,600 and a closing positive fair value of CU20,400; plus receipt of the CU400 funding charge from the prior year).

The fair value change of the derivative is not equivalent to the fair value change of the shares in the period because of the funding charge and the fact that the previously recognised change in credit risk of the counterparty has reversed because the instrument was settled in full at maturity. In accordance with IFRS 9:6.5.8(a) all of the fair value change in the total return swap is recognised in other comprehensive income.

Consequently, hedge ineffectiveness of CU200 (credit) is recognised in other comprehensive income.

Over the life of the hedge relationship, the net amount of hedge ineffectiveness recognised in other comprehensive income is CU1,200 (CU900 + CU100 + CU200). This represents the cumulative receipts on the funding leg of the total return swap. Ineffectiveness from changes in counterparty and own credit risk on the total return swap was recognised in each reporting period but cumulatively was nil because all cash flows on the swap were settled in full.

6.4.4 Discontinuation of a fair value hedge

With the exception of hedged items for which the effective interest rate is used (i.e. debt instruments measured at amortised cost or at FVTOCI, see **6.4.2**), no special provisions apply when a fair value hedge is discontinued. An entity simply ceases to adjust the hedged item for changes in the hedged risk, and for hedges of equity investments measured at FVTOCI, an entity ceases to record gains or losses on the hedging instrument in OCI.

6.5 Cash flow hedge

A cash flow hedge is a hedge of the exposure to variability in cash flows that is attributable to a particular risk associated with all, or a component of, a recognised asset or liability (such as all or some future interest payments on variable-rate debt) or a highly probable forecast transaction, and could affect profit or loss [IFRS 9:6.5.2]

Assets and liabilities and forecast transactions that are commonly cash flow hedged include:

- variable rate liabilities such as loans;
- variable rate assets such as investments in bonds;
- highly probable future issuances of fixed or floating rate debt; and
- highly probable forecast sales and purchases.

An example of a cash flow hedge is a hedge of variable rate debt with a floating to fixed interest rate swap. The variability in cash flow arises due to the reset of interest rates. The cash flow hedge reduces future variability of interest cash flows on the debt.

The basic premise of a cash flow hedge is to accumulate in other comprehensive income the effective portion of gains or losses on the hedging instrument with the objective of recognising those amounts in profit or loss later when the hedged item impacts profit or loss. This is achieved through the following cash flow hedge accounting mechanics which apply to cash flow hedges that meet all of the other hedge accounting requirements

6.5.1 Deferral of hedging instrument gains and losses in other comprehensive income

For a qualifying cash flow hedge: [IFRS 9:6.5.11]

(a) the separate component of equity associated with the hedged item ('cash flow hedge reserve') is adjusted to the lower of the following (in absolute amounts):

  (i) the cumulative gain or loss on the hedging instrument from inception of the hedge; and

(ii) the cumulative change in fair value (present value) of the hedged item (i.e. the present value of the cumulative change in the hedged expected future cash flows) from inception of the hedge.

The above comparison of changes in value of the hedged item and hedging instrument is often referred to as the lower of test. This test is applied for cash flow hedges to limit the amount deferred in the cash flow hedge reserve to the cumulative gain or loss on the hedging instrument. The purpose of this is to avoid recognising amounts in other comprehensive income that do not represent actual gains or losses. For example, consider a scenario where from inception of a hedge the gain on the hedging instrument is CU100 but the opposing change in present value of the cash flows of the hedged forecast transaction is CU110. If the lower of test did not apply, the amount deferred in reserves would be CU110 and a debit of C10 (representing ineffectiveness) would be recognised in profit or loss even though the CU10 does not represent an actual loss given the hedged item is a forecast transaction (rather than a contractual item). Applying the lower of test avoids the recognition of gains or losses from forecast transactions, but does also result in hedge ineffectiveness not being recognised in profit or loss when the hedging instrument "under-hedges" the hedged item.

The change in the amount accumulated in the separate component in equity is recognised as follows: [IFRS 9:6.5.11]

(b) the portion of the gain or loss on the hedging instrument that is determined to be an effective hedge (in accordance with (a) above) shall be recognised in other comprehensive income.

(c) any remaining gain or loss on the hedging instrument or any gain or loss required to balance the change in the cash flow hedge reserve (through application of (a) above) is hedge ineffectiveness that shall be recognised in profit or loss.

Since the requirement in IFRS 9:6.5.11(a) focuses on the cumulative gain or loss, and defers only the lower of the cumulative gain or loss on the hedged item and hedging instrument, the amounts deferred in a reporting period and the ineffectiveness recognised in profit or loss may not be representative of the mismatch in offset for that particular period. For example, consider a hedge where there is a difference between the hedged item and hedging instrument due to basis risk and as a result hedge ineffectiveness is expected to arise. Say, from inception of the hedge the cumulative change in value of the hedged item is positive CU100 and the change in value of the hedging instrument is negative CU95. Cumulatively, applying the lower of test, a debit of CU95 will be deferred in the cash flow reserve in equity. In the following reporting period, the hedged item reduces in value by CU40 and the hedging instrument increases in value by CU30. Hence, the cumulative change in value of the hedged item is now positive CU60 (CU100 – CU40) and the cumulative change in value of the hedging instrument is negative CU65 (CU95 – CU30). Through application of the lower of test, the cumulative amount deferred in the cash flow hedge reserve in equity is negative CU60. As a result the amount deferred in the cash flow hedge reserve has reduced in the period by CU35 (CU95 – CU60), of which CU30 represents a reduction in fair value of the hedging instrument (from CU95 to CU65) recognised in other comprehensive income and CU5 represents hedge ineffectiveness recognised in profit or loss. The CU5 of hedge ineffectiveness recognised in the period differs from the CU10 mismatch between the hedged item and hedging instrument experienced in the reporting period.

6.5.2 Removal of amounts deferred in the cash flow hedge reserve

Ultimately the amounts deferred in the cash flow hedge reserve will have to be recognised in profit or loss. The manner in which this is achieved depends partly on the nature of the hedged item.

If a hedged forecast transaction subsequently results in the recognition of a non-financial asset or non-financial liability, or a hedged forecast transaction for a non-financial asset or a non-financial liability becomes a firm commitment for which fair value hedge accounting is applied, the entity shall remove that amount from the cash flow hedge reserve and include it directly in the initial cost or other carrying amount of the asset or the liability. This is sometimes referred to as a basis adjustment as it adjusts the basis of measurement of the asset or liability that arises from the forecast transaction. It should be noted that the amount is removed directly from equity and recognised as part of the asset or liability arising from the hedged forecast transaction. It is not a reclassification adjustment (see IAS 1 *Presentation of Financial Statements*) and does not affect other comprehensive income. [IFRS 9:6.5.11(d)(i)] A detailed illustration of a cash flow hedge of a forecast transaction that results in the recognition of a non-financial asset that is basis adjusted is included in **section 3.2** in **chapter B10**.

For other cash flow hedges, the amount deferred in the cash flow hedge reserve is reclassified to profit or loss as a reclassification adjustment (see IAS 1) in the same period or periods during which the hedged expected future cash flows affect profit or loss (e.g. in the periods that interest income or interest expense is recognised or when a forecast sale occurs). [IFRS 9:6.5.11(d)(ii)]

However, if that amount is a loss and an entity expects that all or a portion of that loss will not be recovered in one or more future periods, it shall immediately reclassify the amount that is not expected to be recovered into profit or loss as a reclassification adjustment (see IAS 1). [IFRS 9:6.5.11(d)(iii)]

IFRS 9:6.5.11(d)(iii) requires that the amount accumulated in equity that is not expected to be recovered in future periods be immediately reclassified into profit or loss. This requirement was also included in IAS 39 and was seen to cater primarily for circumstances when an entity had elected *not* to apply a basis adjustment when a hedged forecast transaction resulted in the recognition of a non-financial asset. The purpose of this requirement is to ensure that an amount deferred in equity is included as part of the impairment test of any non-financial asset to which it relates such that, if it was not deemed to be recoverable, it would be reclassified to profit or loss in the same way that the amount would have been recognised in profit or loss if a basis adjustment to the asset had been applied and the asset was subsequently impaired.

It is reasonable to conclude that IFRS 9:6.5.11(d)(iii) should be applied in the same manner. Consequently, if at the reporting date (1) the amounts deferred in reserves were assumed to be recognised as part of the hedged item in the statement of financial position (i.e. if it was assumed that the basis-adjusted non-financial asset had been recognised at the reporting date), and (2) that the basis-adjusted asset carrying amount would be greater than the recoverable amount of that asset and would have triggered recognition of an impairment loss, then those amounts deferred that are not expected to be recovered should be reclassified to profit or loss immediately. Once the non-financial asset is recognised, IFRS 9 requires a basis adjustment and the normal impairment requirements would apply.

6.5.2.1 Reclassification of amounts deferred in the cash flow hedge reserve when hedging interest rate risk with an 'off-market' swap

When the hedged risk is cash flow variability from changes in interest rates, the hedged item will often consist of multiple cash flows. For example, if an entity issues floating rate debt with five interest payments, it is common to hedge all five interest payments with a single interest rate swap. If the hedging instrument, when designated, is an 'off-market' interest rate swap (i.e. fair value is not nil) (see **5.2.4.4**), care needs to be taken to establish the correct amount to reclassify in relation to each cash flow. This is particularly true in the case of an 'under-hedge' (i.e. when the cumulative gain or loss on the hedging instrument accumulated in equity is less than the cumulative gain or loss on the hedged item) because the total amount deferred in the cash flow hedge reserve will not be sufficient to fully offset the variation in the hedged cash flows.

A basic approach to determine the amount to be reclassified from the cash flow hedge reserve for a particular relationship is to first calculate the amount that should remain in the cash flow hedge reserve at the reporting date for that relationship, and then reclassify the difference between that amount and the previous balance in the cash flow hedge reserve.

In a hedge of variability in interest cash flows due to changes in interest rates, the hedged item affects profit or loss through the interest accrual (e.g. interest accrual on debt). Therefore, although it is the full (or 'dirty') fair value gains or losses on the hedged item and hedging instrument that are used to measure the ineffectiveness for the hedge relationship, it is the 'clean' fair value gains or losses that should be used to determine the amounts that remain in the cash flow hedge reserve. The clean fair value is the fair value excluding any accrued interest.

For a swap that has a clean fair value of zero on the date of designation (i.e. an 'on-market' swap), the cumulative clean fair value gain or loss will be equal to the clean fair value. However, if the swap has a non-zero fair value on the date of designation (i.e. an 'off-market' swap), the calculation of the clean fair value gain or loss is more complex. One method of calculating the clean fair value gain or loss is to split the off-market swap into an on-market component swap and an 'embedded financing' component, where the embedded financing component will be a strip of fixed cash flows equal to the difference between the fixed leg on the off-market swap and the fixed leg of the 'on-market' component swap. The on-market component swap has a floating leg that matches the off-market swap and a fair value of zero on the date of designation. The embedded financing component and on-market component swap are determined as of the designation date and are not subsequently adjusted. The cumulative clean fair value gain or loss on the on-market component swap will be equal to the clean fair value of that component. The cumulative clean fair value gain or loss on the embedded financing component will be the cumulative change in clean fair value of the embedded financing component plus the portion of the designation date fair value of the embedded financing cash flows that have been settled and accrued (but not yet settled) since the inception of the hedge.

Therefore, the cumulative clean fair value gain or loss on the hedging instrument as a whole is the cumulative change in the clean fair value of the hedging instrument plus the portion of the designation date fair value of the embedded financing component that has been settled and accrued since the inception of the hedge. There are other acceptable methods of calculating the clean fair value gain or loss that give the same result as the above. For example, calculating the fair value movement for each individual cash flow and deducting the designation date fair value of the settled and accrued cash flows of the on-market component from the fair value gain and loss of those cash flows of the off-market swap that have yet to be settled or accrued.

Examples illustrating the journal entries for a cash flow hedge of floating rate debt using an off-market interest rate swap are included in **section 3.3** of **chapter B10**.

6.5.3 Discontinuance of cash flow hedge accounting

When an entity discontinues hedge accounting for a cash flow hedge it shall account for the amount that has been accumulated in the cash flow hedge reserve as follows: [IFRS 9:6.5.12]

(a) if the hedged future cash flows are still expected to occur, that amount shall remain in the cash flow hedge reserve and accounted for as discussed in **section 6.5.2**.

(b) if the hedged future cash flows are no longer expected to occur, that amount is immediately reclassified from the cash flow hedge reserve to profit or loss as a reclassification adjustment (see IAS 1). A hedged future cash flow that is no longer highly probable to occur may still be expected to occur.

Example 6.5.3A

Change in term of forecast debt issuance

Entity D, a Euro functional entity, intends to issue Euro denominated debt in six months' time with a maturity of five years that will pay fixed interest semi-annually. The transaction is highly probable and, therefore, there is a stream of 10 highly probable semi-annual interest payments. In order to hedge its future profit or loss exposure as a result of the fixed interest payments on the debt due to changes in the 6-month EURIBOR rate between now and the issuance of the debt (in six months' time), Entity D enters into a forward starting receive 6-month EURIBOR pay fixed interest rate swap with terms matching the critical terms of the forecast debt issuance such as start date, maturity, notional and payment dates. The entity designates the swap as a cash flow hedge of the profit or loss exposure arising from the series of 10 interest payments on the forecast issuance of debt. Assuming all conditions necessary for hedge accounting are satisfied, the effective portion of the gain and loss on the forward starting swap will be recognised in other comprehensive income.

On the forecast issue date, Entity D issues seven-year Euro denominated fixed rate debt, rather than debt with a five-year term as previously anticipated. Entity D closes out the forward starting swap at the date the debt is issued. Ten forecast highly probable interest payments are still expected to occur, even though they will now be interest payments on debt with a seven-year maturity. The gain or loss recognised in other comprehensive income will be reclassified from equity to profit or loss when the individual interest payments for the first five years of the debt affect profit or loss. An allocation of the amount accumulated in equity when the debt is issued will be required in order to determine how to reclassify the amount to profit or loss. Because the effective portion of the fair value of the swap recognised in other comprehensive income consists of the present value of 10 future fixed cash flows, this present value amount is allocated specifically to those 10 future interest periods and, accordingly, is released to profit or loss in those future periods.

Example 6.5.3B

Change in timing of forecast sale of a non-financial item

Entity S designates a derivative as a hedging instrument in a cash flow hedge of a forecast sale of silver. The hedging relationship meets all of the conditions for hedge accounting.

In a subsequent period, S determines that the forecast transaction is expected to occur in an earlier period than originally anticipated.

The change in timing of the forecast transaction does not affect the validity of the designation. Entity S can conclude that the transaction is the same as the one that was designated as being hedged. However, the change in timing of the hedged transaction may affect the assessment of hedge effectiveness going forward because the hedging instrument must continue to be designated for the whole of its remaining period to maturity. Also, the amount recognised in other comprehensive income up to this point will need to be adjusted to be the lower of the cumulative gain or loss on the derivative from inception of the hedge and the cumulative change in fair value of the future cash flows of the forecast transaction.

If the hedged transaction is no longer expected to occur, then the cumulative amounts in other comprehensive income are reclassified from equity to profit or loss. [IFRS 9:6.5.12(b)]

Example 6.5.3C

Change in timing of forecast debt issuance

Entity D is hedging the forecast issuance of £100 million of 10-year, fixed rate debt using a rate lock agreement (a derivative). Entity D designates the rate lock agreement as a hedge of the variability in the total cash flows arising on the forecast debt issuance. Entity D expects to issue the debt in the second quarter of 20X0. Entity D's credit rating is BB. In the first quarter of 20X0, the spreads between government and corporate bond rates widen significantly. As a result, Entity D does not expect to issue its bonds in the second quarter. Entity D's advisers believe that the markets may stabilise in the first quarter of 20X1. Entity D will now make a decision on the type of funding in the first quarter of 20X1 and, therefore, closes out its rate lock agreement. At the time of closure, the fair value of the lock agreement is negative.

Entity D should recognise the entire loss in profit or loss because the forecast debt issuance is not expected to occur.

If Entity D had instead designated the highly probable forecast interest cash flows occurring over the 10-year period from the second quarter of 20X0 (rather than interest cash flows on the specific debt issuance), and still regarded the forecast interest cash flows from the second quarter of 20X1 to be highly probable, part of the original hedge relating to the cash flows no longer expected to occur (i.e. up to the second quarter of 20X1) would be discontinued and amounts deferred in the cash flow hedge reserve in respect of these cash flows would be reclassified to profit or loss. However, the amounts deferred in the cash flow hedge reserve in respect of the remaining 9-years of hedged cash flows would continue to be deferred in the cash flow hedge reserve if the hedged cash flows are still expected to occur.

6.5.4 Reclassification from equity to profit or loss after a business combination

Following a business combination, when the acquiree has applied cash flow hedging and recognised gains or losses in other comprehensive income prior to the acquisition, the acquirer will not be able to reclassify those gains and losses to consolidated profit or loss. This is because the pre-acquisition reserves of the subsidiary do not exist in the consolidated financial statements of its new parent. Thus, the group can only hedge account for the specific relationship prospectively from the date of acquisition and designation at the group level. Only those amounts recognised in other comprehensive income subsequent to the acquisition (i.e. the cash flow hedge reserve that was recorded post-acquisition) will ultimately be reclassified from equity to consolidated profit or loss.

Given that the hedge relationship is new from the perspective of the group, the hypothetical derivative used to measure post-acquisition fair value changes of the hedged item will be determined at acquisition with nil fair value. The difference between the actual hedging instrument and the hypothetical derivative will result in hedge ineffectiveness.

6.5.5 Further illustrations of cash flow hedges

Detailed illustrations of cash flow hedges are included in **chapter B10** in the following sections.

- **3.1** Cash flow hedging a forecast sale for foreign currency risk
- **3.2** Basis adjusting the acquisition of a non-financial item
- **3.3** Cash flow hedging variable rate interest with an interest rate swap
- **3.4** Cash flow hedging foreign currency risk of floating rate debt
- **3.5** Cash flow hedging foreign currency risk of fixed rate debt
- **3.6** Cash flow hedging foreign currency risk of zero coupon debt
- **3.7** Cash flow hedging foreign currency risk of the principal only on interest-bearing debt

6.6 Net investment hedge of a foreign operation

A hedge of a net investment in a foreign operation is a hedge of the foreign currency exposure to changes in the reporting entity's (generally, the group's) share in the net assets of that foreign operation. The hedged foreign operation could be a subsidiary, associate, joint arrangement or branch of the reporting entity [IAS 21.8]. IAS 21 requires that the group's share of the net assets of a foreign operation be translated into the functional currency of the ultimate parent with the translation gain or loss recognised in other comprehensive income. It does not matter which currency the monetary assets and liabilities of the foreign operation are denominated in, because all those monetary items are firstly retranslated into the foreign operation's functional currency. It is the translation of those net assets of the foreign operation into the ultimate parent's functional currency that is the designated hedged risk.

IFRIC 16 *Hedges of a Net Investment in a Foreign Operation* addresses whether the hedged risk in a net investment hedge is the difference between the functional currency of the foreign operation and the presentation currency of the group or rather the difference between the functional currency of the foreign operation and the functional currency of the parent. The IFRIC (now the IFRS Interpretations Committee) consensus was that the hedged risk in a net investment hedge refers to the difference between the functional currency of the foreign operation and the functional currency of the parent. The IFRIC acknowledged that this question is only relevant to the extent that the presentation currency of the group differs from the functional currency of the parent. The IFRIC recognised that there are competing arguments for either view but found that the arguments in favour of looking to the functional currency of the parent were more compelling. The IFRIC concluded that the presentation currency does not create an exposure to which an entity may apply hedge accounting. The functional currency is determined on the basis of the primary economic environment in which the entity operates. Accordingly, functional currencies create an economic exposure to changes in cash flows or fair values; a presentation currency does not. [IFRIC 16:BC14]

A hedge of a net investment in a foreign operation, including a hedge of a monetary item that is accounted for as part of the net investment as defined in IAS 21, assuming it meets all other requirements for hedge accounting, is accounted for similarly to a cash flow hedge:

[IFRS 9:6.5.13]

(a) the portion of the gain or loss on the hedging instrument that is determined to be an effective hedge is recognised in other comprehensive income (see **section 6.5** for the accounting of cash flow hedges); and

(b) the ineffective portion is recognised immediately in profit or loss.

IFRS 9:6.5.13 does not specify where in reserves the deferred amounts should be accumulated, however, IFRS 9:6.5.14 (see below) refers to reclassification of amounts from the foreign currency translation reserve. Therefore, it would be expected that amounts deferred in reserves in respect of a net investment hedge in a foreign operation would be deferred in the foreign currency translation reserve where the foreign currency translation gains or losses on foreign operations are also recognised.

The descriptions of both fair value and cash flow hedges (see **6.1**) make specific reference to the presence of an exposure attributable to a particular risk that could affect profit or loss (with only one exception for equity investments measured at FVTOCI). The equivalent statement is not made with respect to a hedge of a net investment in a foreign operation. However, this can be seen as simply an omission rather than a substantive difference. The hedged risk in a net investment hedge, being the foreign currency exposure on the retranslation of the reporting entity's share of the net assets of the foreign operation under IAS 21, does affect profit or loss because IAS 21:48 & 48C require the cumulative exchange differences relating to a foreign operation to be reclassified from equity to profit or loss on the disposal (or, in some cases, the partial disposal) of that foreign operation.

Goodwill and any fair value adjustments arising on the acquisition of a foreign operation are treated as assets and liabilities of the foreign operation, expressed in the functional currency of the foreign operation and translated at the closing rate, and thus are considered net assets of the foreign operation. [IAS 21:47] Equally, a monetary item that is receivable from or payable to a foreign operation for which settlement is neither planned nor likely to occur in the foreseeable future is, in substance, part of the entity's net investment in that foreign operation and, therefore, forms part of the net assets of that foreign operation. [IAS 21:15]

Example 6.6

Identifying net assets available to be hedged

Parent A (Sterling functional currency) has a wholly-owned Subsidiary B (US dollar functional currency). Parent A heads Group A. The investment in Subsidiary B was made on 1 January 20X0 when Parent A acquired 100 per cent of Subsidiary B's share capital for US$100 million. At the date of acquisition, the fair value of the identifiable net assets of Subsidiary B was US$70 million. In applying acquisition accounting under IFRS 3 *Business Combinations*, US$30 million of goodwill was recognised in the consolidated financial statements of Group A. At the acquisition date, Parent A extended a loan of £10 million to Subsidiary B when the US$/£ spot exchange rate was US$2:£1. Settlement of this loan is neither planned nor likely to occur in the foreseeable future.

At the acquisition date, Group A wishes to designate as a hedged item its net investment in its foreign operation, Subsidiary B, in the consolidated financial statements. The maximum amount of the net investment in the foreign operation that can be designated as a hedged item is US$120 million. This comprises three elements:

- US$70 million of the identifiable net assets of the foreign operation acquired at acquisition;
- US$30 million of goodwill that forms part of the net assets of the foreign operation; and
- US$20 million of additional net assets as a result of the loan extended by Parent A to Subsidiary B, being a monetary item for which settlement is neither planned nor likely to occur in the foreseeable future (i.e. the loan forms part of the net investment in Subsidiary B).

It should be noted that if the loan extended to Subsidiary B was expected to be settled in the foreseeable future, the maximum amount of the net investment in the foreign operation that could be designated would be US$100 million because the loan would not form part of the net investment in Subsidiary B.

The cumulative gain or loss on the hedging instrument relating to the effective portion of the hedge that has been accumulated in the foreign currency translation reserve shall be reclassified from equity to profit or loss as a reclassification adjustment (see IAS 1) in accordance with IAS 21.48 - 49 on the disposal or partial disposal of the foreign operation. [IFRS 9:6.5.14]

The requirement to reclassify amounts from the foreign currency translation reserve makes it necessary to track the amount of gains and losses on hedging instruments recognised in other comprehensive income in relation to the hedge of each individual foreign operation separately, so as to be able to identify how much of the total amount recognised in other comprehensive income should be reclassified from equity to profit or loss on the disposal or partial disposal of a particular foreign operation. This may be complex in large groups with many foreign operations and with many hedging instruments used over different periods of time.

IAS 21 defines a net investment in a foreign operation as the amount of the reporting entity's interest in the net assets of that operation. [IAS 21:8]

Net investment hedging will apply only where the net assets in a foreign operation are included in the financial statements. This most commonly arises in consolidated financial statements, but it can also arise in individual financial statements that include a branch (e.g. branch of the reporting entity that has a functional currency different from the functional currency of the reporting entity). In this case, the investor may apply net investment hedging in its individual financial statements by designating the translation risk of the net assets of the foreign branch. This is acknowledged in IFRIC 16:2.

In August 2014, the IASB issued an amendment to IAS 27 *Separate Financial Statements* to include the equity method as one of the options in IAS 27 to account for an entity's investment in a subsidiary, joint venture or associate in its separate financial statements. As a result, an entity may use the equity method for such investments in its separate financial statements and, to the extent such interests are foreign operations, net investment hedging may be applied. The amendment is effective for annual periods beginning on or after 1 January 2016 (with earlier application permitted).

In the separate financial statements of the investor (as defined by IAS 27), an investment in a subsidiary, associate or jointly venture may alternatively be recognised either at cost or in accordance with IFRS 9 (i.e. as at FVTPL or FVTOCI). [IAS 27:10] In such circumstances, the carrying amount in the separate financial statements will not be equivalent to the net investment in that operation (as defined by IAS 21) and, therefore, net investment hedging cannot be applied.

However, as an alternative, the investor may wish to apply fair value hedge accounting for the foreign exchange risk of its investment in its foreign operation if the investment is not measured at FVTPL under IFRS 9. For example, if an investor makes an investment in a foreign operation that meets the definition of a subsidiary, and the investor recognises the investment at cost in its separate financial statements, the investing entity will be exposed to a risk that will affect profit or loss (i.e. the foreign currency risk that arises upon disposal or impairment of the foreign investment). If the investing entity has a foreign currency derivative, or a foreign currency denominated liability (e.g. that was used to fund the investment in the foreign operation), that instrument could be designated as a hedging instrument in respect of a portion of the foreign currency risk of the investment in the subsidiary equivalent to the notional on the hedging instrument. In order to qualify for this treatment, the entity must be able to determine that foreign currency risk with respect to the investment in the subsidiary exists of an amount equal to at least the notional of the hedging instrument. For the entity to make this claim, it must either be able to measure the fair value of the investment in local currency terms or, at a minimum, be able to determine that the fair value in local currency terms is not below the notional of the hedging instrument. Applying fair value hedge accounting would result in the gain or loss on the hedging instrument being recognised in profit or loss along with the associated movement in the foreign currency risk on the designated portion of the investment in the subsidiary.

It is worth noting that this approach is very different from applying net investment hedging at a consolidated level where both the effective gain or loss on the hedging instrument and the foreign exchange translation on the net assets of the foreign operation are recognised in other comprehensive income. Additionally, it should be noted that fair value hedge accounting cannot be applied in the consolidated financial statements to an equity method investment or an investment in a consolidated subsidiary. Fair value hedge accounting for such items can only be applied in the separate financial statements of the investor.

6.6.1 Hedging net investments with loans

In the absence of hedge accounting, foreign exchange gains and losses on retranslating the net assets in a foreign operation are recognised in other comprehensive income and taken to a separate component of equity (in accordance with IAS 21), while those on the loan are recognised in profit or loss. This creates a mismatch in foreign currency translation. When net investment hedge accounting is applied, this mismatch is eliminated because the gains and losses on the loan, to the extent effective, are recognised in other comprehensive income.

When the hedging instrument in a net investment hedge is a foreign currency denominated non-derivative financial liability (e.g. a foreign currency denominated loan), it is always the spot retranslation risk that is the hedged risk (as opposed to the forward rate) because it is only the spot rate that is recognised from retranslating the foreign currency non-derivative liability.

6.6.1.1 Loan is less than or equal to the net assets of subsidiary

Example 6.6.1.1

Loan is less than or equal to the net assets of subsidiary

Entity A, a UK entity with a Sterling functional currency, has a US subsidiary with a US dollar functional currency, Entity B. To finance this subsidiary, Entity A has a US$50 million US dollar loan with a third-party bank. Entities A and B have the same 31 December year end and the net assets of Entity B at 31 December 20X1 and 31 December 20X2 are US$70 million.

The loan is designated as a hedging instrument of the first US$50 million of net assets of Entity B. The designation is spot retranslation risk only. The hedge is determined to meet the qualifying criteria for hedge accounting. The US$/£ spot rate on 31/12/X1 is 1.6 and on 31/12/X2 it is 1.7.

On 31/12/X2, the following entries are recorded.

		£ million	£ million
Dr	Loan	1.84	
Cr	Other comprehensive income		1.84

To recognise the foreign exchange gain on the loan. This is the difference between US$50 million translated at 1.6 and 1.7.

		£ million	£ million
Dr	Other comprehensive income	2.57	
Cr	Net assets		2.57

To retranslate the net assets. This is the difference between US$70 million translated at 1.6 and 1.7.

The entire exchange difference on retranslating the net assets of the foreign operation is taken to other comprehensive income in accordance with IAS 21. The application of hedge accounting results in the remeasurement of the loan being recognised in other comprehensive income rather than profit or loss. No hedge ineffectiveness has been recognised. Hedge ineffectiveness would have arisen if the net assets of the foreign operation fell below US$50 million at the period end.

6.6.1.2 Loan exceeds net assets of subsidiary

Hedge accounting is still possible when the amount of the loan exceeds the net assets of the foreign operation.

Example 6.6.1.2

Loan exceeds net assets of subsidiary

Assume the same facts as in Example 6.6.1.1 except that the loan is US$100 million.

The entity designates US$70 million of the loan as a hedging instrument of the first US$70 million net assets of Entity B. The designation is spot retranslation risk only. The hedge is determined to meet the qualifying criteria for hedge accounting. The US$/£ spot rate on 31/12/X1 is 1.6 and on 31/12/X2 it is 1.7.

On 31/12/X2, the following entries are recorded.

		£ million	£ million
Dr	Loan	3.68	
Cr	Other comprehensive income		2.57
Cr	Profit or loss		1.11

To recognise the foreign exchange gain on the loan.

The entire loan must be remeasured at the closing rate, giving rise to an exchange gain. The exchange gain that relates to the designated and effective hedging instrument (i.e. US$70 million of the loan) is reported in other comprehensive income. The remainder is reported in profit or loss.

		£ million	£ million
Dr	Other comprehensive income	2.57	
Cr	Net assets		2.57

To retranslate the net assets.

6.6.1.3 Net assets of the foreign operation change

The facts in **examples 6.6.1.1** and **6.6.1.2** were simplified because the net assets of the subsidiary remained the same at the start and at the end of the reporting period. In practice, this will rarely be the case. Because documentation and designation must be in place at inception of the hedge, the hedged item will be based on the opening net asset position. Hedge ineffectiveness arises to the extent to which the net asset position falls below the designated amount of net assets at the end of the hedged period. The end of the hedged period would be the earlier of the end of the reporting period, the end of the life of the hedge or the end of the period until the next hedge effectiveness assessment is performed.

Example 6.6.1.3

Net assets of foreign operation change

Entity A, a UK entity with a Sterling functional currency, has a US subsidiary with a US dollar functional currency, Entity B. To finance this subsidiary, Entity A has a US$80 million US dollar loan with a third-party bank. The year-end of both entities is 31 December. On 31 December 20X1, the net assets of Entity B were US$90 million, and are expected to remain at approximately this level, so the entire loan is designated as hedging the spot retranslation risk associated with the first US$80 million net assets of Entity B. The term of the hedge is up to 31 December 20X2 and no further assessment of hedge effectiveness is due to be performed subsequent to inception of the hedge.

On 31 December 20X2, the net assets of B are US$75 million. The reduction in net assets was not regarded as a significant change in circumstances affecting hedge effectiveness and hence did not prompt a reassessment of the hedge effectiveness requirements since inception of the hedge (i.e. the hedge ratio was not updated to reflect this change in the period). The US$/£ spot rate on 31/12/X1 is 1.6 and on 31/12/X2 is 1.7.

Hedge ineffectiveness arises because US$80 million of net assets are no longer being hedged. Nevertheless, hedge accounting is required for the period and hedge ineffectiveness must be recognised immediately in profit or loss.

		£ million	£ million
Dr	Loan	2.94	
Cr	Other comprehensive income		2.76
Cr	Profit or loss		0.18

To recognise the foreign exchange gain on the loan.

The foreign exchange gain that relates to the designated and effective hedging instrument (i.e. the exchange gain on US$75 million) is recognised in other comprehensive income while the ineffective portion is recognised in profit or loss.

On 31 December 20X2, the group may choose to redesignate prospectively the hedging instrument to be only US$75 million of the loan in order to comply with the hedge effectiveness requirements and designate an appropriate hedge ratio.

In **example 6.6.1.3**, ineffectiveness was caused by the net assets of the foreign operation falling below the level of the loan hedging it. This ineffectiveness can be minimised by monitoring the net assets of the foreign operation and redesignating as appropriate.

6.6.2 Hedging net investments with forward contracts

If no hedge accounting was applied, then the foreign exchange gains and losses on retranslating the net assets of the foreign operation would be taken to other comprehensive income (in accordance with IAS 21:39) and the change in fair value of the forward contract would be recognised in profit or loss.

When hedging net investments with forward contracts, it is important to specify what risk is being hedged (i.e. the forward or the spot exchange rate) and whether any foreign currency basis spread is excluded from the designation of the hedging instrument (see **6.6.3**). If the spot rate is hedged and any foreign currency basis spread is excluded, the spot element of the forward contract is recognised in other comprehensive income (foreign currency translation reserve) and the remainder (being the forward points and foreign currency basis spread) is recognised either directly in profit or loss or deferred in a separate component of other comprehensive income and amortised to profit or loss (see section **6.9**). Any element recognised in the foreign currency translation reserve is reclassified from equity to profit or loss on the disposal (or, in some cases, partial disposal) of the underlying net investment.

A detailed illustration of a net investment hedge using a forward contract is included in the following sections of **chapter B10**.

- **4.1** Net investment hedging the spot foreign currency rate.
- **4.2** Net investment hedging the forward foreign currency rate.

6.6.3 Hedging net investments with currency swaps

When hedging a net investment in a foreign operation using a currency swap there are a number of different scenarios that can arise, each with different accounting outcomes. These variations arise depending on:

- the interest flows on each leg of the currency swap (i.e. float for float, fixed for fixed, float for fixed or fixed for float);
- the nature of foreign currency risk designated in the net investment (i.e. spot or forward);
- the component of currency swap excluded from the hedge (if any) (i.e. excluding foreign currency basis, excluding forward points, or excluding both foreign currency basis and forward points).

When it comes to assessing and measuring effectiveness of the hedge:

- the spot foreign currency risk of the net investment is measured by simply taking the spot retranslation difference on the hedged amount; and
- the forward foreign currency risk of the net investment is usually measured using the hypothetical derivative method where the hypothetical derivative would be a fixed for fixed currency swap (because this locks in the forward rate).

In the latter case, the change in fair value of the hypothetical derivative would not include any change due to foreign currency basis spreads as this is not deemed to exist in the hedged item (IFRS 9:B6.5.5, see **5.4.1**). Consequently, it would usually be preferable to exclude foreign currency basis spreads when designating a currency swap to reduce hedge ineffectiveness (see **6.10**). Depending on the election made with regard to the recognition of the excluded component, this would result in any change in fair value due to foreign currency basis spreads being recognised directly in profit or loss, or recognised in OCI and reclassified to profit or loss on a rational basis which would reduce profit or loss volatility.

6.6.3.1 Hedging a net investment with a float for float currency swap

A float for float currency swap is a good hedge of spot foreign currency risk as the foreign currency leg of the swap resembles a floating rate foreign currency loan. See **section 4.3** of **chapter B10** for an illustration of this type of hedge.

6.6.3.2 Hedging a net investment with a fixed for fixed currency swap

A fixed for fixed currency swap is a good hedge of forward foreign currency risk because the swap locks in the forward foreign currency rate. Similar to a forward contract, the forward element of a fixed for fixed currency swap could be excluded from the designated component of the swap. Where this is done the remaining component could be a good hedge of spot foreign currency risk. See **sections 4.4** and **4.5** of **chapter B10** for illustrative examples of net investment hedges using fixed for fixed currency swaps.

6.6.3.3 Hedging a net investment with a fixed for float or float for fixed currency swap

It may be more difficult to demonstrate an economic relationship for a net investment hedge using currency swaps that combine fixed legs with floating legs. That is because the fixed leg would introduce a mismatch in a hedge of spot foreign currency risk and the floating leg would introduce a mismatch in a hedge of forward foreign currency risk.

6.6.4 Hedging by multiple parent entities

IFRIC 16 clarified that within consolidated financial statements a parent that hedges a foreign operation can be an immediate parent, intermediate parent, or ultimate parent. The fact that the net investment is held through an intermediate parent does not affect the nature of the economic risk arising from the foreign currency exposure to the ultimate parent entity. [IFRIC 16:12] However, an exposure to foreign currency risk arising from a net investment in a foreign operation may qualify for hedge accounting only once in the consolidated financial statements. Therefore, if the same net assets of a foreign operation are hedged by more than one parent entity within the group (e.g. both a direct and an indirect parent entity) for the same risk, only one hedging relationship will qualify for hedge accounting in the consolidated financial statements of the ultimate parent. [IFRIC 16:13]

If a hedging relationship is designated by one parent entity in its consolidated financial statements, it need not be maintained by another higher level parent entity. However, if it is not maintained by the higher level parent entity, the hedge accounting applied by the lower level parent must be reversed before the higher level parent's hedge accounting is recognised. [IFRIC 16:13] This is not unique to net investment hedging because hedge accounting by a subsidiary or by a sub-consolidated group need not be maintained in the consolidated financial statements that include the subsidiary or a sub-consolidated group. Conversely, hedge accounting could be designated in the consolidated financial statements but not designated in the subsidiary only financial statements or the financial statements of a sub-consolidated group that forms part of the larger group. Furthermore, even where a hedge is designated at a subsidiary level and a group level, the two designations need not be consistent. This flexibility is possible because hedge accounting is entirely voluntary.

Example 6.6.4

Hedge designations

The group structure of Group P is as follows.

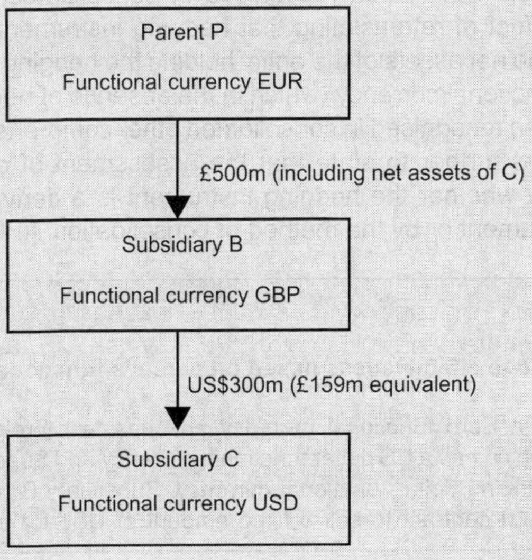

In the consolidated financial statements headed by Group P, the maximum amount of net assets available to be hedged for the respective hedged risk in a qualifying hedge relationship is:

- $300 million net assets for €/US$ risk between P and C; or
- £500 million net assets for €/£ risk between P and B; or
- $300 million net assets for £/US$ risk between B and C; or
- $300 million net assets for £/US$ risk between B and C; and £500 million net assets for €/£ risk between P and B; or
- $300 million net assets for €/US$ risk between P and C; and £341 million net assets for €/£ risk between P and B.

6.6.5 Location of hedging instrument within the group

IFRIC 16:14 states that the hedging instrument(s) may be held by any entity or entities within the group as long as the designation, documentation and effectiveness requirements of IFRS 9:6.4.1 for the net investment hedge are satisfied. IFRIC 16 notes that the hedge strategy must be clearly documented because of the possibility of different designations at different levels of the group.

When the hedging instrument resides in an entity that has the same functional currency as the parent that has the investment in the foreign operation the hedge effectiveness calculations are easier to perform as hedge effectiveness is determined as if the parent that has the investment in the foreign operation also had the hedging instrument. Determining hedge effectiveness is more complex when the entity holding the hedging instrument has a different functional currency to that of the parent that has the exposure to the foreign operation. In such circumstances, IFRIC 16 requires hedge effectiveness to not only reflect the gain/loss residing in the entity holding the hedging instrument (which in the absence of hedge accounting would have been recognised in consolidated profit or loss), but also the effect of retranslating that hedging instrument as part of the translation of the net assets of the entity holding the hedging instrument into the parent's functional currency (which in the absence of hedge accounting would have been recognised in consolidated other comprehensive income). The IFRIC goes further to state that the assessment of effectiveness is not affected by whether the hedging instrument is a derivative or a non-derivative instrument or by the method of consolidation. [IFRIC 16:15]

Example 6.6.5

Assessing hedge effectiveness based on parent's functional currency

Parent P has a Euro functional currency and has two foreign operations, Subsidiary A which has a US dollar functional currency and Subsidiary B which has a New Zealand dollar functional currency. Subsidiary B holds a foreign currency forward contract to sell a fixed amount of US$ for a fixed amount of € at a specific date in the future. Parent P wishes to designate the foreign currency forward as a net investment hedge of its investment in Subsidiary A. The hedged risk is the €/US$ foreign currency exposure with respect to the translation of Subsidiary A's US$ net assets into €.

Parent P wishes to designate the spot foreign currency risk only (not the forward foreign currency risk). The opening net assets of Subsidiary A are US$1,000 and the entire opening net assets are intended to be designated as being hedged by Parent P in its consolidated financial statements. For illustrative purposes the foreign currency forward's fair value is calculated using undiscounted spot rates, the foreign currency spot and forward rate are presumed to be the same and the foreign currency basis spread is assumed to be nil (i.e. there is no gain/loss in respect of fair valuing the forward point differential or foreign currency basis spread).

	Opening spot rate	**Closing spot rate**	**Average spot rate**
€/US$	1.400	1.520	1.460
€/NZ$	2.200	1.850	2.025
US$/NZ$	1.571	1.217	1.394

Parent P's translation of Subsidiary A's designated net assets in the consolidated financial statements:

Opening designated net assets	US$1,000 @ 1.400 =	€714
Closing designated net assets	US$1,000 @ 1.520 =	€658
Loss on translation of Subsidiary A's net assets		€56

Gain/loss on the foreign currency forward with respect to spot rates in Subsidiary B's financial statements:

Receive €	(Buy €714 @ 1.850) =	NZ$1,321
Pay US$	(Sell US$1,000 @ 1.217) =	NZ$1,217
Gain/loss in the period		NZ$104

Impact of the derivative in consolidated profit or loss in the absence of hedge accounting with respect to the hedged risk:

Gain/loss NZ$104 @ 2.025 (average spot rate) = €51

If the translation of the hedging instrument from Subsidiary B's functional currency, NZ$, to the Parent P's functional currency, €, was ignored, the hedge relationship is partly ineffective (€51 compared to €56).

IFRIC 16 requires the effectiveness to be determined by reference to the parent's functional currency. The effect of applying this approach is to include the difference between the average spot rate and the closing spot rate that is recognised in consolidated other comprehensive income with respect to the translation of the derivative in Subsidiary B, as part of the assessment of hedge effectiveness.

Gain/loss	NZ$104 @ 2.025 (average rates) =	€51
Gain/loss	NZ$104 @ 1.850 (closing rates) =	€56
Difference	=	€5

When the additional amount described above is included in the assessment of hedge effectiveness the hedge is fully effective ((€51 + €5) / €56).

Had Parent P held the foreign currency forward, the gain/loss derived from the foreign currency forward would be driven solely by US$ because the € receive leg of the foreign currency forward does not generate foreign currency risk given Parent P has a € functional currency. The gain/loss on the hedging instrument would be an offset to the translation of Subsidiary A's US$ net assets to €. Considered differently, in the group accounts of Parent P the group has a long US$ position being the net assets of Subsidiary A, and a short US$ position being the US$ pay leg of the foreign currency forward contract and, therefore, the derivative would have been fully effective.

In April 2009, the IASB issued *Improvements to IFRSs*, which amended IFRIC 16:14 to allow the hedging instrument to be held by any entity within the group and, thereby, removed the restriction that the foreign operation that is itself being hedged cannot hold the hedging instrument. The Basis for Conclusions states that the IASB believes that, without hedge accounting, part of the foreign exchange difference arising from the hedging instrument would be included in consolidated profit or loss and, therefore, the restriction that the foreign operation being hedged cannot hold the hedging instrument should be removed.

6.6.6 *Hedging a portfolio of net investments with a single instrument*

If a group has multiple foreign operations that have the same functional currency, the group can hedge the foreign operations either as a group, or individually. For example, Parent heads a group that includes two US$ subsidiaries, A and B, each with US$500,000 of net assets, and $1m of third party borrowings. The Parent's interest in subsidiary A and B is held directly, i.e. neither subsidiary is a subsidiary of the other. The group may either designate the borrowings of $1m as a hedge of a group of foreign operations of US$1 million, or designate 50 per cent of the borrowings as hedging US$500,000 of subsidiary A, and 50 per cent of the borrowings as hedging US$500,000 of subsidiary B. When the designation is on a group basis the hedge documentation can be done on a group basis; however, hedge effectiveness must be assessed for each subsidiary individually.

Example 6.6.6

Hedging a portfolio of net investments with a single instrument

Entity P is a Sterling functional currency entity that has US$400 million foreign currency denominated issued debt which it wishes to designate as a hedging instrument of the net investment in its US dollar foreign operations. The group structure is as follows.

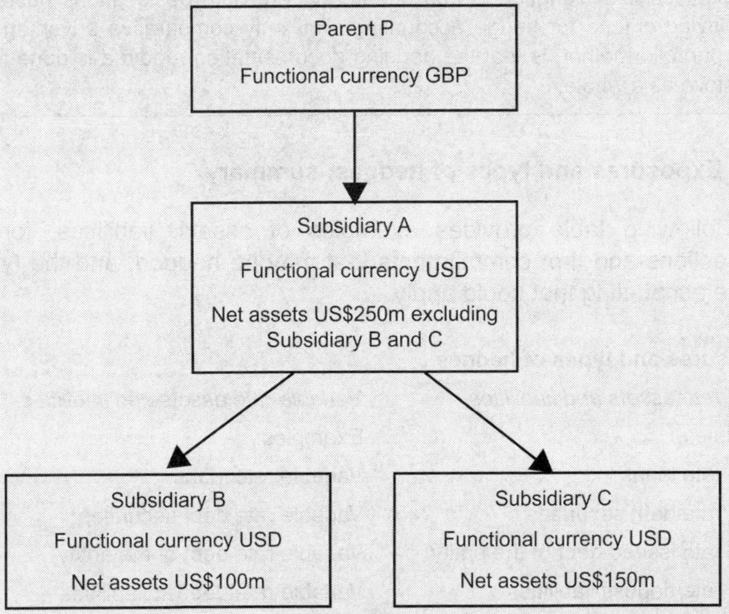

The following designations are permitted by IFRS 9:

1. Entity P may designate US$400m debt as a hedging instrument of a net investment in the consolidated net assets of the sub-group headed by Subsidiary A;
2. Entity P may designate relevant proportions of the US$ debt as hedges of net investments in Subsidiary A, Subsidiary B, and Subsidiary C individually, i.e. 62.5 per cent of the US$ debt as a hedge of the net investment in subsidiary A, 25 per cent of the US$ debt as a hedge of the net investment in Subsidiary B, and 12.5 per cent of the US$ debt as the hedge of the net investment in Subsidiary C; or
3. Entity P may designate US$400 million debt as a hedge of a portfolio of net investments in US$ subsidiaries.

IAS 21 *The Effects of Changes in Foreign Exchange Rates* views a net investment in a foreign operation as "the amount of the reporting entity's interest in the net assets of that operation". [IAS 21:8] The 'operation' is not defined and can be considered to be either the consolidated net assets of the sub-group headed by Entity A, or as a collection of net assets held by each of the three subsidiaries.

> If Entity P chooses to designate a portfolio (designation 3 in the list above) the group must assess and measure hedge effectiveness based on the individual foreign operations within the portfolio. Therefore, to the extent that the net assets of one of the foreign operations fall below the designated net asset amount, or a subsidiary is sold, ineffectiveness will arise.
>
> It should be noted that the amount of ineffectiveness that will be recognised if Entity P were to use the portfolio designation will be the same as that recognised if designation 2 was adopted where both designations pass the qualifying criteria for hedge accounting. The only comparative advantage of the portfolio method is that the hedging documentation required is done for a portfolio as a whole.

6.7 Exposures and types of hedges: summary

The following table provides examples of assets, liabilities, forecast transactions and firm commitments that may be hedged, and the type of hedge accounting that could apply.

Exposures and types of hedges

Fixed rate assets and liabilities		*Variable rate assets and liabilities*	
Examples:		Examples:	
Fixed rate loans		Variable rate loans	
Fixed rate debt securities		Variable rate debt securities	
Fixed rate issued debt of the entity		Variable rate debt of the entity	
Fixed rate deposit liabilities		Variable rate deposit liabilities	
Exposure	*Hedge accounting*	*Exposure*	*Hedge accounting*
Overall fair value	FV (Fair value)	Overall fair value	FV
Interest rates	FV	Interest rates	FV* or CF (Cash flow)
Foreign currency	FV or CF	Foreign currency	FV or CF
Termination options	FV	Termination options	FV
Firm commitments to originate loans		*Forecast purchases and sales of financial instruments*	
Examples:		Examples:	
Issued fixed rate loan commitment		Forecast purchase of debt	
Fixed rate loan commitment held		Forecast loan originations	
Exposure	*Hedge accounting*	*Exposure*	*Hedge accounting*
Overall fair value	FV	Overall variability	CF
Interest rates	FV	Interest rates	CF
Firm commitment to purchase or sell non-financial assets		*Forecast purchases and sales of non-financial assets*	

Exposures and types of hedges

Examples:		Examples:	
Committed sale of inventory		Forecast sale of inventory	
Committed purchase of inventory		Forecast purchase of inventory	
Exposure	*Hedge accounting*	*Exposure*	*Hedge accounting*
Overall fair value	FV	Overall variability	CF
Foreign currency	FV or CF**	Foreign currency	CF
Other risk component (e.g. commodity risk)	FV	Other risk component (e.g. commodity risk)	CF

Other assets

Examples:

Equity investments classified as FVTOCI in IFRS 9

Exposure	*Hedge accounting*
Overall fair value	FV
Foreign currency	FV

* Fair value hedging is generally permitted for hedging the fair value risk associated with the fixing of interest between floating reset dates.

** IFRS 9 recognises that firm commitments create fair value exposure. However, it does allow hedges of the foreign currency risk of a firm commitment to be accounted for as either a fair value hedge or a cash flow hedge. [IFRS 9:6.5.4]

6.8 Accounting for the time value of an option

IFRS 9:6.2.4(a) allows an entity to exclude the time value of an option and designate only the intrinsic value as the hedging instrument. In these cases, the normal hedge accounting mechanics apply to the change in the designated intrinsic value of the option depending on the type of designated hedge relationship (i.e. cash flow hedge, fair value hedge or net investment hedge).

The Standard does not provide a definition of time value or intrinsic value for the purposes of identifying these two elements. This raises the question of what should be taken as intrinsic value, especially in the case of European options where the value of the option is driven from the expected price of the underlying in the future, and not its current price. For example, in the case of a cap on an interest rate index that is exercisable at the maturity of the option, the question arises as to whether intrinsic value at any point in time should be measured based on the current level of the given index (i.e. intrinsic value based on the spot rate) or by reference to the forward rate of the index that coincides with the actual exercise date (i.e. intrinsic value based on the forward rate).

The latter view would seem to be more in line with the economic reality for a European option because the intrinsic value of the option is entirely a function of where the rate of interest is predicted to be at the exercise date as opposed to where it currently is, given that the option cannot be presently exercised. This view of intrinsic value is supported by the fact that there is a readily observable prediction of future interest rates, i.e. the forward rates derived from the yield curve. In this respect European options over interest rate indices are different from those over other underlyings such as equity shares. IFRS 2 *Share-based Payment* Appendix A defines the intrinsic value of a share option as the difference between the fair value of the shares and the exercise price of the option, pointing towards a spot based view of intrinsic value, which is consistent with the fact that for equity shares there is no readily observable prediction of future prices as there is for interest rates.

Consider the case of a purchased European interest rate cap in an environment of an inverted interest rate curve (i.e. a yield curve that predicts that future interest rates will be below current levels). An entity may purchase a European-style interest rate cap at 5 per cent with a maturity of two years when the current spot rate is 6 per cent and the current market prediction as illustrated by the yield curve is that the interest rate is expected to be 4.5 per cent at the exercise date of the option. If intrinsic value is based on the spot rate, the intrinsic value will effectively 'build in' an assumption of the interest rate remaining at 6 per cent, i.e. in excess of the cap even though the yield curve predicts that this will not be the case. This will lead to a value being attributed to intrinsic value that is in excess of the total fair value of the option. As a result 'negative' value will be attributed to the time value in order for the sum of the time and intrinsic values to equal the total fair value of the option. It would seem strange that IFRS 9 would require an entity to attribute 'negative' time value to a purchased option and, therefore, it is reasonable for an entity to assess intrinsic value based on forward rather than spot interest rates, assuming it documents this as part of its risk management strategy and applies this consistently for similar hedging relationships.

In addition, it is necessary to consider whether the intrinsic value of a European option is determined on a discounted or undiscounted basis. For example, where the intrinsic value of an option is determined by comparing the strike price to the forward price, there is no specific guidance in the Standard as to whether that value should be discounted or left undiscounted. In the absence of specific guidance it would be appropriate for an entity to adopt an accounting policy choice applied consistently for similar hedging relationships.

IFRS 9:6.5.15 does not allow changes in the undesignated time value to be recognised directly in profit or loss. Instead the change in time value (some or all of it, depending on how much of it relates to the hedged item) is initially recognised in other comprehensive income. The objective of this approach is to limit the profit or loss volatility that would otherwise arise from fair valuing the time value directly through profit or loss. Since the option is still measured at fair value on the balance sheet, the volatile changes in fair value are captured in other comprehensive income, whilst amounts that would accumulate in equity over the term of the hedge are ultimately recognised in profit or loss on a cost basis. The mechanics for recognising the time value in profit or loss varies depending on:

- how much of the time value relates to the hedged item; and
- the nature of the hedged item and whether it is a *transaction related item* or a *time-period related item*.

The accounting of the time value is not affected by the type of hedging relationship.

To determine how much of the time value of an option relates to the hedged item, an entity is required to value an option that has critical terms that perfectly match the hedged item (e.g. nominal amount, life and underlying). This is referred to as the *aligned time value*. This aligned time value will be the same as that on the actual option used for hedging if the terms perfectly match the hedged item but will be different (higher or lower) if not. [IFRS 9:B6.5.32] Where there is a difference, some of the change in time value of the option will be recognised directly in profit or loss (see **6.8.3**). Where the aligned time value matches the time value on the actual option, the accounting described below for transaction related items and time-period related items would apply to the full fair value change of the time value of the actual option.

An entity determines the aligned time value using the valuation of the option that would have critical terms that perfectly match the hedged item. In determining this, an entity would need to consider which type of option this should be based on. For example, there are different types of options that can be transacted to hedge one-sided risk such as American options where the option can be exercised at any time from the purchase date to the expiry date, European options where the option can only be exercised at expiry, and Bermudan options which can be exercised at set times between the purchase date and expiry date. Because of the additional flexibility, for the same hedged rate, an American option would have a higher premium than a Bermudan option which in turn would have a higher premium than a European option. Hence determining which of these options should be used to determine the aligned time value will require careful assessment of the terms of the hedged item and the risk management objective of the hedge. For example, when a forecast transaction is hedged for a one sided risk, and the potential variability in timing of the transaction is not part of the risk management objective of the hedge, the aligned time value should be based on a European option. Likewise, in a one-sided risk hedge of a firm commitment the aligned time value would be based on a European option because the timing of the transaction is contractually fixed.

The accounting of the time value applies to both purchased and written options (to the extent eligible) as well as combinations of purchased and written options such as collars. It should be noted however that where the designated option is a zero-cost collar with matching critical terms to the hedged item, if the hedge runs to term, there will be no time value recognised in profit or loss as all changes in the time value will be fully recognised in other comprehensive income and would accumulate to nil fair value, see **example 6.8.1**. [IFRS 9:B6.5.31]

Example 6.8A

Actual option same as aligned option

Entity Y, a £ entity, purchases an option contract to sell €10 million in one-year's time at a rate of €1.4 (€:£) when the spot exchange rate is €1.1 (€:£) to protect against foreign currency risk on €10m of net assets in its net investment in foreign operations. It designates the intrinsic value of the option in a hedge of €10m of net assets of its € net investments. The critical terms of the actual option match those of an aligned option; accordingly the time value of the actual option is equal to the aligned time value.

Example 6.8B

Actual option differs from aligned option

Entity Z, a ¥ entity, purchases an option for US$5,000 to hedge a highly probable forecast purchase of copper against increases in the copper price above US$10,000 per tonne. The option is for 1,000 tonnes of copper to be settled on 01/09/20X0. The forecast transaction is for the same tonnage; however, the timing of the purchase is expected to be on 15/07/20X0. Entity Z has designated the intrinsic value of the option in a hedging relationship. In order to determine the hedge accounting journals for changes in the time value of the option, Entity Z needs to determine the aligned time value. This is determined by valuing an option with matching critical terms to the hedged item which means aligning the end date of the option to 15/07/20X0 to match the hedged exposure. Entity Z determines the aligned time value to be US$4,800. As result, Entity Z determines the amount to be deferred in other comprehensive income based on the changes in the aligned time value (i.e. US$4,800) and accounts for any differences in fair value changes between the two time values in profit or loss. Therefore, Entity Z is required to value both the actual hedging instrument and the aligned option to determine the required hedge accounting journal entries. When the hypothetical derivative method is used and the hypothetical option is the same as the aligned option, the intrinsic value of the aligned option can also be used to measure hedge ineffectiveness and determine the amount of the change in intrinsic value of the actual hedging instrument to be deferred in the cash flow hedge reserve (i.e. to apply the 'lower of' test, see **6.5.1**).

Hedged items are determined to be *transaction related items* or *time-period related items* depending on their characteristics, including how and when they affect profit or loss. [IFRS 9:B6.5.29]

IFRS 9:B6.5.29 only refers to the hedged item impacting profit or loss. Therefore, this could be read as prohibiting the use of options as hedging instruments in fair value hedging an investment in an equity instrument designated as at FVTOCI (noting that it is not permissible to cash flow hedge such investments). However, IFRS 9:6.5.15(c) specifically refers to an investment in an equity instrument designated as at FVTOCI being an eligible hedged item when hedging with options and, therefore, there is not a prohibition in using options as hedging instruments when fair value hedging such investments.

The distinction between transaction related and time-period related hedged items is not dependent on the type of hedge they are designated in. For example, transaction related items include many forecast transactions designated in cash flow hedges as well as many firm commitments which could be designated in a fair value hedge. That said, net investments designated in net investment hedges are always time-period related items because there is no underlying transaction.

6.8.1 Transaction related hedged items

The time value of an option relates to a transaction related hedged item if the nature of the hedged item is a transaction for which the time value has the character of costs of that transaction. An example is a hedged item that results in the recognition of an item whose initial measurement includes transaction costs such as a commodity purchase, hedged for commodity price risk that includes transaction costs in the initial measurement of the inventory. [IFRS 9:B6.5.29(a)]

This description of transaction related items is not particularly clear but it could be read as meaning that the hedged item is a future transaction, committed or forecast, where the time value of the option could be regarded as a cost of that transaction, for example, like an insurance cost of that transaction. Despite the example given in IFRS 9:B6.5.29(a), it is not necessary for the hedged item to result in the recognition of an asset or liability for which transaction costs would be capitalised, for example a transaction related item could include a forecast sale in a foreign currency.

Common examples of transaction related items include:

- Forecast purchase of a commodity hedged against price increases;
- Firm commitment to buy property plant and equipment denominated in a foreign currency hedged for foreign currency risk; and

- Forecast sale of goods in a foreign currency hedged for foreign currency risk

For transaction related hedged items, where only the intrinsic value of the option is designated, the change in fair value of the time value (to the extent it relates to the hedged item) is recognised in other comprehensive income and accumulated in a separate component of equity and then accounted for as follows: [IFRS 9:6.5.15(b)]

- If the hedged item results in the recognition of a non-financial asset (e.g. recognition of inventory from a hedged purchase) or non-financial liability, the accumulated amount in equity is reclassified directly from equity (i.e. not as a reclassification adjustment that affects other comprehensive income) and included in the initial carrying amount of the asset or liability, commonly known as a 'basis adjustment'. As a result the time value is recognised in profit or loss when the item impacts profit or loss (e.g. upon the sale of inventory that was hedged).
- If the hedged item results in a firm commitment for which fair value hedge accounting is applied (e.g. fair value hedging foreign currency risk on a firm commitment that was cash flow hedged as a forecast transaction before it became committed) the accumulated amount in equity is reclassified directly from equity (i.e. not as a reclassification adjustment that affects other comprehensive income) and included in the initial carrying amount of the firm commitment, commonly known as a 'basis adjustment'. As a result the time value is recognised in profit or loss when the item impacts profit or loss (e.g. upon the amortisation or sale of the item that was recognised when the firm commitment was settled).
- In all other cases the accumulated amount is reclassified from equity to profit or loss as a reclassification adjustment (see IAS 1) in the same period or periods during which the hedged expected future cash flows affect profit or loss (e.g. when the hedged forecast sale occurs).
- However, if any of the time value is not expected to be recovered in a future period, then the amount not expected to be recovered is immediately reclassified to profit or loss as a reclassification adjustment.

A consequence of the above requirements is that if a hedge of a transaction related item is discontinued part way through the life of the hedge (e.g. due to early termination of the option), but the hedged item is still expected to occur, the time value amounts deferred in equity would remain in equity until the one of the above scenarios arose.

IFRS 9:6.5.15(b)(iii) requires that the amount accumulated in equity that is not expected to be recovered in future periods be immediately reclassified in profit or loss. This requirement was also included in IAS 39 (in the context of amounts deferred in cash flow hedges) and was seen to cater primarily for circumstances where an entity had elected *not* to apply a basis adjustment when a hedged forecast transaction resulted in the recognition of a non-financial asset. The purpose of this requirement is to ensure that the amounts deferred in equity are included as part of the impairment test of any non-financial asset to which it relates such that if it was not deemed to be recoverable, it would be reclassified to profit or loss in the same way that the amount would have been recognised in profit or loss if a basis adjustment to the asset had been applied and the asset was subsequently impaired.

It is reasonable to conclude that IFRS 9:6.5.15(b)(iii) should be applied in the same manner. Consequently, if at the reporting date (1) the amounts deferred in reserves were assumed to be recognised as part of the hedged item in the statement of financial position (i.e. if it was assumed that the basis-adjusted non-financial asset had been recognised at the reporting date), and (2) that the basis-adjusted asset carrying amount would be greater than the recoverable amount of that asset and would have triggered recognition of an impairment loss, then those amounts deferred that are not expected to be recovered should be reclassified to profit or loss immediately. Once the non-financial asset is recognised, IFRS 9 requires a basis adjustment and the normal impairment requirements would apply.

The other purpose of IFRS 9:6.5.15(b)(iii) is to ensure that time value amounts are not deferred in reserves indefinitely, for example when the hedged item is no longer expected to occur. If the time value amounts are not expected to be recovered in a future period, because the future transaction is not expected to occur in a future period, this requirement would result in the deferred amounts being reclassified to profit or loss immediately.

Example 6.8.1

Hedge of a transaction related item using a zero-cost collar

Entity X, with a US$ functional currency, has highly probable forecast € sales due to occur in two years. The Entity X is required to hedge against adverse movements in the US$:€ exchange rate. Under Entity X's risk management policy, the treasurer is permitted to use forward contracts and option contracts to hedge foreign currency risk. At the time of the hedge, the two-year forward rate is 1.05 (US$:€) and the budgeted rate set for the transaction for risk management purposes is 1.10. In this instance, the Entity X chooses to hedge with a zero-cost collar, which hedges the Entity X for increases in the rate above 1.10 and decreases in the rate below 0.95. This hedge strategy protects the Entity X from adverse movements in the exchange rate beyond the budgeted rate of 1.10 but allows it to enjoy the benefits of favourable movements in the rate down to 0.95.

For hedge accounting purposes Entity X designates the intrinsic value of the option in a hedge of the forecast sales for exchange rate changes above 1.10 and below 0.95. Changes in the time value of the option are recognised in other comprehensive income (OCI) and accumulated in a separate component of equity. The hedge is transacted part way through the year and, consequently, spans three annual reporting periods.

Scenario 1 – The value of the option fluctuates, but this is all attributable to the time value because the forward rate never breaches the upper or lower bound of the collar (i.e. the exchange rate remains between 0.95 and 1.1 for the period of the hedge)

	Inception	Year 1	Year 2	Year 3
Option carrying amount (fair value)	Nil	10,000	(4,000)	–
Profit or loss		–	–	–
OCI		(10,000)	14,000	(4,000)
Equity – time value		10,000	(4,000)	–
Equity – cash flow hedge reserve		–	–	–

Scenario 2 – The fluctuations in the value of the option are attributable to both time value and intrinsic value. However, at the end of the term of the hedge the exchange rate is within the 0.95-1.1 collar and hence the option lapses with nil value.

	Inception	Year 1	Year 2	Year 3
Option carrying amount (fair value)	Nil	40,000	80,000	–
Profit or loss		–	–	–
OCI		(40,000)	(40,000)	80,000
Equity – time value		2,000	1,000	–
Equity – cash flow hedge reserve		38,000	79,000	–

Scenario 3 – The value of the option fluctuates in the period which is attributable to both time value and intrinsic value and at the end of the term of the hedge the option terminates in the money. The accumulated intrinsic value at the end of the hedge was US$80,000, which was reclassified and recognised in profit or loss as part of the hedged sales when they arose in year 3.

	Inception	Year 1	Year 2	Year 3
Option carrying amount (fair value)	Nil	40,000	80,000	–
Profit or loss		–	–	(80,000)
OCI		(40,000)	(40,000)	80,000
Equity – time value		2,000	1,000	–
Equity – cash flow hedge reserve		38,000	79,000	–

6.8.2 Time-period related hedged items

The time value of an option relates to a time-period related hedged item if the nature of the hedged item is such that the time value has the character of a cost for obtaining protection against a risk over a particular period of time (but the hedged item does not result in a transaction that involves the notion of a transaction cost in accordance with IFRS 9:B6.5.29(a)). [IFRS 9:B6.5.29(b)]

This description of time-period related items is not particularly clear given that any option could be regarded as giving protection against a risk over a period of time, however, it is clear that the intention is to exclude those items that would be regarded as transaction related items.

Examples of time-period related items include:

- Commodity inventory hedged against commodity price decreases [IFRS 9:B6.5.29(b)]
- Net investment in a foreign operation hedged for adverse changes in foreign exchange rates [IFRS 9:B6.5.29(b)]
- Recognised equity investment (FVTPL or FVTOCI) hedged against equity price decreases
- Issued floating rate bond hedged against increases in interest rates [IFRS 9:B6.5.30]
- Fixed rate foreign bond investment hedged against adverse changes in foreign exchange rates

There are two parts to the accounting for time-period related hedged items where only the intrinsic value of the option is designated. Firstly, the change in time value of the option (to the extent it relates to the hedged item) is recognised in other comprehensive income and accumulated in a separate component of equity. Secondly, the time value at the date of designation of the option (to the extent that it relates to the hedged item) is amortised on a systematic and rational basis over the period during which the hedge adjustment for the option's intrinsic value could affect profit or loss (or other comprehensive income, if the hedged item is an equity instrument at FVTOCI). [IFRS 9:6.5.15(c)]

In practice there may be more than one acceptable basis for amortising deferred costs of hedging for a particular hedge. In some circumstances, simple straight line amortisation may be an acceptable approach. For example, straight-line amortisation could be a reasonable basis for a hedge of foreign currency risk in a net investment using the intrinsic value of a purchased foreign currency option that settles at the end of a two-year period (this could also be appropriate if the hedging instrument was the spot element of a forward or cross-currency interest rate swap excluding the foreign currency basis spread).

In other circumstances, the determination of a systematic and rational basis for amortising deferred costs of hedging from equity to profit or loss will require careful judgement. For example, for a hedge of interest rate risk using a purchased interest rate cap with a single strike price, which hedges 3-month variable cash flows on a fixed principal over a period of say five years, it may also be regarded as appropriate to amortise the total premium on a straight-line basis over the term of the hedge. However, if the principal of the loan varied over the five-year period, or the capped rate is different for different periods over the five years, straight-line amortisation is unlikely to be appropriate.

In each reporting period, the amortisation amount shall be reclassified from the separate component of equity to profit or loss as a reclassification adjustment (see IAS 1). [IFRS 9:6.5.15(c)]

Given the different basis for deferring the time value in and reclassifying from equity, it is possible that at a point in time over the life of the hedge, the amount reclassified from equity to profit or loss will exceed the amount that has been deferred in equity. However, by the end of the full term of the hedge the net amount of time value in equity would be nil and the full time value would have been recognised in profit or loss.

Example 6.8.2A

Hedging foreign currency risk on a net investment in a foreign operation using a purchased foreign exchange option

Entity P, which has a US$ functional currency, has a subsidiary, Entity B, with a € functional currency. In Entity P's consolidated financial statements, €1 million of the net investment in the foreign operation is hedged for unfavourable changes in the foreign exchange rate between US$ and € using a purchased foreign exchange option. The purchase premium for the option was US$24,000. The critical terms of the option and the hedged item match. The term of both the option and the hedge is two years. The change in time value of the option is deferred in other comprehensive income over the life of the hedge. Consequently, over the life of the option and the hedge US$24,000 will be recognised in other comprehensive income.

A hedge of a net investment in a foreign operation is a time-period related hedged item. Consequently, the time value amount is reclassified from equity to profit or loss over the two-year life of the hedge on a rational basis. In this situation, straight-line amortisation is regarded as a rational basis for amortisation, therefore US$1,000 is reclassified from other comprehensive income to profit or loss each month such that, at the end of two years, the net accumulated time value in equity is nil (i.e. US$24,000 is deferred in other comprehensive income and US$24,000 is reclassified from equity to profit or loss).

Example 6.8.2B

Hedging copper inventory for copper price risk using a purchased commodity option

Entity X holds copper inventory which exposes it to copper price risk. To hedge the copper price risk, it purchases, for a premium of US$18,000, an option (a floor) with an 18-month term to protect itself from price declines below US$7,000 per tonne. The critical terms of the option match that of the hedged item. Changes in the time value of the option are recognised in other comprehensive income over the life of the hedge. A hedge of copper inventory is a hedge of a time-period related item. Consequently, the original time value amount of US$18,000 is reclassified from equity to profit or loss on a rational basis. In this situation a straight-line basis, is regarded as a rational basis. Therefore, US$1,000 is reclassified to profit or loss each month such that, over the life of the hedge relationship, the total amount recognised in other comprehensive income of US$18,000 has been reclassified to profit or loss with nothing left in equity at the end of the hedged period.

Although IFRS 9:6.5.15(c) refers to the reclassification occurring in each reporting period, if the period over which the option's intrinsic value could affect profit or loss through the application of hedge accounting has not yet commenced, reclassification of the time value amount from equity would also not yet commence. For example, if an interest rate cap was used to hedge against the risk of interest rates rising above a set rate but only between years two and three on a five year floating rate bond, the option's intrinsic value would only impact profit or loss in years two and three, hence reclassification of the time value amount from equity to profit or loss would only commence at the beginning of year two (see **example 6.8.2C**).

Example 6.8.2C

Hedging interest rate risk on a floating rate bond using an interest rate cap

[IFRS 9:B6.5.30]

A purchased interest rate option (a cap) is used to provide protection against increases in the interest expense on a floating rate bond. The time value of that cap is amortised to profit or loss over the same period over which any intrinsic value of the cap would affect profit or loss.

If the cap hedges increases in interest rates for the first three years out of a total life of the floating rate bond of five years, the time value of that cap is amortised over the first three years.

If the cap is a forward start option that hedges increases in interest rates for years two and three out of a total life of the floating rate bond of five years, the time value of that cap is amortised during years two and three.

If hedge accounting is discontinued the net amount (i.e. including cumulative amortisation) that has been accumulated in the separate component of equity is immediately reclassified into profit or loss as a reclassification adjustment. [IFRS 9:6.5.15(c)]

6.8.3 Actual time value vs aligned time value

As noted in **6.8** above, if the actual time value and the aligned time value differ some of the change in time value of the option will be recognised directly in profit or loss. To determine how much of the change in time value is recognised directly in profit or loss, first it is necessary to determine whether the aligned time value is greater or less than the actual time value of the option designated in the hedge.

If at inception of the hedging relationship, the actual time value is higher than the aligned time value, the entity shall: [IFRS 9:B6.5.33(a)]

(i) determine the amount to be deferred in other comprehensive income based on the aligned time value; and

(ii) account for any differences in fair value changes between the two time values in profit or loss.

If at inception of the hedging relationship, the actual time value is lower than the aligned time value, the entity shall determine the amount to be deferred in other comprehensive income by reference to the lower of the cumulative change in fair value of: [IFRS 9:B6.5.33(b)]

(i) the actual time value; and

(ii) the aligned time value

Any remainder of the change in fair value of the actual time value shall be recognised in profit or loss.

Per IFRS 9:B6.5.33(b), the treatment of the difference between the change in time value of the actual option and the aligned option differs depending on whether at inception of the hedge the time value of the actual option is greater or less than the aligned option. Basing the amounts deferred in reserves on the lower of the change in time value of the actual option and the aligned option (as required when the actual time value is lower than the aligned time value) is logical as it ensures that amounts deferred in reserves can never be greater than the change in time value of the actual option and hence limits the amounts deferred in reserves to actual changes in value. The reason behind basing the amounts deferred in reserves on the aligned time value, in cases where the actual time value is greater than the aligned time value at inception of the hedge, is to avoid, over the full term of the hedge, deferring amounts of the actual time value that are not matched with the aligned time value. However, a consequence of basing the amounts deferred in reserves on the aligned time value can give rise to some unusual accounting outcomes in intervening periods (which would ultimately reverse over the full term of the hedge). For example, where the cumulative change in the aligned time value is greater than the cumulative change in the actual time value part way through the life of the hedge, recording an amount in reserves based on the aligned time value results in a grossing up of the change in value of the actual time value with a debit/credit to other comprehensive income and a corresponding credit/debit to profit or loss. This effectively creates gains or losses in profit or loss and other comprehensive income that do not exist.

6.9 Accounting for the forward element of a forward contract

IFRS 9:6.2.4(b) allows an entity to exclude the forward element of a forward contract and designate only changes in the spot element in a hedging relationship. In these cases, the normal hedge accounting mechanics apply to the designated spot element depending on the type of hedge (i.e. cash flow hedge, fair value hedge or net investment hedge).

For the undesignated forward element of the forward there is a choice over how changes in its value are accounted for which allows the undesignated element to be treated in the same way as the undesignated time value of an option discussed above. [IFRS 9:6.5.16] This choice is made on a hedge-by-hedge basis and applies for the term of the designated hedge. The two alternatives are:

- take changes in value of the undesignated forward element directly to profit or loss; or
- take changes in value of the undesignated forward element (some or all of it, depending on how much of it relates to the hedged item) to other comprehensive income with amounts subsequently removed from equity and ultimately recognised in profit or loss.

If the second of the above two approaches is applied, the mechanics for recognising the change in forward element in profit or loss varies depending on:

- how much of the forward element relates to the hedged item; and
- the nature of the hedged item and whether it is a *transaction related item* or a *time-period related item* (see **6.9.1** and **6.9.2**).

These mechanics are the same as those described above in **section 6.8** when only the intrinsic value of an option is designated as a hedging instrument.

To determine how much of the forward element of a forward relates to the hedged item, an entity is required to value a forward that has critical terms that perfectly match the hedged item (e.g. nominal amount, life and underlying). This is referred to as the *aligned forward element*. This aligned forward element will be the same as that on the forward used for hedging if the terms perfectly match the hedged item but will be different (higher or lower) if not. [IFRS 9:B6.5.37] Where there is a difference, some of the change in value of the forward element will be recognised directly in profit or loss (see **6.9.3**). Where the aligned forward element matches the forward element on the forward, the accounting described below for transaction related items and time-period related items would apply to the full fair value change of the forward element of the actual forward.

Hedged items are determined to be "transaction related items" or "time-period related items" depending on their nature and how and when they affect profit or loss. [IFRS 9:B6.5.34] The distinction between these two types of hedged items is not dependent on the type of hedge they are designated in. For example, transaction related items include many forecast transactions designated in cash flow hedges as well as many firm commitments which could be designated in a fair value hedge. That said, net investments designated in net investment hedges are always time-period related items because there is no underlying transaction. Guidance on distinguishing between transaction related items and time-period related items is provided in **6.9.1** and **6.9.2**.

The accounting for the forward element described below for time period and transaction related items would also apply in the case where the forward element is nil. [IFRS 9:B6.5.36]

6.9.1 Transaction related hedged items

The forward element of a forward contract relates to a transaction related hedged item if the nature of the hedged item is a transaction for which the time value has the character of costs of that transaction. An example is a hedged item that results in the recognition of an item whose initial measurement includes transaction costs such as a future commodity purchase, hedged for foreign currency risk that includes transaction costs in the initial measurement of the inventory. [IFRS 9:B6.5.34(a)]

This description of transaction related items is not particularly clear but it could be read as meaning that the hedged item is a future transaction, committed or forecast, where the forward element of the forward could be regarded as a cost of that transaction, for example, like an insurance cost. Despite the example given in IFRS 9:B6.5.34(a), it is not necessary for the hedged item to result in the recognition of an asset or liability for which transaction costs would be capitalised, for example a transaction related item could include a forecast sale in a foreign currency.

Common examples of transaction related items include:

- Forecast purchase of a commodity hedged for changes in spot commodity prices
- Firm commitment to buy property plant and equipment denominated in a foreign currency hedged for spot foreign currency risk

- Forecast sale of goods in a foreign currency hedged for spot foreign currency risk

For transaction related hedged items, where only the spot element of a forward is designated and the entity has elected not to take the changes in value of the forward element directly to profit or loss, the change in forward element (to the extent it relates to the hedged item) is recognised in other comprehensive income and accumulated in a separate component of equity and then accounted for as follows:

- If the hedged item results in the recognition of a non-financial asset (e.g. recognition of inventory from a hedged purchase) or non-financial liability, the accumulated amount is removed directly from equity (i.e. not as a reclassification adjustment that affects other comprehensive income) and included in the initial carrying amount of the asset or liability, commonly referred to as a 'basis adjustment'. As a result the forward element is recognised in profit or loss when the item impacts profit or loss (e.g. upon the sale of inventory that was hedged).
- If the hedged item results in a firm commitment for which fair value hedge accounting is applied (e.g. fair value hedging foreign currency risk on a firm commitment that was cash flow hedged as a forecast transaction before it became committed) the accumulated amount is removed directly from equity (i.e. not as a reclassification adjustment that affects other comprehensive income) and included in the initial carrying amount of the firm commitment, commonly referred to as a 'basis adjustment'. As a result the forward element is recognised in profit or loss when the item impacts profit or loss (e.g. upon the amortisation or sale of the item that was recognised when the firm commitment was settled).
- In all other cases the accumulated amount is reclassified from equity to profit or loss as a reclassification adjustment (see IAS 1) in the same period or periods during which the hedged expected future cash flows affect profit or loss (e.g. when the hedged forecast sale occurs).
- However, if any of the forward element is not expected to be recovered in a future period, then the amount not expected to be recovered is immediately reclassified to profit or loss as a reclassification adjustment.

A consequence of the above requirements is that if a hedge of a transaction related item is discontinued part way through the life of the hedge (e.g. due to early termination of the forward), but the hedged item is still expected to occur, the amounts deferred in equity would remain in equity until the one of the above scenarios arose.

IFRS 9:6.5.15(b)(iii) & 6.5.16 requires that the forward element amount accumulated in equity that is not expected to be recovered in future periods be immediately reclassified into profit or loss. This requirement was also included in IAS 39 (in the context of amounts deferred in cash flow hedges) and was seen to primarily cater for circumstances where an entity had elected *not* to apply a basis adjustment when a hedged forecast transaction resulted in the recognition of a non-financial asset. The purpose of this requirement is to ensure that the amounts deferred in equity are included as part of the impairment test of any non-financial asset to which it relates such that if it was not deemed to be recoverable it would be reclassified to profit or loss in the same way that the amount would have been recognised in profit or loss if a basis adjustment to the asset had been applied and the asset was subsequently impaired. Based on this it would be reasonable to conclude that the same application would apply in this circumstance. Hence, if at the reporting date (1) the amounts deferred in reserves were assumed to be recognised as part of the hedged item on the balance sheet (i.e. if it was assumed that the basis-adjusted non-financial asset had been recognised at the reporting date) and (2) that basis-adjusted asset balance would be greater than the recoverable amount of that asset and would have triggered an impairment, then those amounts deferred that are not expected to be recovered should be reclassified to profit or loss immediately. Once the non-financial asset is recognised, basis adjustment applies, hence the normal impairment requirements would apply.

The other purpose of this paragraph is to ensure that forward element amounts are not deferred in reserves indefinitely, for example where the hedged item is no longer expected to occur. As the forward element amounts are not expected to recovered in a future period, because the future transaction is not expected to occur in a future period, this requirement would result in the deferred amounts being reclassified to profit or loss immediately.

6.9.2 Time-period related hedged items

The forward element of a forward relates to a time-period related hedged item if the nature of the hedged item is such that the forward element has the character of a cost for obtaining protection against a risk over a particular period of time (but the hedged item does not result in a transaction that involves the notion of a transaction cost in accordance with IFRS 9:B6.5.34(a)). [IFRS 9:B6.5.34(b)]

This description of time-period related items is not particularly clear given that an any forward contract could be regarded as giving protection against a risk over a period of time, however, it is clear that the intention is to exclude those items that would be regarded as transaction related items.

Examples of time-period related items include:

- Commodity inventory hedged for spot commodity price risk [IFRS 9:B6.5.34(b)]

- Net investment in a foreign operation hedged for spot foreign currency risk [IFRS 9:B6.5.34(b)]
- Recognised equity investment hedged for spot equity price risk
- Recognised monetary item hedged for spot foreign currency risk

For time-period related hedged items, where only the spot element of a forward is designated and the entity has elected not to take the changes in value of the forward element directly to profit or loss, the forward element (to the extent it relates to the hedged item) is accounted for in two parts. Firstly the change in forward element recognised in other comprehensive income and accumulated in a separate component of equity. Secondly, the forward element at the date of designation (to the extent that it relates to the hedged item) is amortised on a systematic and rational basis over the period to which the forward element relates. For example, if a forward contract hedges the exposure to variability in three-month interest rates for a three-month period that starts in six months' time, the forward element is amortised during the period that spans months seven to nine. [IFRS 9:B6.5.35]

What is regarded as a systematic and rational basis for amortising the forward element amount from equity to profit or loss may be obvious in some cases but may require careful judgement in others. For example, for a hedge of spot foreign currency risk in a net investment of a foreign operation using a forward contract that settles at the end of a two-year period, straight line amortisation would be a reasonable basis.

In each reporting period, the amortisation amount shall be reclassified from the separate component of equity to profit or loss as a reclassification adjustment (see IAS 1).

Example 6.9.2

Hedging foreign currency risk on a net investment in a foreign operation using a forward contract

Entity X, which has a US$ functional currency, has subsidiary, Entity Y, with € functional currency. In the consolidated financial statements, €1 million of the net investment in the foreign operation is hedged for changes in the foreign exchange rate between US$ and € using a forward contract; the forward points are calculated to be US$2,000. The critical terms of the forward and the hedged item match. The term of the forward and the hedge is two years. The change in value of the undesignated forward element is deferred in other comprehensive income over the life of the hedge. Accordingly, over the life, US$2,000 will be recognised in other comprehensive income. A hedge of a net investment in a foreign operation is a hedge of a time-period related hedged item. Consequently, the forward element amount is reclassified from equity to profit or loss over the two years of the hedge on a rational basis.

In this situation, straight-line amortisation is regarded as a rational basis for amortisation. Therefore US$1,000 is reclassified from other comprehensive income to profit or loss each year such that, at the end of two years, the net accumulated forward element amount in equity is nil (i.e. US$2,000 is deferred in other comprehensive income and US$2,000 is reclassified from equity to profit or loss).

If hedge accounting is discontinued the net amount (i.e. including cumulative amortisation) that has been accumulated in the separate component of equity is immediately reclassified into profit or loss as a reclassification adjustment. [IFRS 9:6.5.15(c)]

6.9.3 Actual forward element vs aligned forward element

If the forward element and the aligned forward element differ, some of the change in the value of the forward element will be recognised directly in profit or loss. To determine how much of the change in value of the forward element is recognised directly in profit or loss, first it is necessary to determine whether the aligned forward element is greater or less than the actual forward element of the forward designated in the hedge.

If, at inception of the hedging relationship, the absolute amount of the actual forward element is higher than that of the aligned forward element the entity shall: [IFRS 9:B6.5.38(a)]

(i) determine the amount that is accumulated in a separate component of equity on the basis of the aligned forward element; and

(ii) account for the differences in the fair value changes between the two forward elements in profit or loss.

If, at inception of the hedging relationship, the absolute amount of the actual forward element is lower than that of the aligned forward element, the entity shall determine the amount that is accumulated in a separate component of equity by reference to the lower of the cumulative change in fair value of: [IFRS 9:B6.5.38(b)]

(i) the absolute amount of the actual forward element; and

(ii) the absolute amount of the aligned forward element.

Any remainder of the change in fair value of the actual forward element shall be recognised in profit or loss.

6.10 Accounting for foreign currency basis spreads of financial instruments

IFRS 9:6.2.4(b) permits the foreign currency basis spread to be excluded from the designation of a financial instrument as the hedging instrument. In these cases, the normal hedge accounting mechanics apply to the designated element of the contract depending on the type of hedge (i.e. cash flow hedge, fair value hedge or net investment hedge).

For the undesignated foreign currency basis spread, the guidance in **section 6.9** applies in the same manner as it is applied to the forward element of a forward contract. [IFRS 9:B6.5.39] That is, for the undesignated basis spread there is a choice over how changes in its value are accounted for which allows the undesignated element to be treated in the same way as the undesignated time value of an option discussed above. [IFRS 9:6.5.16] This choice is made on a hedge-by-hedge basis and applies for the term of the designated hedge. The two alternatives are:

- take changes in value of the undesignated basis spread directly to profit or loss; or
- take changes in value of the undesignated basis spread (some or all of it, depending on how much of it relates to the hedged item) to other comprehensive income with amounts subsequently removed from equity and ultimately recognised in profit or loss.

If the second of the above two approaches is applied, the mechanics for recognising the change in basis spread in profit or loss varies depending on:

- how much of the basis spread relates to the hedged item; and
- the nature of the hedged item and whether it is a *transaction related item* or a *time-period related item* (see **6.9.1** and **6.9.2**)

Cross currency interest rate swaps are commonly held financial instruments that include currency basis spread. In practice these types of instruments are mostly used to hedge time-period related items because such swaps tend to be used to hedge existing recognised items over a period of time rather than future transactions. The following would be examples of cross-currency interest rate swaps being used to hedge time-period related items:

- Recognised foreign currency floating rate issued debt cash flow hedged for foreign currency and interest rate risk using a receive float foreign currency; pay float functional currency cross currency interest rate swap where the currency basis spread is excluded from the hedge. See **example 3.4B** and **example 3.4C**.
- Recognised foreign currency floating rate issued debt cash flow hedged for foreign currency and interest rate risk using a receive float foreign currency; pay fixed functional currency cross currency interest rate swap where the currency basis spread is excluded from the hedge.
- Recognised foreign currency fixed rate issued debt fair value hedged for foreign currency and interest rate risk using a receive fixed foreign currency; pay float functional currency cross currency interest rate swap where the currency basis spread is excluded from the hedge.
- A net investment in a foreign operation hedged for forward foreign currency risk using a receive fixed functional currency, pay fixed foreign

currency cross currency interest rate swap where the currency basis spread is excluded from the hedge.

- A net investment in a foreign operation hedged for spot foreign currency risk using a receive float functional currency, pay float foreign currency cross currency interest rate swap where the currency basis spread is excluded from the hedge. See **example 4.3**.
- A net investment in a foreign operation hedged for spot foreign currency risk using the spot element of a receive fixed functional currency, pay fixed foreign currency cross currency interest rate swap where the currency basis spread is also excluded from the hedge.

For time-period related hedged items, where the currency basis spread is excluded from the hedge and the entity has elected not to take the changes in value of currency basis spread directly to profit or loss, the currency basis spread (to the extent it relates to the hedged item) is accounted for in two parts. Firstly the change in currency basis spread is recognised in other comprehensive income and accumulated in a separate component of equity. Secondly, the currency basis spread at the date of designation (to the extent that it relates to the hedged item) is amortised on a systematic and rational basis over the period during to which the currency basis spread relates.

What is regarded as a systematic and rational basis for amortising the forward element amount from equity to profit or loss may be obvious in some cases but may require careful judgement in others. For example, for a hedge of the foreign currency risk in a net investment in a foreign operation using a five-year cross-currency interest rate swap where the currency basis spread is excluded, straight line amortisation over the five year period would be a reasonable basis.

In each reporting period, the amortisation amount shall be reclassified from the separate component of equity to profit or loss as a reclassification adjustment (see IAS 1).

7 Credit exposures designated at FVTPL

Many financial institutions use credit derivatives (e.g. credit default swaps) to manage their credit risk exposures arising from their lending activities. For example, hedges of credit risk exposures allow financial institutions to transfer the risk of credit loss on a loan, or a loan commitment, to a third party. This might also reduce the regulatory capital requirement for the loan or loan commitment while at the same time allowing the financial institution to retain nominal ownership of the loan and to preserve the relationship with the client. Credit portfolio managers frequently use credit derivatives to hedge the credit risk of a proportion of a particular exposure (e.g. a facility for a particular client) or the bank's overall lending portfolio. [IFRS 9:BC6.469]

Under IFRS 9, the default accounting treatment for credit derivatives is FVTPL. Hence, where the hedged exposure is not measured on the same basis as the credit derivative, an accounting mismatch arises. For example, if a loan asset measured at amortised cost, a written loan commitment outside the scope of IFRS 9, or a written financial guarantee contract not measured at FVTPL is economically hedged for credit risk using a credit derivative, accounting volatility will arise in profit or loss. Mismatches that arise from risk management activities like this are often accommodated by the ability to apply hedge accounting; however, as discussed in more detail in **3.11.6**, the credit risk component of an exposure is not regarded as an eligible risk component under IFRS 9, and therefore hedge accounting is not available for an entity that hedges only the credit risk component of an item using credit derivatives.

To address this issue and allow entities to reflect, to some extent, their credit risk management activities, IFRS 9 provides an alternative to hedge accounting whereby an entity can elect to measure the hedged exposure at FVTPL. This alternative to hedge accounting has specific conditions that must be met before it can be applied (see **7.2**) and is starkly different to the generic fair value option that is available on initial recognition of a financial instrument under IFRS 9 (see **chapter B2**).

Since the designated exposure is measured at its full fair value, it is not equivalent to hedging a specific risk under fair value hedge accounting where the carrying amount of the designated hedged item is adjusted for changes in fair value related to the hedged risk only. Electing the fair value option for the credit exposure results in the hedged credit exposure being revalued for changes in *all* risks, including interest rate risk, and therefore to some extent will result in volatility in profit or loss.

7.1 Option for credit exposures versus general fair value option

A key difference between the fair value option for credit exposures and the general fair value option available under IFRS 9 (see **chapter B2**) is that the fair value option for credit exposures can be elected after initial recognition and can also be revoked during the life of the exposure, whereas the general fair value option can only be chosen on initial recognition and must be retained for the life of the instrument. The fair value option for credit exposures is designed to be more flexible to allow a closer reflection of credit risk management activities where it is common to hedge the credit risk of an exposure sometime after initial recognition (e.g. at the point where the credit risk on the exposure begins to increase). However, this added flexibility introduces some complexities regarding the accounting, which are discussed further below (see **7.3**).

Another key difference is the fact that a credit exposure need not be designated at FVTPL in its entirety if the amount of the exposure managed for credit risk is less than the entire exposure. The IASB permitted this additional flexibility because of the various optional features and drawdown behavioural patterns of loans and loan commitments, which means that credit portfolio managers often engage in a flexible and active risk management strategy, including hedging less than 100 per cent of a loan or loan commitment. [IFRS 9:BC6.471]

7.2 Eligibility of credit exposures for designation at FVTPL

If an entity uses a credit derivative that is measured at fair value through profit or loss to manage the credit risk of all, or a part of, a financial instrument (credit exposure), it may designate that financial instrument to the extent that it is so managed (i.e. all or a proportion of it) as measured at fair value through profit or loss if:

[IFRS 9:6.7.1]

(a) the name of the credit exposure (e.g. the borrower, or the holder of a loan commitment) matches the reference entity of the credit derivative ('name matching'); and

(b) the seniority of the financial instrument matches that of the instruments that can be delivered in accordance with the credit derivative.

An entity may make this designation irrespective of whether the financial instrument that is managed for credit risk is within the scope of IFRS 9. For example, an entity may designate a loan commitment that is outside the scope of IFRS 9. The entity may designate that financial instrument at, or subsequent to, initial recognition, or while it is unrecognised. The entity shall document the designation concurrently. [IFRS 9:6.7.1]

IFRS 9:6.7.1 requires the seniority of the financial instrument hedged for credit risk to *match* that of the instruments that can be delivered under the credit derivative. Therefore, if the instruments that can be delivered under the credit derivative are subordinate to the hedged credit exposure and therefore would result in a pay-out to the holder of the derivative before losses are suffered on the actual exposure, such a credit derivative would not qualify the holder to elect the fair value option for the risk exposure.

Because the fair value option for credit exposures is an alternative to hedge accounting, the eligibility criteria for hedge accounting are not applicable. Accordingly, there is no requirement to demonstrate an economic relationship between the credit derivative and the exposure, nor any specific requirements about the hedge ratio that must be used. However, an entity is required to document the designation so that those credit exposures for which the FVTPL election has been made can be identified because IFRS 9 does not permit retrospective designations.

The IASB determined the eligibility criteria with a view to accommodating economic hedges of credit risk that would otherwise qualify for hedge accounting, but for the fact that the credit risk component within the hedged exposure cannot be separately identified and hence is not a risk component that meets the eligibility criteria for hedged items. The eligibility criteria are also consistent with regulatory requirements and the risk management strategy underlying the current business practice of financial institutions. However, using name matching as a qualifying criterion means that index-based credit default swaps would not meet that criterion. [IFRS 9:BC6.476]

Example 7.2

Hedging a written loan commitment for credit risk

Bank S provides entities with loans and loan facilities. Certain of the loan facilities provided by Bank S, although available for the holder to draw down on, are not expected to be drawn and are used by borrowing entities as a means of securing a line of credit should they need it as a last resort. Given the nature of these loan facilities, they are often drawn down when there is a shortage of financing. Therefore, when they are drawn upon, the risk of default is usually greater than it was when the commitment was issued. Bank S stands to lose the full facility amount of any loan commitment it issues. Consequently, it monitors the credit risk on the loan commitment in the same way as it would had it issued a loan to the holder.

Bank S has issued Entity U a 5-year loan facility of CU200 million. Two years and two months into the term of the facility, the bank's credit risk managers deem it necessary to reduce the bank's credit risk exposure to Entity U. The bank transacts a credit default swap (CDS), with Entity U as the reference entity, to hedge the credit risk on CU50 million of the facility to Entity U. The CDS is for a three-year term and the seniority of the loan facility matches that of the instruments that can be delivered under the credit derivative in the case of a credit event.

Bank S elects to measure CU50 million of the undrawn loan facility at FVTPL to match in profit or loss the subsequent measurement of the CDS. The difference between the carrying amount of the loan commitment for CU50 million (including the loss allowance for expected credit losses on CU50 million of the loan commitment) and its fair value is immediately recognised in profit or loss on the date of designation at FVTPL.

7.3 Accounting for credit exposures designated at FVTPL

The flexibility to allow a credit exposure to be designated at FVTPL after initial recognition (or after issuance, in the case of an unrecognised loan commitment) means that a difference can arise between the exposure's carrying value (if any) and its fair value at the point of designation. IFRS 9 requires that difference to be recognised in profit or loss at the time of designation. [IFRS 9:6.7.2]

For debt instruments measured at FVTOCI, the cumulative gain or loss previously recognised in other comprehensive income is immediately reclassified from equity to profit or loss when the fair value option for the credit exposure is elected. [IFRS 9:6.7.2]

The IASB noted that under this approach there could be concerns about earnings management because on electing fair value accounting the difference to the previous carrying amount of the credit exposure would be immediately recognised in profit or loss. However, the IASB also noted that some would consider that outcome as relevant because it would signal a different approach to managing credit risk and this difference would often be a loss that is a reflection of any lag in the impairment model behind the 'market view'. [IFRS 9: BC6.543(b)]

The IASB also noted that the accounting impact of immediately recognising the measurement change adjustment in profit or loss may also deter an entity from electing fair value through profit or loss accounting. For example, when an entity decides to take out credit protection at a time when the fair value has already moved below the carrying amount of the loan because of credit concerns in the market, it will immediately recognise a loss if it elects fair value through profit or loss accounting. However, it also noted that this approach was operationally simpler than some of the other alternatives that the IASB had considered which would avoid this measurement adjustment upon designation. [IFRS 9:BC6.484 - 5]

Subsequent to the fair value option having been elected for a credit exposure (in its entirety or a proportion of it), that exposure can cease to be measured at FVTPL if:

[IFRS 9:6.7.3]

(a) the qualifying criteria in IFRS 9:6.7.1 are no longer met, for example:
   (i) the credit derivative or the related financial instrument that gives rise to the credit risk expires or is sold, terminated or settled; or
   (ii) the credit risk of the financial instrument is no longer managed using credit derivatives. For example, this could occur because of improvements in the credit quality of the borrower or the loan commitment holder or changes to capital requirements imposed on an entity; and

(b) the financial instrument that gives rise to the credit risk is not otherwise required to be measured at fair value through profit or loss (i.e. the entity's business model has not changed in the meantime so that a reclassification in accordance with IFRS 9:4.4.1 was required). (see **chapter B2**).

When an entity discontinues measuring the financial instrument, or a proportion of it, at FVTPL, the instrument's fair value at the date of discontinuation becomes its new carrying amount. Subsequently, the same measurement that was used before designating it at FVTPL is applied. For example, a financial asset that had originally been classified as amortised cost would revert to that measurement and its effective interest rate would be recalculated based on its new gross carrying amount on the date of discontinuing measurement at FVTPL. [IFRS 9:6.7.4]

Example 7.3A

Hedging a loan for credit risk

Bank Z lends Entity K CU100 million under a 5-year floating rate loan. The loan is held within a business model to collect the contractual cash flows and would be eligible to be measured at amortised cost. Bank Z's credit risk policy requires it to hedge the credit risk on the full €100m for the full loan term. It does so using a credit default swap (CDS).

To reduce the profit or loss volatility arising from measuring the CDS at FVTPL and the loan at amortised cost, Bank Z designates the loan as at FVTPL. To give itself the flexibility to be able to revert to amortised cost accounting, Bank Z clearly documents that the designation is under IFRS 9:6.7.1 rather than the irrevocable fair value option available for financial assets (see **chapter B2**). The reference entity under the CDS contract is Entity K and the seniority of the loan matches that of the instrument that can be delivered under the CDS in the case of a credit event.

After two years, Bank Z deems the credit risk on the loan to have fallen to a level where the CDS is no longer required under the bank's credit risk management policy and the CDS is closed out. At that point, the fair value of the loan is CU110 million.

Bank Z still holds the asset within a business model where the objective is to hold the asset to collect the contractual cash flows.

The qualifying criteria are no longer met for electing to measure the loan at FVTPL and, therefore, Bank Z revokes the fair value option and begins to apply amortised cost accounting. At that point it calculates an effective interest rate for the loan based on the then gross carrying amount of €110 million.

B10 Hedge accounting – examples

Contents

1 Introduction

This chapter includes illustrative examples in addition to those in IFRS 9 on how the hedge accounting mechanics apply to different hedge designations. For these examples, it is assumed that all of the eligibility and qualification criteria have been met. The examples used are simplified for illustrative purposes and unless otherwise stated the effects of own and counterparty credit risk have been ignored. In some examples, the potential effect of foreign currency basis spreads have been ignored which in practice may give rise to hedge ineffectiveness.

2 Fair value hedges

This section illustrates the accounting entries for a fair value hedge.

2.1 Fair value hedging interest rate risk of fixed rate debt

The following example illustrates the accounting entries for a fair value hedge of interest rate risk of fixed rate debt using an interest rate swap.

Example 2.1

Fair value hedging interest rate risk of issued fixed rate debt with an interest rate swap that receives fixed and pays floating.

On 1 January 20X0, Entity B issues GBP fixed rate debt that matures on 30 June 20X2. The principal amount of the debt is £100 million and interest of 6% (per annum) is paid semi-annually in arrears. This includes a credit spread of 123bps. The benchmark rate of interest in the UK is 6M LIBOR.

On 1 January 20X0, Entity B also enters into an interest rate swap that matures on 30 June 20X2. Entity B will receive 4.77% (per annum) and pay 6M LIBOR on £100 million. Interest will be settled net semi-annually in arrears. The fair value of the interest rate swap is nil on 1 January 20X0. The swap is not collateralised.

Period ended	Fair value gain/(loss) during period £ '000s	Fair value of swap before cash settlement £ '000s	Cash settlement £ '000s	Fair value of swap after cash settlement £ '000s
30/06/X0	(1,537)	(1,537)	365	(1,172)
31/12/X0	5,733	4,561	115	4,676
30/06/X1	844	5,520	(1,585)	3,935
31/12/X1	237	4,172	(2,085)	2,087
30/06/X2	48	2,135	(2,135)	0

On 1 January 20X0, Entity B designates the interest rate swap in a fair value hedge of the benchmark interest rate risk of the fixed rate debt. The change in the fair value of the benchmark component of the fixed rate debt due to changes in the hedged risk is calculated for the purposes of hedge accounting by applying the benchmark discount curve to £100 million of the principal and £4.770 million of each interest cash flow of the debt. Other factors, such as changes in the entity's credit spread, could impact the fair value of the debt, but the hedged item is not adjusted for fair value movements in risks other than the hedged risk.

Period ended	6M LIBOR at start of period	Change in hedge adjusted carrying amount of debt (post settlement) during period	Hedge adjusted carrying amount of debt (Post settlement)
		£ '000s	£ '000s
30/06/X0	5.5	1,184	(98,816)
31/12/X0	5.0	(5,956)	(104,772)
30/06/X1	1.6	756	(104,016)
31/12/X1	0.6	1,886	(102,130)
30/06/X2	0.5	2,130	0

The fair value of the interest rate swap is impacted by changes in both Entity B's and the counterparty bank's credit spread which gives rise to ineffectiveness. For example, this is why in the first period the change in the hedge adjusted carrying amount of the debt is £1,184k but the change in the fair value of the swap is £(1,172)k.

The following table illustrates the accounting entries for the transaction during its life in £ '000s. Dr or (Cr) as indicated.

Date		Cash	Derivative	Debt	Profit or loss
01/01/X0	Issue debt	100,000		(100,000)	
30/06/X0	Accrue interest on debt			(3,000)	3,000
	Change in fair value of derivative		(1,537)		1,537
	Settlement of interest on the debt and net settlement of derivative	(3,365)	365	3,000	
	Adjustment to debt for fair value hedge accounting			1,184	(1,184)
31/12/X0	Accrue interest on debt			(3,000)	3,000
	Change in fair value of derivative		5,733		(5,733)

Date		Cash	Derivative	Debt	Profit or loss
	Settlement of interest on the debt and net settlement of derivative	(3,115)	115	3,000	
	Adjustment to debt for fair value hedge accounting			(5,956)	5,956
30/06/X1	Accrue interest on debt			(3,000)	3,000
	Change in fair value of derivative		844		(844)
	Settlement of interest on the debt and net settlement of derivative	(1,415)	(1,585)	3,000	
	Adjustment to debt for fair value hedge accounting			756	(756)
31/12/X1	Accrue interest on debt			(3,000)	3,000
	Change in fair value of derivative		237		(237)
	Settlement of interest on the debt and net settlement of derivative	(915)	(2,085)	3,000	
	Adjustment to debt for fair value hedge accounting			1,886	(1,886)
30/06/X2	Accrue interest on debt			(3,000)	3,000
	Change in fair value derivative		48		(48)
	Settlement of interest on the debt and net settlement of derivative	(865)	(2,135)	3,000	
	Adjustment to debt for fair value hedge accounting			2,130	(2,130)
	Settlement of debt	(100,000)		100,000	
		(9,675)	0	0	9,675
Key		**A**			**B**

A Reflects the total cash settlements on the debt and derivative. The cash settlement in each period is equal to 6M LIBOR at the start of the period + 123bps on £100 million.

B Reflects the total interest expense from the debt and derivative. The interest expense is not equal to the cash settlement in each period because of the ineffectiveness due to credit risk (See journal entries below). However the total ineffectiveness over the life of the hedge is nil.

Journal entries in the financial statements are provided below for illustrative purposes.

1 January 20X0

No entry required for derivative because fair value is nil at inception.

		£ '000s	**£ '000s**
Dr	Cash	100,000	
Cr	Debt		100,000

To recognise the issue of debt.

30 June 20X0

		£ '000s	**£ '000s**
Dr	Interest expense	3,000	
Cr	Debt		3,000

To recognise the accrual of interest on the debt.

		£ '000s	**£ '000s**
Dr	Interest expense	1,537	
Cr	Derivative		1,537
Dr	Debt	1,184	
Cr	Interest expense		1,184

To recognise the change in fair value of the derivative and the corresponding adjustment to the debt.

The net impact on profit or loss of £353k reflects the interest accrual of £365k on the derivative less £12k of ineffectiveness due to credit risk.

		£ '000s	**£ '000s**
Dr	Derivative	365	
Dr	Debt	3,000	
Cr	Cash		3,365

To recognise the settlement of interest on the debt and net settlement of interest on the derivative.

The net cash settlement is equal to 6M LIBOR at the start of the period + 123bps on £100 million * [5.50 + 1.23] % / 2).

Similar entries would be recorded for the remaining term of the hedge relationship.

3 Cash flow hedges

The following cash flow hedges are illustrated in this section.

Section 3.1 Cash flow hedging foreign currency risk of a forecast sale

Section 3.2 Cash flow hedging foreign currency risk of a forecast purchase

Section 3.3 Cash flow hedging floating rate debt

Section 3.4 Cash flow hedging foreign currency risk of floating rate debt

Section 3.5 Cash flow hedging foreign currency risk of fixed rate debt

Section 3.6 Cash flow hedging foreign currency risk of zero coupon debt

Section 3.7 Cash flow hedging foreign currency risk of the principal only of interest-bearing debt

3.1 Cash flow hedging foreign currency risk of a forecast sale

The following example illustrates the entries for a cash flow hedge of foreign currency risk on a forecast sale using a foreign currency forward.

Example 3.1

Cash flow hedging forward foreign currency risk of a forecast sale with a foreign currency forward.

On 1 October 20X3, Entity C with a local functional currency (LC) forecasts a foreign currency (FC) sale that will occur on 31 March 20X4. The amount of the sale is forecasted to be FC3 million.

On 1 October 20X3, Entity C also enters into a foreign currency forward that matures on 31 March 20X4. Entity C will receive LC4.95 million and pay FC3 million. The fair value of the foreign currency forward is nil on 1 October 20X3.

Date	Spot Rate (LC/FC)	Forward Rate for 31/03/X4 (LC/FC)	Fair value gain/ (loss) in period LC	Fair value LC
01/10/X3	1.60	1.65	n/a	0
31/12/X3	1.55	1.62	89,820	89,820
31/03/X4	1.50	1.50	360,180	450,000

On 1 October 20X3, Entity C designates the foreign currency forward in a cash flow hedge of the variability of the FC denominated sale due to changes in the forward rate.

In this example, the hypothetical derivative (which is derived from the hedged item) is the same as the foreign currency forward. The hedge is 100 per cent effective in each period.

Journal entries in the financial statements are provided below for illustrative purposes.

1 October 20X3

No entry required for derivative because fair value is nil at inception.

31 December 20X3

		LC	LC
Dr	Derivative	89,820	
Cr	Equity (cash flow hedge reserve)		89,820

To recognise the change in fair value of the derivative.

31 March 20X4

		LC	LC
Dr	Derivative	360,180	
Cr	Equity (cash flow hedge reserve)		360,180

To recognise the change in fair value of the derivative.

		LC	LC
Dr	Cash	450,000	
Cr	Derivative		450,000

To recognise the settlement of the derivative.

		LC	LC
Dr	Cash	4,500,000	
Cr	Sales		4,500,000

To recognise the receipt of FC 3 million of cash from the sale (at the spot rate).

		LC	LC
Dr	Equity (cash flow hedge reserve)	450,000	
Cr	Sales		450,000

To recognise the reclassification from equity to profit or loss

Because in this example the hedge is perfectly effective, the net effect of reclassifying the amount from equity to profit or loss when the sale occurs is equivalent to recognising the sale translated at the contracted forward rate (FC3 million * 1.65 LC/FC).

Translation of sale at spot rate at 31March 20X4	LC4,500,000
Reclassified from equity to profit or loss at 31 March 20X4	LC450,000
	LC4,950,000

3.2 Cash flow hedging foreign currency risk of a forecast purchase

The following example illustrates the entries for a cash flow hedge of foreign currency risk on a forecast purchase using a foreign currency forward.

Example 3.2

Cash flow hedging forward foreign currency risk of a forecast purchase of a non- financial item with a foreign currency forward.

On 1 October 20X3, Entity C with a local functional currency (LC) forecasts a foreign currency (FC) purchase of inventory that will occur on 31 March 20X4. The amount of the purchase is forecasted to be FC3 million.

On 1 October 20X3, Entity C also enters into a foreign currency forward that matures on 31 March 20X4. Entity C will receive FC3 million and pay LC4.95 million. The fair value of the foreign currency forward is nil on 1 October 20X3.

Date	Spot Rate	Forward Rate for 31/03/X4	Fair value gain/(loss) in period	Fair value
	(LC/FC)	(LC/FC)	LC	LC
01/10/X3	1.60	1.65	n/a	0
31/12/X3	1.55	1.62	(89,820)	(89,820)
31/03/X4	1.50	1.50	(360,180)	(450,000)

On 1 October 20X3, Entity C designates the foreign currency forward in a cash flow hedge of the variability of the FC denominated purchase due to changes in the forward rate.

In this example, the hypothetical derivative (which is derived from the hedged item) is the same as the foreign currency forward. The hedge is 100 per cent effective in each period.

Journal entries in the financial statements are provided below for illustrative purposes.

1 October 20X3

No entry required for derivative because fair value is nil at inception.

31 December 20X3

		LC	LC
Dr	Equity (cash flow hedge reserve)	89,820	
Cr	Derivative		89,820

To recognise the change in fair value of the derivative.

31 March 20X4

		LC	LC
Dr	Equity (cash flow hedge reserve)	360,180	
Cr	Derivative		360,180

To recognise the change in fair value of the derivative.

		LC	LC
Dr	Derivative	450,000	
Cr	Cash		450,000

To recognise the settlement of the derivative.

		LC	LC
Dr	Inventory	4,500,000	
Cr	Cash		4,500,000

To recognise the payment of FC 3 million to purchase the inventory (at the spot rate).

		LC	LC
Dr	Inventory	450,000	
Cr	Equity (cash flow hedge reserve)		450,000

To recognise the removal of amounts from equity and basis adjustment of the inventory.

Because in this example the hedge is perfectly effective, the net effect of removing the amount from equity and including it in the initial carrying amount of the inventory when the purchase occurs is equivalent to recognising the purchase translated at the contracted forward rate (FC3 million * 1.65 LC/FC).

Translation of purchase at spot rate at 31 March 20X4	LC4,500,000
Removal from equity and included in the initial carrying amount of the inventory at 31 March 20X4	LC450,000
	LC4,950,000

3.3 Cash flow hedging floating rate debt

The following three examples illustrate the entries for a cash flow hedge of floating rate debt using an interest rate swap. In the first example (**example 3.3A**) the interest rate swap is 'on-market' (i.e. the interest rate swap has a fair value of nil at the date of designation). In the second and third examples the interest rate swaps are 'off-market' (i.e. the interest rate swaps have a fair value other than nil at the date of designation). In the second example (**example 3.3B**) the interest rate swap is an asset at the date of designation. In the final example (**example 3.3C**) the interest rate swap is a liability at the date of designation.

Example 3.3A

Cash flow hedging the variability in cash flows of issued floating rate debt with an interest rate swap that receives floating and pays fixed.

On 1 January 20X0, Entity B issues GBP floating rate debt that matures on 30 June 20X2. The principal amount of the debt is £100 million and interest of 6M LIBOR + 123bps is paid semi-annually in arrears.

Period ended	6M LIBOR at start of period %	Interest accrual in period £ '000s
30/06/X0	5.5	(3,365)
31/12/X0	5.0	(3,115)
30/06/X1	1.6	(1,415)
31/12/X1	0.6	(915)
30/06/X2	0.5	(865)

On 1 January 20X0, Entity B also enters into an interest rate swap that matures on 30 June 20X2. Entity B will receive 6M LIBOR and pay 4.77 per cent (per annum) on £100 million. Interest will be settled net semi-annually in arrears. The fair value of the interest rate swap is nil on 1 January 20X0.

Period ended	Fair value gain/(loss) during period £ '000s	Fair value of swap before cash settlement £ '000s	Cash settlement £ '000s	Fair value of swap after cash settlement £ '000s
30/06/X0	1,549	1,549	(365)	1,184
31/12/X0	(5,841)	(4,657)	(115)	(4,772)
30/06/X1	(829)	(5,601)	1,585	(4,016)
31/12/X1	(199)	(4,215)	2,085	(2,130)
30/06/X2	(5)	(2,135)	2,135	0

On 1 January 20X0, Entity B designates the interest rate swap in a cash flow hedge of the variability of the interest cash flows of the debt due to changes in the 6M LIBOR rate. In this example, the hypothetical derivative (which is derived from the hedged item) is the same as the interest rate swap. The hedge is 100 per cent effective in each period.

The cumulative amount recognised in the cash flow hedge reserve is the lower of the cumulative fair value gain or loss on the hedging instrument and on the hypothetical derivative. The amount remaining in the cash flow hedge reserve, after reclassification, is the lower of the cumulative clean fair value gain or loss on the hedging instrument and on the hypothetical derivative. The cumulative clean fair value gain or loss on the hypothetical derivative is equal to the clean fair value, because the fair value of the hypothetical derivative at the date of designation is nil.

Period ended	Amount remaining in the cash flow hedge reserve £ '000s	Cumulative amount recognised in the cash flow hedge reserve £ '000s	Cumulative reclassification to offset interest accrual £ '000s	Reclassification in the period to offset interest accrual £ '000s
30/06/X0	1,184	1,549	365	365
31/12/X0	(4,772)	(4,292)	480	115
30/06/X1	(4,016)	(5,121)	(1,105)	(1,585)
31/12/X1	(2,130)	(5,320)	(3,190)	(2,085)
30/06/X2	0	(5,325)	(5,325)	(2,135)

The following table illustrates the accounting entries for the transaction during its life in £ '000s. Dr or (Cr) as indicated.

Date		Cash	Derivative	Debt	Equity	Profit or loss
01/01/X0	Issue debt	100,000		(100,000)		
30/06/X0	Accrue interest on debt			(3,365)		3,365
	Change in fair value of derivative		1,549		(1,549)	
	Reclassify amounts from equity				365	(365)
	Settlement of interest on the debt and net settlement of derivative	(3,000)	(365)	3,365		
31/12/X0	Accrue interest on debt			(3,115)		3,115
	Change in fair value of derivative		(5,841)		5,841	
	Reclassify amounts from equity				115	(115)
	Settlement of interest on the debt and net settlement of derivative	(3,000)	(115)	3,115		
30/06/X1	Accrue interest on debt			(1,415)		1,415
	Change in fair value of derivative		(829)		829	
	Reclassify amounts from equity				(1,585)	1,585
	Settlement of interest on the debt and net settlement of derivative	(3,000)	1,585	1,415		

Date		Cash	Derivative	Debt	Equity	Profit or loss
31/12/X1	Accrue interest on debt			(915)		915
	Change in fair value of derivative		(199)		199	
	Reclassify amounts from equity				(2,085)	2,085
	Settlement of interest on the debt and net settlement of derivative	(3,000)	2,085	915		
30/06/X2	Accrue interest on debt			(865)		865
	Change in fair value of derivative		(5)		5	
	Reclassify amounts from equity				(2,135)	2,135
	Settlement of interest on the debt and net settlement of derivative	(3,000)	2,135	865		
	Settlement of debt	(100,000)		100,000		
		(15,000)	0	0	0	15,000
	Key				**A**	**B**

A Nets to zero reflecting that all amounts in the cash flow hedge reserve in equity have been reclassified to profit or loss to offset recognise interest at the hedged rate.

B Reflects the total interest expense from the debt and derivative. This amount equals the total interest expense that would have been incurred had the entity issued fixed rate debt paying interest at 6 per cent.

Journal entries in the financial statements are provided below for illustrative purposes.

1 January 20X0

No entry required for derivatives because fair value is nil at inception.

		£ '000s	£ '000s
Dr	Cash	100,000	
Cr	Debt		100,000

To recognise the issue of debt.

30 June 20X0

		£ '000s	£ '000s
Dr	Interest expense	3,365	
Cr	Debt		3,365

To recognise the accrual of interest on the debt.

		£ '000s	£ '000s
Dr	Derivative	1,549	
Cr	Equity (cash flow hedge reserve)		1,549

To recognise the change in fair value of the derivative.

		£ '000s	£ '000s
Dr	Equity (cash flow hedge reserve)	365	
Cr	Interest expense		365

To recognise the reclassification from equity to profit or loss.

		£ '000s	£ '000s
Dr	Debt	3,365	
Cr	Derivative		365
Cr	Cash		3,000

To recognise the settlement of interest on the debt and net settlement of interest on the derivative.

Similar entries would be recorded for the remaining term of the hedge relationship.

Example 3.3B

Cash flow hedging the variability in cash flows of issued floating rate debt with an 'off-market' interest rate swap that receives floating and pays fixed, which is an asset at the date of designation.

Assume the same facts as in **example 3.3A** except that on 1 January 20X0, Entity B enters into an 'off-market' interest rate swap that matures on 30 June 20X2. Entity B will receive 6-month LIBOR and pay 3.77 per cent (per annum) on £100 million. Interest will be settled net semi-annually in arrears. Entity B pays £2,323k to enter into the interest rate swap, because the fixed rate on the swap is below the market rate of 4.77 per cent (per annum). Entity B has paid £2,323k in exchange for reducing each net interest settlement on the swap by £500k.

Settlement date	**30/06/X0 £ '000s**	**31/12/X0 £ '000s**	**30/06/X1 £ '000s**	**31/12/X1 £ '000s**	**30/06/X2 £ '000s**	**Total £ '000s**
Reduction in net settlement	500	500	500	500	500	2,500
Fair value on 01/01/X0	487	474	464	454	444	2,232

The fair value of the interest rate swap is £2,323k on 1 January 20X0.

Period ended	Fair value gain/(loss) during period £ '000s	Fair value of swap before cash settlement £ '000s	Cash settlement £ '000s	Fair value of swap after cash settlement* £ '000s
30/06/X0	1,597	3,920	(865)	3,055
31/12/X0	(5,737)	(2,682)	(615)	(3,297)
30/06/X1	(809)	(4,106)	1,085	(3,021)
31/12/X1	(195)	(3,216)	1,585	(1,631)
30/06/X2	(4)	(1,635)	1,635	0

* The fair value of the swap after cash settlement is equal to the 'clean' fair value, i.e. the fair value excluding any accrued interest.

On 1 January 20X0, Entity B designates the interest rate swap in a cash flow hedge of the variability of the interest cash flows of the debt due to changes in the 6-month LIBOR rate. The hypothetical derivative (which is derived from the hedged item) in this example is the same as the interest rate swap except for the fixed rate, which is 4.77 per cent (per annum). The fair value of the hypothetical derivative is nil on 1 January 20X0.

Period ended	Fair value gain/ (loss) during period £ '000s	Fair value gain/(loss) before cash settlement £ '000s	Cash settlement £ '000s	Fair value of swap after cash settlement** £ '000s
30/06/X0	1,549	1,549	(365)	1,184
31/12/X0	(5,841)	(4,657)	(115)	(4,772)
30/06/X1	(829)	(5,601)	1,585	(4,016)
31/12/X1	(199)	(4,215)	2,085	(2,130)
30/06/X2	(5)	(2,135)	2,135	0

** The fair value of the hypothetical derivative after cash settlement is equal to the clean fair value, i.e. the fair value excluding any accrued interest.

The cumulative amount recognised in the cash flow hedge reserve is the lower of the cumulative fair value gain or loss on the hedging instrument and on the hypothetical derivative.

Period ended	Cumulative fair value gain/(loss) on hedging instrument £ '000s	Cumulative fair value gain/ (loss) on hypothetical derivative £ '000s	Cumulative ineffectiveness*** £ '000s	Ineffectiveness during the period £ '000s
30/06/X0	1,597	1,549	48	48
31/12/X0	(4,140)	(4,292)	0	(48)
30/06/X1	(4,949)	(5,121)	0	0
31/12/X1	(5,144)	(5,320)	0	0
30/06/X2	(5,148)	(5,325)	0	0

*** If the cumulative dirty fair value gain or loss on the hedging instrument is less than that on the hypothetical derivative (i.e. there is an under-hedge), the cumulative ineffectiveness will be nil.

The amount remaining in the cash flow hedge reserve, after reclassification, is the lower of the cumulative clean fair value gain or loss on the hedging instrument and on the hypothetical derivative.

Period ended	Cumulative clean fair value gain/ (loss) on hedging instrument**** £ '000s	Cumulative clean fair value gain/ (loss) on hypothetical derivative***** £ '000s	Amount remaining in the cash flow hedge reserve £ '000s	Cumulative amount recognised in the cash flow hedge reserve £ '000s	Cumulative reclassi-fication to offset interest accrual £ '000s	Reclassi-fication in the period to offset interest accrual £ '000s
30/06/X0	1,219	1,184	1,184	1,549	365	365
31/12/X0	(4,659)	(4,772)	(4,659)	(4,140)	519	154
30/06/X1	(3,919)	(4,016)	(3,919)	(4,949)	(1,030)	(1,549)
31/12/X1	(2,075)	(2,130)	(2,075)	(5,144)	(3,069)	(2,039)
30/06/X2	0	0	0	(5,148)	(5,148)	(2,079)

**** The cumulative clean fair value gain or loss on the hedging instrument is the cumulative change in the clean fair value of the hedging instrument plus the portion of the designation date fair value of the off-market component (i.e. the reduction in net interest settlements) that has been settled or accrued since the inception of the hedge, e.g. [£3,055 – £2,323] + £487 = £1,219 in the first period, [£(3,297) – £2,323] + £487 + £474 = £(4,659) in the second and so on.

***** The cumulative clean fair value gain or loss on the hypothetical derivative is equal to the clean fair value because the hypothetical derivative has fair value of nil at the date of designation.

The following table illustrates the accounting entries for the transaction during its life in £ '000s. Dr or (Cr) as indicated.

Date		**Cash**	**Derivative**	**Debt**	**Equity**	**Profit or loss**
01/01/X0	Issue debt	100,000		(100,000)		
	Enter derivative contract	(2,323)	2,323			
30/06/X0	Accrue interest on debt			(3,365)		3,365
	Change in fair value of derivative		1,597		(1,549)	(48)
	Reclassify amounts from equity				365	(365)
	Settlement of interest on the debt and net settlement of derivative	(2,500)	(865)	3,365		
31/12/X0	Accrue interest on debt			(3,115)		3,115
	Change in fair value of derivative		(5,737)		5,689	48
	Reclassify amounts from equity				154	(154)
	Settlement of interest on the debt and net settlement of derivative	(2,500)	(615)	3,115		
30/06/X1	Accrue interest on debt			(1,415)		1,415
	Change in fair value of derivative		(809)		809	
	Reclassify amounts from equity				(1,549)	1,549
	Settlement of interest on the debt and net settlement of derivative	(2,500)	1,085	1,415		
31/12/X1	Accrue interest on debt			(915)		915
	Change in fair value of derivative		(195)		195	
	Reclassify amounts from equity				(2,039)	2,039
	Settlement of interest on the debt and net settlement of derivative	(2,500)	1,585	915		
30/06/X2	Accrue interest on debt			(865)		865
	Change in fair value of derivative		(4)		4	
	Reclassify amounts from equity				(2,079)	2,079

Date		Cash	Derivative	Debt	Equity	Profit or loss
	Settlement of interest on the debt and net settlement of derivative	(2,500)	1,635	865		
	Settlement of debt	(100,000)		100,000		
		(14,823)	0	0	0	14,823
	Key				**A**	**B**

A Nets to zero reflecting that all amounts in the cash flow hedge reserve in equity have been reclassified to profit or loss to offset the interest accrual.

B Reflects the total interest expense from the debt and derivative. This amount equals the total interest expense that would have been incurred had the entity issued fixed rate debt with a par of £100 million paying interest at 5 per cent, at £97,677 (i.e. at a discount).

Journal entries in the financial statements are provided below for illustrative purposes.

1 January 20X0

		£ '000s	£ '000s
Dr	Derivative	2,323	
Cr	Cash		2,323

To recognise the derivative.

		£ '000s	£ '000s
Dr	Cash	100,000	
Cr	Debt		100,000

To recognise the issue of debt.

30 June 20X0

		£ '000s	£ '000s
Dr	Interest expense	3,365	
Cr	Debt		3,365

To recognise the accrual of interest on the debt.

		£ '000s	£ '000s
Dr	Derivative	1,597	
Cr	Equity (cash flow hedge reserve)		1,549
Cr	Interest expense		48

To recognise the change in fair value of the derivative.

		£ '000s	£ '000s
Dr	Equity (cash flow hedge reserve)	365	
Cr	Interest expense		365

To recognise the reclassification from equity to profit or loss.

		£ '000s	£ '000s
Dr	Debt	3,365	
Cr	Derivative		865
Cr	Cash		2,500

To recognise the settlement of interest on the debt and net settlement of interest on the derivative.

Similar entries would be recorded for the remaining term of the hedge relationship.

Example 3.3C

Cash flow hedging the variability in cash flows of issued floating rate debt with an 'off-market' interest rate swap that receives floating and pays fixed, which is a liability at the date of designation.

Assume the same facts as in **example 3.3A** except that on 1 January 20X0, Entity B enters into an 'off-market' interest rate swap that matures on 30 June 20X2. Entity B will receive 6-month LIBOR and pay 5.77 per cent (per annum) on £100 million. Interest will be settled net semi-annually in arrears. Entity B receives £2,323k to enter into the interest rate swap, because the fixed rate on the swap is above the market rate of 4.77 per cent (per annum). Entity B has received £2,323k in exchange for increasing each net interest settlement on the swap by £500k.

Settlement date	30/06/X0 £ '000s	31/12/X0 £ '000s	30/06/X1 £ '000s	31/12/X1 £ '000s	30/06/X2 £ '000s	Total £ '000s
Reduction in net settlement	(500)	(500)	(500)	(500)	(500)	(2,500)
Fair value on 01/01/X0	(487)	(474)	(464)	(454)	(444)	(2,323)

The fair value of the interest rate swap is £(2,323)k on 1 January 20X0.

Period ended	Fair value gain/(loss) during period £ '000s	Fair value of swap before cash settlement £ '000s	Cash settlement £ '000s	Fair value of swap after cash settlement* £ '000s
30/06/X0	1,501	(822)	135	(687)
31/12/X0	(5,945)	(6,632)	385	(6,247)
30/06/X1	(848)	(7,095)	2,085	(5,010)
31/12/X1	(203)	(5,213)	2,585	(2,628)
30/06/X2	(7)	(2,635)	2,635	0

* The fair value of the swap after cash settlement is equal to the clean fair value, i.e. the fair value excluding any accrued interest.

On 1 January 20X0, Entity B designates the interest rate swap in a cash flow hedge of the variability of the interest cash flows of the debt due to changes in the 6-month LIBOR rate.

The hypothetical derivative (which is derived from the hedged item) in this example is the same as the interest rate swap except for the fixed rate, which is 4.77 per cent (per annum). The fair value of the hypothetical derivative is nil on 1 January 20X0.

Period ended	Fair value gain/(loss) during period £ '000s	Fair value of swap before cash settlement £ '000s	Cash settlement £ '000s	Fair value of swap after cash settlement** £ '000s
30/06/X0	1,549	1,549	(365)	1,184
31/12/X0	(5,841)	(4,657)	(115)	(4,772)
30/06/X1	(829)	(5,601)	1,585	(4,016)
31/12/X1	(199)	(4,215)	2,085	(2,130)
30/06/X2	(5)	(2,135)	2,135	0

** The fair value of the hypothetical derivative after cash settlement is equal to the clean fair value, i.e. the fair value excluding any accrued interest.

The cumulative amount recognised in the cash flow hedge reserve is the lower of the cumulative fair value gain or loss on the hedging instrument and on the hypothetical derivative.

Period ended	Cumulative fair value gain/(loss) on hedging instrument £ '000s	Cumulative fair value gain/ (loss) on hypothetical derivative £ '000s	Cumulative ineffectiveness*** £ '000s	Ineffectiveness during the period £ '000s
30/06/X0	1,501	1,549	0	0
31/12/X0	(4,444)	(4,292)	(152)	(152)
30/06/X1	(5,292)	(5,121)	(171)	(19)
31/12/X1	(5,495)	(5,320)	(175)	(4)
30/06/X2	(5,502)	(5,325)	(177)	(2)

*** If the cumulative dirty fair value gain or loss on the hedging instrument is less than that on the hypothetical derivative (i.e. there is an under-hedge), the cumulative ineffectiveness will be nil.

The amount remaining in the cash flow hedge reserve, after reclassification, is the lower of the cumulative clean fair value gain or loss on the hedging instrument and on the hypothetical derivative.

Period ended	Cumulative clean fair value gain/ (loss) on hedging instrument**** £ '000s	Cumulative clean fair value gain/ (loss) on hypothetical derivative***** £ '000s	Amount remaining in the cash flow hedge reserve £ '000s	Cumulative amount recognised in the cash flow hedge reserve £ '000s	Cumulative reclassification to offset interest accrual £ '000s	Reclassification in the period to offset interest accrual £ '000s
30/06/X0	1,149	1,184	1,149	1,501	352	352
31/12/X0	(4,885)	(4,772)	(4,772)	(4,292)	480	128
30/06/X1	(4,112)	(4,016)	(4,016)	(5,121)	(1,105)	(1,585)
31/12/X1	(2,184)	(2,130)	(2,130)	(5,320)	(3,190)	(2,085)
30/06/X2	0	0	0	(5,325)	(5,325)	(2,135)

**** The cumulative clean fair value gain or loss on the hedging instrument is the cumulative change in the clean fair value of the hedging instrument plus the portion of the designation date fair value of the off-market component (i.e. the reduction in net interest settlements) that has been settled or accrued since the inception of the hedge, e.g. [£(687) – £(2,323)] + £(487) = £1,149 in the first period, [£(6,247) – £(2,323)] + £(487) + £(474) = £(4,885) in the second and so on.

***** The cumulative clean fair value gain or loss on the hypothetical derivative is equal to the clean fair value because the hypothetical derivative has fair value of nil at the date of designation.

The following table illustrates the accounting entries for the transaction during its life in £ '000s. Dr or (Cr) as indicated.

Date		Cash	Derivative	Debt	Equity	Profit or loss
01/01/X0	Issue debt	100,000		(100,000)		
	Enter derivative contract	2,323	(2,323)			
30/06/X0	Accrue interest on debt			(3,365)		3,365
	Change in fair value of derivative		1,501		(1,501)	
	Reclassify amounts from equity				352	(352)
	Settlement of interest on the debt and net settlement of derivative	(3,500)	135	3,365		
31/12/X0	Accrue interest on debt			(3,115)		3,115
	Change in fair value of derivative		(5,945)		5,793	152
	Reclassify amounts from equity				128	(128)
	Settlement of interest on the debt and net settlement of derivative	(3,500)	385	3,115		
30/06/X1	Accrue interest on debt			(1,415)		1,415
	Change in fair value of derivative		(848)		829	19

Date		Cash	Derivative	Debt	Equity	Profit or loss
	Reclassify amounts from equity				(1,585)	1,585
	Settlement of interest on the debt and net settlement of derivative	(3,500)	2,085	1,415		
31/12/X1	Accrue interest on debt			(915)		915
	Change in fair value of derivative		(203)		199	4
	Reclassify amounts from equity				(2,085)	2,085
	Settlement of interest on the debt and net settlement of derivative	(3,500)	2,585	915		
30/06/X2	Accrue interest on debt			(865)		865
	Change in fair value of derivative		(7)		5	2
	Reclassify amounts from equity				(2,135)	2,135
	Settlement of interest on the debt and net settlement of derivative	(3,500)	2,635	865		
	Settlement of debt	(100,000)		100,000		
		(15,177)	0	0	0	15,177
	Key				**A**	**B**

A Nets to zero reflecting that all amounts in the cash flow hedge reserve in equity have been reclassified to profit or loss to offset the interest accrual.

B Reflects the total interest expense from the debt and derivative. This amount equals the total interest expense that would have been incurred had the entity issued fixed rate debt with a par of £100 million paying interest at 7 per cent, at £102,323 (i.e. at a premium).

Journal entries in the financial statements are provided below for illustrative purposes.

1 January 20X0

		£ '000s	£ '000s
Dr	Derivative	2,323	
Cr	Cash		2,323

To recognise the derivative.

		£ '000s	£ '000s
Dr	Cash	100,000	
Cr	Debt		100,000

To recognise the issue of debt.

30 June 20X0

		£ '000s	£ '000s
Dr	Interest expense	3,365	
Cr	Debt		3,365

To recognise the accrual of interest on the debt.

		£ '000s	£ '000s
Dr	Derivative	1,501	
Cr	Equity (cash flow hedge reserve)		1,501

To recognise the change in fair value of the derivative.

		£ '000s	£ '000s
Dr	Equity (cash flow hedge reserve)	352	
Cr	Interest expense		352

To recognise the reclassification from equity to profit or loss.

		£ '000s	£ '000s
Dr	Debt	3,365	
Cr	Derivative		135
Cr	Cash		3,500

To recognise the settlement of interest on the debt and net settlement of interest on the derivative.

Similar entries would be recorded for the remaining term of the hedge relationship.

3.4 Cash flow hedging foreign currency risk of floating rate debt

The following three examples illustrate the entries for a cash flow hedge of foreign currency risk on floating rate debt using a floating - floating cross currency interest rate swap. In the first example (**example 3.4A**) the cross currency swap is designated as the hedging instrument in its entirety and the foreign currency basis spread element of the swap gives rise to ineffectiveness. In the second and third examples the foreign currency basis spread element is excluded from the designation of the hedging instrument. In the second example (**example 3.4B**) the excluded element is recognised directly in profit or loss on a fair value basis. In the final example (**example 3.4C**), the entity has elected, in accordance with IFRS 9:6.5.16 to apply IFRS 9:6.5.15 and recognise the excluded element in OCI (to the extent it relates to the hedged item). Because the hedged item is a period related item, the excluded element is amortised from OCI to profit or loss on a rational basis over the period during which the hedge adjustment for the included element could affect profit or loss.

Example 3.4A

Cash flow hedging spot foreign currency risk of issued floating rate foreign currency debt with a cross currency interest rate swap that receives floating foreign currency and pays floating functional currency. The foreign currency basis spread element of the swap is not excluded from the hedge.

On 1 January 20X1, Entity A with a local functional currency (LC), issues foreign currency (FC) floating rate debt that matures on 31 December 20X5. The principal amount of the debt is FC100 million and interest of FC LIBOR is paid annually in arrears. At 1 January 20X1 the FC:LC spot rate is 15.8:1 and so the principal is equivalent to LC6,329,114.

Period ended	Spot rate (FC/LC)	FC LIBOR at start of period	Interest accrual in period	Interest accrual in period (translated at average rate)	Gain/(Loss) on retranslation of debt	Carrying amount of debt before cash settlement	Cash settlement (translated at spot rate)	Carrying amount of debt after cash settlement
			FC '000s	LC '000s	LC '000s	LC '000s	LC '000s	LC '000s
31/12/X1	12.6	12.26	(12,260)	(863)	(1,717)	(8,909)	973	(7,936)
31/12/X2	11.4	7.47	(7,470)	(622)	(869)	(9,427)	655	(8,772)
31/12/X3	11	6.51	(6,510)	(581)	(330)	(9,683)	592	(9,091)
31/12/X4	12.8	5.49	(5,490)	(461)	1,311	(8,241)	428	(7,813)
31/12/X5	15	5.49	(5,490)	(395)	1,175	(7,033)	7,033	0

On 1 January 20X1, Entity A also enters into a floating- floating cross currency interest rate swap that matures on 31 December 20X5. Entity A will receive FC LIBOR interest on FC100 million and pay LC LIBOR -35 bps interest on LC6,329,114. Interest will be exchanged annually in arrears and principal amounts will also be exchanged at maturity. The fair value of the cross currency interest rate swap is nil on 1 January 20X1.

Period ended	LC LIBOR at start of period	Fair value gain/ (loss) during period	Fair value of swap before cash settlement	Cash settlement*	Fair value of swap after cash settlement
		LC '000s	LC '000s	LC '000s	LC '000s
31/12/X1	5.13	2,225	2,225	(670)	1,555
31/12/X2	0.59	1,498	3,053	(640)	2,413
31/12/X3	0.55	922	3,335	(579)	2,756
31/12/X4	0.60	(851)	1,905	(413)	1,492
31/12/X5	0.56	(801)	691	(691)	0

* The cash settlement is the foreign currency cash flow translated at the spot rate plus the local currency cash flow e.g. [-(FC100,000,000 * 12.26%) / (12.6 FC/LC)] + [LC6,329,114 * (5.13 – 0.35)%] = -LC670,484.

On 1 January 20X1, Entity A designates the cross currency interest rate swap in a cash flow hedge of the variability of the interest and principal cash flows of the FC denominated debt due to changes in the spot rate. Entity A does not exclude the foreign currency basis spread element from the designation which gives rise to ineffectiveness.

In this example, the hypothetical derivative (which is derived from the hedged item) is a swap with a foreign currency leg that matches the actual swap and a local currency leg equal to the local currency leg of the actual swap excluding the spread of -35 bps. The change in the present value of the hypothetical derivative is calculated for the purposes of hedge accounting by applying non-currency basis adjusted discount curves (i.e. a LC non- currency basis adjusted discount curve to the LC cash flows and a FC non-currency basis adjusted discount curve to the FC cash flows).

Period ended	Present value gain/(loss) during period LC '000s	Present value before cash settlement LC '000s	Cash settlement** LC '000s	Present value after cash settlement** LC '000s
31/12/X1	2,256	2,256	(648)	1,608
31/12/X2	1,453	3,061	(618)	2,443
31/12/X3	876	3,319	(557)	2,762
31/12/X4	(887)	1,875	(391)	1,484
31/12/X5	(816)	668	(668)	0

** The cash settlement is the foreign currency cash flow translated at the spot rate plus the local currency cash flow e.g. [-(FC100,000,000 * 12.26%) / (12.6 FC/LC)] + (LC6,329,114 * 5.13%) = -LC648,332.

Period ended	Cumulative fair value gain/(loss) hedging instrument LC '000s	Cumulative present value gain/(loss) on hypothetical derivative LC '000s	Cumulative ineffectiveness*** LC '000s	Ineffectiveness during period LC '000s
31/12/X1	2,225	2,256	0	0
31/12/X2	3,723	3,709	14	14
31/12/X3	4,645	4,585	60	46
31/12/X4	3,794	3,698	96	36
31/12/X5	2,993	2,882	111	15

*** If the cumulative fair value gain or loss on the hedging instrument is less than that on the hypothetical derivative (i.e. there is an under-hedge), the cumulative ineffectiveness will be nil.

Amounts are reclassified from the cash flow hedge reserve to profit or loss in the period during which the hedged expected future cash flows affect profit or loss. The cumulative amount reclassified in order to offset the interest accrual on the FC debt is calculated as the difference between the cumulative amount recognised in the cash flow hedge reserve and the lower of the cumulative clean fair value gain or loss on the hedging instrument and the cumulative clean present value gain or loss on the hypothetical derivative.

Period ended	Cumulative amount recognised in the cash flow hedge reserve LC '000s	The lower of the cumulative clean fair value gain/(loss) on the hedging instrument and the cumulative clean present value gain/(loss) on the hypothetical derivative LC '000s	Cumulative reclassification of amounts to offset the interest accrual LC '000s	Reclassification of amounts to offset the interest accrual in period**** LC '000s
31/12/X1	2,225	1,555	670	670
31/12/X2	3,709	2,413	1,296	626
31/12/X3	4,585	2,756	1,829	533
31/12/X4	3,698	1,484	2,214	385
31/12/X5	2,882	338	2,544	330

**** We have chosen to allocate this amount first to offset the retranslation of the interest accrual, then the remainder to offset the accrual of interest at the average rate.

The amount reclassified in order to offset the retranslation of the opening carrying value of the FC debt is equal and opposite to the retranslation gain or loss on the opening carrying value of the FC debt.

The following table illustrates the accounting entries for the transaction during its life in LC '000s. Dr or (Cr) as indicated.

Date		Cash	Derivative	Debt	Equity	Interest expense	Translation loss
01/12/X1	Issue debt	6,329		(6,329)			
31/12/X1	Change in fair value of derivative		2,225		(2,225)		
	Net settlement of derivative (at spot rate)	670	(670)				
	Accrue interest on debt (at average rate)			(863)		863	
	Retranslate debt to spot			(1,717)			1,717
	Reclassify amounts from equity – to offset interest accrual on the FC debt				670	(561)	(109)
	Reclassify amounts from equity – to offset the retranslation of the opening carrying value of the FC debt				1,608		(1,608)

Date		Cash	Derivative	Debt	Equity	Interest expense	Translation loss
	Settlement of interest on the debt (at spot rate)	(973)		973			
31/12/X2	Change in fair value of derivative		1,498		(1,484)	(14)	
	Net settlement of derivatives (at spot rate)	640	(640)				
	Accrue interest on debt (at average rate)			(622)		622	
	Retranslate debt to spot			(869)			869
	Reclassify amounts from equity – to offset interest accrual on the FC debt				626	(592)	(34)
	Reclassify amounts from equity – to offset the retranslation of the opening carrying value of the FC debt				835		(835)
	Settlement of interest on the debt (at spot rate)	(655)		655			
31/12/X3	Change in fair value of derivative		922		(876)	(46)	
	Net settlement of derivative (at spot rate)	579	(579)				
	Accrue interest on debt (at average rate)			(581)		581	
	Retranslate debt to spot			(330)			330
	Reclassify amounts from equity – to offset interest accrual on the FC debt				533	(522)	(11)
	Reclassify amounts from equity – to offset the retranslation of the opening carrying value of the FC debt				319		(319)
	Settlement of interest on the debt (at spot rate)	(592)		592			
31/12/X4	Change in fair value of derivative		(851)		887	(36)	

Date		Cash	Derivative	Debt	Equity	Interest expense	Translation loss
	Net settlement of derivative (at spot rate)	413	(413)				
	Accrue interest on debt (at average rate)			(461)		461	
	Retranslate debt to spot			1,311			(1,311)
	Reclassify amounts from equity – to offset interest accrual on the FC debt				385	(418)	33
	Reclassify amounts from equity – to offset the retranslation of the opening carrying value of the FC debt				(1,278)		1,278
	Settlement of interest on the debt (at spot rate)	(428)		428			
31/12/X5	Change in fair value of derivative		(801)		816	(15)	
	Net settlement of derivative (at spot rate)	353	(353)				
	Accrue interest on debt (at average rate)			(395)		395	
	Retranslate debt to spot			1,175			(1,175)
	Reclassify amounts from equity – to offset interest accrual on the FC debt				330	(359)	29
	Reclassify amounts from equity – to offset the retranslation of the opening carrying value of the FC debt				(1,146)		1,146
	Settlement of interest on the debt (at spot rate)	(366)		366			
	Net settlement of derivative (at spot rate)	338	(338)				
	Settlement of debt	(6,667)		6,667			
		(359)	0	0	0	359	0
Key					**A**	**B**	

A Nets to zero reflecting that all amounts in the cash flow hedge reserve in equity have been reclassified to profit or loss to offset the retranslation of debt to the spot rate each period and recognise interest at the hedged rate.

B Reflects the total interest expense from the FC debt and derivative. This amount equals the total interest expense that would have been incurred had the entity issued LC debt paying interest at LC LIBOR -35 bps (LC6,329,114 * [5.13 + 0.59 + 0.55 + 0.6 + 0.56 - (5 * 0.35)]%). However, because of the impact of hedge ineffectiveness, the expense in each period will not be LC6,329,114 multiplied by LC LIBOR -35bps.

Journal entries in the financial statements are provided below for illustrative purposes.

1 January 20X1

No entry required for derivative because fair value is nil at inception.

		LC '000s	LC '000s
Dr	Cash	6,329	
Cr	Debt		6,329

To recognise the issue of FC denominated debt (translated at spot).

31 December 20X1

		LC '000s	LC '000s
Dr	Derivative	2,225	
Cr	Equity (cash flow hedge reserve)		2,225

To recognise the change in fair value of the derivative.

		LC '000s	LC '000s
Dr	Cash	670	
Cr	Derivative		670

To recognise the net settlement of interest on the derivative (at the spot rate).

		LC '000s	LC '000s
Dr	Interest expense	863	
Cr	Debt		863

To recognise the accrual of interest on the debt (at the average rate).

		LC'000s	LC '000s
Dr	Translation loss	1,717	
Cr	Debt		1,717

To recognise the loss on retranslation of FC debt (at the year end spot rate).

		LC'000s	LC '000s
Dr	Equity (cash flow hedge reserve	2,278	
Cr	Interest expense		561
Cr	Translation loss		1,717

To recognise the reclassification from equity to profit or loss.

		LC'000s	LC '000s
Dr	Debt	973	
Cr	Cash		973

To recognise the payment of interest on the debt in cash (at the spot rate).

Similar entries would be recorded for the remaining term of the hedge relationship.

Example 3.4B

Cash flow hedging spot foreign currency risk of issued floating rate foreign currency debt with a cross currency interest rate swap that receives floating foreign currency and pays floating functional currency. The foreign currency basis spread element of the swap is excluded from the hedge and accounted for at FVTPL.

Assume the same facts as in **example 3.4A** except that on 1 January 20X1, Entity A designates the cross currency interest rate swap excluding the foreign currency basis spread element in a cash flow hedge of the variability of the interest and principal cash flows of the FC denominated debt due to changes in the spot rate. Entity A chooses not to apply the treatment in IFRS 9:6.5.15 to the foreign currency basis spread element of the cross currency swap; consequently, the change in the fair value movement excluded from the hedge relationship is accounted for at FVTPL.

The change in the present value of the cross currency interest rate swap excluding the foreign currency basis spread element is calculated for the purposes of hedge accounting by applying non-currency basis adjusted discount curves to cash flows of a swap with a foreign currency leg that matches the actual swap and a local currency leg equal to the local currency leg of the actual swap excluding the spread of -35 bps. The present value of the foreign currency interest rate swap excluding the foreign currency basis spread is nil on 1 January 20X1.

Period ended	Present value gain/(loss) during period LC '000s	Present value before cash settlement LC '000s	Cash settlement* LC '000s	Present value after cash settlement LC '000s
31/12/X1	2,256	2,256	(648)	1,608
31/12/X2	1,453	3,061	(618)	2,443
31/12/X3	876	3,319	(557)	2,762
31/12/X4	(887)	1,875	(391)	1,484
31/12/X5	(816)	668	(668)	0

* The cash settlement is the foreign currency cash flow translated at the spot rate plus the local currency cash flow e.g. [-(FC100,000,000 * 12.26%) / (12.6 FC/LC)] + (LC6,329,114 * 5.13%) = -LC648,332.

In this example, the hypothetical derivative (which is derived from the hedged item) is the same as in **example 3.4A** (it is the same as the cross currency interest rate swap excluding the foreign currency basis spread element). The hedge is 100 per cent effective in each period as the change in the present value of the cross currency interest rate swap excluding the foreign currency basis spread element is equal to the change in the present value of the hypothetical derivative.

The fair value of the cross currency interest rate swap that is excluded from the hedge relationship is calculated as the balancing figure between the full fair value of the swap and the present value of the spot element of the swap calculated above. It is known on the date of designation that the total change in the value of the excluded component over the life of the hedge will be LC110,760 (LC6,329,114 * 0.35% * 5). We have chosen to present this amount as part of interest expense in the illustrative journal entries below.

The following table illustrates the accounting entries for the transaction during its life in LC '000s. Dr or (Cr) as indicated.

Date		Cash	Derivative	Debt	Equity	Interest expense	Translation loss
01/01/X1	Issue debt	6,329		(6,329)			
31/12/X1	Change in fair value of derivative:						
	- excl. foreign currency basis spread element		2,256		(2,256)		
	- foreign currency basis spread element		(31)			31	
	Net settlement of derivative (at spot rate)	670	(670)				
	Accrue interest on debt (at average rate)			(863)		863	
	Retranslate debt to spot			(1,717)			1,717

Date		Cash	Derivative	Debt	Equity	Interest expense	Translation loss
	Reclassify amounts from equity				2,256	(539)	(1,717)
	Settlement of interest on the debt (at spot rate)	(973)		973			
31/12/X2	Change in fair value of derivative						
	- excl. foreign currency basis spread element		1,453		(1,453)		
	- foreign currency basis spread element		45			(45)	
	Net settlement of derivatives (at spot rate)	640	(640)				
	Accrue interest on debt (at average rate)			(622)		622	
	Retranslate debt to spot			(869)			869
	Reclassify amounts from equity				1,453	(584)	(869)
	Settlement of interest on the debt (at spot rate)	(655)		655			
31/12/X3	Change in fair value of derivative:						
	- excl. foreign currency basis spread element		876		(876)		
	- foreign currency basis spread element		46			(46)	
	Net settlement of derivative (at spot rate)	579	(579)				
	Accrue interest on debt (at average rate)			(581)		581	
	Retranslate debt to spot			(330)			330
	Reclassify amounts from equity				876	(546)	(330)
	Settlement of interest on the debt (at spot rate)	(592)		592			
31/12/X4	Change in fair value of derivative:						
	- excl. foreign currency basis spread		(887)		887		
	- foreign currency basis spread element		36			(36)	
	Net settlement of derivative (at spot rate)	413	(413)				

Date		Cash	Derivative	Debt	Equity	Interest expense	Translation loss
	Accrue interest on debt (at average rate)			(461)		461	
	Retranslate debt to spot			1,311			(1,311)
	Reclassify amounts from equity				(887)	(424)	1,311
	Settlement of interest on the debt (at spot rate)	(428)		428			
31/12/X5	Change in fair value of derivative: - excl. foreign currency basis spread element		(816)		816		
	- foreign currency basis spread element		15			(15)	
	Net settlement of derivative (at spot rate)	353	(353)				
	Accrue interest on debt (at average rate)			(395)		395	
	Retranslate debt to spot			1,175			(1,175)
	Reclassify amounts from equity				(816)	(359)	1,175
	Settlement of interest on the debt (at spot rate)	(366)		366			
	Net settlement of derivative (at spot rate)	338	(338)				
	Settlement of debt	(6,667)		6,667			
		(359)	0	0	0	359	0
Key					**A**	**B**	

A Nets to zero reflecting that all amounts in the cash flow hedge reserve in equity have been reclassified to profit or loss to offset the retranslation of debt to the spot rate each period and recognise interest at the hedged rate.

B Reflects the total interest expense from the FC debt and derivative. This amount equals the total interest expense that would have been incurred had the entity issued LC debt paying interest at LC LIBOR -35 bps (LC6,329,114 * [5.13 + 0.59 + 0.55 + 0.6 + 0.56 – (5 * 0.35)]%). However, the expense in each period will not be LC6,329,114 multiplied by LC LIBOR -35bps.

Journal entries in the financial statements are provided below for illustrative purposes.

1 January 20X1

No entry required for derivative because fair value is nil at inception.

		LC'000s	LC '000s
Dr	Cash	6,329	
Cr	Debt		6,329

To recognise the issue of FC denominated debt (translated at spot).

31 December 20X1

		LC'000s	LC '000s
Dr	Derivative	2,225	
Dr	Interest expense	31	
Cr	Equity (cash flow hedge reserve)		2,256

To recognise the change in fair value of the derivative.

		LC'000s	LC '000s
Dr	Cash	670	
Cr	Derivative		670

To recognise the net settlement of interest on the derivative (at the spot rate).

		LC'000s	LC '000s
Dr	Interest expense	863	
Cr	Debt		863

To recognise the accrual of interest on the debt (at the average rate).

		LC'000s	LC '000s
Dr	Translation loss	1,717	
Cr	Debt		1,717

To recognise the loss on retranslation of FC debt (at the year end spot rate).

		LC'000s	LC '000s
Dr	Equity (cash flow hedge reserve)	2,256	
Cr	Interest expense		539
Cr	Translation loss		1,717

To recognise the reclassification from equity to profit or loss.

		LC'000s	LC '000s
Dr	Debt	973	
Cr	Cash		973

To recognise the payment of interest on the debt in cash(at the spot rate).

Similar entries would be recorded for the remaining term of the hedge relationship.

Example 3.4C

Cash flow hedging spot foreign currency risk of issued floating rate foreign currency debt with a cross currency interest rate swap that receives floating foreign currency and pays floating functional currency. The foreign currency basis spread element of the swap is excluded from the hedge and recognised in OCI and amortised to profit or loss on a rational basis.

Assume the same facts as in **example 3.4A** except that on 1 January 20X1, Entity A designates the cross currency interest rate swap excluding the foreign currency basis spread element in a cash flow hedge of the variability of the interest and principal cash flows of the FC denominated debt due to changes in the spot rate. Entity A chooses to apply the treatment in IFRS 9:6.5.15 to the foreign currency basis spread element of the cross currency swap; consequently, the change in the fair value movement excluded from the hedge relationship is accumulated in other comprehensive income (OCI) to the extent it relates to the hedged item and is then amortised to the profit or loss on a rational basis.

In this example, the hypothetical derivative (which is derived from the hedged item) is the same as in **example 3.4A** (it is the same as the cross currency interest rate swap excluding the foreign currency basis spread element).

As in **example 3.4B**, the change in the present value of the cross currency interest rate swap excluding the foreign currency basis spread element is calculated for the purposes of hedge accounting by applying non-currency basis adjusted discount curves to cash flows of a swap with a foreign currency leg that matches the actual swap and a local currency leg equal to the local currency leg of the actual swap excluding the spread of -35 bps. The present value of the foreign currency interest rate swap excluding the foreign currency basis spread is nil on 1 January 20X1.

The hedge is 100 per cent effective and the excluded element of the cross currency swap is equal to the aligned foreign currency basis spread element. The excluded element of the cross currency interest rate swap is equal to the aligned foreign currency basis spread element.

As in **example 3.4B**, the fair value of the cross currency interest rate swap that is excluded from the hedge relationship is calculated as the balancing figure between the full fair value of the swap and the present value of the swap excluding the foreign currency basis spread element calculated above. It is known on the date of designation that the total change in the value of the excluded component over the life of the hedge will be LC110,760 (LC6,329, 114 * 0.35% * 5). This has been amortised on a straight-line basis to the profit or loss resulting in an additional interest charge of LC22,152 in each period (difference to the numbers in the table is due to rounding). We have chosen to present this amount as part of interest expense in the illustrative journal entries below.

The following table illustrates the accounting entries for the transaction during its life in LC '000s. Dr or (Cr) as indicated.

Date		Cash	Derivative	Debt	Equity	Interest expense	Translation loss
01/01/X1	Issue debt	6,329		(6,329)			
31/12/X1	Change in fair value of derivative: - excl. foreign currency basis spread element		2,256		(2,256)		
	- foreign currency basis spread element		(31)		31		
	Net settlement of derivative (at spot rate)	670	(670)				
	Accrue interest on debt (at average rate)			(863)		863	
	Retranslate debt to spot			(1,717)			1,717
	Reclassify amounts from equity: - cash flow hedge reserve				2,256	(539)	(1,717)
	- separate component of equity				22	(22)	
	Settlement of interest on the debt (at spot rate)	(973)		973			
31/12/X2	Change in fair value of derivative: - excl. foreign currency basis spread element		1,453		(1,453)		
	- foreign currency basis spread element		45		(45)		
	Net settlement of derivatives (at spot rate)	640	(640)				
	Accrue interest on debt (at average rate)			(622)		622	
	Retranslate debt to spot			(869)			869
	Reclassify amounts from equity: - cash flow hedge reserve				1,453	(584)	(869)
	- separate component of equity				23	(23)	
	Settlement of interest on the debt (at spot rate)	(655)		655			
31/12/X3	Change in fair value of derivative: - excl. foreign currency basis spread element		876		(876)		

Date		Cash	Derivative	Debt	Equity	Interest expense	Translation loss
	- foreign currency basis spread element		46		(46)		
	Net settlement of derivative (at spot rate)	579	(579)				
	Accrue interest on debt (at average rate)			(581)		581	
	Retranslate debt to spot			(330)			330
	Reclassify amounts from equity: - cash flow hedge reserve				876	(546)	(330)
	- separate component of equity				22	(22)	
	Settlement of interest on the debt (at spot rate)	(592)		592			
31/12/X4	Change in fair value of derivative: - excl. foreign currency basis spread element		(887)		887		
	- foreign currency basis spread element		36		(36)		
	Net settlement of derivative (at spot rate)	413	(413)				
	Accrue interest on debt (at average rate)			(461)		461	
	Retranslate debt to spot			1,311			(1,311)
	Reclassify amounts from equity: - cash flow hedge reserve				(887)	(424)	1,311
	- separate component of equity				22	(22)	
	Settlement of interest on the debt (at spot rate)	(428)		428			
31/12/X5	Change in fair value of derivative: - excl. foreign currency basis spread element		(816)		816		
	- foreign currency basis spread element		15		(15)		
	Net settlement of derivative (at spot rate)	353	(353)				
	Accrue interest on debt (at average rate)			(395)		395	

Date		Cash	Derivative	Debt	Equity	Interest expense	Translation loss
	Retranslate debt to spot			1,175			(1,175)
	Reclassify amounts from equity: - cash flow hedge reserve				(816)	(359)	1,175
	- separate component of equity				22	(22)	
	Settlement of interest on the debt (at spot rate)	(366)		366			
	Net settlement of derivative (at spot rate)	338	(338)				
	Settlement of debt	(6,667)		6,667			
		(359)	0	0	0	359	0
Key					**A**	**B**	

A Nets to zero reflecting that all amounts recognised in equity have been reclassified to profit or loss either, to offset the retranslation of debt to the spot rate each period and recognise interest at the hedged rate, or through the amortisation of the excluded component on a systematic and rational basis.

B Reflects the total interest expense from the FC debt and derivative. This amount equals the total interest expense that would have been incurred had the entity issued LC debt paying interest at LC LIBOR -35 bps (LC6,329,114 * [5.13 + 0.59 + 0.55 + 0.6 + 0.56 - (5 * 0.35)]%). The expense in each period is LC6,329,114 multiplied by LC LIBOR -35bps.

Journal entries in the financial statements are provided below for illustrative purposes.

1 January 20X1

No entry required for derivative because fair value is nil at inception.

		LC'000s	LC '000s
Dr	Cash	6,329	
Cr	Debt		6,329

To recognise the issue of FC denominated debt (translated at spot).

31 December 20X1

		LC'000s	LC '000s
Dr	Derivative	2,225	
Dr	Equity (separate component of equity)	31	
Cr	Equity (cash flow hedge reserve)		2,256

To recognise the change in fair value of the derivative.

		LC'000s	LC '000s
Dr	Cash	670	
Cr	Derivative		670

To recognise the net settlement of interest on the derivative (at the spot rate).

		LC'000s	LC '000s
Dr	Interest expense	863	
Cr	Debt		863

To recognise the accrual of interest on the debt (at the average rate).

		LC'000s	LC '000s
Dr	Translation loss	1,717	
Cr	Debt		1,717

To recognise the loss on retranslation of FC debt (at the year end spot rate).

		LC'000s	LC '000s
Dr	Equity (cash flow hedge reserve)	2,256	
Dr	Equity (separate component of equity)	22	
Cr	Interest expense		561
Cr	Translation loss		1,717

To recognise the reclassification from equity to profit or loss.

		LC'000s	LC '000s
Dr	Debt	973	
Cr	Cash		973

To recognise the payment of interest on the debt in cash (at the spot rate).

Similar entries would be recorded for the remaining term of the hedge relationship.

3.5 Cash flow hedging foreign currency risk of fixed rate debt

The following two examples illustrate the entries for a cash flow hedge of foreign currency risk on fixed rate debt using a fixed - fixed cross currency interest rate swap. In both examples the foreign currency basis spread and forward elements are excluded from the designation of the hedging instrument. In the first example (**example 3.5A**) these excluded elements are recognised directly in profit or loss on a fair value basis. In the second example (**example 3.5B**), the entity has elected, in accordance with IFRS 9:6.5.16 to apply IFRS 9:6.5.15 and recognise the excluded elements in OCI (to the extent they relate to the hedged item). Because the hedged item is a period related item, the excluded elements are amortised from OCI to profit or loss on a rational basis over the period during which the hedge adjustment for the included element could affect profit or loss.

Example 3.5A

Cash flow hedging spot foreign currency risk of issued fixed rate foreign currency debt with a cross currency interest rate swap that receives fixed foreign currency and pays fixed functional currency. The foreign currency basis spread and forward elements of the swap are excluded from the hedge and accounted for at FVTPL.

On 1 January 20X1, Entity A with a local functional currency (LC), issues foreign currency (FC) fixed rate debt that matures on 31 December 20X5. The principal amount of the debt is FC100 million and interest of 11.93% is paid annually in arrears. At 1 January 20X1 the FC:LC spot rate is 15.8:1 and so the principal is equivalent to LC6,329,114.

Period ended	Spot rate FC/ LC	Interest accrual in period	Interest accrual in period (translated at average rate)	Gain/ (Loss) on retranslation of debt	Carrying amount of debt before cash settlement	Cash settlement (translated at spot rate)	Carrying amount of debt after cash settlement
		FC '000s	LC '000s	LC '000s	LC '000s	LC '000s	LC '000s
31/12/X1	12.6	(11,930)	(840)	(1,714)	(8,883)	947	(7,936)
31/12/X2	11.4	(11,930)	(994)	(888)	(9,818)	1,046	(8,772)
31/12/X3	11	(11,930)	(1,065)	(339)	(10,176)	1,085	(9,091)
31/12/X4	12.8	(11,930)	(1,003)	1,349	(8,745)	932	(7,813)
31/12/X5	15	(11,930)	(858)	1,209	(7,462)	7,462	0

On 1 January 20X1, Entity A also enters into a fixed- fixed cross currency interest rate swap that matures on 31 December 20X5. Entity A will receive 11.93% interest on FC100 million and pay 5.65% (this includes a foreign currency basis spread of -35 bps) interest on LC6,329,114. Interest will be exchanged annually in arrears and principal amounts will also be exchanged at maturity. The fair value of the cross currency interest rate swap is nil on 1 January 20X1.

Period ended	Fair value gain/ (loss) during period	Fair value of swap before cash settlement	Cash settlement*	Fair value of swap after cash settlement
	LC '000s	LC '000s	LC '000s	LC '000s
31/12/X1	2,419	2,419	(589)	1, 830
31/12/X2	1,622	3,452	(689)	2,763
31/12/X3	1,070	3,833	(727)	3,106
31/12/X4	(906)	2,200	(574)	1,626
31/12/X5	(850)	776	(776)	0

* The cash settlement is the foreign currency cash flow translated at the spot rate plus the local currency cash flow e.g. [-(FC100,000,000 * 11.93%)/(12.6 FC/LC)] + (LC6,329,114 * 5.65%) = -LC589,405.

On 1 January 20X1, Entity A designates the spot element of the cross currency interest rate swap (i.e. excluding the foreign currency basis spread and forward elements) in a cash flow hedge of the variability of the interest and principal cash flows of the FC denominated debt due to changes in the spot rate. Entity A chooses not to apply the treatment in IFRS 9:6.5.15 to the foreign currency basis spread and forward elements of the cross currency swap; consequently, the change in the fair value movement excluded from the hedge relationship is accounted for at FVTPL.

The change in the present value of the spot element of the cross currency interest rate swap is calculated for the purposes of hedge accounting using the spot component cash flows of the hedging instrument. The spot component cash flows can be described as a cross currency swap. This cross currency swap has a foreign currency leg that matches the actual swap and a local currency leg equal to the foreign currency leg translated at the spot rate on 1 January 20X1. The foreign currency spot component cash flows are translated into the local currency at the spot rate on the valuation date and discounted in combination with the local currency spot component cash flows. A non- foreign currency basis adjusted curve is used to discount the spot component cash flows. The present value of the spot element of the cross currency interest rate swap is nil on 1 January 20X1.

Period ended	**Present value gain/ (loss) during period LC '000s**	**Present value before cash settlement LC '000s**	**Cash settlement** LC '000s**	**Present value after cash settlement LC '000s**
31/12/X1	2,352	2,352	(192)	2,160
31/12/X2	1,331	3,491	(291)	3,200
31/12/X3	478	3,678	(330)	3,348
31/12/X4	(1,520)	1,828	(177)	1,651
31/12/X5	(1,273)	378	(378)	0

** The cash settlement is the foreign currency cash flow translated at the spot rate plus the local currency cash flow e.g. [-(FC100,000,000 * 11.93%)/(12.6 FC/LC)] + (LC6,329,114 * 11.93%) = - LC191,762.

In this example, the hypothetical derivative (which is derived from the hedged item) is the same as the spot element of the cross currency interest rate swap. The hedge is 100 per cent effective in each period as the change in the present value of the spot element of the cross currency interest rate swap is equal to the change in the present value of the hypothetical derivative.

The fair value of the cross currency interest rate swap that is excluded from the hedge relationship is calculated as the balancing figure between the full fair value of the swap and the present value of the spot element of the swap calculated above. It is known on the date of designation that the total change in the value of the excluded component over the life of the hedge will be LC1,987,342 (LC6,329,114 * [11.93% – 5.65]% * 5). We have chosen to present this amount as part of interest expense in the illustrative journal entries below.

The following table illustrates the accounting entries for the transaction during its life in LC '000s. Dr or (Cr) as indicated.

Date		Cash	Derivative	Debt	Equity	Interest expense	Translation loss
01/01/X1	Issue debt	6,329		(6,329)			
31/12/X1	Change in fair value of derivative:						
	- spot element		2,352		(2,352)		
	- forward and foreign currency basis spread elements		67			(67)	
	Net settlement of derivative (at spot rate)	589	(589)				
	Accrue interest on debt (at average rate)			(840)		840	
	Retranslate debt to spot			(1,714)			1,714
	Reclassify amounts from equity				1,799	(85)	(1,714)
	Settlement of interest on the debt (at spot rate)	(947)		947			
31/12/X2	Change in fair value of derivative:						
	- spot element		1,331		(1,331)		
	- forward and foreign currency basis spread elements		291			(291)	
	Net settlement of derivatives (at spot rate)	689	(689)				
	Accrue interest on debt (at average rate)			(994)		994	
	Retranslate debt to spot			(888)			888
	Reclassify amounts from equity				1,127	(239)	(888)
	Settlement of interest on the debt (at spot rate)	(1,046)		1,046			
31/12/X3	Change in fair value of derivative:						
	- spot element		478		(478)		
	- forward and foreign currency basis spread element		592			(592)	
	Net settlement of derivative (at spot rate)	727	(727)				
	Accrue interest on debt (at average rate)			(1,065)		1,065	

Date		Cash	Derivative	Debt	Equity	Interest expense	Translation loss
	Retranslate debt to spot			(339)			339
	Reclassify amounts from equity				649	(310)	(339)
	Settlement of interest on the debt (at spot rate)	(1,085)		1,085			
31/12/X4	Change in fair value of derivative: - spot element		(1,520)		1,520		
	- forward and foreign currency basis spread elements		614			(614)	
	Net settlement of derivative (at spot rate)	574	(574)				
	Accrue interest on debt (at average rate)			(1,003)		1,003	
	Retranslate debt to spot			1,349			(1,349)
	Reclassify amounts from equity				(1,101)	(248)	1,349
	Settlement of interest on the debt (at spot rate)	(932)		932			
31/12/X5	Change in fair value of derivative: - spot element		(1,273)		1,273		
	- forward and foreign currency basis spread elements		423			(423)	
	Net settlement of derivative (at spot rate)	438	(438)				
	Accrue interest on debt (at average rate)			(858)		858	
	Retranslate debt to spot			1,209			(1,209)
	Reclassify amounts from equity				(1,106)	(103)	1,209
	Settlement of interest on the debt (at spot rate)	(795)		795			
	Net settlement of derivative (at spot rate)	338	(338)				
	Settlement of debt	(6,667)		6,667			
		(1,788)	0	0	0	1,788	0
Key					A	B	

A Nets to zero reflecting that all amounts in the cash flow hedge reserve in equity have been reclassified to profit or loss to offset the retranslation of debt to the spot rate each period and recognise interest at the hedged rate.

B Reflects the total interest expense from the FC debt and derivative. This amount equals the total interest expense that would have been incurred had the entity issued LC debt paying interest at 11.93% (LC6,329,114 * 11.93% * 5) less the movement in the present value of the excluded element over the life of the hedge (LC1,987,342). Although both elements are known from the inception of the hedge, it is not known in advance what the expense in each period will be.

Journal entries in the financial statements are provided below for illustrative purposes.

1 January 20X1

No entry required for derivative because fair value is nil at inception.

		LC '000s	LC '000s
Dr	Cash	6,329	
Cr	Debt		6,329

To recognise the issue of FC denominated debt (translated at spot).

31 December 20X1

		LC '000s	LC '000s
Dr	Derivative	2,419	
Cr	Equity (cash flow hedge reserve)		2,352
Cr	Interest expense		67

To recognise the change in fair value of the derivative.

		LC '000s	LC '000s
Dr	Cash	589	
Cr	Derivative		589

To recognise the net settlement of interest on the derivative (at the spot rate).

		LC '000s	LC '000s
Dr	Interest expense	840	
Cr	Debt		840

To recognise the accrual of interest on the debt (at the average rate).

		LC'000s	LC '000s
Dr	Translation loss	1,714	
Cr	Debt		1,714

To recognise the loss on retranslation of FC debt (at the year end spot rate).

		LC '000s	LC '000s
Dr	Equity (cash flow hedge reserve)	1,799	
Cr	Interest expense		85
Cr	Translation loss		1,714

To recognise the reclassification from equity to profit or loss.

		LC '000s	LC '000s
Dr	Debt	947	
Cr	Cash		947

To recognise the payment of interest on the debt in cash (at the spot rate).

Similar entries would be recorded for the remaining term of the hedge relationship.

Example 3.5B

Cash flow hedging spot foreign currency risk of issued fixed rate foreign currency debt with a cross currency interest rate swap that receives fixed foreign currency and pays fixed functional currency. The foreign currency basis spread and forward elements of the swap are excluded from the hedge and recognised in OCI and amortised to profit or loss on a rational basis.

Assume the same facts as in **example 3.5A** except that on 1 January 20X1, Entity A designates the spot element of the cross currency interest rate swap (i.e. excluding the foreign currency basis spread and forward elements) in a cash flow hedge of the variability of the interest and principal cash flows of the FC denominated debt due to changes in the spot rate. Entity A chooses to apply the treatment in IFRS 9:6.5.15 to the foreign currency basis spread and forward elements of the cross currency swap; consequently, the change in the fair value movement excluded from the hedge relationship is accumulated in other comprehensive income (OCI) to the extent it relates to the hedged item and is then amortised to the profit or loss on a rational basis.

In this example, the hypothetical derivative (which is derived from the hedged item) is the same as in **example 3.5A** (it is the same as the spot element of the cross currency interest rate swap).

As in **example 3.5A**, the change in the present value of the spot element of the cross currency interest rate swap is calculated for the purposes of hedge accounting using the spot component cash flows of the hedging instrument. The spot component cash flows can be described as a cross currency swap. This cross currency swap has a foreign currency leg that matches the actual swap and a local currency leg equal to the foreign currency leg translated at the spot rate on 1 January 20X1. The foreign currency spot component cash flows are translated into the local currency at the spot rate on the valuation date and discounted in combination with the local currency spot component cash flows. A non- foreign currency basis adjusted curve is used to discount the spot component cash flows. The present value of the spot element of the cross currency interest rate swap is nil on 1 January 20X1.

The hedge is 100 per cent effective and the excluded element of the cross currency swap is equal to the aligned foreign currency basis spread and forward elements. The excluded element of the cross currency interest rate swap is equal to the aligned forward and foreign currency basis spread elements.

The fair value of the cross currency interest rate swap that is excluded from the hedge relationship is calculated as the balancing figure between the full fair value of the swap and the present value of the spot element of the swap. It is known on the date of designation that the total change in the value of the excluded component over the life of the hedge will be LC1,987,342 (LC6,329,114 * [11.93 - 5.65]% * 5). This has been amortised on a straight-line basis to the profit or loss resulting in a reduction in the interest charge of LC397,468.36 in each period. We have chosen to present this amount as part of interest expense in the illustrative journal entries below.

The following table illustrates the accounting entries for the transaction during its life in LC '000s. Dr or (Cr) as indicated.

Date		Cash	Derivative	Debt	Equity	Interest expense	Translation loss
01/01/X1	Issue debt	6,329		(6,329)			
31/12/X1	Change in fair value of derivative:						
	- spot element		2,352		(2,352)		
	- forward and foreign currency basis spread elements		67		(67)		
	Net settlement of derivative (at spot rate)	589	(589)				
	Accrue interest on debt (at average rate)			(840)		840	
	Retranslate debt to spot			(1,714)			1,714
	Reclassify amounts from equity:						
	- cash flow hedge reserve				1,799	(85)	(1,714)
	- separate component of equity				397	(397)	
	Settlement of interest on the debt (at spot rate)	(947)		947			
31/12/X2	Change in fair value of derivative:						
	- spot element		1,331		(1,331)		
	- forward and foreign currency basis spread elements		291		(291)		
	Net settlement of derivatives (at spot rate)	689	(689)				
	Accrue interest on debt (at average rate)			(994)		994	

Date		Cash	Derivative	Debt	Equity	Interest expense	Translation loss
	Retranslate debt to spot			(888)			888
	Reclassify amounts from equity: - cash flow hedge reserve				1,127	(239)	(888)
	- separate component of equity				398	(398)	
	Settlement of interest on the debt (at spot rate)	(1,046)		1,046			
31/12/X3	Change in fair value of derivative: - spot element		478		(478)		
	- forward and foreign currency basis spread element		592		(592)		
	Net settlement of derivative (at spot rate)	727	(727)				
	Accrue interest on debt (at average rate)			(1,065)		1,065	
	Retranslate debt to spot			(339)			339
	Reclassify amounts from equity: - cash flow hedge reserve				649	(310)	(339)
	- separate component of equity				398	(398)	
	Settlement of interest on the debt (at spot rate)	(1,085)		1,085			
31/12/X4	Change in fair value of derivative: - spot element		(1,520)		1,520		
	- forward and foreign currency basis spread elements		614		(614)		
	Net settlement of derivative (at spot rate)	574	(574)				
	Accrue interest on debt (at average rate)			(1,003)		1,003	
	Retranslate debt to spot			1,349			(1,349)
	Reclassify amounts from equity: - cash flow hedge reserve				(1,101)	(248)	1,349
	- separate component of equity				397	(397)	

Date		Cash	Derivative	Debt	Equity	Interest expense	Translation loss
	Settlement of interest on the debt (at spot rate)	(932)		932			
31/12/X5	Change in fair value of derivative: - spot element		(1,273)		1,273		
	- forward and foreign currency basis spread elements		423		(423)		
	Net settlement of derivative (at spot rate)	438	(438)				
	Accrue interest on debt (at average rate)			(858)		858	
	Retranslate debt to spot			1,209			(1,209)
	Reclassify amounts from equity: - cash flow hedge reserve				(1,106)	(103)	1,209
	- separate component of equity				397	(397)	
	Settlement of interest on the debt (at spot rate)	(795)		795			
	Net settlement of derivative (at spot rate)	338	(338)				
	Settlement of debt	(6,667)		6,667			
		(1,788)	0	0	0	1,788	0
Key					A	B	

A Nets to zero reflecting that all amounts in equity have been reclassified to profit or loss either, to offset the retranslation of debt to the spot rate each period and recognise interest at the hedged rate, or through the amortisation of the excluded component on a systematic and rational basis.

B Reflects the total interest expense from the FC debt and derivative. This amount equals the total interest expense that would have been incurred had the entity issued LC debt paying interest at 5.65% (LC6,329,114 * 5.65% * 5). The amount recognised in profit or loss each period is LC357,595 (difference to the numbers in the table is due to rounding).

Journal entries in the financial statements are provided below for illustrative purposes.

1 January 20X1

No entry required for derivative because fair value is nil at inception.

		LC '000s	LC '000s
Dr	Cash	6,329	
Cr	Debt		6,329

To recognise the issue of FC denominated debt (translated at spot).

31 December 20X1

		LC '000s	LC '000s
Dr	Derivative	2,419	
Cr	Equity (cash flow hedge reserve)		2,352
Cr	Equity (separate component of equity)		67

To recognise the change in fair value of the derivative.

		LC '000s	LC '000s
Dr	Cash	589	
Cr	Derivative		589

To recognise the net settlement of interest on the derivative (at the spot rate).

		LC '000s	LC '000s
Dr	Interest expense	840	
Cr	Debt		840

To recognise the accrual of interest on the debt (at the average rate).

		LC'000s	LC '000s
Dr	Translation loss	1,714	
Cr	Debt		1,714

To recognise the loss on retranslation of FC debt (at the year end spot rate).

		LC '000s	LC '000s
Dr	Equity (cash flow hedge reserve)	1,799	
Dr	Equity (separate component of equity)	397	
Cr	Interest expense		482
Cr	Translation loss		1,714

To recognise the reclassification from equity to profit or loss.

	LC '000s	LC '000s
Dr Debt	947	
Cr Cash		947

To recognise the payment of interest on the debt in cash (at the spot rate).

Similar entries would be recorded for the remaining term of the hedge relationship.

3.6 Cash flow hedging foreign currency risk of zero coupon debt

The following two examples illustrate the entries for a cash flow hedge of foreign currency risk on zero coupon debt using a foreign currency forward. In both examples the foreign currency basis spread and forward elements are excluded from the designation of the hedging instrument. In the first example (**example 3.6A**) these excluded elements are recognised directly in profit or loss on a fair value basis. In the second example (**example 3.6B**), the entity has elected, in accordance with IFRS 9:6.5.16 to apply IFRS 9:6.5.15 and recognise the excluded element in OCI (to the extent it relates to the hedged item). Because the hedged item is a time-period related item, the excluded element is amortised from OCI to profit or loss on a rational basis over the period during which the hedge adjustment for the included element could affect profit or loss.

Example 3.6A

Cash flow hedging spot foreign currency risk of issued zero coupon foreign currency debt with a foreign currency forward. The foreign currency basis spread and forward elements of the forward are excluded from the hedge and accounted for at FVTPL.

On 1 January 20X1, Entity A with a local functional currency (LC), issues foreign currency (FC) zero coupon debt that matures on 31 December 20X5. The principal amount of the debt is FC100 million. At 1 January 20X1 the fair value of the debt is FC57,224,312 and so the effective interest rate ('EIR') is 11.81%. The FC:LC spot rate is 15.8:1 on 1 January 20X1.

Period ended	Spot rate FC/LC	Carrying amount of debt before cash settlement FC '000s	Interest accrual in period FC '000s	Interest income (translated at average rate) LC '000s	Gain/ (Loss) on retranslation of debt LC '000s	Carrying amount of debt before cash settlement LC '000s
31/12/X1	12.6	(63,983)	(6,759)	(476)	(980)	(5,078)
31/12/X2	11.4	(71,540)	(7,557)	(630)	(568)	(6,276)
31/12/X3	11	(79,989)	(8,449)	(754)	(242)	(7,272)
31/12/X4	12.8	(89,437)	(9,448)	(794)	1,079	(6,987)
31/12/X5	15	(100,000)	(10,563)	(760)	1,080	(6,667)

On 1 January 20X1, Entity A also enters into a foreign currency forward that matures on 31 December 20X5. Entity A will receive FC100 million and pay LC4,761,905 (on 1 January 20X1 the five year FC:LC forward rate is 21:1). The fair value of the foreign currency forward is nil on 1 January 20X1.

Period ended	**Fair value gain/ (loss) during period LC '000s**	**Fair value of forward before cash settlement LC '000s**
31/12/X1	1,485	1,485
31/12/X2	1,102	2,587
31/12/X3	778	3,365
31/12/X4	(706)	2,659
31/12/X5	(755)	1,904

On 1 January 20X1, Entity A designates the spot element of the foreign currency forward (i.e. excluding the foreign currency basis spread and forward elements) in a cash flow hedge of the variability of the principal cash flow of the FC denominated debt due to changes in the spot rate. Entity A chooses not to apply the treatment in IFRS 9:6.5.15 to the foreign currency basis spread and forward elements of the foreign currency forward; consequently, the change in the fair value movement excluded from the hedge relationship is accounted for at FVTPL.

The change in the present value of the spot element of the foreign currency forward is calculated for the purposes of hedge accounting using the spot component cash flows of the hedging instrument. The spot component cash flows can be described as a forward. This forward has a foreign currency leg that matches the actual forward (i.e. receive FC100 million) and a local currency leg equal to the foreign currency leg translated at the spot rate on 1 January 20X1 (i.e. pay LC6,329,114). The foreign currency spot component cash flows are translated into the local currency at the spot rate on the valuation date and discounted in combination with the local currency spot component cash flows. A non- foreign currency basis adjusted curve is used to discount the spot component cash flows. The present value of the spot element of the foreign currency forward is nil on 1 January 20X1.

Period ended	**Present value gain/ (loss) during period LC '000s**	**Present value before cash settlement LC '000s**
31/12/X1	1,431	1,431
31/12/X2	913	2,344
31/12/X3	354	2,698
31/12/X4	(1,223)	1,475
31/12/X5	(1,137)	338

In this example, the hypothetical derivative (which is derived from the hedged item) is the same as the spot element of the foreign currency forward. The hedge is 100 per cent effective in each period as the change in the present value of the spot element of the foreign currency forward is equal to the change in the present value of the hypothetical derivative.

The fair value of the foreign currency forward that is excluded from the hedge relationship is calculated as the balancing figure between the full fair value of the forward and the present value of the spot element of the forward calculated above. It is known on the date of designation that the total change in the value of the excluded component over the life of the hedge will be LC1,567,209 (FC100,000,000 * [1/15.8 - 1/21]LC/FC). We have chosen to present this amount as part of interest expense in the illustrative journal entries below.

The following table illustrates the accounting entries for the transaction during its life in LC '000s. Dr or (Cr) as indicated.

Date		Cash	Derivative	Debt	Equity	Interest expense	Translation loss
01/01/X1	Issue debt	3,622		(3,622)			
31/12/X1	Change in fair value of derivative:						
	- spot element		1,431		(1,431)		
	- forward and foreign currency basis spread elements		54			(54)	
	Accrue interest on debt (at average rate)			(476)		476	
	Retranslate debt to spot			(980)			980
	Reclassify amounts from equity				1,028	(48)	(980)
31/12/X2	Change in fair value of derivative:						
	- spot element		913		(913)		
	- forward and foreign currency basis spread elements		189			(189)	
	Accrue interest on debt (at average rate)			(630)		630	
	Retranslate debt to spot			(568)			568
	Reclassify amounts from equity				720	(152)	(568)
31/12/X3	Change in fair value of derivative:						
	- spot element		354		(354)		
	- forward and foreign currency basis spread element		424			(424)	
	Accrue interest on debt (at average rate)			(754)		754	
	Retranslate debt to spot			(242)			242

Date		Cash	Derivative	Debt	Equity	Interest expense	Translation loss
	Reclassify amounts from equity				462	(220)	(242)
31/12/X4	Change in fair value of derivative:						
	- spot element		(1,223)		1,223		
	- forward and foreign currency basis spread elements		517			(517)	
	Accrue interest on debt (at average rate)			(794)		794	
	Retranslate debt to spot			1,079			(1,079)
	Reclassify amounts from equity				(883)	(196)	1,079
31/12/X5	Change in fair value of derivative:						
	- spot element		(1,137)		1,137		
	- forward and foreign currency basis spread elements		382			(382)	
	Accrue interest on debt (at average rate)			(760)		760	
	Retranslate debt to spot			1,080			(1,080)
	Reclassify amounts from equity				(989)	(91)	1,080
	Net settlement of derivative (at spot rate)	1,904	(1,904)				
	Settlement of debt (at spot rate)	(6,667)		6,667			
		(1,141)	0	0	0	1,141	0
Key					A	B	

A Nets to zero reflecting that all amounts in the cash flow hedge reserve in equity have been reclassified to profit or loss to offset the retranslation of debt to the spot rate each period and recognise interest at the hedged rate.

B Reflects the total interest expense from the FC debt and derivative. This amount equals the total interest expense that would have been incurred had the entity translated the FC interest accrual at the spot rate on the date of designation throughout the hedge (see table below) less the movement in the present value of the excluded element over the life of the hedge (LC1,567,209). Although both elements are known from the inception of the hedge, it is not known in advance what the expense in each period will be.

Translating the FC carrying amount and interest accrual (EIR 11.81%) at the spot rate on 1 January 20X1 would give the following:

Period ended	Interest accrual in period LC '000s	Carrying amount before cash settlement LC '000s
31/12/X1	(428)	(4,050)
31/12/X2	(478)	(4,528)
31/12/X3	(534)	(5,062)
31/12/X4	(598)	(5,660)
31/12/X5	(669)	(6,329)

Journal entries in the financial statements are provided below for illustrative purposes.

1 January 20X1

No entry required for derivative because fair value is nil at inception.

	LC '000s	LC '000s
Dr Cash	3,622	
Cr Debt		3,622

To recognise the issue of FC denominated debt (translated at spot).

31 December 20X1

	LC '000s	LC '000s
Dr Derivative	1,485	
Cr Equity (cash flow hedge reserve)		1,431
Cr Interest expense		54

To recognise the change in fair value of the derivative.

	LC '000s	LC '000s
Dr Interest expense	476	
Cr Debt		476

To recognise the accrual interest on the debt (at the average rate).

	LC '000s	LC '000s
Dr Translation loss	980	
Cr Debt		980

To recognise the loss on retranslation of FC debt (at the year end spot rate).

	LC '000s	LC '000s
Dr Equity (cash flow hedge reserve)	1,028	
Cr Interest expense		48
Cr Translation loss		980

To recognise the reclassification from equity to profit or loss.

Similar entries would be recorded for the remaining term of the hedge relationship.

Example 3.6B

Cash flow hedging spot foreign currency risk of issued zero coupon foreign currency debt with a foreign currency forward to buy foreign currency and sell functional currency. The foreign currency basis spread and forward elements of the forward are excluded from the hedge and recognised in OCI and amortised to profit or loss on a rational basis.

Assume the same facts as in **example 3.6A** except that Entity A chooses to apply the treatment in IFRS 9:6.5.15 to the foreign currency basis spread and forward elements of the foreign currency forward; consequently, the change in the fair value movement excluded from the hedge relationship is accumulated in other comprehensive income (OCI) to the extent it relates to the hedged item and is then amortised to the profit or loss on a rational basis.

In this example, the hypothetical derivative (which is derived from the hedged item) is the same as in **example 3.6A** (it is the same as the spot element of the foreign currency forward).

As in **example 3.6A**, the change in the present value of the spot element of the foreign currency forward is calculated for the purposes of hedge accounting using the spot component cash flows of the hedging instrument. The spot component cash flows can be described as a forward. This forward has a foreign currency leg that matches the actual forward (i.e. receive FC100 million) and a local currency leg equal to the foreign currency leg translated at the spot rate on 1 January 20X1 (i.e. pay LC6,329,114). The foreign currency spot component cash flows are translated into the local currency at the spot rate on the valuation date and discounted in combination with the local currency spot component cash flows. A non- foreign currency basis adjusted curve is used to discount the spot component cash flows. The present value of the spot element of the foreign currency forward is nil on 1 January 20X1.

The hedge is 100 per cent effective and the excluded element of the foreign currency forward is equal to the aligned foreign currency basis spread and forward elements. The excluded element of the foreign currency forward is equal to the aligned forward and foreign currency basis spread elements.

The fair value of the foreign currency forward that is excluded from the hedge relationship is calculated as the balancing figure between the full fair value of the forward and the present value of the spot element of the forward. It is known on the date of designation that the total change in the value of the excluded component over the life of the hedge will be LC1,567,209 (FC100,000,000 * [1/15.8 – 1/21]LC/FC). This has been amortised to the P&L on a rational basis that achieves a constant rate of interest on the synthetic LC debt throughout the term of the hedge of 5.63%. We have chosen to present this amount as part of interest expense in the illustrative journal entries below.

The following table illustrates the accounting entries for the transaction during its life in LC '000s. Dr or (Cr) as indicated.

Date		Cash	Derivative	Debt	Equity	Interest expense	Translation loss
01/01/X1	Issue debt	3,622		(3,622)			
31/12/X1	Change in fair value of derivative:						
	- spot element		1,431		(1,431)		
	- forward and foreign currency basis spread elements		54		(54)		
	Accrue interest on debt (at average rate)			(476)		476	
	Retranslate debt to spot			(980)			980
	Reclassify amounts from equity:						
	- cash flow hedge reserve				1,028	(48)	(980)
	- separate component of equity				224	(224)	
31/12/X2	Change in fair value of derivative:						
	- spot element		913		(913)		
	- forward and foreign currency basis spread elements		189		(189)		
	Accrue interest on debt (at average rate)			(630)		630	
	Retranslate debt to spot			(568)			568
	Reclassify amounts from equity:						
	- cash flow hedge reserve				720	(152)	(568)
	- separate component of equity				262	(262)	
31/12/X3	Change in fair value of derivative:						
	- spot element		354		(354)		
	- forward and foreign currency basis spread element		424		(424)		
	Accrue interest on debt (at average rate)			(754)		754	
	Retranslate debt to spot			(242)			242
	Reclassify amounts from equity:						
	- cash flow hedge reserve				462	(220)	(242)
	- separate component of equity				307	(307)	

Date		Cash	Derivative	Debt	Equity	Interest expense	Translation loss
31/12/X4	Change in fair value of derivative:						
	- spot element		(1,223)		1,223		
	- forward and foreign currency basis spread elements		517		(517)		
	Accrue interest on debt (at average rate)			(794)		794	
	Retranslate debt to spot			1,079			(1,079)
	Reclassify amounts from equity:						
	- cash flow hedge reserve				(883)	(196)	1,079
	- separate component of equity				358	(358)	
31/12/X5	Change in fair value of derivative:						
	- spot element		(1,137)		1,137		
	- forward and foreign currency basis spread elements		382		(382)		
	Accrue interest on debt (at average rate)			(760)		760	
	Retranslate debt to spot			1,080			(1,080)
	Reclassify amounts from equity:						
	- cash flow hedge reserve				(989)	(91)	1,080
	- separate component of equity				415	(415)	
	Net settlement of derivative (at spot rate)	1,904	(1,904)				
	Settlement of debt (at spot rate)	(6,667)		6,667			
		(1,141)	0	0	0	1,141	0
Key					**A**	**B**	

A Nets to zero reflecting that all amounts in equity have been reclassified to profit or loss either, to offset the retranslation of debt to the spot rate each period and recognise interest at the hedged rate, or through the amortisation of the excluded component on a systematic and rational basis.

B Reflects the total interest expense from the FC debt and derivative. This amount equals the total interest expense that would have been incurred had the entity issued LC zero coupon debt (see table below).

Had Entity A issued zero coupon LC debt with notional of LC4,761,905 (EIR 5.63%) the carrying amount and interest accrual would have been as follows:

Period ended	Interest accrual in period LC '000s	Carrying amount before cash settlement LC '000s
31/12/X1	(204)	(3,825)
31/12/X2	(216)	(4,041)
31/12/X3	(227)	(4,268)
31/12/X4	(240)	(4,508)
31/12/X5	(254)	(4,762)

Journal entries in the financial statements are provided below for illustrative purposes.

1 January 20X1

No entry required for derivative because fair value is nil at inception.

		LC '000s	LC '000s
Dr	Cash	3,622	
Cr	Debt		3,622

To recognise the issue of FC denominated debt (translated at spot).

31 December 20X1

		LC '000s	LC '000s
Dr	Derivative	1,485	
Cr	Equity (cash flow hedge reserve)		1,431
Cr	Equity (separate component of equity)		54

To recognise the change in fair value of the derivative.

		LC '000s	LC '000s
Dr	Interest expense	476	
Cr	Debt		476

To recognise the accrual interest on the debt (at the average rate).

		LC '000s	LC '000s
Dr	Translation loss	980	
Cr	Debt		980

To recognise the loss on retranslation of FC debt (at the year end spot rate).

		LC '000s	LC '000s
Dr	Equity (cash flow hedge reserve)	1,028	
Dr	Equity (separate component of equity)	224	
Cr	Interest expense		272
Cr	Translation loss		980

To recognise the reclassification from equity to profit or loss.

Similar entries would be recorded for the remaining term of the hedge relationship.

3.7 Cash flow hedging foreign currency risk of the principal only of interest-bearing debt

The following example illustrates the entries for a cash flow hedge of foreign currency risk on the principal only of interest-bearing debt using a foreign currency forward. In this example the foreign currency basis spread and forward elements are excluded from the designation of the hedging instrument. The entity has elected, in accordance with IFRS 9:6.5.16 to apply IFRS 9:6.5.15 and recognise the excluded element in OCI (to the extent it relates to the hedged item). Because the hedged item is a period related item, it is amortised to profit or loss on a rational basis over the period during which the hedge adjustment for the included element could affect profit or loss.

Example 3.7

Cash flow hedging spot foreign currency risk of the principal only of issued interest-bearing foreign currency debt with a foreign currency forward. The foreign currency basis spread and forward elements of the forward are excluded from the hedge and recognised in OCI and amortised to profit or loss on a rational basis.

On 1 January 20X1, Entity A with a local functional currency (LC), issues foreign currency (FC) fixed rate debt that matures on 31 December 20X5. The principal amount of the debt is FC100 million and interest of 11.93% is paid annually in arrears. At 1 January 20X1 the FC:LC spot rate is 15.8:1 and so the principal is equivalent to LC6,329,114.

Period ended	Spot rate FC/ LC	Interest accrual in period FC '000s	Interest income (translated at average rate) LC '000s	Gain/ (Loss) on retranslation of debt LC '000s	Carrying amount of debt before cash settlement LC '000s	Cash settlement (translated at spot rate) LC '000s	Carrying amount of debt after cash settlement LC '000s
31/12/X1	12.6	(11,930)	(840)	(1,714)	(8,883)	947	(7,936)
31/12/X2	11.4	(11,930)	(994)	(888)	(9,818)	1,046	(8,772)
31/12/X3	11	(11,930)	(1,065)	(339)	(10,176)	1,085	(9,091)
31/12/X4	12.8	(11,930)	(1,003)	1,349	(8,745)	932	(7,813)
31/12/X5	15	(11,930)	(858)	1,209	(7,462)	7,462	0

On 1 January 20X1, Entity A also enters into a foreign currency forward that matures on 31 December 20X5. Entity A will receive FC100 million and pay LC4,761,905 (on 1 January 20X1 the five year FC:LC forward rate is 21:1). The fair value of the foreign currency forward is nil on 1 January 20X1.

Period ended	Fair value gain/ (loss) during period LC '000s	Fair value of forward before cash settlement LC '000s
31/12/X1	1,485	1,485
31/12/X2	1,102	2,587
31/12/X3	778	3,365
31/12/X4	(706)	2,659
31/12/X5	(755)	1,904

On 1 January 20X1, Entity A designates the spot element of the foreign currency forward (i.e. excluding the foreign currency basis spread and forward elements) in a cash flow hedge of the variability of the principal cash flow of the FC denominated debt due to changes in the spot rate. Entity A chooses to apply the treatment in IFRS 9:6.5.15 to the foreign currency basis spread and forward elements of the foreign currency forward; consequently, the change in the fair value movement excluded from the hedge relationship is accumulated in other comprehensive income (OCI) to the extent it relates to the hedged item and is then amortised to the profit or loss on a rational basis.

The change in the present value of the spot element of the foreign currency forward is calculated for the purposes of hedge accounting using the spot component cash flows of the hedging instrument. The spot component cash flows can be described as a forward. This forward has a foreign currency leg that matches the actual forward (i.e. receive FC100 million) and a local currency leg equal to the foreign currency leg translated at the spot rate on 1 January 20X1 (i.e. pay LC6,329,114). The foreign currency spot component cash flows are translated into the local currency at the spot rate on the valuation date and discounted in combination with the local currency spot component cash flows. A non- foreign currency basis adjusted curve is used to discount the spot component cash flows. The present value of the spot element of the foreign currency forward is nil on 1 January 20X1.

Period ended	Present value gain/ (loss) during period LC '000s	Present value before cash settlement LC '000s
31/12/X1	1,431	1,431
31/12/X2	913	2,344
31/12/X3	354	2,698
31/12/X4	(1,223)	1,475
31/12/X5	(1,137)	338

In this example, the hypothetical derivative (which is derived from the hedged item) is the same as the spot element of the foreign currency forward. The hedge is 100 per cent effective in each period as the change in the present value of the spot element of the foreign currency forward is equal to the change in the present value of the hypothetical derivative. The excluded element of the foreign currency forward is equal to the aligned foreign currency basis spread and forward elements.

The fair value of the foreign currency forward that is excluded from the hedge relationship is calculated as the balancing figure between the full fair value of the forward and the present value of the spot element of the forward calculated above. It is known on the date of designation that the total change in the value of the excluded component over the life of the hedge will be LC1,567,209 (FC100,000,000 * [1/15.8 - 1/21]LC/FC). This has been amortised to the P&L on a rational basis that achieves a constant rate of interest on the synthetic LC debt throughout the term of the hedge of 5.63%. We have chosen to present this amount as part of interest expense in the illustrative journal entries below.

The following table illustrates the accounting entries for the transaction during its life in LC '000s. Dr or (Cr) as indicated.

Date		Cash	Derivative	Debt	Equity	Interest expense	Translation loss
01/01/X1	Issue debt	6,329		(6,329)			
31/12/X1	Change in fair value of derivative:						
	- spot element		1,431		(1,431)		
	- forward and foreign currency basis spread elements		54		(54)		
	Accrue interest on debt (at average rate)			(840)		840	
	Retranslate debt to spot			(1,714)			1,714
	Reclassify amounts from equity:						
	- cash flow hedge reserve				1,028	(48)	(980)
	- separate component of equity				224	(224)	
	Settlement of interest on the debt (at spot rate)	(947)		947			
31/12/X2	Change in fair value of derivative:						
	- spot element		913		(913)		
	- forward and foreign currency basis spread elements		189		(189)		
	Accrue interest on debt (at average rate)			(994)		994	
	Retranslate debt to spot			(888)			888
	Reclassify amounts from equity:						
	- cash flow hedge reserve				720	(152)	(568)
	- separate component of equity				262	(262)	
	Settlement of interest on the debt (at spot rate)	(1,046)		1,046			

Date		Cash	Derivative	Debt	Equity	Interest expense	Translation loss
31/12/X3	Change in fair value of derivative:						
	- spot element		354		(354)		
	- forward and foreign currency basis spread element		424		(424)		
	Accrue interest on debt (at average rate)			(1,065)		1,065	
	Retranslate debt to spot			(339)			339
	Reclassify amounts from equity:						
	- cash flow hedge reserve				462	(220)	(242)
	- separate component of equity				307	(307)	
	Settlement of interest on the debt (at spot rate)	(1,085)		1,085			
31/12/X4	Change in fair value of derivative:						
	- spot element		(1,223)		1,223		
	- forward and foreign currency basis spread elements		517		(517)		
	Accrue interest on debt (at average rate)			(1,003)		1,003	
	Retranslate debt to spot			1,349			(1,349)
	Reclassify amounts from equity:						
	- cash flow hedge reserve				(883)	(196)	1,079
	- separate component of equity				358	(358)	
	Settlement of interest on the debt (at spot rate)	(932)		932			
31/12/X5	Change in fair value of derivative:						
	- spot element		(1,137)		1,137		
	- forward and foreign currency basis spread elements		382		(382)		
	Accrue interest on debt (at average rate)			(858)		858	
	Retranslate debt to spot			1,209			(1,209)
	Reclassify amounts from equity:						
	- cash flow hedge reserve				(989)	(91)	1,080

Date		Cash	Derivative	Debt	Equity	Interest expense	Translation loss
	- separate component of equity				415	(415)	
	Settlement of interest on the debt (at spot rate)	(795)		795			
	Net settlement of derivative (at spot rate)	1,904	(1,904)				
	Settlement of debt (at spot rate)	(6,667)		6,667			
		(3,239)	0	0	0	2,487	752
Key					A	B	C

A Nets to zero reflecting that all amounts in equity have been reclassified to profit or loss either, to offset the retranslation of the principal only portion of debt to the spot rate each period and recognise interest at the hedged rate, or through the amortisation of the excluded component on a systematic and rational basis.

B Reflects the total interest expense from the FC debt and derivative. This amount equals the total interest expense that would have been incurred had the entity issued LC zero coupon debt with notional of LC4,761,561 (see **example 3.6B**) and a FC interest strip paying FC11,930,000 in each period.

C Reflects the retranslation of the interest only portion of the debt to spot each period.

Because Entity A only hedged the principal amount of the FC denominated debt this is equivalent to hedging a FC zero coupon bond with the same maturity and so the amounts reclassified from equity in this example are the same as those in **example 3.6B**.

Journal entries in the financial statements are provided below for illustrative purposes.

1 January 20X1

No entry required for derivative because fair value is nil at inception.

		LC '000s	LC '000s
Dr	Cash	6,329	
Cr	Debt		6,329

To recognise the issue of FC denominated debt (translated at spot).

31 December 20X1

		LC '000s	LC '000s
Dr	Derivative	1,485	
Cr	Equity (cash flow hedge reserve)		1,431
Cr	Equity (separate component of equity)		54

To recognise the change in fair value of the derivative.

		LC '000s	LC '000s
Dr	Interest expense	840	
Cr	Debt		840

To recognise the accrual interest on the debt (at the average rate).

		LC '000s	LC '000s
Dr	Translation loss	1,714	
Cr	Debt		1,714

To recognise the loss on retranslation of FC debt (at the year end spot rate).

		LC '000s	LC '000s
Dr	Equity (cash flow hedge reserve)	1,028	
Dr	Equity (separate component of equity)	224	
Cr	Interest expense		272
Cr	Translation loss		980

To recognise the appropriate reclassification from equity to profit or loss.

		LC '000s	LC '000s
Dr	Debt	947	
Cr	Cash		947

To recognise the payment of interest on the debt in cash (at the spot rate).

Similar entries would be recorded for the remaining term of the hedge relationship.

4 Net investment hedges

The following net investment hedges are illustrated in this section.

Section 4.1 Net investment hedging spot foreign currency risk using a foreign currency forward

Section 4.2 Net investment hedging forward foreign currency risk using a foreign currency forward

Section 4.3 Net investment hedging spot foreign currency risk using a floating - floating cross currency interest rate swap

Section 4.4 Net investment hedging spot foreign currency risk using a fixed – fixed cross currency interest rate swap

Section 4.5 Net investment hedging forward foreign currency risk using a fixed – fixed cross currency interest rate swap

4.1 Net investment hedging spot foreign currency risk using a foreign currency forward

The following two examples illustrate the entries for a net investment hedge of spot foreign currency risk using a foreign currency forward. In the first example (**example 4.1A**) the foreign currency forward is designated as a hedging instrument in its entirety and the foreign currency basis and the forward element of the foreign currency forward give rise to ineffectiveness. In the second example (**example 4.1B**) the entity has excluded the foreign currency basis and forward elements from the designation and has elected, in accordance with IFRS 9:6.5.16 to apply IFRS 9:6.5.15 and recognise the excluded elements in OCI (to the extent it relates to the hedged item). Because the hedged item is a period related item, the excluded element is amortised from OCI to profit or loss on a rational basis over the period during which the hedge adjustment for the included element could affect profit or loss.

Example 4.1A

Net investment hedging spot foreign currency risk with a foreign currency forward to buy functional currency and sell foreign currency. The foreign currency basis spread and forward elements of the forward are not excluded from the hedge.

On 1 January 20X1, Entity A with a local functional currency (LC), acquires a foreign subsidiary with a foreign functional currency (FC). Entity A will be subject to foreign currency risk (between FC and LC) on retranslation of the net investment in the consolidated financial statements. At 1 January 20X1 the FC:LC spot rate is 15.8:1 and the net assets of the subsidiary are FC200 million.

Period ended	Spot rate (FC/LC)	Total net assets FC '000s
31/12/X1	12.6	210,000
31/12/X2	11.4	190,000
31/12/X3	11	150,000
31/12/X4	12.8	140,000
31/12/X5	15	125,000

On 1 January 20X1, Entity A also enters into a foreign currency forward that matures on 31 December 20X5. Entity A will receive LC4,761,905 and pay FC100 million (on 1 January 20X1 the five year FC:LC forward rate is 21:1). The fair value of the foreign currency forward is nil on 1 January 20X1.

Period ended	Fair value gain/ (loss) during period LC '000s	Fair value of forward before cash settlement LC '000s
31/12/X1	(1,485)	(1,485)
31/12/X2	(1,102)	(2,587)
31/12/X3	(778)	(3,365)
31/12/X4	706	(2,659)
31/12/X5	755	(1,904)

On 1 January 20X1, Entity A designates the foreign currency forward in a net investment hedge of the foreign exchange translation risk on the first FC100 million of the net assets of the foreign subsidiary associated with movements in the spot rate. Entity A does not exclude the foreign currency basis spread and forward elements from the designation which gives rise to ineffectiveness.

Period ended	Retranslation gain/ (loss) on hedged net assets during period LC '000s	Carrying amount of hedged net assets LC '000s
31/12/X1	1,608	7,937
31/12/X2	835	8,772
31/12/X3	319	9,091
31/12/X4	(1,278)	7,813
31/12/X5	(1,146)	6,667

Entity A designates the undiscounted spot component of these net assets as the hedged item.

Period ended	Cumulative fair value gain/ (loss) hedging instrument LC '000s	Cumulative retranslation gain/(loss) on net assets LC '000s	Cumulative ineffectiveness* LC '000s	Ineffectiveness during the period LC '000s
31/12/X1	(1,485)	1,608	0	0
31/12/X2	(2,587)	2,443	(144)	(144)
31/12/X3	(3,365)	2,762	(603)	(459)
31/12/X4	(2,659)	1,484	(1,175)	(716)
31/12/X5	(1,904)	338	(1,566)	(850)

* If the cumulative fair value gain or loss on the hedging instrument is less than that on the retranslation of the hedged net assets (i.e. there is an under-hedge), the cumulative ineffectiveness will be nil.

The following table illustrates the accounting entries for the transaction during its life in LC '000s. Dr or (Cr) as indicated. For illustrative purposes only, the entries have recognised only FC100 million of net assets and not the actual net assets. IAS 21 *The Effects of Foreign Exchange Rates* would require the retranslation of all net assets of the foreign operation.

Date		Cash	Derivative	Consolidated net assets	Equity	Profit or loss
31/12/X1	Retranslate net assets to spot			1,608	(1,608)	
	Change in fair value of derivative		(1,485)		1,485	
31/12/X2	Retranslate net assets to spot			835	(835)	
	Change in fair value of derivative		(1,102)		958	144
31/12/X3	Retranslate net assets to spot			319	(319)	
	Change in fair value of derivative		(778)		319	459
31/12/X4	Retranslate net assets to spot			(1,278)	1,278	
	Change in fair value of derivative		706		(1,278)	572
31/12/X5	Retranslate debt to spot			(1,146)	1,146	
	Change in fair value of derivative		755		(1,146)	391
	Net settlement of derivative (at spot rate)	(1,904)	1,904			
		(1,904)	0	338	0	1,566
Key				**A**	**B**	**C**

A Reflects the retranslation of the hedged portion of the net assets of the subsidiary, which is equal to the movement in the spot element of the foreign currency forward over the life of the hedge.

B Nets to zero reflecting that all amounts remaining in the net investment hedge reserve in equity are offset by the spot retranslation of the hedged net assets of the subsidiary.

C Reflects the change in present value of the foreign currency basis spread and forward elements of the foreign currency forward over the life of the hedge. The total amount, LC1,567,209.16 (FC100,000,000 * [1/15.8 – 1/21]LC/FC) is known at the date of designation (difference to the number in the table is due to rounding). Although known from the inception of the hedge, it is not known in advance what the expense in each period will be.

Journal entries in the financial statements are provided below for illustrative purposes.

1 January 20X1

No entry required for derivative because fair value is nil at inception.

31 December 20X1

		LC '000s	LC '000s
Dr	Consolidated net assets	1,608	
Cr	Equity		1,608

To recognise the gain on retranslation of the net assets of the subsidiary (at the year end spot rate).

		LC '000s	LC '000s
Dr	Equity	1,485	
Cr	Derivative		1,485

To recognise the change in fair value of the derivative.

Similar entries would be recorded for the remaining term of the hedge relationship.

On 31 December 20X5, Entity A disposes of its entire interest in the foreign subsidiary for LC8.75 million (LC7 million for the hedged portion of net assets). The following journals are required in respect of the hedged portion of the net assets; additional journals (not shown below) would be necessary in respect of the disposal of the unhedged portion.

		LC '000s	LC '000s
Dr	Cash	7,000	
Dr	Equity	338	
Cr	Profit or loss		671
Cr	Consolidated net assets		6,667

To recognise the sale proceeds and profit on disposal.

		LC '000s	LC '000s
Dr	Profit or loss	338	
Cr	Equity		338

To recognise the reclassification from equity to profit or loss.

The total, post hedge, profit on disposal for the hedged portion of net assets is LC333,333 (LC7,000,000 – LC6,666,667).

It is assumed for the purposes of illustration that the total net assets of the foreign operation are unaffected by the application of the IFRS 5 *Non-current Assets Held for Sale and Discontinued Operations* to the disposal group, i.e. the carrying amount of the net assets is lower than the fair value less costs to sell.

Example 4.1B

Net investment hedging spot foreign currency risk with a foreign currency forward to buy functional currency and sell foreign currency. The foreign currency basis spread and forward elements of the forward are excluded from the hedge and recognised in OCI and amortised to profit or loss on a rational basis.

Assume the same facts as in **example 4.1A** except that on 1 January 20X1, Entity A designates the spot element of the foreign currency forward (i.e. excluding the foreign currency basis spread and forward elements) in a net investment hedge of the foreign exchange translation risk on the first FC100 million of the net assets of the foreign subsidiary associated with movements in the spot rate. Entity A designates the discounted spot component of these net assets as the hedged item. Entity A chooses to apply the treatment in IFRS 9:6.5.15 to the foreign currency basis spread and forward elements of the foreign currency forward; accordingly, the change in the fair value movement excluded from the hedge relationship is accumulated in other comprehensive income (OCI) to the extent it relates to the hedged item and is then amortised to the profit or loss on a rational basis.

The change in the present value of the spot element of the foreign currency forward is calculated for the purposes of hedge accounting using the spot component cash flows of the hedging instrument. The spot component cash flows can be described as a forward. This forward has a foreign currency leg that matches the actual forward (i.e. pay FC100 million) and a local currency leg equal to the foreign currency leg translated at the spot rate on 1 January 20X1 (i.e. receive LC6,329,114). The foreign currency spot component cash flows are translated into the local currency at the spot rate on the valuation date and discounted in combination with the local currency spot component cash flows. A non- foreign currency basis adjusted curve is used to discount the spot component cash flows. The present value of the spot element of the foreign currency forward is nil on 1 January 20X1.

Period ended	**Present value gain/ (loss) during period LC '000s**	**Present value before cash settlement LC '000s**
31/12/X1	(1,431)	(1,431)
31/12/X2	(913)	(2,344)
31/12/X3	(354)	(2,698)
31/12/X4	1,223	(1,475)
31/12/X5	1,137	(338)

In this example, the hypothetical derivative (which is derived from the hedged item) is the same as the spot element of the foreign currency forward. The hedge is 100 per cent effective in each period because the change in the present value of the spot element of the foreign currency forward is equal to the change in the present value of the hypothetical derivative. The excluded element of the foreign currency forward is equal to the aligned foreign currency basis spread and forward elements.

The fair value of the foreign currency forward that is excluded from the hedge relationship is calculated as the balancing figure between the full fair value of the forward and the present value of the spot element of the forward calculated above. It is known on the date of designation that the total change in the value of the excluded component over the life of the hedge will be LC1,567,209 (FC100,000,000 * [1/15.8 – 1/21]LC/FC). This has been amortised on a straight-line basis to the profit or loss resulting in a charge of LC313,442 in each period.

The following table illustrates the accounting entries for the transaction during its life in LC '000s. Dr or (Cr) as indicated. For illustrative purposes only, the entries have recognised only FC100 million of net assets and not the actual net assets. IAS 21 *The Effects of Foreign Exchange Rates* would require the retranslation of all net assets of the foreign operation.

Date		Cash	Derivative	Consolidated net assets	Equity	Profit or loss
31/12/X1	Retranslate net assets to spot			1,608	(1,608)	
	Change in fair value of derivative:					
	- spot element		(1,431)		1,431	
	- forward and foreign currency basis spread elements		(54)		54	
	Reclassify amounts from equity				(313)	313
31/12/X2	Retranslate net assets to spot			835	(835)	
	Change in fair value of derivative:					
	- spot element		(913)		913	
	- forward and foreign currency basis spread elements		(189)		189	
	Reclassify amounts from equity				(313)	313
31/12/X3	Retranslate net assets to spot			319	(319)	
	Change in fair value of derivative:					
	- spot element		(354)		354	
	- forward and foreign currency basis spread element		(424)		424	
	Reclassify amounts from equity				(313)	313
31/12/X4	Retranslate net assets to spot			(1,278)	1,278	
	Change in fair value of derivative:					
	- spot element		1,223		(1,223)	
	- forward and foreign currency basis spread elements		(517)		517	
	Reclassify amounts from equity				(313)	313
31/12/X5	Retranslate debt to spot			(1,146)	1,146	
31/12/X5	Change in fair value of derivative:					
	- spot element		1,137		(1,137)	
	- forward and foreign currency basis spread elements		(382)		382	
	Reclassify amounts from equity				(314)	314

Date		Cash	Derivative	Consolidated net assets	Equity	Profit or loss
	Net settlement of derivative (at spot rate)	(1,904)	1,904			
		(1,904)	0	338	0	1,566
Key				A	B	C

A Reflects the retranslation of the hedged portion of the net assets of the subsidiary, which is equal to the movement in the spot element of the foreign currency forward over the life of the hedge.

B Nets to zero reflecting that all amounts remaining in the net investment hedge reserve in equity are offset by the spot retranslation of the hedged net assets of the subsidiary.

C Reflects the change in present value of the foreign currency basis spread and forward elements of the foreign currency forward over the life of the hedge. The total amount, LC1,567,209, is known at the date of designation. The amount recognised in profit or loss each period is LC313,442 (difference to the numbers in the table is due to rounding).

Journal entries in the financial statements are provided below for illustrative purposes.

1 January 20X1

No entry required for derivative because fair value is nil at inception.

31 December 20X1

		LC '000s	LC '000s
Dr	Consolidated net assets	1,608	
Cr	Equity		1,608

To recognise the gain on retranslation of the net assets of the subsidiary (at the year end spot rate).

		LC '000s	LC '000s
Dr	Equity	1,431	
Dr	Equity (separate component of equity)	54	
Cr	Derivative		1,485

To recognise the change in fair value of the derivative.

		LC '000s	LC '000s
Dr	Profit or loss	313	
Cr	Equity (separate component of equity)		313

To recognise the appropriate reclassification from equity to profit or loss.

Similar entries would be recorded for the remaining term of the hedge relationship.

On 31 December 20X5, Entity A disposes of its entire interest in the foreign subsidiary for LC8.75 million (LC7 million for the hedged portion of net assets). The following journals are required in respect of the hedged portion of the net assets; additional journals (not shown below) would be necessary in respect of the disposal of the unhedged portion.

The total, post hedge, profit on disposal for the hedged portion of net assets is LC333,333 (LC7,000,000 – LC6,666,667). It is assumed for the purposes of illustration that the total net assets of the foreign operation are unaffected by the application of the IFRS 5 *Non-current Assets Held for Sale and Discontinued Operations* to the disposal group, i.e. that no adjustment is required to reduce the carrying amount of the net assets to fair value less costs to sell.

		LC '000s	LC '000s
Dr	Cash	7,000	
Dr	Equity	338	
Cr	Profit or loss		671
Cr	Consolidated net assets		6,667

To recognise the sale proceeds and profit on disposal.

		LC '000s	LC '000s
Dr	Profit or loss	338	
Cr	Equity		338

To recognise the reclassification from equity to profit or loss.

The total, post hedge, profit on disposal for the hedged portion of net assets is LC333,333 (LC7,000,000 - LC6,666,667).

It is assumed for the purposes of illustration that the total net assets of the foreign operation are unaffected by the application of the IFRS 5 *Non-current Assets Held for Sale and Discontinued Operations* to the disposal group, i.e. the carrying amount of the net assets is lower than the fair value less costs to sell.

4.2 Net investment hedging forward foreign currency risk using a foreign currency forward

The following example illustrates the entries for a net investment hedge of forward foreign currency risk using a foreign currency forward. In this example the foreign currency basis spread element is excluded from the designation of the hedging instrument. The entity has elected, in accordance with IFRS 9:6.5.16 to apply IFRS 9:6.5.15 and recognise the excluded element in OCI (to the extent it relates to the hedged item). Because the hedged item is a period related item, the excluded element is amortised from OCI to profit or loss on a rational basis over the period during which the hedge adjustment for the included element could affect profit or loss.

Example 4.2

Net investment hedging forward foreign currency risk with a foreign currency forward to buy functional currency and sell foreign currency. The foreign currency basis spread element of the forward is excluded from the hedge and recognised in OCI and amortised to profit or loss on a rational basis.

Assume the same facts as in **example 4.1A** except that on 1 January 20X1, Entity A designates the foreign currency forward excluding the foreign currency basis spread element in a net investment hedge of the foreign exchange translation risk on the first FC100 million of the net assets of the foreign subsidiary associated with movements in the forward rate. Entity A designates the forward component of these net assets as the hedged item (the forward component relates to the life of the hedge). Entity A chooses to apply the treatment in IFRS 9:6.5.15 to the foreign currency basis spread element of the foreign currency forward; accordingly, the change in the fair value movement excluded from the hedge relationship is accumulated in other comprehensive income (OCI) to the extent it relates to the hedged item and is then amortised to the profit or loss on a rational basis.

The change in the present value of the foreign currency forward excluding the foreign currency basis spread element is calculated for the purposes of hedge accounting by applying non-currency basis adjusted discount curves to cash flows of a forward with a foreign currency leg that matches the actual forward (i.e. pay FC100 million) and a local currency leg that brings the present value calculated using non-currency basis adjusted curves to nil on 1 January 20X1 (i.e. receive LC4,847,310).

Period ended	Present value gain/ (loss) during period LC '000s	Fair value before cash settlement LC '000s
31/12/X1	(1,510)	(1,510)
31/12/X2	(1,069)	(2,579)
31/12/X3	(743)	(3,322)
31/12/X4	736	(2,586)
31/12/X5	767	(1,819)

In this example, the hypothetical derivative (which is derived from the hedged item) is the same as the foreign currency forward excluding the foreign currency basis spread element. The hedge is 100 per cent effective in each period as the change in the present value of the foreign currency forward excluding the foreign currency basis spread element is equal to the change in the present value of the hypothetical derivative. The excluded element of the foreign currency forward is equal to the aligned foreign currency basis spread element.

The fair value of the foreign currency forward that is excluded from the hedge relationship is calculated as the balancing figure between the full fair value of the forward and the present value of the forward excluding the foreign currency basis spread element calculated above. It is known on the date of designation that the total change in the value of the excluded component over the life of the hedge will be LC85,405 (LC4,847,310 – LC4,761,905). This has been amortised on a straight-line basis to the profit or loss resulting in a charge of LC17,081 in each period.

The following table illustrates the accounting entries for the transaction during its life in LC '000s. Dr or (Cr) as indicated. For illustrative purposes only, the entries have recognised only FC100 million of net assets and not the actual net assets. IAS 21 *The Effects of Foreign Exchange Rates* would require the retranslation of all net assets of the foreign operation.

Date		**Cash**	**Derivative**	**Consolidated net assets**	**Equity**	**Profit or loss**
31/12/X1	Retranslate net assets to spot			1,608	(1,608)	
	Change in fair value of derivative:					
	- excl. foreign currency basis spread element		(1,510)		1,510	
	- foreign currency basis spread element		25		(25)	
	Reclassify amounts from equity				(17)	17
31/12/X2	Retranslate net assets to spot			835	(835)	
	Change in fair value of derivative:					
	- excl. foreign currency basis spread element		(1,069)		1,069	
	- foreign currency basis spread element		(33)		33	
	Reclassify amounts from equity				(17)	17
31/12/X3	Retranslate net assets to spot			319	(319)	
	Change in fair value of derivative:					
	- excl. foreign currency basis spread element		(742)		742	
	- foreign currency basis spread element		(36)		36	
	Reclassify amounts from equity				(17)	17
31/12/X4	Retranslate net assets to spot			(1,278)	1,278	
	Change in fair value of derivative:					
	- excl. foreign currency basis spread element		736		(736)	

Date		Cash	Derivative	Consolidated net assets	Equity	Profit or loss
	- foreign currency basis spread element		(30)		30	
	Reclassify amounts from equity				(17)	17
31/12/X5	Retranslate net assets to spot			(1,146)	1,146	
	Change in fair value of derivative:					
	- excl. foreign currency basis spread element		766		(766)	
	- foreign currency basis spread element		(11)		11	
	Reclassify amounts from equity				(17)	17
	Net settlement of derivative (at spot rate)	(1,904)	1,904			
		(1,904)	0	338	1,481	85
Key				A	B	C

A Reflects the retranslation of the hedged portion of the net assets of the subsidiary, which is equal to the movement in the spot element of the foreign currency forward over the life of the hedge.

B Reflects the change in present value of the forward element of the foreign currency forward over the life of the hedge. The movement in the forward element of the foreign currency forward is not offset by the spot retranslation of the hedged net assets of the subsidiary. The total amount, LC1,481,804 (LC6,329,114 – LC4,847,310), is known at the date of designation (difference to the numbers in the table is due to rounding).

C Reflects the change in present value of the foreign currency basis spread element of the foreign currency forward over the life of the hedge. The total amount, LC85,405, is known at the date of designation (difference to the numbers in the table is due to rounding). The amount recognised in profit or loss each period is LC17,081.

Journal entries in the financial statements are provided below for illustrative purposes.

1 January 20X1

No entry required for derivative because fair value is nil at inception.

31 December 20X1

		LC '000s	LC '000s
Dr	Consolidated net assets	1,608	
Cr	Equity		1,608

To recognise the gain on retranslation of the net assets of the subsidiary (at the year end spot rate).

		LC '000s	LC '000s
Dr	Equity	1,510	
Cr	Equity (separate component of equity)		25
Cr	Derivative		1,485

To recognise the change in fair value of the derivative.

		LC '000s	LC '000s
Dr	Profit or loss	17	
Cr	Equity (separate component of equity)		17

To recognise the appropriate reclassification from equity to profit or loss.

Similar entries would be recorded for the remaining term of the hedge relationship.

On 31 December 20X5, Entity A disposes of its entire interest in the foreign subsidiary for LC 8.75 million (LC7 million for the hedged portion of net assets) the following journals would be required in relation to the hedged portion of the net assets; additional journals (not shown below) would be necessary in relation to the disposal of the unhedged portion.

		LC '000s	LC '000s
Dr	Cash	7,000	
Dr	Equity	338	
Cr	Profit or loss		671
Cr	Consolidated net assets		6,667

To recognise the sale proceeds and profit on disposal.

		LC '000s	LC '000s
Dr	Profit or loss	1,819	
Cr	Equity		1,819

To recognise the reclassification from equity to profit or loss.

The total, post hedge, loss on disposal for the hedged portion of net assets is LC1,148,471 (LC6,666,667 – LC7,000,000 + LC1,481,804).

Compared to **examples 4.1** and **4.1B** above, the profit/(loss) on disposal is LC1,481,804 less because in those examples the fair value of the forward points were recognised in profit or loss throughout the life of the hedge relationship.

It is assumed for the purposes of illustration that the total net assets of the foreign operation are unaffected by the application of the IFRS 5 *Non-current Assets Held for Sale and Discontinued Operations* to the disposal group, i.e. the carrying amount of the net assets is lower than the fair value less costs to sell.

4.3 Net investment hedging spot foreign currency risk using a floating – floating cross currency interest rate swap

The following example illustrates the entries for a net investment hedge of spot foreign currency risk using a floating – floating cross currency interest rate swap. In this example the foreign currency basis spread element is excluded from the designation of the hedging instrument. The entity has elected, in accordance with IFRS 9:6.5.16 to apply IFRS 9:6.5.15 and recognise the excluded element in OCI (to the extent it relates to the hedged item). Because the hedged item is a period related item, it is amortised to profit or loss on a rational basis over the period during which the hedge adjustment for the included element could affect profit or loss.

Example 4.3

Net investment hedging spot foreign currency risk with a cross currency interest rate swap that receives floating functional currency and pays floating foreign currency. The foreign currency basis spread element of the swap is excluded from the hedge and recognised in OCI and amortised to profit or loss on a rational basis.

On 1 January 20X1, Entity A with a local functional currency (LC), acquires a foreign subsidiary with a foreign currency (FC) functional currency. Entity A will be subject to foreign currency risk (between FC and LC) on retranslation of the net investment in the consolidated financial statements. At 1 January 20X1 the FC:LC spot rate is 15.8:1 and the net assets of the subsidiary are FC200 million.

Period ended	Spot rate (FC/LC)	Total net assets FC '000s
31/12/X1	12.6	210,000
31/12/X2	11.4	190,000
31/12/X3	11	150,000
31/12/X4	12.8	140,000
31/12/X5	15	125,000

On 1 January 20X1, Entity A also enters into a floating – floating cross currency interest rate swap that matures on 31 December 20X5. Entity A will receive LC LIBOR -35 bps interest on LC6,329,114 and pay FC LIBOR interest on FC100 million. Interest will be exchanged annually in arrears and principal amounts will also be exchanged at maturity. The fair value of the cross currency interest rate swap is nil on 1 January 20X1.

Period ended	LC LIBOR at start of period	FC LIBOR at start of period	Fair value gain/ (loss) during period LC '000s	Fair value of swap before cash settlement LC '000s	Cash settlement* LC '000s	Fair value of swap after cash settlement LC '000s
31/12/X1	5.13	12.26	(2,225)	(2,225)	670	(1,555)
31/12/X2	0.59	7.47	(1,498)	(3,053)	640	(2,413)
31/12/X3	0.55	6.51	(922)	(3,335)	579	(2,756)
31/12/X4	0.60	5.49	851	(1,905)	413	(1,492)
31/12/X5	0.56	5.49	801	(691)	691	0

* The cash settlement is the foreign currency cash flow translated at the spot rate plus the local currency cash flow e.g.[(FC100,000,000 * 12.26%) / (12.6 FC/LC)] – [LC6,329,114 * (5.13 – 0.35)%] = LC670,484.

On 1 January 20X1, Entity A designates the cross currency interest rate swap excluding the foreign currency basis spread element in a net investment hedge of the foreign exchange translation risk on the first FC100 million of the net assets of the foreign subsidiary associated with movements in the spot rate.

Period ended	Retranslation gain on hedged net assets in period LC '000s	Carrying amount of hedged net assets LC '000s
31/12/X1	1,608	7,937
31/12/X2	835	8,772
31/12/X3	319	9,091
31/12/X4	(1,278)	7,813
31/12/X5	(1,146)	6,667

Entity A designates the discounted spot component of these net assets as the hedged item (the net assets are discounted over the life of the hedge). Entity A chooses to apply the treatment in IFRS 9:6.5.15 to the foreign currency basis spread element of the cross currency swap; accordingly, the change in the fair value movement excluded from the hedge relationship is accumulated in other comprehensive income (OCI) to the extent it relates to the hedged item and is then amortised to the profit or loss on a rational basis.

The change in the present value of the cross currency interest rate swap excluding the foreign currency basis spread element is calculated for the purposes of hedge accounting by applying non-currency basis adjusted discount curves to cash flows of a swap with a foreign currency leg that matches the foreign currency leg of the actual swap and a local currency leg equal to the local currency leg of the actual swap excluding the spread of -35 bps. The present value of the foreign currency interest rate swap excluding the foreign currency basis spread is nil on 1 January 20X1.

Period ended	Present value gain/ (loss) during period LC '000s	Present value before cash settlement LC '000s	Cash settlement** LC '000s	Present value after cash settlement LC '000s
31/12/X1	(2,256)	(2,256)	648	(1,608)
31/12/X2	(1,453)	(3,061)	618	(2,443)
31/12/X3	(876)	(3,319)	557	(2,762)
31/12/X4	887	(1,875)	391	(1,484)
31/12/X5	816	(668)	668	0

** The cash settlement is the foreign currency cash flow translated at the spot rate plus the local currency cash flow e.g. [(FC100,000,000 * 12.26%) / (12.6 FC/LC)] – (LC6,329,114 * 5.13%) = LC648,332.

The fair value of the cross currency swap is impacted by the fixing of the FC and LC LIBOR payments at the start of each period. This gives rise to ineffectiveness equal to the cash settlement of the interest payments on the spot component of the cross currency swap in each period. The excluded element of the cross currency swap is equal to the aligned foreign currency basis spread element.

The fair value of the cross currency interest rate swap that is excluded from the hedge relationship is calculated as the balancing figure between the full fair value of the swap and the present value of the swap excluding the foreign currency basis spread element calculated above. It is known on the date of designation that the total change in the value of the excluded component over the life of the hedge will be LC110,760 (LC6,329,114 * 0.35% * 5). This has been amortised on a straight-line basis to the profit or loss resulting in an additional charge of LC22,152 in each period.

The following table illustrates the accounting entries for the transaction during its life in LC '000s. Dr or (Cr) as indicated. For illustrative purposes only, the entries have recognised only FC100 million of net assets and not the actual net assets. IAS 21 *The Effects of Foreign Exchange Rates* would require the retranslation of all net assets of the foreign operation.

Date		Cash	Derivative	Consolidated net assets	Equity	Profit or loss
31/12/X1	Retranslate net assets to spot			1,608	(1,608)	
	Change in fair value of derivative:					
	- excl. foreign currency basis spread element		(2,256)		1,608	648
	- foreign currency basis spread element		31		(31)	
	Net settlement of derivative (at spot rate)	(670)	670			
	Reclassify amounts from equity				(22)	22

Date		Cash	Derivative	Consolidated net assets	Equity	Profit or loss
31/12/X2	Retranslate net assets to spot			835	(835)	
	Change in fair value of derivative - excl. foreign currency basis spread element		(1,453)		835	618
	- foreign currency basis spread element		(45)		45	
	Net settlement of derivative (at spot rate)	(640)	640			
	Reclassify amounts from equity				(22)	22
31/12/X3	Retranslate net assets to spot			319	(319)	
	Change in fair value of derivative: - excl. foreign currency basis spread element		(876)		319	557
	- foreign currency basis spread element		(46)		46	
	Net settlement of derivative (at spot rate)	(579)	579			
	Reclassify amounts from equity				(22)	22
31/12/X4	Retranslate net assets to spot			(1,278)	1,278	
	Change in fair value of derivative: - excl. foreign currency basis spread element		887		(1,278)	391
	- foreign currency basis spread element		(36)		36	
	Net settlement of derivative (at spot rate)	(413)	413			
	Reclassify amounts from equity				(22)	22
31/12/X5	Retranslate net assets to spot			(1,146)	1,146	
	Change in fair value of derivative: - excl. foreign currency basis spread element		815		(1,146)	331
	- foreign currency basis spread element		(14)		14	

Date		Cash	Derivative	Consolidated net assets	Equity	Profit or loss
	Net settlement of derivative (at spot rate)	(353)	353			
	Net settlement of derivative (at spot rate)	(338)	338			
	Reclassify amounts from equity				(22)	22
		(2,993)	0	338	0	2,655
Key				A	B	C

A Reflects the retranslation of the hedged portion of the net assets of the subsidiary.

B Nets to zero reflecting that all amounts remaining in the net investment hedge reserve in equity are offset by the spot retranslation of the hedged net assets of the subsidiary.

C Reflects the change in present value of the foreign currency basis spread element of the cross currency swap over the life of the hedge plus the ineffectiveness due to the accrual of interest. The total amount recognised in profit or loss each period is equal to the cash settlement of interest payments on the swap.

Journal entries in the financial statements are provided below for illustrative purposes.

1 January 20X1

No entry required for derivative because fair value is nil at inception.

31 December 20X1

		LC '000s	LC '000s
Dr	Consolidated net assets	1,608	
Cr	Equity		1,608

To recognise the gain on retranslation of the net assets of the subsidiary (at the year end spot rate)

		LC '000s	LC '000s
Dr	Profit or loss	648	
Dr	Equity	1,608	
Cr	Equity (separate component of equity)		31
Cr	Derivative		2,225

To recognise the change in fair value of the derivative.

		LC '000s	LC '000s
Dr	Derivative	670	
Cr	Cash		670

To recognise the net settlement of interest on the derivative (at the spot rate).

	LC '000s	LC '000s
Dr Profit or loss	22	
Cr Equity (separate component of equity)		22

To recognise the appropriate reclassification from equity to profit or loss.

Similar entries would be recorded for the remaining term of the hedge relationship.

4.4 Net investment hedging spot foreign currency risk using a fixed – fixed cross currency interest rate swap

The following example illustrates the entries for a net investment hedge of spot foreign currency risk using a fixed – fixed cross currency interest rate swap. In this example the foreign currency basis spread and forward elements are excluded from the designation of the hedging instrument. The entity has elected, in accordance with IFRS 9:6.5.16 to apply IFRS 9:6.5.15 and recognise the excluded elements in OCI (to the extent it relates to the hedged item). Because the hedged item is a period related item, it is amortised to profit or loss on a rational basis over the period during which the hedge adjustment for the included element could affect profit or loss.

Example 4.4

Net investment hedging spot foreign currency risk with a cross currency interest rate swap that receives fixed functional currency and pays fixed foreign currency. The net assets hedged are equal to the foreign currency principal cash flow of the cross currency swap. The foreign currency basis spread and forward elements of the swap are excluded from the hedge and recognised in OCI and amortised to profit or loss on a rational basis.

On 1 January 20X1, Entity A with a local functional currency (LC), acquires a foreign subsidiary with a foreign currency (FC) functional currency. Entity A will be subject to foreign currency risk (between FC and LC) on retranslation of the net investment in the consolidated financial statements. At 1 January 20X1, the FC:LC spot rate is 15.8:1 and the net assets of the subsidiary are FC200 million.

Period ended	Spot rate (FC/LC)	Total net assets FC '000s
31/12/X1	12.6	210,000
31/12/X2	11.4	190,000
31/12/X3	11	150,000
31/12/X4	12.8	140,000
31/12/X5	15	125,000

On 1 January 20X1, Entity A also enters into a fixed-fixed cross currency interest rate swap that matures on 31 December 20X5. Entity A will receive 5.65 per cent (this includes a foreign currency basis spread of -35 bps) interest on LC6,329,114 and pay 11.93 per cent interest on FC100 million. Interest will be exchanged annually in arrears and principal amounts will also be exchanged at maturity. The fair value of the cross currency interest rate swap is nil on 1 January 20X1.

Period ended	LC LIBOR at start of period	FC LIBOR at start of period	Fair value gain/ (loss) during period	Fair value of swap before cash settlement	Cash settlement*	Fair value of swap after cash settlement
			LC '000s	LC '000s	LC '000s	LC '000s
31/12/X1	5.13	12.26	(2,419)	(2,419)	589	(1,830)
31/12/X2	0.59	7.47	(1,622)	(3,452)	689	(2,763)
31/12/X3	0.55	6.51	(1,070)	(3,833)	727	(3,106)
31/12/X4	0.60	5.49	906	(2,200)	574	(1,626)
31/12/X5	0.56	5.49	850	(776)	776	0

* The cash settlement is the foreign currency cash flow translated at the spot rate plus the local currency cash flow e.g. [(FC100,000,000 * 11.93%) / (12.6 FC/LC)] – (LC6,329,114 * 5.65%) = LC589,405.

On 1 January 20X1, Entity A designates the spot element of the cross currency interest rate swap (i.e. excluding the foreign currency basis spread and forward elements) in a net investment hedge of the foreign exchange translation risk on the first FC100 million of the net assets of the foreign subsidiary associated with movements in the spot rate.

Period ended	Retranslation gain on hedged net assets in period	Carrying amount of hedged net assets
	LC '000s	LC '000s
31/12/X1	1,608	7,937
31/12/X2	835	8,772
31/12/X3	319	9,091
31/12/X4	(1,278)	7,813
31/12/X5	(1,146)	6,667

Entity A designates the discounted spot component of these net assets as the hedged item (the net assets are discounted over the life of the hedge). Entity A chooses to apply the treatment in IFRS 9:6.5.15 to the foreign currency basis spread and forward elements of the cross currency swap; accordingly, the change in the fair value movement excluded from the hedge relationship is accumulated in other comprehensive income (OCI) to the extent that it relates to the hedged item and is then amortised to the profit or loss on a rational basis.

The change in the present value of the spot element of the cross currency interest rate swap is calculated for the purposes of hedge accounting using the spot component cash flows of the hedging instrument. The spot component cash flows can be described as a forward (i.e. the principal exchange corresponds to the spot element and the interest cash flows correspond to the forward and the foreign currency basis spread elements).This forward has a foreign currency leg that matches the foreign currency principal cash flow of the actual swap and a local currency leg equal to the foreign currency leg translated at the spot rate on 1 January 20X1 (i.e. receive LC6,329,114). The foreign currency spot component cash flows are translated into the local currency at the spot rate on the valuation date and discounted in combination with the local currency spot component cash flows. A non-foreign currency basis adjusted curve is used to discount the spot component cash flows. The present value of the spot element of the cross currency interest rate swap is nil on 1 January 20X1.

Period ended	Present value gain/ (loss) during period LC '000s	Present value before cash settlement LC '000s
31/12/X1	(1,431)	(1,431)
31/12/X2	(913)	(2,344)
31/12/X3	(354)	(2,698)
31/12/X4	1,223	(1,475)
31/12/X5	1,137	(338)

In this example, the hypothetical derivative (which is derived from the hedged item) is the same as the spot element of the cross currency interest rate swap. The hedge is 100 per cent effective in each period because the change in the present value of the spot element of the cross currency interest rate swap is equal to the change in the present value of the hypothetical derivative. The excluded element of the cross currency swap is equal to the aligned foreign currency basis spread and forward elements.

The fair value of the cross currency interest rate swap that is excluded from the hedge relationship is calculated as the balancing figure between the full fair value of the swap and the present value of the spot element of the swap calculated above. It is known on the date of designation that the total change in the value of the excluded component over the life of the hedge will be FC59,650,000 (FC100,000,000 * 11.93% * 5) translated at the average of the closing rates less LC1,787,975 (LC6,329,114 * 5.65% * 5). These two separate amounts have been amortised on a straight-line basis to the profit or loss in the currency in which they are denominated (the foreign currency amount translated at the spot rate at the end of each period), resulting in a charge equal to the cash settlements on the swap.

The following table illustrates the accounting entries for the transaction during its life in LC '000s. Dr or (Cr) as indicated. For illustrative purposes only, the entries have recognised only FC100 million of net assets and not the actual net assets. IAS 21 *The Effects of Foreign Exchange Rates* would require the retranslation of all net assets of the foreign operation.

Date		Cash	Derivative	Consolidated net assets	Equity	Profit or loss
31/12/X1	Retranslate net assets to spot			1,608	(1,608)	
	Change in fair value of derivative:					
	- spot element		(1,431)		1,431	
	- foreign currency basis spread element		(988)		988	
	Net settlement of derivative (at spot rate)	(589)	589			
	Reclassify amounts from equity				(589)	589
31/12/X2	Retranslate net assets to spot			835	(835)	
	Change in fair value of derivative:					
	- spot element		(913)		913	
	- foreign currency basis spread element		(709)		709	
	Net settlement of derivative (at spot rate)	(689)	689			
	Reclassify amounts from equity				(689)	689
31/12/X3	Retranslate net assets to spot			319	(319)	
	Change in fair value of derivative:					
	- spot element		(354)		354	
	- foreign currency basis spread element		(716)		716	
	Net settlement of derivative (at spot rate)	(727)	727			
	Reclassify amounts from equity				(727)	727
31/12/X4	Retranslate net assets to spot			(1,278)	1,278	
	Change in fair value of derivative:					
	- spot element		1,223		(1,223)	
	- foreign currency basis spread element		(317)		317	
	Net settlement of derivative (at spot rate)	(574)	574			
	Reclassify amounts from equity				(574)	574

Date		Cash	Derivative	Consolidated net assets	Equity	Profit or loss
31/12/X5	Retranslate net assets to spot			(1,146)	1,146	
	Change in fair value of derivative:					
	- spot element		1,137		(1,137)	
	- foreign currency basis spread element		(287)		287	
	Net settlement of derivative (at spot rate)	(438)	438			
	Reclassify amounts from equity				(438)	438
	Net settlement of derivative (at spot rate)	(338)	338			
		(3,355)	0	338	0	3,017
Key				A	B	C

A Reflects the retranslation of the hedged portion of the net assets of the subsidiary, which is equal to the movement in the spot element of the cross currency swap over the life of the hedge.

B Nets to zero reflecting that all amounts remaining in the net investment hedge reserve in equity are offset by the spot retranslation of the hedged net assets of the subsidiary.

C Reflects the change in present value of the foreign currency basis spread and forward elements of the cross currency swap over the life of the hedge. The total amount, LC3,017,252 ([FC100,000,000 * 11.93% * (1/12.6 + 1/11.4 + 1/11 + 1/12.8 + 1/15)LC/FC] + [LC6,239,114 * 5.65% * 5]), is not known in local currency at the date of designation because it is partially fixed in foreign currency rather than local currency. The amount recognised in profit or loss each period is equal to the cash settlement of interest payments on the swap.

Journal entries in the financial statements are provided below for illustrative purposes.

1 January 20X1

No entry required for derivative because fair value is nil at inception.

31 December 20X1

		LC '000s	LC '000s
Dr	Consolidated net assets	1,608	
Cr	Equity		1,608

To recognise the gain on retranslation of the net assets of the subsidiary (at the year end spot rate).

		LC '000s	LC '000s
Dr	Equity	1,431	
Dr	Equity (separate component of equity)	988	
Cr	Derivative		2,419

To recognise the change in fair value of the derivative.

		LC '000s	LC '000s
Dr	Derivative	589	
Cr	Cash		589

To recognise the net settlement of interest on the derivative (at the spot rate).

		LC '000s	LC '000s
Dr	Profit or loss	589	
Cr	Equity (separate component of equity)		589

To recognise the appropriate reclassification from equity to profit or loss.

Similar entries would be recorded for the remaining term of the hedge relationship.

4.5 Net investment hedging forward foreign currency risk using a fixed – fixed cross currency interest rate swap

The following two examples illustrate the entries for a net investment hedge of forward foreign currency risk using a fixed - fixed cross currency interest rate swap. In both examples the entity has excluded foreign currency basis spread element of the swap and elected, in accordance with IFRS 9:6.5.16 to apply IFRS 9:6.5.15 and recognise the excluded element in OCI (to the extent it relates to the hedged item). In the first example (**example 4.5A**) the net assets designated equal to foreign currency principal cash flow of the cross currency swap and the settlements of the swap are recorded in profit or loss. In the second example (**example 4.5B**) the net assets designated are equal to the future foreign currency cash flows of the cross currency swap. Because the hedged item is a period related item, it is amortised to profit or loss on a rational basis over the period during which the hedge adjustment for the included element could affect profit or loss. This has the result that the interest settlements are recognised in other comprehensive income.

Example 4.5A

Net investment hedging forward foreign currency risk with a cross currency interest rate swap that receives fixed functional currency and pays fixed foreign currency. The net assets hedged are equal to the foreign currency principal cash flow of the cross currency swap. The foreign currency basis spread element of the swap is excluded from the hedge and recognised in OCI and amortised to profit or loss on a rational basis.

Assume the same facts as in **example 4.4** except that on 1 January 20X1, Entity A designates the cross currency interest rate swap excluding the foreign currency basis spread element, in a net investment hedge of the foreign exchange translation risk on the first FC100 million of the net assets of the foreign subsidiary associated with movements in the forward rate.

Period ended	Retranslation gain on hedged net assets in period FC '000s	Carrying amount of hedged net assets FC '000s
31/12/X1	1,608	7,937
31/12/X2	835	8,772
31/12/X3	319	9,091
31/12/X4	(1,278)	7,813
31/12/X5	(1,146)	6,667

Entity A designates the forward component of these net assets as the hedged item (the forward component relates to the life of the hedge). Entity A chooses to apply the treatment in IFRS 9:6.5.15 to the foreign currency basis spread element of the cross currency swap; accordingly, the change in the fair value movement excluded from the hedge relationship is accumulated in other comprehensive income (OCI) to the extent that it relates to the hedged item and is then amortised to the profit or loss on a rational basis.

The change in the present value of the cross currency interest rate swap excluding the foreign currency basis spread element is calculated for the purposes of hedge accounting by applying non-currency basis adjusted discount curves to cash flows of a swap with a foreign currency leg that matches the foreign currency leg of actual swap and a local currency leg equal to the local currency leg of the actual swap excluding the spread of -35 bps. The present value of the foreign currency interest rate swap excluding the foreign currency basis spread is nil on 1 January 20X1.

Period ended	Cash settlement* LC '000s	Present value after cash settlement LC '000s	Present value change during period LC '000s
31/12/X1	567	(1,891)	(1,891)
31/12/X2	667	(2,800)	(909)
31/12/X3	705	(3,114)	(314)
31/12/X4	552	(1,618)	1,496
31/12/X5	753	0	1,618

* The cash settlement is the foreign currency cash flow translated at the spot rate plus the local currency cash flow e.g. [(FC100,000,000 * 11.93%)/(12.6 FC/LC)] – [LC6,329,114 * (5.65 + 0.35)%] = LC567,079.

In this example, the hypothetical derivative (which is derived from the hedged item) is the same as the cross currency interest rate swap excluding the foreign currency basis spread element. The hedge is 100 per cent effective in each period because the change in the present value of the cross currency interest rate swap excluding the foreign currency basis spread element is equal to the change in the present value of the hypothetical derivative. The excluded element of the cross currency swap is equal to the aligned foreign currency basis spread element.

The fair value of the cross currency interest rate swap that is excluded from the hedge relationship is calculated as the balancing figure between the full fair value of the swap and the present value of the cross currency interest rate swap excluding the foreign currency basis spread element calculated above. It is known on the date of designation that the total change in the value after cash settlements of the excluded component over the life of the hedge will be nil and so no amortisation is necessary.

The following table illustrates the accounting entries for the transaction during its life in LC '000s. Dr or (Cr) as indicated. For illustrative purposes only, the entries have recognised only FC100 million of net assets and not the actual net assets. IAS 21 *The Effects of Foreign Exchange Rates* would require the retranslation of all net assets of the foreign operation.

Date		Cash	Derivative	Consolidated net assets	Equity	Profit or loss
31/12/X1	Retranslate net assets to spot			1,608	(1,608)	
	Change in fair value of derivative:					
	- excl. foreign currency basis spread element		(1,891)		1,891	
	- foreign currency basis spread element		61		(61)	
	Net settlement of derivative (at spot rate)	(589)				589
31/12/X2	Retranslate net assets to spot			835	(835)	
	Change in fair value of derivative:					
	- excl. foreign currency basis spread element		(909)		909	
	- foreign currency basis spread element		(24)		24	
	Net settlement of derivative (at spot rate)	(689)				689
31/12/X3	Retranslate net assets to spot			319	(319)	
	Change in fair value of derivative:					

Date		Cash	Derivative	Consolidated net assets	Equity	Profit or loss
	- excl. foreign currency basis spread element		(314)		314	
	- foreign currency basis spread element		(29)		29	
	Net settlement of derivative (at spot rate)	(727)				727
31/12/X4	Retranslate net assets to spot			(1,278)	1,278	
	Change in fair value of derivative:					
	- excl. foreign currency basis spread element		1,496		(1,496)	
	- foreign currency basis spread element		(16)		16	
	Net settlement of derivative (at spot rate)	(574)				574
31/12/X5	Retranslate net assets to spot			(1,146)	1,146	
	Change in fair value of derivative:					
	- excl. foreign currency basis spread element		1,280		(1,280)	
	- foreign currency basis spread element		8		(8)	
	Net settlement of derivative (at spot rate)	(438)				438
	Net settlement of derivative (at spot rate)	(338)	338			
		(3,355)	0	338	0	3,017
Key				A	B	C

A Reflects the retranslation of the hedged portion of the net assets of the subsidiary, which is equal to the movement in the spot element of the cross currency swap over the life of the hedge.

B Nets to zero reflecting that all amounts remaining in the net investment hedge reserve in equity are offset by the spot retranslation of the hedged net assets of the subsidiary.

C The amount recognised in profit or loss each period is equal to the cash settlement of interest payments on the swap.

Journal entries in the financial statements are provided below for illustrative purposes.

1 January 20X1

No entry required for derivative because fair value is nil at inception.

31 December 20X1

		LC '000s	LC '000s
Dr	Consolidated net assets	1,608	
Cr	Equity		1,608

To recognise the gain on retranslation of the net assets of the subsidiary (at the year end spot rate).

		LC '000s	LC '000s
Dr	Equity	1,891	
Dr	Equity (separate component of equity)		61
Cr	Derivative		1,830

To recognise the change in fair value of the derivative.

		LC '000s	LC '000s
Dr	Profit or loss	589	
Cr	Cash		589

To recognise the net settlement of interest on the derivative (at the spot rate).

Similar entries would be recorded for the remaining term of the hedge relationship.

Example 4.5B

Net investment hedging forward foreign currency risk with a cross currency interest rate swap that receives fixed functional currency and pays fixed foreign currency. The net assets hedged are equal to the foreign currency interest and principal cash flows of the cross currency swap. The foreign currency basis spread element of the swap is excluded from the hedge and recognised in OCI and amortised to profit or loss on a rational basis.

Assume the same facts as in **example 4.4** except that on 1 January 20X1, Entity A designates the cross currency interest rate swap excluding the foreign currency basis spread element in a net investment hedge of the foreign exchange translation risk on a portion of the net assets of the foreign subsidiary associated with movements in the forward rate. The portion of the net assets hedged is equal to the future FC (i.e. both interest and principal) cash flows on the cross currency swap. The portion of the net assets designated decreases at each settlement date as follows.

Period ended	Hedged net assets FC '000s	Opening carrying amount of hedged net assets FC '000s	Retranslation gain on hedged net assets in period FC '000s	Closing carrying amount of hedged net assets FC '000s
31/12/X1	159,650	10,104	2,566	12,670
31/12/X2	147,720	11,724	1,234	12,958
31/12/X3	135,790	11,911	433	12,344
31/12/X4	123,860	11,260	(1,583)	9,677
31/12/X5	111,930	8,745	(1,283)	7,462

Entity A designates the forward component of these net assets as the hedged item (the forward component relates to the life of the hedge). Entity A chooses to apply the treatment in IFRS 9:6.5.15 to the foreign currency basis spread element of the cross currency swap; accordingly, the change in the fair value movement excluded from the hedge relationship is accumulated in other comprehensive income (OCI) to the extent that it relates to the hedged item and is then amortised to the profit or loss on a rational basis.

The change in the present value of the cross currency interest rate swap excluding the foreign currency basis spread element is calculated for the purposes of hedge accounting by applying non-currency basis adjusted discount curves to cash flows of a swap with a foreign currency leg that matches the foreign currency leg of actual swap and a local currency leg equal to the local currency leg of the actual swap excluding the spread of -35 bps. The present value of the foreign currency interest rate swap excluding the foreign currency basis spread is nil on 1 January 20X1.

Period ended	Present value gain/ (loss) during period LC '000s	Present value before cash settlement LC '000s	Cash settlement* LC '000s	Present value after cash settlement LC '000s
31/12/X1	(2,458)	(2,458)	567	(1,891)
31/12/X2	(1,576)	(3,467)	667	(2,800)
31/12/X3	(1,019)	(3,819)	705	(3,114)
31/12/X4	944	(2,170)	552	(1,618)
31/12/X5	865	(753)	753	0

* The cash settlement is the foreign currency cash flow translated at the spot rate plus the local currency cash flow e.g. [(FC100,000,000 * 11.93%) / (12.6 FC/LC)] – [LC6,329,114 * (5.65 + 0.35)%] = LC567,079.

In this example, the hypothetical derivative (which is derived from the hedged item) is same as the cross currency interest rate swap excluding the foreign currency basis spread element. The hedge is 100 per cent effective in each period because the change in the present value of the cross currency interest rate swap excluding the foreign currency basis spread element is equal to the change in the present value of the hypothetical derivative. The excluded element of the cross currency swap is equal to the aligned foreign currency basis spread element.

The fair value of the cross currency interest rate swap that is excluded from the hedge relationship is calculated as the balancing figure between the full fair value of the swap and the present value of the spot element of the swap calculated above. It is known on the date of designation that the total change in the value of the excluded component over the life of the hedge will be LC110,760 (LC6,329,114 * 0.35% * 5). This has been amortised on a straight line basis to the profit or loss resulting in a charge of LC22,152 in each period.

The following table illustrates the accounting entries for the transaction during its life in LC '000s. Dr or (Cr) as indicated. For illustrative purposes only, the entries have recognised only FC100 million of net assets and not the actual net assets. IAS 21 *The Effects of Foreign Exchange Rates* would require the retranslation of all net assets of the foreign operation.

Date		Cash	Derivative	Consolidated net assets	Equity	Profit or loss
31/12/X1	Retranslate net assets to spot			2,566	(2,566)	
	Change in fair value of derivative:					
	- spot element		(2,352)		2,352	
	- foreign currency basis spread element		(67)		67	
	Net settlement of derivative (at spot rate)	(589)	589			
	Reclassify amounts from equity				(22)	22
31/12/X2	Retranslate net assets to spot			1,234	(1,234)	
	Change in fair value of derivative:					
	- spot element		(1,331)		1,331	
	- foreign currency basis spread element		(291)		291	
	Net settlement of derivative (at spot rate)	(689)	689			
	Reclassify amounts from equity				(22)	22
31/12/X3	Retranslate net assets to spot			433	(433)	
	Change in fair value of derivative:					
	- spot element		(478)		478	
	- foreign currency basis spread element		(592)		592	

Date		Cash	Derivative	Consolidated net assets	Equity	Profit or loss
	Net settlement of derivative (at spot rate)	(727)	727			
	Reclassify amounts from equity				(22)	22
31/12/X4	Retranslate net assets to spot			(1,583)	1,583	
	Change in fair value of derivative:					
	- spot element		1,520		(1,520)	
	- foreign currency basis spread element		(614)		614	
	Net settlement of derivative (at spot rate)	(574)	574			
	Reclassify amounts from equity				(22)	22
31/12/X5	Retranslate net assets to spot			(1,283)	1,283	
	Change in fair value of derivative:					
	- spot element		1,273		(1,273)	
	- foreign currency basis spread element		(423)		423	
	Net settlement of derivative (at spot rate)	(438)	438			
	Reclassify amounts from equity				(22)	22
	Net settlement of derivative (at spot rate)	(338)	338			
		(3,355)	0	1,367	1,878	110
Key				A	B	C

A Reflects the retranslation of the hedged portion of the net assets of the subsidiary, which is equal to the movement in the spot element of the cross currency swap over the life of the hedge.

B Reflects the change in present value of the forward element of the cross currency swap over the life of the hedge. The movement in the forward element of the cross currency swap is not offset by the spot retranslation of the hedged net assets of the subsidiary. The total amount, LC1,876,582 (LC6,329,114 * [11.93 – 6]% * 5), is known at the date of designation (difference to the number in the table is due to rounding).

C Reflects the change in present value of the foreign currency basis spread element of the cross currency swap over the life of the hedge. The total amount, LC110,760, is known at the date of designation (difference to the number in the table is due to rounding). The amount recognised in profit or loss each period is LC22,132.

Journal entries in the financial statements are provided below for illustrative purposes.

1 January 20X1

No entry required for derivative because fair value is nil at inception.

31 December 20X1

		LC '000s	LC '000s
Dr	Consolidated net assets	2,566	
Cr	Equity		2,566

To recognise the gain on retranslation of the net assets of the subsidiary (at the year end spot rate).

		LC '000s	LC '000s
Dr	Equity	2,352	
Dr	Equity (separate component of equity)	67	
Cr	Derivative		2,419

To recognise the change in fair value of the derivative.

		LC '000s	LC '000s
Dr	Derivative	589	
Cr	Cash		589

To recognise the net settlement of interest on the derivative (at the spot rate).

		LC '000s	LC '000s
Dr	Profit or loss	22	
Cr	Equity (separate component of equity)		22

To recognise the appropriate reclassification from equity to profit or loss.

Similar entries would be recorded for the remaining term of the hedge relationship.

5 Aggregated exposures

The examples in this section are taken from the IFRS 9 implementation guidance. They illustrate hedge accounting for aggregated exposures. The following examples have been included in this section:

Section 5.1 Combined commodity price risk and foreign currency risk hedge (cash flow hedge/cash flow hedge combination)

Section 5.2 Combined interest rate risk and foreign currency risk hedge (fair value hedge/cash flow hedge combination)

Section 5.3 Combined interest rate risk and foreign currency risk hedge (cash flow hedge/fair value hedge combination)

5.1 Combined commodity price risk and foreign currency risk hedge (cash flow hedge/cash flow hedge combination)

Example 5.1

Combined commodity price risk and foreign currency risk hedge (cash flow hedge/cash flow hedge combination)

[*IFRS 9:IE116 - IE127, Example 16*]

Fact Pattern

Entity A wants to hedge a highly probable forecast coffee purchase (which is expected to occur at the end of Period 5). Entity A's functional currency is its Local Currency (LC). Coffee is traded in Foreign Currency (FC). Entity A has the following risk exposures:

a. commodity price risk: the variability in cash flows for the purchase price, which results from fluctuations of the spot price of coffee in FC; and

b. foreign currency (FX) risk: the variability in cash flows that result from fluctuations of the spot exchange rate between LC and FC.

Entity A hedges its risk exposures using the following risk management strategy:

a. Entity A uses benchmark commodity forward contracts, which are denominated in FC, to hedge its coffee purchases four periods before delivery. The coffee price that Entity A actually pays for its purchase is different from the benchmark price because of differences in the type of coffee, the location and delivery arrangement.[1] This gives rise to the risk of changes in the relationship between the two coffee prices (sometimes referred to as 'basis risk'), which affects the effectiveness of the hedging relationship. Entity A does not hedge this risk because it is not considered economical under cost/benefit considerations.

b. Entity A also hedges its FX risk. However, the FX risk is hedged over a different horizon- only three periods before delivery. Entity A considers the FX exposure from the variable payments for the coffee purchase in FC and the gain or loss on the commodity forward contract in FC as one aggregated FX exposure. Hence, Entity A uses one single FX forward contract to hedge the FX cash flows from a forecast coffee purchase and the related commodity forward contract.

The following table sets out the parameters used for Example 1 (the 'basis spread' is the differential, expressed as a percentage, between the price of the coffee that Entity A actually buys and the price for the benchmark coffee):

Example 1 – Parameters

Period	**1**	**2**	**3**	**4**	**5**
Interest rates for remaining maturity [FC]	0.26%	0.21%	0.16%	0.06%	0.00%
Interest rates for remaining maturity [LC]	1.12%	0.82%	0.46%	0.26%	0.00%
Forward price [FC/lb]	1.25	1.01	1.43	1.22	2.15
Basis spread	–5.00%	–5.50%	–6.00%	–3.40%	–7.00%
FX rate (spot) [FC/LC]	1.3800	1.3300	1.4100	1.4600	1.4300

Accounting mechanics

Entity A designates as cash flow hedges the following two hedging relationships:[2]

a. A commodity price risk hedging relationship between the coffee price related variability in cash flows attributable to the forecast coffee purchase in FC as the hedged item and a commodity forward contract denominated in FC as the hedging instrument (the 'first level relationship'). This hedging relationship is designated at the end of Period 1 with a term to the end of Period 5. Because of the basis spread between the price of the coffee that Entity A actually buys and the price for the benchmark coffee, Entity A designates a volume of 112,500 pounds (lbs) of coffee as the hedging instrument and a volume of 118,421 lbs as the hedged item.[3]

b. An FX risk hedging relationship between the aggregated exposure as the hedged item and an FX forward contract as the hedging instrument (the 'second level relationship'). This hedging relationship is designated at the end of Period 2 with a term to the end of Period 5. The aggregated exposure that is designated as the hedged item represents the FX risk that is the effect of exchange rate changes, compared to the forward FX rate at the end of Period 2 (ie the time of designation of the FX risk hedging relationship), on the combined FX cash flows in FC of the two items designated in the commodity price risk hedging relationship, which are the forecast coffee purchase and the commodity forward contract. Entity A's long- term view of the basis spread between the price of the coffee that it actually buys and the price for the benchmark coffee has not changed from the end of Period 1. Consequently, the actual volume of hedging instrument that Entity A enters into (the nominal amount of the FX forward contract of FC140,625) reflects the cash flow exposure associated with a basis spread that had remained at -5 per cent. However, Entity A's actual aggregated exposure is affected by changes in the basis spread. Because the basis spread has moved from -5 per cent to -5.5 per cent during Period 2, Entity A's actual aggregated exposure at the end of Period 2 is FC140,027.

The following table sets out the fair values of the derivatives, the changes in the value of the hedged items and the calculation of the cash flow hedge reserves and hedge ineffectiveness:[4]

Example 1 – Calculations

		Period	1	2	3	4	5
Commodity price risk hedging relationship (first level relationship)							
Forward purchase contract for coffee							
Volume (lbs)	112,500						
Forward price [FC/lb]	1.25	Price (fwd) [FC/lb]	1.25	1.01	1.43	1.22	2.15
		Fair value [FC]	0	(26,943)	20,219	(3,373)	101,250
		Fair value [LC]	0	(20,258)	14,339	(2,310)	70,804
		Change in fair value [LC]		(20,258)	34,598	(16,650)	73,114
Hedged forecast coffee purchase							
Hedge ratio	105.26%	Basis spread	-5.00%	-5.50%	-6.00%	-3.40%	-7.00%
Hedged volume	118.421	Price (fwd) [FC/lb]	1.19	0.95	1.34	1.18	2.00
Implied forward price	1.1875	Present value [FC]	0	27,540	(18,528)	1,063	(96,158)
		Present value [LC]	0	20,707	(13,140)	728	(67,243)
		Change in present value [LC]		20,707	(33,847)	13,868	(67,971)
Accounting			LC	LC	LC	LC	LC
Derivative			0	(20,258)	14,339	(2,310)	70,804
Cash flow hedge reserve			0	(20,258)	13,140	(728)	67,243
Change in cash flow hedge reserve				(20,258)	33,399	(13,868)	67,971
Profit or loss				0	1,199	(2,781)	5,143
Retained earnings			0	0	1,199	(1,582)	3,561
FX risk hedging relationship (second level relationship)							
FX rate [FC/LC]		Spot	1.3800	1.3300	1.4100	1.4600	1.4300
		Forward	1.3683	1.3220	1.4058	1.4571	1.4300
Commodity price risk hedging relationship (first level relationship)							
FX forward contract (buy FC/sell LC)							
Volume [FC]	140,625						
Forward rate (in P_2)	1,3220	Fair value [LC]		0	(6,313)	(9,840)	(8,035)
		Change in fair value [LC]			(6,313)	(3,528)	1,805
Hedged FX							
Aggregated FX exposure		Hedged volume [FC]		140,027	138,932	142,937	135,533
		Present value [LC]		0	6,237	10,002	7,744
		Change in fair value [LC]			6,237	3,765	(2,258)

Example 1 – Calculations

	Period 1	2	3	4	5
Accounting		*LC*	*LC*	*LC*	*LC*
Derivative		0	(6,313)	(9,840)	(8,035)
Cash flow hedge reserve		0	(6,237)	(9,840)	(7,744)
Change in cash flow hedge reserve			(6,237)	(3,604)	2,096
Profit or loss			(76)	76	(291)
Retained earnings		0	(76)	0	(291)

The commodity price risk hedging relationship is a cash flow hedge of a highly probable forecast transaction that starts at the end of Period 1 and remains in place when the FX risk hedging relationship starts at the end of Period 2, ie the first level relationship continues as a separate hedging relationship.

The volume of the aggregated FX exposure (in FC), which is the hedged volume of the FX risk hedging relationship, is the total of:[5]

(a) the hedged coffee purchase volume multiplied by the current forward price (this represents the expected spot price of the actual coffee purchase); and

(b) the volume of the hedging instrument (designated nominal amount) multiplied by the difference between the contractual forward rate and the current forward rate (this represents the expected price differential from benchmark coffee price movements in FC that Entity A will receive or pay under the commodity forward contract).

The present value (in LC) of the hedged item of the FX risk hedging relationship (ie the aggregated exposure) is calculated as the hedged volume (in FC) multiplied by the difference between the forward FX rate at the measurement date and the forward FX rate at the designation date of the hedging relationship (ie the end of Period 2).[6]

Using the present value of the hedged item and the fair value of the hedging instrument, the cash flow hedge reserve and the hedge ineffectiveness are then determined (see paragraph 6.5.11 of IFRS 9).

The following table shows the effect on Entity A's statement of profit or loss and other comprehensive income and its statement of financial position (for the sake of transparency the line items[7] are disaggregated on the face of the statements by the two hedging relationships, i.e. for the commodity price risk hedging relationship and the FX risk hedging relationship):

Example 1 – Overview of effect on statements of financial performance and financial position

[All amounts in LC]

Period	**1**	**2**	**3**	**4**	**5**
Hedge ineffectiveness					
Commodity hedge		0	(1,199)	2,781	(5,143)
FX hedge		0	76	(76)	291
Profit or loss	0	0	(1,123)	2,705	(4,852)
Other comprehensive income (OCI)					
Commodity hedge		20,258	(33,399)	13,868	(67,971)
FX hedge		0	6,237	3,604	(2,096)
Total other comprehensive income	0	20,258	(27,162)	17,472	(70,067)
Comprehensive income	0	20,258	(28,285)	20,177	(74,920)
Statement of financial position					
Commodity forward	0	(20,258)	14,339	(2,310)	70,804
FX forward		0	(6,313)	(9,840)	(8,035)
Total net assets	0	(20,258)	8,027	(12,150)	62,769
Equity					
Accumulated OCI	0	20,258			
Commodity hedge		0	(13,140)	728	(67,243)
FX hedge			6,237	9,840	7,744
	0	20,258	(6,904)	10,568	(59,499)
Retained earnings					
Commodity hedge	0	0	(1,199)	1,582	(3,561)
FX hedge		0	76	0	291
	0	0	(1,123)	1,582	(3,270)
Total equity	0	20,258	(8,027)	12,150	(62,769)

The total cost of inventory after hedging is as follows:[8]

Cost of inventory [all amounts in LC]	
Cash price (at spot for commodity price risk and FX risk)	165,582
Gain/loss from CFHR for commodity price risk	(67,243)
Gain/loss from CFHR for FX risk	7,744
Cost of inventory	106,083

The total overall cash flow from all transactions (the actual coffee purchase at the spot price and the settlement of the two derivatives) is LC102,813. It differs from the hedge adjusted cost of inventory by LC3,270, which is the net amount of cumulative hedge ineffectiveness from the two hedging relationships. This hedge ineffectiveness has a cash flow effect but is excluded from the measurement of the inventory.

[1] For the purpose of this example it is assumed that the hedged risk is not designated based on a benchmark coffee price risk component. Consequently, the entire coffee price risk is hedged.

[2] This example assumes that all qualifying criteria for hedge accounting are met (see IFRS 9:6.4.1). The following description of the designation is solely for the purpose of understanding this example (ie it is not an example of the complete formal documentation required in accordance with IFRS 9:6.4.1(b)).

[3] In this example, the current basis spread at the time of designation is coincidentally the same as Entity A's long- term view of the basis spread (-5 per cent) that determines the volume of coffee purchases that it actually hedges. Also, this example assumes that Entity A designates the hedging instrument in its entirety and designates as much of its highly probable forecast purchases as it regards as hedged. That results in a hedge ratio of 1/(100%-5%). Other entities might follow different approaches when determining what volume of their exposure they actually hedge, which can result in a different hedge ratio and also designating less than a hedging instrument in its entirety (see IFRS 9:B6.4.10).

[4] In the following table for the calculations all amounts (including the calculations for accounting purposes of amounts for assets, liabilities, equity and profit or loss) are in the format of positive (plus) and negative (minus) numbers (eg a profit or loss amount that is a negative number is a loss).

[5] For example, at the end of Period 3 the aggregated FX exposure is determined as: 118,421 lbs × 1.34 FC/lb = FC159,182 for the expected price of the actual coffee purchase and 112,500 lbs × (1.25 [FC/lb] – 1.43 [FC/lb]) = FC(20,250) for the expected price differential under the commodity forward contract, which gives a total of FC138,932—the volume of the aggregated FX exposure at the end of Period 3.

[6] For example, at the end of Period 3 the present value of the hedged item is determined as the volume of the aggregated exposure at the end of Period 3 (FC138,932) multiplied by the difference between the forward FX rate at the end of Period 3 (1/1.4058) and the forward FX rate and the time of designation (ie the end of Period 2: 1/1.3220) and then discounted using the interest rate (in LC) at the end of Period 3 with a term of 2 periods (ie until the end of Period 5 – 0.46 per cent). The calculation is: FC138,932 × (1/(1.4058[FC/LC]) – 1/(1.3220 [FC/LC]))/(1 + 0.46%) = LC6,237.

[7] The line items used in this example are a possible presentation. Different presentation formats using different line items (including line items that include the amounts shown here) are also possible (IFRS 7 *Financial Instruments: Disclosures* sets out disclosure requirements for hedge accounting that include disclosures about hedge ineffectiveness, the carrying amount of hedging instruments and the cash flow hedge reserve).

[8] 'CFHR' is the cash flow hedge reserve, ie the amount accumulated in other comprehensive income for a cash flow hedge.

5.2 Combined interest rate risk and foreign currency risk hedge (fair value hedge/cash flow hedge combination)

Example 5.2

Combined interest rate risk and foreign currency risk hedge (fair value hedge/cash flow hedge combination)

[*IFRS 9:IE128 - IE137, Example 17*]

Fact Pattern

Entity B wants to hedge a fixed rate liability that is denominated in Foreign Currency (FC). The liability has a term of four periods from the start of Period 1 to the end of Period 4. Entity B's functional currency is its Local Currency (LC). Entity B has the following risk exposures:

a. fair value interest rate risk and FX risk: the changes in fair value of the fixed rate liability attributable to interest rate changes, measured in LC.

b. cash flow interest rate risk: the exposure that arises as a result of swapping the combined fair value interest rate risk and FX risk exposure associated with the fixed rate liability (see (a) above) into a variable rate exposure in LC in accordance with Entity B's risk management strategy for FC denominated fixed rate liabilities (see (a) of the next paragraph).

Entity B hedges its risk exposures using the following risk management strategy:

a. Entity B uses cross currency interest rate swaps to swap its FC denominated fixed rate liabilities into a variable rate exposure in LC. Entity B hedges its FC denominated liabilities (including the interest) for their entire life. Consequently, Entity B enters into a cross currency interest rate swap at the same time as it issues an FC denominated liability. Under the cross currency interest rate swap Entity B receives fixed interest in FC (used to pay the interest on the liability) and pays variable interest in LC.

b. Entity B considers the cash flows on a hedged liability and on the related cross currency interest rate swap as one aggregated variable rate exposure in LC. From time to time, in accordance with its risk management strategy for variable rate interest rate risk (in LC), Entity B decides to lock in its interest payments and hence swaps its aggregated variable rate exposure in LC into a fixed rate exposure in LC. Entity B seeks to obtain as a fixed rate exposure a single blended fixed coupon rate (ie the uniform forward coupon rate for the hedged term that exists at the start of the hedging relationship).[9] Consequently, Entity B uses interest rate swaps (denominated entirely in LC) under which it receives variable interest (used to pay the interest on the pay leg of the cross currency interest rate swap) and pays fixed interest.

The following table sets out the parameters used for Example 2:

Example 2 – Parameters

	t_0	Period 1	Period 2	Period 3	Period 4
FX spot rate [LC/FC]	1.2000	1.0500	1.4200	1.5100	1.3700
Interest curves					
(vertical presentation of rates for each quarter of a period on a per annum basis)					
LC	2.50%	5.02%	6.18%	0.34%	[N/A]
	2.75%	5.19%	6.26%	0.49%	
	2.91%	5.47%	6.37%	0.94%	
	3.02%	5.52%	6.56%	1.36%	
	2.98%	5.81%	6.74%		
	3.05%	5.85%	6.93%		
	3.11%	5.91%	7.19%		
	3.15%	6.06%	7.53%		
	3.11%	6.20%			
	3.14%	6.31%			
	3.27%	6.36%			
	3.21%	6.40%			
	3.21%				
	3.25%				
	3.29%				
	3.34%				
FC	3.74%	4.49%	2.82%	0.70%	[N/A]
	4.04%	4.61%	2.24%	0.79%	
	4.23%	4.63%	2.00%	1.14%	
	4.28%	4.34%	2.18%	1.56%	
	4.20%	4.21%	2.34%		
	4.17%	4.13%	2.53%		
	4.27%	4.07%	2.82%		
	4.14%	4.09%	3.13%		
	4.10%	4.17%			
	4.11%	4.13%			
	4.11%	4.24%			
	4.13%	4.34%			
	4.14%				
	4.06%				
	4.12%				
	4.19%				

Accounting mechanics

Entity B designates the following hedging relationships:[10]

(a) As a fair value hedge, a hedging relationship for fair value interest rate risk and FX risk between the FC denominated fixed rate liability (fixed rate FX liability) as the hedged item and a cross currency interest rate swap as the hedging instrument (the 'first level relationship'). This hedging relationship is designated at the beginning of Period 1 (i.e. t_0) with a term to the end of Period 4.

(b) As a cash flow hedge, a hedging relationship between the aggregated exposure as the hedged item and an interest rate swap as the hedging instrument (the 'second level relationship'). This hedging relationship is designated at the end of Period 1, when Entity B decides to lock in its interest payments and hence swaps its aggregated variable rate exposure in LC into a fixed rate exposure in LC, with a term to the end of Period 4. The aggregated exposure that is designated as the hedged item represents, in LC, the variability in cash flows that is the effect of changes in the combined cash flows of the two items designated in the fair value hedge of the fair value interest rate risk and FX risk (see (a) above), compared to the interest rates at the end of Period 1 (i.e. the time of designation of the hedging relationship between the aggregated exposure and the interest rate swap).

The following table[11] sets out the overview of the fair values of the derivatives, the changes in the value of the hedged items and the calculation of the cash flow hedge reserve and hedge ineffectiveness.[12] In this example, hedge ineffectiveness arises on both hedging relationships.[13]

Example 2 – Calculations

	t_0	Period 1	Period 2	Period 3	Period 4
Fixed rate FX liability					
Fair value [FC]	(1,000,000)	(995,522)	(1,031,008)	(1,030,193)	(1,000,000)
Fair value [LC]	(1,200,000)	(1,045,298)	(1,464,031)	(1,555,591)	(1,370,000)
Change in fair value [LC]		154,702	(418,733)	(91,560)	185,591
CCIRS (receive fixed FC/pay variable LC)					
Fair value [FC]	0	(154,673)	264,116	355,553	170,000
Change in fair value [LC]		(154,673)	418,788	91,437	(185,553)

Example 2 – Calculations

	t_0	Period 1	Period 2	Period 3	Period 4
IRS (receive variable/pay fixed)					
Fair value [LC]		0	18,896	(58,767)	0
Change in fair value [LC]			18,896	(77,663)	58,767
CF variability of the aggregated exposure					
Present value [LC]		0	(18,824)	58,753	0
Change in present value [LC]			(18,824)	77,577	(58,753)
CFHR					
Balance (end of period) [LC]		0	18,824	(58,753)	0
Change [LC]			18,824	(77,577)	58,753

The hedging relationship between the fixed rate FX liability and the cross currency interest rate swap starts at the beginning of Period 1 (i.e. t_0) and remains in place when the hedging relationship for the second level relationship starts at the end of Period 1, i.e. the first level relationship continues as a separate hedging relationship.

The cash flow variability of the aggregated exposure is calculated as follows:

a. At the point in time from which the cash flow variability of the aggregated exposure is hedged (i.e. the start of the second level relationship at the end of Period 1), all cash flows expected on the fixed rate FX liability and the cross currency interest rate swap over the hedged term (i.e. until the end of Period 4) are mapped out and equated to a single blended fixed coupon rate so that the total present value (in LC) is nil. This calculation establishes the single blended fixed coupon rate (reference rate) that is used at subsequent dates as the reference point to measure the cash flow variability of the aggregated exposure since the start of the hedging relationship. This calculation is illustrated in the following table:

Example 2 – Cash flow variability of the aggregated exposure (calibration)

Variability in cash flows of the aggregated exposure

		FX liability		CCIRS FC leg		CCIRS LC leg		Calibration	PV
		CF(s)	PV	CF(s)	PV	CF(s)	PV	1,200,000 Nominal 5.6963% Rate 4 frequency	
		[FC]	[FC]	[FC]	[FC]	[LC]	[LC]	[LC]	[LC]
	Time								
	t_0								
	t_1								
Period 1	**t_2**								
	t_3								
	t_4								
	t_5	0	0	0	0	(14,771)	(14,591)	17,089	16,881
Period 2	**t_6**	(20,426)	(19,977)	20,246	19,801	(15,271)	(14,896)	17,089	16,669
	t_7	0	0	0	0	(16,076)	(15,473)	17,089	16,449
	t_8	(20,426)	(19,543)	20,582	19,692	(16,241)	(15,424)	17,890	16,229
	t_9	0	0	0	0	(17,060)	(15,974)	17,089	16,002
Period 3	**t_{10}**	(20,426)	(19,148)	20,358	19,084	(17,182)	(15,862)	17,089	15,776
	t_{11}	0	0	0	0	(17,359)	(15,797)	17,089	15,551
	t_{12}	(20,426)	(18,769)	20,582	18,912	(17,778)	(15,942)	17,089	15,324
	t_{13}	0	0	0	0	(18,188)	(16,066)	17,089	15,095
Period 4	**t_{14}**	(20,426)	(18,391)	20,246	18,229	(18,502)	(16,095)	17,089	14,866
	t_{15}	0	0	0	0	(18,646)	(15,972)	17,089	14,638
	t_{16}	(1,020,426)	(899,695)	1,020,582	899,832	(1,218,767)	(1,027,908)	1,217,089	1,026,493
	Totals		(995,522)		955,550		(1,200,000)		1,199,971
Totals in LC			(1,045,298)		1,045,327		(1,200,000)		1,199,971

PV of all CF(s) [LC] 0 ← Σ

The nominal amount that is used for the calibration of the reference rate is the same as the nominal amount of aggregated exposure that creates the variable cash flows in LC (LC1,200,000), which coincides with the nominal amount of the cross currency interest rate swap for the variable rate leg in LC. This results in a reference rate of 5.6963 per cent (determined by iteration so that the present value of all cash flows in total is nil).

b. At subsequent dates, the cash flow variability of the aggregated exposure is determined by comparison to the reference point established at the end of Period 1. For that purpose, all remaining cash flows expected on the fixed rate FX liability and the cross currency interest rate swap over the remainder of the hedged term (i.e. from the effectiveness measurement date until the end of Period 4) are updated (as applicable) and then discounted. Also, the reference rate of 5.6963 per cent is applied to the nominal amount that was used for the calibration of that rate at the end of Period 1 (LC1,200,000) in order to generate a set of cash flows over the remainder of the hedged term that is then also discounted. The total of all those present values represents the cash flow variability of the aggregated exposure. This calculation is illustrated in the following table for the end of Period 2:

Example 2 – Cash flow variability of the aggregated exposure (calibration)

	Variability in cash flows of the aggregated exposure							
	FX liability		CCIRS FC leg		CCIRS LC leg		Calibration	PV
	CF(s)	PV	CF(s)	PV	CF(s)	PV	1,200,000 Nominal 5.6963% Rate 4 frequency	
	[FC]	[FC]	[FC]	[FC]	[LC]	[LC]	[LC]	[LC]
Time								
t_0								
t_1								
Period 1 t_2								
t_3								
t_4								
t_5	0	0	0	0	0	0	0	0
Period 2 t_6	0	0	0	0	0	0	0	0
t_7	0	0	0	0	0	0	0	0
t_8	0	0	0	0	0	0	0	0
t_9	0	0	0	0	(18,120)	(17,850)	17,089	16,835
Period 3 t_{10}	(20,426)	(20,173)	20,358	20,106	(18,360)	(17,814)	17,089	16,581
t_{11}	0	0	0	0	(18,683)	(17,850)	17,089	16,327
t_{12}	(20,426)	(19,965)	20,582	20,117	(19,203)	(18,058)	17,089	16,070
t_{13}	0	0	0	0	(19,718)	(18,243)	17,089	15,810
Period 4 t_{14}	(20,426)	19,726)	20,246	19,553	(20,279)	(18,449)	17,089	15,547
t_{15}	0	0	0	0	(21,014)	(18,789)	17,089	15,280
t_{16}	(1,020,426)	(971,144)	1,020,582	971,292	(1,221,991)	(1,027,947)	1,217,089	1,068,643
Totals		(1,031,008)		1,031,067		(1,200,000)		1,181,092
Totals in LC		(1,464,031)		1,464,116		(1,200,000)		1,181,092

PV of all CF(s) [LC] (18,824) ← Σ

The changes in interest rates and the exchange rate result in a change of the cash flow variability of the aggregated exposure between the end of Period 1 and the end of Period 2 that has a present value of LC- 18,824.[14]

Using the present value of the hedged item and the fair value of the hedging instrument, the cash flow hedge reserve and the hedge ineffectiveness are then determined (see paragraph 6.5.11 of IFRS 9).

The following table shows the effect on Entity B's statement of profit or loss and other comprehensive income and its statement of financial position (for the sake of transparency some line items[15] are disaggregated on the face of the statements by the two hedging relationships, i.e. for the fair value hedge of the fixed rate FX liability and the cash flow hedge of the aggregated exposure):[16]

Example 2 – Overview of effect on statements of financial performance and financial position

[*All amounts in LC*]

	t_0	Period 1	Period 2	Period 3	Period 4
Statement of profit or loss and other comprehensive income					
Interest expense					
FX liability		45,958	50,452	59,848	58,827
FVH adjustment		(12,757)	11, 941	14,385	(49,439)
		33,202	62,393	74,233	9,388
Reclassifications (CFH)			5,990	(5,863)	58,982
Total interest expense		33,202	68,383	68,370	68,370
Other gains/losses					
Change in fair value of the CCIRS		154,673	(418,788)	(91,437)	185,553
FVH adjustment (FX liability)		(154,702)	418,733	91,560	(185,591)
Hedge ineffectiveness		25	(72)	(54)	(19)
Total other gains/losses		(4)	(127)	68	(57)
Profit or loss		33,198	68,255	68,438	68,313
Other comprehensive income (OCI)					
Effective CFH gain/loss			(12,834)	71,713	229
Reclassification			(5,990)	5,863	(58,982)
Total other comprehensive income			(18,824)	77,577	(58,753)
Comprehensive income		33,198	49,432	146,015	9,560
Statement of financial position					
FX liability	(1,200,000)	(1,045,298)	(1,464,031)	(1,555,591)	(1,397,984)
CCIRS	0	(154,673)	264,116	355,553	194,141
IRS		0	18,896	(58,767)	(13,004)
Cash	1,200,000	1,166,773	1,098,390	1,030,160	978,641
Total net assets	0	(33,198)	(82,630)	(228,645)	(238,205)
Equity					
Accumulated OCI		0	(18,824)	58,753	0
Retained earnings	0	33,198	101,454	169,892	238,205
Total equity	0	33,198	82,630	228,645	238,205

The total interest expense in profit or loss reflects Entity B's interest expense that results from its risk management strategy:

(a) In Period 1 the risk management strategy results in interest expense reflecting variable interest rates in LC after taking into account the effect of the cross currency interest rate swap. There is also some hedge ineffectiveness that results from a difference in the changes in fair value for the fixed rate FX liability (as represented by the fair value hedge adjustment) and the cross currency interest rate swap as well as from differences between the cash flows on the two instruments that were settled during Period 1.

(b) For Periods 2 to 4 the risk management strategy results in interest expense that reflects, after taking into account the effect of the interest rate swap entered into at the end of Period 1, fixed interest rates in LC (i.e. locking in a single blended fixed coupon rate for a three-period term based on the interest rate environment at the end of Period 1). However, Entity B's interest expense is affected by the hedge ineffectiveness that arises on its hedging relationships. In Period 2 the interest expense is slightly higher than the fixed rate payments locked in with the interest rate swap because the variable payments received under the interest rate swap are less than the total of the cash flows resulting from the aggregated exposure.[17] In Periods 3 and 4 the interest expense is equal to the locked in rate because the variable payments received under the swap are more than the total of the cash flows resulting from the aggregated exposure.[18]

[9] An entity may have a different risk management strategy whereby it seeks to obtain a fixed rate exposure that is not a single blended rate but a series of forward rates that are each fixed for the respective individual interest period. For such a strategy the hedge effectiveness is measured based on the difference between the forward rates that existed at the start of the hedging relationship and the forward rates that exist at the effectiveness measurement date for the individual interest periods. For such a strategy a series of forward contracts corresponding with the individual interest periods would be more effective than an interest rate swap (that has a fixed payment leg with a single blended fixed rate).

[10] This example assumes that all qualifying criteria for hedge accounting are met (see IFRS 9:6.4.1). The following description of the designation is solely for the purpose of understanding this example (i.e. it is not an example of the complete formal documentation required in accordance with IFRS 9:6.4.1(b)).

[11] Tables in this example use the following acronyms: 'CCIRS' for cross currency interest rate swap, 'CF(s)' for cash flow(s), 'CFH' for cash flow hedge, 'CFHR' for cash flow hedge reserve, 'FVH' for fair value hedge, 'IRS' for interest rate swap and 'PV' for present value.

[12] In the following table for the calculations all amounts (including the calculations for accounting purposes of amounts for assets, liabilities and equity) are in the format of positive (plus) and negative (minus) numbers (eg an amount in the cash flow hedge reserve that is in brackets is a loss).

[13] For a situation such as in this example, hedge ineffectiveness can result from various factors, for example credit risk, differences in the day count method or, depending on whether it is included in the designation of the hedging instrument, the charge for exchanging different currencies that is included in cross currency interest rate swaps (commonly referred to as the 'currency basis').

[14] This is the amount that is included in the table with the overview of the calculations as the present value of the cash flow variability of the aggregated exposure at the end of Period 2.

[15] The line items used in this example are a possible presentation. Different presentation formats using different line items (including line items that include the amounts shown here) are also possible (IFRS 7 *Financial Instruments: Disclosures* sets out disclosure requirements for hedge accounting that include disclosures about hedge

ineffectiveness, the carrying amount of hedging instruments and the cash flow hedge reserve).

16 For Period 4 the values in the table with the overview of the calculations differ from those in the following table. For Periods 1 to 3 the 'dirty' values (i.e. including interest accruals) equal the 'clean' values (i.e. excluding interest accruals) because the period end is a settlement date for all legs of the derivatives and the fixed rate FX liability. At the end of Period 4 the table with the overview of the calculations uses clean values in order to calculate the value changes consistently over time. For the following table the dirty values are presented, i.e. the maturity amounts including accrued interest immediately before the instruments are settled (this is for illustrative purposes as otherwise all carrying amounts other than cash and retained earnings would be nil).

17 In other words, the cash flow variability of the interest rate swap was lower than, and consequently did not fully offset, the cash flow variability of the aggregated exposure as a whole (sometimes called an 'under-hedge' situation). In those situations the cash flow hedge does not contribute to the hedge ineffectiveness that is recognised in profit or loss because the hedge ineffectiveness is not recognised (see IFRS 9:6.5.11). The hedge ineffectiveness arising on the fair value hedge affects profit or loss in all periods.

18 In other words, the cash flow variability of the interest rate swap was lower than, and consequently did not fully offset, the cash flow variability of the aggregated exposure as a whole (sometimes called an 'under-hedge' situation). In those situations the cash flow hedge does not contribute to the hedge ineffectiveness that is recognised in profit or loss because the hedge ineffectiveness is not recognised (see IFRS 9:6.5.11). The hedge ineffectiveness arising on the fair value hedge affects profit or loss in all periods.

5.3 Combined interest rate risk and foreign currency risk hedge (cash flow hedge/ fair value hedge combination)

Example 5.3

Combined interest rate risk and foreign currency risk hedge (cash flow hedge/ fair value hedge combination)

[*IFRS 9:IE138 - IE147, Example 18*]

Fact Pattern

Entity C wants to hedge a variable rate liability that is denominated in Foreign Currency (FC). The liability has a term of four periods from the start of Period 1 to the end of Period 4. Entity C's functional currency is its Local Currency (LC). Entity C has the following risk exposures:

a. cash flow interest rate risk and FX risk: the changes in cash flows of the variable rate liability attributable to interest rate changes, measured in LC.

b. fair value interest rate risk: the exposure that arises as a result of swapping the combined cash flow interest rate risk and FX risk exposure associated with the variable rate liability (see (a) above) into a fixed rate exposure in LC in accordance with Entity C's risk management strategy for FC denominated variable rate liabilities (see (a) of the next paragraph).

Entity C hedges its risk exposures using the following risk management strategy:

a. Entity C uses cross currency interest rate swaps to swap its FC denominated variable rate liabilities into a fixed rate exposure in LC. Entity C hedges its FC denominated liabilities (including the interest) for their entire life. Consequently, Entity C enters into a cross currency interest rate swap at the same time as it issues an FC denominated liability. Under the cross currency interest rate swap Entity C receives variable interest in FC (used to pay the interest on the liability) and pays fixed interest in LC.

b. Entity C considers the cash flows on a hedged liability and on the related cross currency interest rate swap as one aggregated fixed rate exposure in LC. From time to time, in accordance with its risk management strategy for fixed rate interest rate risk (in LC), Entity C decides to link its interest payments to current variable interest rate levels and hence swaps its aggregated fixed rate exposure in LC into a variable rate exposure in LC. Consequently, Entity C uses interest rate swaps (denominated entirely in LC) under which it receives fixed interest (used to pay the interest on the pay leg of the cross currency interest rate swap) and pays variable interest.

The following table sets out the parameters used for Example 3:

Example 3 – Parameter overview

	t_0	Period 1	Period 2	Period 3	Period 4
FX spot rate [LC/FC]	1.2	1.05	1.42	1.51	1.37
Interest curves					
(vertical presentation of rates for each quarter of a period on a per annum basis)					
LC	2.50%	1.00%	3.88%	0.34%	[N/A]
	2.75%	1.21%	4.12%	0.49%	
	2.91%	1.39%	4.22%	0.94%	
	3.02%	1.58%	5.11%	1.36%	
	2.98%	1.77%	5.39%		
	3.05%	1.93%	5.43%		
	3.11%	2.09%	5.50%		
	3.15%	2.16%	5.64%		
	3.11%	2.22%			
	3.14%	2.28%			
	3.27%	2.30%			
	3.21%	2.31%			
	3.21%				
	3.25%				
	3.29%				
	3.34%				

Example 3 – Parameter overview

	t_0	Period 1	Period 2	Period 3	Period 4
FC	3.74%	4.49%	2.82%	0.70%	[N/A]
	4.04%	4.61%	2.24%	0.79%	
	4.23%	4.63%	2.00%	1.14%	
	4.28%	4.34%	2.18%	1.56%	
	4.20%	4.21%	2.34%		
	4.17%	4.13%	2.53%		
	4.27%	4.07%	2.82%		
	4.14%	4.09%	3.13%		
	4.10%	4.17%			
	4.11%	4.13%			
	4.11%	4.24%			
	4.13%	4.34%			
	4.14%				
	4.06%				
	4.12%				
	4.19%				

Accounting mechanics

Entity C designates the following hedging relationships:[19]

a. As a cash flow hedge, a hedging relationship for cash flow interest rate risk and FX risk between the FC denominated variable rate liability (variable rate FX liability) as the hedged item and a cross currency interest rate swap as the hedging instrument (the 'first level relationship'). This hedging relationship is designated at the beginning of Period 1 (i.e. t0) with a term to the end of Period 4.

b. As a fair value hedge, a hedging relationship between the aggregated exposure as the hedged item and an interest rate swap as the hedging instrument (the 'second level relationship'). This hedging relationship is designated at the end of Period 1, when Entity C decides to link its interest payments to current variable interest rate levels and hence swaps its aggregated fixed rate exposure in LC into a variable rate exposure in LC, with a term to the end of Period 4. The aggregated exposure that is designated as the hedged item represents, in LC, the change in value that is the effect of changes in the value of the combined cash flows of the two items designated in the cash flow hedge of the cash flow interest rate risk and FX risk (see (a) above), compared to the interest rates at the end of Period 1 (i.e. the time of designation of the hedging relationship between the aggregated exposure and the interest rate swap).

The following table[20] sets out the overview of the fair values of the derivatives, the changes in the value of the hedged items and the calculation of the cash flow hedge reserve.[21] In this example no hedge ineffectiveness arises on either hedging relationship because of the assumptions made.[22]

Example 3 – Calculations

	t_0	Period 1	Period 2	Period 3	Period 4
Variable rate FX liability					
Fair value [FC]	(1,000,000)	(1.000,000)	(1,000,000)	(1,000,000)	(1,000,000)
Fair value [LC]	(1,200,000)	(1,050,000)	(1,420,000)	(1,510,000)	(1,370,000)
Change in fair value [LC]		150,000	(370,000)	(90,000)	140,000
PV of change in variable CF(s) [LC]	0	192,310	(260,346)	(282,979)	(170,000)
Change in PV [LC]		192,310	(452,656)	(22,633)	112,979
CCIRS (receive variable FC/pay fixed LC)					
Fair value [LC]	0	(192,310)	260,346	282,979	170,000
Change in fair value [LC]		(192,310)	452,656	22,633	(112,979)
CFHR					
Opening balance	0	0	(42,310)	(28,207)	(14,103)
Reclassification FX risk		153,008	(378,220)	(91,030)	140,731
Reclassification (current period CF)		(8,656)	(18,410)	2,939	21,431
Effective CFH gain/loss		(186,662)	479,286	20,724	(135,141)
Reclassification of interest rate risk		0	(82,656)	67,367	(27,021)
Amortisation of CFHR		0	14,103	14,103	14,103
Ending balance		(42,310)	(28,207)	(14,103)	0
IRS (receive fixed/pay variable)					
Fair value [LC]		0	(82,656)	(15,289)	(42,310)
Change in fair value			(82,656)	67,367	(27,021)
Change in present value of the aggregated exposure					
Present value [LC]		(1,242,310)	(1,159,654)	(1,227,021)	(1,200,000)
Change in present value [LC]			82,656	(67,367)	27,021

The hedging relationship between the variable rate FX liability and the cross currency interest rate swap starts at the beginning of Period 1 (i.e. t_0) and remains in place when the hedging relationship for the second level relationship starts at the end of Period 1, i.e. the first level relationship continues as a separate hedging relationship. However, the hedge accounting for the first level relationship is affected by the start of hedge accounting for the second level relationship at the end of Period 1. The fair value hedge for the second level relationship affects the timing of the reclassification to profit or loss of amounts from the cash flow hedge reserve for the first level relationship:

a. The fair value interest rate risk that is hedged by the fair value hedge is included in the amount that is recognised in other comprehensive income as a result of the cash flow hedge for the first level hedging relationship (i.e. the gain or loss on the cross currency interest rate swap that is determined to be an effective hedge).[23] This means that from the end of Period 1 the part of the effective cash flow hedging gain or loss that represents the fair value interest rate risk (in LC), and is recognised in other comprehensive income in a first step, is in a second step immediately (i.e. in the same period) transferred from the cash flow hedge reserve to profit or loss. That reclassification adjustment offsets the gain or loss on the interest rate swap that is recognised in profit or loss.[24] In the context of accounting for the aggregated exposure as the hedged item, that reclassification adjustment is the equivalent of a fair value hedge adjustment because in contrast to a hedged item that is a fixed rate debt instrument (in LC) at amortised cost, the aggregated exposure is already remeasured for changes regarding the hedged risk but the resulting gain or loss is recognised in other comprehensive income because of applying cash flow hedge accounting for the first level relationship. Consequently, applying fair value hedge accounting with the aggregated exposure as the hedged item does not result in changing the hedged item's measurement but instead affects where the hedging gains and losses are recognised (i.e. reclassification from the cash flow hedge reserve to profit or loss).

b. The amount in the cash flow hedge reserve at the end of Period 1 (LC42,310) is amortised over the remaining life of the cash flow hedge for the first level relationship (i.e. over Periods 2 to 4).[25]

The change in value of the aggregated exposure is calculated as follows:

a. At the point in time from which the change in value of the aggregated exposure is hedged (i.e. the start of the second level relationship at the end of Period 1), all cash flows expected on the variable rate FX liability and the cross currency interest rate swap over the hedged term (i.e. until the end of Period 4) are mapped out and their combined present value, in LC, is calculated. This calculation establishes the present value that is used at subsequent dates as the reference point to measure the change in present value of the aggregated exposure since the start of the hedging relationship. This calculation is illustrated in the following table:

Example 3 – Present value of the aggregated exposure (starting point)

Present value of the aggregated exposure

	Time	FX liability CF(s) [FC]	FX liability PV [FC]	CCIRS FC leg CF(s) [FC]	CCIRS FC leg PV [FC]	CCIRS LC leg CF(s) [LC]	CCIRS LC leg PV [LC]
	t_0						
	t_1						
Period 1	t_2						
	t_3						
	t_4						
	t_5	(11,039)	(10,918)	11,039	10,918	(9,117)	(9,094)
Period 2	t_6	(11,331)	(11,082)	11,331	11,082	(9,117)	(9,067)
	t_7	(11,375)	(11,000)	11,375	11,000	(9,117)	(9,035)
	t_8	(10,689)	(10,227)	10,689	10,227	(9,117)	(9,000)
	t_9	(10,375)	(9,824)	10,375	9,824	(9,117)	(8,961)
Period 3	t_{10}	(10,164)	(9,528)	10,164	9,528	(9,117)	(8,918)
	t_{11}	(10,028)	(9,307)	10,028	9,307	(9,117)	(8,872)
	t_{12}	(10,072)	(9,255)	10,072	9,255	(9,117)	(8,825)
	t_{13}	(10,256)	(9,328)	10,256	9,328	(9,117)	(8,776)
Period 4	t_{14}	(10,159)	(9,147)	10,159	9,147	(9,117)	(8,727)
	t_{15}	(10,426)	(9,290)	10,426	9,290	(9,117)	(8,678)
	t_{16}	(1,010,670)	(891,093)	1,010,670	891,093	(1,209,117)	(1,144,358)
	Totals		(1,000,000)		(1,000,000)		(1,242,310)
	Totals in LC		(1,050,000)		(1,050,000)		(1,242,310)

PV of aggregated exposure [LC] (1,242,310) ← Σ

The present value of all cash flows expected on the variable rate FX liability and the cross currency interest rate swap over the hedged term at the end of Period 1 is LC- 1,242,310.[26]

b. At subsequent dates, the present value of the aggregated exposure is determined in the same way as at the end of Period 1 but for the remainder of the hedged term. For that purpose, all remaining cash flows expected on the variable rate FX liability and the cross currency interest rate swap over the remainder of the hedged term (i.e. from the effectiveness measurement date until the end of Period 4) are updated (as applicable) and then discounted. The total of those present values represents the present value of the aggregated exposure. This calculation is illustrated in the following table for the end of Period 2:

Example 3 – Present value of the aggregated exposure (at the end of Period 2)

		Present value of the aggregated exposure					
		FX liability		CCIRS FC leg		CCIRS LC leg	
		CF(s) [FC]	PV [FC]	CF(s) [FC]	PV [FC]	CF(s) [LC]	PV [LC]
	Time						
	t_0						
	t_1						
Period 1	t_2						
	t_3						
	t_4						
	t_5	0	0	0	0	0	0
Period 2	t_6	0	0	0	0	0	0
	t_7	0	0	0	0	0	0
	t_8	0	0	0	0	0	0
	t_9	(6,969)	(6,921)	6,969	6,921	(9,117)	(9,030)
Period 3	t_{10}	(5,544)	(5,475)	5,544	5,475	(9,117)	(8,939)
	t_{11}	(4,971)	(4,885)	4,971	4,885	(9,117)	(8,847)
	t_{12}	(5,401)	(5,280)	5,401	5,280	(9,117)	(8,738)
	t_{13}	(5,796)	(5,632)	5,796	5,632	(9,117)	(8,624)
Period 4	t_{14}	(6,277)	(6,062)	6,277	6,062	(9,117)	(8,511)
	t_{15}	(6,975)	(6,689)	6,975	6,689	(9,117)	(8,397)
	t_{16}	(1,007,725)	(959,056)	1,007,725	956,056	(1,209,117)	(1,098,568)
	Totals		(1,000,000)		1,000,000		(1,159,654)
	Totals in LC		(1,420,000)		1,420,000		(1,159,654)

PV of aggregated exposure [LC] (1,159,654) ← Σ

The changes in interest rates and the exchange rate result in a present value of the aggregated exposure at the end of Period 2 of LC-1,159,654. Consequently, the change in the present value of the aggregated exposure between the end of Period 1 and the end of Period 2 is a gain of LC82,656.[27]

Using the change in present value of the hedged item (i.e. the aggregated exposure) and the fair value of the hedging instrument (i.e. the interest rate swap), the related reclassifications from the cash flow hedge reserve to profit or loss (reclassification adjustments) are then determined.

The following table shows the effect on Entity C's statement of profit or loss and other comprehensive income and its statement of financial position (for the sake of transparency some line items[28] are disaggregated on the face of the statements by the two hedging relationships, i.e. for the cash flow hedge of the variable rate FX liability and the fair value hedge of the aggregated exposure):[29]

Example 3 – Overview of effect on statements of financial performance and financial position

[All amounts in LC]

	t_0	Period 1	Period 2	Period 3	Period 4
Statement of profit or loss and other comprehensive income					
Interest expense					
FX liability		45,122	54,876	33,527	15,035
FVH adjustment		0	(20,478)	16,517	(26,781)
		45,122	34,398	50,045	(11,746)
Reclassifications (CFH)		(8,656)	(18,410)	2,939	21,431
		36,466	15,989	52,983	9,685
Amortisation of CFHR		0	14,103	14,103	14,103
Total interest expense		36,466	30,092	67,087	23,788
Other gains/losses					
IRS		0	82,656	(67,367)	27,021
FX gain/loss (liability)		(150,000)	370,000	90,000	(140,000)
FX gain/loss (interest)		(3,008)	8,220	1,030	(731)
Reclassification for FX risk		153,008	(378,220)	(91,030)	140,731
Reclassification for interest rate risk		0	(82,656)	67,367	(27,021)
Total other gains/losses		0	0	0	0
Profit or loss		36,466	30,092	67,087	23,788
Other comprehensive income (OCI)					
Effective gain/loss		186,662	(479,286)	(20,724)	135,141
Reclassification (current period CF)		8,656	18,410	(2,939)	(21,431)
Reclassification for FX risk		(153,008)	378,220	91,030	(140,731)
Reclassification for interest rate risk		0	82,656	(67,367)	27,021
Amortisation of CFHR		0	(14,103)	(14,103)	(14,103)
Total other comprehensive income		42,310	(14,103)	(14,103)	(14,103)
Comprehensive income		78,776	15,989	52,983	9,685

Example 3 – Overview of effect on statements of financial performance and financial position

[All amounts in LC]

	t_0	Period 1	Period 2	Period 3	Period 4
Statement of financial position					
FX liability	(1,200,000)	(1,050,000)	(1,420,000)	(1,510,000)	(1,375,306)
CCIRS	0	(192,310)	260,346	262,979	166,190
IRS		0	(82,656)	(15,289)	(37,392)
Cash	1,200,000	1,163,534	1,147,545	1,094,562	1,089,076
Total net assets	0	(78,776)	(94,765)	(147,748)	(157,433)
Accumulated OCI	0	42,310	28,207	14,103	0
Retained earnings	0	36,466	66,558	133,645	157,433
Total equity	0	78,776	94,765	147,748	157,433

The total interest expense in profit or loss reflects Entity C's interest expense that results from its risk management strategy:

a. In Period 1 the risk management strategy results in interest expense reflecting fixed interest rates in LC after taking into account the effect of the cross currency interest rate swap.

b. For Periods 2 to 4, after taking into account the effect of the interest rate swap entered into at the end of Period 1, the risk management strategy results in interest expense that changes with variable interest rates in LC (i.e. the variable interest rate prevailing in each period). However, the amount of the total interest expense is not equal to the amount of the variable rate interest because of the amortisation of the amount that was in the cash flow hedge reserve for the first level relationship at the end of Period 1.[30]

[19] This example assumes that all qualifying criteria for hedge accounting are met (see IFRS 9:6.4.1). The following description of the designation is solely for the purpose of understanding this example (i.e. it is not an example of the complete formal documentation required in accordance with IFRS 9:6.4.1(b)).

[20] Tables in this example use the following acronyms: 'CCIRS' for cross currency interest rate swap, 'CF(s)' for cash flow(s), 'CFH' for cash flow hedge, 'CFHR' for cash flow hedge reserve, 'FVH' for fair value hedge, 'IRS' for interest rate swap and 'PV' for present value.

[21] In the following table for the calculations all amounts (including the calculations for accounting purposes of amounts for assets, liabilities and equity) are in the format of positive (plus) and negative (minus) numbers (eg an amount in the cash flow hedge reserve that is a negative number is a loss).

[22] Those assumptions have been made for didactical reasons, in order to better focus on illustrating the accounting mechanics in a cash flow hedge/fair value hedge combination. The measurement and recognition of hedge ineffectiveness has already been demonstrated in Example 1 and Example 2. However, in reality such hedges are typically not perfectly effective because hedge ineffectiveness can result from various factors, for example credit risk, the charge for exchanging different currencies that is included in cross currency interest rate swaps (commonly referred to as the 'currency basis') or differences in the day count method.

[23] As a consequence of hedging its exposure to cash flow interest rate risk by entering into the cross currency interest rate swap that changed the cash flow interest rate risk of the variable rate FX liability into a fixed rate exposure (in LC), Entity C in effect assumed an exposure to fair value interest rate risk.

[24] In the table with the overview of the calculations this reclassification adjustment is the line item "Reclassification for interest rate risk" in the reconciliation of the cash flow hedge reserve (eg at the end of Period 2 a reclassification of a gain of LC82,656 from the cash flow hedge reserve to profit or loss).

[25] In the table with the overview of the calculations this amortisation results in a periodic reclassification adjustment of LC14,103 that is included in the line item "Amortisation of CFHR" in the reconciliation of the cash flow hedge reserve.

[26] In this example no hedge ineffectiveness arises on either hedging relationship because of the assumptions made. Consequently, the absolute values of the variable rate FX liability and the FC denominated leg of the cross currency interest rate are equal (but with opposite signs). In situations in which hedge ineffectiveness arises, those absolute values would not be equal so that the remaining net amount would affect the present value of the aggregated exposure.

[27] This is the amount that is included in the table with the overview of the calculations as the change in present value of the aggregated exposure at the end of Period 2.

[28] The line items used in this example are a possible presentation. Different presentation formats using different line items (including line items that include the amounts shown here) are also possible (IFRS 7 *Financial Instruments: Disclosures* sets out disclosure requirements for hedge accounting that include disclosures about hedge ineffectiveness, the carrying amount of hedging instruments and the cash flow hedge reserve).

[29] For Period 4 the values in the table with the overview of the calculations differ from those in the following table. For Periods 1 to 3 the 'dirty' values (i.e. including interest accruals) equal the 'clean' values (i.e. excluding interest accruals) because the period end is a settlement date for all legs of the derivatives and the fixed rate FX liability. At the end of Period 4 the table with the overview of the calculations uses clean values in order to calculate the value changes consistently over time. For the following table the dirty values are presented, i.e. the maturity amounts including accrued interest immediately before the instruments are settled (this is for illustrative purposes as otherwise all carrying amounts other than cash and retained earnings would be nil).

B11 Disclosure

Contents

1 Introduction

IFRS 7 *Financial Instruments: Disclosures* sets out comprehensive disclosure requirements for financial instruments that apply to all entities complying with IFRSs. The requirements of IFRS 7 apply to an entity's annual financial statements. IAS 34 *Interim Financial Reporting* establishes general principles regarding disclosures in interim financial reports and includes a number of specific requirements regarding financial instruments. These requirements are not included in this chapter.

Since IFRS 7 was originally issued in 2005, the Standard has been subject to a number of amendments, the most significant of which were as follows.

- *Improving Disclosures about Financial Instruments* issued in March 2009 amended the required disclosures for fair value measurement and liquidity risk.
- *Improvements to IFRSs* issued in May 2010 included amendments to IFRS 7 that mostly clarified and refined certain disclosure requirements.
- *Transfers of Financial Assets* issued in October 2010 amended the required disclosures for transfers of financial assets that resulted in continued recognition or derecognition.
- *IFRS 13 Fair Value Measurement* issued in May 2011 removed the fair value disclosures from IFRS 7 and included them, with limited amendment, in IFRS 13.
- *Disclosures – Offsetting Financial Assets and Financial Liabilities* introduced new disclosures for financial assets and financial liabilities that are set-off in accordance with IAS 32 as well as recognised financial instruments subject to an enforceable master netting arrangement or similar agreement, irrespective of whether they are off set in the statement of financial position. These requirements are described in **section 6.7**.
- Consequential amendments arising from the issue of IFRS 9 which introduced a number of new disclosures particularly in respect of hedge accounting (see **section 4.3.2**) and credit risk (see **section 5.2.1**).

This chapter assumes the reporting entity is applying IFRS 9 *Financial Instruments* and therefore the chapter includes the consequential amendments to IFRS 7 that arose when IFRS 9 was issued in July 2014.

The objective of IFRS 7 is to require entities to provide disclosures in their financial statements that enable users to evaluate:

[IFRS 7:1]

(i) the significance of financial instruments for the entity's financial position and performance; and

(ii) the nature and extent of risks arising from financial instruments to which the entity is exposed during the period and at the end of the reporting period, and how the entity manages those risks.

These disclosures are designed to provide users of financial statements with additional information that may influence their assessment of the financial position, financial performance and of the amount, timing and uncertainty of future cash flows for the reporting entity. Further disclosures are required to enable users to determine what accounting elections and judgements have been made when applying the requirements of IAS 32 and IFRS 9, and their impact on the financial statements.

IFRS 7 includes mandatory application guidance (in Appendix B) and is accompanied by non-mandatory Implementation Guidance, with the latter providing illustrative examples and guidance on how the requirements of IFRS 7 may be met.

The extent to which an entity will provide financial instrument disclosures will depend on the entity's use of financial instruments and the associated risks. Because many of the requirements of IFRS 7 are based on information provided internally to key management personnel, the depth of disclosure will reflect partly the information provided for use within the business. Entities with few financial instruments and associated risks will provide less disclosure than those entities that have significant financial instruments and related exposures to financial risk.

2 Scope

IFRS 7 is applicable to *all* entities and to *all* risks arising from *all* financial instruments, whether recognised or unrecognised, except where specifically mentioned below. Recognised financial instruments include financial assets and financial liabilities that are within the scope of IFRS 9.

Even though IFRS 9 supersedes IAS 39, IFRS 9(2013 & 2014) permits an accounting policy choice to apply all the hedge accounting requirements of IAS 39 instead of the hedge accounting requirements of IFRS 9, or the requirements on portfolio fair value hedges of interest rate risk in IAS 39 and the remaining hedge accounting requirements in IFRS 9. Irrespective of whether an entity applies the hedge accounting requirements in IFRS 9, or in part or in full in IAS 39, the requirements for disclosures on hedge accounting in IFRS 7 that were consequentially amended when IFRS 9(2013) was issued, which are also included in IFRS 9(2014) still apply. [IFRS 7:BC6.104]

IFRS 7 applies to the financial statements of subsidiaries. There is no exemption even if full disclosures are provided in the consolidated financial statements in which the subsidiary is included. The IASB considers when an entity prepares any financial statements in accordance with IFRSs, users of those financial statements should receive information of the same quality as users of general purpose financial statements prepared in accordance with IFRSs. [IFRS 7:BC11]

2.1 Summary of arrangements

The table included in **section 2** of **chapter B1** summarises whether certain arrangements are in the scope of IFRS 7 or not.

2.2 Unrecognised financial instruments

Unrecognised financial instruments include some financial instruments that, although outside the scope of IFRS 9, are within the scope of IFRS 7, such as certain loan commitments that are not designated or required to be carried at FVTPL. [IFRS 7:4]

While a loan commitment may eventually give rise to a recognised financial asset for the lender, to the extent that funds have not been drawn down by the counterparty, the commitment to lend meets the definition of a financial liability because the lender is *contractually obligated to deliver cash or another financial asset to another entity*. [IAS 32:11] When this commitment is not recognised and measured in accordance with IFRS 9, it is considered to be an unrecognised financial liability to which IFRS 7's disclosure requirements apply. Similarly, the party with the right to draw down funds (the borrower) under a loan commitment has an unrecognised financial asset (to the extent that the funds have not yet been drawn down) to which IFRS 7 disclosure requirements apply.

It is important to note that even though the loan commitments may not always be recognised in accordance with IFRS 9, there will be specific accounting requirements to meet in respect of the expected credit losses (see **5.1** of **chapter B6**). IFRS 7 sets out detailed disclosure requirements specifically for expected credit losses that have to be met in addition to disclosure requirements for the unrecognised financial instrument.

Regular way sales and purchases of financial assets accounted for using a settlement date accounting policy may also give rise to unrecognised financial assets or liabilities that are within the scope of IFRS 7 (see **2.2** in **chapter B8** for settlement date accounting).

2.3 Leases

IFRS 7 includes within its scope any lease which meets the definition of a financial instrument. Finance leases are financial instruments whereas operating leases are not (except as regards individual payments currently due and payable). For further discussion see **3.4** in **chapter B1**.

2.4 Interests in subsidiaries, associates and joint arrangements

IFRS 7 applies to all contracts linked to interests in subsidiaries, associates or joint ventures that meet the definition of a derivative unless they meet the definition of an equity instrument in IAS 32. [IFRS 7:3(a)]

IFRS 7 scopes out derivatives over own equity that meet the definition of equity. This will include derivatives over shares in a subsidiary that meet the definition of equity in the consolidated financial statements. IFRS 7 does not appear to have a scope exception for non-derivative instruments classified as equity from the perspective of the issuer, such as ordinary shares and certain preference shares. This appears to be an oversight in the drafting of the Standard because IFRS 7:BC8 states that the scope of IFRS 7 is intended to be the same as IAS 32 (which included disclosure requirements for financial instruments prior to IFRS 7 being issued) with one exception, namely "derivatives based on interests in subsidiaries, associates or joint ventures if the derivatives meet the definition of an equity instrument in IAS 32". The Basis for Conclusions justifies the exclusion of such derivatives by stating that these instruments are not remeasured and hence "do not expose the issuer to balance sheet and income statement risk", and that the disclosures about the significance of financial instruments for financial position and performance are not relevant to equity instruments. In addition, IFRS 7:BC8 states that these instruments are excluded from the scope of IFRS 7, but they are within the scope of IAS 32 for the purpose of determining whether they meet the definition of equity instruments. It seems reasonable that the scope exclusions for derivatives over own equity that meet the definition of equity would also apply to non-derivatives that meet the definition of equity because the justification in the Basis for Conclusions would be equally relevant.

IFRS 7 excludes from its scope those interests in subsidiaries, associates and joint ventures that are accounted for in accordance with IAS 27 *Separate Financial Statements*, IAS 28 *Investments in Associates and Joint Ventures* or IFRS 10 *Consolidated Financial Statements*. [IFRS 7:3(a)] The only exception is when an entity applies IFRS 9 for measuring its interests in a subsidiary, joint venture or associate as specifically permitted by those standards.

Consolidated financial statements include all financial instruments of subsidiaries except those intragroup financial instruments that are fully eliminated on consolidation. Only if the financial instrument is fully eliminated on consolidation is it excluded from the scope of IFRS 7 in the consolidated financial statements.

IFRS 7 does not apply to an investment in an associate or joint venture accounted for under the equity method because the carrying amount represents the investor's initial cost adjusted for the post-acquisition changes in the investor's share of net assets of the investee.

It is less clear whether IFRS 7 applies to the share of any financial instruments of a joint operator held in a joint operation under IFRS 11. The application of IFRS 11 on joint operations means that the statement of financial position of the joint operator includes its share of the assets that it jointly holds and its share of the liabilities for which it is jointly responsible. [IFRS 11:20] Because the assets and liabilities will include the joint operator's share of financial instruments that are recognised and measured in accordance with IFRS 9, it would seem reasonable that these financial instruments are subject to the disclosure requirements of IFRS 7.

2.5 Non-current assets held for sale or discontinued operations

IFRS 5 *Non-current Assets Held for Sale and Discontinued Operations* specifically states in paragraph 2 that the classification and presentation requirements of IFRS 5 apply to all non-current assets (or disposal groups) classified as held for sale and discontinued operations. A question arises as to whether IFRS 7 disclosures are also required for financial assets and financial liabilities classified as held for sale or that form part of disposal groups because there is no scope exemption in IFRS 7 in this respect. The IASB issued *Improvements to IFRSs* in April 2009, which clarified that IFRS 5 specifies the disclosures required in respect of non-current assets (or disposal groups) classified as held for sale or discontinued operations. IFRS 5:5B states that disclosures in other IFRSs do not apply to such assets (or disposal groups) unless those IFRSs require:

[IFRS 5:5B]

(a) specific disclosures in respect of non-current assets (or disposal groups) classified as held for sale or discontinued operations; or

(b) disclosures about measurement of assets and liabilities within a disposal group that are not within the scope of the measurement requirement of IFRS 5 and such disclosures are not already provided in the other notes to the financial statements.

Additional disclosures about non-current assets (or disposal groups) classified as held for sale or discontinued operations may be necessary to comply with the general requirements of IAS 1 *Presentation of Financial Statements*, in particular IAS 1:15 & 125. [IFRS 5:5B]

Therefore, in the context of IFRS 7, IFRS 5.5B means that the disclosure requirements of IFRS 7 apply to stand-alone non-current financial assets held for sale and to financial assets/liabilities that form part of a disposal group *to the extent that those disclosure requirements relate to measurement.*

The specific disclosure requirements of IFRS 7 that apply should be determined as a matter of judgement. In some circumstances, the applicable disclosures about measurement may be limited to:

- the accounting policies and measurement bases for financial assets and liabilities; [IFRS 7:21] and
- the carrying amount of each category of financial asset and liability; [IFRS 7:8]

In some cases it could be argued that, for example, the liquidity risk, credit risk and market risk disclosures, amongst others, are not relevant to financial assets held for sale and financial assets/liabilities within a disposal group in the scope of IFRS 5's presentation and disclosure requirements.

2.6 Contracts to buy or sell non-financial items

It is important to remember that contracts to buy or sell non-financial items that may not be typically considered financial instruments are within the scope of IFRS 7 if they are in the scope of IFRS 9. Guidance on the recognition and measurement of contracts over non-financial items is set out at **2.5** in **chapter B1**.

2.7 Contract assets under IFRS 15

The credit risk disclosure requirements contained in IFRS 7:35A-35N (see **section 5.2.1**) apply to those rights that IFRS 15 *Revenue from Contracts with Customers* specifies are accounted for under IFRS 9 for the purposes of recognising impairment losses. Consequently, any reference to financial assets or financial instruments should include those rights unless otherwise specified. [IFRS 7:5A]

3 Classes of financial instruments

IFRS 7 specifies a number of disclosure requirements to be provided by 'class of financial instrument'. These include:

- derecognition of financial assets (see **4.1.6**);
- impairment losses in the period (see **4.2.5**);
- hedge accounting (see **section 4.3.2**);
- 'day 1 profit or loss' (see **4.3.3.8**); and
- credit risk (see **section 5.2.1**).

IFRS 13 also requires fair value disclosures by class of assets and liabilities (see **4.3.3**).

IFRS 7 requires entities to group financial instruments into classes that are appropriate to the nature of the information disclosed and that take into account the characteristics of those financial instruments. The classes are to be reconciled to the line items presented in the statement of financial position. [IFRS 7:6]

The classes are determined by the entity and are distinct from the categories of financial instruments specified by IFRS 9. [IFRS 7:B1] At a minimum, the classes are required to distinguish between those financial instruments that are measured at amortised cost and those that are measured at fair value. The entity should treat as a separate class or classes those financial instruments that are outside the scope of IFRS 7 (when the entity wishes to provide disclosures regarding such financial instruments in addition to the requirements of IFRS 7). [IFRS 7:B2] In many instances, classes of financial instruments will be more granular than the categories of financial instruments specified by IFRS 9. For example, amortised cost financial assets are a financial instrument category in IFRS 9 that could comprise various classes such as home loans, credit card loans, unsecured medium-term loans, etc.

IFRS 13 provides some additional guidance on determining classes for the basis of fair value disclosures. In addition to considering the nature, characteristics and risks of the asset and liability (as with IFRS 7) it states that consideration should be given to the level of the fair value hierarchy within which the fair value measurement is categorised. The number of classes may need to be greater for fair value measurements categorised within Level 3 of the fair value hierarchy because those measurements have a greater degree of uncertainty and subjectivity. IFRS 13 notes that where classes of assets and liabilities differ to line items in the statement of financial position an entity shall provide information sufficient to permit reconciliation to the line items presented in the statement of financial position. [IFRS 13:94]

The preparer of the financial statements must strike a balance between providing excessive detail and obscuring information as a result of too much aggregation. [IFRS 7:B3]

IFRS 7 is not clear whether the same classes of financial instruments are applied universally to all the disclosures that IFRS 7 requires by class. An advantage of using the same classification for financial instruments across all the required disclosures is that it enhances comparability and understanding between disclosures. However, such an approach may be in conflict with IFRS 7 in the following instances.

(i) Disclosure by class is required for certain quantitative disclosures, and IFRS 7:34 requires this information to be consistent with that provided internally to key management personnel. If the information provided to key management for the quantitative disclosures required by the Standard is aggregated differently, depending on the applicable risk disclosure, this information must be disclosed. It would be inappropriate to aggregate classes differently to the aggregation provided to key management personnel.

(ii) IFRS 7:IG21 indicates that in determining classes for credit risk disclosures, entities should group financial instruments that share economic characteristics with respect to the risk being disclosed, e.g. residential mortgages, unsecured consumer loans and commercial loans. This implies that classes vary depending on the type of information being disclosed. The classes applied to credit risk disclosure, therefore, may not be appropriate for the classes of financial instruments applied to fair value disclosure (e.g. the specific disclosures required for 'day 1 profit or loss' – see **4.3.3.8**). If only a small number of items are included in the day 1 profit or loss disclosure, but the characteristics of the instruments or valuation techniques differ, an entity may consider it more appropriate to choose classes for the specific disclosure that differ to other required disclosures.

Care should be taken to ensure that the determination of classes is relevant to the disclosure requirement and provides the most meaningful information. If different classifications of financial instruments are used for different disclosures, then the entity should place greater emphasis on making clear how the classes are reconciled to the statement of financial position and between notes.

Because IFRSs do not prescribe line items for the statement of financial position, other than specified minimum requirements set out in IAS 1 and a number of other Standards, an entity could choose to use its IFRS 7 classes of financial instruments as the basis for the line items in its statement of financial position. Such an approach would be likely to result in the presentation of many more line items in the statement of financial position that would be the case if the entity uses IFRS 9's categories for financial assets as the basis for line items in its statement of financial position.

4 Significance of financial instruments

One of the two key objectives of IFRS 7 is to require entities to provide disclosures in their financial statements that enable users to evaluate the significance of financial instruments for the entity's financial position and performance. To achieve this objective, disclosures are required relating to the statement of financial position, statement of comprehensive income and equity.

4.1 Disclosures relating to the statement of financial position

IFRS 7 requires specific disclosures in respect of items included in the statement of financial position. Some are very broad (e.g. disclosing financial asset and financial liabilities by classification category) and others are very specific (e.g. disclosures regarding collateral and derecognition).

4.1.1 Categories of financial assets and financial liabilities

An entity is required to disclose the carrying amount for each financial instrument category as defined by IFRS 9 either in the statement of financial position or in the notes to the financial statements. The carrying amounts of each of the following categories are specifically required to be disclosed:

[IFRS 7:8]

(a) financial assets measured at fair value through profit or loss, showing separately (i) those designated as such upon initial recognition or where a credit exposure is subsequently measured at FVTPL in accordance with IFRS 9:6.7.1 and (ii) those mandatorily measured at fair value in accordance with IFRS 9;

(b)-(d) [deleted]

(e) financial liabilities at fair value through profit or loss, showing separately (i) those designated as such upon initial recognition or where a credit exposure is subsequently measured at FVTPL in accordance with IFRS 9:6.7.1 and (ii) those that meet the definition of held for trading in IFRS 9;

(f) financial assets measured at amortised cost;

(g) financial liabilities measured at amortised cost; and

(h) financial assets measured at fair value through other comprehensive income, showing separately:

  (i) financial assets that are measured at fair value through other comprehensive income in accordance with IFRS 9:4.1.2A (e.g. debt instruments that are held within a business model that is collecting contractual cash flows and selling financial assets) (see **section 5** in **chapter B2**); and

  (ii) investments in equity instruments designated as such upon initial recognition in accordance with IFRS 9:5.7.5 (see **5.3.2** in **chapter B2**).

These disclosures are intended to assist users in understanding the extent to which accounting policies affect the amounts at which financial assets and financial liabilities are recognised. [IFRS 7:BC14] Together with the disclosure of gains and losses by category of financial instrument, the disclosure of the carrying amounts for each category of financial instrument allows users to appraise management on its decisions to buy, sell or hold financial assets and to incur, maintain or discharge financial liabilities.

A derivative that is designated in a hedging relationship in which the derivative is not measured at FVTPL (e.g. in a cash flow hedge or hedge of a net investment in a foreign operation) does not appear to fit with the classification categories in IFRS 7:8 reproduced above. Similarly, financial liabilities that are written financial guarantee contracts that are not designated as at FVTPL and certain written loan commitments at a below-market interest rate that are not designated as at FVTPL do not fit in with the financial liability classification categories of amortised cost and FVTPL described above. It is reasonable, therefore, to include such items as a separate category in order to facilitate reconciliation between disclosures by category and the statement of financial position. Some entities may choose to show derivatives in effective hedging relationships, written financial guarantee contracts and loan commitments in separate captions both in the statement of financial position and in the notes.

4.1.2 Financial assets at FVTPL

An entity that designates certain debt instruments (or a group of debt instruments) as at fair value through profit or loss (FVTPL) (see **5.5.3** in **chapter B2**) is required to provide extensive disclosures. These disclosures are required because the application of the fair value option to these instruments may have a significant impact on the financial statements as a result of fair value movements and, in particular, those movements caused by changes in credit risk.

IFRS 7 requires disclosure of the following information for financial assets (or groups of financial assets) that have been designated as measured at fair value through profit or loss:

[IFRS 7:9]

(a) the maximum exposure to *credit risk* of the financial asset (or group of financial assets) designated as at fair value through profit or loss, or group of financial assets, at the end of the reporting period;

(b) the amount by which any related credit derivatives or similar instruments mitigate that maximum exposure to credit risk;

(c) the amount of change, during the period and cumulatively, in the fair value of the financial asset (or group of financial assets), that is attributable to changes in the credit risk of the financial asset determined either:

   (i) as the amount of change in its fair value that is not attributable to changes in market conditions that give rise to *market risk*; or

   (ii) using an alternative method the entity believes more faithfully represents the amount of change in its fair value that is attributable to changes in the credit risk of the asset.

   Changes in market conditions that give rise to market risk include changes in an observed (benchmark) interest rate, commodity price, foreign exchange rate or index of prices or rates; and

(d) the amount of the change in the fair value of any related credit derivatives or similar instruments that has occurred during the period and cumulatively since the financial asset was designated.

In addition, an entity should disclose:

[IFRS 7:11]

(a) the methods used to comply with the requirements in (c) above; and

(b) if the entity believes that the disclosure it has given to comply with the requirements in (c) above does not faithfully represent the change in the fair value of the financial asset attributable to changes in its credit risk, the reasons for reaching this conclusion and the factors it believes are relevant.

The maximum exposure to credit risk for a derivative is its carrying amount. [IFRS 7:BC50] The Standard is not clear whether the maximum exposure to credit risk for financial assets can also equal the carrying amount, which is fair value, when an entity designates those assets as at FVTPL.

The information to be disclosed regarding the maximum exposure to credit risk depends on whether exposure to credit loss is viewed as a 'cash loss' or a loss that will be recognised in the statement of comprehensive income. Credit risk is defined as "the risk that one party to a financial instrument will cause a financial loss for the other party by failing to discharge an obligation". [IFRS 7:Appendix A] If the maximum exposure to credit risk is viewed as a cash loss, then the amount to be disclosed would be the amount owed (e.g. if the fair value of the debt is CU70 and the amount owed is CU100, then the maximum 'cash loss' is CU100). If, however, the maximum exposure to credit risk is viewed as a loss that will be recognised in the statement of comprehensive income, then the carrying amount (i.e. the fair value of the assets in this instance) will be the amount that is required to be disclosed.

While either approach is supportable, an entity must apply a consistent policy in disclosing the maximum exposure to credit risk for financial assets that are designated as at FVTPL.

Example 4.1.2

Portfolio of assets designated at FVTPL

Entity A acquired at the beginning of the prior period a portfolio of non-amortising unsecured long-term loans with a fixed interest rate of 9 per cent and five years remaining to maturity. The loans meet the amortised cost criteria in IFRS 9:4.1.2. Entity A chooses to designate the loans as at FVTPL. The loans were acquired for CU905 million when the effective interest rate was 10 per cent, consisting of 8 per cent benchmark interest rate and 2 per cent credit spread. The par amount of the loans is CU1 billion. At the date of acquisition, Entity A entered into a credit default swap with a financial institution to provide credit protection on the loans with a notional of CU500 million. The credit default swap had an initial fair value of zero and remains outstanding at the end of the reporting period.

At the end of the reporting period:

- the fair value of the loans is CU896 million (prior year: CU852 million);
- benchmark interest rates for the remaining maturity are 8 per cent and credit spreads are 2.5 per cent (prior year: 9 per cent and 3 per cent respectively); and
- the fair value of the credit default swap is CU35 million (prior year: CU46 million).

The items to be disclosed in accordance with IFRS 7:9 are as follows.

(a) Maximum exposure to credit risk at the end of the reporting period

If maximum exposure to credit risk is viewed as being the loss that will be recognised in the statement of comprehensive income, then the amount to be disclosed would be CU896 million (prior year: CU852 million), being the fair value of the loans at the end of the reporting period.

If the maximum exposure to credit risk is viewed as being equal to a cash loss, then the amount to be disclosed would be CU1 billion (prior year: CU1 billion), being the amount owed by the borrower at the end of the reporting period.

Note: the entity cannot offset the loans and the credit default swaps because there is no right of set-off and the financial instruments are with different counterparties.

(b) Amount by which any related credit derivatives or similar instruments mitigate that maximum exposure to credit risk

The credit default swap provides credit protection for half of the loans. On a fair value basis, the maximum protection is equivalent to 56 per cent (prior year: 59 per cent) and on a cash loss basis is equivalent to 50 per cent (prior year: 50 per cent).

(c) Amount of change, during the period and cumulatively, in the fair value of loans that is attributable to changes in credit risk

The cumulative change in fair value due to credit risk of the loans is a CU16 million loss (prior year: CU27 million loss). The change in fair value due to credit risk for the period is a CU11 million gain.

4.1.3 Financial liabilities at FVTPL

When an entity has designated financial liabilities as at FVTPL, IFRS 7:10 & 10A require extensive disclosures, in particular regarding the reporting entity's creditworthiness. The disclosure requirements vary depending on whether all of the fair value gains or losses are recognised in profit or loss or whether only part of the fair value gains or losses are recognised in profit or loss because the effects of changes in the liability's credit risk are recognised in other comprehensive income (see **7.1.2.5** in **chapter B3**).

If the entity has designated a financial liability as at FVTPL and is required to present the effects of changes in that liability's credit risk in other comprehensive income, it is required to disclose:

[IFRS 7:10]

(a) the cumulative change in the fair value of the financial liability that is attributable to changes in the credit risk of that liability;

(b) the difference between the financial liability's carrying amount and the amount the entity would be contractually required to pay at maturity to the holder of the obligation;

(c) any transfers of the cumulative gain or loss within equity during the period, including the reason for such transfers;

(d) if a liability is derecognised during the period, the amount (if any) presented in other comprehensive income that was realised at derecognition.

If an entity has designated a financial liability as at FVTPL and is required to present all changes in the fair value of that liability (including the effects of changes in the credit risk of the liability) in profit or loss, it is required to disclose:

[IFRS 7:10A]

(a) the amount of change, during the period and cumulatively, in the fair value of the financial liability that is attributable to changes in the credit risk of that liability; and

(b) the difference between the financial liability's carrying amount and the amount the entity would be contractually required to pay at maturity to the holder of the obligation.

IFRS 7:BC22 states that the fair value may differ significantly from the settlement amount (i.e. the amount contractually required to be paid at maturity), in particular for financial liabilities with a long duration when an entity has experienced a significant deterioration in creditworthiness since the issue of those financial liabilities. In order to comply with the requirements of IFRS 7:10(b) (see above) the amount contractually required to be paid at maturity should be an undiscounted amount, not affected by the entity's own credit risk. To the extent that the amount payable at maturity is subject to variability (e.g. because the principal is index-linked), an estimation of this amount should also be included, whether or not the index-linked feature is a separately accounted for embedded derivative. This is consistent with the principle applied for liquidity risk disclosures (as discussed in **section 5.2.2**) where the effects of any embedded derivatives are included on an undiscounted basis based on conditions existing at the end of the reporting period (incorporating forward rates as applicable).

The Standard also requires disclosure of:

[IFRS 7:11]

(a) a detailed description of the methods used to comply with IFRS 7:9(c), 10(a), 10A(a) & IFRS 9:5.7.7(a), including an explanation of why the method is appropriate;

(b) if the entity believes that the disclosures it has made, either in the statement of financial position or in the notes, to comply with the requirements in IFRS 7:9(c), 10(a), 10A(a) or IFRS 9:5.7.7(a) does not faithfully represent the change in the fair value of the financial asset or financial liability attributable to changes in its credit risk, the reasons for reaching this conclusion and the factors it believes are relevant;

(c) a detailed description of the methodology or methodologies used to determine whether presenting the effects of changes in a liability's credit risk in other comprehensive income would create or enlarge an accounting mismatch in profit or loss. If an entity is required to present the effects of changes in a liability's credit risk in profit or loss, the disclosure must include a detailed description of the economic relationship described in IFRS 9:B5.7.6.

Example 4.1.3

Financial liabilities designated as at FVTPL

On the first day of its current financial period, Entity B issued a 5-year bond in order to finance the expansion of its operations. The bond trades on a recognised bond exchange. Entity B's year end is 31 December 20X1.

Details of the bond are as follows.

Maturity date:	31 December 20X5
Nominal value:	CU500 million
Coupon:	9%, payable annually on 31 December in arrears
Issue price (1 January 20X1):	CU450 million
Fair value (31 December 20X1):	CU400 million
5-year LIBOR (1 January 20X1):	10.5%
4-year LIBOR (31 December 20X1):	12.75%

IFRS 7 requires disclosure of the amount of change in the fair value of the financial liability that is attributable to changes in the liability's credit risk. As permitted by IFRS 9:B5.7.18, Entity B determines the amount of change in the fair value of the financial liability that is attributable to changes in the liability's credit risk as the change in the liability's fair value that is not attributable to changes in market conditions that give rise to market risk. This is appropriate as the only relevant changes in market conditions for the liability are changes in the observed (benchmark) interest rate. Entity B calculates the amount of change in the fair value of the financial liability that is attributable to changes in the liability's credit risk as follows.

(a) Determine the liability's internal rate of return (IRR) at the start of the period using the fair value of the liability and the liability's contractual cash flows at the start of the period.

Year 0	Year 1	Year 2	Year 3	Year 4	Year 5
(450,000,000)[1]	45,000,000[2]	45,000,000[2]	45,000,000[2]	45,000,000[2]	545,000,000[3]

[1] The bonds are recognised initially at fair value (CU450 million).

[2] Yearly cash flows are determined as being 9% x CU500 million.

[3] The terminal cash flow is determined as the nominal value of the bonds plus the interest coupon.

The IRR, equal to the effective interest rate, at the issue date is 11.76%.

(b) Deduct the observed (benchmark) interest rate at the start of the period from the IRR to arrive at an instrument-specific component of the IRR (i.e. the portion of the effective interest that relates to credit risk).

11.76% − 10.5% = 1.26% instrument specific component of the IRR

(c) Compute the present value of the cash flows of the liability using the liability's contractual cash flows at the end of the period and a discount rate equal to the sum of the observed benchmark interest rate at the end of the period and the instrument-specific component of the internal rate of return determined in (b).

Remaining cash flows to be discounted using an IRR of 14.01% (12.75% + 1.26%)

Year 2	Year 3	Year 4	Year 5
45,000,000	45,000,000	45,000,000	545,000,000

Present value is equal to CU427,059,828 as at the end of the reporting period.

(d) Compute the change in the fair value of the liability that is not attributable to changes in the observed (benchmark) interest rate as the difference between the fair value of the liability and the amount determined above.

Change in fair value due to changes in credit risk is determined as CU27,059,828 (CU427,059,828 – CU400,000,000).

The required disclosures may be provided as follows.

Financial liabilities

During the year, the group issued a commercial bond with a nominal value of CU500 million with a maturity of five years that was designated as at fair value through profit or loss at initial recognition. The fair value and the change in that fair value that can be ascribed to changes in underlying credit risk are set out below.

	31 December 20X1	31 December 20X0
Fair value of commercial bond	CU400,000,000	–
Change in fair value of commercial bond not attributable to changes in market conditions	CU(27,059,828)	–
Difference between carrying amount and amount contractually required to be paid at maturity	CU100,000,000	–

The group estimates changes in fair value due to credit risk by estimating the amount of change in the fair value that is not due to changes in market conditions that give rise to market risk.

Example 4.1.3 assumes that changes in the fair value arising from factors other than changes in the bond's credit risk or changes in interest rates are not significant. Irrespective of whether IFRS 9 requires separation of the embedded derivative the effects of the embedded derivative need to be excluded.

The methodology illustrated in **example 4.1.3** is a reasonable approach to determining the extent to which fair value movements are attributable to changes in credit risk for vanilla debt instruments. When other factors affect the change in the instrument's fair value (e.g. embedded derivatives), then alternative methods may be used to calculate the amount of change in the fair value attributable to changes in credit risk of the liability. Such methods are required to be disclosed, as well as why those methods provide a more faithful representation than the method described in IFRS 7. [IFRS 7:BC21(a)] Liabilities, such as unit-linked insurance contracts (for which the amount of the liability reflects the performance of a defined pool of assets) present particular challenges.

4.1.4 Reclassification

IFRS 7 requires extensive disclosures when financial assets are reclassified (e.g. from amortised cost to FVTPL or vice versa) as a result of a change in the entity's business model for managing financial assets. If an entity reclassifies financial assets in the current or previous reporting periods, the entity is required to disclose:

[IFRS 7:12B]

(a) the date of reclassification;

(b) a detailed explanation of the change in business model and a qualitative description of its effect on the entity's financial statements; and

(c) the amount reclassified into and out of each category.

For each reporting period following reclassification until derecognition, when a financial asset is reclassified from FVTPL to amortised cost, an entity is required to disclose the effective interest rate determined on the date of reclassification and the interest income or expense recognised. [IFRS 7:12C]

If since its last annual reporting date an entity has reclassified financial assets so that they are measured at amortised cost, it is required to disclose:

[IFRS 7:12D]

(a) the fair value of the financial assets at the end of the reporting period; and

(b) the fair value gain or loss that would have been recognised in profit or loss during the reporting period if the financial assets had not been reclassified.

In May 2010, the IASB issued *Improvements to IFRSs*, which includes an amendment to IAS 34 *Interim Financial Reporting* to make specific reference to including in interim financial statements disclosures where there are changes in the classification of assets as a result of a change in the purpose or use of those assets since the end of the last annual reporting period.

4.1.5 Investments in equity instruments designated at fair value through other comprehensive income

If an entity chooses to designate an investment in an equity instrument as at fair value through comprehensive income (FVTOCI) as permitted by IFRS 9:4.1.4 an entity is required to disclose:

[IFRS 7:11A]

(a) which investments in equity instruments have been designated to be measured at FVTOCI;

(b) the reasons for using this presentation alternative;

(c) the fair value of each such investment at the end of the reporting period;

(d) dividends recognised during the period, showing separately those related to investments derecognised during the reporting period and those related to investments held at the end of the reporting period; and

(e) any transfers of the cumulative gain or loss within equity during the period including the reason for such transfers.

In addition, in the reporting period in which an investment is derecognised, the entity is required to disclose:

[IFRS 7:11B]

(a) the reasons for disposing of the investments;

(b) the fair value of the investments at the date of derecognition; and

(c) the cumulative gain or loss on disposal.

4.1.6 Transfers of financial assets

When an entity transfers financial assets they may continue to be recognised, derecognised in full, or partly derecognised to the extent of the transferor's continuing involvement. The derecognition requirements of IFRS 9 are extensive and are discussed at length in **chapter B8**.

IFRS 7 requires specific disclosures relating to transfers of financial assets because it is considered to be important for users of financial statements to be able to evaluate the significance of such transactions and the risks retained, the nature of the risks and rewards to which the entity continues to be exposed, and the extent of its continuing involvement with the transferred asset.

IAS 1.122 requires an entity to disclose the judgements that management has made in the process of applying its accounting policies. IAS 1:123(b) makes specific reference to disclosure of the judgements made in determining when substantially all the significant risks and rewards of ownership of financial assets and lease assets are transferred to other entities.

The disclosures for transfers of financial assets required by IFRS 7 are by class of financial asset and can be provided either by type of financial assets (i.e. differentiating by characteristics of the assets) or by type of risks or rewards of ownership to which the entity remains exposed.

In October 2010, the IASB issued amendments to IFRS 7, *Disclosures – Transfers of Financial Assets*, which substantially changed the disclosure requirements regarding transfers of financial assets. These extensive disclosures are required to be presented in a single note in the financial statements for all transferred financial assets that are not derecognised and for any continuing involvement in a transferred asset, existing at the reporting date, irrespective of when the related transfer transaction occurred. [IFRS 7:42A] This has the effect of requiring extensive disclosures regarding transfers that arose in periods prior to the comparative period.

The objective of the disclosures is to help users of financial statements:

[IFRS 7:42B]

(a) to understand the relationship between transferred financial assets that are not derecognised in their entirety and the associated liabilities; and

(b) to evaluate the nature of and risks associated with the entity's continuing involvement in derecognised financial assets.

In addition to the specific disclosures required under IFRS 7:42D-42G, an entity is required to disclose any information that it considers necessary to meet the disclosure objective described in IFRS 7:42B. [IFRS 7:42H] The scope of the disclosure requirements extend to all transfers of all or part of a financial asset ('the transferred asset') if, and only if, either the transferor:

[IFRS 7:42A]

(a) transfers the contractual rights to receive the cash flows of that financial asset; or

(b) retains the contractual rights to receive the cash flows of that financial asset, but assumes a contractual obligation to pay the cash flows to one or more recipients in an arrangement.

The scope of IFRS 7's disclosure requirements regarding transferred financial assets (as set out in IFRS 7:42A immediately above) differs from the definition of a transfer in IFRS 9:3.2.4 (see **3.1.4** in **chapter B8**) for the purposes of determining whether the transferred asset is derecognised; IFRS 7:42A(a) is the same as IFRS 9:3.2.4(a), but IFRS 7:42A(b) is not the same as IFRS 9:3.2.4(b). An arrangement whereby the transferor retains the contractual rights to receive the cash flows of the financial asset but assumes an obligation to pay the cash flows to one or more recipients is only regarded as a transfer under IFRS 9 if it passes all three of the pass-through tests in IFRS 9:3.2.5. Meeting the pass-through tests is not a requirement for the arrangement to fall within the scope of IFRS 7:42A because the IFRS 7 disclosure requirements are intended to be broader and to capture transactions where the all three of the pass-through tests are not necessarily met.

The disclosure requirements in IFRS 7 prior to the October 2010 amendments relating to assets that continue to be recognised in part or in full, were retained in the revised IFRS 7 because the Board considers that these requirements still provide relevant information to users of financial statements. The amendments to IFRS 7 introduce additional disclosure requirements regarding the nature of the relationship between transferred assets and associated liabilities, including restrictions on the transferor's use of the transferred asset, and additional disclosures when the transferee has recourse only to the transferred assets. Following the October 2010 amendments, all of these requirements are set out in IFRS 7:42D.

When a transferred asset is not derecognised in its entirety, the transferor is required to disclose:

[IFRS 7:42D]

(a) the nature of the transferred assets;

(b) the nature of the risks and rewards of ownership to which the entity is exposed;

(c) a description of the nature of the relationship between the transferred assets and the associated liabilities, including restrictions arising from the transfer on the reporting entity's use of the transferred assets;

(d) when the counterparty (counterparties) to the associated liabilities has (have) recourse only to the transferred assets, a schedule that sets out the fair value of the transferred assets, the fair value of the associated liabilities and the net position (the difference between the fair value of the transferred assets and the associated liabilities);

(e) when the entity continues to recognise all of the transferred assets, the carrying amounts of the transferred assets and the associated liabilities; and

(f) when the entity continues to recognise the assets to the extent of its continuing involvement (see IFRS 9:3.2.6(c)(ii) & 3.2.16, see **3.4** in **chapter B8**), the total carrying amount of the original assets before the transfer, the carrying amount of the assets that the entity continues to recognise, and the carrying amount of the associated liabilities.

The Board considered that additional disclosures regarding the nature of the relationship between the transferred assets and associated liabilities was necessary in order for users to understand the economic benefit generated by assets of an entity that cannot be used in an unrestricted manner. Without this disclosure, users could incorrectly conclude that, because transferred assets continue to be recognised, the transferor has unlimited rights to the economic benefits from those assets, even though as a result of the transfer the transferee has a part or a full beneficial interest in the economic benefits of the transferred assets. Further, requiring additional disclosures when associated liabilities will be settled entirely from the proceeds received from the transferred assets ensures that users understand whether a transferee only has claims against the transferred assets as opposed to having claims against the assets of the transferor in general. [IFRS 7:BC65H]

Prior to the October 2010 amendments to IFRS 7, the disclosure requirements in IFRS 7 only related to transfers of assets where the transferred asset continued to be recognised either in full or partly to the extent of the transferor's continuing involvement. The amendments to IFRS 7 retain this focus but also add extensive disclosure requirements for transfers of financial assets that are derecognised. The introduction of disclosures regarding derecognised assets where the transferor retains some continuing exposure to the transferred asset provides a more comprehensive picture of the entity's exposure to risk as a result of transferring financial assets.

Example 4.1.6A

Transferred financial assets that are not derecognised in their entirety

[IFRS 7:IG40B]

Illustrating the application of IFRS 7:42D(d) and (e)

	Financial assets at fair value through profit or loss		**Amortised cost**		**Fair value through other comprehensive income**
	CU million		**CU million**		**CU million**
	Trading securities	**Derivatives**	**Mortgages**	**Consumer loans**	**Equity investments**
Carrying amount of assets	X	X	X	X	X
Carrying amount of associated liabilities	(X)	(X)	(X)	(X)	(X)
For those liabilities that recourse only to the transferred assets:					
Fair value of assets	X	X	X	X	X
Fair value of associated liabilities	(X)	(X)	(X)	(X)	(X)
Net position	X	X	X	X	X

The disclosure requirements of IFRS 7:42D apply only in respect of transferred assets that have not been derecognised in full. A transferred asset will not be derecognised in full if either (a) the transferor retains substantially all the risks and rewards of ownership of the transferred asset, or (b) the transferor neither transfers nor retains substantially all the risks of rewards of ownership of the transferred asset but continues to control the transferred asset. Examples of arrangements that would meet these requirements and, therefore, be subject to the disclosures requirements of IFRS 7:42D are:

- a transfer of a financial asset with an obligation to repurchase the transferred asset in the future at a fixed price;
- a transfer of a financial asset where the transferor has an option to buy the transferred asset back at a fixed price and, at the date of transfer, the option strike price is deeply in the money;
- a transfer of a financial asset where the transferee has the right to require the transferor to repurchase the transferred asset back at a fixed price and, at the date of transfer, the option strike price is deeply in the money.
- a transfer of a financial asset where the transferor has an option to buy the transferred asset back at a fixed price and, at the date of transfer, the option strike price is neither deeply in nor deeply out of the money and the asset is not readily obtainable in the market;
- a transfer of a financial asset where the transferee has the right to require the transferor to repurchase the transferred asset back at a fixed price and, at the date of transfer, the option strike price is neither deeply in nor deeply out of the money and the asset is not readily obtainable in the market;
- a transfer of a financial asset where the transferor has written a financial guarantee (or provided other credit enhancement) to the transferee agreeing to reimburse the transferee for credit losses suffered on the transferred asset and, at the date of transfer, the financial guarantee contract results in the transferor retaining substantially all the risks and rewards of ownership; and
- a transfer of a financial asset where the transferor has written a financial guarantee (or providing other credit enhancement) to the transferee agreeing to reimburse the transferee for credit losses suffered on the transferred asset and, at the date of transfer, the financial guarantee contract results in the transferor neither retaining nor transferring substantially all the risks and rewards of ownership of the transferred asset, and the transferor controls the transferred assets.

If a transferred asset is derecognised and the transferor retains a 'continuing involvement' in the transferred financial asset IFRS 7 requires the transferor to provide extensive disclosures. A transferor has a continuing involvement in the transferred asset if, as part of the transfer, the transferor retains any of the contractual rights or obligations inherent in the transferred financial asset or obtains any new contractual rights or obligations relating to the transferred financial asset. The following do not constitute continuing involvement:

[IFRS 7:42C]

(a) normal representations and warranties relating to fraudulent transfer and concepts of reasonableness, good faith and fair dealings that could invalidate a transfer as a result of legal action;

(b) forward, option and other contracts to reacquire the transferred financial asset for which the contract price (or exercise price) is the fair value of the transferred financial asset; or

(c) an arrangement whereby an entity retains the contractual rights to receive the cash flows of a financial asset but assumes a contractual obligation to pay the cash flows to one or more entities and the conditions in IFRS 9:3.2.5(a)-(c) are met (see **3.1.4** in **chapter B8**).

In September 2014 the IASB issued *Annual Improvements to IFRSs 2012-2014 Cycle*. The amendment clarifies how an entity should apply the guidance in IFRS 7:42C to a servicing contract in order to decide whether a servicing contract is 'continuing involvement' for the purposes of applying the disclosure requirements in IFRS 7:42E-H. Servicing agreements can arise when an entity transfers a financial asset but retains the right to service that asset for a fee. The amendment provides an example where a servicer will have continuing involvement in the transferred asset if the servicing fee is dependent on the amount or timing of the cash flows collected from the transferred asset. Another example provided notes that a servicer has continuing involvement if a fixed fee would not be paid in full because of non-performance of the transferred financial asset. In these two examples, the servicer has an interest in the future performance of the transferred asset.

The amendments apply retrospectively for annual periods beginning on or after 1 January 2016, except for any period presented that begins before the annual period for which the entity first applies the amendments. To avoid the risk of hindsight being applied, the Board decided to require the application of the amendment only to annual periods beginning on or after this date. The Board has characterised the transition provisions as retrospective despite this relief, because entities are required to look back to past derecognition events to determine whether a servicing asset or servicing liability needs to be disclosed. Earlier application is permitted in which case an entity shall disclose that it has applied those amendments for an earlier period. [IFRS 7:44AA and BC72A]

The use of the term 'continuing involvement' for IFRS 7 disclosures should not be confused with the continuing involvement derecognition requirements in IFRS 9:3.2.6(c)(ii) & 3.2.16 (see **3.4** in **chapter B8**). An asset that is derecognised to the extent of the transferor's continuing involvement in accordance with IFRS 9 would be subject to the disclosure requirements in IFRS 7:42D described above because the transferred asset is not derecognised in its entirety. This compares with the specific disclosures required in IFRS 7:42E-H when an asset is derecognised but the transferor retains some continuing involvement. It is unfortunate that both terms are used to apply to transfers of financial assets, one for applying the derecognition requirements and one for applying the disclosure requirements, but their application applies to different subsets of transferred assets.

When the transferor derecognises the transferred asset in its entirety but has some continuing involvement in the asset, the transferor is required to disclose, as a minimum, for each type of continuing involvement at each reporting date:

[IFRS 7:42E]

(a) the carrying amount of the assets and liabilities that are recognised in the entity's statement of financial position and represent the entity's continuing involvement in the derecognised financial assets, and the line items in which the carrying amount of those assets and liabilities are recognised;

(b) the fair value of the assets and liabilities that represent the entity's continuing involvement in the derecognised financial assets;

(c) the amount that best represents the entity's maximum exposure to loss from its continuing involvement in the derecognised financial assets, and information showing how the maximum exposure to loss is determined;

(d) the undiscounted cash outflows that would or may be required to repurchase derecognised financial assets (e.g. the strike price in an option agreement) or other amounts payable to the transferee in respect of the transferred assets. If the cash outflow is variable, then the amount disclosed should be based on the conditions that exist at each reporting date;

Example 4.1.6B

Transferred financial assets that are derecognised in their entirety

[IFRS 7:IG40B]

Illustrating the application of IFRS 7:42E(a) - (d)

	Cash outflows to repurchase transferred (derecognised) assets	Carrying amount of continuing involvement in statement of financial position			Fair value of continuing involvement		Maximum exposure to loss
	CU million	CU million			CU million		CU million
Type of continuing involvement		Financial assets at fair value through profit or loss	Financial assets at fair value through other comprehensive income	Financial liabilities at fair value through profit or loss	Assets	Liabilities	
Written put options	(X)			(X)		(X)	X
Purchased call options	(X)	X			X		X
Securities lending	(X)			(X)	X	(X)	X
Total		X		(X)	X	(X)	X

(e) a maturity analysis of the undiscounted cash outflows that would or may be required to repurchase the derecognised financial assets or other amounts payable to the transferee in respect of the transferred assets, showing the remaining contractual maturities of the entity's continuing involvement;

Example 4.1.6C

Transferred financial assets that are derecognised in their entirety

[IFRS 7:IG40B]

Illustrating the application of IFRS 7:42E(e)

Undiscounted cash flows to repurchase transferred assets

	Maturity of continuing involvement CU million							
Type of continuing involvement	Total	less than 1 month	1–3 months	3–6 months	6 months – 1 year	1–3 years	3–5 years	more than 5 years
Written put options	X		X	X	X	X		
Purchased call options	X			X	X	X		X
Securities lending	X	X	X					

(f) qualitative information that explains and supports the quantitative disclosures required in (a)-(e).

The disclosures required by IFRS 7:42E may be aggregated in respect of a particular asset if the transferor has more than one type of continuing involvement in that derecognised financial asset, and reported under one type of continuing involvement. [IFRS 7:42F]

In many cases, the existence of a continuing exposure to a transferred asset will result in the asset not being derecognised, in which case the disclosure requirements of IFRS 7:42E-H do not apply. The disclosure requirements of IFRS 7:42E-H should be applied in circumstances where, even though the transferor retains a continuing exposure to the transferred asset, the transferred asset is still derecognised. This is the case when the transferor either (a) does not retain substantially all the risks and rewards of ownership of the transferred asset following the transfer or, (b) if it did not transfer or retain substantially all the risks of rewards of ownership of the transferred asset, it also does not control the transferred asset. Examples of arrangements that would result in derecognition of the transferred asset despite some continuing involvement and which, therefore, would be subject to the disclosure requirements of IFRS 7:42E-H are:

- a transfer of a financial asset where the transferor has an option to buy the transferred asset back at a fixed price but, at the date of transfer, the option strike price is deeply out of the money;
- a transfer of a financial asset where the transferee has the right to require the transferor to repurchase the transferred asset back at a fixed price but, at the date of transfer, the option strike price is deeply out of the money;
- a transfer of a financial asset where the transferor has an option to buy the transferred asset back at a fixed price but, at the date of transfer, the option strike price is neither deeply in nor deeply out of the money and the asset is readily obtainable in the market;
- a transfer of a financial asset where the transferee has the right to require the transferor to repurchase the transferred asset back at a fixed price but, at the date of transfer, the option strike price is neither deeply in nor deeply out of the money and the asset is readily obtainable in the market;
- a transfer of a financial asset where the transferor has written a financial guarantee (or other credit enhancement) to the transferee agreeing to reimburse the transferee for credit losses suffered on the transferred asset, but, at the date of transfer, the financial guarantee contract does not prevent the transferor from transferring substantially all the risks and rewards of ownership; and

- a transfer of a financial asset where the transferor has written a financial guarantee (or other credit enhancement) to the transferee agreeing to reimburse the transferee for credit losses suffered on the transferred asset, but, at the date of transfer, the financial guarantee contract results in the transferor neither retaining nor transferring substantially all the risks and rewards of ownership of the transferred asset and the transferor does not control the transferred assets.

For each type of continuing involvement, the transferor is also required to disclose:

[IFRS 7:42G]

(a) the gain or loss recognised at the date of transfer of the assets;

(b) income and expenses recognised, both in the reporting period and cumulatively, from the entity's continuing involvement in the derecognised financial assets (e.g. fair value changes in derivative instruments); and

(c) if the total amount of proceeds from transfer activity (that qualifies for derecognition) in a reporting period is not evenly distributed throughout the reporting period (e.g. if a substantial proportion of the total amount of transfer activity takes place in the closing days of a reporting period):

  (i) when the greatest transfer activity took place within that reporting period (e.g. the last five days before the end of the reporting period);

  (ii) the amount (e.g. related gains or losses) recognised from transfer activity in that part of the reporting period; and

  (iii) the total amount of proceeds from transfer activity in that part of the reporting period.

Entities are required to provide this information for each period for which a statement of comprehensive income is presented.

The Board considered that disclosure of the gain or loss on derecognition and the timing of recognition of that gain or loss as required by IFRS 7:42G(a) is useful information because it illustrates the proportion of an entity's profit or loss that arises from transferred financial assets in which the entity also has a continuing involvement. This information is useful in assessing the extent to which an entity generates profits from transferring financial assets while retaining some form of continuing involvement and thus exposure to risk. [IFRS 7:BC65M]

The requirement for extensive disclosure if the transfer activity during the period is not evenly distributed was introduced to highlight instances of potential 'window dressing' where the transfer transaction might have been undertaken for the purpose of altering the appearance of the statement of financial position at the reporting date rather than for an ongoing commercial or financing purpose. [IFRS 7:BC65N]

4.1.7 Collateral

An entity is required to disclose the carrying amount of financial assets it has pledged as collateral (non-cash financial assets) for liabilities or contingent liabilities, including amounts the transferor has reclassified when the transferee has the right to sell or pledge the collateral (see **3.5** in **chapter B8**). The entity is also required to disclose the terms and conditions relating to its pledge. [IFRS 7:14] The terms and conditions may include:

- how much collateral needs to be maintained as security for the loans; and
- the type of collateral that needs to be provided as security for the loans.

When an entity holds collateral (both financial and non-financial assets) as security for financial assets loaned to another entity and it is permitted to sell or repledge in the absence of default by the owner of the collateral, the entity is required to disclose:

[IFRS 7:15]

- the fair value of the collateral held;
- the fair value of any such collateral that has been sold or repledged, and whether the entity has an obligation to return it; and
- the terms and conditions associated with its use of the collateral.

The disclosure of the existence of such collateral is important because it provides information to users of the financial statements regarding the amount of collateral used and available for use that may not be recognised in the statement of financial position of the entity.

Disclosure of collateral that the entity does not have the right to sell or pledge in the absence of default by the borrower is required in the credit risk disclosures note – see **5.2.1.2**.

4.1.8 Allowance account for credit losses

For assets measured FVTOCI in accordance with IFRS 9:4.1.2A (i.e. those debt instruments held which meet the cash flow characteristics tests and are held in a business with an objective to collect contractual cash flows and selling financial assets) the carrying value is equal to fair value and is therefore not reduced by an allowance for credit losses. Consequently, the loss allowance shall be disclosed in the notes to the financial statements. [IFRS 7:16A]

See **section 5.2.1** for detailed disclosures around expected credit losses.

4.1.9 Compound financial instruments with multiple embedded derivatives

IAS 32 prescribes how a compound financial instrument should be separated into its liability and equity components. For a compound financial instrument, the value of the debt or equity component may be affected by the other component. For instance, for convertible debt, the value of the debt component may depend in part on the relative attractiveness of early conversion. Therefore, the aggregate fair value of the convertible bond could differ from the sum of the estimated fair values of the debt and equity components if these were valued independently of each other. IAS 32 assigns the full value of these interdependencies to the liability component and treats equity as the residual. This allocation is arbitrary and could be argued to misstate the amount of the liability and, thereby, misstate the 'true' interest cost.

The interdependencies become even more significant when a compound instrument contains multiple embedded features whose values are also interdependent. For example, the values of an embedded purchased call option and a written equity conversion option in a callable convertible debt instrument depend in part on each other; because the equity conversion option is extinguished if the issuer exercises its purchased call option to redeem early, and vice versa, the value of the issuer purchased call option depends on the likelihood that the holder will exercise its right to convert early into shares. Because of the importance of these features, IFRS 7:17 requires an issuer of a compound instrument that has multiple embedded derivatives whose values are interdependent to disclose the existence of those features.

4.1.10 Defaults and breaches

For loans payable recognised at the end of the reporting period, disclosure is required of any defaults during the period of principal, interest, sinking fund, or redemption terms. In addition, the entity is required to disclose the carrying amount of any such loans that are in default at the end of the reporting period and whether the default was remedied, or the terms of the loans payable were renegotiated, before the financial statements were authorised for issue. [IFRS 7:18] Loans payable are defined as "financial liabilities, other than short-term trade payables on normal credit terms". [IFRS 7:Appendix A] It is important to note that disclosure regarding defaults is required even when those defaults were rectified by the end of the reporting period.

If, during the period, there were breaches of loan agreement terms other than those described in the IFRS 7:18 (see previous paragraph), the entity is required to disclose the same information as required by IFRS 7:18 if those breaches permitted the lender to demand accelerated repayment (unless the breaches were remedied, or the terms of the loan were renegotiated, on or before the end of the reporting period). [IFRS 7:19] Examples of such defaults include breaches of collateral requirements or loan covenant features, or a failure to administer the loan in terms of the loan agreement.

Such disclosures are designed to provide the users with relevant information about the entity's creditworthiness and its prospects for obtaining future loans. [IFRS 7:BC32]

The presentation of such loans as either current or non-current in accordance with the requirements of IAS 1 may also be affected by such defaults.

4.2 Disclosures relating to the statement of comprehensive income

IFRS 7 requires disclosure of specified income, expense, gains or loss items either in the statement of comprehensive income or in the notes to the financial statements.

4.2.1 Net gains or net losses

An entity is required to disclose in the statement of comprehensive income or in the notes the net gains or net losses for:

[IFRS 7:20(a)]

(i) financial assets or financial liabilities measured at fair value through profit or loss, showing separately those relating to financial assets or financial liabilities designated as such upon initial recognition, and those relating to financial assets or financial liabilities that are mandatorily measured at fair value in accordance with IFRS 9. For financial liabilities designated at FVTPL, an entity shall show separately the amount of gain or loss recognised in other comprehensive income and the amount recognised in profit or loss;

(ii)-(iv) [deleted]

(v) financial liabilities measured at amortised cost;

(vi) financial assets measured at amortised cost;

(vii) investments in equity instruments designated at fair value through other comprehensive income in accordance with IFRS 9:5.7.5 (see **5.3.2** in **chapter B2**)

(viii) financial assets measured at fair value through other comprehensive income in accordance with IFRS 9:4.1.2A (see **section 5** in **chapter B2**), showing separately the amount of gain or loss recognised in other comprehensive income during the period and the amount reclassified upon derecognition from accumulated other comprehensive income to profit or loss for the period.

The disclosures required by IFRS 7:20(a) are intended to assist users in understanding the extent to which accounting policies affect the performance of the entity and in understanding the nature of such gains and losses.

[IFRS 7:BC33] The disclosures also provide useful financial information, together with the disclosure of the carrying amounts by category of financial instruments, which is designed to allow users to appraise management on the manner in which it has classified financial instruments and, ultimately, its decisions to buy, sell or hold financial assets and to incur, maintain or discharge financial liabilities.

IFRS 7:BC33 states that the above disclosure of gains and losses analysed by IFRS 9's measurement categories complements the disclosures regarding the statement of financial position disclosures described in **section 4.1**. Despite this claim, it would appear that there is a difference between the disclosure requirements regarding the statement of financial position and the statement of comprehensive income. As explained in **section 4.1**, IFRS 7:8 requires disclosure of the carrying amounts of: financial assets *and* financial liabilities designated at FVTPL upon initial recognition, as well as financial assets *and* financial liabilities mandatorily measured at fair value with IFRS 9. The equivalent requirements regarding the statement of comprehensive income refer to financial assets *or* financial liabilities. It is reasonable to presume this difference in wording was an oversight in the drafting and, therefore, an entity should disclose information on net gain or net losses in relation to *both* financial assets *and* financial liabilities.

Financial instruments that have been designated as effective hedging instruments are not included in any of the financial instrument categories. Instead, any fair value movements relating to those instruments will be reported under the hedge accounting disclosure requirements.

4.2.2 Interest income and interest expense

IFRS 7 requires the disclosure of total interest income and total interest expense, determined using the effective interest method, for:

[IFRS 7:20(b)]

- financial assets measured at amortised cost; or
- financial assets measured at fair value through other comprehensive income in accordance with IFRS 9:4.1.2A (see **section 5** in **chapter B2**); or
- financial liabilities not at fair value through profit or loss.

Total interest expense is a component of the finance costs that are required to be disclosed as a line item in the statement of comprehensive income in accordance with IAS 1:82(b). Finance costs that are required to be disclosed in accordance with IAS 1 may also include amounts that arise on non-financial liabilities such as pension liabilities and income taxes. Separate disclosure of total interest expense allows users of the financial statements to understand the extent to which financial instruments contribute to finance costs.

4.2.3 Fee income and expense

IFRS 7 requires disclosure of fee income and expense, other than those amounts that are included in determining the effective interest rate, from financial assets and financial liabilities that are not at fair value through profit or loss. [IFRS 7:20(c)(i)] Such items include:

[IFRS 9:B5.4.3]

(a) fees charged for servicing a loan;

(b) commitment fees to originate a loan when the loan commitment is outside the scope of IFRS 9 and it is unlikely that a specific lending arrangement will be entered into; and

(c) loan syndication fees received by an entity that arranges a loan and retains no part of the loan package for itself (or retains a part at the same effective interest rate for comparable risk as other participants).

In addition, disclosure is required of trust and other fiduciary activities that result in the holding or investing of assets on behalf of individuals, trusts, retirement benefit plans, and other institutions. [IFRS 7:20(c)(ii)] This information indicates the level of such activities and helps users to estimate possible future income of the entity. [IFRS 7:BC35]

The extent of disclosure required under IFRS 7:20(c)(i) will depend on the type of business. Lenders are likely to be subject to a significant level of disclosure. Examples of fees will include annual membership fee income for credit cards (payable irrespective of whether the card holder uses the card); interchange fees received each time a credit card is used; merchant service commission fees for processing debit and credit transactions; fees for withdrawing cash on a credit card; overdraft fee income received irrespective of whether the borrower utilises the overdraft facility, etc. Many fees with respect to specific borrowing and lending will meet the definition of a transaction cost and, therefore, will form part of the effective interest rate (and, thereby, will not be subject to separate disclosure).

4.2.5 Amortised cost assets derecognised

IFRS 7 requires disclosure of an analysis of the gain or loss recognised in the statement of comprehensive income arising from the derecognition of financial assets measured at amortised cost, showing separately gains and losses arising from derecognition of financial assets. This disclosure is required to include the reasons for derecognising those financial assets. [IFRS 7:20A]

The disclosures required by IFRS 7:20A help to illustrate the degree to which, and the reasons why, assets are derecognised prior to their maturity in light of the entity asserting, as part of the amortised cost criteria, that the assets are held in a business with the objective of collecting the contractual cash flows.

Further, when IFRS 9 was issued, an additional disclosure requirement was added at IAS 1:82(aa) to require a line item in the statement of comprehensive income for "gains and losses arising from the derecognition of financial assets measured at amortised cost". This line item can be the sum of all gains and losses arising from derecognising financial assets measured at amortised cost. This compares with the disclosure required by IFRS 7:20A where, at a minimum, the analysis must show separately the total gains on derecognition of financial assets measured at amortised cost from the total losses.

4.3 Other disclosures

4.3.1 Accounting policies

IAS 1.117 requires disclosure of the measurement bases used in preparing the financial statements and the other accounting policies used that are relevant to an understanding of the financial statements. For financial instruments these would normally include:

[IFRS 7:B5]

(a) for financial liabilities designated as at fair value through profit or loss:
   - (i) the nature of the financial liabilities that have been designated as at fair value through profit or loss;
   - (ii) the criteria for so designating such financial liabilities on initial recognition; and
   - (iii) how the entity has satisfied the criteria in IFRS 9:4.2.2 for such designation. That disclosure includes a narrative description of the circumstances underlying the measurement or recognition inconsistency that would otherwise arise and a narrative description of how designation at fair value through profit or loss is consistent with the entity's documented risk management or investment strategy where applicable.

(aa) for financial assets designated as at fair value through profit or loss:
   - (i) the nature of the financial assets the entity has designated as at fair value through profit or loss; and
   - (ii) how the entity satisfied the criteria in IFRS 9:4.1.5 for such designation. That disclosure includes a narrative description of the circumstances underlying the measurement or recognition inconsistency that would otherwise arise;

(b) [deleted]

(c) whether regular way purchases and sales of financial assets are accounted for at trade date or at settlement date;

(d) [deleted]

(e) how net gains or net losses on each category of financial instrument are determined (e.g. whether the net gains or net losses on items at fair value through profit or loss include interest or dividend income);

It appears that the objective of the Standard in requiring an entity to disclose whether interest or dividends are shown separately from other fair value gains/losses is to make clear how interest and dividends are presented in income for non-derivative instruments that are carried at FVTPL. It is reasonable that if a derivative is not in a qualifying hedge relationship and, therefore, is required to be measured at FVTPL, movements in its fair value is a single number recognised in income and should not be split further across other profit or loss captions. This view is consistent with the SEC's view of US GAAP that if a derivative does not qualify for hedge accounting, income, expenses and fair value changes related to that derivative (whether realised or unrealised) must be presented in one line item in the financial statements and this line item must not change.

For non-derivative financial instruments carried at FVTPL, some entities include interest income and expense and dividend income in gains and losses on financial assets and financial liabilities respectively and others include them in separate line items for interest and dividends. The disclosure regarding whether net gains and losses on financial assets or financial liabilities that are carried as at FVTPL include interest income and expense or dividend income is designed to aid comparability between entities.

It seems reasonable to have a separate policy for interest-bearing instruments (e.g. debt) and non-interest-bearing instruments that earn a dividend (e.g. equity securities), but it is not acceptable to have a separate policy for interest-bearing assets and a separate policy for interest-bearing liabilities because this could result in overstating or understating interest income and expense.

(f) [deleted]

(g) [deleted]

4.3.2 Hedge accounting

The hedge accounting disclosure requirements set out in IFRS 7 apply equally to entities choosing to use the hedge accounting requirements in IFRS 9 and those that on adoption of IFRS 9 elect to continue to apply the hedge accounting requirements of IAS 39. [IFRS 9:BC6.104]

If an entity that applies IFRS 9 chooses to apply the hedge accounting requirements of IAS 39 there will be additional hedge accounting information to disclose under IFRS 7 relative to an entity that applies the IAS 39 hedge accounting requirements and does not apply IFRS 9. Some of the disclosure requirements will require careful consideration and might be difficult to apply when using IAS 39 as the basis for hedge accounting. An example would be the requirements in IFRS 7:23C to provide information about risk management strategies and descriptions of how risk management strategies are achieved through designating hedge relationships that frequently reset. IAS 39 does not necessarily look to risk management strategies as the basis for hedge accounting requirements. Consequently, more work would be required to link risk management strategies and the hedge accounting requirements in IAS 39 to provide useful information to users of financial statements.

Hedging activities are integral to an entity's financial risk management and are often significant. Hedge accounting for such activities can have a significant impact on the financial statements. In the absence of hedge accounting, changes in fair value of all derivatives would be reflected in profit or loss as they arise, often creating a mismatch with timing and recognition of gains or losses on the exposure that is being hedged. Hedge accounting attempts to overcome this measurement and recognition mismatch. Consequently, the hedge accounting disclosures in IFRS 7 provides a link between the accounting information and the risk management information.

The IFRS 7 disclosure requirements apply only for those risk exposures that an entity hedges and for which it elects to apply hedge accounting. [IFRS 7:21A]

Because hedge accounting is a choice and the decision to apply hedge accounting can have a significant effect on an entity's reported financial position and performance, IFRS 7 requires in-depth disclosures about the impact of applying hedge accounting. In addition, to provide context to the hedge accounting applied, IFRS 7 requires disclosures about the risk management strategy and how it affects the amount and timing of cash flows. Some of these disclosures may overlap with the quantitative disclosures required in respect of each type of risk by IFRS 7:34 (see **section 5.2**), and therefore an entity will need to consider how the two sets of disclosures are best provided consistently and without unnecessary repetition.

Hedge accounting disclosures provide users of financial statements with information about: [IFRS7:21A]

(a) an entity's risk management strategy and how it is applied to manage risk;

(b) how the entity's hedging activities may affect the amount, timing and uncertainty of its future cash flows; and

(c) the effect that hedge accounting has had on the entity's statement of financial position, statement of comprehensive income and statement of changes in equity.

IFRS 7 requires that an entity present the required disclosures in a single note or a separate section in its financial statements. However, an entity need not duplicate information that is already presented elsewhere, provided that the information is incorporated by cross-reference from the financial statements to some other statement, such as a management commentary or risk report, which is available to users of financial statements on the same terms as the financial statements and at the same time. Without the information incorporated by cross reference, the financial statements are incomplete. [IFRS 7:21B]

In practice, where audit requirements apply to the financial statements, it is likely that entities would include the necessary information within the (audited) financial statements rather than by reference to another audited statement.

A number of the hedge accounting disclosures require disclosure by risk category. In these cases, an entity must determine each risk category on the basis of the risk exposure it hedges and for which hedge accounting is applied and they should be applied consistently for all the hedge accounting disclosures. [IFRS 7:21C]

IFRS 7 does not prescribe the risk categories by which disclosures need to be disaggregated. Judgement will be required in categorising risks based on how an entity manages its risks through hedging. These categories should not be generic, but rather specific to the entity and how it manages its risks through hedging.

For example, an entity manages its floating interest rate risk using interest rate swaps (to change it to a fixed interest rate) for some hedging relationships, while it also uses cross-currency interest rate swaps to manage both floating interest rate and foreign exchange risk of other hedging relationships. Consequently, the entity would have one risk category for floating interest rate risk and another risk category for foreign exchange risk combined with floating interest rate risk. Whatever risk categories an entity decides to use, must be applied consistently throughout all hedge accounting disclosures. [IFRS 7:BC35O]

When presenting the hedge accounting disclosures, entities should determine (subject to the specific disclosures required):

- the level of detail to disclose;
- how much emphasis to place on different aspects of the disclosure requirements;

- the appropriate level of aggregation and disaggregation (which should be the same as that used for related information disclosed under IFRS 13 *Fair Value Measurement*); and
- whether users of financial statements need additional explanations to evaluate the quantitative information disclosed. [IFRS 7:21D]

By using the same level of aggregation or disaggregation for hedge accounting disclosures under IFRS 7 and related information disclosed under IFRS 13, users should be able to identify the financial instruments not designated as hedging instruments by simply comparing the disclosures with each other. In addition, users of financial statements should be able to understand how entities manage the risks it is exposed to as a result of financial instruments using the disclosure requirements in IFRS 7 that are not related to the hedge accounting disclosures. [IFRS 7:BC35MM]

4.3.2.1 Risk management strategy

The hedge accounting disclosures in IFRS 7 do not simply focus on the effect of the decision to apply hedge accounting on the financial statements. They also aim to provide context by requiring entities to explain their risk management strategy for each risk category of risk exposure that it decides to hedge and for which hedge accounting is applied. There is some flexibility in how such explanations are provided, however, IFRS 7:22A states that "the explanation should enable users of financial statements to evaluate (for example):

(a) how each risk arises.

(b) how the entity manages each risk; this includes whether the entity hedges an item in its entirety for all risks or hedges a risk component (or components) of an item and why.

(c) the extent of risk exposures that the entity manages."

IFRS 7:22A states that "the explanation *should* enable users of financial statements to evaluate (*for example*): ..." (emphasis added). The use of both "should" and "for example" make it ambiguous as to whether the list of items are just examples of what *could* be covered by the explanation of the risk management strategy or whether they are items that *should* be covered as a minimum requirement. That said, it would seem reasonable that any explanation of risk management strategy would at least include these items. See **example 4.3.2.1A** for an example of disclosures for foreign currency risk.

To meet the above requirement, the information should include (but is not limited to) a description of:

[IFRS 7:22B]

(a) the hedging instruments that are used (and how they are used) to hedge risk exposures;

(b) how the entity determines the economic relationship between the hedged item and the hedging instrument for the purpose of assessing hedge effectiveness; and

(c) how the entity establishes the hedge ratio and what the sources of hedge ineffectiveness are.

In addition to the above requirements, when an entity designates a specific risk component as a hedged item it is required to provide qualitative or quantitative information about:

[IFRS 7:22C]

(a) how the entity determined the risk component that is designated as the hedged item (including a description of the nature of the relationship between the risk component and the item as a whole);

(b) how the risk component relates to the item in its entirety (e.g. the designated risk component historically covered 80 per cent of the changes in fair value of the item as a whole).

Example 4.3.2.1A

Example disclosure of the risk management strategy for foreign exchange risk for a Japanese shipping entity

Company A (a Japanese shipping entity) is exposed to foreign exchange risk from international sales and from purchases of fuel, ships and spare parts. The foreign currencies the company is exposed to are the US dollar, euro and pound sterling. The Company hedges its forecast foreign currency cash flows out to 24 months. A net exposure for each currency is determined first to allow for any natural offset. Of the three currencies it is a net payer of US dollars and net receiver of euro and pound sterling. The following proportion of each net exposure in each currency is hedged:

0-3 months	100%
3-6 months	90%
6-12 months	80%
12-18 months	60%
18-24 months	40%

The risk management strategy allows for up to 10% deviation from the above proportions for exposures beyond 12 months and 5% deviation for exposures within the next 12 months.

The Company uses a combination of over-the-counter foreign currency forward contracts and foreign currency bank accounts (in credit or debit positions) to economically hedge its foreign currency risk. When forward contracts are used, the term of the forward matches the month in which the net exposure is forecast to occur.

When applying hedge accounting the company designates a gross position of foreign sales or purchases in a cash flow hedge relationship. The hedge ratio is 100 per cent because the critical terms of the hedging instrument match those of the hedged item. The primary source of hedge ineffectiveness arises from credit risk on the forward contracts since these are uncollateralised. However, the amount of hedge ineffectiveness recognised in the current year and prior year was not material.

4.3.2.2 The amount, timing and uncertainty of future cash flows

To supplement the qualitative information about the entity's risk management strategy, IFRS 7 requires quantitative information to be disclosed, by risk category, to allow the evaluation of the terms and conditions of hedging instruments and how they affect the amount, timing and uncertainty of future cash flows of the entity. [IFRS 7:23A]

To meet the above objective, an entity must provide a breakdown that discloses:

[IFRS 7:23B]

(a) a profile of the timing of the nominal amount of the hedging instrument; and

(b) if applicable, the average price or rate (for example strike or forward prices, etc.) of the hedging instrument.

Example 4.3.2.2A

Disclosure of amount, timing and uncertainty of future cash flows

The following table presents the Yen nominal amounts (thousands) of the foreign currency forwards contracts used to hedge foreign currency risk along with the average exchange rate.

	0 – 6 months	***6 – 12 months***	***Beyond 12 months***
USD Forward contracts	**125,000**	**105,000**	**150,000**
Average exchange rate to JPY	90	100	124
EUR Forward contracts	**(53,000)**	**(40,000)**	**(35,000)**
Average exchange rate to JPY	136	145	140
GBP Forward contracts	**(82,000)**	**(64,000)**	**(90,000)**
Average exchange rate to JPY	150	170	192

In situations in which an entity frequently resets (i.e. discontinue and restart) hedging relationships because both the hedging instrument and the hedged item frequently change (i.e. an entity uses a dynamic process in which both the exposure and the hedging instruments used to manage the exposure do not remain the same for long), the above disclosures about the terms and conditions of hedging instruments (IFRS 7:23A) and the profile of timing of nominal amounts and average rates (IFRS 7:23B) are not required.

The Board did not require these disclosures for entities hedging on a dynamic basis because it felt in those circumstances, providing information about the terms and conditions of the hedging instruments would not be useful given that the hedging instruments are in a hedge relationship only for a short period at a time before being redesignated or left undesignated. [IFRS 7:BC35Z]

In place of these disclosures, for dynamic hedges an entity is required to expand its discussion of the risk management strategy and how it uses hedge accounting to reflect this by requiring the following to be disclosed:

[IFRS 7:23C]

(a) information about what the ultimate risk management strategy is in relation to those hedging relationships;

(b) a description of how it reflects its risk management strategy by using hedge accounting and designating those particular hedging relationships; and

(c) an indication of how frequently the hedging relationships are discontinued and restarted as part of the entity's process in relation to those hedging relationships.

Because the designated hedging relationship changes frequently, the specific relationships at the reporting date might not be representative of the normal volumes during the period. In situations when the volume of hedging relationships is unrepresentative of normal volumes during the period IFRS 7 requires disclosure of that fact and the reason the volumes are unrepresentative. [IFRS 7:24D]

Furthermore, for all types or hedges, including dynamic hedges, IFRS 7 requires:

- by risk category, a description of the sources of hedge ineffectiveness that are expected to affect the hedging relationship during its term. If other sources of hedge ineffectiveness emerge in a hedging relationship, an entity shall disclose those sources by risk category and explain the resulting hedge ineffectiveness. [IFRS 7:23D and 23E]
- for cash flow hedges, a description of any forecast transaction for which hedge accounting had been used in the previous period, but which is no longer expected to occur. [IFRS 7:23F]

It is noted that some of the disclosure requirements in IFRS 7:23D and 23E overlap with the requirements in IFRS 7:22B(c) which also require disclosures about sources of hedge ineffectiveness.

4.3.2.3 *Effects of hedge accounting on financial position and performance*

IFRS 7 requires that the effects of hedge accounting on an entity's financial position and performance be disclosed in tabular format reflecting the accounting treatment applied (e.g. cash flow hedge accounting or fair value hedge accounting).

Even though users of financial statements do not necessarily evaluate an entity's hedging activities by the accounting treatment applied, providing information in this format provides a sufficient link between the accounting information and the risk management information. [IFRS 7:BC35EE]

The disclosure requirements about the effects of hedge accounting are extensive and, depending on the level of aggregation, could provide a user of the financial statements the ability to reverse out the effects of hedge accounting on the financial position and performance of the entity. This is because the disclosures require detailed information about the amounts recognised in respect of hedging instruments, hedged items, including any hedge ineffectiveness, as well as disclosure of the line items affected by hedge accounting.

With respect to hedging instruments, entities are required to provide the following information, in tabular format, separately by risk category for each type of hedge (i.e. fair value hedge, cash flow hedge or hedge of a net investment in a foreign operation):

[IFRS 7:24A]

(a) the carrying amount of the hedging instruments (financial assets separately from financial liabilities);

(b) the line in the statement of financial position that includes the hedging instrument;

(c) the change in fair value of the hedging instrument used as the basis for recognising hedge ineffectiveness for the period; and

(d) the nominal amount (including quantities such as tonnes or cubic metres) of the hedging instruments.

Example 4.3.2.3A

Disclosure of amounts related to designated hedging instruments

[Extract from IFRS 7:IG13C]

	Nominal amount of the hedging instrument	Carrying amount of the hedging instrument		Line item in the statement of financial position where the hedging instrument is located	Changes in fair value used for calculating hedge ineffectiveness for 20X1
		Assets	Liabilities		
Cash flow hedges					
Commodity price risk – Forecast sales contracts	xx	xx	xx	Line item xx	xx
Fair value hedges					
Interest rate risk – Interest rate swaps	xx	xx	xx	Line item xx	xx
Foreign exchange risk – Foreign currency loan	xx	xx	xx	Line item xx	xx

With respect to hedged items, entities are required to provide the following, extensive information, in tabular format, separately by risk category for each type of hedge:

[IFRS 7:24B]

(a) For fair value hedges:

i. the carrying amount of the hedged item recognised in the statement of financial position (presenting assets separately from liabilities);

ii. the accumulated amount of fair value hedge adjustments included in the carrying amount of the hedged item recognised in the statement of financial position (presenting assets separately from liabilities);

iii. the line item in the statement of financial position that includes the hedged item;

iv. the change in value of the hedged item used as the basis for recognising hedge ineffectiveness for the period; and

v. the accumulated amount of fair value hedge adjustments remaining in the statement of financial position for any hedged items that have ceased to be adjusted for hedging gains and losses in accordance with IFRS 9:6.5.10 (see **6.4.2** in **chapter B9**).

(b) For cash flow hedges and hedges of a net investment in a foreign operation:

i. the change in value of the hedged item used as the basis for recognising hedge ineffectiveness for the period (i.e. for cash flow hedges the change in value used to determine the recognised hedge ineffectiveness in accordance with IFRS 9:6.5.11(c) (see **6.5.1** in **chapter B9**);

ii. the balances in the cash flow hedge reserve and the foreign currency translation reserve for continuing hedges that are accounted for as cash flow hedges operation in accordance with IFRS 9:6.5.11 (see **6.5.1** in **chapter B9**) and hedges of a net investment in a foreign in accordance with IFRS 9:6.5.13(a) (see **6.6** in **chapter B9**); and

iii. the balances remaining in the cash flow hedge reserve and the foreign currency translation reserve from any hedging relationships for which hedge accounting is no longer applied.

Example 4.3.2.3B

Disclosure of amounts related to designated hedged items

[Extract from IFRS 7:IG13D]

	Carrying amount of the hedged item		**Accumulated amount of fair value hedge adjustments on the hedged item included in the carrying amount of the hedged item**		**Line item in the statement of financial position in which the hedged item is included**	**Change in value used for calculating hedge ineffectiveness for 20X1**	**Cash flow hedge reserve**
	Assets	**Liabilities**	**Assets**	**Liabilities**			
Cash flow hedges							
Commodity price risk							
– Forecast sales	n/a	n/a	n/a	n/a	n/a	xx	xx
– Discontinued hedges (forecast sales)	n/a	n/a	n/a	n/a	n/a	n/a	xx
Fair value hedges							
Interest rate risk							
– Loan payable	-	xx	-	xx	Line item XX	n/a	n/a
– Discontinued hedges (Loan payable)	-	xx	-	xx	Line item XX	n/a	n/a

	Carrying amount of the hedged item		Accumulated amount of fair value hedge adjustments on the hedged item included in the carrying amount of the hedged item		Line item in the statement of financial position in which the hedged item is included	Change in value used for calculating hedge ineffectiveness for 20X1	Cash flow hedge reserve
	Assets	**Liabilities**	**Assets**	**Liabilities**			
Foreign exchange risk							
– Firm commitment	xx	xx	xx	xx	Line item XX	n/a	n/a

Furthermore, in addition to the extensive quantitative disclosures about the hedging instrument and hedged item discussed above, further disclosures are required about hedge ineffectiveness recognised and also about amounts reclassified in respect of cash flow hedges and hedges of a net investment in a foreign operation. IFRS 7:24C requires that an entity provide the following amounts, in tabular format separately by risk category for each type of hedge:

(a) for fair value hedges:

i. hedge ineffectiveness, i.e. the difference between the hedging gains or losses of the hedging instrument and the hedged item-recognised in profit or loss (or other comprehensive income for hedges of an equity instrument for which an entity has elected to present changes in fair value in other comprehensive income in accordance with IFRS 9:5.7.5 (see **5.3.2** in **chapter B2**)); and

ii. the line item in the statement of comprehensive income that includes the recognised hedge ineffectiveness.

(b) for cash flow hedges and hedges of a net investment in a foreign operation:

i. hedging gains or losses of the reporting period that were recognised in other comprehensive income;

ii. hedge ineffectiveness recognised in profit or loss;

iii. the line item in the statement of comprehensive income that includes the recognised hedge ineffectiveness;

iv. the amount reclassified from the cash flow hedge reserve or the foreign currency translation reserve into profit or loss as a reclassification adjustment (see IAS 1). Differentiating between:

- amounts for which hedge accounting had previously been used, but for which the hedged future cash flows are no longer expected to occur, and
- amounts that have been transferred because the hedged item has affected profit or loss;

v. the line item in the statement of comprehensive income that includes the reclassification adjustment (see IAS 1); and

vi. for hedges of net positions, the hedging gains or losses recognised in a separate line item in the statement of comprehensive income.

Example 4.3.2.3C

Disclosure of effects of hedge accounting on the statement of comprehensive income

[Extract from IFRS 7:IG13E]

Cash flow hedges[(a)]	**Separate line item recognised in profit or loss as a result of a hedge of a net position**[(b)]	**Change in the value of the hedging instrument recognised in other comprehensive income**	**Hedge ineffectiveness recognised in profit or loss**	**Line item in profit or loss (that includes hedge ineffectiveness)**	**Amount reclassified from the cash flow hedge reserve to profit or loss**	**Line item affected in profit or loss because of the reclassi-fication**
Commodity price risk Commodity X	n/a	xx	xx	Line item XX	xx	Line item XX
- Discontinued hedge	n/a	n/a	n/a	n/a	xx	Line item XX

(a) The information disclosed in the statement of changes in equity (cash flow hedge reserve) should have the same level of detail as these disclosures.

(b) This disclosure only applies to cash flow hedges of foreign currency risk.

Fair value hedges	**Ineffectiveness recognised in profit or loss**	**Line item(s) in profit or loss (that include(s) hedge ineffectiveness)**
Interest rate risk	xx	Line item XX
Foreign exchange risk	xx	Line item XX

Given that the mechanics of hedge accounting often use separate components of equity to defer gains or losses on hedging instruments, equity can be significantly affected by the application of hedge accounting.

IAS 1:106 requires a reconciliation of each component of equity in the statement of changes in equity. However, to supplement this, IFRS 7 requires a reconciliation of other comprehensive income separated by risk category for the items that relate to hedge accounting. The detailed information can be provided either in the statement of changes in equity or in the notes to the financial statements. [IFRS 7:24F]

The reconciliation should have the same level of detail as the information that identifies the effects of hedge accounting on the statement of profit or loss and other comprehensive income. Consequently, the reconciliation should differentiate separately by risk category, at a minimum, between:

[IFRS 7:24E]

(a) hedging gains or losses of the reporting period that were recognised in other comprehensive income in respect of cash flow hedges and hedges of a net investment in a foreign operations;

(b) the amount reclassified from the cash flow hedge reserve or the foreign currency translation reserve into profit or loss as a reclassification adjustment, differentiating between:

- amounts for which hedge accounting was previously used but for which the hedged future cash flows are no longer expected to occur, and
- amounts that have been transferred because the hedged item has effected profit or loss;

(c) the amount removed from the cash flow hedge reserve and included directly in the initial cost or other carrying amount of:
   i. a non-financial asset or a non-financial liability that is recognised subsequent to a hedged forecast transaction; or
   ii. a firm commitment that results from a hedged forecast transaction for a non-financial asset or non-financial liability for which fair value hedge accounting is applied.

(d) the amount reclassified from the cash flow hedge reserve into profit or loss as a reclassification adjustment in relation to a loss (or a portion of it) that the entity does not expect to recover in one or more future periods;

(e) the amounts associated with the time value of purchased option that hedge transaction-related hedged items and amounts associated with the time value of purchased options that hedge time period-related hedged items (when an entity designates as the hedging instrument only the change in intrinsic value of the option) (see **6.8** in **chapter B9**); and

(f) the amounts associated with the forward elements of forward contracts and the foreign currency basis spreads of financial instruments that hedge transaction-related hedged items and amounts associated with the forward elements of forward contracts and the foreign currency basis spreads of financial instruments that hedge time period-related hedged items (when an entity designates as the hedging instrument only the change in the value of the spot element of the forward contract or excludes the foreign currency basis spreads) (see **6.9** & **6.10** in **chapter B9**).

4.3.2.4 Option to designate a credit exposure as measured at fair value through profit or loss

Under IFRS 9, the credit risk component of an exposure (e.g. a bond asset) is not an eligible hedged item and therefore hedge accounting is not available for an entity that hedges only the credit risk component of an item using credit derivatives (see **3.11.6** in **chapter B9**). As an alternative to hedge accounting, IFRS 9 allows an entity to designate a credit exposure at FVTPL when it uses a credit derivative measured at FVTPL to hedge the credit risk of that exposure (see **7.2** in **chapter B9**). Such designations will not be captured by the required hedge accounting disclosures discussed above because the accounting applied is not hedge accounting.

Furthermore, as a consequence of measuring the exposure at FVTPL, the IFRS 9 impairment requirements would not apply to the exposure because the requirements scope out financial instruments measured at FVTPL which also means the IFRS 7 credit risk disclosures in IFRS 7:35F to 35N would not apply.

In such cases IFRS 7 requires the following disclosures: [IFRS 7:24G]

(a) a reconciliation of each of the nominal amount and the fair value, at the beginning and end of the period, of the credit derivatives that have been used to manage the credit risk;

(b) the gain or loss recognised in profit or loss on designation of a financial instrument (or a proportion of it) as measured at FVTPL; and

(c) on discontinuation of measuring a financial instrument (or a proportion of it) at FVTPL, that financial instrument's fair value that has become the new carrying amount and the related nominal or principal amount.

Except for providing comparative information under IAS 1, an entity does not need to continue the disclosure requirement in (c) above in reporting periods subsequent to the period in which the financial instrument (or a proportion of it) ceased to be measured at FVTPL.

4.3.3 Fair value

IFRS 7 requires fair value information to be provided for all financial assets and liabilities (with limited exceptions, see **4.3.3.1**). An entity is required to disclose the fair value of that class of assets and liabilities in a way that permits it to be compared with its carrying amount. In disclosing fair values, an entity shall group financial assets and financial liabilities into classes, but shall offset them only to the extent that their carrying amounts are offset in the statement of financial position. [IFRS 7:25 & 26]

IFRS 13 requires disclose of information that helps users of its financial statements assess both of the following:

[IFRS 13:91]

(a) for assets and liabilities that are measured at fair value on a recurring or non-recurring basis in the statement of financial position after initial recognition, the valuation techniques and inputs used to develop those measurements.

(b) for recurring fair value measurements using significant unobservable inputs (Level 3) (see **7.3** in **chapter B7**), the effect of the measurements on profit or loss or other comprehensive income for the period.

To meet the objectives above, an entity shall consider all the following:

[IFRS 13:92]

(a) the level of detail necessary to satisfy the disclosure requirements;

(b) how much emphasis to place on each of the various requirements;

(c) how much aggregation or disaggregation to undertake; and

(d) whether users of financial statements need additional information to evaluate the quantitative information disclosed.

To meet the objectives in IFRS 13:91 the standard requires minimum disclosures that are aggregated by class of assets and liabilities. If the disclosures provided in accordance with IFRS 13 and other IFRSs are insufficient to meet the objectives described above in IFRS 13:91, an entity shall disclose additional information necessary to meet those objectives.

The amount of the disclosure required by IFRS 13 depends on whether IFRS 9 requires the financial asset or financial liability to be measured at fair value in the statement of financial position. The greatest amount of disclosure is required for those assets or liabilities subsequently measured at fair value in the statement of financial position on a recurring basis. Most, but not all, of these disclosures are required for those assets and liabilities that are measured at fair value on a non-recurring basis. A recurring fair value measurement is where IFRSs require or permit in the statement of financial position the asset or liability to be subsequently measured at fair value at the end of each reporting period. A non-recurring fair value is where IFRSs require or permit in the statement of financial position the asset or liability to be subsequently measured at fair value in particular circumstances, i.e. not necessarily at the end of each reporting period. [IFRS 13:93(a)]

Financial instruments subsequently measured in the statement of financial position at fair value are generally recurring fair value measurements.

Recurring and non-recurring fair value measurements include only those assets or liabilities measured at fair value in the statement of financial position. Financial instruments measured at amortised cost that are fair value hedge adjusted are not recurring or non-recurring fair value measurements because they are not measured at fair value.

4.3.3.1 Exceptions from fair value disclosures for financial instruments

IFRS 7 provides limited exceptions from fair value disclosures for financial instruments. IFRS 7:29 does not require disclosure of fair value:

- when the carrying amount is a reasonable approximation of fair value, for example, for financial instruments such as short-term trade receivables and payables;
- for a contract containing a discretionary participation feature (as described in IFRS 4) if the fair value of that feature cannot be measured reliably.

However, when fair value cannot be measured reliably, additional disclosures are required to assist users of the financial statements in making their own judgements about the extent of possible differences between the carrying amount of those financial assets or financial liabilities and their fair value. These disclosures include:

[IFRS 7:30]

- a statement that fair value information has not been disclosed for these instruments because their fair value cannot be measured reliably;
- a description of the financial instruments, their carrying amount, and an explanation of why fair value cannot be measured reliably;
- information about the market for the instruments;
- information about whether and how the entity intends to dispose of the financial instruments; and
- if such instruments are subsequently derecognised, the carrying amount at the date of disposal, the fact that fair value could not be reliably measured, and the gain or loss that results.

4.3.3.2 Summary of fair value disclosures

The minimum disclosures required by IFRS 13 that relate to financial instruments are summarised below. Many of the disclosures are based on the fair value hierarchy as described in IFRS 13 which is described in detail in **section 7** in **chapter B7**.

	Assets and liabilities measured at fair value in the statement of financial position after the date of initial recognition		
Required disclosure:	**Recurring**	**Non-recurring**	**Fair value disclosed in the notes to the financial statements**
Fair value at the reporting date [IFRS 13:93(a) & 97, IFRS 7:25]	✓	✓	✓
Reason for the fair value measurement [IFRS 13:93(a)]		✓	
The level of the fair value measurement in the fair value hierarchy [IFRS 13:93(b)]	✓	✓	✓
For assets and liabilities held at the end of the reporting period, amounts of any transfers between Levels 1 and 2 (separately for transfers into and out of each level), the reasons for those transfers, and the entity's policy for determining that a transfer has occurred [IFRS 13:93(c)]	✓		
For Levels 2 and 3 measurements, a description of the valuation techniques and inputs used [IFRS 13:93(d)]	✓	✓	✓
For Level 2 and 3 measurements for which there has been a change in valuation technique, the nature of that change and the reason for it [IFRS 13:93(d)]	✓	✓	✓
Information sufficient to permit reconciliation between the amounts disclosed for classes of assets and liabilities by level of the fair value hierarchy and the line items presented in the statement of financial position [IFRS 13:94]	✓	✓	Not required by IFRS 13 but for financial instruments required by IFRS 7:6
If an entity chooses as its accounting policy to use the portfolio valuation exception permitted by IFRS 13:48, that fact [IFRS 13:96]	✓		
For a liability measured at fair value, the existence of any credit enhancement and whether it is reflected in the fair value measurement of the liability [IFRS 13:98]	✓	✓	

	Assets and liabilities measured at fair value in the statement of financial position after the date of initial recognition		
Required disclosure:	**Recurring**	**Non-recurring**	**Fair value disclosed in the notes to the financial statements**
The following disclosures only apply to Level 3 fair value measurements			
Quantitative information about the significant unobservable inputs used in the fair value measurement [IFRS 13:93(d)]	✓	✓	
Reconciliation of movements in fair value from opening to closing balances, showing separately: • total gains and losses recognised in profit or loss (including the line items in profit or loss); • total gains and losses recognised in other comprehensive income (including the line items in other comprehensive income); • purchases, sales, issues, settlements (each disclosed separately); and • the amounts of transfers into and out of Level 3 separately (including the reasons for those transfers and the entity's policy for determining that a transfer has occurred) [IFRS 13:93(e)].	✓		
Amount of total gains or losses for the period recognised in profit or loss that is attributable to the change in unrealised gains or losses for those assets and liabilities held at the end of the reporting period, and the line items in profit or loss in which the gains or losses are recognised [IFRS 13:93(f)]	✓		
Description of the valuation processes used, including a description of how an entity the entity decides on valuation policies and procedures and how it analyses changes in fair value from period to period [IFRS 13:93(g)]	✓	✓	

	Assets and liabilities measured at fair value in the statement of financial position after the date of initial recognition		
Required disclosure:	**Recurring**	**Non-recurring**	**Fair value disclosed in the notes to the financial statements**
Narrative description of the sensitivity of the fair value measurement to changes in unobservable inputs if a change in those inputs might result in a significantly different fair value measurement and a description of the interrelationships between those inputs, if any, including how those interrelationships might magnify or mitigate the impact on fair value arising from changes in such inputs. The narrative description of the sensitivity should include, at a minimum, all significant unobservable inputs used in the fair value measurement [IFRS 13:93(h)(i)]	✓		
For financial assets and liabilities, when a change in one or more of the unobservable inputs to reflect reasonably possible alternative assumptions would change fair value significantly, that fact, the effect of those changes, and how the effect of such a change is calculated [IFRS 13:93(h)(ii)]	✓		

The quantitative disclosures required by IFRS 13 shall be presented in a tabular format unless another format is more appropriate. [IFRS 13:99]

In addition, IFRS 7 requires specific disclosures in respect of 'day 1 profit or loss' which are detailed in **4.3.3.8**.

4.3.3.3 Financial instruments measured at fair value

For recurring and non-recurring fair value measurements an entity is required to disclose the fair value at the end of the reporting period and level within the fair value hierarchy within which the fair value measurement is categorised in their entirety (i.e. Level 1, 2 or 3). For non-recurring fair value measurements the reason for the measurement shall be disclosed. [IFRS 13:93(a) & (b)]

IFRS 13:IE60 provides an illustrative example of the disclosures required by IFRS 13:93(a) & (b) in the case of assets measured at fair value. The example has been reproduced below, however, excludes non-financial items that are not within the scope of this volume.

Example 4.3.3.3

Financial assets measured at fair value

[IFRS 13:IE60]

(CU in millions)	**Fair value measurements at the end of the reporting period using**			
Description	**31/12/X9**	**Quoted prices in active markets for identical assets (Level 1)**	**Significant other observable inputs (Level 2)**	**Significant unobservable inputs (Level 3)**
Recurring fair value measurements				
Trading equity securities[(a)]:				
Real estate industry	93	70	23	
Oil and gas industry	45	45		
Other	15	15		
Total trading equity securities	153	130	23	
Other equity securities[(a)]:				
Financial services industry	150	150		
Healthcare industry	163	110		53
Energy industry	32			32
Private equity fund investments[(b)]:	25			25
Other	15	15		
Total other equity securities	385	275		110
Debt securities:				
Residential mortgage-backed securities	149		24	125
Commercial mortgage-backed securities	50			50
Collateralised debt obligations	35			35
Risk-free government securities	85	85		
Corporate bonds	93	9	84	
Total debt securities	412	94	108	210
Hedge fund investments:				
Equity long/short	55		55	
Global opportunities	35		35	
High-yield debt securities	90			90
Total hedge fund investments	180		90	90

(CU in millions)		Fair value measurements at the end of the reporting period using		
Description	**31/12/X9**	**Quoted prices in active markets for identical assets (Level 1)**	**Significant other observable inputs (Level 2)**	**Significant unobservable inputs (Level 3)**
Derivatives:				
Interest rate contracts	57		57	
Foreign exchange contracts	43		43	
Credit contracts	38			38
Commodity futures contracts	78	78		
Commodity forward contracts	20		20	
Total derivatives	236	78	120	38

(a) On the basis of its analysis of the nature, characteristics and risks of the securities, the entity has determined that presenting them by industry is appropriate.

(b) On the basis of its analysis of the nature, characteristics and risks of the investments, the entity has determined that presenting them as a single class is appropriate.

(Note: A similar would be presented for liabilities unless another format is deemed more appropriate by the entity.)

IFRS 13 also requires that the amounts of transfers between Levels 1 and 2, the reasons for those transfers, and the entity's policy for determining when transfers between levels are deemed to have occurred shall be disclosed. [IFRS 13:93(c)]

The Standard provides guidance on what policy may be applied in determining when within the reporting period a transfer between levels of the fair value hierarchy occurs. An entity is required to disclose and consistently follow its policy for determining when those transfers have deemed to occur. This applies to both transfers in and out the levels. Examples of policies for determining the timing of transfers include the following:

[IFRS 13:95]

(a) the date of the event or change in circumstances that caused the transfer;

(b) the beginning of the reporting period; and

(c) the end of the reporting period.

The policy chosen should be applied consistently to transfer in and out of the levels in the hierarchy with transfers in and transfers out disclosed and discussed separately.

In the case of a compound financial instrument (i.e. an instrument including a financial liability and equity component as described in **section 3** of **chapter B3**), the disclosures regarding fair value will relate only to the financial liability component of the compound instrument because the equity component is scoped out of IFRS 7 (see **section 2**). The fair value of the financial liability component will incorporate interest rate risk and the entity's own credit risk but will exclude any consideration of equity price risk.

4.3.3.4 Valuation techniques and inputs

IFRS 13 requires certain disclosures about valuation techniques which are used in fair valuing both recurring and non-recurring fair value measurements for assets and liabilities. The Standard requires a description of the valuation technique(s) and inputs used as well as disclosure if there has been a change in valuation technique, disclosing the change and the reason(s) for making the change. [IFRS 13:93(d)]

4.3.3.5 Level 3 fair value measurements

In addition to the disclosures on valuation techniques described in **4.3.3.4**, IFRS 13 requires further disclosure for Level 3 fair value measurements. IFRS 13 requires greater disclosure for Level 3 fair value measurements compared with Levels 1 and 2 fair value measurements because determining their measurement is more subjective.

For recurring and non-recurring fair value measurements that are categorised within Level 3 of the fair value hierarchy an entity shall provide quantitative information about the significant unobservable inputs used in the fair value measurement. An entity is not required to create quantitative information to comply with this disclosure requirement if quantitative unobservable inputs are not developed by the entity when measuring fair value (e.g. when an entity uses prices from prior transactions or third-party pricing information without adjustment). However, when providing this disclosure an entity cannot ignore quantitative unobservable inputs that are significant to the fair value measurement and are reasonably available to the entity. [IFRS 13:93(d)]

In addition to the quantitative information required by IFRS 13 it states an entity shall consider whether additional information shall be disclosed in order for users of financial statements to evaluate the quantitative information disclosed. [IFRS 13:92(d)] The illustrative examples contained in IFRS 13 describe some or all of the following information an entity must disclose in order to meet the requirement.

[IFRS 13:IE64]

(a) the nature of the item being measured at fair value, including the characteristics of the item being measured that are taken into account in the determination of relevant inputs. For example, for residential mortgage-backed securities, an entity might disclose the following:

(i) the types of underlying loans (e.g. prime loans or sub-prime loans)
(ii) collateral
(iii) guarantees or other credit enhancements
(iv) seniority level of the tranches of securities
(v) the year of issue
(vi) the weighted-average coupon rate of the underlying loans and the securities
(vii) the weighted-average maturity of the underlying loans and the securities
(viii) the geographical concentration of the underlying loans
(ix) information about the credit ratings of the securities.

(b) how third-party information such as broker quotes, pricing services, net asset values and relevant market data was taken into account when measuring fair value.

For recurring Level 3 fair value IFRS 13 requires a reconciliation of the opening and closing balances. The Standard requires the following to be included in that reconciliation:

[IFRS 13:93(e)]

(i) total gains or losses for the period recognised in profit or loss, and the line item(s) in profit or loss in which those gains or losses are recognised.
(ii) total gains or losses for the period recognised in other comprehensive income, and the line item(s) in other comprehensive income in which those gains or losses are recognised.
(iii) purchases, sales, issues and settlements (each of those types of changes disclosed separately).
(iv) the amounts of any transfers into or out of Level 3 of the fair value hierarchy, the reasons for those transfers and the entity's policy for determining when transfers between levels are deemed to have occurred (see **4.3.3.3**). Transfers into Level 3 shall be disclosed and discussed separately from transfers out of Level 3.

Physically settled commodity derivative instruments within the scope of IFRS 9 that do not meet the 'own-use' exception or elected to be measured at FVTPL (see **2.5** in **chapter B1**) are treated the same as financial commodity derivatives.

For financial commodity derivatives, economic performance is demonstrated by the changes in fair value and results in net settlement or settlements that occur over the life of the instrument. Gains or losses for net-settled financial derivatives are determined based on the cash settlement activity. In contrast, physically settled commodity derivatives feature a gross exchange of a physical commodity and cash or another financial asset based on a pre-determined price. However, the objective of the Level 3 roll forward reconciliation remains the same – that is, to provide information about the economic performance and position of the derivative in value terms, irrespective of the settlement provisions. Consequently, for physically settled commodity derivative contracts "settlements" includes the cash or another financial asset paid or received under the contract as well as the physical commodity delivered in exchange.

Example 4.3.3.5

Level 3 reconciliation

Entity A has the following two financial derivatives.

	Financial derivative 1 (CU)	**Financial derivative 2 (CU)**
Beginning balance	100	Not applicable as entered into during the period
Change in fair value	10	250
Cash received	110	Not applicable
Closing fair value	–	250

The contracts are part of the same class for the purposes of IFRS 13:94 and, consequently, are reported in a single column of the reconciliation table.

	Financial contracts CU
Beginning balance	100
Total gains or losses (realised and unrealised) recognised in profit or loss [(i)] [(ii)]	260
Total gains or losses recognised in other comprehensive income [(i)]	–
Purchases	–
Sales	–
Issuances	–
Settlements [(iii)]	(110)
Transfers into Level 3	–
Transfers out of Level 3	–
Closing balance	250

(i) The entity should also disclose the line item in profit or loss/other comprehensive income in which these gains or losses are recognised

(ii) Represents the change in fair value of Derivative 1 (CU10) and change in fair value of Derivative 2 (CU250).

(iii) Represents cash received on settlement

Entity A also has two physically settled commodity derivatives. Physical derivative 1 is a sale of 100 mmbtu of Natural Gas at CU8 per mmbtu. Physical derivative 2 is a sale of 100 mmbtu of Natural Gas at CU12 per mmbtu.

	Physical derivative 1 (CU)	**Physical derivative 2 (CU)**
Beginning balance	100	Not applicable as entered into during the period
Change in fair value	10	250
Cash received	800	Not applicable
Market value of commodity delivered	690	Not applicable
Closing fair value	–	250

The contracts are part of the same class for the purposes of IFRS 13:94 and, consequently, are reported in a single column of the reconciliation table.

	Physical contracts CU
Beginning balance	100
Total gains or losses (realised and unrealised) recognised in profit or loss (i) (ii)	260
Total gains or losses recognised in other comprehensive income (i)	–
Purchases	–
Sales	–
Issuances	–
Settlements (iii)	(110)
Transfers into Level 3	–
Transfers out of Level 3	–
Closing balance	250

(i) The entity should also disclose the line item in profit or loss/other comprehensive income in which these gains or losses are recognised.

(ii) Represents the change in fair value of Derivative 1 (CU10) and change in fair value of Derivative 2 (CU250).

(iii) Represents settlement of the fixed price forward component of the physical derivative. The fixed price is the cash received on gross settlement (CU800) that is offset against the market spot price for gas (underlying the physical derivative) at settlement. In this example, the spot price is assumed to be CU6.9 per mmbtu or CU690

In addition, an entity is required to disclose the amount of the total gains or losses recognised in profit or loss in the period that is included in the Level 3 reconciliation that is attributable to the change in unrealised gains or losses relating to those assets and liabilities held at the end of the reporting period, and the line item(s) in profit or loss in which those unrealised gains or losses are recognised. [IFRS 13:93(f)]

4.3.3.6 Valuation processes for Level 3 fair value measurements

For recurring and non-recurring fair value measurements categorised within Level 3 of the fair value hierarchy an entity is required to disclose a description of the valuation processes used by the entity (including, for example, how an entity decides its valuation policies and procedures and analyses changes in fair value measurements from period to period). [IFRS 13:93(g)] The illustrative examples contained in IFRS 13 contain an example of the disclosures an entity might include in order to meet the requirement:

[IFRS 13:IE65]

(a) for the group within the entity that decides the entity's valuation policies and procedures:
   (i) its description;
   (ii) to whom that group reports; and
   (iii) the internal reporting procedures in place (e.g. whether and, if so, how pricing, risk management or audit committees discuss and assess the fair value measurements);
(b) the frequency and methods for calibration, back testing and other testing procedures of pricing models;
(c) the process for analysing changes in fair value measurements from period to period;
(d) how the entity determined that third-party information, such as broker quotes or pricing services, used in the fair value measurement was developed in accordance with the IFRS; and
(e) the methods used to develop and substantiate the unobservable inputs used in a fair value measurement.

4.3.3.7 Information about sensitivity to changes in significant unobservable inputs for Level 3 fair value measurements

For recurring fair value measurements categorised within Level 3 of the fair value hierarchy an entity must disclose a narrative description of the sensitivity of the fair value measurement to changes in unobservable inputs if a change in those inputs to a different amount might result in a significantly higher or lower fair value measurement. If there are interrelationships between those inputs and other unobservable inputs used in the fair value measurement, an entity shall also provide a description of those interrelationships and of how they might magnify or mitigate the effect of changes in the unobservable inputs on the fair value measurement. To comply with that disclosure requirement, the narrative description of the sensitivity to changes in unobservable inputs shall include, at a minimum, the unobservable inputs disclosed when complying with IFRS 13:93(d) (see **4.3.3.5**). [IFRS 13:93(h)(i)]

Example 4.3.3.7

Information about sensitivity to changes in significant observable inputs

[IFRS 13:IE66]

The significant unobservable inputs used in the fair value measurement of the entity's residential mortgage-backed securities are prepayment rates, probability of default and loss severity in the event of default. Significant increases (decreases) in any of those inputs in isolation would result in a significantly lower (higher) fair value measurement. Generally, a change in the assumption used for the probability of default is accompanied by a directionally similar change in the assumption used for the loss severity and a directionally opposite change in the assumption used for prepayment rates.

For financial assets and financial liabilities, if changing one or more of the unobservable inputs to reflect reasonably possible alternative assumptions would change fair value significantly, an entity shall state that fact and disclose the effect of those changes. The entity shall disclose how the effect of a change to reflect a reasonably possible alternative assumption was calculated. For that purpose, significance shall be judged with respect to profit or loss, and total assets or total liabilities, or, when changes in fair value are recognised in other comprehensive income, total equity. [IFRS 13:93(h)(ii)]

4.3.3.8 Day 1 profit or loss

IFRS 9 requires that no gain or loss should be recognised on initial recognition of a financial instrument if the fair value at initial recognition is neither evidenced by a quoted price in an active market for an identical asset or liability (i.e. a Level 1 input) nor based on a valuation technique that uses data from observable markets. A gain or loss should be recognised subsequently only to the extent that it arises from a change in factor (including time) that market participants would take into account when pricing the asset or liability. As noted at **7.1** in **chapter B7** there is little clarity as to when day 1 profit or loss should be recognised because the Standard does not specify how entities should account for those initial differences in subsequent periods. Disclosure is required, by class of financial instrument, of:

- The accounting policy for recognising in profit or loss the difference between the fair value at initial recognition and the transaction price to reflect a change in factors (including time) that market participants would take into account when pricing the financial instrument. [IFRS 7:28(a)]

- The aggregate difference yet to be recognised in profit or loss at the beginning and end of the period should be disclosed together with a reconciliation of the changes in the balance during the period. [IFRS 7:28(b)]
- Why the entity concluded that the transaction price was not the best evidence of fair value, including a description of the evidence that supports the fair value. [IFRS 7:28(c)]

5 Nature and extent of risks arising from financial instruments

IFRS 7 has two key objectives: firstly to show the significance of financial instruments as discussed in **section 4**; and, secondly, to require entities to disclose information that enables users of its financial statements to evaluate the nature and extent of risks arising from financial instruments to which the entity is exposed at the end of the reporting period as discussed below.

Both qualitative and quantitative disclosures are required regarding the risks that arise from financial instruments and how those risks have been managed. The risks typically include, but are not limited to, credit risk, liquidity risk and market risk. [IFRS 7:32] The disclosures provided should depend on the extent of an entity's use of financial instruments and the extent to which it assumes associated risks, although certain minimum disclosures are required for all entities. The guidance on how the disclosures should be provided has been developed so as to be consistent with the Basel Committee disclosure requirements for banks (generally referred to as 'Pillar 3' of Basel II) to allow banks to prepare a single set of co-ordinated disclosures about financial risk. [IFRS 7:BC41] It is of note that Pillar 3 disclosures are broader than those required under IFRS 7 because they include operational risks.

The disclosures should either be provided in the financial statements or incorporated by clear cross-reference from the financial statements to some other statement (e.g. a management commentary or risk report). Such a report must be available to users on the same terms as the financial statements and be available at the same time. Without such information, the financial statements are incomplete. [IFRS 7:B6]

If the disclosures are provided in a separate statement, the information should be clearly referenced as being part of the IFRS financial statements.

5.1 Qualitative disclosures

For each type of risk to which an entity is exposed, disclosure is required regarding:

[IFRS 7:33]

- the exposures to the risk and how those exposures arose;
- the entity's objectives, policies and processes for managing the risk and the methods used to measure it; and
- any changes in the information disclosed under the previous two bullets from the previous period.

Providing qualitative disclosures in the context of quantitative disclosures enables users to link related disclosures and, as a result, to form an overall picture of the nature and extent of risks arising from financial instruments. The interaction between qualitative and quantitative disclosures contributes to disclosure of information in a way that better enables users to evaluate an entity's exposure to risks. [IFRS 7:32A]

Disclosures may be provided on both a gross basis and net of any risk transfer and other risk-mitigating transactions. [IFRS 7:IG15(a)] Such information is useful because it highlights the relationships between financial instruments and provides users of the financial statements with information to understand the effect of those relationships on the nature, timing and uncertainty of future cash flows.

Disclosure of the entity's policies and processes for accepting, measuring, monitoring and controlling risk may include disclosure of the following:

[IFRS 7:IG15(b) & (c)]

- the structure and organisation of the entity's risk management function;
- the scope and nature of risk reporting or measurement systems;
- policies for hedging or mitigating risk, including policies and procedures for taking collateral;
- the entity's processes for monitoring the continuing effectiveness of such hedges or mitigating devices; and
- disclosure of the policies and procedures that are undertaken to avoid excessive concentrations of risk.

An entity is required to disclose any changes in the qualitative information from the previous period. Such changes may result from changes in the entity's exposure to risk or from changes in the way in which the exposures are managed. [IFRS 7:IG17] This information is important because users of the financial statements need to understand the effect that such changes have on the nature, timing and uncertainty of future cash flows.

One of the objectives of the disclosure requirements is to enable users to evaluate an entity's ability to generate returns, and to appreciate the risks and uncertainties of those expected returns. This evaluation can only be meaningful if it is carried out in the context of the entity's risk management policies.

5.2 Quantitative disclosures

For each type of risk arising from financial instruments, IFRS 7 requires an entity to provide quantitative information about exposure to that risk at the end of the reporting period, based on information reported internally to key management personnel. [IFRS 7:34(a)] If more than one method is used to manage and report information about risk exposures, then the method that provides the most relevant and reliable information should be disclosed. [IFRS 7:B7] The advantages of basing disclosures on management information are that such disclosures:

[IFRS 7:BC47]

- provide a useful insight into how risk is viewed and managed by the entity;
- are based on information that has a more predictive value than information based on assumptions and methods that management does not use; and
- adapt to changes in the manner in which risk is measured and managed and allows users to use the same data that management uses to measure and manage risk.

Key management personnel are defined as "those persons having authority and responsibility for planning, directing and controlling the activities of the entity, directly or indirectly, including any director (whether executive or otherwise) of that entity". [IAS 24:9]

Following the definition, any director, whether executive or non-executive, will be considered to be key management personnel. The definition of key management personnel is, however, wider than just directors of an entity. Key management personnel might, in some instances, include directors of subsidiaries who are not directors of the parent entity and senior managers who are not directors. Other managers may be included as key management personnel in some circumstances, and not in others. Consideration needs to be given to the relative autonomy of management and whether their decisions are subject to the approval of the board of directors. For example, a Treasury Manager in an organisation may unilaterally review exposures and act independently following only guidelines and objectives established by the board of directors. In such circumstances, the Treasury Manager may be considered to be part of the key management personnel of that entity. In contrast, if the Treasury Manager operates purely in accordance with detailed treasury risk policies set out and approved by the board of directors, then that person is more likely to be excluded from the definition of key management personnel. In order to arrive at an appropriate determination, it is always necessary to obtain a thorough understanding of the manager's role within the organisation and the extent of his or her authority.

In addition to the disclosures under IFRS 7:34(a) (see above), which are based on information provided to key management personnel, IFRS 7:34(b) requires disclosures regarding credit, liquidity and market risk to the extent that these are not covered by the disclosures under IFRS 7:34(a) (see **5.2.1** to **5.2.3**).

Disclosures regarding concentrations of risk are also required to be provided if not apparent from the disclosures provided in accordance with IFRS 7:34(a) & (b). [IFRS 7:34(c)] Concentrations of risk arise from financial instruments that have similar characteristics and are affected similarly by changes in economic or other conditions. The identification of concentrations of risk requires judgement and must take into account the specific circumstances of the entity. Disclosures may include:

[IFRS 7:B8]

- a description of how management determines concentrations;
- a description of the shared characteristic that identifies each concentration (e.g. counterparty credit rating, geographical distribution, industry sector and other risks such as liquidity and market risks); and
- the amount of the risk exposure associated with all financial instruments that share that risk characteristic.

In all circumstances, the quantitative information should be provided for the risk exposures that exist at the end of the reporting period. When such information is unrepresentative of the exposure to financial risk during the period, an entity should provide additional information, which may include, but not be limited to, disclosure of the highest, lowest and average amount of risk the entity was exposed to during the period. [IFRS 7:IG20]

5.2.1 Credit risk

Credit risk is defined as "the risk that one party to a financial instrument will cause a financial loss for the other party by failing to discharge an obligation". [IFRS 7:Appendix A] IFRS 7 disclosure requirements regarding credit risk are substantial and are discussed in detail below.

When applying the IFRS 9 impairment model there are many judgements for management to take. For example, a key judgement is how to determine when there has been a significant increase in credit risk. This is an important judgement because it determines when an allowance for lifetime expected losses should be recognised instead of 12-month expected losses. Other judgements include an entity's definition of default and determination of low credit risk; both of which can have a significant effect on the recognition and measurement of expected losses. Furthermore, any measurement of expected losses is inherently subjective because it uses forward looking information, management assumptions and estimates and entity specific inputs, all of which can give rise to measurement uncertainty. The methods and approaches used to determine expected losses will also vary amongst entities depending, in part, on their approach to risk management but also due to availability of information without undue cost and effort (see **5.3.5** in **chapter B6**).

Given all of these factors influencing the application of the IFRS 9 impairment model, it is no surprise that IFRS 7 requires in-depth disclosures about *how* an entity has applied the model, *what* the results of applying the model have been for each class of financial instrument, and the reasons *why* for any changes in expected losses.

5.2.1.1 Scope and objective

The IFRS 7 credit risk disclosures are designed to enable users of financial statements to understand the effect of credit risk on the amount, timing and uncertainty of future cash flows. This is achieved by requiring disclosures in the following three areas for financial instruments to which the IFRS 9 impairment requirements are applied (see **section 5.1** in **chapter B6**):

- **credit risk management practices** – requiring information on some of the key judgements, inputs, assumptions and estimation techniques used to apply the IFRS 9 impairment model and in essence explains *how* the entity has applied the model (see **5.2.1.2**);
- **quantitative and qualitative information about amounts arising from expected credit losses** – requiring a detailed reconciliation of changes in the loss allowance by class, with a number of specific requirements, in essence explaining *what* the results of applying the model were, supplemented by narrative explaining *why* the results were as they were (i.e. giving cause and effect analysis) (see **5.2.1.3**); and
- **credit risk exposures** – requiring information about the entity's exposure to credit risk and significant credit risk concentrations (see **5.2.1.4**).

When providing the above disclosures consideration should be given as to:

- how much detail to disclose, how much emphasis to place on different aspects of the disclosure requirements;
- the appropriate level of aggregation or disaggregation; and

- whether users of financial statements need additional explanations to evaluate the quantitative information disclosed. [IFRS 7:35D]

If the specific credit risk disclosures required by IFRS 7 (see **5.2.1.2** to **5.2.1.7**) are insufficient to enable users of financial statements to understand the effect of credit risk on the amount, timing and uncertainty of future cash flows, an entity is required to disclose additional information as necessary. [IFRS 7:35E]

As with other IFRS 7 disclosures, credit risk information may be disclosed outside the notes to the financial statements as long as there is cross-reference from the financial statements to other statements, such as a management commentary or risk report that are available to users of the financial statements on the same terms as the financial statements and at the same time. Without the information incorporated by cross-reference, the financial statements are incomplete. [IFRS 7:35C]

IFRS 7 also requires some disclosures about credit exposures not in scope of the IFRS 9 impairment requirements, see **5.2.1.5** and **5.2.1.6**.

5.2.1.2 Credit risk management practices

An explanation of an entity's credit risk management practices, including how they relate to the recognition and measurement of expected credit losses, is a key component of the credit risk disclosures. IFRS 7 specifically requires the disclosure of information that enables users of financial statements to understand and evaluate:

[IFRS 7:35F]

(a) how an entity determined whether the credit risk of financial instruments has increased significantly since initial recognition, including, if and how:
   (i) financial instruments are considered to have low credit risk in accordance with IFRS 9:5.5.10 (and therefore presumed not have exhibited a significant increase in credit risk, see **5.2.5.1** in **chapter B6**), including the classes of financial instruments to which it applies; and
   (ii) the presumption in IFRS 9:5.5.11, that there have been significant increases in credit risk since initial recognition when financial assets are more than 30 days past due, has been rebutted (and therefore the instrument still has a 12-month expected loss allowance, see **5.2.2.8** in **chapter B6**);

IFRS 7:35F(a)(i) requires disclosure of the classes of financial instruments to which the low credit risk simplification applies, however, as noted at **5.2.5.1** in **chapter B6** the low credit risk simplification can be applied on an instrument by instrument basis, and therefore it may not apply to a whole class of financial instruments. When this is the case the disclosures should provide sufficient information to make this clear.

(b) an entity's definitions of default, including the reasons for selecting those definitions;

Given that the definition of default is fundamental to the application of the impairment model and that it can be defined in different ways (e.g. based on qualitative and/or quantitative factors), this disclosure will be important for users to allow them to compare impairment results across different entities. Disclosures could include the qualitative and quantitative factors considering in defining default and whether different default definitions are applied to different financial instruments. Also, disclosure of the assumptions about the cure rate (being the extent that financial assets return to a performing status from a non-performing status) could be provided. [IFRS 7:B8A]

(c) how the instruments were grouped if expected credit losses were measured on a collective basis;

(d) how an entity determined that financial assets are credit-impaired financial assets;

(e) an entity's write-off policy, including the indicators that there is no reasonable expectation of recovery and information about the policy for financial assets that are written-off but are still subject to enforcement activity; and

An entity is required to directly reduce the gross carrying amount of a financial asset when there is no reasonable expectation of recovery (see **3.11** in **chapter B8**). This disclosure therefore assists users to understand an entity's policy for determining when there is no reasonable expectation of recovery and continuing with enforcement activity despite there being no reasonable expectation of recovery.

In addition to this, IFRS 7:35L requires an entity to disclose the contractual amount outstanding on financial assets that were written off during the reporting period and are still subject to enforcement activity.

(f) how the requirements in IFRS 9:5.5.12 (see **5.2.3.2** in **chapter B6**) for the modification of contractual cash flows of financial instruments have been applied, including how an entity:

  (i) determines whether the credit risk on a financial asset that has been modified while the loss allowance was measured at an amount equal to lifetime expected credit losses, has decreased to the extent that the loss allowance reverts to being measured at an amount equal to 12-month expected credit losses in accordance with IFRS 9:5.5.5 (see **5.2.1** in **chapter B6**); and

(ii) monitors the extent to which the loss allowance on financial assets meeting the criteria in (i) are subsequently remeasured at an amount equal to lifetime expected credit losses in accordance with IFRS 9:5.5.3 (see **5.2.1** in **chapter B6**).

IFRS 7:B8A refers to disclosure of the 'deterioration rate', being the rate at which modified loans that revert to 12 month expected losses on modification then subsequently move to lifetime expected credit losses. The deterioration rate may help users of financial statements understand the extent to which the lender is successful at managing the credit risk through its restructuring and modification policies.

To apply the IFRS 9 impairment model, an entity will have to determine the inputs, assumptions and estimation techniques to use and these could be different to those used by other entities with similar credit risk exposures. Therefore to aid comparison across different entities IFRS 7 requires the following:

[IFRS 7:35G]

(a) the basis of inputs and assumptions and the estimation techniques used to:
   (i) measure the 12-month and lifetime expected credit losses;
   (ii) determine whether the credit risk of financial instruments have increased significantly since initial recognition; and
   (iii) determine whether a financial asset is a credit-impaired financial asset.

(b) how forward-looking information has been incorporated into the determination of expected credit losses, including the use of macroeconomic information; and

(c) changes in the estimation techniques or significant assumptions made during the reporting period and the reasons for those changes.

An entity's assumptions and inputs used to measure expected credit losses or determine the extent of increases in credit risk since initial recognition may include information obtained from internal historical information or rating reports and assumptions about the expected life of financial instruments and the timing of the sale of collateral. [IFRS 7:B8C]

5.2.1.3 Quantitative and qualitative information about amounts arising from expected credit losses

From period to period the amount of the loss allowance could vary for a variety of reasons. For example, it could go up because of an increase in lending activity or because of an increase in credit risk on existing lending; or they could go down because of write-offs or sales, or a reduction in credit risk on existing lending. Each of these different reasons has important information value and therefore IFRS 7 requires an explanation of the changes in the loss allowance and the reasons for those changes. In particular it requires a reconciliation from the opening balance to the closing balance of the loss allowance, by class of financial instrument in a table, showing separately the changes during the period for:

[IFRS 7:35H]

(a) the loss allowance measured at an amount equal to 12-month expected credit losses;

(b) the loss allowance measured at an amount equal to lifetime expected credit losses for:

  (i) financial instruments for which credit risk has increased significantly since initial recognition but that are not credit-impaired financial assets; and

  (ii) financial assets that are credit-impaired at the reporting date (but that are not purchased or originated credit-impaired);

  (iii) trade receivables, contract assets or lease receivables for which the loss allowance is measured at an amount equal to lifetime expected losses using the simplified approach (see **5.2.5.2** in **chapter B6**).

(c) financial assets that are purchased or originated credit-impaired. In addition to the reconciliation, an entity shall disclose the total amount of undiscounted expected credit losses at initial recognition on financial assets initially recognised during the reporting period.

IFRS 7:BC48W explains that the disclosure requirement in IFRS 7:35H(c) is to enhance the comparability of financial assets that are credit-impaired on initial recognition with those that are not. Disclosure of the undiscounted expected credit losses that are implicit in the pricing at initial recognition of purchased or originated credit-impaired financial assets should allow users to see the possible contractual cash flows that an entity could collect if there was a favourable change in expectations of credit losses for such assets.

It may be necessary to provide a narrative explanation of the change in the loss allowance in the period. This could include analysis of the:

[IFRS 7:B8D]

(a) portfolio composition;

(b) volume of financial instruments purchased or originated; and

(c) severity of the loss.

The loss allowance for loan commitments and financial guarantee contracts is recognised as a provision. The change in the loss allowance recognised as a provision should be disclosed separately from the loss allowance for financial assets. However, when a financial instrument includes both a loan (i.e. financial asset) and an undrawn commitment (i.e. loan commitment) component and it may not be possible to separately identify the expected credit losses on the loan commitment component from those on the financial asset component. In such cases, the expected credit losses on the loan commitment are required to be recognised together with the loss allowance for the financial asset. In some cases this could result in the combined expected credit losses exceeding the gross carrying amount of the financial asset (e.g. when the drawn down amount is small relative to the undrawn amount). In such cases the expected credit losses should be presented as a provision to avoid the recognition of a negative asset. [IFRS 7:B8E]

Example 5.2.1.3A

Changes in loss allowance

[Extract from IFRS 7:IG20B]

The following example illustrates one way of providing information about the changes in the loss allowance. This example does not illustrate the requirements for financial assets that are purchased or originated credit-impaired.

Mortgage loans-loss allowance	**12-month expected credit losses**	**Lifetime expected credit losses (collectively assessed)**	**Lifetime expected credit losses (individually assessed)**	**Credit-impaired financial assets (lifetime expected credit losses**
CU'000				
Loss allowance as at 1 January	**X**	**X**	**X**	**X**
Changes due to financial instruments recognised as at 1 January:				
– Transfer to lifetime expected credit losses	(X)	X	X	–
– Transfer to credit-impaired financial assets	(X)	–	(X)	X
– Transfer to 12-month expected credit losses	X	(X)	(X)	–
Financial assets that have been derecognised during the period	(X)	(X)	(X)	(X)

Mortgage loans-loss allowance	**12-month expected credit losses**	**Lifetime expected credit losses (collectively assessed)**	**Lifetime expected credit losses (individually assessed)**	**Credit-impaired financial assets (lifetime expected credit losses**
New financial assets originated or purchased	X	–	–	–
Write-offs	–	–	(X)	(X)
Changes in models/ risk parameters	X	X	X	X
Foreign exchange and other movements	X	X	X	X
Loss allowance as at 31 December	**X**	**X**	**X**	**X**

Significant changes in the gross carrying amount of mortgage loans that contributed to changes in the loss allowance were:

- The acquisition of the ABC prime mortgage portfolio increased the residential mortgage book by x per cent, with a corresponding increase in the loss allowance measured on a 12-month basis.
- The write-off of the CUXX DEF portfolio following the collapse of the local market reduced the loss allowance for financial assets with objective evidence of impairment by CUX.
- The expected increase in unemployment in the Region X caused a net increase in financial assets whose loss allowance is equal to lifetime expected credit losses and drove a net increase of CUX in the lifetime expected credit losses allowance.

To supplement the reconciliation of the loss allowance, IFRS 7 requires an explanation of how significant changes in the gross carrying amount of financial instruments during the period contributed to changes in the loss allowance. [IFRS 7:35I] The information, both qualitative and quantitative, should be provided separately for financial instruments:

(a) for which the loss allowance is measured at an amount equal to 12-month expected credit losses;

(b) for which the loss allowance is measured at an amount equal to lifetime expected credit losses and that are:

(i) financial instruments for which credit risk has increased significantly since initial recognition but that are not credit-impaired financial assets; and

(ii) financial assets that are credit-impaired at the reporting date (but that are not purchased or originated credit-impaired);

(iii) trade receivables, contract assets or lease receivables for which the loss allowance is measured at an amount equal to lifetime expected losses using the simplified approach (see **5.2.5.2** in **chapter B6**).

(c) that are purchased or originated credit-impaired assets.

Examples of changes in the gross carrying amount of financial instruments that contributed to the changes in the loss allowance may include:

[IFRS 7:35I]

(a) changes because of financial instruments originated or acquired during the reporting period;

(b) the modification of contractual cash flows on financial assets that do not result in a derecognition of those financial assets in accordance with IFRS 9;

(c) changes because of financial instruments that were derecognised or written-off during the reporting period; and

(d) changes arising from whether the loss allowance is measured at an amount equal to 12-month or lifetime expected credit losses.

IFRS 7:35I(d) refers to changes arising from whether the loss allowance is measured at an amount equal to 12-month or lifetime expected losses. It should be noted that moving between 12-month and lifetime expected losses does not give rise to a change in the gross carrying amount for the particular asset (i.e. the gross amount of the asset remains the same and only the loss allowance changes). However, moving between 12-month and lifetime expected losses changes the proportion of all of the gross amounts that are subject to 12-month or lifetime expected losses.

Example 5.2.1.3B

Changes in gross carrying amount

[Extract from IFRS 7:IG20B]

The following example illustrates one way of providing information about the significant changes in the gross carrying amount of financial assets during the period that contributed to changes in the loss allowance. This example does not illustrate the requirements for financial assets that are purchased or originated credit-impaired.

Mortgage loans-gross carrying amount	**12-month expected credit losses**	**Lifetime expected credit losses (collectively assessed)**	**Lifetime expected credit losses (individually assessed)**	**Credit-impaired financial assets (lifetime expected credit losses**
CU'000				
Gross carrying amount as at 1 January	**X**	**X**	**X**	**X**
Individual financial assets transferred to lifetime expected credit losses	(X)	–	X	–
Individual financial assets transferred to credit-impaired financial assets	(X)	–	(X)	X
Individual financial assets transferred from credit-impaired financial assets	X	–	X	(X)
Financial assets assessed on collective basis	(X)	X	–	–
New financial assets originated or purchased	X	–	–	–
Write-offs	–	–	(X)	(X)
Financial assets that have been derecognised	(X)	(X)	(X)	(X)
Changes due to modifications that did not result in derecognition	(X)	–	(X)	(X)
Other changes	X	X	X	X
Gross carrying amount as at 31 December	**X**	**X**	**X**	**X**

Because the allowance for expected losses is derived from the difference between all the contractual cash flows that are due and the contractual cash flows expected to be received, a modification of a financial asset which does not result in derecognition can give rise to a change in the amount of the loss allowance. Furthermore, a modification could change the credit risk of a financial asset such that the loss allowance is measured on a different basis (e.g. moving from lifetime to 12-month expected losses). Consequently, IFRS 7 requires disclosures on the nature and effect of modifications and how they impact the measurement of expected credit losses. These disclosures cover all modifications that have not resulted in derecognition of the financial asset and not only those that arise from financial difficulty of the borrower. The following disclosures are required:

[IFRS 7:35J]

(a) the amortised cost before the modification and the net modification gain or loss recognised for financial assets for which the contractual cash flows have been modified during the reporting period while they had a loss allowance measured at an amount equal to lifetime expected credit losses; and

(b) the gross carrying amount at the end of the reporting period of financial assets that have been modified since initial recognition at a time when the loss allowance was measured at an amount equal to lifetime expected credit losses and for which the loss allowance has changed during the reporting period to an amount equal to 12-month expected credit losses.

When lifetime expected credit losses are recognised for trade receivables, contract assets (under IFRS 15 *Revenue from Contracts with Customers*) and lease receivables using the simplified approach (see **5.2.5.2** in **chapter B6**) and those assets are modified while more than 30 days past due, the disclosures in paragraph (a) immediately above applies to those assets. [IFRS 7:35A(a)]

The disclosures in IFRS 7:35J specifically apply to assets which had a lifetime expected loss allowance when they were modified. This would appear to exclude purchase or originated credit-impaired financial assets which have a loss allowance measured at an amount equal to the *change* in lifetime expected losses since initial recognition (see **5.2.5.3** in **chapter B6**). This is reasonable given IFRS 7:35J(b) refers to a 12-month expected loss provision which is not relevant for purchased credit-impaired financial assets. However, the information required by IFRS 7:35J(a) would appear to be equally relevant for purchased or originated credit-impaired financial assets. Consequently, an entity should consider whether this information should be provided for purchased or originated credit-impaired financial assets in order to meet the credit risk disclosure objectives (see **5.2.1.1**).

For a financial asset measured at FVTOCI, the loan loss allowance is the same as if the asset was measured at amortised cost, except that it is recognised in accumulated other comprehensive income rather than as a reduction in the carrying value of the asset. Although the disclosures required by IFRS 7:35J are based on amortised cost they are not specifically restricted to those assets measured at amortised cost and the disclosures required would be equally relevant to assets measured at FVTOCI. Therefore the disclosures in IFRS 7:35J are required for assets measured at amortised cost and FVTOCI.

Collateral and other credit enhancements (e.g. guarantees, credit derivatives and netting agreements that do not qualify for offset in accordance with IAS 32 *Financial Instruments: Presentation*) can have a significant effect on the measurement of expected losses and the expected cash flows from them can vary from period to period (e.g. due to a change in the value of collateral or change in credit quality of the guarantor). Consequently, IFRS 7 requires the following disclosure by class of financial instrument:

[IFRS 7:35K]

(a) the amount that best represents its maximum exposure to credit risk at the end of the reporting period without taking account of any collateral held or other credit enhancements;

For financial assets exposed to credit risk, an entity's maximum exposure to credit risk is typically the gross carrying amount of those financial assets, net of any amounts offset in accordance with IAS 32 and any loss allowance recognised in accordance with IFRS 9. [IFRS 7:B9]

(b) a narrative description of collateral held as security and other credit enhancements, including:
   (i) a description of the nature and quality of the collateral held;
   (ii) an explanation of any significant changes in the quality of that collateral or credit enhancements as a result of deterioration or changes in the collateral policies of the entity during the reporting period; and
   (iii) information about financial instruments for which an entity has not recognised a loss allowance because of the collateral.

(c) quantitative information about the collateral held as security and other credit enhancements (for example, quantification of the extent to which collateral and other credit enhancements mitigate credit risk) for financial assets that are credit-impaired at the reporting date.

The narrative description could include information about:

[IFRS 7:B8G]

(a) the main types of collateral held as security and other credit enhancements;

(b) the volume of collateral held and other credit enhancements and its significance in terms of the loss allowance;

(c) the policies and processes for valuing and managing collateral and other credit enhancements;

(d) the main types of counterparties to collateral and other credit enhancements and their creditworthiness; and

(e) information about risk concentrations within the collateral and other credit enhancements.

When providing the above disclosures, it is not a requirement that the fair value of collateral and other credit enhancements nor the value of the collateral that was included in the calculation of expected credit losses be disclosed [IFRS 7:B8F] Furthermore, the narrative disclosure of the description of collateral held as security and other credit enhancements required by IFRS 7:35K(b) are not required for lease receivables. [IFRS 7:35A]

Under IFRS 9, an entity is required to directly reduce the gross carrying amount of a financial asset when there is no reasonable expectation of recovery (see **3.11** in **chapter B8**). When an entity has written off some or all of an asset but it is required to disclose the contractual amount outstanding on financial assets that were written off during the reporting period and are still subject to enforcement activity. [IFRS 7:35L]

Information about assets written off but still subject to enforcement activity provides users with insight about potential future recoveries.

5.2.1.4 Credit risk exposure

For some entities, a concentration of credit risk can arise when a number of counterparties are located in a geographical region or are engaged in similar activities and have similar economic characteristics that would cause their ability to meet contractual obligations to be similarly affected by changes in economic or other conditions. [IFRS 7:B8H]

To aid an assessment of an entity's credit risk exposure and an understanding of its significant credit risk concentrations, disclosure of the gross carrying amount of financial assets and the exposure to credit risk on loan commitments and financial guarantee contracts is required by credit risk rating grade (i.e. the rating of credit risk based on the risk of a default occurring on the financial instrument).

This information is provided separately for financial instruments:

[IFRS 7:35M]

(a) for which the loss allowance is measured at an amount equal to 12-month expected credit losses; and

(b) for which the loss allowance is measured at an amount equal to lifetime expected credit losses and that are:

(i) financial instruments for which credit risk has increased significantly since initial recognition but that are not credit-impaired financial assets;

(ii) financial assets that are credit-impaired at the reporting date (but that are not purchased or originated credit-impaired); and

(iii) trade receivables, contract assets or lease receivables for which the loss allowance is measured at an amount equal to lifetime expected losses using the simplified approach (see **5.2.5.2** in **chapter B6**).

(c) that are purchased or originated credit-impaired financial assets.

When the loss allowance for trade receivables, contract assets and lease receivables is based on lifetime expected credit losses the information required by IFRS 7:35M(b)(iii) may be based on a provision matrix (see **5.3.5.5** in **chapter B6**). [IFRS 7:35N].

The number of credit risk rating grades used should be consistent with the number reported to key management personnel for credit risk management purposes. For some entities, delinquency information may be the only borrower-specific information available without undue cost or effort and past due information may be used to assess whether credit risk has increased significantly since initial recognition (see **5.2.2.1** in **chapter B6**). In such cases an entity is required to provide an analysis of those financial assets by past due status. [IFRS 7:B8]

When expected credit losses are measured on a collective basis and it is not possible to allocate the gross carrying amount of individual financial assets or the exposure to credit risk on loan commitments and financial guarantee contracts to the credit risk rating grades, separate disclosure of the gross carrying amount of financial instruments for which lifetime expected credit losses have been measured on a collective basis is required. [IFRS 7:B8J]

Example 5.2.1.4A

Information about credit risk exposure and significant credit risk concentrations

[Extract from IFRS 7:IG20C]

The following example illustrates some ways of providing information about an entity's credit risk exposure and significant credit risk concentrations in accordance with IFRS 7:35M. The number of grades used to disclose the information in accordance with IFRS 7:35M shall be consistent with the number that the entity uses to report internally to key management personnel for internal credit risk management purposes. However, if information about credit risk rating grades is not available without undue cost or effort and an entity uses past due information to assess whether credit risk has increased significantly since initial recognition in accordance with IFRS 9:5.5.11, the entity shall provide an analysis by past-due status for those financial assets.

Consumer loan credit risk exposure by internal rating grades				
20XX	**Consumer – credit card**		**Consumer – automotive**	
CU'000	**Gross carrying amount**		**Gross carrying amount**	
	Lifetime	**12-month**	**Lifetime**	**12-month**
Internal Grade 1-2	X	X	X	X
Internal Grade 3-4	X	X	X	X
Internal Grade 5-6	X	X	X	X
Internal Grade 7	X	X	X	X
Total	**X**	**X**	**X**	**X**

Corporate loan credit risk profile by external rating grades				
20XX	**Corporate – equipment**		**Corporate – construction**	
CU'000	**Gross carrying amount**		**Gross carrying amount**	
	Lifetime	**12-month**	**Lifetime**	**12-month**
AAA-AA	X	X	X	X
A	X	X	X	X
BBB-BB	X	X	X	X
B	X	X	X	X
CCC-CC	X	X	X	X
C	X	X	X	X
D	X	X	X	X
Total	**X**	**X**	**X**	**X**

Corporate loan risk profile by probability of default				
20XX	**Corporate – unsecured**		**Corporate – secured**	
CU'000	**Gross carrying amount**		**Gross carrying amount**	
	Lifetime	**12-month**	**Lifetime**	**12-month**
0.00 - 0.10	X	X	X	X
0.11 - 0.40	X	X	X	X
0.41 - 1.00	X	X	X	X
1.01 - 3.00	X	X	X	X
3.01 - 6.00	X	X	X	X
6.01 - 11.00	X	X	X	X
11.01 - 17.00	X	X	X	X
17.01 - 25.00	X	X	X	X
25.01 - 50.00	X	X	X	X
50.01 +	X	X	X	X
Total	**X**	**X**	**X**	**X**

Example 5.2.1.4B

Information about credit risk exposure and significant credit risk concentrations for trade receivables

[Extract from IFRS 7:IG20D]

Entity A manufactures cars and provides financing to both dealers and end customers. Entity A discloses its dealer financing and customer financing as separate classes of financial instruments and applies the simplified approach to its trade receivables so that the loss allowance is always measured at an amount equal to lifetime expected credit losses. The following table illustrates the use of a provision matrix as a risk profile disclosure under the simplified approach:

20XXCU'000	**Trade receivables days past due**				
Dealer financing	**Current**	**More than 30 days**	**More than 60 days**	**More than 90 days**	**Total**
Expected credit loss rate	0.10%	2%	5%	13%	
Estimated total gross carrying amount at default	CU20,777	CU1,416	CU673	CU235	CU23,101
Lifetime expected credit losses - dealer financing	CU21	CU28	CU34	CU31	CU114
Customer financing Expected credit loss rate	0.20%	3%	8%	15%	
Estimated total gross carrying amount at default	CU19,222	CU2,010	CU301	CU154	CU21,687
Lifetime expected credit losses – customer financing	CU38	CU60	CU24	CU23	CU145

5.2.1.5 Exposure to credit risk on instruments to which the impairment requirements in IFRS 9 are not applied

For all financial instruments within the scope of IFRS 7, but to which the impairment requirements in IFRS 9 are not applied, an entity is required to disclose by class of financial instrument the amount that best represents the entity's maximum credit risk exposure at the end of the reporting period, *excluding* the effect of any collateral and other amounts that do not qualify for offset in accordance with IAS 32. This disclosure is not required for financial instruments whose carrying amount best represents the maximum exposure to credit risk. [IFRS 7:36(a)]

Examples of financial instruments in scope of IFRS 7 but not subject to the IFRS 9 impairment requirements include:

- Financial assets measured at FVTPL;
- Financial guarantee contracts issued measured at FVTPL;
- Loan commitments issued measured at FVTPL;
- Derivative financial instruments measured at FVTPL; and
- Forward contracts between an acquirer and a vendor in a business combination to buy or sell an acquiree at a future date.

Equity investments are also in scope of IFRS 7 but not subject to the IFRS 9 impairment requirements, however, they do not give rise to an exposure to credit risk and therefore are not subject to the IFRS 7 credit risk disclosures. Credit risk is defined as "the risk that one party to a financial instrument will cause a financial loss for the other party by failing to discharge an obligation". [IFRS 7:Appendix A]

These disclosures are designed to provide users of the financial statements with a consistent measure of the amounts exposed to credit risk and to allow for the possibility that the maximum exposure to loss may differ from the carrying amount of financial assets recognised at the end of the reporting period. [IFRS 7:BC49] The disclosure requirement focuses on the entity's exposure to credit risk that is not already reflected in the statement of financial position. [IFRS 7:BC49A]

For financial assets exposed to credit risk, an entity's maximum exposure to credit risk is typically the gross carrying amount of those financial assets, net of any amounts offset in accordance with IAS 32 and any loss allowance recognised in accordance with IFRS 9. [IFRS 7:B9]

Although IFRS 7:B9 refers to the maximum exposure to credit risk being net of any loss allowance, this would not be relevant for the financial instruments not subject to the IFRS 9 impairment requirements.

In the case of a derivative that is measured at fair value, an entity's maximum exposure to credit risk at the end of the reporting period will equal its carrying amount. [IFRS 7:B10(b)]

The maximum exposure to credit risk for financial guarantees that have been granted is equal to the maximum amount the entity would have to pay if the guarantee is called upon, irrespective of the likelihood of the guarantee being exercised. This amount will generally be significantly greater than the amount recognised as a liability. [IFRS 7:B10(c)]

Irrespective of whether a financial guarantee is accounted for under IFRS 4 or IFRS 9, similar disclosures are required. IFRS 4 requires disclosure of information about the credit risk associated with such contracts in the same manner as IFRS 7 requires credit risk disclosures for instruments that are measured in accordance with IFRS 9. [IFRS 4:39(d)]

The maximum exposure to credit risk for a loan commitment that is irrevocable over the life of the facility, or is revocable only in response to a material adverse change, and that cannot be settled net in cash or another financial asset, is the full amount of the commitment. This is because it is uncertain whether the amount of any undrawn portion may be drawn upon in the future. Therefore, the amount of the maximum exposure to credit risk for a loan commitment may be significantly greater than the amount recognised as a liability. [IFRS 7:B10(d)] Loan commitments that can be settled net in cash or other financial instruments are treated as derivative financial instruments and, consequently, an entity's maximum exposure to credit risk in respect of such loan commitments will be equal to their carrying amount.

While loan commitments at FVTPL (e.g. designated at FVTPL) that cannot be settled net in cash or other financial instruments are outside the scope of the IFRS 9 impairment requirements, they are within the scope of IFRS 7 because they are unrecognised financial assets or financial liabilities. [IFRS 7:4] For such loan commitments IFRS 7 is not clear whether it is possible to consider the entity's maximum exposure to credit risk in respect of that loan commitment as being its fair value (as is the case for other derivative financial assets). Because a loan commitment that cannot be settled net will always result in the origination of a loan if the commitment is exercised by the borrower, the most appropriate amount representing the entity's maximum exposure to credit risk would seem to be the maximum that can be borrowed under the commitment. Disclosing this amount is consistent with the disclosures for loan commitments in scope of the IFRS 9 impairment requirements.

The exposure on a loan to be originated under a loan commitment is the same as the exposure under a financial guarantee over the same loan, should it be drawn under the loan commitment. Both the lender and guarantor are exposed to the same risk of non-payment by the borrower.

IFRS 7:B10(c) states that the maximum exposure to credit risk for a written guarantee is the amount the entity could have to pay if the guarantee is called upon. It is reasonable to conclude that this amount should be based on what could be required to be paid if the guarantee was called upon in respect of a fully drawn loan (i.e. not only based on the drawn down amount at the end of the reporting period).

Example 5.2.1.5A

Maximum exposure to credit risk: loan commitment

Bank A issues a loan commitment to Entity B for US$100 million. The maximum exposure to credit risk that will be disclosed in Bank A's financial statements with respect to the loan commitment will be equal to the full amount of the loan that has been offered (i.e. US$100 million). Assume that Entity C issues a financial guarantee to Bank A relating to Bank A's loan commitment to Entity B over US$100 million. The guarantee will provide protection against Entity B defaulting on its loan to Bank A should Entity B draw down on the loan commitment. The maximum exposure to credit risk for Bank A is US$100 million, being the maximum potential loss under the loan ignoring the guarantee it has acquired to reduce this potential loss. This amount will be disclosed at the end of the reporting period even if no draw down on the loan commitment is made by Entity B.

Entity C has credit risk on the financial guarantee written to Bank A. The maximum exposure to credit risk is also US$100 million because this is the maximum amount Entity C could have to pay to Bank A if the guarantee is called upon.

Example 5.2.1.5B

Maximum exposure to credit risk: financial guarantee contracts

Entity B is a wholly-owned operating subsidiary of Entity A, the ultimate parent of Group A. To finance its working capital requirements, Entity B has short-term banking facilities of €300 million with various banks. Entity A has issued a variety of guarantees on behalf of its subsidiary and in favour of the banks which meet the definition of financial guarantee contracts. The schedule below details the drawn down banking facilities of Entity B and the amounts guaranteed by Entity A at 30 June 20X2 and 30 June 20X1.

	30 June 20X2	**30 June 20X1**
	€ million	**€ million**
Short term banking facilities drawn down at year end	100	100
Guarantees issued by Entity A to lenders	250	250

The following amount will be disclosed as the maximum exposure to credit risk in Entity B's financial statements, Entity A's separate financial statements, and Group A's consolidated financial statements in relation to the above amounts.

- Entity B: € nil (20X1: € nil) because Entity B is the borrower, it does not have an exposure to credit risk.
- Entity A (separate financial statements): €250 million (20X1: €250 million) being the full amount of the guarantee that would be required to be paid if the guarantee is called upon. [IFRS 7:B10(c)]
- Group A: € nil (20X1: € nil) because, from a group perspective, the group is the borrower and it does not have exposure to credit risk. The amount repayable is the same irrespective of whether Entity B repays the debt or Entity A pays under the financial guarantee contract.

5.2.1.6 Collateral held as security and other credit enhancements for financial instruments to which the impairment requirements in IFRS 9 are not applied

IFRS 7 requires disclosures regarding collateral held as security and other credit enhancements for all financial instruments within the scope of IFRS 7, but to which the impairment requirements in IFRS 9 are not applied.

More specifically, IFRS 7 requires a description of collateral held as security and other credit enhancements (e.g. guarantees, credit derivatives, and netting agreements that do not qualify for offset in accordance with IAS 32), and their financial effect (e.g. quantification of the extent to which collateral and other credit enhancements mitigate credit risk) in respect of the amount that best represents the maximum exposure to credit risk. [IFRS 7:36(b)]

These requirements may be met by disclosing:

[IFRS 7:IG22]

- the policies and processes for valuing and managing collateral and other credit enhancements obtained;
- a description of the main types of collateral and other credit enhancements;
- the main types of counterparties to collateral and other credit enhancements and their creditworthiness; and
- information about risk concentrations within the collateral or other credit enhancements.

5.2.1.7 Disclosures regarding collateral and other credit enhancements obtained

When an entity obtains financial or non-financial assets by taking possession of collateral or calling on other credit enhancements (e.g. financial guarantee contracts) at foreclosure, and such assets are required to be recognised at the reporting date in accordance with IFRS 9 or another standard, disclosure should be provided regarding the nature and carrying amount of such assets held at the reporting date. If the assets are not readily convertible into cash, the entity's policies for disposing of the assets or using them in its operations should also be disclosed. [IFRS 7:38] Disclosures regarding collateral are useful in such circumstances because they provide information about the frequency of such events and the entity's ability to obtain and realise the value of the collateral.

Consideration should be given to the type of assets that are obtained as collateral and the ability to sell those assets. The mere fact that the collateral consists of listed securities does not indicate that it is readily convertible to cash because the liquidity of those assets and the size of the holding should be considered.

Example 5.2.1.7

Collateral and other credit enhancements obtained

Scenario 1

Bank A lends CU100,000 to a homeowner with property specified as collateral for the loan. During the period, the homeowner defaults under the loan and the property meets the criteria for recognition in the statement of financial position of Bank A before being disposed of. Bank A must comply with the disclosure requirements of IFRS 7:38 as noted above.

Scenario 2

Bank B lends CU1,000 to a retail customer. Concurrently, it purchases a financial guarantee from Entity C under which, if the retail customer fails to make payments under the loan agreement when due, Entity C will reimburse Bank B the CU1,000 in cash. During the period, the retail customer defaults under the loan. At the reporting date, Bank B has a claim under the financial guarantee contract and recognises a receivable from Entity C for CU1,000. The amount of CU1,000 is required to be disclosed under the requirements of IFRS 7:38.

5.2.2 Liquidity risk

Liquidity risk is defined as "the risk that an entity will encounter difficulty in meeting obligations associated with financial liabilities that are settled by delivering cash or another financial asset". [IFRS 7:Appendix A]

If a financial liability is exclusively settled in the issuer's own equity instruments (e.g. a variable number of equity shares equal to a fixed monetary amount), then the financial liability will not be included in the liquidity risk disclosures. Equally, if the issuer has the right to deliver its own equity instruments instead of cash or another financial asset, the financial liability is deemed not to have liquidity risk because the issuer can avoid the delivery of cash or another financial asset by electing to deliver its own equity instruments. If the counterparty to the financial liability can demand cash or another financial asset, even if there is an equity-settlement alternative, the financial liability must be included in the liquidity risk disclosures because the issuer cannot avoid settlement in cash or another financial asset if the counterparty chooses this settlement alternative.

If an entity has a contractual arrangement recognised as a financial liability where the entity is required to deliver a non-financial item only (e.g. gold), or the entity has a choice of delivering a non-financial item instead of cash or another financial asset, then the financial liability is excluded from the liquidity risk disclosures, because the non-financial item is not cash or another financial asset (even if the non-financial item is regarded as readily convertible into cash). This will typically be the case for contracts for the delivery of non-financial assets that are included within the scope of IFRS 9 because they are deemed net settled in accordance with IFRS 9:2.4-2.7 (see **2.5** in **chapter B1**). Such instruments are generally classified as derivatives as at FVTPL and may be financial liabilities at the reporting period end.

Liquidity risk also arises because of the possibility (which may often be remote) that the entity could be required to pay its financial liabilities earlier than expected.

5.2.2.1 Quantitative liquidity risk disclosures

IFRS 7 requires an entity to disclose summary quantitative information provided internally to key management personnel regarding its exposure to liquidity risk and how this data is determined. If the outflows of cash or another financial asset included in the data could occur significantly earlier or be for significantly different amounts than indicated in the data, this fact should be disclosed and additional quantitative information should be provided to enable users of the financial statements to evaluate the risk. [IFRS 7:B10A] The example provided in IFRS 7 is where data on derivatives assumes net settlement but where the counterparty has the option to require gross settlement. However, additional quantitative information is not required if it is already included in the maturity analysis disclosure.

5.2.2.2 Maturity analysis

IFRS 7:39 requires disclosure of:

(a) a maturity analysis for non-derivative financial liabilities (including issued financial guarantee contracts) that shows the remaining contractual maturities;

(b) a maturity analysis for derivative financial liabilities. The maturity analysis should include the remaining contractual maturities for those derivative financial liabilities for which contractual maturities are essential for an understanding of the timing of the cash flows (see IFRS 7:B11B); and

(c) a description of how the entity manages the liquidity risk inherent in (a) and (b).

IFRS 7:B11B provides two examples where a quantitative maturity analysis for derivative financial liabilities showing remaining contractual maturities is deemed essential for an understanding of the timing of the cash flows. The first example is an interest rate swap with a remaining maturity of five years in a cash flow hedge of a variable rate financial asset or liability. The second example is all loan commitments.

A contractual maturity analysis is not required in respect of derivative liabilities if the information is not essential for an understanding of the timing of cash flows. This may be the case when an entity frequently buys and sells derivatives (e.g. derivative liabilities included in a trading book in a financial institution). Showing the contractual maturities may not be essential for understanding the timing of cash flows because the derivative liabilities will be settled through sale rather than through the payment/receipt of the contractual cash flows under the instrument until its contractual maturity. In such circumstances, the entity is still required to show a maturity analysis for derivative financial liabilities, but the analysis could be presented on an alternative basis; for example, it could be based on expected maturities, or even on fair values at the end of the reporting period when the entity's expectation is that the carrying amount of the derivative liability (i.e. its fair value) will be payable as a result of a disposal shortly after the reporting date.

An entity should exercise its judgement in determining the appropriate number of the time bands in the maturity analysis prescribed in IFRS 7:39 (a) and (b) (see above).

Because quantitative information is required to be reported based on information reported to key management personnel, the time bands should, where applicable, be equivalent to those reported internally. Some entities may have many more time bands than others; for example, some banks disclose liquidity for 1 day, 1-3 days, 3-7 days, 7-30 days etc.

In any event, the entity should evaluate whether the liquidity analysis provides sufficient disclosure regarding its liquidity requirements by considering the relative timing of its liquidity needs. For example, an entity may have significant obligations due in a month's time, in which case aggregating all obligations for the first year into one band will not be appropriate.

5.2.2.3 Contractual maturity analysis: determining which time band

When a counterparty has a choice regarding when an amount is required to be paid, the liability is included on the basis of the earliest date on which the entity can be required to pay (e.g. demand deposits should be included in the earliest time band because the deposit holder can require repayment on demand). [IFRS 7:B11C(a)] Therefore, American-style written options that can be exercised by the holder at any time should be disclosed in the earliest time band in which the holder can exercise, while a European-style option, which is only exercisable by the holder at maturity, should be included in the time period equivalent to its maturity date.

When the counterparty has the choice regarding when an amount is to be paid, the liquidity analysis should be based on the 'worst case' scenario, i.e. the earliest date on which the entity could be required to pay. [IFRS 7:BC57] This also has implications for the treatment of financial liabilities that are callable by the issuer. IFRS 7:BC57 would seem to imply that an issuer call option is not taken into account for the purposes of the liquidity analysis. Therefore, for liquidity risk purposes, perpetual fixed rate debt that can be called by the issuer will be presented as if the call feature were absent and, therefore, the issuer has an obligation to pay cash flows into perpetuity. Similarly, if a financial liability has a maturity of 10 years but is callable by the issuer after 5 years, the cash flows included in the liquidity analysis would assume the instrument will remain outstanding until its contractual maturity. This approach applies even if it is highly likely that the issuer's call option will be exercised and also if the effect of the call option has been included in the determining the effective interest rate of the liability for the purpose of its measurement at amortised cost (see **4.1** of **chapter B6** for details).

When an entity is committed to make amounts available in instalments, each instalment is allocated to the earliest period in which the entity can be required to pay it (e.g. an undrawn loan commitment should be included in the time band containing the earliest date that it can be drawn down). [IFRS 7:B11C(b)] If loan commitments can be drawn by the holder at any time, they should be included in the earliest time period.

While the loan commitment is undrawn, it is generally an unrecognised financial liability. However, IFRS 7:4 is clear that unrecognised financial liabilities are included within its scope. The requirement for the writer of the loan commitment (i.e. the potential lender) to include in the contractual maturity analysis of liquidity risk its potential obligation to pay cash under undrawn loan commitments in the time band that reflects the earliest period the holder can draw down under the loan commitment is reasonable because it demonstrates the timing and amount of cash that the entity may be committed to pay to a borrower.

The approach applied to written loan commitments is equally applied to written financial guarantee contracts. The maximum amount that the writer could be required to pay to the holder of the guarantee should be included in the time band that reflects the earliest period in which the guarantee could be called. [IFRS 7:B11C(c)]

If an entity has issued perpetual debt, the entity must consider how the cash flows that are due to perpetuity will be included in the maturity analysis. Because the cash flows are perpetual, it would be reasonable to determine the number of time bands based on all other financial liabilities that are not perpetual (i.e. that are term liabilities) and include undiscounted interest cash flows in relation to perpetual liabilities as appropriate in these time bands. In addition, it will be necessary to make clear through additional disclosure (in narrative form or a combination of an additional column with narrative disclosure) that the entity is subject to a stream of interest cash flows in relation to the perpetual instrument into infinity with disclosure of the key terms of the perpetual instrument (such as the rate of interest and the notional amount).

5.2.2.4 Contractual maturity analysis: amount to include in the time band

The amounts to be presented in the contractual maturity analysis are contractual, undiscounted cash flows. These amounts will differ from the amounts disclosed in the statement of financial position for financial liabilities, which are typically discounted amounts. [IFRS 7:B11D]

Although not specifically mentioned in IFRS 7, the financial liabilities to be disclosed as part of the liquidity risk analysis should be after any amounts offset in accordance with IAS 32.

Examples of amounts included on an undiscounted basis include:

[IFRS 7:B11D]

- gross finance lease obligations, before deduction of finance charges;
- prices specified in forward agreements to purchase financial assets for cash;
- net amounts for pay (receive) floating/receive (pay) fixed interest rate swaps for which net cash flows are exchanged;
- contractual amounts to be exchanged in a derivative financial instrument, such as a cross-currency swap, for which gross cash flows are exchanged; and
- gross cash flows in respect of loan commitments.

For foreign currency denominated fixed- or floating-rate debt instruments, the disclosure of principal and interest in the appropriate time bands is determined based on the interest rates curves in the foreign currency interest rate environment. These amounts may be disclosed in the foreign currency. Alternatively, they may be disclosed in the functional currency when preparing entity-only financial statements, or alternatively disclosed in the group presentation currency when preparing consolidated financial statements.

When the amount payable is not fixed, as is the case for issued debt that has a variable interest rate, the amount to be disclosed should be determined by reference to the conditions existing at the end of the reporting period. If the amount payable varies with changes in an index, the amount disclosed may be based on the level of the index at the end of the reporting period. [IFRS 7:B11D]

What is not clear from IFRS 7:B11D is whether "conditions existing at the end of the reporting period" is referring solely to the absolute level of the index at the end of the reporting period (e.g. the LIBOR rate at the end of the reporting period), or whether it is referring to conditions relating to future LIBOR that exist at the end of the reporting period. The former would result in, say, a five-year LIBOR-based issued debt having five interest payments of the same amount, whereas the latter would have five interest payments based on the prevailing forward curve at the end of the reporting period (i.e. based on expectations of future LIBOR). The most appropriate disclosure would seem to be the latter because it recognises the conditions at the period end relating to the entity's expected payments of cash or another financial asset.

A derivative may be an asset in one period and a liability in another period depending on its fair value at each reporting date. In order to provide some comparability, an entity may choose to project the undiscounted cash flows on the derivative (whether it is settled net or gross) and disclose these undiscounted cash flows in the appropriate time bands, irrespective of whether in a particular time band the entity is expecting a net cash inflow or a net cash outflow.

In the case of gross-settled derivatives that are liabilities at the end of the reporting period, the Standard only requires disclosure of the gross outflow leg. However, an entity may wish to disclose these derivatives separately from net-settled derivatives so that users of the financial statements can distinguish the derivatives that will be accompanied by a gross inflow. An entity may also choose to provide the information in relation to the accompanying gross inflow to make clear the total cash flows on derivative instruments.

Disclosure of the gross outflow leg of gross-settled derivative liabilities is required even if the outflow leg is not a cash leg, but the outflow is still the delivery of a financial instrument. For example, an entity may have entered into a forward contract to sell a particular corporate bond in exchange for CU100 million cash in 9 months' time with the contract being exclusively gross-settled through delivery of the bond and receipt of the cash.

Consideration needs to be given as to how to present optional derivative financial liabilities that are not written loan commitments or financial guarantee contracts (whether stand-alone or embedded) in the maturity analysis. For example, if a written credit default option that does not meet the definition of a financial guarantee contract because the payout under the contract is driven not only by non-payment of a debtor but also by the credit rating of the borrower, it will be measured at FVTPL. The fair value of the written option will, at each reporting date, comprise intrinsic value and time value. In determining the amount to be included in the liquidity analysis, it would seem reasonable to draw on the principle in IFRS 7:B11D and disclose an undiscounted amount that represents the expected payout under the option based on conditions at the end of the reporting period. Under this, an amount of nil would be disclosed for options that are out of the money (based on forward rates, if applicable) at the end of the reporting period. For options that are in the money (based on forward rates, if applicable) the amount of the expected payout would be included in the liquidity risk analysis. It should be noted that this amount will not take account of any of the option's time value because the time value is not payable by the writer to the counterparty, and will also differ from the intrinsic value of the option because this will include the effect of discounting.

If an entity is preparing a contractual maturity analysis and has a hybrid (combined) financial instrument, it should not separate an embedded derivative for the purposes of including cash flows in the maturity analysis. [IFRS 7:B11A] The entity will instead include the cash flows in the maturity analysis based on the terms of the whole arrangement (i.e. based on it being a non-derivative financial liability, whether or not embedded derivatives in the instrument are separately accounted for). If the hybrid (combined) financial instrument is a recognised financial asset, an entity should disclose cash flows in the maturity analysis based on the terms of the whole arrangement if that information is necessary to enable users of its financial statements to evaluate the nature and extent of liquidity risk (see **5.2.2.5**). [IFRS 7:B11E]

The guidance in IFRS 7:B11A applies to hybrid (combined) financial instruments. An example would be an issued equity-linked bond or an issued debt instrument where the interest payments breach the 'double-double' test (see **7.3** in **chapter B5**).

IFRS 7 does not refer to the inclusion or exclusion of an embedded derivative that is a financial liability at the reporting date that is embedded in a non-financial arrangement that is outside the scope of IFRS 7 (e.g. a separately recognised embedded derivative in an unrecognised executory contract to receive a non-financial item). Because the embedded derivative financial liability is fully within the scope of IFRS 7, it would appear that it should be included within the maturity analysis if the embedded derivative results in the entity delivering cash or another financial asset. However, including the embedded derivative in the maturity analysis would appear to be in conflict with the principle in IFRS 7:B11A that requires an entity to consider the outflows of the whole contractual arrangement. Because the whole contractual arrangement is not in the scope of IFRS 7 (only the embedded derivative liability is) and the embedded derivative liability recognised may include imputed (not contractual) cash flows as a result of separating out part of the arrangement from the host contract, it is reasonable to exclude the embedded derivative from the maturity analysis.

Example 5.2.2.4

Liquidity risk disclosure: maturity analysis of financial liabilities

Bank M is a financial institution with a 31 December 20X1 reporting date. Bank M accepts deposits from a wide range of investors with a variety of rates and maturities. The bank manages its exposure to liquidity risk through a separate and independent liquidity risk management board which reports monthly to the board of directors with a maturity analysis based on the term structure of its deposit book. Bank M uses interest rate swaps to economically hedge its net interest margin. The interest rate swaps are not part of a trading book where there is frequent buying or selling. Bank M considers that the inclusion of cash flows on its interest rate swaps in its liquidity risk maturity analysis is essential in order for users of the financial statements to understand the timing of cash flows.

The schedule below sets out the financial liabilities at 31 December 20X1 (ignores comparative amounts and assumes that all figures quoted in the table are the notional amounts only, where applicable).

Instrument type	**CU'000**
5.35% 15-day notice deposits[1]	4,550
4.5% demand deposits[2]	6,750
Fixed rate deposits[3]	6,200
10% preference shares[4]	5,000
LIBOR-based financial liabilities[5]	10,000
Interest rate swaps[6]	1,200
Total	**33,700**

[1] The notice deposits have a clause that allows for a depositor to elect to liquidate his/her deposit within 15 days. At the end of the reporting period, 40 per cent of the outstanding balance is in respect of depositors who have made this election.

[2] The demand deposits are repayable within 30 days of notice being given. No persons had given notice at the end of the reporting period.

[3] The fixed rate deposits are for periods ranging between 60 days, 90 days and 120 days at varying rates. The balance at the reporting date is made up as follows.

[4] The preference shares are redeemable after five years. The interest on the preference shares is paid yearly on 31 December.

[5] The LIBOR-based financial liabilities pay interest monthly with the interest rate resetting to LIBOR in advance, with a bullet repayment of principal in one year's time. The forward curve at the reporting date was as follows:

[6] The interest rate swaps are settled net on a quarterly basis. The undiscounted future cash flows for all interest rate swap liabilities based on the forward curve at the reporting date were as follows (negatives represent cash inflows)

Maturity	Rate	Notional amount (CU'000)
60 days	4.90%	1,240
90 days	6.50%	1,860
120 days	7.36%	3,100

Interest is payable on maturity.

Month	Interest rate
January 20X2	5.53%
February 20X2	5.61%
March 20X2	6.12%
April 20X2	6.57%
May 20X2	6.59%
June 20X2	6.69%
July 20X2	6.71%
August 20X2	6.95%
September 20X2	7.06%
October 20X2	7.06%
November 20X2	7.30%
December 20X2	7.18%

Month	Net cash flow CU'000
March 20X2	600
June 20X2	500
September 20X2	400
December 20X2	350
March 20X3	300
June 20X3	200
September 20X3	100
December 20X3	50
March 20X4	(100)
June 20X4	(150)
September 20X4	(250)
December 20X4	(300)

Liquidity risk – maturity analysis CU'000

	≤1 month	1–≤3 months	3–≤12 months	1–≤3 years	3–≤5 years
Notice deposits	4,560[1]				
Demand deposits	6,775[2]				
Fixed deposits		3,140[3]	3,175[3]		
Preference shares			500[4]	1,000[4]	6,000[4]
LIBOR-based financial liabilities		142[5]	10,520[5]		
Interest rate swaps		600[6]	1,250[6]	(150)[6]	
Total	11,335	3,882	15,445	850	6,000

[1] (4,550 × 5.35% × 40% × 15/365) + (4,550 × 5.35% × 60% × 16/365) + 4,550 = CU4,560

While 40% of the depositors have indicated they will liquidate their deposits, on a worst case scenario basis, the remaining 60% will also all liquidate their deposits by giving notice the next day for their funds to be repaid within the following 15 days. Therefore, the total liability would be settled within a month, and the disclosure will need to include the principal plus interest due.

[2] (6,750 × 4.5% × 30/365) + 6,750 = CU6,775

On a worst case basis, all of the demand deposits will be called within the following month. The amount to be disclosed will be the principal plus the interest for 30 days.

[3] 60 days: (1,240 x 4.90% x 60/365) + 1,240 = CU1,250

90 days: (1,860 x 6.50% x 90/365) + 1,860 = CU1,890

The fixed deposit is payable in tranches. The first two tranches fall due within the first 3 months. Total for 1-3 month time period = CU3,140.

120 days: (3,100 x 7.36% x 120/365) + 3,100 = CU3,175

The fixed deposit is payable in tranches. The last tranche falls due in 120 days' time, i.e.: 3-12 month period.

[4] 1 year: (5,000 x 10%) = CU500

2, 3 years: (5,000 x 10% x 2) = CU1,000

4, 5 years: (5,000 x 10% x 2) +5,000 = CU6,000

The interest payment for the preference share falls due at the end of each year, with the capital being repaid at the end of 5 years.

[5] Interest due is determined using the yield curve at the end of the reporting period, and is calculated as the product of the notional of the loan, the interest rate and the number of days.

[6] The undiscounted forecasted cash flow for:

March 20X2 =	CU600
June, September and December 20X2 =	CU1,250
March 20X3 to December 20X4	(CU150)

Amounts determined as follows.

Total for 1-3 months.

Month	Days	Time band	Rate	Cash flow CU'000
January 20X2	31	1–3 months	5.53%	47.00
February 20X2	28	1–3 months	5.61%	43.00
March 20X2	31	1–3 months	6.12%	52.00
Total				142.00

Total for 3-12 months

Month	Days	Time band	Rate	Cash flow CU'000
April 20X2	30	3–12 months	6.57%	54
May 20X2	31	3–12 months	6.59%	56
June 20X2	30	3–12 months	6.69%	55
July 20X2	31	3–12 months	6.71%	57
August 20X2	31	3–12 months	6.95%	59
September 20X2	30	3–12 months	7.06%	58
October 20X2	31	3–12 months	7.06%	60
November 20X2	30	3–12 months	7.30%	60
December 20X2	31	3–12 months	7.18%	61
December 20X2	–	3–12 months	–	10,000
Total				**10,520**

5.2.2.5 Liquidity risk management

An entity is required to describe how it manages the liquidity risk inherent in the financial liabilities included in the maturity analysis (see **5.2.2.2**). An entity should disclose a maturity analysis of financial assets it holds for managing liquidity risk (e.g. financial assets that are readily saleable or expected to generate cash inflows to meet cash outflows on financial liabilities), if that information is necessary to enable users of its financial statements to evaluate the nature and extent of liquidity risk. [IFRS 7:B11E]

There is an apparent conflict between IFRS 7 which requires the disclosure of a liquidity analysis for all *financial liabilities* and IAS 1:65 which states that "IFRS 7 requires disclosure of the maturity dates of *financial assets and financial liabilities*" [emphasis added]. An entity is not required to disclose a maturity analysis for financial assets in all cases. The minimum required disclosure is for a maturity analysis for financial liabilities only. However, a maturity analysis should be disclosed for financial assets if the entity holds financial assets for managing liquidity risk and that information is necessary to enable users of its financial statements to evaluate the nature and extent of liquidity risk. [IFRS 7:B11E]

Other factors that an entity may wish to disclose in describing how it manages its liquidity risk include, but are not limited to, whether the entity:

[IFRS 7:B11F]

(a) has committed borrowing facilities (e.g. commercial paper facilities) or other lines of credit (e.g. stand-by credit facilities) that it can access to meet liquidity needs;

(b) holds deposits at central banks to meet liquidity needs;

(c) has very diverse funding sources;

(d) has significant concentrations of liquidity risk in either its assets or its funding sources;

(e) has internal control processes and contingency plans for managing liquidity risk;

(f) has instruments that include accelerated repayment terms (e.g. on the downgrade of the entity's credit rating);

(g) has instruments that could require the posting of collateral (e.g. margin calls for derivatives);

(h) has instruments that allows the entity to choose whether it settles its financial liabilities by delivering cash (or another financial asset) or by delivering its own shares; or

(i) has instruments that are subject to master netting agreements.

5.2.3 Market risk

Market risk is defined as "the risk that the fair value or future cash flows of a financial instrument will fluctuate because of changes in market prices. Market risk comprises three types of risk: currency risk, interest rate risk and other price risk". [IFRS 7:Appendix A] Each of these risks is defined as follows.

[IFRS 7:Appendix A]

(a) **Currency risk:** the risk that the fair value or future cash flows of a financial instrument will fluctuate because of changes in foreign exchange rates. Currency risk arises on financial instruments that are denominated in a different currency to the entity's functional currency.

(b) **Interest rate risk:** the risk that the fair value or future cash flows of a financial instrument will fluctuate because of changes in market interest rates. Interest rate risk arises on interest-bearing financial instruments that are recognised in the statement of financial position (e.g. debt instruments acquired or issued), and on some financial instruments that are not recognised in the statement of financial position (e.g. some loan commitments).

(c) **Other price risk:** the risk that the fair value or future cash flows of a financial instrument will fluctuate because of changes in market prices (other than those arising from interest rate risk or currency risk), whether those changes are caused by factors specific to the individual financial instrument or its issuer, or factors affecting all similar financial instruments traded in the market.

Examples of other price risks include equity price risk, commodity price risk, prepayment risk and residual value risk.

Market risk sensitivity analysis is required for each type of market risk to which the entity is exposed at the end of the reporting period showing how profit or loss and equity would have been affected by changes in the relevant risk variable that were reasonably possible at the end of the reporting period. In addition, disclosure should be provided of the methods and assumptions that were used in preparing the sensitivity analysis, any changes from the previous period in the methods and assumptions used, and the reasons for those changes. [IFRS 7:40]

An entity will need to decide how it should aggregate information to present a comprehensive analysis without combining information with different characteristics about exposures to risks from significantly different economic environments. For example:

(a) an entity that trades financial instruments might disclose this information separately for financial instruments held for trading and those not held for trading; and

(b) an entity is exposed to market risks from areas of hyperinflation and areas of very low inflation would disclose the information sensitivity for the two areas.

If an entity is exposed to only one type of market risk in only one economic environment, it would not show disaggregated information. [IFRS 7:B17]

The sensitivity analysis provides useful information because it is relatively easy to calculate and understand, is suitable for all entities, and highlights the nature and extent of risks that arise from financial instruments. [IFRS 7:BC59]

It is not necessary to prepare an analysis that reflects inter-dependencies between risk variables (e.g. in preparing an interest rate sensitivity analysis, an entity does not need to determine the impact of changes in interest rates would have on the relative strengthening and weakening of the currency with other currencies). Rather a simple sensitivity analysis that shows the change in only one variable is sufficient. [IFRS 7:BC60]

The preparation of a market risk sensitivity analysis requires the following steps.

(i) Identify risk exposures

(ii) Identify the exposures at the end of the reporting period and how those exposures affect the sensitivity analysis

(iii) Determine what is a reasonably possible change in the relevant risk variable

(iv) Determine the appropriate level of aggregation that should be provided in the disclosures

(v) Calculate and present the sensitivity analyses

Each of these steps in considered in detail below.

(i) Identify risk exposures

All market risks to which the entity is exposed need to be identified.

(ii) Identify the exposures at the end of the reporting period and how those exposures affect the sensitivity analysis

All financial instruments at the end of the reporting period whose fair value and/or cash flows are affected by changes in risk factors need to be identified.

Examples of financial instruments and their impact on profit or loss are set out below.

- Floating rate debt instruments, whether assets or liabilities, are sensitive to interest rates. The entity will flex interest rates for floating rate instruments outstanding at the period end showing how profit or loss would have varied in the period assuming the instruments at the reporting date were outstanding for the entire period.
- Foreign currency denominated debt instruments are sensitive to foreign currency rates because monetary items are retranslated into the functional currency of the entity at the reporting date. The sensitivity to foreign currency rates applies irrespective of whether the instrument is an asset or a liability, and whether it is measured at fair value or amortised cost. This includes intragroup foreign currency denominated loans that are expected to be repaid in the foreseeable future when the foreign currency risk does not eliminate on consolidation.
- For financial instruments held at the reporting date that are designated as at FVTPL or are held for trading, sensitivities will depend on the underlying risks of the instrument. A debt instrument may be sensitive to changes in interest rate and foreign currency risk, whereas an equity instrument may be sensitive to changes in equity prices and foreign currency risk.
- All derivatives in designated and qualifying fair value hedge accounting relationships are sensitive to the underlying risks of the instrument.

- Fixed rate debt instruments that are hedged items in qualifying fair value hedges of interest rate risk are sensitive to changes in interest rates.

Examples of financial instruments and their impact in other comprehensive income are set out below:

- Foreign currency denominated debt instruments that are designated as a qualifying hedging instrument in a foreign currency cash flow or net investment hedge are sensitive to foreign currency rates.
- Intragroup foreign currency denominated debt instruments to or from a foreign operation that are not expected to be repaid in the foreseeable future in accordance with IAS 21:15 are sensitive to foreign currency rates when the foreign currency risk does not eliminate on consolidation. Even though the debt instrument may form part of the foreign operation in accordance with IFRS 9:6.5.13, it remains within the scope of IFRS 7 and IFRS 9 and, therefore, should be included in the sensitivity analysis.
- Derivatives and embedded derivatives designated as effective hedging instruments in a cash flow hedge or a hedge of a net investment in a foreign operation are sensitive to the underlying risks of the instrument.
- Foreign currency denominated equity securities classified as at FVTOCI are sensitive to foreign currency rates and equity prices.

Any recognised financial instrument at the end of the reporting period whose cash flows are contractually linked to a variable or whose fair value is dependent on a variable should be included in a sensitivity analysis to the extent that changes in the variable will affect profit or loss or equity. For example, if an entity has issued debt that is contractually linked to inflation, where the inflation linkage is considered a closely related embedded derivative, the carrying amount of the debt and its impact on profit or loss will depend on the level of inflation throughout the reporting period and at the period end. Alternatively, if the inflation linkage is not closely related, the instrument will affect profit or loss through its remeasurement as a derivative at FVTPL.

An example of a financial instrument that has no impact on profit or loss or equity is a fixed rate debt instrument, whether an asset or a liability, measured at amortised cost, that is denominated in the entity's functional currency and, in the case of a financial liability, does not have embedded derivatives that are separated. Changes in interest rates or currency rates in respect of this instrument do not impact profit or loss or equity.

IFRS 7:Appendix A defines currency risk as "the risk that the fair value or future cash flows of a financial instrument will fluctuate because of changes in foreign exchange rates. IFRS 7:B23 states that currency risk (or foreign exchange risk) arises on financial instruments that are denominated in a foreign currency, i.e. in a currency other than the functional currency in which they are measured". The Standard is clear that any foreign currency monetary item held at the reporting date should be included in the foreign currency risk sensitivity analysis. What is less clear is whether IFRS 7 requires an entity to also include in the foreign currency risk sensitivity analysis the extent to which the effective interest rate that is recognised in profit or loss in the period in respect of the monetary item held at the reporting date would have differed had foreign currency rates differed. The foreign currency interest recognised in profit or loss is usually translated using the average monthly foreign currency rate and, therefore, profit or loss is sensitive to changes in foreign currency rates irrespective of whether the loan has fixed or floating foreign currency interest. Because the monetary item affects profit or loss through the recognition of interest, as well as the translation of the carrying amount at the reporting date, it would be meaningful to include both interest and principal of a monetary item within the foreign currency sensitivity analysis. This approach is consistent with the view that foreign currency interest is variable in the functional currency of the entity.

Financial instruments that are classified as equity in accordance with IAS 32 are not remeasured and, therefore, do not affect profit or loss or equity when sensitivity analysis is performed. [IFRS 7:B28]

It should be noted that if the entity is party to derivatives over own equity that are not classified as equity (e.g. if the entity has issued warrants with an exercise price in a currency other than the functional currency of the entity), then its own equity price risk will be a relevant example of an 'other price risk'. Because the instruments will be accounted for as derivatives at FVTPL with the underlying being the entity's own equity price, they will need to be considered for the purposes of the sensitivity analysis.

(iii) Determine what is a reasonably possible change in the relevant risk variable

An entity needs to determine what it considers to be a reasonably possible change in the relevant risk variable, and should consider both the economic environment in which it operates and the time frame over which it is making the assessment. A reasonably possible change in a relevant risk variable in one environment may not be the same in another environment (e.g. a reasonably possible change in interest rates may be 100bp for Sterling denominated debt, but the same could not be said for Yen denominated debt, for which a reasonably possible change may be substantially smaller). Entities are required to judge what those reasonably possible changes are and should not include remote or 'worse case scenarios' or 'stress tests'. A reasonably possible change in the relevant risk variable should be assessed over the time frame until the entity will next present these disclosures, which is usually until the end of the entity's next annual reporting period. [IFRS 7:B19]

While the range of reasonably possible changes may be wide, disclosure is not required for each change within that range. It is sufficient to disclose the effects of the changes at the limits of the reasonably possible range. [IFRS 7:B18(b)]

IFRS 7 requires comparative information to be presented. If the volatility of a given risk variable changes and, therefore, an entity alters its view of what is a reasonably possible change, this would not prompt restatement of the comparative risk disclosures. The entity should, however, carefully disclose the fact that there has been a change in what is considered to be a reasonably possible change in the risk variable.

(iv) Determine the appropriate level of aggregation that should be provided in the disclosures

An entity should aggregate the output from sensitivity analysis in order to provide a broad view of the entity's overall sensitivity to market risk but without combining information with different characteristics about exposures to risks from significantly different economic environments. Disclosures may, for example, be provided separately for financial instruments that are held for trading from those that are not. Alternatively, disclosures may be disclosed for each risk. As a minimum, sensitivity analyses for each currency to which an entity has a significant exposure should be provided. [IFRS 7:B24]

An entity should provide sensitivity analysis for the whole of its business but may provide different types of sensitivity analyses for different classes of financial instruments. [IFRS 7:B21]

An entity could provide different types of sensitivity analysis for different parts of its business if this is consistent with how it manages risk internally. For example, a financial institution may comprise a retail banking division and an investment banking division. The entity could choose to provide a conventional sensitivity analysis, as described in the steps above, in relation to the retail banking division and a value-at-risk (VaR) analysis in relation to the investment banking division, if the latter analysis is used for internal risk management purposes within the investment banking division. However, the entity in this case would need to consider carefully how to treat any transactions and exposures between the two divisions so that the disclosure is not misleading (see (vi) below for discussion of VaR as an alternative disclosure of market risk).

(v) Calculate and present the sensitivity analyses

Entities should disclose the effect on profit or loss and equity for exposures at the end of the reporting period assuming that a reasonably possible change in the relevant risk variable had been applied to those exposures at the end of the reporting period. [IFRS 7:B18]

The sensitivity may be reported separately for different lines in profit or loss or for consolidated profit or loss and equity. An entity might disclose a sensitivity analysis for interest rate risk for each currency in which the entity has material exposures to interest rate risk. [IFRS 7:IG34]

The sensitivity of profit or loss and the sensitivity of other comprehensive income should be disclosed separately (for example, investments in equity instruments whose changes in fair value are presented in other comprehensive income). [IFRS 7:B27]

The sensitivity analysis is prepared based on financial instruments that are recognised at the end of the reporting period. This is the case even when those exposures did not exist for the entire period or when the exposure changed materially during the period.

For example, an entity is building a road. To finance the construction of the road, it negotiates a floating rate debt facility. The entity starts to draw down on the facility half-way through the year and, by year end, it has fully drawn down the facility. A sensitivity analysis will be prepared for the loan showing profit or loss sensitivity assuming that the loan was in place for the entire period. A similar situation would arise in the case of an amortising loan where the exposure has reduced over the period due to part repayment of the principal. In that instance, the sensitivity analysis would be prepared on the basis of the exposure at the end of the reporting period, notwithstanding the significantly higher exposures during the period.

IFRS 7:35 does state that if the quantitative data disclosed as at the end of the reporting period is unrepresentative of an entity's exposure to risk during the period, the entity should provide further information that is representative. For sensitivity analysis, an entity may provide supplementary disclosures illustrating the impact on profit or loss and equity based on the timing of recognition and derecognition of financial instruments in the period, in addition to the analysis based on financial instruments recognised at the period end.

While IFRS 7 provides some guidance on the determination of reasonably possible changes in the relevant risk variable, no guidance is available on whether the degree of change at the end of the reporting period in the relevant risk variable should be extrapolated to the risk variables during the period, or whether the change should be determined as a fixed amount of change.

For example, an entity has a floating rate liability at the reporting date. The current LIBOR rate is 5 per cent, and the entity estimates that a reasonably possible change in LIBOR is 100bp. During the year, LIBOR was 2 per cent in the first half of the year, 3 per cent at half-year and 4 per cent during the second 6 months. The volatility in cash flows during the year may either be expressed as:

(a) an *absolute change* of 100bp's to all rates. Thus, the sensitivity would be of 100bp increase and decrease to the loan's cash flows during the year; or

(b) a *percentage change*, where the change at the end of the reporting period is 20 per cent (1/5) and, hence, all rates should change by 20 per cent during the period. Thus, the volatility in cash flows will be determined as the change of the above interest rate of 1.6 and 2.4 per cent, 2.4 and 3.6 per cent and 3.2 and 4.8 per cent (all increased and decreased by 20 per cent).

While either approach would be acceptable under IFRS 7, approach (a) provides information that seems more relevant and reliable than approach (b), because the sensitivity analysis will be more comparable with past periods. Whichever approach is used, the methods and assumptions used should be disclosed.

IFRS 7 requires disclosure of a sensitivity analysis showing how profit or loss and equity would have been affected by changes in the relevant risk variable. The Standard is not clear whether sensitivity analysis should be provided on a pre- or post-tax basis. Because equity is defined in IAS 32 as the residual interest in the assets of the entity after deducting all of its liabilities, and tax on gains or losses recognised in other comprehensive income (and accumulated in equity) will also be recognised in other comprehensive income (and accumulated in equity), it is reasonable to assume that for the purposes of the sensitivity analysis the analysis should be net of tax. Additionally, IFRS 7:IG36 provides an example of a sensitivity analysis that is determined on an after-tax basis.

Example 5.2.3A

Market risk disclosures: sensitivity analysis

Company D (ZAR functional currency) is a diversified oil and gas group. The earnings of the group are exposed to movements due to changes in market interest rates, equity prices, exchange rates and commodity prices. The entity expects the following to be reasonably possible changes in the relevant risk variable at the end of the reporting period.

ZAR market interest rates =	**100 basis points**
ZAR equity prices =	8%
ZAR/USD exchange rate =	15%
USD Brent crude price =	25%

Assume a tax rate of 30%. Profit after tax for the year ended 31 December 20X0 was ZAR 2,750 million and equity was ZAR 1,000 million. Company D has the following financial instruments that have an exposure to the relevant risk variable at the end of the reporting period.

1. USD denominated short term accounts receivable with a carrying amount of ZAR 235 million are measured at amortised cost.
2. ZAR denominated listed equity investments that are classified as at FVTPL with a carrying amount of ZAR 500 million.
3. ZAR denominated listed equity investments that are designated as at FVTOCI with a carrying amount of ZAR 200 million.
4. ZAR denominated fixed rate cash deposits with a carrying amount ZAR 1,245 million. The cash deposits are measured at amortised cost and return a rate of 10 per cent per annum. The deposits were initially recognised at the beginning of the year.
5. ZAR denominated treasury bonds that have a fixed rate of interest of 12 per cent per annum with a carrying amount of ZAR 765 million. The bonds are designated as at FVTPL. A 100 basis point change in market interest rates is equivalent to a 4 per cent change in the fair value of the bond.
6. Purchased Brent crude futures denominated in USD that are classified as at FVTPL and have a carrying amount of ZAR 490 million. A 100 basis point change in the ZAR market interest rate is equivalent to a 1 per cent change in the fair value of the futures and a 25 per cent change in the Brent crude oil price is equivalent to a 20 per cent change in the fair value of the futures.
7. USD denominated fixed rate borrowings initially recognised at the beginning of the year. The interest rate is 10 per cent. The borrowings have been classified as a liability to be carried at amortised cost. The weighted average exchange rate during the reporting period was ZAR7:$1.These borrowings were designated as a hedge of a net investment of its foreign operation and had a carrying amount at year end of ZAR 730 million (USD100 million at a closing exchange rate of ZAR7.3:$1)
8. ZAR denominated floating rate borrowings of ZAR 350 million that are classified as a financial liability held at amortised cost and were entered into at the beginning of the year for an amount of ZAR 350 million. The floating interest resets on a quarterly basis in advance, with the quarterly rates during the past reporting period being as follows.

Month	Rate
1 January 20X0	14%
1 April 20X0	13%
1 July 20X0	12%
1 October 20X0	13%
1 January 20X1	14%

Company D wishes to present its sensitivity analysis by risk variable. Comparative financial data has been ignored for the purposes of this example.

The following represents the calculation of the market risk sensitivity analysis as required by IFRS 7:40.

Market interest rates

Items (1), (2), (3) and (4) do not affect profit or loss or equity, if market interest rates change. In the case of item (4), the ZAR denominated fixed rate cash deposits that are measured at amortised cost do not affect profit or loss or equity given a reasonably possible change in market interest rates since they are neither measured at fair value nor do they contain variable cash flows.

Item (5), the ZAR denominated fixed rate bonds that are designated at fair value through profit or loss will result in sensitivity in profit or loss of ZAR765 million x 4% = **+/-ZAR 30.60 million**.

Item (6), the Brent crude futures will result in sensitivity in profit or loss of +/-ZAR 490 million x 1% = **+/-ZAR 4.90 million**.

Item (7), the USD denominated fixed rate liability is designated as a hedging instrument for foreign currency risk only, with the carrying amount in foreign currency measured at amortised cost. This liability does not affect profit or loss or equity if market interest rates change since it is neither measured at fair value nor does it contain variable cash flows.

Item (8), the ZAR denominated floating rate borrowings are subject to floating interest rates. If market rates changed by 100 basis points during the period the sensitivity in interest cash flows would be 1.0% x ZAR 350million = **+/-ZAR 3.50 million**

The treasury bond assets and the issued floating rate borrowings have the same directional sensitivity to interest rates with respect to their impact on profit or loss. As interest rates rise, the treasury bond assets fall in value, resulting in a loss in profit or loss, and the floating rate borrowing results in a higher interest expense in profit or loss. The reverse is equally true when interest rates fall. Total profit or loss sensitivity as a result of changes in ZAR market interest rates is **+/-ZAR 27.30 million** after tax (30.60+4.90+3.50) x (1-30%).

ZAR Equity prices

Items (1), (4) – (8) do not affect profit or loss or equity if ZAR equity prices change.

Item (2), the ZAR listed investments that have been classified as held for trading will result in profit or loss sensitivity of ZAR 500 million x 8% = +/-ZAR 40.00 million.

Item (3), the ZAR listed investments that have been designated as at FVTOCI will result in equity sensitivity of ZAR 200 million x 8% = +/-ZAR 16.00 million.

Total profit or loss sensitivity as a result of changes in ZAR equity prices is **+/-ZAR 28.00 million** after tax 40.00 x (1-30%).

Total equity sensitivity as a result of changes in ZAR equity prices is **+/-ZAR 11.20 million** after tax 16.00 x (1-30%).

ZAR/USD exchange rate

Items (2), (3), (4), (5) and (8) do not affect profit or loss or equity if ZAR/USD exchange rates change.

Item (1), the USD denominated accounts receivable will result in profit or loss sensitivity of ZAR 235 million x 15% = +/-ZAR 35.25 million.

Item (6), the USD denominated Brent crude derivatives will result in profit or loss sensitivity of ZAR 490 million x 15% = +/-ZAR 73.50 million.

Item (7), the USD denominated borrowings will result in equity sensitivity of ZAR 730 million x 15% = +/-ZAR 109.50 million, being the retranslation of the borrowings at the end of the reporting period. Sensitivity of profit or loss due to recording interest cash flows during the year at a different exchange rate is determined as USD 100million x 10% interest rate x weighted average exchange rate during the year of ZAR7:$1 x sensitivity of 15% = ZAR 10.50 million

Total profit or loss sensitivity as a result of changes in the ZAR/USD exchange rate is **+/-ZAR 68.78 million** after tax (35.25+73.5-10.5) x (1-30%).

Total equity sensitivity as a result of changes in the ZAR/USD exchange rate is **+/-ZAR 76.65 million** after tax (109.5) x (1-30%).

USD Brent crude price

Items (1) – (5), (7) and (8) do not affect profit or loss or equity if USD Brent crude prices change.

Item (6), the USD denominated Brent crude futures will result in profit or loss sensitivity of ZAR 490million x 20% = +/- ZAR 98.00 million.

Total profit or loss sensitivity as a result of changes in the Brent crude price is +/-ZAR 68.60 million after tax 98.00 x (1-30%).

Disclosure

For financial instruments held, the entity has used a sensitivity analysis technique that measures the change in the fair value and cash flows of the entity's financial instruments for hypothetical changes in all relevant market risk variables.

The amounts generated from the sensitivity analysis are forward-looking estimates of market risk assuming certain market conditions. Actual results in the future may differ materially from those projected results due to the inherent uncertainty of global financial markets. The methods and assumptions used are the same as those applied in the previous reporting period.

The sensitivity of profit or loss and equity due to changes in the relevant risk variables as at 31 December 20X0 are set out in the table below. The methods and assumptions used in calculating are set out in note X1 to the financial statements.

The estimated change in fair values and cash flows for changes in market interest rates are based on an instantaneous increase or decrease of 100 basis points at the end of the reporting period, with all other variables remaining constant.

The estimated change in fair values for changes in ZAR equity prices are based on an instantaneous increase or decrease of 8 per cent for instruments at the end of the reporting period, with all other variables remaining constant.

The estimated change in fair values for changes in the ZAR/USD exchange rate are based on an instantaneous increase or decrease of 15 per cent for instruments at the end of the reporting period, with all other variables remaining constant.

The estimated change in fair values for changes in Brent crude prices are based on an instantaneous increase or decrease of 25 per cent for instruments at the end of the reporting period, with all other variables remaining constant.

The above-mentioned changes in the risk variables may result in non-proportional changes in fair values or cash flows due to the specific terms and nature of the relevant risk exposures.

The sensitivity analysis is for illustrative purposes only – in practice market rates rarely change in isolation and are likely to be interdependent.

The sensitivity of the relevant risk variables, on an after tax basis is as follows.

Market risk exposure	**Profit or loss sensitivity ZAR million**	**Equity sensitivity ZAR million**
Market interest rates	+/–27.30	–
ZAR equity prices	+/–28.00	+/–11.20
ZAR/USD exchange rates	+/–68.78	+/–76.65
USD Brent crude	+/–68.60	–

Example 5.2.3A includes only non-optional derivatives (in this case, Brent crude oil futures). Other non-optional derivatives include swaps and forward contracts. If non-optional derivatives do not contain options embedded within their contractual terms (such as knock-out or knock-in options, early termination clauses that terminate at an amount other than at fair value), the sensitivity to the underlying is likely to be the same irrespective of whether the price of the underlying moves up or down. This would not be the case for optional derivatives like options, or derivatives that are constructed using combinations of options (e.g. collars). Because an option addresses one-directional exposure (e.g. protection against rising interest rates), the fair value sensitivity of the option to increasing interest rates will be different from the sensitivity to falling interest rates. The fair value sensitivity of optional derivatives will vary depending on the directional movement in the underlying market risk. The fair value sensitivity of an option to the underlying market risk will also depend on the price of the underlying at the

end of the reporting period compared to the strike price of the option. If an option is nearly at the money, it will have a greater sensitivity to changes in market risk when compared to an option that is deeply out of the money.

(vi) Provide additional disclosures

When the sensitivity analysis is unrepresentative of a risk inherent in a financial instrument, that fact is required to be disclosed together with the reason why the entity believes the sensitivity analysis is unrepresentative. [IFRS 7:42] Examples of circumstances where this may occur include the following.

[IFRS 7:IG37 – IG 39]

(a) Financial instruments contain terms and conditions whose effects are not apparent from the sensitivity analysis (e.g. options that are deeply out of (or in) the money for the chosen change in risk variable). In this situation, additional disclosures might include the terms and conditions of the financial instruments, the effect on profit or loss if the option were exercised

(b) Financial assets are illiquid so that the calculated changes in profit or loss are difficult to realise when there are low volumes of transactions or lack of counterparties to trade at those prices or rates. In this situation, additional disclosures might include the reasons for the reasons for the lack of liquidity and how the entity hedges the risk.

(c) An entity has a large holding of a financial asset that would be sold at a discount or premium to the quoted market price. In this situation, additional disclosures might include the nature of the security (e.g. the entity name), the extent of holding, the effect on profit or loss and how the entity hedges the risk.

IFRS 7:IG38(b) states that when financial instruments contain terms and conditions whose effects are not apparent from the sensitivity analysis, an entity may wish to state the effect on profit or loss if the term or condition were met. An entity may also wish to state the impact on equity because this is consistent with the objective of sensitivity analysis of providing users of financial statements with the impact on profit or loss and equity. For example, an entity may have designated a purchased interest cap as a cash flow hedge of highly probable forecast floating interest payments where the option is so deeply out of the money at the period end that no intrinsic value is recognised in other comprehensive income. Because the option is so deeply out of the money, a moderate change in interest rates has little fair value sensitivity. If interest rates were to increase significantly, movements in the option's fair value would be reflected in profit or loss, and potentially would result in part of the fair value being recognised in other comprehensive income (and accumulated in equity) if interest rates are higher than the strike price of the cap. Because the derivative is an effective hedging instrument in a cash flow hedge, illustrating the impact on equity is equally appropriate to illustrating the impact in profit or loss.

The sensitivity analysis may not give a true presentation of exposure to risk in cases where the hedging instrument is in the scope of IFRS 7 but the hedged item is not. An example is a hedge of a net investment in a foreign operation. Changes in the sensitivity of the fair value of derivatives or foreign currency risk for non-derivative financial instruments will be reported in other comprehensive income if it is a qualifying hedging instrument in a net investment hedge. The changes in the hedged item, being the retranslation of the net assets in accordance with IAS 21 *The Effects of Changes in Foreign Exchange Rates*, is not required to be reported in the sensitivity analysis because it is not a financial instrument within the scope of IFRS 7. An entity may choose to provide additional disclosure to explain that the retranslation of the net assets of the foreign operation would reduce the sensitivity of the hedging instrument in equity. For example, if the entity designates spot foreign currency risk as being hedged and the hedge is fully effective, the gains and losses on the hedging instrument recognised in other comprehensive income (and accumulated in equity) will be offset by the losses and gains on foreign currency translation on the net assets of the foreign operation, which are also recognised in other comprehensive income (and accumulated in equity). Similarly, additional disclosure may be appropriate for cash flow hedges or fair value hedges of non-financial items (including unrecognised off balance sheet' items). An entity may designate a foreign exchange forward contract in a highly effective hedge of a firm commitment to acquire plant and equipment, with the hedged risk being spot foreign currency risk. The forward contract will be included in the sensitivity analysis, while the fair value adjustment to the firm commitment to acquire a non-financial item will be outside the scope of IFRS 7. Additional disclosures may be useful to explain that the retranslation of the firm commitment at spot rates reduces the sensitivity of the hedging instrument in profit or loss.

Example 5.2.3B

Interest rate risk

[IFRS 7:IG36]

At 31 December 20X2, if interest rates at that date had been 10 basis points lower with all other variables held constant, post-tax profit for the year would have been CU1.7 million (20X1 - CU2.4 million) higher, arising mainly as a result of lower interest expense on variable borrowings. If interest rates had been 10 basis points higher, with all other variables held constant, post-tax profit would have been CU1.5 million (20X1 – CU2.1 million) lower, arising mainly as a result of higher interest expense on variable borrowings. Profit is more sensitive to interest rate decreases than increases because of borrowings with capped interest rates. The sensitivity is lower in 20X2 than in 20X1 because of a reduction in outstanding borrowings that has occurred as the entity's debt has matured (see note X).

Foreign currency exchange rate risk

At 31 December 20X2, if the CU had weakened 10 per cent against the US dollar with all other variables held constant, post-tax profit for the year would have been CU2.8 million (20X1 - CU6.4 million) lower, and other comprehensive income would have been CU1.2 million (20X1 – CU1.1 million) higher. Conversely, if the CU had strengthened 10 per cent against the US dollar with all other variables held constant, post-tax profit would have been CU2.8 million (20X1 – CU6.4 million) higher, and other comprehensive income would have been CU1.2 million (20X1 – CU1.1 million) lower. The lower foreign currency exchange rate sensitivity in profit in 20X2 compared with 20X1 is attributable to a reduction in foreign currency denominated debt. Equity is more sensitive in 20X2 than in 20X1 because of the increased use of hedges of foreign currency purchases, offset by the reduction in foreign currency debt.

As an alternative to sensitivity analysis, disclosure may be provided of a value-at-risk (VaR) analysis that reflects interdependencies between risk variables. An entity may only disclose value-at-risk analysis when the entity uses such a model to manage risk internally. Disclosures should include an explanation of the method used in preparing such an analysis, how the model works (such as whether the model is based on a delta-normal variance-covariance approach, historical simulation or Monte Carlo simulation), the main parameters and assumptions underlying the data provided such as the holding period, confidence interval, historical observation period and weightings assigned to the observations, how options are dealt with and which volatilities and correlations are used. The objective of the method used and the limitations that may result in the information not fully reflecting the fair value of the assets and liabilities involved should also be disclosed. [IFRS 7:41 & B20]

The value-at-risk analysis used internally may measure the potential for loss or gain including the effects of items that are outside the scope of IFRS 7 (e.g. contracts to buy or sell non-financial items outside the scope of IFRS 9, hedged items that are outside the scope of IFRS 7 or risks such as credit risk that are not market risks). In contrast to conventional sensitivity analysis as described above, a value-at-risk analysis including such items would, if used as a model to manage risk internally, satisfy the requirements of the Standard. If such items are included, this fact should be clearly disclosed as part of the method used in preparing the analysis.

Example 5.2.3C

Market risk disclosures: value at risk

The Group manages the market risk in its trading and treasury portfolios through the use of value-at-risk (VaR) limits as well as stress testing, position and sensitivity limits. VaR is a technique that produces estimates of the potential negative change in the market value of a portfolio over a specified time horizon at a given confidence level. The table below sets out the trading and treasury VaR for the Group, which assumes a 95 per cent confidence level and a one-day time horizon. The VAR model uses largely historical data from the preceding three years to simulate scenarios of the future.

Year	Period end	Minimum	Maximum	Average
	CUm	CUm	CUm	CUm
Trading VaR				
20X1	17.2	13.4	24.3	19.1
20X0	16.2	14.0	22.3	18.1
Treasury VaR				
20X1	8.1	6.6	12.1	9.5
20X0	8.0	6.9	13.1	8.5

The Group's VaR should be interpreted in light of the limitations of the methodologies used. These limitations include the following.

- Historical data may not provide the best estimate of the joint distribution of risk factor changes in the future and may fail to capture the risk of possible extreme adverse market movements which have not occurred in the historical window used in the calculations.
- VaR using a one-day time horizon does not fully capture the market risk of positions that cannot be liquidated or hedged within one day.
- The Group largely computes the VaR of the trading portfolios at the close of business and positions may change substantially during the course of the trading day. Controls are in place to limit the Group's intra-day exposure such as the calculation of VaR for selected portfolios.
- VaR using a 95 per cent confidence level does not reflect the extent of potential losses beyond that percentile.

These limitations and the nature of the VaR measure mean that the Group can neither guarantee that losses will not exceed the VaR amounts indicated nor that losses in excess of the VaR amounts will not occur more frequently than once in 20 business days.

6 Offsetting financial assets and financial liabilities

6.1 General principle

IAS 32 requires that a financial asset and a financial liability should be offset as a net amount in the statement of financial position when, and only when, both of the following conditions are satisfied:

- the entity currently has a legally enforceable right to set off the recognised amounts of the asset and liability; and
- the entity intends to settle on a net basis, or to realise the asset and settle the liability simultaneously.

In the case of a transfer of a financial asset that does not qualify for derecognition under IFRS 9, the entity should not offset the transferred asset and the associated liability (for further details on derecognition refer to **3.3** in **chapter B8**). [IAS 32:42]

When offset is applied, the entity has the right to pay or receive a single net amount in relation to the two instruments, and intends to do so; therefore, in effect, the entity only has a single financial asset or financial liability. If the conditions for offset are not met, the two financial instruments are presented separately. Whether or not a financial asset and a financial liability are offset, they should be measured in accordance with the normal measurement principles with respect to financial assets and financial liabilities.

It should be noted that offsetting a financial asset and a financial liability (and the consequent net presentation in the statement of financial position) is different from derecognition of those financial instruments. In contrast to offsetting, derecognition of a financial asset or a financial liability not only removes the financial instrument from the statement of financial position, but also may give rise to a gain or loss on derecognition. [IAS 32:44] Offset does not result in the asset or liability being removed from the statement of financial position, but in net presentation of the asset and liability as either a net asset or a net liability. A gain or loss does not arise because of the offsetting requirements, although it may arise because of the measurement requirements applicable to the asset or liability, respectively.

In December 2011 the IASB issued amendments to IAS 32 *Offsetting Financial Assets and Financial Liabilities*. Concurrently the IASB introduced new offsetting disclosures by amending IFRS 7. The amendments to IAS 32 introduce further application guidance which was intended to address inconsistencies in applying some of the offsetting criteria. This included clarifying the meaning of 'currently has a legally enforceable right of set-off' and that some gross settlement systems may be considered equivalent to net settlement. [IAS 32:BC78] These amendments are reflected in the sections below. The amendments are effective for annual periods beginning on or after 1 January 2013.

In September 2014 the IASB issued *Annual Improvements to IFRSs 2012-2014 Cycle*, which amended IFRS 7:44R to clarify that the additional disclosure required by the amendments to IFRS 7 *Disclosure – Offsetting Financial Assets and Financial Liabilities* is not specifically required in condensed interim financial statements that are prepared in accordance with IAS 34 *Interim Financial Reporting*. However, the additional disclosure is given when its inclusion would be required in accordance with the general principles in IAS 34. The amendment applies retrospectively for annual periods beginning on or after 1 January 2016. Earlier application is permitted in which case an entity shall disclose that it has applied those amendments for an earlier period.

The amendments to IAS 32 are effective for annual periods beginning on or after 1 January 2014 and must be retrospectively applied. An entity that early applies the IAS 32 amendments must state this fact and also early apply the IFRS 7 amendments at the same time. [IAS 32:97L]

6.2 Legal right of offset

The first part of the offset criteria is that the reporting entity 'currently has a legally enforceable right to set off the recognised amounts' [IAS 32:42]

IAS 32 defines the right of offset as a debtor's legal right, by contract or otherwise, to settle or otherwise eliminate all or a portion of an amount due to a creditor by applying against that amount an amount due from the creditor. Because the right is specifically a legal right, the circumstances that give rise to such a right will vary from one legal jurisdiction to another. Thus, for each relationship between the two parties (the debtor and the creditor), it will be necessary to consider the particular laws applicable to it. [IAS 32:45]

The amendments to IAS 32 acknowledge that a right of set-off may be currently available or it may be contingent on a future event (for example, the right may be triggered or exercisable only on the occurrence of some future event, such as the default, insolvency or bankruptcy of one of the counterparties). Even if the right of set-off is not contingent on a future event, it may only be legally enforceable in the normal course of business, or in the event of default, or in the event of insolvency or bankruptcy, of one or all of the counterparties. [IAS 32:AG38A]

The Standard makes clear the characteristics that a currently legally enforceable right to set-off the recognised amounts should have. The right of set-off:

[IAS 32:AG38B]

(a) must not be contingent on a future event; and

(b) must be legally enforceable in all of the following circumstances:

(i) the normal course of business;
(ii) the event of default; and
(iii) the event of insolvency or bankruptcy

of the entity and all of the counterparties.

The nature and extent of the right of set-off, including any conditions attached to its exercise and whether it would remain in the event of default or insolvency or bankruptcy, may vary from one legal jurisdiction to another. Consequently, it cannot be assumed that the right of set-off is automatically available outside of the normal course of business. For example, the bankruptcy or insolvency laws of a jurisdiction may prohibit, or restrict, the right of set-off in the event of bankruptcy or insolvency in some circumstances. [IAS 32:AG38C] The reference to default, insolvency or bankruptcy are broad and are intended to describe scenarios where an entity will not or cannot perform under the contract. [IAS 32:BC81]

The laws applicable to the relationships between the parties (for example, contractual provisions, the laws governing the contract, or the default, insolvency or bankruptcy laws applicable to the parties) need to be considered to ascertain whether the right of set-off is enforceable in the normal course of business, in an event of default, and in the event of insolvency or bankruptcy, of the entity and all of the counterparties (as specified in IAS 32:AG38B(b)). [IAS 32:AG38D]

The amendments to IAS 32 in this area arose following feedback on the exposure draft that revealed inconsistencies in the application of this criterion. In amending IAS 32 the IASB made clear that where set-off only arises if a contingent event occurs it is not acceptable to offset financial assets and financial liabilities. Even where the right to set-off is not dependent on a contingent event the right to set-off must apply in all circumstances, i.e. not just in the normal course of business but also in bankruptcy, default or insolvency. This means that the right must apply in cases where the reporting entity (or counterparty) ceases to operate as a going concern.

Uncertainties about the amount to be paid (and/or received) under the set-off arrangement do not preclude an entity from currently having a legally enforceable right to set-off. Similarly, the passage of time is not considered a contingent right that would prevent offsetting. [IAS 32:BC83]

For example, if a receivable and payable are contractually due on the same date and there is an enforceable right to set-off on that date, the fact there is no right to enforce net settlement (and potentially simultaneous settlement) prior to that date does not prevent offset as prior to that the receivable and payable are not due. However, in order for the offset criteria to be met the reporting entity must be able to demonstrate that there is a currently enforceable right to set-off the recognised amounts on the settlement date which would apply in all circumstances, i.e. in the normal course of business or in the case of default, insolvency or bankruptcy of either party.

If the right of set-off is not exercisable during a period when amounts are due and payable, then the entity does not meet the offsetting criterion as it has no right to set off those payments. [IAS 32:BC84] For example, a right to set-off the recognised amount that only applies say at the reporting period end, but not throughout the reporting period(s) would not meet the offset criterion.

Similarly, a right of set-off that could disappear or that would no longer be enforceable after a future event that could take place in the normal course of business or in the event of default, or in the event of insolvency or bankruptcy, such as a ratings downgrade, would not meet the currently legally enforceable criterion in IAS 32:42(a). [IAS 32:BC84]

In some circumstances, the debtor may have a legal right to apply an amount due from a third party against the amount due to a creditor provided that there is an agreement between the three parties that clearly establishes the debtor's right to offset. [IAS 32:45]

Legal rights do not need to be established in a single document between the three parties. For example, a debtor might obtain set-off rights separately from the third party and from the creditor. In establishing the validity of the legal right to set-off, it is necessary to understand the terms of the particular contracts, as well as the context within which set-off is to be applied. The legal right to set-off could, inter alia, be evidenced with reference to a legal opinion, or be established by statutory or regulatory provisions which have been clearly demonstrated as applicable to and governing the particular transaction.

Assessing whether the entity has a legal right to set off the recognised amounts is independent from assessing how the reporting entity intends to settle the arrangement. The requirement to have a currently legally enforceable right to set off the recognised amounts in effect means that the reporting entity can enforce settlement of the net amount and can do so in all situations (i.e. the exercise of this right is not contingent on a future event). The Board clarified in the Basis for Conclusions that the ability to exercise this right 'is assured' [IAS 32:BC86]. This right must exist and be assured irrespective if the entity does not intend to settle the net amount, but instead (as permitted by IAS 32) intends to settle the asset and liability simultaneously (see **6.3**).

For a discussion of considerations surrounding master netting agreements refer to **6.6**.

6.3 Intention to settle on a net basis, or to realise the asset and settle the liability simultaneously

The second part of the offset criteria is that the reporting entity 'intends to settle on a net basis, or to realise the asset and settle the liability simultaneously'. [IAS 32:42]

The existence of the legal right of offset (while it affects the entity's rights and obligations and may affect its credit exposure) is not sufficient in itself for offsetting. When there is a legal right, and an entity intends to exercise the right of offset (i.e. to settle net), or to settle simultaneously, the entity is, in effect, exposed to a net amount, which reflects the timing of the expected cash flows and the risks to which those cash flows are exposed and, therefore, presentation of the financial instruments on a net basis is appropriate. [IAS 32:46]

The intention by one or both parties to settle on a net basis without the legal right to do so is not sufficient to justify offsetting a financial asset and a financial liability. This is due to the fact that the legal rights and obligations pertaining to the individual financial assets and financial liabilities are not altered. [IAS 32:45]

Intention may be demonstrated through management representations that are not contradicted by past experience or other relevant circumstances (e.g. normal business practices, requirements of financial markets, circumstances that limit the ability to settle net) and also may take into account reference to the entity's risk management policies, if appropriate. There is no requirement for an assessment of the counterparty's intent, however, if the counterparty was able to restrict the reporting entity's right to enforce the set-off of the recognised amounts this prevents the reporting entity from meeting the offset criteria.

Example 6.3

Offset: unmatched payments and receipts

Assume that the legal right of offset exists in the following scenario.

Company X owes Company Y four payments of CU10 million each at the end of each calendar quarter (31 March, 30 June, 30 September, 31 December), totalling CU40 million. As part of another contract, Company Y owes Company X two payments of CU15 million at 30 June and 31 December, totalling CU30 million.

The intention to settle simultaneously can only be demonstrated in respect of the 30 June and 31 December cash flows. At the beginning of the year, Company X will, therefore, reflect a financial liability of CU20 million (being the 31 March and 30 September payments) and a separate financial asset of CU10 million (representing the difference between the CU10 million payable and CU15 million receivable from Company Y on 30 June and 31 December). Although Company

X's net position over the whole year is a financial liability of CU10 million, because it cannot demonstrate the intention to settle net or simultaneously for all payments, the criteria for offset are not satisfied in respect of those unmatched payments and separate presentation is required. Company Y correspondingly has an asset of CU20 million and a liability of CU10 million.

It is common for entities to have amounts on deposit with a financial institution and simultaneously have a drawn-down borrowing facility, sometimes referred to as an 'overdraft', with the same financial institution. The entity has a separate financial asset and a financial liability with the same counterparty. It is usually not possible to achieve offset for the asset and the liability because, in most cases, the entity cannot assert that the asset will be used to settle the liability. The asset will rise and fall as the entity places further cash on deposit or withdraws cash to settle other obligations. Although the asset at the reporting date could be used to settle the overdraft, the entity cannot claim offset because the entity does not have the intention at the reporting date to settle the overdraft liability with the deposit asset. Rather, the entity's intention is to use the deposit asset at the reporting date, and potentially draw down more borrowings if needed to meet its working capital needs.

The amendments to IAS 32 clarified when simultaneous settlement of gross amounts can meet the second part of the offset criterion in IAS 32:42. This will be the case where the gross settlement mechanism has features that eliminate or result in insignificant credit and liquidity risk, and that will process receivables and payables in a single settlement process or cycle. For example, a gross settlement system that has all of the following characteristics would meet the net settlement criterion in IAS 32:42(b):

(a) financial assets and financial liabilities eligible for set-off are submitted at the same point in time for processing;

(b) once the financial assets and financial liabilities are submitted for processing, the parties are committed to fulfil the settlement obligation;

(c) there is no potential for the cash flows arising from the assets and liabilities to change once they have been submitted for processing (unless the processing fails – see (d) below);

(d) assets and liabilities that are collateralised with securities will be settled on a securities transfer or similar system (for example, delivery versus payment), so that if the transfer of securities fails, the processing of the related receivable or payable for which the securities are collateral will also fail (and vice versa);

(e) any transactions that fail, as outlined in (d), will be re-entered for processing until they are settled;

(f) settlement is carried out through the same settlement institution (for example, a settlement bank, a central bank or a central securities depository); and

(g) an intraday credit facility is in place that will provide sufficient overdraft amounts to enable the processing of payments at the settlement date for each of the parties, and it is virtually certain that the intraday credit facility will be honoured if called upon.

[IAS 32:AG38F]

The Basis for Conclusions recognises that simultaneous settlement is included as a practical exception to net settlement as there may be cases when an entity currently has a legally enforceable right and desire to settle net, but may not have the operational capabilities to effect net settlement. The gross positions would be settled at the same moment such that the outcome would not be distinguishable from net settlement. [IAS 32:BC95] The requirements introduced in IAS 32:AG38F were included to clarify that certain gross settlement mechanism with features that both (i) eliminate credit and liquidity risk; and (ii) process receivables and payables in a single settlement process may meet the simultaneous settlement criteria in IAS 32:42(b). [IAS 32:BC99].

The Board was conscious not to mandate that arrangements with all clearing houses or other similar organisations would meet the simultaneous settlement criteria as arrangements will vary with different organisations. Therefore care should be taken in analysing the contractual arrangements with clearing houses and other similar organisations against the strict criteria in IAS 32:AG38F.

6.4 Unit of account to which offsetting applies

IAS 32 does not provide specific guidance whether the offset requirements are to be applied to the unit of account as included in the statement of financial position (i.e. the entire financial instrument) or whether it is applied to individual identifiable contractual cash flows that make up the financial instrument.

The IASB considered this issue when developing the amendments to IAS 32 but decided to provide no further guidance. The IASB acknowledges that some industries, e.g. energy producers and traders, apply the offsetting criteria to individual identifiable cash flows whereas others do not. The Board noted that some entities such as financial institutions would find it impractical and burdensome to apply offsetting to individual identifiable cash flows. [IAS 32:BC106]

The Board acknowledged that the focus of the offsetting model is the entity's net exposure and expected future cash flows from settling the related financial instruments. [IAS 32:BC107] The Board did consider clarifying the application guidance in IAS 32 to indicate that offsetting should apply to individual identifiable cash flows of financial instruments, however, it decided against such an approach because of the need to add an exemption from this requirement for some entities on the grounds of operational complexity. The Board concluded that applying either approach, being the entire financial instrument or individual identifiable cash flows of the financial instrument, does not result in inappropriate application of the offsetting criteria and therefore chose to not provide any further guidance. [IAS 32:BC110 & BC111]

In light of the IASB's view that it is appropriate to apply offsetting to either an entire financial instrument or individual identifiable cash flows, entities should apply one of these approaches as a consistently applied accounting policy.

There may be circumstances where the offset requirements are met only in relation to some of the cash flows of a contractually single financial asset and a contractually single financial liability. In such circumstances, the offset requirements are applied to the extent that the conditions are met. This is illustrated in the following example.

Example 6.4

Offset: partial offset of cash flows

Company A and Company B are independent entities. On 1 January 20X1, Company A borrows CU100 from Company B (Instrument 1). The terms of Instrument 1 require repayment after six years (at 31 December 20X6) of CU100 and annual interest of 6 per cent on the notional of CU100. One year later, on 1 January 20X2, Company A lends CU50 to Company B (Instrument 2) on terms that require repayment of CU50 after five years (at 31 December 20X6) and annual interest of 6 per cent on the notional of CU50.

The terms of the instruments give both parties the legally enforceable right to settle the principal amounts repayable on a net basis on maturity of the instruments (i.e. through Company A paying a net amount of CU50 to Company B on 31 December 20X6). Both parties intend to settle the principal amounts on this basis. In respect of the 6 per cent interest payments/receipts over the life of the two instruments there is no ability to settle on a net basis.

Company A measures both the financial liability (Instrument 1) and the financial asset (Instrument 2) at amortised cost, using the effective interest method.

Company A should offset the financial asset and financial liability to the extent that the financial asset and financial liability meet the conditions for offset. The offset conditions are met in respect of a proportion of the principal payments on the two instruments at 1 January 20X2 onwards. Therefore, offsetting is appropriate in respect of these amounts. However, offsetting is not appropriate in respect of the interest amounts.

Assume the amortised cost carrying amount of Instrument 1 (before considering offset) at 1 January 20X2 is CU100, which comprises an amount of CU75 being the present value of the principal payment and an amount of CU25 being the present value of the interest payments. Similarly, the amortised cost carrying amount of Instrument 2 (before considering offset) comprises an amount of CU37.50, representing the present value of the principal payment and an amount of CU12.50 representing the present value of the interest payments.

Applying offset to the proportion of principal payments but not to the interest components of the financial asset and financial liability will result in a liability of CU62.50 and asset of CU12.50 being shown in the statement of financial position of Company A. This balance is summarised below.

	CU	CU
Asset		
Present value of interest flows on Instrument 2		12.50
Liability		
Present value of interest flows on Instrument 1		25
Present value of principal flow on Instrument 1	75	
Less offset of principal flow on Instrument 2	(37.50)	
Net principal flow		37.50
		62.50

The offset that is achieved by Company A can equally apply to Company B; Company B will present a liability of CU12.50 to Company A, and a loan and receivable of CU62.50 from Company A.

6.5 Circumstances in which offsetting is usually not appropriate

Because the conditions outlined in **6.1** are not met, offsetting is specifically identified in IAS 32 as not being appropriate when:

[IAS 32:49]

(a) several different financial instruments are used to emulate the features of a single financial instrument (known as 'synthetic instrument');

Example 6.5

Offset: synthetic instrument accounting

Assume an entity issues long-term floating rate debt in the market and concurrently enters into an interest rate swap with the bank that involves receiving floating rate payments and making fixed rate payments with a maturity equal to that of the debt. The combination of the issued debt and the interest rate swap could be seen as synthetically amounting to fixed rate long-term debt.

Each of the two instruments (floating rate liability and receive floating rate pay fixed rate interest rate swap) represent contractually separate arrangements with their own terms and conditions and each may be transferred or settled separately. Moreover, each of the two instruments will be exposed to risks that differ from those to which the other instrument is exposed. The offset conditions are not met because there is no legal right of set-off and, while the cash flows under the two instruments may occur within a short space of time, they are not simultaneous. Therefore, the debt and the swap are not presented on a net basis in the entity's statement of financial position.

(b) financial assets and financial liabilities arise from financial instruments with the same primary risk exposure (e.g. assets and liabilities within a portfolio of forward contracts or other derivative instruments) but with different counterparties;

(c) financial or other assets are pledged as collateral for non-recourse financial liabilities;

(d) financial assets are set aside in trust by a debtor for the purpose of discharging an obligation without those assets having been accepted by the creditor in settlement of the obligation (e.g. a sinking fund arrangement); or

(e) obligations incurred as a result of events giving rise to losses are expected to be recovered from a third party by virtue of a claim made under an insurance policy.

6.6 Master netting agreements

An entity that undertakes a number of financial instrument transactions with a single counterparty may enter into a 'master netting agreement' covering all of its transactions with that counterparty. Such an agreement creates a legally enforceable right of offset that comes into effect and affects the realisation of individual financial assets and settlement of individual financial liabilities only on the occurrence of a specified event of default, or other events not expected to happen in the normal course of business. Such agreements are typically used by financial institutions to provide a degree of protection in the event of bankruptcy or other circumstances that render a counterparty unable to meet its obligations. Once the triggering event takes place, the contract will typically provide for a single net settlement of all financial instruments covered by the agreement.

The existence of a master netting agreement does not in itself provide a basis for offsetting assets and liabilities covered by the agreement: firstly, the master netting agreement creates only a conditional right to set off recognised amounts, which falls short of the IAS 32 requirement that the entity must have a *currently enforceable* legal right to set off recognised amounts; and secondly, the entity may not have the intention or ability to either settle on a net basis or realise the asset and settle the liability simultaneously. [IAS 32:50]

Example 6.6A

Offset: master netting agreement

Bank X, an investment bank, enters into several swap transactions with different reset dates to manage the interest rate risk arising from its corporate loans portfolio. Although these transactions are with a range of other banks as counterparties, Bank X's systems aggregate all exposures on a daily basis to enable them to recognise the net profit or loss due to the change in fair value of all open (i.e. unexpired) contracts. Certain contracts have a positive fair value while others are in a loss position. ISDA (International Swaps and Derivatives Association) Master Netting Agreements are in place with some, but not all, of these counterparties. Bank X does not net the settlements across swap positions with counterparties on reset dates.

Bank X does not meet the criteria for offsetting financial assets and liabilities related to its swap positions. It does not settle on a net basis and, due to the mismatch in reset dates across its swaps book, cannot demonstrate the simultaneous settlement of swap cash flows. Additionally, the ISDA Master Netting Agreements are not, in themselves, sufficient to provide Bank X with the legal right to set off its settlement cash flows across contracts except in the conditional event of default or termination by one of the parties.

Example 6.6B

Offset: options

Company X, a gold producer in South Africa, manages its exposure to changes in the gold price and locks in the cost of funding future capital expenditure by entering into option strategies with several investment banks. These strategies require Company X to both purchase call options and to write put options at various strike prices and with various maturity dates. The transactions are expected to be settled in cash and, therefore, are measured at FVTPL in IFRS 9.

The investment banks require Company X to enter into ISDA Master Netting agreements which give either party the legal right of offset on termination of the contract, or on default of the other party. These agreements do not provide for the offset of settlements in the ordinary course of business.

Company X may not offset the financial assets and financial liabilities arising from the premiums paid and received and subsequent measurement of these options to fair value. The master netting agreement establishes a legally enforceable right of offset only in the event of a contingent event (i.e. default or on termination by one of the parties) and not in respect of ongoing settlements. Additionally, by virtue of the different maturity dates, Company X does not demonstrate the intention to settle on a net basis or to realise the asset and settle the liability simultaneously. Therefore, the requirements in IAS 32 are not satisfied. Even in the case where the premiums are settled on the same date, the continuing exposure to credit risk on the party writing the option precludes set-off.

6.7 Offset disclosures

The amendments to the offsetting requirements in IAS 32 that were issued in December 2011 were accompanied with amendments to IFRS 7 that introduced specific offsetting disclosure requirements. Prior to these amendments IFRS 7 did not have any specific disclosure requirements for offsetting financial assets and financial liabilities. The aim of the disclosures is to enable users of an entity's financial statements to evaluate the effect or potential effect of netting arrangements, including rights of set-off associated with the entity's recognised financial assets and financial liabilities, on the entity's financial position. [IFRS 7:IN9]

An entity shall retrospectively apply the amendments to IFRS 7 for annual periods beginning on or after 1 January 2013 and interim periods within those annual periods. [IFRS 7:44R]

The transition guidance as stated in IFRS 7:44R does not address whether it permits early application. However, the transition guidance as stated in IAS 32:97L does require an entity to apply the IFRS 7 amendments if it early applies the amendments to IAS 32. Therefore, an entity that early applies the IAS 32 amendments must also early apply the IFRS 7 amendments at the same time. The standards do not address whether they permit an entity to apply the IFRS 7 amendments on their own, i.e., without also applying the IAS 32 amendments at the same time. However, in light of the IFRS 7 amendments not being in conflict with the pre-amended disclosure requirements in IFRS 7 it would be reasonable for an entity to provide such information as additional information without stating that it has early applied those amendments.

6.7.1 Scope

The scope of the offsetting disclosure requirements are designed to be broad. The disclosure requirements have been designed to capture not only financial assets and financial liabilities that are offset in the statement of financial position but also recognised financial instruments that are subject to an enforceable master netting arrangement or similar agreement where the financial assets and financial liabilities are not offset. [IFRS 7:13A] As the amendments to IFRS 7 arose out of a convergence project with the U.S. Financial Accounting Standards Board (FASB) one of the aims of broadening the scope of the disclosures was to ensure that users of IFRS and US GAAP financial statements would benefit from converged disclosures even though the requirements to achieve offsetting in the statement of financial position were not the same.

However, following stakeholder feedback, the FASB issued ASU No. 2013-01, *Clarifying the scope of disclosures about offsetting assets and liabilities*, which limits the scope of the offsetting disclosure requirements to derivatives (including bifurcated embedded derivatives), (reverse) sale and repurchase agreements, and securities borrowing and lending transactions. IFRS 7 was not subject to an equivalent amendment and therefore following the amendment by the FASB, IFRS 7 has a broader scope.

Typical enforceable master netting arrangements arise with derivative financial instruments where multiple derivatives with the same counterparty are subject to an agreement that dictates the netting of these multiple contracts in the case either party defaults on its obligations. The 'similar arrangements' referred to in IFRS 7:13A includes derivatives clearing arrangements, global master repurchase agreements, global master securities lending arrangements, and any related rights to financial collateral. [IFRS 7:B41]

The types of financial instruments and transactions that would typically be subject to the disclosures if subject to an enforceable master netting arrangement or similar arrangement would be derivatives, sale and repurchase agreements, reverse sale and repurchase agreements, securities borrowing, and securities lending agreements. Financial instruments that are not within the scope are loans and customer deposits at the same institution (unless they are set off in the statement of financial position), and financial instruments that are subject only to a collateral agreement. [IFRS 7:B41]

6.7.2 Offsetting disclosure requirements

An entity shall disclose information to enable users of its financial statements to evaluate the effect or potential effect of netting arrangements on the entity's financial position. This includes the effect or potential effect of rights of set-off associated with the entity's recognised financial assets and recognised financial liabilities that are within the scope as described above. [IFRS 7:13B] To meet this objective, an entity shall disclose, at the end of the reporting period, the following quantitative information separately for recognised financial assets and recognised financial liabilities:

[IFRS 7:13C]

(a) the gross amounts of those recognised financial assets and recognised financial liabilities;

(b) the amounts that are set off in accordance with the criteria in IAS 32:42 when determining the net amounts presented in the statement of financial position;

(c) the net amounts presented in the statement of financial position;

(d) the amounts subject to an enforceable master netting arrangement or similar agreement that are not otherwise included in paragraph (b) above, including:

(i) amounts related to recognised financial instruments that do not meet some or all of the offsetting criteria in IAS 32:42; and

(ii) amounts related to financial collateral (including cash collateral); and

(e) the net amount after deducting the amounts in (d) from the amounts in (c) above.

The information above shall be presented in a tabular format, separately for financial assets and financial liabilities, unless another format is more appropriate.

The total amount for an instrument that is disclosed in accordance with (d) above is limited to the amount in (c) above for that instrument. [IFRS 7:13D] For example, if the amount in (c) is a net financial asset, then deducting the amount in (d) will not result in the balance being disclosed as a net financial liability. Conversely, if the amount in (c) is a net financial liability, then deducting the amount in (d) will not result in the balance being disclosed as a net financial asset. By limiting the amount in (d) to be less or equal to the amount in (c) for financial instruments subject to an enforceable master netting arrangement or similar arrangement the amounts in (e) represent the net credit exposure after reflecting the impact of the netting arrangement as the amounts in (d) act as a credit risk mitigant for the amount in (c).

A description and the nature of the rights of set-off associated with the entity's recognised financial assets and recognised financial liabilities subject to enforceable master netting arrangements and similar agreements that are disclosed in accordance IFRS 7:13C(d) shall be disclosed [IFRS 7:13E]

If the information required by IFRS 7:13B-13E is disclosed in more than one note to the financial statements, an entity shall cross-refer between those notes. [IFRS 7:13F]

IFRS 7 includes some illustrative examples within its implementation guidance:

Example 6.7.2

Disclosures (paragraphs 13A-13F and B40-B53)

[IFRS 7:IG40D]

Background

An entity has entered into transactions subject to an enforceable master netting arrangement or similar agreement with the following counterparties. The entity has the following recognised financial assets and financial liabilities resulting from those transactions that meet the scope of the disclosure requirements in paragraph 13A.

Counterparty A:

The entity has a derivative asset (fair value of CU100 million) and a derivative liability (fair value of CU80 million) with Counterparty A that meet the offsetting criteria in paragraph 42 of IAS 32.

Consequently, the gross derivative liability is set off against the gross derivative asset, resulting in the presentation of a net derivative asset of CU20 million in the entity's statement of financial position.

Cash collateral has also been received from Counterparty A for a portion of the net derivative asset (CU10 million). The cash collateral of CU10 million does not meet the offsetting criteria in paragraph 42 of IAS 32, but it can be set off against the net amount of the derivative asset and derivative liability in the case of default and insolvency or bankruptcy, in accordance with an associated collateral arrangement.

Counterparty B:

The entity has a derivative asset (fair value of CU100 million) and a derivative liability (fair value of CU80 million) with Counterparty B that do not meet the offsetting criteria in paragraph 42 of IAS 32, but which the entity has the right to set off in the case of default and insolvency or bankruptcy. Consequently, the gross amount of the derivative asset (CU100 million) and the gross amount of the derivative liability (CU80 million) are presented separately in the entity's statement of financial position. Cash collateral has also been received from Counterparty B for the net amount of the derivative asset and derivative liability (CU20 million). The cash collateral of CU20 million does not meet the offsetting criteria in paragraph 42 of IAS 32, but it can be set off against the net amount of the derivative asset and derivative liability in the case of default and insolvency or bankruptcy, in accordance with an associated collateral arrangement.

Counterparty C:

The entity has entered into a sale and repurchase agreement with Counterparty C that is accounted for as a collateralised borrowing. The carrying amount of the financial assets (bonds) used as collateral and posted by the entity for the transaction is CU79 million and their fair value is CU85 million. The carrying amount of the collateralised borrowing (repo payable) is CU80 million.

The entity has also entered into a reverse sale and repurchase agreement with Counterparty C that is accounted for as a collateralised lending. The fair value of the financial assets (bonds) received as collateral (and not recognised in the entity's statement of financial position) is CU105 million. The carrying amount of the collateralised lending (reverse repo receivable) is CU90 million.

The transactions are subject to a global master repurchase agreement with a right of set-off only in default and insolvency or bankruptcy and therefore do not meet the offsetting criteria in paragraph 42 of IAS 32. Consequently, the related repo payable and repo receivable are presented separately in the entity's statement of financial position.

Illustrating the application of IFRS 7:13C(a) - (e) by type of financial instrument

Financial assets subject to offsetting, enforceable master netting arrangements and similar arrangements

CU million						
As at 31 December 20XX	**(a)**	**(b)**	**(c)=(a)–(b)**	**(d)**		**(e)=(c)–(d)**
				Related amounts not set off in the statement of financial position		
	Gross amounts of recognised financial assets	**Gross amounts of recognised financial liabilities set off in the statement of financial position**	**Net amounts of financial assets presented in the statement of financial position**	**(d)(i), (d)(ii) Financial instru-ments**	**(d)(ii) Cash collateral received**	**Net amount**
Description						
Derivatives	200	(80)	120	(80)	(30)	10
Reverse repurchase, securities borrowing and similar agreements	90	–	90	(90)	–	–
Other financial instruments	–	–	–	–	–	–
Total	290	(80)	210	(170)	(30)	10

Financial liabilities subject to offsetting, enforceable master netting arrangements and similar arrangements

CU million

As at 31 December 20XX	**(a)**	**(b)**	**(c)=(a)–(b)**	**(d)**		**(e)=(c)–(d)**
				Related amounts not set off in the statement of financial position		
	Gross amounts of recognised financial liabilities	**Gross amounts of recognised financial assets set off in the statement of financial position**	**Net amounts of financial liabilities presented in the statement of financial position**	**(d)(i), (d)(ii) Financial instru-ments**	**(d)(ii) Cash collateral pledged**	**Net amount**
Description						
Derivatives	160	(80)	80	(80)	–	–
Repurchase, securities lending and similar agreements	80	–	80	(80)	–	–
Other financial instruments	–	–	–	–	–	–
Total	240	(80)	160	(160)	–	–

Illustrating the application of IFRS 7:13C(a)-(c) by type of financial instrument and IFRS 7:13C(c)-(e) by counterparty

Financial assets subject to offsetting, enforceable master netting arrangements and similar arrangements

CU million As at 31 December 20XX	(a) Gross amounts of recognised financial assets	(b) Gross amounts of recognised financial liabilities set off in the statement of financial position	(c)=(a)–(b) Net amounts of financial assets presented in the statement of financial position
Description			
Derivatives	200	(80)	120
Reverse repurchase, securities borrowing and similar agreements	90	–	90
Other financial instruments	–	–	–
Total	290	(80)	210

Net financial assets subject to offsetting, enforceable master netting arrangements and similar arrangements

CU million As at 31 December 20XX	(a) Net amounts of financial assets presented in the statement of financial position	(d) Related amounts not set off in the statement of financial position (d)(i), (d)(ii) Financial instruments	 (d)(ii) Cash collateral received	(e)=(c)–(d) Net amount
Counterparty A	20	–	(10)	10
Counterparty B	100	(80)	(20)	–
Counterparty C	90	(90)	–	–
Other	–	–	–	–
Total	210	(170)	(30)	10

Financial liabilities subject to offsetting, enforceable master netting arrangements and similar arrangements

CU million As at 31 December 20XX	(a)	(b)	(c)=(a)–(b)
	Gross amounts of recognised financial liabilities	Gross amounts of recognised financial assets set off in the statement of financial position	Net amounts of financial liabilities presented in the statement of financial position
Description			
Derivatives	160	(80)	80
Repurchase, securities lending and similar agreements	80	–	80
Other financial instruments	–	–	–
Total	240	(80)	160

Net financial liabilities subject to enforceable master netting arrangements and similar agreements, by counterparty

CU million As at 31 December 20XX	(c)	(d)		(e)=(c)–(d)
		Related amounts not set off in the statement of financial position		
	Net amounts of financial liabilities presented in the statement of financial position	(d)(i), (d)(ii) Financial instruments	(d)(ii) Cash collateral pledged	Net amount
Counterparty A	–	–	–	–
Counterparty B	80	(80)	–	–
Counterparty C	80	(80)	–	–
Other	–	–	–	–
Total	160	(160)	–	–

B12 First-time adoption of IFRSs

Contents

1 Introduction

A first-time adopter of IFRSs is an entity that prepares its first IFRS annual financial statements containing an explicit and unreserved statement of compliance with IFRSs. [IFRS 1:3] The date of transition to IFRSs for a first-time adopter is the beginning of the earliest period for which an entity presents full comparative information under IFRSs in its first IFRS financial statements. [IFRS 1:Appendix A]

In general, IFRS 1 *First-time Adoption of International Financial Reporting Standards* requires a first-time adopter to comply retrospectively with each IFRS effective at the end of the reporting period for its first IFRS financial statements. [IFRS 1:7] IFRS 1 grants limited exemptions from these requirements in specified areas, including financial instruments (see **2.7**) and prohibits retrospective application in others, also including financial instruments (see **section 3**).

The general requirements of IFRS 1 are dealt with in detail in **chapter A3** of **Volume A**, Deloitte's companion volume for this manual. These include the requirements regarding the information to be disclosed in order to explain how the transition from previous GAAP to IFRSs has affected the entity's reported financial position, financial performance and cash flows. The scope of this chapter is limited to an exploration of the impact of some of the requirements of IFRS 1 on an entity's accounting for financial instruments that are within the scope of IAS 32 and IFRS 9, namely:

- the requirement to identify, recognise, classify and measure as appropriate all financial instruments in the scope of IAS 32 and IFRS 9 (see **sections 2** to **2.6**, and **2.8**);
- IFRS 1's elective exemption from retrospective application of IAS 32 to compound instruments when the liability component is no longer outstanding (see **2.7**);
- IFRS 1's mandatory prohibitions from retrospective application of IFRS 9 in respect of derecognition and hedge accounting (see **3.1** and **3.3**); and
- IFRS 1's exemption from restatement of comparative amounts if a first-time adopter of IFRSs applies IFRS 9 in its first IFRS financial statements for an annual period beginning before 1 January 2019 (see **section 4**).

2 Transition to IFRSs with respect to financial instruments

At the date of transition to IFRSs, a first-time adopter is required to identify, recognise, classify and measure as appropriate all financial assets and financial liabilities that qualify for recognition in accordance with IAS 32 and IFRS 9, and to treat any adjustment to the carrying amount of a financial asset or financial liability resulting from the adoption of these Standards as a transition adjustment to be recognised in the opening balance of retained earnings at the date of transition to IFRSs. [IFRS 1:IG58A]

At the date of transition to IFRSs, a first-time adopter is required to derecognise assets and liabilities that do not qualify for recognition in accordance with IAS 32 and IFRS 9 (e.g. gains and losses deferred as assets and/or liabilities in the statement of financial position in respect of hedge relationships under previous GAAP that do not qualify for recognition as assets and liabilities under IFRSs – see **3.3**).

2.1 The key steps to conversion to IFRSs for financial instruments

The key steps to ensure that an entity complies with IAS 32 and IFRS 9 on first-time adoption can be summarised as follows:

(a) identify all financial instruments and other contracts that fall within the scope of IAS 32 and IFRS 9 which may or may not be accounted for as financial instruments under previous GAAP, including embedded derivatives and other contracts scoped into those Standards (see **chapter B1** and **2.2**);

(b) recognise and classify all financial instruments in accordance with the financial asset and liability classifications in IFRS 9 and the rules on equity and liability classification in IAS 32 (see **chapters B2** and **B3**);

(c) derecognise items if IAS 32 and IFRS 9 do not permit their recognition (e.g. gains and losses deferred as assets and/or liabilities in the statement of financial position in respect of hedge relationships under previous GAAP that do not qualify for recognition as assets and liabilities under IFRSs – see **3.1**);

(d) designate and document qualifying hedge relationships on or before the date of transition to IFRSs to ensure these comply with IFRS 9's hedge accounting criteria should an entity wish to apply hedge accounting prospectively from the date of transition to IFRSs (see **3.3** and **chapter B9**);

(e) apply IAS 32 and IFRS 9 in measuring all financial assets and financial liabilities in accordance with their classification (**2.4** and **chapters B2**, **B3**, **B6** and **B7**); and

(f) design and implement controls and procedures for continued compliance with (a) to (e) above.

2.2 Identification of all financial assets and financial liabilities on first-time adoption

Depending on an entity's previous GAAP a number of items would *not* have been recognised under previous GAAP compared to IFRSs. These may include:

(a) all derivatives, including:
   (i) contracts to buy or sell a non-financial item, scoped into IFRS 9 if they can be settled net in cash or another financial instrument, or by exchanging financial instruments, and are not entered into or held in accordance with the entity's expected purchase, sale or usage requirements (see **2.5** in **chapter B1**);
   (ii) issued guarantees falling within the scope of IFRS 9 that do not meet the definition of a financial guarantee contract (see **2.3.3** in **chapter B1**);
   (iii) derivatives on an interest in a subsidiary, associate or joint venture unless they meet the definition of an equity instrument of the entity in accordance with IAS 32 or because they will result in a business combination at a future date (see **2.1** and **3.2** in **chapter B1**);
   (iv) derivatives based on climatic, geological or other physical variables unless they meet the definition of an insurance contract and are within the scope of IFRS 4 (see **2.3** and **2.3.8** in **chapter B1**); and
   (v) loan commitments that can be settled net in cash or another financial instrument, loan commitments that the issuer designates as financial assets or liabilities at FVTPL or loan commitments to provide a loan at a below-market interest rate (see **3.5** in **chapter B1**);

(b) all embedded derivatives that are required to be separately accounted for as required by IFRS 9 (e.g. an embedded derivative in a financial liability that is not measured at FVTPL when the embedded derivative is not closely related to the non-derivative financial liability host contract – see **chapter B5**);

(c) other interests, such as servicing rights or servicing liabilities, retained after a derecognition transaction and still existing at the date of transition to IFRSs (see **chapter B8**); and

(d) financial instruments that are held by subsidiaries that were not consolidated under the previous GAAP, but are consolidated under IFRSs because the entity controls the entity at the date of transition to IFRSs (see **3.1.1** in **chapter B8**).

2.2.1 Embedded derivatives

First-time adopters need to assess all contractual arrangements for embedded derivatives (although in the case of host contracts that are financial assets in IFRS 9 they do not require separation). IFRS 9 requires separate accounting for embedded derivatives not closely related to the host contract, where the entire contract is not one measured at FVTPL.

IFRS 1:B9 states that a first-time adopter should make its assessment as to whether an embedded derivative is to be separated on the basis of conditions that existed at the later of the date it first became party to the contract and the date (if any) a reassessment is required by IFRS 9:B4.3.11, i.e. when the contract is significantly modified (for a discussion of the 'significantly modified' criterion, see **section 3** of **chapter B5**).

If there has been no significant modification of the arrangement, the assessment as to whether the embedded derivative is closely related is made on the basis of conditions that existed at the date when the entity first became party to the contract and not on the date of transition to IFRSs. The initial carrying amounts of the embedded derivative and the host contract reflect circumstances at the date the whole instrument satisfied the recognition criteria of IFRS 9. [IFRS 1:IG55] Once the carrying amount at initial recognition of an embedded derivative that is not closely related to the host contract is separately determined (see **section 12** of **chapter B5**), it is then possible to determine the appropriate carrying amounts at the date of transition. These adjustments are recognised in the opening balance of retained earnings at the date of transition to IFRSs.

If the entity cannot determine the initial carrying amounts of the embedded derivative and host contract reliably, it treats the entire combined contract as a financial instrument as at FVTPL (see **section 12** of **chapter B5**). [IFRS 1:IG55]

2.3 Recognition of all financial instruments on first-time adoption

Subject to the exception discussed in **3.1** relating to the retrospective application of IFRS 9's derecognition rules, at the date of transition to IFRSs an entity is required to recognise all financial assets and financial liabilities that qualify for recognition under IFRS 9 (e.g. certain derivative instruments) that have not yet qualified for derecognition under IFRS 9 except for non-derivative financial assets and non-derivative financial liabilities derecognised in accordance with previous GAAP before the date of transition to IFRSs. For example, an entity that does not apply IFRS 1:B3 (see **3.1**) does not recognise assets transferred in a securitisation, transfer or other derecognition transaction that occurred before the date of transition to IFRSs if those transactions qualified for derecognition in accordance with previous GAAP. However, if the entity uses the same securitisation arrangement or other derecognition arrangement for further transfers after the date of transition to IFRSs, those further transfers qualify for derecognition only if they meet the derecognition criteria of IFRS 9. [IFRS 1:IG52-54]

In December 2010 the IASB issued amendments to IFRS 1, *Severe Hyperinflation and Removal of Fixed Dates for First-time Adopters*. Prior to these amendments to IFRS 1:IG53 first time adopters were required to assess transactions as far back as 1 January 2004 to determine whether under IFRS they would have led to derecognition of financial assets and financial liabilities. This fixed date was removed and replaced with the 'date of transition to IFRSs'.

It appears when IFRS 9(2014) was published in July 2014 it incorrectly included as part of its consequential amendments to IFRS 1 reference to the fixed date of 1 January 2004 rather than the date of transition to IFRSs. This appears to be an error and in conflict with IFRS 1:B2 (which is consistent with the amendments made to IFRS 1 in 2010). Consequently, IFRS 1:IG53 should be read as not including the fixed date, rather the date should be read as the 'date of transition to IFRSs'.

An entity does not recognise financial assets and financial liabilities that do not qualify for recognition in accordance with IFRS 9, or have already qualified for derecognition in accordance with IFRS 9. [IFRS 1:IG54]

2.4 Classification and measurement of financial assets and financial liabilities on transition

The classification and measurement requirement for financial assets and financial liabilities are not applied fully retrospectively. Rather, a first-time adopter applies the criteria in IFRS 9 to identify on the basis of the facts and circumstances that exist at the date of transition to IFRSs those financial assets and financial liabilities that are measured at fair value through profit or loss, those that are measured at fair value through other comprehensive income and those that are measured at amortised cost. The resulting classifications are applied retrospectively. [IFRS 1:IG56]

IFRS 1:B8 is explicit that an entity shall assess whether a financial asset meets the amortised cost criteria in IFRS 9:4.1.2 and fair value through other comprehensive income criteria in IFRS 9:4.1.2A on the basis of the facts and circumstances that exist at the date of transition to IFRSs.

The criteria for qualification for amortised cost and fair value through other comprehensive income measurement under IFRS 9 are discussed in detail in **chapter B2**. In summary, IFRS 9:4.1.2 requires an entity to assess whether the objective of its business model is to manage financial assets so as to collect the contractual cash flows for amortised cost measurement; IFRS 9:4.1.2A requires an entity to assess whether the business model is achieved by both collecting contractual cash flows and selling financial assets for fair value through other comprehensive income measurement. The requirement in IFRS 1:B8 for first-time adopters to make this assessment on the basis of facts and circumstances at the date of transition is consistent with the general transition requirement for continuing IFRS reporters in IFRS 9:7.2.3 (which requires that the assessment be carried out at the date of initial application of the Standard). IFRS 9:BC7.18 explains that the IASB believes that it would be "difficult, and perhaps impossible," to make the assessment on the basis of circumstances when the financial asset first qualified for recognition as a financial asset.

Once the classification of a financial asset has been determined on the basis described in IFRS 1:B8, that classification is applied retrospectively irrespective of the entity's business model in prior reporting periods.

For those financial assets and financial liabilities classified at the date of transition in an amortised cost category, an entity determines their amortised cost on the basis of circumstances existing when the assets and liabilities first satisfied the recognition criteria in IFRS 9. However, if the entity acquired those financial assets and financial liabilities in a past business combination, their carrying amount under previous GAAP immediately following the business combination is their deemed cost under IFRSs at that date. [IFRS 1:IG57]

Example 2.4A

Determining classification and measurement at date of transition to IFRSs

Entity ABC has a 31 December year end and is a first-time adopter in 20X2. Its date of transition to IFRSs is 1 January 20X1. It chooses to apply IFRS 9 and to restate comparative amounts in accordance with IFRS 9.

How does Entity ABC apply the requirements of IFRS 9 in respect of the classification and measurement of its financial assets and financial liabilities?

At 1 January 20X1, Entity ABC applies the classification and measurement criteria in IFRS 9 to its financial assets and financial liabilities as if it had initially recognised those financial assets and financial liabilities in accordance with the Standard as illustrated.

- Entity ABC must assess whether a financial asset meets the amortised cost criteria in IFRS 9:4.1.2 on the basis of the facts and circumstances that exist at the date of transition to IFRSs. [IFRS 1:B8] Entity ABC recognises any adjustment to financial assets classified and measured at amortised cost, as if that measurement basis had been applied since the date the asset first qualified for recognition at amortised cost in accordance with IFRS 9, directly in retained earnings. If it is impracticable (as defined in IAS 8) to apply retrospectively the effective interest method in IFRS 9, the fair value of the financial asset or the financial liability at the date of transition to IFRSs is the new gross carrying value of that financial asset or the new amortised cost of that financial liability at the date of transition to IFRSs. [IFRS 1:B8C]
- Entity ABC must assess whether a financial asset meets the fair value through other comprehensive income criteria in IFRS 9:4.1.2A on the basis of the facts and circumstances that exist at the date of transition to IFRSs. [IFRS 1:B8] Entity ABC recognises any adjustment to financial assets classified and measured at fair value through other comprehensive income, as if that measurement basis had been applied since the date the asset first qualified for recognition at fair value through other comprehensive income in accordance with IFRS 9, in a separate component of equity. [IFRS 1:IG59] If it is impracticable (as defined in

IAS 8) to apply retrospectively the effective interest method in IFRS 9, the fair value of the financial asset at the date of transition to IFRSs is the new gross carrying value of that financial asset at the date of transition to IFRSs. [IFRS 1:B8C]

- If a financial asset meets the amortised cost criteria in IFRS 9:4.1.2 or fair value through other comprehensive income criteria in IFRS 9:4.1.2A, Entity ABC may designate that financial asset as at FVTPL in accordance with IFRS 9:4.1.5. The designation shall be on the basis of the facts and circumstances that exist at the date of transition to IFRSs. [IFRS 1:D19A] Entity ABC recognises directly in retained earnings any adjustment to financial assets classified as at FVTPL as if that measurement basis had been applied since the date the asset first qualified for recognition as at FVTPL in accordance with IFRS 9. Entity ABC must disclose the fair value of any financial assets designated into the FVTPL category and their classification and carrying amount in its previous financial statements. [IFRS 1:29]
- Entity ABC can designate an investment in an equity instrument as at FVTOCI in accordance with IFRS 9:5.7.5. The designation shall be on the basis of facts and circumstances that exist at the date of transition to IFRSs. [IFRS 1:D19B] The designation in this category on transition to IFRSs is irrevocable. The fair value gain or loss on transition for assets designated as at FVTOCI is taken to a separate component of equity as if those assets had been accounted for since initial recognition as at FVTOCI. [IFRS 1:IG59]
- Entity ABC recognises any derivative financial assets and derivative financial liabilities that are in the scope of IFRS 9 at fair value with fair value gains or losses on transition accounted for as an adjustment to retained earnings, except for derivatives that were part of a net investment hedge or cash flow hedge under previous GAAP of a type that qualifies under IFRS 9. [IFRS 1:B5 & IG60B]
- At the date of transition to IFRS 9, Entity ABC is permitted to designate any financial liability as one to be measured at FVTPL if specified criteria are met, i.e. the 'fair value option' (see **7.1.2** in **chapter B3**) is available as a one-off choice on transition. [IFRS 1:D19] The fair value gain or loss on transition for financial liabilities designated as at FVTPL at the date of transition is accounted for as an adjustment through retained earnings, i.e. the liabilities are accounted for as if designated as at FVTPL from the date of initial recognition. It should be noted that the application of IFRS 9:5.7.7 generally results in changes in the fair value of a financial liability attributable to credit risk being presented in other comprehensive income with other gains or losses recognised in profit or loss. Entity ABC must disclose the fair value of any financial liabilities designated into the 'financial liabilities at fair value through profit or loss' category and their classification and carrying amount in its previous financial statements. [IFRS 1:29A] If Entity ABC wishes to designate a financial liability at FVTPL under the fair value option but does not wish to recognise changes in the fair value associated with changes in own credit risk in other comprehensive income, rather it wishes for these gains or losses to be recognised in profit or loss, Entity ABC must determine whether the presentation of changes in the fair value of a financial liability attributable to changes in credit risk in other comprehensive income would create or enlarge an accounting

mismatch in profit or loss (see **7.1.2.5** in **chapter B3**) based on the facts and circumstances that exist at the date of transition to IFRSs.

- Entity ABC classifies financial liabilities that are not measured at FVTPL, either because the 'fair value option' has not been applied or because the items are not held for trading, as other financial liabilities measured at amortised cost (see **section 7** in **chapter B3**). It recognises in retained earnings any adjustment to measure them at the appropriate amortised cost amount as if that measurement basis had been applied since the date they first qualified for recognition in accordance with IFRS 9. If it is impracticable (as defined in IAS 8) to apply retrospectively the effective interest method in IFRS 9, the fair value of the financial liability at the date of transition to IFRSs is the new amortised cost of that financial liability at the date of transition to IFRSs. [IFRS 1:B8C]

Example 2.4B

Derivative not measured at fair value under previous GAAP

Entity P is a first-time adopter of IFRSs and is preparing its first annual IFRS financial statements for the year ended 31 December 20X2.

Entity P has some derivative financial instruments. Under previous GAAP, these instruments were not recognised at fair value in the statement of financial position because they were considered to be hedging instruments. The derivatives were instead held on an accruals basis and were included in the carrying amount of the item being hedged. At the date of transition the instruments have a fair value of CU(2) million and do not qualify as hedging instruments in accordance with IFRS 9 as they are net written options.

On Entity P's date of transition to IFRSs (1 January 20X1), it recognises the derivative liability in its statement of financial position with the corresponding entry recognised in retained earnings. The entity cannot include the loss in a cash flow hedge accounting reserve because the derivative is not a qualifying hedging instrument under IFRS 9.

Under previous GAAP, the derivatives had been netted against the item being hedged. Not only is the measurement basis not compliant with IFRSs, but also the financial instruments could not be offset unless the criteria for offset in IAS 32 were met (see **section 6** of **chapter B11**). An adjustment will be required to the hedged items to recognise them at the appropriate carrying amounts.

Example 2.4C

Determining amortised cost

Entity MNO is a first-time adopter of IFRSs and is preparing its first annual IFRS financial statements for the year ended 31 December 20X8. Therefore, its date of transition to IFRSs is 1 January 20X7. Entity MNO has the following two zero coupon bond assets.

- Bond 1 was purchased at original issuance on 1 January 20X5 for €1,000. It is redeemable in 5 years' time at €1,250. The effective interest rate on this instrument is 4.56 per cent.
- Bond 2 has the same terms as Bond 1, but the bond was acquired in a business combination on 1 January 20X6. The fair value of the bond on the date of the business combination was €1,100. The bond has risen in value since it was issued because of the unwinding of discount and because interest rates have fallen since the bond was issued. The effective interest rate calculated at the time of the business combination is 3.25 per cent.

Whether the bonds are quoted in an active market or not is not relevant in classifying financial assets under IFRS 9. Instead, Entity MNO will assess whether the amortised cost criteria in IFRS 9:4.1.2 are met at the date of transition to IFRSs. If the bonds are held within a business model whose objective is to hold assets in order to collect contractual cash flows and the contractual terms of the financial asset give rise on specified dates to cash flows that are solely payments of principal and interest on the principal amount outstanding then the bonds are eligible for amortised cost measurement.

In determining amortised cost, Entity MNO determines the carrying amount of Bond 1 as if it had been accounted for at amortised cost since acquisition using the bond's effective interest rate of 4.56 per cent. The amortised cost on 1 January 20X7 is €1,093, reflecting two years of amortisation at 4.56 per cent.

In determining amortised cost, Entity MNO determines the carrying amount of Bond 2 as if it had been accounted for at amortised cost since it was acquired in the business combination using the bond's effective interest rate of 3.25 per cent. The amortised cost on 1 January 20X7 is €1,136, reflecting 1 year of amortisation at 3.25 per cent.

Alternatively, the fair value option could be applied to the bonds on transition to IFRSs if the bonds meet the amortised cost criteria and the specified criteria in IFRS 9:4.1.5 on the basis of the facts and circumstances that exist at the date of transition to IFRSs. [IFRS 1:D19A]

If it is impracticable to assess a modified time value of money element in accordance with IFRS 9:B4.1.9B - B4.1.9D on the basis of the facts and circumstances that exist at the date of transition to IFRSs, an entity shall assess the contractual cash flow characteristics of that financial asset on the basis of the facts and circumstances that existed at the date of transition to IFRSs without taking into account the requirements related to the modification of the time value of money element in IFRS 9:B4.1.9B - B4.1.9D. (In this case, the entity shall also apply IFRS 7:42R but references to 'paragraph 7.2.4 of IFRS 9' shall be read to mean this paragraph and references to 'initial recognition of the financial asset' shall be read to mean 'at the date of transition to IFRSs'.) [IFRS 1:B8A]

If it is impracticable to assess whether the fair value of a prepayment feature is insignificant in accordance with IFRS 9:B4.1.12(c) on the basis of the facts and circumstances that exist at the date of transition to IFRSs, an entity shall assess the contractual cash flow characteristics of that financial asset on the basis of the facts and circumstances that existed at the date of transition to IFRSs without taking into account the exception for prepayment features in paragraph B4.1.12 of IFRS 9. (In this case, the entity shall also apply IFRS 7:42S of IFRS 7 but references to 'paragraph 7.2.5 of IFRS 9' shall be read to mean this paragraph and references to 'initial recognition of the financial asset' shall be read to mean 'at the date of transition to IFRSs'.)

An asset that meets the amortised cost criteria or fair value through comprehensive income criteria at the date of transition to IFRSs may be designated as at FVTPL if it meets the criteria in IFRS 9:4.1.5 on the basis of the facts and circumstances that exist at the date of transition to IFRSs. [IFRS 1:D19A] Entities are required to disclose the fair value of financial assets so designated at the date of designation and their classification and carrying amount in the previous financial statements. [IFRS 1:29]

An entity is also permitted to designate a financial liability that meets the amortised cost criteria at the date of transition to IFRSs as at FVTPL if it meets the criteria in IFRS 9:4.2.2. [IFRS 1:D19] For a financial liability that is designated as a financial liability at fair value through profit or loss, an entity shall determine whether the treatment in IFRS 9:5.7.7 of fair valuing changes in own credit risk in other comprehensive income would create an accounting mismatch in profit or loss on the basis of the facts and circumstances that exist at the date of transition to IFRSs. Entities are required to disclose the fair value of financial liabilities so designated at the date of designation and their classification and carrying amount in the previous financial statements. [IFRS 1:29A]

Example 2.4D

Date of designation for instruments acquired after the date of transition

Entity B prepares its first set of IFRS financial statements for the year ended 31 December 20X2; its date of transition to IFRSs is 1 January 20X1. In February 20X1, Entity B issued fixed rate debentures that were measured at amortised cost on initial recognition. At the same time, Entity B used the proceeds of the debt to acquire a portfolio of fixed rate assets which failed the amortised cost criteria and, therefore, were measured at FVTPL. The fair value changes on the assets tend to offset the fair value movements on the debenture liabilities. During 20X1, Entity B realises that there is a measurement and recognition inconsistency in measuring the fixed rate debt liability at amortised cost while measuring the fixed rate assets at FVTPL.

Entity B cannot re-designate the fixed rate debentures after initial recognition. At initial recognition, in February 20X1, Entity B chose to designate the fixed rate debentures at amortised cost and not at FVTPL. A designation as at FVTPL must be made at the later of initial recognition and date of transition to IFRSs.

If the fixed rate debentures were acquired prior to the date of transition to IFRSs (i.e. prior to 1 January 20X1), Entity B could have designated those fixed rate debentures as at FVTPL at the date of transition to IFRSs if the specified criteria were met.

A first-time adopter is permitted to designate an investment in an equity instrument as at fair value through other comprehensive income at the date of transition to IFRSs if the criteria in IFRS 9:5.7.5 (see **5.3** in **chapter B3**) are met on the basis of the facts and circumstances that exist at the date of transition to IFRSs. [IFRS 1:D19B]

A first-time adopter of IFRSs must de-designate financial assets and financial liabilities that under previous GAAP were designated as at FVTPL but that do not qualify for such designation under IFRS 9 and apply the measurement requirements of IFRSs retrospectively. A financial asset or financial liability that was recognised at fair value under previous GAAP and qualifies for the fair value option under IFRS 9 does not need to be measured at FVTPL as the fair value option only applies under IFRS 9 if it is designated as such.

2.5 Impairment

The requirements for first time adoption of impairment of financial assets are the same as the IFRS 9 transitional requirements for entities that adopt IFRS 9 that are already IFRS reporters, i.e. are not first time adopters of IFRSs.

IFRS 1:B8D requires that the impairment requirements in Section 5.5 of IFRS 9 are applied retrospectively subject to IFRS 9:7.2.15 (on whether to restate comparative information) and 7.2.18 - 7.2.20.

At the date of transition to IFRSs, an entity shall use reasonable and supportable information that is available without undue cost or effort to determine the credit risk at the date that financial instruments were initially recognised (or for loan commitments and financial guarantee contracts the date that the entity became a party to the irrevocable commitment in accordance with IFRS 9:5.5.6) and compare that to the credit risk at the date of transition to IFRSs (also see IFRS 9:B7.2.2 - B7.2.3 of IFRS 9). [IFRS 1:B8E & IFRS 9:7.2.18]

When determining whether there has been a significant increase in credit risk since initial recognition, an entity may apply:

[IFRS 1:B8F & IFRS 9:7.2.19]

(a) the requirements in IFRS 9:5.5.10 and B5.5.22 - B5.5.24 in assuming the credit risk on the financial instrument is 'low'; and

(b) the rebuttable presumption in IFRS 9:5.5.11 for contractual payments that are more than 30 days past due if an entity will apply the impairment requirements by identifying significant increases in credit risk since initial recognition for those financial instruments on the basis of past due information.

If, at the date of initial application, determining whether there has been a significant increase in credit risk since initial recognition would require undue cost or effort, an entity shall recognise a loss allowance at an amount equal to lifetime expected credit losses at each reporting date until that financial instrument is derecognised (unless that financial instrument is low credit risk at a reporting date, in which case IFRS 1:B8F(a) (reproduced above) applies). [IFRS 1:B8G & IFRS 9:7.2.20]

2.6 Classification as a financial liability or equity

In its opening IFRS statement of financial position, an entity applies the criteria in IAS 32 to classify financial instruments issued (or components of compound instruments issued) as either financial liabilities or equity instruments in accordance with the substance of the contractual arrangement when the instrument first satisfied the recognition criteria in IAS 32:15, without considering events after that date other than changes to the terms of the instruments. [IFRS 1:IG35]

Example 2.6

Assessing terms at date of transition to IFRSs

Entity P issued a capital instrument on 1 January 20X1 which is required to be settled in cash in specified circumstances. Entity P's date of transition to IFRSs is 1 January 20X3. If IAS 32 had been applied at the date of issue of the instrument, the instrument would have been classified as a liability because the instrument's contingent settlement provision (requiring redemption in cash) would have been judged to be genuine (i.e. the event that would trigger redemption would not have been considered to be extremely rare). At 1 January 20X3, circumstances have changed such that it is now considered that the event that would trigger redemption is now extremely rare (there has been no change in the terms of the instrument).

In accordance with IFRS 1:IG35 (see above), the classification of the instrument as either a financial liability or as equity should be determined based on conditions at the date of issue (1 January 20X1). Entity P should classify the instrument as a financial liability on transition notwithstanding the fact that if it issued an instrument with the same terms at 1 January 20X3 it would recognise an equity instrument.

2.7 Compound instruments

IFRS 1 provides some relief for first-time adopters when applying IAS 32 for the first time. To the extent that the liability component of a compound instrument is no longer outstanding at the date of transition to IFRSs, retrospective application of IAS 32's requirement to split the instrument is not required. [IFRS 1:D18]

This exemption is justified on the basis of expediency. The only effect of retrospective application of IAS 32 in the circumstances described would be the separation of two components of equity for compound instruments that have matured: one portion would include the cumulative interest accrued on the liability component during its life using the effective interest method (which would normally reside in retained earnings) and the second portion would include the original equity component that would have been separated on initial recognition of the instrument.

Example 2.7A

Convertible debt: outstanding at date of transition to IFRSs

Entity H is a first-time adopter in 20X4. Entity H issued 2,000 convertible bonds on 1 January 20X1. The bonds have a four-year term, and were issued at par with a face value of CU1,000 per bond, giving total proceeds of CU2 million. Interest is payable annually in arrears at an annual interest rate of 6 per cent. Each bond is convertible, at the holder's discretion, at any time up to maturity into 250 ordinary shares. When the bonds were issued, the market interest rate for similar debt without the conversion option was 9 per cent.

How should Entity H account for its convertible debt on first-time adoption of IFRSs?

An entity that has an issued compound instrument outstanding at the date of transition to IFRSs determines the initial carrying amounts of the liability and equity components based on circumstances existing when the instrument was issued. [IFRS 1:IG36]

IAS 32 requires that the liability component be valued first. The liability component is calculated as the present value of the contractual cash flows using the discount rate of 9 per cent, which was the market interest rate for similar bonds with the same credit standing having no conversion rights when the bonds were issued. The difference between the proceeds of the bond issue and the fair value of the liability at the time of original issuance is assigned to the equity component. The equity component is not remeasured. An adjustment in the opening balance of retained earnings is required to measure the liability component at its appropriate amortised cost at the date of transition.

Example 2.7B

Convertible debt: not outstanding at date of transition to IFRSs

Entity Q is adopting IFRSs for the first time in its annual financial statements for the year ending 31 December 20X7, with a date of transition to IFRSs of 1 January 20X6. Entity Q issued a convertible bond on 1 January 20X1. The bond had a three-year term, was convertible at any time up to maturity into 250 ordinary shares of the entity, and was redeemed at maturity.

How should Entity Q account for its convertible bond on first-time adoption of IFRSs?

The liability component of Entity Q's convertible bond is no longer outstanding at Entity Q's date of transition to IFRSs. Therefore, Entity Q is not required to separate the two components of equity that would have resulted if full retrospective application had been applied. [IFRS 1:D18]

Example 2.7C

Convertible debt: redeemed after date of transition to IFRSs

Using the facts as in **example 2.7B**, if Entity Q's convertible bond had a maturity of 1 January 20X7 (i.e. it had a six-year term and was expected to be redeemed on its maturity on 1 January 20X7), would Entity Q be exempted from full retrospective application of IAS 32 for its convertible bond?

No. Entity Q's date of transition to IFRSs is 1 January 20X6. In this example, the liability component of Entity Q's convertible bond is still outstanding at the date of transition. Therefore, Entity Q would be required to apply IAS 32 retrospectively to its convertible bond and to separate out the equity component that would have been separated on initial recognition of the instrument in accordance with IAS 32.

2.8 Fair value measurement of financial assets or financial liabilities

Because all financial assets and financial liabilities, except for trade receivables that do not have a significant financing component (determined in accordance with IFRS 15 *Revenue from Contracts with Customers*), are required to be initially recognised at fair value, an entity must consider the specific guidance in IFRS 13 on fair value at initial recognition when determining the carrying amount of financial assets and financial liabilities at the date of transition to IFRSs.

IFRS 9 has very specific guidance on the accounting for differences between fair value and the transaction price on initial recognition of financial assets and financial liabilities. The Standard limits upfront gain/ loss recognition unless the fair value of the instrument is evidenced by comparison with other observable current market transactions in the same instrument (i.e. without modification or repackaging) or based on a valuation technique whose variables include only data from observable markets. This is often referred to as "day 1 P&L" and is discussed in more depth at **7.1** in **chapter B7**. IFRS 1:D20 has specific transition requirements when applying the day 1 P&L guidance. IFRS 1 permits an entity to apply the day 1 P&L guidance (with specific reference from IFRS 1 to the last sentence of IFRS 9:B5.1.2A(b)) prospectively to transactions entered into on or after the date of transition to IFRSs. Alternatively the requirements are applied retrospectively.

2.9 Designating contracts to buy or sell a non-financial item at FVTPL

IFRS 9:2.5 permits some contracts to buy or sell a non-financial item to be designated at inception as measured at fair value through profit or loss. Despite this requirement an entity is permitted to designate, at the date of transition to IFRSs, contracts that already exist on that date as measured at fair value through profit or loss but only if they meet the requirements of IFRS 9:2.5 at that date and the entity designates all similar contracts. [IFRS 1:D33]

2.10 Extinguishing financial liabilities with equity instruments

IFRIC 19 *Extinguishing Financial Liabilities with Equity Instruments* addresses the accounting for entities that issue equity instruments in order to extinguish all or part of a financial liability (often referred to as 'debt for equity swaps'). The requirements of IFRIC 19 are discussed in **4.2** of **chapter B8**.

IFRS 1 permits first-time adopters to apply the transition provisions in IFRIC 19. [IFRS 1:D25]

The transition provisions of IFRIC 19 require that an entity should apply any change in accounting policy arising from the application of the Interpretation from the beginning of the earliest comparative period presented.

First-time adopters therefore have a choice between full retrospective application of IFRIC 19 and application of the transition provisions of IFRIC 19. The option selected will have no impact on amounts reported for the first IFRS reporting period and for the comparative period, but full retrospective application could result in some additional reclassifications within equity.

In finalising IFRIC 19, the IFRIC (now the IFRS Interpretations Committee) concluded that it was preferable to require entities that could apply the Interpretation retrospectively to do so, rather than requiring all entities to apply it prospectively to future transactions; the Committee made specific reference to IAS 8's guidance on circumstances in which retrospective application might be impracticable. To simplify transition, the IFRIC also concluded that it should require retrospective application only from the beginning of the earliest comparative period presented because application to earlier periods would result only in a reclassification of amounts within equity. [IFRIC 19:BC33]

3 Exceptions to retrospective application of IAS 32 and IFRS 9

IFRS 1:B1 requires retrospective application of IFRSs with the following exceptions that relate to financial instruments:

- classification and measurement of financial assets (see **2.4**);
- impairment of financial assets (see **2.5**);
- derecognition of financial assets and financial liabilities (see **3.2**);
- hedge accounting (see **3.3**); and
- government grants (see **3.4**).

3.1 Transitional requirements on derecognition for first-time adopters

A first-time adopter is required by IFRS 1:B2 to apply the derecognition rules in IFRS 9 prospectively from the date of transition to IFRSs unless it chooses to apply the derecognition rules of IFRS 9 retrospectively from a date of its choosing in accordance with IFRS 1:B3 (see **3.2**). Therefore, if a first-time adopter derecognised financial assets under its previous GAAP in a securitisation, transfer or other derecognition transaction that occurred before the date of transition to IFRSs, it does not recognise those assets and liabilities at the date of transition (even if they would not have qualified for derecognition under IFRS 9), unless they qualify for recognition as a result of a later transaction or event.

However, a first-time adopter must recognise any financial interest retained as a result of a derecognition transaction prior to the date of transition to IFRSs that still exists at the date of transition to IFRSs (e.g. any derivatives and other interests, such as servicing rights or servicing liabilities).

Furthermore, the exemptions from retrospective application of the derecognition requirements do not extend to consolidation. A first-time adopter must consolidate all subsidiaries (as defined in IFRS 10 *Consolidated Financial Statements*), unless IFRS 10 requires otherwise. [IFRS 1:IG26] Therefore, although a group may have derecognised financial assets under its previous GAAP before the date of transition to IFRSs (or before a different date of its choosing in accordance with IFRS 1:B3) by transferring the assets to an unconsolidated transferee, if the transferee is consolidated into the group's statement of financial position under IFRS 10 and the transferee did not derecognise the transferred assets under previous GAAP, then the IFRS 9 derecognition decision tree will be applied to the new group, including the transferred assets, as defined by IFRSs.

Example 3.1

Transfers to a structured entity

Entity X is part of Group Y. The date of transition to IFRSs for Entity X and for Group Y is 1 January 20X5. The entity and the group do not apply the election available under IFRS 1:B3 (see **3.2**) to apply the derecognition rules to transactions derecognised prior to the date of transition to IFRSs.

Entity X derecognised financial assets under its previous GAAP on 30 September 20X3. These assets were transferred to Entity Z. Entity Z was not considered a member of Group Y under previous GAAP. Entity Z is a structured entity that issues beneficial interests in the underlying financial assets transferred to it by Entity X to unrelated third-party investors, and provides servicing of those financial assets.

On the date of transition to IFRSs, in accordance with IFRS 10, Entity Z is now considered to be part of Group Y and must be consolidated by Group Y.

Individual financial statements of Entity X under IFRSs

Because Entity X derecognised the financial assets under its previous GAAP in a transaction occurring prior to the date of transition to IFRSs, the transferred assets continue to be derecognised under IFRSs.

Group Y's financial statements under IFRSs

Because Group Y now includes Entity Z, the derecognition requirements must be applied to the enlarged group. If Entity Z could not derecognise the financial assets under its previous GAAP, and the assets continue to be recognised under IFRSs, then Group Y continues to recognise those assets. If Entity Z did derecognise the financial assets under its previous GAAP, the assets will remain derecognised under IFRSs because they were derecognised under previous GAAP in a transaction occurring prior to the date of transition to IFRSs.

When the entity and group have made the election available under IFRS 1:B3 to apply the derecognition requirements of IFRS 9 to derecognition transactions occurring before the date of transition to IFRSs (see **3.2**), the derecognition requirements of IFRS 9 would apply to the transaction on 30 September 20X3.

3.2 Option to apply derecognition rules retrospectively from a chosen date

Notwithstanding the requirement to apply IFRS 9's rules on derecognition prospectively from the date of transition to IFRSs, an entity may choose to apply them retrospectively from a date of the entity's choosing, provided that the information needed to apply IFRS 9 to financial assets and financial liabilities derecognised as a result of past transactions was obtained at the time of initially accounting for those transactions (see **example 3.1B**). [IFRS 1:B3]

3.3 Hedge accounting

IFRS 1 prohibits retrospective application of IFRS 9 in respect of hedge accounting. [IFRS 1:B4 - B6] This is consistent with the general hedging requirements of IFRS 9 under which hedge accounting is only ever available prospectively if the hedge relationship is appropriately designated, documented and satisfies all other hedge accounting criteria (see **chapter B9**).

At the date of transition to IFRSs, an entity must measure all derivatives at fair value and eliminate all deferred gains and losses arising on derivatives that were reported under previous GAAP as assets or liabilities in the statement of financial position in respect of hedge relationships under previous GAAP because these do not qualify for recognition as assets and liabilities under IFRSs. [IFRS 1:B4]

If, before the date of transition to IFRSs, a transaction had been designated as a hedge of a type that qualifies for hedge accounting under IFRS 9 but the hedge does not meet all the specific conditions for hedge accounting in IFRS 9, the requirements of IFRS 9:6.5.6 and IFRS 9:6.5.7 should be applied to discontinue hedge accounting. [IFRS 1:B6]

The designation and documentation of a hedge relationship must be completed on or before the date of transition to IFRSs if the hedge relationship is to qualify for hedge accounting from that date. Hedge accounting can be applied prospectively only from the date that the hedge relationship is fully designated and documented. [IFRS 1:IG60]

When an entity first applies IFRS 9, it may choose as its accounting policy to continue to apply the hedge accounting requirements of IAS 39 *Financial Instruments: Recognition and Measurement* instead of the requirements in Chapter 6 of IFRS 9. [IFRS 9:7.2.21] In other words, IFRS 9:7.2.21 permits entities that already apply IFRSs and that are applying IFRS 9 for the first time to continue to use the hedge accounting requirements in IAS 39.

This raises the question of whether a first-time adopter of IFRSs applying IFRS 9 in its first IFRS financial statements is permitted to apply IFRS 9:7.2.21 so that it effectively has an accounting policy choice between applying the hedge accounting requirements in IAS 39 or IFRS 9.

Because the transition provisions in IFRSs apply to changes in accounting policies made by entities that already use IFRSs, they do not apply to a first-time adopter's transition to IFRSs except in the circumstances specified in IFRS 1, Appendices B to E. [IFRS 1:9]

IFRS 1, Appendices B to E do not provide any exception equivalent to the requirements of IFRS 9:7.2.21. Therefore, the choice between applying the hedge accounting requirements of IAS 39 or IFRS 9 is not available to a first-time adopter of IFRSs applying IFRS 9.

It is worth noting that if a first-time adopter of IFRSs wishes to apply the hedge accounting requirements of IAS 39, instead of those in IFRS 9, this can be achieved if the first-time adopter's date of transition to IFRSs is prior to the effective date of IFRS 9 (1 January 2018). The first-time adopter could in that case adopt IAS 39 in full in its first IFRS financial statements and then adopt IFRS 9, applying IFRS 9's transition provisions, in a subsequent period (either at or before IFRS 9's effective date). However, this approach is unlikely to be attractive to most first-time adopters because it may be burdensome to adopt IAS 39 in full and transition to IFRS 9 at a later date.

3.3.1 Re-designation or discontinuation of hedge relationships of a type that do not comply with IFRS 9

When a first-time adopter has a hedge relationship of a type that does not qualify for hedge accounting under IFRS 9 (e.g. when the hedging instrument is a stand-alone written option or a net written option; or where the hedged item is a net position in a cash flow hedge of a risk other than foreign currency risk), the entity should not reflect that hedge relationship in its opening IFRS statement of financial position. However, if an entity designated a net position as a hedged item under previous GAAP, it may designate as a hedged item in accordance with IFRSs within that net position, or a net position that meets the requirements in IFRS 9:6.6.1, provided that it does so no later than the date of transition to IFRSs and provided that all other hedge accounting criteria are met. [IFRS 1:B5]

3.3.1.1 Fair value hedge under previous GAAP of a type that does not qualify as a fair value hedge under IFRSs

Example 3.3.1.1

Non-qualifying hedge (1)

Entity J is fair value hedging issued fixed rate, non-prepayable debt for interest rate risk under previous GAAP with an interest rate swap whereby Entity J receives a fixed rate of interest and pays LIBOR. The interest rate swap contains an option for the Bank to cancel the swap at any time at a settlement amount of zero (the bank will cancel the swap when it is unfavourable to them). Under IFRSs, the debt instrument will be carried at amortised cost.

How should this relationship be accounted for on first-time adoption of IFRSs?

Entity J has written an option embedded in the swap. A stand-alone written option or net written option does not qualify as a hedging instrument unless it is designated as an offset to a purchased option, including one that is embedded in another financial instrument. [IFRS 9:B6.2.4] Because the debt is non-prepayable and, therefore, does not have an equal and opposite embedded purchased option, the hedging instrument is not a qualifying instrument. The difference between the fair value of the interest rate swap and its previously reported carrying amount, together with the difference between the debt's amortised cost and its previously reported carrying amount, should be recognised directly in opening retained earnings. No fair value hedging adjustment to the hedged debt is allowed.

3.3.1.2 Cash flow hedge under previous GAAP that does not qualify as a cash flow hedge under IFRSs

Example 3.3.1.2

Non-qualifying hedge (2)

If a forecasted transaction is not expected to occur at the date of transition to IFRSs, how should any net cumulative gains or losses arising on measurement at fair value of the hedging instrument be accounted for at the date of transition?

If, at the date of transition to IFRSs, the forecasted transaction is not expected to occur the hedge does not qualify as a cash flow hedge. A first-time adopter reclassifies any net cumulative gain or loss reported in other comprehensive income under previous GAAP to retained earnings at the date of transition in accordance with IFRS 1:11.

If the derivative instrument was carried at cost, and no changes in value of the derivative were recognised in other comprehensive income, the full amount of the adjustment to the derivative asset or liability necessary to recognise the derivative at fair value should be recognised in retained earnings if hedge accounting is not permitted. If the derivative instrument was carried at an amount other than fair value with a deferred debit or credit in the statement of financial position recognised as an offset, that deferred debit or credit should be reversed through retained earnings if it does not meet the appropriate recognition criteria under IFRSs, and the value of the derivative brought up to its fair value at the date of transition.

3.3.2 Hedge relationships of a type that continue to qualify under IFRS 9

For a hedge relationship to continue to qualify as a hedge relationship at the date of transition to IFRSs, it must meet all of the hedge accounting criteria (see **chapters B9** and **B10**). In particular, the designation and documentation of a hedge relationship must be completed on or before the date of transition to IFRSs if the hedge relationship is to qualify for hedge accounting from that date. Hedge accounting can be applied prospectively only from the date that the hedge relationship is fully designated and documented.

For a first-time adopter of IFRSs, this may be a significant change from previous GAAP which may not have required such rigorous hedge designation and documentation. Hedge accounting under IFRS 9, and hence on first-time adoption of IFRSs, can only be applied prospectively from the date that the hedge relationship is fully designated and documented, subject to all other hedge accounting requirements of IFRS 9 being met.

If an entity designates and documents a hedge relationship in accordance with IFRS 9 on or before the date of transition to IFRSs the effective start date of the hedge relationship for the purpose of deriving the hypothetical derivative (used to measure the hedged item, see **5.4.1** in **chapter B9**) could be a date before the date of transition to IFRSs. This is because the combination of the hedge accounting transition adjustments posted for qualifying cash flow hedges (see **3.3.2.2**) and application of hedge accounting from the date of transition to IFRSs has a similar effect to applying hedge accounting from the point the hedge relationship first arose. However, if the hedge relationship is documented and designated on a date after the date of transition to IFRSs the date of documentation and designation would be used as the start date of the hedge for the purpose of deriving the hypothetical derivative. This is illustrated in the following example.

Example 3.3.2

Determining the hypothetical derivative

Entity A is a first time adopter of IFRSs. Its date of transition to IFRSs is 1 January 20X8. At the date of transition, Entity A has an issued 1-month LIBOR floating rate bond outstanding which will be measured at amortised cost under IFRS 9 and an interest rate swap with matching critical terms that pays fixed interest and receives 1-month LIBOR which in the absence of hedge accounting would be measured at FVTPL. The bond was issued, and the swap was entered into, on 1 September 20X5 and under its previous GAAP the entity accounted for the swap by only accruing the net cash flows of the swap (i.e. it did not recognise the swap at FVTPL).

Entity A wishes to apply cash flow hedge accounting from the date of transition to IFRSs and documents and designates the cash flow hedge on 1 January 20X8. Consequently, from the date of transition to IFRSs the IFRS 9 cash flow hedge accounting requirements apply (see **6.5** in **chapter B9**). For the period up to the date of transition to IFRSs, the cash flow hedge accounting transition requirements apply (see **3.3.2.2**).

To measure the change in present value of the hedged item for changes in the hedged risk from the date of transition, Entity A uses the hypothetical derivative method. A critical feature of the hypothetical derivative is that it has nil fair value on the date of designation. In this scenario, because of the transition adjustments for the cash flow hedge and the fact that the hedge was designated under IFRS 9 on the date of transition to IFRSs it could be argued that the hedge relationship is effectively a continuing hedge from 1 September 20X5. Consequently it would be appropriate to use 1 September 20X5 as the designation date for the purpose of deriving the hypothetical derivative.

> This treatment would not be appropriate if Entity A had not documented and designated the hedge on or before the date of transition to IFRSs. For example, if Entity A designated the hedge on 1 February 20X8, then it could not be argued that the hedge is effectively a continuing hedge since 1 September 20X5 because of the break in the hedge relationship between 1 January 20X8 and 1 February 20X8. Instead, the hypothetical derivative would be derived using the designation date of 1 February 20X8.

3.3.2.1 Qualifying fair value hedges

Under its previous GAAP, an entity may have deferred or not recognised gains and losses on a fair value hedge of a hedged item that is not measured at fair value. In these circumstances, IFRS 1 requires an adjustment (in the opening balance of retained earnings) to the carrying amount of the hedged item at the date of transition provided that the hedge is of a type that would be a qualifying hedge relationship under IFRS 9. This adjustment is the lower of:

[IFRS 1:IG60A]

(a) that portion of the cumulative change in the fair value of the hedged item that reflects the designated hedged risk and was not recognised under previous GAAP; and

(b) that portion of the cumulative change in the fair value of the hedging instrument that reflects the designated hedged risk and, under previous GAAP, was either (i) not recognised or (ii) deferred in the statement of financial position as an asset or liability.

These requirements result in the hedged item being adjusted by the cumulative change in the fair value of the hedged item due to the designated risk when the fair value of the hedging instrument is more than the exposure on the hedged item. This entry is equivalent to the entry that would have been recognised had the entity always applied IFRSs. The difference between the carrying value of the hedged item under IFRSs and previous GAAP will be recognised in retained earnings if the item is measured at amortised cost, or if measured at fair value through other comprehensive income partly in retained earnings (for the fair value hedge adjustment element) and in a separate component of equity for the remaining revaluation element.

If the fair value of the derivative is less than the exposure of the hedged item, the hedged item is adjusted to the value of the derivative which would have been different had the entity always applied IFRSs.

Example 3.3.2.1

Qualifying fair value hedges

Assume for both of the following scenarios that the hedge relationship is one that is a qualifying hedge relationship under IFRS 9 and, therefore, qualifies for hedge accounting at the date of transition to IFRSs.

Scenario A

Entity D has an issued fixed rate bond (CU100 million) and a receive fixed rate CU pay floating 3-month CU LIBOR interest rate swap that it has designated in a fair value hedge of the fixed rate bond (with the designated risk being fair value interest rate exposure due to changes in 3-month CU LIBOR). Under Entity D's previous GAAP, changes in the fair value of the swap were not recognised in the financial statements and the carrying amount of the debt was not adjusted for changes in fair value attributable to the designated risk (3-month CU LIBOR). There were no transaction costs on issue of the debt and the debt was measured under previous GAAP at CU100 million.

At the date of transition to IFRSs, the fair value of the bond is CU70 million. Of the CU30 million cumulative changes in the value of the bond since its issue (when its fair value was CU100 million), CU20 million is determined to be due to changes in the 3-month CU LIBOR interest rate while CU10 million relates to changes in Entity D's credit risk. At the date of transition to IFRSs, the cumulative changes in the fair value of the swap (not reflected in the financial statements under previous GAAP) amount to CU21 million of which CU19.5 million is attributable to the hedged risk (changes in the 3-month CU LIBOR rate).

In accordance with IFRS 1:IG60A, on transition to IFRSs, the hedged item (the fixed rate bond) is adjusted by CU19.5 million such that its carrying amount in the opening statement of financial position is CU80.5 million (CU100 million less the adjustment of CU19.5 million). The CU19.5 million adjustment is the lower of the portion of the cumulative change in the fair value of the hedged item due to the designated hedged risk and the portion of the cumulative change in the fair value of the hedging instrument due to the designated hedged risk (CU20 million and CU19.5 million respectively).

At the date of transition Entity F makes the following entries.

		CU million	CU million
Dr	Fixed rate bond	19.5	
Cr	Retained earnings		19.5

To adjust the hedged item for the designated risk.

		CU million	CU million
Dr	Retained earnings	21.0	
Cr	Derivative liability		21.0

To recognise the swap at fair value.

Scenario B

Entity F has a fixed rate investment that is measured at amortised cost under previous GAAP that it originally acquired at its par amount for CU100 million some years ago. There were no transaction costs at acquisition. On acquisition of the investment, Entity F also entered into a receive floating 1-month CU LIBOR pay fixed CU interest rate swap that it designated under previous GAAP as a hedging instrument in a fair value hedge of the fixed rate investment (with the hedged risk being fair value interest rate risk due to changes in the 1-month CU LIBOR rate).

At the date of transition to IFRSs, the fair value of the fixed rate investment is CU115 million. Under IFRSs the asset will be measured at amortised cost. Changes in the fair value of the investment have not been recognised under previous GAAP. Of the CU15 million cumulative change in the value of the fixed rate investment since it was acquired (when its fair value was CU100 million), CU13 million is determined to be due to fair value changes due to changes in the 1-month CU LIBOR rate while CU2 million relates to changes in the issuer's credit risk. At the date of transition, the cumulative change in the fair value of the swap (not reflected in the financial statements under previous GAAP) amounts to CU12 million, all of which is determined to relate to the hedged risk (changes in the 1-month CU LIBOR rate).

At the date of transition, the fixed rate investment is adjusted by CU12 million such that its carrying amount in the opening statement of financial position is CU112 million (CU100 million plus the adjustment of CU12 million). This adjustment is the lower of the portion of the cumulative change in the fair value of the hedged item due to the designated hedged risk and the portion of the cumulative change in the fair value of the hedging instrument due to the designated hedged risk (CU13 million and CU12 million respectively).

On transition Entity F makes the following entries.

		CU million	**CU million**
Dr	Fixed rate investment	12	
Cr	Retained earnings		12

To adjust the hedged item.

		CU million	**CU million**
Dr	Retained earnings	12	
Cr	Derivative liability		12

To recognise the swap at fair value.

3.3.2.2 Qualifying cash flow hedges

An entity may have deferred gains and losses on a cash flow hedge of a forecast transaction. If, at the date of transition to IFRSs, the hedge relationship is of a type that would be a qualifying hedge relationship under IFRS 9 and it is still expected to occur, the entire deferred gain or loss on the hedging instrument is recognised in equity. [IFRS 1:IG60B] Note that this initial entry in or reclassification into equity (depending on whether the gains and losses were either previously not recognised or deferred in the statement of financial position outside of equity) comprises the entire cumulative gain or loss on the hedging instrument as at the date of transition regardless of its effectiveness up to that date.

The amount recognised in equity in the cash flow hedge reserve has to be reclassified out of the cash flow hedge reserve in accordance with the requirements for cash flow hedge accounting in IFRS 9 (see **chapter B9**).

Example 3.3.2.2

Qualifying cash flow hedges

Prior to the date of transition, a Sterling functional currency entity expects, with a high degree of probability, to sell goods to one of its customers for €1 million on a date after the date of transition to IFRSs. The entity enters into a forward contract to sell €1 million and buy £ at a forward rate of £0.7:€1 on the expected date of sale of the goods. Under previous GAAP, the entity did not recognise the fair value of the forward contract in its statement of financial position.

Assume that on date of transition:

- the fair value of the forward contract is £(200,000), i.e. it is a liability; and
- the sale of goods for €1 million at the date originally forecast is still a highly probable forecast transaction.

At the date of transition, the entire cumulative loss on the forward contract to date is recognised in equity as follows.

		£	£
Dr	Equity	200,000	
Cr	Forward contract		200,000

To recognise the fair value of the forward contract.

After the date of transition to IFRSs, the accounting treatment depends on the whether the hedge accounting conditions are still met (including whether the forecast transaction is highly probable).

(a) If the forecast transaction is no longer expected to occur then the hedge accounting conditions are not met and so the entire cumulative gain/loss on the forward contract deferred in equity until that date (including that portion deferred on transition) is immediately reclassified from equity to profit or loss. [IFRS 9:6.5.12(b)]

(b) If the forecast transaction is not highly probable but is still expected to occur then the hedge accounting conditions are not met and so subsequent gains and losses on the forward contract are recognised in profit or loss. However, the cumulative gain/loss on the forward contract deferred in equity (including that portion deferred on transition) up until the forecast transaction is no longer highly probable, remains in equity until either the transaction takes place (see (c) below) or it is no longer expected to occur (see (a) above). [IFRS 9:6.5.12(a)]

(c) The highly probable forecast transaction takes place as expected. The cumulative gains/losses on the hedging instrument (including that portion deferred on transition) will be released to profit or loss at the same time as the highly probable forecast transaction (in the form of Euro denominated revenues) affects profit or loss (i.e. when the Euro denominated sale occurs).

3.3.2.3 Qualifying net investment hedges

Neither IFRS 9 nor IFRS 1 contains any explicit guidance as to the transitional requirements in respect of hedges of a net investment in a foreign operation.

IFRS 9:6.5.13(a) states that the portion of the gain or loss on the hedging instrument that is determined to be an effective hedge shall be recognised in other comprehensive income in accordance with IFRS 9:6.5.11, which is a paragraph on cash flow hedging. It may, therefore, be argued that similar transitional provisions to those for cash flow hedging should be applied in the case of hedges of a net investment in a foreign operation. This would imply that, provided that the hedge relationship qualifies for hedge accounting under IFRS 9, the cumulative gain/loss on the hedging instrument at the date of transition (that under previous GAAP may or may not have been recorded in the statement of financial position) is recognised in equity in the net investment hedging reserve. Therefore, for a derivative hedging instrument (e.g. cross-currency swap or foreign currency forward contract) not previously reflected in the statement of financial position under previous GAAP, the following journal entry is required.

Dr/Cr	Fair value of derivative (statement of financial position)	X
Cr/Dr	Equity (net investment hedging reserve)	X

This amount classified in equity is reclassified to profit or loss upon disposal of the foreign operation in accordance with the requirements of IFRS 9:6.5.14 (see **chapter B9** for more details on hedging a net investment in a foreign operation). The reclassification of the deferred fair value gains/losses on the hedging instrument from equity to profit or loss will offset either fully or partially the foreign exchange gains/losses recognised in other comprehensive income arising on the retranslation of the net assets of the foreign operation in accordance with IAS 21 *The Effects of Changes in Foreign Exchange Rates*.

Pre-transition gains and losses recognised in equity will not be reclassified from equity to profit or loss in accordance with IFRS 9:6.5.13 when an entity has elected to reset the cumulative translation reserve in equity to zero in accordance with IFRS 1:D13. Applying the exemption in IFRS 1:D13, the cumulative translation differences for all foreign operations are deemed to be zero at the date of transition and, therefore, only subsequent translation differences that arise after the date of the transition will be reclassified from equity to profit or loss on disposal of the foreign operation. If an entity has applied net investment hedge accounting in the consolidated financial statements under previous GAAP, and the related hedging reserve is set to zero at the date of transition to IFRSs, the gains and losses on the hedging instrument prior to the date of transition should be recognised in the opening balance of retained earnings.

3.4 Government grants

A first-time adopter shall classify all government loans received as a financial liability or an equity instrument in accordance with IAS 32 *Financial Instruments: Presentation*. Except as permitted by IFRS:B11, a first-time adopter shall apply the requirements in IFRS 9 *Financial Instruments* and IAS 20 *Accounting for Government Grants and Disclosure of Government Assistance* prospectively to government loans existing at the date of transition to IFRSs and shall not recognise the corresponding benefit of a government loan at a below-market rate of interest as a government grant. Consequently, if a first-time adopter did not, under its previous GAAP, recognise and measure a government loan at a below-market rate of interest on a basis consistent with IFRS requirements, it shall use its previous GAAP carrying amount of the loan at the date of transition to IFRSs as the carrying amount of the loan in the opening IFRS statement of financial position. An entity shall apply IFRS 9 to the measurement of such loans after the date of transition to IFRSs. [IFRS 1:B10]

Despite IFRS 1:B10, an entity may apply the requirements in IFRS 9 and IAS 20 retrospectively to any government loan originated before the date of transition to IFRSs, provided that the information needed to do so had been obtained at the time of initially accounting for that loan. [IFRS 1:B11]

The requirements and guidance in IFRS 1:B10 and B11 do not preclude an entity from being able to use the exemptions described in IFRS 1:D19 - D19D (see **2.4**) relating to the designation of previously recognised financial instruments at fair value through profit or loss. [IFRS 1:B12]

4 Exemption from requirement to present comparative information in accordance with IFRS 9

If an entity is a first-time adopter of IFRSs in an annual period beginning before 1 January 2019 and applies the completed version of IFRS 9 (issued in 2014), the comparative information in the entity's first IFRS financial statements need not comply with IFRS 7 *Financial Instruments: Disclosure* or the completed version of IFRS 9, to the extent that the disclosures required by IFRS 7 relate to items within the scope of IFRS 9. For such entities, references to the 'date of transition to IFRSs' shall mean, in the case of IFRS 9 and IFRS 7 only, the beginning of the first IFRS reporting period. [IFRS 1:E1] In effect, an entity that adopts IFRSs for annual periods beginning before 1 January 2019 and chooses to apply IFRS 9 has the choice of whether or not to apply IFRS 9 (and the related disclosures in IFRS 7) to the comparative period(s) in the first year of adoption of IFRSs.

If a first-time adopter of IFRSs chooses not to present comparative information in accordance with IFRS 9 (and the related disclosures in IFRS 7), the entity is required to:

[IFRS 1:E2]

(a) apply the recognition and measurement requirements of its previous GAAP in place of the requirements of IFRS 9 to comparative information about financial instruments within the scope of IFRS 9;

(b) disclose this fact together with the basis used to prepare this information;

(c) treat any adjustment between the statement of financial position at the comparative period's reporting date (i.e. the statement of financial position that includes comparative information under previous GAAP) and the statement of financial position at the start of the first IFRS reporting period (i.e. the first period that includes information that complies with IFRS 9 and IFRS 7) as arising from a change in accounting policy and give the disclosures required by IAS 8:28(a) - (e) & (f)(i). IAS 8:28(f)(i) applies only to amounts presented in the statement of financial position at the comparative period's reporting date; and

(d) apply IAS 1:17(c) to provide additional disclosures when compliance with the specific requirements in IFRSs is insufficient to enable users to understand the impact of particular transactions, other events and conditions on the entity's financial position and financial performance.

B13 Transition to IFRS 9

Contents

1 Introduction

When an IFRS reporter applies IFRS 9 for the first time, it is required to comply with the specific transitional provisions detailed in IFRS 9 and other Standards that were consequentially amended when IFRS 9 was issued. These transitional provisions, which are discussed in detail in this chapter, apply only to continuing IFRS reporters; entities preparing their first IFRS financial statements should instead refer to the requirements of IFRS 1 *First-time Adoption of IFRSs* which are described in **chapter B12**.

Transitioning to IFRS 9 is complex, because the requirements of IFRS 9 are generally applied retrospectively. However, there are various practical expedients and elections with respect to classification, measurement, impairment and hedge accounting available at the date of transition to IFRS 9 which can make transition less onerous.

IFRS 9 has been issued in stages. The first instalment was issued in November 2009 (IFRS 9(2009)) and it only dealt with the classification and measurement of financial assets. In October 2010, the Standard was reissued (IFRS 9(2010)) to include the classification and measurement of financial liabilities, recognition and derecognition, and the requirements for separating embedded derivatives.

In 2013, IFRS 9 was reissued to include the new general hedge accounting model and in 2014 the Standard was finalised to include impairment as well as amendments to classification and measurement of financial assets.

The finalised version of IFRS 9 issued in 2014 has an effective date of 1 January 2018. That version also supersedes IFRS 9(2009), IFRS 9(2010) and IFRS (2013). However, for annual periods beginning before 1 January 2018, an entity may elect to apply earlier version instead of applying IFRS 9(2014) if, and only if, the entity's relevant date of initial application is before 1 February 2015. [IFRS 9:7.3.2]

In practice, there are only two differences in accounting treatment between applying IFRS 9(2009) (combined with the relevant requirements of IAS 39) and IFRS 9(2010). If IFRS 9(2009) is applied, all fair value gains and losses on financial liabilities that are designated as at FVTPL will be recognised in profit or loss, whereas IFRS 9(2010) requires that in most cases the change in fair value associated with the credit risk of the liability is recognised in other comprehensive income (see **7.1.2.5** in **chapter B3**). The other difference is that if IFRS 9(2009) is applied, certain derivative financial liabilities that result in the delivery of an unquoted equity instrument will be measured at cost, whereas IFRS 9(2010) requires them to be measured at fair value.

The publication of IFRS 9(2013) made substantial changes to the general hedge accounting model that was previously included in IAS 39, though

IFRS 9:7.2.21 allows entities the choice when they first apply IFRS 9 to choose as an accounting policy to continue to apply the hedge accounting requirements of IAS 39 instead of the hedge accounting requirements of IFRS 9. All the hedge accounting requirements in IFRS 9(2013) were then carried over into IFRS 9(2014) which introduced a new model for impairment of financial assets as well as amended the classification and measurement requirements for financial assets that were firstly introduced in IFRS 9(2009). Also, IFRS 9:6.1.3 permits an entity that applies the hedge accounting requirements of IFRS 9 to apply the requirements of IAS 39 when designating a fair value hedge of interest rate of a portfolio of financial assets or financial liabilities, with all other hedge accounting designations following the IFRS 9 hedge accounting requirements.

This volume assumes that an entity is applying the final and complete version of IFRS 9 (i.e. IFRS 9(2014)) in full and has therefore chosen as its accounting policy to apply the hedge accounting requirements of IFRS 9(2014). For the remainder of this chapter, and throughout this volume, unless otherwise stated, references to IFRS 9 are to the 2014 version of the Standard.

2 Summary of significant differences

The impact of the transition from IAS 39 to IFRS 9 will vary for different entities depending on the nature and complexity of financial instruments held and issued. It is not practicable to summarise all of the differences between the Standards, and entities will need to understand the detailed requirements of IFRS 9 before they can determine the impact of transition in their particular circumstances. As an overview, the following table provides a very high level comparison of IAS 39 and IFRS 9.

Accounting requirement	Comparison of IAS 39 and IFRS 9
Scope	The scope of IAS 39 and IFRS 9 are broadly similar. The main difference is the ability in IFRS 9 to irrevocably designate as measured at FVTPL certain contracts to buy or sell a non-financial item even if it was entered into for the purpose of the receipt or delivery of a non-financial item in accordance with the entity's expected purchase, sale or usage requirements. Also the measurement of certain written loan commitments and written financial guarantee contracts has changed as previously they were partly measured in accordance with IAS 37 *Provisions, Contingent Liabilities and Contingent Asset* whereas under IFRS 9 they are partly measured using the impairment measurement requirements of IFRS 9.

Accounting requirement	Comparison of IAS 39 and IFRS 9
Classification – assets	IAS 39 has four classification categories: (i) FVTPL, (ii) held to maturity, (iii) available-for-sale and (iv) loans and receivables. IFRS 9 has three measurement categories (i) FVTPL, (ii) FVTOCI and (iii) amortised cost. The classification approach in IFRS 9 prohibits financial assets in the scope of IFRS 9 to be assessed for embedded derivatives, whereas this is required for all financial assets in the scope of IAS 39 that are not measured at FVTPL. Like IAS 39, the FVTPL category in IFRS 9 consists of financial assets that are automatically classified as FVTPL because they meet the FVTPL criteria and those that the entity chooses to designate at FVTPL under a 'fair value option'. Assets that are held for trading will be measured at FVTPL under both Standards. However, IFRS 9 requires all assets to automatically be classified at FVTPL if they fail the amortised cost or FVTOCI criteria. IAS 39 has a different approach, as assets that meet the loans and receivables criteria may be elected, without restriction, to be classified as available for sale at initial recognition. Further, the criterion for designation at fair value option under IFRS 9 is more restrictive. Both IAS 39 and IFRS 9 require, and in some cases permit, debt and equity instruments to be measured at FVTOCI. In IAS 39 this is the default measurement categories for non-held for trading equity instruments, with an election to be measured at FVTPL if the criteria are met. In IFRS 9 the default category for holdings of equity instruments is FVTPL, with an election for non-held for trading equity instruments to be measured at FVTOCI if the criteria are met. Under IFRS 9, the criteria for measuring debt instruments at FVTOCI is partly based on the business model for holding the asset, whereas in IAS 39 it is not. Further, fair value movements on assets measured at FVTOCI under IAS 39 are reclassified from equity to profit or loss on impairment or disposal under IAS 39. Under IFRS 9, all gains or losses (except for dividend income) arising on equity investments designated at FVTOCI under IFRS 9 are never reclassified; for debt instruments amounts are reclassified from equity to profit or loss on disposal.
Classification – liabilities	The classification of financial liabilities is broadly the same under the two Standards; the default is measurement at amortised cost, with some liabilities being classified as FVTPL either because they are held for trading or because they meet specified criteria for designation at FVTPL under the fair value option.

Accounting requirement	Comparison of IAS 39 and IFRS 9
	The two differences are: • derivative liabilities that will result in the delivery of an unquoted equity investment must be measured at cost under IAS 39 if the fair value of the unquoted equity investments cannot be determined reliably whereas, under IFRS 9, they are required to be measured at FVTPL; and • the change in fair value that is attributable to changes in credit risk of a financial liability designated at FVTPL will generally be recognised in other comprehensive income under IFRS 9, whereas under IAS 39 these amounts are always recognised in profit or loss.
Distinction between liabilities and equity	Requirements are specified in IAS 32 and are not affected by the transition from IAS 39 to IFRS 9.
Measurement basis	IAS 39 and IFRS 9 both measure financial assets and financial liabilities at amortised cost and fair value (though amortised cost measurement differs because the impairment requirements for debt instruments differ). IAS 39 also permits measurement at cost for certain equity investments and derivatives over such investments, but IFRS 9 does not permit any instruments to be measured at cost.
Impairment	IAS 39 requires an assessment and measurement of impairment of assets measured at cost, amortised cost and classified as AFS. IFRS 9 requires the same measurement basis for impairment for all items in the scope of the impairment requirements. This differs to IAS 39 where impairment was calculated differently for amortised cost assets and available-for-sale assets. Further, IFRS 9 applies the same impairment measurement approach to certain loan commitments and financial guarantee contracts where previously these were measured differently in accordance with IAS 37 *Provisions, Contingent Liabilities and Contingent Assets*. The impairment model under IFRS 9 is based on expected credit losses while the model under IAS 39 was based on incurred losses. Under IFRS 9, the loan loss allowance is for either 12-month expected credit losses or lifetime expected credit losses. The latter applies if credit risk has increased significantly since initial recognition of the financial instrument. A different approach applies for purchased or originated credit-impaired financial assets (e.g. distressed debt).

Accounting requirement	Comparison of IAS 39 and IFRS 9
Hedge accounting	Entities have an accounting policy choice under IFRS 9 as to whether to continue to apply the hedge accounting model in IAS 39 or IFRS 9. They also have a choice whether, for fair value hedges of interest rate risk on a portfolio of financial assets or financial liabilities only, to apply the specific requirements in IAS 39 for those types of hedges or use the requirements in IFRS 9. The new requirements aim to have a greater link between hedge accounting and an entity's risk management policies. Therefore, IFRS 9 does not contain as many restrictions as IAS 39 and has expanded the scope of eligible hedging relationships. There are fewer restrictions on hedging non-financial items, hedging group of items and net positions compared with IAS 39. IAS 39 defines a hedge as highly effective if the offset between the changes in fair value or cash flows of the hedging instrument and the hedged item is in the range of 80-125 per cent. This range was not included in IFRS 9 and instead emphasis is put on the economic relationship between the hedging instrument and the hedged item, taking into account the credit risk and the hedge ratio. As opposed to IAS 39, it is not appropriate for an entity to voluntarily discontinue hedge accounting when the risk management objective has not changed for the hedging relationship. This means, an entity cannot elect to revoke the designation of a hedging relationship for as long as the hedge accounting criteria are met.

3 Effective date

Entities are required to apply IFRS 9 for annual periods beginning on or after 1 January 2018. Earlier application is permitted. If an entity applies IFRS 9 in its financial statements for a period beginning before 1 January 2018, it is required to disclose that fact and must apply all of the requirements in IFRS 9 at the same time. [IFRS 9:7.1.1] Despite this, for annual periods beginning before 1 January 2018, an entity may elect to early apply only the requirements for the presentation of gains and losses on financial liabilities designated as at FVTPL in IFRS 9:5.7.1(c), 5.7.7 - 5.7.9, 7.2.14 and B5.7.5 - B5.7.20 without applying the other requirements in the Standard. This permits an entity to early adopt the presentation of fair value changes in own credit risk on financial liabilities designated as at FVTPL in other comprehensive income (see **7.1.2** in **chapter B3**). If this element is early adopted this fact must be disclosed along with ongoing related disclosures set out in IFRS 7:10 - 11 (see **4.1.3** in **chapter B11**).

An entity with a date of initial application before 1 February 2015 can apply earlier versions of IFRS 9 in the annual periods that begin prior to 1 January 2018. The exemption is explained in **section 1**. This gives early adopters of IFRS 9 an array of different choices as to how they may apply IFRS 9 in the annual periods that begin prior to 1 January 2018. The following table summarises the various alternatives available to those early applying IFRS 9 assuming the entity is transitioning from applying IAS 39 in full and the annual period of the entity begins on 1 January.

Alternative	Early adoption	Available post 1 January 2018?	General hedge accounting (excluding macro fair value hedge accounting)	Macro fair value hedge accounting	Fair value changes in own credit risk on financial liabilities designated at FVTPL	Financial assets classif-ication and measure-ment	Impairment model
Apply IAS 39 in full except early adopt IFRS 9 own credit risk [IFRS 9 (2010):7.1.1A; IFRS 9 (2013):7.1.2; or IFRS 9 (2014):7.1.2]	Early adoption of own credit risk permitted up to IFRS 9 (2014) effective date of 1 January 2018	No	IAS 39	IAS 39	IFRS 9 (fair value gains/ losses in OCI)	IAS 39	IAS 39 (incurred loss)
Apply all of IFRS 9(2014) [IFRS 9 (2014):7.1.1]	Early adoption available until IFRS 9 (2014) effective date of 1 January 2018	Yes	IFRS 9	IFRS 9	IFRS 9 (fair value gains/ losses in OCI)	IFRS 9 (2014)	IFRS 9 (expected loss)
Apply all of IFRS 9 (2014) except for all of hedge accounting [IFRS 9 (2014):7.1.1 & 7.2.21]	Early adoption available until IFRS 9 (2014) effective date of 1 January 2018 but only for those transitioning from IAS 39	Yes	IAS 39	IAS 39	IFRS 9 (fair value gains/ losses in OCI)	IFRS 9 (2014)	IFRS 9 (expected loss)
Apply all of IFRS 9 (2014) except for macro fair value hedge accounting [IFRS 9 (2014):7.1.1 & 6.1.3]	Available for all adopters of IFRS 9 (2014)	Yes	IFRS 9	IAS 39	IFRS 9 (fair value gains/ losses in OCI)	IFRS 9 (2014)	IFRS 9 (expected loss)

Alternative	Early adoption	Available post 1 January 2018?	General hedge accounting (excluding macro fair value hedge accounting)	Macro fair value hedge accounting	Fair value changes in own credit risk on financial liabilities designated at FVTPL	Financial assets classif-ication and measure-ment	Impairment model
Apply IFRS 9 (2013) [IFRS 9 (2013):7.3.2]	Only available if date of initial application is before 1 February 2015	No	IFRS 9	IFRS 9	IFRS 9 (fair value gains/ losses in OCI)	IFRS 9 (2009)	IAS 39 (incurred loss)
Apply all of IFRS 9 (2013) except for all of hedge accounting [IFRS 9 (2014):7.3.2 and IFRS 9 (2013):7.2.16]	Available for those transitioning from IAS 39 whose date of initial application is before 1 February 2015	No	IAS 39	IAS 39	IFRS 9 (fair value gains/ losses in OCI)	IFRS 9 (2009)	IAS 39 (incurred loss)
Apply all of IFRS 9 (2013) except for macro fair value hedge accounting [IFRS 9 (2014):7.3.2 and IFRS 9 (2013):6.1.3]	Available for all adopters of IFRS 9 (2013)	No	IFRS 9	IAS 39	IFRS 9 (fair value gains/ losses in OCI)	IFRS 9 (2009)	IAS 39 (incurred loss)
Apply IFRS 9 (2010) [IFRS 9 (2010):7.3.2]	Only available if date of initial application is before 1 February 2015	No	IAS 39	IAS 39	IFRS 9 (fair value gains/ losses in OCI)	IFRS 9 (2009)	IAS 39 (incurred loss)
Apply IFRS 9 (2009) [IFRS 9 (2009):8.1.1]	Only available if date of initial application is before 1 February 2015	No	IAS 39	IAS 39	IAS 39 (fair value gains/ losses in profit or loss)	IFRS 9 (2009)	IAS 39 (incurred loss)

Alternative	Early adoption	Available post 1 January 2018?	General hedge accounting (excluding macro fair value hedge accounting)	Macro fair value hedge accounting	Fair value changes in own credit risk on financial liabilities designated at FVTPL	Financial assets classification and measurement	Impairment model
Apply IFRS 9 (2009) and provisions for fair value of own credit risk in OCI [IFRS 9 (2009):8.1.1 & IFRS 9 (2010):7.1.1A; IFRS 9 (2013):7.1.2; or IFRS 9 (2014):7.1.2]	Only available if date of initial application is before 1 February 2015	No	IAS 39	IAS 39	IFRS 9 (fair value gains/ losses in OCI)	IFRS 9 (2009)	IAS 39 (incurred loss)

This volume assumes an entity is applying IFRS 9(2014) in full, including all aspects of hedge accounting.

4 Application

4.1 General requirements

An entity that applies IFRS 9 for the first time is required to apply the Standard retrospectively in accordance with IAS 8 *Accounting Policies, Changes in Accounting Estimates and Errors*, subject to certain exemptions and exceptions in applying the effective interest method (see **6.3.3**); impairment measurement requirements (see **6.4**); and hedge accounting requirements (see **4.2** and **6.5**). Furthermore, IFRS 9 is not applied to items that have already been derecognised at the date of initial application. [IFRS 9:7.2.1]

As noted in **section 6**, the date of initial application is the date an entity first applies IFRS 9 and must be the beginning of a reporting period after the issue of the Standard. Therefore, if an entity chooses to restate comparatives (see **section 5**), IFRS 9 would not apply to items in the comparative period that are derecognised before the date of initial application as the date of initial application of IFRS 9 cannot be in the comparative period in the financial statements in which IFRS 9 is first applied. For these items an entity is required to apply IAS 39 in the comparative period. The exception was first introduced in IFRS 9(2009) for financial assets to provide some transition relief and was extended to financial liabilities derecognised at the date of initial application for consistency. [IFRS 9:BC7.29] However, this transition relief was not included as an election but as a requirement. Consequently, an entity choosing to restate comparatives to allow a consistent comparison of its financial performance for the current and prior period(s) would be constrained in respect of items derecognised by the date of initial application. In these circumstances an entity could choose to provide additional disclosures if it wished.

Example 4.1A

Retrospective application

In November 20X3, Entity S reclassified certain debt instruments from FVTPL to amortised cost as permitted by IAS 39. The assets were acquired in 20X2. Entity S's annual reporting period end is 31 December.

Entity S applies IFRS 9 for the first time in its annual financial statements for the year ending 31 December 20X5. Entity S's date of initial application of IFRS 9 (see **section 6**) is 1 January 20X5. The assets that were reclassified in November 20X3 continue to be recognised at the date of initial application of IFRS 9. The financial assets meet the criteria for amortised cost measurement. Entity S chooses to restate comparative information.

Because Entity S must apply IFRS 9 retrospectively to financial assets recognised at the date of initial application of IFRS 9, it must determine what the amortised cost carrying amount of the reclassified assets would have been at the start of the first comparative period (1 January 20X4) assuming the entity had measured the assets at amortised cost since their initial recognition in 20X2. Entity S must restate the results for 20X4 as if the assets were measured at amortised cost since initial recognition. This will have the effect of reversing the impact of the reclassification that occurred on November 20X3 as well as reversing the impact of the FVTPL classification prior to November 20X3.

If Entity S had elected not to restate the comparative period when first applying IFRS 9 (see **section 5**), the results for 20X4 would be unchanged from previously published, i.e. the classification that resulted from the reclassification in November 20X3 would be retained in the comparative information in the financial statements ending 31 December 20X4. However, Entity S would need to determine the amount of the adjustment needed to restate the carrying amount of the reclassified assets at the start of the current reporting period, 1 January 20X5, to reflect the classification requirements of IFRS 9. The financial assets that were reclassified in 20X3 would be restated at 1 January 20X5, with an adjustment to retained earnings or other appropriate equity component, as if the entity had classified the financial assets at amortised cost when they were initially recognised in 20X2.

Example 4.1B

Derecognition exemption

Entity W applies IFRS 9 for the first time in its financial statements for the year ending 31 March 20X5. Entity W chooses to restate comparative information when it applies IFRS for the first time (see **section 5**).

Entity W's date of initial application of IFRS 9 is 1 April 20X4 (i.e. the beginning of the first annual period in which it applies IFRS 9).

Entity W derecognised some available-for-sale debt and equity securities in August 20X3 and, in accordance with IAS 39, reclassified the associated gains and losses relating to those securities from equity to profit or loss.

Because the available-for-sale securities were derecognised prior to the date of initial application of IFRS 9, the accounting for these securities is unchanged, i.e. IAS 39 continues to apply for the comparative period, even though the entity is applying IFRS 9 in its annual period ending 31 March 20X5. The classification and measurement requirement in IAS 39 (including the requirements regarding effective interest rate, impairment, reclassification of gains and losses and derecognition) will apply to those assets in the comparative period, whilst IFRS 9 will apply to all other items not derecognised at 1 April 20X4 (i.e. the date of initial application).

4.2 Hedge accounting

On initial application of IFRS 9, an entity can decide to continue applying the hedge accounting requirements of IAS 39 instead of the requirements set out in IFRS 9. This decision applies to all of the entity's hedging relationships. If an entity chooses to continue applying IAS 39 for hedge accounting, it also applies IFRIC 16 *Hedges of a Net Investment in a Foreign Operation* without the consequential amendments that were made when IFRS 9 was published. Alternatively, an entity can apply the hedge accounting requirements of IFRS 9 except for fair value hedges of interest rate risk on a portfolio of financial assets or financial liabilities where the specific requirements of IAS 39 can be applied instead. [IFRS 9:6.1.3]

Except for some specific transition requirements (see **6.5**) the hedge accounting requirements of IFRS 9 shall be applied prospectively.

5 Comparative information on initial application

To reduce the burden for preparers when an entity first applies IFRS 9 it is not required to restate prior periods. [IFRS 9:7.2.15]

However, it is required to provide comprehensive disclosures about financial assets and liabilities at the date of initial application (see **section 7**). These disclosures aim to provide the necessary information for investors to understand the effect of the transition from IAS 39 to IFRS 9 and are required regardless of whether an entity restates comparative information.

An entity may restate prior periods if it is possible without the use of hindsight. If an entity does not restate prior periods, it is required to recognise any difference between the previous carrying amount and the carrying amount at the beginning of the annual reporting period that includes the date of initial application in the opening retained earnings (or other component of equity, as appropriate) of the annual reporting period that includes the date of initial application.

If an entity restates prior periods, the restated financial statements must reflect all of the requirements of IFRS 9.

Example 5

Exemption from restating prior periods

Entity A applies IFRS 9 for the first time in its annual reporting period ending 31 December 20X5. Entity A elects not to apply IFRS 9 to its comparative information. Entity A's date of initial application of IFRS 9 is 1 January 20X5.

At 31 December 20X4, Entity A had investments in equity instruments classified as available-for-sale financial assets in accordance with IAS 39. Their fair value is CU150 and the cumulative gain accumulated in the available-for-sale reserve in equity is CU40. At the date of initial application of IFRS 9, Entity A did not choose to designate the investment in equity instruments as at FVTOCI, rather they were classified as at FVTPL. Therefore, at 1 January 20X5, Entity A eliminates the available-for-sale reserve to nil and recognises a corresponding gain in retained earnings of CU40 to reflect the retrospective application of IFRS 9 to the investment in equity instruments held at the date of initial application of IFRS 9.

6 Initial application of IFRS 9

The date of initial application for IFRS 9 is the date when an entity first applies the Standard. IFRS 9 requires the date of initial application to be the beginning of a reporting period after the issue of the Standard [IFRS 9:7.2.2].

Example 6

Date of initial application

Entity A applies IFRS 9 for the first time in its financial statements for the year ending 31 December 20X8. Entity A will choose to restate one year of comparative information when it applies IFRS 9 for the first time.

Entity X's date of initial application of IFRS 9 is 1 January 20X8 (i.e. the beginning of the first annual period in which it applies IFRS 9). This date is significant when transitioning to IFRS 9 as many of the transition requirements require assessments to be performed as at, and elections to be made on, the date of initial application (see **section 6.2**).

In this scenario, the date of initial application is different to the beginning of the earliest reporting period presented under IFRS 9 which will be 1 January 20X7 because the entity is choosing to provide one year of comparative information.

Depending on the entity's chosen approach to applying IFRS 9, the transition can involve more than one date of initial application for different requirements in the case when some requirements are early adopted where others are not (see **section 1**).

6.1 Interim comparative information

If an entity prepares interim financial reports in accordance with IAS 34 *Interim Financial Reporting*, the entity need not apply the requirements in IFRS 9 to interim periods prior to the date of initial application if it is impracticable (as defined in IAS 8). [IFRS 9:7.2.16]

6.2 Classifications and designations at the date of initial application

The date of initial application of IFRS 9 is significant because it is the date at which certain conditions for classification and measurement are assessed.

6.2.1 Debt instruments held

At the date of initial application, an entity assesses whether a financial asset meets the business model test for amortised cost and FVTOCI measurement (see **chapter B2**) on the basis of the facts and circumstances that exist at that date. The resulting classification is applied retrospectively irrespective of the entity's business model in prior reporting periods. [IFRS 9:7.2.3]

The IASB chose to require the business model assessment to be performed as at the date of initial application because it believed it would be difficult, perhaps impossible, to assess that condition on the basis of circumstances that existed when the instrument first satisfied the recognition criterion in IAS 39. [IFRS 9:BC7.18]

Example 6.2.1

Business model assessment date

Entity D applies IFRS 9 for the first time in its annual financial statements for the year ending 31 December 20X5. Entity D's date of initial application of IFRS 9 is 1 January 20X5. In the first quarter of 20X4, Entity D changed its business model. Previously, its business objective in holding financial assets was to realise their fair value by disposing of the financial assets before their contractual maturity. Following a strategic review by key management personnel, that objective was changed to holding financial assets with a view to collecting the contractual cash flows from those assets.

For the purpose of classifying financial assets, Entity D's business model is assessed at the date of initial application (i.e. 1 January 20X5) and, therefore, the assessment will take account of the change in business model that occurred in the first quarter of 20X4.

If, instead, the change in business model occurred in the second quarter of 20X5, the impact would be different. Entity D would initially classify its financial assets based on its business model at 1 January 20X5, i.e. its date of initial application of IFRS 9. The change in business model in the second quarter (i.e. after the date of initial application) would potentially result in the reclassification of financial assets (as required by IFRS 9:4.4.1 & 5.6.1), which would take effect from the start of the next reporting period, i.e. the period starting 1 January 20X6 (see **section 7** in **chapter B2**).

If it is impracticable to assess a modified time value of money element on the basis of the facts and circumstances at initial recognition of the financial asset (see **5.4.3** in **chapter B2**), the contractual cash flow characteristics test is applied without taking into account that requirement. [IFRS 9:7.2.4]

If it is impracticable to assess whether the fair value of a prepayment feature was insignificant on the basis of the facts and circumstances at initial recognition of the financial asset (see **5.4.4** in **chapter B2**), an entity applies the contractual cash flow characteristics test without taking into account the exception for prepayment features.[IFRS 9:7.2.5]

6.2.2 Designation of equity investments as at FVTOCI

At the date of initial application, an entity may designate an investment in an equity instrument as at FVTOCI if it meets the specified criterion (see **5.3** in **chapter B2**). The designation should be made on the basis of the facts and circumstances at the date of initial application. [IFRS 9:7.2.8(b)]

For the purpose of designating an equity investment as at FVTOCI, an entity determines whether a financial asset falls outside the definition of held for trading as if the entity had acquired the assets at the date of initial application. [IFRS 9:B7.2.1] The classification is required to be applied retrospectively.

Example 6.2.2

Date of designation as at FVTOCI

Entity K has an investment in an equity instrument held for many years. Entity K first applies IFRS 9 in the annual reporting period ending 31 December 20X4. Entity K's date of initial application is 1 January 20X4 and, therefore, it makes its assessment regarding whether its equity investment meets the definition of held for trading at that date. Only if the investment does not meet the definition of held for trading at 1 January 20X4 can Entity K designate the investment as at FVTOCI.

6.2.3 Designation of financial assets as at FVTPL

At the date of initial application, an entity may designate a financial asset that would otherwise be accounted for at amortised cost or FVTOCI as at FVTPL if doing so eliminates or significantly reduces a measurement or recognition inconsistency ('accounting mismatch') (see **5.5.3** in **chapter B2**). The designation should be made on the basis of the facts and circumstances at the date of initial application. [IFRS 9:7.2.8]

Example 6.2.3A

Designation of financial assets as at FVTPL (1)

Entity P holds a fixed rate loan asset that is economically hedged with a pay fixed receive floating interest rate swap. The loan was initially recognised in May 20X3 but the interest rate swap was not entered into until February 20X4. Entity P first applies IFRS 9 in the annual reporting period ending 30 June 20X4. Entity P's date of initial application for IFRS 9 is 1 July 20X3.

The fixed rate loan meets the amortised cost criteria at the date of initial application of IFRS 9 and, therefore, in the absence of designation at FVTPL will be measured at amortised cost. Entity P cannot designate the fixed rate loan as at FVTPL because the interest rate swap was entered into after the date of initial application and, therefore, at the date of initial application of IFRS 9 there is no accounting mismatch. The accounting mismatch arises only after the initial recognition of the interest rate swap.

If, however, the interest rate swap was entered into prior to the date of initial application (i.e. before 1 July 20X3), Entity P might have been able to claim that the measurement of the interest rate swap at FVTPL and the fixed rate loan at amortised cost created an accounting mismatch which could be significantly reduced by designating the fixed rate loan as at FVTPL at the date of initial application of IFRS 9.

IAS 39 permitted designation as at FVTPL only in the following circumstances:

(a) designation would eliminate or significantly reduce a measurement or recognition inconsistency that would otherwise arise from measuring assets or liabilities or recognising the gains and losses on them on different bases (commonly referred to as an 'accounting mismatch');

(b) a group of financial assets, financial liabilities or both was managed and its performance was evaluated on a fair value basis, in accordance with a documented risk management or investment strategy, and information about the group was provided internally on that basis to the entity's key management personnel; or

(c) in the case of a hybrid contract containing one or more embedded derivatives, an entity could designate the entire hybrid (combined) contract as a financial asset or financial liability as at FVTPL unless:

- the embedded derivative did not significantly modify the cash flows that otherwise would be required by the contract; or
- it is clear with little or no analysis when a similar hybrid instrument was first considered that separation of the embedded derivative is

prohibited, for example a prepayment option embedded in a loan that permits the holder to prepay the loan for approximately its amortised cost (see **7.1** in **chapter B5**).

Only the first of these three criteria (the 'accounting mismatch') has been carried forward to IFRS 9 for financial assets. A financial asset designated as at FVTPL under IAS 39 (prior to it being consequentially amended by IFRS 9) on the basis of an accounting mismatch can only continue to be designated as at FVTPL on adoption of IFRS 9 if the accounting mismatch continues to exist at the date of initial application of IFRS 9. [IFRS 9:7.2.9(a)]

If a financial asset had been designated as at FVTPL under IAS 39 based on one of the other criteria, it would no longer be eligible for designation as at FVTPL on initial application of IFRS 9 unless it also satisfied the 'accounting mismatch' condition. However, the asset may be *required* to be measured at FVTPL (e.g. because the asset fails the contractual cash flow characteristics test or is not held in a business model whose objective includes holding assets to collect contractual cash flows).

Example 6.2.3B

Designation of financial assets as at FVTPL (2)

Entity J invests in a series of non-held for trading structured loans which, in accordance with IAS 39, had non-closely related embedded derivatives. However, Entity J chose to apply the fair value option at initial recognition as permitted by IAS 39:11A and, therefore, designated the loans as at FVTPL.

At the date of initial application of IFRS 9, Entity J must determine whether the loans meet the amortised cost or fair value through other comprehensive income criteria in IFRS 9 (see **chapter B2**).

If the loans do not meet the amortised cost or fair value through other comprehensive income criteria at the date of initial application of IFRS 9, the loans would continue to be measured at FVTPL under IFRS 9. More importantly, the loans are mandatorily *classified* as at FVTPL, and are not *designated* as at FVTPL, because the loans by default fail the amortised cost and fair value through other comprehensive income criteria in IFRS 9.

If the loans meet the amortised cost criteria at the date of initial application of IFRS 9, the loans would by default be measured at amortised cost under IFRS 9. If the loans meet the fair value through other comprehensive income criteria at the date of initial application of IFRS 9, the loans would by default be measured at fair value through other comprehensive under IFRS 9. However, Entity J can consider whether at the date of initial application it wishes to designate the loans as at FVTPL in accordance with IFRS 9:4.1.5 if doing so would eliminate or significantly reduce an accounting mismatch. If an accounting mismatch would be eliminated or significantly reduced by designating the loans as at FVTPL, Entity J may designate the loans as at FVTPL even if no such basis for applying the fair value option existed upon initial recognition of the loans under IAS 39. If, on initial application of IFRS 9, an accounting mismatch would not be eliminated or significantly reduced by designating the loans as at FVTPL, the loans must be measured at amortised cost or fair value through other comprehensive income under IFRS 9 depending on which classification criteria is met. The loans would be restated from FVTPL under IAS 39 to amortised cost or fair value through other comprehensive income as required by IFRS 9 on a retrospective basis.

Furthermore, at the date of initial application, an entity is required to revoke a previous designation of a financial asset as measured at FVTPL if that designation had previously been made to eliminate or significantly reduce an accounting mismatch but the condition is no longer met on the basis of the facts and circumstances that exist at the date of initial application of IFRS 9. If the conditions for the fair value option are met at the date of initial application (i.e. continuing to measure the asset at FVTPL eliminates or significantly reduces a measurement mismatch) an entity can choose to revoke the designation but is not required to. The revised measurement is required to be applied retrospectively. [IFRS 9:7.2.9]

Example 6.2.3C

Designation of financial assets as at FVTPL (3)

Entity L has previously invested in a series of fixed rate bonds that meet the amortised cost criteria at the date of initial application of IFRS 9. Entity L economically hedged the interest rate risk of these bonds with pay fixed receive floating interest rate swaps. Entity L applied the fair value option in IAS 39 to designate the bonds as at FVTPL based on the fair value option eliminating or significantly reducing an accounting mismatch. In the absence of the fair value option, an accounting mismatch would have arisen because the bonds would have been classified as available-for-sale and measured at fair value with fair value gains or losses recognised in other comprehensive income and the interest rate swaps would have been classified as at FVTPL.

At the date of initial application of IFRS 9, the bonds and the interest rate swaps continue to be recognised and, in the absence of designating the bonds as at FVTPL, an accounting mismatch would continue because the bonds meet the amortised cost criteria. Entity L is not forced to continue to designate the bonds as at FVTPL under IFRS 9 even though the accounting mismatch would still exist absent the fair value option. At the date of initial application of IFRS 9, Entity L has a choice as to whether it wishes to designate the bonds as at FVTPL under IFRS 9 (thereby continuing the application of the fair value option) or not to designate the bonds as at FVTPL under IFRS 9 and instead, by default, classify the bonds at amortised cost.

Had there not been an accounting mismatch eliminated or significantly reduced at the date of initial application by measuring the bonds at FVTPL, Entity L would be required to revoke the previous FVTPL designation on transition to IFRS 9 and measure the bonds at amortised cost.

6.2.4 Designation of financial liabilities as at FVTPL

At the date of initial application, an entity may designate an existing financial liability as at FVTPL if doing so eliminates or significantly reduces an accounting mismatch (see **7.1.2.1** in **chapter B3**). [IFRS 9:7.2.10(a)] This designation can be made when applying IFRS 9 for the first time even if the equivalent designation was not made when the entity initially recognised the financial liability under IAS 39. In other words, it is not a requirement that the entity also chose to make the same election, if it was available, when applying IAS 39.

Example 6.2.4A

Designation of financial liabilities as at FVTPL (1)

Entity U has issued fixed rate debt instruments in the past which continue to be recognised at the date of initial application of IFRS 9. At the date the debt was issued, Entity U designated a receive fixed pay floating interest rate swap in a fair value hedge of interest rate risk. The hedge accounting designation remains in place at the date of initial application of IFRS 9.

On the date of initial application of IFRS 9, Entity U chooses to cease hedge accounting and designates the issued fixed rate debt as at FVTPL because it reduces an accounting mismatch that would arise if the debt were not designated as at FVTPL (given that Entity U has discontinued the use of hedge accounting). Ceasing hedge accounting would result in the issued debt being measured at amortised cost and the interest rate swap being classified as at FVTPL, creating an accounting mismatch which can be significantly reduced if the debt is designated as at FVTPL.

In this case, applying IFRS 9 for the first time allows Entity U to apply the fair value option to a financial liability even though it would not have been able to do so under IAS 39 because the fair value option can only be applied at initial recognition.

A financial liability designated as at FVTPL under IAS 39 on the basis of an accounting mismatch can only continue to be designated as at FVTPL on adoption of IFRS 9 if the accounting mismatch criteria for applying the fair value option is met at the date of initial application of IFRS 9. [IFRS 9:7.2.10(b)]

Example 6.2.4B

Designation of financial liabilities as at FVTPL (2)

Prior to the date of initial application of IFRS 9, Entity T issued a fixed rate debt instrument on which the interest rate risk was economically hedged with a receive fixed pay floating interest rate swap. Entity T did not apply hedge accounting when the instruments were first recognised because it instead chose to designate the issued debt as at FVTPL under the fair value option in IAS 39:9; by designating the issued debt as at FVTPL, Entity T significantly reduced an accounting mismatch that would have resulted if the interest rate swap was measured at FVTPL and the issued debt was measured at amortised cost. Both instruments remain outstanding at the date of initial application of IFRS 9.

At the date of initial application of IFRS 9, Entity T chooses to continue with the existing accounting treatment under IAS 39 (i.e. the issued debt continues to be designated as at FVTPL) and is entitled to do so because the accounting mismatch continues to exist.

Furthermore, at the date of initial application, an entity may choose to revoke a previous designation of a financial liability as measured at FVTPL that was designated when the entity applied IAS 39 and was designated on the basis of an accounting mismatch. Such revocation is made on the basis of the facts and circumstances that exist at the date of initial application and is required to be applied retrospectively. [IFRS 9:7.2.10(c)] Revocation of the FVTPL designation is not permitted for those financial liabilities that were previously designated at FVTPL at their initial recognition in accordance with IAS 39:11A, based on having an embedded derivative that significantly modifies the cash flows of the contract, or IAS 39:9(b)(ii), where groups of financial liabilities or financial assets and financial liabilities are managed and their performance is evaluated on a fair value basis.

Example 6.2.4C

Revocation of designation of financial liabilities as at FVTPL

Prior to the date of initial application of IFRS 9, Entity V issued a fixed rate debt instrument where the interest rate risk was economically hedged with a receive fixed pay floating interest rate swap. Entity V did not apply hedge accounting when the instruments were first recognised because it instead chose to designate the issued debt as at FVTPL under the fair value option in IAS 39:9; by designating the issued debt as at FVTPL, Entity V significantly reduced an accounting mismatch that would have resulted if the interest rate swap was measured at FVTPL and the issued debt was measured at amortised cost. Both instruments remain outstanding at the date of initial application of IFRS 9.

At the date of initial application of IFRS 9, Entity V chooses to revoke the fair value option and therefore de-designates the issued debt as at FVTPL. Assuming the debt meets the amortised cost criteria at the date of initial application of IFRS 9, it will be measured at amortised cost. Entity V will retrospectively apply the new amortised cost classification, thereby reversing the previous fair value gains or losses recognised in profit or loss (and retained earnings) to reflect the accounting that would have applied had the instrument been measured at amortised cost since its initial recognition. It is not possible for Entity V to retrospectively apply fair value hedge accounting, and, thereby, reflect in the measurement of the issued debt any fair value hedge adjustments because hedge accounting in these circumstances is required to be applied prospectively.

6.2.5 Assessment of accounting mismatch for own credit risk

IFRS 9 requires in some limited circumstances that all gains and losses for financial liabilities designated as at FVTPL should be recognised in profit or loss, as opposed to recognising the fair value gains and losses with respect to changes in the credit risk of the liability in other comprehensive income and the remainder in profit or loss (see **7.1.2.5** in **chapter B3**). Whether the fair value gains or losses due to changes in credit risk are presented in profit or loss depends on whether the fair value gains or losses would create or enlarge an accounting mismatch in profit or loss if they were presented in other comprehensive income. When IFRS 9 is first applied, this assessment should be based on the facts and circumstances that exist at the date of initial application of IFRS 9 and the resulting measurement applied retrospectively. [IFRS 9:7.2.14]

6.3 Measurement exceptions

The transitional requirements in IFRS 9 permit certain practical expedients when determining the measurement of certain financial instruments. These exceptions are limited to (i) measuring an instrument at fair value for the first time that was previously under IAS 39 only partly measured at fair value as it was regarded as a hybrid financial instrument (see **6.3.1**); (ii) measuring an unquoted equity instrument at fair value for the first time that was previously under IAS 39 measured at cost; and, (iii) not applying the effective interest rate retrospectively if it is impracticable.

6.3.1 Hybrid contracts measured at fair value

If an entity measures a hybrid contract at fair value, and its fair value had not been previously determined in the comparative reporting periods, its fair value in the comparative reporting periods is taken to be the sum of the fair values of the components (i.e. the non-derivative host and the embedded derivative) at the end of each comparative reporting period. [IFRS 9:7.2.6]

An entity will measure a hybrid contract that is a financial asset at fair value under IFRS 9 when it does not meet the amortised cost or FVTOCI criteria (see **chapter B2**), or when it meets the amortised cost or FVTOCI criteria but the entity has elected to designate the financial asset as at FVTPL. The hybrid contract may not have been measured at FVTPL in its entirety prior to applying IFRS 9 because IAS 39 required an embedded derivative to be separated from the host contract and measured as at FVTPL whereas the host contract was not required to be measured as at FVTPL.

An entity may not have previously determined the fair value of a hybrid contract in its entirety. Moreover, an entity may not have the necessary information to determine fair value retrospectively without using hindsight. However, an entity would have been required to measure both the embedded derivative and host separately at fair value to apply the disclosure requirements in IFRS 7. Therefore, in comparative periods, IFRS 9 requires the sum of the fair value of the embedded derivative and the host to be used as an approximation of the fair value of the entire hybrid contract. [IFRS 9:BC7.16]

At the date of initial application of IFRS 9, entities are required to recognise any difference between the fair value of the entire hybrid contract at the date of initial application and the sum of the fair values of the components of the hybrid contract at the date of initial application in opening retained earnings of the reporting period of initial application. [IFRS 9:7.2.7]

Example 6.3.1

Fair valuation of hybrid contracts

Entity Q acquired an investment in an equity-linked note on 1 January 20X1. Under IAS 39, the equity-linked note was not classified as at FVTPL; rather, it was separated into a non-closely related embedded derivative (the equity-linked feature) which was classified as at FVTPL, and a debt host contract which was classified as an available-for-sale financial asset measured at fair value with fair value gains and losses recognised in other comprehensive income.

Entity Q applies IFRS 9 for the first time in the annual reporting period ending 31 December 20X5. Entity Q's date of initial application of IFRS 9 is 1 January 20X5 and the equity-linked note continues to be recognised at this date. Entity Q has chosen not to apply IFRS 9 to its comparative period.

The fair value of the hybrid contract had not been measured in the statement of financial position in the comparative period when IAS 39 was applied as only the embedded derivative was measured at FVTPL. Consequently in accordance with IFRS 9:7.2.6 the fair value for the hybrid contract in the comparative period is the sum of the fair values of the components (i.e. the non-derivative host and the embedded derivative) at the end of the comparative period. Entity Q determines this to be CU10.7 million.

At the date of initial application, Entity Q determines that the fair value of the equity-linked note in its entirety is CU10.9 million. Entity Q recognises the difference of CU0.2m in opening retained earnings at 1 January 20X5.

At the start of the comparative period, as comparatives are being restated, Entity Q will eliminate the available-for-sale reserve and recognise the cumulative gain or loss in that reserve in retained earnings. The gain or loss recognised in the available-for-sale reserve in the annual period ending 31 December 20X4 when IAS 39 was applied will be restated so the gain or loss is recognised in profit or loss.

6.3.2 Unquoted equity instrument previously measured at cost

If an entity previously accounted for an investment in an unquoted equity instrument (or a derivative asset or liability that is linked to, and must be settled by delivery of, an unquoted equity instrument) at cost in accordance with IAS 39, it is required to measure that instrument at fair value at the date of initial application of IFRS 9. Any difference between the previous carrying amount of the equity instrument and its fair value is recognised in the opening retained earnings of the reporting period that includes the date of initial application. [IFRS 9:7.2.12 & 13]

Example 6.3.2

Fair valuation of unquoted equity instruments

Entity K acquired an investment in an unlisted equity instrument on 1 January 20X0. Under IAS 39, the investment was measured at cost in accordance with IAS 39:46(c) because the investment did not have a quoted market price in an active market and fair value could not be reliably measured in accordance with IAS 39:AG80-81. The cost at 1 January 20X0 was CU10 million; however, in 20X1, Entity K recognised an impairment loss of CU3 million in profit or loss in accordance with IAS 39:66. Since 20X1, the carrying amount has remained at CU7 million.

Entity K applies IFRS 9 for the first time in the annual reporting period ending 31 December 20X5. Entity K has chosen not to apply IFRS 9 to its comparative period. Entity K's date of initial application of IFRS 9 is 1 January 20X5. Entity K determines that the fair value of the investment in the unlisted equity instrument at the date of initial application of IFRS 9 is CU8m. In accordance with IFRS 9:7.2.12, the difference between the carrying amount under IAS 39 (CU7 million), and the fair value (CU8 million), at the date of initial application of IFRS 9 is recognised in opening retained earnings in the reporting period that includes the date of initial application, i.e. at 1 January 20X5.

6.3.3 Impracticability override for the application of the effective interest method

If it is impracticable for an entity to apply retrospectively the effective interest method, the entity treats the fair value of the financial asset or financial liability at the end of each comparative period as the gross carrying amount of the financial asset or the amortised cost of the financial liability if the entity restates prior periods. If it is impracticable (as defined in IAS 8) for an entity to apply retrospectively the effective interest method, the fair value of the financial asset or financial liability at the date of initial application is treated as the new gross carrying amount of that financial asset or the new amortised cost of that financial liability at the date of initial application of IFRS 9. [IFRS 9:7.2.11]

Applying a requirement is impracticable when the entity cannot apply it after making every reasonable effort to do so. [IAS 8:5] The IASB acknowledged that retrospective application of the effective interest method would be cumbersome in some situations, in particular for an entity with a large number of financial assets that were previously measured at fair value but are measured at amortised cost in accordance with the approach in IFRS 9. [IFRS 9:BC7.14]

IFRS 9:BC7.14 also states that "[s]everal loss events and reversals might have occurred between the date when the asset was initially recognised and the date of initial application of the Standard. IFRS 9 requires that if applying the impairment requirements is impracticable or requires the use of hindsight, an entity should use previously determined fair value information to determine whether a financial asset was impaired in comparative periods. IFRS 9 also requires that the fair value at the date of initial application of the new requirements should be treated as the new amortised cost carrying amount of that financial asset in that case."

This implies that if there had potentially been several past loss events and reversals for assets measured at FVTPL it may be impracticable for the entity to apply the effective interest method on initial application of IFRS 9. However, the loss allowance is determined separately from the gross carrying amount under IFRS 9. Therefore, the gross carrying amount of an asset is not affected by loss events or reversals because the gross carrying amount does not include the loss allowance. Consequently, the potential for several past loss events or reversals would not make it impracticable to retrospectively apply the effective interest method. The reason IFRS 9:BC7.14 refers to loss events and reversals is because it relates to the original impracticability exception in IFRS 9(2009):8.2.10 which provided relief if it was impracticable for an entity to retrospectively apply the effective interest method or the impairment requirements *in IAS 39* under which the loss allowance is not required to be separate (rather than the impairment requirements *in IFRS 9*). This also explains why IFRS 9:BC7.14 states "an entity should use previously determined fair value information to determine whether a financial asset was impaired in comparative periods" as this is relevant for IFRS 9(2009) (but not IFRS 9(2014) which includes a new impairment model with different transition requirements, see **6.4**).

Example 6.3.3

Exemption from retrospectively applying effective interest method

Entity Q has a portfolio of debt instruments that were classified as held for trading under IAS 39 at initial recognition. At the date of initial application of IFRS 9, a significant portion of the portfolio of debt instruments continue to be recognised and remain classified as held for trading under IAS 39.

When IFRS 9 is first applied, Entity Q assesses the classification of its portfolio of debt instruments. The portfolio meets the FVTOCI criteria based on conditions existing at the date of initial application of IFRS 9.

When Entity Q applied IAS 39, it did not determine the effective interest rate for its portfolio of debt instruments because the gain or loss recognised in profit or loss was some movement only. Entity Q is aware that some of the debt instruments had contractual terms that were modified but because they were measured at FVTPL under IAS 39 both before and after the modification because they met the definition of held for trading in all cases, Entity Q did not perform a derecognition assessment for each modification.

If Entity Q were to determine the effective interest rate retrospectively it would have to first identify those that were modified to determine whether the modification would have resulted in derecognition (and a revised effective interest rate). Entity Q determines that it is impracticable to apply retrospectively the effective interest method in restating the portfolio of held for trading debt instruments at the date of initial application of IFRS 9.

The fair value of the portfolio of debt instruments at the start and end of the comparative period was CU12 million and CU9 million respectively. Entity Q regards the fair values at the start and end of the comparative period as the deemed amortised cost, in effect, not restating the amounts previously recognised when they were classified as held for trading under IAS 39. The carrying amount reported for the comparative period when first applying IFRS 9 will be the same as previously reported when applying IAS 39. The fair value at the end of the comparative period is also the fair value at the date of initial application of IFRS 9 because the date of initial application is the beginning of the first annual period that the entity first applies IFRS 9. Therefore, the gross carrying amount is deemed to be CU9 million at the date of initial application. At that date Entity Q determines the expected contractual cash flows on the debt instruments and in doing so calculates an effective interest rate. This effective interest rate is the basis for recognising interest in the period(s) after the date of initial application of IFRS 9.

6.4 Transition for the expected loss impairment model

The impairments requirements of IFRS 9 are applied retrospectively in accordance with IAS 8 subject to meeting specific exceptions as described below. [IFRS 9:7.2.17]

At the date of initial application, an entity shall use reasonable and supportable information that is available without undue cost or effort to determine the credit risk at the date that a financial instrument was initially recognised (or for loan commitments and financial guarantee contracts the date that the entity became a party to the irrevocable commitment) and compare that to the credit risk at the date of initial application of IFRS 9. [IFRS 9:7.2.18]

An entity is not required to undertake an exhaustive search for information when determining, at the date of transition, whether there have been significant increases in credit risk since initial recognition. [IFRS 9:B7.2.2] To determine the loss allowance on financial instruments initially recognised prior to the date of initial application, an entity should consider information (internal and external, including portfolio information) that is relevant in determining or approximating the credit risk at initial recognition. [IFRS 9:B7.2.3] An entity with little historical information may use information from internal reports and statistics, information about similar products or peer group experience for comparable financial instruments, if relevant. [IFRS 9:B7.2.4]

If it would require undue cost or effort at the date of initial application to determine whether there has been a significant increase in credit risk since initial recognition, an entity should recognise a loss allowance at an amount equal to lifetime expected credit losses at each reporting date until that financial instrument is derecognised. However, if the financial instrument is low credit risk at a reporting date, the entity may assume that the credit risk has not increased significantly since initial recognition. [IFRS 9:7.2.20]

Example 6.4

Determining whether there has been a significant increase in credit risk since initial recognition

Entity K had entered into a series of loan agreements many years ago that were measured at amortised cost in the loans and receivables category of IAS 39. Entity K chooses to initially apply IFRS 9 for the reporting period beginning on 1 January 20X5.

Entity K introduced a credit risk management system in 20X4 and has very limited data on the credit quality of the loans entered into many years ago. On the date of initial application of IFRS 9 it would require undue cost and effort for Entity K to determine whether there has been a significant increase in credit risk since initial recognition of each loan.

Therefore, if the credit risk for a loan is more than low, it recognises a loss allowance at an amount equal to the lifetime expected credit losses at each reporting date subsequent to initial application of IFRS 9.

If Entity K determines that the credit risk is low at the date of initial application of IFRS 9, the entity may assume that the credit risk has not increased significantly since initial recognition. In this case, the loan loss allowance will reflect 12 months of expected credit losses.

6.5 Hedge accounting

The requirements for hedge accounting in IFRS 9 are generally applied prospectively. [IFRS 9:7.2.22]

To apply hedge accounting from the date of initial application all qualifying criteria must be met at that date. [IFRS 9:7.2.23]

However, an entity should apply retrospectively the accounting for the time value of options if, in accordance with IAS 39, only the change in an option's intrinsic value was designated as a hedging instrument in a hedging relationship. This only applies to hedging relationships that existed at the beginning of the earliest comparative period or were designated thereafter. [IFRS 9:7.2.26(a)]

Example 6.5

Accounting for the time value of options

In May 20X1, Entity R acquired bonds issued by Entity T, which are measured at amortised cost. To protect itself against a decrease in the bond price, Entity R purchased a net cash settled put option over the bonds in July 20X1.

In July 20X1, Entity R designated the intrinsic value of the put option as a hedging instrument in a fair value hedge of the bonds.

Entity R initially applies IFRS 9 for the annual reporting period ending on 31 December 20X5. The hedging relationship existed at the start of the earliest comparative period (i.e. 1 January 20X4). Therefore, the entity is required to retrospectively apply the accounting for the time value (see **6.8** in **chapter B9**).

Under the same provision, an entity may apply the accounting for the forward element of forward contracts retrospectively, if, in accordance with IAS 39, only the change in the spot element of a forward contract was designated as a hedging instrument in a hedging relationship. If electing retrospective application this should be applied to all hedging relationships that qualify for this election. An election on a hedging-relationship-by-hedging-relationship basis is not available on transition. [IFRS 9:7.2.26(b)]

The accounting for foreign currency basis spreads in IFRS 9:6.5.16 (see **6.10** in **chapter B9**) may be applied retrospectively for those hedging relationships that existed at the beginning of the earliest reporting period or were designated thereafter. [IFRS 9:7.2.26(b)]

Under IAS 39 an entity could exclude the time value of an option or the forward element of a forward from the designation of a hedging instrument and this is required for the retrospective application to apply. However, IAS 39 did not allow excluding foreign currency basis spreads from the designation of a hedging instrument. Consequently, the retrospective application of the accounting for foreign currency basis spreads effectively permits a change in the designation of the hedging instrument to exclude the foreign currency basis spread provided the accounting for foreign currency basis spreads in IFRS 9:6.5.16 (see **6.10** in **chapter B9**) is applied retrospectively.

The restriction that retrospective application is available only on an 'all-or-nothing' basis does not apply to foreign currency basis spreads because of the variety of hedging instruments that involve those spreads. [IFRS 9:BC7.49]

Hedging relationships that qualified for hedge accounting in accordance with IAS 39 that also qualify for hedge accounting in accordance with IFRS 9 should be treated as continuing hedging relationships, i.e. the existing hedging relationship is not discontinued at transition. If necessary, an entity needs to rebalance the hedging relationship on initial application of IFRS 9 [IFRS 9:7.2.24].

As a starting point for rebalancing existing hedging relationships, an entity should consider the hedge ratio in accordance with IAS 39. Any gain or loss from such a rebalancing should be recognised in profit or loss [IFRS 9:7.2.25(b)].

7 Disclosures on first time application

When IFRS 9 was finalised it made consequential amendments to IFRS 7 to require certain disclosures when an entity first applies IFRS 9. The disclosures, which are extensive, apply regardless of whether an entity restates comparatives.

On first time application of IFRS 9, the following disclosures are required for each class of financial assets and financial liabilities at the date of initial application:

[IFRS 7:42I]

(a) the original measurement category and carrying amount determined under IAS 39 (or under a previous version of IFRS 9, if the entity's chosen approach to applying IFRS 9 involves more than one date of initial application for different requirements);

(b) the new measurement category and carrying amount determined under IFRS 9; and

(c) the amount of any financial assets and financial liabilities in the statement of financial position that were previously designated as measured at fair value through profit or loss but are no longer so designated, distinguishing between those that IFRS 9 requires an entity to reclassify and those that an entity elects to reclassify.

These quantitative disclosures, as well as those discussed below, are required to be presented in a table unless another format is more appropriate.

In addition, the following disclosures are also required which need not be made in subsequent reporting periods unless otherwise stated:

- the changes in the classifications of financial assets and financial liabilities as at the date of initial application of IFRS 9, showing separately:
  - (a) the changes in the carrying amounts on the basis of their measurement categories in accordance with IAS 39 (i.e. not resulting from a change in measurement attribute on transition to IFRS 9); and

(b) the changes in the carrying amounts arising from a change in measurement attribute on transition to IFRS 9. [IFRS 7:42L]

- for financial assets and financial liabilities that have been reclassified to amortised cost on transition to IFRS 9:
  (a) the fair value of the financial assets or financial liabilities at the end of the reporting period; and
  (b) the fair value gain or loss that would have been recognised in profit or loss or other comprehensive income during the reporting period if the financial assets or financial liabilities had not been reclassified. [IFRS 7:42M]
- for financial assets reclassified out of FVTPL to FVTOCI on transition to IFRS 9:
  (a) the fair value at the end of the reporting period; and
  (b) the fair value gain or loss that would have been recognised in profit or loss during the reporting period if the financial assets had not been reclassified. [IFRS 7:42M]
- for financial assets and financial liabilities reclassified out of FVTPL on transition to IFRS 9:
  (a) the effective interest rate determined on the date of initial application; and
  (b) the interest revenue or expense recognised.

  If the fair value of a financial asset or a financial liability has been treated as the new (gross) carrying amount at the date of initial application (see **6.3.3**), this disclosure is required for each reporting period until derecognition. [IFRS 7:42N]

When the disclosures listed immediately above are provided they must permit reconciliation between:

(a) the measurement categories presented in accordance with IAS 39 and IFRS 9; and

(b) the class of financial instrument as at the date of initial application.

In addition to the quantitative disclosures, qualitative disclosures are also required to enable users to understand:

[IFRS 7:42J]

(a) how the entity applied the classification requirements of IFRS 9 to those financial assets whose classification changed as a result of applying IFRS 9; and

(b) the reasons for any designation or de-designation of financial assets or financial liabilities as measured at fair value through profit or loss at the date of initial application.

Example 7

First time application disclosures

The following illustration is an example of one possible way to meet the quantitative disclosure requirements in IFRS 7:42K to 42O at the date of initial application of IFRS 9. However, this illustration does not address all possible ways of applying the disclosure requirements of IFRS 9. [IFRS 7:IG40E]

Reconciliation of statement of financial position balances from IAS 39 to IFRS 9 at 1 January 2018

Financial assets	**(i)** **IAS 39 carrying amount 31 December 2017** [1]	**(ii)** **Reclassifications**	**(iii)** **Remeasurements**	**(iv) = (i) + (ii) + (iii)** **IFRS 9 carrying amount 1 January 2018**	**(v) = (iii)** **Retained earnings effect on 1 January 2018** [2], [3]
FVTPL					
Additions:					
From AFS (IAS 39)		(a)			(c)
From amortised cost (IAS 39)					
- required reclassification		(b)			
- fair value option elected at 1 January 2018					
Subtractions:					
To amortised cost (IFRS 9)					
To FVTOCI					
- debt instruments (IFRS 9)					
- equity instruments (IFRS 9)					
Total change to FVTPL					
FVTOCI					
Additions – debt instruments:					
From AFS (IAS 39)					(g)
From amortised cost (IAS 39)					(h)
From FVTPL					
- required classification based on classification criteria					(i)

Financial assets	(i) IAS 39 carrying amount 31 December 2017 [1]	(ii) Reclassifications	(iii) Remeasurements	(iv) = (i) + (ii) + (iii) IFRS 9 carrying amount 1 January 2018	(v) = (iii) Retained earnings effect on 1 January 2018 [2], [3]
- fair value option criteria not met at 1 January 2018					(j)
- fair value option revoked at 1 January 2018 by choice					(k)
Additions – equity instruments:					
From AFS (IAS 39)					
From FVTPL (fair value option under IAS 39) – FVTOCI elected at 1 January 2018					
From cost (IAS 39)					
Subtractions – debt and equity instruments:					
AFS (IAS 39) to FVTPL (IFRS 9)					
- required reclassification based on classification criteria					(d)
- fair value option elected at 1 January 2018					
AFS (IAS 39) to amortised cost (IFRS 9)					(e)
Total change to FVTOCI					
Amortised cost					
Additions:					
From AFS (IAS 39)					(f)
From FVTPL (IAS 39)					
- required reclassification					
- fair value option criteria not met at 1 January 2018					
- fair value option revoked at 1 January 2018 by choice					
Subtractions:					
To FVTOCI (IFRS 9)					

Financial assets	**(i)** IAS 39 carrying amount 31 December 2017 [1]	**(ii)** Reclassifications	**(iii)** Remeasurements	**(iv) = (i) + (ii) + (iii)** IFRS 9 carrying amount 1 January 2018	**(v) = (iii)** Retained earnings effect on 1 January 2018 [2], [3]
To FVTPL (IFRS 9)					
- required reclassification based on classification criteria					
- fair value option elected at 1 January 2018					
Total change to amortised cost					
Total financial asset balances, reclassifications and remeasurements at 1 January 2018					

[1] Includes the effect of reclassifying hybrid instruments that were bifurcated under IAS 39 with host contract components of (a), which had associated embedded derivatives with a fair value of X at 31 December 2017, and (b), which had associated embedded derivatives with a fair value of Y at 31 December 2017.

[2] Includes (c), (d), (e) and (f), which are amounts reclassified from other comprehensive income to retained earnings at the date of initial application.

[3] Includes (g), (h), (i), (j), (k) and (l) which are amounts reclassified from retained earnings to accumulated other comprehensive income at the date of initial application

On the date of initial application of the impairment requirements of IFRS 9, an entity is required to disclose information that would permit the reconciliation of the ending impairment allowances under IAS 39 and provisions under IAS 37 (for certain loan commitments and financial guarantee contracts) to the opening loss allowances determined under IFRS 9. For financial assets, this disclosure is required by the assets' measurement categories under IAS 39 and IFRS 9, showing separately the effect of the changes in the measurement category on the loss allowance at that date. [IFRS 7:42P]

An entity is not required to disclose the line item amounts that would have been reported in accordance with the classification and measurement requirements (including the requirements related to amortised cost measurement of financial assets and impairment, see **chapter B6**) of:

[IFRS 7:42Q]

(a) IFRS 9 for prior periods; and

(b) IAS 39 for the current period.

As discussed in **6.2.1**, IFRS 9 provides exceptions (based on impracticability) in respect of assessing:

- the modified time value of money element based on the facts and circumstances that existed at the initial recognition of the financial asset; and
- whether the fair value of a prepayment feature was insignificant based on the facts and circumstances that existed at the initial recognition of the financial asset.

For financial assets to which either exception has been applied, IFRS 7 requires disclosure of the carrying amount at the reporting date (separately for each exception) of the financial assets until those financial assets are derecognised. [IFRS 7:42R and 42S]

Index